The Sporting News

PRO FOOTBALL REGISTER

1991 EDITION

Editor/Pro Football Register
MARK SHIMABUKURO

Contributing Editors/Pro Football Register
CRAIG CARTER, TOM DIENHART, JOE HOPPEL, DAVE SLOAN

Publisher
THOMAS G. OSENTON

Director, Specialized Publications
GARY LEVY

Managing Editor, Specialized Publications
MIKE NAHRSTEDT

Published by

The Sporting News

1212 North Lindbergh Boulevard ● P.O. Box 56 ● St. Louis, MO 63166

Copyright © 1991
The Sporting News Publishing Company

A Times Mirror
Company

ISBN 0-89204-397-0   ISSN 0071-7258

CONTENTS

EXPLANATION OF ABBREVIATIONS

LEAGUES: AFL—American Football League. Arena Football—Arena Football League. CFL—Canadian Football League. CoFL—Continental Football League. EFL—Eastern Football League. NFL—National Football League. USFL—United States Football League. WFL—World Football League. WLAF—World League of American Football.

TEAMS: Atl.—Atlanta. Buf.—Buffalo. Cal.—Calgary. Chi.—Chicago. Cin.—Cincinnati. Cle.—Cleveland. Dal.—Dallas. Den.—Denver. Det.—Detroit. Edm.—Edmonton. G.B.—Green Bay. Ham.—Hamilton. Hou.—Houston. Ind.—Indianapolis. K.C.—Kansas City. Rai.—Los Angeles Raiders. Rams—Los Angeles Rams. Mia.—Miami. Min.—Minnesota. Mon.—Montreal. N.E.—New England. N.Y./N.J.—New York/New Jersey. N.O.—New Orleans. N.Y.G.—New York Giants. N.Y.J.—New York Jets. Ott.—Ottawa. Phi.—Philadelphia. Pho.—Phoenix. Pit.—Pittsburgh. S.D.—San Diego. Sask.—Saskatchewan. S.F.—San Francisco. Sea.—Seattle. St.L.—St. Louis. T.B.—Tampa Bay. Tor.—Toronto. Was.—Washington. Win.—Winnipeg.

STATISTICS: Att.—Attempts. Avg.—Average. Blk.—Blocked punts. Cmp.—Completions. F.—Fumbles. FGA—Field goals attempted. FGM—Field goals made. G—Games. Int.—Interceptions. L—Lost. No.—Number. Pct.—Percentage. Pts.—Points scored. T—Tied. TD—Touchdowns. W—Won. XPA—Extra points attempted. XPM—Extra points made. Yds.—Yards (net).

ON THE COVER: Kansas City linebacker Derrick Thomas led the National Football League with 20 sacks in 1990, including a league-record seven in one game against Seattle. (Photo by Jon SooHoo/Bernstein Associates)

VETERAN PLAYERS

Please note for statistical comparisons: In 1982, only nine of 16 games were played due to the cancellation of games because of a players' strike. In 1987, only 15 of 16 games were played due to the cancellation of games in the third week because of a players' strike. Most NFL players also missed games scheduled in the fourth, fifth and sixth weeks.

*Indicates led league or tied for league lead.

ABRAMS, BOBBY
LB, GIANTS

PERSONAL: Born April 12, 1967, at Detroit.... 6-3/230.... Full name: Robert Abrams Jr.
HIGH SCHOOL: Henry Ford (Detroit).
COLLEGE: Michigan.
TRANSACTIONS/CAREER NOTES: Signed as free agent by New York Giants (April 26, 1990).
PLAYING EXPERIENCE: New York Giants NFL, 1990.... Games: 1990 (16).
CHAMPIONSHIP GAME EXPERIENCE: Played in NFC championship game after 1990 season.... Played in Super Bowl XXV after 1990 season.

ADAMS, GEORGE
RB, PATRIOTS

PERSONAL: Born December 22, 1962, at Lexington, Ky.... 6-1/225.... Full name: George Wallace Adams.... Cousin of Dermontti Dawson, center with Pittsburgh Steelers.
HIGH SCHOOL: Lafayette (Lexington, Ky.).
COLLEGE: Kentucky.
TRANSACTIONS/CAREER NOTES: Selected by Orlando Renegades in third round (33rd pick overall) of 1985 USFL draft.... Selected by New York Giants in first round (19th pick overall) of 1985 NFL draft.... Signed by Giants (July 22, 1985).... On injured reserve with hip injury (September 1, 1986-entire season).... On injured reserve with hip injury (January 6, 1990-remainder of 1989 season playoffs).... Granted unconditional free agency (February 1, 1990).... Signed by New England Patriots (March 23, 1990).
PRO STATISTICS: 1985—Attempted one pass with no completions and recovered two fumbles. 1987—Recovered one fumble.

Year	Team	G	Att.	Yds.	Avg.	TD	No.	Yds.	Avg.	TD	No.	Yds.	Avg.	TD	TD	Pts.	F.
			RUSHING				RECEIVING				KICKOFF RETURNS				TOTAL		
1985—	N.Y. Giants NFL	16	128	498	3.9	2	31	389	12.5	2	14	241	17.2	0	4	24	7
1987—	N.Y. Giants NFL	12	61	169	2.8	1	35	298	8.5	1	9	166	18.4	0	2	12	3
1988—	N.Y. Giants NFL	16	29	76	2.6	0	27	174	6.4	0	0	0		0	0	0	0
1989—	N.Y. Giants NFL	14	9	29	3.2	0	2	7	3.5	0	0	0		0	0	0	0
1990—	New England NFL	16	28	111	4.0	0	16	146	9.1	1	1	7	7.0	0	1	6	1
Pro totals (5 years)		74	255	883	3.5	3	111	1014	9.1	4	24	414	17.3	0	7	42	11

ADAMS, STEFON
WR, RAIDERS

PERSONAL: Born August 11, 1963, at High Point, N.C.... 5-10/185.... Full name: Stefon Lee Adams.
HIGH SCHOOL: Southwest Guilford (High Point, N.C.).
COLLEGE: East Carolina.
TRANSACTIONS/CAREER NOTES: Selected by Baltimore Stars in fourth round (58th pick overall) of 1985 USFL draft.... Selected by Los Angeles Raiders in third round (80th pick overall) of 1985 NFL draft.... Signed by Raiders (July 17, 1985).... On injured reserve with hamstring injury (September 2, 1985-entire season).... Released by Raiders (August 26, 1988).... Re-signed by Raiders (September 14, 1988).... Released by Raiders (September 3, 1990).... Awarded on waivers to Cleveland Browns (September 4, 1990).... Released by Browns (November 24, 1990).... Signed by Miami Dolphins (December 19, 1990).... Granted unconditional free agency (February 1, 1991).... Signed by Los Angeles Raiders (April 1, 1991).
PRO STATISTICS: 1986—Intercepted one pass for 32 yards and recovered two fumbles. 1987—Intercepted one pass for eight yards. 1988—Recovered three fumbles for one yard. 1989—Credited with a safety and recovered one fumble.

Year	Team	G	No.	Yds.	Avg.	TD	No.	Yds.	Avg.	TD	TD	Pts.	F.
			PUNT RETURNS				KICKOFF RETURNS				TOTAL		
1986—	L.A. Raiders NFL	16	0	0		0	27	573	21.2	0	0	0	0
1987—	L.A. Raiders NFL	9	5	39	7.8	0	3	61	20.3	0	0	0	0
1988—	L.A. Raiders NFL	14	6	45	7.5	0	8	132	16.5	0	0	0	0
1989—	L.A. Raiders NFL	14	19	156	8.2	0	22	425	19.3	0	0	2	2
1990—	Cle (10)-Mia (2) NFL	12	13	81	6.2	0	5	49	9.8	0	0	0	2
Pro totals (5 years)		65	43	321	7.5	0	65	1240	19.1	0	0	2	4

ADICKES, MARK
G, REDSKINS

PERSONAL: Born April 22, 1961, at Badconstadt, West Germany.... 6-4/275.... Full name: Mark Stephen Adickes.... Name pronounced ADD-dix.... Brother of John Adickes, center with Chicago Bears and Minnesota Vikings, 1987-1989.
HIGH SCHOOL: Killeen (Tex.).
COLLEGE: Baylor.
TRANSACTIONS/CAREER NOTES: Selected by Houston Gamblers in 1984 USFL territorial draft.... USFL rights traded by Gamblers with rights to center Mike Ruether to Los Angeles Express for second-round pick in 1985 and 1986 draft (February 13, 1984).... Signed by Express (February 13, 1984).... Granted roster exemption (February 13-February 24, 1984).... On injured reserve with knee injury (March 6, 1984-remainder of season).... Selected by Kansas City Chiefs in first round (fifth pick overall) of 1984 NFL supplemental draft.... Released by Los Angeles Express (August 1, 1985).... Re-signed by Express (August 2, 1985).... Released by Express (April 3, 1986).... Signed by Kansas City Chiefs (June 5, 1986).... On injured reserve with back injury (August 22-October 15, 1988).... Granted unconditional free agency (February 1, 1990).... Signed by Washington Redskins (March 29, 1990).... On inactive list (September 9, 16, 30; and October 14, 21 and 28, 1990).

PLAYING EXPERIENCE: Los Angeles USFL, 1984 and 1985; Kansas City NFL, 1986-1989; Washington NFL, 1990.... Games: 1984 (2), 1985 (11), 1986 (15), 1987 (12), 1988 (10), 1989 (16), 1990 (8). Total USFL: 13. Total NFL: 61. Total Pro: 74.
RECORDS/HONORS: Named as offensive tackle on THE SPORTING NEWS college All-America team, 1983.
PRO STATISTICS: 1987—Caught one pass for three yards and a touchdown and recovered one fumble. 1989—Recovered one fumble.

AGEE, TOMMIE
FB, COWBOYS

PERSONAL: Born February 22, 1964, at Chilton, Ala.... 6-0/223.... Full name: Tommie Lee Agee.
HIGH SCHOOL: Maplesville (Ala.).
COLLEGE: Auburn (degree in criminal justice).
TRANSACTIONS/CAREER NOTES: Selected by Seattle Seahawks in fifth round (119th pick overall) of 1987 NFL draft.... Signed by Seahawks (July 21, 1987).... On injured reserve with knee injury (September 1, 1987-entire season).... Granted unconditional free agency (February 1, 1989).... Signed by Kansas City Chiefs (February 24, 1989).... On injured reserve with finger injury (September 13-October 24, 1989).... Granted unconditional free agency (February 1, 1990).... Signed by Dallas Cowboys (March 3, 1990).
PRO STATISTICS: 1988—Had only pass attempt intercepted and recovered one fumble.

		RUSHING				RECEIVING				TOTAL		
Year Team	G	Att.	Yds.	Avg.	TD	No.	Yds.	Avg.	TD	TD	Pts.	F.
1988— Seattle NFL	16	1	2	2.0	0	3	31	10.3	0	0	0	0
1989— Kansas City NFL	9	1	3	3.0	0	0	0		0	0	0	0
1990— Dallas NFL	16	53	213	4.0	0	30	272	9.1	1	1	6	0
Pro totals (3 years)	41	55	218	4.0	0	33	303	9.2	1	1	6	0

AGNEW, RAY
DE, PATRIOTS

PERSONAL: Born December 9, 1967, at Winston-Salem, N.C.... 6-3/272.... Full name: Raymond Mitchell Agnew.
HIGH SCHOOL: Carver (Winston-Salem, N.C.).
COLLEGE: North Carolina State.
TRANSACTIONS/CAREER NOTES: Selected by New England Patriots in first round (10th pick overall) of 1990 NFL draft.... Signed by Patriots (July 19, 1990).... On inactive list (December 23, 1990).... On injured reserve with knee injury (December 29, 1990-remainder of season).
PLAYING EXPERIENCE: New England NFL, 1990.... Games: 1990 (12).
PRO STATISTICS: 1990—Recovered one fumble.

AHRENS, DAVE
LB, SEAHAWKS

PERSONAL: Born December 5, 1958, at Cedar Falls, Ia.... 6-4/247.... Full name: David Iver Ahrens.... Name pronounced AIR-ens.
HIGH SCHOOL: Oregon (Wis.).
COLLEGE: Wisconsin.
TRANSACTIONS/CAREER NOTES: Selected by St. Louis Cardinals in sixth round (143rd pick overall) of 1981 NFL draft.... Traded by Cardinals to Indianapolis Colts for 10th-round pick in 1986 draft (August 27, 1985).... Released by Colts (August 24, 1988).... Signed as free agent by Detroit Lions (October 20, 1988).... Granted unconditional free agency (February 1, 1989). ... Signed by Miami Dolphins (March 23, 1989).... On injured reserve with knee injury (November 29, 1989-remainder of season).... Granted unconditional free agency (February 1, 1990).... Signed by Seattle Seahawks (March 5, 1990).... Released by Seahawks (August 27, 1990).... Re-signed by Seahawks (October 10, 1990).... On injured reserve with leg injury (December 23, 1990-remainder of season).
PLAYING EXPERIENCE: St. Louis NFL, 1981-1984; Indianapolis NFL, 1985-1987; Detroit NFL, 1988; Miami NFL, 1989; Seattle NFL, 1990.... Games: 1981 (16), 1982 (9), 1983 (16), 1984 (16), 1985 (16), 1986 (16), 1987 (12), 1988 (8), 1989 (11), 1990 (10). Total: 130.
PRO STATISTICS: 1981—Intercepted one pass for 14 yards. 1982—Returned one kickoff for five yards and recovered one fumble. 1983—Caught one pass for four yards. 1985—Recovered one fumble. 1987—Returned one punt for no yards and recovered two fumbles. 1989—Returned one kickoff for 10 yards.

AIKMAN, TROY
QB, COWBOYS

PERSONAL: Born November 21, 1966, at West Covina, Calif.... 6-4/218.... Full name: Troy Kenneth Aikman.
HIGH SCHOOL: Henryetta (Okla.).
COLLEGE: Oklahoma, then UCLA.
TRANSACTIONS/CAREER NOTES: Selected by Dallas Cowboys in first round (first pick overall) of 1989 NFL draft.... Signed by Cowboys (April 20, 1989).... On injured reserve with shoulder injury (December 28, 1990-remainder of season).
RECORDS/HONORS: Named as quarterback on THE SPORTING NEWS college All-America team, 1988.
PRO STATISTICS: Passer rating points: 1989 (55.7), 1990 (66.6). Career: 62.0.... 1989—Caught one pass for minus 13 yards and recovered three fumbles. 1990—Recovered one fumble.

		PASSING							RUSHING				TOTAL		
Year Team	G	Att.	Cmp.	Pct.	Yds.	TD	Int.	Avg.	Att.	Yds.	Avg.	TD	TD	Pts.	F.
1989— Dallas NFL	11	293	155	52.9	1749	9	18	5.97	38	302	7.9	0	0	0	6
1990— Dallas NFL	15	399	226	56.6	2579	11	18	6.46	40	172	4.3	1	1	6	5
Pro totals (2 years)	26	692	381	55.1	4328	20	36	6.25	78	474	6.1	1	1	6	11

ALBRITTON, VINCE
S, COWBOYS

PERSONAL: Born July 23, 1962, at Oakland, Calif. . . . 6-2/212. . . . Full name: Vince Denader Albritton.
HIGH SCHOOL: McClymond (Oakland, Calif.).
COLLEGE: Washington.
TRANSACTIONS/CAREER NOTES: Selected by Philadelphia Stars in 16th round (326th pick overall) of 1984 USFL draft. . . . Signed as free agent by Dallas Cowboys (May 3, 1984). . . . On injured reserve with hamstring injury (August 20-November 7, 1985). . . . Activated after clearing procedural waivers (November 9, 1985). . . . On injured reserve with thigh injury (August 23-October 29, 1988). . . . On inactive list (November 4, 11, 18 and 22, 1990). . . . On injured reserve with leg injury (November 29, 1990-remainder of season).
PLAYING EXPERIENCE: Dallas NFL, 1984-1990. . . . Games: 1984 (16), 1985 (7), 1986 (16), 1987 (11), 1988 (6), 1989 (16), 1990 (8). Total: 80.
PRO STATISTICS: 1984—Recovered two fumbles. 1986—Recovered two fumbles. 1989—Intercepted one pass for three yards and recovered one fumble. 1990—Recovered two fumbles.

ALEXANDER, BRUCE
CB, LIONS

PERSONAL: Born September 17, 1965, at Lufkin, Tex. . . . 5-9/169. . . . Full name: Bruce E. Alexander. . . . Cousin of Benny Barnes, safety with Dallas Cowboys, 1972-1982.
HIGH SCHOOL: Lufkin (Tex.).
COLLEGE: Stephen F. Austin State.
TRANSACTIONS/CAREER NOTES: Signed as free agent by Detroit Lions (May 1, 1989). . . . Released by Lions (August 30, 1989). . . . Re-signed by Lions to developmental squad (September 6, 1989). . . . On developmental squad (September 6-November 1, 1989). . . . Activated after clearing procedural waivers (November 3, 1989). . . . On injured reserve with sprained knee (September 4-December 7, 1990). . . . On inactive list (December 16, 22 and 30, 1990).
PLAYING EXPERIENCE: Detroit NFL, 1989 and 1990. . . . Games: 1989 (8), 1990 (1). Total: 9.
PRO STATISTICS: 1989—Returned five kickoffs for 100 yards.

ALEXANDER, DAVID
C, EAGLES

PERSONAL: Born July 28, 1964, at Silver Spring, Md. . . . 6-3/275.
HIGH SCHOOL: Broken Arrow (Okla.).
COLLEGE: Tulsa.
TRANSACTIONS/CAREER NOTES: Selected by Philadelphia Eagles in fifth round (121st pick overall) of 1987 NFL draft. . . . Signed by Eagles (August 5, 1987).
PLAYING EXPERIENCE: Philadelphia NFL, 1987-1990. . . . Games: 1987 (12), 1988 (16), 1989 (16), 1990 (16). Total: 60.
PRO STATISTICS: 1988—Recovered one fumble. 1989—Recovered one fumble and fumbled once for minus four yards.

ALEXANDER, MIKE
WR, RAIDERS

PERSONAL: Born March 19, 1965, at Manhattan, N.Y. . . . 6-3/185. . . . Full name: Michael Fitzgerald Alexander.
HIGH SCHOOL: Piscataway (N.J.).
COLLEGE: Nassau Community College (N.Y.), then Penn State.
TRANSACTIONS/CAREER NOTES: Selected by Los Angeles Raiders in eighth round (199th pick overall) of 1988 NFL draft. . . . Signed by Raiders (July 14, 1988). . . . On injured reserve with knee injury (August 22, 1988-entire season). . . . On injured reserve with hamstring injury (September 4, 1990-entire season).

| | | | RECEIVING | | |
Year Team	G	No.	Yds.	Avg.	TD
1989— L.A. Raiders NFL	16	15	295	19.7	1
Pro totals (1 year)	16	15	295	19.7	1

ALLEN, ERIC
CB, EAGLES

PERSONAL: Born November 22, 1965, at San Diego. . . . 5-10/180. . . . Full name: Eric Andre Allen.
HIGH SCHOOL: Point Loma (San Diego).
COLLEGE: Arizona State (degree in broadcasting, 1988).
TRANSACTIONS/CAREER NOTES: Selected by Philadelphia Eagles in second round (30th pick overall) of 1988 NFL draft. . . . Signed by Eagles (July 19, 1988).
RECORDS/HONORS: Played in Pro Bowl after 1989 season.
PRO STATISTICS: 1989—Fumbled once for seven yards. 1990—Returned one kickoff for two yards and recovered one fumble.

| | | | INTERCEPTIONS | | |
Year Team	G	No.	Yds.	Avg.	TD
1988— Philadelphia NFL	16	5	76	15.2	0
1989— Philadelphia NFL	15	8	38	4.8	0
1990— Philadelphia NFL	16	3	37	12.3	1
Pro totals (3 years)	47	16	151	9.4	1

ALLEN, MARCUS
RB, RAIDERS

PERSONAL: Born March 26, 1960, at San Diego. . . . 6-2/210 . . . Brother of Damon Allen, quarterback with Edmonton Eskimos (CFL), 1985-1988.
HIGH SCHOOL: Lincoln (San Diego).
COLLEGE: Southern California.
TRANSACTIONS/CAREER NOTES: Selected by Los Angeles Raiders in first round (10th pick overall) of 1982 NFL draft. . . . On reserve/did not report list (July 26-August 30, 1989). . . . On injured reserve with knee injury (October 13-November 29, 1989). . . . Transferred to developmental squad (November 30, 1989). . . . Activated (December 2, 1989). . . . Granted free agency

(February 1, 1990).... Re-signed by Raiders (July 27, 1990).
CHAMPIONSHIP GAME EXPERIENCE: Played in AFC championship game after 1983 and 1990 seasons.... Played in Super Bowl XVIII after 1983 season.
RECORDS/HONORS: Established NFL record for most combined yards, season (2,314), 1985; most consecutive games, 100 yards rushing (11), 1985-1986.... Heisman Trophy winner, 1981.... Named THE SPORTING NEWS College Football Player of the Year, 1981.... Named as running back on THE SPORTING NEWS college All-America team, 1981.... Named THE SPORTING NEWS NFL Rookie of the Year, 1982.... Played in Pro Bowl after 1982, 1984, 1985 and 1987 seasons.... Named to play in Pro Bowl after 1986 season; replaced due to injury by Sammy Winder.... Named THE SPORTING NEWS NFL Player of the Year, 1985.... Named to THE SPORTING NEWS NFL All-Pro team, 1985.
PRO STATISTICS: 1982—Completed one of four pass attempts for 47 yards and recovered two fumbles. 1983—Attempted seven passes with four completions for 111 yards and three touchdowns and recovered two fumbles (including one in end zone for a touchdown). 1984—Attempted four passes with one completion for 38 yards and recovered three fumbles. 1985—Attempted two passes with one completion for 16 yards and recovered two fumbles. 1986—Recovered one fumble. 1987—Attempted two passes with one completion for 23 yards. 1988—Attempted two passes with one completion for 21 yards. 1990—Attempted one pass with no completions and recovered one fumble.

Year Team	G	Att.	Yds.	Avg.	TD	No.	Yds.	Avg.	TD	TD	Pts.	F.
		RUSHING				RECEIVING				TOTAL		
1982— L.A. Raiders NFL	9	160	697	4.4	*11	38	401	10.6	3	*14	*84	5
1983— L.A. Raiders NFL	15	266	1014	3.8	9	68	590	8.7	2	12	72	*14
1984— L.A. Raiders NFL	16	275	1168	4.2	13	64	758	11.8	5	*18	108	8
1985— L.A. Raiders NFL	16	380	*1759	4.6	11	67	555	8.3	3	14	84	3
1986— L.A. Raiders NFL	13	208	759	3.6	5	46	453	9.8	2	7	42	7
1987— L.A. Raiders NFL	12	200	754	3.8	5	51	410	8.0	0	5	30	3
1988— L.A. Raiders NFL	15	223	831	3.7	7	34	303	8.9	1	8	48	5
1989— L.A. Raiders NFL	8	69	293	4.2	2	20	191	9.6	0	2	12	2
1990— L.A. Raiders NFL	16	179	682	3.8	12	15	189	12.6	1	13	78	1
Pro totals (9 years)	120	1960	7957	4.1	75	403	3850	9.6	17	93	558	48

ALLEN, MARVIN
RB, PATRIOTS

PERSONAL: Born November 23, 1965, at Wichita Falls, Tex. ... 5-10/208. ... Full name: Marvin Ray Allen.
HIGH SCHOOL: Hirschi (Wichita Falls, Tex.).
COLLEGE: Tyler Junior College (Tex.), then Tulane (degree in sports administration, 1988).
TRANSACTIONS/CAREER NOTES: Selected by New England Patriots in 11th round (294th pick overall) of 1988 NFL draft. ... Signed by Patriots (July 13, 1988).... Released by Patriots (August 29, 1988).... Re-signed by Patriots (August 30, 1988). ... On injured reserve with fractured shoulder (November 16, 1988-remainder of season).... On injured reserve with foot injury (November 9, 1989-remainder of season).... Granted free agency (February 1, 1990).... Re-signed by Patriots (July 18, 1990).... Released by Patriots (September 3, 1990).... Re-signed by Patriots (October 29, 1990).
PRO STATISTICS: 1988—Recovered two fumbles. 1989—Recovered one fumble. 1990—Recovered three fumbles.

Year Team	G	Att.	Yds.	Avg.	TD	No.	Yds.	Avg.	TD	No.	Yds.	Avg.	TD	TD	Pts.	F.
		RUSHING				RECEIVING				KICKOFF RETURNS				TOTAL		
1988— New England NFL..	11	7	40	5.7	0	0	0		0	18	391	21.7	0	0	0	0
1989— New England NFL..	3	11	51	4.6	1	0	0		0	6	124	20.7	0	1	6	0
1990— New England NFL..	8	63	237	3.8	1	6	48	8.0	0	11	168	15.3	0	1	6	1
Pro totals (3 years)	22	81	328	4.1	2	6	48	8.0	0	35	683	19.5	0	2	12	1

ALLEN, PATRICK
CB, CHIEFS

PERSONAL: Born August 26, 1961, at Seattle. ... 5-10/182. ... Full name: Lloyd Patrick Allen. ... Brother of Anthony Allen, wide receiver with Los Angeles Express (USFL), Michigan Panthers (USFL), Portland Breakers (USFL), Atlanta Falcons, Washington Redskins and San Diego Chargers, 1983-1989.
HIGH SCHOOL: Garfield (Seattle).
COLLEGE: Utah State.
TRANSACTIONS/CAREER NOTES: Selected by Washington Federals in second round (27th pick overall) of 1984 USFL draft.... Selected by Houston Oilers in fourth round (100th pick overall) of 1984 NFL draft.... Signed by Oilers (July 18, 1984).... Granted free agency (February 1, 1988).... Re-signed by Oilers (August 29, 1988).... Granted roster exemption (August 29-September 5, 1988).... Granted free agency (February 1, 1990).... Re-signed by Oilers (September 4, 1990).... Activated (September 7, 1990).... Granted unconditional free agency (February 1, 1991).... Rights relinquished (April 4, 1991). ... Signed by Kansas City Chiefs (June 4, 1991).
PRO STATISTICS: 1984—Returned 11 kickoffs for 210 yards (19.1 avg.). 1985—Recovered two fumbles. 1987—Recovered one fumble. 1988—Recovered one fumble for seven yards. 1989—Recovered one fumble.

Year Team	G	No.	Yds.	Avg.	TD
		INTERCEPTIONS			
1984— Houston NFL	16	1	2	2.0	0
1985— Houston NFL	16	0	0		0
1986— Houston NFL	16	3	20	6.7	0
1987— Houston NFL	11	1	37	37.0	0
1988— Houston NFL	15	1	23	23.0	0
1989— Houston NFL	16	0	0		0
1990— Houston NFL	16	1	27	27.0	0
Pro totals (7 years)	106	7	109	15.6	0

ALM, JEFF
DT, OILERS

PERSONAL: Born March 31, 1968, at New York. . . . 6-6/269. . . . Full name: Jeffrey Lawrence Alm. **HIGH SCHOOL:** Carl Sandburg (Orland Park, Ill.). **COLLEGE:** Notre Dame (bachelor's degree in marketing, 1990). **TRANSACTIONS/CAREER NOTES:** Selected by Houston Oilers in second round (41st pick overall) of 1990 NFL draft. . . . Signed by Oilers (July 27, 1990). **PLAYING EXPERIENCE:** Houston NFL, 1990. . . . Games: 1990 (16).

ALPHIN, GERALD
WR, SAINTS

PERSONAL: Born May 21, 1964, at Portland, Ore. . . . 6-3/215. **HIGH SCHOOL:** University City (St. Louis). **COLLEGE:** Kansas State. **TRANSACTIONS/CAREER NOTES:** Signed as free agent by Los Angeles Raiders (May 2, 1986). . . . Released by Raiders (August 8, 1986). . . . Signed as free agent by Montreal Alouettes of CFL (September 30, 1986). . . . Released by Alouettes (June 15, 1987). . . . Signed as free agent by Ottawa Rough Riders of CFL (June 30, 1987). . . . Granted free agency (March 1, 1990). . . . Signed by New Orleans Saints (March 30, 1990). . . . On inactive list (September 10, 16, 23, 30; and October 14, 1990).
PRO STATISTICS: CFL: 1986—Fumbled once. 1987—Returned 10 kickoffs for 189 yards, rushed four times for 12 yards, attempted one pass with one completion for 14 yards and fumbled four times. 1988—Rushed once for minus two yards, credited with one 2-point conversion and fumbled twice. 1989—Rushed three times for nine yards and attempted one pass with one completion for 14 yards and a touchdown.

			RECEIVING		
Year	Team	G	No.	Yds.	Avg.	TD
1986— Montreal CFL		6	20	409	20.5	2
1987— Ottawa CFL		14	67	1029	15.4	8
1988— Ottawa CFL		15	64	1307	20.4	5
1989— Ottawa CFL		17	68	1471	21.6	10
1990— New Orleans NFL		11	4	57	14.3	0
CFL totals (4 years)		52	219	4216	19.3	25
NFL totals (1 year)		11	4	57	14.3	0
Pro totals (5 years)		63	223	4273	19.2	25

ALSTON, O'BRIEN
LB, RAIDERS

PERSONAL: Born December 21, 1965, at New Haven, Conn. . . . 6-6/245. . . . Full name: O'Brien Darwin Alston. **HIGH SCHOOL:** Oxon Hill (Md.). **COLLEGE:** Maryland.
TRANSACTIONS/CAREER NOTES: Selected by Indianapolis Colts in 10th round (270th pick overall) of 1988 NFL draft. . . . Signed by Colts (July 13, 1988). . . . On injured reserve with knee injury (October 3, 1989-remainder of season). . . . Granted free agency (February 1, 1990). . . . Re-signed by Colts (August 8, 1990). . . . On injured reserve with knee injury (September 5-October 22, 1990). . . . Transferred to practice squad (October 22-November 29, 1990). . . . On injured reserve with knee injury (November 29, 1990-remainder of season). . . . Granted unconditional free agency (February 1, 1991). . . . Signed by Los Angeles Raiders (offseason, 1991).
PLAYING EXPERIENCE: Indianapolis NFL, 1988 and 1989. . . . Games: 1988 (15), 1989 (4). Total: 19.

ALT, JOHN
OT, CHIEFS

PERSONAL: Born May 30, 1962, at Stuttgart, West Germany. . . . 6-8/296. . . . Full name: John Michael Alt. **HIGH SCHOOL:** Columbia Heights (Minn.). **COLLEGE:** Iowa (degree in business, 1984).
TRANSACTIONS/CAREER NOTES: Selected by Oklahoma Outlaws in third round (46th pick overall) of 1984 USFL draft. . . . Selected by Kansas City Chiefs in first round (21st pick overall) of 1984 NFL draft. . . . Signed by Chiefs (July 18, 1984). . . . On injured reserve with back injury (December 6, 1985-remainder of season). . . . On reserve/physically unable to perform list with back injury (August 18-November 8, 1986). . . . On injured reserve with knee injury (December 9, 1987-remainder of season).
PLAYING EXPERIENCE: Kansas City NFL, 1984-1990. . . . Games: 1984 (15), 1985 (13), 1986 (7), 1987 (9), 1988 (14), 1989 (16), 1990 (16). Total: 90.
RECORDS/HONORS: Named to THE SPORTING NEWS NFL All-Pro team, 1990.

ANDERSEN, MORTEN
PK, SAINTS

PERSONAL: Born August 19, 1960, at Struer, Denmark. . . . 6-2/221. **HIGH SCHOOL:** Davis (Indianapolis). **COLLEGE:** Michigan State. **TRANSACTIONS/CAREER NOTES:** Selected by New Orleans Saints in fourth round (86th pick overall) of 1982 NFL draft. . . . On injured reserve with sprained ankle (September 15-November 20, 1982).
RECORDS/HONORS: Tied NFL record for most field goals, 50 or more yards, game (2), against Philadelphia Eagles (December 11, 1983). . . . Named as place-kicker on THE SPORTING NEWS college All-America team, 1981. . . . Played in Pro Bowl after 1985-1988 and 1990 seasons. . . . Named to THE SPORTING NEWS NFL All-Pro team, 1985-1987.

			PLACE-KICKING			
Year	Team	G	XPM	XPA	FGM	FGA	Pts.
1982— New Orleans NFL		8	6	6	2	5	12
1983— New Orleans NFL		16	37	38	18	24	91
1984— New Orleans NFL		16	34	34	20	27	94

Year	Team		G	XPM	XPA	FGM	FGA	Pts.
				—	PLACE-KICKING	—		
1985— New Orleans NFL		......	16	27	29	31	35	120
1986— New Orleans NFL		......	16	30	30	26	30	108
1987— New Orleans NFL		......	12	37	37	*28	*36	121
1988— New Orleans NFL		......	16	32	33	26	36	110
1989— New Orleans NFL		......	16	44	45	20	29	104
1990— New Orleans NFL		......	16	29	29	21	27	92
Pro totals (9 years)		....	132	276	281	192	249	852

ANDERSON, ALFRED
RB, VIKINGS

PERSONAL: Born August 4, 1961, at Waco, Tex. . . . 6-1/214. . . . Full name: Alfred Anthony Anderson.
HIGH SCHOOL: Richfield (Waco, Tex.).
COLLEGE: Baylor.
TRANSACTIONS/CAREER NOTES: Selected by San Antonio Gunslingers in 1984 USFL territorial draft. . . . Selected by Minnesota Vikings in third round (67th pick overall) of 1984 NFL draft. . . . Signed by Vikings (May 18, 1984). . . . On inactive list (September 9, 1990). . . . On injured reserve with knee injury (September 12-October 15, 1990).
CHAMPIONSHIP GAME EXPERIENCE: Played in NFC championship game after 1987 season.
PRO STATISTICS: 1984—Attempted seven passes with three completions for 95 yards with two touchdowns and one interception and recovered two fumbles. 1986—Attempted two passes with one completion for 17 yards and recovered two fumbles. 1989—Recovered one fumble.

Year	Team		G	Att.	Yds.	Avg.	TD	No.	Yds.	Avg.	TD	No.	Yds.	Avg.	TD	TD	Pts.	F.
				—	RUSHING	—		—	RECEIVING	—		—	KICKOFF RETURNS	—		—	TOTAL	—
1984— Minnesota NFL		......	16	201	773	3.8	2	17	102	6.0	1	30	639	21.3	0	3	18	8
1985— Minnesota NFL		......	12	50	121	2.4	4	16	175	10.9	1	0	0		0	5	30	0
1986— Minnesota NFL		......	16	83	347	4.2	2	17	179	10.5	2	3	38	12.7	0	4	24	3
1987— Minnesota NFL		......	10	68	319	4.7	2	7	69	9.9	0	0	0		0	2	12	1
1988— Minnesota NFL		......	16	87	300	3.4	7	23	242	10.5	1	0	0		0	8	48	3
1989— Minnesota NFL		......	11	52	189	3.6	2	20	193	9.7	0	5	75	15.0	0	2	12	3
1990— Minnesota NFL		......	11	59	207	3.5	2	13	80	6.2	0	0	0		0	2	12	1
NFL totals (7 years)		......	92	600	2256	3.8	21	113	1040	9.2	5	38	752	19.8	0	26	156	19

ANDERSON, EDDIE
S, RAIDERS

PERSONAL: Born July 22, 1963, at Warner Robins, Ga. . . . 6-1/205. . . . Full name: Eddie Lee Anderson Jr.
HIGH SCHOOL: Warner Robins (Ga.).
COLLEGE: Fort Valley State College (Ga.).
TRANSACTIONS/CAREER NOTES: Selected by Seattle Seahawks in sixth round (153rd pick overall) of 1986 NFL draft. . . . Signed by Seahawks (July 16, 1986). . . . On injured reserve with back injury (September 11-November 21, 1986). . . . Released by Seahawks (September 1, 1987). . . . Signed as free agent replacement player by Los Angeles Raiders (September 24, 1987).
CHAMPIONSHIP GAME EXPERIENCE: Played in AFC championship game after 1990 season.
PRO STATISTICS: 1987—Recovered one fumble. 1990—Recovered one fumble.

Year	Team		G	No.	Yds.	Avg.	TD
				—	INTERCEPTIONS	—	
1986— Seattle NFL		....	5	0	0		0
1987— L.A. Raiders NFL		......	13	1	58	58.0	0
1988— L.A. Raiders NFL		......	16	2	-6	-3.0	0
1989— L.A. Raiders NFL		......	15	5	*233	46.6	*2
1990— L.A. Raiders NFL		......	16	3	49	16.3	0
Pro totals (5 years)		....	65	11	334	30.4	2

ANDERSON, GARY
PK, STEELERS

PERSONAL: Born July 16, 1959, at Parys, Orange Free State, South Africa. . . . 5-11/184. . . . Full name: Gary Allan Anderson. . . . Son of Rev. Douglas Anderson, former pro soccer player in England.
HIGH SCHOOL: Brettonwood (Durban, South Africa).
COLLEGE: Syracuse (bachelor of science degree in management and accounting, 1982).
TRANSACTIONS/CAREER NOTES: Selected by Buffalo Bills in seventh round (171st pick overall) of 1982 NFL draft. . . . Released by Bills (September 6, 1982). . . . Awarded on waivers to Pittsburgh Steelers (September 7, 1982).
CHAMPIONSHIP GAME EXPERIENCE: Played in AFC championship game after 1984 season.
RECORDS/HONORS: Played in Pro Bowl after 1983 and 1985 seasons.

Year	Team		G	XPM	XPA	FGM	FGA	Pts.
				—	PLACE-KICKING	—		
1982— Pittsburgh NFL		....	9	22	22	10	12	52
1983— Pittsburgh NFL		....	16	38	39	27	31	119
1984— Pittsburgh NFL		....	16	45	45	24	32	117
1985— Pittsburgh NFL		....	16	40	40	*33	*42	139
1986— Pittsburgh NFL		....	16	32	32	21	32	95
1987— Pittsburgh NFL		....	12	21	21	22	27	87
1988— Pittsburgh NFL		....	16	34	35	28	36	118
1989— Pittsburgh NFL		....	16	28	28	21	30	91
1990— Pittsburgh NFL		....	16	32	32	20	25	92
Pro totals (9 years)		....	133	292	294	206	267	910

ANDERSON, GARY
RB, BUCCANEERS

PERSONAL: Born April 18, 1961, at Columbia, Mo. . . . 6-1/190. . . . Full name: Gary Wayne Anderson.
HIGH SCHOOL: Hickman (Columbia, Mo.).
COLLEGE: Arkansas.
TRANSACTIONS/CAREER NOTES: Selected by New Jersey Generals in first round (fifth pick overall) of 1983 USFL draft. . . . Selected by San Diego Chargers in first round (20th pick overall) of 1983 NFL draft. . . . USFL rights traded by New Jersey Generals to Tampa Bay Bandits for first-round pick in 1984 draft (May 9, 1983). . . . Signed by Bandits (May 9, 1983). . . . Granted roster exemption (May 9-May 14, 1983). . . . Released by Bandits (September 27, 1985). . . . Signed by San Diego Chargers (September 30, 1985). . . . Granted roster exemption (September 30-October 5, 1985). . . . Granted free agency (February 1, 1989). . . . On reserve/unsigned list (entire 1989 season). . . . Re-signed by Chargers and traded to Tampa Bay Buccaneers for third-round pick in 1990 NFL draft and conditional third-round pick in 1991 NFL draft (April 21, 1990).
RECORDS/HONORS: Named as running back on THE SPORTING NEWS USFL All-Star team, 1985. . . . Played in Pro Bowl after 1986 season.
PRO STATISTICS: USFL: 1983—Attempted one pass with no completions and recovered one fumble. 1984—Attempted three passes with two completions for 44 yards, one touchdown and one interception and recovered two fumbles. 1985—Attempted three passes with two completions for three yards, a touchdown and recovered five fumbles. . . . NFL: 1985—Recovered three fumbles. 1986—Attempted one pass with one completion for four yards and a touchdown and recovered two fumbles. 1987—Recovered one fumble. 1988—Recovered three fumbles.

Year — Team	G	Att.	RUSHING Yds.	Avg.	TD	No.	RECEIVING Yds.	Avg.	TD	No.	PUNT RETURNS Yds.	Avg.	TD	No.	KICKOFF RETURNS Yds.	Avg.	TD	TOTALS TD	Pts.	F.
1983— Tampa Bay USFL	8	97	516	5.3	4	29	347	12.0	0	2	-1	-.5	0	3	47	15.7	0	4	24	7
1984— Tampa Bay USFL	18	268	1008	3.8	*19	66	682	10.3	2	4	22	5.5	0	0	0		0	*21	126	8
1985— Tampa Bay USFL	18	276	1207	4.4	16	72	678	9.4	4	0	0		0	0	2		0	20	120	11
1985— San Diego NFL	12	116	429	3.7	4	35	422	12.1	2	0	0		0	13	302	23.2	1	7	42	5
1986— San Diego NFL	16	127	442	3.5	1	80	871	10.9	8	25	227	9.1	0	24	482	20.1	0	9	54	5
1987— San Diego NFL	12	80	260	3.3	3	47	503	10.7	2	0	0		0	22	433	19.7	0	5	30	4
1988— San Diego NFL	14	225	1119	5.0	3	32	182	5.7	0	0	0		0	0	0		0	3	18	5
1990— Tampa Bay NFL	16	166	646	3.9	3	38	464	12.2	2	0	0		0	6	123	20.5	0	5	30	7
USFL totals (3 years)	44	641	2731	4.3	39	167	1707	10.2	6	6	21	3.5	0	3	49	16.3	0	45	270	26
NFL totals (5 years)	70	714	2896	4.1	14	232	2442	10.5	14	25	227	9.1	0	65	1340	20.6	1	29	174	26
Pro totals (8 years)	114	1355	5627	4.2	53	399	4149	10.4	20	31	248	8.0	0	68	1389	20.4	1	74	444	52

ANDERSON, JESSE
TE, BUCCANEERS

PERSONAL: Born July 26, 1966, at West Point, Miss. . . . 6-2/245. . . . Full name: Jesse Lemond Anderson.
HIGH SCHOOL: West Point (Miss.).
COLLEGE: Mississippi State.
TRANSACTIONS/CAREER NOTES: Selected by Tampa Bay Buccaneers in fourth round (87th pick overall) of 1990 NFL draft. . . . Signed by Buccaneers (July 20, 1990).

Year — Team	G	RECEIVING No.	Yds.	Avg.	TD
1990— Tampa Bay NFL	16	5	77	15.4	0
Pro totals (1 year)	16	5	77	15.4	0

ANDERSON, NEAL
RB, BEARS

PERSONAL: Born August 14, 1964, at Graceville, Fla. . . . 5-11/210. . . . Full name: Charles Neal Anderson.
HIGH SCHOOL: Graceville (Fla.).
COLLEGE: Florida (degree in public relations, 1986).
TRANSACTIONS/CAREER NOTES: Selected by Tampa Bay Bandits in 1986 USFL territorial draft. . . . Selected by Chicago Bears in first round (27th pick overall) of 1986 NFL draft. . . . Signed by Bears (August 15, 1986). . . . Granted free agency (February 1, 1990). . . . Re-signed by Bears (March 23, 1990).
CHAMPIONSHIP GAME EXPERIENCE: Played in NFC championship game after 1988 season.
RECORDS/HONORS: Played in Pro Bowl after 1988 season. . . . Named to play in Pro Bowl after 1989 and 1990 seasons; replaced due to injury after 1989 season by Brent Fullwood; replaced due to injury after 1990 season by Emmitt Smith.
PRO STATISTICS: 1986—Returned four kickoffs for 26 yards. 1988—Attempted one pass with no completions and recovered two fumbles.

Year — Team	G	Att.	RUSHING Yds.	Avg.	TD	No.	RECEIVING Yds.	Avg.	TD	TOTAL TD	Pts.	F.
1986— Chicago NFL	14	35	146	4.2	0	4	80	20.0	1	1	6	1
1987— Chicago NFL	11	129	586	4.5	3	47	467	9.9	3	6	36	2
1988— Chicago NFL	16	249	1106	4.4	12	39	371	9.5	0	12	72	8
1989— Chicago NFL	16	274	1275	4.7	11	50	434	8.7	4	15	90	5
1990— Chicago NFL	15	260	1078	4.2	10	42	484	11.5	3	13	78	2
Pro totals (5 years)	72	947	4191	4.4	36	182	1836	10.1	11	47	282	18

ANDERSON, O.J.
RB, GIANTS

PERSONAL: Born January 19, 1957, at West Palm Beach, Fla. . . . 6-2/225. . . . Full name: Ottis Jerome Anderson. . . . Step-brother of Mike Taliferro, defensive lineman with Denver Gold (USFL), 1985.
HIGH SCHOOL: Forest Hill (West Palm Beach, Fla.).
COLLEGE: Miami, Fla. (degree in physical education).
TRANSACTIONS/CAREER NOTES: Selected by St. Louis Cardinals in first round (eighth pick overall) of 1979 NFL draft. . . . Traded

by Cardinals to New York Giants for second- and seventh-round picks in 1987 draft (October 8, 1986).... Granted unconditional free agency (February 1, 1989).... Received no qualifying offer (April 15, 1989).... Re-signed by Giants (April 21, 1989).

CHAMPIONSHIP GAME EXPERIENCE: Played in NFC championship game after 1986 and 1990 seasons.... Played in Super Bowl XXI after 1986 season and Super Bowl XXV after 1990 season.

RECORDS/HONORS: Tied NFL record for most 100-yard games by rookie, season (9), 1979.... Played in Pro Bowl after 1979 and 1980 seasons.... Named THE SPORTING NEWS NFC Player of the Year, 1979.... Named THE SPORTING NEWS NFC Rookie of the Year, 1979.... Named to THE SPORTING NEWS NFC All-Star team, 1979.

PRO STATISTICS: 1979—Attempted one pass with no completions and recovered one fumble. 1980—Recovered four fumbles. 1981—Recovered three fumbles. 1982—Recovered one fumble. 1983—Recovered three fumbles. 1984—Recovered one fumble. 1985—Recovered one fumble. 1988—Recovered one fumble for five yards. 1990—Recovered two fumbles and fumbled once for 22 yards.

| | | | RUSHING | | | | RECEIVING | | | | TOTAL | |
Year Team	G	Att.	Yds.	Avg.	TD	No.	Yds.	Avg.	TD	TD	Pts.	F.
1979— St. Louis NFL	16	331	1605	4.9	8	41	308	7.5	2	10	60	10
1980— St. Louis NFL	16	301	1352	4.5	9	36	308	8.6	0	9	54	5
1981— St. Louis NFL	16	328	1376	4.2	9	51	387	7.6	0	9	54	13
1982— St. Louis NFL	8	145	587	4.1	3	14	106	7.6	0	3	18	2
1983— St. Louis NFL	15	296	1270	4.3	5	54	459	8.5	1	6	36	10
1984— St. Louis NFL	15	289	1174	4.1	6	70	611	8.7	2	8	48	8
1985— St. Louis NFL	9	117	479	4.1	4	23	225	9.8	0	4	24	3
1986— St.L. (4)-N.Y. Giants (8) NFL	12	75	237	3.2	3	19	137	7.2	0	3	18	2
1987— N.Y. Giants NFL	4	2	6	3.0	0	2	16	8.0	0	0	0	0
1988— N.Y. Giants NFL	16	65	208	3.2	8	9	57	6.3	0	8	48	0
1989— N.Y. Giants NFL	16	325	1023	3.2	14	28	268	9.6	0	14	84	2
1990— N.Y. Giants NFL	16	225	784	3.5	11	18	139	7.7	0	11	66	1
Pro totals (12 years)	159	2499	10101	4.0	80	365	3021	8.3	5	85	510	56

ANDERSON, WILLIE
WR, RAMS

PERSONAL: Born March 7, 1965, at Philadelphia.... 6-0/175.... Full name: Willie Lee Anderson Jr.
HIGH SCHOOL: Paulsboro (N.J.).
COLLEGE: UCLA.

TRANSACTIONS/CAREER NOTES: Selected by Los Angeles Rams in second round (46th pick overall) of 1988 NFL draft.... Signed by Rams (July 17, 1988).

CHAMPIONSHIP GAME EXPERIENCE: Played in NFC championship game after 1989 season.

RECORDS/HONORS: Established NFL record for pass reception yards, game (336), against New Orleans Saints (November 26, 1989).

PRO STATISTICS: 1989—Rushed once for minus one yard. 1990—Rushed once for 13 yards and recovered one fumble.

| | | RECEIVING | | | |
Year Team	G	No.	Yds.	Avg.	TD
1988— L.A. Rams NFL	16	11	319	29.0	0
1989— L.A. Rams NFL	16	44	1146	*26.0	5
1990— L.A. Rams NFL	16	51	1097	*21.5	4
Pro totals (3 years)	48	106	2562	24.2	9

ANDOLSEK, ERIC
G, LIONS

PERSONAL: Born August 22, 1966, at Thibodaux, La.... 6-2/286.... Full name: Eric Thomas Andolsek.
HIGH SCHOOL: Thibodaux (La.).
COLLEGE: Louisiana State.

TRANSACTIONS/CAREER NOTES: Selected by Detroit Lions in fifth round (111th pick overall) of 1988 NFL draft.... Signed by Lions (July 16, 1988).

PLAYING EXPERIENCE: Detroit NFL, 1988-1990.... Games: 1988 (13), 1989 (16), 1990 (16). Total: 45.

PRO STATISTICS: 1988—Returned one kickoff for three yards. 1990—Returned one kickoff for 12 yards and recovered one fumble.

ANDREWS, RICKY
LB, SEAHAWKS

PERSONAL: Born April 14, 1966, at Western Samoa.... 6-2/236.... Full name: Richard Guy Andrews.
HIGH SCHOOL: University (Mililani, Hawaii).
COLLEGE: Washington.

TRANSACTIONS/CAREER NOTES: Selected by San Diego Chargers in 10th round (260th pick overall) of 1989 NFL draft.... Signed by Chargers (July 24, 1989).... Released by Chargers (September 4, 1989).... Re-signed by Chargers to developmental squad (September 7, 1989).... Released by Chargers (November 8, 1989).... Signed by Seattle Seahawks (March 3, 1990). ... On injured reserve with shoulder injury (December 23, 1990-remainder of season).

PLAYING EXPERIENCE: Seattle NFL, 1990.... Games: 1990 (15).

ANNO, SAM
LB, BUCCANEERS

PERSONAL: Born January 26, 1965, at Silver Springs, Md.... 6-2/235... Name pronounced AH-no. ... Last name originally was Aono.
HIGH SCHOOL: Santa Monica (Calif.).
COLLEGE: Southern California.

TRANSACTIONS/CAREER NOTES: Signed as free agent by Los Angeles Rams (May 14, 1987).... Released by Rams (September 7,

1987).... Re-signed by Rams (September 8, 1987).... Released by Rams (November 3, 1987).... Signed as free agent by Minnesota Vikings (November 18, 1987).... Released by Vikings (August 30, 1988).... Re-signed by Vikings (September 17, 1988).... Released by Vikings (December 17, 1988).... Re-signed by Vikings (December 21, 1988).... Granted unconditional free agency (February 1, 1989).... Signed by Tampa Bay Buccaneers (March 27, 1989).

PLAYING EXPERIENCE: Los Angeles Rams (3)-Minnesota (6) NFL, 1987; Minnesota NFL, 1988; Tampa Bay NFL, 1989 and 1990. ...Games: 1987 (9), 1988 (13), 1989 (16), 1990 (16). Total: 54.

CHAMPIONSHIP GAME EXPERIENCE: Played in NFC championship game after 1987 season.

ANTHONY, TERRY
WR, BUCCANEERS

PERSONAL: Born July 26, 1966, at Daytona Beach, Fla.... 6-0/200.... Full name: Terrence Anthony.
HIGH SCHOOL: Mainland (Daytona Beach, Fla.).
COLLEGE: Florida State.
TRANSACTIONS/CAREER NOTES: Selected by Tampa Bay Buccaneers in 11th round (281st pick overall) of 1990 NFL draft.... Signed by Buccaneers (July 9, 1990).... Released by Buccaneers (September 2, 1990).... Re-signed by Buccaneers to practice squad (November 14, 1990).... Activated (November 16, 1990).... Released by Buccaneers (November 23, 1990).... Re-signed by Buccaneers to practice squad (November 27, 1990).... On practice squad (November 27, 1990-remainder of season).
PLAYING EXPERIENCE: Tampa Bay NFL, 1990.... Games: 1990 (1).

ARCHAMBEAU, LESTER
DE, PACKERS

PERSONAL: Born June 27, 1967, at Montville, N.J.... 6-5/271.... Full name: Lester Milward Archambeau.
HIGH SCHOOL: Montville (N.J.).
COLLEGE: Stanford (degree in industrial engineering).
TRANSACTIONS/CAREER NOTES: Selected by Green Bay Packers in seventh round (186th pick overall) of 1990 NFL draft.... Signed by Packers (July 22, 1990).... On injured reserve with back injury (October 6, 1990-remainder of season).
PLAYING EXPERIENCE: Green Bay NFL, 1990.... Games: 1990 (4).

ARD, BILLY
G, PACKERS

PERSONAL: Born March 12, 1959, at East Orange, N.J.... 6-3/273.... Full name: William Donovan Ard.
HIGH SCHOOL: Watchung (N.J.).
COLLEGE: Wake Forest.
TRANSACTIONS/CAREER NOTES: Selected by New York Giants in eighth round (221st pick overall) of 1981 NFL draft.... On injured reserve with knee injury (December 11, 1984-remainder of season).... Granted unconditional free agency (February 1, 1989).... Signed by Green Bay Packers (February 27, 1989).
PLAYING EXPERIENCE: New York Giants NFL, 1981-1988; Green Bay NFL, 1989 and 1990.... Games: 1981 (13), 1982 (9), 1983 (16), 1984 (15), 1985 (16), 1986 (16), 1987 (12), 1988 (16), 1989 (15), 1990 (15). Total: 143.
CHAMPIONSHIP GAME EXPERIENCE: Played in NFC championship game after 1986 season.... Played in Super Bowl XXI after 1986 season.
RECORDS/HONORS: Named as guard on THE SPORTING NEWS college All-America team, 1980.
PRO STATISTICS: 1981—Recovered one fumble. 1986—Recovered one fumble for one yard.

ARMSTRONG, BRUCE
OT, PATRIOTS

PERSONAL: Born September 7, 1965, at Miami.... 6-4/284.
HIGH SCHOOL: Central (Miami).
COLLEGE: Louisville.
TRANSACTIONS/CAREER NOTES: Selected by New England Patriots in first round (23rd pick overall) of 1987 NFL draft.... Signed by Patriots (July 23, 1987).
PLAYING EXPERIENCE: New England NFL, 1987-1990.... Games: 1987 (12), 1988 (16), 1989 (16), 1990 (16). Total: 60.
RECORDS/HONORS: Named to THE SPORTING NEWS NFL All-Pro team, 1988.... Played in Pro Bowl after 1990 season.
PRO STATISTICS: 1990—Recovered two fumbles for four yards.

ARMSTRONG, TRACE
DE, BEARS

PERSONAL: Born October 5, 1965, at Bethesda, Md.... 6-4/259.... Full name: Raymond Lester Armstrong.
HIGH SCHOOL: John Carroll (Birmingham, Ala.).
COLLEGE: Arizona State, then Florida (bachelor of science degree in psychology, 1989).
TRANSACTIONS/CAREER NOTES: Selected by Chicago Bears in first round (12th pick overall) of 1989 NFL draft.... Signed by Bears (August 18, 1989).
PLAYING EXPERIENCE: Chicago NFL, 1989 and 1990.... Games: 1989 (15), 1990 (16). Total: 31.
RECORDS/HONORS: Named as defensive lineman on THE SPORTING NEWS college All-America team, 1988.
PRO STATISTICS: 1989—Recovered one fumble. 1990—Recovered two fumbles.

ARNOLD, JIM
P, LIONS

PERSONAL: Born January 31, 1961, at Dalton, Ga.... 6-3/211.... Full name: James Edward Arnold.
HIGH SCHOOL: Dalton (Ga.).
COLLEGE: Vanderbilt.
TRANSACTIONS/CAREER NOTES: Selected by Kansas City Chiefs in fifth round (119th pick overall) of 1983 NFL draft.... Released by Chiefs (August 26, 1986).... Signed as free agent by Detroit Lions (November 5, 1986).... Released by Lions (Sep-

tember 7, 1987).... Re-signed by Lions (September 14, 1987).
RECORDS/HONORS: Led NFL in punting yards with 4,397, 1984.... Led NFL in net punting average with 39.6, 1987.... Led NFL in punting yards with 4,110, 1988.... Named as punter on THE SPORTING NEWS college All-America team, 1982.... Played in Pro Bowl after 1987 and 1988 seasons.... Named to THE SPORTING NEWS NFL All-Pro team, 1987.
PRO STATISTICS: 1984—Rushed once for no yards and recovered two fumbles and fumbled once for minus nine yards. 1988—Attempted one pass with no completions.

		— PUNTING—		
Year Team	G	No.	Avg.	Blk.
1983— Kansas City NFL	16	93	39.9	0
1984— Kansas City NFL	16	*98	*44.9	0
1985— Kansas City NFL	16	*93	41.2	*2
1986— Detroit NFL	7	36	42.6	1
1987— Detroit NFL	11	46	43.6	0
1988— Detroit NFL	16	97	42.4	0
1989— Detroit NFL	16	82	43.1	1
1990— Detroit NFL	16	63	40.6	1
Pro totals (8 years)	114	608	42.3	5

ASHE, RICHARD
TE, GIANTS

PERSONAL: Born March 14, 1967, at Chicago.... 6-5/252.... Full name: Richard Anthony Ashe.
HIGH SCHOOL: Birmingham (Moreno Valley, Calif.).
COLLEGE: Humboldt State (Calif.).
TRANSACTIONS/CAREER NOTES: Signed as free agent by Los Angeles Rams (offseason, 1989).... Released by Rams (September 5, 1989).... Re-signed by Rams to developmental squad (September 6, 1989).... Released by Rams (January 29, 1990).... Re-signed by Rams (March 9, 1990).... On inactive list (September 16, 1990).... On injured reserve with foot injury (September 21-October 18, 1990).... Released by Rams (October 18, 1990).... Re-signed by Rams to practice squad (October 18, 1990).... Signed as free agent by New York Giants (April, 1991).
PLAYING EXPERIENCE: Los Angeles Rams NFL, 1990.... Games: 1990 (1).

ATKINS, GENE
S, SAINTS

PERSONAL: Born November 22, 1964, at Tallahassee, Fla.... 6-1/200.... Full name: Gene Reynard Atkins.
HIGH SCHOOL: James S. Rickards (Tallahassee, Fla.).
COLLEGE: Florida A&M.
TRANSACTIONS/CAREER NOTES: Selected by New Orleans Saints in seventh round (179th pick overall) of 1987 NFL draft.... Signed by Saints (July 25, 1987).... On injured reserve with eye injury (September 7-October 1, 1987).... Crossed picket line during players' strike (October 1, 1987).... Granted free agency (February 1, 1990).... Re-signed by Saints (July 15, 1990).
PRO STATISTICS: 1987—Recovered one fumble. 1988—Recovered two fumbles. 1989—Recovered two fumbles. 1990—Recovered three fumbles.

Year Team	G	— INTERCEPTIONS—				— KICKOFF RETURNS—				— TOTAL —		
		No.	Yds.	Avg.	TD	No.	Yds.	Avg.	TD	TD	Pts.	F.
1987— New Orleans NFL	13	3	12	4.0	0	0	0		0	0	0	0
1988— New Orleans NFL	16	4	42	10.5	0	20	424	21.2	0	0	0	1
1989— New Orleans NFL	14	1	-2	-2.0	0	12	245	20.4	0	0	0	1
1990— New Orleans NFL	16	2	15	7.5	0	19	471	24.8	0	0	0	1
Pro totals (4 years)	59	10	67	6.7	0	51	1140	22.4	0	0	0	3

ATWATER, STEVE
S, BRONCOS

PERSONAL: Born October 28, 1966, at Chicago.... 6-3/231.... Full name: Stephen Dennis Atwater.... Cousin of Mark Ingram, wide receiver with New York Giants.
HIGH SCHOOL: Lutheran North (St. Louis).
COLLEGE: Arkansas (bachelor of science degree in business administration, 1989).
TRANSACTIONS/CAREER NOTES: Selected by Denver Broncos in first round (20th pick overall) of 1989 NFL draft.... Signed by Broncos (August 1, 1989).
CHAMPIONSHIP GAME EXPERIENCE: Played in AFC championship game after 1989 season.... Played in Super Bowl XXIV after 1989 season.
RECORDS/HONORS: Played in Pro Bowl after 1990 season.
PRO STATISTICS: 1989—Recovered one fumble for 29 yards. 1990—Returned one kickoff for no yards.

		— INTERCEPTIONS—			
Year Team	G	No.	Yds.	Avg.	TD
1989— Denver NFL	16	3	34	11.3	0
1990— Denver NFL	15	2	32	16.0	0
Pro totals (2 years)	31	5	66	13.2	0

AWALT, ROB
TE, COWBOYS

PERSONAL: Born April 9, 1964, at Landsthul, West Germany.... 6-5/238.... Full name: Robert Mitchell Awalt.... Name pronounced AY-walt.
HIGH SCHOOL: Valley (Sacramento, Calif.).
COLLEGE: Nevada at Reno (did not play football), then Sacramento City College (Calif.), then San Diego State.
TRANSACTIONS/CAREER NOTES: Selected by St. Louis Cardinals in third round (62nd pick overall) of 1987 NFL draft.... Signed

by Cardinals (July 31, 1987).... Franchise transferred to Phoenix (March 15, 1988).... Traded by Phoenix Cardinals to Dallas Cowboys for eighth-round pick in 1991 NFL draft (August 29, 1990).... On inactive list (December 16, 23 and 30, 1990).
RECORDS/HONORS: Named THE SPORTING NEWS NFL Rookie of the Year, 1987.
PRO STATISTICS: 1987—Rushed twice for minus nine yards and recovered one fumble. 1988—Fumbled once. 1989—Had only pass attempt intercepted. 1990—Fumbled once.

Year Team	G	No.	Yds.	Avg.	TD
			RECEIVING		
1987— St. Louis NFL	12	42	526	12.5	6
1988— Phoenix NFL	16	39	454	11.6	4
1989— Phoenix NFL	16	33	360	10.9	0
1990— Dallas NFL	13	13	133	10.2	0
Pro totals (4 years)	57	127	1473	11.6	10

BAAB, MIKE
C, BROWNS

PERSONAL: Born December 6, 1959, at Fort Worth, Tex.... 6-4/275.... Full name: Micheal James Baab.
HIGH SCHOOL: Trinity (Euless, Tex.).
COLLEGE: Tarrant County Junior College, then Austin Community College (Minn.), then Texas (bachelor of science degree in political science).
TRANSACTIONS/CAREER NOTES: Selected by Cleveland Browns in fifth round (115th pick overall) of 1982 NFL draft.... Traded by Browns to New England Patriots for fifth-round pick in 1989 draft (August 29, 1988).... Granted unconditional free agency (February 1, 1990).... Signed by Cleveland Browns (March 6, 1990).
PLAYING EXPERIENCE: Cleveland NFL, 1982-1987; New England NFL, 1988 and 1989; Cleveland NFL, 1990.... Games: 1982 (7), 1983 (15), 1984 (16), 1985 (16), 1986 (16), 1987 (12), 1988 (15), 1989 (16), 1990 (16). Total: 129.
CHAMPIONSHIP GAME EXPERIENCE: Played in AFC championship game after 1986 and 1987 seasons.
PRO STATISTICS: 1984—Fumbled once for minus 11 yards. 1985—Rushed once for no yards and fumbled once for minus two yards. 1989—Recovered one fumble.

BAHR, MATT
PK, GIANTS

PERSONAL: Born July 6, 1956, at Philadelphia.... 5-10/175.... Full name: Matthew David Bahr. ... Brother of Chris Bahr, placekicker with Cincinnati Bengals, Oakland-Los Angeles Raiders and San Diego Chargers, 1976-1989.
HIGH SCHOOL: Neshaminy Langhorne (Langhorne, Pa.).
COLLEGE: Penn State (bachelor of science degree in electrical engineering, 1979).
TRANSACTIONS/CAREER NOTES: Played with Colorado Caribous and Tulsa Roughnecks of North American Soccer League, 1978 (26 games, 3 assists).... Selected by Pittsburgh Steelers in sixth round (165th pick overall) of 1979 NFL draft.... Released by Steelers (August 31, 1981).... Signed as free agent by San Francisco 49ers (September 8, 1981).... Traded by 49ers to Cleveland Browns for ninth-round pick in 1983 draft (October 6, 1981).... On injured reserve with knee injury (November 26, 1986-remainder of season).... On reserve/physically unable to perform list with knee injury (September 1-December 11, 1987).... Released by Browns (September 3, 1990).... Signed by New York Giants (September 28, 1990).
CHAMPIONSHIP GAME EXPERIENCE: Played in AFC championship game after 1979, 1987 and 1989 seasons.... Played in NFC championship game after 1990 season.... Played in Super Bowl XIV after 1979 season and Super Bowl XXV after 1990 season.
PRO STATISTICS: 1988—Rushed once for minus eight yards.

Year Team	G	XPM	XPA	FGM	FGA	Pts.
			PLACE-KICKING			
1979— Pittsburgh NFL	16	*50	52	18	30	104
1980— Pittsburgh NFL	16	39	42	19	28	96
1981— SF (4)-Cle (11) NFL	15	34	34	15	26	79
1982— Cleveland NFL	9	17	17	7	15	38
1983— Cleveland NFL	16	38	40	21	24	101
1984— Cleveland NFL	16	25	25	24	32	97
1985— Cleveland NFL	16	35	35	14	18	77
1986— Cleveland NFL	12	30	30	20	26	90
1987— Cleveland NFL	3	9	10	4	5	21
1988— Cleveland NFL	16	32	33	24	29	104
1989— Cleveland NFL	16	40	40	16	24	88
1990— N.Y. Giants NFL	13	29	30	17	23	80
Pro totals (12 years)	164	378	388	199	280	975

BAILEY, CARLTON
LB, BILLS

PERSONAL: Born December 15, 1964, at Baltimore.... 6-2/237.... Full name: Carlton Wilson Bailey.
HIGH SCHOOL: Woodlawn (Baltimore).
COLLEGE: North Carolina (bachelor of arts degree in sociology, 1988).
TRANSACTIONS/CAREER NOTES: Selected by Buffalo Bills in ninth round (235th pick overall) of 1988 NFL draft.... Signed by Bills (July 15, 1988).... On injured reserve with knee injury (August 30-November 14, 1988).
PLAYING EXPERIENCE: Buffalo NFL, 1988-1990.... Games: 1988 (6), 1989 (16), 1990 (16). Total: 38.
CHAMPIONSHIP GAME EXPERIENCE: Played in AFC championship game after 1988 and 1990 seasons.... Played in Super Bowl XXV after 1990 season.
PRO STATISTICS: 1989—Intercepted one pass for 16 yards. 1990—Recovered one fumble.

BAILEY, DAVID
DE, CHIEFS

PERSONAL: Born September 3, 1965, at Coatesville, Pa. . . . 6-4/225.
HIGH SCHOOL: U.S. Grant (Oklahoma City).
COLLEGE: Oklahoma State.
TRANSACTIONS/CAREER NOTES: Signed as free agent by Philadelphia Eagles (April, 1989). . . .
Released by Eagles (September 5, 1989). . . . Signed by Eagles to developmental squad (September 6, 1989). . . . Released by Eagles (January 9, 1990). . . . Re-signed by Eagles (February 13, 1990). . . . On inactive list (December 9, 1990). . . . Released by Eagles (December 21, 1990). . . . Signed by WLAF (January 31, 1991). . . . Selected by San Antonio Riders in second round (20th defensive lineman) of 1991 WLAF positional draft. . . . Signed by Kansas City Chiefs (June 14, 1991).
PLAYING EXPERIENCE: Philadelphia NFL, 1990; San Antonio WLAF, 1991. . . . Games: 1990 (13), 1991 (10). Total NFL: 13. Total Pro: 23.

BAILEY, EDWIN
G, SEAHAWKS

PERSONAL: Born May 15, 1959, at Savannah, Ga. . . . 6-4/279. . . . Full name: Edwin Raymond Bailey.
HIGH SCHOOL: Tompkins (Savannah, Ga.).
COLLEGE: South Carolina State.
TRANSACTIONS/CAREER NOTES: Selected by Seattle Seahawks in fifth round (114th pick overall) of 1981 NFL draft. . . . On injured reserve with knee injury (November 10-December 8, 1984). . . . On injured reserve with knee injury (September 11-October 11, 1986). . . . On injured reserve with knee injury (November 28, 1990-remainder of season).
PLAYING EXPERIENCE: Seattle NFL, 1981-1990. . . . Games: 1981 (16), 1982 (9), 1983 (16), 1984 (12), 1985 (16), 1986 (12), 1987 (12), 1988 (16), 1989 (16), 1990 (11). Total: 136.
CHAMPIONSHIP GAME EXPERIENCE: Played in AFC championship game after 1983 season.
PRO STATISTICS: 1982—Recovered one fumble. 1986—Caught one pass for three yards. 1988—Recovered two fumbles. 1989—Recovered one fumble. 1990—Recovered two fumbles for three yards.

BAILEY, JOHNNY
RB, BEARS

PERSONAL: Born March 17, 1967, at Houston. . . . 5-8/180. . . . Full name: Johnny Lee Bailey.
HIGH SCHOOL: Jack Yates (Houston).
COLLEGE: Texas A&I.
TRANSACTIONS/CAREER NOTES: Selected by Chicago Bears in ninth round (228th pick overall) of 1990 NFL draft. . . . Signed by Bears (July 24, 1990).
PRO STATISTICS: 1990—Attempted one pass with one completion for 22 yards and recovered four fumbles.

		RUSHING				PUNT RETURNS				KICKOFF RETURNS				TOTAL		
Year Team	G	Att.	Yds.	Avg.	TD	No.	Yds.	Avg.	TD	No.	Yds.	Avg.	TD	TD	Pts.	F.
1990—Chicago NFL	16	26	86	3.3	0	36	399	11.1	1	23	363	15.8	0	1	6	8
NFL totals (1 year)	16	26	86	3.3	0	36	399	11.1	1	23	363	15.8	0	1	6	8

BAILEY, STACEY
WR, RAMS

PERSONAL: Born February 10, 1960, at San Rafael, Calif. . . . 6-1/163. . . . Full name: Stacey Dwayne Bailey.
HIGH SCHOOL: Terra Linda (San Rafael, Calif.).
COLLEGE: San Jose State.
TRANSACTIONS/CAREER NOTES: Selected by Atlanta Falcons in third round (63rd pick overall) of 1982 NFL draft. . . . On inactive list (September 12 and 19, 1982). . . . On injured reserve with hamstring injury (September 2-November 1, 1986). . . . On injured reserve with shoulder injury (October 29-December 10, 1988). . . . Granted unconditional free agency (February 1, 1990). . . . Re-signed by Falcons (June 28, 1990). . . . Released by Falcons (September 3, 1990). . . . Re-signed by Falcons (September 4, 1990). . . . On injured reserve with ankle injury (October 6-October 31, 1990). . . . Transferred to practice squad (October 31, 1990). . . . Activated after clearing procedural recall waivers (November 2, 1990). . . . On inactive list (November 12 and 19, 1990). . . . On injured reserve (November 23-December 19, 1990). . . . Transferred to practice squad (December 19, 1990-remainder of season). . . . Granted unconditional free agency (February 1, 1991). . . . Signed as free agent by Los Angeles Rams after Falcons relinquished rights (April 15, 1991).
PRO STATISTICS: 1982—Fumbled once. 1983—Rushed twice for minus five yards, recovered one fumble and fumbled once. 1984—Fumbled once. 1985—Rushed once for minus three yards and fumbled once. 1986—Rushed once for six yards. 1987—Fumbled once.

		RECEIVING			
Year Team	G	No.	Yds.	Avg.	TD
1982—Atlanta NFL	5	2	24	12.0	1
1983—Atlanta NFL	15	55	881	16.0	6
1984—Atlanta NFL	16	67	1138	17.0	6
1985—Atlanta NFL	15	30	364	12.1	0
1986—Atlanta NFL	6	3	39	13.0	0
1987—Atlanta NFL	7	20	325	16.3	3
1988—Atlanta NFL	10	17	437	25.7	2
1989—Atlanta NFL	15	8	170	21.3	0
1990—Atlanta NFL	3	4	44	11.0	0
Pro totals (9 years)	92	206	3422	16.6	18

BAKER, STEPHEN
WR, GIANTS

PERSONAL: Born August 30, 1964, at San Antonio. . . . 5-8/160.
HIGH SCHOOL: Hamilton (Los Angeles).
COLLEGE: West Los Angeles College (Calif.), then Fresno State.
TRANSACTIONS/CAREER NOTES: Selected by New York Giants in third round (83rd pick

overall) of 1987 NFL draft. . . . Signed by Giants (July 27, 1987).
CHAMPIONSHIP GAME EXPERIENCE: Played in NFC championship game after 1990 season. . . . Played in Super Bowl XXV after 1990 season.
PRO STATISTICS: 1987—Rushed once for 18 yards, returned three punts for 16 yards and fumbled once. 1988—Returned five punts for 34 yards and recovered one fumble. 1990—Rushed once for three yards.

Year Team	G	No.	RECEIVING Yds.	Avg.	TD
1987— N.Y. Giants NFL	12	15	277	18.5	2
1988— N.Y. Giants NFL	16	40	656	16.4	7
1989— N.Y. Giants NFL	15	13	255	19.6	2
1990— N.Y. Giants NFL	16	26	541	20.8	4
Pro totals (4 years)	59	94	1729	18.4	15

BALDINGER, BRIAN
G, COLTS

PERSONAL: Born January 7, 1959, at Pittsburgh. . . . 6-4/278. . . . Full name: Brian D. Baldinger. . . . Brother of Rich Baldinger, offensive tackle with Kansas City Chiefs; and brother of Gary Baldinger, nose tackle with Buffalo Bills.
HIGH SCHOOL: Massapequa (N.Y.).
COLLEGE: Nassau Community College (N.Y.), then Duke (bachelor of science degree in psychology, 1982).
TRANSACTIONS/CAREER NOTES: Signed as free agent by Dallas Cowboys (April 30, 1982). . . . On inactive list (September 13 and 19, 1982). . . . On injured reserve with knee injury (August 27, 1985-entire season). . . . On injured reserve with knee injury (September 2-October 24, 1987). . . . Granted free agency with option not exercised (February 1, 1988). . . . Signed by Indianapolis Colts (July 19, 1988).
PLAYING EXPERIENCE: Dallas NFL, 1982-1984, 1986 and 1987; Indianapolis NFL, 1988-1990. . . . Games: 1982 (4), 1983 (16), 1984 (16), 1986 (16), 1987 (3), 1988 (16), 1989 (16), 1990 (16). Total: 103.
CHAMPIONSHIP GAME EXPERIENCE: Played in NFC championship game after 1982 season.
PRO STATISTICS: 1988—Caught one pass for 37 yards and recovered one fumble. 1989—Recovered one fumble.

BALDINGER, GARY
NT, BILLS

PERSONAL: Born October 4, 1963, at Philadelphia. . . . 6-3/270. . . . Full name: Gary Thomas Baldinger. . . . Brother of Brian Baldinger, guard with Indianapolis Colts; and brother of Rich Baldinger, offensive tackle with Kansas City Chiefs.
HIGH SCHOOL: Massapequa (N.Y.).
COLLEGE: Wake Forest (degree in history, 1986).
TRANSACTIONS/CAREER NOTES: Selected by Kansas City Chiefs in ninth round (229th pick overall) of 1986 NFL draft. . . . Signed by Chiefs (July 17, 1986). . . . Released by Chiefs (September 1, 1986). . . . Re-signed by Chiefs (September 2, 1986). . . . Released by Chiefs (October 10, 1986). . . . Re-signed by Chiefs (February 12, 1987). . . . On injured reserve with back injury (October 30-December 5, 1987). . . . On injured reserve with broken thumb (November 16, 1988-remainder of season). . . . Granted unconditional free agency (February 1, 1989). . . . Signed by Atlanta Falcons (March 30, 1989). . . . Released by Falcons (September 5, 1989). . . . Signed as free agent by Indianapolis Colts (May 1, 1990). . . . Released by Colts (September 14, 1990). . . . Signed by Buffalo Bills (October 10, 1990). . . . On inactive list (December 23 and 30, 1990).
PLAYING EXPERIENCE: Kansas City NFL, 1986-1988; Indianapolis (1)-Buffalo (9) NFL, 1990. . . . Games: 1986 (5), 1987 (7), 1988 (11), 1990 (10). Total: 33.
CHAMPIONSHIP GAME EXPERIENCE: Played in AFC championship game after 1990 season. . . . Played in Super Bowl XXV after 1990 season.

BALDINGER, RICH
OT, CHIEFS

PERSONAL: Born December 31, 1959, at Camp Le Jeune, N.C. . . . 6-4/293. . . . Full name: Richard L. Baldinger. . . . Brother of Brian Baldinger, guard with Indianapolis Colts; and brother of Gary Baldinger, nose tackle with Buffalo Bills.
HIGH SCHOOL: Massapequa (N.Y.).
COLLEGE: Wake Forest (degree in history, 1982).
TRANSACTIONS/CAREER NOTES: Selected by New York Giants in 10th round (270th pick overall) of 1982 NFL draft. . . . On inactive list (September 12, 1982). . . . Released by Giants (August 29, 1983). . . . Re-signed by Giants (September 8, 1983). . . . Released by Giants (October 7, 1983). . . . Signed as free agent by Kansas City Chiefs (October 26, 1983).
PLAYING EXPERIENCE: New York Giants NFL, 1982; New York Giants (2)-Kansas City (6) NFL, 1983; Kansas City NFL, 1984-1990. . . . Games: 1982 (1), 1983 (8), 1984 (14), 1985 (16), 1986 (16), 1987 (12), 1988 (14), 1989 (16), 1990 (16). Total: 113.
PRO STATISTICS: 1987—Recovered one fumble. 1988—Recovered one fumble. 1990—Recovered one fumble.

BALL, ERIC
RB, BENGALS

PERSONAL: Born July 1, 1966, at Cleveland. . . . 6-2/214. . . . Full name: Eric Clinton Ball.
HIGH SCHOOL: Ypsilanti (Mich.).
COLLEGE: UCLA.
TRANSACTIONS/CAREER NOTES: Selected by Cincinnati Bengals in second round (35th pick overall) of 1989 NFL draft. . . . Signed by Bengals (July 21, 1989). . . . On inactive list (October 22 and 28, 1990).

Year Team	G	RUSHING Att.	Yds.	Avg.	TD	RECEIVING No.	Yds.	Avg.	TD	KICKOFF RETURNS No.	Yds.	Avg.	TD	TOTAL TD	Pts.	F.
1989— Cincinnati NFL	15	98	391	4.0	3	6	44	7.3	0	1	19	19.0	0	3	18	3
1990— Cincinnati NFL	13	22	72	3.3	1	2	46	23.0	1	16	366	22.9	0	2	12	1
Pro totals (2 years)	28	120	463	3.9	4	8	90	11.3	1	17	385	22.7	0	5	30	4

BALL, JERRY
NT, LIONS

PERSONAL: Born December 15, 1964, at Beaumont, Tex. . . . 6-1/298. . . . Full name: Jerry Lee Ball. . . . Related to Mel Farr Sr., running back with Detroit Lions, 1967-1973; cousin of Mel Farr Jr., running back with Detroit Lions; and cousin of Mike Farr, wide receiver with Detroit Lions. **HIGH SCHOOL:** Westbrook (Tex.).
COLLEGE: Southern Methodist.
TRANSACTIONS/CAREER NOTES: Selected by Detroit Lions in third round (63rd pick overall) of 1987 NFL draft. . . . Signed by Lions (July 6, 1987).
PLAYING EXPERIENCE: Detroit NFL, 1987-1990. . . . Games: 1987 (12), 1988 (16), 1989 (16), 1990 (15). Total: 59.
RECORDS/HONORS: Played in Pro Bowl after 1989 and 1990 seasons.
PRO STATISTICS: 1987—Returned two kickoffs for 23 yards. 1989—Recovered three fumbles.

BALL, MICHAEL
DB, COLTS

PERSONAL: Born August 5, 1964, at New Orleans. . . . 6-0/220. . . . Full name: Michael Ball Jr.
HIGH SCHOOL: Booker T. Washington (New Orleans).
COLLEGE: Southern.
TRANSACTIONS/CAREER NOTES: Selected by Indianapolis Colts in fourth round (104th pick overall) of 1988 NFL draft. . . . Signed by Colts (July 20, 1988). . . . Granted free agency (February 1, 1991). . . . Re-signed by Colts (June 28, 1991).
PLAYING EXPERIENCE: Indianapolis NFL, 1988-1990. . . . Games: 1988 (16), 1989 (16), 1990 (16). Total: 48.
PRO STATISTICS: 1988—Recovered one fumble. 1989—Intercepted one pass for five yards. 1990—Returned one kickoff for no yards.

BALLARD, HOWARD
OT, BILLS

PERSONAL: Born November 3, 1963, at Ashland, Ala. . . . 6-6/315. . . . Full name: Howard Louis Ballard.
HIGH SCHOOL: Clay County (Ashland, Ala.).
COLLEGE: Alabama A&M.
TRANSACTIONS/CAREER NOTES: Selected by Buffalo Bills in 11th round (283rd pick overall) of 1987 NFL draft (elected to return to college for final year of eligibility). . . . Signed by Bills (March 30, 1988).
PLAYING EXPERIENCE: Buffalo NFL, 1988-1990. . . . Games: 1988 (16), 1989 (16), 1990 (16). Total: 48.
CHAMPIONSHIP GAME EXPERIENCE: Played in AFC championship game after 1988 and 1990 seasons. . . . Played in Super Bowl XXV after 1990 season.

BANES, JOEY
OT, OILERS

PERSONAL: Born April 7, 1967, at Houston. . . . 6-7/282.
HIGH SCHOOL: Klein (Houston).
COLLEGE: Houston.
TRANSACTIONS/CAREER NOTES: Selected by Houston Oilers in 11th round (295th pick overall) of 1990 NFL draft. . . . Signed by Oilers (July 20, 1990). . . . Released by Oilers (September 2, 1990). . . . Signed by Oilers to practice squad (October 3, 1990). . . . Signed by Indianapolis Colts (November 8, 1990). . . . Released by Colts (November 27, 1990). . . . Re-signed by Houston Oilers (May 10, 1991).
PLAYING EXPERIENCE: Indianapolis NFL, 1990. . . . Games: 1990 (1).

BANKS, CARL
LB, GIANTS

PERSONAL: Born August 29, 1962, at Flint, Mich. . . . 6-4/235.
HIGH SCHOOL: Beecher (Flint, Mich.).
COLLEGE: Michigan State.
TRANSACTIONS/CAREER NOTES: Selected by Michigan Panthers in 1984 USFL territorial draft. . . . Selected by New York Giants in first round (third pick overall) of 1984 NFL draft. . . . Signed by Giants (July 12, 1984). . . . On injured reserve with knee injury (October 12-November 9, 1985). . . . Granted free agency (February 1, 1988). . . . Re-signed by Giants (August 29, 1988). . . . Granted roster exemption (August 29-September 5, 1988). . . . On injured reserve with dislocated wrist (October 17-December 1, 1990). . . . On inactive list (December 30, 1990).
PLAYING EXPERIENCE: New York Giants NFL, 1984-1990. . . . Games: 1984 (16), 1985 (12), 1986 (16), 1987 (12), 1988 (14), 1989 (16), 1990 (9). Total: 95.
CHAMPIONSHIP GAME EXPERIENCE: Played in NFC championship game after 1986 and 1990 seasons. . . . Played in Super Bowl XXI after 1986 season and Super Bowl XXV after 1990 season.
RECORDS/HONORS: Named as linebacker on THE SPORTING NEWS college All-America team, 1983. . . . Played in Pro Bowl after 1987 season. . . . Named to THE SPORTING NEWS NFL All-Pro team, 1987.
PRO STATISTICS: 1984—Recovered one fumble. 1985—Recovered one fumble. 1986—Recovered two fumbles for five yards. 1987—Intercepted one pass for no yards. 1988—Intercepted one pass for 15 yards and a touchdown. 1989—Caught one pass for 22 yards and a touchdown and intercepted one pass for six yards and recovered one fumble. 1990—Recovered one fumble.

BANKS, CHIP
LB, COLTS

PERSONAL: Born September 18, 1959, at Fort Lawton, Okla. . . . 6-4/254. . . . Full name: William Chip Banks.
HIGH SCHOOL: Lucy Laney (Augusta, Ga.).
COLLEGE: Southern California.
TRANSACTIONS/CAREER NOTES: Selected by Cleveland Browns in first round (third pick overall) of 1982 NFL draft. . . . Traded by Browns with third-round pick in 1985 draft and first- and sixth-round picks in 1986 draft to Buffalo Bills for first-round pick in 1985 supplemental draft (April 9, 1985); Bills later received first-round pick in 1985 draft from Browns when Banks did not report). . . . On reserve/did not report list (August 18-September 1, 1986). . . . Granted roster exemption (September 1-September 6, 1986). . . . Traded by Browns with first- and second-round picks in 1987 draft to San Diego Chargers for first- and second-round picks in 1987 draft (April 28, 1987). . . . On reserve free agent/asked to re-sign list (August 22, 1988-entire season). . . . Re-signed by Chargers and traded to Indianapolis Colts for third-round pick in 1990 NFL draft (October 17, 1989).

CHAMPIONSHIP GAME EXPERIENCE: Played in AFC championship game after 1986 season.
RECORDS/HONORS: Named as linebacker on THE SPORTING NEWS college All-America team, 1981. . . . Played in Pro Bowl after 1982, 1983 and 1986 seasons. . . . Named to play in Pro Bowl after 1985 season; replaced due to injury by Clay Matthews.
PRO STATISTICS: 1983—Recovered one fumble. 1984—Recovered three fumbles for 17 yards. 1986—Recovered two fumbles. 1987—Recovered two fumbles. 1989—Recovered one fumble. 1990—Recovered one fumble.

			INTERCEPTIONS		
Year Team	G	No.	Yds.	Avg.	TD
1982— Cleveland NFL	9	1	14	14.0	0
1983— Cleveland NFL	16	3	95	31.7	1
1984— Cleveland NFL	16	1	8	8.0	0
1985— Cleveland NFL	16	0	0		0
1986— Cleveland NFL	16	0	0		0
1987— San Diego NFL	12	1	20	20.0	0
1989— Indianapolis NFL	10	2	13	6.5	0
1990— Indianapolis NFL	16	0	0		0
Pro totals (8 years)	111	8	150	18.8	1

BANKS, FRED
WR, DOLPHINS

PERSONAL: Born May 26, 1962, at Columbus, Ga. . . . 5-10/185. . . . Full name: Frederick Ray Banks.
HIGH SCHOOL: Baker (Columbus, Ga.).
COLLEGE: Chowan College (N.C.), then Liberty Baptist College.
TRANSACTIONS/CAREER NOTES: Selected by Denver Gold in eighth round (107th pick overall) of 1985 USFL draft. . . . Selected by Cleveland Browns in eighth round (203rd pick overall) of 1985 NFL draft. . . . Signed by Browns (July 11, 1985). . . . On injured reserve with pulled hamstring (October 9-November 16, 1985). . . . On reserve/physically unable to perform list with ankle injury (August 19-September 15, 1986). . . . Released by Browns (September 16, 1986). . . . Signed as free agent by Miami Dolphins for 1987 (November 24, 1986). . . . Released by Dolphins (December 12, 1987). . . . Re-signed by Dolphins (December 15, 1987). . . . On injured reserve with ribs injury (September 2-October 1, 1988). . . . On injured reserve with broken foot (November 16, 1990-remainder of 1990 season playoffs).
PRO STATISTICS: 1989—Recovered one fumble and fumbled once. 1990—Rushed once for three yards and recovered two fumbles.

			RECEIVING		
Year Team	G	No.	Yds.	Avg.	TD
1985— Cleveland NFL	10	5	62	12.4	2
1987— Miami NFL.................	3	1	10	10.0	1
1988— Miami NFL.................	11	23	430	18.7	2
1989— Miami NFL.................	15	30	520	17.3	1
1990— Miami NFL.................	8	13	131	10.1	0
Pro totals (5 years)	47	72	1153	16.0	6

BANKS, ROBERT
DE, OILERS

PERSONAL: Born December 10, 1963, at Williamsburg, Va. . . . 6-5/260. . . . Full name: Robert Nathan Banks.
HIGH SCHOOL: Peninsula Catholic (Newport News, Va.) and Hampton (Va.).
COLLEGE: Notre Dame (degree in psychology).
TRANSACTIONS/CAREER NOTES: Selected by Houston Oilers in seventh round (176th pick overall) of 1987 NFL draft. . . . Signed by Oilers (July 12, 1987). . . . On injured reserve with finger injury (September 6, 1987-entire season). . . . Granted unconditional free agency (February 1, 1989). . . . Signed by Cleveland Browns (March 16, 1989). . . . Granted unconditional free agency (February 1, 1991). . . . Signed by Houston Oilers (April 1, 1991).
PLAYING EXPERIENCE: Houston NFL, 1988; Cleveland NFL, 1989 and 1990. . . . Games: 1988 (14), 1989 (15), 1990 (15). Total: 44.
CHAMPIONSHIP GAME EXPERIENCE: Played in AFC championship game after 1989 season.
PRO STATISTICS: 1989—Recovered two fumbles.

BARBER, MIKE
WR, BENGALS

PERSONAL: Born June 19, 1967, at Winfield, W.Va. . . . 5-11/172. . . . Full name: Michael Dale Barber Jr.
HIGH SCHOOL: Winfield (W.Va.).
COLLEGE: Marshall.
TRANSACTIONS/CAREER NOTES: Selected by San Francisco 49ers in fourth round (112th pick overall) of 1989 NFL draft. . . . Signed by 49ers (July 14, 1989). . . . Released by 49ers (October 12, 1989). . . . Re-signed by 49ers to developmental squad (October 14, 1989). . . . On developmental squad (October 14-November 22, 1989). . . . Activated after clearing procedural waivers (November 24, 1989). . . . Released by 49ers (December 13, 1989). . . . Awarded on waivers to Phoenix Cardinals (December 14, 1989). . . . Active for two games with Cardinals in 1989; did not play. . . . Granted unconditional free agency (February 1, 1990). . . . Signed by Cincinnati Bengals (March 8, 1990). . . . Released by Bengals (September 3, 1990). . . . Re-signed by Bengals (September 6, 1990).

		RUSHING				RECEIVING				KICKOFF RETURNS				TOTAL		
Year Team	G	Att.	Yds.	Avg.	TD	No.	Yds.	Avg.	TD	No.	Yds.	Avg.	TD	TD	Pts.	F.
1989— S.F. (8)-Pho. (0) NFL	8	0	0		0	0	0		0	0	0		0	0	0	0
1990— Cincinnati NFL.......	16	1	-13	-13.0	0	14	196	14.0	1	1	14	14.0	0	1	6	0
Pro totals (2 years)	24	1	-13	-13.0	0	14	196	14.0	1	1	14	14.0	0	1	6	0

BARKER, BRYAN
P, CHIEFS

PERSONAL: Born June 28, 1964, at Jacksonville Beach, Fla. . . . 6-1/187. . . . Full name: Bryan Christopher Barker.
HIGH SCHOOL: Miramonte (Orinda, Calif.).
COLLEGE: Santa Clara (degree in economics).
TRANSACTIONS/CAREER NOTES: Signed as free agent by Denver Broncos (May, 1988). . . . Released by Broncos (July 19, 1988). . . . Signed by Seattle Seahawks (offseason, 1989). . . . Released by Seahawks (August 30, 1989). . . . Signed as free agent by Kansas City Chiefs (May 1, 1990). . . . Released by Chiefs (August 28, 1990). . . . Re-signed by Chiefs (September 26, 1990).

Year Team	G	No.	Avg.	Blk.
		PUNTING		
1990— Kansas City NFL	13	64	38.7	0
Pro totals (1 year)	13	64	38.7	0

BARKER, LEO
LB, BENGALS

PERSONAL: Born November 7, 1959, at Cristobal, Panama. . . . 6-2/230.
HIGH SCHOOL: Cristobal (Panama).
COLLEGE: New Mexico State.
TRANSACTIONS/CAREER NOTES: Selected by Arizona Wranglers in 1984 USFL territorial draft. . . . Selected by Cincinnati Bengals in seventh round (177th pick overall) of 1984 NFL draft. . . . Signed by Bengals (June 26, 1984). . . . On inactive list (November 4, 1990).
PLAYING EXPERIENCE: Cincinnati NFL, 1984-1990. . . . Games: 1984 (16), 1985 (16), 1986 (16), 1987 (12), 1988 (16), 1989 (16), 1990 (14). Total: 106.
CHAMPIONSHIP GAME EXPERIENCE: Played in AFC championship game after 1988 season. . . . Played in Super Bowl XXIII after 1988 season.
PRO STATISTICS: 1986—Intercepted two passes for seven yards. 1988—Returned one fumble for 34 yards and a touchdown. 1990—Recovered one fumble.

BARNES, LEW
WR/KR, CHIEFS

PERSONAL: Born December 27, 1962, at Long Beach, Calif. . . . 5-8/165. . . . Full name: Lew Eric Barnes.
HIGH SCHOOL: Abraham Lincoln (San Diego).
COLLEGE: San Diego Mesa College (Calif.), then Oregon.
TRANSACTIONS/CAREER NOTES: Selected by Chicago Bears in fifth round (138th pick overall) of 1986 NFL draft. . . . Signed by Bears (July 16, 1986). . . . On injured reserve with broken leg (August 27, 1987-entire season). . . . Released by Bears (August 23, 1988). . . . Awarded on waivers to Detroit Lions (August 24, 1988). . . . Released by Lions (August 30, 1988). . . . Signed as free agent by Atlanta Falcons (September 14, 1988). . . . Granted unconditional free agency (February 1, 1989). . . . Signed by Kansas City Chiefs (March 31, 1989). . . . Released by Chiefs (September 4, 1989). . . . Re-signed by Chiefs (September 5, 1989). . . . Released by Chiefs (September 20, 1989). . . . Signed as free agent by Buffalo Bills (February 6, 1990). . . . Released by Bills (August 22, 1990). . . . Signed by Kansas City Chiefs (March 13, 1991).
RECORDS/HONORS: Established NFL record for most punt returns, rookie season (57), 1986.
PRO STATISTICS: 1986—Recovered three fumbles.

Year Team	G	No.	Yds.	Avg.	TD	No.	Yds.	Avg.	TD	No.	Yds.	Avg.	TD	TD	Pts.	F.
		RECEIVING				**PUNT RETURNS**				**KICKOFF RETURNS**				**TOTAL**		
1986— Chicago NFL	16	4	54	13.5	0	*57	482	8.5	0	3	94	31.3	*1	1	6	5
1988— Atlanta NFL	13	0	0		0	34	307	9.0	0	6	142	23.7	0	0	0	4
1989— Kansas City NFL	2	0	0		0	2	41	20.5	0	0	0		0	0	0	0
Pro totals (3 years)	31	4	54	13.5	0	93	830	8.9	0	9	236	26.2	1	1	6	9

BARNETT, FRED
WR, EAGLES

PERSONAL: Born June 17, 1966, at Shelby, Miss. . . . 6-0/199. . . . Full name: Fred Lee Barnett Jr. . . . Nephew of John Barnett, running back with Los Angeles Express of USFL, 1983; and cousin of Tim Barnett, rookie wide receiver with Kansas City Chiefs.
HIGH SCHOOL: Rosedale (Miss.).
COLLEGE: Arkansas State.
TRANSACTIONS/CAREER NOTES: Selected by Philadelphia Eagles in third round (77th pick overall) of 1990 NFL draft. . . . Signed by Eagles (August 13, 1990).

Year Team	G	Att.	Yds.	Avg.	TD	No.	Yds.	Avg.	TD	No.	Yds.	Avg.	TD	TD	Pts.	F.
		RUSHING				**RECEIVING**				**KICKOFF RETURNS**				**TOTAL**		
1990— Philadelphia NFL	16	2	13	6.5	0	36	721	20.0	8	4	65	16.3	0	8	48	0
Pro totals (1 year)	16	2	13	6.5	0	36	721	20.0	8	4	65	16.3	0	8	48	0

BARNETT, HARLON
S, BROWNS

PERSONAL: Born January 2, 1967, at Cincinnati. . . . 5-11/200.
HIGH SCHOOL: Princeton (Cincinnati).
COLLEGE: Michigan State.
TRANSACTIONS/CAREER NOTES: Selected by Cleveland Browns in fourth round (101st pick overall) of 1990 NFL draft. . . . Signed by Browns (July 22, 1990). . . . On injured reserve with back injury (September 8-November 24, 1990).
PLAYING EXPERIENCE: Cleveland NFL, 1990. . . . Games: 1990 (6).
RECORDS/HONORS: Named as defensive back to THE SPORTING NEWS college All-America team, 1989.
PRO STATISTICS: 1990—Returned one kickoff for 15 yards.

BARNETT, OLIVER
DT, FALCONS

PERSONAL: Born April 9, 1966, at Louisville, Ky. . . . 6-3/285. . . . Full name: Oliver Wesley Barnett.
HIGH SCHOOL: Jeffersontown (Ky.).
COLLEGE: Kentucky.
TRANSACTIONS/CAREER NOTES: Selected by Atlanta Falcons in third round (55th pick overall) of 1990 NFL draft. . . . Signed by Falcons (July 27, 1990). . . . On inactive list (November 18, 1990).
PLAYING EXPERIENCE: Atlanta NFL, 1990. . . . Games: 1990 (15).

BARNHARDT, TOMMY
P, SAINTS

PERSONAL: Born June 11, 1963, at Salisbury, N.C. . . . 6-2/207. . . . Full name: Tommy Ray Barnhardt.
HIGH SCHOOL: South Rowan (China Grove, N.C.).
COLLEGE: East Carolina, then North Carolina (degree in industrial relations, 1986).
TRANSACTIONS/CAREER NOTES: Selected by Baltimore Stars in 1986 USFL territorial draft. . . . Selected by Tampa Bay Buccaneers in ninth round (223rd pick overall) of 1986 NFL draft. . . . Signed by Buccaneers (July 16, 1986). . . . Released by Buccaneers (August 25, 1986). . . . Re-signed by Buccaneers (February 6, 1987). . . . Released by Buccaneers (August 5, 1987). . . . Signed as free agent replacement player by New Orleans Saints (September 23, 1987). . . . Released by Saints (November 3, 1987). . . . Signed as free agent by Chicago Bears (December 16, 1987). . . . Released by Bears (August 24, 1988). . . . Signed as free agent by Washington Redskins (September 9, 1988). . . . On injured reserve with pulled quadricep (October 11, 1988-remainder of season). . . . Granted unconditional free agency (February 1, 1989). . . . Re-signed by Redskins (May 11, 1989). . . . Released by Redskins (June 27, 1989). . . . Signed as free agent by Detroit Lions (July 20, 1989). . . . Released by Lions (August 30, 1989). . . . Signed as free agent by New Orleans Saints (October 11, 1989).
PRO STATISTICS: 1987—Rushed once for minus 13 yards.

| | | —PUNTING— | | |
Year Team	G	No.	Avg.	Blk.
1987— N.O. (3)-Chi. (2) NFL	5	17	42.3	0
1988— Washington NFL	4	15	41.9	0
1989— New Orleans NFL	11	55	39.6	0
1990— New Orleans NFL	16	70	42.7	1
Pro totals (4 years)	36	157	41.6	1

BARTLEWSKI, RICH
TE, FALCONS

PERSONAL: Born August 15, 1967, at Butler, Pa. . . . 6-5/255. . . . Full name: Richard Stanley Bartlewski Jr.
HIGH SCHOOL: Chowchilla Union (Chowchilla, Calif.).
COLLEGE: Fresno State.
TRANSACTIONS/CAREER NOTES: Signed as free agent by Los Angeles Raiders (May 1, 1990). . . . Released by Raiders (August 23, 1990). . . . Re-signed by Raiders to practice squad (October 3, 1990). . . . Released by Raiders (October 18, 1990). . . . Re-signed by Raiders to practice squad (October 25, 1990). . . . Activated (December 10, 1990). . . . Released by Raiders (January 10, 1991). . . . Signed by Atlanta Falcons (April 18, 1991).
PLAYING EXPERIENCE: Los Angeles Raiders NFL, 1990. . . . Games: 1990 (4).

BARTON, HARRIS
G/OT, 49ERS

PERSONAL: Born April 19, 1964, at Atlanta. . . . 6-4/280. . . . Full name: Harris Scott Barton.
HIGH SCHOOL: Dunwoody (Ga.).
COLLEGE: North Carolina (bachelor of science degree, 1987).
TRANSACTIONS/CAREER NOTES: Selected by San Francisco 49ers in first round (22nd pick overall) of 1987 NFL draft. . . . Signed by 49ers (July 22, 1987). . . . Granted free agency (February 1, 1990). . . . Re-signed by 49ers (July 30, 1990).
PLAYING EXPERIENCE: San Francisco NFL, 1987-1990. . . . Games: 1987 (12), 1988 (16), 1989 (16), 1990 (16). Total: 60.
CHAMPIONSHIP GAME EXPERIENCE: Played in NFC championship game after 1988-1990 seasons. . . . Played in Super Bowl XXIII after 1988 season and Super Bowl XXIV after 1989 season.
PRO STATISTICS: 1987—Recovered one fumble.

BATES, BILL
S, COWBOYS

PERSONAL: Born June 6, 1961, at Knoxville, Tenn. . . . 6-1/204. . . . Full name: William Frederick Bates.
HIGH SCHOOL: Farragut (Knoxville, Tenn.).
COLLEGE: Tennessee.
TRANSACTIONS/CAREER NOTES: Selected by New Jersey Generals in 1983 USFL territorial draft. . . . Signed as free agent by Dallas Cowboys (April 28, 1983). . . . On injured reserve with hip injury (September 3-September 28, 1984).
RECORDS/HONORS: Played in Pro Bowl after 1984 season.
PRO STATISTICS: 1983—Recovered two fumbles. 1984—Recovered one fumble. 1988—Recovered one fumble. 1989—Rushed once for no yards. 1990—Rushed once for four yards.

| | | —INTERCEPTIONS— | | | | —PUNT RETURNS— | | | | —TOTAL— | | |
Year Team	G	No.	Yds.	Avg.	TD	No.	Yds.	Avg.	TD	TD	Pts.	F.
1983— Dallas NFL	16	1	29	29.0	0	0	0		0	0	0	1
1984— Dallas NFL	12	1	3	3.0	0	0	0		0	0	0	0
1985— Dallas NFL	16	4	15	3.8	0	22	152	6.9	0	0	0	0
1986— Dallas NFL	15	0	0		0	0	0		0	0	0	0
1987— Dallas NFL	12	3	28	9.3	0	0	0		0	0	0	0
1988— Dallas NFL	16	1	0	.0	0	0	0		0	0	0	0
1989— Dallas NFL	16	1	18	18.0	0	0	0		0	0	0	0
1990— Dallas NFL	16	1	4	4.0	0	0	0		0	0	0	0
Pro totals (8 years)	119	12	97	8.1	0	22	152	6.9	0	0	0	1

BATY, GREG
TE, DOLPHINS

PERSONAL: Born August 28, 1964, at Hastings, Mich. . . . 6-5/240. . . . Full name: Gregory James Baty.
HIGH SCHOOL: Sparta (N.J.).
COLLEGE: Stanford (bachelor of arts degree in human biology, 1986).
TRANSACTIONS/CAREER NOTES: Selected by New England Patriots in eighth round (220th pick overall) of 1986 NFL draft. . . . Signed by Patriots (July 18, 1986). . . . Released by Patriots (November 12, 1987). . . . Awarded on waivers to Los Angeles Rams (November 13, 1987). . . . Granted free agency (February 1, 1988). . . . Withdrew qualifying offer (August 1, 1988). . . . Signed by San Francisco 49ers (August 4, 1988). . . . On injured reserve with thigh injury (August 23-September 19, 1988). . . . Released by 49ers (September 20, 1988). . . . Signed as free agent by Phoenix Cardinals (September 30, 1988). . . . Released by Cardinals (October 19, 1988). . . . Signed as free agent by New York Giants (April 25, 1989). . . . Released by Giants (August 28, 1989). . . . Awarded on waivers to Tampa Bay Buccaneers (August 29, 1989). . . . Released by Buccaneers (September 5, 1989). . . . Signed as free agent by Miami Dolphins (November 15, 1989). . . . Released by Dolphins (November 20, 1989). . . . Re-signed by Dolphins (May 4, 1990). . . . Released by Dolphins (September 3, 1990). . . . Re-signed by Dolphins (October 4, 1990).
PRO STATISTICS: 1990—Recovered one fumble.

			RECEIVING		
Year Team	G	No.	Yds.	Avg.	TD
1986— New England NFL	16	37	331	9.0	2
1987— N.E. (5)-Rams (4) NFL .	9	18	175	9.7	2
1988— Phoenix NFL	1	0	0		0
1990— Miami NFL.................	12	0	0		0
Pro totals (4 years)	38	55	506	9.2	4

BAVARO, DAVID
LB, BILLS

PERSONAL: Born March 27, 1967, at Danvers, Mass. . . . 6-0/235. . . . Full name: David Anthony Bavaro. . . . Brother of Mark Bavaro, tight end with New York Giants, 1985-1990.
HIGH SCHOOL: Danvers (Mass.).
COLLEGE: Syracuse (degree in history, 1990).
TRANSACTIONS/CAREER NOTES: Selected by Phoenix Cardinals in ninth round (225th pick overall) of 1990 NFL draft. . . . Signed by Cardinals (July 18, 1990). . . . Released by Cardinals (September 27, 1990). . . . Re-signed by Cardinals to practice squad (October 1, 1990). . . . Activated (October 13, 1990). . . . Granted unconditional free agency (February 1, 1991). . . . Signed by Buffalo Bills (March 30, 1991).
PLAYING EXPERIENCE: Phoenix NFL, 1990. . . . Games: 1990 (14).

BAX, CARL
OL, BUCCANEERS

PERSONAL: Born January 5, 1966, at St. Charles, Mo. . . . 6-4/290. . . . Full name: Carl William Bax.
HIGH SCHOOL: St. Charles (Mo.).
COLLEGE: Missouri (degree in management, 1989).
TRANSACTIONS/CAREER NOTES: Selected by Tampa Bay Buccaneers in eighth round (200th pick overall) of 1989 NFL draft. . . . Signed by Buccaneers (July 11, 1989). . . . On suspended list for steroid use (August 31-September 28, 1990). . . . On inactive list (December 16, 23 and 30, 1990).
PLAYING EXPERIENCE: Tampa Bay NFL, 1989 and 1990. . . . Games: 1989 (6), 1990 (9). Total: 15.

BAXTER, BRAD
RB, JETS

PERSONAL: Born May 5, 1967, at Dothan, Ala. . . . 6-1/235. . . . Full name: Herman Bradley Baxter.
HIGH SCHOOL: Slocomb (Ala.).
COLLEGE: Alabama State.
TRANSACTIONS/CAREER NOTES: Selected by Minnesota Vikings in 11th round (303rd pick overall) of 1989 NFL draft. . . . Signed by Vikings (July 26, 1989). . . . Released by Vikings (August 30, 1989). . . . Signed as free agent by New York Jets to developmental squad (October 5, 1989). . . . On developmental squad (October 5-December 18, 1989). . . . Activated after clearing procedural waivers (December 20, 1989).
PRO STATISTICS: 1990—Recovered one fumble.

		RUSHING				RECEIVING				TOTAL		
Year Team	G	Att.	Yds.	Avg.	TD	No.	Yds.	Avg.	TD	TD	Pts.	F.
1989— N.Y. Jets NFL	1	0	0		0	0	0		0	0	0	0
1990— N.Y. Jets NFL	16	124	539	4.4	6	8	73	9.1	0	6	36	4
Pro totals (2 years)	17	124	539	4.4	6	8	73	9.1	0	6	36	4

BAYLESS, MARTIN
S, CHARGERS

PERSONAL: Born October 11, 1962, at Dayton, O. . . . 6-2/212. . . . Name pronounced BAY-liss.
HIGH SCHOOL: Belmont (Dayton, O.).
COLLEGE: Bowling Green State.
TRANSACTIONS/CAREER NOTES: Selected by Memphis Showboats in first round (20th pick overall) of 1984 USFL draft. . . . Selected by St. Louis Cardinals in fourth round (101st pick overall) of 1984 NFL draft. . . . Signed by Cardinals (July 20, 1984). . . . Released by Cardinals (September 19, 1984). . . . Awarded on waivers to Buffalo Bills (September 20, 1984). . . . On injured reserve with pinched nerve in neck (December 6, 1985-remainder of season). . . . Traded by Bills to San Diego Chargers for cornerback Wayne Davis (August 26, 1987). . . . On inactive list (October 28 and November 4, 1990).
PRO STATISTICS: 1985—Recovered one fumble. 1989—Recovered one fumble. 1990—Recovered one fumble.

Year	Team	G	— INTERCEPTIONS —			
			No.	Yds.	Avg.	TD
1984— S.L.(3)-Buf.(13) NFL ...		16	0	0		0
1985— Buffalo NFL..............		12	2	10	5.0	0
1986— Buffalo NFL..............		16	1	0	.0	0
1987— San Diego NFL..........		12	0	0		0
1988— San Diego NFL..........		15	0	0		0
1989— San Diego NFL..........		16	1	0	.0	0
1990— San Diego NFL..........		14	1	0	.0	0
Pro totals (7 years)		101	5	10	2.0	0

BAYLOR, JOHN
DB, COLTS

PERSONAL: Born March 5, 1965, at Meridian, Miss. ... 6-0/203. ... Full name: John Martin Baylor.
HIGH SCHOOL: Meridian (Miss.).
COLLEGE: Southern Mississippi.
TRANSACTIONS/CAREER NOTES: Selected by Indianapolis Colts in fifth round (129th pick overall) of 1988 NFL draft. ... Signed by Colts (July 13, 1988). ... On injured reserve with wrist injury (August 29, 1988-entire season). ... Granted free agency (February 1, 1990). ... Re-signed by Colts (August 4, 1990). ... On inactive list (September 30, 1990). ... On injured reserve with hamstring injury (November 28-December 26, 1990).
PLAYING EXPERIENCE: Indianapolis NFL, 1989 and 1990. ... Games: 1989 (16), 1990 (10). Total: 26.

BEACH, PAT
TE, COLTS

PERSONAL: Born December 28, 1959, at Grant's Pass, Ore. ... 6-4/249. ... Full name: Patrick Jesse Beach.
HIGH SCHOOL: Pullman (Wash.).
COLLEGE: Washington State.
TRANSACTIONS/CAREER NOTES: Selected by Baltimore Colts in sixth round (140th pick overall) of 1982 NFL draft. ... Franchise transferred to Indianapolis (March 31, 1984). ... On non-football injury list with ankle injury (August 10-August 21, 1984). ... On injured reserve with ankle injury (August 22, 1984-entire season).
RECORDS/HONORS: Named as tight end on THE SPORTING NEWS college All-America team, 1981.
PRO STATISTICS: 1983—Returned one kickoff for no yards. 1985—Recovered one fumble and fumbled three times for five yards. 1986—Recovered one fumble and fumbled twice. 1988—Returned one kickoff for 35 yards and fumbled once. 1989—Fumbled once.

Year	Team	G	— RECEIVING —			
			No.	Yds.	Avg.	TD
1982— Baltimore NFL............		9	4	45	11.3	1
1983— Baltimore NFL............		16	5	56	11.2	1
1985— Indianapolis NFL		16	36	376	10.4	6
1986— Indianapolis NFL		16	25	265	10.6	1
1987— Indianapolis NFL		12	28	239	8.5	0
1988— Indianapolis NFL		16	26	235	9.0	0
1989— Indianapolis NFL		16	14	87	6.2	2
1990— Indianapolis NFL		16	12	124	10.3	1
Pro totals (8 years)		117	150	1427	9.5	12

BEACH, SANJAY
WR, 49ERS

PERSONAL: Born February 21, 1966, at Clark A.F.B., Philippines. ... 6-1/190. ... Full name: Sanjay Ragiv Beach.
HIGH SCHOOL: Chandler (Ariz.).
COLLEGE: Colorado State (bachelor's degree in speech communications).
TRANSACTIONS/CAREER NOTES: Signed as free agent by Dallas Cowboys (April 28, 1988). ... Released by Cowboys (August 19, 1988). ... Signed as free agent by New York Jets (April 11, 1989). ... Released by Jets (August 29, 1989). ... Re-signed by Jets to developmental squad (September 6, 1989). ... On developmental squad (September 6-October 11, 1989). ... Activated after clearing procedural waivers (October 13, 1989). ... Released by Jets (October 17, 1989). ... Re-signed by Jets to developmental squad (October 18, 1989). ... On developmental squad (October 18-December 26, 1989). ... Released by Jets (December 27, 1989). ... Signed as free agent by San Francisco 49ers (March 20, 1990). ... Released by 49ers (August 31, 1990). ... Signed by 49ers to practice squad (October 1, 1990). ... On practice squad (October 1, 1990-remainder of season). ... Signed by 49ers for 1991 (February 25, 1991).
PLAYING EXPERIENCE: New York Jets NFL, 1989. ... Games: 1989 (1).

BEAVERS, SCOTT
OL, BRONCOS

PERSONAL: Born February 17, 1967, at Atlanta. ... 6-4/277. ... Full name: Scott Travis Beavers.
HIGH SCHOOL: Campbell (Smyrna, Ga.).
COLLEGE: Georgia Tech.
TRANSACTIONS/CAREER NOTES: Signed as free agent by Denver Broncos (May, 1990). ... Released by Broncos (September 3, 1990). ... Re-signed by Broncos (September 4, 1990). ... On inactive list (September 9, 17, 23, 30; and October 8 and 14, 1990). ... Released by Broncos (October 17, 1990). ... Re-signed to practice squad and later activated (December 1, 1990). ... Released by Broncos (December 11, 1990). ... Re-signed by Broncos (December 19, 1990).
PLAYING EXPERIENCE: Denver NFL, 1990. ... Games: 1990 (2).

BECKLES, IAN

G, BUCCANEERS

PERSONAL: Born July 20, 1967, at Montreal, Que.... 6-1/295.... Full name: Ian Harold Beckles.
HIGH SCHOOL: Lindsay Place (Montreal, Que.).
COLLEGE: Waldorf Junior College (Ia.), then Indiana (bachelor's degree in general studies).
TRANSACTIONS/CAREER NOTES: Selected by Tampa Bay Buccaneers in fifth round (114th pick overall) of 1990 NFL draft.... Signed by Buccaneers (July 19, 1990).
PLAYING EXPERIENCE: Tampa Bay NFL, 1990.... Games: 1990 (16).

BEEBE, DON

WR, BILLS

PERSONAL: Born December 18, 1964, at Aurora, Ill.... 5-11/177.... Full name: Don Lee Beebe.... Name pronounced bee-bee.
HIGH SCHOOL: Kaneland (Maple Park, Ill.).
COLLEGE: Western Illinois, Aurora University (did not play football), then Chadron State College (Neb.).
TRANSACTIONS/CAREER NOTES: Selected by Buffalo Bills in third round (82nd pick overall) of 1989 NFL draft.... Signed by Bills (May 8, 1989).... On inactive list (September 24 and 30; and October 7, 1990).... On injured reserve with broken leg (December 29-remainder of 1990 season playoffs).

		RUSHING				RECEIVING				KICKOFF RETURNS				TOTAL		
Year Team	G	Att.	Yds.	Avg.	TD	No.	Yds.	Avg.	TD	No.	Yds.	Avg.	TD	TD	Pts.	F.
1989—Buffalo NFL	14	0	0		0	17	317	18.6	2	16	353	22.1	0	2	12	1
1990—Buffalo NFL	12	1	23	23.0	0	11	221	20.1	1	6	119	19.8	0	1	6	0
Pro totals (2 years)	26	1	23	23.0	0	28	538	19.2	3	22	472	21.5	0	3	18	1

BELL, ANTHONY

LB, CARDINALS

PERSONAL: Born July 2, 1964, at Miami.... 6-4/250.... Full name: Anthony Dewitt Bell.
HIGH SCHOOL: Boyd H. Anderson (Fort Lauderdale, Fla.).
COLLEGE: Michigan State.
TRANSACTIONS/CAREER NOTES: Selected by St. Louis Cardinals in first round (fifth pick overall) of 1986 NFL draft.... Signed by Cardinals (August 11, 1986).... Franchise transferred to Phoenix (March 15, 1988). ... Granted free agency (February 1, 1990).... Re-signed by Cardinals (August 20, 1990).
PLAYING EXPERIENCE: St. Louis NFL, 1986 and 1987; Phoenix NFL, 1988-1990.... Games: 1986 (16), 1987 (12), 1988 (16), 1989 (16), 1990 (16). Total: 76.
PRO STATISTICS: 1987—Intercepted one pass for 13 yards and fumbled once. 1988—Recovered three fumbles. 1990—Intercepted one pass for no yards.

BELL, BILLY

CB, CHIEFS

PERSONAL: Born January 16, 1961, at Dayton, Tex.... 5-10/170.... Full name: Billy Ray Bell.
HIGH SCHOOL: Dayton (Tex.).
COLLEGE: Lamar.
TRANSACTIONS/CAREER NOTES: Signed as free agent by New Jersey Generals of USFL (May 28, 1986).... Granted free agency when USFL suspended operations (August 7, 1986).... Signed by Houston Oilers (May 4, 1989).... Released by Oilers (September 5, 1989).... Re-signed by Oilers to developmental squad (September 8, 1989).... On developmental squad (September 8-November 4, 1989).... Released by Oilers (November 21, 1989).... Re-signed by Oilers to developmental squad (November 24, 1989).... On developmental squad (November 24-December 8, 1989).... Released by Oilers (September 2, 1990).... Signed by B.C. Lions (September, 1990).... Signed by Kansas City Chiefs (May 5, 1991).
PLAYING EXPERIENCE: Houston NFL, 1989; B.C. CFL, 1990.... Games: 1989 (4), 1990 (4). Total NFL: 4. Total Pro: 8.
PRO STATISTICS: CFL: 1990—Intercepted one pass for 16 yards.

BELL, GREG

RB, RAIDERS

PERSONAL: Born August 1, 1962, at Columbus, O.... 5-10/210.... Full name: Greg Leon Bell.
HIGH SCHOOL: South (Columbus, O.).
COLLEGE: Notre Dame (bachelor of arts degree in economics, 1984).
TRANSACTIONS/CAREER NOTES: Selected by Chicago Blitz in 1984 USFL territorial draft.... Selected by Buffalo Bills in first round (26th pick overall) of 1984 NFL draft.... Signed by Bills (July 23, 1984).... On injured reserve with groin injury (October 18-December 13, 1986).... On injured reserve with groin injury (December 20, 1986-remainder of season).... Traded by Bills with first-round pick in 1988 draft and first- and second-round picks in 1989 draft to Los Angeles Rams in exchange for Indianapolis Colts trading rights to linebacker Cornelius Bennett (October 31, 1987); Rams also acquired first- and second-round picks in 1988 draft, second-round pick in 1989 draft and running back Owen Gill from Colts for running back Eric Dickerson.... On injured reserve with shoulder injury (December 4, 1987-remainder of season).... Traded by Los Angeles Rams to Los Angeles Raiders for an undisclosed draft pick (June 20, 1990).... On injured reserve (October 21, 1990-remainder of regular season).
CHAMPIONSHIP GAME EXPERIENCE: Played in NFC championship game after 1989 season.... Played in AFC championship game after 1990 season.
RECORDS/HONORS: Played in Pro Bowl after 1984 season.
PRO STATISTICS: 1984—Returned one kickoff for 15 yards and recovered three fumbles. 1985—Attempted one pass with no completions and recovered two fumbles. 1986—Recovered two fumbles. 1988—Recovered two fumbles. 1989—Recovered one fumble.

		RUSHING				RECEIVING				TOTAL		
Year Team	G	Att.	Yds.	Avg.	TD	No.	Yds.	Avg.	TD	TD	Pts.	F.
1984—Buffalo NFL	16	262	1100	4.2	7	34	277	8.2	1	8	48	5
1985—Buffalo NFL	16	223	883	4.0	8	58	576	9.9	1	9	54	8
1986—Buffalo NFL	6	90	377	4.2	4	12	142	11.8	2	6	36	2
1987—Buff. (2)-Rams (2) NFL	4	22	86	3.9	0	9	96	10.7	1	1	6	1

Year	Team	G	Att.	Yds.	Avg.	TD	No.	Yds.	Avg.	TD	TD	Pts.	F.
			RUSHING				**RECEIVING**				**TOTAL**		
1988—L.A. Rams NFL		16	288	1212	4.2	*16	24	124	5.2	2	*18	108	6
1989—L.A. Rams NFL		16	272	1137	4.2	*15	19	85	4.5	0	15	90	7
1990—L.A. Raiders NFL		6	47	164	3.5	1	1	7	7.0	0	1	6	0
Pro totals (7 years)		80	1204	4959	4.1	51	157	1307	8.3	7	58	348	29

BELL, MIKE
DE, CHIEFS

PERSONAL: Born August 30, 1957, at Wichita, Kan. . . . 6-4/265. . . . Full name: Mike J. Bell. . . . Twin brother of Mark E. Bell, tight end with Seattle Seahawks and Baltimore-Indianapolis Colts, 1979, 1980 and 1982-1984.
HIGH SCHOOL: Bishop Carroll (Wichita, Kan.).
COLLEGE: Colorado State.
TRANSACTIONS/CAREER NOTES: Selected by Kansas City Chiefs in first round (second pick overall) of 1979 NFL draft. . . . On injured reserve with knee injury (October 9-November 17, 1979). . . . On injured reserve with torn bicep (September 20, 1980-remainder of season). . . . On injured reserve with groin injury (December 14, 1982-remainder of season). . . . On injured reserve with knee injury (December 13, 1984-remainder of season). . . . Granted roster exemption/leave of absence with drug problem (November 20, 1985-remainder of season). . . . On reserve/did not report (August 11, 1986-entire season; included prison term on drug charges, August 11-December 10, 1986). . . . Reinstated (March 25, 1987). . . . On reserve/non-football injury list with substance abuse (October 22-November 16, 1988).
PLAYING EXPERIENCE: Kansas City NFL, 1979-1985 and 1987-1990. . . . Games: 1979 (11), 1980 (2), 1981 (16), 1982 (6), 1983 (16), 1984 (15), 1985 (11), 1987 (12), 1988 (12), 1989 (15), 1990 (16). Total: 132.
RECORDS/HONORS: Named as defensive lineman on THE SPORTING NEWS college All-America team, 1978.
PRO STATISTICS: 1979—Recovered one fumble. 1981—Recovered one fumble. 1983—Recovered one fumble. 1984—Recovered two fumbles and fumbled once. 1985—Recovered one fumble. 1987—Recovered two fumbles. 1988—Recovered one fumble. 1990—Recovered one fumble.

BELL, RICHARD
RB, CHIEFS

PERSONAL: Born May 3, 1967, at Los Angeles. . . . 6-0/206. . . . Full name: Richard Arron Bell.
HIGH SCHOOL: John Muir (Pasadena, Calif.).
COLLEGE: Nebraska (degree in communications).
TRANSACTIONS/CAREER NOTES: Selected by Pittsburgh Steelers in 12th round (319th pick overall) of 1990 NFL draft. . . . Signed by Steelers (July 10, 1990). . . . Granted unconditional free agency (February 1, 1991). . . . Signed by Kansas City Chiefs (April 2, 1991).

Year	Team	G	Att.	Yds.	Avg.	TD	No.	Yds.	Avg.	TD	TD	Pts.	F.
			RUSHING				**RECEIVING**				**TOTAL**		
1990—Pittsburgh NFL		16	5	18	3.6	0	12	137	11.4	1	1	6	0
Pro totals (1 year)		16	5	18	3.6	0	12	137	11.4	1	1	6	0

BELLAMY, MIKE
WR, EAGLES

PERSONAL: Born June 28, 1966, at New York. . . . 6-0/195. . . . Full name: Michael Sinclair Bellamy II.
HIGH SCHOOL: Kenwood Academy (Chicago).
COLLEGE: College of DuPage (Ill.), then Illinois (degree in speech communications).
TRANSACTIONS/CAREER NOTES: Selected by Philadelphia Eagles in second round (50th pick overall) of 1990 NFL draft. . . . Signed by Eagles (August 1, 1990). . . . On injured reserve with groin injury (September 11-November 5, 1990). . . . On inactive list (November 12, 18 and 25, 1990).
PRO STATISTICS: 1990—Recovered one fumble.

Year	Team	G	No.	Yds.	Avg.	TD	No.	Yds.	Avg.	TD	TD	Pts.	F.
			PUNT RETURNS				**KICKOFF RETURNS**				**TOTAL**		
1990—Philadelphia NFL		6	2	22	11.0	0	1	17	17.0	0	0	0	1
Pro totals (1 year)		6	2	22	11.0	0	1	17	17.0	0	0	0	1

BENNETT, CORNELIUS
LB, BILLS

PERSONAL: Born August 25, 1966, at Birmingham, Ala. . . . 6-2/235. . . . Full name: Cornelius O'Landa Bennett.
HIGH SCHOOL: Ensley (Birmingham, Ala.).
COLLEGE: Alabama.
TRANSACTIONS/CAREER NOTES: Selected by Indianapolis Colts in first round (second pick overall) of 1987 NFL draft. . . . Placed on reserve/unsigned list (August 31-October 30, 1987). . . . Rights traded by Colts to Buffalo Bills in exchange for Bills trading first-round pick in 1988 draft, first- and second-round picks in 1989 draft and running back Greg Bell to Los Angeles Rams (October 31, 1987); Rams also traded running back Eric Dickerson to Colts for first- and second-round picks in 1988 draft, second-round pick in 1989 draft and running back Owen Gill. . . . Signed by Buffalo Bills (October 31, 1987). . . . Granted roster exemption (October 31-November 7, 1987).
PLAYING EXPERIENCE: Buffalo NFL, 1987-1990. . . . Games: 1987 (8), 1988 (16), 1989 (12), 1990 (16). Total: 52.
CHAMPIONSHIP GAME EXPERIENCE: Played in AFC championship game after 1988 and 1990 seasons. . . . Played in Super Bowl XXV after 1990 season.
RECORDS/HONORS: Named as linebacker on THE SPORTING NEWS college All-America team, 1984-1986. . . . Played in Pro Bowl after 1988 and 1990 seasons. . . . Named to THE SPORTING NEWS NFL All-Pro team, 1988.
PRO STATISTICS: 1988—Intercepted two passes for 30 yards and recovered three fumbles. 1989—Intercepted two passes for five yards and recovered two fumbles for five yards. 1990—Returned blocked field-goal attempt 80 yards for a touchdown and recovered two fumbles.

BENNETT, TONY
LB, PACKERS

PERSONAL: Born July 1, 1967, at Alligator, Miss.... 6-2/242. **HIGH SCHOOL:** Coahoma County (Clarksdale, Miss.). **COLLEGE:** Mississippi (degree in physical education and recreation). **TRANSACTIONS/CAREER NOTES:** Selected by Green Bay Packers in first round (18th pick overall) of 1990 NFL draft.... Signed by Packers (July 22, 1990).... On inactive list (December 9 and 16, 1990). **PLAYING EXPERIENCE:** Green Bay NFL, 1990.... Games: 1990 (14). **PRO STATISTICS:** 1990—Recovered one fumble.

BENSON, MITCHELL
DT, CHARGERS

PERSONAL: Born May 30, 1967, at Fort Worth, Tex.... 6-4/300.... Full name: Mitchell Oswell Benson. **HIGH SCHOOL:** Eastern Hills (Fort Worth, Tex.). **COLLEGE:** Texas Christian.
TRANSACTIONS/CAREER NOTES: Selected by Indianapolis Colts in third round (72nd pick overall) of 1989 NFL draft.... Signed by Colts (July 25, 1989).... On inactive list (September 9, 1990).... Released by Colts (November 20, 1990).... Signed by San Diego Chargers (March 12, 1991). **PLAYING EXPERIENCE:** Indianapolis NFL, 1989 and 1990.... Games: 1989 (16), 1990 (9). Total: 25.

BENSON, TOM
LB, RAIDERS

PERSONAL: Born September 6, 1961, at Ardmore, Okla.... 6-2/240.... Full name: Thomas Carl Benson.... Cousin of Rich Turner, defensive tackle with Green Bay Packers, 1981-1983. **HIGH SCHOOL:** Ardmore (Okla.). **COLLEGE:** Oklahoma.
TRANSACTIONS/CAREER NOTES: Selected by Oklahoma Outlaws in 1984 USFL territorial draft.... Selected by Atlanta Falcons in second round (36th pick overall) of 1984 NFL draft.... Signed by Falcons (July 22, 1984).... Traded by Falcons to San Diego Chargers for sixth-round pick in 1987 draft (July 25, 1986).... Granted free agency (February 1, 1987).... Re-signed by Chargers (September 8, 1987).... Granted roster exemption (September 8-September 19, 1987).... On physically unable to perform/active list with shoulder injury (July 25-July 31, 1988).... Passed physical (August 1, 1988).... Traded by Chargers to New England Patriots for seventh-round pick in 1989 draft (August 22, 1988).... On injured reserve with thigh injury (August 30-September 30, 1988).... Granted unconditional free agency (February 1, 1989).... Signed by Los Angeles Raiders (April 1, 1989). **PLAYING EXPERIENCE:** Atlanta NFL, 1984 and 1985; San Diego NFL, 1986 and 1987; New England NFL, 1988; Los Angeles Raiders NFL, 1989 and 1990.... Games: 1984 (16), 1985 (16), 1986 (16), 1987 (11), 1988 (12), 1989 (16), 1990 (16). Total: 103. **CHAMPIONSHIP GAME EXPERIENCE:** Played in AFC championship game after 1990 season. **PRO STATISTICS:** 1985—Recovered two fumbles. 1986—Recovered two fumbles. 1987—Recovered one fumble. 1989—Intercepted two passes for 36 yards and recovered two fumbles.

BENTLEY, ALBERT
RB, COLTS

PERSONAL: Born August 15, 1960, at Naples, Fla.... 5-11/217.... Full name: Albert Timothy Bentley. **HIGH SCHOOL:** Immokalee (Fla.). **COLLEGE:** Miami (Fla.).
TRANSACTIONS/CAREER NOTES: Selected by Chicago Blitz in first round (seventh pick overall) of 1984 USFL draft.... USFL rights traded by Blitz to Michigan Panthers for safety John Arnaud (April 17, 1984).... Signed by Panthers (April 17, 1984).... Granted roster exemption (April 17-May 5, 1984).... Selected by Indianapolis Colts in second round (36th pick overall) of 1984 NFL supplemental draft.... Not protected in merger of Michigan Panthers and Oakland Invaders.... Selected by Invaders in USFL dispersal draft (December 6, 1984).... Released by Invaders (August 1, 1985).... Signed by Indianapolis Colts (September 3, 1985).... Granted roster exemption (September 3-September 12, 1985).... On injured reserve with ankle injury (October 20-November 21, 1986). **CHAMPIONSHIP GAME EXPERIENCE:** Played in USFL championship game after 1985 season. **PRO STATISTICS:** USFL: 1984—Recovered two fumbles. 1985—Attempted one pass with no completions and recovered two fumbles.... NFL: 1985—Attempted one pass with one completion for six yards and recovered one fumble. 1986—Recovered one fumble for nine yards. 1987—Recovered three fumbles. 1988—Attempted one pass with no completions. 1989—Attempted one pass with no completions, recovered blocked punt in end zone for a touchdown and recovered three fumbles for seven yards. 1990—Recovered one fumble and fumbled twice for 11 yards.

Year Team	G	RUSHING Att.	Yds.	Avg.	TD	RECEIVING No.	Yds.	Avg.	TD	KICKOFF RETURNS No.	Yds.	Avg.	TD	TOTAL TD	Pts.	F.
1984— Michigan USFL......	8	18	60	3.3	0	2	7	3.5	0	19	425	22.4	0	0	0	1
1985— Oakland USFL........	18	191	1020	5.3	4	42	441	10.5	3	7	177	25.3	0	7	42	6
1985— Indianapolis NFL ...	15	54	288	5.3	2	11	85	7.7	0	27	674	25.0	0	2	12	1
1986— Indianapolis NFL ...	12	73	351	4.8	3	25	230	9.2	0	32	687	21.5	0	3	18	2
1987— Indianapolis NFL ...	12	142	631	4.4	7	34	447	13.1	2	22	500	22.7	0	9	54	3
1988— Indianapolis NFL ...	16	45	230	5.1	2	26	252	9.7	1	39	775	19.9	0	3	18	2
1989— Indianapolis NFL ...	16	75	299	4.0	1	52	525	10.1	3	17	328	19.3	0	5	30	3
1990— Indianapolis NFL ...	16	137	556	4.1	4	71	664	9.4	2	11	211	19.2	0	6	36	2
USFL totals (2 years)	26	209	1080	5.2	4	44	448	10.2	3	26	602	23.2	0	7	42	7
NFL totals (6 years)	87	526	2355	4.5	19	219	2203	10.1	8	148	3175	21.5	0	28	168	13
Pro totals (8 years)	113	735	3435	4.7	23	263	2651	10.1	11	174	3777	21.7	0	35	210	20

DID YOU KNOW...

...that only 13 of the 169 overtime games played since 1974 have ended in ties?

BENTLEY, RAY
LB, BILLS

PERSONAL: Born November 25, 1960, at Grand Rapids, Mich. . . . 6-2/235. . . . Full name: Ray Russell Bentley.
HIGH SCHOOL: Hudsonville (Mich.).
COLLEGE: Central Michigan.
TRANSACTIONS/CAREER NOTES: Selected by Michigan Panthers in 1983 USFL territorial draft. . . . Signed by Panthers (January 24, 1983). . . . On developmental squad for five games (May 4-June 5, 1983). . . . Protected in merger of Michigan Panthers and Oakland Invaders (December 6, 1984). . . . Sold by Oakland Invaders to Arizona Outlaws (August 14, 1985). . . . Traded by Outlaws to Memphis Showboats for rights to linebacker Steve Hathaway (September 17, 1985). . . . Granted free agency when USFL suspended operations (August 7, 1986). . . . Signed as free agent by Tampa Bay Buccaneers (August 12, 1986). . . . Granted roster exemption (August 12-August 22, 1986). . . . Released by Buccaneers (August 30, 1986). . . . Signed as free agent by Buffalo Bills (September 17, 1986). . . . Released by Bills (October 18, 1986). . . . Re-signed by Bills (October 21, 1986).
CHAMPIONSHIP GAME EXPERIENCE: Played in USFL championship game after 1983 and 1985 seasons. . . . Played in AFC championship game after 1988 and 1990 seasons. . . . Played in Super Bowl XXV after 1990 season.
RECORDS/HONORS: Named as inside linebacker on THE SPORTING NEWS USFL All-Star team, 1983.
PRO STATISTICS: USFL: 1983—Credited with one sack for nine yards and recovered one fumble. 1984—Credited with 1½ sacks for 12½ yards and recovered one fumble. 1985—Credited with two sacks for 20 yards and recovered one fumble. . . . NFL: 1988—Recovered one fumble. 1990—Recovered one fumble for 10 yards.

			INTERCEPTIONS		
Year Team	G	No.	Yds.	Avg.	TD
1983— Michigan USFL	14	2	11	5.5	0
1984— Michigan USFL	18	2	10	5.0	0
1985— Oakland USFL	18	2	9	4.5	0
1986— Buffalo NFL	13	0	0		0
1987— Buffalo NFL	9	0	0		0
1988— Buffalo NFL	16	1	0	.0	0
1989— Buffalo NFL	15	0	0		0
1990— Buffalo NFL	16	1	13	13.0	0
USFL totals (3 years)	50	6	30	5.0	0
NFL totals (5 years)	69	2	13	6.5	0
Pro totals (8 years)	119	8	43	5.4	0

BERGESON, ERIC
S, OILERS

PERSONAL: Born January 1, 1966, at Salt Lake City. . . . 5-11/192. . . . Full name: Eric Scott Bergeson.
HIGH SCHOOL: Timpview (Provo, Utah).
COLLEGE: Brigham Young.
TRANSACTIONS/CAREER NOTES: Signed as free agent by Atlanta Falcons (April 26, 1990). . . . Released by Falcons (October 22, 1990). . . . Re-signed by Falcons to practice squad (October 23, 1990). . . . Activated (October 25, 1990). . . . Released by Falcons (November 6, 1990). . . . Re-signed by Falcons to practice squad (November 7, 1990). . . . Activated (November 23, 1990). . . . Granted unconditional free agency (February 1, 1991). . . . Signed by Houston Oilers (April 1, 1991).
PLAYING EXPERIENCE: Atlanta NFL, 1990. . . . Games: 1990 (13).

BERNSTINE, ROD
TE, CHARGERS

PERSONAL: Born February 8, 1965, at Fairfield, Calif. . . . 6-3/238. . . . Full name: Rod Earl Bernstine.
HIGH SCHOOL: Bryan (Tex.).
COLLEGE: Texas A&M.
TRANSACTIONS/CAREER NOTES: Selected by San Diego Chargers in first round (24th pick overall) of 1987 NFL draft. . . . Signed by Chargers (August 11, 1987). . . . On injured reserve with hamstring injury (September 8-October 24, 1987). . . . On injured reserve with knee injury (December 9, 1988-remainder of season). . . . On injured reserve with knee injury (November 25, 1989-remainder of season). . . . On inactive list (November 11, 1990). . . . On injured reserve with hamstring injury (November 21-December 22, 1990).
PRO STATISTICS: 1987—Returned one kickoff for 13 yards and recovered one fumble.

		RUSHING				RECEIVING				TOTAL		
Year Team	G	Att.	Yds.	Avg.	TD	No.	Yds.	Avg.	TD	TD	Pts.	F.
1987— San Diego NFL	10	1	9	9.0	0	10	76	7.6	1	1	6	0
1988— San Diego NFL	14	2	7	3.5	0	29	340	11.7	0	0	0	0
1989— San Diego NFL	5	15	137	9.1	1	21	222	10.6	1	2	12	0
1990— San Diego NFL	12	124	589	4.8	4	8	40	5.0	0	4	24	1
Pro totals (4 years)	41	142	742	5.2	5	68	678	10.0	2	7	42	1

BERRY, LATIN
CB, RAMS

PERSONAL: Born January 13, 1967, at Lakeview Terrace, Calif. . . . 5-10/196. . . . Full name: Latin Dafonso Berry.
HIGH SCHOOL: Milwaukie (Ore.).
COLLEGE: Oregon.
TRANSACTIONS/CAREER NOTES: Selected by Los Angeles Rams in third round (78th pick overall) of 1990 NFL draft. . . . Signed by Rams (July 13, 1990).

		KICKOFF RETURNS			
Year Team	G	No.	Yds.	Avg.	TD
1990— L.A. Rams NFL	16	17	315	18.5	0
Pro totals (1 year)	16	17	315	18.5	0

BERRY, RAY

LB, VIKINGS

PERSONAL: Born October 28, 1963, at Lovington, N.M. . . . 6-2/226. . . . Full name: Raymond Lenn Berry.
HIGH SCHOOL: Cooper (Abilene, Tex.).
COLLEGE: Baylor (degree in business management and real estate, 1987).
TRANSACTIONS/CAREER NOTES: Selected by Minnesota Vikings in second round (44th pick overall) of 1987 NFL draft. . . . Signed by Vikings (August 10, 1987).
PLAYING EXPERIENCE: Minnesota NFL, 1987- 1990. . . . Games: 1987 (11), 1988 (15), 1989 (16), 1990 (16). Total: 58.
CHAMPIONSHIP GAME EXPERIENCE: Played in NFC championship game after 1987 season.
PRO STATISTICS: 1987—Recovered one fumble. 1989—Credited with a safety.

BETHUNE, GEORGE

LB, RAMS

PERSONAL: Born March 30, 1967, at Fort Walton Beach, Fla. . . . 6-4/240. . . . Full name: George Edward Bethune.
HIGH SCHOOL: Choctawhatchee (Fort Walton Beach, Fla.).
COLLEGE: Alabama (degree in criminal justice, 1990).
TRANSACTIONS/CAREER NOTES: Selected by Los Angeles Rams in seventh round (188th pick overall) of 1989 NFL draft. . . . Signed by Rams (July 13, 1989).
PLAYING EXPERIENCE: Los Angeles Rams NFL, 1989 and 1990. . . . Games: 1989 (16), 1990 (16). Total: 32.
CHAMPIONSHIP GAME EXPERIENCE: Played in NFC championship game after 1989 season.
PRO STATISTICS: 1989—Recovered one fumble.

BEUERLEIN, STEVE

QB, RAIDERS

PERSONAL: Born March 7, 1965, at Hollywood, Calif. . . . 6-2/210. . . . Full name: Stephen Taylor Beuerlein. . . . Name pronounced BURR-line.
HIGH SCHOOL: Servite (Anaheim, Calif.).
COLLEGE: Notre Dame (bachelor of arts degree in American studies, 1987).
TRANSACTIONS/CAREER NOTES: Selected by Los Angeles Raiders in fourth round (110th pick overall) of 1987 NFL draft. . . . Signed by Raiders (July 24, 1987). . . . On injured reserve with elbow and shoulder injuries (September 7, 1987-entire season). . . . Granted free agency (February 1, 1990). . . . Re-signed by Raiders (September 3, 1990). . . . Granted roster exemption (September 3-September 16, 1990). . . . On inactive list (September 16, 23, 30; October 7, 14, 21, 28; November 4, 11, 19, 25; and December 2, 10, 16, 22 and 30, 1990).
CHAMPIONSHIP GAME EXPERIENCE: Member of Los Angeles Raiders for AFC championship game after 1990 season; inactive.
PRO STATISTICS: Passer rating points: 1988 (66.6), 1989 (78.4). Career: 72.2. 1988—Caught one pass for 21 yards and recovered two fumbles and fumbled six times for minus one yard. 1989—Recovered three fumbles and fumbled six times for minus eight yards.

				PASSING						RUSHING				TOTAL		
Year	Team	G	Att.	Cmp.	Pct.	Yds.	TD	Int.	Avg.	Att.	Yds.	Avg.	TD	TD	Pts.	F.
1988— L.A. Raiders NFL		10	238	105	44.1	1643	8	7	6.90	30	35	1.2	0	0	0	6
1989— L.A. Raiders NFL		10	217	108	49.8	1677	13	9	7.73	16	39	2.4	0	0	0	6
Pro totals (2 years)		20	455	213	46.8	3320	21	16	7.30	46	74	1.6	0	0	0	12

BIASUCCI, DEAN

PK, COLTS

PERSONAL: Born July 25, 1962, at Niagara Falls, N.Y. . . . 6-0/190.
HIGH SCHOOL: Miramar (Fla.).
COLLEGE: Western Carolina.
TRANSACTIONS/CAREER NOTES: Signed as free agent by Atlanta Falcons (May 16, 1984). . . . Released by Falcons (August 14, 1984). . . . Signed as free agent by Indianapolis Colts (September 8, 1984). . . . Released by Colts (August 27, 1985). . . . Re-signed by Colts (April 22, 1986). . . . Granted free agency (February 1, 1990). . . . Re-signed by Colts (July 27, 1990).
RECORDS/HONORS: Established NFL record for most field goals, 50 or more yards, season (6), 1988. . . . Played in Pro Bowl after 1987 season. . . . Named to THE SPORTING NEWS NFL All-Pro team, 1988.
PRO STATISTICS: 1988—Recovered one fumble.

			PLACE-KICKING			
Year	Team	G	XPM	XPA	FGM	FGA	Pts.
1984— Indianapolis NFL		15	13	14	3	5	22
1986— Indianapolis NFL		16	26	27	13	25	65
1987— Indianapolis NFL		12	24	24	24	27	96
1988— Indianapolis NFL		16	39	40	25	32	114
1989— Indianapolis NFL		16	31	32	21	27	94
1990— Indianapolis NFL		16	32	33	17	24	83
Pro totals (6 years)		91	165	170	103	140	474

BICKETT, DUANE

LB, COLTS

PERSONAL: Born December 1, 1962, at Los Angeles. . . . 6-5/251. . . . Full name: Duane Clair Bickett. . . . Name pronounced BIK-ett.
HIGH SCHOOL: Glendale (Calif.).
COLLEGE: Southern California (degree in accounting, 1986).
TRANSACTIONS/CAREER NOTES: Selected by Los Angeles Express in 1985 USFL territorial draft. . . . Selected by Indianapolis Colts in first round (fifth pick overall) of 1985 NFL draft. . . . Signed by Colts (August 7, 1985).
RECORDS/HONORS: Named as linebacker on THE SPORTING NEWS college All-America team, 1984. . . . Played in Pro Bowl after 1987 season.
PRO STATISTICS: 1985—Recovered two fumbles. 1986—Recovered one fumble. 1987—Recovered two fumbles for 32 yards and fumbled once. 1988—Recovered one fumble. 1989—Recovered three fumbles for two yards. 1990—Recovered two fumbles.

Year	Team	G	INTERCEPTIONS No.	Yds.	Avg.	TD
1985—	Indianapolis NFL	16	1	0	.0	0
1986—	Indianapolis NFL	16	2	10	5.0	0
1987—	Indianapolis NFL	12	0	0		0
1988—	Indianapolis NFL	16	3	7	2.3	0
1989—	Indianapolis NFL	16	1	6	6.0	0
1990—	Indianapolis NFL	15	1	9	9.0	0
	Pro totals (6 years)	91	8	32	4.0	0

BILLUPS, LEWIS
CB, BENGALS

PERSONAL: Born October 10, 1963, at Tampa, Fla. . . . 5- 11/ 182. . . . Full name: Lewis Kenneth Billups.
HIGH SCHOOL: Niceville (Fla.).
COLLEGE: North Alabama.

TRANSACTIONS/CAREER NOTES: Selected by Birmingham Stallions in 1986 USFL territorial draft. . . . Selected by Cincinnati Bengals in second round (38th pick overall) of 1986 NFL draft. . . . Signed by Bengals (August 13, 1986). . . . On injured reserve with knee injury (October 17-November 10, 1986). . . . Granted free agency (February 1, 1990). . . . Re-signed by Bengals (September 5, 1990). . . . Activated (September 6, 1990). . . . On inactive list (December 16, 1990).
CHAMPIONSHIP GAME EXPERIENCE: Played in AFC championship game after 1988 season. . . . Played in Super Bowl XXIII after 1988 season.
PRO STATISTICS: 1986—Recovered one fumble for two yards. 1987—Recovered one fumble. 1988—Recovered two fumbles for 26 yards and a touchdown. 1990—Recovered two fumbles for four yards.

Year	Team	G	INTERCEPTIONS No.	Yds.	Avg.	TD
1986—	Cincinnati NFL..........	12	0	0		0
1987—	Cincinnati NFL..........	11	0	0		0
1988—	Cincinnati NFL..........	16	4	47	11.8	0
1989—	Cincinnati NFL..........	16	2	0	.0	0
1990—	Cincinnati NFL..........	15	3	39	13.0	0
	Pro totals (5 years)	70	9	86	9.6	0

BINGHAM, GUY
C, FALCONS

PERSONAL: Born February 25, 1958, at Koiaumi Gumma Ken, Japan. . . . 6-3/260. . . . Full name: Guy Richard Bingham.
HIGH SCHOOL: Weatherwax (Aberdeen, Wash.).
COLLEGE: Montana (degree in physical education).

TRANSACTIONS/CAREER NOTES: Selected by New York Jets in 10th round (260th pick overall) of 1980 NFL draft. . . . On injured reserve with knee injury (September 7-November 19, 1982). . . . On injured reserve with knee injury (December 16, 1988-remainder of season). . . . Traded by Jets to Atlanta Falcons for seventh-round pick in 1990 NFL draft (September 4, 1989). . . . Granted roster exemption (September 3-September 8, 1990).
PLAYING EXPERIENCE: New York Jets NFL, 1980- 1988; Atlanta NFL, 1989 and 1990. . . . Games: 1980 (16), 1981 (16), 1982 (7), 1983 (16), 1984 (16), 1985 (16), 1986 (16), 1987 (12), 1988 (10), 1989 (16), 1990 (16). Total: 157.
CHAMPIONSHIP GAME EXPERIENCE: Played in AFC championship game after 1982 season.
PRO STATISTICS: 1980—Returned one kickoff for 19 yards. 1984—Recovered one fumble. 1986—Recovered one fumble.

BIRDEN, J.J.
WR/KR, CHIEFS

PERSONAL: Born June 16, 1965, at Portland, Ore. . . . 5-9/ 170. . . . Full name: LaJourdain J. Birden.
HIGH SCHOOL: Lakeridge (Lake Oswego, Ore.).
COLLEGE: Oregon (degree in leisure studies and services).
TRANSACTIONS/CAREER NOTES: Selected by Cleveland Browns in eighth round (216th pick overall) of 1988 NFL draft. . . . On physically unable to perform list with knee injury (August 23, 1988-entire season). . . . Released by Browns (September 5, 1989). . . . Signed by Dallas Cowboys to developmental squad (November 1, 1989). . . . Released by Cowboys (January 5, 1990). . . . Signed by Kansas City Chiefs (April 3, 1990). . . . Released by Chiefs (September 3, 1990). . . . Re-signed by Chiefs to practice squad (October 1, 1990). . . . Activated (October 10, 1990).

Year Team	G	RECEIVING No.	Yds.	Avg.	TD	PUNT RETURNS No.	Yds.	Avg.	TD	KICKOFF RETURNS No.	Yds.	Avg.	TD	TOTAL TD	Pts.	F.
1990— Kansas City NFL.	11	15	352	23.5	3	10	72	7.2	0	1	14	14.0	0	3	18	1
Pro totals (1 year)	11	15	352	23.5	3	10	72	7.2	0	1	14	14.0	0	3	18	1

BLACKMON, ROBERT
S, SEAHAWKS

PERSONAL: Born May 12, 1967, at Bay City, Tex. . . . 6-0/ 198. . . . Full name: Robert James Blackmon.
HIGH SCHOOL: Van Vleck (Tex.).
COLLEGE: Baylor (degree in therapy recreation).

TRANSACTIONS/CAREER NOTES: Selected by Seattle Seahawks in second round (34th pick overall) of 1990 NFL draft. . . . Signed by Seahawks (July 29, 1990). . . . On inactive list (October 21, 1990).
PLAYING EXPERIENCE: Seattle NFL, 1990. . . . Games: 1990 (15).
PRO STATISTICS: 1990—Recovered one fumble.

BLADES, BENNIE
S, LIONS

PERSONAL: Born September 3, 1966, at Fort Lauderdale, Fla. . . . 6-1/221. . . . Full name: Horatio Benedict Blades. . . . Brother of Brian Blades, wide receiver with Seattle Seahawks.
HIGH SCHOOL: Piper (Sunrise, Fla.).
COLLEGE: Miami (Fla.).
TRANSACTIONS/CAREER NOTES: Selected by Detroit Lions in first round (third pick overall) of 1988 NFL draft. . . . Signed by Lions (July 14, 1988). . . . On inactive list (September 23, 30; and October 7 and 14, 1990).
RECORDS/HONORS: Named as defensive back on THE SPORTING NEWS college All-America team, 1986 and 1987.
PRO STATISTICS: 1988—Recovered four fumbles for 22 yards. 1989—Recovered one fumble. 1990—Recovered one fumble.

		INTERCEPTIONS			
Year Team	G	No.	Yds.	Avg.	TD
1988— Detroit NFL	15	2	12	6.0	0
1989— Detroit NFL	16	0	0		0
1990— Detroit NFL	12	2	25	12.5	0
Pro totals (3 years)	43	4	37	9.3	0

BLADES, BRIAN
WR, SEAHAWKS

PERSONAL: Born July 24, 1965, at Fort Lauderdale, Fla. . . . 5-11/191. . . . Full name: Brian Keith Blades. . . . Brother of Bennie Blades, safety with Detroit Lions.
HIGH SCHOOL: Piper (Sunrise, Fla.).
COLLEGE: Miami (Fla.).
TRANSACTIONS/CAREER NOTES: Selected by Seattle Seahawks in second round (49th pick overall) of 1988 NFL draft. . . . Signed by Seahawks (May 19, 1988).
RECORDS/HONORS: Played in Pro Bowl after 1989 season.
PRO STATISTICS: 1988—Recovered one fumble. 1989—Recovered one fumble.

		RUSHING				RECEIVING				TOTAL		
Year Team	G	Att.	Yds.	Avg.	TD	No.	Yds.	Avg.	TD	TD	Pts.	F.
1988— Seattle NFL	16	5	24	4.8	0	40	682	17.1	8	8	48	1
1989— Seattle NFL	16	1	3	3.0	0	77	1063	13.8	5	5	30	3
1990— Seattle NFL	16	3	19	6.3	0	49	525	10.7	3	3	18	0
Pro totals (3 years)	48	9	46	5.1	0	166	2270	13.7	16	16	96	4

BLADOS, BRIAN
G, BENGALS

PERSONAL: Born January 11, 1962, at Arlington, Va. . . . 6-5/296. . . . Full name: Brian Timothy Blados.
HIGH SCHOOL: Washington Lee (Arlington, Va.).
COLLEGE: North Carolina.
TRANSACTIONS/CAREER NOTES: Selected by Philadelphia Stars in 1984 USFL territorial draft. . . . Selected by Cincinnati Bengals in first round (28th pick overall) of 1984 NFL draft. . . . Signed by Bengals (June 28, 1984). . . . On inactive list (October 7, 1990). . . . On injured reserve with neck injury (October 12, 1990-entire season).
PLAYING EXPERIENCE: Cincinnati NFL, 1984-1990. . . . Games: 1984 (16), 1985 (16), 1986 (16), 1987 (11), 1988 (16), 1989 (13), 1990 (4). Total: 92.
CHAMPIONSHIP GAME EXPERIENCE: Played in AFC championship game after 1988 season. . . . Played in Super Bowl XXIII after 1988 season.
PRO STATISTICS: 1985—Caught one pass for four yards.

BLAND, CARL
WR, PACKERS

PERSONAL: Born August 17, 1961, at Fluvanna County, Va. . . . 5-11/178. . . . Full name: Carl Nathaniel Bland.
HIGH SCHOOL: Thomas Jefferson (Richmond, Va.).
COLLEGE: Virginia Union.
TRANSACTIONS/CAREER NOTES: Signed as free agent by Detroit Lions (May 3, 1984). . . . On injured reserve with hamstring injury (August 20-November 7, 1984). . . . Activated after clearing procedural waivers (November 9, 1984). . . . Released by Lions (September 3, 1985). . . . Re-signed by Lions (October 17, 1985). . . . Released by Lions (October 31, 1985). . . . Re-signed by Lions (November 4, 1985). . . . On injured reserve with knee injury (September 7-October 24, 1987). . . . Granted unconditional free agency (February 1, 1989). . . . Signed by Green Bay Packers (March 27, 1989). . . . Released by Packers (September 8, 1990). . . . Re-signed by Packers (September 22, 1990).
PRO STATISTICS: 1986—Recovered two fumbles for eight yards. 1988—Rushed once for four yards and returned five punts for 59 yards. 1989—Recovered three fumbles for four yards (including one in end zone for a touchdown). 1990—Recovered one fumble.

		RECEIVING				KICKOFF RETURNS				TOTAL		
Year Team	G	No.	Yds.	Avg.	TD	No.	Yds.	Avg.	TD	TD	Pts.	F.
1984— Detroit NFL	3	0	0		0	0	0		0	0	0	0
1985— Detroit NFL	8	12	157	13.1	0	0	0		0	0	0	0
1986— Detroit NFL	16	44	511	11.6	2	6	114	19.0	0	2	12	1
1987— Detroit NFL	10	2	14	7.0	1	2	44	22.0	0	1	6	0
1988— Detroit NFL	16	21	307	14.6	2	8	179	22.4	0	2	12	1
1989— Green Bay NFL	16	11	164	14.9	1	13	256	19.7	0	2	12	0
1990— Green Bay NFL	14	0	0		0	7	104	14.9	0	0	0	0
Pro totals (7 years)	83	90	1153	12.8	6	36	697	19.4	0	7	42	2

BLANKENSHIP, BRIAN

G, STEELERS

PERSONAL: Born April 7, 1963, at Omaha, Neb. . . . 6-1/277. . . . Full name: Brian Patrick Blankenship.
HIGH SCHOOL: Daniel J. Gross (Omaha, Neb.).
COLLEGE: Nebraska-Omaha, then Nebraska.
TRANSACTIONS/CAREER NOTES: Selected by Memphis Showboats in 1986 USFL territorial draft. . . . Signed as free agent by Pittsburgh Steelers (May 13, 1986). . . . Released by Steelers (September 1, 1986). . . . Signed as free agent by Indianapolis Colts (May 11, 1987). . . . Released by Colts (August 7, 1987). . . . Signed as free agent replacement player by Pittsburgh Steelers (September 24, 1987). . . . Released by Steelers (August 30, 1988). . . . Re-signed by Steelers (September 21, 1988).
PLAYING EXPERIENCE: Pittsburgh NFL, 1987-1990. . . . Games: 1987 (13), 1988 (13), 1989 (16), 1990 (16). Total: 58.
PRO STATISTICS: 1988—Returned one kickoff for five yards and recovered one fumble. 1990—Fumbled once.

BLAYLOCK, TONY

CB, BROWNS

PERSONAL: Born February 21, 1965, at Raleigh, N.C. . . . 5-11/190. . . . Full name: Anthony Darius Blaylock.
HIGH SCHOOL: Garner (N.C.).
COLLEGE: Winston-Salem State.
TRANSACTIONS/CAREER NOTES: Selected by Cleveland Browns in fourth round (103rd pick overall) of 1988 NFL draft. . . . Signed by Browns (July 17, 1988). . . . On injured reserve with back injury (December 12, 1988-remainder of season).
PLAYING EXPERIENCE: Cleveland NFL, 1988-1990. . . . Games: 1988 (12), 1989 (16), 1990 (16). Total: 44.
CHAMPIONSHIP GAME EXPERIENCE: Member of Cleveland Browns for AFC championship game after 1989 season; did not play.
PRO STATISTICS: 1990—Intercepted two passes for 45 yards and recovered one fumble for 30 yards and a touchdown.

BOLCAR, NED

LB, DOLPHINS

PERSONAL: Born January 12, 1967, at Phillipsburg, N.J. . . . 6-1/235. . . . Full name: Ned Francis Bolcar.
HIGH SCHOOL: Phillipsburg (N.J.).
COLLEGE: Notre Dame (bachelor of arts degree in liberal arts, 1990).
TRANSACTIONS/CAREER NOTES: Selected by Seattle Seahawks in sixth round (146th pick overall) of 1990 NFL draft. . . . Signed by Seahawks (July 16, 1990). . . . On injured reserve with knee injury (October 10, 1990-remainder of season). . . . Granted unconditional free agency (February 1, 1991). . . . Signed by Miami Dolphins (March 26, 1991).
PLAYING EXPERIENCE: Seattle NFL, 1990. . . . Games: 1990 (5).
PRO STATISTICS: 1990—Intercepted one pass for no yards.

BONO, STEVE

QB, 49ERS

PERSONAL: Born May 11, 1962, at Norristown, Pa. . . . 6-4/215. . . . Full name: Steven Christopher Bono.
HIGH SCHOOL: Norristown (Pa.).
COLLEGE: UCLA.
TRANSACTIONS/CAREER NOTES: Selected by Memphis Showboats in 1985 USFL territorial draft. . . . Selected by Minnesota Vikings in sixth round (142nd pick overall) of 1985 NFL draft. . . . Signed by Vikings (July 10, 1985). . . . Released by Vikings (October 4, 1986). . . . Re-signed by Vikings (November 19, 1986). . . . Released by Vikings (December 9, 1986). . . . Signed as free agent by Pittsburgh Steelers (March 25, 1987). . . . Released by Steelers (September 7, 1987). . . . Re-signed as replacement player by Steelers (September 24, 1987). . . . Released by Steelers (April 13, 1989). . . . Signed by San Francisco 49ers (June 13, 1989). . . . On inactive list (September 10, 16; October 7, 14, 21, 28; November 4; and December 3 and 17, 1990). . . . Active for seven games with 49ers in 1990; did not play.
CHAMPIONSHIP GAME EXPERIENCE: Member of San Francisco 49ers for NFC championship game after 1989 and 1990 seasons; inactive. . . . Member of 49ers for Super Bowl XXIV after 1989 season; inactive.
PRO STATISTICS: Passer rating points: 1985 (39.6), 1986 (79.2), 1987 (76.3), 1988 (25.9), 1989 (157.9). Career: 61.4. . . . 1987—Caught one pass for two yards and recovered three fumbles.

			PASSING						RUSHING				TOTAL		
Year Team	G	Att.	Cmp.	Pct.	Yds.	TD	Int.	Avg.	Att.	Yds.	Avg.	TD	TD	Pts.	F.
1985— Minnesota NFL	1	10	1	10.0	5	0	0	.50	0	0		0	0	0	0
1986— Minnesota NFL	1	1	1	100.0	3	0	0	3.00	0	0		0	0	0	0
1987— Pittsburgh NFL	3	74	34	45.9	438	5	2	5.92	8	27	3.4	1	1	6	5
1988— Pittsburgh NFL	2	35	10	28.6	110	1	2	3.14	0	0		0	0	0	0
1989— San Francisco NFL....	1	5	4	80.0	62	1	0	12.40	0	0		0	0	0	0
Pro totals (5 years)	8	125	50	40.0	618	7	4	4.94	8	27	3.4	1	1	6	5

BOOTY, JOHN

DB, EAGLES

PERSONAL: Born October 9, 1965, at Deberry, Tex. . . . 6-0/180. . . . Full name: John Fitzgerald Booty.
HIGH SCHOOL: Carthage (Tex.).
COLLEGE: Cisco Junior College (Tex.), then Texas Christian (bachelor of arts degree in speech communications, 1988).
TRANSACTIONS/CAREER NOTES: Selected by New York Jets in 10th round (257th pick overall) of 1988 NFL . Signed by Jets (June 7, 1988). . . . On injured reserve with neck injury (September 5-October 17, 1989). . . . Granted free agency (February 1, 1990). . . . Re-signed by Jets (July 17, 1990). . . . On injured reserve with knee injury (December 1-December 28, 1990). . . . Granted unconditional free agency (February 1, 1991). . . . Signed by Philadelphia Eagles (April 1, 1991).
PRO STATISTICS: 1988—Recovered two fumbles.

		INTERCEPTIONS			
Year Team	G	No.	Yds.	Avg.	TD
1988— N.Y. Jets NFL..............	16	3	0	.0	0
1989— N.Y. Jets NFL..............	9	1	13	13.0	0
1990— N.Y. Jets NFL..............	13	0	0		0
Pro totals (3 years)	38	4	13	3.3	0

BORTZ, MARK
G, BEARS

PERSONAL: Born February 12, 1961, at Pardeeville, Wis. . . . 6-6/272. . . . Full name: Mark Steven Bortz.
HIGH SCHOOL: Pardeeville (Wis.).
COLLEGE: Iowa.
TRANSACTIONS/CAREER NOTES: Selected by Los Angeles Express in fourth round (48th pick overall) of 1983 USFL draft. . . . Selected by Chicago Bears in eighth round (219th pick overall) of 1983 NFL draft. . . . Signed by Bears (June 2, 1983).
PLAYING EXPERIENCE: Chicago NFL, 1983-1990. Games: 1983 (16), 1984 (15), 1985 (16), 1986 (15), 1987 (12), 1988 (16), 1989 (16), 1990 (16). Total: 122.
CHAMPIONSHIP GAME EXPERIENCE: Played in NFC championship game after 1984, 1985 and 1988 seasons. . . . Played in Super Bowl XX after 1985 season.
RECORDS/HONORS: Played in Pro Bowl after 1988 season. . . . Named to play in Pro Bowl after 1990 season; replaced due to injury by William Roberts.
PRO STATISTICS: 1986—Caught one pass for eight yards. 1989—Recovered one fumble.

BOSA, JOHN
DE, JETS

PERSONAL: Born January 10, 1964, at Keene, N.H. . . . 6-4/275. . . . Full name: John Wilfred Bosa.
HIGH SCHOOL: Keene (N.H.).
COLLEGE: Boston College (bachelor of science degree in marketing, 1987).
TRANSACTIONS/CAREER NOTES: Selected by Miami Dolphins in first round (16th pick overall) of 1987 NFL draft. . . . Signed by Dolphins (September 1, 1987). . . . Granted roster exemption (September 1 and 2, 1987). . . . On injured reserve with knee injury (October 19, 1988-remainder of season). . . . Released by Dolphins (August 8, 1990). . . . Re-signed by Dolphins (August 9, 1990). . . . On injured reserve with knee injury (August 9, 1990-entire season). . . . Granted unconditional free agency (February 1, 1991). . . . Signed by New York Jets (March 15, 1991).
PLAYING EXPERIENCE: Miami NFL, 1987-1989. . . . Games: 1987 (12), 1988 (6), 1989 (13). Total: 31.
PRO STATISTICS: 1987—Recovered two fumbles.

BOSO, CAP
TE, BEARS

PERSONAL: Born September 10, 1963, at Kansas City, Mo. . . . 6-4/240. . . . Full name: Casper N. Boso. . . . Name pronounced BO-so.
HIGH SCHOOL: Bishop Chatard (Indianapolis, Ind.).
COLLEGE: Joliet Junior College (Ill.), then Illinois (liberal arts and sciences degree in sociology, 1986).
TRANSACTIONS/CAREER NOTES: Selected by Orlando Renegades in 1986 USFL territorial draft. . . . Selected by Pittsburgh Steelers in eighth round (207th pick overall) of 1986 NFL draft. . . . Signed by Steelers (July 18, 1986). . . . Released by Steelers (September 1, 1986). . . . Signed as free agent by St. Louis Cardinals (December 10, 1986). . . . Released by Cardinals (September 7, 1987). . . . Awarded on waivers to Chicago Bears (September 8, 1987). . . . On injured reserve with neck injury (August 31-November 11, 1988). . . . On inactive list (November 25, 1990). . . . On injured reserve with ankle injury (December 21, 1990-remainder of season).
CHAMPIONSHIP GAME EXPERIENCE: Member of Chicago Bears for NFC championship game after 1988 season; inactive.

| | | | RECEIVING | | |
Year Team	G	No.	Yds.	Avg.	TD
1986— St. Louis NFL	2	0	0		0
1987— Chicago NFL	12	17	188	11.1	2
1988— Chicago NFL	6	6	50	8.3	0
1989— Chicago NFL	16	17	182	10.7	1
1990— Chicago NFL	13	11	135	12.3	1
Pro totals (5 years)	49	51	555	10.9	4

BOSTIC, JEFF
C, REDSKINS

PERSONAL: Born September 18, 1958, at Greensboro, N.C. . . . 6-2/260. . . . Brother of Joe Bostic, guard with St. Louis-Phoenix Cardinals, 1979-1988.
HIGH SCHOOL: Benjamin L. Smith (Greensboro, N.C.).
COLLEGE: Clemson.
TRANSACTIONS/CAREER NOTES: Signed as free agent by Philadelphia Eagles (May 20, 1980). . . . Released by Eagles (August 26, 1980). . . . Signed as free agent by Washington Redskins (September 1, 1984). . . . On injured reserve with knee injury (October 23, 1984-remainder of season). . . . On injured reserve with knee injury (August 24-October 19, 1985).
PLAYING EXPERIENCE: Washington NFL, 1980-1990. . . . Games: 1980 (16), 1981 (16), 1982 (9), 1983 (16), 1984 (8), 1985 (10), 1986 (16), 1987 (12), 1988 (13), 1989 (16), 1990 (16). Total: 148.
CHAMPIONSHIP GAME EXPERIENCE: Played in NFC championship game after 1982, 1983, 1986 and 1987 seasons. . . . Played in Super Bowl XVII after 1982 season, Super Bowl XVIII after 1983 season and Super Bowl XXII after 1987 season.
RECORDS/HONORS: Played in Pro Bowl after 1983 season.
PRO STATISTICS: 1981—Caught one pass for minus four yards and recovered one fumble. 1983—Recovered three fumbles. 1984—Recovered two fumbles. 1985—Recovered one fumble. 1986—Recovered one fumble for one yard.

BOWLES, TODD
S, 49ERS

PERSONAL: Born November 18, 1963, at Elizabeth, N.J. . . . 6-2/205. . . . Full name: Todd Robert Bowles.
HIGH SCHOOL: Elizabeth (N.J.).
COLLEGE: Temple.
TRANSACTIONS/CAREER NOTES: Selected by Baltimore Stars in 1986 USFL territorial draft. . . . Signed as free agent by Washington Redskins (May 6, 1986). . . . Granted free agency (February 1, 1990). . . . Re-signed by Redskins (July 30, 1990). . . . Granted unconditional free agency (February 1, 1991). . . . Signed by San Francisco 49ers (April 1, 1991).
CHAMPIONSHIP GAME EXPERIENCE: Played in NFC championship game after 1986 and 1987 seasons. . . . Played in Super Bowl XXII after 1987 season.
PRO STATISTICS: 1987—Recovered one fumble. 1989—Recovered one fumble. 1990—Returned one kickoff for no yards and recovered one fumble.

Year	Team	G	No.	Yds.	Avg.	TD
			INTERCEPTIONS			
1986—	Washington NFL	15	2	0	.0	0
1987—	Washington NFL	12	4	24	6.0	0
1988—	Washington NFL	16	1	20	20.0	0
1989—	Washington NFL	16	3	25	8.3	0
1990—	Washington NFL	16	3	74	24.7	0
Pro totals (5 years)		75	13	143	11.0	0

BOYER, MARK

TE, JETS

PERSONAL: Born September 16, 1962, at Huntington Beach, Calif. . . . 6-4/242. . . . Full name: Mark Hearn Boyer.
HIGH SCHOOL: Edison (Huntington Beach, Calif.).
COLLEGE: Southern California.
TRANSACTIONS/CAREER NOTES: Selected by Los Angeles Express in 1985 USFL territorial draft. . . . Selected by Indianapolis Colts in ninth round (229th pick overall) of 1985 NFL draft. . . . Signed by Colts (July 18, 1985). . . . On injured reserve with broken arm (October 26-December 4, 1987). . . . Granted free agency (February 1, 1988). . . . Re-signed by Colts (August 23, 1988). . . . Granted unconditional free agency (February 1, 1990). . . . Signed by New York Jets (March 20, 1990).
PRO STATISTICS: 1985—Recovered one fumble. 1986—Fumbled once. 1989—Recovered one fumble and fumbled octe. 1990—Returned one kickoff for 14 yards and fumbled once.

Year	Team	G	No.	Yds.	Avg.	TD
			RECEIVING			
1985—	Indianapolis NFL	16	25	274	11.0	0
1986—	Indianapolis NFL	16	22	237	10.8	1
1987—	Indianapolis NFL	7	10	73	7.3	0
1988—	Indianapolis NFL	16	27	256	9.5	2
1989—	Indianapolis NFL	16	11	58	5.3	2
1990—	N.Y. Jets NFL	16	40	334	8.4	1
Pro totals (6 years)		87	135	1232	9.1	6

BRACKEN, DON

P, PACKERS

PERSONAL: Born February 16, 1962, at Coalinga, Calif. . . . 6-1/211. . . . Full name: Donald Craig Bracken.
HIGH SCHOOL: Hot Springs County (Thermopolis, Wyo.).
COLLEGE: Michigan (bachelor of science degree in physical education).
TRANSACTIONS/CAREER NOTES: Selected by Michigan Panthers in 1984 USFL territorial draft. . . . Signed by Panthers (January 8, 1984). . . . Released by Panthers (February 16, 1984). . . . Signed as free agent by Kansas City Chiefs (May 4, 1984). . . . Released by Chiefs (June 1, 1984). . . . Signed as free agent by Indianapolis Colts (June 14, 1984). . . . Released by Colts (August 6, 1984). . . . Signed as free agent by Denver Broncos (January 30, 1985). . . . Released by Broncos (August 26, 1985). . . . Signed as free agent by Green Bay Packers (November 6, 1985). . . . On injured reserve with dislocated elbow (December 5, 1986-remainder of season). . . . Released by Packers (September 7, 1987). . . . Re-signed by Packers (September 8, 1987).

Year	Team	G	No.	Avg.	Blk.
			PUNTING		
1985—	Green Bay NFL	7	26	40.5	0
1986—	Green Bay NFL	13	55	40.1	2
1987—	Green Bay NFL	12	72	40.9	1
1988—	Green Bay NFL	16	85	38.7	1
1989—	Green Bay NFL	16	66	40.6	0
1990—	Green Bay NFL	16	64	38.0	1
Pro totals (6 years)		80	368	39.8	5

BRADY, ED

LB, BENGALS

PERSONAL: Born June 17, 1960, at Morris, Ill. . . . 6-2/236. . . . Full name: Ed John Brady.
HIGH SCHOOL: Morris (Ill.).
COLLEGE: Illinois.
TRANSACTIONS/CAREER NOTES: Selected by Chicago Blitz in 1984 USFL territorial draft. . . . Selected by Los Angeles Rams in eighth round (215th pick overall) of 1984 NFL draft. . . . Signed by Rams (July 14, 1984). . . . Released by Rams (August 27, 1984). . . . Re-signed by Rams (August 28, 1984). . . . Released by Rams (September 1, 1986). . . . Awarded on waivers to Cincinnati Bengals (September 2, 1986).
PLAYING EXPERIENCE: Los Angeles Rams NFL, 1984 and 1985; Cincinnati NFL, 1986-1990. . . . Games: 1984 (16), 1985 (16), 1986 (16), 1987 (12), 1988 (16), 1989 (16), 1990 (16). Total: 108.
CHAMPIONSHIP GAME EXPERIENCE: Played in NFC championship game after 1985 season. . . . Played in AFC championship game after 1988 season. . . . Played in Super Bowl XXIII after 1988 season.
PRO STATISTICS: 1985—Recovered one fumble. 1986—Fumbled once for minus seven yards. 1987—Recovered one fumble. 1990—Recovered one fumble.

BRAGGS, STEPHEN

DB, BROWNS

PERSONAL: Born August 29, 1965, at Houston. . . . 5-9/180.
HIGH SCHOOL: Smiley (Tex.).
COLLEGE: Texas.
TRANSACTIONS/CAREER NOTES: Selected by Cleveland Browns in sixth round (165th pick overall) of 1987 NFL draft. . . . Signed by Browns (July 26, 1987). . . . On injured reserve with stress fracture of foot (Octo-

ber 27, 1989-remainder of season).... On inactive list (November 25, 1990).
PLAYING EXPERIENCE: Cleveland NFL, 1987-1990.... Games: 1987 (12), 1988 (16), 1989 (7), 1990 (15). Total: 50.
CHAMPIONSHIP GAME EXPERIENCE: Played in AFC championship game after 1987 season.
PRO STATISTICS: 1988—Returned one kickoff for 27 yards. 1989—Returned two kickoffs for 20 yards. 1990—Intercepted two passes for 13 yards and recovered two fumbles for 16 yards.

BRANDES, JOHN
TE, REDSKINS

PERSONAL: Born April 2, 1964, at Fort Riley, Kan.... 6-2/250.... Full name: John Wesley Brandes.
HIGH SCHOOL: Lamar (Arlington, Tex.).
COLLEGE: Cameron, Okla. (bachelor of science degree in health).
TRANSACTIONS/CAREER NOTES: Signed as free agent by Indianapolis Colts (May 11, 1987).... Crossed picket line during players' strike (October 7, 1987).... Granted unconditional free agency (February 1, 1990).... Signed by Washington Redskins (March 15, 1990).

			—— RECEIVING ——		
Year	Team	G	No.	Yds.	Avg.	TD
1987— Indianapolis NFL	12	5	35	7.0	0
1988— Indianapolis NFL	16	0	0		0
1989— Indianapolis NFL	16	0	0		0
1990— Washington NFL	16	0	0		0
Pro totals (4 years)	60	5	35	7.0	0

BRANDON, DAVID
LB, BROWNS

PERSONAL: Born February 9, 1965, at Memphis, Tenn.... 6-4/230.... Full name: David Sherrod Brandon.
HIGH SCHOOL: Mitchell (Memphis, Tenn.).
COLLEGE: Memphis State.
TRANSACTIONS/CAREER NOTES: Selected by Buffalo Bills in third round (60th pick overall) of 1987 NFL draft.... Signed by Bills (July 25, 1987).... Traded by Bills with fourth-round pick in 1988 draft to San Diego Chargers for wide receiver Trumaine Johnson and seventh-round pick in 1988 NFL draft (August 31, 1987).... On injured reserve with knee injury (July 23, 1990-entire season).... Granted unconditional free agency (February 1, 1991).... Signed by Cleveland Browns (April 1, 1991).
PLAYING EXPERIENCE: San Diego NFL, 1987-1989.... Games: 1987 (8), 1988 (8), 1989 (13). Total: 29.
PRO STATISTICS: 1987—Recovered blocked punt in end zone for a touchdown.

BRANTLEY, JOHN
LB, CARDINALS

PERSONAL: Born October 23, 1965, at Ocala, Fla.... 6-1/230.... Full name: John Phillip Brantley Jr.
HIGH SCHOOL: Wildwood (Fla.).
COLLEGE: Georgia.
TRANSACTIONS/CAREER NOTES: Selected by Houston Oilers in 12th round (325th pick overall) of 1988 NFL draft.... Signed by Oilers (July 15, 1988).... Released by Oilers (August 24, 1988).... Re-signed by Oilers (March 20, 1989).... On injured reserve with quadricep injury (November 4-December 11, 1989).... Released by Oilers (December 12, 1989).... Re-signed by Oilers to developmental squad (December 13, 1989).... On developmental squad (December 13, 1989-January 1, 1990).... Released by Oilers (January 2, 1990).... Re-signed by Oilers (April 30, 1990).... Released by Oilers (September 2, 1990).... Signed by WLAF (January 12, 1991).... Selected by Birmingham Fire in second round (15th linebacker) of 1991 WLAF positional draft.... Signed by Phoenix Cardinals (July 17, 1991).
PLAYING EXPERIENCE: Houston NFL, 1989; Birmingham WLAF, 1991.... Games: 1989 (8), 1991 (10). Total NFL: 8. Total Pro: 18.

BRATTON, MELVIN
RB, BRONCOS

PERSONAL: Born February 2, 1965, at Miami.... 6-1/225.... Full name: Melvin Torrence Bratton.
HIGH SCHOOL: Northwestern (Miami).
COLLEGE: Miami, Fla. (bachelor of business administration degree in business management).
TRANSACTIONS/CAREER NOTES: Selected by Miami Dolphins in sixth round (153rd pick overall) of 1988 NFL draft.... Selected by Denver Broncos in seventh round (180th pick overall) of 1989 NFL draft.... Signed by Broncos (August 15, 1989).
CHAMPIONSHIP GAME EXPERIENCE: Played in AFC championship game after 1989 season.... Played in Super Bowl XXIV after 1989 season.
PRO STATISTICS: 1990—Recovered three fumbles.

		—— RUSHING ——				—— RECEIVING ——				– KICKOFF RETURNS –				—— TOTAL ——		
Year	Team	G	Att.	Yds.	Avg.	TD	No.	Yds.	Avg.	TD	No.	Yds.	Avg.	TD	TD	Pts.	F.
1989— Denver NFL	16	30	108	3.6	1	10	69	6.9	3	2	19	9.5	0	4	24	0
1990— Denver NFL	16	27	82	3.0	3	29	276	9.5	1	3	37	12.3	0	4	24	3
Pro totals (2 years)	32	57	190	3.3	4	39	345	8.9	4	5	56	11.2	0	8	48	3

BRAXTON, DAVID
LB, CARDINALS

PERSONAL: Born May 26, 1965, at Omaha, Neb.... 6-2/230.... Full name: David Harold Braxton.
HIGH SCHOOL: Jacksonville (N.C.).
COLLEGE: Wake Forest.
TRANSACTIONS/CAREER NOTES: Selected by Minnesota Vikings in second round (52nd pick overall) of 1989 NFL draft.... Signed

by Vikings (July 28, 1989)....On injured reserve with groin injury (September 5-October 30, 1989)....On injured reserve with thigh injury (November 10-December 22, 1989)....On injured reserve (September 15-October 2, 1990)....Released by Vikings (October 2, 1990)....Signed by Phoenix Cardinals (October 17, 1990).
PLAYING EXPERIENCE: Minnesota NFL, 1989; Minnesota (1)-Phoenix (11) NFL, 1990....Games: 1989 (3), 1990 (12). Total: 15.

BRAXTON, TYRONE
CB, BRONCOS

PERSONAL: Born December 12, 1964, at Madison, Wis....5-11/185....Full name: Tyrone Scott Braxton....Related to Jim Braxton, fullback with Buffalo Bills and Miami Dolphins, 1971-1978.
HIGH SCHOOL: James Madison (Madison, Wis.).
COLLEGE: North Dakota State.
TRANSACTIONS/CAREER NOTES: Selected by Denver Broncos in 12th round (334th pick overall) of 1987 NFL draft....Signed by Broncos (July 18, 1987)....On injured reserve with shoulder injury (September 1-December 18, 1987)....On injured reserve with knee injury (September 25, 1990-remainder of season).
CHAMPIONSHIP GAME EXPERIENCE: Played in AFC championship game after 1987 and 1989 seasons....Played in Super Bowl XXII after 1987 season and Super Bowl XXIV after 1989 season.
PRO STATISTICS: 1988—Recovered one fumble. 1989—Recovered two fumbles for 35 yards.

			INTERCEPTIONS		
Year Team	G	No.	Yds.	Avg.	TD
1987— Denver NFL	2	0	0		0
1988— Denver NFL	16	2	6	3.0	0
1989— Denver NFL	16	6	103	17.2	1
1990— Denver NFL	3	1	10	10.0	0
Pro totals (4 years)	37	9	119	13.2	1

BREECH, JIM
PK, BENGALS

PERSONAL: Born April 11, 1956, at Sacramento, Calif....5-6/161....Full name: James Thomas Breech.
HIGH SCHOOL: Sacramento (Calif.).
COLLEGE: California.
TRANSACTIONS/CAREER NOTES: Selected by Detroit Lions in eighth round (206th pick overall) of 1978 NFL draft....Released by Lions (August 23, 1978)....Signed as free agent by Oakland Raiders (December 12, 1978)....Active for one game with Raiders in 1978; did not play....Released by Raiders (September 1, 1980)....Signed as free agent by Cincinnati Bengals (November 25, 1980)....Released by Bengals (September 5, 1989)....Re-signed by Bengals (October 2, 1989).
CHAMPIONSHIP GAME EXPERIENCE: Played in AFC championship game after 1981 and 1988 seasons....Played in Super Bowl XVI after 1981 season and Super Bowl XXIII after 1988 season.
PRO STATISTICS: 1980—Punted twice for 33.5 avg. 1983—Fumbled once. 1985—Punted five times for 30.6 avg. 1988—Punted three times for 21.3 avg. 1989—Punted twice for 29.0 avg. 1990—Punted once for 34 yards.

			PLACE-KICKING			
Year Team	G	XPM	XPA	FGM	FGA	Pts.
1979— Oakland NFL	16	41	45	18	27	95
1980— Cincinnati NFL	4	11	12	4	7	23
1981— Cincinnati NFL	16	49	51	22	32	115
1982— Cincinnati NFL	9	25	26	14	18	67
1983— Cincinnati NFL	16	39	41	16	23	87
1984— Cincinnati NFL	16	37	37	22	31	103
1985— Cincinnati NFL	16	48	50	24	33	120
1986— Cincinnati NFL	16	50	51	17	32	101
1987— Cincinnati NFL	12	25	27	24	30	97
1988— Cincinnati NFL	16	*56	59	11	16	89
1989— Cincinnati NFL	12	37	38	12	14	73
1990— Cincinnati NFL	16	41	44	17	21	92
Pro totals (12 years)	165	459	481	201	284	1062

BRENNAN, BRIAN
WR, BROWNS

PERSONAL: Born February 15, 1962, at Bloomfield, Mich....5-10/185....Full name: Brian Michael Brennan.
HIGH SCHOOL: Brother Rice (Birmingham, Mich.).
COLLEGE: Boston College (bachelor of science degree in finance, 1984).
TRANSACTIONS/CAREER NOTES: Selected by Denver Gold in 16th round (324th pick overall) in 1984 USFL draft....Selected by Cleveland Browns in fourth round (104th pick overall) of 1984 NFL draft....Signed by Browns (May 18, 1984)....On injured reserve with separated shoulder (September 4-October 2, 1985)....Crossed picket line during players' strike (October 14, 1987).
CHAMPIONSHIP GAME EXPERIENCE: Played in AFC championship game after 1986, 1987 and 1989 seasons.
PRO STATISTICS: 1985—Attempted one pass with one completion for 33 yards and a touchdown. 1986—Recovered fumble in end zone for a touchdown, attempted one pass with one completion for 35 yards and fumbled once. 1987—Recovered one fumble. 1989—Recovered one fumble.

		RECEIVING				PUNT RETURNS				TOTAL		
Year Team	G	No.	Yds.	Avg.	TD	No.	Yds.	Avg.	TD	TD	Pts.	F.
1984— Cleveland NFL	15	35	455	13.0	3	25	199	8.0	0	3	18	1
1985— Cleveland NFL	12	32	487	15.2	0	19	153	8.1	1	1	6	3
1986— Cleveland NFL	16	55	838	15.2	6	0	0		0	7	42	0

Year Team	G	No.	RECEIVING Yds.	Avg.	TD	PUNT RETURNS No.	Yds.	Avg.	TD	TOTAL TD	Pts.	F.
1987— Cleveland NFL	13	43	607	14.1	6	0	0		0	6	36	1
1988— Cleveland NFL	16	46	579	12.6	1	0	0		0	1	6	0
1989— Cleveland NFL	14	28	289	10.3	0	0	0		0	0	0	1
1990— Cleveland NFL	16	45	568	12.6	2	9	72	8.0	0	2	12	1
Pro totals (7 years)	102	284	3823	13.5	18	53	424	8.0	1	20	120	7

BRENNAN, MIKE
G, BENGALS

PERSONAL: Born March 22, 1967, at Los Angeles. . . . 6-5/274. . . . Full name: Michael Sean Brennan.
HIGH SCHOOL: Mount St. Joseph (Baltimore, Md.).
COLLEGE: Notre Dame (degree in business, 1990).
TRANSACTIONS/CAREER NOTES: Selected by Cincinnati Bengals in fourth round (91st pick overall) of 1990 NFL draft. . . . Signed by Bengals (July 23, 1990).
PLAYING EXPERIENCE: Cincinnati NFL, 1990. . . . Games: 1990 (16).

BRENNER, HOBY
TE, SAINTS

PERSONAL: Born June 2, 1959, at Linwood, Calif. . . . 6-5/245. . . . Full name: Hoby F.J. Brenner.
HIGH SCHOOL: Fullerton (Calif.).
COLLEGE: Southern California.
TRANSACTIONS/CAREER NOTES: Selected by New Orleans Saints in third round (71st pick overall) of 1981 NFL draft. . . . On injured reserve with turf toe (September 1-October 23, 1981). . . . On injured reserve with knee injury (December 31, 1982-remainder of season). . . . On injured reserve with separated shoulder (September 27-October 24, 1987).
RECORDS/HONORS: Played in Pro Bowl after 1987 season.
PRO STATISTICS: 1981—Fumbled once. 1982—Recovered one fumble and fumbled once. 1985—Fumbled once. 1989—Fumbled once.

Year Team	G	No.	RECEIVING Yds.	Avg.	TD
1981— New Orleans NFL	9	7	143	20.4	0
1982— New Orleans NFL	8	16	171	10.7	0
1983— New Orleans NFL	16	41	574	14.0	3
1984— New Orleans NFL	16	28	554	19.8	6
1985— New Orleans NFL	16	42	652	15.5	3
1986— New Orleans NFL	15	18	286	15.9	0
1987— New Orleans NFL	12	20	280	14.0	2
1988— New Orleans NFL	10	5	67	13.4	0
1989— New Orleans NFL	16	34	398	11.7	4
1990— New Orleans NFL	16	17	213	12.5	2
Pro totals (10 years)	134	228	3338	14.6	20

BRILZ, DARRICK
G, SEAHAWKS

PERSONAL: Born February 14, 1964, at Richmond, Calif. . . . 6-3/281. . . . Full name: Darrick Joseph Brilz.
HIGH SCHOOL: Pinole Valley (Pinole, Calif.).
COLLEGE: Oregon State.
TRANSACTIONS/CAREER NOTES: Signed as free agent by Washington Redskins (May 1, 1987). . . . Released by Redskins (August 31, 1987). . . . Re-signed as replacement player by Redskins (September 23, 1987). . . . On injured reserve with pinched nerve in neck (December 12, 1987-remainder of season). . . . Released by Redskins (August 29, 1988). . . . Awarded on waivers to San Diego Chargers (August 30, 1988). . . . Released by Chargers (August 1, 1989). . . . Signed as free agent by Seattle Seahawks (August 16, 1989). . . . Released by Seahawks (September 5, 1989). . . . Re-signed by Seahawks (September 21, 1989).
PLAYING EXPERIENCE: Washington NFL, 1987; San Diego NFL, 1988; Seattle NFL, 1989 and 1990. . . . Games: 1987 (7), 1988 (14), 1989 (14), 1990 (16). Total: 51.

BRIM, MIKE
CB, JETS

PERSONAL: Born January 23, 1966, at Danville, Va. . . . 6-0/192. . . . Full name: Michael Anthony Brim.
HIGH SCHOOL: George Washington (Danville, Va.).
COLLEGE: Virginia Union (degree in history, 1988).
TRANSACTIONS/CAREER NOTES: Selected by Phoenix Cardinals in fourth round (95th pick overall) of 1988 NFL draft. . . . Signed by Cardinals (July 10, 1988). . . . On injured reserve with cracked ribs (August 29-November 25, 1988). . . . Released by Cardinals (September 5, 1989). . . . Signed as free agent by Detroit Lions (September 20, 1989). . . . Released by Lions (October 25, 1989). . . . Signed as free agent by Minnesota Vikings (November 8, 1989). . . . Granted free agency (February 1, 1990). . . . Re-signed by Vikings (July 30, 1990). . . . Granted unconditional free agency (February 1, 1991). . . . Signed by New York Jets (March 11, 1991).
PLAYING EXPERIENCE: Phoenix NFL, 1988; Detroit (2)-Minnesota (7) NFL, 1989; Minnesota NFL, 1990. . . . Games: 1988 (4), 1989 (9), 1990 (16). Total: 29.
PRO STATISTICS: 1990—Intercepted two passes for 11 yards.

BRISTER, BUBBY

QB, STEELERS

PERSONAL: Born August 15, 1962, at Alexandria, La. . . . 6-3/208. . . . Full name: Walter Andrew Brister III.
HIGH SCHOOL: Neville (Monroe, La.).
COLLEGE: Tulane, then Northeast Louisiana.
TRANSACTIONS/CAREER NOTES: Selected by Pittsburgh Steelers in third round (67th pick overall) of 1986 NFL draft. . . . Selected by New Jersey Generals in 11th round (80th pick overall) of 1986 USFL draft. . . . Signed by Pittsburgh Steelers (July 25, 1986).
PRO STATISTICS: Passer rating points: 1986 (37.6), 1987 (2.8), 1988 (65.3), 1989 (73.1), 1990 (81.6). Career: 70.2. . . . 1988—Recovered two fumbles. 1989—Caught one pass for minus 10 yards and recovered one fumble.

		PASSING							RUSHING				TOTAL		
Year Team	G	Att.	Cmp.	Pct.	Yds.	TD	Int.	Avg.	Att.	Yds.	Avg.	TD	TD	Pts.	F.
1986— Pittsburgh NFL	2	60	21	35.0	291	0	2	4.85	6	10	1.7	1	1	6	1
1987— Pittsburgh NFL	2	12	4	33.3	20	0	3	1.67	0	0		0	0	0	0
1988— Pittsburgh NFL	13	370	175	47.3	2634	11	14	7.12	45	209	4.6	6	6	36	8
1989— Pittsburgh NFL	14	342	187	54.7	2365	9	10	6.92	27	25	.9	0	0	0	4
1990— Pittsburgh NFL	16	387	223	57.6	2725	20	14	7.04	25	64	2.6	0	0	0	9
Pro totals (5 years)	47	1171	610	52.1	8035	40	43	6.86	103	308	3.0	7	7	42	22

BASEBALL TRANSACTIONS: Selected by Detroit Tigers' organization in fourth round of free-agent draft (June 8, 1981). . . . On suspended list (June 22, 1982-entire season). . . . Placed on restricted list (October 7, 1982).

BASEBALL RECORD AS PLAYER

Year Team	League	Pos.	G	AB	R	H	2B	3B	HR	RBI	Avg.	PO	A	E	F.A.
1981— Bristol.....................Appal.		OF/SS	39	111	12	20	7	0	0	10	.180	46	11	9	.864
1982— Bristol.....................Appal.					Did not play										

BROCK, MATT

DE/NT, PACKERS

PERSONAL: Born January 14, 1966, at Ogden, Utah. . . . 6-5/290. . . . Full name: Matthew Lee Brock. . . . Son of Clyde Brock, defensive tackle with Dallas Cowboys and San Francisco 49ers, 1962 and 1963.
HIGH SCHOOL: University City (San Diego).
COLLEGE: Oregon.
TRANSACTIONS/CAREER NOTES: Selected by Green Bay Packers in third round (58th pick overall) of 1989 NFL draft. . . . Signed by Packers (July 24, 1989). . . . On injured reserve with broken bone in hand (November 14, 1989-remainder of season).
PLAYING EXPERIENCE: Green Bay NFL, 1989 and 1990. . . . Games: 1989 (7), 1990 (16). Total: 23.

BROCK, STAN

OT, SAINTS

PERSONAL: Born June 8, 1958, at Portland, Ore. . . . 6-6/278. . . . Full name: Stanley James Brock. . . . Brother of Pete Brock, center with New England Patriots, 1976-1987; and brother of Willie Brock, center with Detroit Lions, 1978.
HIGH SCHOOL: Jesuit (Beaverton, Ore.).
COLLEGE: Colorado.
TRANSACTIONS/CAREER NOTES: Selected by New Orleans Saints in first round (12th pick overall) of 1980 NFL draft. . . . On injured reserve with knee injury (December 5, 1984-remainder of season). . . . On injured reserve with knee injury (October 22, 1988-remainder of season). . . . Granted free agency (February 1, 1990). . . . Re-signed by Saints (August 12, 1990).
PLAYING EXPERIENCE: New Orleans NFL, 1980-1990. . . . Games: 1980 (16), 1981 (16), 1982 (9), 1983 (16), 1984 (14), 1985 (16), 1986 (16), 1987 (12), 1988 (7), 1989 (16), 1990 (16). Total: 154.
RECORDS/HONORS: Named as offensive tackle on THE SPORTING NEWS college All-America team, 1979.
PRO STATISTICS: 1980—Recovered one fumble. 1981—Returned two kickoffs for 18 yards and recovered two fumbles. 1983—Returned one kickoff for 15 yards and recovered one fumble. 1985—Recovered one fumble. 1987—Returned one kickoff for 11 yards. 1989—Recovered one fumble. 1990—Recovered one fumble.

BROOKS, BILL

WR, COLTS

PERSONAL: Born April 6, 1964, at Boston. . . . 6-0/189. . . . Full name: William Brooks Jr.
HIGH SCHOOL: North (Framingham, Mass.).
COLLEGE: Boston University (bachelor of science degree in business administration, 1986).
TRANSACTIONS/CAREER NOTES: Selected by Indianapolis Colts in fourth round (86th pick overall) of 1986 NFL draft. . . . Signed by Colts (June 23, 1986).
PRO STATISTICS: 1986—Returned eight kickoffs for 143 yards and recovered one fumble. 1988—Recovered two fumbles.

		RUSHING				RECEIVING				PUNT RETURNS				TOTAL		
Year Team	G	Att.	Yds.	Avg.	TD	No.	Yds.	Avg.	TD	No.	Yds.	Avg.	TD	TD	Pts.	F.
1986— Indianapolis NFL ...	16	4	5	1.3	0	65	1131	17.4	8	18	141	7.8	0	8	48	2
1987— Indianapolis NFL ...	12	2	-2	-1.0	0	51	722	14.2	3	22	136	6.2	0	3	18	3
1988— Indianapolis NFL ...	16	5	62	12.4	0	54	867	16.1	3	3	15	5.0	0	3	18	1
1989— Indianapolis NFL ...	16	2	-3	-1.5	0	63	919	14.6	4	0	0		0	4	24	1
1990— Indianapolis NFL ...	16	0	0		0	62	823	13.3	5	0	0		0	5	30	0
Pro totals (5 years)	76	13	62	4.8	0	295	4462	15.1	23	43	292	6.8	0	23	138	7

BROOKS, JAMES

RB, BENGALS

PERSONAL: Born December 28, 1958, at Warner Robins, Ga. . . . 5-10/182. . . . Full name: James Robert Brooks. . . . Cousin of Kevin Porter, safety with Kansas City Chiefs.
HIGH SCHOOL: Warner Robins (Ga.).
COLLEGE: Auburn.

TRANSACTIONS/CAREER NOTES: Selected by San Diego Chargers in first round (24th pick overall) of 1981 NFL draft.... Traded by Chargers to Cincinnati Bengals for running back Pete Johnson (May 29, 1984).
CHAMPIONSHIP GAME EXPERIENCE: Played in AFC championship game after 1981 and 1988 seasons.... Played in Super Bowl XXIII after 1988 season.
RECORDS/HONORS: Played in Pro Bowl after 1986 and 1988-1990 seasons.
PRO STATISTICS: 1981—Recovered two fumbles. 1982—Recovered one fumble. 1983—Recovered three fumbles. 1985—Attempted one pass with one completion for eight yards and a touchdown and recovered one fumble. 1986—Attempted one pass with no completions. 1989—Recovered one fumble. 1990—Recovered one fumble.

Year Team	G	RUSHING Att	Yds	Avg	TD	RECEIVING No	Yds	Avg	TD	PUNT RETURNS No	Yds	Avg	TD	KICKOFF RETURNS No	Yds	Avg	TD	TOTALS TD	Pts	F
1981—San Diego NFL....	14	109	525	4.8	3	46	329	7.2	3	22	290	13.2	0	40	949	23.7	0	6	36	7
1982—San Diego NFL....	9	87	430	4.9	6	13	66	5.1	0	12	138	11.5	0	*33	*749	22.7	0	6	36	4
1983—San Diego NFL....	15	127	516	4.1	3	25	215	8.6	0	18	137	7.6	0	32	607	19.0	0	3	18	8
1984—Cincinnati NFL....	15	103	396	3.8	2	34	268	7.9	2	0	0		0	7	144	20.6	0	4	24	4
1985—Cincinnati NFL....	16	192	929	4.8	7	55	576	10.5	5	0	0		0	3	38	12.7	0	12	72	7
1986—Cincinnati NFL....	16	205	1087	*5.3	5	54	686	12.7	4	0	0		0	0	0			9	54	2
1987—Cincinnati NFL....	9	94	290	3.1	1	22	272	12.4	2	0	0		0	2	42	21.0	0	3	18	0
1988—Cincinnati NFL....	15	182	931	5.1	8	29	287	9.9	6	0	0		0	1	-6	-6.0	0	14	84	1
1989—Cincinnati NFL....	16	221	1239	5.6	7	37	306	8.3	2	0	0		0	0	0			9	54	9
1990—Cincinnati NFL....	16	195	1004	5.2	5	26	269	10.4	4	0	0		0	0	0			9	54	3
Pro totals (10 years).....	141	1515	7347	4.9	47	341	3274	9.6	28	52	565	10.9	0	118	2523	21.4	0	75	450	45

BROOKS, MICHAEL
LB, BRONCOS

PERSONAL: Born October 2, 1964, at Ruston, La.... 6-1/235.
HIGH SCHOOL: Ruston (La.).
COLLEGE: Louisiana State.
TRANSACTIONS/CAREER NOTES: Selected by Denver Broncos in third round (86th pick overall) of 1987 NFL draft.... Signed by Broncos (July 24, 1987).... Granted free agency (February 1, 1990).... Re-signed by Broncos (July 29, 1990).
PLAYING EXPERIENCE: Denver NFL, 1987-1990.... Games: 1987 (12), 1988 (16), 1989 (16), 1990 (16). Total: 60.
CHAMPIONSHIP GAME EXPERIENCE: Played in AFC championship game after 1987 and 1989 seasons.... Played in Super Bowl XXII after 1987 season and Super Bowl XXIV after 1989 season.
PRO STATISTICS: 1987—Recovered one fumble. 1989—Credited with a safety and recovered two fumbles.

BROOKS, MICHAEL
S, COWBOYS

PERSONAL: Born March 12, 1967, at Greensboro, N.C.... 6-0/195.... Full name: Michael Antonio Brooks.
HIGH SCHOOL: Page (Greensboro, N.C.).
COLLEGE: North Carolina State.
TRANSACTIONS/CAREER NOTES: Signed as free agent by San Diego Chargers (May 2, 1989).... Released by Chargers (August 30, 1989).... Re-signed by Chargers (September 1, 1989).... Released by Chargers (September 5, 1989).... Re-signed by Chargers to developmental squad (September 7, 1989).... On developmental squad (September 7-December 13, 1989).... Activated after clearing procedural waivers (December 15, 1989).... Released by Chargers (September 3, 1990).... Re-signed by Chargers (September 26, 1990).... On inactive list (October 7, 1990).... Released by Chargers (October 10, 1990). ... Signed by Dallas Cowboys to practice squad (November 7, 1990).... Activated (December 10, 1990).
PLAYING EXPERIENCE: San Diego NFL, 1989; San Diego (1)-Dallas (3) NFL, 1990.... Games: 1989 (1), 1990 (4). Total: 5.

BROSTEK, BERN
G/C, RAMS

PERSONAL: Born September 11, 1966, at Honolulu.... 6-3/300.... Name pronounced BRAH-stek.
HIGH SCHOOL: Iolani (Honolulu).
COLLEGE: Washington.
TRANSACTIONS/CAREER NOTES: Selected by Los Angeles Rams in first round (23rd pick overall) of 1990 NFL draft.... Signed by Rams (July 29, 1990).
PLAYING EXPERIENCE: Los Angeles Rams NFL, 1990.... Games: 1990 (16).
RECORDS/HONORS: Named as center on The Sporting News college All-America team, 1989.

BROUGHTON, WILLIE
DT, COWBOYS

PERSONAL: Born September 9, 1964, at Fort Pierce, Fla.... 6-5/280.... Full name: Willie Lee Broughton.... Brother of Dock Luckie, nose tackle with Winnipeg Blue Bombers (CFL), 1981.
HIGH SCHOOL: Central (Fort Pierce, Fla.).
COLLEGE: Miami (Fla.).
TRANSACTIONS/CAREER NOTES: Selected by Orlando Renegades in 1985 USFL territorial draft.... Selected by Indianapolis Colts in fourth round (88th pick overall) of 1985 NFL draft.... Signed by Colts (August 9, 1985).... On injured reserve with knee injury (August 5, 1987-entire season).... Crossed picket line during players' strike (September 29, 1987).... Released by Colts (August 24, 1988).... Signed as free agent by Dallas Cowboys (July 18, 1989).... On inactive list (October 7, 1990). ... On injured reserve with back injury (October 8, 1990-remainder of season).
PLAYING EXPERIENCE: Indianapolis NFL, 1985 and 1986; Dallas NFL, 1989 and 1990.... Games: 1985 (15), 1986 (15), 1989 (16), 1990 (4). Total: 50.
PRO STATISTICS: 1986—Recovered one fumble.

BROUSSARD, STEVE
RB, FALCONS

PERSONAL: Born February 22, 1967, at Los Angeles. . . . 5-7/201. . . . Full name: Steve N. Broussard.
HIGH SCHOOL: Manual Arts (Los Angeles).
COLLEGE: Washington State.
TRANSACTIONS/CAREER NOTES: Selected by Atlanta Falcons in first round (20th pick overall) of 1990 NFL draft. . . . Signed by Falcons (July 12, 1990). . . . On inactive list (December 2, 16, and 23, 1990).

		—RUSHING—				—RECEIVING—				– KICKOFF RETURNS –				—TOTAL—		
Year	Team	G	Att.	Yds.	Avg.	TD	No.	Yds.	Avg.	TD	No.	Yds.	Avg.	TD	TD	Pts.	F.
1990— Atlanta NFL		13	126	454	3.6	4	24	160	6.7	0	3	45	15.0	0	4	24	6
Pro totals (1 year)		13	126	454	3.6	4	24	160	6.7	0	3	45	15.0	0	4	24	6

BROWN, A.B.
RB, JETS

PERSONAL: Born December 4, 1965, at Salem, N.J. . . . 5-9/215. . . . Full name: Anthony James Brown.
HIGH SCHOOL: Salem (N.J.).
COLLEGE: Pittsburgh, then West Virginia.
TRANSACTIONS/CAREER NOTES: Selected by New York Jets in eighth round (209th pick overall) of 1989 NFL draft. . . . Signed by Jets (July 21, 1989). . . . On injured reserve with knee injury (September 11, 1990-remainder of season).

		—RUSHING—				—RECEIVING—				– KICKOFF RETURNS –				—TOTAL—		
Year	Team	G	Att.	Yds.	Avg.	TD	No.	Yds.	Avg.	TD	No.	Yds.	Avg.	TD	TD	Pts.	F.
1989— N.Y. Jets NFL		16	12	63	5.3	0	4	10	2.5	0	0	0		0	0	0	0
1990— N.Y. Jets NFL		1	1	8	8.0	0	0	0		0	1	63	63.0	0	0	0	0
Pro totals (2 years)		17	13	71	5.5	0	4	10	2.5	0	1	63	63.0	0	0	0	0

BROWN, ANDRE
WR, DOLPHINS

PERSONAL: Born August 21, 1966, at Chicago. . . . 6-3/210. . . . Full name: Andre L. Brown.
HIGH SCHOOL: Fenger (Chicago).
COLLEGE: Miami (Fla.).
TRANSACTIONS/CAREER NOTES: Signed as free agent by Miami Dolphins (April 27, 1989). . . . On inactive list (November 4, 1990). . . . On injured reserve with groin injury (November 7, 1990-remainder of regular season and playoffs).
PRO STATISTICS: 1989—Returned two kickoffs for nine yards, recovered one fumble and fumbled once.

		—RECEIVING—			
Year	Team	G	No.	Yds.	Avg.	TD
1989— Miami NFL		16	24	410	17.1	5
1990— Miami NFL		6	3	49	16.3	0
Pro totals (2 years)		22	27	459	17.0	5

BROWN, DENNIS
DE, 49ERS

PERSONAL: Born November 6, 1967, at Los Angeles. . . . 6-4/290. . . . Full name: Dennis Trammel Brown.
HIGH SCHOOL: Long Beach Jordan (Long Beach, Calif.).
COLLEGE: Washington.
TRANSACTIONS/CAREER NOTES: Selected by San Francisco 49ers in second round (47th pick overall) of 1990 NFL draft. . . . Signed by 49ers (July 27, 1990). . . . On inactive list (September 16, 1990).
PLAYING EXPERIENCE: San Francisco NFL, 1990. . . . Games: 1990 (15).
CHAMPIONSHIP GAME EXPERIENCE: Played in NFC championship game after 1990 season.

BROWN, EDDIE
WR, BENGALS

PERSONAL: Born December 17, 1962, at Miami. . . . 6-0/185. . . . Full name: Eddie Lee Brown.
HIGH SCHOOL: Senior (Miami).
COLLEGE: Navarro College (Tex.), then Miami (Fla.).
TRANSACTIONS/CAREER NOTES: Selected by Orlando Renegades in 1985 USFL territorial draft. . . . Selected by Cincinnati Bengals in first round (13th pick overall) of 1985 NFL draft. . . . Signed by Bengals (August 7, 1985). . . . On inactive list (October 7 and 14, 1990).
CHAMPIONSHIP GAME EXPERIENCE: Played in AFC championship game after 1988 season. . . . Played in Super Bowl XXIII after 1988 season.
RECORDS/HONORS: Named THE SPORTING NEWS NFL Rookie of the Year, 1985. . . . Played in Pro Bowl after 1988 season.
PRO STATISTICS: 1985—Returned one kickoff for six yards and recovered one fumble. 1986—Recovered two fumbles. 1987—Recovered one fumble. 1988—Returned 10 punts for 48 yards and recovered one fumble.

		—RUSHING—				—RECEIVING—				—TOTAL—		
Year	Team	G	Att.	Yds.	Avg.	TD	No.	Yds.	Avg.	TD	TD	Pts.	F.
1985— Cincinnati NFL		16	14	129	9.2	0	53	942	17.8	8	8	48	2
1986— Cincinnati NFL		16	8	32	4.0	0	58	964	16.6	4	4	24	0
1987— Cincinnati NFL		12	1	0	.0	0	44	608	13.8	3	3	18	3
1988— Cincinnati NFL		16	1	-5	-5.0	0	53	1273	*24.0	9	9	54	1
1989— Cincinnati NFL		15	0	0		0	52	814	15.7	6	6	36	0
1990— Cincinnati NFL		14	0	0		0	44	706	16.1	9	9	54	0
Pro totals (6 years)		89	24	156	6.5	0	304	5307	17.5	39	39	234	6

BROWN, J.B.
CB, DOLPHINS

PERSONAL: Born January 5, 1967, at Washington, D.C. . . . 6-0/192. . . . Full name: James Harold Brown.
HIGH SCHOOL: DeMatha (Hyattsville, Md.).
COLLEGE: Maryland.
TRANSACTIONS/CAREER NOTES: Selected by Miami Dolphins in 12th round (315th pick overall) of 1989 NFL draft. . . . Signed by Dolphins (July 16, 1989).
PLAYING EXPERIENCE: Miami NFL, 1989 and 1990. . . . Games: 1989 (16), 1990 (16). Total: 32.

BROWN, JEROME
DT, EAGLES

PERSONAL: Born February 4, 1965, at Brooksville, Fla. . . . 6-2/295. . . . Cousin of Maulty Moore, offensive tackle with Miami Dolphins, Cincinnati Bengals and Tampa Bay Buccaneers, 1972-1976.
HIGH SCHOOL: Hernando (Brooksville, Fla.).
COLLEGE: Miami (Fla.).
TRANSACTIONS/CAREER NOTES: Selected by Philadelphia Eagles in first round (ninth pick overall) of 1987 NFL draft. . . . Signed by Eagles (August 21, 1987).
PLAYING EXPERIENCE: Philadelphia NFL, 1987-1990. . . . Games: 1987 (12), 1988 (16), 1989 (16), 1990 (16). Total: 60.
RECORDS/HONORS: Named as defensive lineman on THE SPORTING NEWS college All-America team, 1986. . . . Named to play in Pro Bowl after 1990 season; replaced due to injury by Erik Howard.
PRO STATISTICS: 1987—Intercepted two passes for seven yards and recovered one fumble for 37 yards. 1988—Intercepted one pass for minus five yards. 1989—Recovered two fumbles for 17 yards. 1990—Recovered five fumbles for 10 yards.

BROWN, LOMAS
OT, LIONS

PERSONAL: Born March 30, 1963, at Miami. . . . 6-4/287. . . . Full name: Lomas Brown Jr. . . . Cousin of Joe Taylor, defensive back with Chicago Bears, 1967-1974; and Guy McIntyre, guard with San Francisco 49ers.
HIGH SCHOOL: Miami Springs (Fla.).
COLLEGE: Florida.
TRANSACTIONS/CAREER NOTES: Selected by Orlando Renegades in second round (18th pick overall) of 1985 USFL draft. . . . Selected by Detroit Lions in first round (sixth pick overall) of 1985 NFL draft. . . . Signed by Lions (August 9, 1985).
PLAYING EXPERIENCE: Detroit NFL, 1985-1990. . . . Games: 1985 (16), 1986 (16), 1987 (11), 1988 (16), 1989 (16), 1990 (16). Total: 91.
RECORDS/HONORS: Named as tackle on THE SPORTING NEWS college All-America team, 1984. . . . Played in Pro Bowl after 1990 season.
PRO STATISTICS: 1989—Rushed once for three yards and recovered one fumble.

BROWN, MARK
LB, LIONS

PERSONAL: Born July 18, 1961, at New Brunswick, N.J. . . . 6-2/240. . . . Full name: Mark Anthony Brown.
HIGH SCHOOL: Inglewood (Calif.).
COLLEGE: Los Angeles Southwest Community College, then Purdue.
TRANSACTIONS/CAREER NOTES: Selected by Boston Breakers in 10th round (115th pick overall) of 1983 USFL draft. . . . Selected by Miami Dolphins in ninth round (250th pick overall) of 1983 NFL draft. . . . Signed by Dolphins (June 15, 1983). . . . On suspended list (November 30-December 5, 1988). . . . Granted free agency (February 1, 1989). . . . Re-signed by Dolphins (September 25, 1989). . . . Granted roster exemption (September 25-September 28, 1989). . . . Transferred to suspended list (September 29-October 22, 1989). . . . Reinstated and released by Dolphins (October 23, 1989). . . . Awarded on waivers to Detroit Lions (October 24, 1989). . . . On inactive list (October 28, 1990).
PLAYING EXPERIENCE: Miami NFL, 1983-1988; Detroit NFL, 1989 and 1990. . . . Games: 1983 (14), 1984 (16), 1985 (15), 1986 (14), 1987 (12), 1988 (13), 1989 (6), 1990 (15). Total: 105.
CHAMPIONSHIP GAME EXPERIENCE: Played in AFC championship game after 1984 and 1985 seasons. . . . Played in Super Bowl XIX after 1984 season.
PRO STATISTICS: 1983—Intercepted one pass for no yards, returned one kickoff for no yards and recovered one fumble. 1985—Intercepted one pass for five yards and recovered two fumbles. 1986—Recovered four fumbles for 11 yards. 1987—Recovered one fumble for one yard. 1988—Intercepted two passes for 13 yards.

BROWN, RAY
OT, REDSKINS

PERSONAL: Born December 12, 1962, at West Memphis, Ark. . . . 6-5/280. . . . Full name: Leonard Ray Brown Jr.
HIGH SCHOOL: Marion (Ark.).
COLLEGE: Memphis State, then Arizona State, then Arkansas State.
TRANSACTIONS/CAREER NOTES: Selected by St. Louis Cardinals in eighth round (201st pick overall) of 1986 NFL draft. . . . Signed by Cardinals (July 14, 1986). . . . On injured reserve with knee injury (October 17-November 21, 1986). . . . Released by Cardinals (September 7, 1987). . . . Re-signed as free agent replacement player by Cardinals (September 25, 1987). . . . On injured reserve with disclosed finger (November 12-December 12, 1987). . . . Franchise transferred to Phoenix (March 15, 1988). . . . Granted unconditional free agency (February 1, 1989). . . . Signed by Washington Redskins (March 10, 1989). . . . On injured reserve with knee injury (September 5-November 4, 1989). . . . On injured reserve with knee injury (September 4, 1990-January 4, 1991).
PLAYING EXPERIENCE: St. Louis NFL, 1986 and 1987; Phoenix NFL, 1988; Washington NFL, 1989 and 1990. . . . Games: 1986 (11), 1987 (7), 1988 (15), 1989 (7), 1990 (0). Total: 40.

BROWN, RICHARD
LB, BROWNS

PERSONAL: Born September 21, 1965, at Western Samoa. . . . 6-3/240. . . . Full name: Richard Solomon Brown.
HIGH SCHOOL: Westminster (Calif.).
COLLEGE: San Diego State.

TRANSACTIONS/CAREER NOTES: Signed as free agent by Los Angeles Rams (May 14, 1987).... On injured reserve with hamstring injury (August 31-November 3, 1987).... Released by Los Angeles Rams (August 30, 1988).... Re-signed by Rams (March 10, 1989).... Released by Rams (September 4, 1989).... Re-signed by Rams (September 5, 1989).... Released by Rams (December 15, 1989).... Signed by San Diego Chargers (May 18, 1990).... On injured reserve with hamstring injury (November 21, 1990-remainder of season).... Granted unconditional free agency (February 1, 1991).... Signed by Cleveland Browns (March 29, 1991).
PLAYING EXPERIENCE: Los Angeles Rams NFL, 1987 and 1989; San Diego NFL, 1990.... Games: 1987 (8), 1989 (13), 1990 (11). Total: 32.
PRO STATISTICS: 1989—Recovered two fumbles. 1990—Recovered one fumble.

BROWN, ROBERT
DE, PACKERS

PERSONAL: Born May 21, 1960, at Edenton, N.C.... 6-3/278.... Full name: Robert Lee Brown.
HIGH SCHOOL: John A. Holmes (Edenton, N.C.).
COLLEGE: Chowan Junior College (N.C.), then Virginia Tech.
TRANSACTIONS/CAREER NOTES: Selected by Green Bay Packers in fourth round (98th pick overall) of 1982 NFL draft.... On inactive list (September 20, 1982).
PLAYING EXPERIENCE: Green Bay NFL, 1982-1990.... Games: 1982 (8), 1983 (16), 1984 (16), 1985 (16), 1986 (16), 1987 (12), 1988 (16), 1989 (16), 1990 (16). Total: 132.
PRO STATISTICS: 1982—Recovered one fumble. 1984—Intercepted one pass for five yards and a touchdown. 1985—Credited with one safety and recovered four fumbles. 1986—Recovered one fumble. 1987—Recovered four fumbles. 1990—Recovered one fumble.

BROWN, ROGER
CB, GIANTS

PERSONAL: Born December 16, 1966, at Baltimore.... 6-0/196.
HIGH SCHOOL: Cardinal Gibbons (Baltimore).
COLLEGE: Virginia Tech.
TRANSACTIONS/CAREER NOTES: Selected by Green Bay Packers in eighth round (215th pick overall) of 1990 NFL draft.... Signed by Packers (July 22, 1990).... Released by Packers (September 3, 1990).... Signed by New York Giants (September 19, 1990).... On practice squad (October 21-December 23, 1990).
PLAYING EXPERIENCE: New York Giants NFL, 1990.... Games: 1990 (5).
CHAMPIONSHIP GAME EXPERIENCE: Played in NFC championship game after 1990 season.... Played in Super Bowl XXV after 1990 season.

BROWN, RON
CB, RAIDERS

PERSONAL: Born March 31, 1961, at Los Angeles.... 5-11/185.... Full name: Ronald James Brown.
HIGH SCHOOL: Baldwin Park (Calif.).
COLLEGE: Arizona State.
TRANSACTIONS/CAREER NOTES: Selected by Arizona Wranglers in 1983 USFL territorial draft.... Selected by Cleveland Browns in second round (41st pick overall) of 1983 NFL draft.... NFL rights traded by Browns to Los Angeles Rams for second-round pick in 1984 draft (April 27, 1984).... Signed by Rams (August 16, 1984).... Granted free agency (February 1, 1988).... Re-signed by Rams (October 17, 1988).... Granted roster exemption (October 17-October 31, 1988).... Granted unconditional free agency (February 1, 1990).... Signed by Los Angeles Raiders (March 26, 1990).
CHAMPIONSHIP GAME EXPERIENCE: Played in NFC championship game after 1985 and 1989 seasons.... Played in AFC championship game after 1990 season.
RECORDS/HONORS: Tied NFL record for most touchdowns scored by kickoff return, game (2), against Green Bay Packers (November 24, 1985); most touchdowns by combined kick return, game (2), against Green Bay Packers (November 24, 1985).... Played in Pro Bowl after 1985 season.... Named as kick returner to THE SPORTING NEWS NFL All-Pro team, 1985.
MISCELLANEOUS: Won gold medal in 4x100 relay during 1984 summer Olympics.... Switched positions from wide receiver to defensive back (1990).
PRO STATISTICS: 1986—Recovered two fumbles. 1987—Recovered one fumble.

| | | | RUSHING | | | | RECEIVING | | | | — KICKOFF RETURNS — | | | | — TOTAL — | |
Year Team	G	Att.	Yds.	Avg.	TD	No.	Yds.	Avg.	TD	No.	Yds.	Avg.	TD	TD	Pts.	F.
1984—L.A. Rams NFL.......	16	2	25	12.5	0	23	478	20.8	4	0	0		0	4	24	0
1985—L.A. Rams NFL.......	13	2	13	6.5	0	14	215	15.4	3	28	918	*32.8	*3	6	36	2
1986—L.A. Rams NFL.......	14	4	5	1.3	0	25	396	15.8	0	36	794	22.1	0	3	18	1
1987—L.A. Rams NFL.......	12	2	22	11.0	0	26	521	20.0	2	27	581	21.5	1	3	18	2
1988—L.A. Rams NFL.......	7	3	24	8.0	0	2	16	8.0	0	19	401	21.1	0	0	0	1
1989—L.A. Rams NFL.......	16	6	27	4.5	0	5	113	22.6	1	*47	968	20.6	0	1	6	3
1990—L.A. Raiders NFL ...	16	0	0		0	0	0		0	30	575	19.2	0	0	0	1
Pro totals (7 years).......	94	19	116	6.1	0	95	1739	18.3	13	187	4237	22.7	4	17	102	10

BROWN, STEVE
CB, 49ERS

PERSONAL: Born March 20, 1960, at Sacramento, Calif.... 6-0/187.
HIGH SCHOOL: C.K. McClatchy (Sacramento, Calif.).
COLLEGE: Oregon.
TRANSACTIONS/CAREER NOTES: Selected by Arizona Wranglers in seventh round (74th pick overall) of 1983 USFL draft.... Selected by Houston Oilers in third round (83rd pick overall) of 1983 NFL draft.... Signed by Oilers (June 28, 1983).... Granted unconditional free agency (February 1, 1991).... Signed by San Francisco 49ers (April 1, 1991).
PRO STATISTICS: 1984—Recovered one fumble. 1985—Recovered one fumble. 1987—Recovered one fumble.

Year Team	G	No.	Yds.	Avg.	TD	No.	Yds.	Avg.	TD	TD	Pts.	F.
		INTERCEPTIONS				**KICKOFF RETURNS**				**TOTAL**		
1983— Houston NFL	16	1	16	16.0	0	31	795	25.7	*1	1	6	2
1984— Houston NFL	16	1	26	26.0	0	3	17	5.7	0	0	0	1
1985— Houston NFL	15	5	41	8.2	0	2	45	22.5	0	0	0	1
1986— Houston NFL	16	2	34	17.0	0	0	0		0	0	0	0
1987— Houston NFL	10	2	45	22.5	0	0	0		0	0	0	1
1988— Houston NFL	14	2	48	24.0	1	0	0		0	1	6	0
1989— Houston NFL	16	5	54	10.8	0	0	0		0	0	0	0
1990— Houston NFL	16	0	0		0	0	0		0	0	0	0
Pro totals (8 years)	119	18	264	14.7	1	36	857	23.8	1	2	12	5

BROWN, TIM
WR, RAIDERS

PERSONAL: Born July 22, 1966, at Dallas. . . . 6-0/ 195. . . . Full name: Timothy Donell Brown. **HIGH SCHOOL:** Woodrow Wilson (Dallas). **COLLEGE:** Notre Dame (undergraduate degree). **TRANSACTIONS/CAREER NOTES:** Selected by Los Angeles Raiders in first round (sixth pick overall) of 1988 NFL draft. . . . Signed by Raiders (July 14, 1988). . . . On injured reserve with knee injury (September 12, 1989-remainder of season).
CHAMPIONSHIP GAME EXPERIENCE: Played in AFC championship game after 1990 season.
RECORDS/HONORS: Established NFL record for most yards gained, rookie, season (2,317), 1988. . . . Heisman Trophy winner, 1987. . . . Named as wide receiver on THE SPORTING NEWS college All-America team, 1986 and 1987. . . . Named as kick returner to THE SPORTING NEWS NFL All-Pro team, 1988. . . . Played in Pro Bowl after 1988 season.
PRO STATISTICS: 1988—Recovered seven fumbles (including one in end zone for a touchdown).

Year Team	G	Att.	Yds.	Avg.	TD	No.	Yds.	Avg.	TD	No.	Yds.	Avg.	TD	No.	Yds.	Avg.	TD	TD	Pts.	F.
		RUSHING				**RECEIVING**				**PUNT RETURNS**				**KICKOFF RETURNS**				**TOTALS**		
1988— L.A. Raiders NFL	16	14	50	3.6	1	43	725	16.9	5	49	444	9.1	0	*41	*1098	*26.8	*1	7	42	5
1989— L.A. Raiders NFL	1	0	0		0	1	8	8.0	0	4	43	10.8	0	3	63	21.0	0	0	0	1
1990— L.A. Raiders NFL	16	0	0		0	18	265	14.7	3	34	295	8.7	0	0	0		0	3	18	3
Pro totals (3 years)	33	14	50	3.6	1	62	998	16.1	8	87	782	9.0	0	44	1161	26.4	1	10	60	9

BROWN, VINCENT
LB, PATRIOTS

PERSONAL: Born January 9, 1965, at Atlanta. . . . 6-2/245. . . . Full name: Vincent Bernard Brown. **HIGH SCHOOL:** Walter F. George (Atlanta). **COLLEGE:** Mississippi Valley State (degree in criminal justice, 1988).
TRANSACTIONS/CAREER NOTES: Selected by New England Patriots in second round (43rd pick overall) of 1988 NFL draft. . . . Signed by Patriots (July 20, 1988).
PLAYING EXPERIENCE: New England NFL, 1988-1990. . . . Games: 1988 (16), 1989 (14), 1990 (16). Total: 46.
PRO STATISTICS: 1989—Intercepted one pass for minus one yard and recovered two fumbles.

BROWNER, JOEY
S, VIKINGS

PERSONAL: Born May 15, 1960, at Warren, O. . . . 6-2/228. . . . Full name: Joey Matthew Browner. . . . Brother of Ross Browner, defensive end with Cincinnati Bengals, Houston Gamblers (USFL) and Green Bay Packers, 1978-1988; brother of Jim Browner, defensive back with Cincinnati Bengals, 1979 and 1980; and brother of Keith Browner, linebacker with Tampa Bay Buccaneers, San Francisco 49ers, Los Angeles Raiders and San Diego Chargers, 1984-1988.
HIGH SCHOOL: Warren Reserve (Warren, O.), then Southwest (Atlanta).
COLLEGE: Southern California.
TRANSACTIONS/CAREER NOTES: Selected by Los Angeles Express in 1983 USFL territorial draft. . . . Selected by Minnesota Vikings in first round (19th pick overall) of 1983 NFL draft. . . . Signed by Vikings (April 30, 1983).
CHAMPIONSHIP GAME EXPERIENCE: Played in NFC championship game after 1987 season.
RECORDS/HONORS: Tied NFL record for most opponents' fumbles recovered, game (3), against San Francisco 49ers (September 8, 1985). . . . Played in Pro Bowl after 1985-1990 seasons. . . . Named to THE SPORTING NEWS NFL All-Pro team, 1987, 1988 and 1990.
PRO STATISTICS: 1983—Recovered four fumbles for four yards and fumbled once. 1984—Recovered three fumbles for 63 yards and a touchdown. 1985—Returned one kickoff for no yards and recovered three fumbles for five yards and fumbled once. 1986—Recovered four fumbles. 1987—Recovered one fumble. 1988—Recovered two fumbles for nine yards.

Year Team	G	No.	Yds.	Avg.	TD
		INTERCEPTIONS			
1983— Minnesota NFL	16	2	0	.0	0
1984— Minnesota NFL	16	1	20	20.0	0
1985— Minnesota NFL	16	2	17	8.5	*1
1986— Minnesota NFL	16	4	62	15.5	1
1987— Minnesota NFL	12	6	67	11.2	0
1988— Minnesota NFL	16	5	29	5.8	0
1989— Minnesota NFL	16	5	70	14.0	0
1990— Minnesota NFL	16	7	103	14.7	1
Pro totals (8 years)	124	32	368	11.5	3

BRUCE, AUNDRAY
LB, FALCONS

PERSONAL: Born April 30, 1966, at Montgomery, Ala. . . . 6-5/250. . . . Uncle of Ricky Shaw, linebacker with Kansas City Chiefs.
HIGH SCHOOL: George Washington Carver (Montgomery, Ala.).
COLLEGE: Auburn.
TRANSACTIONS/CAREER NOTES: Signed by Atlanta Falcons (April 6, 1988). . . . Selected officially by Falcons in first round (first pick overall) of 1988 NFL draft.
PLAYING EXPERIENCE: Atlanta NFL, 1988-1990. . . . Games: 1988 (16), 1989 (16), 1990 (16). Total: 48.
RECORDS/HONORS: Named as linebacker on THE SPORTING NEWS college All-America team, 1987.
PRO STATISTICS: 1988—Intercepted two passes for 10 yards and recovered one fumble. 1989—Intercepted one pass for no yards and returned one kickoff for 15 yards.

BRUHIN, JOHN
G, BUCCANEERS

PERSONAL: Born December 9, 1964, at Knoxville, Tenn. . . . 6-3/285. . . . Full name: John Glenn Bruhin. . . . Name pronounced BRUIN.
HIGH SCHOOL: Powell (Tenn.).
COLLEGE: Tennessee.
TRANSACTIONS/CAREER NOTES: Selected by Tampa Bay Buccaneers in fourth round (86th pick overall) of 1988 NFL draft. . . . Signed by Buccaneers (July 10, 1988). . . . On injured reserve with knee injury (October 24-December 15, 1989). . . . On inactive list (November 25 and December 2, 1990).
PLAYING EXPERIENCE: Tampa Bay NFL, 1988-1990. . . . Games: 1988 (16), 1989 (9), 1990 (14). Total: 39.

BRYAN, RICK
DE, FALCONS

PERSONAL: Born March 20, 1962, at Tulsa, Okla. . . . 6-4/265. . . . Full name: Rick Don Bryan. . . . Brother of Steve Bryan, linebacker with Denver Broncos, 1987 and 1988.
HIGH SCHOOL: Coweta (Okla.).
COLLEGE: Oklahoma.
TRANSACTIONS/CAREER NOTES: Selected by Oklahoma Outlaws in 1984 USFL territorial draft. . . . Selected by Atlanta Falcons in first round (ninth pick overall) of 1984 NFL draft. . . . Signed by Falcons (July 20, 1984). . . . Granted free agency (February 1, 1988). . . . Re-signed by Falcons (August 29, 1988). . . . On injured reserve with neck injury (September 23, 1989-remainder of season).
PLAYING EXPERIENCE: Atlanta NFL, 1984-1990. . . . Games: 1984 (16), 1985 (16), 1986 (16), 1987 (9), 1988 (16), 1989 (2), 1990 (16). Total: 91.
RECORDS/HONORS: Named as defensive lineman on THE SPORTING NEWS college All-America team, 1983.
PRO STATISTICS: 1984—Credited with one safety. 1985—Caught extra point and ran four yards with lateral on fumble recovery. 1987—Recovered one fumble. 1988—Recovered one fumble. 1990—Recovered one fumble.

BRYANT, JEFF
DT, SEAHAWKS

PERSONAL: Born May 22, 1960, at Atlanta. . . . 6-5/281. . . . Full name: Jeff Dwight Bryant.
HIGH SCHOOL: Gordon (Decatur, Ga.).
COLLEGE: Clemson.
TRANSACTIONS/CAREER NOTES: Selected by Seattle Seahawks in first round (sixth pick overall) of 1982 NFL draft. . . . On injured reserve with ankle injury (November 14-December 13, 1986). . . . Granted free agency (February 1, 1988). . . . Re-signed by Seahawks (August 31, 1988). . . . On inactive list (October 21, 1990).
PLAYING EXPERIENCE: Seattle NFL, 1982-1990. . . . Games: 1982 (9), 1983 (16), 1984 (16), 1985 (16), 1986 (12), 1987 (12), 1988 (16), 1989 (15), 1990 (15). Total: 127.
CHAMPIONSHIP GAME EXPERIENCE: Played in AFC championship game after 1983 season.
PRO STATISTICS: 1983—Recovered one fumble. 1984—Intercepted one pass for one yard, credited with a safety and recovered two fumbles. 1985—Recovered four fumbles. 1987—Recovered one fumble. 1988—Recovered two fumbles.

BUCK, JASON
DE, BENGALS

PERSONAL: Born July 27, 1963, at Moses Lake, Wash. . . . 6-5/264. . . . Full name: Jason Ogden Buck.
HIGH SCHOOL: South Fremont (St. Anthony, Idaho).
COLLEGE: Ricks College (Idaho), then Brigham Young.
TRANSACTIONS/CAREER NOTES: Selected by Cincinnati Bengals in first round (17th pick overall) of 1987 NFL draft. . . . Signed by Bengals (September 8, 1987). . . . Granted roster exemption (September 8, 1987).
PLAYING EXPERIENCE: Cincinnati NFL, 1987-1990. . . . Games: 1987 (12), 1988 (16), 1989 (16), 1990 (16). Total: 60.
CHAMPIONSHIP GAME EXPERIENCE: Played in AFC championship game after 1988 season. . . . Played in Super Bowl XXIII after 1988 season.
RECORDS/HONORS: Outland Trophy winner, 1986. . . . Named as defensive lineman on THE SPORTING NEWS college All-America team, 1986.
PRO STATISTICS: 1989—Recovered one fumble.

BUCK, MIKE
QB, SAINTS

PERSONAL: Born April 22, 1967, at Long Island, N.Y. . . . 6-3/227. . . . Full name: Mike Eric Buck.
HIGH SCHOOL: Sayville (N.Y.).
COLLEGE: Maine (degree in physical education).
TRANSACTIONS/CAREER NOTES: Selected by New Orleans Saints in sixth round (156th pick overall) of 1990 NFL draft. . . . Signed by Saints (July 16, 1990). . . . On inactive list (September 16, 23; October 14, 21, 28; and December 9, 16 and 31, 1990). . . . Active for eight games in 1990; did not play.
PLAYING EXPERIENCE: New Orleans NFL, 1990. . . . Games: 1990 (0).

BUCK, VINCE

CB, SAINTS

PERSONAL: Born January 12, 1968, at Owensboro, Ky. . . . 6-/198. . . . Full name: Vincent Lamont Buck.
HIGH SCHOOL: Owensboro (Ky.).
COLLEGE: Central State (O.).
TRANSACTIONS/CAREER NOTES: Selected by New Orleans Saints in second round (44th pick overall) of 1990 NFL draft. . . . Signed by Saints (May 7, 1990).
PRO STATISTICS: 1990—Recovered two fumbles.

			— PUNT RETURNS—				— KICKOFF RETURNS—				— TOTAL —		
Year	Team	G	No.	Yds.	Avg.	TD	No.	Yds.	Avg.	TD	TD	Pts.	F.
1990— New Orleans NFL		16	37	305	8.2	0	3	38	12.7	0	0	0	2
Pro totals (1 year)		16	37	305	8.2	0	3	38	12.7	0	0	0	2

BUCZKOWSKI, BOB

DE, SEAHAWKS

PERSONAL: Born May 5, 1964, at Pittsburgh. . . . 6-5/261. . . . Full name: John Robert Buczkowski.
HIGH SCHOOL: Gateway (Monroeville, Pa.).
COLLEGE: Pittsburgh.
TRANSACTIONS/CAREER NOTES: Selected by Los Angeles Raiders in first round (24th pick overall) of 1986 NFL draft. . . . Signed by Raiders (July 17, 1986). . . . On injured reserve with back injury (August 26, 1986-entire season). . . . On non-football injury list with hepatitis (September 10-October 14, 1987). . . . Crossed picket line during players' strike (October 14, 1987). . . . On injured reserve with ankle injury (November 11-December 12, 1987). . . . Released by Raiders (August 30, 1988). . . . Signed as free agent by San Diego Chargers (May 25, 1989). . . . Released by Chargers (September 4, 1989). . . . Signed as free agent by Phoenix Cardinals (October 25, 1989). . . . Released by Cardinals (December 15, 1989). . . . Signed as free agent by Cleveland Browns (March 29, 1990). . . . Traded by Browns to Seattle Seahawks for ninth-round pick in 1991 NFL draft (April 22, 1991).
PLAYING EXPERIENCE: Los Angeles Raiders NFL, 1987; Phoenix NFL, 1989; Cleveland NFL, 1990. . . . Games: 1987 (2), 1989 (4), 1990 (15). Total: 21.
PRO STATISTICS: 1989—Recovered one fumble.

BUFORD, MAURY

P, BEARS

PERSONAL: Born February 18, 1960, at Mount Pleasant, Tex. . . . 6-0/198. . . . Full name: Maury Anthony Buford.
HIGH SCHOOL: Mount Pleasant (Tex.).
COLLEGE: Texas Tech (degree in business administration and marketing, 1982).
TRANSACTIONS/CAREER NOTES: Selected by San Diego Chargers in eighth round (215th pick overall) of 1982 NFL draft. . . . Traded by Chargers to Chicago Bears for 12th-round pick in 1986 NFL draft (August 20, 1985). . . . Released by Bears (September 7, 1987). . . . Signed as free agent by Denver Broncos (April 28, 1988). . . . Released by Broncos (July 22, 1988). . . . Awarded on waivers to Atlanta Falcons (July 26, 1988). . . . Released by Falcons (August 25, 1988). . . . Signed as free agent by New York Giants (September 7, 1988). . . . Granted unconditional free agency (February 1, 1989). . . . Signed by Green Bay Packers (March 30, 1989). . . . Released by Packers (July 28, 1989). . . . Awarded on waivers to Chicago Bears (August 1, 1989).
CHAMPIONSHIP GAME EXPERIENCE: Played in NFC championship game after 1985 season. . . . Played in Super Bowl XX after 1985 season.
PRO STATISTICS: 1983—Attempted one pass with no completions. 1985—Attempted one pass with one completion for five yards. 1986—Rushed once for minus 13 yards and fumbled once. 1989—Rushed once for six yards. 1990—Rushed once for minus nine yards and fumbled once.

		— PUNTING—		
Year	Team	G	No.	Avg.	Blk.
1982— San Diego NFL	9	21	41.3	*2
1983— San Diego NFL	16	63	43.9	0
1984— San Diego NFL	16	66	42.0	0
1985— Chicago NFL	16	68	42.2	1
1986— Chicago NFL	16	69	41.3	1
1988— N.Y. Giants NFL	15	73	41.3	2
1989— Chicago NFL	16	72	39.5	0
1990— Chicago NFL	16	76	40.4	2
Pro totals (8 years)	120	508	41.5	8

BURBAGE, CORNELL

WR, STEELERS

PERSONAL: Born February 22, 1965, at Lexington, Ky. . . . 5-10/189. . . . Full name: Cornell Rodney Burbage.
HIGH SCHOOL: Bryan Station (Lexington, Ky.).
COLLEGE: Kentucky (bachelor of science degree in mathematics, 1987).
TRANSACTIONS/CAREER NOTES: Signed as free agent by Dallas Cowboys (April 30, 1987). . . . Released by Cowboys (September 7, 1987). . . . Re-signed as replacement player by Cowboys (September 23, 1987). . . . Released by Cowboys (October 26, 1987). . . . Re-signed by Cowboys for 1988 season (December 24, 1987). . . . Released by Cowboys (August 30, 1988). . . . Re-signed by Cowboys (October 11, 1988). . . . On injured reserve with shoulder injury (September 18-October 31, 1989). . . . Activated after clearing procedural waivers (November 2, 1989). . . . Granted unconditional free agency (February 1, 1990). . . . Signed by Minnesota Vikings (March 28, 1990). . . . Released by Vikings (August 28, 1990). . . . Signed by WLAF (January 10, 1991). . . . Selected by New York/New Jersey Knights in first round (seventh wide receiver) of 1991 WLAF positional draft. . . . Signed by Pittsburgh Steelers (July 11, 1991).

Year	Team	G	RECEIVING				PUNT RETURNS				KICKOFF RETURNS				TOTAL		
			No.	Yds.	Avg.	TD	No.	Yds.	Avg.	TD	No.	Yds.	Avg.	TD	TD	Pts.	F.
1987— Dallas NFL		3	7	168	24.0	2	5	29	5.8	0	0	0		0	0	2	12	0
1988— Dallas NFL		10	2	50	25.0	0	0	0		0	20	448	22.4	0	0	0	1
1989— Dallas NFL		10	17	134	7.9	0	3	5	1.7	0	3	55	18.3	0	0	0	0
1990— N.Y./N.J. WLAF		10	22	419	19.1	1	11	48	4.4	0	8	136	17.0	0	1	6	—
NFL totals (3 years) ...		23	26	352	13.5	2	8	34	4.3	0	23	503	21.9	0	2	12	1
WLAF totals (1 year) ..		10	22	419	19.1	1	11	48	4.4	0	8	136	17.0	0	1	6	—
Pro totals (4 years)		33	48	771	16.1	3	19	82	4.3	0	31	639	20.6	0	3	18	1

BURKETT, CHRIS
WR, JETS

PERSONAL: Born August 21, 1962, at Laurel, Miss. . . . 6-4/200.
HIGH SCHOOL: Collins (Miss.).
COLLEGE: Jackson State.
TRANSACTIONS/CAREER NOTES: Selected by Baltimore Stars in first round (14th pick overall) of 1985 USFL draft. . . . Selected by Buffalo Bills in second round (42nd pick overall) of 1985 NFL draft. . . . Signed by Bills (July 23, 1985). . . . Released by Bills (September 21, 1989). . . . Awarded on waivers to New York Jets (September 22, 1989). . . . Granted free agency with option not exercised (September 23, 1989). . . . Signed by Jets (September 25, 1989).
CHAMPIONSHIP GAME EXPERIENCE: Played in AFC championship game after 1988 season.
PRO STATISTICS: 1986—Fumbled once. 1987—Fumbled once. 1989—Rushed once for minus four yards. 1990—Recovered one fumble.

Year	Team	G	RECEIVING			
			No.	Yds.	Avg.	TD
1985— Buffalo NFL		16	21	371	17.7	0
1986— Buffalo NFL		14	34	778	*22.9	4
1987— Buffalo NFL		12	56	765	13.7	4
1988— Buffalo NFL		11	23	354	15.4	1
1989— Buf. (2)-NYJ (13) NFL..		15	24	298	12.4	1
1990— N.Y. Jets NFL		16	14	204	14.6	0
Pro totals (6 years)		84	172	2770	16.1	10

BURNETT, ROB
DL, BROWNS

PERSONAL: Born August 27, 1967, at Livingston, N.J. . . . 6-4/270. . . . Full name: Robert Barry Burnett.
HIGH SCHOOL: Newfield (Selden, N.Y.).
COLLEGE: Syracuse.
TRANSACTIONS/CAREER NOTES: Selected by Cleveland Browns in fifth round (129th pick overall) of 1990 NFL draft. . . . Signed by Browns (July 22, 1990).
PLAYING EXPERIENCE: Cleveland NFL, 1990. . . . Games: 1990 (16).

BURRUSS, LLOYD
S, CHIEFS

PERSONAL: Born October 31, 1957, at Charlottesville, Va. . . . 6-0/214. . . . Full name: Lloyd Earl Burruss Jr.
HIGH SCHOOL: Charlottesville (Va.).
COLLEGE: Maryland (bachelor of arts degree in general studies, 1981).
TRANSACTIONS/CAREER NOTES: Selected by Kansas City Chiefs in third round (78th pick overall) of 1981 NFL draft. . . . On injured reserve with knee injury (December 23, 1987-remainder of season). . . . On injured reserve with thigh injury (September 5-October 28, 1989).
RECORDS/HONORS: Tied NFL record for most touchdowns scored by interception, game (2), against San Diego Chargers (October 19, 1986). . . . Played in Pro Bowl after 1986 season.
PRO STATISTICS: 1981—Returned five kickoffs for 91 yards, recovered one fumble for four yards and fumbled once. 1983—Recovered two fumbles for 26 yards. 1984—Recovered one fumble. 1986—Returned blocked field goal 78 yards for a touchdown and recovered one fumble. 1990—Recovered one fumble for two yards.

Year	Team	G	INTERCEPTIONS			
			No.	Yds.	Avg.	TD
1981— Kansas City NFL		14	4	75	18.8	1
1982— Kansas City NFL		9	1	25	25.0	0
1983— Kansas City NFL		12	4	46	11.5	0
1984— Kansas City NFL		16	2	16	8.0	0
1985— Kansas City NFL		15	1	0	.0	0
1986— Kansas City NFL		15	5	*193	38.6	*3
1987— Kansas City NFL		11	0	0		
1988— Kansas City NFL		10	2	57	28.5	0
1989— Kansas City NFL		9	1	0	.0	0
1990— Kansas City NFL		16	1	14	14.0	0
Pro totals (10 years)		127	21	426	20.3	4

BURTON, LEONARD
C, BILLS

PERSONAL: Born June 18, 1964, at Memphis, Tenn. . . . 6-3/277. . . . Full name: Leonard Bernard Burton.
HIGH SCHOOL: Oakhaven (Memphis, Tenn.).
COLLEGE: Northwest Mississippi Junior College, then South Carolina.

TRANSACTIONS/CAREER NOTES: Selected by Jacksonville Bulls in 1986 USFL territorial draft. . . . Selected by Buffalo Bills in third round (77th pick overall) of 1986 NFL draft. . . . USFL rights traded by Jacksonville Bulls with rights to offensive tackle Doug Williams to Memphis Showboats for rights to wide receiver Tim McGee (May 6, 1986). . . . Signed by Buffalo Bills (July 24, 1986). . . . On injured reserve with knee injury (December 17, 1986-remainder of season). . . . On injured reserve with knee injury (September 4, 1990-entire season).
PLAYING EXPERIENCE: Buffalo NFL, 1986-1989. . . . Games: 1986 (14), 1987 (12), 1988 (16), 1989 (16). Total: 58.
CHAMPIONSHIP GAME EXPERIENCE: Played in AFC championship game after 1988 season.

BUSH, BLAIR
C, PACKERS

PERSONAL: Born November 25, 1956, at Fort Hood, Tex. . . . 6-3/275. . . . Full name: Blair Walter Bush.
HIGH SCHOOL: Palos Verdes (Calif.).
COLLEGE: Washington (degree in education).
TRANSACTIONS/CAREER NOTES: Selected by Cincinnati Bengals in first round (16th pick overall) of 1978 NFL draft. . . . Traded by Bengals to Seattle Seahawks for first-round pick in 1985 draft (June 29, 1983). . . . On injured reserve with knee injury (October 22, 1986-remainder of season). . . . Crossed picket line during players' strike (October 14, 1987). . . . On injured reserve with broken hand (December 18, 1987-remainder of season). . . . Granted unconditional free agency (February 1, 1989). . . . Signed by Green Bay Packers (March 10, 1989).
PLAYING EXPERIENCE: Cincinnati NFL, 1978-1982; Seattle, NFL, 1983-1988; Green Bay NFL, 1989 and 1990. . . . Games: 1978 (16), 1979 (12), 1980 (16), 1981 (16), 1982 (8), 1983 (16), 1984 (16), 1985 (16), 1986 (7), 1987 (11), 1988 (16), 1989 (16), 1990 (16). Total: 182.
CHAMPIONSHIP GAME EXPERIENCE: Played in AFC championship game after 1981 and 1983 seasons. . . . Played in Super Bowl XVI after 1981 season.
PRO STATISTICS: 1981—Recovered one fumble for 12 yards. 1985—Recovered one fumble. 1989—Recovered one fumble.

BUSSEY, BARNEY
S, BENGALS

PERSONAL: Born May 20, 1962, at Lincolnton, Ga. . . . 6-0/210. . . . Full name: Barney A. Bussey.
HIGH SCHOOL: Lincoln County (Lincolnton, Ga.).
COLLEGE: South Carolina State.
TRANSACTIONS/CAREER NOTES: Selected by Memphis Showboats in first round (fourth pick overall) of 1984 USFL draft. . . . Selected by Cincinnati Bengals in fifth round (119th pick overall) of 1984 NFL draft. . . . Signed by Memphis Showboats (May 8, 1984). . . . Granted roster exemption (May 8-May 15, 1984). . . . On developmental squad for one game (March 16-March 24, 1985). . . . Granted free agency when USFL suspended operations (August 7, 1986). . . . Signed by Cincinnati Bengals (August 12, 1986).
CHAMPIONSHIP GAME EXPERIENCE: Played in AFC championship game after 1988 season. . . . Played in Super Bowl XXIII after 1988 season.
RECORDS/HONORS: Named as strong safety on THE SPORTING NEWS USFL All-Star team, 1985.
PRO STATISTICS: USFL: 1984—Recovered one fumble. 1985—Credited with one sack for four yards and recovered one fumble for 12 yards. . . . NFL: 1988—Recovered one fumble. 1989—Recovered blocked punt in end zone for a touchdown. 1990—Recovered one fumble for 70 yards and a touchdown.

		—INTERCEPTIONS—				—KICKOFF RETURNS—				—TOTAL—		
Year Team	G	No.	Yds.	Avg.	TD	No.	Yds.	Avg.	TD	TD	Pts.	F.
1984—Memphis USFL	6	0	0		0	0	0		0	0	0	0
1985—Memphis USFL	17	3	11	3.7	0	0	0		0	0	0	0
1986—Cincinnati NFL	16	1	19	19.0	0	0	0		0	0	0	0
1987—Cincinnati NFL	12	1	0	.0	0	21	406	19.3	0	0	0	1
1988—Cincinnati NFL	16	0	0		0	7	83	11.9	0	0	0	1
1989—Cincinnati NFL	16	1	0	.0	0	0	0		0	1	6	0
1990—Cincinnati NFL	16	4	37	9.3	0	0	0		0	1	6	0
USFL totals (2 years)	23	3	11	3.7	0	0	0		0	0	0	0
NFL totals (5 years)	76	7	56	8.0	0	28	489	17.5	0	2	12	2
Pro totals (7 years)	99	10	67	6.7	0	28	489	17.5	0	2	12	2

BUTCHER, PAUL
LB, RAMS

PERSONAL: Born November 8, 1963, at Detroit. . . . 6-0/230. . . . Full name: Paul Martin Butcher.
HIGH SCHOOL: St. Alphonsus (Dearborn, Mich.).
COLLEGE: Wayne State, Mich. (degree in mechanical engineering, 1986).
TRANSACTIONS/CAREER NOTES: Signed as free agent by Detroit Lions (July 23, 1986). . . . Released by Lions (August 18, 1986). . . . Re-signed by Lions (October 3, 1986). . . . Granted unconditional free agency (February 1, 1989). . . . Signed by Philadelphia Eagles (March 27, 1989). . . . Released by Eagles (August 30, 1989). . . . Signed by Los Angeles Rams (January 4, 1990). . . . On injured reserve with groin injury (January 10, 1990-remainder of 1989 season playoffs).
PLAYING EXPERIENCE: Detroit NFL, 1986-1988. . . . Los Angeles Rams NFL, 1990. . . . Games: 1986 (12), 1987 (12), 1988 (16), 1990 (16). Total: 56.

BUTLER, BOBBY
CB, FALCONS

PERSONAL: Born May 28, 1959, at Boynton Beach, Fla. . . . 5-11/175. . . . Full name: Robert Calvin Butler. . . . Cousin of James (Cannonball) Butler, running back with Pittsburgh Steelers, Atlanta Falcons and St. Louis Cardinals, 1965-1972.
HIGH SCHOOL: Atlantic (Delray Beach, Fla.).
COLLEGE: Florida State.
TRANSACTIONS/CAREER NOTES: Selected by Atlanta Falcons in first round (25th pick overall) of 1981 NFL draft. . . . On injured

reserve with broken leg (October 20, 1986 - remainder of season).
PRO STATISTICS: 1983—Returned one kickoff for 17 yards and recovered one fumble. 1984—Recovered one fumble for 10 yards. 1988—Recovered three fumbles for 29 yards. 1989—Recovered one fumble for 29 yards and a touchdown. 1990—Recovered two fumbles (including one in the end zone for a touchdown) and returned blocked punt 62 yards for a touchdown.

			INTERCEPTIONS		
Year Team	G	No.	Yds.	Avg.	TD
1981— Atlanta NFL	16	5	86	17.2	0
1982— Atlanta NFL	9	2	0	.0	0
1983— Atlanta NFL	16	4	12	3.0	0
1984— Atlanta NFL	15	2	25	12.5	0
1985— Atlanta NFL	16	5	-4	-.8	0
1986— Atlanta NFL	7	1	33	33.0	1
1987— Atlanta NFL	12	4	48	12.0	0
1988— Atlanta NFL	16	1	22	22.0	0
1989— Atlanta NFL	16	0	0		0
1990— Atlanta NFL	16	3	0	.0	0
Pro totals (10 years)	139	27	222	8.2	1

BUTLER, KEVIN
PK, BEARS

PERSONAL: Born July 24, 1962, at Savannah, Ga. . . . 6-1/190. . . . Full name: Kevin Gregory Butler.
HIGH SCHOOL: Redan (Ga.).
COLLEGE: Georgia.
TRANSACTIONS/CAREER NOTES: Selected by Jacksonville Bulls in 1985 USFL territorial draft. . . . Selected by Chicago Bears in fourth round (105th pick overall) of 1985 NFL draft. . . . Signed by Bears (July 23, 1985).
CHAMPIONSHIP GAME EXPERIENCE: Played in NFC championship game after 1985 and 1988 seasons. . . . Played in Super Bowl XX after 1985 season.
RECORDS/HONORS: Established NFL record for most points, rookie season (144), 1985; most consecutive field goals (24), 1988-89. Tied NFL record for most field goals, 50 or more yards, game (2): against Minnesota Vikings (September 23, 1990) and Green Bay Packers (October 7, 1990).

			PLACE-KICKING		
Year Team	G	XPM	XPA	FGM	FGA	Pts.
1985— Chicago NFL	16	51	51	31	37	*144
1986— Chicago NFL	16	36	37	28	*41	120
1987— Chicago NFL	12	28	30	19	28	85
1988— Chicago NFL	16	37	38	15	19	82
1989— Chicago NFL	16	43	45	15	19	88
1990— Chicago NFL	16	36	37	26	37	114
Pro totals (6 years)	92	231	238	134	181	633

BUTLER, LEROY
CB, PACKERS

PERSONAL: Born July 19, 1968, at Jacksonville, Fla. . . . 6-0/ 195.
HIGH SCHOOL: Robert E. Lee Sr. (Jacksonville, Fla.).
COLLEGE: Florida State (degree in social science).
TRANSACTIONS/CAREER NOTES: Selected by Green Bay Packers in second round (48th pick overall) of 1990 NFL draft. . . . Signed by Packers (July 25, 1990).

			INTERCEPTIONS		
Year Team	G	No.	Yds.	Avg.	TD
1990— Green Bay NFL..........	16	3	42	14.0	0
Pro totals (1 year)	16	3	42	14.0	0

BUTTS, MARION
RB, CHARGERS

PERSONAL: Born August 1, 1966, at Sylvester, Ga. . . . 6-1/248. . . . Full name: Marion Stevenson Butts Jr.
HIGH SCHOOL: Worth Academy (Sylvester, Ga.).
COLLEGE: Northeastern Oklahoma A&M, then Florida State.
TRANSACTIONS/CAREER NOTES: Selected by San Diego Chargers in seventh round (183rd pick overall) of 1989 NFL draft. . . . Signed by Chargers (July 21, 1989). . . . On inactive list (December 23 and 30, 1990).
RECORDS/HONORS: Named to play in Pro Bowl after 1990 season; replaced due to injury by James Brooks.
PRO STATISTICS: 1989—Recovered one fumble. 1990—Recovered one fumble.

		RUSHING				RECEIVING				TOTAL		
Year Team	G	Att.	Yds.	Avg.	TD	No.	Yds.	Avg.	TD	TD	Pts.	F.
1989— San Diego NFL	15	170	683	4.0	9	7	21	3.0	0	9	54	2
1990— San Diego NFL	14	265	1225	4.6	8	16	117	7.3	0	8	48	0
Pro totals (2 years)	29	435	1908	4.4	17	23	138	6.0	0	17	102	2

BYARS, KEITH
RB, EAGLES

PERSONAL: Born October 14, 1963, at Dayton, O. . . . 6-1/238.
HIGH SCHOOL: Nettie Lee Roth (Dayton, O.).
COLLEGE: Ohio State.
TRANSACTIONS/CAREER NOTES: Selected by New Jersey Generals in 1986 USFL territorial draft.

... Selected by Philadelphia Eagles in first round (10th pick overall) of 1986 NFL draft.... Signed by Eagles (July 25, 1986).
... Granted free agency (February 1, 1990).... Re-signed by Eagles (August 10, 1990).
RECORDS/HONORS: Named as running back on THE SPORTING NEWS college All-America team, 1984.
PRO STATISTICS: 1986—Returned two kickoffs for 47 yards, attempted two passes with one completion for 55 yards and one touchdown and recovered two fumbles. 1987—Recovered two fumbles. 1988—Returned two kickoffs for 20 yards, recovered two fumbles for 14 yards and attempted two passes with no completions. 1989—Returned one kickoff for 27 yards and recovered four fumbles for six yards. 1990—Attempted four passes with four completions for 53 yards and four touchdowns and recovered one fumble.

		——— RUSHING ———				——— RECEIVING ———				— TOTAL —		
Year Team	G	Att.	Yds.	Avg.	TD	No.	Yds.	Avg.	TD	TD	Pts.	F.
1986— Philadelphia NFL	16	177	577	3.3	1	11	44	4.0	0	1	6	3
1987— Philadelphia NFL	10	116	426	3.7	3	21	177	8.4	1	4	24	3
1988— Philadelphia NFL	16	152	517	3.4	6	72	705	9.8	4	10	60	5
1989— Philadelphia NFL	16	133	452	3.4	5	68	721	10.6	0	5	30	4
1990— Philadelphia NFL	16	37	141	3.8	0	81	819	10.1	3	3	18	4
Pro totals (5 years)	74	615	2113	3.4	15	253	2466	9.8	8	23	138	19

BYNER, EARNEST
RB, REDSKINS

PERSONAL: Born September 15, 1962, at Milledgeville, Ga.... 5-10/215.... Full name: Earnest Alexander Byner.
HIGH SCHOOL: Baldwin (Milledgeville, Ga.).
COLLEGE: East Carolina.
TRANSACTIONS/CAREER NOTES: Selected by Cleveland Browns in 10th round (280th pick overall) of 1984 NFL draft.... On injured reserve with ankle injury (October 21, 1986-January 10, 1987).... Granted free agency (February 1, 1989).... Re-signed by Browns and traded to Washington Redskins for running back Mike Oliphant (April 23, 1989).
CHAMPIONSHIP GAME EXPERIENCE: Played in AFC championship game after 1986 and 1987 seasons.
RECORDS/HONORS: Played in Pro Bowl after 1990 season.
PRO STATISTICS: 1984—Recovered two fumbles for 55 yards and a touchdown. 1985—Recovered four fumbles. 1987—Recovered one fumble. 1988—Recovered two fumbles. 1989—Attempted one pass with no completions and recovered two fumbles. 1990—Attempted two passes with one completion for 31 yards and a touchdown and recovered one fumble.

		——— RUSHING ———				——— RECEIVING ———				– KICKOFF RETURNS –				— TOTAL —		
Year Team	G	Att.	Yds.	Avg.	TD	No.	Yds.	Avg.	TD	No.	Yds.	Avg.	TD	TD	Pts.	F.
1984— Cleveland NFL	16	72	426	5.9	2	11	118	10.7	0	22	415	18.9	0	3	18	3
1985— Cleveland NFL	16	244	1002	4.1	8	45	460	10.2	2	0	0		0	10	60	5
1986— Cleveland NFL	7	94	277	2.9	2	37	328	8.9	2	0	0		0	4	24	1
1987— Cleveland NFL	12	105	432	4.1	8	52	552	10.6	2	1	2	2.0	0	10	60	5
1988— Cleveland NFL	16	157	576	3.7	3	59	576	9.8	2	0	0		0	5	30	5
1989— Washington NFL	16	134	580	4.3	7	54	458	8.5	2	0	0		0	9	54	2
1990— Washington NFL	16	*297	1219	4.1	6	31	279	9.0	1	0	0		0	7	42	2
Pro totals (7 years)	99	1103	4512	4.1	36	289	2771	9.6	11	23	417	18.1	0	48	288	23

BYRD, DENNIS
DT, JETS

PERSONAL: Born October 5, 1966, at Oklahoma City. ... 6-5/270. ... Full name: Dennis DeWayne Byrd.
HIGH SCHOOL: Mustang (Okla.).
COLLEGE: Tulsa (degree in communications, 1990).
TRANSACTIONS/CAREER NOTES: Selected by New York Jets in second round (42nd pick overall) of 1989 NFL draft.... Signed by Jets (July 25, 1989).
PLAYING EXPERIENCE: New York Jets NFL, 1989 and 1990.... Games: 1989 (16), 1990 (16). Total: 32.
PRO STATISTICS: 1989—Returned one kickoff for one yard. 1990—Credited with a safety.

BYRD, GILL
DB, CHARGERS

PERSONAL: Born February 20, 1961, at San Francisco.... 5-11/198.... Full name: Gill Arnette Byrd. ... Nephew of MacArthur Byrd, linebacker with Los Angeles Rams, 1965.
HIGH SCHOOL: Lowell (San Francisco).
COLLEGE: San Jose State (degree in business administration and finance, 1982).
TRANSACTIONS/CAREER NOTES: Selected by Oakland Invaders in 1983 USFL territorial draft.... Selected by San Diego Chargers in first round (22nd pick overall) of 1983 NFL draft.... Signed by Chargers (May 20, 1983).... On injured reserve with pulled hamstring (December 12, 1984-remainder of season).
RECORDS/HONORS: Named to THE SPORTING NEWS NFL All-Pro team, 1989.
PRO STATISTICS: 1985—Recovered one fumble. 1987—Recovered one fumble. 1988—Fumbled once.

		——— INTERCEPTIONS ———			
Year Team	G	No.	Yds.	Avg.	TD
1983— San Diego NFL	14	1	0	.0	0
1984— San Diego NFL	13	4	157	39.3	*2
1985— San Diego NFL	16	1	25	25.0	0
1986— San Diego NFL	15	5	45	9.0	0
1987— San Diego NFL	12	0	0		0
1988— San Diego NFL	16	7	82	11.7	0
1989— San Diego NFL	16	7	38	5.4	0
1990— San Diego NFL	16	7	63	9.0	0
Pro totals (8 years)	118	32	410	12.8	2

CADIGAN, DAVE
G/OT, JETS

PERSONAL: Born April 6, 1965, at Needham, Mass. . . . 6-4/285.
HIGH SCHOOL: Newport Harbor (Newport Beach, Calif.).
COLLEGE: Southern California (degree in communications, 1988).
TRANSACTIONS/CAREER NOTES: Selected by New York Jets in first round (eighth pick over-all) of 1988 NFL draft. . . . Signed by Jets (July 26, 1988). . . . On injured reserve with foot injury (October 17, 1988-remainder of season). . . . On injured reserve with knee injury (October 10, 1990-remainder of season).
PLAYING EXPERIENCE: New York Jets NFL, 1988-1990. . . . Games: 1988 (5), 1989 (13), 1990 (5). Total: 23.
RECORDS/HONORS: Named as offensive tackle on THE SPORTING NEWS college All-America team, 1987.
PRO STATISTICS: 1988—Recovered one fumble.

CAIN, JOE
LB, SEAHAWKS

PERSONAL: Born June 11, 1965, at Los Angeles. . . . 6-1/233. . . . Full name: Joseph Harrison Cain Jr.
HIGH SCHOOL: Compton (Calif.).
COLLEGE: Stanford, then Oregon Tech.
TRANSACTIONS/CAREER NOTES: Selected by Minnesota Vikings in eighth round (210th pick overall) of 1988 NFL draft. . . . Signed by Vikings (July 24, 1988). . . . Released by Vikings (August 30, 1988). . . . Signed as free agent by Seattle Seahawks (March 31, 1989). . . . Released by Seahawks (September 5, 1989). . . . Re-signed by Seahawks to develop-mental squad (September 6, 1989). . . . On developmental squad (September 6-October 11, 1989). . . . Activated after clearing procedural waivers (October 13, 1989).
PLAYING EXPERIENCE: Seattle NFL, 1989 and 1990. . . . Games: 1989 (9), 1990 (16). Total: 25.

CALDWELL, RAVIN
LB, REDSKINS

PERSONAL: Born August 4, 1963, at Port Arthur, Tex. . . . 6-3/229. . . . Full name: Ravin Caldwell Jr. . . . First name pronounced RAY-vin.
HIGH SCHOOL: Northside (Fort Smith, Ark.).
COLLEGE: Arkansas.
TRANSACTIONS/CAREER NOTES: Selected by Memphis Showboats in 1986 USFL territorial draft. . . . Selected by Washington Red-skins in fifth round (113th pick overall) of 1986 NFL draft. . . . Signed by Redskins (July 18, 1986). . . . On injured reserve with knee injury (August 23, 1986-entire season).
PLAYING EXPERIENCE: Washington NFL, 1987-1990. . . . Games: 1987 (12), 1988 (16), 1989 (15), 1990 (16). Total: 59.
CHAMPIONSHIP GAME EXPERIENCE: Played in NFC championship game after 1987 season. . . . Played in Super Bowl XXII after 1987 season.
PRO STATISTICS: 1988—Returned one punt for no yards and credited with a safety. 1990—Recovered one fumble.

CALL, KEVIN
OT, COLTS

PERSONAL: Born November 13, 1961, at Boulder, Colo. . . . 6-7/308. . . . Full name: Kevin Bradley Call.
HIGH SCHOOL: Fairview (Boulder, Colo.).
COLLEGE: Colorado State.
TRANSACTIONS/CAREER NOTES: Selected by Denver Gold in 1984 USFL territorial draft. . . . Selected by Indianapolis Colts in fifth round (130th pick overall) of 1984 NFL draft. . . . Signed by Colts (July 24, 1984). . . . On injured reserve with shoulder injury (November 7, 1990-remainder of season).
PLAYING EXPERIENCE: Indianapolis NFL, 1984-1990. . . . Games: 1984 (15), 1985 (14), 1986 (16), 1987 (12), 1988 (8), 1989 (15), 1990 (8). Total: 88
PRO STATISTICS: 1989—Recovered one fumble.

CALLOWAY, CHRIS
WR, STEELERS

PERSONAL: Born March 29, 1968, at Chicago. . . . 5-10/185. . . . Full name: Christo-pher Fitzpatrick Calloway.
HIGH SCHOOL: Mt. Carmel (Chicago).
COLLEGE: Michigan (bachelor general studies degree in communications and film, 1990).
TRANSACTIONS/CAREER NOTES: Selected by Pittsburgh Steelers in fourth round (97th pick overall) of 1990 NFL draft. . . . Signed by Steelers (July 18, 1990).

Year Team	G	No.	RECEIVING Yds.	Avg.	TD
1990—Pittsburgh NFL	16	10	124	12.4	1
Pro totals (1 year)	16	10	124	12.4	1

CAMARILLO, RICH
P, CARDINALS

PERSONAL: Born November 29, 1959, at Whittier, Calif. . . . 5-11/195. . . . Full name: Ri-chard Jon Camarillo. . . . Nephew of Leo Camarillo, professional on rodeo circuit.
HIGH SCHOOL: El Rancho (Pico Rivera, Calif.).
COLLEGE: Cerritos Junior College (Calif.), then Washington.
TRANSACTIONS/CAREER NOTES: Signed as free agent by New England Patriots (May 11, 1981). . . . Released by Patriots (August 24, 1981). . . . Re-signed by Patriots after clearing procedural waivers (October 20, 1981). . . . On injured reserve with knee in-jury (August 28-November 3, 1984). . . . Released by Patriots (August 30, 1988). . . . Signed as free agent by Los Angeles Rams (August 31, 1988). . . . Released by Rams (November 2, 1988). . . . Signed as free agent by Phoenix Cardinals (April 7, 1989). . . . Granted free agency (February 1, 1990). . . . Re-signed by Cardinals (August 1, 1990).
CHAMPIONSHIP GAME EXPERIENCE: Played in AFC championship game after 1985 season. . . . Played in Super Bowl XX after 1985 season.
RECORDS/HONORS: Led NFL in net punting average (37.1), 1983. . . . Led NFL in punting yards (3,953), 1985. . . . Played in Pro Bowl after 1983 and 1989 seasons. . . . Named to THE SPORTING NEWS NFL All-Pro team, 1983.

PRO STATISTICS: 1981—Recovered one fumble and fumbled once. 1987—Rushed once for no yards. 1989—Attempted one pass with one completion for no yards. 1990—Rushed once for minus 11 yards and fumbled once.

| | | | — PUNTING — | | |
Year	Team	G	No.	Avg.	Blk.
1981— New England NFL		9	47	41.7	0
1982— New England NFL		9	49	43.7	0
1983— New England NFL		16	81	44.6	0
1984— New England NFL		7	48	42.1	0
1985— New England NFL		16	92	43.0	0
1986— New England NFL		16	89	42.1	*3
1987— New England NFL		12	62	40.1	1
1988— L.A. Rams NFL		9	40	39.5	0
1989— Phoenix NFL		15	76	*43.4	0
1990— Phoenix NFL		16	67	42.8	0
Pro totals (10 years)		125	651	42.3	4

CAMPBELL, JEFF
WR, LIONS

PERSONAL: Born March 29, 1968, at Denver.... 5-8/167.
HIGH SCHOOL: Battle Mountain (Minturn, Colo.).
COLLEGE: Colorado (bachelor of arts degree in sociology, 1991).
TRANSACTIONS/CAREER NOTES: Selected by Detroit Lions in fifth round (118th pick overall) of 1990 NFL draft.... Signed by Lions (July 16, 1990).

| | | | — RECEIVING — | | | | — PUNT RETURNS — | | | | – KICKOFF RETURNS – | | | | — TOTAL — | | |
Year	Team	G	No.	Yds.	Avg.	TD	No.	Yds.	Avg.	TD	No.	Yds.	Avg.	TD	TD	Pts.	F.
1990— Detroit NFL		16	19	236	12.4	2	1	0	.0	0	12	238	19.8	0	2	12	1
Pro totals (1 year)		16	19	236	12.4	2	1	0	.0	0	12	238	19.8	0	2	12	1

CAMPBELL, SCOTT
QB, FALCONS

PERSONAL: Born April 15, 1962, at Hershey, Pa.... 6-0/195.... Full name: Robert Scott Campbell.... Son of Ken Campbell, wide receiver with New York Titans (AFL), 1960.
HIGH SCHOOL: Hershey (Pa.).
COLLEGE: Purdue.
TRANSACTIONS/CAREER NOTES: Selected by Philadelphia Stars in fourth round (76th pick overall) of 1984 USFL draft.... Selected by Pittsburgh Steelers in seventh round (191st pick overall) of 1984 NFL draft.... Signed by Steelers (May 19, 1984). ... Released by Steelers (September 24, 1986).... Signed as free agent by Atlanta Falcons for 1987 (November 7, 1986).... Signed by Falcons for 1986 season (November 17, 1986).... On injured reserve with knee injury (August 22, 1988-entire season).... On inactive list (December 31, 1990).
CHAMPIONSHIP GAME EXPERIENCE: Member of Pittsburgh Steelers for AFC championship game after 1984 season; did not play.
PRO STATISTICS: Passer rating points: 1984 (71.3), 1985 (53.8), 1986 (39.6), 1987 (65.0), 1990 (61.7). Career: 61.6.... 1984—Recovered one fumble. 1985—Recovered three fumbles. 1987—Recovered two fumbles.

| | | | — PASSING — | | | | | | | | — RUSHING — | | | | — TOTAL — | | |
Year	Team	G	Att.	Cmp.	Pct.	Yds.	TD	Int.	Avg.	Att.	Yds.	Avg.	TD	TD	Pts.	F.
1984— Pittsburgh NFL		5	15	8	53.3	109	1	1	7.27	3	-5	-1.7	0	0	0	1
1985— Pittsburgh NFL		16	96	43	44.8	612	4	6	6.38	9	28	3.1	0	0	0	3
1986— Pitt.(3)-Atl.(1) NFL.		4	7	1	14.3	7	0	0	1.00	1	7	7.0	0	0	0	0
1987— Atlanta NFL		12	260	136	52.3	1728	11	14	6.65	21	102	4.9	2	2	12	4
1989— Atlanta NFL		1	0	0		0	0	0		0	0		0	0	0	0
1990— Atlanta NFL		7	76	36	47.4	527	3	4	6.93	9	38	4.2	0	0	0	1
Pro totals (6 years)		45	454	224	49.3	2983	19	25	6.57	43	170	4.0	2	2	12	9

CAMPEN, JAMES
C, PACKERS

PERSONAL: Born June 11, 1964, at Sacramento, Calif.... 6-3/275.... Full name: James F. Campen.
HIGH SCHOOL: Ponderosa (Shingle Springs, Calif.).
COLLEGE: Sacramento City College (Calif.), then Tulane.
TRANSACTIONS/CAREER NOTES: Signed as free agent by New Orleans Saints (May 13, 1986).... Released by Saints (August 25, 1986).... Re-signed by Saints for 1987 (October 23, 1986).... On injured reserve with rotator cuff injury (September 7-September 28, 1987).... Crossed picket line during players' strike (September 28, 1987).... Released by Saints (August 30, 1988).... Re-signed by Saints (September 9, 1988).... On injured reserve with back injury (December 10, 1988-remainder of season).... Granted unconditional free agency (February 1, 1989).... Signed by Green Bay Packers (February 24, 1989).
PLAYING EXPERIENCE: New Orleans NFL, 1987 and 1988; Green Bay NFL, 1989 and 1990.... Games: 1987 (3), 1988 (3), 1989 (15), 1990 (16). Total: 37.
PRO STATISTICS: 1987—Recovered one fumble. 1990—Fumbled twice for minus 21 yards.

CAREY, RICHARD
CB, FALCONS

PERSONAL: Born May 6, 1968, at Seattle. ... 5-9/185. ... Full name: Richard Andre Carey.
HIGH SCHOOL: James A. Garfield (Seattle).
COLLEGE: Idaho.
TRANSACTIONS/CAREER NOTES: Signed as free agent by Cincinnati Bengals (April 27, 1989).... Released by Bengals (September 5, 1989).... Re-signed by Bengals to developmental squad (September 6-November 8, 1989).... Activated after clearing

procedural waivers (November 10, 1989). . . . Released by Bengals (September 6, 1990). . . . Signed as free agent by Buffalo Bills (November 7, 1990). . . . On inactive list (November 11, 1990). . . . Released by Bills (December 5, 1990). . . . Signed as free agent by Atlanta Falcons (March 14, 1991).
PLAYING EXPERIENCE: Cincinnati NFL, 1989; Buffalo NFL, 1990. . . . Games: 1989 (7), 1990 (3). Total: 10.
PRO STATISTICS: 1989—Intercepted one pass for five yards, returned six kickoffs for 104 yards, returned three punts for 29 yards, recovered one fumble and fumbled once.

CARLSON, CODY
QB, OILERS

PERSONAL: Born November 5, 1963, at Dallas. . . . 6-3/202. . . . Full name: Matthew Cody Carlson.
HIGH SCHOOL: Winston Churchill (San Antonio).
COLLEGE: Baylor (bachelor of science degree in marketing management, 1987).
TRANSACTIONS/CAREER NOTES: Selected by Houston Oilers in third round (64th pick overall) of 1987 NFL draft. . . . Signed by Oilers (June 3, 1987). . . . Active for four games with Oilers in 1987; did not play. . . . Granted free agency (February 1, 1990). . . . Re-signed by Oilers (August 6, 1990).
PRO STATISTICS: Passer rating points: 1988 (59.2), 1989 (49.8), 1990 (96.3). Career: 68.0. . . . 1988—Fumbled five times for minus 12 yards. 1989—Recovered one fumble and fumbled once for minus six yards.

				PASSING					RUSHING				TOTAL		
Year Team	G	Att.	Cmp.	Pct.	Yds.	TD	Int.	Avg.	Att.	Yds.	Avg.	TD	TD	Pts.	F.
1988— Houston NFL	6	112	52	46.4	775	4	6	6.92	12	36	3.0	1	1	6	5
1989— Houston NFL	6	31	15	48.4	155	0	1	5.00	3	-3	-1.0	0	0	0	1
1990— Houston NFL	6	55	37	67.3	383	4	2	6.96	11	52	4.7	0	0	0	0
Pro totals (3 years)	18	198	104	52.5	1313	8	9	6.63	26	85	3.3	1	1	6	6

CARLSON, JEFF
QB, BUCCANEERS

PERSONAL: Born May 23, 1966, at Long Beach, Calif. . . . 6-3/215. . . . Full name: Jeffrey Allen Carlson.
HIGH SCHOOL: Pacifica (Garden Grove, Calif.).
COLLEGE: Weber State (bachelor of arts degree in communications).
TRANSACTIONS/CAREER NOTES: Selected by Los Angeles Rams in fourth round (102nd pick overall) of 1989 NFL draft. . . . Released by Rams (September 4, 1989). . . . Signed by Rams to developmental squad (September 6, 1989). . . . Released by Rams (January 29, 1990). . . . Signed by Tampa Bay Buccaneers (March 20, 1990). . . . On inactive list (September 9, 16, 23, 30; October 7, 21; November 4, 11, 25; and December 16, 23 and 30, 1990).
PLAYING EXPERIENCE: Tampa Bay NFL, 1990. . . . Games: 1990 (1).
PRO STATISTICS: 1990—Rushed once for no yards and fumbled once.

CARNEY, JOHN
PK, CHARGERS

PERSONAL: Born April 20, 1964, at Hartford, Conn. . . . 5-11/170. . . . Full name: John Michael Carney.
HIGH SCHOOL: Cardinal Newman (West Palm Beach, Fla.).
COLLEGE: Notre Dame (bachelor of business administration degree in marketing, 1987).
TRANSACTIONS/CAREER NOTES: Signed as free agent by Cincinnati Bengals (May 1, 1987). . . . Released by Bengals (August 10, 1987). . . . Signed as free agent replacement player by Tampa Bay Buccaneers (September 24, 1987). . . . Released by Buccaneers (October 14, 1987). . . . Re-signed by Buccaneers (April 5, 1988). . . . Released by Buccaneers (August 23, 1988). . . . Re-signed by Buccaneers (November 22, 1988). . . . Granted unconditional free agency (February 1, 1989). . . . Re-signed by Buccaneers (April 13, 1989). . . . Released by Buccaneers (September 5, 1989). . . . Re-signed by Buccaneers (December 13, 1989). . . . Granted unconditional free agency (February 1, 1990). . . . Signed by San Diego Chargers (April 1, 1990). . . . Released by Chargers (August 28, 1990). . . . Signed by Los Angeles Rams (September 21, 1990). . . . Released by Rams (September 26, 1990). . . . Re-signed by San Diego Chargers (October 3, 1990).

		PLACE-KICKING				
Year Team	G	XPM	XPA	FGM	FGA	Pts.
1988— Tampa Bay NFL	4	6	6	2	5	12
1989— Tampa Bay NFL	1	0	0	0	0	0
1990— Rams (1)-S.D. (12) NFL	13	27	28	19	21	84
Pro totals (3 years)	18	33	34	21	26	96

CARREKER, ALPHONSO
DE, BRONCOS

PERSONAL: Born May 25, 1962, at Columbus, O. . . . 6-6/272 . . . Name pronounced CARE-uh-ker.
HIGH SCHOOL: Marion Franklin (Columbus, O.).
COLLEGE: Florida State.
TRANSACTIONS/CAREER NOTES: Selected by Tampa Bay Bandits in 1984 USFL territorial draft. . . . Selected by Green Bay Packers in first round (12th pick overall) of 1984 NFL draft. . . . Signed by Packers (June 20, 1984). . . . Granted unconditional free agency (February 1, 1989). . . . Signed by Denver Broncos (March 15, 1989). . . . On injured reserve with knee injury (September 3, 1990-entire season).
PLAYING EXPERIENCE: Green Bay NFL, 1984-1988; Denver NFL, 1989. . . . Games: 1984 (14), 1985 (16), 1986 (16), 1987 (12), 1988 (14), 1989 (16). Total: 88.
CHAMPIONSHIP GAME EXPERIENCE: Played in AFC championship game after 1989 season. . . . Played in Super Bowl XXIV after 1989 season.
PRO STATISTICS: 1986—Recovered two fumbles. 1987—Intercepted one pass for six yards. 1988—Recovered one fumble.

CARRIER, MARK
S, BEARS

PERSONAL: Born April 28, 1968, at Lake Charles, La. . . . 6-1/180. . . . Full name: Mark Anthony Carrier.
HIGH SCHOOL: Long Beach Polytechnic (Long Beach, Calif.).
COLLEGE: Southern California (bachelor of arts degree in communications).

TRANSACTIONS/CAREER NOTES: Selected by Chicago Bears in first round (sixth pick overall) of 1990 NFL draft. . . . Signed by Bears (April 22, 1990).
RECORDS/HONORS: Named as defensive back on THE SPORTING NEWS college All-America team, 1989. . . . Played in Pro Bowl after 1990 season.
PRO STATISTICS: 1990—Recovered two fumbles for 16 yards.

			INTERCEPTIONS		
Year Team	G	No.	Yds.	Avg.	TD
1990— Chicago NFL	16	* 10	39	3.9	0
Pro totals (1 year)	16	10	39	3.9	0

CARRIER, MARK
WR, BUCCANEERS

PERSONAL: Born October 28, 1965, at Lafayette, La. . . . 6-0/185. . . . Full name: John Mark Carrier.
HIGH SCHOOL: Church Point (La.).
COLLEGE: Nicholls State.
TRANSACTIONS/CAREER NOTES: Selected by Tampa Bay Buccaneers in third round (57th pick overall) of 1987 NFL draft. . . . Signed by Buccaneers (July 18, 1987). . . . Granted free agency (February 1, 1990). . . . Re-signed by Buccaneers (August 13, 1990).
RECORDS/HONORS: Played in Pro Bowl after 1989 season.
PRO STATISTICS: 1987—Returned one kickoff for no yards. 1988—Fumbled twice. 1989—Fumbled once.

			RECEIVING		
Year Team	G	No.	Yds.	Avg.	TD
1987— Tampa Bay NFL.........	10	26	423	16.3	3
1988— Tampa Bay NFL.........	16	57	970	17.0	5
1989— Tampa Bay NFL.........	16	86	1422	16.5	9
1990— Tampa Bay NFL.........	16	49	813	16.6	4
Pro totals (4 years)........	58	218	3628	16.6	21

CARRINGTON, DARREN
DB, CHARGERS

PERSONAL: Born October 10, 1966, at Bronx, N.Y. . . . 6-2/200. . . . Full name: Darren Russell Carrington.
HIGH SCHOOL: James Monroe (Bronx, N.Y.).
COLLEGE: Northern Arizona.
TRANSACTIONS/CAREER NOTES: Selected by Denver Broncos in fifth round (134th pick overall) of 1989 NFL draft. . . . Signed by Broncos (July 19, 1989). . . . Released by Broncos (September 8, 1990). . . . Signed by Detroit Lions (September 21, 1990). . . . Granted unconditional free agency (February 1, 1991). . . . Signed by San Diego Chargers (March 29, 1991).
PLAYING EXPERIENCE: Denver NFL, 1989; Detroit NFL, 1990. . . . Games: 1989 (16), 1990 (12). Total: 28.
CHAMPIONSHIP GAME EXPERIENCE: Played in AFC championship game after 1989 season. . . . Played in Super Bowl XXIV after 1989 season.
PRO STATISTICS: 1989—Intercepted one pass for two yards, returned six kickoffs for 152 yards (25.3 avg.), returned one punt for no yards and fumbled once. 1990—Recovered one fumble.

CARTER, ANTHONY
WR, VIKINGS

PERSONAL: Born September 17, 1960, at Riviera Beach, Fla. . . . 5-11/178 . . . Cousin of Leonard Coleman, defensive back with Memphis Showboats (USFL), Indianapolis Colts and San Diego Chargers, 1985-1989.
HIGH SCHOOL: Sun Coast (Riviera Beach, Fla.).
COLLEGE: Michigan.
TRANSACTIONS/CAREER NOTES: Selected by Michigan Panthers in 1983 USFL territorial draft. . . . Signed by Panthers (February 26, 1983). . . . Selected by Miami Dolphins in 12th round (334th pick overall) of 1983 NFL draft. . . . On injured reserve with broken arm (April 5, 1984-remainder of season). . . . Protected in merger of Michigan Panthers and Oakland Invaders (December 6, 1984). . . . On developmental squad for one game with Invaders (June 24-June 30, 1985). . . . NFL rights traded by Miami Dolphins to Minnesota Vikings for linebacker Robin Sendlein and second-round pick in 1986 NFL draft (August 15, 1985). . . . Released by Oakland Invaders (August 23, 1985). . . . Signed by Minnesota Vikings (August 25, 1985). . . . Granted roster exemption (August 25-August 29, 1985). . . . On injured reserve with knee injury (September 5-October 4, 1986). . . . Granted free agency (February 1, 1990). . . . Re-signed by Vikings (July 30, 1990).
CHAMPIONSHIP GAME EXPERIENCE: Played in USFL championship game after 1983 and 1985 seasons. . . . Played in NFC championship game after 1987 season.
RECORDS/HONORS: Named as wide receiver on THE SPORTING NEWS college All-America team, 1981 and 1982. . . . Named as punt returner on THE SPORTING NEWS USFL All-Star team, 1983. . . . Named as wide receiver on THE SPORTING NEWS USFL All-Star team, 1985. . . . Played in Pro Bowl after 1987 and 1988 seasons.
PRO STATISTICS: USFL: 1983—Recovered three fumbles. 1984—Recovered one fumble. 1985—Recovered one fumble in end zone for a touchdown and attempted one pass with no completions. . . . NFL: 1985—Recovered one fumble. 1988—Returned one kickoff for no yards and recovered one fumble. 1989—Returned one kickoff for 19 yards and recovered one fumble.

		RUSHING				RECEIVING				PUNT RETURNS				TOTAL		
Year Team	G	Att.	Yds.	Avg.	TD	No.	Yds.	Avg.	TD	No.	Yds.	Avg.	TD	TD	Pts.	F.
1983— Michigan USFL	18	3	1	.3	0	60	1181	19.7	9	40	387	9.7	* 1	10	60	6
1984— Michigan USFL	6	0	0		0	30	538	17.9	4	5	21	4.2	0	4	24	2
1985— Oakland USFL	17	0	0		0	70	1323	18.9	14	0	0		0	15	90	0
1985— Minnesota NFL	16	0	0		0	43	821	19.1	8	9	117	13.0	0	8	48	1
1986— Minnesota NFL	12	1	12	12.0	0	38	686	18.1	7	0	0		0	7	42	1
1987— Minnesota NFL	12	0	0		0	38	922	24.3	7	3	40	13.3	0	7	42	0
1988— Minnesota NFL	16	4	41	10.3	0	72	1225	17.0	6	1	3	3.0	0	6	36	1

Year	Team	G	RUSHING Att.	Yds.	Avg.	TD	RECEIVING No.	Yds.	Avg.	TD	PUNT RETURNS No.	Yds.	Avg.	TD	TOTAL TD	Pts.	F.
1989—	Minnesota NFL	16	3	18	6.0	0	65	1066	16.4	4	1	2	2.0	0	4	24	0
1990—	Minnesota NFL	15	3	16	5.3	0	70	1003	14.3	8	0	0		0	8	48	2
	USFL totals (3 years)	41	3	1	.3	0	160	3042	19.0	27	45	408	9.1	1	29	174	8
	NFL totals (6 years)	87	11	87	7.9	0	326	5723	17.6	40	14	162	11.6	0	40	240	5
	Pro totals (9 years)	128	14	88	6.3	0	486	8765	18.0	67	59	570	9.7	1	69	414	13

CARTER, CARL
CB, BENGALS

PERSONAL: Born March 7, 1964, at Fort Worth, Tex. . . . 5-11/180. . . . Full name: Carl Anthony Carter.
HIGH SCHOOL: O.D. Wyatt (Fort Worth, Tex.).
COLLEGE: Texas Tech.
TRANSACTIONS/CAREER NOTES: Selected by St. Louis Cardinals in fourth round (89th pick overall) of 1986 NFL draft. . . . Signed by Cardinals (July 12, 1986). . . . Franchise transferred to Phoenix (March 15, 1988). . . . Traded by Phoenix Cardinals to Cincinnati Bengals for linebacker Chris Chenault (August 21, 1990). . . . On inactive list (October 22, 1990).
PRO STATISTICS: 1986—Returned two kickoffs for 21 yards, returned one punt for no yards, recovered one fumble and fumbled once. 1987—Recovered one fumble. 1990—Recovered three fumbles.

Year	Team	G	INTERCEPTIONS No.	Yds.	Avg.	TD
1986—	St. Louis NFL	14	2	12	6.0	0
1987—	St. Louis NFL	12	1	0	.0	0
1988—	Phoenix NFL	16	3	0	.0	0
1989—	Phoenix NFL	15	1	0	.0	0
1990—	Cincinnati NFL...........	15	0	0		0
	Pro totals (5 years)	72	7	12	1.7	0

CARTER, CRIS
WR, VIKINGS

PERSONAL: Born November 25, 1965, at Middletown, O. . . . 6-3/200.
HIGH SCHOOL: Middletown (O.).
COLLEGE: Ohio State.
TRANSACTIONS/CAREER NOTES: Selected by Philadelphia Eagles in fourth round of 1987 NFL supplemental draft (September 4, 1987). . . . Signed by Eagles (September 17, 1987). . . . Granted roster exemption (September 17-October 26, 1987). . . . Released by Eagles (September 3, 1990). . . . Awarded on waivers to Minnesota Vikings (September 4, 1990).
PRO STATISTICS: 1987—Attempted one pass with no completions. 1988—Recovered one fumble in end zone for a touchdown. 1989—Recovered one fumble.

Year	Team	G	RUSHING Att.	Yds.	Avg.	TD	RECEIVING No.	Yds.	Avg.	TD	KICKOFF RETURNS No.	Yds.	Avg.	TD	TOTAL TD	Pts.	F.
1987—	Philadelphia NFL ...	9	0	0		0	5	84	16.8	2	12	241	20.1	0	2	12	0
1988—	Philadelphia NFL ...	16	1	1	1.0	0	39	761	19.5	6	0	0		0	7	42	0
1989—	Philadelphia NFL ...	16	2	16	8.0	0	45	605	13.4	11	0	0		0	11	66	1
1990—	Minnesota NFL	16	2	6	3.0	0	27	413	15.3	3	0	0		0	3	18	0
	Pro totals (4 years)	57	5	23	4.6	0	116	1863	16.1	22	12	241	20.1	0	23	138	1

CARTER, DEXTER
RB, 49ERS

PERSONAL: Born September 15, 1967, at Baxley, Ga. . . . 5-9/170. . . . Full name: Dexter Anthony Carter.
HIGH SCHOOL: Appling County (Baxley, Ga.).
COLLEGE: Florida State (degree in child development).
TRANSACTIONS/CAREER NOTES: Selected by San Francisco 49ers in first round (25th pick overall) of 1990 NFL draft. . . . Signed by 49ers (July 26, 1990).
CHAMPIONSHIP GAME EXPERIENCE: Played in NFC championship game after 1990 season.
PRO STATISTICS: 1990—Recovered two fumbles.

Year	Team	G	RUSHING Att.	Yds.	Avg.	TD	RECEIVING No.	Yds.	Avg.	TD	KICKOFF RETURNS No.	Yds.	Avg.	TD	TOTAL TD	Pts.	F.
1990—	San Francisco NFL	16	114	460	4.0	1	25	217	8.7	0	41	783	19.1	0	1	6	8
	Pro totals (1 year)	16	114	460	4.0	1	25	217	8.7	0	41	783	19.1	0	1	6	8

CARTER, MICHAEL
NT, 49ERS

PERSONAL: Born October 29, 1960, at Dallas. . . . 6-2/285. . . . Full name: Michael D'Andrea Carter.
HIGH SCHOOL: Thomas Jefferson (Dallas).
COLLEGE: Southern Methodist (bachelor of science degree in sociology, 1984).
TRANSACTIONS/CAREER NOTES: Selected by Los Angeles Express in 10th round (194th pick overall) of 1984 USFL draft. . . . Selected by San Francisco 49ers in fifth round (121st pick overall) of 1984 NFL draft. . . . USFL rights traded by Los Angeles Express to New Orleans Breakers for past considerations (June 19, 1984). . . . Signed by San Francisco 49ers (August 14, 1984). . . . On injured reserve with torn hamstring (September 28-October 26, 1985). . . . On injured reserve with foot injury (December 2, 1989-remainder of season). . . . On inactive list (September 10, 1990).
PLAYING EXPERIENCE: San Francisco NFL, 1984-1990. . . . Games: 1984 (16), 1985 (12), 1986 (15), 1987 (12), 1988 (16), 1989 (8), 1990 (15). Total: 94.

CHAMPIONSHIP GAME EXPERIENCE: Played in NFC championship game after 1984 and 1988-1990 seasons. . . . Played in Super Bowl XIX after 1984 season, Super Bowl XXIII after 1988 season and Super Bowl XXIV after 1989 season.
RECORDS/HONORS: Played in Pro Bowl after 1985, 1987 and 1988 seasons. . . . Named to THE SPORTING NEWS NFL All-Pro team, 1987.
MISCELLANEOUS: Won silver medal in shot put during 1984 Summer Olympics.
PRO STATISTICS: 1988—Intercepted one pass for no yards.

CARTER, PAT
TE, RAMS

PERSONAL: Born August 1, 1966, at Sarasota, Fla. . . . 6-3/255. . . . Full name: Wendell Patrick Carter.
HIGH SCHOOL: Riverview (Sarasota, Fla.).
COLLEGE: Florida State.
TRANSACTIONS/CAREER NOTES: Selected by Detroit Lions in second round (32nd pick overall) of 1988 NFL draft. . . . Signed by Lions (June 13, 1988). . . . Traded by Lions to Los Angeles Rams for fourth-round pick in 1990 NFL draft (August 18, 1989).
CHAMPIONSHIP GAME EXPERIENCE: Played in NFC championship game after 1989 season.
RECORDS/HONORS: Named as tight end on THE SPORTING NEWS college All-America team, 1987.

			RECEIVING		
Year Team	G	No.	Yds.	Avg.	TD
1988— Detroit NFL	15	13	145	11.2	0
1989— L.A. Rams NFL	16	0	0		0
1990— L.A. Rams NFL	16	8	58	7.3	0
Pro totals (3 years)	47	21	203	9.7	0

CARTHON, MAURICE
RB, GIANTS

PERSONAL: Born April 24, 1961, at Chicago. . . . 6-1/225.
HIGH SCHOOL: Osceola (Ark.).
COLLEGE: Arkansas State.
TRANSACTIONS/CAREER NOTES: Selected by New Jersey Generals in eighth round (94th pick overall) of 1983 USFL draft. . . . Signed by Generals (January 19, 1983). . . . On developmental squad for three games (June 17, 1983-remainder of season). . . . Signed by New York Giants (March 7, 1985), for contract to take effect after being granted free agency after 1985 USFL season. . . . On did not report list (January 21-January 28, 1985). . . . Granted roster exemption (January 28-February 4, 1985). . . . Granted free agency (February 1, 1990). . . . Re-signed by Giants (August 10, 1990).
CHAMPIONSHIP GAME EXPERIENCE: Played in NFC championship game after 1986 and 1990 seasons. . . . Played in Super Bowl XXI after 1986 season and Super Bowl XXV after 1990 season.
PRO STATISTICS: includes three 2-point conversions. 1984—Recovered one fumble.

		RUSHING				RECEIVING				TOTAL		
Year Team	G	Att.	Yds.	Avg.	TD	No.	Yds.	Avg.	TD	TD	Pts.	F.
1983— New Jersey USFL	11	90	334	3.7	3	20	170	8.5	0	3	24	4
1984— New Jersey USFL	18	238	1042	4.4	11	26	194	7.5	1	12	72	4
1985— New Jersey USFL	18	175	726	4.2	6	18	154	8.6	0	6	36	3
1985— N.Y. Giants NFL	16	27	70	2.6	0	8	81	10.1	0	0	0	1
1986— N.Y. Giants NFL	16	72	260	3.6	0	16	67	4.2	0	0	0	1
1987— N.Y. Giants NFL	11	26	60	2.3	0	8	71	8.9	0	0	0	0
1988— N.Y. Giants NFL	16	46	146	3.2	2	19	194	10.2	1	3	18	1
1989— N.Y. Giants NFL	16	57	153	2.7	0	15	132	8.8	0	0	0	1
1990— N.Y. Giants NFL	16	36	143	4.0	0	14	151	10.8	0	0	0	1
USFL totals (3 years)	47	503	2102	4.2	20	64	518	8.1	1	21	132	11
NFL totals (6 years)	91	264	832	3.2	2	80	696	8.7	1	3	18	5
Pro totals (9 years)	138	767	2934	3.8	22	144	1214	8.4	2	24	150	16

CASE, SCOTT
S, FALCONS

PERSONAL: Born May 17, 1962, at Waynoka, Okla. . . . 6-1/188. . . . Full name: Jeffrey Scott Case.
HIGH SCHOOL: Alva (Okla.) and Memorial (Edmond, Okla.).
COLLEGE: Northeastern Oklahoma A&M, then Oklahoma.
TRANSACTIONS/CAREER NOTES: Selected by Oklahoma Outlaws in 1984 USFL territorial draft. . . . Selected by Atlanta Falcons in second round (32nd pick overall) of 1984 NFL draft. . . . Signed by Falcons (July 20, 1984). . . . Granted free agency (February 1, 1988). . . . Re-signed by Falcons (August 29, 1988). . . . On injured reserve with foot injury (December 23, 1989-remainder of season).
RECORDS/HONORS: Played in Pro Bowl after 1988 season.
PRO STATISTICS: 1985—Credited with one safety and recovered one fumble for 13 yards. 1990—Returned one kickoff for 13 yards and recovered two fumbles.

			INTERCEPTIONS		
Year Team	G	No.	Yds.	Avg.	TD
1984— Atlanta NFL	16	0	0		0
1985— Atlanta NFL	14	4	78	19.5	0
1986— Atlanta NFL	16	4	41	10.3	0
1987— Atlanta NFL	11	1	12	12.0	0
1988— Atlanta NFL	16	*10	47	4.7	0
1989— Atlanta NFL	14	2	13	6.5	0
1990— Atlanta NFL	16	3	38	12.7	1
Pro totals (7 years)	103	24	229	9.5	1

CASILLAS, TONY
NT, COWBOYS

PERSONAL: Born October 26, 1963, at Tulsa, Okla. . . . 6-3/280. . . . Full name: Tony Steven Casillas.
HIGH SCHOOL: East Central (Tulsa, Okla.).
COLLEGE: Oklahoma (bachelor's degree, 1986).
TRANSACTIONS/CAREER NOTES: Selected by Atlanta Falcons in first round (second pick overall) of 1986 NFL draft. . . . Selected by Arizona Outlaws in first round (second pick overall) of 1986 USFL draft. . . . Signed by Atlanta Falcons (July 20, 1986). . . . Granted roster exemption (September 13-September 24, 1990). . . . On inactive list (October 22, 1990). . . . On reserve/suspended list (October 23-November 5, 1990). . . . On injured reserve with fractured elbow (December 27, 1990-remainder of season). . . . Traded by Falcons to Dallas Cowboys for second-round and conditional pick in 1992 NFL draft (July 21, 1991).
PLAYING EXPERIENCE: Atlanta NFL, 1986-1990. . . . Games: 1986 (16), 1987 (9), 1988 (16), 1989 (16), 1990 (9). Total: 66.
RECORDS/HONORS: Named as defensive lineman on THE SPORTING NEWS college All-America team, 1984 and 1985.
PRO STATISTICS: 1986—Recovered one fumble. 1987—Recovered one fumble. 1988—Recovered one fumble. 1989—Recovered three fumbles.

CASTON, TOBY
LB, LIONS

PERSONAL: Born July 17, 1965, at Monroe, La. . . . 6-1/243. . . . Full name: Sebastian Tobias Caston.
HIGH SCHOOL: Neville (Monroe, La.).
COLLEGE: Louisiana State.
TRANSACTIONS/CAREER NOTES: Selected by Houston Oilers in sixth round (159th pick overall) of 1987 NFL draft. . . . Signed by Oilers (July 27, 1987). . . . On injured reserve with foot and arch injuries (November 24, 1987-remainder of season). . . . Granted unconditional free agency (February 1, 1989). . . . Signed by Detroit Lions (March 15, 1989). . . . On injured reserve with knee and shoulder injuries (November 8-December 7, 1990).
PLAYING EXPERIENCE: Houston NFL, 1987 and 1988; Detroit NFL, 1989 and 1990. . . . Games: 1987 (6), 1988 (16), 1989 (16), 1990 (12). Total: 50.
PRO STATISTICS: 1990—Recovered one fumble.

CAVANAUGH, MATT
QB, GIANTS

PERSONAL: Born October 27, 1956, at Youngstown, O. . . . 6-2/212. . . . Full name: Matthew Andrew Cavanaugh.
HIGH SCHOOL: Chaney (Youngstown, O.).
COLLEGE: Pittsburgh (bachelor of science degree in administration of justice).
TRANSACTIONS/CAREER NOTES: Selected by New England Patriots in second round (50th pick overall) of 1978 NFL draft. . . . Active for 16 games with Patriots in 1978; did not play. . . . Traded by Patriots to San Francisco 49ers for seventh-round pick in 1984 draft, eighth-round pick in 1985 draft and seventh-round in 1986 draft (August 10, 1983). . . . Traded by 49ers to Philadelphia Eagles for third-round pick in 1986 draft and second-round pick in 1987 draft (April 29, 1986). . . . Released by Eagles (September 3, 1990). . . . Signed by New York Giants (September 5, 1990). . . . On inactive list (September 9, 16, 23, 30; October 21; November 11; and December 3 and 9, 1990). . . . Active for seven games with Giants in 1990; did not play.
CHAMPIONSHIP GAME EXPERIENCE: Member of San Francisco 49ers for NFC championship game after 1983 season; did not play. . . . Played in NFC championship game after 1984 and 1990 seasons. . . . Member of San Francisco 49ers for Super Bowl XIX after 1984 season; did not play. . . . Member of New York Giants for Super Bowl XXV after 1990 season; did not play.
PRO STATISTICS: Passer rating points: 1979 (108.3), 1980 (95.9), 1981 (60.0), 1982 (66.7), 1984 (99.7), 1985 (69.5), 1986 (53.6), 1988 (59.6), 1989 (79.6). Career: 71.7. . . . 1980—Recovered one fumble and fumbled once for minus four yards. 1981—Caught one pass for nine yards.

			PASSING							RUSHING				TOTAL		
Year	Team	G	Att.	Cmp.	Pct.	Yds.	TD	Int.	Avg.	Att.	Yds.	Avg.	TD	TD	Pts.	F.
1979— New England NFL		13	1	1	100.0	10	0	0	10.00	1	-2	-2.0	0	0	0	0
1980— New England NFL		16	105	63	60.0	885	9	5	8.43	19	97	5.1	0	0	0	1
1981— New England NFL		16	219	115	52.5	1633	5	13	7.46	17	92	5.4	3	3	18	2
1982— New England NFL		7	60	27	45.0	490	5	5	8.17	2	3	1.5	0	0	0	1
1983— San Francisco NFL		5	0	0		0	0	0		1	8	8.0	0	0	0	0
1984— San Francisco NFL		8	61	33	54.1	449	4	0	7.36	4	-11	-2.8	0	0	0	0
1985— San Francisco NFL		16	54	28	51.9	334	1	1	6.19	4	5	1.3	0	0	0	0
1986— Philadelphia NFL		10	58	28	48.3	397	2	4	6.84	9	26	2.9	0	0	0	2
1987— Philadelphia NFL		3	0	0		0	0	0		1	-2	-2.0	0	0	0	0
1988— Philadelphia NFL		5	16	7	43.8	101	1	1	6.31	0	0		0	0	0	0
1989— Philadelphia NFL		9	5	3	60.0	33	1	1	6.60	2	-3	-1.5	0	0	0	1
Pro totals (11 years)		108	579	305	52.7	4332	28	30	7.48	60	213	3.6	3	3	18	7

CECIL, CHUCK
S, PACKERS

PERSONAL: Born November 8, 1964, at Red Bluff, Calif. . . . 6-0/190. . . . Full name: Charles Douglas Cecil.
HIGH SCHOOL: Helix (La Mesa, Calif.).
COLLEGE: Arizona.
TRANSACTIONS/CAREER NOTES: Selected by Green Bay Packers in fourth round (89th pick overall) of 1988 NFL draft. . . . Signed by Packers (July 17, 1988). . . . On inactive list (September 9, 1990). . . . On injured reserve with hamstring injury (September 15-October 12, 1990). . . . On injured reserve (December 20, 1990-remainder of season).
PRO STATISTICS: 1988—Recovered one fumble.

			INTERCEPTIONS			
Year	Team	G	No.	Yds.	Avg.	TD
1988— Green Bay NFL		16	4	56	14.0	0
1989— Green Bay NFL		9	1	16	16.0	0
1990— Green Bay NFL		9	1	0	.0	0
Pro totals (3 years)		34	6	72	12.0	0

CENTERS, LARRY
RB, CARDINALS

PERSONAL: Born June 1, 1968, at Tatum, Tex. . . . 5-10/203. . . . Full name: Larry E. Centers.
HIGH SCHOOL: Tatum (Tex.).
COLLEGE: Stephen F. Austin State.
TRANSACTIONS/CAREER NOTES: Selected by Phoenix Cardinals in fifth round (115th pick overall) of 1990 NFL draft. . . . Signed by Cardinals (July 23, 1990). . . . On inactive list (September 9, 23, 30; October 14, 21, 28; November 18, 25; and December 2, 1990).
PRO STATISTICS: 1990—Fumbled once.

			— KICKOFF RETURNS —		
Year Team	G	No.	Yds.	Avg.	TD
1990— Phoenix NFL	6	16	272	17.0	0
Pro totals (1 year)	6	16	272	17.0	0

CHADWICK, JEFF
WR, SEAHAWKS

PERSONAL: Born December 16, 1960, at Detroit. . . . 6-3/189. . . . Full name: Jeffrey Allan Chadwick.
HIGH SCHOOL: Divine Child (Dearborn, Mich.).
COLLEGE: Grand Valley State (Mich.).
TRANSACTIONS/CAREER NOTES: Signed as free agent by Detroit Lions (May 15, 1983). . . . On injured reserve with broken collarbone (November 4, 1985-remainder of season). . . . On injured reserve with achilles heal injury (December 17, 1986-remainder of season). . . . On injured reserve with broken hand (December 1, 1987-remainder of season). . . . On injured reserve with achilles heel injury (August 23-October 15, 1988). . . . Granted unconditional free agency (February 1, 1989). . . . Re-signed by Lions (April 26, 1989). . . . Released by Lions (September 12, 1989). . . . Signed as free agent by Seattle Seahawks (September 27, 1989). . . . Granted free agency (February 1, 1990). . . . Re-signed by Seahawks (June 10, 1990).
PRO STATISTICS: 1984—Rushed once for 12 yards and a touchdown. 1986—Fumbled once. 1987—Rushed once for minus six yards. 1990—Rushed once for minus three yards, recovered two fumbles and fumbled once.

			— RECEIVING —		
Year Team	G	No.	Yds.	Avg.	TD
1983— Detroit NFL	16	40	617	15.4	4
1984— Detroit NFL	16	37	540	14.6	2
1985— Detroit NFL	7	25	478	19.1	3
1986— Detroit NFL	15	53	995	18.8	5
1987— Detroit NFL	8	30	416	13.9	0
1988— Detroit NFL	10	20	304	15.2	3
1989— Det. (1)-Sea. (11) NFL .	12	9	104	11.6	0
1990— Seattle NFL	16	27	478	17.7	4
Pro totals (8 years)	100	241	3932	16.3	21

CHANDLER, CHRIS
QB, BUCCANEERS

PERSONAL: Born October 12, 1965, at Everett, Wash. . . . 6-4/220. . . . Full name: Christopher Mark Chandler. . . . Brother of Greg Chandler, catcher in San Francisco Giants' organization, 1978.
HIGH SCHOOL: Everett (Wash.).
COLLEGE: Washington (degree in economics, 1988).
TRANSACTIONS/CAREER NOTES: Selected by Indianapolis Colts in third round (76th pick overall) of 1988 NFL draft. . . . Signed by Colts (July 23, 1988). . . . On injured reserve with broken hand (October 3, 1989-remainder of season). . . . Traded by Colts to Tampa Bay Buccaneers for conditional draft pick in 1991 NFL draft (August 7, 1990).
PRO STATISTICS: Passer rating points: 1988 (67.2), 1989 (63.4), 1990 (41.4). Career: 61.0. . . . 1988—Recovered five fumbles and fumbled eight times for minus six yards. 1990—Recovered one fumble and fumbled five times for minus two yards.

		PASSING							RUSHING				TOTAL		
Year Team	G	Att.	Cmp.	Pct.	Yds.	TD	Int.	Avg.	Att.	Yds.	Avg.	TD	TD	Pts.	F.
1988— Indianapolis NFL	15	233	129	55.4	1619	8	12	6.95	46	139	3.0	3	3	18	8
1989— Indianapolis NFL	3	80	39	48.8	537	2	3	6.71	7	57	8.1	1	1	6	0
1990— Tampa Bay NFL.........	7	83	42	50.6	464	1	6	5.59	13	71	5.5	1	1	6	5
Pro totals (3 years)	25	396	210	53.0	2620	11	21	6.62	66	267	4.1	5	5	30	13

CHAPURA, DICK
DT, OILERS

PERSONAL: Born June 15, 1964, at Sarasota, Fla. . . . 6-3/277. . . . Full name: Richard Harry Chapura Jr. . . . Name pronounced sha-POOR-uh.
HIGH SCHOOL: Riverview (Sarasota, Fla.).
COLLEGE: Missouri.
TRANSACTIONS/CAREER NOTES: Selected by Chicago Bears in 10th round (277th pick overall) of 1987 NFL draft. . . . Signed by Bears (July 27, 1987). . . . On injured reserve with knee injury (August 27-November 16, 1987). . . . Released by Bears (September 3, 1990). . . . Signed by Phoenix Cardinals (September 11, 1990). . . . Released by Cardinals (October 13, 1990). . . . Signed by Philadelphia Eagles (October 31, 1990). . . . On inactive list (November 25 and December 2, 1990). . . . Traded by Eagles to Houston Oilers for pick in 1992 draft (August 8, 1991).
PLAYING EXPERIENCE: Chicago NFL, 1987-1989; Phoenix (3)-Philadelphia (7) NFL, 1990. . . . Games: 1987 (2), 1988 (15), 1989 (16), 1990 (10). Total: 43.
CHAMPIONSHIP GAME EXPERIENCE: Played in NFC championship game after 1988 season.
PRO STATISTICS: 1989—Returned one kickoff for eight yards. 1990—Recovered one fumble.

CHARLES, MIKE
DT, RAIDERS

PERSONAL: Born September 23, 1962, at Newark, N.J. . . . 6-4/315. . . . Full name: Michael William Charles.
HIGH SCHOOL: Central (Newark, N.J.).
COLLEGE: Syracuse (bachelor of science degree in speech communications).
TRANSACTIONS/CAREER NOTES: Selected by New Jersey Generals in 1983 USFL territorial draft. . . . Selected by Miami Dolphins in second round (55th pick overall) of 1983 NFL draft. . . . Signed by Dolphins (July 12, 1983). . . . On injured reserve with knee injury (November 17-December 28, 1984). . . . On suspended list (September 6-September 26, 1986). . . . On injured reserve with knee injury (October 1-November 1, 1986). . . . Released by Dolphins (July 31, 1987). . . . Awarded on waivers to Tampa Bay Buccaneers (August 3, 1987). . . . Released by Buccaneers (August 17, 1987). . . . Awarded on waivers to San Diego Chargers (August 18, 1987). . . . Released by Chargers (October 23, 1989). . . . Signed as free agent by Los Angeles Raiders (May 21, 1990). . . . On inactive list (November 25, 1990). . . . Released by Raiders (November, 1990). . . . Re-signed by Raiders (February 10, 1991).
PLAYING EXPERIENCE: Miami NFL, 1983-1986; San Diego NFL, 1987-1989; Los Angeles Raiders NFL, 1990. . . . Games: 1983 (16), 1984 (10), 1985 (16), 1986 (9), 1987 (11), 1988 (16), 1989 (6), 1990 (10). Total: 94.
CHAMPIONSHIP GAME EXPERIENCE: Played in AFC championship game after 1984 and 1985 seasons. . . . Played in Super Bowl XIX after 1984 season.
PRO STATISTICS: 1983—Recovered one fumble and credited with a safety. 1986—Intercepted one pass for two yards.

CHARLTON, CLIFFORD
LB, CHIEFS

PERSONAL: Born February 16, 1965, at Tallahassee, Fla. . . . 6-3/233. . . . Full name: Clifford Tyrone Charlton.
HIGH SCHOOL: Leon (Tallahassee, Fla.).
COLLEGE: Florida.
TRANSACTIONS/CAREER NOTES: Selected by Cleveland Browns in first round (21st pick overall) of 1988 NFL draft. . . . Signed by Browns (July 22, 1988). . . . Released by Browns (September 3, 1990). . . . Awarded on waivers to Miami Dolphins (September 4, 1990). . . . Released by Dolphins (September 7, 1990). . . . Signed by Kansas City Chiefs (April 4, 1991).
PLAYING EXPERIENCE: Cleveland NFL, 1988 and 1989. . . . Games: 1988 (16), 1989 (15). Total: 31.
CHAMPIONSHIP GAME EXPERIENCE: Played in AFC championship game after 1989 season.
RECORDS/HONORS: Named as linebacker on THE SPORTING NEWS college All-America team, 1987.

CHEEK, LOUIS
G/OT, PACKERS

PERSONAL: Born October 6, 1964, at Galveston, Tex. . . . 6-7/286. . . . Full name: Louis Ray Cheek Jr.
HIGH SCHOOL: Fairfield (Tex.).
COLLEGE: Texas A&M (bachelor of science degree in agricultural economics, 1988).
TRANSACTIONS/CAREER NOTES: Selected by Miami Dolphins in eighth round (220th pick overall) of 1988 NFL draft. . . . Signed by Dolphins (July 15, 1988). . . . Granted unconditional free agency (February 1, 1990). . . . Signed by Dallas Cowboys (March 29, 1990). . . . Suspended for steroid use (August 13-August 24, 1990). . . . On reserve/non-football injury list (September 2-September 28, 1990). . . . On injured reserve with knee injury (September 28-October 26, 1990). . . . On inactive list (October 28 and November 4, 1990). . . . Released by Cowboys (December 10, 1990). . . . Awarded on waivers to Philadelphia Eagles (December 12, 1990). . . . On inactive list (December 16 and 23, 1990). . . . Granted unconditional free agency (February 1, 1991). . . . Signed by Green Bay Packers (March 29, 1991).
PLAYING EXPERIENCE: Miami NFL, 1988 and 1989; Dallas (4)-Philadelphia (1) NFL, 1990. . . . Games: 1988 (15), 1989 (13), 1990 (5). Total: 33.

CHERRY, DERON
S, CHIEFS

PERSONAL: Born September 12, 1959, at Riverside, N.J. . . . 5-11/203. . . . Full name: Deron Leigh Cherry. . . . First name pronounced da-RON. . . . Related to Raphel Cherry, safety with Washington Redskins and Detroit Lions, 1985, 1987 and 1988.
HIGH SCHOOL: Palmyra (N.J.).
COLLEGE: Rutgers (degree in biology, 1981).
TRANSACTIONS/CAREER NOTES: Signed as free agent by Kansas City Chiefs (May 4, 1981). . . . Released by Chiefs (August 31, 1981). . . . Re-signed by Chiefs (September 23, 1981). . . . On inactive list (September 19, 1982). . . . On injured reserve with shoulder separation (December 30, 1982-remainder of season). . . . On injured reserve with knee injury (December 21, 1989-remainder of season). . . . On reserve/physically unable to perform list with knee injury (August 28-November 3, 1990).
RECORDS/HONORS: Tied NFL record for most interceptions, game (4), against Seattle Seahawks (September 29, 1985). . . . Played in Pro Bowl after 1983-1988 seasons. . . . Named to THE SPORTING NEWS NFL All-Pro team, 1986 and 1988.
PRO STATISTICS: 1981—Returned three kickoffs for 52 yards. 1982—Returned one kickoff for 39 yards. 1983—Returned two kickoffs for 54 yards, recovered two fumbles for four yards and fumbled twice. 1984—Returned one kickoff for no yards. 1986—Recovered blocked punt in end zone twice for two touchdowns and recovered two fumbles for seven yards. 1987—Recovered one fumble. 1988—Recovered six fumbles for 10 yards. 1989—Recovered two fumbles.

| | | | —— INTERCEPTIONS —— | | |
Year Team	G	No.	Yds.	Avg.	TD
1981— Kansas City NFL........	13	1	4	4.0	0
1982— Kansas City NFL........	7	0	0		0
1983— Kansas City NFL........	16	7	100	14.3	0
1984— Kansas City NFL........	16	7	140	20.0	0
1985— Kansas City NFL........	16	7	87	12.4	*1
1986— Kansas City NFL........	16	9	150	16.7	0
1987— Kansas City NFL........	8	3	58	19.3	0
1988— Kansas City NFL........	16	7	51	7.3	0
1989— Kansas City NFL........	15	2	27	13.5	0
1990— Kansas City NFL........	9	3	40	13.3	0
Pro totals (10 years)......	132	46	657	14.3	1

CHILDRESS, RAY

DT/DE, OILERS

PERSONAL: Born October 20, 1962, at Memphis, Tenn.... 6-6/272.
HIGH SCHOOL: J.J. Pearce (Richardson, Tex.).
COLLEGE: Texas A&M.
TRANSACTIONS/CAREER NOTES: Selected by Houston Gamblers in 1985 USFL territorial draft.... Selected by Houston Oilers in first round (third pick overall) of 1985 NFL draft.... Signed by Oilers (August 24, 1985).... Granted roster exemption (August 24-August 30, 1985).... Crossed picket line during players' strike (October 14, 1987).... Granted free agency (February 1, 1989).... Tendered offer sheet by Chicago Bears (March 30, 1989).... Matched by Oilers (April 3, 1989).
PLAYING EXPERIENCE: Houston NFL, 1985-1990.... Games: 1985 (16), 1986 (16), 1987 (13), 1988 (16), 1989 (14), 1990 (16). Total: 91.
RECORDS/HONORS: Tied NFL record for most opponents' fumbles recovered, game (3), against Washington Redskins (October 30, 1988).... Named as defensive lineman on THE SPORTING NEWS college All-America team, 1984.... Played in Pro Bowl after 1988 and 1990 seasons.... Named to THE SPORTING NEWS NFL All-Pro team, 1990.
PRO STATISTICS: 1985—Recovered one fumble. 1986—Recovered one fumble. 1987—Recovered one fumble for one yard. 1988—Recovered seven fumbles. 1989—Recovered one fumble. 1990—Credited with safety and recovered one fumble.

CHILTON, GENE

C, PATRIOTS

PERSONAL: Born March 27, 1964, at Houston.... 6-3/286.... Full name: Gene Alan Chilton.
HIGH SCHOOL: Memorial (Houston).
COLLEGE: Texas.
TRANSACTIONS/CAREER NOTES: Selected by St. Louis Cardinals in third round (59th pick overall) of 1986 NFL draft.... Signed by Cardinals (July 25, 1986).... Franchise transferred to Phoenix (March 15, 1988). ...Released by Phoenix Cardinals (August 30, 1988).... Signed as free agent by Kansas City Chiefs (March 3, 1989).... Released by Chiefs (September 3, 1990).... Awarded on waivers to New England Patriots (September 4, 1990).... On injured reserve with knee injury (October 8, 1990-remainder of season).
PLAYING EXPERIENCE: St. Louis NFL, 1986 and 1987; Kansas City NFL, 1989; New England NFL, 1990.... Games: 1986 (16), 1987 (11), 1989 (16), 1990 (4). Total: 47.
PRO STATISTICS: 1986—Recovered one fumble.

CHRISTIE, STEVE

PK, BUCCANEERS

PERSONAL: Born November 13, 1967, at Hamilton, Ont. ... 6-0/185. ... Full name: Geoffrey Stephen Christie.
HIGH SCHOOL: Oakville Trafalgar (Oakville, Ont.).
COLLEGE: William & Mary.
TRANSACTIONS/CAREER NOTES: Signed as free agent by Tampa Bay Buccaneers (May 8, 1990).

		——— PLACE-KICKING ———				
Year Team	G	XPM	XPA	FGM	FGA	Pts.
1990— Tampa Bay NFL.........	16	27	27	23	27	96
Pro totals (1 year)............	16	27	27	23	27	96

CLANCY, SAM

DE, COLTS

PERSONAL: Born May 29, 1958, at Pittsburgh.... 6-7/300.
HIGH SCHOOL: Brashear (Pittsburgh).
COLLEGE: Pittsburgh.
TRANSACTIONS/CAREER NOTES: Selected by Seattle Seahawks in 11th round (284th pick overall) of 1982 NFL draft.... On injured reserve with knee injury (August 16, 1982-entire season).... Granted free agency (February 1, 1984).... Signed by Pittsburgh Maulers of USFL (February 10, 1984).... Franchise disbanded (October 25, 1984)... ..Selected by Memphis Showboats in USFL dispersal draft (December 6, 1984).... Granted free agency (August 1, 1985).... Re-signed by Seattle Seahawks and traded to Cleveland Browns for seventh-round pick in 1986 draft (August 27, 1985).... Granted roster exemption (August 27-September 6, 1985).... Crossed picket line during players' strike (October 14, 1987)... . Granted unconditional free agency (February 1, 1989).... Signed by Indianapolis Colts (March 31, 1989).
PLAYING EXPERIENCE: Seattle NFL, 1983; Pittsburgh USFL, 1984; Memphis USFL, 1985; Cleveland NFL, 1985-1988; Indianapolis NFL, 1989 and 1990.... Games: 1983 (13), 1984 (18), 1985 USFL (18), 1985 NFL (14), 1986 (16), 1987 (13), 1988 (16), 1989 (16), 1990 (16). Total NFL: 104. Total USFL: 36. Total Pro: 140.
CHAMPIONSHIP GAME EXPERIENCE: Played in AFC championship game after 1986 and 1987 seasons.
PRO STATISTICS: USFL: 1984—Credited with 15 sacks for 136 yards and recovered two fumbles. 1985—Credited with four sacks for 28 yards.... NFL: 1986—Recovered one fumble. 1987—Recovered two fumbles. 1989—Recovered three fumbles.
BASKETBALL TRANSACTIONS: Selected by Phoenix Suns in third round (62nd pick overall) of 1981 NBA draft.... Released by Suns (October 19, 1981).... Signed by Billings Volcanos of CBA (November 12, 1981).

BASKETBALL RECORD AS PLAYER

Year Team	G	Min.	FGM	FGA	Pct.	FTM	FTA	Pct.	—3-pt.—Made	Att.	Pts.	Avg.	Reb.	Avg.	Ast.	PF	Blk.Shots	St.
81-82—Billings CBA	41	1170	190	355	53.5	89	128	69.5	1	5	472	11.5	342	8.3	50	144	41	67
Totals	41	1170	190	355	53.5	89	128	69.5	1	5	472	11.5	342	8.3	50	144	41	67

PLAYOFF RECORD

Year Team	G	Min.	FGM	FGA	Pct.	FTM	FTA	Pct.	—3-pt.—Made	Att.	Pts.	Avg.	Reb.	Avg.	Ast.	PF	Blk.Shots	St.
81-82—Billings CBA	5	167	24	46	52.1	12	19	63.1	1	1	63	12.6	54	10.8	8	23	5	8

CLARK, BERNARD

LB, BENGALS

PERSONAL: Born January 12, 1967, at Tampa, Fla.... 6-2/248.
HIGH SCHOOL: Leto Comprehensive (Tampa, Fla.).
COLLEGE: Miami (Fla.).
TRANSACTIONS/CAREER NOTES: Selected by Cincinnati Bengals in third round (65th pick

overall) of 1990 NFL draft. . . . Signed by Bengals (July 24, 1990).
PLAYING EXPERIENCE: Cincinnati NFL, 1990. . . . Games: 1990 (14).

CLARK, GARY
WR, REDSKINS

PERSONAL: Born May 1, 1962, at Radford, Va. . . . 5-9/173. . . . Full name: Gary C. Clark.
HIGH SCHOOL: Pulaski County (Dublin, Va.).
COLLEGE: James Madison.
TRANSACTIONS/CAREER NOTES: Selected by Jacksonville Bulls in first round (sixth pick overall) of 1984 USFL draft. . . . Signed by Bulls (January 16, 1984). . . . On developmental squad (May 9-May 16, 1984). . . . On developmental squad for two games (June 4-June 12, 1984). . . . Selected by Washington Redskins in second round (55th pick overall) of 1984 NFL supplemental draft. . . . On developmental squad for one game with Jacksonville Bulls (March 17-March 20, 1985). . . . Released by Bulls (May 1, 1985). . . . Signed by Washington Redskins (May 13, 1985).
CHAMPIONSHIP GAME EXPERIENCE: Played in NFC championship game after 1986 and 1987 seasons. . . . Played in Super Bowl XXII after 1987 season.
RECORDS/HONORS: Played in Pro Bowl after 1986, 1987 and 1990 seasons.
PRO STATISTICS: USFL: 1984—Recovered four fumbles. 1985—Recovered one fumble. . . . NFL: 1986—Recovered one fumble.

		RUSHING				RECEIVING				PUNT RETURNS				KICKOFF RETURNS				TOTALS		
Year Team	G	Att.	Yds.	Avg.	TD	No.	Yds.	Avg.	TD	No.	Yds.	Avg.	TD	No.	Yds.	Avg.	TD	TD	Pts.	F.
1984—Jack. USFL	16	2	9	4.5	0	56	760	13.6	2	20	84	4.2	0	19	341	18.0	0	2	12	5
1985—Jack. USFL	9	0	0		0	10	61	6.1	1	7	44	6.3	0	3	56	18.7	0	1	6	1
1985—Washington NFL	16	0	0		0	72	926	12.9	5	0	0		0	0	0		0	5	30	0
1986—Washington NFL	15	2	10	5.0	0	74	1265	17.1	7	1	14	14.0	0	0	0		0	7	42	1
1987—Washington NFL	12	1	0	.0	0	56	1066	19.0	7	0	0		0	0	0		0	7	42	3
1988—Washington NFL	16	2	6	3.0	0	59	892	15.1	7	8	48	6.0	0	0	0		0	7	42	2
1989—Washington NFL	15	2	19	9.5	0	79	1229	15.6	9	0	0		0	0	0		0	9	54	1
1990—Washington NFL	16	1	1	1.0	0	75	1112	14.8	8	0	0		0	0	0		0	8	48	0
USFL totals (2 years)	25	2	9	4.5	0	66	821	12.4	3	27	128	4.7	0	22	397	18.1	0	3	18	6
NFL totals (6 years)	90	8	36	4.5	0	415	6490	15.6	43	9	62	6.9	0	0	0			43	258	7
Pro totals (8 years)	115	10	45	4.5	0	481	7311	15.2	46	36	190	5.3	0	22	397	18.1	0	46	276	13

CLARK, GREG
LB, PACKERS

PERSONAL: Born March 5, 1965, at Los Angeles. . . . 6-0/226. . . . Full name: Gregory Klondike Clark.
HIGH SCHOOL: North (Torrance, Calif.).
COLLEGE: Arizona State.
TRANSACTIONS/CAREER NOTES: Selected by Chicago Bears in 12th round (329th pick overall) of 1988 NFL draft. . . . Signed by Bears (July 21, 1988). . . . Granted unconditional free agency (February 1, 1989). . . . Signed by Miami Dolphins (March 16, 1989). . . . Granted unconditional free agency (February 1, 1990). . . . Signed by Green Bay Packers (March 31, 1990). . . . Released by Packers (September 3, 1990). . . . Signed by Los Angeles Rams (September 5, 1990). . . . On injured reserve with leg injury (November 28, 1990-remainder of season). . . . Granted unconditional free agency (February 1, 1991). . . . Signed by Green Bay Packers (April 1, 1991).
PLAYING EXPERIENCE: Chicago NFL, 1988; Miami NFL, 1989; Los Angeles Rams NFL, 1990. . . . Games: 1988 (15), 1989 (16), 1990 (11). Total: 42.
CHAMPIONSHIP GAME EXPERIENCE: Played in NFC championship game after 1988 season.
PRO STATISTICS: 1988—Recovered one fumble. 1989—Recovered one fumble.

CLARK, KEN
RB, COLTS

PERSONAL: Born June 11, 1966, at Evergreen, Ala. . . . 5-9/204. . . . Full name: Kenneth Clark.
HIGH SCHOOL: Bryan (Omaha, Neb.).
COLLEGE: Nebraska.
TRANSACTIONS/CAREER NOTES: Selected by Indianapolis Colts in eighth round (206th pick overall) of 1990 NFL draft. . . . Signed by Colts (July 26, 1990). . . . Released by Colts (October 16, 1990). . . . Signed by Colts to practice squad (October 18, 1990). . . . On practice squad (October 18, 1990-remainder of season).

		RUSHING				RECEIVING				TOTAL		
Year Team	G	Att.	Yds.	Avg.	TD	No.	Yds.	Avg.	TD	TD	Pts.	F.
1990—Indianapolis NFL	5	7	10	1.4	0	5	23	4.6	0	0	0	0
Pro totals (1 year)	5	7	10	1.4	0	5	23	4.6	0	0	0	0

CLARK, KEVIN
DB, BRONCOS

PERSONAL: Born June 8, 1964, at Sacramento, Calif. . . . 5-10/185. . . . Full name: Kevin Randall Clark.
HIGH SCHOOL: C.K. McClatchy (Sacramento, Calif.).
COLLEGE: San Jose State.
TRANSACTIONS/CAREER NOTES: Signed as free agent by Denver Broncos (May 1, 1987). . . . Released by Broncos (September 7, 1987). . . . Re-signed as replacement player by Broncos (September 25, 1987). . . . Released by Broncos (September 22, 1988). . . . Signed as free agent by Dallas Cowboys (February 3, 1989). . . . Released by Cowboys (July, 1989). . . . Signed as free agent by Edmonton Eskimos of CFL (April 11, 1990). . . . Released by Eskimos (July 8, 1990). . . . Re-signed by Eskimos (July 17, 1990). . . . Released by Eskimos (August 29, 1990). . . . Signed by B.C. Lions to practice roster (September 9, 1990). . . . Activated (September 20, 1990). . . . Released by Lions (October 13, 1990). . . . Signed by Denver Broncos (October 17, 1990).
CHAMPIONSHIP GAME EXPERIENCE: Played in AFC championship game after 1987 season. . . . Played in Super Bowl XXII after 1987 season.
MISCELLANEOUS: Served as defensive backs coach for Frankfurt Galaxy of WLAF, 1991.
PRO STATISTICS: NFL: 1987—Recovered one fumble. . . . CFL: 1990—Recovered three fumbles for no yards.

Year Team	G	No.	INTERCEPTIONS Yds.	Avg.	TD	No.	PUNT RETURNS Yds.	Avg.	TD	No.	KICKOFF RETURNS Yds.	Avg.	TD	TD	TOTAL Pts.	F.
1987— Denver NFL	11	3	105	35.0	0	18	233	12.9	1	2	33	16.5	0	1	6	1
1988— Denver NFL	3	0	0		0	13	115	8.9	0	0	0		0	0	0	0
1990— Edm. (7)-B.C. (3) CFL	10	2	48	24.0	0	0	32		0	1	25	25.0	0	0	0	0
1990— Denver NFL	8	0	0		0	21	159	7.6	0	20	505	*25.3	0	0	0	0
NFL totals (3 years)	22	3	105	35.0	0	52	507	9.8	1	22	538	24.5	0	1	6	1
CFL totals (1 year)	10	2	48	24.0	0	0	32		0	1	25	25.0	0	0	0	0
Pro totals (4 years)	32	5	153	30.6	0	52	539	10.4	1	23	563	24.5	0	1	6	1

CLARK, LOUIS
WR, SEAHAWKS

PERSONAL: Born July 3, 1964, at Shannon, Miss.... 6-0/198.... Full name: Louis Steven Clark. ... Brother of Dave Clark, former outfielder with Cleveland Indians and Chicago Cubs.
HIGH SCHOOL: Shannon (Miss.).
COLLEGE: Mississippi State.
TRANSACTIONS/CAREER NOTES: Selected by Seattle Seahawks in 10th round (270th pick overall) of 1987 NFL draft.... Signed by Seahawks (July 21, 1987).... On injured reserve with pulled hamstring (November 16, 1987-remainder of season).... On injured reserve with hamstring injury (August 29-October 22, 1988).
PRO STATISTICS: 1989—Returned one kickoff for 31 yards and fumbled once.

Year Team	G	No.	RECEIVING Yds.	Avg.	TD
1987— Seattle NFL	2	0	0		0
1988— Seattle NFL	7	1	20	20.0	1
1989— Seattle NFL	16	25	260	10.4	1
1990— Seattle NFL	4	0	0		0
Pro totals (4 years)	29	26	280	10.8	2

CLARK, ROBERT
WR, LIONS

PERSONAL: Born August 8, 1965, at Brooklyn, N.Y.... 5-11/173.
HIGH SCHOOL: Maggie L. Walker (Richmond, Va.).
COLLEGE: North Carolina Central.
TRANSACTIONS/CAREER NOTES: Selected by New Orleans Saints in 10th round (263rd pick overall) of 1987 NFL draft.... Signed by Saints (July 24, 1987).... On injured reserve with stress fracture of leg (October 30, 1987-remainder of season).... Granted unconditional free agency (February 1, 1989).... Signed by Detroit Lions (February 27, 1989).
PRO STATISTICS: 1988—Recovered one fumble and fumbled once. 1989—Fumbled twice.

Year Team	G	No.	RECEIVING Yds.	Avg.	TD
1987— New Orleans NFL	2	3	38	12.7	0
1988— New Orleans NFL	16	19	245	12.9	2
1989— Detroit NFL	16	41	748	18.2	2
1990— Detroit NFL	16	52	914	17.6	8
Pro totals (4 years)	50	115	1945	16.9	12

CLARKE, KEN
DT, VIKINGS

PERSONAL: Born August 28, 1956, at Savannah, Ga.... 6-2/280.... Full name: Kenneth Maurice Clarke.
HIGH SCHOOL: English (Boston).
COLLEGE: Syracuse (bachelor of science degree in psychology, 1978).
TRANSACTIONS/CAREER NOTES: Signed as free agent by Philadelphia Eagles (May 4, 1978).... Released by Eagles (May 9, 1988).... Signed as free agent by Seattle Seahawks (July 18, 1988).... Released by Seahawks (September 8, 1989).... Signed as free agent by Minnesota Vikings (September 13, 1989).... Released by Vikings (August 28, 1990).... Re-signed by Vikings (October 2, 1990).
PLAYING EXPERIENCE: Philadelphia NFL, 1978-1987; Seattle NFL, 1988; Minnesota NFL, 1989 and 1990.... Games: 1978 (16), 1979 (16), 1980 (16), 1981 (16), 1982 (9), 1983 (16), 1984 (16), 1985 (16), 1986 (16), 1987 (11), 1988 (16), 1989 (11), 1990 (12). Total: 187.
CHAMPIONSHIP GAME EXPERIENCE: Played in NFC championship game after 1980 season.... Played in Super Bowl XV after 1980 season.
PRO STATISTICS: 1978—Recovered one fumble. 1980—Returned one kickoff for no yards and fumbled once. 1981—Returned one kickoff for no yards and credited with a safety. 1982—Recovered one fumble. 1983—Recovered three fumbles for five yards. 1985—Recovered two fumbles. 1990—Recovered one fumble.

CLAYBORN, RAYMOND
CB, BROWNS

PERSONAL: Born January 2, 1955, at Fort Worth, Tex.... 6-1/190.... Full name: Raymond De Wayne Clayborn.
HIGH SCHOOL: Trimble (Fort Worth, Tex.).
COLLEGE: Texas (degree in communications).
TRANSACTIONS/CAREER NOTES: Selected by New England Patriots in first round (16th pick overall) of 1977 NFL draft.... Crossed picket line during players' strike (October 2, 1987).... On injured reserve with knee injury (November 23, 1987-remainder of season).... Granted unconditional free agency (February 1, 1990).... Signed by Cleveland Browns (March 15, 1990).

CHAMPIONSHIP GAME EXPERIENCE: Played in AFC championship game after 1985 season. . . . Played in Super Bowl XX after 1985 season.
RECORDS/HONORS: Named as cornerback on THE SPORTING NEWS college All-America team, 1976. . . . Played in Pro Bowl after 1983, 1985 and 1986 seasons. . . . Named to THE SPORTING NEWS NFL All-Pro team, 1983.
PRO STATISTICS: 1977—Credited with a safety. 1978—Recovered one fumble. 1980—Recovered one fumble. 1981—Recovered two fumbles for four yards. 1982—Recovered one fumble. 1986—Recovered two fumbles. 1987—Returned blocked field goal attempt 71 yards for a touchdown and recovered one fumble.

		— INTERCEPTIONS—				— KICKOFF RETURNS—				— TOTAL —		
Year Team	G	No.	Yds.	Avg.	TD	No.	Yds.	Avg.	TD	TD	Pts.	F.
1977— New England NFL	14	0	0		0	28	869	*31.0	*3	3	20	1
1978— New England NFL	16	4	72	18.0	0	27	636	23.6	0	0	0	0
1979— New England NFL	16	5	56	11.2	0	2	33	16.5	0	0	0	0
1980— New England NFL	16	5	87	17.4	0	0	0		0	0	0	0
1981— New England NFL	16	2	39	19.5	0	0	0		0	0	0	0
1982— New England NFL	9	1	26	26.0	0	0	0		0	0	0	0
1983— New England NFL	16	0	0		0	0	0		0	0	0	0
1984— New England NFL	16	3	102	34.0	0	0	0		0	0	0	0
1985— New England NFL	16	6	80	13.3	*1	0	0		0	1	6	0
1986— New England NFL	16	3	4	1.3	0	0	0		0	0	0	0
1987— New England NFL	10	2	24	12.0	0	0	0		0	1	6	0
1988— New England NFL	16	4	65	16.3	0	0	0		0	0	0	0
1989— New England NFL	14	1	0	.0	0	0	0		0	0	.0	0
1990— Cleveland NFL	16	0	0		0	0	0		0	0	0	0
Pro totals (14 years)	207	36	555	15.4	1	57	1538	27.0	3	5	32	1

CLAYTON, MARK
WR, DOLPHINS

PERSONAL: Born April 8, 1961, at Indianapolis. . . . 5-9/185. . . . Full name: Mark Gregory Clayton.
HIGH SCHOOL: Cathedral (Indianapolis).
COLLEGE: Louisville.
TRANSACTIONS/CAREER NOTES: Selected by Miami Dolphins in eighth round (223rd pick overall) of 1983 NFL draft. . . . On reserve/did not report list (July 28-September 11, 1989). . . . On inactive list (September 9, 1990). . . . On injured reserve with knee injury (November 13-December 19, 1990). . . . Transferred to practice squad (December 19, 1990). . . . Activated (December 22, 1990).
CHAMPIONSHIP GAME EXPERIENCE: Played in AFC championship game after 1984 and 1985 seasons. . . . Played in Super Bowl XIX after 1984 season.
RECORDS/HONORS: Played in Pro Bowl after 1984-1986 and 1988 seasons.
PRO STATISTICS: 1983—Attempted one pass with one completion for 48 yards and a touchdown and recovered one fumble. 1984—Attempted one pass with one interception and recovered one fumble. 1985—Recovered one fumble.

		— RUSHING—				— RECEIVING—				–PUNT RETURNS–				KICKOFF RETURNS				– TOTALS –		
Year Team	G	Att.	Yds.	Avg.	TD	No.	Yds.	Avg.	TD	No.	Yds.	Avg.	TD	No.	Yds.	Avg.	TD	TD	Pts.	F.
1983— Miami NFL	14	2	9	4.5	0	6	114	19.0	1	41	392	9.6	*1	1	25	25.0	0	2	12	3
1984— Miami NFL	15	3	35	11.7	0	73	1389	19.0	*18	8	79	9.9	0	2	15	7.5	0	*18	108	2
1985— Miami NFL	16	1	10	10.0	0	70	996	14.2	4	2	14	7.0	0	0	0			4	24	2
1986— Miami NFL	15	2	33	16.5	0	60	1150	19.2	10	1	0	.0	0	0	0			10	60	1
1987— Miami NFL	12	2	8	4.0	0	46	776	16.9	7	0	0			0	0			7	42	0
1988— Miami NFL	16	1	4	4.0	0	86	1129	13.1	*14	0	0			0	0			14	84	0
1989— Miami NFL	15	3	9	3.0	0	64	1011	15.8	9	0	0			0	0			9	54	1
1990— Miami NFL	10	0	0		0	32	406	12.7	3	0	0			0	0			3	18	1
Pro totals (8 years)	113	14	108	7.7	0	437	6971	16.0	66	52	485	9.3	1	3	40	13.3	0	67	402	10

CLAYTON, STAN
OT/G, PATRIOTS

PERSONAL: Born January 31, 1965, at Philadelphia. . . . 6-3/265. . . . Full name: Stanley David Clayton.
HIGH SCHOOL: East (Cherry Hill, N.J.).
COLLEGE: Penn State.
TRANSACTIONS/CAREER NOTES: Selected by Atlanta Falcons in 10th round (250th pick overall) of 1988 NFL draft. . . . Signed by Falcons (July 16, 1988). . . . On injured reserve with knee injury (August 31-December 10, 1988). . . . Granted free agency (February 1, 1990). . . . Re-signed by Falcons (July 27, 1990). . . . Released by Falcons (September 3, 1990). . . . Awarded on waivers to New England Patriots (September 4, 1990). . . . On inactive list (December 2, 9 and 15, 1990).
PLAYING EXPERIENCE: Atlanta NFL, 1988 and 1989; New England NFL, 1990. . . . Games: 1988 (2), 1989 (13), 1990 (11). Total: 26.
PRO STATISTICS: 1989—Recovered one fumble.

CLIFTON, KYLE
LB, JETS

PERSONAL: Born August 23, 1962, at Onley, Tex. . . . 6-4/236.
HIGH SCHOOL: Bridgeport (Tex.).
COLLEGE: Texas Christian (degree in business management).
TRANSACTIONS/CAREER NOTES: Selected by Birmingham Stallions in first round (12th pick overall) of 1984 USFL draft. . . . Selected by New York Jets in third round (64th pick overall) of 1984 NFL draft. . . . Signed by Jets (July 12, 1984).
PRO STATISTICS: 1984—Recovered one fumble. 1986—Recovered one fumble. 1985—Recovered two fumbles. 1988—Recovered two fumbles for six yards. 1989—Recovered one fumble. 1990—Recovered one fumble.

Year	Team		G	No.	Yds.	Avg.	TD
					INTERCEPTIONS		
1984—	N.Y. Jets NFL		16	1	0	.0	0
1985—	N.Y. Jets NFL		16	3	10	3.3	0
1986—	N.Y. Jets NFL		16	2	8	4.0	0
1987—	N.Y. Jets NFL		12	0	0		0
1988—	N.Y. Jets NFL		16	0	0		0
1989—	N.Y. Jets NFL		16	0	0		0
1990—	N.Y. Jets NFL		16	3	49	16.3	0
Pro totals (7 years)			108	9	67	7.4	0

COBB, REGGIE
RB, BUCCANEERS

PERSONAL: Born July 7, 1968, at Knoxville, Tenn. . . . 6-0/215. . . . Full name: Reginald John Cobb.
HIGH SCHOOL: Central (Knoxville, Tenn.).
COLLEGE: Tennessee.
TRANSACTIONS/CAREER NOTES: Selected by Tampa Bay Buccaneers in second round (30th pick overall) of 1990 NFL draft. . . . Signed by Buccaneers (August 6, 1990).
PRO STATISTICS: 1990—Recovered six fumbles.

			RUSHING				RECEIVING				KICKOFF RETURNS				TOTAL		
Year	Team	G	Att.	Yds.	Avg.	TD	No.	Yds.	Avg.	TD	No.	Yds.	Avg.	TD	TD	Pts.	F.
1990—	Tampa Bay NFL	16	151	480	3.2	2	39	299	7.7	0	11	223	20.3	0	2	12	8
Pro totals (1 year)		16	151	480	3.2	2	39	299	7.7	0	11	223	20.3	0	2	12	8

COFER, MICHAEL
LB, LIONS

PERSONAL: Born April 7, 1960, at Knoxville, Tenn. . . . 6-5/244. . . . Full name: Michael Lynn Cofer. . . . Brother of James Cofer, linebacker with Baltimore Stars (USFL), 1985.
HIGH SCHOOL: Rule (Knoxville, Tenn.).
COLLEGE: Tennessee.
TRANSACTIONS/CAREER NOTES: Selected by New Jersey Generals in 1983 USFL territorial draft. . . . Selected by Detroit Lions in third round (67th pick overall) of 1983 NFL draft. . . . Signed by Lions (July 1, 1983). . . . On injured reserve with hip injury (October 25, 1985-remainder of season).
PLAYING EXPERIENCE: Detroit NFL, 1983-1990. . . . Games: 1983 (16), 1984 (16), 1985 (7), 1986 (16), 1987 (11), 1988 (16), 1989 (15), 1990 (16). Total: 113.
RECORDS/HONORS: Played in Pro Bowl after 1988 season.
PRO STATISTICS: 1983—Recovered one fumble. 1984—Recovered one fumble. 1986—Recovered three fumbles. 1987—Recovered one fumble. 1988—Recovered two fumbles. 1990—Intercepted one pass for no yards and recovered two fumbles.

COFER, MIKE
PK, 49ERS

PERSONAL: Born February 19, 1964, at Columbia, S.C. . . . 6-1/190. . . . Full name: James Michael Cofer.
HIGH SCHOOL: Country Day (Charlotte, N.C.).
COLLEGE: North Carolina State (bachelor of arts degree in business management and political science).
TRANSACTIONS/CAREER NOTES: Signed as free agent by Cleveland Browns (May 5, 1987). . . . Released by Browns (September 1, 1987). . . . Signed as free agent replacement player by New Orleans Saints (September 24, 1987). . . . Released by Saints (October 16, 1987). . . . Signed as free agent by San Francisco 49ers (April 5, 1988). . . . Granted free agency (February 1, 1990). . . . Re-signed by 49ers (May 8, 1990).
CHAMPIONSHIP GAME EXPERIENCE: Played in NFC championship game after 1988-1990 seasons. . . . Played in Super Bowl XXIII after 1988 season and Super Bowl XXIV after 1989 season.

			PLACE-KICKING			
Year	Team	G	XPM	XPA	FGM	FGA	Pts.
1987—	New Orleans NFL	2	5	7	1	1	8
1988—	San Francisco NFL	16	40	41	27	*38	121
1989—	San Francisco NFL	16	49	51	29	36	*136
1990—	San Francisco NFL	16	39	39	24	36	111
Pro totals (4 years)		50	133	138	81	111	376

COFIELD, TIM
LB, RAIDERS

PERSONAL: Born May 18, 1963, at Murfreesboro, N.C. . . . 6-2/240. . . . Full name: Timmy Lee Cofield.
HIGH SCHOOL: Murfreesboro (N.C.).
COLLEGE: Elizabeth City State (N.C.).
TRANSACTIONS/CAREER NOTES: Selected by Baltimore Stars in sixth round (45th pick overall) of 1986 USFL draft. . . . Signed as free agent by Kansas City Chiefs (May 8, 1986). . . . Granted unconditional free agency (February 1, 1989). . . . Signed by New York Jets (March 9, 1989). . . . Released by Jets (October 24, 1989). . . . Awarded on waivers to Buffalo Bills (October 25, 1989). . . . Released by Bills (September 4, 1990). . . . Signed by Los Angeles Raiders (February 10, 1991).
PLAYING EXPERIENCE: Kansas City NFL, 1986-1988; New York Jets (6)-Buffalo (5) NFL, 1989. . . . Games: 1986 (15), 1987 (12), 1988 (16), 1989 (11). Total: 54.
PRO STATISTICS: 1986—Recovered one fumble. 1987—Recovered one fumble. 1988—Intercepted one pass for no yards and recovered one fumble.

COLEMAN, MONTE

PERSONAL: Born November 4, 1957, at Pine Bluff, Ark. . . . 6-2/230. **HIGH SCHOOL:** Pine Bluff (Ark.). **COLLEGE:** Central Arkansas.

TRANSACTIONS/CAREER NOTES: Selected by Washington Redskins in 11th round (289th pick overall) of 1979 NFL draft. . . . On injured reserve with thigh injury (September 16-October 17, 1983). . . . On injured reserve with strained hamstring (September 25-November 9, 1985). . . . On injured reserve with pulled hamstring (October 8-November 8, 1986).

CHAMPIONSHIP GAME EXPERIENCE: Played in NFC championship game after 1982, 1983, 1986 and 1987 seasons. . . . Played in Super Bowl XVII after 1982 season, Super Bowl XVIII after 1983 season and Super Bowl XXII after 1987 season.

PRO STATISTICS: 1979—Recovered three fumbles. 1980—Caught one pass for 12 yards and recovered two fumbles. 1981—Recovered one fumble for two yards. 1983—Recovered two fumbles. 1984—Ran 27 yards with lateral on punt return and recovered one fumble. 1988—Recovered one fumble for nine yards. 1989—Rushed once for minus one yard, recovered one fumble and fumbled once.

			INTERCEPTIONS		
Year Team	G	No.	Yds.	Avg.	TD
1979— Washington NFL	16	1	13	13.0	0
1980— Washington NFL	16	3	92	30.7	0
1981— Washington NFL	12	3	52	17.3	1
1982— Washington NFL	8	0	0		0
1983— Washington NFL	10	0	0		0
1984— Washington NFL	16	1	49	49.0	1
1985— Washington NFL	10	0	0		0
1986— Washington NFL	11	0	0		0
1987— Washington NFL	12	2	53	26.5	0
1988— Washington NFL	13	1	11	11.0	0
1989— Washington NFL	15	2	24	12.0	1
1990— Washington NFL	15	1	0	.0	0
Pro totals (12 years)	154	14	294	21.0	3

COLEMAN, PAT

PERSONAL: Born April 8, 1967, at Cleveland, Miss. . . . 5-7/173. . . . Full name: Patrick Darryl Coleman. **HIGH SCHOOL:** Cleveland (Miss.). **COLLEGE:** Mississippi.

TRANSACTIONS/CAREER NOTES: Selected by Houston Oilers in ninth round (237th pick overall) of 1990 NFL draft. . . . Signed by Oilers (July 20, 1990). . . . On inactive list (September 9, 1990). . . . Released by Oilers (September 11, 1990). . . . Signed by Oilers to practice squad (October 3, 1990). . . . Signed by New England Patriots (November 21, 1990). . . . Released by Patriots (November 27, 1990). . . . Re-signed by Houston Oilers to practice squad (November 28, 1990). . . . Re-signed by Oilers for 1991 (May 20, 1991).

PLAYING EXPERIENCE: New England NFL, 1990. . . . Games: 1990 (1).

PRO STATISTICS: 1990—Returned two kickoffs for 18 yards.

COLEMAN, SIDNEY

PERSONAL: Born January 14, 1964, at Gulfport, Miss. . . . 6-2/250. **HIGH SCHOOL:** Harrison Central (Gulfport, Miss.). **COLLEGE:** Southern Mississippi.

TRANSACTIONS/CAREER NOTES: Signed as free agent by Tampa Bay Buccaneers (April 29, 1988). . . . On injured reserve with knee injury (October 4-November 28, 1989). . . . Transferred to developmental squad (November 29, 1989-remainder of season). . . . Granted unconditional free agency (February 1, 1991). . . . Signed by Phoenix Cardinals (February 26, 1991).

PLAYING EXPERIENCE: Tampa Bay NFL, 1988-1990. . . . Games: 1988 (16), 1989 (4), 1990 (16). Total: 36.

PRO STATISTICS: 1988—Recovered one fumble. 1990—Returned one kickoff for nine yards.

COLEY, JAMES

PERSONAL: Born April 13, 1967, at Jacksonville, Fla. . . . 6-3/270. . . . Full name: James Lester Coley. **HIGH SCHOOL:** Robert E. Lee Sr. (Jacksonville, Fla.). **COLLEGE:** Clemson.

TRANSACTIONS/CAREER NOTES: Signed as free agent by Chicago Bears (May 4, 1989). . . . Released by Bears (September 5, 1989). . . . Re-signed by Bears to developmental squad (September 6, 1989). . . . Released by Bears (January 4, 1990). . . . Re-signed by Bears (March 15, 1990).

			RECEIVING		
Year Team	G	No.	Yds.	Avg.	TD
1990— Chicago NFL	16	1	7	7.0	0
Pro totals (1 year)	16	1	7	7.0	0

COLLIE, BRUCE

PERSONAL: Born June 27, 1962, at Nuremburg, Germany. . . . 6-6/270. . . . Full name: Bruce Stokes Collie. **HIGH SCHOOL:** Robert E. Lee (San Antonio). **COLLEGE:** Texas-Arlington.

TRANSACTIONS/CAREER NOTES: Selected by Baltimore Stars in sixth round (78th pick overall) of 1985 USFL draft. . . . Selected

by San Francisco 49ers in fifth round (140th pick overall) of 1985 NFL draft. . . . Signed by 49ers (June 25, 1985). . . . Released by 49ers (September 3, 1990). . . . Awarded on waivers to Philadelphia Eagles (September 4, 1990). . . . On inactive list (September 9, 1990).
PLAYING EXPERIENCE: San Francisco NFL, 1985-1989; Philadelphia NFL, 1990. . . . Games: 1985 (16), 1986 (16), 1987 (11), 1988 (15), 1989 (16), 1990 (12). Total: 86.
CHAMPIONSHIP GAME EXPERIENCE: Played in NFC championship game after 1988 and 1989 seasons. . . . Played in Super Bowl XXIII after 1988 season and Super Bowl XXIV after 1989 season.

COLLINS, ANDRE
LB, REDSKINS

PERSONAL: Born May 4, 1968, at Riverside, N.J. . . . 6-1/230. . . . Full name: Andre Pierre Collins.
HIGH SCHOOL: Cinnaminson (N.J.).
COLLEGE: Penn State (bachelor of arts degree in health planning and administration, 1991).
TRANSACTIONS/CAREER NOTES: Selected by Washington Redskins in second round (46th pick overall) of 1990 NFL draft. . . . Signed by Redskins (July 22, 1990).
PLAYING EXPERIENCE: Washington NFL, 1990. . . . Games: 1990 (16).

COLLINS, MARK
CB, GIANTS

PERSONAL: Born January 16, 1964, at San Bernardino, Calif. . . . 5-10/190.
HIGH SCHOOL: Pacific (San Bernardino, Calif.).
COLLEGE: Cal State Fullerton.
TRANSACTIONS/CAREER NOTES: Selected by New York Giants in second round (44th pick overall) of 1986 NFL draft. . . . Signed by Giants (July 30, 1986). . . . On injured reserve with back injury (December 23, 1987-remainder of season). . . . On injured reserve with pulled groin (December 3, 1988-remainder of season). . . . On injured reserve with sprained ankle (September 19-October 19, 1990).
CHAMPIONSHIP GAME EXPERIENCE: Played in NFC championship game after 1986 and 1990 seasons. . . . Played in Super Bowl XXI after 1986 season and Super Bowl XXV after 1990 season.
RECORDS/HONORS: Named as defensive back on THE SPORTING NEWS college All-America team, 1985.
PRO STATISTICS: 1986—Returned three punts for 11 yards and recovered three fumbles for five yards. 1988—Credited with a safety. 1989—Recovered two fumbles for eight yards.

| | | — INTERCEPTIONS— | | | — KICKOFF RETURNS— | | | | — TOTAL — | | |
Year Team	G	No.	Yds.	Avg.	TD	No.	Yds.	Avg.	TD	TD	Pts.	F.
1986— N.Y. Giants NFL	15	1	0	.0	0	11	204	18.5	0	0	0	2
1987— N.Y. Giants NFL	11	2	28	14.0	0	0	0		0	0	0	0
1988— N.Y. Giants NFL	11	1	13	13.0	0	4	67	16.8	0	0	2	0
1989— N.Y. Giants NFL	16	2	12	6.0	0	1	0	.0	0	0	0	0
1990— N.Y. Giants NFL	13	2	0	.0	0	0	0		0	0	0	0
Pro totals (5 years)	66	8	53	6.6	0	16	271	16.9	0	0	2	2

COLLINS, SHAWN
WR, FALCONS

PERSONAL: Born February 20, 1967, at San Diego. . . . 6-2/204.
HIGH SCHOOL: Kearny (San Diego).
COLLEGE: Northern Arizona.
TRANSACTIONS/CAREER NOTES: Selected by Atlanta Falcons in first round (27th pick overall) of 1989 NFL draft. . . . Signed by Falcons (July 24, 1989).
PRO STATISTICS: 1990—Recovered two fumbles and fumbled once.

| | | — RECEIVING — | | | |
Year Team	G	No.	Yds.	Avg.	TD
1989— Atlanta NFL	16	58	862	14.9	3
1990— Atlanta NFL	16	34	503	14.8	2
Pro totals (2 years)	32	92	1365	14.8	5

COMEAUX, DARREN
LB, SEAHAWKS

PERSONAL: Born April 15, 1960, at San Diego. . . . 6-1/239. . . . Name pronounced CO-MO.
HIGH SCHOOL: San Diego.
COLLEGE: San Diego Mesa College, then Arizona State.
TRANSACTIONS/CAREER NOTES: Signed as free agent by Denver Broncos (April 30, 1982). . . . On injured reserve with broken foot (September 7-December 16, 1982). . . . Released by Broncos (August 29, 1983). . . . Re-signed by Broncos (September 13, 1983). . . . Released by Broncos (September 2, 1985). . . . Re-signed by Broncos (September 3, 1985). . . . On injured reserve with broken thumb (October 16-November 22, 1985). . . . Released by Broncos (September 7, 1987). . . . Signed as free agent replacement player by San Francisco 49ers (October 8, 1987). . . . Released by 49ers (November 3, 1987). . . . Re-signed by 49ers (November 6, 1987). . . . On injured reserve with knee and hamstring injuries (August 29-October 12, 1988). . . . Released by 49ers after clearing procedural waivers (October 13, 1988). . . . Awarded on waivers to Seattle Seahawks (October 14, 1988). . . . Granted free agency (February 1, 1990). . . . Re-signed by Seahawks (August 12, 1990). . . . On injured reserve with knee injury (November 14, 1990-remainder of season).
PLAYING EXPERIENCE: Denver NFL, 1982-1986; San Francisco NFL, 1987; Seattle NFL, 1988-1990. . . . Games: 1982 (3), 1983 (14), 1984 (16), 1985 (11), 1986 (16), 1987 (8), 1988 (9), 1989 (16), 1990 (9). Total: 102.
CHAMPIONSHIP GAME EXPERIENCE: Played in AFC championship game after 1986 season. . . . Played in Super Bowl XXI after 1986 season.
PRO STATISTICS: 1984—Intercepted one pass for five yards and recovered one fumble. 1986—Recovered one fumble. 1988—In-

tercepted one pass for 18 yards and fumbled once. 1989—Intercepted one pass for no yards, returned one kickoff for nine yards and recovered one fumble.

CONLAN, SHANE
LB, BILLS

PERSONAL: Born April 3, 1964, at Frewsburg, N.Y. . . . 6-3/235. . . . Full name: Shane Patrick Conlan.
HIGH SCHOOL: Central (Frewsburg, N.Y.).
COLLEGE: Penn State (degree in administration of justice, 1987).
TRANSACTIONS/CAREER NOTES: Selected by Buffalo Bills in first round (eighth pick overall) of 1987 draft. . . . Signed by Bills (August 9, 1987). . . . On injured reserve with knee injury (September 21-November 3, 1989).
PLAYING EXPERIENCE: Buffalo NFL, 1987-1990. . . . Games: 1987 (12), 1988 (13), 1989 (10), 1990 (16). Total: 51.
CHAMPIONSHIP GAME EXPERIENCE: Played in AFC championship game after 1988 and 1990 seasons. . . . Played in Super Bowl XXV after 1990 season.
RECORDS/HONORS: Named to THE SPORTING NEWS NFL All-Pro team, 1988. . . . Member of Pro Bowl squad after 1988 season; did not play. . . . Played in Pro Bowl after 1989 and 1990 seasons.
PRO STATISTICS: 1988—Intercepted one pass for no yards and recovered one fumble. 1989—Intercepted one pass for no yards.

CONLIN, CHRIS
C, COLTS

PERSONAL: Born June 7, 1965, at Philadelphia. . . . 6-4/290. . . . Full name: Christopher Howard Conlin.
HIGH SCHOOL: Bishop McDevitt (Wyncote, Pa.).
COLLEGE: Penn State.
TRANSACTIONS/CAREER NOTES: Selected by Miami Dolphins in fifth round (132nd pick overall) of 1987 NFL draft. . . . Signed by Dolphins (July 23, 1987). . . . On injured reserve with knee injury (December 4, 1987-remainder of season). . . . On physically unable to perform/active list with knee injury (July 12-August 12, 1988). . . . Transferred to reserve/physically unable to perform list with knee injury (August 23, 1988-entire season). . . . On injured reserve with knee injury (August 29-October 24, 1989). . . . Released by Dolphins (October 25, 1989). . . . Signed by Indianapolis Colts (April 16, 1990).
PLAYING EXPERIENCE: Miami NFL, 1987; Indianapolis NFL, 1990. . . . Games: 1987 (3), 1990 (16). Total: 19.

CONNER, DARION
LB, FALCONS

PERSONAL: Born September 28, 1967, at Macon, Ga. . . . 6-2/250.
HIGH SCHOOL: Noxubee County (Macon, Ga.).
COLLEGE: Jackson State.
TRANSACTIONS/CAREER NOTES: Selected by Atlanta Falcons in second round (27th pick overall) of 1990 NFL draft. . . . Signed by Falcons (July 12, 1990).
PLAYING EXPERIENCE: Atlanta NFL, 1990. . . . Games: 1990 (16).

COOK, MARV
TE, PATRIOTS

PERSONAL: Born February 24, 1966, at Iowa City, Ia. . . . 6-4/234. . . . Full name: Marvin Eugene Cook.
HIGH SCHOOL: West Branch (Ia.).
COLLEGE: Iowa.
TRANSACTIONS/CAREER NOTES: Selected by New England Patriots in third round (63rd pick overall) of 1989 NFL draft. . . . Signed by Patriots (August 1, 1989).
PRO STATISTICS: 1990—Fumbled twice.

			RECEIVING		
Year Team	G	No.	Yds.	Avg.	TD
1989— New England NFL......	16	3	13	4.3	0
1990— New England NFL......	16	51	455	8.9	5
Pro totals (2 years)........	32	54	468	8.7	5

COOK, TOI
CB, SAINTS

PERSONAL: Born December 3, 1964, at Chicago. . . . 5-11/188. . . . Full name: Toi Fitzgerald Cook. . . . First name pronounced TOY.
HIGH SCHOOL: Montclair (Calif.).
COLLEGE: Stanford.
TRANSACTIONS/CAREER NOTES: Selected by New Orleans Saints in eighth round (207th pick overall) of 1987 NFL draft. . . . Signed by Saints (July 24, 1987). . . . Granted free agency (February 1, 1990). . . . Re-signed by Saints (August 13, 1990).
MISCELLANEOUS: Selected by Minnesota Twins' organization in 38th round of 1987 free-agent baseball draft (June 2, 1987).
PRO STATISTICS: 1987—Returned one punt for three yards. 1989—Caught one pass for eight yards and fumbled once.

			INTERCEPTIONS		
Year Team	G	No.	Yds.	Avg.	TD
1987— New Orleans NFL.......	7	0	0		0
1988— New Orleans NFL.......	16	1	0	.0	0
1989— New Orleans NFL.......	16	3	81	27.0	1
1990— New Orleans NFL.......	16	2	55	27.5	0
Pro totals (4 years)........	55	6	136	22.7	1

COOKS, JOHNIE
LB, GIANTS

PERSONAL: Born November 23, 1958, at Leland, Miss. . . . 6-4/251. . . . Full name: Johnie Earl Cooks.
HIGH SCHOOL: Leland (Miss.).
COLLEGE: Mississippi State (degree in physical education).

TRANSACTIONS/CAREER NOTES: Selected by Baltimore Colts in first round (second pick overall) of 1982 NFL draft. . . . Franchise transferred to Indianapolis (March 31, 1984). . . . Released by Indianapolis Colts (September 13, 1988). . . . Awarded on waivers to New York Giants (September 15, 1988).
PLAYING EXPERIENCE: Baltimore NFL, 1982 and 1983; Indianapolis NFL, 1984-1987; Indianapolis (1)-New York Giants (13) NFL, 1988; New York Giants NFL, 1989 and 1990. . . . Games: 1982 (9), 1983 (16), 1984 (16), 1985 (16), 1986 (15), 1987 (10), 1988 (14), 1989 (16), 1990 (14). Total: 126.
CHAMPIONSHIP GAME EXPERIENCE: Member of New York Giants for NFC championship game after 1990 season; did not play. . . . Played in Super Bowl XXV after 1990 season.
RECORDS/HONORS: Named as linebacker on THE SPORTING NEWS college All-America team, 1981.
PRO STATISTICS: 1982—Recovered one fumble. 1983—Intercepted one pass for 15 yards, recovered two fumbles for 52 yards and a touchdown and fumbled once. 1985—Intercepted one pass for seven yards. 1986—Intercepted one pass for one yard. 1987—Intercepted one pass for two yards, recovered one fumble and fumbled once. 1988—Recovered one fumble.

COOPER, LOUIS
LB, DOLPHINS

PERSONAL: Born August 5, 1963, at Marion, S.C. . . . 6-2/238. . . . Full name: Alexander Louis Cooper.
HIGH SCHOOL: Marion (S.C.).
COLLEGE: West Carolina (degree in sports management, 1985).
TRANSACTIONS/CAREER NOTES: Selected by Orlando Renegades in sixth round (76th pick overall) of 1985 USFL draft. . . . Selected by Seattle Seahawks in 11th round (305th pick overall) of 1985 NFL draft. . . . Signed by Seahawks (July 17, 1985). . . . Released by Seahawks (August 27, 1985). . . . Signed as free agent by Kansas City Chiefs (September 17, 1985). . . . On injured reserve with ankle injury (October 14-November 20, 1985). . . . Activated after clearing procedural waivers (November 22, 1985). . . . Released by Chiefs (August 26, 1986). . . . Re-signed by Chiefs (September 2, 1986). . . . On injured reserve with elbow injury (November 10-December 12, 1988). . . . Released by Chiefs (September 4, 1989). . . . Re-signed by Chiefs (September 5, 1989). . . . Granted roster exemption (September 3-September 8, 1990). . . . Granted unconditional free agency (February 1, 1991). . . . Signed by Miami Dolphins (April 1, 1991).
PLAYING EXPERIENCE: Kansas City NFL, 1985-1990. . . . Games: 1985 (8), 1986 (16), 1987 (12), 1988 (11), 1989 (16), 1990 (16). Total: 79.
PRO STATISTICS: 1986—Recovered one fumble. 1987—Intercepted one pass for no yards. 1989—Recovered one fumble for six yards.

COOPER, RICHARD
OT, SAINTS

PERSONAL: Born November 1, 1964, at Memphis, Tenn. . . . 6-5/290. . . . Full name: Richard Warren Cooper.
HIGH SCHOOL: Melrose (Tenn.).
COLLEGE: Tennessee.
TRANSACTIONS/CAREER NOTES: Signed as free agent by Seattle Seahawks (May, 1988). . . . Released by Seahawks (August 1, 1988). . . . Signed as free agent by New Orleans Saints (February 2, 1989). . . . Released by Saints (September 5, 1989). . . . Signed by Saints to developmental squad (September 6, 1989). . . . Released by Saints (December 29, 1989). . . . Re-signed by Saints (February 2, 1990).
PLAYING EXPERIENCE: New Orleans NFL, 1990. . . . Games: 1990 (2).

COPELAND, DANNY
S, REDSKINS

PERSONAL: Born January 24, 1966, at Camilla, Ga. . . . 6-2/210. . . . Full name: Danny Lamar Copeland.
HIGH SCHOOL: Central (Thomasville, Ga.).
COLLEGE: Eastern Kentucky.
TRANSACTIONS/CAREER NOTES: Selected by Cleveland Browns in ninth round (244th pick overall) of 1988 NFL draft. . . . Signed by Browns (July 21, 1988). . . . On injured reserve with hamstring injury (August 23, 1988-entire season). . . . Granted unconditional free agency (February 1, 1989). . . . Signed by Kansas City Chiefs (March 27, 1989). . . . On inactive list (October 7 and 14, 1990). . . . Granted unconditional free agency (February 1, 1991). . . . Signed by Washington Redskins (April 1, 1991).
PRO STATISTICS: 1989—Recovered one fumble and fumbled once.

		— KICKOFF RETURNS —			
Year Team	G	No.	Yds.	Avg.	TD
1989—Kansas City NFL........	16	26	466	17.9	0
1990—Kansas City NFL........	14	0	0	0	0
Pro totals (2 years)........	30	26	466	17.9	0

CORNISH, FRANK
C/G, CHARGERS

PERSONAL: Born September 24, 1967, at Chicago. . . . 6-4/295. . . . Full name: Frank Edgar Cornish.
HIGH SCHOOL: Mt. Carmel (Ill.).
COLLEGE: UCLA.
TRANSACTIONS/CAREER NOTES: Selected by San Diego Chargers in sixth round (143rd pick overall) of 1990 NFL draft. . . . Signed by Chargers (July 19, 1990).
PLAYING EXPERIENCE: San Diego NFL, 1990. . . . Games: 1990 (16).

CORRINGTON, KIP
S, BRONCOS

PERSONAL: Born April 12, 1965, at Ames, Ia. . . . 6-0/175. . . . Full name: Kip Alan Corrington.
HIGH SCHOOL: A&M Consolidated (College Station, Tex.).
COLLEGE: Texas A&M (degree in philosophy, 1989).

TRANSACTIONS/CAREER NOTES: Selected by Detroit Lions in ninth round (223rd pick overall) of 1988 NFL draft.... Failed physical with knee injury (May 1, 1988).... Rights traded by Lions to Denver Broncos for conditional ninth-round pick in NFL draft (May 13, 1988).... Signed by Broncos (June 26, 1988).... On injured reserve with hip injury (August 22, 1988-entire season).
PLAYING EXPERIENCE: Denver NFL, 1989 and 1990.... Games: 1989 (16), 1990 (16). Total: 32.
CHAMPIONSHIP GAME EXPERIENCE: Played in AFC championship after 1989 season.... Played in Super Bowl XXIV after 1989 season.
PRO STATISTICS: 1989—Intercepted one pass for eight yards. 1990—Recovered one fumble.

COTTON, MARCUS
LB, SEAHAWKS

PERSONAL: Born August 11, 1966, at Los Angeles.... 6-3/237.... Full name: Marcus Glenn Cotton.
HIGH SCHOOL: Castlemont (Oakland, Calif.).
COLLEGE: Southern California.
TRANSACTIONS/CAREER NOTES: Selected by Atlanta Falcons in second round (28th pick overall) of 1988 NFL draft.... Signed by Falcons (May 27, 1988).... On inactive list (October 7 and 14, 1990).... Released by Falcons (November 13, 1990).... Awarded on waivers to Cleveland Browns (November 14, 1990).... Granted unconditional free agency (February 1, 1991).... Signed by Seattle Seahawks (April 1, 1991).
PLAYING EXPERIENCE: Atlanta NFL, 1988 and 1989; Atlanta (7)-Cleveland (7) NFL, 1990.... Games: 1988 (11), 1989 (16), 1990 (14). Total: 41.

COVERT, JIM
OT, BEARS

PERSONAL: Born March 22, 1960, at Conway, Pa.... 6-4/278.... Full name: James Paul Covert.
HIGH SCHOOL: Area (Freedom, Pa.).
COLLEGE: Pittsburgh.
TRANSACTIONS/CAREER NOTES: Selected by Tampa Bay Bandits in first round (12th pick overall) of 1983 USFL draft.... Selected by Chicago Bears in first round (sixth pick overall) of 1983 NFL draft.... Signed by Bears (July 20, 1983).... On injured reserve with back injury (September 30-November 5, 1988).... Granted free agency (February 1, 1990).... Re-signed by Bears (July 29, 1990).
PLAYING EXPERIENCE: Chicago NFL, 1983-1990.... Games: 1983 (16), 1984 (16), 1985 (15), 1986 (16), 1987 (9), 1988 (9), 1989 (15), 1990 (15). Total: 111.
CHAMPIONSHIP GAME EXPERIENCE: Played in NFC championship game after 1984, 1985 and 1988 seasons.... Played in Super Bowl XX after 1985 season.
RECORDS/HONORS: Played in Pro Bowl after 1985 and 1986 seasons.... Named to THE SPORTING NEWS NFL All-Pro team, 1985 and 1986.
PRO STATISTICS: 1983—Recovered one fumble. 1984—Recovered two fumbles. 1986—Recovered one fumble. 1987—Recovered one fumble. 1989—Recovered one fumble.

COX, AARON
WR, RAMS

PERSONAL: Born March 13, 1965, at Los Angeles.... 5-10/178.... Full name: Aaron Dion Cox.
HIGH SCHOOL: Dorsey (Los Angeles).
COLLEGE: Arizona State.
TRANSACTIONS/CAREER NOTES: Selected by Los Angeles Rams in first round (20th pick overall) of 1988 NFL draft.... Signed by Rams (July 19, 1988).... On inactive list (October 7 and December 2, 1990).
CHAMPIONSHIP GAME EXPERIENCE: Played in NFC championship game after 1989 season.
PRO STATISTICS: 1989—Recovered two fumbles for four yards and fumbled once.

| | | —— RECEIVING —— | | | |
Year	Team	G	No.	Yds.	Avg.	TD
1988— L.A. Rams NFL		16	28	590	21.1	5
1989— L.A. Rams NFL		16	20	340	17.0	3
1990— L.A. Rams NFL		14	17	266	15.6	0
Pro totals (3 years)		46	65	1196	18.4	8

COX, ARTHUR
TE, CHARGERS

PERSONAL: Born February 5, 1961, at Plant City, Fla.... 6-2/270.... Full name: Arthur Dean Cox.
HIGH SCHOOL: Plant City (Fla.).
COLLEGE: Texas Southern.
TRANSACTIONS/CAREER NOTES: Signed as free agent by Atlanta Falcons (May 4, 1983).... Granted free agency (February 1, 1988).... Withdrew qualifying offer (May 2, 1988).... Signed by San Diego Chargers (May 10, 1988).
PRO STATISTICS: 1983—Fumbled once. 1984—Fumbled once. 1986—Recovered two fumbles and fumbled once. 1987—Returned one kickoff for 11 yards and fumbled twice. 1990—Fumbled twice.

| | | —— RECEIVING —— | | | |
Year	Team	G	No.	Yds.	Avg.	TD
1983— Atlanta NFL		15	9	83	9.2	1
1984— Atlanta NFL		16	34	329	9.7	3
1985— Atlanta NFL		16	33	454	13.8	2
1986— Atlanta NFL		16	24	301	12.5	1
1987— Atlanta NFL		12	11	101	9.2	0
1988— San Diego NFL		16	18	144	8.0	0
1989— San Diego NFL		16	22	200	9.1	2
1990— San Diego NFL		16	14	93	6.6	1
Pro totals (8 years)		123	165	1705	10.3	10

COX, GREG

S/LB, 49ERS

PERSONAL: Born January 6, 1965, at Niagara Falls, N.Y. . . . 6-0/217. . . . Full name: Gregory Mark Cox. **HIGH SCHOOL:** Walnut Ridge (Columbus, O.). **COLLEGE:** Hartnell Community College (Calif.), then San Jose State. **TRANSACTIONS/CAREER NOTES:** Signed as free agent by San Francisco 49ers (May 23, 1988). . . . Granted unconditional free agency (February 1, 1989). . . . Signed by New York Giants (March 16, 1989). . . . Granted unconditional free agency (February 1, 1990). . . . Signed by San Francisco 49ers (March 29, 1990). . . . Released by 49ers (September 3, 1990). . . . Re-signed by 49ers (October 3, 1990). . . . On injured reserve with hamstring injury (January 11, 1991-remainder of 1990 season playoffs). **PLAYING EXPERIENCE:** San Francisco NFL, 1988; New York Giants NFL, 1989; San Francisco NFL, 1990. . . . Games: 1988 (15), 1989 (16), 1990 (13). Total: 44. **CHAMPIONSHIP GAME EXPERIENCE:** Played in NFC championship game after 1988 season. . . . Played in Super Bowl XXIII after 1988 season.

COX, ROBERT

OT, RAMS

PERSONAL: Born December 30, 1963, at San Francisco. . . . 6-5/285. . . . Full name: Robert Lloyd Cox. **HIGH SCHOOL:** Dublin (Calif.). **COLLEGE:** Chabot College (Calif.), then UCLA. **TRANSACTIONS/CAREER NOTES:** Selected by Arizona Outlaws in 1986 USFL territorial draft. . . . Selected by Los Angeles Rams in sixth round (144th pick overall) of 1986 NFL draft. . . . Signed by Rams (July 22, 1986). . . . On injured reserve with ankle injury (August 27, 1986-entire season). . . . On inactive list (October 14, 21, 29; and November 4 and 11, 1990). **PLAYING EXPERIENCE:** Los Angeles Rams NFL, 1987-1990. . . . Games: 1987 (10), 1988 (16), 1989 (16), 1990 (11). Total: 53. **CHAMPIONSHIP GAME EXPERIENCE:** Played in NFC championship game after 1989 season. **PRO STATISTICS:** 1987—Returned one kickoff for 12 yards.

COX, RON

LB, BEARS

PERSONAL: Born February 27, 1968, at Fresno, Calif. . . . 6-2/242. . . . Full name: Ron E. Cox. **HIGH SCHOOL:** Washington Union (Fresno, Calif.). **COLLEGE:** Fresno State. **TRANSACTIONS/CAREER NOTES:** Selected by Chicago Bears in second round (33rd pick overall) of 1990 NFL draft. . . . Signed by Bears (July 25, 1990). . . . On inactive list (December 2, 23 and 29, 1990). **PLAYING EXPERIENCE:** Chicago NFL, 1990. . . . Games: 1990 (13).

CRAIG, ROGER

RB, RAIDERS

PERSONAL: Born July 10, 1960, at Davenport, Ia. . . . 6-0/225. . . . Full name: Roger Timothy Craig. **HIGH SCHOOL:** Central (Davenport, Ia.). **COLLEGE:** Nebraska. **TRANSACTIONS/CAREER NOTES:** Selected by Boston Breakers in 1983 USFL territorial draft. . . . Selected by San Francisco 49ers in second round (49th pick overall) of 1983 NFL draft. . . . Signed by 49ers (June 13, 1983). . . . Crossed picket line during players' strike (October 7, 1987). . . . On inactive list (October 14, 21, 28; and December 23 and 30, 1990). . . . Granted unconditional free agency (February 1, 1991). . . . Signed by Los Angeles Raiders (April 1, 1991). **CHAMPIONSHIP GAME EXPERIENCE:** Played in NFC championship game after 1983, 1984 and 1988-1990 seasons. . . . Played in Super Bowl XIX after 1984 season, Super Bowl XXIII after 1988 season and Super Bowl XXIV after 1989 season. **RECORDS/HONORS:** Established NFL record for most pass receptions by running back, season (92), 1985. . . . Played in Pro Bowl after 1985 and 1987-1989 seasons. . . . Named to THE SPORTING NEWS NFL All-Pro team, 1988. **PRO STATISTICS:** 1983—Recovered one fumble. 1984—Recovered one fumble. 1986—Recovered one fumble. 1987—Recovered two fumbles. 1988—Returned two kickoffs for 32 yards and recovered two fumbles. 1989—Recovered one fumble.

		RUSHING				RECEIVING				TOTAL		
Year Team	G	Att.	Yds.	Avg.	TD	No.	Yds.	Avg.	TD	TD	Pts.	F.
1983— San Francisco NFL	16	176	725	4.1	8	48	427	8.9	4	12	72	6
1984— San Francisco NFL	16	155	649	4.2	7	71	675	9.5	3	10	60	3
1985— San Francisco NFL	16	214	1050	4.9	9	*92	1016	11.0	6	15	90	5
1986— San Francisco NFL	16	204	830	4.1	7	81	624	7.7	0	7	42	4
1987— San Francisco NFL	14	215	815	3.8	3	66	492	7.5	1	4	24	5
1988— San Francisco NFL	16	310	1502	4.8	9	76	534	7.0	1	10	60	8
1989— San Francisco NFL	16	271	1054	3.9	6	49	473	9.7	1	7	42	4
1990— San Francisco NFL	11	141	439	3.1	1	25	201	8.0	0	1	6	2
Pro totals (8 years)	121	1686	7064	4.2	49	508	4442	8.7	16	66	396	37

CRAWFORD, ELBERT

C/G, PATRIOTS

PERSONAL: Born June 20, 1966, at Chicago. . . . 6-3/280. **HIGH SCHOOL:** Hall (Little Rock, Ark.). **COLLEGE:** Arkansas (degree in communications). **TRANSACTIONS/CAREER NOTES:** Selected by Los Angeles Rams in eighth round (216th pick overall) of 1990 NFL draft. . . . Signed by Rams (July 11, 1990). . . . Released by Rams (September 3, 1990). . . . Signed by New England Patriots (September 12, 1990). **PLAYING EXPERIENCE:** New England NFL, 1990. . . . Games: 1990 (14).

CRISWELL, JEFF

OT, JETS

PERSONAL: Born March 7, 1964, at Grinnell, Ia. . . . 6-7/291. . . . Full name: Jeffrey L. Criswell. **HIGH SCHOOL:** Lynnville-Sully (Sully, Ia.). **COLLEGE:** Graceland, Ia. (bachelor of arts degree in physical education, health and sec-

ondary education).
TRANSACTIONS/CAREER NOTES: Signed as free-agent replacement player by Indianapolis Colts (September 26, 1987).... Released by Colts (October 19, 1987).... Signed as free agent by New York Jets (May 3, 1988).
PLAYING EXPERIENCE: Indianapolis NFL, 1987; New York Jets NFL, 1988-1990.... Games: 1987 (3), 1988 (15), 1989 (16), 1990 (16). Total: 50.
PRO STATISTICS: 1989—Recovered one fumble. 1990—Recovered one fumble.

CROCKETT, RAY
CB, LIONS

PERSONAL: Born January 5, 1967, at Dallas.... 5-9/181.... Full name: Donald Ray Crockett.
HIGH SCHOOL: Duncanville (Tex.).
COLLEGE: Baylor.
TRANSACTIONS/CAREER NOTES: Selected by Detroit Lions in fourth round (86th pick overall) of 1989 NFL draft.... Signed by Lions (July 18, 1989).
PRO STATISTICS: 1989—Returned one kickoff for eight yards and recovered one fumble. 1990—Recovered two fumbles for 22 yards and a touchdown.

| | | | — INTERCEPTIONS — | | |
Year	Team	G	No.	Yds.	Avg.	TD
1989—	Detroit NFL	16	1	5	5.0	0
1990—	Detroit NFL	16	3	17	5.7	0
	Pro totals (2 years)	32	4	22	5.5	0

CROCKETT, WILLIS
LB, COWBOYS

PERSONAL: Born August 25, 1966, at Douglas, Ga.... 6-3/234.... Full name: Willis Robert Crockett.
HIGH SCHOOL: Coffee County (Douglas, Ga.).
COLLEGE: Georgia Tech.
TRANSACTIONS/CAREER NOTES: Selected by Dallas Cowboys in fifth round (119th pick overall) of 1989 NFL draft.... Signed by Cowboys (July 27, 1989).... On injured reserve with knee injury (August 28, 1989-entire season).... Released by Cowboys (September 2, 1990).... Re-signed by Cowboys (September 13, 1990).... On inactive list (October 14 and 28, 1990).
PLAYING EXPERIENCE: Dallas NFL, 1990.... Games: 1990 (13).

CROSS, HOWARD
TE, GIANTS

PERSONAL: Born August 8, 1967, at Huntsville, Ala.... 6-5/245.... Full name: Howard E. Cross.
HIGH SCHOOL: New Hope (Ala.).
COLLEGE: Alabama.
TRANSACTIONS/CAREER NOTES: Selected by New York Giants in sixth round (158th pick overall) of 1989 NFL draft.... Signed by Giants (July 24, 1989).
CHAMPIONSHIP GAME EXPERIENCE: Played in NFC championship game after 1990 season.... Played in Super Bowl XXV after 1990 season.
PRO STATISTICS: 1989—Fumbled once. 1990—Returned one kickoff for 10 yards.

| | | | — RECEIVING — | | |
Year	Team	G	No.	Yds.	Avg.	TD
1989—	N.Y. Giants NFL	16	6	107	17.8	1
1990—	N.Y. Giants NFL	16	8	106	13.3	0
	Pro totals (2 years)	32	14	213	15.2	1

CROSS, JEFF
DE, DOLPHINS

PERSONAL: Born March 25, 1966, at Riverside, Calif.... 6-4/272.... Full name: Jeffrey Allen Cross.
HIGH SCHOOL: Palo Verde Valley (Blythe, Calif.).
COLLEGE: Riverside City College (Calif.), then Missouri.
TRANSACTIONS/CAREER NOTES: Selected by Miami Dolphins in ninth round (239th pick overall) of 1988 NFL draft.... Signed by Dolphins (July 11, 1988).
PLAYING EXPERIENCE: Miami NFL, 1988-1990.... Games: 1988 (16), 1989 (16), 1990 (16). Total: 48.
RECORDS/HONORS: Played in Pro Bowl after 1990 season.
PRO STATISTICS: 1990—Recovered two fumbles.

CRUDUP, DERRICK
S, RAIDERS

PERSONAL: Born February 15, 1965, at Delray Beach, Fla.... 6-2/215.
HIGH SCHOOL: Boca Raton (Fla.).
COLLEGE: Florida, then Oklahoma.
TRANSACTIONS/CAREER NOTES: Selected by Los Angeles Raiders in seventh round (171st pick overall) of 1988 NFL draft.... Signed by Raiders (July 13, 1988).... On injured reserve with back injury (August 29, 1988-entire season).... Released by Raiders (September 27, 1989).... Re-signed by Raiders to developmental squad (October 4, 1989).... On developmental squad (October 4-October 11, 1989).... Activated after clearing procedural waivers (October 13, 1989)... Released by Raiders (October 19, 1989).... Re-signed by Raiders to developmental squad (October 23, 1989).... On developmental squad (October 23-November 29, 1989).... Released by Raiders (November 30, 1989).... Re-signed by Raiders to developmental squad (December 6, 1989).... On developmental squad (December 6, 1989-remainder of season).... Released by Raiders (January 29, 1990).... Re-signed by Raiders (April 2, 1990).... Released by Raiders (September 3, 1990).... Re-signed by Raiders (May 27, 1991).
PLAYING EXPERIENCE: Los Angeles Raiders NFL, 1989.... Games: 1989 (4).

CUNNINGHAM, PAT

OT, COLTS

PERSONAL: Born January 4, 1969, at Los Angeles. . . . 6-6/312. . . . Full name: Patrick Dante Ross Cunningham.
HIGH SCHOOL: Beverly Hills (Calif.).
COLLEGE: Sacramento Community College (Calif.), then Texas A&M.
TRANSACTIONS/CAREER NOTES: Selected by Indianapolis Colts in fourth round (106th pick overall) of 1990 NFL draft. . . . Signed by Colts (July 17, 1990). . . . On inactive list (September 16, 23; October 7, 21, 28; November 5, 11, 18, 25; and December 9 and 16, 1990).
PLAYING EXPERIENCE: Indianapolis NFL, 1990. . . . Games: 1990 (2).

CUNNINGHAM, RANDALL

QB, EAGLES

PERSONAL: Born March 27, 1963, at Santa Barbara, Calif. . . . 6-4/205. . . . Brother of Sam Cunningham, running back with New England Patriots, 1973-1979, 1981 and 1982.
HIGH SCHOOL: Santa Barbara (Calif.).
COLLEGE: UNLV.
TRANSACTIONS/CAREER NOTES: Selected by Arizona Outlaws in 1985 USFL territorial draft. . . . Selected by Philadelphia Eagles in second round (37th pick overall) of 1985 NFL draft. . . . Signed by Eagles (July 22, 1985).
RECORDS/HONORS: Tied NFL record for most own fumbles recovered, game (4), against Los Angeles Raiders (November 30, 1986); most fumbles recovered, own and opponents', game (4), against Los Angeles Raiders (November 30, 1986). . . . Named as punter on THE SPORTING NEWS college All-America team, 1984. . . . Played in Pro Bowl after 1988-1990 seasons.
PRO STATISTICS: Passer rating points: 1985 (29.8), 1986 (72.9), 1987 (83.0), 1988 (77.6), 1989 (75.5), 1990 (91.6). Career: 78.8. . . . 1986—Punted twice for 27.0 avg. and recovered four fumbles. 1987—Caught one pass for minus three yards and recovered six fumbles and fumbled 12 times for minus seven yards. 1988—Punted three times for 55.7 avg. and recovered six fumbles. 1989—Punted six times for 53.2 avg. and recovered four fumbles and fumbled 17 times for minus six yards. 1990—Recovered three fumbles and fumbled nine times for minus four yards.

				PASSING						RUSHING				TOTAL	
Year Team	G	Att.	Cmp.	Pct.	Yds.	TD	Int.	Avg.	Att.	Yds.	Avg.	TD	TD	Pts.	F.
1985— Philadelphia NFL	6	81	34	42.0	548	1	8	6.77	29	205	7.1	0	0	0	3
1986— Philadelphia NFL	15	209	111	53.1	1391	8	7	6.66	66	540	8.2	5	5	30	7
1987— Philadelphia NFL	12	406	223	54.9	2786	23	12	6.86	76	505	6.6	3	3	18	*12
1988— Philadelphia NFL	16	560	301	53.8	3808	24	16	6.80	93	624	6.7	6	6	36	*12
1989— Philadelphia NFL	16	532	290	54.5	3400	21	15	6.39	104	621	*6.0	4	4	24	17
1990— Philadelphia NFL	16	465	271	58.3	3466	30	13	7.45	118	942	*8.0	5	5	30	9
Pro totals (6 years)	81	2253	1230	54.6	15399	107	71	6.83	486	3437	7.1	23	23	138	60

CURTIS, SCOTT

LB, BRONCOS

PERSONAL: Born December 26, 1964, at Burlington, Vt. . . . 6-1/230. . . . Full name: Alston Scott Curtis.
HIGH SCHOOL: Lynnfield (Mass.).
COLLEGE: New Hampshire.
TRANSACTIONS/CAREER NOTES: Signed as free agent by Philadelphia Eagles (April 27, 1988). . . . Granted unconditional free agency (February 1, 1989). . . . Signed by Denver Broncos (February 28, 1989). . . . On inactive list (November 18, 1990). . . . On injured reserve with knee injury (November 20, 1990-remainder of season).
PLAYING EXPERIENCE: Philadelphia NFL, 1988; Denver NFL, 1989 and 1990. . . . Games: 1988 (16), 1989 (16), 1990 (9). Total: 41.
CHAMPIONSHIP GAME EXPERIENCE: Played in AFC championship game after 1989 season. . . . Played in Super Bowl XXIV after 1989 season.

CURTIS, TRAVIS

S, JETS

PERSONAL: Born September 27, 1965, at Washington, D.C. . . . 5-10/180. . . . Full name: Travis Fennell Curtis.
HIGH SCHOOL: Winston Churchill (Potomac, Md.).
COLLEGE: West Virginia (degree in graphic design).
TRANSACTIONS/CAREER NOTES: Signed as free agent by St. Louis Cardinals (May 20, 1987). . . . Released by Cardinals (September 7, 1987). . . . Re-signed by Cardinals (September 9, 1987). . . . Crossed picket line during players' strike (October 14, 1987). . . . Franchise transferred to Phoenix (March 15, 1988). . . . On injured reserve with ankle injury (November 22-December 7, 1988). . . . Re-signed after clearing procedural waivers (December 8, 1988). . . . Lost to Washington Redskins in procedural waivers (December 9, 1988). . . . Granted unconditional free agency (February 1, 1989). . . . Signed by Minnesota Vikings (March 16, 1989). . . . Granted unconditional free agency (February 1, 1990). . . . Signed by New York Jets (March 8, 1990). . . . On inactive list (December 22, 1990). . . . On injured reserve with shoulder injury (December 28, 1990-remainder of season).
PRO STATISTICS: 1989—Returned one kickoff for 18 yards. 1990—Recovered one fumble.

		INTERCEPTIONS			
Year Team	G	No.	Yds.	Avg.	TD
1987— St. Louis NFL	13	5	65	13.0	0
1988— Pho.(12)-Was.(1) NFL	13	1	18	18.0	0
1989— Minnesota NFL	16	0	0		0
1990— N.Y. Jets NFL	14	2	45	22.5	0
Pro totals (4 years)	56	8	128	16.0	0

DID YOU KNOW. . .

. . .that the Washington Redskins have had just four No. 1 draft picks since 1968?

DALLAFIOR, KEN
G/C, LIONS

PERSONAL: Born August 26, 1959, at Royal Oak, Mich. . . . 6-4/279. . . . Full name: Kenneth Ray Dallafior. . . . Name pronounced DAL-uh-for.
HIGH SCHOOL: Madison (Madison Heights, Mich.).
COLLEGE: Minnesota (bachelor of arts and science degree in business studies, 1982).
TRANSACTIONS/CAREER NOTES: Selected by Pittsburgh Steelers in fifth round (124th pick overall) of 1982 NFL draft. . . . On injured reserve with sprained neck (September 6, 1982-entire season). . . . Released by Steelers (August 29, 1983). . . . Signed as free agent by Michigan Panthers of USFL (October 26, 1983). . . . Not protected in merger of Michigan Panthers and Oakland Invaders. . . . Selected by New Jersey Generals (December 6, 1984). . . . Released by Generals (January 28, 1985). . . . Signed as free agent by San Diego Chargers (June 21, 1985). . . . Released by Chargers (September 2, 1985). . . . Re-signed by Chargers (December 4, 1985). . . . On injured reserve with knee injury (August 26-October 4, 1986). . . . Activated after clearing procedural waivers (October 6, 1986). . . . Released by Chargers (August 30, 1988). . . . Re-signed by Chargers (September 21, 1988). . . . Granted unconditional free agency (February 1, 1989). . . . Signed by Detroit Lions (April 1, 1989).
PLAYING EXPERIENCE: Michigan USFL, 1984: San Diego NFL, 1985-1988; Detroit NFL, 1989 and 1990. . . . Games: 1984 (18), 1985 (3), 1986 (12), 1987 (8), 1988 (13), 1989 (16), 1990 (16). Total NFL: 68. Total Pro: 86.
PRO STATISTICS: 1988—Recovered two fumbles. 1989—Returned two kickoffs for 13 yards. 1990—Recovered one fumble.

DANIEL, EUGENE
DB, COLTS

PERSONAL: Born May 4, 1961, at Baton Rouge, La. . . . 5-11/188. . . . Full name: Eugene Daniel Jr.
HIGH SCHOOL: Robert E. Lee (Baton Rouge, La.).
COLLEGE: Louisiana State (degree in marketing).
TRANSACTIONS/CAREER NOTES: Selected by New Orleans Breakers in 1984 USFL territorial draft. . . . Selected by Indianapolis Colts in eighth round (205th pick overall) of 1984 NFL draft. . . . Signed by Colts (June 21, 1984). . . . On inactive list (October 7, 1990).
PRO STATISTICS: 1985—Returned one punt for six yards, recovered three fumbles for 25 yards and fumbled once. 1986—Returned blocked punt 13 yards for a touchdown and recovered one fumble. 1989—Recovered one fumble for five yards. 1990—Returned one punt for no yards.

			— INTERCEPTIONS —			
Year	Team	G	No.	Yds.	Avg.	TD
1984—	Indianapolis NFL	15	6	25	4.2	0
1985—	Indianapolis NFL	16	8	53	6.6	0
1986—	Indianapolis NFL	15	3	11	3.7	0
1987—	Indianapolis NFL	12	2	34	17.0	0
1988—	Indianapolis NFL	16	2	44	22.0	1
1989—	Indianapolis NFL	15	1	34	34.0	0
1990—	Indianapolis NFL	15	0	0		0
Pro totals (7 years)		104	22	201	9.1	1

DARWIN, MATT
OT, EAGLES

PERSONAL: Born March 11, 1963, at Houston. . . . 6-4/275. . . . Full name: Matthew Wayne Darwin.
HIGH SCHOOL: Cheyenne Mountain (Colorado Springs, Colo.) and Klein (Houston).
COLLEGE: Texas A&M.
TRANSACTIONS/CAREER NOTES: Selected by Houston Gamblers in 1985 USFL territorial draft. . . . Selected by Dallas Cowboys in fifth round (119th pick overall) of 1985 NFL draft. . . . On reserve/did not sign list (entire 1985 season-April 28, 1986). . . . Selected by Philadelphia Eagles in fourth round (106th pick overall) of 1986 NFL draft. . . . Signed by Eagles (July 31, 1986). . . . On injured reserve with knee injury (December 21, 1989-remainder of season). . . . On physically unable to perform list with knee injury (August 2-August 15, 1990). . . . On inactive list (September 23, 1990). . . . On injured reserve with knee injury (September 28, 1990-remainder of regular season and playoffs).
PLAYING EXPERIENCE: Philadelphia NFL, 1986-1990. . . . Games: 1986 (16), 1987 (12), 1988 (16), 1989 (15), 1990 (2). Total: 61.
PRO STATISTICS: 1987—Recovered one fumble. 1988—Recovered one fumble.

DAVIDSON, JEFF
G, BRONCOS

PERSONAL: Born October 3, 1967, at Akron, O. . . . 6-5/309. . . . Full name: Jeffrey John Davidson.
HIGH SCHOOL: Westerville North (Westerville, O.).
COLLEGE: Ohio State.
TRANSACTIONS/CAREER NOTES: Selected by Denver Broncos in fifth round (111th pick overall) of 1990 NFL draft. . . . Signed by Broncos (July 18, 1990). . . . On inactive list (November 4, 11; and December 23 and 30, 1990).
PLAYING EXPERIENCE: Denver NFL, 1990. . . . Games: 1990 (12).

DAVIDSON, KENNY
DE, STEELERS

PERSONAL: Born August 17, 1967, at Shreveport, La. . . . 6-5/272. . . . Full name: Kenneth Darrell Davidson.
HIGH SCHOOL: Huntington (Shreveport, La.).
COLLEGE: Louisiana State (bachelor of science degree in business administration, 1991).
TRANSACTIONS/CAREER NOTES: Selected by Pittsburgh Steelers in second round (43rd pick overall) of 1990 NFL draft. . . . Signed by Steelers (July 19, 1990).
PLAYING EXPERIENCE: Pittsburgh NFL, 1990. . . . Games: 1990 (14).

DAVIS, BRIAN
CB, SEAHAWKS

PERSONAL: Born August 31, 1963, at Phoenix.... 6-2/190.
HIGH SCHOOL: Cortez (Phoenix).
COLLEGE: Glendale Community College (Ariz.), then Nebraska.
TRANSACTIONS/CAREER NOTES: Selected by Washington Redskins in second round (30th pick overall) of 1987 NFL draft.... Signed by Redskins (July 26, 1987).... On injured reserve with hamstring injury (November 3-December 5, 1987).... On injured reserve with quadricep injury (November 24, 1988-remainder of season).... On inactive list (November 4, 1990).... Released by Redskins (November 16, 1990).... Signed by Seattle Seahawks (July 12, 1991).
PLAYING EXPERIENCE: Washington NFL, 1987-1990.... Games: 1987 (7), 1988 (9), 1989 (15), 1990 (7). Total: 38.
CHAMPIONSHIP GAME EXPERIENCE: Played in NFC championship game after 1987 season.... Played in Super Bowl XXII after 1987 season.
PRO STATISTICS: 1987—Recovered one fumble for 11 yards. 1988—Intercepted one pass for 11 yards. 1989—Intercepted four passes for 40 yards and returned one punt for three yards.

DAVIS, DARRELL
DE, JETS

PERSONAL: Born March 10, 1966, at Houston.... 6-2/264.... Full name: Darrell O. Davis.
HIGH SCHOOL: Midland Senior (Midland, Tex.).
COLLEGE: Texas Christian (bachelor of science degree in criminal justice, 1990).
TRANSACTIONS/CAREER NOTES: Selected by New York Jets in 12th round (306th pick overall) of 1990 NFL draft.... Signed by Jets (July 12, 1990).... On inactive list (October 7, 1990).
PLAYING EXPERIENCE: New York Jets NFL, 1990.... Games: 1990 (15).
PRO STATISTICS: 1990—Recovered one fumble in end zone for a touchdown.

DAVIS, ERIC
CB, 49ERS

PERSONAL: Born January 26, 1968, at Anniston, Ala.... 5-11/178.... Full name: Eric Wayne Davis.
HIGH SCHOOL: Anniston (Ala.).
COLLEGE: Jacksonville State.
TRANSACTIONS/CAREER NOTES: Selected by San Francisco 49ers in second round (53rd pick overall) of 1990 NFL draft.... Signed by 49ers (July 28, 1990).
CHAMPIONSHIP GAME EXPERIENCE: Played in NFC championship game after 1990 season.
PRO STATISTICS: 1990—Recovered one fumble for 34 yards.

		—INTERCEPTIONS—				—PUNT RETURNS—				—TOTAL—		
Year Team	G	No.	Yds.	Avg.	TD	No.	Yds.	Avg.	TD	TD	Pts.	F.
1990— San Francisco NFL	16	1	13	13.0	0	5	38	7.6	0	0	0	0
Pro totals (1 year)	16	1	13	13.0	0	5	38	7.6	0	0	0	0

DAVIS, GREG
PK, CARDINALS

PERSONAL: Born October 29, 1965, at Rome, Ga.... 6-0/200.... Full name: Gregory Brian Davis.
HIGH SCHOOL: Lakeside (Atlanta).
COLLEGE: The Citadel (degree in physical education, 1987).
TRANSACTIONS/CAREER NOTES: Selected by Tampa Bay Buccaneers in ninth round (246th pick overall) of 1987 NFL draft.... Signed by Buccaneers (July 18, 1987).... Released by Buccaneers (September 7, 1987).... Signed as free agent replacement player by Atlanta Falcons (September 24, 1987).... Released by Falcons (October 19, 1987).... Awarded on waivers to Tampa Bay Buccaneers (October 20, 1987).... Released by Buccaneers (November 2, 1987).... Signed as free agent by Atlanta Falcons for 1988 (December 24, 1987).... Granted unconditional free agency (February 1, 1989).... Signed by New England Patriots (March 9, 1989).... Released by Patriots (November 8, 1989).... Signed by Atlanta Falcons (November 15, 1989).... Granted unconditional free agency (February 1, 1991).... Signed by Phoenix Cardinals (February 21, 1991).
PRO STATISTICS: 1987—Punted six times for 31.8 avg.

		—— PLACE-KICKING ——				
Year Team	G	XPM	XPA	FGM	FGA	Pts.
1987— Atlanta NFL	3	6	6	3	4	15
1988— Atlanta NFL	16	25	27	19	30	82
1989— N.E. (9)-Atl. (6) NFL	15	25	28	23	34	94
1990— Atlanta NFL	16	40	40	22	33	106
Pro totals (4 years)	50	96	101	67	101	297

DAVIS, JOHN
OT, BILLS

PERSONAL: Born August 22, 1965, at Ellijay, Ga.... 6-4/310.... Full name: John Henry Davis.
HIGH SCHOOL: Gilmer (Ellijay, Ga.).
COLLEGE: Georgia Tech.
TRANSACTIONS/CAREER NOTES: Selected by Houston Oilers in 11th round (287th pick overall) of 1987 NFL draft.... Signed by Oilers (July 24, 1987).... On injured reserve with ankle injury (December 19, 1987-remainder of season).... Granted unconditional free agency (February 1, 1989).... Signed by Buffalo Bills (March 3, 1989).
PLAYING EXPERIENCE: Houston NFL, 1987 and 1988; Buffalo NFL, 1989 and 1990.... Games: 1987 (6), 1988 (13), 1989 (16), 1990 (16). Total: 51.
CHAMPIONSHIP GAME EXPERIENCE: Played in AFC championship game after 1990 season.... Played in Super Bowl XXV after 1990 season.

DAVIS, KENNETH
RB, BILLS

PERSONAL: Born April 10, 1962, at Williamson County, Tex.... 5-10/209.... Full name: Kenneth Earl Davis.
HIGH SCHOOL: Temple (Tex.).
COLLEGE: Texas Christian.

TRANSACTIONS/CAREER NOTES: Selected by Green Bay Packers in second round (41st pick overall) of 1986 NFL draft.... Signed by Packers (May 17, 1986).... On injured reserve with ankle injury (October 21-December 10, 1988).... Granted unconditional free agency (February 1, 1989).... Signed by Buffalo Bills (March 3, 1989).
CHAMPIONSHIP GAME EXPERIENCE: Played in AFC championship game after 1990 season. ... Played in Super Bowl XXV after 1990 season.
RECORDS/HONORS: Named as running back on THE SPORTING NEWS college All-America team, 1984.
PRO STATISTICS: 1990—Recovered one fumble.

Year	Team	G	Att.	Yds.	Avg.	TD	No.	Yds.	Avg.	TD	No.	Yds.	Avg.	TD	TD	Pts.	F.
			RUSHING				RECEIVING				KICKOFF RETURNS				TOTAL		
1986— Green Bay NFL.......		16	114	519	4.6	0	21	142	6.8	1	12	231	19.3	0	1	6	2
1987— Green Bay NFL.......		10	109	413	3.8	3	14	110	7.9	0	0	0		0	3	18	2
1988— Green Bay NFL.......		9	39	121	3.1	1	11	81	7.4	0	0	0		0	1	6	0
1989— Buffalo NFL............		16	29	149	5.1	1	6	92	15.3	2	3	52	17.3	0	3	18	2
1990— Buffalo NFL............		16	64	302	4.7	4	9	78	8.7	1	0	0		0	5	30	1
Pro totals (5 years)		67	355	1504	4.2	9	61	503	8.2	4	15	283	18.9	0	13	78	7

DAVIS, LORENZO
WR, STEELERS

PERSONAL: Born February 12, 1968, at Ft. Lauderdale, Fla.... 5-11/188.... Full name: Lorenzo Edward Davis.
HIGH SCHOOL: Dillard (Ft. Lauderdale, Fla.).
COLLEGE: Youngstown State.
TRANSACTIONS/CAREER NOTES: Signed as free agent by Pittsburgh Steelers (May 3, 1990).... Released by Steelers (September 4, 1990).... Signed by Steelers to practice squad (October 1, 1990).... Activated (October 29, 1990).... Released by Steelers (November 30, 1990).... Re-signed by Steelers to practice squad (December 4, 1990).... Signed by Steelers for 1991 (February 14, 1991).
PLAYING EXPERIENCE: Pittsburgh NFL, 1990.... Games: 1990 (4).

DAVIS, REUBEN
DL, BUCCANEERS

PERSONAL: Born May 7, 1965, at Greensboro, N.C.... 6-4/295.... Full name: Reuben Cordell Davis.
HIGH SCHOOL: Grimsley (Greensboro, N.C.).
COLLEGE: North Carolina (degree in journalism and mass communications, 1988).
TRANSACTIONS/CAREER NOTES: Selected by Tampa Bay Buccaneers in ninth round (225th pick overall) of 1988 NFL draft.... Signed by Buccaneers (July 6, 1988).... Granted free agency (February 1, 1990).... Re-signed by Buccaneers (July 22, 1990).
PLAYING EXPERIENCE: Tampa Bay NFL, 1988-1990.... Games: 1988 (16), 1989 (16), 1990 (16). Total: 48.
PRO STATISTICS: 1989—Intercepted one pass for 13 yards and a touchdown and recovered two fumbles. 1990—Recovered one fumble.

DAVIS, SCOTT
DE, RAIDERS

PERSONAL: Born August 7, 1965, at Joliet, Ill.... 6-7/275.
HIGH SCHOOL: Plainfield (Ill.).
COLLEGE: Illinois (degree in marketing, 1988).
TRANSACTIONS/CAREER NOTES: Selected by Los Angeles Raiders in first round (25th pick overall) of 1988 NFL draft.... Signed by Raiders (July 14, 1988).
PLAYING EXPERIENCE: Los Angeles Raiders NFL, 1988-1990.... Games: 1988 (15), 1989 (14), 1990 (16). Total: 45.
CHAMPIONSHIP GAME EXPERIENCE: Played in AFC championship game after 1990 season.
PRO STATISTICS: 1989—Recovered one fumble.

DAVIS, TRAVIS
NT, COLTS

PERSONAL: Born May 10, 1966, at Warren, O.... 6-2/285.... Full name: Travis Neil Davis.
HIGH SCHOOL: Warren G. Harding (Warren, O.).
COLLEGE: Michigan State (degree in marketing management).
TRANSACTIONS/CAREER NOTES: Selected by Phoenix Cardinals in fourth round (85th pick overall) of 1990 NFL draft.... Signed by Cardinals (July 29, 1990).... Released by Cardinals (September 3, 1990).... Signed by New Orleans Saints to practice squad (October 1, 1990).... Activated (December 19, 1990).... Granted unconditional free agency (February 1, 1991).... Signed by Indianapolis Colts (April 1, 1991).
PLAYING EXPERIENCE: New Orleans NFL, 1990.... Games: 1990 (2).

DAVIS, WENDELL
WR, BEARS

PERSONAL: Born January 3, 1966, at Shreveport, La.... 5-11/188.... Full name: Wendell Tyrone Davis.
HIGH SCHOOL: Fair Park (Shreveport, La.).
COLLEGE: Louisiana State.
TRANSACTIONS/CAREER NOTES: Selected by Chicago Bears in first round (27th pick overall) of 1988 NFL draft.... Signed by Bears (July 20, 1988).... On inactive list (September 30 and October 7, 1990).
CHAMPIONSHIP GAME EXPERIENCE: Played in NFC championship game after 1988 season.
RECORDS/HONORS: Named as wide receiver on THE SPORTING NEWS college All-America team, 1986 and 1987.
PRO STATISTICS: 1988—Rushed once for three yards, returned three punts for 17 yards, recovered one fumble and fumbled twice. 1990—Fumbled once.

Year	Team	G	No.	Yds.	Avg.	TD
				RECEIVING		
1988— Chicago NFL		16	15	220	14.7	0
1989— Chicago NFL		14	26	397	15.3	3
1990— Chicago NFL		14	39	572	14.7	3
Pro totals (3 years)		44	80	1189	14.9	6

DAWKINS, DALE
WR, JETS

PERSONAL: Born October 30, 1966, at Vero Beach, Fla. . . . 6-1/190. . . . Full name: Dale V. Dawkins.
HIGH SCHOOL: Vero Beach Senior (Vero Beach, Fla.).
COLLEGE: Miami, Fla. (degree in sociology, 1990).
TRANSACTIONS/CAREER NOTES: Selected by New York Jets in ninth round (223rd pick overall) of 1990 NFL draft. . . . Signed by Jets (July 20, 1990). . . . On injured reserve with knee injury (September 4-October 13, 1990).

Year	Team	G	No.	Yds.	Avg.	TD
				RECEIVING		
1990— N.Y. Jets NFL		11	5	68	13.6	0
Pro totals (1 year)		11	5	68	13.6	0

DAWSON, DERMONTTI
C, STEELERS

PERSONAL: Born July 17, 1965, at Lexington, Ky. . . . 6-2/274. . . . Full name: Dermontti Farra Dawson. . . . Cousin of George Adams, running back with New England Patriots; and Marc Logan, fullback with Miami Dolphins.
HIGH SCHOOL: Bryan Station (Lexington, Ky.).
COLLEGE: Kentucky (bachelor of science degree in education, 1988).
TRANSACTIONS/CAREER NOTES: Selected by Pittsburgh Steelers in second round (44th pick overall) of 1988 NFL draft. . . . Signed by Steelers (August 1, 1988). . . . On injured reserve with knee injury (September 26-November 26, 1988).
PLAYING EXPERIENCE: Pittsburgh NFL, 1988-1990. . . . Games: 1988 (8), 1989 (16), 1990 (16). Total: 40.

DAWSON, DOUG
G/C, OILERS

PERSONAL: Born December 27, 1961, at Houston. . . . 6-3/288. . . . Full name: Douglas Arlin Dawson.
HIGH SCHOOL: Memorial (Houston).
COLLEGE: Texas.
TRANSACTIONS/CAREER NOTES: Selected by San Antonio Gunslingers in 1984 USFL territorial draft. . . . Selected by St. Louis Cardinals in second round (45th pick overall) of 1984 NFL draft. . . . Signed by Cardinals (July 28, 1984). . . . On injured reserve with Achilles' heel injury (September 12, 1986-remainder of season). . . . Released by Cardinals after failing physical (August 10, 1987). . . . Awarded on waivers to Houston Oilers (August 11, 1987). . . . Released by Oilers after failing physical (August 20, 1987). . . . Re-signed by Oilers (May 3, 1990).
PLAYING EXPERIENCE: St. Louis NFL, 1984-1986; Houston NFL, 1990. . . . Games: 1984 (15), 1985 (16), 1986 (1), 1990 (16). Total: 48.
PRO STATISTICS: 1985—Recovered one fumble.

DeBERG, STEVE
QB, CHIEFS

PERSONAL: Born January 19, 1954, at Oakland. . . . 6-3/217. . . . Full name: Steven L. DeBerg.
HIGH SCHOOL: Savanna (Anaheim, Calif.).
COLLEGE: Fullerton College (Calif.), then San Jose State (bachelor of science degree, 1980).
TRANSACTIONS/CAREER NOTES: Selected by Dallas Cowboys in 10th round (275th pick overall) of 1977 NFL draft. . . . Awarded on waivers from Cowboys to San Francisco 49ers (September 12, 1977). . . . Active for five games with 49ers in 1977; did not play. . . . Traded by 49ers to Denver Broncos for fourth-round pick in 1983 draft (August 31, 1981). . . . USFL rights traded by Oakland Invaders to Denver Gold for rights to tight end John Thompson and offensive tackle Randy Van Divier (October 7, 1983). . . . On injured reserve with separated shoulder (November 16-December 22, 1983). . . . Granted free agency (February 1, 1984). . . . Re-signed by Broncos and traded to Tampa Bay Buccaneers for fourth-round pick in 1984 draft and second-round pick in 1985 draft (April 24, 1984). . . . Granted free agency (February 1, 1988). . . . Re-signed by Buccaneers and traded to Kansas City Chiefs for safety Mark Robinson and fourth- and eighth-round picks in 1988 draft (March 31, 1988).
PRO STATISTICS: Passer rating points: 1978 (39.8), 1979 (73.1), 1980 (66.5), 1981 (77.6), 1982 (67.2), 1983 (79.9), 1984 (79.3), 1985 (71.3), 1986 (49.7), 1987 (85.3), 1988 (73.5), 1989 (75.8), 1990 (96.3). Career: 73.7. . . . 1978—Recovered two fumbles and fumbled nine times for minus five yards. 1979—Recovered two fumbles and fumbled six times for minus 17 yards. 1980—Fumbled four times for minus six yards. 1984—Recovered two fumbles and fumbled 15 times for minus eight yards. 1986—Recovered one fumble and fumbled twice for minus five yards. 1987—Recovered two fumbles and fumbled seven times for minus two yards. 1989—Recovered three fumbles and fumbled four times for minus 26 yards. 1990—Recovered three fumbles and fumbled nine times for minus 31 yards.

Year	Team	G	Att.	Cmp.	Pct.	Yds.	TD	Int.	Avg.	Att.	Yds.	Avg.	TD	TD	Pts.	F.
					PASSING						RUSHING				TOTAL	
1978— San Francisco NFL		12	302	137	45.4	1570	8	22	5.20	15	20	1.3	1	1	6	9
1979— San Francisco NFL		16	*578	*347	60.0	3652	17	21	6.32	17	10	.6	0	0	0	6
1980— San Francisco NFL		11	321	186	57.9	1998	12	17	6.22	6	4	.7	0	0	0	4
1981— Denver NFL		14	108	64	59.3	797	6	6	7.38	9	40	4.4	0	0	0	2
1982— Denver NFL		9	223	131	58.7	1405	7	11	6.30	8	27	3.4	1	1	6	4
1983— Denver NFL		10	215	119	55.4	1617	9	7	7.52	13	28	2.2	1	1	6	5
1984— Tampa Bay NFL		16	509	308	60.5	3554	19	18	6.98	28	59	2.1	2	2	12	15

			PASSING						RUSHING				TOTAL		
Year Team	G	Att.	Cmp.	Pct.	Yds.	TD	Int.	Avg.	Att.	Yds.	Avg.	TD	TD	Pts.	F.
1985— Tampa Bay NFL........	11	370	197	53.2	2488	19	18	6.72	9	28	3.1	0	0	0	3
1986— Tampa Bay NFL........	16	96	50	52.1	610	5	12	6.35	2	1	.5	1	1	6	2
1987— Tampa Bay NFL........	12	275	159	57.8	1891	14	7	6.88	8	-8	-1.0	0	0	0	7
1988— Kansas City NFL.......	13	414	224	54.1	2935	16	16	7.09	18	30	1.7	1	1	6	1
1989— Kansas City NFL.......	12	324	196	60.5	2529	11	16	7.81	14	-8	-.6	0	0	0	4
1990— Kansas City NFL.......	16	444	258	58.1	3444	23	4	7.76	21	-5	-.2	0	0	0	9
Pro totals (13 years)...........	168	4179	2376	56.9	28490	166	175	6.82	168	226	1.4	7	7	42	71

DEL GRECO, AL
PK, CARDINALS

PERSONAL: Born March 2, 1962, at Providence, R.I.... 5-10/200.... Full name: Albert Louis Del Greco Jr.
HIGH SCHOOL: Coral Gables (Fla.).
COLLEGE: Auburn.
TRANSACTIONS/CAREER NOTES: Signed as free agent by Miami Dolphins (May 17, 1984).... Released by Dolphins (August 27, 1984).... Signed as free agent by Green Bay Packers (October 17, 1984).... Released by Packers (November 25, 1987).... Signed as free agent by St. Louis Cardinals (December 8, 1987).... Franchise transferred to Phoenix (March 15, 1988).
PRO STATISTICS: 1988—Rushed once for eight yards. 1990—Recovered one fumble.

		PLACE-KICKING				
Year Team	G	XPM	XPA	FGM	FGA	Pts.
1984— Green Bay NFL...........	9	34	34	9	12	61
1985— Green Bay NFL...........	16	38	40	19	26	95
1986— Green Bay NFL...........	16	29	29	17	27	80
1987— G.B.(5)-S.L.(3) NFL	8	19	20	9	15	46
1988— Phoenix NFL	16	42	44	12	21	78
1989— Phoenix NFL	16	28	29	18	26	82
1990— Phoenix NFL	16	31	31	17	27	82
Pro totals (7 years)..........	97	221	227	101	154	524

DELLENBACH, JEFF
OT/C, DOLPHINS

PERSONAL: Born February 14, 1963, at Wausau, Wis.... 6-6/285.... Full name: Jeffrey Alan Dellenbach.... Name pronounced del-en-BOK.
HIGH SCHOOL: East (Wausau, Wis.).
COLLEGE: Wisconsin.
TRANSACTIONS/CAREER NOTES: Selected by Jacksonville Bulls in 1985 USFL territorial draft.... Selected by Miami Dolphins in fourth round (111th pick overall) of 1985 NFL draft.... Signed by Dolphins (July 15, 1985).... Granted free agency (February 1, 1990).... Re-signed by Dolphins (August 30, 1990).... Granted roster exemption (August 30-September 8, 1990).
PLAYING EXPERIENCE: Miami NFL, 1985-1990.... Games: 1985 (11), 1986 (13), 1987 (11), 1988 (16), 1989 (16), 1990 (15). Total: 82.
CHAMPIONSHIP GAME EXPERIENCE: Played in AFC championship game after 1985 season.
PRO STATISTICS: 1987—Fumbled once for minus 13 yards. 1988—Fumbled once for minus nine yards.

DeLONG, KEITH
LB, 49ERS

PERSONAL: Born August 14, 1967, at San Diego.... 6-2/235.... Full name: Keith Allen De-Long.... Son of Steve DeLong, nose tackle with San Diego Chargers and Chicago Bears, 1965-1972.
HIGH SCHOOL: Lawrence (Kan.).
COLLEGE: Tennessee.
TRANSACTIONS/CAREER NOTES: Selected by San Francisco 49ers in first round (28th pick overall) of 1989 NFL draft.... Signed by 49ers (August 1, 1989).
PLAYING EXPERIENCE: San Francisco NFL, 1989 and 1990.... Games: 1989 (15), 1990 (16). Total: 31.
CHAMPIONSHIP GAME EXPERIENCE: Played in NFC championship game after 1989 and 1990 seasons.... Played in Super Bowl XXIV after 1989 season.
RECORDS/HONORS: Named as linebacker on THE SPORTING NEWS college All-America team, 1988.
PRO STATISTICS: 1989—Intercepted one pass for one yard. 1990—Recovered three fumbles.

DELPINO, ROBERT
FB, RAMS

PERSONAL: Born November 2, 1965, at Dodge City, Kan.... 6-0/205.... Full name: Robert Lewis Delpino.... Name pronounced del-PEE-no.
HIGH SCHOOL: Dodge City (Kan.).
COLLEGE: Dodge City Community College (Kan.), then Missouri.
TRANSACTIONS/CAREER NOTES: Selected by Los Angeles Rams in fifth round (117th pick overall) of 1988 NFL draft.... Signed by Rams (July 12, 1988).... On inactive list (November 4, 1990).
CHAMPIONSHIP GAME EXPERIENCE: Played in NFC championship game after 1989 season.
PRO STATISTICS: 1988—Recovered one fumble. 1990—Recovered one fumble.

		RUSHING				RECEIVING				KICKOFF RETURNS				TOTAL		
Year Team	G	Att.	Yds.	Avg.	TD	No.	Yds.	Avg.	TD	No.	Yds.	Avg.	TD	TD	Pts.	F.
1988— L.A. Rams NFL.......	15	34	147	4.3	0	30	312	10.4	2	14	333	23.8	0	2	12	2
1989— L.A. Rams NFL.......	16	78	368	4.7	1	34	334	9.8	1	17	334	19.7	0	2	12	1
1990— L.A. Rams NFL.......	15	13	52	4.0	0	15	172	11.5	4	20	389	19.5	0	4	24	1
Pro totals (3 years).......	46	125	567	4.5	1	79	818	10.4	7	51	1056	20.7	0	8	48	4

DEL RIO, JACK

LB, COWBOYS

PERSONAL: Born April 4, 1963, at Castro Valley, Calif. . . . 6-4/240. **HIGH SCHOOL:** Hayward (Calif.). **COLLEGE:** Southern California.
TRANSACTIONS/CAREER NOTES: Selected by Los Angeles Express in 1985 USFL territorial draft. . . . Selected by New Orleans Saints in third round (68th pick overall) of 1985 NFL draft. . . . Signed by Saints (July 31, 1985). . . . Traded by Saints to Kansas City Chiefs for fifth-round pick in 1988 draft (August 17, 1987). . . . On injured reserve with knee injury (December 13, 1988-remainder of season). . . . Released by Chiefs (August 30, 1989). . . . Awarded on waivers to Dallas Cowboys (August 31, 1989).
PLAYING EXPERIENCE: New Orleans NFL, 1985 and 1986; Kansas City NFL, 1987 and 1988; Dallas NFL, 1989 and 1990. . . . Games: 1985 (16), 1986 (16), 1987 (10), 1988 (15), 1989 (14), 1990 (16). Total: 87.
MISCELLANEOUS: Selected by Toronto Blue Jays' organization in 22nd round of free-agent baseball draft (June 8, 1981).
PRO STATISTICS: 1985—Recovered five fumbles for 22 yards and a touchdown and intercepted two passes for 13 yards. 1986—Rushed once for 16 yards. 1988—Intercepted one pass for no yards and recovered one fumble. 1989—Returned two fumbles for 57 yards and a touchdown.

DENNIS, MARK

OT, DOLPHINS

PERSONAL: Born April 15, 1965, at Junction City, Kan. . . . 6-6/295. . . . Full name: Mark Francis Dennis. **HIGH SCHOOL:** Washington (Ill.). **COLLEGE:** Illinois.
TRANSACTIONS/CAREER NOTES: Selected by Miami Dolphins in eighth round (212th pick overall) of 1987 NFL draft. . . . Signed by Dolphins (July 23, 1987). . . . On injured reserve with knee injury (November 28, 1988-remainder of season). . . . On reserve/physically unable to perform list with knee injury (August 29-November 4, 1989). . . . Granted unconditional free agency (February 1, 1990). . . . Re-signed by Dolphins (July 31, 1990).
PLAYING EXPERIENCE: Miami NFL, 1987-1990. . . . Games: 1987 (5), 1988 (13), 1989 (8), 1990 (16). Total: 42.

DENNISON, RICK

LB, BRONCOS

PERSONAL: Born June 22, 1958, at Kalispell, Mont. . . . 6-3/220. . . . Full name: Rick Steven Dennison. **HIGH SCHOOL:** Rocky Mountain (Fort Collins, Colo.). **COLLEGE:** Colorado State (bachelor of science degree in civil engineering, 1980).
TRANSACTIONS/CAREER NOTES: Signed as free agent by Buffalo Bills (May 9, 1980). . . . Released by Bills (August 20, 1980). . . . Signed as free agent by Denver Broncos (December 29, 1980). . . . Released by Broncos (August 31, 1981). . . . Signed as free agent by Buffalo Bills (February 26, 1982). . . . Released by Bills (August 31, 1982). . . . Signed as free agent by Denver Broncos (September 7, 1982). . . . Released by Broncos (September 3, 1990). . . . Re-signed by Broncos (September 25, 1990).
PLAYING EXPERIENCE: Denver NFL, 1982-1990. . . . Games: 1982 (9), 1983 (16), 1984 (16), 1985 (15), 1986 (16), 1987 (12), 1988 (16), 1989 (15), 1990 (13). Total: 128.
CHAMPIONSHIP GAME EXPERIENCE: Played in AFC championship game after 1986, 1987 and 1989 seasons. . . . Played in Super Bowl XXI after 1986 season, Super Bowl XXII after 1987 season and Super Bowl XXIV after 1989 season.
PRO STATISTICS: 1984—Returned two kickoffs for 27 yards and recovered one fumble. 1986—Intercepted one pass for five yards. 1987—Intercepted one pass for 10 yards. 1988—Intercepted one pass for 29 yards and recovered three fumbles. 1989—Intercepted one pass for one yard and recovered one fumble.

DENT, BURNELL

LB, PACKERS

PERSONAL: Born March 16, 1963, at New Orleans. . . . 6-1/233. . . . Full name: Burnell Joseph Dent. **HIGH SCHOOL:** Destrehan (La.). **COLLEGE:** Tulane (bachelor of science degree in physical education, 1986).
TRANSACTIONS/CAREER NOTES: Selected by Green Bay Packers in sixth round (143rd pick overall) of 1986 NFL draft. . . . Signed by Packers (July 18, 1986). . . . On injured reserve with knee injury (September 1-October 24, 1987). . . . On injured reserve with knee injury (October 4-November 19, 1988). . . . On inactive list (October 14, 1990).
PLAYING EXPERIENCE: Green Bay NFL, 1986-1990. . . . Games: 1986 (16), 1987 (9), 1988 (10), 1989 (16), 1990 (15). Total: 66.
PRO STATISTICS: 1988—Recovered one fumble. 1989—Intercepted one pass for 53 yards.

DENT, RICHARD

DE, BEARS

PERSONAL: Born December 13, 1960, at Atlanta. . . . 6-5/268. . . . Full name: Richard Lamar Dent. **HIGH SCHOOL:** Murphy (Atlanta). **COLLEGE:** Tennessee State.
TRANSACTIONS/CAREER NOTES: Selected by Philadelphia Stars in eighth round (89th pick overall) of 1983 USFL draft. . . . Selected by Chicago Bears in eighth round (203rd pick overall) of 1983 NFL draft. . . . Signed by Bears (May 12, 1983). . . . On non-football injury list with substance abuse (September 8, 1988). . . . Activated (September 9, 1988). . . . On injured reserve with fractured fibula (November 29, 1988-remainder of season).
PLAYING EXPERIENCE: Chicago NFL, 1983-1990. . . . Games: 1983 (16), 1984 (16), 1985 (16), 1986 (15), 1987 (12), 1988 (13), 1989 (15), 1990 (16). Total: 119.
CHAMPIONSHIP GAME EXPERIENCE: Played in NFC championship game after 1984 and 1985 seasons. . . . Played in Super Bowl XX after 1985 season.
RECORDS/HONORS: Played in Pro Bowl after 1984, 1985 and 1990 seasons.
PRO STATISTICS: 1984—Recovered one fumble. 1985—Intercepted two passes for 10 yards and a touchdown and recovered two fumbles. 1987—Recovered two fumbles for 11 yards. 1988—Recovered one fumble. 1989—Intercepted one pass for 30 yards and recovered two fumbles. 1990—Intercepted three passes for 21 yards and recovered three fumbles for 45 yards and a touchdown.

DeOSSIE, STEVE
LB, GIANTS

PERSONAL: Born November 22, 1962, at Tacoma, Wash. . . . 6-2/248. . . . Full name: Steven Leonard DeOssie.
HIGH SCHOOL: Don Bosco Technical (Boston).
COLLEGE: Boston College (bachelor of science degree in communications, 1984).
TRANSACTIONS/CAREER NOTES: Selected by New Jersey Generals in first round (14th pick overall) of 1984 USFL draft. . . . Selected by Dallas Cowboys in fourth round (110th pick overall) of 1984 NFL draft. . . . Signed by Cowboys (May 3, 1984). . . . Traded by Cowboys to New York Giants for sixth-round pick in 1990 NFL draft (June 2, 1989). . . . On injured reserve with broken toe (September 27-November 15, 1989). . . . Transferred to developmental squad (November 16-November 18, 1989).
PLAYING EXPERIENCE: Dallas NFL, 1984-1988; New York Giants NFL, 1989 and 1990. . . . Games: 1984 (16), 1985 (16), 1986 (16), 1987 (11), 1988 (16), 1989 (9), 1990 (16). Total: 100.
CHAMPIONSHIP GAME EXPERIENCE: Played in NFC championship game after 1990 season. . . . Played in Super Bowl XXV after 1990 season.
PRO STATISTICS: 1989—Intercepted one pass for 10 yards. 1990—Recovered one fumble.

DERBY, GLENN
OT/G, PACKERS

PERSONAL: Born June 27, 1964, at Oconomowoc, Wis. . . . 6-6/289. . . . Full name: Glenn E. Derby Jr.
HIGH SCHOOL: Oconomowoc (Wis.).
COLLEGE: Wisconsin (degree in general studies, 1989).
TRANSACTIONS/CAREER NOTES: Selected by New Orleans Saints in eighth round (218th pick overall) of 1988 NFL draft. . . . Signed by Saints (July 17, 1988). . . . On injured reserve with foot injury (August 29, 1988-entire season). . . . Released by Saints (September 5, 1989). . . . Re-signed by Saints to developmental squad (October 4, 1989). . . . On developmental squad (October 4-October 10, 1989). . . . Released by Saints (October 11, 1989). . . . Re-signed by Saints to developmental squad (October 18, 1989). . . . On developmental squad (October 18-November 11, 1989). . . . Granted unconditional free agency (February 1, 1991). . . . Signed by Green Bay Packers (March 28, 1991).
PLAYING EXPERIENCE: New Orleans NFL, 1989 and 1990. . . . Games: 1989 (3), 1990 (4). Total: 7.

DeRIGGI, FRED
NT, PATRIOTS

PERSONAL: Born January 15, 1967, at Scranton, Pa. . . . 6-2/268. . . . Full name: Fred John DeRiggi. . . . Name pronounced dee-RIJ-ee.
HIGH SCHOOL: West Scranton (Scranton, Pa.).
COLLEGE: Syracuse (degree in retailing).
TRANSACTIONS/CAREER NOTES: Selected by Buffalo Bills in seventh round (181st pick overall) of 1990 NFL draft. . . . Signed by Bills (July 28, 1990). . . . Released by Bills (August 27, 1990). . . . Signed by New England Patriots to practice squad (November 11, 1990). . . . Activated (December 22, 1990).
PLAYING EXPERIENCE: New England NFL, 1990. . . . Games: 1990 (2).

DICKERSON, ERIC
RB, COLTS

PERSONAL: Born September 2, 1960, at Sealy, Tex. . . . 6-3/224. . . . Full name: Eric Demetric Dickerson. . . . Cousin of Dexter Manley, defensive end with Phoenix Cardinals.
HIGH SCHOOL: Sealy (Tex.).
COLLEGE: Southern Methodist.
TRANSACTIONS/CAREER NOTES: Selected by Arizona Wranglers in first round (sixth pick overall) of 1983 USFL draft. . . . Selected by Los Angeles Rams in first round (second pick overall) of 1983 NFL draft. . . . Signed by Rams (July 12, 1983). . . . On did not report list (August 20-September 12, 1985). . . . Reported and granted roster exemption (September 13-September 20, 1985). . . . Traded by Rams to Indianapolis Colts for first- and second-round picks in 1988 draft, second-round pick in 1989 draft and running back Owen Gill (October 31, 1987); Rams also acquired first-round pick in 1988 draft, first- and second-round picks in 1989 draft and running back Greg Bell from Buffalo Bills in exchange for Colts trading rights to linebacker Cornelius Bennett to Bills. . . . On reserve/non-football injury list (August 28-October 17, 1990).
CHAMPIONSHIP GAME EXPERIENCE: Played in NFC championship game after 1985 season.
RECORDS/HONORS: Established NFL records for most yards rushing, rookie season (1,808), 1983; most rushing attempts, rookie season (390), 1983; most touchdowns rushing, rookie season (18), 1983; most combined attempts, rookie season (442), 1983; most yards rushing, season (2,105), 1984; most games, 100 yards rushing, season (12), 1984; most consecutive seasons, 1,000 or more yards rushing (7), 1983-1989. Tied NFL record for most seasons, 2,000 yards rushing and receiving combined (4). . . . Named as running back on THE SPORTING NEWS college All-America team, 1982. . . . Played in Pro Bowl after 1983, 1984 and 1986-1989 seasons. . . . Named THE SPORTING NEWS NFL Player of the Year, 1983. . . . Named to THE SPORTING NEWS NFL All-Pro team, 1983, 1984 and 1986-1988.
PRO STATISTICS: 1983—Recovered one fumble. 1984—Attempted one pass with one interception and recovered four fumbles. 1985—Recovered three fumbles. 1986—Attempted one pass with one completion for 15 yards and a touchdown and recovered two fumbles. 1987—Recovered three fumbles. 1988—Recovered one fumble.

		— RUSHING —				— RECEIVING —				— TOTAL —		
Year	Team	G	Att.	Yds.	Avg.	TD	No.	Yds.	Avg.	TD	TD	Pts.	F.
1983— L.A. Rams NFL		16	*390	*1808	4.6	18	51	404	7.9	2	20	120	13
1984— L.A. Rams NFL		16	379	*2105	5.6	*14	21	139	6.6	0	14	84	14
1985— L.A. Rams NFL		14	292	1234	4.2	12	20	126	6.3	0	12	72	10
1986— L.A. Rams NFL		16	*404	*1821	4.5	11	26	205	7.9	0	11	66	12
1987— Rams (3)-Ind. (9) NFL		12	283	1288	4.6	6	18	171	9.5	0	6	36	7
1988— Indianapolis NFL		16	*388	*1659	4.3	14	36	377	10.5	1	15	90	5
1989— Indianapolis NFL		15	314	1311	4.2	7	30	211	7.0	1	8	48	10
1990— Indianapolis NFL		11	166	677	4.1	4	18	92	5.1	0	4	24	0
Pro totals (8 years)		116	2616	11903	4.6	86	220	1725	7.8	4	90	540	71

DILL, SCOTT
OT, BUCCANEERS

PERSONAL: Born April 5, 1966, at Birmingham, Ala. . . . 6-5/285. . . . Full name: Gerald Scott Dill. **HIGH SCHOOL:** W.A. Berry (Birmingham, Ala.). **COLLEGE:** Memphis State.
TRANSACTIONS/CAREER NOTES: Selected by Phoenix Cardinals in ninth round (233rd pick overall) of 1988 NFL draft. . . . Signed by Cardinals (July 13, 1988). . . . Granted unconditional free agency (February 1, 1990). . . . Signed by Tampa Bay Buccaneers (March 16, 1990). . . . On inactive list (October 14, 1990). . . . On injured reserve with back injury (October 19, 1990-remainder of season).
PLAYING EXPERIENCE: Phoenix NFL, 1988 and 1989; Tampa Bay NFL, 1990. . . . Games: 1988 (13), 1989 (16), 1990 (3). Total: 32.
PRO STATISTICS: 1989—Recovered one fumble.

DILWEG, ANTHONY
QB, PACKERS

PERSONAL: Born March 28, 1965, at Washington, D.C. . . . 6-3/192. . . . Full name: Anthony Hume Dilweg. . . . Grandson of Lavvie Dilweg, end with Green Bay Packers, 1927-1934; and Eleanor Dilweg, former Olympic swimmer and world-record holder. **HIGH SCHOOL:** Walt Whitman (Bethesda, Md.).
COLLEGE: Duke (degrees in psychology and drama, 1989).
TRANSACTIONS/CAREER NOTES: Selected by Green Bay Packers in third round (74th pick overall) of 1989 NFL draft. . . . Signed by Packers (July 23, 1989).
PRO STATISTICS: Passer rating points: 1989 (95.8), 1990 (72.1). Career: 72.3. . . . 1990—Recovered four fumbles and fumbled 10 times for minus nine yards.

Year Team	G	Att.	Cmp.	Pct.	Yds.	TD	Int.	Avg.	Att.	Yds.	Avg.	TD	TD	Pts.	F.
				PASSING						RUSHING				TOTAL	
1989— Green Bay NFL	1	1	1	100.0	7	0	0	7.00	0	0		0	0	0	0
1990— Green Bay NFL	9	192	101	52.6	1267	8	7	6.60	21	114	5.4	0	0	0	10
Pro totals (2 years)	10	193	102	52.9	1274	8	7	6.60	21	114	5.4	0	0	0	10

DIMRY, CHARLES
CB, BRONCOS

PERSONAL: Born January 31, 1966, at San Diego. . . . 6-0/175. . . . Full name: Charles Louis Dimry III. **HIGH SCHOOL:** Oceanside (Calif.). **COLLEGE:** UNLV.
TRANSACTIONS/CAREER NOTES: Selected by Atlanta Falcons in fifth round (110th pick overall) of 1988 NFL draft. . . . Signed by Falcons (July 16, 1988). . . . Granted unconditional free agency (February 1, 1991). . . . Signed by Denver Broncos (March 28, 1991).

Year Team	G	No.	Yds.	Avg.	TD
		INTERCEPTIONS			
1988— Atlanta NFL	16	0	0		0
1989— Atlanta NFL	16	2	72	36.0	0
1990— Atlanta NFL	16	3	16	5.3	0
Pro totals (3 years)	48	5	88	17.6	0

DISHMAN, CRIS
CB, OILERS

PERSONAL: Born August 13, 1965, at Louisville, Ky. . . . 6-0/178. . . . Full name: Cris Edward Dishman. **HIGH SCHOOL:** DeSales (Louisville, Ky.). **COLLEGE:** Purdue.
TRANSACTIONS/CAREER NOTES: Selected by Houston Oilers in fifth round (125th pick overall) of 1988 NFL draft. . . . Signed by Oilers (July 15, 1988).
PRO STATISTICS: 1988—Returned blocked punt 10 yards for a touchdown and recovered one fumble. 1989—Returned blocked punt seven yards for a touchdown and recovered one fumble.

Year Team	G	No.	Yds.	Avg.	TD
		INTERCEPTIONS			
1988— Houston NFL	15	0	0		0
1989— Houston NFL	16	4	31	7.8	0
1990— Houston NFL	16	4	50	12.5	0
Pro totals (3 years)	47	8	81	10.1	0

DIXON, FLOYD
WR, FALCONS

PERSONAL: Born April 9, 1964, at Beaumont, Tex. . . . 5-9/170. . . . Full name: Floyd Eugene Dixon. **HIGH SCHOOL:** Hebert (Beaumont, Tex.). **COLLEGE:** Stephen F. Austin State (bachelor's degree, 1987).
TRANSACTIONS/CAREER NOTES: Selected by Atlanta Falcons in sixth round (154th pick overall) of 1986 NFL draft. . . . Signed by Falcons (July 17, 1986).
PRO STATISTICS: 1986—Returned one kickoff for 13 yards and recovered two fumbles. 1990—Returned one kickoff for no yards.

Year Team	G	Att.	Yds.	Avg.	TD	No.	Yds.	Avg.	TD	No.	Yds.	Avg.	TD	TD	Pts.	F.
		RUSHING				RECEIVING				PUNT RETURNS				TOTAL		
1986— Atlanta NFL	16	11	67	6.1	0	42	617	14.7	2	26	151	5.8	0	2	12	3
1987— Atlanta NFL	12	3	-3	-1.0	0	36	600	16.7	5	0	0		0	5	30	0
1988— Atlanta NFL	14	7	69	9.9	0	28	368	13.1	2	0	0		0	2	12	1

Year	Team		G	Att.	RUSHING Yds.	Avg.	TD	No.	RECEIVING Yds.	Avg.	TD	No.	PUNT RETURNS Yds.	Avg.	TD	TD	TOTAL Pts.	F.
1989—	Atlanta NFL		16	2	-23	-11.5	0	25	357	14.3	2	0	0		0	2	12	0
1990—	Atlanta NFL		16	0	0		0	38	399	10.5	4	0	0		0	4	24	0
	Pro totals (5 years)		74	23	110	4.8	0	169	2341	13.9	15	26	151	5.8	0	15	90	4

DIXON, JAMES
WR, COWBOYS

PERSONAL: Born February 2, 1967, at Vernon, Tex. . . . 5-10/184. . . . Full name: James A. Dixon.
HIGH SCHOOL: Vernon (Tex.).
COLLEGE: Cisco Junior College (Tex.), then Houston.
TRANSACTIONS/CAREER NOTES: Signed as free agent by Detroit Lions (April 26, 1989). . . . Released by Lions (August 29, 1989). . . . Awarded on waivers to Dallas Cowboys (August 30, 1989).
PRO STATISTICS: 1989—Recovered one fumble.

Year	Team		G	Att.	RUSHING Yds.	Avg.	TD	No.	RECEIVING Yds.	Avg.	TD	No.	KICKOFF RETURNS Yds.	Avg.	TD	TD	TOTAL Pts.	F.
1989—	Dallas NFL		16	3	30	10.0	0	24	477	19.9	2	*47	*1181	25.1	*1	3	18	4
1990—	Dallas NFL		15	11	43	3.9	0	2	26	13.0	0	36	736	20.4	0	0	0	2
	Pro totals (2 years)		31	14	73	5.2	0	26	503	19.4	2	83	1917	23.1	1	3	18	6

DIXON, RANDY
G, COLTS

PERSONAL: Born March 12, 1965, at Clewiston, Fla. . . . 6-3/302. . . . Full name: Randy C. Dixon. . . . Related to Titus Dixon, wide receiver with Kansas City Chiefs.
HIGH SCHOOL: Clewiston (Fla.).
COLLEGE: Pittsburgh.
TRANSACTIONS/CAREER NOTES: Selected by Indianapolis Colts in fourth round (85th pick overall) of 1987 NFL draft. . . . Signed by Colts (July 24, 1987). . . . Granted free agency (February 1, 1990). . . . Re-signed by Colts (September 12, 1990). . . . Activated (September 14, 1990).
PLAYING EXPERIENCE: Indianapolis NFL, 1987-1990. . . . Games: 1987 (3), 1988 (16), 1989 (16), 1990 (15). Total: 50.
RECORDS/HONORS: Named as offensive tackle on THE SPORTING NEWS college All-America team, 1986.
PRO STATISTICS: 1989—Recovered one fumble in end zone for a touchdown,

DIXON, RICKEY
S, BENGALS

PERSONAL: Born December 26, 1966, at Dallas. . . . 5-11/191.
HIGH SCHOOL: Wilmer-Hutchins (Dallas).
COLLEGE: Oklahoma.
TRANSACTIONS/CAREER NOTES: Selected by Cincinnati Bengals in first round (fifth pick overall) of 1988 NFL draft. . . . Signed by Bengals (September 3, 1988). . . . On injured reserve with broken leg (December 14, 1990-remainder of season).
CHAMPIONSHIP GAME EXPERIENCE: Played in AFC championship game after 1988 season. . . . Played in Super Bowl XXIII after 1988 season.
PRO STATISTICS: 1988—Returned one kickoff for 18 yards and recovered one fumble for minus three yards.

Year	Team	G	No.	INTERCEPTIONS Yds.	Avg.	TD
1988—	Cincinnati NFL	15	1	13	13.0	0
1989—	Cincinnati NFL	16	3	47	15.7	0
1990—	Cincinnati NFL	13	0	0		0
	Pro totals (3 years)	44	4	60	15.0	0

DIXON, TITUS
WR, CHIEFS

PERSONAL: Born June 15, 1966, at Clewiston, Fla. . . . 5-6/152. . . . Full name: Titus L. Dixon. . . . Related to Randy Dixon, guard with Indianapolis Colts.
HIGH SCHOOL: Cleiston (Fla.).
COLLEGE: Troy State, Ala. (degree in criminal justice, 1989).
TRANSACTIONS/CAREER NOTES: Selected by New York Jets in sixth round (153rd pick overall) of 1989 NFL draft. . . . Signed by Jets (July 23, 1989). . . . Released by Jets (September 26, 1989). . . . Signed as free agent by Indianapolis Colts (October 4, 1989). . . . Released by Colts (October 16, 1989). . . . Awarded on waivers to Detroit Lions (October 17, 1989). . . . Released by Lions (October 25, 1989). . . . Active for one game with Lions in 1989; did not play. . . . Signed as free agent by Atlanta Falcons (April 6, 1990). . . . Released by Falcons (August 28, 1990). . . . Signed by Kansas City Chiefs (April 4, 1991).
PLAYING EXPERIENCE: New York Jets (3)-Indianapolis (1)-Detroit (0) NFL, 1989. . . . Games: 1989 (4).
PRO STATISTICS: 1989—Returned four kickoffs for 67 yards and fumbled once.

DOLEMAN, CHRIS
DE, VIKINGS

PERSONAL: Born October 16, 1961, at Indianapolis. . . . 6-5/263. . . . Full name: Christopher John Doleman.
HIGH SCHOOL: Valley Forge Military Academy (Wayne, Pa.), then William Penn (York, Pa.).
COLLEGE: Pittsburgh.
TRANSACTIONS/CAREER NOTES: Selected by Baltimore Stars in 1985 USFL territorial draft. . . . Selected by Minnesota Vikings in first round (fourth pick overall) of 1985 NFL draft. . . . Signed by Vikings (August 8, 1985).
PLAYING EXPERIENCE: Minnesota NFL, 1985-1990. . . . Games: 1985 (16), 1986 (16), 1987 (12), 1988 (16), 1989 (16), 1990 (16). Total: 92.

CHAMPIONSHIP GAME EXPERIENCE: Played in NFC championship game after 1987 season.
RECORDS/HONORS: Played in Pro Bowl after 1987-1990 seasons. . . . Named to THE SPORTING NEWS NFL All-Pro team, 1989.
PRO STATISTICS: 1985—Intercepted one pass for five yards and recovered three fumbles. 1986—Intercepted one pass for 59 yards and a touchdown. 1989—Recovered five fumbles for seven yards. 1990—Intercepted one pass for 30 yards and credited with a safety.

DOMBROWSKI, JIM
G/OT, SAINTS

PERSONAL: Born October 19, 1963, at Williamsville, N.Y. . . . 6-5/298. . . . Full name: James Matthew Dombrowski. . . . Name pronounced dum-BROW-skee.
HIGH SCHOOL: South (Williamsville, N.Y.).
COLLEGE: Virginia (bachelor's degree in biology, 1986).
TRANSACTIONS/CAREER NOTES: Selected by Orlando Renegades in 1986 USFL territorial draft. . . . Selected by New Orleans Saints in first round (sixth pick overall) of 1986 NFL draft. . . . Signed by Saints (August 1, 1986). . . . On injured reserve with broken foot (September 22, 1986-remainder of season). . . . Granted free agency (February 1, 1990). . . . Re-signed by Saints (July 17, 1990).
PLAYING EXPERIENCE: New Orleans NFL, 1986-1990. . . . Games: 1986 (3), 1987 (10), 1988 (16), 1989 (16), 1990 (16). Total: 61.
RECORDS/HONORS: Named as offensive tackle on THE SPORTING NEWS college All-America team, 1985.
PRO STATISTICS: 1988—Recovered one fumble. 1989—Recovered one fumble.

DONALDSON, JEFF
S, FALCONS

PERSONAL: Born April 19, 1962, at Fort Collins, Colo. . . . 6-0/188. . . . Full name: Jeffery Michael Donaldson.
HIGH SCHOOL: Fort Collins (Colo.).
COLLEGE: Colorado.
TRANSACTIONS/CAREER NOTES: Selected by Denver Gold in 1984 USFL territorial draft. . . . Selected by Houston Oilers in ninth round (228th pick overall) of 1984 NFL draft. . . . Signed by Oilers (July 17, 1984). . . . Granted unconditional free agency (February 1, 1990). . . . Signed by Kansas City Chiefs (March 26, 1990). . . . Granted unconditional free agency (February 1, 1991). . . . Signed by Atlanta Falcons (April 1, 1991).
PRO STATISTICS: 1985—Returned six punts for 35 yards, returned five kickoffs for 93 yards, recovered two fumbles and fumbled once. 1986—Recovered two fumbles for one yard and a touchdown. 1987—Recovered two fumbles. 1988—Recovered two fumbles and returned one kickoff for five yards.

			—— INTERCEPTIONS ——			
Year	Team	G	No.	Yds.	Avg.	TD
1984—Houston NFL		16	0	0		0
1985—Houston NFL		16	0	0		0
1986—Houston NFL		16	1	0	.0	0
1987—Houston NFL		12	4	16	4.0	0
1988—Houston NFL		16	4	29	7.3	0
1989—Houston NFL		14	0	14		0
1990—Kansas City NFL		16	3	28	9.3	0
Pro totals (7 years)		106	12	87	7.3	0

DONALDSON, RAY
C, COLTS

PERSONAL: Born May 18, 1958, at Rome, Ga. . . . 6-3/300. . . . Full name: Raymond Canute Donaldson. . . . Step-brother of John Tutt, outfielder in Baltimore Orioles' and San Diego Padres' organizations, 1981-1986; and Aguas of Mexican league, 1983; and cousin of Robert Lavette, running back with Dallas Cowboys and Philadelphia Eagles, 1985-1987.
HIGH SCHOOL: East (Rome, Ga.).
COLLEGE: Georgia.
TRANSACTIONS/CAREER NOTES: Selected by Baltimore Colts in second round (32nd pick overall) of 1980 NFL draft. . . . Franchise transferred to Indianapolis (March 31, 1984).
PLAYING EXPERIENCE: Baltimore NFL, 1980-1983; Indianapolis NFL, 1984-1990. . . . Games: 1980 (16), 1981 (16), 1982 (9), 1983 (16), 1984 (16), 1985 (16), 1986 (16), 1987 (12), 1988 (16), 1989 (16), 1990 (16). Total: 165.
RECORDS/HONORS: Played in Pro Bowl after 1986-1989 seasons.
PRO STATISTICS: 1981—Recovered one fumble. 1982—Recovered one fumble. 1983—Fumbled once. 1985—Recovered one fumble. 1986—Fumbled twice for minus four yards. 1988—Caught one pass for minus three yards. 1989—Recovered one fumble and fumbled once for minus 22 yards.

DONNELLY, RICK
P, SEAHAWKS

PERSONAL: Born May 17, 1962, at Miller Place, N.Y. . . . 6-0/203.
HIGH SCHOOL: Miller Place (N.Y.).
COLLEGE: Wyoming.
TRANSACTIONS/CAREER NOTES: Selected by San Antonio Gunslingers in 14th round (192nd pick overall) of 1985 USFL draft. . . . Signed as free agent by New England Patriots (May 8, 1985). . . . Released by Patriots (August 19, 1985). . . . Signed as free agent by Atlanta Falcons (August 23, 1985). . . . On injured reserve with knee injury (November 18, 1985-remainder of season). . . . Granted free agency (February 1, 1988). . . . Re-signed by Falcons (August 31, 1988). . . . On reserve/physically unable to perform list with back injury (August 29, 1989-entire season). . . . Granted unconditional free agency (February 1, 1990). . . . Signed by Seattle Seahawks (March 27, 1990).
PRO STATISTICS: 1985—Rushed twice for minus five yards and recovered one fumble. 1986—Successful on only extra point attempt. 1987—Rushed three times for minus six yards and recovered one fumble and fumbled twice for minus four yards.

Year	Team	G	No.	Avg.	Blk.
			PUNTING		
1985— Atlanta NFL		11	59	43.6	0
1986— Atlanta NFL		16	78	43.9	1
1987— Atlanta NFL		12	61	*44.0	*2
1988— Atlanta NFL		16	*98	40.0	0
1990— Seattle NFL		16	67	40.6	0
Pro totals (5 years)		71	363	42.4	3

DORN, TORIN
CB, RAIDERS

PERSONAL: Born February 28, 1968, at Greenwood, S.C. . . . 6-0/190.
HIGH SCHOOL: Southfield Senior (Southfield, Mich.).
COLLEGE: North Carolina.
TRANSACTIONS/CAREER NOTES: Selected by Los Angeles Raiders in fourth round (95th pick overall) of 1990 NFL draft. . . . Signed by Raiders (June 9, 1990).
PLAYING EXPERIENCE: Los Angeles Raiders NFL, 1990. . . . Games: 1990 (16).
CHAMPIONSHIP GAME EXPERIENCE: Played in AFC championship game after 1990 season.

DORSEY, ERIC
DE, GIANTS

PERSONAL: Born August 5, 1964, at Washington, D.C. . . . 6-5/280. . . . Full name: Eric Hall Dorsey. . . . Cousin of Allen Pinkett, running back with Houston Oilers.
HIGH SCHOOL: McLean (Va.).
COLLEGE: Notre Dame (bachelor of business administration degree in marketing, 1988).
TRANSACTIONS/CAREER NOTES: Selected by Orlando Renegades in 1986 USFL territorial draft. . . . Selected by New York Giants in first round (19th pick overall) of 1986 NFL draft. . . . Signed by Giants (August 8, 1986). . . . On injured reserve with broken bone in foot (September 23-December 11, 1989). . . . Transferred to developmental squad (December 12, 1989-January 6, 1990). . . . Granted free agency (February 1, 1990). . . . Re-signed by Giants (August 7, 1990).
PLAYING EXPERIENCE: New York Giants NFL, 1986-1990. . . . Games: 1986 (16), 1987 (12), 1988 (16), 1989 (2), 1990 (16). Total: 62.
CHAMPIONSHIP GAME EXPERIENCE: Played in NFC championship game after 1986 and 1990 seasons. . . . Played in Super Bowl XXI after 1986 season and Super Bowl XXV after 1990 season.
PRO STATISTICS: 1987—Returned one kickoff for 13 yards. 1988—Recovered two fumbles. 1989—Recovered one fumble.

DOUGLASS, MAURICE
CB, BEARS

PERSONAL: Born February 12, 1964, at Muncie, Ind. . . . 5-11/200. . . . Full name: Maurice Gerrard Douglass.
HIGH SCHOOL: Madison (Trotwood, O.).
COLLEGE: Coffeyville Community College (Kan.), then Kentucky.
TRANSACTIONS/CAREER NOTES: Selected by Chicago Bears in eighth round (221st pick overall) of 1986 NFL draft. . . . Signed by Bears (June 22, 1986). . . . Released by Bears (September 1, 1986) . . . Re-signed by Bears (November 28, 1986). . . . On reserve/non-football injury with steroids (August 29-September 25, 1989). . . . Reinstated and granted roster exemption (September 28-October 2, 1989). . . . On injured reserve with neck injury (December 14, 1989-remainder of season). . . . On inactive list (October 14, 1990). . . . On injured reserve with ankle injury (October 23-November 24, 1990).
CHAMPIONSHIP GAME EXPERIENCE: Played in NFC championship game after 1988 season.
PRO STATISTICS: 1987—Recovered one fumble. 1988—Recovered three fumbles and fumbled once. 1989—Recovered one fumble. 1990—Recovered one fumble.

Year	Team	G	No.	Yds.	Avg.	TD
			INTERCEPTIONS			
1986— Chicago NFL		4	0	0		0
1987— Chicago NFL		12	2	0	.0	0
1988— Chicago NFL		15	1	35	35.0	0
1989— Chicago NFL		10	1	0	.0	0
1990— Chicago NFL		11	0	0		0
Pro totals (5 years)		52	4	35	8.8	0

DOZIER, D.J.
RB, VIKINGS

PERSONAL: Born September 21, 1965, at Norfolk, Va. . . . 6-0/205. . . . Full name: William Henry Dozier Jr.
HIGH SCHOOL: Kempsville (Virginia Beach, Va.).
COLLEGE: Penn State.
TRANSACTIONS/CAREER NOTES: Selected by Minnesota Vikings in first round (14th pick overall) of 1987 NFL draft. . . . Signed by Vikings (July 6, 1987). . . . On injured reserve with hip injury (September 9-October 22, 1988). . . . Granted free agency (February 1, 1990). . . . Re-signed by Vikings (November 7, 1990). . . . Granted roster exemption (November 7-November 19, 1990).
CHAMPIONSHIP GAME EXPERIENCE: Played in NFC championship game after 1987 season.
PRO STATISTICS: 1989—Attempted one pass with one completion for 19 yards and a touchdown and recovered two fumbles.

Year	Team	G	Att.	Yds.	Avg.	TD	No.	Yds.	Avg.	TD	No.	Yds.	Avg.	TD	TD	Pts.	F.
			RUSHING				RECEIVING				KICKOFF RETURNS				TOTAL		
1987— Minnesota NFL		9	69	257	3.7	5	12	89	7.4	2	2	23	11.5	0	7	42	2
1988— Minnesota NFL		8	42	167	4.0	2	5	49	9.8	0	5	105	21.0	0	2	12	0
1989— Minnesota NFL		14	46	207	4.5	0	14	148	10.6	0	12	258	21.5	0	0	0	2
1990— Minnesota NFL		6	6	12	2.0	0	1	12	12.0	0	0	0		0	0	0	0
Pro totals (4 years)		37	163	643	3.9	7	32	298	9.3	2	19	386	20.3	0	9	54	4

BASEBALL TRANSACTIONS: Selected by Detroit Tigers' organization in 18th round of free-agent draft (June 6, 1983).... Signed as free agent by New York Mets' organization (March 26, 1990).

BASEBALL RECORD AS PLAYER

Year	Team	League	Pos.	G	AB	R	H	2B	3B	HR	RBI	Avg.	PO	A	E	F.A.
1990— St. Lucie	....	Fla. St.	OF	93	317	56	94	11	3	13	57	.297	116	6	2	.984
1990— Jackson	....	Texas	OF	29	102	20	33	5	7	2	23	.324	44	4	0	1.000

DRANE, DWIGHT
S, BILLS

PERSONAL: Born May 6, 1962, at Miami.... 6-2/205.
HIGH SCHOOL: Central (Miami).
COLLEGE: Oklahoma.
TRANSACTIONS/CAREER NOTES: Selected by Oklahoma Outlaws in 1984 USFL territorial draft.... Rights traded by Outlaws to Los Angeles Express for rights to running back Andrew Lazarus (February 29, 1984).... Signed by Express (March 2, 1984).... Granted roster exemption (March 2-March 9, 1984).... Selected by Buffalo Bills in first round (14th pick overall) of 1984 NFL supplemental draft.... On developmental squad for three games with Los Angeles Express (June 9, 1985-remainder of season).... Traded by Express with running back Mel Gray, guard Wayne Jones, tight end Ken O'Neal, defensive backs John Warren and Troy West and linebacker Howard Carson to Arizona Outlaws for past considerations (August 1, 1985).... Granted free agency when USFL suspended operations (August 7, 1986).... Signed by Buffalo Bills (September 10, 1986).... Granted roster exemption (September 10-September 22, 1986).... On injured reserve with dislocated ankle (September 26-November 3, 1990).
PLAYING EXPERIENCE: Los Angeles USFL, 1984 and 1985; Buffalo NFL, 1986-1990.... Games: 1984 (16), 1985 (15), 1986 (13), 1987 (11), 1988 (16), 1989 (16), 1990 (12). Total USFL: 31. Total NFL: 68. Total Pro: 99.
CHAMPIONSHIP GAME EXPERIENCE: Played in AFC championship game after 1988 and 1990 seasons.... Played in Super Bowl XXV after 1990 season.
PRO STATISTICS: USFL: 1984—Intercepted three passes for 43 yards and a touchdown and recovered one fumble for 50 yards. ...NFL: 1987—Recovered one fumble. 1989—Intercepted one pass for 25 yards.

DRESSEL, CHRIS
TE, JETS

PERSONAL: Born February 7, 1961, at Placentia, Calif.... 6-4/239.
HIGH SCHOOL: El Dorado (Placentia, Calif.).
COLLEGE: Stanford.
TRANSACTIONS/CAREER NOTES: Selected by Oakland Invaders in 1983 USFL territorial draft.... Selected by Houston Oilers in third round (69th pick overall) of 1983 NFL draft.... Signed by Oilers (June 22, 1983). ... Traded by Oilers to Washington Redskins for conditional 1988 draft choice (June 22, 1987).... Released by Redskins (September 1, 1987).... Signed as free agent replacement player by San Francisco 49ers (September 24, 1987).... Released by 49ers (October 14, 1987).... Signed as free agent by Cleveland Browns (November 19, 1987).... Released by Browns (December 10, 1987).... Re-signed by Browns (April 30, 1988).... Released by Browns (November 14, 1988).... Active for four games with Browns in 1988; did not play.... Signed as free agent by Kansas City Chiefs (April 6, 1989).... Released by Chiefs (October 28, 1989).... Awarded on waivers to New York Jets (October 30, 1989).... On inactive list (December 30, 1990).
PRO STATISTICS: 1983—Returned four kickoffs for 40 yards and rushed once for three yards. 1984—Fumbled once. 1985—Recovered one fumble. 1989—Fumbled once. 1990—Returned one kickoff for seven yards and fumbled once.

			RECEIVING		
Year	Team	G	No.	Yds.	Avg.	TD
1983— Houston NFL	....	16	32	316	9.9	4
1984— Houston NFL	....	16	40	378	9.5	2
1985— Houston NFL	....	16	3	17	5.7	1
1986— Houston NFL	....	16	0	0		0
1987— San Francisco NFL	....	1	1	8	8.0	0
1989— KC (7)-NYJ (8) NFL		15	12	191	15.9	1
1990— N.Y. Jets NFL	....	15	6	66	11.0	0
Pro totals (7 years)	....	95	94	976	10.4	8

DREWREY, WILLIE
WR, BUCCANEERS

PERSONAL: Born April 28, 1963, at Columbus, N.J.... 5-7/170.
HIGH SCHOOL: Northern Burlington (Columbus, N.J.).
COLLEGE: West Virginia.
TRANSACTIONS/CAREER NOTES: Selected by Birmingham Stallions in 1985 USFL territorial draft.... Selected by Houston Oilers in 11th round (281st pick overall) of 1985 NFL draft.... Signed by Oilers (July 18, 1985).... On injured reserve with dislocated elbow (December 6, 1988-remainder of season).... Granted unconditional free agency (February 1, 1989).... Signed by Tampa Bay Buccaneers (March 27, 1989).
RECORDS/HONORS: Named as kick returner on THE SPORTING NEWS college All-America team, 1984.
PRO STATISTICS: 1985—Rushed twice for minus four yards. 1986—Recovered one fumble.

			RECEIVING				PUNT RETURNS				KICKOFF RETURNS				TOTAL		
Year	Team	G	No.	Yds.	Avg.	TD	No.	Yds.	Avg.	TD	No.	Yds.	Avg.	TD	TD	Pts.	F.
1985— Houston NFL	....	14	2	28	14.0	0	24	215	9.0	0	26	642	24.7	0	0	0	2
1986— Houston NFL	....	15	18	299	16.6	0	34	262	7.7	0	25	500	20.0	0	0	0	3
1987— Houston NFL	....	12	11	148	13.5	0	3	11	3.7	0	8	136	17.0	0	0	0	0
1988— Houston NFL	....	14	11	172	15.6	1	2	8	4.0	0	1	10	10.0	0	1	6	0
1989— Tampa Bay NFL	..	16	14	157	11.2	1	20	220	11.0	0	1	26	26.0	0	1	6	0
1990— Tampa Bay NFL	..	16	7	182	26.0	1	23	184	8.0	0	14	244	17.4	0	1	6	1
Pro totals (6 years)	....	87	63	986	15.7	3	106	900	8.5	0	75	1558	20.8	0	3	18	6

DRUMMOND, ROBERT
RB, EAGLES

PERSONAL: Born June 21, 1967, at Apopka, Fla. . . . 6-1/205. . . . Full name: Robert C. Drummond.
HIGH SCHOOL: Jamesville-DeWitt (DeWitt, N.Y.).
COLLEGE: Syracuse.
TRANSACTIONS/CAREER NOTES: Selected by Philadelphia Eagles in third round (76th pick overall) of 1989 NFL draft. . . . Signed by Eagles (July 26, 1989). . . . On inactive list (September 30 and October 15, 1990). . . . On injured reserve with hand injury (October 24, 1990-December 24, 1990). . . . On practice squad (December 24, 1990-remainder of regular season and play-offs).
PRO STATISTICS: 1989—Recovered one fumble.

		RUSHING				RECEIVING				TOTAL		
Year Team	G	Att.	Yds.	Avg.	TD	No.	Yds.	Avg.	TD	TD	Pts.	F.
1989— Philadelphia NFL	16	32	127	4.0	0	17	180	10.6	1	1	6	0
1990— Philadelphia NFL	4	8	33	4.1	1	5	39	7.8	0	1	6	0
Pro totals (2 years)	20	40	160	4.0	1	22	219	10.0	1	2	12	0

DUCKENS, MARK
DE, LIONS

PERSONAL: Born March 4, 1965, at Wichita, Kan. . . . 6-4/270. . . . Full name: Mark Anthony Duckens.
HIGH SCHOOL: North (Wichita, Kan.).
COLLEGE: Wichita State, then Arizona State.
TRANSACTIONS/CAREER NOTES: Signed as free agent by Washington Redskins (April 26, 1988). . . . On injured reserve with hand injury (August 23, 1988-entire season). . . . Released by Redskins (September 4, 1989). . . . Awarded on waivers to New York Giants (September 5, 1989). . . . Granted unconditional free agency (February 1, 1990). . . . Signed by Detroit Lions (March 7, 1990). . . . On inactive list (October 14, 1990).
PLAYING EXPERIENCE: New York Giants NFL, 1989; Detroit NFL, 1990. . . . Games: 1989 (15), 1990 (15). Total: 30.
PRO STATISTICS: 1990—Recovered one fumble.

DUERSON, DAVE
S, GIANTS

PERSONAL: Born November 28, 1960, at Muncie, Ind. . . . 6-1/208. . . . Full name: David Russell Duerson. . . . Cousin of Allen Leavell, guard with Houston rockets, 1979-80 through 1988-89.
HIGH SCHOOL: Northside (Muncie, Ind.).
COLLEGE: Notre Dame (bachelor of arts degree in economics and communications, 1983).
TRANSACTIONS/CAREER NOTES: Selected by Chicago Blitz in 1983 USFL territorial draft. . . . Selected by Chicago Bears in third round (64th pick overall) of 1983 NFL draft. . . . Signed by Bears (June 25, 1983). . . . Released by Bears (August 26, 1990). . . . Signed by New York Giants (September 4, 1990).
CHAMPIONSHIP GAME EXPERIENCE: Played in NFC championship game after 1984, 1985, 1988 and 1990 seasons. . . . Played in Super Bowl XX after 1985 season. . . . Played in Super Bowl XXV after 1990 season.
RECORDS/HONORS: Played in Pro Bowl after 1985-1988 seasons. . . . Named to THE SPORTING NEWS NFL All-Pro team, 1986.
PRO STATISTICS: 1983—Returned three kickoffs for 66 yards. 1984—Returned four kickoffs for 95 yards. 1985—Recovered one fumble. 1986—Recovered two fumbles for six yards. 1987—Recovered one fumble for 10 yards. 1990—Recovered one fumble for 31 yards and a touchdown.

		INTERCEPTIONS				PUNT RETURNS				TOTAL		
Year Team	G	No.	Yds.	Avg.	TD	No.	Yds.	Avg.	TD	TD	Pts.	F.
1983— Chicago NFL	16	0	0		0	0	0		0	0	0	0
1984— Chicago NFL	16	1	9	9.0	0	1	4	4.0	0	0	0	0
1985— Chicago NFL	15	5	53	10.6	0	6	47	7.8	0	0	0	1
1986— Chicago NFL	16	6	139	23.2	0	0	0		0	0	0	0
1987— Chicago NFL	12	3	0	.0	0	1	10	10.0	0	0	0	0
1988— Chicago NFL	15	2	18	9.0	0	0	0		0	0	0	0
1989— Chicago NFL	12	1	2	2.0	0	0	0		0	0	0	0
1990— N.Y. Giants NFL	16	1	0	.0	0	0	0		0	0	0	0
Pro totals (8 years)	118	19	221	11.6	0	8	61	7.6	0	0	0	1

DUFFY, ROGER
C, JETS

PERSONAL: Born July 16, 1967, at Pittsburgh. . . . 6-3/285. . . . Full name: Roger Thomas Duffy.
HIGH SCHOOL: Canton Central Catholic (Canton, O.).
COLLEGE: Penn State (bachelor of arts degree in communications, 1990).
TRANSACTIONS/CAREER NOTES: Selected by New York Jets in eighth round (196th pick overall) of 1990 NFL draft. . . . Signed by Jets (July 18, 1990).
PLAYING EXPERIENCE: New York Jets NFL, 1990. . . . Games: 1990 (16).
PRO STATISTICS: 1990—Returned one kickoff for eight yards.

DUKES, JAMIE
C, FALCONS

PERSONAL: Born June 14, 1964, at Schnectady, N.Y. . . . 6-1/285. . . . Full name: Jamie Donnell Dukes.
HIGH SCHOOL: Evans (Orlando, Fla.).
COLLEGE: Florida State.
TRANSACTIONS/CAREER NOTES: Selected by Tampa Bay Bandits in 1986 USFL territorial draft. . . . Signed as free agent by Atlanta Falcons (May 4, 1986). . . . On injured reserve with toe injury (November 23, 1988-remainder of season). . . . Granted free agency (February 1, 1990). . . . Re-signed by Falcons (July 17, 1990).
PLAYING EXPERIENCE: Atlanta NFL, 1986-1990. . . . Games: 1986 (14), 1987 (4), 1988 (12), 1989 (16), 1990 (16). Total: 62.
PRO STATISTICS: 1986—Recovered one fumble. 1988—Returned one kickoff for 13 yards. 1990—Recovered one fumble and fumbled once for minus six yards.

DUNCAN, CURTIS
WR, OILERS

PERSONAL: Born January 26, 1965, at Detroit....5-11/184....Full name: Curtis Everett Duncan.
HIGH SCHOOL: Redford (Detroit).
COLLEGE: Northwestern (bachelor of science degree in business/pre-law, 1987).
TRANSACTIONS/CAREER NOTES: Selected by Houston Oilers in 10th round (258th pick overall) of 1987 NFL draft....Signed by Oilers (July 30, 1987).
PRO STATISTICS: 1989—Rushed once for no yards.

		— RECEIVING —				— PUNT RETURNS —				– KICKOFF RETURNS –				— TOTAL —		
Year	Team	G	No.	Yds.	Avg.	TD	No.	Yds.	Avg.	TD	No.	Yds.	Avg.	TD	TD	Pts.	F.
1987—Houston NFL	10	13	237	18.2	5	8	23	2.9	0	28	546	19.5	0	5	30	0
1988—Houston NFL	16	22	302	13.7	1	4	47	11.8	0	1	34	34.0	0	1	6	0
1989—Houston NFL	16	43	613	14.3	5	0	0		0	0	0		0	5	30	1
1990—Houston NFL	16	66	785	11.9	1	0	0		0	0	0		0	1	6	1
Pro totals (4 years)	58	144	1937	13.5	12	12	70	5.8	0	29	580	20.0	0	12	72	2

DUNN, K.D.
TE, BROWNS

PERSONAL: Born April 28, 1963, at Fort Hood, Tex....6-3/213....Full name: Keldrick A. Dunn.
HIGH SCHOOL: Gordon (Decatur, Ga.).
COLLEGE: Clemson.
TRANSACTIONS/CAREER NOTES: Selected by Orlando Renegades in 1985 USFL territorial draft....Selected by St. Louis Cardinals in fifth round (116th pick overall) of 1985 NFL draft....Signed by Cardinals (July 3, 1985)....Released by Cardinals (August 26, 1985)....Signed by Tampa Bay Buccaneers (November 5, 1985)....Released by Buccaneers (August 22, 1986)....Re-signed by Buccaneers (November 4, 1986)....Released by Buccaneers (August 24, 1987)....Signed as free agent replacement player by Washington Redskins (September 23, 1987)....Released by Redskins (October 20, 1987)....Signed by New York Jets (May 3, 1988)....Released by Jets (September 5, 1989)....Re-signed by Jets (October 24, 1989)....On injured reserve, then released by Jets (December 4, 1989)....Signed by Cleveland Browns for 1990....Released by Browns (March 1, 1990)....Signed by WLAF (January 31, 1991)....Selected by Montreal Machine in second round (20th tight end) of 1991 WLAF positional draft....Signed by Cleveland Browns (June 8, 1991).
PRO STATISTICS: NFL: 1986—Returned one kickoff for no yards.

		— RECEIVING —			
Year	Team	G	No.	Yds.	Avg.	TD
1985—Tampa Bay NFL	7	0	0		0
1986—Tampa Bay NFL	7	3	83	27.7	0
1987—Washington NFL	3	0	0		0
1988—N.Y. Jets NFL	15	6	67	11.2	0
1989—N.Y. Jets NFL	1	2	13	6.5	0
1991—Montreal WLAF	10	31	321	10.4	1
NFL totals (5 years)	33	11	163	14.8	0
WLAF totals (1 year)	10	31	321	10.4	1
Pro totals (6 years)	43	42	484	11.5	1

DUPER, MARK
WR, DOLPHINS

PERSONAL: Born January 25, 1959, at Pineville, La....5-9/192....Full name: Mark Super Duper....Given name at birth was Mark Kirby Dupas.
HIGH SCHOOL: Moreauville (La.).
COLLEGE: Northwestern (La.) State.
TRANSACTIONS/CAREER NOTES: Selected by Miami Dolphins in second round (52nd pick overall) of 1982 NFL draft....On inactive list (September 12 and 19, 1982)....On injured reserve with broken leg (September 16-November 9, 1985)....Granted free agency (February 1, 1988)....Re-signed by Dolphins (August 21, 1988)....On non-football injury list with substance abuse (November 30, 1988-remainder of season).
CHAMPIONSHIP GAME EXPERIENCE: Member of Miami Dolphins for AFC championship game and Super Bowl XVII after 1982 season; did not play....Played in AFC championship game after 1984 and 1985 seasons....Played in Super Bowl XIX after 1984 season.
RECORDS/HONORS: Played in Pro Bowl after 1983 and 1984 seasons....Named to play in Pro Bowl after 1986 season; replaced due to injury by Mark Clayton.
PRO STATISTICS: 1984—Recovered one fumble. 1985—Recovered one fumble for three yards and fumbled once. 1986—Rushed once for minus 10 yards. 1990—Fumbled once.

		— RECEIVING —			
Year	Team	G	No.	Yds.	Avg.	TD
1982—Miami NFL	2	0	0		0
1983—Miami NFL	16	51	1003	19.7	10
1984—Miami NFL	16	71	1306	18.4	8
1985—Miami NFL	9	35	650	18.6	3
1986—Miami NFL	16	67	1313	19.6	11
1987—Miami NFL	11	33	597	18.1	8
1988—Miami NFL	13	39	626	16.1	1
1989—Miami NFL	15	49	717	14.6	1
1990—Miami NFL	16	52	810	15.6	5
Pro totals (9 years)	114	397	7022	17.7	47

DUPREE, MARCUS
RB, RAMS

PERSONAL: Born May 22, 1964, at Philadelphia, Miss....6-2/225....Full name: Marcus L. Dupree.
HIGH SCHOOL: Philadelphia (Miss.).
COLLEGE: Oklahoma, then Southern Mississippi.

TRANSACTIONS/CAREER NOTES: USFL rights traded by New Jersey Generals to New Orleans Breakers for draft choice (March 5, 1984).... Signed by New Orleans Breakers (March 3, 1984).... Granted roster exemption (March 3-March 8, 1984).... On developmental squad for one game (June 15-June 22, 1984).... Breakers franchise transferred to Portland (November 13, 1984).... Selected by Los Angeles Rams in 12th round (327th pick overall) of 1986 NFL draft.... Signed by Rams (October 3, 1990).... On injured reserve with knee injury (October 5-November 7, 1990).

PRO STATISTICS: USFL: 1984—Attempted three passes with one completion for 19 yards and recovered one fumble. 1985—Attempted one pass with no completions.

			— RUSHING —			— RECEIVING —				— TOTAL —		
Year	Team	G	Att.	Yds.	Avg.	TD	No.	Yds.	Avg.	TD	TD	Pts.	F.
1984— New Orleans USFL	15	145	684	4.7	9	28	182	6.5	0	9	54	5
1985— Portland USFL	1	17	69	4.1	1	2	7	3.5	0	1	6	0
1990— L.A. Rams NFL	7	19	72	3.8	0	0	0		0	0	0	0
USFL totals (2 years)	16	162	753	4.7	10	30	189	6.3	0	10	60	5
NFL totals (1 year)	7	19	72	3.8	0	0	0		0	0	0	0
Pro totals (3 years)	23	181	825	4.6	10	30	189	6.3	0	10	60	5

DUSBABEK, MARK
LB, VIKINGS

PERSONAL: Born June 23, 1964, at Faribault, Minn.... 6-3/230.... Full name: Mark Edward Dusbabek.
HIGH SCHOOL: Faribault (Minn.).
COLLEGE: Minnesota.
TRANSACTIONS/CAREER NOTES: Selected by Houston Oilers in fourth round (105th pick overall) of 1987 NFL draft.... Signed by Oilers (July 28, 1987).... On injured reserve with shoulder injury (August 31, 1987-entire season).... On injured reserve with shoulder injury (August 29, 1988-entire season).... Granted unconditional free agency (February 1, 1989).... Signed by Minnesota Vikings (April 1, 1989).... On inactive list (September 23 and 30, 1990).
PLAYING EXPERIENCE: Minnesota NFL, 1989 and 1990.... Games: 1989 (16), 1990 (14). Total: 30.
PRO STATISTICS: 1989—Intercepted one pass for two yards and recovered two fumbles. 1990—Credited with safety and recovered one fumble.

DYAL, MIKE
TE, RAIDERS

PERSONAL: Born May 20, 1966, at San Antonio.... 6-2/240.
HIGH SCHOOL: Tivy (Kerrville, Tex.).
COLLEGE: Texas A&I.
TRANSACTIONS/CAREER NOTES: Signed as free agent by Los Angeles Raiders (April 28, 1988).... On injured reserve with ankle injury (August 22, 1988-entire season).... Placed on injured reserve with hamstring injury (September 19, 1990).... Activated for game (December 2, 1990).... On injured reserve (December 4, 1990-remainder of season).
CHAMPIONSHIP GAME EXPERIENCE: Played in AFC championship game after 1990 season.

			— RECEIVING —			
Year	Team	G	No.	Yds.	Avg.	TD
1989— L.A. Raiders NFL	16	27	499	18.5	2
1990— L.A. Raiders NFL	3	3	51	17.0	0
Pro totals (2 years)	19	30	550	18.3	2

DYKES, HART LEE
WR, PATRIOTS

PERSONAL: Born September 2, 1966, at Bay City, Tex.... 6-4/218.... Full name: Hart Lee Dykes Jr.
HIGH SCHOOL: Bay City (Tex.).
COLLEGE: Oklahoma State.
TRANSACTIONS/CAREER NOTES: Selected by New England Patriots in first round (16th pick overall) of 1989 NFL draft.... Signed by Patriots (August 20, 1989).... On reserve/non-football injury list (October 27-December 1, 1990).
RECORDS/HONORS: Named as wide receiver on THE SPORTING NEWS college All-America team, 1988.
MISCELLANEOUS: Selected by Chicago White Sox' organization in 54th round of free-agent baseball draft (June 1, 1988).
PRO STATISTICS: 1989—Recovered one fumble and fumbled three times.

			— RECEIVING —			
Year	Team	G	No.	Yds.	Avg.	TD
1989— New England NFL	16	49	795	16.2	5
1990— New England NFL	10	34	549	16.2	2
Pro totals (2 years)	26	83	1344	16.2	7

DYKO, CHRIS
OT, SEAHAWKS

PERSONAL: Born March 16, 1966, at Champaign, Ill.... 6-6/295.... Full name: Christopher Edward Dyko.
HIGH SCHOOL: University (Spokane, Wash.).
COLLEGE: Washington State (bachelor of arts degree in recreation sports and leisure, 1989).
TRANSACTIONS/CAREER NOTES: Selected by Chicago Bears in eighth round (221st pick overall) of 1989 NFL draft.... Signed by Bears (July 27, 1989).... Released by Bears (September 3, 1990).... Signed by Seattle Seahawks (September 18, 1990).... On injured reserve with ankle injury (September 19, 1990-remainder of season).
PLAYING EXPERIENCE: Chicago NFL, 1989.... Games: 1989 (8).

EARLY, QUINN
WR, SAINTS

PERSONAL: Born April 13, 1965, at West Hempstead, N.Y. . . . 6-0/190. . . . Full name: Quinn Remar Early.
HIGH SCHOOL: Great Neck (N.Y.).
COLLEGE: Iowa (degree in art, 1988).
TRANSACTIONS/CAREER NOTES: Selected by San Diego Chargers in third round (60th pick overall) of 1988 NFL draft. . . . Signed by Chargers (July 11, 1988). . . . On injured reserve with knee injury (October 21-December 13, 1989). . . . Transferred to developmental squad (December 14 and 15, 1989). . . . Activated (December 16, 1989). . . . Granted unconditional free agency (February 1, 1991). . . . Signed by New Orleans Saints (April 1, 1991).

Year Team	G	RUSHING				RECEIVING				TOTAL		
		Att.	Yds.	Avg.	TD	No.	Yds.	Avg.	TD	TD	Pts.	F.
1988— San Diego NFL	16	7	63	9.0	0	29	375	12.9	4	4	24	1
1989— San Diego NFL	6	1	19	19.0	0	11	126	11.5	0	0	0	0
1990— San Diego NFL	14	0	0		0	15	238	15.9	1	1	6	0
Pro totals (3 years)	36	8	82	10.3	0	55	739	13.4	5	5	30	1

EATMAN, IRV
OT, JETS

PERSONAL: Born January 1, 1961, at Birmingham, Ala. . . . 6-7/298. . . . Full name: Irvin Humphrey Eatman.
HIGH SCHOOL: Meadowdale (Dayton, O.).
COLLEGE: UCLA.
TRANSACTIONS/CAREER NOTES: Selected by Philadelphia Stars in first round (eighth pick overall) of 1983 USFL draft. . . . Signed by Stars (February 8, 1983). . . . Selected by Kansas City Chiefs in eighth round (204th pick overall) of 1983 NFL draft. . . . Philadelphia Stars franchise transferred to Baltimore (November 1, 1984). . . . Granted free agency when USFL suspended operations (August 7, 1986). . . . Signed by Kansas City Chiefs (August 10, 1986). . . . Granted free agency (February 1, 1990). . . . Re-signed by Chiefs (August 15, 1990). . . . On inactive list (September 9, 17 and 30, 1990). . . . Traded by Chiefs to New York Jets for defensive lineman Ron Stallworth (February 1, 1991).
PLAYING EXPERIENCE: Philadelphia USFL, 1983 and 1984; Baltimore USFL, 1985; Kansas City NFL, 1986-1990. . . . Games: 1983 (18), 1984 (18), 1985 (18), 1986 (16), 1987 (12), 1988 (16), 1989 (13), 1990 (12). Total USFL: 54. Total NFL: 69. Total Pro: 123.
CHAMPIONSHIP GAME EXPERIENCE: Played in USFL championship game after 1983-1985 seasons.
RECORDS/HONORS: Named as offensive tackle on THE SPORTING NEWS USFL All-Star team, 1983 and 1984.
PRO STATISTICS: 1989—Recovered one fumble.

EATON, TRACEY
S, FALCONS

PERSONAL: Born July 19, 1965, at Medford, Ore. . . . 6-1/195 . . . Son of Scott Eaton, defensive back with New York Giants, 1967-1971.
HIGH SCHOOL: Medford (Ore.).
COLLEGE: Portland (Ore.) State.
TRANSACTIONS/CAREER NOTES: Selected by Houston Oilers in seventh round (187th pick overall) of 1988 NFL draft. . . . Signed by Oilers (July 18, 1988). . . . On injured reserve with shoulder injury (August 23-December 17, 1988). . . . Granted unconditional free agency (February 1, 1990). . . . Signed by Phoenix Cardinals (March 2, 1990). . . . On injured reserve with shoulder injury (November 28, 1990-remainder of season). . . . Granted unconditional free agency (February 1, 1991). . . . Signed by Atlanta Falcons (April 1, 1991).
PLAYING EXPERIENCE: Houston NFL, 1988 and 1989; Phoenix NFL, 1990. . . . Games: 1988 (1), 1989 (16), 1990 (11). Total: 28.
PRO STATISTICS: 1989—Intercepted three passes for 33 yards.

EDMUNDS, FERRELL
TE, DOLPHINS

PERSONAL: Born April 16, 1965, at South Boston, Va. . . . 6-6/254. . . . Full name: Ferrell Edmunds Jr. . . . First name pronounced FAIR-el.
HIGH SCHOOL: George Washington (Danville, Va.).
COLLEGE: Maryland.
TRANSACTIONS/CAREER NOTES: Selected by Miami Dolphins in third round (73rd pick overall) of 1988 NFL draft. . . . Signed by Dolphins (July 12, 1988).
RECORDS/HONORS: Played in Pro Bowl after 1989 and 1990 seasons.
PRO STATISTICS: 1988—Rushed once for minus eight yards, returned one kickoff for 20 yards and fumbled four times. 1989—Recovered one fumble and fumbled once. 1990—Rushed once for minus seven yards, recovered two fumbles and fumbled twice.

Year Team	G	RECEIVING			
		No.	Yds.	Avg.	TD
1988— Miami NFL	16	33	575	17.4	3
1989— Miami NFL	16	32	382	11.9	3
1990— Miami NFL	16	31	446	14.4	1
Pro totals (3 years)	48	96	1403	14.6	7

EDWARDS, AL
WR, BILLS

PERSONAL: Born May 18, 1967, at New Orleans. . . . 5-8/168. . . . Full name: Albert Edwards Jr.
HIGH SCHOOL: Bonnabel (Metairie, La.).
COLLEGE: Northwestern State (La.).
TRANSACTIONS/CAREER NOTES: Selected by Buffalo Bills in 11th round (292nd pick overall) of 1990 NFL draft. . . Signed by Bills (June 18, 1990). . . . On inactive list (October 28 and November 4, 1990).
CHAMPIONSHIP GAME EXPERIENCE: Played in AFC championship game after 1990 season. . . . Played in Super Bowl XXV after 1990 season.

Year	Team	G	RECEIVING				PUNT RETURNS				KICKOFF RETURNS				TOTAL		
			No.	Yds.	Avg.	TD	No.	Yds.	Avg.	TD	No.	Yds.	Avg.	TD	TD	Pts.	F.
1990— Buffalo NFL		14	2	11	5.5	0	14	92	6.6	0	11	256	23.3	0	0	0	0
Pro totals (1 year)		14	2	11	5.5	0	14	92	6.6	0	11	256	23.3	0	0	0	0

EDWARDS, ANTHONY
WR, CARDINALS

PERSONAL: Born May 26, 1966, at Casa Grande, Ariz. . . . 5-9/190.
HIGH SCHOOL: Union (Casa Grande, Ariz.).
COLLEGE: New Mexico Highlands.
TRANSACTIONS/CAREER NOTES: Signed as free agent by Philadelphia Eagles (July 7, 1989). . . . Released by Eagles (September 5, 1989). . . . Re-signed by Eagles to developmental squad (September 6, 1989). . . . On developmental squad (September 6-October 18, 1989). . . . Activated after clearing procedural waivers (October 20, 1989). . . . On injured reserve with knee injury (September 4-October 1, 1990). . . . On practice squad (October 1-October 30, 1990). . . . Released by Eagles (October 30, 1990). . . . Re-signed by Eagles (October 31, 1990). . . . On inactive list (December 9, 1990). . . . Released by Eagles (December 12, 1990). . . . Signed by Phoenix Cardinals (May, 1991).
PRO STATISTICS: 1989—Recovered one fumble.

Year	Team	G	RECEIVING				PUNT RETURNS				KICKOFF RETURNS				TOTAL		
			No.	Yds.	Avg.	TD	No.	Yds.	Avg.	TD	No.	Yds.	Avg.	TD	TD	Pts.	F.
1989— Philadelphia NFL		9	2	74	37.0	0	7	64	9.1	0	3	23	7.7	0	0	0	2
1990— Philadelphia NFL		5	0	0		0	8	60	7.5	0	3	36	12.0	0	0	0	2
Pro totals (2 years)		14	2	74	37.0	0	15	124	8.3	0	6	59	9.8	0	0	0	4

EDWARDS, BRAD
S, REDSKINS

PERSONAL: Born February 22, 1966, at Lumberton, N.C. . . . 6-2/196. . . . Full name: Bradford Wayne Edwards. . . . Son of Wayne Edwards, infielder in Baltimore Orioles' organization, 1962-1965.
HIGH SCHOOL: Douglas Byrd (Fayetteville, N.C.).
COLLEGE: South Carolina (degree in business management, 1988).
TRANSACTIONS/CAREER NOTES: Selected by Minnesota Vikings in second round (54th pick overall) of 1988 NFL draft. . . . Signed by Vikings (July 20, 1988). . . . On injured reserve with neck injury (September 14-November 4, 1989). . . . Granted unconditional free agency (February 1, 1990). . . . Signed by Washington Redskins (March 7, 1990).

Year	Team	G	INTERCEPTIONS			
			No.	Yds.	Avg.	TD
1988— Minnesota NFL		16	2	47	23.5	1
1989— Minnesota NFL		9	1	18	18.0	0
1990— Washington NFL		16	2	33	16.5	0
Pro totals (3 years)		41	5	98	19.6	1

EGU, PATRICK
RB, JETS

PERSONAL: Born February 20, 1967, at Owerri, Nigeria. . . . 5-11/206. . . . Full name: Okechukwu Patrick Egu. . . . Name pronounced E-gu. . . . First name means "God's gift."
HIGH SCHOOL: John F. Kennedy (Richmond, Calif.).
COLLEGE: Contra Costa College (Calif.), then Nevada-Reno.
TRANSACTIONS/CAREER NOTES: Selected by Tampa Bay Buccaneers in ninth round (230th pick overall) of 1989 NFL draft. . . . Signed by Buccaneers (July 15, 1989). . . . Released by Buccaneers (September 5, 1989). . . . Signed as free agent by New England Patriots to developmental squad (September 14, 1989). . . . On developmental squad (September 14-November 8, 1989). . . . Activated after clearing procedural waivers (November 10, 1989). . . . Granted unconditional free agency (February 1, 1990). . . . Signed by New York Jets (April 1, 1990). . . . On injured reserve with arm injury (September 4, 1990-entire season).
PRO STATISTICS: 1989—Recovered one fumble.

Year	Team	G	RUSHING				KICKOFF RETURNS				TOTAL		
			No.	Yds.	Avg.	TD	No.	Yds.	Avg.	TD	TD	Pts.	F.
1989— New England NFL		7	3	20	6.7	1	2	26	13.0	0	1	6	1
Pro totals (1 year)		7	3	20	6.7	1	2	26	13.0	0	1	6	1

EILERS, PAT
S, VIKINGS

PERSONAL: Born September 3, 1966, at St. Paul, Minn. . . . 5-11/195. . . . Full name: Patrick Christopher Eilers.
HIGH SCHOOL: St. Thomas Academy (St. Paul, Minn.).
COLLEGE: Notre Dame (bachelor of science degrees in mechanical engineering and biology).
TRANSACTIONS/CAREER NOTES: Signed as free agent by Minnesota Vikings (April 27, 1990). . . . Released by Vikings (September 3, 1990). . . . Re-signed by Vikings to practice squad (October 1, 1990). . . . Activated (November 9, 1990).
PLAYING EXPERIENCE: Minnesota NFL, 1990. . . . Games: 1990 (8).
PRO STATISTICS: 1990—Recovered one fumble.

EISENHOOTH, STAN
C, SEAHAWKS

PERSONAL: Born July 8, 1963, at Harrisburg, Pa. . . . 6-5/291. . . . Full name: Stanley Emerson Eisenhooth. . . . Brother of John Eisenhooth, defensive tackle with Seattle Seahawks, 1987.
HIGH SCHOOL: Bald Eagle Area (Wingate, Pa.).
COLLEGE: Arizona Western College, then Towson State.

TRANSACTIONS/CAREER NOTES: Signed as free agent by Seattle Seahawks (May 8, 1986).... On injured reserve with shoulder injury (September 3, 1986-entire season).... On injured reserve with broken hand (September 1-December 18, 1987).... Crossed picket line during players' strike (September 28, 1987).... Returned to picket line (October 1, 1987).... Active for two games with Seahawks in 1987; did not play.... Granted unconditional free agency (February 1, 1989).... Signed by Indianapolis Colts (March 29, 1989).... Released by Colts (September 3, 1990).... Signed by Seattle Seahawks (May 3, 1991).
PLAYING EXPERIENCE: Seattle NFL, 1987 and 1988; Indianapolis NFL, 1989.... Games: 1988 (13), 1989 (16). Total: 29.

ELDER, DONNIE
CB, CHARGERS

PERSONAL: Born December 13, 1963, at Chattanooga, Tenn. .... 5-9/178. .... Full name: Donald Eugene Elder.
HIGH SCHOOL: Brainerd (Chattanooga, Tenn.).
COLLEGE: Memphis State.

TRANSACTIONS/CAREER NOTES: Selected by Memphis Showboats in 1985 USFL territorial draft.... Selected by New York Jets in third round (67th pick overall) of 1985 NFL draft.... Signed by Jets (July 17, 1985).... On injured reserve with hip injury (November 16, 1985-remainder of season).... Released by Jets (August 25, 1986).... Awarded on waivers to Pittsburgh Steelers (August 26, 1986).... Released by Steelers (November 28, 1986).... Signed as free agent by Detroit Lions (December 3, 1986).... On injured reserve with knee injury (September 7-November 16, 1987).... Released by Lions (November 17, 1987).... Signed as free agent by Tampa Bay Buccaneers (February 18, 1988).... Granted unconditional free agency (February 1, 1990).... Signed by Miami Dolphins (March 29, 1990).... On injured reserve with hamstring injury (September 3-October 1, 1990).... Released by Dolphins (October 1, 1990).... Signed by San Diego Chargers (October 3, 1990).
PRO STATISTICS: 1986—Recovered one fumble. 1988—Returned one punt for no yards and recovered one fumble for six yards. 1989—Recovered one fumble. 1990—Recovered two fumbles.

		—INTERCEPTIONS—				—KICKOFF RETURNS—				—TOTAL—		
Year	Team	G	No.	Yds.	Avg.	TD	No.	Yds.	Avg.	TD	TD	Pts.	F.
1985—	N.Y. Jets NFL	10	0	0		0	3	42	14.0	0	0	0	1
1986—	Pitt. (9)-Det. (3) NFL	12	0	0		0	22	435	19.8	0	0	0	1
1988—	Tampa Bay NFL	16	3	9	3.0	0	34	772	22.7	0	0	0	1
1989—	Tampa Bay NFL	16	1	0	.0	0	40	685	17.1	0	0	0	2
1990—	San Diego NFL	12	1	0	.0	0	24	571	23.8	0	0	0	2
Pro totals (5 years)		66	5	9	1.8	0	123	2505	20.4	0	0	0	7

ELKINS, MIKE
QB, CHIEFS

PERSONAL: Born July 20, 1966, at Greensboro, N.C. .... 6-3/225. .... Full name: Michael David Elkins.... Son of Jack Elkins, minor league catcher, 1945, 1947-1954 and 1956.
HIGH SCHOOL: Grimsley (Greensboro, N.C.).
COLLEGE: Wake Forest (degree in speech-communications, 1989).

TRANSACTIONS/CAREER NOTES: Selected by Kansas City Chiefs in second round (32nd pick overall) of 1989 NFL draft.... Signed by Chiefs (August 9, 1989).... On injured reserve with back injury (September 5-October 16, 1989).... On developmental squad (October 17-November 25, 1989).... On inactive list for all 16 games in 1990.... Assigned to Sacramento Surge in 1991 WLAF enhancement allocation program (March 4, 1991).
PRO STATISTICS: Passer rating points: NFL: 1989 (16.7). WLAF: 1991 (67.1).

			—————PASSING—————							—————RUSHING—————				———TOTAL———		
Year	Team	G	Att.	Cmp.	Pct.	Yds.	TD	Int.	Avg.	Att.	Yds.	Avg.	TD	TD	Pts.	F.
1989—	Kansas City NFL	1	2	1	50.0	5	0	1	2.50	0	0		0	0	0	0
1991—	Sacramento WLAF	10	312	153	49.0	2068	13	13	6.63	20	71	3.6	0	0	0	—
NFL totals (1 year)		1	2	1	50.0	5	0	1	2.50	0	0		0	0	0	0
WLAF totals (1 year)		10	312	153	49.0	2068	13	13	6.63	20	71	3.6	0	0	0	—
Pro totals (2 years)		11	314	154	49.0	2073	13	14	6.60	20	71	3.6	0	0	0	0

ELLARD, HENRY
WR, RAMS

PERSONAL: Born July 21, 1961, at Fresno, Calif. .... 5-11/182 ... Name pronounced EL-lard.
HIGH SCHOOL: Hoover (Fresno, Calif.).
COLLEGE: Fresno State.

TRANSACTIONS/CAREER NOTES: Selected by Oakland Invaders in 1983 USFL territorial draft.... Selected by Los Angeles Rams in second round (32nd pick overall) of 1983 NFL draft.... Signed by Rams (July 22, 1983).... Granted free agency (February 1, 1986).... Re-signed by Rams (October 22, 1986).... Granted roster exemption (October 22-October 25, 1986).... On inactive list (November 25, 1990).
CHAMPIONSHIP GAME EXPERIENCE: Played in NFC championship game after 1985 and 1989 seasons.
RECORDS/HONORS: Played in Pro Bowl after 1984, 1988 and 1989 seasons.... Named as punt returner to THE SPORTING NEWS NFL All-Pro team, 1984 and 1985.... Named to THE SPORTING NEWS NFL All-Pro team, 1988.
PRO STATISTICS: 1983—Recovered two fumbles. 1984—Recovered two fumbles. 1985—Recovered five fumbles. 1986—Recovered one fumble. 1987—Recovered one fumble.

		———RUSHING———				———RECEIVING———				—PUNT RETURNS—				KICKOFF RETURNS				– TOTALS –		
Year	Team	G	Att.	Yds.	Avg.	TD	No.	Yds.	Avg.	TD	No.	Yds.	Avg.	TD	No.	Yds.	Avg.	TD	TD	Pts.	F.
1983—	L.A. Rams NFL	12	3	7	2.3	0	16	268	16.8	0	16	217	*13.6	*1	15	314	20.9	0	1	6	2
1984—	L.A. Rams NFL	16	3	-5	-1.7	0	34	622	18.3	6	30	403	13.4	*2	2	24	12.0	0	8	48	4
1985—	L.A. Rams NFL	16	3	8	2.7	0	54	811	15.0	5	37	501	13.5	1	0	0		0	6	36	3
1986—	L.A. Rams NFL	9	1	-15	-15.0	0	34	447	13.2	4	14	127	9.1	0	1	18	18.0	0	4	24	3
1987—	L.A. Rams NFL	12	1	4	4.0	0	51	799	15.7	3	15	107	7.1	0	1	8	8.0	0	3	18	3
1988—	L.A. Rams NFL	16	1	7	7.0	0	86	*1414	16.4	10	17	119	7.0	0	0	0		0	10	60	3
1989—	L.A. Rams NFL	14	2	10	5.0	0	70	1382	19.7	8	2	20	10.0	0	0	0		0	8	48	0
1990—	L.A. Rams NFL	15	2	21	10.5	0	76	1294	17.0	4	2	15	7.5	0	0	0		0	4	24	4
Pro totals (8 years)		110	16	37	2.3	0	421	7037	16.7	40	133	1509	11.4	4	19	364	19.2	0	44	264	22

ELLIOTT, JOHN

OT, GIANTS

PERSONAL: Born April 1, 1965, at Lake Ronkonkoma, N.Y. . . . 6-7/305.
HIGH SCHOOL: Sachem (Lake Ronkonkoma, N.Y.).
COLLEGE: Michigan (degree, 1988).
TRANSACTIONS/CAREER NOTES: Selected by New York Giants in second round (36th pick overall) of 1988 NFL draft. . . . Signed by Giants (July 18, 1988). . . . On inactive list (October 14, 21, 28; November 5, 11, 18, 25; and December 3, 1990).
PLAYING EXPERIENCE: New York Giants NFL, 1988-1990. . . . Games: 1988 (16), 1989 (13), 1990 (8). Total: 37.
CHAMPIONSHIP GAME EXPERIENCE: Played in NFC championship game after 1990 season. . . . Played in Super Bowl XXV after 1990 season.
PRO STATISTICS: 1988—Recovered one fumble.

ELLISON, RIKI

LB, RAIDERS

PERSONAL: Born August 15, 1960, at Christchurch, New Zealand. . . . 6-2/230. . . . Full name: Riki Morgan Ellison. . . . Formerly known as Riki Gray.
HIGH SCHOOL: Amphitheater (Tucson, Ariz.).
COLLEGE: Southern California (bachelor of arts degree in international relations, certificate of defense and strategic studies and physical education, 1983).
TRANSACTIONS/CAREER NOTES: Selected by Los Angeles Express in 1983 USFL territorial draft. . . . Selected by San Francisco 49ers in fifth round (117th pick overall) of 1983 NFL draft. . . . Signed by 49ers (June 1, 1983). . . . On injured reserve with broken arm (September 14-December 17, 1987). . . . On injured reserve with broken arm (September 4, 1989-entire season). . . . Granted unconditional free agency (February 1, 1990). . . . Rights relinquished (April 13, 1990). . . . Signed by Los Angeles Raiders (May 7, 1990).
PLAYING EXPERIENCE: San Francisco NFL, 1983-1989; Los Angeles Raiders NFL, 1990. . . . Games: 1983 (16), 1984 (16), 1985 (16), 1986 (16), 1987 (3), 1988 (13), 1990 (16). Total: 96.
CHAMPIONSHIP GAME EXPERIENCE: Played in NFC championship game after 1983 and 1984 seasons. . . . Member of San Francisco 49ers for NFC championship game after 1988 season; inactive. . . . Played in AFC championship game after 1990 season. . . . Played in Super Bowl XIX after 1984 season and Super Bowl XXIII after 1988 season.
PRO STATISTICS: 1985—Recovered two fumbles for seven yards. 1986—Recovered one fumble. 1990—Intercepted one pass for seven yards.

ELWAY, JOHN

QB, BRONCOS

PERSONAL: Born June 28, 1960, at Port Angeles, Wash. . . . 6-3/215. . . . Full name: John Albert Elway. . . . Son of Jack Elway, former head football coach at Stanford and head coach of Frankfurt Galaxy of WLAF.
HIGH SCHOOL: Granada Hills (Calif.).
COLLEGE: Stanford (bachelor of arts degree in economics, 1983).
TRANSACTIONS/CAREER NOTES: Selected by Oakland Invaders in 1983 USFL territorial draft. . . . Selected by Baltimore Colts in first round (first pick overall) of 1983 NFL draft. . . . Rights traded by Colts to Denver Broncos for quarterback Mark Herrmann, rights to offensive lineman Chris Hinton and first-round pick in 1984 draft (May 2, 1983). . . . Signed by Broncos (May 2, 1983).
CHAMPIONSHIP GAME EXPERIENCE: Played in AFC championship game after 1986, 1987 and 1989 seasons. . . . Played in Super Bowl XXI after 1986 season, Super Bowl XXII after 1987 season and Super Bowl XXIV after 1989 season.
RECORDS/HONORS: Named as quarterback on THE SPORTING NEWS college All-America team, 1980 and 1982. . . . Played in Pro Bowl after 1986 and 1987 seasons. . . . Named to play in Pro Bowl after 1989 season; replaced due to injury by Dave Krieg. . . . Named to THE SPORTING NEWS NFL All-Pro team, 1987.
PRO STATISTICS: Passer rating points: 1983 (54.9), 1984 (76.8), 1985 (70.2), 1986 (79.0), 1987 (83.4), 1988 (71.4), 1989 (73.7), 1990 (78.5). Career: 74.3. . . . 1983—Recovered three fumbles. 1984—Recovered five fumbles and fumbled 14 times for minus 10 yards. 1985—Recovered two fumbles and fumbled seven times for minus 35 yards. 1986—Caught one pass for 23 yards and a touchdown and recovered one fumble and fumbled eight times for minus 13 yards. 1987—Punted once for 31 yards and fumbled twice for minus one yard. 1988—Punted three times for 39.0 avg. and recovered five fumbles and fumbled seven times for minus nine yards. 1989—Punted once for 34 yards and recovered two fumbles and fumbled nine times for minus four yards. 1990—Punted once for 37 yards and recovered one fumble and fumbled eight times for minus three yards.

					PASSING						RUSHING			TOTAL		
Year	Team	G	Att.	Cmp.	Pct.	Yds.	TD	Int.	Avg.	Att.	Yds.	Avg.	TD	TD	Pts.	F.
1983— Denver NFL		11	259	123	47.5	1663	7	14	6.42	28	146	5.2	1	1	6	6
1984— Denver NFL		15	380	214	56.3	2598	18	15	6.84	56	237	4.2	1	1	6	14
1985— Denver NFL		16	*605	327	54.0	3891	22	23	6.43	51	253	5.0	0	0	0	7
1986— Denver NFL		16	504	280	55.6	3485	19	13	6.91	52	257	4.9	1	2	12	8
1987— Denver NFL		12	410	224	54.6	3198	19	12	7.80	66	304	4.6	4	4	24	2
1988— Denver NFL		15	496	274	55.2	3309	17	19	6.67	54	234	4.3	1	1	6	7
1989— Denver NFL		15	416	223	53.6	3051	18	18	7.33	48	244	5.1	3	3	18	9
1990— Denver NFL		16	502	294	58.6	3526	15	14	7.02	50	258	5.2	3	3	18	8
Pro totals (8 years)		116	3572	1959	54.8	24721	135	128	6.92	405	1933	4.8	14	15	90	61

BASEBALL TRANSACTIONS: Selected by Kansas City Royals' organization in 18th round of free-agent draft (June 5, 1979). . . . Selected by New York Yankees' organization in second round of free-agent draft (June 8, 1981).

BASEBALL RECORD AS PLAYER

Year	Team	League	Pos.	G	AB	R	H	2B	3B	HR	RBI	Avg.	PO	A	E	F.A.
1982— Oneonta	NYP	OF	42	151	26	48	6	2	4	25	.318	69	8	0	1.000

ENGLISH, KEITH

P, RAMS

PERSONAL: Born March 10, 1966, at Denver. . . . 6-3/220. . . . Full name: Keith Alan English.
HIGH SCHOOL: West (Greeley, Colo.).
COLLEGE: Colorado (bachelor of arts degree in business).
TRANSACTIONS/CAREER NOTES: Signed as free agent by Los Angeles Raiders (May 15,

1989).... Released by Raiders (August 29, 1989).... Awarded on waivers to Atlanta Falcons (August 30, 1989).... Released by Falcons (September 5, 1989).... Signed by San Diego Chargers (April 16, 1990).... Traded by Chargers to Los Angeles Rams for undisclosed draft choice (August 28, 1990).

RECORDS/HONORS: Named as punter to THE SPORTING NEWS college All-America team, 1988.

PRO STATISTICS: 1990—Rushed twice for minus 19 yards.

Year Team	G	No.	Avg.	Blk.
1990— L.A. Rams NFL	16	68	39.2	1
Pro totals (1 year)	16	68	39.2	1

—PUNTING— (spanning No., Avg., Blk.)

EPPS, TORY
NT, FALCONS

PERSONAL: Born May 28, 1967, at Uniontown, Pa.... 6-0/270.... Full name: Torrean D. Epps.
HIGH SCHOOL: Uniontown Area (Uniontown, Pa.).
COLLEGE: Memphis State.
TRANSACTIONS/CAREER NOTES: Selected by Atlanta Falcons in eighth round (195th pick overall) of 1990 NFL draft.... Signed by Falcons (July 27, 1990).
PLAYING EXPERIENCE: Atlanta NFL, 1990.... Games: 1990 (16).

ESIASON, BOOMER
QB, BENGALS

PERSONAL: Born April 17, 1961, at West Islip, N.Y.... 6-5/220.... Full name: Norman Julius Esiason.
HIGH SCHOOL: East Islip (Islip Terrace, N.Y.).
COLLEGE: Maryland.
TRANSACTIONS/CAREER NOTES: Selected by Washington Federals in 1984 USFL territorial draft.... Selected by Cincinnati Bengals in second round (38th pick overall) of 1984 NFL draft.... Signed by Bengals (June 19, 1984).
CHAMPIONSHIP GAME EXPERIENCE: Played in AFC championship game after 1988 season.... Played in Super Bowl XXIII after 1988 season.
RECORDS/HONORS: Led NFL quarterbacks in passing with 97.4 points in 1988.... Played in Pro Bowl after 1986 season.... Named to play in Pro Bowl after 1988 season; replaced due to injury by Jim Kelly.... Named to play in Pro Bowl after 1989 season; replaced due to injury by John Elway.... Named THE SPORTING NEWS NFL Player of the Year, 1988.... Named to THE SPORTING NEWS NFL All-Pro team, 1988.
PRO STATISTICS: Passer rating points: 1984 (62.9), 1985 (93.2), 1986 (87.7), 1987 (73.1), 1988 (97.4), 1989 (92.1), 1990 (77.0). Career: 85.8.... 1984—Recovered two fumbles and fumbled four times for minus two yards. 1985—Recovered four fumbles and fumbled nine times for minus five yards. 1986—Punted once for 31 yards and recovered five fumbles and fumbled 12 times for minus 10 yards. 1987—Punted twice for a 34.0 average and recovered four fumbles and fumbled 10 times for minus eight yards. 1988—Punted once for 21.0 avg. and recovered four fumbles. 1989—Recovered two fumbles and fumbled eight times for minus four yards. 1990—Recovered two fumbles and fumbled 11 times for minus 23 yards.

Year Team	G	Att.	Cmp.	Pct.	Yds.	TD	Int.	Avg.	Att.	Yds.	Avg.	TD	TD	Pts.	F.
1984— Cincinnati NFL	10	102	51	50.0	530	3	3	5.20	19	63	3.3	2	2	12	4
1985— Cincinnati NFL	15	431	251	58.2	3443	27	12	7.99	33	79	2.4	1	1	6	9
1986— Cincinnati NFL	16	469	273	58.2	3959	24	17	*8.44	44	146	3.3	1	1	6	12
1987— Cincinnati NFL	12	440	240	54.5	3321	16	19	7.55	52	241	4.6	0	0	0	10
1988— Cincinnati NFL	16	388	223	57.5	3572	28	14	*9.21	43	248	5.8	1	1	6	5
1989— Cincinnati NFL	16	455	258	56.7	3525	28	11	7.75	47	278	5.9	0	0	0	8
1990— Cincinnati NFL	16	402	224	55.7	3031	24	*22	7.54	49	157	3.2	0	0	0	11
Pro totals (7 years)	101	2687	1520	56.6	21381	150	98	7.96	287	1212	4.2	5	5	30	59

—PASSING— (Att. through Avg.); *—RUSHING—* (Att. through TD); *—TOTAL—* (TD, Pts., F.)

ETIENNE, LeROY
LB, 49ERS

PERSONAL: Born July 25, 1966, at Lafayette, La.... 6-2/245.... Full name: LeRoy Joseph Etienne.
HIGH SCHOOL: New Iberia (Lafayette, La.).
COLLEGE: Nebraska.
TRANSACTIONS/CAREER NOTES: Signed as free agent by New York Giants (May 5, 1989).... Released by Giants (September 4, 1989).... Signed by San Francisco 49ers (July 26, 1990).... Released by 49ers (September 3, 1990).... Signed by 49ers to practice squad (October 1, 1990).... Activated (October 17, 1990).... On inactive list (November 4, 1990).
PLAYING EXPERIENCE: San Francisco NFL, 1990.... Games: 1990 (10).
CHAMPIONSHIP GAME EXPERIENCE: Member of San Francisco 49ers for NFC championship game after 1990 season; inactive.

EVANS, BYRON
LB, EAGLES

PERSONAL: Born February 23, 1964, at Phoenix.... 6-2/235.... Full name: Byron Nelson Evans.
HIGH SCHOOL: South Mountain (Phoenix).
COLLEGE: Arizona.
TRANSACTIONS/CAREER NOTES: Selected by Philadelphia Eagles in fourth round (93rd pick overall) of 1987 NFL draft.... Signed by Eagles (August 6, 1987).... Granted free agency (February 1, 1990).... Re-signed by Eagles (August 24, 1990).
PRO STATISTICS: 1987—Recovered one fumble. 1988—Recovered two fumbles. 1989—Recovered three fumbles for 21 yards. 1990—Ran 21 yards with lateral from interception.

Year Team	G	No.	Yds.	Avg.	TD
1987— Philadelphia NFL	12	1	12	12.0	0
1988— Philadelphia NFL	16	0	0		0
1989— Philadelphia NFL	16	3	23	7.7	0
1990— Philadelphia NFL	16	1	43	43.0	1
Pro totals (4 years)	60	5	78	15.6	1

—INTERCEPTIONS— (No., Yds., Avg., TD)

EVANS, DONALD
DE, STEELERS

PERSONAL: Born March 14, 1964, at Raleigh, N.C. . . . 6-2/280. . . . Full name: Donald Lee Evans.
HIGH SCHOOL: Athens Drive (Raleigh, N.C.).
COLLEGE: Winston-Salem State.
TRANSACTIONS/CAREER NOTES: Selected by Los Angeles Rams in second round (47th pick overall) of 1987 NFL draft. . . . Signed by Rams (August 1, 1987). . . . On injured reserve with strained abdomen (September 7-December 8, 1987). . . . Released by Rams (August 30, 1988). . . . Signed as free agent by Philadelphia Eagles (September 8, 1988). . . . On injured reserve with fractured jaw (October 13, 1988-remainder of season). . . . Released by Eagles (September 5, 1989). . . . Signed as free agent by Pittsburgh Steelers (April 24, 1990).
PLAYING EXPERIENCE: Los Angeles Rams NFL, 1987; Philadelphia NFL, 1988; Pittsburgh NFL, 1990. . . . Games: 1987 (1), 1988 (5), 1990 (16). Total: 22.
PRO STATISTICS: 1987—Rushed three times for 10 yards. 1990—Recovered three fumbles for 59 yards.

EVANS, VINCE
QB, RAIDERS

PERSONAL: Born June 14, 1955, at Greensboro, N.C. . . . 6-2/210. . . . Full name: Vincent Tobias Evans.
HIGH SCHOOL: Benjamin L. Smith (Greensboro, N.C.).
COLLEGE: Los Angeles City College, then Southern California.
TRANSACTIONS/CAREER NOTES: Selected by Chicago Bears in sixth round (140th pick overall) of 1977 NFL draft. . . . On injured reserve with staph infection (October 12, 1979-remainder of season). . . . USFL rights traded by Los Angeles Express to Washington Federals for rights to cornerback Johnny Lynn (November 11, 1983). . . . Signed by Chicago Blitz of USFL (November 14, 1983), for contract to take effect after being granted free agency February 1, 1984. . . . USFL rights traded by Washington Federals to Chicago Blitz for linebacker Ben Apuna and rights to wide receiver Waddell Smith (December 27, 1983). . . . Blitz franchise disbanded (November 20, 1984). . . . Traded by Blitz with linebackers Kelvin Atkins, Jay Wilson and Ed Thomas to Denver Gold for past consideration (December 6, 1984). . . . Contract rights returned to Chicago Blitz (August 2, 1985). . . . Granted free agency when USFL suspended operations (August 7, 1986). . . . Signed as replacement player by Los Angeles Raiders (September 24, 1987). . . . Released by Raiders (October 10, 1988). . . . Re-signed by Raiders (November 30, 1988). . . . Active for six games with Raiders in 1988; did not play. . . . Released by Raiders (September 3, 1990). . . . Re-signed by Raiders (September 4, 1990).
CHAMPIONSHIP GAME EXPERIENCE: Played in AFC championship game after 1990 season.
PRO STATISTICS: NFL Passer rating points: 1978 (42.3), 1979 (66.1), 1980 (66.1), 1981 (51.0), 1982 (16.8), 1983 (69.0), 1987 (72.9), 1989 (118.8), 1990 (118.8). Total: 59.0. . . . USFL Passer rating points: 1984 (58.3), 1985 (63.1). Total: 60.1. . . . NFL: 1977—Returned 13 kickoffs for 253 yards (19.5 average) and recovered two fumbles. 1979—Fumbled once for minus two yards. 1980—Fumbled four times for minus three yards. 1981—Recovered two fumbles and fumbled 13 times for minus 10 yards. 1982—Fumbled once for minus 24 yards. . . . USFL: 1984—Recovered two fumbles.

			PASSING						RUSHING				TOTAL		
Year Team	G	Att.	Cmp.	Pct.	Yds.	TD	Int.	Avg.	Att.	Yds.	Avg.	TD	TD	Pts.	F.
1977— Chicago NFL	13	0	0		0	0	0		1	0	.0	0	0	0	3
1978— Chicago NFL	3	3	1	33.3	38	0	1	12.67	6	23	3.8	0	0	0	0
1979— Chicago NFL	4	63	32	50.8	508	4	5	8.06	12	72	6.0	1	1	6	1
1980— Chicago NFL	13	278	148	53.2	2039	11	16	7.34	60	306	5.1	8	8	48	4
1981— Chicago NFL	16	436	195	44.7	2354	11	20	5.40	43	218	5.1	3	3	18	13
1982— Chicago NFL	4	28	12	42.9	125	0	4	4.46	2	0	.0	0	0	0	1
1983— Chicago NFL	9	145	76	52.4	1108	5	7	7.64	22	142	6.5	1	1	6	4
1984— Chicago USFL	15	411	200	48.7	2624	14	22	6.38	30	144	4.8	6	6	36	6
1985— Denver USFL	14	325	157	48.3	2259	12	16	6.95	43	283	6.6	7	7	42	3
1987— L.A. Raiders NFL	3	83	39	47.0	630	5	4	7.59	11	144	13.1	1	1	6	0
1989— L.A. Raiders NFL	1	2	2	100.0	50	0	0	25.00	1	16	16.0	0	0	0	1
1990— L.A. Raiders NFL	5	1	1	100.0	36	0	0	36.00	1	-2	-2.0	0	0	0	0
NFL totals (10 years)	71	1039	506	48.7	6888	36	57	6.63	159	919	5.8	14	14	84	27
USFL totals (2 years)	29	736	357	48.5	4883	26	38	6.64	73	427	5.9	13	13	78	9
Pro totals (12 years)	100	1775	863	48.6	11771	62	95	6.63	232	1346	5.8	27	27	162	36

EVERETT, ERIC
DB, BUCCANEERS

PERSONAL: Born July 13, 1966, at Daingerfield, Tex. . . . 5-10/170. . . . Full name: Eric Eugene Everett. . . . Brother of Thomas Everett, safety with Pittsburgh Steelers.
HIGH SCHOOL: Daingerfield (Tex.).
COLLEGE: Texas Tech.
TRANSACTIONS/CAREER NOTES: Selected by Philadelphia Eagles in fifth round (122nd pick overall) of 1988 NFL draft. . . . Signed by Eagles (July 21, 1988). . . . Granted unconditional free agency (February 1, 1990). . . . Signed by Tampa Bay Buccaneers (March 1, 1990).
PRO STATISTICS: 1990—Recovered one fumble.

		INTERCEPTIONS			
Year Team	G	No.	Yds.	Avg.	TD
1988— Philadelphia NFL	16	1	0	.0	0
1989— Philadelphia NFL	16	4	64	16.0	1
1990— Tampa Bay NFL	16	3	28	9.3	0
Pro totals (3 years)	48	8	92	11.5	1

EVERETT, JIM
QB, RAMS

PERSONAL: Born January 3, 1963, at Emporia, Kan. . . . 6-5/212. . . . Full name: James Samuel Everett III.
HIGH SCHOOL: Eldorado (Albuquerque, N.M.).
COLLEGE: Purdue (degree in finance, 1986).

TRANSACTIONS/CAREER NOTES: Selected by Houston Oilers in first round (third pick overall) of 1986 NFL draft. . . . Selected by Memphis Showboats in first round (fourth pick overall) of 1986 USFL draft. . . . NFL rights traded by Houston Oilers to Los Angeles Rams for guard Kent Hill, defensive end William Fuller, first- and fifth-round picks in 1987 draft and first-round pick in 1988 draft (September 18, 1986). . . . Signed by Rams (September 25, 1986). . . . Granted roster exemption (September 25-September 30, 1986). . . . Crossed picket line during players' strike (October 14, 1987).
CHAMPIONSHIP GAME EXPERIENCE: Played in NFC championship game after 1989 season.
RECORDS/HONORS: Named to play in Pro Bowl after 1989 season; replaced due to injury by Randall Cunningham. . . . Played in Pro Bowl after 1990 season.
PRO STATISTICS: Passer rating points: 1986 (67.8), 1987 (68.4), 1988 (89.2), 1989 (90.6), 1990 (79.3). Career: 82.2. . . . 1986—Fumbled twice for minus two yards. 1987—Recovered one fumble. 1988—Fumbled seven times for minus 17 yards. 1989—Recovered four fumbles and fumbled four times for minus one yard. 1990—Fumbled four times for minus 12 yards.

				PASSING						RUSHING				TOTAL	
Year	Team	G	Att.	Cmp.	Pct.	Yds.	TD	Int.	Avg.	Att.	Yds.	Avg.	TD	TD	Pts.	F.
1986— L.A. Rams NFL		6	147	73	49.7	1018	8	8	6.93	16	46	2.9	1	1	6	2
1987— L.A. Rams NFL		11	302	162	53.6	2064	10	13	6.83	18	83	4.6	1	1	6	2
1988— L.A. Rams NFL		16	517	308	59.6	3964	*31	18	7.67	34	104	3.1	0	0	0	7
1989— L.A. Rams NFL		16	518	304	58.7	4310	*29	17	8.32	25	31	1.2	1	1	6	4
1990— L.A. Rams NFL		16	554	307	55.4	3989	23	17	7.20	20	31	1.6	1	1	6	4
Pro totals (5 years)		65	2038	1154	56.6	15345	101	73	7.53	113	295	2.6	4	4	24	19

EVERETT, THOMAS
S, STEELERS

PERSONAL: Born November 21, 1964, at Daingerfield, Tex. . . . 5-9/182. . . . Full name: Thomas Gregory Everett. . . . Brother of Eric Everett, defensive back with Tampa Bay Buccaneers.
HIGH SCHOOL: Daingerfield (Tex.).
COLLEGE: Baylor.
TRANSACTIONS/CAREER NOTES: Selected by Pittsburgh Steelers in fourth round (94th pick overall) of 1987 NFL draft. . . . Signed by Steelers (July 26, 1987). . . . On inactive list (September 16, 1990).
RECORDS/HONORS: Named as defensive back on THE SPORTING NEWS college All-America team, 1986.
PRO STATISTICS: 1987—Returned four punts for 22 yards, recovered two fumbles for seven yards and fumbled once. 1988—Recovered two fumbles for 38 yards. 1989—Recovered one fumble and fumbled once for 21 yards.

			INTERCEPTIONS		
Year	Team	G	No.	Yds.	Avg.	TD
1987— Pittsburgh NFL		12	3	22	7.3	0
1988— Pittsburgh NFL		14	3	31	10.3	0
1989— Pittsburgh NFL		16	3	68	22.7	0
1990— Pittsburgh NFL		15	3	2	.7	0
Pro totals (4 years)		57	12	123	10.3	0

EVERS, WILLIAM
CB, FALCONS

PERSONAL: Born September 24, 1968, at Cairo, Ga. . . . 5-10/175.
HIGH SCHOOL: Cairo (Ga.).
COLLEGE: Florida A&M.
TRANSACTIONS/CAREER NOTES: Signed as free agent by Atlanta Falcons (April 30, 1990). . . . Released by Falcons (August 28, 1990). . . . Re-signed by Falcons (September 14, 1990). . . . Released by Falcons (September 18, 1990). . . . Re-signed by Falcons (September 20, 1990). . . . Released by Falcons, then re-signed (October 3, 1990). . . . On injured reserve with broken finger (December 12, 1990-remainder of season).
PLAYING EXPERIENCE: Atlanta NFL, 1990. . . . Games: 1990 (2).

EZOR, BLAKE
RB, BRONCOS

PERSONAL: Born October 11, 1966, at Las Vegas. . . . 5-9/183.
HIGH SCHOOL: Bishop Gorman (Las Vegas).
COLLEGE: Michigan State.
TRANSACTIONS/CAREER NOTES: Signed as free agent by Denver Broncos (May, 1990). . . . Released by Broncos (September 3, 1990). . . . Signed by Broncos to practice squad (October 1, 1990). . . . Activated (October 19, 1990).

			RUSHING				KICKOFF RETURNS				TOTAL	
Year	Team	G	No.	Yds.	Avg.	TD	No.	Yds.	Avg.	TD	TD	Pts.	F.
1990— Denver NFL		9	23	81	3.5	0	13	214	16.5	0	0	0	1
Pro totals (1 year)		9	23	81	3.5	0	13	214	16.5	0	0	0	1

FAGAN, KEVIN
DE, 49ERS

PERSONAL: Born April 25, 1963, at Lake Worth, Fla. . . . 6-3/260.
HIGH SCHOOL: John I. Leonard (Lake Worth, Fla.).
COLLEGE: Miami (Fla.).
TRANSACTIONS/CAREER NOTES: Selected by Orlando Renegades in 1986 USFL territorial draft. . . . Selected by San Francisco 49ers in fourth round (102nd pick overall) of 1986 NFL draft. . . . Signed by 49ers (July 20, 1986). . . . On non-football injury list with knee injury (July 22, 1986-entire season).
PLAYING EXPERIENCE: San Francisco NFL, 1987-1990. . . . Games: 1987 (7), 1988 (14), 1989 (16), 1990 (16). Total: 53.
CHAMPIONSHIP GAME EXPERIENCE: Played in NFC championship game after 1988-1990 seasons. . . . Played in Super Bowl XXIII after 1988 season and Super Bowl XXIV after 1989 season.
PRO STATISTICS: 1987—Recovered one fumble for six yards. 1989—Recovered two fumbles.

FAIRS, ERIC

LB, OILERS

PERSONAL: Born February 17, 1964, at Memphis, Tenn.... 6-3/244.... Full name: Eric Jerome Fairs.
HIGH SCHOOL: Northside (Memphis, Tenn.).
COLLEGE: Memphis State.
TRANSACTIONS/CAREER NOTES: Selected by Memphis Showboats in 1986 USFL territorial draft.... Signed as free agent by Houston Oilers (May 21, 1986).... Released by Oilers (August 26, 1986).... Re-signed by Oilers (October 2, 1986).... Granted free agency (February 1, 1990).... Re-signed by Oilers (June 25, 1990).
PLAYING EXPERIENCE: Houston NFL, 1986-1990.... Games: 1986 (12), 1987 (12), 1988 (16), 1989 (16), 1990 (16). Total: 72.
PRO STATISTICS: 1988—Credited with a safety and recovered one fumble. 1989—Returned one kickoff for one yard and recovered two fumbles. 1990—Recovered one fumble.

FAISON, DERRICK

WR, RAMS

PERSONAL: Born August 24, 1967, at Lake City, S.C.... 6-4/200 ... Name pronounced FAY-son.
HIGH SCHOOL: Lake City (S.C.).
COLLEGE: Howard.
TRANSACTIONS/CAREER NOTES: Signed as free agent by Los Angeles Rams (March 9, 1990).... On inactive list (December 9, 1990).

Year Team	G	No.	Yds.	Avg.	TD
			RECEIVING		
1990— L.A. Rams NFL	15	3	27	9.0	1
Pro totals (1 year)	15	3	27	9.0	1

FARR, MEL

RB, LIONS

PERSONAL: Born August 12, 1966, at Santa Monica, Calif.... 6-0/237.... Full name: Melvin Farr Jr. ... Son of Mel Farr Sr., running back with Detroit Lions, 1967-1973; nephew of Miller Farr, cornerback with Denver Broncos, San Diego Chargers, Houston Oilers, St. Louis Cardinals and Detroit Lions, 1965-1973; brother of Mike Farr, wide receiver with Detroit Lions; and cousin of Jerry Ball, nose tackle with Detroit Lions.
HIGH SCHOOL: Brother Rice (Birmingham, Mich.).
COLLEGE: UCLA.
TRANSACTIONS/CAREER NOTES: Selected by Denver Broncos in ninth round (248th pick overall) of 1988 NFL draft.... Signed by Broncos (July 12, 1988).... Released by Broncos (August 23, 1988).... Signed as free agent by Los Angeles Rams (April 11, 1989).... Released by Rams (September 5, 1989).... Re-signed by Rams to developmental squad (September 6, 1989).... On developmental squad (September 6-December 20, 1989).... Activated after clearing procedural waivers (December 22, 1989).... Released by Rams (September 3, 1990).... Signed by WLAF (January 7, 1991).... Selected by Sacramento Surge in fifth round (46th running back) of 1991 WLAF positional draft.... Signed by Detroit Lions (June 27, 1991).
CHAMPIONSHIP GAME EXPERIENCE: Played in NFC championship game after 1989 season.

Year Team	G	RUSHING Att.	Yds.	Avg.	TD	RECEIVING No.	Yds.	Avg.	TD	KICKOFF RETURNS No.	Yds.	Avg.	TD	TOTAL TD	Pts.	F.
1989— L.A. Rams NFL	1	0	0		0	0	0		0	0	0		0	0	0	0
1991— Sacramento WLAF	10	1	10	10.0	0	23	309	13.4	1	2	24	12.0	0	1	6	—
NFL totals (1 year)	1	0	0		0	0	0		0	0	0		0	0	0	0
WLAF totals (1 year)	10	1	10	10.0	0	23	309	13.4	1	2	24	12.0	0	1	6	—
Pro totals (2 years)	11	1	10	10.0	0	23	309	13.4	1	2	24	12.0	0	1	6	0

FARR, MIKE

WR, LIONS

PERSONAL: Born August 8, 1967, at Santa Monica, Calif.... 5-10/192.... Full name: Michael Anthony Farr.... Son of Mel Farr Sr., running back with Detroit Lions, 1967-1973; nephew of Miller Farr, cornerback with Denver Broncos, San Diego Chargers, Houston Oilers, St. Louis Cardinals and Detroit Lions, 1965-1973; brother of Mel Farr Jr., running back with Detroit Lions; and cousin of Jerry Ball, nose tackle with Detroit Lions.
HIGH SCHOOL: Brother Rice (Birmingham, Mich.).
COLLEGE: UCLA (degree in sociology).
TRANSACTIONS/CAREER NOTES: Signed as free agent by Detroit Lions (April 26, 1990).... Released by Lions (September 3, 1990).... Re-signed by Lions (September 4, 1990).... On inactive list (September 16 and 23, 1990).... Granted unconditional free agency (February 1, 1991).... Re-signed by Detroit (April 8, 1991).

Year Team	G	No.	Yds.	Avg.	TD
			RECEIVING		
1990— Detroit NFL	12	12	170	14.2	0
Pro totals (1 year)	12	12	170	14.2	0

FARRELL, SEAN

G, BRONCOS

PERSONAL: Born May 25, 1960, at Southampton, N.Y.... 6-3/260.... Full name: Sean Ward Farrell.
HIGH SCHOOL: Westhampton Beach (N.Y.).
COLLEGE: Penn State (bachelor of arts degree in general arts and sciences, 1982).
TRANSACTIONS/CAREER NOTES: Selected by Tampa Bay Buccaneers in first round (17th pick overall) of 1982 NFL draft.... Granted free agency (February 1, 1987).... Re-signed by Buccaneers and traded to New England Patriots for second-, seventh- and ninth-round picks in 1987 draft (February 19, 1987).... Crossed picket line during players' strike (October 2, 1987).... On injured reserve with shoulder injury (September 4-November 28, 1990).... Released by Patriots (November 28, 1990).... Awarded on waivers to Denver Broncos (November 30, 1990).

PLAYING EXPERIENCE: Tampa Bay NFL, 1982-1986; New England NFL, 1987-1989; New England (0)-Denver (5) NFL, 1990....
Games: 1982 (9), 1983 (10), 1984 (15), 1985 (14), 1986 (16), 1987 (14), 1988 (15), 1989 (14), 1990 (5). Total: 112.
RECORDS/HONORS: Named as guard on THE SPORTING NEWS college All-America .. Named to THE SPORTING
NEWS NFL All-Pro team, 1984.
PRO STATISTICS: 1983—Recovered one fumble. 1984—Recovered two fumbles. 1988—Caught one pass for four yards.

FARREN, PAUL
OT/G, BROWNS

PERSONAL: Born December 24, 1960, at Weymouth, Mass.... 6-6/270.... Full name: Paul V. Farren.
HIGH SCHOOL: Cohasset (Mass.).
COLLEGE: Boston University (bachelor of arts degree in marketing finance, 1983).
TRANSACTIONS/CAREER NOTES: Selected by Boston Breakers in 1983 USFL territorial draft.... Selected by Cleveland Browns in 12th round (316th pick overall) of 1983 NFL draft.... Signed by Browns (May 31, 1983).... On injured reserve with knee injury (December 30, 1985-remainder of 1985 season playoffs).... Granted free agency (February 1, 1990).... Re-signed by Browns (August 28, 1990).... Granted roster exemption (September 3-September 8, 1990).
PLAYING EXPERIENCE: Cleveland NFL, 1983-1990.... Games: 1983 (16), 1984 (15), 1985 (13), 1986 (16), 1987 (12), 1988 (15), 1989 (16), 1990 (16). Total: 119.
CHAMPIONSHIP GAME EXPERIENCE: Played in AFC championship game after 1986, 1987 and 1989 seasons.
PRO STATISTICS: 1984—Recovered one fumble. 1987—Recovered one fumble. 1989—Recovered one fumble. 1990—Recovered one fumble.

FARYNIARZ, BRETT
LB, RAMS

PERSONAL: Born July 23, 1965, at Carmichael, Calif.... 6-3/232.... Full name: Brett Allen Faryniarz.... Name pronounced FAIR-in-nezz.
HIGH SCHOOL: Cordova (Rancho Cordova, Calif.).
COLLEGE: San Diego State.
TRANSACTIONS/CAREER NOTES: Signed as free agent by Los Angeles Rams (June 17, 1988).... Granted free agency (February 1, 1990).... Re-signed by Rams (July 27, 1990).
PLAYING EXPERIENCE: Los Angeles Rams NFL, 1988-1990.... Games: 1988 (15), 1989 (16), 1990 (16). Total: 47.
CHAMPIONSHIP GAME EXPERIENCE: Played in NFC championship game after 1989 season.
PRO STATISTICS: 1989—Recovered two fumbles.

FAULKNER, JEFF
DE, CARDINALS

PERSONAL: Born April 4, 1964, at St. Thomas, Virgin Islands.... 6-4/305.... Full name: Jeff E. Faulkner.
HIGH SCHOOL: American (Miami).
COLLEGE: Southern (bachelor of arts degree in business management).
TRANSACTIONS/CAREER NOTES: Signed as free agent by Kansas City Chiefs for 1987.... Released by Chiefs (August, 1987).... Re-signed as replacement player by Chiefs (1987).... Signed by Chicago Bruisers of Arena Football League (1988).... Signed by Minnesota Vikings (August, 1988).... Released by Vikings (August, 1988).... Signed by Minnesota Vikings for 1989.... Released by Vikings (September, 1989).... Signed as free agent by Miami Dolphins (February 22, 1990).... Released by Dolphins (September 3, 1990).... Re-signed by Dolphins (October 9, 1990).... Released by Dolphins (October 27, 1990).... Active for one game with Dolphins in 1990; did not play.... Signed by Indianapolis Colts (November 7, 1990).... Granted unconditional free agency (February 1, 1991).... Signed by Phoenix Cardinals (February 27, 1991).
PLAYING EXPERIENCE: Kansas City NFL, 1987; Chicago Arena Football, 1988; Miami (0)-Indianapolis (7) NFL, 1990.... Games: 1987 (3), 1988 (12), 1990 (7). Total NFL: 10. Total Pro: 22.

FEAGLES, JEFF
P, EAGLES

PERSONAL: Born March 7, 1966, at Scottsdale, Ariz.... 6-1/205.... Full name: Jeffrey Allan Feagles.
HIGH SCHOOL: Gerard Catholic (Phoenix).
COLLEGE: Scottsdale Community College (Ariz.), then Miami, Fla. (bachelor of business administration degree, 1988).
TRANSACTIONS/CAREER NOTES: Signed as free agent by New England Patriots (May 1, 1988).... Released by Patriots (May 24, 1990).... Awarded on waivers to Philadelphia Eagles (June 5, 1990).
PRO STATISTICS: 1988—Rushed once for no yards and recovered one fumble. 1989—Attempted two passes with no completions, recovered one fumble and fumbled once. 1990—Attempted one pass with no completion and rushed twice for three yards.

			—PUNTING—		
Year	Team	G	No.	Avg.	Blk.
1988— New England NFL		16	91	38.3	0
1989— New England NFL		16	63	38.0	1
1990— Philadelphia NFL		16	72	42.0	2
Pro totals (3 years)		48	226	39.4	3

FEARS, WILLIE
DE/NT, CHIEFS

PERSONAL: Born June 4, 1964, at Chicago.... 6-4/298.
HIGH SCHOOL: Barton (Ark.).
COLLEGE: Holmes Junior College (Miss.), then Northwestern State (La.).
TRANSACTIONS/CAREER NOTES: Signed as free agent by Ottawa Rough Riders of CFL (June, 1986).... Released by Rough Riders (July, 1986).... Signed as free agent replacement player by Cincinnati Bengals (September 25, 1987).... Released by Bengals (October 19, 1987).... Signed as free agent by New York Jets (April 15, 1988).... Released by Jets (August 30, 1988).... Signed as free agent by Winnipeg Blue Bombers of CFL (September, 1988).... Released by Blue Bombers (August 14, 1989).... Awarded on waivers to Ottawa Rough Riders of CFL (August 15, 1989).... Re-

leased by Rough Riders (September 25, 1989).... Signed as free agent by Toronto Argonauts of CFL (October 31, 1989)....
Granted free agency (March 1, 1990).... Signed by Green Bay Packers (March 16, 1990).... Released by Packers (August
27, 1990).... Signed by Minnesota Vikings (September 3, 1990).... Released by Vikings (October 26, 1990).... Re-signed
by Vikings (October 30, 1990).... Released by Vikings (November 3, 1990).... Signed by Kansas City Chiefs (April 4, 1991).
PLAYING EXPERIENCE: Cincinnati NFL, 1987; Winnipeg CFL, 1988; Ottawa (6)-Toronto (1) CFL, 1989; Minnesota NFL, 1990....
Games: 1987 (3), 1988 (9), 1989 (7), 1990 (2). Total NFL: 5. Total CFL: 16. Total Pro: 21.
CHAMPIONSHIP GAME EXPERIENCE: Played in Grey Cup (CFL championship game) after 1988 season.
PRO STATISTICS: CFL: 1988—Recovered three fumbles. 1989—Intercepted one pass for no yards.

FEASEL, GRANT
C, SEAHAWKS

PERSONAL: Born June 28, 1960, at Barstow, Calif. ... 6-7/279. ... Full name: Grant Earl
Feasel. ... Name pronounced FEE-zel. ... Brother of Greg Feasel, offensive tackle with
Denver Gold (USFL), Green Bay Packers and San Diego Chargers, 1983-1987.
HIGH SCHOOL: Barstow (Calif.).

COLLEGE: Abilene Christian (bachelor of science degree in biology, 1983).
TRANSACTIONS/CAREER NOTES: Selected by Baltimore Colts in sixth round (161st pick overall) of 1983 NFL draft.... Franchise
transferred to Indianapolis (March 31, 1984).... Released by Indianapolis Colts (October 10, 1984).... Signed as free agent
by Minnesota Vikings (October 17, 1984).... On injured reserve with knee injury (August 29, 1985-entire season).... Granted free agency with option not exercised (February 1, 1986).... Re-signed by Vikings (June 21, 1986).... On injured reserve
with knee injury (August 19-October 27, 1986).... Released by Vikings (October 28, 1986).... Re-signed by Vikings after
clearing procedural waivers (November 20, 1986).... Released by Vikings (November 28, 1986).... Active for one game with
Vikings in 1986; did not play.... Signed as free agent by Seattle Seahawks (February 25, 1987).... Granted free agency (February 1, 1990).... Re-signed by Seahawks (June 10, 1990).
PLAYING EXPERIENCE: Baltimore NFL, 1983; Indianapolis (6)-Minnesota (9) NFL, 1984; Minnesota NFL, 1986; Seattle NFL,
1987-1990.... Games: 1983 (11), 1984 (15), 1986 (0), 1987 (12), 1988 (16), 1989 (16), 1990 (16). Total: 86.
PRO STATISTICS: 1987—Recovered one fumble and fumbled once for minus 19 yards. 1988—Recovered four fumbles and fumbled once for minus 22 yards. 1989—Caught one pass for five yards and recovered one fumble. 1990—Recovered one fumble.

FENERTY, GILL
RB, SAINTS

PERSONAL: Born August 24, 1963, at New Orleans. ... 6-0/205. ... Full name: Lawrence Gill
Fenerty.
HIGH SCHOOL: Jesuit (New Orleans).
COLLEGE: Holy Cross.

TRANSACTIONS/CAREER NOTES: Selected by New Orleans Saints in seventh round (173rd pick overall) of 1986 NFL draft....
Played semi-pro football in Italy (1986).... Signed as free agent by Toronto Argonauts of CFL (March 21, 1987).... Granted
free agency (March 1, 1990).... Signed by New Orleans Saints (April 19, 1990).... On inactive list (October 7, 1990).
CHAMPIONSHIP GAME EXPERIENCE: Played in Grey Cup (CFL championship game) after 1987 season.
PRO STATISTICS: CFL: 1987—Recovered one fumble. 1989—Recovered two fumbles.

			RUSHING				RECEIVING				KICKOFF RETURNS				TOTAL		
Year	Team	G	Att.	Yds.	Avg.	TD	No.	Yds.	Avg.	TD	No.	Yds.	Avg.	TD	TD	Pts.	F.
1987— Toronto CFL		16	178	879	4.9	*12	53	456	8.6	3	10	190	19.0	0	*15	90	8
1988— Toronto CFL		13	202	968	4.8	10	51	443	8.7	2	0	0		0	12	72	2
1989— Toronto CFL		16	245	1247	5.1	10	36	291	8.1	2	1	15	15.0	0	12	72	5
1990— New Orleans NFL		15	73	355	4.9	2	18	209	11.6	0	28	572	20.4	0	2	12	4
CFL totals (3 years)		45	625	3094	5.0	32	140	1190	8.5	7	11	205	18.6	0	39	234	15
NFL totals (1 year)		15	73	355	4.9	2	18	209	11.6	0	28	572	20.4	0	2	12	4
Pro totals (4 years)		60	698	3449	4.9	34	158	1399	8.9	7	39	777	19.9	0	41	246	19

FENNER, DERRICK
RB, SEAHAWKS

PERSONAL: Born April 6, 1967, at Washington, D.C. ... 6-3/228. ... Full name: Derrick
Steven Fenner.
HIGH SCHOOL: Oxon Hill, Md.
COLLEGE: North Carolina, then Gardner-Webb College, N.C. (did not play football).

TRANSACTIONS/CAREER NOTES: Selected by Seattle Seahawks in 10th round (268th pick overall) of 1989 NFL draft.... Signed
by Seahawks (July 22, 1989).
PRO STATISTICS: 1990—Recovered one fumble.

			RUSHING				RECEIVING				TOTAL		
Year	Team	G	Att.	Yds.	Avg.	TD	No.	Yds.	Avg.	TD	TD	Pts.	F.
1989— Seattle NFL		5	11	41	3.7	1	3	23	7.7	0	1	6	0
1990— Seattle NFL		16	215	859	4.0	*14	17	143	8.4	1	15	90	3
Pro totals (2 years)		21	226	900	4.0	15	20	166	8.3	1	16	96	3

FENNEY, RICK
RB, VIKINGS

PERSONAL: Born December 7, 1964, at Everett, Wash. ... 6-1/231. ... Full name: Ricky Dale
Fenney.
HIGH SCHOOL: Snohomish (Wash.).
COLLEGE: Washington.

TRANSACTIONS/CAREER NOTES: Selected by Minnesota Vikings in eighth round (211th pick overall) of 1987 NFL draft.... Signed
by Vikings (July 30, 1987).... On inactive list (November 18, 25; and December 2, 1990).... On injured reserve with knee injury (December 28, 1990-remainder of season).
CHAMPIONSHIP GAME EXPERIENCE: Played in NFC championship game after 1987 season.
PRO STATISTICS: 1989—Returned one kickoff for 12 yards and recovered one fumble. 1990—Recovered one fumble.

Year Team	G	RUSHING				RECEIVING				TOTAL		
		Att.	Yds.	Avg.	TD	No.	Yds.	Avg.	TD	TD	Pts.	F.
1987— Minnesota NFL	11	42	174	4.1	2	7	27	3.9	0	2	12	0
1988— Minnesota NFL	13	55	271	4.9	3	15	224	14.9	0	3	18	0
1989— Minnesota NFL	16	151	588	3.9	4	30	254	8.5	2	6	36	4
1990— Minnesota NFL	12	87	376	4.3	2	17	112	6.6	0	2	12	3
Pro totals (4 years)	52	335	1409	4.2	11	69	617	8.9	2	13	78	7

FERNANDEZ, MERVYN
WR, RAIDERS

PERSONAL: Born December 29, 1959, at Merced, Calif.... 6-3/205.
HIGH SCHOOL: Andrew Hill (San Jose, Calif.).
COLLEGE: De Anza College (Calif.), then San Jose State.
TRANSACTIONS/CAREER NOTES: Signed as free agent by British Columbia Lions of CFL (March 11, 1982).... Selected by Los Angeles Raiders in 10th round (277th pick overall) of 1983 NFL draft.... On injured list (July 1-September 2, 1986).... Granted free agency (March 1, 1987).... Signed by Los Angeles Raiders (March 4, 1987).... Crossed picket line during players' strike (October 14, 1987).... On injured reserve with shoulder injury (November 21, 1987-remainder of season).
CHAMPIONSHIP GAME EXPERIENCE: Played in AFC championship game after 1990 season.
PRO STATISTICS: CFL: 1982—Scored one two-point conversion, returned 20 punts for 179 yards and one touchdown, returned one kickoff for 32 yards, rushed twice for one yard and fumbled twice. 1983—Scored one two-point conversion, returned two punts for 19 yards and fumbled twice. 1985—Rushed three times for 33 yards, returned one kickoff for three yards, attempted one pass with one completion for 55 yards and fumbled once. 1986—Punted 14 times for 34.0 yard average and attempted one pass with one completion for 86 yards.... NFL: 1987—Fumbled once. 1988—Rushed once for nine yards. 1989—Rushed twice for 16 yards and fumbled three times. 1990—Rushed three times for 10 yards.

Year Team	G	RECEIVING			
		No.	Yds.	Avg.	TD
1982— B.C. CFL	16	64	1046	16.3	8
1983— B.C. CFL	16	78	1284	16.5	10
1984— B.C. CFL	15	89	*1486	16.7	17
1985— B.C. CFL	16	95	*1727	18.2	*15
1986— B.C. CFL	11	48	865	18.0	5
1987— L.A. Raiders NFL	7	14	236	16.9	0
1988— L.A. Raiders NFL	16	31	805	26.0	4
1989— L.A. Raiders NFL	16	57	1069	18.8	9
1990— L.A. Raiders NFL	16	52	839	16.1	5
CFL totals (5 years)	74	374	6408	17.1	55
NFL totals (4 years)	55	154	2949	19.1	18
Pro totals (9 years)	129	528	9357	17.7	73

FIGARO, CEDRIC
LB, COLTS

PERSONAL: Born August 17, 1966, at Lafayette, La.... 6-3/258.... Full name: Cedric Noah Figaro.
HIGH SCHOOL: Lafayette (La.).
COLLEGE: Notre Dame.
TRANSACTIONS/CAREER NOTES: Selected by San Diego Chargers in sixth round (152nd pick overall) of 1988 NFL draft.... Signed by Chargers (July 13, 1988).... On injured reserve with back injury (August 29-November 12, 1988).... Granted free agency (February 1, 1990).... Re-signed by Chargers (August 1, 1990).... Granted unconditional free agency (February 1, 1991).... Signed by Indianapolis Colts (April 1, 1991).
PLAYING EXPERIENCE: San Diego NFL, 1988-1990.... Games: 1988 (6), 1989 (16), 1990 (16). Total: 38.
PRO STATISTICS: 1989—Intercepted one pass for two yards, returned one kickoff for 21 yards, returned one punt for no yards and recovered one fumble.

FIKE, DAN
G, BROWNS

PERSONAL: Born June 16, 1961, at Mobile, Ala.... 6-7/285.... Full name: Dan Clement Fike Jr.
HIGH SCHOOL: Pine Forest (Pensacola, Fla.).
COLLEGE: Florida.
TRANSACTIONS/CAREER NOTES: Selected by Tampa Bay Bandits in 1984 USFL territorial draft.... Selected by New York Jets in 10th round (274th pick overall) of 1983 NFL draft.... Signed by Jets (June 10, 1983).... Released by Jets (August 29, 1983).... Signed by Tampa Bay Bandits (November 13, 1983).... Signed by Cleveland Browns to take effect after being granted free agency following 1985 USFL season (January 20, 1985).... On injured reserve with knee injury (December 7, 1989-remainder of season).... On reserve/physically unable to perform list with knee injury (August 28-October 22, 1990).
PLAYING EXPERIENCE: Tampa Bay USFL, 1984 and 1985; Cleveland NFL, 1985-1990.... Games: 1984 (18), 1985 USFL (18), 1985 NFL (13), 1986 (16), 1987 (12), 1988 (16), 1989 (13), 1990 (10). Total USFL: 36. Total NFL: 80. Total Pro: 116.
CHAMPIONSHIP GAME EXPERIENCE: Played in AFC championship game after 1986 and 1987 seasons.
PRO STATISTICS: USFL: 1985—Recovered one fumble.... NFL: 1986—Recovered one fumble.

FitzPATRICK, JAMES
OT, RAIDERS

PERSONAL: Born February 1, 1964, at Heidelberg, Germany.... 6-7/320.... Full name: James Joseph FitzPatrick III.
HIGH SCHOOL: Beaverton (Ore.).
COLLEGE: Southern California.
TRANSACTIONS/CAREER NOTES: Selected by New Jersey Generals in 1986 USFL territorial draft. ... Selected by San Diego

Chargers in first round (13th pick overall) of 1986 NFL draft. . . . Signed by Chargers (July 25, 1986). . . . On injured reserve with back injury (October 6, 1986-remainder of season). . . . On injured reserve with back injury (August 30-October 8, 1988). . . . Granted unconditional free agency (February 1, 1990). . . . Signed by Los Angeles Raiders (April 1, 1990). . . . On inactive list (December 2, 10, 16, 22 and 30, 1990).
PLAYING EXPERIENCE: San Diego NFL, 1986-1989; Los Angeles Raiders NFL, 1990. . . . Games: 1986 (4), 1987 (10), 1988 (11), 1989 (13), 1990 (11). Total: 49.

FLAGLER, TERRENCE
RB, 49ERS

PERSONAL: Born September 24, 1964, at New York. . . . 6-0/200. . . . Full name: R. Terrence Flagler.
HIGH SCHOOL: Fernandina Beach (Fla.).
COLLEGE: Clemson.

TRANSACTIONS/CAREER NOTES: Selected by San Francisco 49ers in first round (25th pick overall) of 1987 NFL draft. . . . Signed by 49ers (July 24, 1987). . . . On injured reserve with foot injury (September 10-November 5, 1988). . . . Traded by 49ers with defensive end Dan Stubbs and third- and 11th-round picks in 1990 NFL draft to Dallas Cowboys for second- and third-round picks in 1990 draft (April 19, 1990). . . . Released by Cowboys (September 3, 1990). . . . Signed by Phoenix Cardinals (September 27, 1990). . . . Traded by Cardinals to San Francisco 49ers for an undisclosed draft pick (August 12, 1991).
CHAMPIONSHIP GAME EXPERIENCE: Played in NFC championship game after 1988 and 1989 seasons. . . . Member of San Francisco 49ers for Super Bowl XXIII after 1988 season; inactive. . . . Played in Super Bowl XXIV after 1989 season.
PRO STATISTICS: 1987—Recovered one fumble. 1989—Recovered one fumble.

		RUSHING				RECEIVING				KICKOFF RETURNS				TOTAL	
Year Team	G	Att.	Yds.	Avg.	TD	No.	Yds.	Avg.	TD	No.	Yds.	Avg.	TD	TD	Pts.	F.
1987— San Francisco NFL	3	6	11	1.8	0	2	28	14.0	0	3	31	10.3	0	0	0	2
1988— San Francisco NFL	3	3	5	1.7	0	4	72	18.0	0	0	0		0	0	0	0
1989— San Francisco NFL	15	33	129	3.9	1	6	51	8.5	0	32	643	20.1	0	1	6	5
1990— Phoenix NFL	13	13	85	6.5	1	13	130	10.0	1	10	167	16.7	0	2	12	0
Pro totals (4 years)	34	55	230	4.2	2	25	281	11.2	1	45	841	18.7	0	3	18	7

FLETCHER, SIMON
LB, BRONCOS

PERSONAL: Born February 18, 1962, at Bay City, Tex. . . . 6-5/240. . . . Full name: Simon Raynard Fletcher. . . . Related to Pat Franklin, running back with Tampa Bay Buccaneers and Cincinnati Bengals, 1986 and 1987.
HIGH SCHOOL: Bay City, Tex.
COLLEGE: Houston.
TRANSACTIONS/CAREER NOTES: Selected by Houston Gamblers in 1985 USFL territorial draft. . . . Selected by Denver Broncos in second round (54th pick overall) of 1985 NFL draft. . . . Signed by Broncos (July 16, 1985).
PLAYING EXPERIENCE: Denver NFL, 1985-1990. . . . Games: 1985 (16), 1986 (16), 1987 (12), 1988 (16), 1989 (16), 1990 (16). Total: 92.
CHAMPIONSHIP GAME EXPERIENCE: Played in AFC championship game after 1986, 1987 and 1989 seasons. . . . Played in Super Bowl XXI after 1986 season, Super Bowl XXII after 1987 season and Super Bowl XXIV after 1989 season.
PRO STATISTICS: 1986—Recovered two fumbles. 1987—Recovered one fumble. 1988—Intercepted one pass for four yards and recovered one fumble. 1989—Recovered one fumble. 1990—Credited with safety and recovered one fumble.

FLOYD, ERIC
G/OT, CHARGERS

PERSONAL: Born October 28, 1965, at Rome, Ga. . . . 6-5/300. . . . Full name: Eric Cunningham Floyd.
HIGH SCHOOL: West Rome (Rome, Ga.).
COLLEGE: Auburn.
TRANSACTIONS/CAREER NOTES: Signed as free agent by San Diego Chargers (May, 1988). . . . Released by Chargers (August 25, 1988). . . . Re-signed by Chargers (off-season, 1989). . . . Released by Chargers (August 30, 1989). . . . Signed by Chargers to developmental squad (September 7, 1989). . . . Released by Chargers (December 7, 1989). . . . Re-signed by Chargers (March 5, 1990).
PLAYING EXPERIENCE: San Diego NFL, 1990. . . . Games: 1990 (16).

FLUTIE, DARREN
WR, CARDINALS

PERSONAL: Born November 18, 1966, at Baltimore. . . . 5-10/188. . . . Full name: Darren Paul Flutie. . . . Brother of Doug Flutie, quarterback with B.C. Lions (CFL) and former quarterback with New Jersey Generals (USFL), Chicago Bears and New England Patriots.
HIGH SCHOOL: Natick (Mass.).
COLLEGE: Boston College (bachelor of science degree in speech communication, 1988).
TRANSACTIONS/CAREER NOTES: Signed as free agent by San Diego Chargers (May 4, 1988). . . . Released by Chargers (September 6, 1989). . . . Signed as free agent by Phoenix Cardinals (May 1, 1990). . . . On injured reserve with foot injury (August 27, 1990-entire season).

		RECEIVING				PUNT RETURNS				KICKOFF RETURNS				TOTAL	
Year Team	G	No.	Yds.	Avg.	TD	No.	Yds.	Avg.	TD	No.	Yds.	Avg.	TD	TD	Pts.	F.
1988— San Diego NFL	16	18	208	11.6	2	7	36	5.1	0	1	10	10.0	0	2	12	2
Pro totals (1 year)	16	18	208	11.6	2	7	36	5.1	0	1	10	10.0	0	2	12	2

FOLSOM, STEVE
TE, COWBOYS

PERSONAL: Born March 21, 1958, at Los Angeles. . . . 6-5/240. . . . Full name: Steve Mark Folsom.
HIGH SCHOOL: Santa Fe Springs (Calif.).
COLLEGE: California State at Long Beach, then Utah (bachelor of science degree in commercial recreation, 1981).

TRANSACTIONS/CAREER NOTES: Selected by Miami Dolphins in 10th round (261st pick overall) of 1981 NFL draft.... Released by Dolphins (August 17, 1981).... Signed as free agent by Philadelphia Eagles (November 25, 1981).... On injured reserve with pulled hamstring (December 26, 1981-remainder of 1981 season playoffs).... On injured reserve with neck injury (September 6, 1982).... Released by Eagles (September 7, 1982).... Signed as free agent by New York Giants (September 13, 1982).... On inactive list (September 20, 1982).... Released by Giants (November 30, 1982).... USFL rights traded by Los Angeles Express to Philadelphia Stars for rights to defensive back Chuck Scicli (September 9, 1982).... Signed by Stars (January 27, 1983).... On developmental squad for one game (June 21, 1984-remainder of season).... Franchise transferred to Baltimore (November 1, 1984).... On reserve/physically unable to perform (February 18-April 6, 1985).... On developmental squad for four games (May 15-June 14, 1985).... Granted free agency when USFL suspended operations (August 7, 1986).... Signed as free agent by Dallas Cowboys (April 30, 1987).... Released by Cowboys (September 7, 1987).... Re-signed by Cowboys (October 20, 1987).... Released by Cowboys (September 3, 1990).... Re-signed by Cowboys (December 18, 1990).
CHAMPIONSHIP GAME EXPERIENCE: Played in USFL championship game after 1983 and 1985 seasons.... On developmental squad for USFL championship game after 1984 season.
PRO STATISTICS: 1983—Fumbled once. 1984—Returned one kickoff for three yards.

| | | | — RECEIVING — | | |
Year	Team	G	No.	Yds.	Avg.	TD
1981— Philadelphia NFL		3	0	0		0
1983— Philadelphia USFL		18	26	286	11.0	1
1984— Philadelphia USFL		17	46	485	10.5	6
1985— Baltimore USFL		8	1	4	4.0	0
1987— Dallas NFL		9	0	0		0
1988— Dallas NFL		16	9	84	9.3	2
1989— Dallas NFL		16	28	265	9.5	2
1990— Dallas NFL		1	0	0		0
NFL totals (5 years)		45	37	349	9.4	4
USFL totals (3 years)		43	73	775	10.6	7
Pro totals (8 years)		88	110	1124	10.2	11

FONTENOT, HERMAN
RB, PACKERS

PERSONAL: Born September 12, 1963, at St. Elizabeth, Tex.... 6-0/221.
HIGH SCHOOL: Charlton-Pollard (Beaumont, Tex.).
COLLEGE: Louisiana State.
TRANSACTIONS/CAREER NOTES: Selected by New Jersey Generals in ninth round (127th pick overall) of 1985 USFL draft.... Signed as free agent by Cleveland Browns (May 6, 1985).... On injured reserve with broken bone in back (August 27-October 25, 1985).... Granted unconditional free agency (February 1, 1989)..... Traded by Browns with third- and fifth-round picks in 1989 draft and first-round pick in 1990 draft to Green Bay Packers for second- and third-round picks in 1989 draft (April 23, 1989).... Granted roster exemption (September 5-September 15, 1990).... On suspended list (October 5-October 8, 1990).
CHAMPIONSHIP GAME EXPERIENCE: Played in AFC championship game after 1986 and 1987 seasons.
PRO STATISTICS: 1985—Attempted one pass with no completions. 1986—Attempted one pass with one completion for 46 yards and a touchdown and recovered one fumble. 1987—Attempted one pass with one completion for 14 yards. 1988—Attempted one pass with no completions and returned blocked punt one yard for a touchdown. 1989—Recovered two fumbles. 1990—Recovered one fumble.

| | | | — RUSHING — | | | | — RECEIVING — | | | | — KICKOFF RETURNS — | | | | — TOTAL — | | |
Year	Team	G	Att.	Yds.	Avg.	TD	No.	Yds.	Avg.	TD	No.	Yds.	Avg.	TD	TD	Pts.	F.
1985— Cleveland NFL		9	0	0		0	2	19	9.5	0	8	215	26.9	0	0	0	1
1986— Cleveland NFL		16	25	105	4.2	1	47	559	11.9	1	7	99	14.1	0	2	12	2
1987— Cleveland NFL		12	15	33	2.2	0	4	40	10.0	0	9	130	14.4	0	0	0	0
1988— Cleveland NFL		16	28	87	3.1	0	19	170	9.0	0	21	435	20.7	0	2	12	0
1989— Green Bay NFL		16	17	69	4.1	1	40	372	9.3	3	2	30	15.0	0	4	24	0
1990— Green Bay NFL		14	17	76	4.5	0	31	293	9.5	1	3	88	29.3	0	1	6	1
Pro totals (6 years)		83	102	370	3.6	2	143	1453	10.2	6	50	997	19.9	0	9	54	4

FONTENOT, JERRY
C, BEARS

PERSONAL: Born November 21, 1966, at Lafayette, La.... 6-3/272.... Full name: Jerry Paul Fontenot.
HIGH SCHOOL: Lafayette (La.).
COLLEGE: Texas A&M.
TRANSACTIONS/CAREER NOTES: Selected by Chicago Bears in third round (65th pick overall) of 1989 NFL draft.... Signed by Bears (July 27, 1989).
PLAYING EXPERIENCE: Chicago NFL, 1989 and 1990.... Games: 1989 (16), 1990 (16). Total: 32.
PRO STATISTICS: 1989—Recovered one fumble. 1990—Fumbled once.

FOOTE, CHRIS
C, VIKINGS

PERSONAL: Born December 2, 1956, at Louisville, Ky.... 6-4/266.... Full name: Chris D. Foote.
HIGH SCHOOL: Fairview (Boulder, Colo.).
COLLEGE: Southern California (bachelor of arts degree in communications, 1980).
TRANSACTIONS/CAREER NOTES: Selected by Baltimore Colts in sixth round (144th pick overall) of 1980 NFL draft.... Released by Colts (September 6, 1982).... Signed as free agent by New York Giants (September 17, 1982).... Traded by Giants to New York Jets for future draft pick (August 23, 1983).... Released by Jets (August 29, 1983).... Signed as free agent by New York Giants (September 13, 1983).... Signed by Los Angeles Express of USFL (November 13, 1983), for contract to take effect after being granted free agency, February 1, 1984.... Traded by Express to Tampa Bay Ban-

dits for past considerations (March 12, 1984). . . . On developmental squad for two games with Bandits (April 5-April 19, 1985). . . . Granted free agency when USFL suspended operations (August 7, 1986). . . . Re-signed by New York Giants and traded to Minnesota Vikings for conditional pick in 1988 NFL draft (May 7, 1987). . . . On injured reserve with broken hand (September 1-November 9, 1987). . . . Released by Vikings (November 10, 1987). . . . Re-signed by Vikings after clearing procedural waivers (November 17, 1987).
PLAYING EXPERIENCE: Baltimore NFL, 1980 and 1981; New York Giants NFL, 1982 and 1983; Los Angeles (3)-Tampa Bay (15) USFL, 1984; Tampa Bay USFL, 1985; Minnesota NFL, 1987-1990. . . . Games: 1980 (16), 1981 (16), 1982 (7), 1983 (11), 1984 (18), 1985 (16), 1987 (6), 1988 (16), 1989 (16), 1990 (16). Total NFL: 104. Total USFL: 34. Total Pro: 138.
CHAMPIONSHIP GAME EXPERIENCE: Played in NFC championship game after 1987 season.
PRO STATISTICS: NFL: 1980—Returned one kickoff for nine yards and recovered one fumble. 1981—Returned one kickoff for no yards. . . . USFL: 1985—Recovered one fumble.

FORD, BERNARD
WR, OILERS

PERSONAL: Born February 27, 1966, at Cordele, Ga. . . . 5-10/171. . . . Full name: K. Bernard Ford.
HIGH SCHOOL: Crisp County (Cordele, Ga.).
COLLEGE: Marion Military Institute (Ala.), then Central Florida.
TRANSACTIONS/CAREER NOTES: Selected by Buffalo Bills in third round (65th pick overall) of 1988 NFL draft. . . . Signed by Bills (July 16, 1988). . . . On injured reserve with separated shoulder (August 15, 1988-entire season). . . . Released by Bills (September 5, 1989). . . . Signed as free agent by Dallas Cowboys to developmental squad (September 7, 1989). . . . On developmental squad (September 7-October 19, 1989). . . . Granted unconditional free agency (February 1, 1990). . . . Signed by Houston Oilers (March 26, 1990). . . . On inactive list (September 16, 1990).

		RECEIVING				KICKOFF RETURNS				TOTAL		
Year	Team	G	No.	Yds.	Avg.	TD	No.	Yds.	Avg.	TD	TD	Pts.	F.
1989— Dallas NFL		10	7	78	11.1	1	0	0	0	0	1	6	0
1990— Houston NFL		14	10	98	9.8	1	14	219	15.6	0	1	6	2
Pro totals (2 years)		24	17	176	10.4	2	14	219	15.6	0	2	12	2

FORD, CHRIS
WR, BUCCANEERS

PERSONAL: Born May 20, 1967, at Houston. . . . 6-1/185. . . . Full name: Christopher David Ford.
HIGH SCHOOL: St. Thomas (Houston).
COLLEGE: Lamar.
TRANSACTIONS/CAREER NOTES: Signed as free agent by Tampa Bay Buccaneers (April 26, 1990). . . . Released by Buccaneers (September 2, 1990). . . . Signed by Buccaneers to practice squad (October 1, 1990). . . . Activated (October 19, 1990). . . . Released by Buccaneers (October 26, 1990). . . . Re-signed by Buccaneers to practice squad (October 30, 1990). . . . Activated (November 2, 1990). . . . On inactive list (November 11, 1990).
PLAYING EXPERIENCE: Tampa Bay NFL, 1990. . . . Games: 1990 (1).

FORD, JOHN
WR, SEAHAWKS

PERSONAL: Born July 31, 1966, at Belle Glade, Fla. . . . 6-2/204. . . . Full name: John Allen Ford.
HIGH SCHOOL: Glade Central (Belle Glade, Fla.).
COLLEGE: Virginia (degree in sociology, 1989).
TRANSACTIONS/CAREER NOTES: Selected by Detroit Lions in second round (30th pick overall) of 1989 NFL draft. . . . Signed by Lions (August 4, 1989). . . . On injured reserve with hamstring injury (September 14-November 7, 1989). . . . Traded by Lions to Seattle Seahawks for undisclosed draft pick (August 27, 1990). . . . Released by Seahawks (September 3, 1990). . . . Re-signed by Seahawks (March 4, 1991).

		RECEIVING			
Year	Team	G	No.	Yds.	Avg.	TD
1989— Detroit NFL		7	5	56	11.2	0
Pro totals (1 year)		7	5	56	11.2	0

FORDE, BRIAN
LB, SAINTS

PERSONAL: Born November 1, 1963, at Montreal, Que. . . . 6-3/235. . . . Name pronounced FORD.
HIGH SCHOOL: Champlain Regional College Prep (Montreal, Que.).
COLLEGE: Washington State.
TRANSACTIONS/CAREER NOTES: Selected by New Orleans Saints in seventh round (190th pick overall) of 1988 NFL draft. . . . Signed by Saints (July 17, 1988). . . . Granted free agency (February 1, 1990). . . . Re-signed by Saints (August 14, 1990).
PLAYING EXPERIENCE: New Orleans NFL, 1988-1990. . . . Games: 1988 (16), 1989 (16), 1990 (16). Total: 48.
PRO STATISTICS: 1989—Credited with a safety and recovered one fumble. 1990—Recovered one fumble.

FOSTER, BARRY
RB, STEELERS

PERSONAL: Born December 8, 1968, at Hurst, Tex. . . . 5-10/223.
HIGH SCHOOL: Duncanville (Tex.).
COLLEGE: Arkansas.
TRANSACTIONS/CAREER NOTES: Selected by Pittsburgh Steelers in fifth round (128th pick overall) of 1990 NFL draft. . . . Signed by Steelers (July 18, 1990).
PRO STATISTICS: 1990—Recovered one fumble.

		RUSHING					RECEIVING				KICKOFF RETURNS				TOTAL		
Year	Team	G	Att.	Yds.	Avg.	TD	No.	Yds.	Avg.	TD	No.	Yds.	Avg.	TD	TD	Pts.	F.
1990— Pittsburgh NFL		16	36	203	5.6	1	1	2	2.0	0	3	29	9.7	0	1	6	2
Pro totals (1 year)		16	36	203	5.6	1	1	2	2.0	0	3	29	9.7	0	1	6	2

FOSTER, ROY
G, 49ERS

PERSONAL: Born May 24, 1960, at Los Angeles. . . . 6-4/290. . . . Full name: Roy Allen Foster.
HIGH SCHOOL: Taft (Woodland Hills, Calif.), then Shawnee Mission West (Overland Park, Kan.).
COLLEGE: Southern California.
TRANSACTIONS/CAREER NOTES: Selected by Miami Dolphins in first round (24th pick overall) of 1982 NFL draft. . . . Granted free agency (February 1, 1990). . . . Re-signed by Dolphins (September 4, 1990). . . . Granted roster exemption (September 4-September 8, 1990). . . . Granted unconditional free agency (February 1, 1991). . . . Signed by San Francisco 49ers (March 25, 1991).
PLAYING EXPERIENCE: Miami NFL, 1982-1990. . . . Games: 1982 (9), 1983 (16), 1984 (16), 1985 (16), 1986 (16), 1987 (12), 1988 (15), 1989 (16), 1990 (16). Total: 132.
CHAMPIONSHIP GAME EXPERIENCE: Played in AFC championship game after 1982, 1984 and 1985 seasons. . . . Played in Super Bowl XVII after 1982 season and Super Bowl XIX after 1984 season.
RECORDS/HONORS: Named as guard on THE SPORTING NEWS college All-America team, 1981. . . . Played in Pro Bowl after 1985 and 1986 seasons.
PRO STATISTICS: 1984—Recovered one fumble. 1986—Recovered two fumbles. 1987—Recovered one fumble.

FOX, MIKE
DE, GIANTS

PERSONAL: Born August 5, 1967, at Akron, O. . . . 6-6/275.
HIGH SCHOOL: Akron North (Akron, O.).
COLLEGE: West Virginia.
TRANSACTIONS/CAREER NOTES: Selected by New York Giants in second round (51st pick overall) of 1990 NFL draft. . . . Signed by Giants (July 31, 1990).
PLAYING EXPERIENCE: New York Giants NFL, 1990. . . . Games: 1990 (16).
CHAMPIONSHIP GAME EXPERIENCE: Played in NFC championship game after 1990 season. . . . Played in Super Bowl XXV after 1990 season.

FRALIC, BILL
G, FALCONS

PERSONAL: Born October 31, 1962, at Penn Hills, Pa. . . . 6-5/280. . . . Full name: William P. Fralic Jr.
HIGH SCHOOL: Penn Hills (Pittsburgh).
COLLEGE: Pittsburgh.
TRANSACTIONS/CAREER NOTES: Selected by Baltimore Stars in 1985 USFL territorial draft. . . . Selected by Atlanta Falcons in first round (second pick overall) of 1985 NFL draft. . . . Signed by Falcons (July 22, 1985). . . . On injured reserve with knee injury (December 14, 1988-remainder of season).
PLAYING EXPERIENCE: Atlanta NFL, 1985-1990. . . . Games: 1985 (15), 1986 (16), 1987 (12), 1988 (14), 1989 (15), 1990 (16). Total: 88.
RECORDS/HONORS: Named as offensive tackle on THE SPORTING NEWS college All-America team, 1983 and 1984. . . . Named to THE SPORTING NEWS NFL All-Pro team, 1986 and 1987. . . . Played in Pro Bowl after 1986, 1987 and 1989 seasons. . . . Named to play in Pro Bowl after 1988 season; replaced due to injury by Mark Bortz.

FRANCIS, JAMES
LB, BENGALS

PERSONAL: Born August 4, 1968, at Houston. . . . 6-5/252 . . . Brother of Ron Francis, cornerback with New England Patriots.
HIGH SCHOOL: La Marque (Tex.).
COLLEGE: Baylor.
TRANSACTIONS/CAREER NOTES: Selected by Cincinnati Bengals in first round (12th pick overall) of 1990 NFL draft. . . . Signed by Bengals (July 19, 1990).
RECORDS/HONORS: Named as special-teams player on THE SPORTING NEWS college All-America team, 1989.
PRO STATISTICS: 1990—Credited with a safety.

| | | INTERCEPTIONS | | | |
Year Team	G	No.	Yds.	Avg.	TD
1990— Cincinnati NFL	16	1	17	17.0	1
Pro totals (1 year)	16	1	17	17.0	1

FRANCIS, JEFF
QB, BROWNS

PERSONAL: Born July 7, 1966, at Park Ridge, Ill. . . . 6-4/225. . . . Full name: Jeffrey Lee Francis.
HIGH SCHOOL: Prospect (Mount Prospect, Ill.).
COLLEGE: Tennessee.
TRANSACTIONS/CAREER NOTES: Selected by Los Angeles Raiders in sixth round (140th pick overall) of 1989 NFL draft. . . . On developmental squad (entire 1989 season). . . . Released by Raiders (September 4, 1990). . . . Signed by Cleveland Browns to practice squad (October 10, 1990) . . . Activated (December 19, 1990).
PRO STATISTICS: Passer rating points: 1990 (118.8). . . . 1990—Recovered one fumble.

| | | PASSING | | | | | | | RUSHING | | | | TOTAL | | |
Year Team	G	Att.	Cmp.	Pct.	Yds.	TD	Int.	Avg.	Att.	Yds.	Avg.	TD	TD	Pts.	F.
1990— Cleveland NFL	1	2	2	1.000	26	0	0	13.0	0	0		0	0	0	0
NFL totals (1 year)	1	2	2	1.000	26	0	0	13.0	0	0		0	0	0	0

FRANCIS, RON
CB, PATRIOTS

PERSONAL: Born April 7, 1964, at LaMarque, Tex. . . . 5-9/186. . . . Full name: Ronald Bernard Francis. . . . Brother of James Francis, linebacker with Cincinnati Bengals.
HIGH SCHOOL: LaMarque (Tex.).
COLLEGE: Baylor.

TRANSACTIONS/CAREER NOTES: Selected by Dallas Cowboys in second round (39th pick overall) of 1987 NFL draft.... Signed by Cowboys (July 24, 1987).... Traded by Cowboys with linebackers Eugene Lockhart and David Howard to New England Patriots (April 22, 1991), to complete deal in which Dallas traded first- and second-round 1991 draft picks to New England for first-round pick in 1991 draft (April 20, 1991).
PRO STATISTICS: 1987—Recovered one fumble for two yards. 1990—Recovered two fumbles.

		—	INTERCEPTIONS	—	
Year Team	G	No.	Yds.	Avg.	TD
1987— Dallas NFL	11	2	18	9.0	1
1988— Dallas NFL	13	1	29	29.0	0
1989— Dallas NFL	15	1	2	2.0	0
1990— Dallas NFL	15	0	0		0
Pro totals (4 years)	54	4	49	12.3	1

FRANK, DONALD
CB, CHARGERS
PERSONAL: Born October 24, 1965, at Edgcombe County, N.C.... 6-0/200.... Full name: Donald Lee Frank.... Cousin of Kelvin Bryant, former running back with Baltimore Stars (USFL), Philadelphia Stars (USFL) and Washington Redskins.
HIGH SCHOOL: Tarboro (N.C.).
COLLEGE: Winston-Salem State.
TRANSACTIONS/CAREER NOTES: Signed as free agent by San Diego Chargers (April 26, 1990).

		— INTERCEPTIONS—				— KICKOFF RETURNS—				— TOTAL —		
Year Team	G	No.	Yds.	Avg.	TD	No.	Yds.	Avg.	TD	TD	Pts.	F.
1990— San Diego NFL	16	2	8	4.0	0	8	172	21.5	0	0	0	0
Pro totals (1 year)	16	2	8	4.0	0	8	172	21.5	0	0	0	0

FRASE, PAUL
DT/DE, JETS
PERSONAL: Born May 6, 1965, at Elmira, N.Y.... 6-5/270.... Full name: Paul Miles Frase.... Name pronounced FRAZE.
HIGH SCHOOL: Spaulding (Rochester, N.H.).
COLLEGE: Syracuse (degree in psychology).
TRANSACTIONS/CAREER NOTES: Selected by New York Jets in sixth round (146th pick overall) of 1988 NFL draft.... Signed by Jets (June 21, 1988).... On reserve/non-football illness list with hyperthyroidism (August 27, 1990-entire season).
PLAYING EXPERIENCE: New York Jets NFL, 1988 and 1989.... Games: 1988 (16), 1989 (16). Total: 32.

FRAZIER, PAUL
RB, COWBOYS
PERSONAL: Born November 12, 1967, at Beaumont, Tex.... 5-8/197.... Full name: Daniel Paul Frazier.
HIGH SCHOOL: Coushatta (La.).
COLLEGE: Northwestern State (La.).
TRANSACTIONS/CAREER NOTES: Signed as free agent by New Orleans Saints (May 3, 1989).... Granted unconditional free agency (February 1, 1990).... Signed by Green Bay Packers (March 17, 1990).... Released by Packers (September 3, 1990).... Signed by WLAF (January 31, 1991).... Selected by Sacramento Surge in first round (sixth running back) of 1991 WLAF positional draft.... Signed by Dallas Cowboys (July 3, 1991).

		—	RUSHING	—		—	RECEIVING	—		— KICKOFF RETURNS—				— TOTAL —		
Year Team	G	Att.	Yds.	Avg.	TD	No.	Yds.	Avg.	TD	No.	Yds.	Avg.	TD	TD	Pts.	F.
1989— New Orleans NFL	15	25	112	4.5	1	3	25	8.3	0	8	157	19.6	0	1	6	1
1991— Sacramento WLAF	7	90	308	3.4	3	15	106	7.1	0	7	123	17.6	0	3	18	—
NFL totals (1 year)	15	25	112	4.5	1	3	25	8.3	0	8	157	19.6	0	1	6	1
WLAF totals (1 year)	7	90	308	3.4	3	15	106	7.1	0	7	123	17.6	0	3	18	—
Pro totals (2 years)	22	115	420	3.7	4	18	131	7.3	0	15	280	18.7	0	4	24	1

FREEMAN, LORENZO
DL, STEELERS
PERSONAL: Born May 23, 1964, at East Camden, N.J.... 6-5/319.... Full name: Lorenzo Z. Freeman.
HIGH SCHOOL: Woodrow Wilson (Camden, N.J.).
COLLEGE: Pittsburgh.
TRANSACTIONS/CAREER NOTES: Selected by Green Bay Packers in fourth round (89th pick overall) of 1987 NFL draft.... Signed by Packers (July 25, 1987).... On injured reserve with ankle injury (September 7-September 22, 1987).... Released by Packers (November 3, 1987).... Signed as free agent by Pittsburgh Steelers (November 18, 1987).... On injured reserve (October 13-November 17, 1990).... On injured reserve with foot injury (December 28, 1990-remainder of season).
PLAYING EXPERIENCE: Pittsburgh NFL, 1987-1990.... Games: 1987 (6), 1988 (13), 1989 (16), 1990 (11). Total: 46.
PRO STATISTICS: 1990—Recovered one fumble.

FREROTTE, MITCH
G, BILLS
PERSONAL: Born March 30, 1965, at Kittanning, Pa.... 6-3/280.... Full name: Paul Mitchael Frerotte.... Name pronounced fur-ROT.
HIGH SCHOOL: Kittanning (Pa.).
COLLEGE: Penn State.
TRANSACTIONS/CAREER NOTES: Signed as free agent by Buffalo Bills (July 22, 1987).... Released by Bills (August 30, 1988). ... Re-signed by Bills (January 10, 1989).... On injured reserve with back injury (August 29, 1989-entire season).
PLAYING EXPERIENCE: Buffalo NFL, 1987 and 1990.... Games: 1987 (12), 1990 (16). Total: 28.

CHAMPIONSHIP GAME EXPERIENCE: Played in AFC championship game after 1990 season. . . . Played in Super Bowl XXV after 1990 season.

FRIESZ, JOHN
QB, CHARGERS

PERSONAL: Born May 19, 1967, at Missoula, Mont. . . . 6-4/209. . . . Full name: John Melvin Friesz. . . . Name pronounced FREEZE.
HIGH SCHOOL: Coeur D'Alene (Idaho).
COLLEGE: Idaho.
TRANSACTIONS/CAREER NOTES: Selected by San Diego Chargers in sixth round (138th pick overall) of 1990 NFL draft. . . . Signed by Chargers (July 20, 1990). . . . On injured reserve with elbow injury (September 4-October 3, 1990). . . . On practice squad (October 3-December 28, 1990).
PRO STATISTICS: Passer rating points: 1990 (58.5).

		PASSING							RUSHING				TOTAL		
Year Team	G	Att.	Cmp.	Pct.	Yds.	TD	Int.	Avg.	Att.	Yds.	Avg.	TD	TD	Pts.	F.
1990— San Diego NFL	1	22	11	50.0	98	1	1	4.46	1	3	3.0	0	0	0	0
Pro totals (1 year)................	1	22	11	50.0	98	1	1	4.46	1	3	3.0	0	0	0	0

FRIZZELL, WILLIAM
DB, BUCCANEERS

PERSONAL: Born September 8, 1962, at Greenville, N.C. . . . 6-3/205. . . . Full name: William Jasper Frizzell. . . . Name pronounced fri-ZELL.
HIGH SCHOOL: J.H. Rose (Greenville, N.C.).
COLLEGE: North Carolina Central.
TRANSACTIONS/CAREER NOTES: Selected by Detroit Lions in 10th round (259th pick overall) of 1984 NFL draft. . . . On injured reserve with ankle injury (September 2-November 2, 1985). . . . Released by Lions (August 26, 1986). . . . Signed as free agent by Philadelphia Eagles (October 8, 1986). . . . Released by Eagles (November 6, 1986). . . . Re-signed by Eagles (November 26, 1986). . . . Granted unconditional free agency (February 1, 1991). . . . Signed by Tampa Bay Buccaneers (March 29, 1991).
PRO STATISTICS: 1987—Recovered one fumble. 1989—Recovered three fumbles for 12 yards.

		INTERCEPTIONS			
Year Team	G	No.	Yds.	Avg.	TD
1984— Detroit NFL	16	0	0		0
1985— Detroit NFL	8	1	3	3.0	0
1986— Philadelphia NFL	8	0	0		0
1987— Philadelphia NFL	12	0	0		0
1988— Philadelphia NFL	16	3	19	6.3	0
1989— Philadelphia NFL	16	4	58	14.5	0
1990— Philadelphia NFL	16	3	91	30.3	1
Pro totals (7 years)	92	11	171	15.6	1

FRYAR, IRVING
WR/KR, PATRIOTS

PERSONAL: Born September 28, 1962, at Mount Holly, N.J. . . . 6-0/200. . . . Full name: Irving Dale Fryar.
HIGH SCHOOL: Rancocas Valley Regional (Mount Holly, N.J.).
COLLEGE: Nebraska.
TRANSACTIONS/CAREER NOTES: Selected by Chicago Blitz in first round (third pick overall) of 1984 USFL draft. . . . Signed by New England Patriots (April 11, 1984). . . . Selected officially by Patriots in first round (first pick overall) of 1984 NFL draft.
CHAMPIONSHIP GAME EXPERIENCE: Played in Super Bowl XX after 1985 season.
RECORDS/HONORS: Named as wide receiver on THE SPORTING NEWS college All-America team, 1983. . . . Played in Pro Bowl after 1985 season.
PRO STATISTICS: 1984—Recovered one fumble. 1986—Recovered one fumble. 1990—Recovered one fumble.

		RUSHING				RECEIVING				PUNT RETURNS				KICKOFF RETURNS				TOTALS		
Year Team	G	Att.	Yds.	Avg.	TD	No.	Yds.	Avg.	TD	No.	Yds.	Avg.	TD	No.	Yds.	Avg.	TD	TD	Pts.	F.
1984— New Eng. NFL	14	2	-11	-5.5	0	11	164	14.9	1	36	347	9.6	0	5	95	19.0	0	1	6	4
1985— New Eng. NFL	16	7	27	3.9	1	39	670	17.2	7	37	520	*14.1	*2	3	39	13.0	0	10	60	4
1986— New Eng. NFL	14	4	80	20.0	0	43	737	17.1	6	35	366	10.5	1	10	192	19.2	0	7	42	4
1987— New Eng. NFL	12	9	52	5.8	0	31	467	15.1	5	18	174	9.7	0	6	119	19.8	0	5	30	2
1988— New Eng. NFL	15	6	12	2.0	0	33	490	14.9	5	38	398	10.5	0	1	3	3.0	0	5	30	2
1989— New Eng. NFL	11	2	15	7.5	0	29	537	18.5	3	12	107	8.9	0	1	47	47.0	0	3	18	2
1990— New Eng. NFL	16	0	0		0	54	856	15.9	4	28	133	4.8	0	0	0		0	4	24	1
Pro totals (7 years)	98	30	175	5.8	1	240	3921	16.3	31	204	2045	10.0	3	26	495	19.0	0	35	210	19

FULCHER, DAVID
S, BENGALS

PERSONAL: Born September 28, 1964, at Los Angeles. . . . 6-3/238. . . . Full name: David Dwayne Fulcher.
HIGH SCHOOL: John C. Fremont (Los Angeles).
COLLEGE: Arizona State.
TRANSACTIONS/CAREER NOTES: Selected by Cincinnati Bengals in third round (78th pick overall) of 1986 NFL draft. . . . Selected by Arizona Outlaws in 1986 USFL supplemental territorial draft. . . . Signed by Cincinnati Bengals (July 19, 1986). . . . On injured reserve with back injury (December 26, 1987-remainder of season). . . . Granted free agency (February 1, 1990). . . . Re-signed by Bengals (July 26, 1990). . . . On injured reserve with separated shoulder (November 6-December 7, 1990).
CHAMPIONSHIP GAME EXPERIENCE: Played in AFC championship game after 1988 season. . . . Played in Super Bowl XXIII after 1988 season.
RECORDS/HONORS: Named as defensive back on THE SPORTING NEWS college All-America team, 1984 and 1985. . . . Played in

Pro Bowl after 1988-1990 seasons.... Named to THE SPORTING NEWS NFL All-Pro team, 1989.
PRO STATISTICS: 1986—Recovered one fumble. 1987—Returned one kickoff for no yards and recovered one fumble. 1988—Fumbled once. 1989—Recovered four fumbles. 1990—Credited with a safety.

			INTERCEPTIONS		
Year	Team	G	No.	Yds.	Avg.	TD
1986— Cincinnati NFL	16	4	20	5.0	0
1987— Cincinnati NFL	11	3	30	10.0	0
1988— Cincinnati NFL	16	5	38	7.6	1
1989— Cincinnati NFL	16	8	87	10.9	0
1990— Cincinnati NFL	13	4	20	5.0	0
Pro totals (5 years)	72	24	195	8.1	1

FULHAGE, SCOTT
P, FALCONS

PERSONAL: Born November 17, 1961, at Beloit, Kan. ... 6-0/193. ... Full name: Scott Alan Fulhage.
HIGH SCHOOL: Beloit (Kan.).
COLLEGE: Kansas State (bachelor of science degree in agricultural economics, 1985).
TRANSACTIONS/CAREER NOTES: Signed as free agent by Buffalo Bills (June 20, 1985).... Released by Bills (August 5, 1985).... Signed as free agent by Washington Redskins (June 29, 1986).... Released by Redskins (August 18, 1986).... Signed as free agent by Cincinnati Bengals (February 4, 1987).... Released by Bengals (September 7, 1987).... Re-signed as replacement player by Bengals (September 25, 1987).... Released by Bengals (October 19, 1987).... Awarded on waivers to Green Bay Packers (October 20, 1987).... Released by Packers (November 3, 1987).... Signed as free agent by Bengals (November 5, 1987).... On injured reserve with back injury (December 21, 1988-remainder of season and playoffs).... Released by Bengals (August 16, 1989).... Signed as free agent by Atlanta Falcons (August 23, 1989).... Granted free agency (February 1, 1990).... Re-signed by Falcons (June 28, 1990).
PRO STATISTICS: 1989—Attempted one pass with one completion for 12 yards, rushed once for no yards, recovered one fumble and fumbled once for minus 20 yards.

			PUNTING		
Year	Team	G	No.	Avg.	Blk.
1987— Cincinnati NFL	11	52	41.7	0
1988— Cincinnati NFL	13	44	38.0	2
1989— Atlanta NFL	16	84	41.3	1
1990— Atlanta NFL	16	70	41.6	0
Pro totals (4 years)	56	250	40.7	3

FULLER, JOE
CB, PACKERS

PERSONAL: Born September 25, 1964, at Minneapolis, Minn. ... 5-11/186.
HIGH SCHOOL: Central (Minneapolis, Minn.).
COLLEGE: Northern Iowa.
TRANSACTIONS/CAREER NOTES: Signed as free agent by Saskatchewan Roughriders of CFL (March, 1986).... Granted free agency (March 1, 1989).... Signed as free agent by Minnesota Vikings (March 16, 1989).... Released by Vikings (September 5, 1989).... Re-signed by Vikings to developmental squad (September 7, 1989).... On developmental squad (September 7-October 2, 1989).... Released by Vikings (October 3, 1989).... Signed as free agent by San Diego Chargers (February 21, 1990).... On injured reserve with hamstring injury (October 3-December 7, 1990).... Released by Chargers (December 7, 1990).... Signed by Green Bay Packers (April 23, 1991).
PRO STATISTICS: CFL: 1988—Recovered one fumble.

			INTERCEPTIONS				PUNT RETURNS				KICKOFF RETURNS				TOTAL		
Year	Team	G	No.	Yds.	Avg.	TD	No.	Yds.	Avg.	TD	No.	Yds.	Avg.	TD	TD	Pts.	F.
1986— Sask. CFL	7	0	0		0	6	34	5.7	0	5	106	21.2	0	0	0	0
1987— Sask. CFL	18	5	41	8.2	0	52	403	7.8	0	18	289	16.1	0	0	0	2
1988— Sask. CFL	18	7	131	18.7	1	54	426	7.9	0	4	55	13.8	0	1	6	3
1990— San Diego NFL	4	1	5	5.0	0	0	0		0	0	0		0	0	0	0
CFL totals (3 years)	43	12	172	14.3	1	112	863	7.7	0	27	450	16.7	0	1	6	5
NFL totals (1 year)	4	1	5	5.0	0	0	0		0	0	0		0	0	0	0
Pro totals (4 years)	47	13	177	13.6	1	112	863	7.7	0	27	450	16.7	0	1	6	5

FULLER, WILLIAM
DE, OILERS

PERSONAL: Born March 8, 1962, at Norfolk, Va. ... 6-3/265. ... Full name: William Henry Fuller Jr.
HIGH SCHOOL: Indian River (Chesapeake, Va.).
COLLEGE: North Carolina.
TRANSACTIONS/CAREER NOTES: Selected by Philadelphia Stars in 1984 USFL territorial draft.... Signed by Stars (February 6, 1984).... On injured reserve with fractured ankle (May 18-June 23, 1984).... Selected by Los Angeles Rams in first round (21st pick overall) of 1984 NFL supplemental draft.... Philadelphia Stars franchise transferred to Baltimore (November 1, 1984).... Granted free agency when USFL suspended operations (August 7, 1986).... Signed by Los Angeles Rams (September 10, 1986).... Traded by Rams with guard Kent Hill, first- and fifth-round picks in 1987 draft and first-round pick in 1988 draft to Houston Oilers for rights to quarterback Jim Everett (September 8, 1986).... Granted roster exemption (September 18-September 22, 1986).
PLAYING EXPERIENCE: Philadelphia USFL, 1984; Baltimore USFL, 1985; Houston NFL, 1986-1990.... Games: 1984 (13), 1985 (18), 1986 (13), 1987 (12), 1988 (16), 1989 (15), 1990 (16). Total USFL: 31. Total NFL: 72. Total Pro: 103.
CHAMPIONSHIP GAME EXPERIENCE: Played in USFL championship game after 1984 and 1985 seasons.
RECORDS/HONORS: Named as defensive tackle on THE SPORTING NEWS college All-America team, 1983.... Named as defen-

sive end on THE SPORTING NEWS USFL All-Star team, 1985.
PRO STATISTICS: USFL: 1984—Credited with two sacks for 18 yards and recovered one fumble. 1985—Credited with 8 ½ sacks for 102 yards, intercepted one pass for 35 yards and recovered four fumbles for 17 yards.... NFL: 1987—Recovered one fumble and returned one kickoff for no yards. 1988—Intercepted one pass for nine yards. 1990—Recovered one fumble.

FULLINGTON, DARRELL
S, VIKINGS

PERSONAL: Born April 17, 1964, at New Smyrna Beach, Fla.... 6-1/195.
HIGH SCHOOL: New Smyrna Beach (Fla.).
COLLEGE: Miami, Fla. (degree in business management organization, 1988).

TRANSACTIONS/CAREER NOTES: Selected by Minnesota Vikings in fifth round (124th pick overall) of 1988 NFL draft.... Signed by Vikings (July 19, 1988).
PRO STATISTICS: 1988—Recovered one fumble. 1990—Recovered one fumble.

| | | | INTERCEPTIONS | | |
Year Team	G	No.	Yds.	Avg.	TD
1988— Minnesota NFL	15	3	57	19.0	0
1989— Minnesota NFL	16	1	0	.0	0
1990— Minnesota NFL	16	1	10	10.0	0
Pro totals (3 years)	47	5	67	13.4	0

FULLWOOD, BRENT
RB, DOLPHINS

PERSONAL: Born October 10, 1963, at Kissimmee, Fla. ... 5-11/210.... Full name: Brent Lanard Fullwood.
HIGH SCHOOL: St. Cloud (Fla.).
COLLEGE: Auburn.

TRANSACTIONS/CAREER NOTES: Selected by Green Bay Packers in first round (fourth pick overall) of 1987 NFL draft.... Signed by Packers (August 4, 1987).... Granted free agency (February 1, 1990).... Re-signed by Packers (August 2, 1990).... Traded by Packers to Cleveland Browns for undisclosed draft pick (October 9, 1990).... On inactive list (October 14, 21, 28; November 4, 18; and December 2 and 9, 1990).... Released by Browns (December 24, 1990).... Signed by Miami Dolphins (February 12, 1991).
RECORDS/HONORS: Named as running back on THE SPORTING NEWS college All-America team, 1986.... Played in Pro Bowl after 1989 season.
PRO STATISTICS: 1987—Recovered one fumble. 1988—Recovered one fumble. 1989—Recovered one fumble.

| | | RUSHING | | | | RECEIVING | | | | KICKOFF RETURNS | | | | TOTAL | | |
Year Team	G	Att.	Yds.	Avg.	TD	No.	Yds.	Avg.	TD	No.	Yds.	Avg.	TD	TD	Pts.	F.
1987— Green Bay NFL.......	11	84	274	3.3	5	2	11	5.5	0	24	510	21.3	0	5	30	2
1988— Green Bay NFL.......	14	101	483	4.8	7	20	128	6.4	1	21	421	20.1	0	8	48	6
1989— Green Bay NFL.......	15	204	821	4.0	5	19	214	11.3	0	11	243	22.1	0	5	30	6
1990— G.B. (5)-Cle.(1) NFL.	6	44	124	2.8	1	3	17	5.7	0	6	119	19.8	0	1	6	1
Pro totals (4 years)	46	433	1702	3.9	18	44	370	8.4	1	62	1293	20.9	0	19	114	15

FUTRELL, BOBBY
DB, LIONS

PERSONAL: Born August 4, 1962, at Ahoskie, N.C. ... 5-11/185.... Full name: Bobby Lee Futrell.... Name pronounced few-TRELL.
HIGH SCHOOL: Ahoskie (N.C.).
COLLEGE: Elizabeth City State (N.C.).

TRANSACTIONS/CAREER NOTES: Selected by Michigan Panthers in fifth round (93rd pick overall) of 1984 USFL draft.... Signed by Panthers (January 23, 1984).... Not protected in merger of Michigan Panthers and Oakland Invaders; selected by Tampa Bay Bandits in USFL dispersal draft (December 6, 1984).... Released by Bandits (February 18, 1985).... Re-signed by Bandits (February 19, 1985).... Released by Bandits (April 19, 1985).... Awarded on waivers to Oakland Invaders (April 23, 1985).... On developmental squad for three games (May 23-June 15, 1985).... Released by Invaders (August 2, 1985).... Signed as free agent by Tampa Bay Buccaneers (April 2, 1986).... Granted unconditional free agency (February 1, 1990).... Re-signed by Buccaneers (July 17, 1990).... Released by Buccaneers (September 14, 1990).... Signed by Detroit Lions (April 25, 1991).
CHAMPIONSHIP GAME EXPERIENCE: On developmental squad for USFL championship game after 1985 season.
PRO STATISTICS: USFL: 1984—Recovered two fumbles.... NFL: 1986—Recovered one fumble. 1987—Recovered two fumbles. 1988—Recovered one fumble. 1989—Recovered one fumble.

| | | INTERCEPTIONS | | | | PUNT RETURNS | | | | KICKOFF RETURNS | | | | TOTAL | | |
Year Team	G	No.	Yds.	Avg.	TD	No.	Yds.	Avg.	TD	No.	Yds.	Avg.	TD	TD	Pts.	F.
1984— Michigan USFL	18	1	29	29.0	0	3	17	5.7	0	27	576	21.3	0	0	0	4
1985— T.B.(8)-Oak.(6) USFL.	14	0	0		0	0	0		0	10	199	19.9	0	0	0	0
1986— Tampa Bay NFL.....	16	0	0		0	14	67	4.8	0	5	115	23.0	0	0	0	1
1987— Tampa Bay NFL.....	12	2	46	23.0	0	24	213	8.9	0	31	609	19.7	0	0	0	2
1988— Tampa Bay NFL.....	16	1	26	26.0	0	27	283	10.5	0	2	38	19.0	0	0	0	4
1989— Tampa Bay NFL.....	16	1	1	1.0	0	12	76	6.3	0	4	58	14.5	0	0	0	1
1990— Tampa Bay NFL.....	1	0	0		0	0	0		0	0	0		0	0	0	0
USFL totals (2 years)	32	1	29	29.0	0	3	17	5.7	0	37	775	21.0	0	0	0	4
NFL totals (5 years)	61	4	73	18.3	0	77	639	8.3	0	42	820	19.5	0	0	0	8
Pro totals (7 years)	93	5	102	20.4	0	80	656	8.2	0	79	1595	20.2	0	0	0	12

GAGLIANO, BOB
QB, CHARGERS

PERSONAL: Born September 5, 1958, at Los Angeles. . . . 6-3/205. . . . Full name: Robert Frank Gagliano. . . . Name pronounced GAL-e-ON-o.
HIGH SCHOOL: Hoover (Glendale, Calif.).
COLLEGE: Glendale Junior College (Calif.), then U.S. International, then Utah State (degree in psychology).
TRANSACTIONS/CAREER NOTES: Selected by Kansas City Chiefs in 12th round (319th pick overall) of 1981 NFL draft. . . . Released by Chiefs (August 25, 1981). . . . Re-signed by Chiefs (August 27, 1981). . . . Active for 16 games with Chiefs in 1981; did not play. . . . On inactive list (September 12 and 19, 1982). . . . USFL rights traded by New Jersey Generals with rights to wide receiver Dave Dorn to Chicago Blitz to offensive tackle Jeff Weston and linebacker Bobby Leopold (November 23, 1983). . . . USFL rights traded by Chicago Blitz to San Antonio Gunslingers for defensive tackle Broderick Thompson and first-round pick in 1984 draft (January 3, 1984). . . . Signed by Gunslingers (January 6, 1984), for contract to take effect after being granted free agency February 1, 1984. . . . Traded by Gunslingers to Denver Gold for linebacker Putt Choate and ninth-round pick in 1985 draft (February 13, 1984). . . . On developmental squad for 10 games (February 24-March 17, 1984; April 28-May 25, 1984; June 2-June 8, 1984; and June 15, 1984-remainder of season). . . . Denver Gold franchise merged with Jacksonville Bulls (February 19, 1986). . . . Released by Bulls (March 18, 1986). . . . Signed as free agent by San Francisco 49ers (October 29, 1986). . . . Released by 49ers (November 7, 1986). . . . Active for one game with 49ers in 1986; did not play. . . . Re-signed by 49ers for 1987 (November 13, 1986). . . . Released by 49ers (September 7, 1987). . . . Re-signed as replacement player by 49ers (September 24, 1987). . . . Released by 49ers (August 9, 1988). . . . Signed as free agent by Tampa Bay Buccaneers (August 15, 1988). . . . Released by Buccaneers (August 29, 1988). . . . Signed as free agent by Houston Oilers (September 13, 1988). . . . Released by Oilers (September 19, 1988). . . . Signed as free agent by Indianapolis Colts (October 11, 1988). . . . Active for game with Colts in 1988; did not play. . . . Released by Colts (October 26, 1988). . . . Signed as free agent by Detroit Lions (March 16, 1989). . . . Granted free agency (February 1, 1990). . . . Re-signed by Lions (July 25, 1990). . . . Granted unconditional free agency (February 1, 1991). . . . Signed by San Diego Chargers (March 30, 1991).
PRO STATISTICS: USFL Passer rating points: 1984 (95.6), 1985 (73.5). Career: 75.5. . . . NFL Passer rating points: 1987 (78.1), 1989 (61.2), 1990 (73.6). Career: 67.2. . . . USFL: 1984—Recovered two fumbles and credited with one 2-point conversion. 1985—Recovered three fumbles. . . . NFL: 1989—Recovered two fumbles and fumbled three times for minus one yard. 1990—Fumbled five times for minus ten yards.

| | | PASSING | | | | | | | RUSHING | | | | TOTAL | | |
Year Team	G	Att.	Cmp.	Pct.	Yds.	TD	Int.	Avg.	Att.	Yds.	Avg.	TD	TD	Pts.	F.
1982— Kansas City NFL	1	1		100.0	7	0	0	7.00	0	0		0	0	0	0
1983— Kansas City NFL	1	0	0		0	0	0		0	0		0	0	0	0
1984— Denver USFL	8	31	20	64.5	236	2	1	7.61	1	7	7.0	0	0	2	2
1985— Denver USFL	18	358	205	57.3	2695	13	17	7.53	34	111	3.3	2	2	12	5
1987— San Francisco NFL	3	29	16	55.2	229	1	1	7.90	0	0		0	0	0	0
1989— Detroit NFL	11	232	117	50.4	1671	6	12	7.20	41	192	4.7	4	4	24	3
1990— Detroit NFL	9	159	87	54.7	1190	10	10	7.48	46	145	3.2	0	0	0	5
NFL totals (5 years)	25	421	221	52.5	3097	17	23	7.36	87	337	3.9	4	4	24	8
USFL totals (2 years)	26	389	225	57.8	2931	15	18	7.54	35	118	3.4	2	2	14	7
Pro totals (7 years)	51	810	446	55.1	6028	32	41	7.44	122	455	3.7	6	6	38	15

GAINER, DERRICK
RB, BROWNS

PERSONAL: Born August 15, 1966, at Plant City, Fla. . . . 5-11/235. . . . Full name: Derrick Luther Gainer.
HIGH SCHOOL: Plant City (Fla.).
COLLEGE: Florida A&M (degree in criminology).
TRANSACTIONS/CAREER NOTES: Selected by Los Angeles Raiders in eighth round (205th pick overall) of 1989 NFL draft. . . . Released by Raiders (September 8, 1989). . . . Re-signed by Raiders to developmental squad (September 9, 1989). . . . Released by Raiders (November 30, 1989). . . . Signed by Cleveland Browns to developmental squad (December 12, 1989). . . . Released by Browns (January 29, 1990). . . . Re-signed by Browns (February 5, 1990).

| | | RUSHING | | | | RECEIVING | | | | KICKOFF RETURNS | | | | TOTAL | | |
Year Team	G	Att.	Yds.	Avg.	TD	No.	Yds.	Avg.	TD	No.	Yds.	Avg.	TD	TD	Pts.	F.
1990— Cleveland NFL	16	30	81	2.7	1	7	85	12.1	0	1	0	.0	0	1	6	0
Pro totals (1 year)	16	30	81	2.7	1	7	85	12.1	0	1	0	.0	0	1	6	0

GALBRAITH, SCOTT
TE, BROWNS

PERSONAL: Born January 7, 1967, at Sacramento, Calif. . . . 6-3/260. . . . Full name: Alan Scott Galbraith.
HIGH SCHOOL: Highlands (North Highlands, Calif.).
COLLEGE: Southern California.
TRANSACTIONS/CAREER NOTES: Selected by Cleveland Browns in seventh round (178th pick overall) of 1990 NFL draft. . . . Signed by Browns (July 17, 1990).
PRO STATISTICS: 1990—Recovered one fumble.

| | | RECEIVING | | | | KICKOFF RETURNS | | | | TOTAL | | |
Year Team	G	No.	Yds.	Avg.	TD	No.	Yds.	Avg.	TD	TD	Pts.	F.
1990— Cleveland NFL	16	4	62	15.5	0	3	16	5.3	0	0	0	0
Pro totals (1 year)	16	4	62	15.5	0	3	16	5.3	0	0	0	0

GALBREATH, HARRY
G, DOLPHINS

PERSONAL: Born January 1, 1965, at Clarksville, Tenn. . . . 6-1/275. . . . Full name: Harry Curtis Galbreath.
HIGH SCHOOL: Clarksville (Tenn.).
COLLEGE: Tennessee (received undergraduate degree).

TRANSACTIONS/CAREER NOTES: Selected by Miami Dolphins in eighth round (212nd pick overall) of 1988 NFL draft.... Signed by Dolphins (July 12, 1988).
PLAYING EXPERIENCE: Miami NFL, 1988-1990.... Games: 1988 (16), 1989 (14), 1990 (16). Total: 46.
RECORDS/HONORS: Named as guard on THE SPORTING NEWS college All-America team, 1987.
PRO STATISTICS: 1989—Recovered one fumble.

GALLOWAY, DAVID
DE, BRONCOS

PERSONAL: Born February 16, 1959, at Tampa, Fla.... 6-3/265.... Full name: David Lawrence Galloway.
HIGH SCHOOL: Brandon, Fla.
COLLEGE: Florida.
TRANSACTIONS/CAREER NOTES: Selected by St. Louis Cardinals in second round (38th pick overall) of 1982 NFL draft.... On injured reserve with dislocated elbow (September 8-December 1, 1982).... On injured reserve with broken arm (September 1-December 5, 1987).... Franchise transferred to Phoenix (March 15, 1988).... On injured reserve with broken thumb (August 30-October 22, 1988).... On injured reserve with ankle injury (September 4-October 16, 1990).... Traded by Phoenix Cardinals to Denver Broncos for undisclosed draft pick (October 16, 1990).... Activated (October 19, 1990).
PLAYING EXPERIENCE: St. Louis NFL, 1982-1987; Phoenix NFL, 1988 and 1989; Phoenix (0)-Denver (10) NFL, 1990.... Games: 1982 (5), 1983 (16), 1984 (14), 1985 (16), 1986 (14), 1987 (4), 1988 (8), 1989 (12), 1990 (10). Total: 99.
PRO STATISTICS: 1983—Intercepted one pass for 17 yards, credited with one safety and recovered one fumble. 1985—Recovered one fumble. 1986—Recovered two fumbles. 1988—Recovered one fumble.

GALVIN, JOHN
LB, JETS

PERSONAL: Born July 9, 1965, at Lowell, Mass.... 6-3/230.... Full name: John Blake Galvin Jr.
HIGH SCHOOL: Lowell (Mass.).
COLLEGE: Boston College (degree in speech communications, 1988).
TRANSACTIONS/CAREER NOTES: Selected by New York Jets in 11th round (287th pick overall) of 1988 NFL draft.... Signed by Jets (July 12, 1988).... Granted unconditional free agency (February 1, 1989).... Signed by Minnesota Vikings (March 29, 1989).... On injured reserve with back injury (September 12-October 10, 1989).... Released by Vikings (October 11, 1989). ... Re-signed by Vikings after clearing procedural waivers (October 12, 1989).... Released by Vikings (November 1, 1989). ... Re-signed by Vikings (November 9, 1989).... Released by Vikings (August 15, 1990).... Awarded on waivers to New York Jets (August 18, 1990).
PLAYING EXPERIENCE: New York Jets NFL, 1988; Minnesota NFL, 1989; New York Jets NFL, 1990.... Games: 1988 (16), 1989 (11), 1990 (16). Total: 43.
PRO STATISTICS: 1988—Recovered one fumble.

GAMBLE, KENNY
RB/KR, CHIEFS

PERSONAL: Born March 8, 1965, at Holyoke, Mass.... 5-10/204.... Full name: Kenneth Patrick Gamble.
HIGH SCHOOL: Holyoke (Mass.) and Cushing Academy (Ashburnham, Mass.).
COLLEGE: Colgate (degree in international relations, 1988).
TRANSACTIONS/CAREER NOTES: Selected by Kansas City Chiefs in 10th round (251st pick overall) of 1988 NFL draft.... Signed by Chiefs (July 12, 1988).... On injured reserve with foot and shoulder injuries (September 22, 1989-remainder of season). ... On injured reserve with knee injury (September 17, 1990-remainder of season).
PRO STATISTICS: 1988—Intercepted one pass for two yards.

Year Team	G	RUSHING				RECEIVING				KICKOFF RETURNS				TOTAL		
		Att.	Yds.	Avg.	TD	No.	Yds.	Avg.	TD	No.	Yds.	Avg.	TD	TD	Pts.	F.
1988— Kansas City NFL....	16	0	0		0	1	-7	-7.0	0	15	291	19.4	0	0	0	1
1989— Kansas City NFL....	2	6	24	4.0	1	2	2	1.0	0	3	55	18.3	0	0	0	0
1990— Kansas City NFL....	1	0	0		0	0	0		0	0	0		0	0	0	0
Pro totals (3 years)	19	6	24	4.0	1	3	-5	-1.7	0	18	346	19.2	0	0	0	1

GAMBOL, CHRIS
G/OT, PATRIOTS

PERSONAL: Born September 14, 1964, at Pittsburgh.... 6-6/303.... Full name: Christopher Hughes Gambol.
HIGH SCHOOL: Oxford (Mich.).
COLLEGE: Iowa (bachelor of business administration degree in finance, 1988).
TRANSACTIONS/CAREER NOTES: Selected by Indianapolis Colts in third round (58th pick overall) of 1987 NFL draft.... Signed by Colts (July 23, 1987).... On injured reserve with back injury (September 7, 1987-entire season).... Released by Colts (September 22, 1988).... Awarded on waivers to San Diego Chargers (September 23, 1988).... Granted unconditional free agency (February 1, 1989).... Signed by Detroit Lions (March 22, 1989).... Released by Lions (September 5, 1989).... Re-signed by Lions (November 15, 1989).... Granted unconditional free agency (February 1, 1990).... Signed by New England Patriots (April 1, 1990).
PLAYING EXPERIENCE: Indianapolis (1)-San Diego (11) NFL, 1988; Detroit NFL, 1989; New England NFL, 1990.... Games: 1988 (12), 1989 (6), 1990 (16). Total: 34.

GANN, MIKE
DE, FALCONS

PERSONAL: Born October 19, 1963, at Stillwater, Okla.... 6-5/270.... Full name: Mike Alan Gann.
HIGH SCHOOL: Lakewood (Colo.).
COLLEGE: Notre Dame (bachelor of business administration degree, 1985).
TRANSACTIONS/CAREER NOTES: Selected by Tampa Bay Bandits in first round (12th pick overall) of 1985 USFL draft.... Selected by Atlanta Falcons in second round (45th pick overall) of 1985 NFL draft.... Signed by Falcons (July 23, 1985).

PLAYING EXPERIENCE: Atlanta NFL, 1985-1990. . . . Games: 1985 (16), 1986 (16), 1987 (12), 1988 (16), 1989 (16), 1990 (16). Total: 92.
PRO STATISTICS: 1985—Recovered one fumble for 42 yards and a touchdown. 1986—Credited with a safety and recovered three fumbles for 12 yards. 1988—Recovered two fumbles for 36 yards and a touchdown. 1990—Recovered three fumbles.

GANNON, CHRIS
DE, PATRIOTS

PERSONAL: Born January 20, 1966, at Brandon, Fla. . . . 6-6/260. . . . Full name: Christopher Stephen Gannon.
HIGH SCHOOL: Orange Park (Fla.).
COLLEGE: Southwestern Louisiana.
TRANSACTIONS/CAREER NOTES: Selected by New England Patriots in third round (73rd pick overall) of 1989 NFL draft. . . . Signed by Patriots (July 24, 1989). . . . Released by Patriots (September 4, 1989). . . . Awarded on waivers to San Diego Chargers (September 5, 1989). . . . On injured reserve with knee injury (November 16, 1989-remainder of season). . . . Granted unconditional free agency (February 1, 1990). . . . Signed by New England Patriots (April 1, 1990). . . . On reserve/physically unable to perform list with knee injury (August 28-November 6, 1990).
PLAYING EXPERIENCE: San Diego NFL, 1989; New England NFL, 1990. . . . Games: 1989 (10), 1990 (6). Total: 16.
PRO STATISTICS: 1989—Recovered one fumble. 1990—Rushed once for no yards and fumbled once for minus 25 yards.

GANNON, RICH
QB, VIKINGS

PERSONAL: Born December 20, 1965, at Philadelphia. . . . 6-3/202. . . . Full name: Richard Joseph Gannon.
HIGH SCHOOL: St. Joseph's Prep (Philadelphia).
COLLEGE: Delaware (degree in criminal justice, 1987).
TRANSACTIONS/CAREER NOTES: Selected by New England Patriots in fourth round (98th pick overall) of 1987 NFL draft. . . . Rights traded by Patriots to Minnesota Vikings for 4th- and 11th-round picks in 1988 NFL draft (May 6, 1987). . . . Signed by Minnesota Vikings (July 30, 1987). . . . Active for 13 games with Vikings in 1989; did not play. . . . Granted free agency (February 1, 1990). . . . Re-signed by Vikings (July 30, 1990).
CHAMPIONSHIP GAME EXPERIENCE: Member of Minnesota Vikings for NFC championship game after 1987 season; did not play.
PRO STATISTICS: Passer rating points: 1987 (2.8), 1988 (66.0), 1990 (68.9). Career: 67.2. . . . 1990—Recovered six fumbles and fumbled 10 times for minus three yards.

			PASSING						RUSHING				TOTAL		
Year Team	G	Att.	Cmp.	Pct.	Yds.	TD	Int.	Avg.	Att.	Yds.	Avg.	TD	TD	Pts.	F.
1987— Minnesota NFL	4	6	2	33.3	18	0	1	3.00	0	0		0	0	0	0
1988— Minnesota NFL	3	15	7	46.7	90	0	0	6.00	4	29	7.3	0	0	0	0
1990— Minnesota NFL	14	349	182	52.2	2278	16	16	6.53	52	268	5.2	1	1	6	10
Pro totals (3 years)	21	370	191	51.6	2386	16	17	6.45	56	297	5.3	1	1	6	10

GANT, KENNETH
CB, COWBOYS

PERSONAL: Born April 18, 1967, at Lakeland, Fla. . . . 5-11/188. . . . Full name: Kenneth Dwayne Gant.
HIGH SCHOOL: Kathleen (Lakeland, Fla.).
COLLEGE: Albany State.
TRANSACTIONS/CAREER NOTES: Selected by Dallas Cowboys in ninth round (221 pick overall) of 1990 NFL draft. . . . Signed by Cowboys (July 18, 1990). . . . On injured reserve with hamstring injury (September 6-October 1, 1990).
PLAYING EXPERIENCE: Dallas NFL, 1990. . . . Games: 1990 (12).

		INTERCEPTIONS			
Year Team	G	No.	Yds.	Avg.	TD
1990— Dallas NFL	12	1	26	26.0	0
Pro totals (1 year)	12	1	26	26.0	0

GARCIA, TEDDY
PK, OILERS

PERSONAL: Born June 4, 1964, at Caddo Parish, La. . . . 5-9/172. . . . Full name: Alfonso Teddy Garcia.
HIGH SCHOOL: Lewisville (Tex.).
COLLEGE: Northeast Louisiana.
TRANSACTIONS/CAREER NOTES: Selected by New England Patriots in fourth round (100th pick overall) of 1988 NFL draft. . . . Signed by Patriots (July 15, 1988). . . . Granted unconditional free agency (February 1, 1989). . . . Signed by Phoenix Cardinals (March 9, 1989). . . . Released by Cardinals (August 28, 1989). . . . Awarded on waivers to Minnesota Vikings (August 29, 1989). . . . Released by Vikings (September 27, 1989). . . . Signed as free agent by Seattle Seahawks (April 26, 1990). . . . Released by Seahawks (September 4, 1990). . . . Signed by Houston Oilers (October 25, 1990). . . . Signed by WLAF (February 18, 1991). . . . Assigned to San Antonio Riders in 1991 WLAF enhancement allocation program. . . . Released by Riders (April 4, 1991).

		PLACE-KICKING				
Year Team	G	XPM	XPA	FGM	FGA	Pts.
1988— New England NFL	16	11	16	6	13	29
1989— Minnesota NFL	3	8	8	1	5	11
1990— Houston NFL	9	26	28	14	20	68
1991— San Antonio WLAF	2	4	5	1	4	7
NFL totals (3 years)	28	45	52	21	38	108
WLAF totals (1 year)	2	4	5	1	4	7
Pro totals (4 years)	30	49	57	22	42	115

GARDNER, CARWELL
FB, BILLS

PERSONAL: Born November 27, 1966, at Louisville, Ky. . . . 6-2/235. . . . Full name: Carwell Ernest Gardner.
HIGH SCHOOL: Trinity High School for Boys (Louisville, Ky.).
COLLEGE: Louisville.

TRANSACTIONS/CAREER NOTES: Selected by Buffalo Bills in second round (42nd pick overall) of 1990 NFL draft. . . . Signed by Bills (July 28, 1990). . . . On injured reserve with knee injury (September 4-November 3, 1990).
CHAMPIONSHIP GAME EXPERIENCE: Played in AFC championship game after 1990 season. . . . Played in Super Bowl XXV after 1990 season.

Year Team	G	Att.	RUSHING Yds.	Avg.	TD
1990— Buffalo NFL	7	15	41	2.7	0
Pro totals (1 year)	7	15	41	2.7	0

GARNER, HAL
LB, BILLS

PERSONAL: Born January 18, 1962, at New Iberia, La. . . . 6-4/235. . . . Full name: Hal E. Garner Jr.
HIGH SCHOOL: Logan (Utah).
COLLEGE: Utah State.

TRANSACTIONS/CAREER NOTES: Selected by Baltimore Stars in third round (44th pick overall) of 1985 USFL draft. . . . Selected by Buffalo Bills in third round (63rd pick overall) of 1985 NFL draft. . . . Signed by Bills (July 19, 1985). . . . On injured reserve with toe injury (December 6, 1985-remainder of season). . . . On injured reserve with knee injury (September 1, 1987-entire season). . . . On non-football injury list with substance abuse (November 10-December 7, 1988). . . . Announced retirement (June 13, 1989). . . . Reinstated by NFL and signed by Buffalo Bills (August 2, 1990). . . . On injured reserve with dislocated toe (September 26-November 3, 1990). . . . On inactive list (December 9 and 15, 1990).
PLAYING EXPERIENCE: Buffalo NFL 1985, 1986, 1988 and 1990. . . . Games: 1985 (13), 1986 (16), 1988 (12), 1990 (10). Total: 51.
CHAMPIONSHIP GAME EXPERIENCE: Played in AFC championship game after 1988 and 1990 seasons. . . . Played in Super Bowl XXV after 1990 season.

GARRETT, JOHN
WR, BILLS

PERSONAL: Born March 2, 1965, at Danville, Pa. . . . 5-11/172. . . . Full name: John Morgan Garrett. . . . Brother of Judd Garrett, first-year running back with Buffalo Bills; brother of Jason Garrett, quarterback with San Antonio Riders (WLAF), 1991; and son of Jim Garrett, scout for Dallas Cowboys.
HIGH SCHOOL: University (Cleveland).
COLLEGE: Columbia, then Princeton (bachelor of arts degree).
TRANSACTIONS/CAREER NOTES: Signed as free agent by Dallas Cowboys (May 3, 1988). . . . . Released by Cowboys (August 9, 1988). . . . Signed as free agent by Cincinnati Bengals for 1989 (October 26, 1988). . . . Released by Bengals (August 30, 1989). . . . Re-signed by Bengals to developmental squad (September 7, 1989). . . . On developmental squad (September 7-December 16, 1989). . . . Released by Bengals (September 3, 1990). . . . Signed by WLAF (January 4, 1991). . . . Selected by San Antonio Riders of WLAF in second round (17th wide receiver) of 1991 WLAF positional draft. . . . Signed by Buffalo Bills (June 12, 1991).

Year Team	G	No.	RECEIVING Yds.	Avg.	TD
1989— Cincinnati NFL	1	2	29	14.5	0
1991— San Antonio WLAF	10	23	386	16.8	3
NFL totals (1 year)	1	2	29	14.5	0
WLAF totals (1 year)	10	23	386	16.8	3
Pro totals (2 years)	11	25	415	16.6	3

GARY, CLEVELAND
RB, RAMS

PERSONAL: Born May 4, 1966, at Stuart, Fla. . . . 6-0/226. . . . Full name: Cleveland Everette Gary.
HIGH SCHOOL: South Fork (Indiantown, Fla.).
COLLEGE: Miami (Fla.).

TRANSACTIONS/CAREER NOTES: Selected by Los Angeles Rams in first round (26th pick overall) of 1989 NFL draft. . . . Signed by Rams (September 6, 1989). . . . Granted roster exemption (September 6-September 18, 1989).
CHAMPIONSHIP GAME EXPERIENCE: Played in NFC championship game after 1989 season.
PRO STATISTICS: 1989—Returned one kickoff for four yards.

Year Team	G	Att.	RUSHING Yds.	Avg.	TD	No.	RECEIVING Yds.	Avg.	TD	TOTAL TD	Pts.	F.
1989— L.A. Rams NFL	10	37	163	4.4	1	2	13	6.5	0	1	6	1
1990— L.A. Rams NFL	15	204	808	4.0	*14	30	150	5.0	1	15	90	12
Pro totals (2 years)	25	241	971	4.0	15	32	163	5.1	1	16	96	13

GASH, THANE
S, BROWNS

PERSONAL: Born September 1, 1965, at Hendersonville, N.C. . . . 6-0/195. . . . Full name: Thane Alvin Gash.
HIGH SCHOOL: Henderson (N.C.).
COLLEGE: East Tennessee State (bachelor of science degree, 1988).
TRANSACTIONS/CAREER NOTES: Selected by Cleveland Browns in seventh round (188th pick overall) of 1988 NFL draft. . . . Signed by Browns (July 13, 1988).

CHAMPIONSHIP GAME EXPERIENCE: Played in AFC championship game after 1989 season.
PRO STATISTICS: 1989—Recovered one fumble for 15 yards. 1990—Recovered two fumbles.

			—INTERCEPTIONS—		
Year	Team	G	No.	Yds.	Avg.	TD
1988— Cleveland NFL	16	0	0		0
1989— Cleveland NFL	16	3	65	21.7	*2
1990— Cleveland NFL	16	1	16	16.0	0
Pro totals (3 years)	48	4	81	20.3	2

GAULT, WILLIE
WR, RAIDERS

PERSONAL: Born September 5, 1960, at Griffin, Ga. . . . 6-1/180. . . . Full name: Willie James Gault.
HIGH SCHOOL: Griffin (Ga.).
COLLEGE: Tennessee.
TRANSACTIONS/CAREER NOTES: Selected by New Jersey Generals in 1983 USFL territorial draft. . . . Selected by Chicago Bears in first round (18th pick overall) of 1983 NFL draft. . . . Signed by Bears (August 16, 1983). . . . Granted free agency (February 1, 1988). . . . Re-signed by Bears and traded to Los Angeles Raiders for first-round pick in 1989 draft and third-round pick in 1990 NFL draft (July 28, 1988).
CHAMPIONSHIP GAME EXPERIENCE: Played in NFC championship game after 1984 and 1985 seasons. . . . Played in AFC championship game after 1990 season. . . . Played in Super Bowl XX after 1985 season.
PRO STATISTICS: 1983—Returned nine punts for 60 yards and recovered one fumble. 1987—Recovered one fumble.

			—RUSHING—				—RECEIVING—				—KICKOFF RETURNS—				—TOTAL—		
Year	Team	G	Att.	Yds.	Avg.	TD	No.	Yds.	Avg.	TD	No.	Yds.	Avg.	TD	TD	Pts.	F.
1983— Chicago NFL	16	4	31	7.8	0	40	836	20.9	8	13	276	21.2	0	8	48	1
1984— Chicago NFL	16	0	0		0	34	587	17.3	6	1	12	12.0	0	6	36	1
1985— Chicago NFL	16	5	18	3.6	0	33	704	21.3	1	22	577	26.2	1	2	12	0
1986— Chicago NFL	16	8	79	9.9	0	42	818	19.5	5	1	20	20.0	0	5	30	1
1987— Chicago NFL	12	2	16	8.0	0	35	705	20.1	7	0	0		0	7	42	0
1988— L.A. Raiders NFL ...	15	1	4	4.0	0	16	392	24.5	2	0	0		0	2	12	1
1989— L.A. Raiders NFL ...	16	0	0		0	28	690	24.6	4	1	16	16.0	0	4	24	0
1990— L.A. Raiders NFL ...	16	0	0		0	50	985	19.7	3	0	0		0	3	18	1
Pro totals (8 years)	123	20	148	7.4	0	278	5717	20.6	36	38	901	23.7	1	37	222	5

GAYLE, SHAUN
S, BEARS

PERSONAL: Born March 8, 1962, at Newport News, Va. . . . 5-11/194. . . . Full name: Shaun Lanard Gayle.
HIGH SCHOOL: Bethel (Hampton, Va.).
COLLEGE: Ohio State (bachelor of science degree in education, 1984).
TRANSACTIONS/CAREER NOTES: Selected by Michigan Panthers in 14th round (288th pick overall) of 1984 USFL draft. . . . Selected by Chicago Bears in 10th round (271st pick overall) of 1984 NFL draft. . . . Signed by Bears (June 21, 1984). . . . On injured reserve with broken ankle (December 12, 1984-remainder of season). . . . On injured reserve with ankle injury (September 8-November 6, 1987). . . . On injured reserve with neck injury (October 14, 1988-remainder of season).
CHAMPIONSHIP GAME EXPERIENCE: Played in NFC championship game after 1985 season. . . . Played in Super Bowl XX after 1985 season.
PRO STATISTICS: 1985—Recovered one fumble. 1986—Recovered one fumble. 1989—Recovered two fumbles for 11 yards. 1990—Recovered three fumbles for two yards.

			—INTERCEPTIONS—		
Year	Team	G	No.	Yds.	Avg.	TD
1984— Chicago NFL	15	1	- 1	- 1.0	0
1985— Chicago NFL	16	0	0		0
1986— Chicago NFL	16	1	13	13.0	0
1987— Chicago NFL	8	1	20	20.0	1
1988— Chicago NFL	4	1	0	.0	0
1989— Chicago NFL	14	3	39	13.0	0
1990— Chicago NFL	16	2	5	2.5	0
Pro totals (7 years)	89	9	76	8.4	1

GEATHERS, JAMES
DE, REDSKINS

PERSONAL: Born June 26, 1960, at Georgetown, S.C. . . . 6-7/290 . . . Brother of Robert Geathers, defensive end with Boston Breakers (USFL), 1983.
HIGH SCHOOL: Choppee (Georgetown, S.C.).
COLLEGE: Paducah Community College (Ky.), then Wichita State.
TRANSACTIONS/CAREER NOTES: Selected by Oklahoma Outlaws in 1984 USFL territorial draft. . . . Selected by New Orleans Saints in second round (42nd pick overall) of 1984 NFL draft. . . . Signed by Saints (May 30, 1984). . . . On injured reserve with knee injury (September 1-December 26, 1987). . . . On injured reserve with knee injury (December 21, 1989-remainder of season). . . . Granted unconditional free agency (February 1, 1990). . . . Signed by Washington Redskins (March 30, 1990). . . . On reserve/physically unable to perform list (August 28-November 3, 1990).
PLAYING EXPERIENCE: New Orleans NFL, 1984- 1989; Washington NFL, 1990. . . . Games: 1984 (16), 1985 (16), 1986 (16), 1987 (1), 1988 (16), 1989 (15), 1990 (9). Total: 89.
PRO STATISTICS: 1986—Recovered one fumble. 1988—Recovered three fumbles. 1989—Recovered five fumbles.

GELBAUGH, STAN
QB, CHIEFS

PERSONAL: Born December 4, 1962, at Carlisle, Pa.... 6-3/207.... Full name: Stanley Morris Gelbaugh.
HIGH SCHOOL: Cumberland Valley (Mechanicsburg, Pa.).
COLLEGE: Maryland (bachelor of science degree in marketing, 1986).
TRANSACTIONS/CAREER NOTES: Selected by Baltimore Stars in 1986 USFL territorial draft.... Selected by Dallas Cowboys in sixth round (150th pick overall) of 1986 NFL draft.... Signed by Cowboys (July 5, 1986).... Released by Cowboys (August 18, 1986).... Signed as free agent by Saskatchewan Roughriders (August 27, 1986).... Released by Roughriders (October 7, 1986).... Signed as free agent by Buffalo Bills (November 18, 1986).... Active for five games with Bills in 1986; did not play.... On injured reserve with elbow injury (September 8, 1987-entire season).... Released by Bills (September 16, 1988).... Re-signed by Bills (September 20, 1988).... Released by Bills (September 5, 1989).... Re-signed by Bills (October 11, 1989).... Released by Bills (October 24, 1989).... Re-signed by Bills (October 25, 1989).... Released by Bills (November 6, 1989).... Active for three games with Bills in 1988; did not play.... Signed as free agent by Cincinnati Bengals (March 5, 1990).... Released by Bengals prior to 1990 season.... Signed by WLAF for 1991.... Selected by London Monarchs in first round (eighth pick overall) of 1991 WLAF supplemental draft (February 28, 1991).... Signed by Hamilton Tiger-Cats of CFL (July 29, 1991).... Released by Tiger-Cats (August, 1991).... Signed by Kansas City Chiefs (August 12, 1991).
CHAMPIONSHIP GAME EXPERIENCE: Member of Buffalo Bills for AFC championship game after 1988 season; inactive.

			PASSING							RUSHING				TOTAL		
Year Team	G	Att.	Cmp.	Pct.	Yds.	TD	Int.	Avg.	Att.	Yds.	Avg.	TD	TD	Pts.	F.
1986— Saskatchewan CFL ...	5	0	0		0	0	0		0	0		0	0	0	0
1989— Buffalo NFL.............	1	0	0		0	0	0		1	-3	-3.0	0	0	0	0
1991— London WLAF............	10	303	189	62.4	2655	17	12	8.76	9	66	7.3	0	0	0	—
CFL totals (1 year).............	5	0	0		0	0	0		0	0		0	0	0	0
NFL totals (1 year).............	1	0	0		0	0	0		1	-3	-3.0	0	0	0	0
WLAF totals (1 year)............	10	303	189	62.4	2655	17	12	8.76	9	66	7.3	0	0	0	—
Pro totals (3 years).............	16	303	189	62.4	2655	17	12	8.76	10	63	6.3	0	0	0	0

GENTRY, DENNIS
WR, BEARS

PERSONAL: Born February 10, 1959, at Lubbock, Tex.... 5-8/180.... Full name: Dennis Louis Gentry.
HIGH SCHOOL: Dunbar (Lubbock, Tex.).
COLLEGE: Baylor.
TRANSACTIONS/CAREER NOTES: Selected by Chicago Bears in fourth round (89th pick overall) of 1982 NFL draft.... On inactive list (December 2, 1990).
CHAMPIONSHIP GAME EXPERIENCE: Played in NFC championship game after 1984, 1985 and 1988 seasons.... Played in Super Bowl XX after 1985 season.
PRO STATISTICS: 1982—Recovered one fumble. 1986—Recovered blocked punt in end zone for a touchdown.

		RUSHING				RECEIVING				PUNT RETURNS				KICKOFF RETURNS				TOTALS		
Year Team	G	Att.	Yds.	Avg.	TD	No.	Yds.	Avg.	TD	No.	Yds.	Avg.	TD	No.	Yds.	Avg.	TD	TD	Pts.	F.
1982— Chicago NFL	9	4	21	5.3	0	1	9	9.0	0	17	89	5.2	0	9	161	17.9	0	0	0	4
1983— Chicago NFL	15	16	65	4.1	0	2	8	4.0	0	0	0		0	7	130	18.6	0	0	0	1
1984— Chicago NFL	16	21	79	3.8	1	4	29	7.3	0	0	0		0	11	209	19.0	0	1	6	0
1985— Chicago NFL	16	30	160	5.3	2	5	77	15.4	0	0	47		0	18	466	25.9	1	3	18	0
1986— Chicago NFL	15	11	103	9.4	1	19	238	12.5	0	0	0		0	20	576*28.8	*1	3	18	0
1987— Chicago NFL	12	6	41	6.8	0	17	183	10.8	1	0	0		0	25	621	24.8	1	2	12	2
1988— Chicago NFL	16	7	86	12.3	1	33	486	14.7	3	0	0		0	27	578	21.4	0	4	24	2
1989— Chicago NFL	16	17	106	6.2	0	39	463	11.9	1	0	0		0	28	667	23.8	0	1	6	1
1990— Chicago NFL	14	11	43	3.9	0	23	320	13.9	2	0	0		0	18	388	21.6	0	2	12	1
Pro totals (9 years)	129	123	704	5.7	5	143	1813	12.7	7	17	136	8.0	0	163	3796	23.3	3	16	96	11

GEORGE, JEFF
QB, COLTS

PERSONAL: Born December 8, 1967, at Indianapolis.... 6-4/221.... Full name: Jeffrey Scott George.
HIGH SCHOOL: Warren Central (Indianapolis).
COLLEGE: Purdue, then Illinois (degree in speech communications, 1991).
TRANSACTIONS/CAREER NOTES: Signed by Indianapolis Colts (April 20, 1990).... Selected officially by Colts in first round (first pick overall) of 1990 NFL draft.
PRO STATISTICS: Passer rating points: 1990 (73.8).... 1990—Recovered two fumbles.

			PASSING							RUSHING			TOTAL		
Year Team	G	Att.	Cmp.	Pct.	Yds.	TD	Int.	Avg.	Att.	Yds.	Avg.	TD	TD	Pts.	F.
1990— Indianapolis NFL	13	334	181	54.2	2152	16	13	6.44	11	2	.2	1	1	6	4
Pro totals (1 year)................	13	334	181	54.2	2152	16	13	6.44	11	2	.2	1	1	6	4

GESEK, JOHN
G, COWBOYS

PERSONAL: Born February 18, 1963, at San Francisco.... 6-5/283.... Full name: John Christian Gesek Jr.
HIGH SCHOOL: San Ramon Valley (Danville, Calif.) and Bellflower (Calif.).
COLLEGE: Diablo Valley College, Calif. (did not play football), then California State at Sacramento.
TRANSACTIONS/CAREER NOTES: Selected by Los Angeles Raiders in 10th round (265th pick overall) of 1987 NFL draft.... Signed by Raiders (July 11, 1987).... On injured reserve with back injury (September 7-October 14, 1987).... Crossed picket line during players' strike (October 13, 1987).... On injured reserve with knee injury (October 19-December 5, 1987).... On injured reserve with knee injury (November 30, 1988-remainder of season).... Traded by Raiders to Dallas Cowboys for fifth-round pick in 1991 draft (September 3, 1990).... On inactive list (September 9, 1990).

PLAYING EXPERIENCE: Los Angeles Raiders NFL, 1987-1989; Dallas NFL, 1990. . . . Games: 1987 (3), 1988 (12), 1989 (16), 1990 (15). Total: 46.
PRO STATISTICS: 1988—Fumbled once. 1990—Recovered two fumbles.

GIBSON, DENNIS
LB, LIONS

PERSONAL: Born February 8, 1964, at Des Moines, Ia. . . . 6-2/243. . . . Full name: Dennis Michael Gibson.
HIGH SCHOOL: Ankeny (Ia.).
COLLEGE: Iowa State.
TRANSACTIONS/CAREER NOTES: Selected by Detroit Lions in eighth round (203rd pick overall) of 1987 NFL draft. . . . Signed by Lions (July 25, 1987). . . . On injured reserve with shoulder injury (September 18-November 6, 1989). . . . Transferred to developmental squad (November 7-November 22, 1989). . . . On inactive list (December 2 and 10, 1990). . . . On injured reserve with arch injury (December 14, 1990-remainder of season).
PLAYING EXPERIENCE: Detroit NFL, 1987-1990. . . Games: 1987 (12), 1988 (16), 1989 (6), 1990 (11). Total: 45.
PRO STATISTICS: 1987—Intercepted one pass for five yards. 1988—Recovered one fumble. 1989—Intercepted one pass for 10 yards and recovered three fumbles for minus four yards. 1990—Recovered one fumble.

GIBSON, TOM
DL, BROWNS

PERSONAL: Born December 20, 1963, at San Fernando, Calif. . . . 6-8/275. . . . Full name: Tom A. Gibson.
HIGH SCHOOL: Saugus (Calif.).
COLLEGE: Northern Arizona (degree in criminal justice, 1990).
TRANSACTIONS/CAREER NOTES: Selected by New England Patriots in fifth round (116th pick overall) of 1987 NFL draft. . . . Signed by Patriots (July 21, 1987). . . . On injured reserve with groin injury (September 8, 1987-entire season). . . . On injured reserve with groin injury (August 29, 1988-entire season). . . . Granted unconditional free agency (February 1, 1989). . . . Signed by Cleveland Browns (March 17, 1989). . . . On injured reserve with hernia (September 4-October 3, 1990).
PLAYING EXPERIENCE: Cleveland NFL, 1989 and 1990. . . . Games: 1989 (16), 1990 (12). Total: 28.
CHAMPIONSHIP GAME EXPERIENCE: Played in AFC championship game after 1989 season.

GILBERT, GALE
QB, BILLS

PERSONAL: Born December 20, 1961, at Red Bluff, Calif. . . . 6-3/210.
HIGH SCHOOL: Red Bluff, Calif.
COLLEGE: California.
TRANSACTIONS/CAREER NOTES: Selected by Oakland Invaders in 1985 USFL territorial draft. . . . Signed as free agent by Seattle Seahawks (May 2, 1985). . . . On injured reserve with knee injury (September 8, 1987-entire season). . . . Granted free agency (February 1, 1988). . . . Rights relinquished (June 8, 1988). . . . Signed by Buffalo Bills (May 11, 1989). . . . On injured reserve with ribs injury (September 14, 1989-remainder of season). . . . Inactive for one game with Bills in 1989. . . . On inactive list (September 9, 16, 24, 30; October 21; November 4, 11, 18, 26; and December 2, 15, 1990).
CHAMPIONSHIP GAME EXPERIENCE: Member of Buffalo Bills for AFC championship game and Super Bowl XXV after 1990 season; did not play.
PRO STATISTICS: Passer rating points: 1985 (51.9), 1986 (71.4), 1990 (76.0). Career: 64.7. . . . 1985—Recovered one fumble and fumbled once for minus five yards.

				PASSING					RUSHING				TOTAL	
Year Team	G	Att.	Cmp.	Pct.	Yds.	TD	Int.	Avg.	Att.	Yds.	Avg.	TD	TD	Pts. F.
1985—Seattle NFL	9	40	19	47.5	218	1	2	5.45	7	4	.6	0	0	0 1
1986—Seattle NFL	16	76	42	55.3	485	3	3	6.38	3	8	2.7	0	0	0 1
1990—Buffalo NFL	1	15	8	53.3	106	2	2	7.07	0	0		0	0	0 0
Pro totals (3 years)	26	131	69	52.7	809	6	7	6.18	10	12	1.2	0	0	0 2

GIVINS, ERNEST
WR, OILERS

PERSONAL: Born September 3, 1964, at St. Petersburg, Fla. . . . 5-9/172. . . . Full name: Ernest P. Givins.
HIGH SCHOOL: Lakewood (St. Petersburg, Fla.).
COLLEGE: Northeastern Oklahoma A&M, then Louisville.
TRANSACTIONS/CAREER NOTES: Selected by Houston Oilers in second round (34th pick overall) of 1986 NFL draft. . . . Selected by Tampa Bay Bandits in first round (eighth pick overall) of 1986 USFL draft. . . . Signed by Houston Oilers (August 1, 1986).
RECORDS/HONORS: Played in Pro Bowl after 1990 season.
PRO STATISTICS: 1986—Attempted two passes with no completions and returned eight punts for 80 yards. 1989—Recovered one fumble.

		RUSHING				RECEIVING				TOTAL	
Year Team	G	Att.	Yds.	Avg.	TD	No.	Yds.	Avg.	TD	TD	Pts. F.
1986—Houston NFL	15	9	148	16.4	1	61	1062	17.4	3	4	24 0
1987—Houston NFL	12	1	-13	-13.0	0	53	933	17.6	6	6	36 2
1988—Houston NFL	16	4	26	6.5	0	60	976	16.3	5	5	30 1
1989—Houston NFL	15	0	0		0	55	794	14.4	3	3	18 0
1990—Houston NFL	16	3	65	21.7	0	72	979	13.6	9	9	54 1
Pro totals (5 years)	74	17	226	13.3	1	301	4744	15.8	26	27	162 4

GLASGOW, NESBY
S, SEAHAWKS

PERSONAL: Born April 15, 1957, at Los Angeles. . . . 5-10/187. . . . Full name: Nesby Lee Glasgow.
HIGH SCHOOL: Gardena (Calif.).
COLLEGE: Washington.

TRANSACTIONS/CAREER NOTES: Selected by Baltimore Colts in eighth round (207th pick overall) of 1979 NFL draft.... Franchise transferred to Indianapolis (March 31, 1984).... Released by Indianapolis Colts (August 4, 1988).... Signed as free agent by Seattle Seahawks (August 8, 1988).

RECORDS/HONORS: Tied NFL record for most combined kick returns, game (12), against Denver Broncos (September 2, 1979).

PRO STATISTICS: 1979—Recovered two fumbles. 1980—Recovered two fumbles. 1981—Recovered two fumbles. 1984—Recovered one fumble. 1986—Recovered two fumbles. 1987—Recovered one fumble. 1989—Caught one pass for four yards and recovered five fumbles for 38 yards and a touchdown. 1990—Recovered one fumble for six yards.

			— INTERCEPTIONS —			— PUNT RETURNS —				— KICKOFF RETURNS —				— TOTAL —		
Year	Team	G	No.	Yds.	Avg.	TD	No.	Yds.	Avg.	TD	No.	Yds.	Avg.	TD	TD	Pts.	F.
1979— Baltimore NFL........		16	1	-1	-1.0	0	44	352	8.0	1	50	1126	22.5	0	1	6	8
1980— Baltimore NFL........		16	4	65	16.3	0	23	187	8.1	0	33	743	22.5	0	0	0	5
1981— Baltimore NFL........		14	2	35	17.5	0	0	0		0	1	35	35.0	0	0	0	0
1982— Baltimore NFL........		9	0	0		0	4	24	6.0	0	0	0		0	0	0	0
1983— Baltimore NFL........		16	3	35	11.7	0	1	9	9.0	0	0	0		0	0	0	0
1984— Indianapolis NFL ...		16	1	8	8.0	0	7	79	11.3	0	0	0		0	0	0	1
1985— Indianapolis NFL ...		16	0	0		0	0	0		0	0	0		0	0	0	0
1986— Indianapolis NFL ...		14	0	0		0	0	0		0	0	0		0	0	0	0
1987— Indianapolis NFL ...		11	1	0	.0	0	0	0		0	0	0		0	0	0	0
1988— Seattle NFL		16	2	19	9.5	0	1	0	.0	0	0	0		0	0	0	1
1989— Seattle NFL		16	0	0		0	0	0		0	0	0		0	1	6	0
1990— Seattle NFL		16	0	0		0	0	0		0	1	2	2.0	0	0	0	1
Pro totals (12 years).....		176	14	161	11.5	0	80	651	8.1	1	85	1906	22.4	0	2	12	16

GLENN, KERRY

CB, DOLPHINS

PERSONAL: Born January 3, 1962, at East St. Louis, Ill. ... 5-9/178. ... Full name: Kerry R. Glenn.

HIGH SCHOOL: East St. Louis (Ill.).

COLLEGE: Minnesota.

TRANSACTIONS/CAREER NOTES: Selected by Orlando Renegades in fourth round (46th pick overall) of 1985 USFL draft.... Selected by New York Jets in 10th round (262nd pick overall) of 1985 NFL draft.... Signed by Jets (July 26, 1985).... On injured reserve with sprained foot (September 10, 1986-remainder of season).... On injured reserve with knee injury (December 4, 1987-remainder of season).... On physically unable to perform/active list with knee injury (July 25-August 21, 1988).... Transferred to reserve/physically unable to perform list with knee injury (August 22, 1988-entire season).... Granted unconditional free agency (February 1, 1989).... Signed by Cleveland Browns (April 1, 1989).... Released by Browns (September 5, 1989).... Signed as free agent by New York Jets (September 21, 1989).... Granted unconditional free agency (February 1, 1990).... Signed by Miami Dolphins (March 30, 1990).

PRO STATISTICS: 1985—Returned five kickoffs for 71 yards and recovered two fumbles for 31 yards. 1986—Recovered one fumble.

			— INTERCEPTIONS —			
Year	Team	G	No.	Yds.	Avg.	TD
1985— N.Y. Jets NFL		16	4	15	3.8	1
1986— N.Y. Jets NFL		1	0	0		0
1987— N.Y. Jets NFL		8	0	0		0
1989— N.Y. Jets NFL		14	1	0	.0	0
1990— Miami NFL.................		16	2	31	15.5	1
Pro totals (5 years)		55	7	46	6.6	2

GLENN, VENCIE

S, RAIDERS

PERSONAL: Born October 26, 1964, at Grambling, La. ... 6-0/190. ... Full name: Vencie Leonard Glenn.

HIGH SCHOOL: John F. Kennedy (Silver Spring, Md.).

COLLEGE: Indiana State.

TRANSACTIONS/CAREER NOTES: Selected by New England Patriots in second round (54th pick overall) of 1986 NFL draft.... Signed by Patriots (July 29, 1986).... Traded by Patriots to San Diego Chargers for fifth-round pick in 1987 draft and cash (September 29, 1986).... Granted free agency (February 1, 1990).... Re-signed by Chargers (August 7, 1990).... On inactive list (September 30 and October 21, 1990).... Granted unconditional free agency (February 1, 1991).... Signed by Los Angeles Raiders (March, 1991).

RECORDS/HONORS: Established NFL record for longest interception return (103 yards), against Denver Broncos (November 29, 1987).

PRO STATISTICS: 1986—Recovered two fumbles for 32 yards. 1987—Recovered one fumble. 1988—Recovered two fumbles. 1989—Recovered one fumble for 81 yards and a touchdown.

			— INTERCEPTIONS —			
Year	Team	G	No.	Yds.	Avg.	TD
1986— San Diego NFL		12	2	31	15.5	0
1987— San Diego NFL		12	4	*166	41.5	1
1988— San Diego NFL		16	1	0	.0	0
1989— San Diego NFL		16	4	52	13.0	0
1990— San Diego NFL		14	1	0	.0	0
Pro totals (5 years)		70	12	249	20.8	1

GLOVER, KEVIN
C, LIONS

PERSONAL: Born June 17, 1963, at Washington, D.C. . . . . 6-2/282. . . . Full name: Kevin Bernard Glover.
HIGH SCHOOL: Largo (Md.).
COLLEGE: Maryland.
TRANSACTIONS/CAREER NOTES: Selected by Tampa Bay Bandits in 1985 USFL territorial draft. . . . Selected by Detroit Lions in second round (34th pick overall) of 1985 NFL draft. . . . Signed by Lions (July 23, 1985). . . . On injured reserve with knee injury (December 7, 1985-remainder of season). . . . On injured reserve with knee injury (September 29-December 20, 1986).
PLAYING EXPERIENCE: Detroit NFL, 1985-1990. . . . Games: 1985 (10), 1986 (4), 1987 (12), 1988 (16), 1989 (16), 1990 (16). Total: 74.
RECORDS/HONORS: Named as center on THE SPORTING NEWS college All-America team, 1984.
PRO STATISTICS: 1987—Returned one kickoff for 19 yards. 1988—Recovered two fumbles. 1990—Recovered one fumble.

GOAD, TIM
NT, PATRIOTS

PERSONAL: Born February 28, 1966, at Claudville, Va. . . . 6-3/280. . . . Full name: Timothy Ray Goad. . . . Name pronounced GODE.
HIGH SCHOOL: Patrick County (Stuart, Va.).
COLLEGE: North Carolina.
TRANSACTIONS/CAREER NOTES: Selected by New England Patriots in fourth round (87th pick overall) of 1988 NFL draft. . . . Signed by Patriots (July 15, 1988).
PLAYING EXPERIENCE: New England NFL, 1988-1990. . . . Games: 1988 (16), 1989 (16), 1990 (16). Total: 48.
PRO STATISTICS: 1990—Recovered one fumble.

GOEAS, LEO
G/OT, CHARGERS

PERSONAL: Born August 15, 1966, at Honolulu. . . . 6-4/285. . . . Full name: Leo Douglas Goeas. . . . Name pronounced GO-az.
HIGH SCHOOL: Kamehameha (Honolulu).
COLLEGE: Hawaii.
TRANSACTIONS/CAREER NOTES: Selected by San Diego Chargers in third round (60th pick overall) of 1990 NFL draft. . . . Signed by Chargers (July 19, 1990). . . . On inactive list (September 9, 1990).
PLAYING EXPERIENCE: San Diego NFL, 1990. . . . Games: 1990 (15).
PRO STATISTICS: 1990—Recovered one fumble.

GOFF, ROBERT
NT, SAINTS

PERSONAL: Born October 2, 1965, at Rochester, N.Y. . . . 6-3/270. . . . Full name: Robert Lamar Goff.
HIGH SCHOOL: Bayshore (Bradenton, Fla.).
COLLEGE: Butler County Community College (Kan.), then Auburn.
TRANSACTIONS/CAREER NOTES: Selected by Tampa Bay Buccaneers in fourth round (83rd pick overall) of 1988 NFL draft. . . . Signed by Buccaneers (July 10, 1988). . . . Traded by Buccaneers to New Orleans Saints for 10th-round pick in 1991 NFL draft (September 3, 1990). . . . On inactive list (September 10, 1990).
PLAYING EXPERIENCE: Tampa Bay NFL, 1988 and 1989; New Orleans NFL, 1990. . . . Games: 1988 (16), 1989 (12), 1990 (15). Total: 43.
PRO STATISTICS: 1988—Recovered three fumbles. 1989—Recovered one fumble. 1990—Recovered one fumble for 13 yards.

GOGAN, KEVIN
G/OT, COWBOYS

PERSONAL: Born November 2, 1964, at San Francisco. . . . 6-7/311. . . . Full name: Kevin Patrick Gogan.
HIGH SCHOOL: Sacred Heart (San Francisco).
COLLEGE: Washington (degree in sociology, 1987).
TRANSACTIONS/CAREER NOTES: Selected by Dallas Cowboys in eighth round (206th pick overall) of 1987 NFL draft. . . . Signed by Cowboys (July 18, 1987). . . . On non-football injury list with substance abuse (August 5-August 31, 1988). . . . Granted roster exemption (August 31-September 5, 1988).
PLAYING EXPERIENCE: Dallas NFL, 1987-1990. . . . Games: 1987 (11), 1988 (15), 1989 (13), 1990 (16). Total: 55.
PRO STATISTICS: 1987—Recovered one fumble. 1990—Recovered one fumble.

GOLIC, BOB
DT, RAIDERS

PERSONAL: Born October 26, 1957, at Cleveland. . . . 6-2/275. . . . Full name: Robert Perry Golic. . . . Name pronounced GO-lik. . . . Son of Louis Golic, former player with Montreal Alouettes, Hamilton Tiger-Cats and Saskatchewan Roughriders of CFL; and brother of Mike Golic, defensive tackle with Philadelphia Eagles.
HIGH SCHOOL: St. Joseph (Cleveland).
COLLEGE: Notre Dame (bachelor of business administration degree in management, 1979).
TRANSACTIONS/CAREER NOTES: Selected by New England Patriots in second round (52nd pick overall) of 1979 NFL draft. . . . On injured reserve with shoulder injury (August 28-December 15, 1979). . . . Released by Patriots (August 31, 1982). . . . Signed as free agent by Cleveland Browns (September 2, 1982). . . . On inactive list (September 12, 1982). . . . On injured reserve with broken arm (December 30, 1987-remainder of 1987 season playoffs). . . . Granted unconditional free agency (February 1, 1989). . . . Signed by Los Angeles Raiders (April 1, 1989).
PLAYING EXPERIENCE: New England NFL, 1979-1982; Cleveland NFL, 1983-1988; Los Angeles Raiders NFL, 1989 and 1990. . . . Games: 1979 (1), 1980 (16), 1981 (16), 1982 (6), 1983 (16), 1984 (15), 1985 (16), 1986 (16), 1987 (12), 1988 (16), 1989 (16), 1990 (16). Total: 162.
CHAMPIONSHIP GAME EXPERIENCE: Played in AFC championship game after 1986 and 1990 seasons.
RECORDS/HONORS: Played in Pro Bowl after 1985 and 1986 seasons. . . . Named to play in Pro Bowl after 1987 season; replaced due to injury by Tim Krumrie. . . . Named to THE SPORTING NEWS NFL All-Pro team, 1985.

PRO STATISTICS: 1981—Recovered one fumble. 1983—Intercepted one pass for seven yards and a touchdown. 1984—Recovered one fumble for 18 yards. 1990—Recovered two fumbles.

GOLIC, MIKE
DT, EAGLES

PERSONAL: Born December 12, 1962, at Willowick, O. . . . 6-5/275. . . . Name pronounced GO-lik. . . . Son of Louis Golic, former player with Montreal Alouettes, Hamilton Tiger-Cats and Saskatchewan Roughriders of CFL; and brother of Bob Golic, defensive tackle with Los Angeles Raiders. **HIGH SCHOOL:** St. Joseph (Cleveland).
COLLEGE: Notre Dame (bachelor of business administration degree in management, 1985).
TRANSACTIONS/CAREER NOTES: Selected by Orlando Renegades in 15th round (204th pick overall) of 1985 USFL draft. . . . Selected by Houston Oilers in 10th round (255th pick overall) of 1985 NFL draft. . . . Signed by Oilers (July 18, 1985). . . . On injured reserve with ankle injury (August 27, 1985-entire season). . . . Released by Oilers (November 3, 1987). . . . Signed as free agent by Philadelphia Eagles (November 11, 1987). . . . On injured reserve with ankle injury (November 4-December 2, 1988).
PLAYING EXPERIENCE: Houston NFL, 1986; Houston (2)-Philadelphia (6) NFL, 1987; Philadelphia NFL, 1988-1990. . . . Games: 1986 (16), 1987 (8), 1988 (12), 1989 (16), 1990 (16). Total: 68.
PRO STATISTICS: 1986—Recovered two fumbles for four yards. 1989—Intercepted one pass for 23 yards and ran eight yards on lateral from fumble recovery. 1990—Intercepted one pass for 12 yards.

GOODBURN, KELLY
P, REDSKINS

PERSONAL: Born April 14, 1962, at Cherokee, Ia. . . . 6-2/202. . . . Full name: Kelly Joe Goodburn.
HIGH SCHOOL: Eastwood Community (Correctionville, Ia.).
COLLEGE: Iowa State, then Emporia State, Kan. (degree in physical education, 1987).
TRANSACTIONS/CAREER NOTES: Signed as free agent by Kansas City Chiefs (May 3, 1986). . . . Released by Chiefs (August 19, 1986). . . . Re-signed by Chiefs (April 7, 1987). . . . Released by Chiefs (August 31, 1987). . . . Re-signed as replacement player by Chiefs (September 25, 1987). . . . Released by Chiefs (September 26, 1990). . . . Signed by Washington Redskins (December 4, 1990).
PRO STATISTICS: 1987—Rushed once for 16 yards. 1988—Rushed once for 15 yards. 1990—Rushed once for five yards.

			—— PUNTING——		
Year Team	G	No.	Avg.	Blk.
1987— Kansas City NFL	13	59	40.9	0
1988— Kansas City NFL	16	76	40.3	0
1989— Kansas City NFL	16	67	40.1	0
1990— K.C. (3)-Wash. (4) NFL	7	28	36.8	0
Pro totals (4 years)	52	230	39.5	0

GOODE, CHRIS
DB, COLTS

PERSONAL: Born September 17, 1963, at Town Creek, Ala. . . . 6-0/196. . . . Full name: Chris K. Goode. . . . Name pronounced Good. . . . Brother of Kerry Goode, running back with Tampa Bay Buccaneers and Miami Dolphins, 1988 and 1989; and cousin of Robert Penchion, offensive lineman with Buffalo Bills, San Francisco 49ers and Seattle Seahawks, 1972-1976.
HIGH SCHOOL: Hazelwood (Town Creek, Ala.).
COLLEGE: North Alabama, then Alabama.
TRANSACTIONS/CAREER NOTES: Selected by Indianapolis Colts in 10th round (253rd pick overall) of 1987 NFL draft. . . . Signed by Colts (July 23, 1987). . . . On injured reserve with strained abdomen (September 7-November 6, 1987). . . . On injured reserve with knee injury (December 2, 1988-remainder of season). . . . Granted free agency (February 1, 1990). . . . Re-signed by Colts (August 11, 1990).
PLAYING EXPERIENCE: Indianapolis NFL, 1987-1990. . . . Games: 1987 (8), 1988 (13), 1989 (15), 1990 (16). Total: 52.
PRO STATISTICS: 1988—Intercepted two passes for 53 yards and recovered four fumbles for 16 yards. 1990—Intercepted one pass for 10 yards and recovered two fumbles for 63 yards (including returning one fumble 54 yards for a touchdown).

GORDON, ALEX
LB, BENGALS

PERSONAL: Born September 14, 1964, at Jacksonville, Fla. . . . 6-5/245. . . . Full name: Alex Groncier Gordon.
HIGH SCHOOL: Englewood (Jacksonville, Fla.).
COLLEGE: Cincinnati.
TRANSACTIONS/CAREER NOTES: Selected by New York Jets in second round (42nd pick overall) of 1987 NFL draft. . . . Signed by Jets (July 22, 1987). . . . On injured reserve (September, 1990-October 15, 1990). . . . Traded by Jets to Los Angeles Raiders for cornerback Dennis Price (October 15, 1990). . . . Granted unconditional free agency (February 1, 1991). . . . Signed by Cincinnati Bengals (March 25, 1991).
PLAYING EXPERIENCE: New York Jets NFL, 1987-1989; Los Angeles Raiders NFL, 1990. . . . Games: 1987 (12), 1988 (13), 1989 (16), 1990 (10). Total: 51.
CHAMPIONSHIP GAME EXPERIENCE: Played in AFC championship game after 1990 season.
PRO STATISTICS: 1988—Recovered one fumble. 1989—Intercepted one pass for two yards and recovered one fumble.

GORDON, TIM
S, PATRIOTS

PERSONAL: Born May 7, 1965, at Ardmore, Okla. . . . 6-0/188. . . . Full name: Tim Carvelle Gordon. **HIGH SCHOOL:** Ardmore (Okla.).
COLLEGE: Tulsa.
TRANSACTIONS/CAREER NOTES: Signed as free agent by Atlanta Falcons (May 6, 1987). . . . Released by Falcons (September 1, 1987). . . . Re-signed by Falcons (September 16, 1987). . . . On injured reserve with shoulder injury (September 4-October 3, 1990). . . . Transferred to practice squad (October 3-October 20, 1990). . . . On injured reserve (November 20-December 19, 1990). . . . Awarded on waivers to New England Patriots (December 22, 1990). . . . On inactive list (December 23 and 30, 1990).
PRO STATISTICS: 1987—Recovered one fumble. 1988—Recovered one fumble.

Year	Team	G	INTERCEPTIONS				KICKOFF RETURNS				TOTAL		
			No.	Yds.	Avg.	TD	No.	Yds.	Avg.	TD	TD	Pts.	F.
1987—	Atlanta NFL	11	2	28	14.0	0	0	0		0	0	0	0
1988—	Atlanta NFL	16	2	10	5.0	0	14	209	14.9	0	0	0	1
1989—	Atlanta NFL	14	4	60	15.0	0	0	0		0	0	0	0
1990—	Atl. (5)-N.E. (0) NFL	5	0	0		0	1	43	43.0	0	0	0	0
	Pro totals (4 years)	46	8	98	12.3	0	15	252	16.8	0	0	0	1

GOSS, ANTONIO
LB, 49ERS

PERSONAL: Born August 11, 1966, at Randleman, N.C. . . . 6-4/228. . . . Full name: Antonio Derrell Goss.
HIGH SCHOOL: Randleman (N.C.).
COLLEGE: North Carolina.
TRANSACTIONS/CAREER NOTES: Selected by San Francisco 49ers in 12th round (319th pick overall) of 1989 NFL draft. . . . Signed by 49ers (July 20, 1989). . . . Released by 49ers (September 5, 1989). . . . Re-signed by 49ers to developmental squad (September 7, 1989). . . . On developmental squad (September 7-November 4, 1989). . . . Released by 49ers (September 3, 1990). . . . Signed by San Diego Chargers (November 21, 1990). . . . On inactive list (November 25 and December 2, 1990). . . . Released by Chargers (December 5, 1990). . . . Signed by San Francisco 49ers (April 12, 1991).
PLAYING EXPERIENCE: San Francisco NFL, 1989; San Diego NFL, 1990. . . . Games: 1989 (8), 1990 (0). Total: 8.
CHAMPIONSHIP GAME EXPERIENCE: Member of San Francisco 49ers for NFC championship game and Super Bowl XXIV after 1989 season; inactive.
PRO STATISTICS: 1989—Recovered one fumble.

GOSSETT, JEFF
P, RAIDERS

PERSONAL: Born January 25, 1957, at Charleston, Ill. . . . 6-2/195. . . . Full name: Jeffery Alan Gossett.
HIGH SCHOOL: Charleston (Ill.).
COLLEGE: Eastern Illinois (bachelor of science degree in physical education, 1982).
TRANSACTIONS/CAREER NOTES: Signed as free agent by Dallas Cowboys (May, 1980). . . . Released by Cowboys (August 25, 1980). . . . Signed as free agent by San Diego Chargers (April 6, 1981). . . . Released by Chargers (August 31, 1981). . . . Signed as free agent by Kansas City Chiefs (November 5, 1981). . . . Released by Chiefs (December 14, 1982). . . . Re-signed by Chiefs (December 21, 1982). . . . Released by Chiefs (August 29, 1983). . . . Awarded on waivers to Cleveland Browns (August 30, 1983). . . . Signed by Chicago Blitz of USFL (December 20, 1983), for contract to take effect after being granted free agency, February 1, 1984. . . . USFL rights traded by Pittsburgh Maulers with place-kicker Efren Herrera to Chicago Blitz for rights to linebacker Bruce Huther (December 30, 1983). . . . Blitz franchise disbanded (November 20, 1984). . . . Signed as free agent by Portland Breakers (February 4, 1985). . . . Signed by Cleveland Browns for 1985 season (May 20, 1985). . . . Released by Portland Breakers (June 26, 1985). . . . Crossed picket line during players' strike (October 14, 1987). . . . Released by Cleveland Browns (November 17, 1987). . . . Signed as free agent by Houston Oilers (December 3, 1987). . . . Traded by Houston Oilers to Los Angeles Raiders for past considerations (August 16, 1988).
CHAMPIONSHIP GAME EXPERIENCE: Played in AFC championship game after 1986 and 1990 seasons.
PRO STATISTICS: NFL: 1982—recovered one fumble. 1985—Attempted one pass with no completions. 1986—Attempted two passes with one completion for 30 yards and one interception. 1989—Attempted one pass with no completions. . . . USFL: 1984—Rushed once for no yards. 1985—Attempted one pass with one interception, rushed once for minus four yards, recovered one fumble and fumbled once.

Year	Team	G	PUNTING		
			No.	Avg.	Blk.
1981—	Kansas City NFL	7	29	39.3	0
1982—	Kansas City NFL	8	33	41.4	0
1983—	Cleveland NFL	16	70	40.8	0
1984—	Chicago USFL	18	85	*42.5	—
1985—	Portland USFL	18	74	42.2	—
1985—	Cleveland NFL	16	81	40.3	0
1986—	Cleveland NFL	16	83	41.2	0
1987—	Cle. (5)-Hou. (4) NFL	9	44	40.4	1
1988—	L.A. Raiders NFL	16	91	41.8	0
1989—	L.A. Raiders NFL	16	67	40.5	0
1990—	L.A. Raiders NFL	16	60	38.6	2
	NFL totals (9 years)	120	558	40.5	3
	USFL totals (2 years)	36	159	42.4	—
	Pro totals (11 years)	156	717	40.8	3

BASEBALL TRANSACTIONS: Selected by New York Mets' organization in fifth round of free-agent draft (June 6, 1978). . . . Placed on restricted list (April 30, 1980).

RECORD AS BASEBALL PLAYER

Year	Team	League	Pos.	G	AB	R	H	2B	3B	HR	RBI	Avg.	PO	A	E	F.A.
1978—	Lynchburg	Carol.	3B/OF	10	21	1	5	1	0	0	4	.238	6	8	6	.700
1978—	Little Falls	NYP	3B/OF	61	233	30	59	12	4	4	36	.253	54	102	19	.891
1979—	Lynchburg	Carol.	3B	112	386	56	98	25	2	13	53	.254	71	200	*32	.894

GOUVEIA, KURT
LB, REDSKINS

PERSONAL: Born September 14, 1964, at Honolulu. . . . 6-1/227. . . . Full name: Kurt Keola Gouveia. . . . Name pronounced goo-VAY-uh.
HIGH SCHOOL: Waianae (Hawaii).
COLLEGE: Brigham Young.

TRANSACTIONS/CAREER NOTES: Selected by Washington Redskins in eighth round (213th pick overall) of 1986 NFL draft. . . . Signed by Redskins (July 18, 1986). . . . On injured reserve with knee injury (August 25, 1986-entire season).
PLAYING EXPERIENCE: Washington NFL, 1987-1990. . . . Games: 1987 (11), 1988 (16), 1989 (15), 1990 (16). Total: 58.
CHAMPIONSHIP GAME EXPERIENCE: Played in NFC championship game after 1987 season. . . . Played in Super Bowl XXII after 1987 season.
PRO STATISTICS: 1989—Intercepted one pass for one yard and returned one kickoff for no yards. 1990—Returned two kickoffs for 23 yards and recovered one fumble for 39 yards and a touchdown.

GRADDY, SAM
WR, RAIDERS

PERSONAL: Born February 10, 1964, at Gaffney, S.C. . . . 5-10/180. . . . Full name: Samuel Louis Graddy.
HIGH SCHOOL: Northside (Atlanta).
COLLEGE: Tennessee (bachelor of arts degree in economics, 1987).
TRANSACTIONS/CAREER NOTES: Signed as free agent by Denver Broncos (May 1, 1987). . . . On injured reserve with hamstring injury (September 1-December 12, 1987). . . . Released by Broncos (September 8, 1988). . . . Re-signed by Broncos (September 12, 1988). . . . On injured reserve with back injury (October 31, 1988-remainder of season). . . . Granted unconditional free agency (February 1, 1989). . . . Signed by Los Angeles Raiders (April 1, 1989). . . . On injured reserve with broken leg (September 6-November 29, 1989). . . . Transferred to developmental squad (November 30, 1989-remainder of season).
PLAYING EXPERIENCE: Denver NFL, 1987 and 1988; Los Angeles Raiders NFL, 1990. . . . Games: 1987 (1), 1988 (7), 1990 (16). Total: 24.
CHAMPIONSHIP GAME EXPERIENCE: Member of Denver Broncos for Super Bowl XXII after 1987 season; inactive. . . . Played in AFC championship game after 1990 season.
MISCELLANEOUS: Won gold medal in 4x100 relay during 1984 Summer Olympics.
PRO STATISTICS: 1988—Caught one pass for 30 yards. 1990—Caught one pass for 47 yards and a touchdown.

GRAF, RICK
LB, OILERS

PERSONAL: Born August 29, 1964, at Iowa City, Ia. . . . 6-5/250. . . . Full name: Richard Glenn Graf.
HIGH SCHOOL: James Madison Memorial (Madison, Wis.).
COLLEGE: Wisconsin (bachelor of arts degree in communication arts, 1987).
TRANSACTIONS/CAREER NOTES: Selected by Miami Dolphins in second round (43rd pick overall) of 1987 NFL draft. . . . Signed by Dolphins (August 1, 1987). . . . On injured reserve with broken thumb (October 4-November 28, 1989). . . . Transferred to developmental squad (November 29, 1989-remainder of season). . . . Granted free agency (February 1, 1990). . . . Re-signed by Dolphins (September 26, 1990). . . . Granted roster exemption (September 26-October 6, 1990). . . . On injured reserve with groin injury (December 8, 1990-January 4, 1991). . . . Deactivated for remainder of 1990 season playoffs (January 11, 1991). . . . Granted unconditional free agency (February 1, 1991). . . . Signed by Houston Oilers (March 21, 1991).
PLAYING EXPERIENCE: Miami NFL, 1987-1990. . . . Games: 1987 (12), 1988 (16), 1989 (4), 1990 (8). Total: 40.
PRO STATISTICS: 1987—Recovered one fumble. 1988—Intercepted one pass for 14 yards and recovered three fumbles for five yards. 1990—Returned one kickoff for six yards and recovered one fumble for three yards.

GRAHAM, DERRICK
OT, CHIEFS

PERSONAL: Born March 18, 1967, at Groveland, Fla. . . . 6-4/306. . . . Full name: Detrice Andrew Graham.
HIGH SCHOOL: Groveland (Fla.).
COLLEGE: Appalachian State.
TRANSACTIONS/CAREER NOTES: Selected by Kansas City Chiefs in fifth round (124th pick overall) of 1990 NFL draft. . . . Signed by Chiefs (July 28, 1990). . . . On inactive list (October 21, 1990). . . . On injured reserve with ankle injury (November 3, 1990-remainder of season).
PLAYING EXPERIENCE: Kansas City NFL, 1990. . . . Games: 1990 (6).

GRANT, AFRICAN
S, DOLPHINS

PERSONAL: Born August 2, 1965, at New York. . . . 6-0/200. . . . Full name: African Nigeria Grant.
HIGH SCHOOL: Dwight Morrow (Englewood, N.J.).
COLLEGE: Illinois (bachelor of arts degree in communications).
TRANSACTIONS/CAREER NOTES: Selected as free agent by Washington Redskins (May, 1988). . . . Released by Redskins (August 24, 1988). . . . Signed by Miami Dolphins (April, 1989). . . . On injured reserve with thumb injury (September 6, 1989-entire season). . . . Released by Dolphins (September 3, 1990). . . . Re-signed by Dolphins (September 14, 1990). . . . On injured reserve with knee injury (October 9, 1990-remainder of regular season and playoffs).
PLAYING EXPERIENCE: Miami NFL, 1990. . . . Games: 1990 (4).

GRANT, ALAN
DB, COLTS

PERSONAL: Born October 1, 1966, at Pasadena, Calif. . . . 5-10/187.
HIGH SCHOOL: St. Francis (La Canada, Calif.).
COLLEGE: Stanford.
TRANSACTIONS/CAREER NOTES: Selected by Indianapolis Colts in fourth round (103rd pick overall) of 1990 NFL draft. . . . Signed by Colts (July 20, 1990).
PRO STATISTICS: 1990—Recovered two fumbles and fumbled once for five yards.

		— INTERCEPTIONS—				— PUNT RETURNS —				– KICKOFF RETURNS–				— TOTAL —		
Year	Team	G	No.	Yds.	Avg.	TD	No.	Yds.	Avg.	TD	No.	Yds.	Avg.	TD	TD	Pts.	F.
1990— Indianapolis NFL ...		16	1	25	25.0	1	2	6	3.0	0	15	280	18.7	0	1	6	1
Pro totals (1 year)		16	1	25	25.0	1	2	6	3.0	0	15	280	18.7	0	1	6	1

GRANT, DARRYL
DT, REDSKINS

PERSONAL: Born November 22, 1959, at San Antonio. . . . 6-1/275.
HIGH SCHOOL: Highlands (San Antonio).
COLLEGE: Rice.
TRANSACTIONS/CAREER NOTES: Selected by Washington Redskins in ninth round (231st pick overall) of 1981 NFL draft. . . . On injured reserve with knee injury (November 2, 1985-remainder of season). . . . Granted free agency (February 1, 1990). . . . Re-signed by Redskins (August 21, 1990).
PLAYING EXPERIENCE: Washington NFL, 1981-1990. . . . Games: 1981 (15), 1982 (9), 1983 (16), 1984 (15), 1985 (8), 1986 (16), 1987 (12), 1988 (16), 1989 (16), 1990 (16). Total: 139.
CHAMPIONSHIP GAME EXPERIENCE: Played in NFC championship game after 1982, 1983, 1986 and 1987 seasons. . . . Played in Super Bowl XVII after 1982 season, Super Bowl XVIII after 1983 season and Super Bowl XXII after 1987 season.
PRO STATISTICS: 1981—Returned one kickoff for 20 yards. 1983—Recovered two fumbles. 1984—Recovered four fumbles for 22 yards and a touchdown. 1987—Recovered one fumble. 1988—Recovered one fumble. 1989—Intercepted two passes for no yards and recovered one fumble. 1990—Recovered two fumbles for two yards.

GRANT, DAVID
DE, BENGALS

PERSONAL: Born September 17, 1965, at Belleville, N.J. . . . 6-5/278.
HIGH SCHOOL: Belleville (N.J.).
COLLEGE: West Virginia.
TRANSACTIONS/CAREER NOTES: Selected by Cincinnati Bengals in fourth round (84th pick over-all) of 1988 NFL draft. . . . Signed by Bengals (July 10, 1988).
PLAYING EXPERIENCE: Cincinnati NFL, 1988-1990. . . . Games: 1988 (16), 1989 (16), 1990 (16). Total: 48.
CHAMPIONSHIP GAME EXPERIENCE: Played in AFC championship game after 1988 season. . . . Played in Super Bowl XXIII after 1988 season.
PRO STATISTICS: 1988—Recovered one fumble. 1990—Recovered one fumble.

GRAVES, RORY
OT, RAIDERS

PERSONAL: Born July 21, 1963, at Atlanta. . . . 6-6/295. . . . Full name: Rory Anthony Graves.
HIGH SCHOOL: Columbia (Decatur, Ga.).
COLLEGE: Ohio State.
TRANSACTIONS/CAREER NOTES: Selected by New Jersey Generals in 1986 USFL territorial draft. . . . Signed as free agent by Seattle Seahawks (May 12, 1986). . . . On injured reserve with back injury (August 19, 1986-entire season). . . . Released by Seahawks (September 1, 1987). . . . Signed as free agent by Los Angeles Raiders for 1988 (November 5, 1987). . . . On inactive list (November 4, 1990).
PLAYING EXPERIENCE: Los Angeles Raiders NFL, 1988-1990. . . . Games: 1988 (16), 1989 (15), 1990 (15). Total: 46.
CHAMPIONSHIP GAME EXPERIENCE: Played in AFC championship game after 1990 season.
PRO STATISTICS: 1988—Recovered one fumble.

GRAY, CECIL
G/OT, EAGLES

PERSONAL: Born February 16, 1968, at Harlem, N.Y. . . . 6-4/275. . . . Full name: Cecil Talik Gray. . . . First name pronounced SEE-sil.
HIGH SCHOOL: Norfolk Catholic (Norfolk, Va.).
COLLEGE: North Carolina (degree in journalism).
TRANSACTIONS/CAREER NOTES: Selected by Philadelphia Eagles in ninth round (245th pick overall) of 1990 NFL draft. . . . Signed by Eagles (August 1, 1990). . . . On inactive list (October 28; and December 23 and 29, 1990).
PLAYING EXPERIENCE: Philadelphia NFL, 1990. . . . Games: 1990 (12).

GRAY, JERRY
CB, RAMS

PERSONAL: Born December 16, 1962, at Lubbock, Tex. . . . 6-0/185.
HIGH SCHOOL: Estacado (Lubbock, Tex.).
COLLEGE: Texas.
TRANSACTIONS/CAREER NOTES: Selected by San Antonio Gunslingers in 1985 USFL territorial draft. . . . Selected by Los Angeles Rams in first round (21st pick overall) of 1985 NFL draft. . . . Signed by Rams (August 1, 1985). . . . On injured reserve with knee injury (September 4-October 1, 1990). . . . On practice squad (October 1-October 5, 1990).
CHAMPIONSHIP GAME EXPERIENCE: Played in NFC championship game after 1985 and 1989 seasons.
RECORDS/HONORS: Named as defensive back on THE SPORTING NEWS college All-America team, 1984. . . . Played in Pro Bowl after 1986-1989 seasons.
PRO STATISTICS: 1986—Recovered one fumble. 1987—Recovered blocked punt in end zone for a touchdown and recovered one fumble. 1988—Returned one punt for one yard and recovered one fumble. 1989—Recovered one fumble. 1990—Recovered one fumble.

| | | | INTERCEPTIONS | | |
Year Team	G	No.	Yds.	Avg.	TD
1985— L.A. Rams NFL	16	0	0		0
1986— L.A. Rams NFL	16	8	101	12.6	0
1987— L.A. Rams NFL	12	2	35	17.5	0
1988— L.A. Rams NFL	16	3	83	27.7	1
1989— L.A. Rams NFL	16	6	48	8.0	1
1990— L.A. Rams NFL	12	0	0		0
Pro totals (6 years)	88	19	267	14.1	2

GRAY, MEL
WR/KR, LIONS

PERSONAL: Born March 16, 1961, at Williamsburg, Va. . . . 5-9/162.
HIGH SCHOOL: Lafayette (Williamsburg, Va.).
COLLEGE: Coffeyville Junior College, then Purdue.
TRANSACTIONS/CAREER NOTES: Selected by Chicago Blitz in seventh round (132nd pick overall) of

1984 USFL draft.... USFL rights traded by Blitz to Los Angeles Express for wide receiver Kris Haines (February 11, 1984)....
Signed by Express (February 16, 1984).... On developmental squad for four games (February 24-March 9, 1984; and May
26-June 9, 1984).... Selected by New Orleans Saints in second round (42nd pick overall) of 1984 NFL supplemental draft....
Traded by Los Angeles Express with defensive backs Dwight Drane, John Warren and Troy West, guard Wayne Jones, linebacker Howard Carson and tight end Ken O'Neal to Arizona Outlaws for past considerations (August 1, 1985).... Granted free
agency when USFL suspended operations (August 7, 1986).... Signed by New Orleans Saints (August 18, 1986).... Granted
roster exemption (August 18-August 29, 1986).... Granted unconditional free agency (February 1, 1989).... Signed by Detroit Lions (March 1, 1989).

RECORDS/HONORS: Named as kickoff returner to THE SPORTING NEWS NFL All-Pro team, 1986.... Named as punt returner to
THE SPORTING NEWS NFL All-Pro team, 1987.... Named as kick returner to THE SPORTING NEWS NFL All-Pro team, 1990.
... Played in Pro Bowl after 1990 season.

PRO STATISTICS: USFL: 1984—Attempted one pass with one completion for 29 yards and recovered two fumbles. 1985—Recovered one fumble.... NFL: 1987—Recovered one fumble. 1988—Recovered two fumbles. 1990—Recovered three fumbles.

Year	Team	G	RUSHING				RECEIVING				PUNT RETURNS				KICKOFF RETURNS				TOTALS		
			Att.	Yds.	Avg.	TD	No.	Yds.	Avg.	TD	No.	Yds.	Avg.	TD	No.	Yds.	Avg.	TD	TD	Pts.	F.
1984—	Los Ang. USFL....	15	133	625	4.7	3	27	288	10.7	1	0	0		0	20	332	16.6	0	4	24	10
1985—	Los Ang. USFL....	16	125	526	4.2	1	20	101	5.1	0	0	0		0	11	203	18.5	0	1	6	7
1986—	New Orleans NFL	16	6	29	4.8	0	2	45	22.5	0	0	0		0	31	866	27.9	*1	1	6	0
1987—	New Orleans NFL	12	8	37	4.6	1	6	30	5.0	0	24	352	*14.7	0	30	636	21.2	0	1	6	0
1988—	New Orleans NFL	14	0	0		0	0	0		0	25	305	12.2	1	32	670	20.9	0	0	0	5
1989—	Detroit NFL	10	3	22	7.3	0	2	47	23.5	0	11	76	6.9	0	24	640	26.7	0	0	0	0
1990—	Detroit NFL	16	0	0		0	0	0		0	34	361	10.6	0	41	939	22.9	0	0	0	4
	USFL totals (2 years)....	31	258	1151	4.5	4	47	389	8.3	1	0	0		0	31	535	17.3	0	5	30	17
	NFL totals (5 years)......	68	17	88	5.2	1	10	122	12.2	0	94	1094	11.6	1	158	3751	23.7	1	2	12	12
	Pro totals (7 years).......	99	275	1239	4.5	5	57	511	9.0	1	94	1094	11.6	1	189	4286	22.7	1	7	42	29

GRAYBILL, MICHAEL
OT, LIONS

PERSONAL: Born October 14, 1966, at Washington, D.C. ... 6-7/280. ... Full
name: Michael Alton Graybill. ... Nephew of Harvey Graybill, minor league pitcher, 1946.

HIGH SCHOOL: DeMatha Catholic (Hyattsville, Md.).

COLLEGE: Boston University (bachelor of science degree in business administration, 1989).
TRANSACTIONS/CAREER NOTES: Selected by Cleveland Browns in seventh round (187th pick overall) of 1989 NFL draft. ...
Signed by Browns (July 18, 1989). ... Released by Browns (September 5, 1989). ... Re-signed by Browns to developmental
squad (September 6, 1989). ... On developmental squad (September 6-September 28, 1989). ... On injured reserve with back
injury (November 7, 1989-remainder of season). ... Released by Browns (August 23, 1990). ... Awarded on waivers to Dallas
Cowboys (August 24, 1990). ... Released by Cowboys (September 2, 1990). ... Signed by Phoenix Cardinals (November 27,
1990). ... On inactive list (December 2, 16, 23 and 29, 1990). ... Active for one game with Cardinals in 1990; did not play. ...
Granted unconditional free agency (February 1, 1991). ... Signed by Detroit Lions (March 22, 1991).
PLAYING EXPERIENCE: Cleveland NFL, 1989; Phoenix NFL, 1990. ... Games: 1989 (6), 1990 (0). Total: 6.

GRAYSON, DAVID
LB, BROWNS

PERSONAL: Born February 27, 1964, at San Diego. ... 6-3/230. ... Full name: David Lee
Grayson Jr. ... Son of Dave Grayson, defensive back with Dallas Texans-Kansas City
Chiefs and Oakland Raiders, 1961-1970.

HIGH SCHOOL: Abraham Lincoln (San Diego).

COLLEGE: California State Poly, then Fresno State.
TRANSACTIONS/CAREER NOTES: Selected by San Francisco 49ers in eighth round (217th pick overall) of 1987 NFL draft. ...
Signed by 49ers (July 15, 1987). ... Released by 49ers (August 28, 1987). ... Signed as free agent replacement player by
Cleveland Browns (September 23, 1987). ... Granted free agency (February 1, 1990). ... Re-signed by Browns (August 15,
1990).
PLAYING EXPERIENCE: Cleveland NFL, 1987-1990. ... Games: 1987 (11), 1988 (16), 1989 (10), 1990 (16). Total: 53.
CHAMPIONSHIP GAME EXPERIENCE: Played in AFC championship game after 1987 and 1989 seasons.
PRO STATISTICS: 1987—Recovered one fumble for 17 yards and a touchdown and returned one kickoff for six yards. 1989—In-
tercepted two passes for 25 yards and a touchdown and recovered two fumbles for 31 yards and a touchdown. 1990—Intercepted one pass for three yards and recovered one fumble.

GREEN, DARRELL
CB, REDSKINS

PERSONAL: Born February 15, 1960, at Houston. ... 5-8/170.
HIGH SCHOOL: Jesse Jones (Houston).
COLLEGE: Texas A&I.
TRANSACTIONS/CAREER NOTES: Selected by Denver Gold in 10th round (112th pick over-
all) of 1983 USFL draft. ... Selected by Washington Redskins in first round (28th pick overall) of 1983 NFL draft. ... Signed by
Redskins (June 10, 1983). ... On injured reserve with broken hand (December 13, 1988-remainder of season). ... On injured
reserve with broken bone in wrist (October 24, 1989-remainder of season).
CHAMPIONSHIP GAME EXPERIENCE: Played in NFC championship game after 1983, 1986 and 1987 seasons. ... Played in Super
Bowl XVIII after 1983 season and Super Bowl XXII after 1987 season.
RECORDS/HONORS: Played in Pro Bowl after 1984, 1986, 1987 and 1990 seasons.
PRO STATISTICS: 1983—Recovered one fumble. 1985—Rushed once for six yards and recovered one fumble. 1986—Recovered
one fumble and fumbled once. 1987—Recovered one fumble for 26 yards and a touchdown. 1988—Recovered one fumble.
1989—Recovered one fumble.

Year	Team	G	INTERCEPTIONS				PUNT RETURNS				TOTAL		
			No.	Yds.	Avg.	TD	No.	Yds.	Avg.	TD	TD	Pts.	F.
1983—	Washington NFL..............................	16	2	7	3.5	0	4	29	7.3	0	0	0	1
1984—	Washington NFL..............................	16	5	91	18.2	1	2	13	6.5	0	1	6	0

Year	Team	G	No.	INTERCEPTIONS Yds.	Avg.	TD	No.	PUNT RETURNS Yds.	Avg.	TD	TD	TOTAL Pts.	F.
1985— Washington NFL		16	2	0	.0	0	16	214	13.4	0	0	0	2
1986— Washington NFL		16	5	9	1.8	0	12	120	10.0	0	0	0	0
1987— Washington NFL		12	3	65	21.7	0	5	53	10.6	0	1	6	0
1988— Washington NFL		15	1	12	12.0	0	9	103	11.4	0	0	0	1
1989— Washington NFL		7	2	0	.0	0	1	11	11.0	0	0	0	1
1990— Washington NFL		16	4	20	5.0	1	1	6	6.0	0	1	6	0
Pro totals (8 years)		114	24	204	8.5	2	50	549	11.0	0	3	18	5

GREEN, ERIC
TE, STEELERS

PERSONAL: Born June 22, 1967, at Savannah, Ga.... 6-5/274.... Full name: Bernard Eric Green. **HIGH SCHOOL:** A.E. Beach (Savannah, Ga.). **COLLEGE:** Liberty (bachelor of science degree in finance, 1991). **TRANSACTIONS/CAREER NOTES:** Selected by Pittsburgh Steelers in first round (21st pick overall) of 1990 NFL draft.... Signed by Steelers (September 10, 1990).... Granted roster exemption (September 10-September 24, 1990).

PRO STATISTICS: 1990—Returned one kickoff for 16 yards, recovered one fumble and fumbled once.

Year	Team	G	No.	RECEIVING Yds.	Avg.	TD
1990— Pittsburgh NFL		13	34	387	11.4	7
Pro totals (1 year)		13	34	387	11.4	7

GREEN, GASTON
RB, BRONCOS

PERSONAL: Born August 1, 1966, at Los Angeles.... 5-11/192.... Full name: Gaston Alfred Green III. **HIGH SCHOOL:** Gardena (Calif.). **COLLEGE:** UCLA.

TRANSACTIONS/CAREER NOTES: Selected by Los Angeles Rams in first round (14th pick overall) of 1988 NFL draft.... Signed by Rams (July 20, 1988).... On injured reserve with hamstring injury (January 4, 1990-remainder of 1989 season playoffs).... Traded by Rams with fourth-round pick in 1991 NFL draft to Denver Broncos for offensive tackle Gerald Perry and 12th-round pick in 1991 draft (April 22, 1991).

PRO STATISTICS: 1988—Recovered three fumbles. 1990—Recovered two fumbles.

Year	Team	G	Att.	RUSHING Yds.	Avg.	TD	No.	RECEIVING Yds.	Avg.	TD	No.	KICKOFF RETURNS Yds.	Avg.	TD	TD	TOTAL Pts.	F.
1988— L.A. Rams NFL		10	35	117	3.3	0	6	57	9.5	0	17	345	20.3	0	0	0	1
1989— L.A. Rams NFL		6	26	73	2.8	0	1	-5	-5.0	0	0	0		0	0	0	1
1990— L.A. Rams NFL		15	68	261	3.8	0	2	23	11.5	1	25	560	22.4	1	2	12	1
Pro totals (3 years)		31	129	451	3.5	0	9	75	8.3	1	42	905	21.6	1	2	12	3

GREEN, HAROLD
RB, BENGALS

PERSONAL: Born January 29, 1968, at Ladson, S.C.... 6-2/222. **HIGH SCHOOL:** Stratford (Goose Creek, S.C.). **COLLEGE:** South Carolina. **TRANSACTIONS/CAREER NOTES:** Selected by Cincinnati Bengals in second round (38th pick overall) of 1990 NFL draft.... Signed by Bengals (August 1, 1990).... On inactive list (November 25; December 2 and 9, 1990).

PRO STATISTICS: 1990—Recovered two fumbles.

Year	Team	G	Att.	RUSHING Yds.	Avg.	TD	No.	RECEIVING Yds.	Avg.	TD	TD	TOTAL Pts.	F.
1990— Cincinnati NFL		12	83	353	4.3	1	12	90	7.5	1	2	12	2
Pro totals (1 year)		12	83	353	4.3	1	12	90	7.5	1	2	12	2

GREEN, HUGH
LB, DOLPHINS

PERSONAL: Born July 27, 1959, at Natchez, Miss.... 6-2/230.... Full name: Hugh Donell Green. **HIGH SCHOOL:** North (Natchez, Miss.). **COLLEGE:** Pittsburgh. **TRANSACTIONS/CAREER NOTES:** Selected by Tampa Bay Buccaneers in first round (seventh pick overall) of 1981 NFL draft.... On non-football injury list with eye and wrist injury (November 1-November 30, 1984).... Traded by Buccaneers to Miami Dolphins for first- and second-round picks in 1986 draft (October 9, 1985).... On injured reserve with knee injury (September 23, 1986-remainder of season).... On injured reserve with knee injury (September 7-October 24, 1987).... Granted unconditional free agency (February 1, 1989).... Received no qualifying offer (April 15, 1989). ... Re-signed by Dolphins (May 5, 1989).

CHAMPIONSHIP GAME EXPERIENCE: Played in AFC championship game after 1985 season.

RECORDS/HONORS: Named as defensive end on THE SPORTING NEWS college All-America team, 1979 and 1980.... Named THE SPORTING NEWS College Football Player of the Year, 1980.... Played in Pro Bowl after 1982 and 1983 seasons.... Named to THE SPORTING NEWS NFL All-Pro team, 1983.

PRO STATISTICS: 1981—Recovered one fumble. 1983—Recovered two fumbles for 11 yards and fumbled once. 1985—Recovered one fumble. 1988—Recovered one fumble for five yards. 1989—Recovered two fumbles.

Year	Team	G	No.	Yds.	Avg.	TD
1981— Tampa Bay NFL		16	2	56	28.0	0
1982— Tampa Bay NFL		9	1	31	31.0	0
1983— Tampa Bay NFL		16	2	54	27.0	*2
1984— Tampa Bay NFL		8	0	0		0
1985— T.B.(5)-Mia.(11) NFL...		16	1	28	28.0	0
1986— Miami NFL		3	0	0		0
1987— Miami NFL		9	0	0		0
1988— Miami NFL		16	0	0		0
1989— Miami NFL		16	0	0		0
1990— Miami NFL		16	0	0		0
Pro totals (10 years)		125	6	169	28.2	2

GREEN, JACOB
DE, SEAHAWKS

PERSONAL: Born January 21, 1957, at Pasadena, Tex. . . . 6-3/256. . . . Full name: Jacob Carl Green. . . . Cousin of George Small, defensive tackle with New York Giants and Calgary Stampeders (CFL), 1980-1983.
HIGH SCHOOL: Kashmere (Houston).
COLLEGE: Texas A&M.
TRANSACTIONS/CAREER NOTES: Selected by Seattle Seahawks in first round (10th pick overall) of 1980 NFL draft.
PLAYING EXPERIENCE: Seattle NFL, 1980-1990. . . . Games: 1980 (14), 1981 (16), 1982 (9), 1983 (16), 1984 (16), 1985 (16), 1986 (16), 1987 (12), 1988 (16), 1989 (15), 1990 (16). Total: 162.
CHAMPIONSHIP GAME EXPERIENCE: Played in AFC championship game after 1983 season.
RECORDS/HONORS: Named to THE SPORTING NEWS NFL All-Pro team, 1984. . . . Played in Pro Bowl after 1986 and 1987 seasons.
PRO STATISTICS: 1981—Recovered one fumble. 1983—Intercepted one pass for 73 yards and a touchdown and recovered two fumbles. 1984—Recovered four fumbles. 1985—Recovered two fumbles for 79 yards and a touchdown and intercepted one pass for 19 yards and a touchdown. 1986—Recovered one fumble. 1987—Recovered one fumble. 1988—Recovered two fumbles (including one in end zone for a touchdown). 1989—Recovered one fumble. 1990—Recovered one fumble.

GREEN, MARK
RB, BEARS

PERSONAL: Born March 22, 1967, at Riverside, Calif. . . . 5-11/195. . . . Full name: Mark Anthony Green.
HIGH SCHOOL: Polytechnic (Riverside, Calif.).
COLLEGE: Notre Dame (bachelor of American studies degree, 1989).
TRANSACTIONS/CAREER NOTES: Selected by Chicago Bears in fifth round (130th pick overall) of 1989 NFL draft. . . . Signed by Bears (July 26, 1989). . . . On injured reserve with knee injury (November 2-December 14, 1989). . . . On injured reserve with knee injury (September 26-November 2, 1990).

			RUSHING				RECEIVING				PUNT RETURNS				KICKOFF RETURNS				TOTALS		
Year	Team	G	Att.	Yds.	Avg.	TD	No.	Yds.	Avg.	TD	No.	Yds.	Avg.	TD	No.	Yds.	Avg.	TD	TD	Pts.	F.
1989— Chicago NFL		10	5	46	9.2	1	5	48	9.6	0	16	141	8.8	0	11	239	21.7	0	1	6	0
1990— Chicago NFL		12	27	126	4.7	0	4	26	6.5	1	0	0		0	7	112	16.0	0	1	6	0
Pro totals (2 years)		22	32	172	5.4	1	9	74	8.2	1	16	141	8.8	0	18	351	19.5	0	2	12	0

GREEN, ROY
WR, BROWNS

PERSONAL: Born June 30, 1957, at Magnolia, Ark. . . . 6-0/195.
HIGH SCHOOL: Magnolia (Ark.).
COLLEGE: Henderson State (Ark.).
TRANSACTIONS/CAREER NOTES: Selected by St. Louis Cardinals in fourth round (89th pick overall) of 1979 NFL draft. . . . On injured reserve with knee injury (December 15, 1980-remainder of season). . . . On injured reserve with ankle injury (September 23-October 24, 1986). . . . Crossed picket line during players' strike (September 30, 1987). . . . Franchise transferred to Phoenix (March 15, 1988). . . . Granted free agency (February 1, 1990). . . . Re-signed by Phoenix Cardinals (July 23, 1990). . . . Traded by Cardinals to Cleveland Browns for an undisclosed draft pick (June 8, 1991).
RECORDS/HONORS: Tied NFL record for longest kickoff return, game (106 yards), against Dallas Cowboys (October 21, 1979). . . . Named as kick returner to THE SPORTING NEWS NFC All-Star team, 1979. . . . Played in Pro Bowl after 1983 and 1984 seasons. . . . Named to THE SPORTING NEWS NFL All-Pro team, 1983 and 1984.
MISCELLANEOUS: Began career as defensive back (1979-1981), played both defensive back and wide receiver (1981) and has played wide receiver since 1981.
PRO STATISTICS: 1979—Recovered two fumbles. 1980—Intercepted one pass for 10 yards. 1981—Intercepted two passes for 44 yards. 1982—Attempted one pass with no completions and recovered one fumble for two yards. 1983—Recovered one fumble. 1990—Attempted one pass with one completion for 20 yards.

			RUSHING				RECEIVING				PUNT RETURNS				KICKOFF RETURNS				TOTALS		
Year	Team	G	Att.	Yds.	Avg.	TD	No.	Yds.	Avg.	TD	No.	Yds.	Avg.	TD	No.	Yds.	Avg.	TD	TD	Pts.	F.
1979— St. Louis NFL		16	0	0		0	1	15	15.0	0	8	42	5.3	0	41	1005	24.5	*1	1	6	4
1980— St. Louis NFL		15	0	0		0	0	0		0	16	168	10.5	1	32	745	23.3	0	1	6	2
1981— St. Louis NFL		16	3	60	20.0	1	33	708	21.5	4	0	0		0	8	135	16.9	0	5	30	2
1982— St. Louis NFL		9	6	8	1.3	0	32	453	14.2	3	3	20	6.7	0	0	0		0	3	18	1
1983— St. Louis NFL		16	4	49	12.3	0	78	1227	15.7	*14	0	0		0	1	14	14.0	0	14	84	3
1984— St. Louis NFL		16	1	-10	-10.0	0	78	*1555	19.9	12	0	0		0	1	18	18.0	0	12	72	1
1985— St. Louis NFL		13	1	2	2.0	0	50	693	13.9	5	0	0		0	0	0		0	5	30	2
1986— St. Louis NFL		11	2	-4	-2.0	0	42	517	12.3	6	0	0		0	0	0		0	6	36	1
1987— St. Louis NFL		12	2	34	17.0	0	43	731	17.0	4	0	0		0	0	0		0	4	24	1
1988— Phoenix NFL		16	4	1	.3	0	68	1097	16.1	7	0	0		0	0	0		0	7	42	0

Year	Team	G	Att.	RUSHING Yds.	Avg.	TD	No.	RECEIVING Yds.	Avg.	TD	No.	PUNT RETURNS Yds.	Avg.	TD	No.	KICKOFF RETURNS Yds.	Avg.	TD	TOTALS TD	Pts.	F.
1989— Phoenix NFL		12	0	0		0	44	703	16.0	7	0	0		0	0	0		0	7	42	2
1990— Phoenix NFL		16	0	0		0	53	797	15.0	4	0	0		0	1	15	15.0	0	4	24	1
Pro totals (12 years)		168	23	140	6.1	1	522	8496	16.3	66	27	230	8.5	1	84	1932	23.0	1	69	414	20

GREENE, TIM
DE, FALCONS

PERSONAL: Born December 16, 1963, at Liverpool, N.Y. . . . 6-2/245. . . . Full name: Timothy John Green.
HIGH SCHOOL: Liverpool (N.Y.).
COLLEGE: Syracuse (degree in English literature, 1986).
TRANSACTIONS/CAREER NOTES: Selected by New Jersey Generals in 1986 USFL territorial draft. . . . Selected by Atlanta Falcons in first round (17th pick overall) of 1986 NFL draft. . . . Signed by Falcons (August 14, 1986). . . . Granted roster exemption (August 14-August 22, 1986). . . . On injured reserve with pulled calf (September 6-October 11, 1986). . . . Crossed picket line during players strike (October 2, 1987). . . . On injured reserve with knee injury (November 17, 1987-remainder of season). . . . On injured reserve with elbow injury (September 3-October 15, 1988). . . . Granted free agency (February 1, 1990). . . . Re-signed by Falcons (June 18, 1990).
PLAYING EXPERIENCE: Atlanta NFL, 1986-1990. . . . Games: 1986 (11), 1987 (9), 1988 (10), 1989 (16), 1990 (16). Total: 62.
RECORDS/HONORS: Named as defensive lineman on THE SPORTING NEWS college All-America team, 1984 and 1985.
PRO STATISTICS: 1987—Recovered two fumbles for 35 yards. 1989—Recovered two fumbles and fumbled once for five yards. 1990—Recovered one fumble.

GREENE, KEVIN
DE, RAMS

PERSONAL: Born July 31, 1962, at New York. . . . 6-3/247. . . . Full name: Kevin Darwin Greene.
HIGH SCHOOL: South (Granite City, Ill.).
COLLEGE: Auburn.
TRANSACTIONS/CAREER NOTES: Selected by Birmingham Stallions in 1985 USFL territorial draft. . . . Selected by Los Angeles Rams in fifth round (113th pick overall) of 1985 NFL draft. . . . Signed by Rams (July 12, 1985). . . . Crossed picket line during players' strike (October 14, 1987). . . . Granted free agency (February 1, 1990). . . . Re-signed by Rams (September 1, 1990). . . . Activated (September 7, 1990).
PLAYING EXPERIENCE: Los Angeles Rams NFL, 1985-1990. . . . Games: 1985 (15), 1986 (16), 1987 (9), 1988 (16), 1989 (16), 1990 (15). Total: 87.
CHAMPIONSHIP GAME EXPERIENCE: Played in NFC championship game after 1985 and 1989 seasons.
RECORDS/HONORS: Played in Pro Bowl after 1989 season. . . . Named to THE SPORTING NEWS NFL All-Pro team, 1989.
PRO STATISTICS: 1986—Recovered one fumble for 13 yards. 1987—Intercepted one pass for 25 yards and a touchdown. 1988—Intercepted one pass for 10 yards and credited with a safety. 1989—Recovered two fumbles. 1990—Recovered four fumbles.

GREENE, TIGER
S, PACKERS

PERSONAL: Born February 15, 1962, at Hendersonville, N.C. . . . 6-0/192. . . . Full name: George Greene.
HIGH SCHOOL: East Henderson (Flat Rock, N.C.).
COLLEGE: Western Carolina.
TRANSACTIONS/CAREER NOTES: Selected by Memphis Showboats in 14th round (191st pick overall) of 1985 USFL draft. . . . Signed as free agent by Atlanta Falcons (May 3, 1985). . . . On injured reserve with knee injury (September 16-October 19, 1985). . . . On injured reserve with ankle injury (December 10, 1985-remainder of season). . . . Released by Falcons (August 22, 1986). . . . Signed as free agent by Green Bay Packers (September 25, 1986).
PRO STATISTICS: 1987—Recovered two fumbles. 1989—Recovered one fumble and fumbled once. 1990—Returned blocked punt 36 yards for a touchdown.

Year	Team	G	INTERCEPTIONS No.	Yds.	Avg.	TD
1985— Atlanta NFL		10	2	27	13.5	0
1986— Green Bay NFL..........		13	2	0	.0	0
1987— Green Bay NFL..........		11	1	11	11.0	0
1988— Green Bay NFL..........		16	0	0		0
1989— Green Bay NFL..........		16	1	0	.0	0
1990— Green Bay NFL..........		16	0	0		0
Pro totals (6 years)		82	6	38	6.3	0

GRIFFIN, DON
CB, 49ERS

PERSONAL: Born March 17, 1964, at Pelham, Ga. . . . 6-0/176. . . . Full name: Donald Frederick Griffin. . . . Brother of James Griffin, safety with Cincinnati Bengals and Detroit Lions, 1983-1989.
HIGH SCHOOL: Mitchell-Baker (Pelham, Ga.).
COLLEGE: Middle Tennessee State.
TRANSACTIONS/CAREER NOTES: Selected by Memphis Showboats in 1986 USFL territorial draft. . . . Selected by San Francisco 49ers in sixth round (162nd pick overall) of 1986 NFL draft. . . . Signed by 49ers (July 21, 1986).
CHAMPIONSHIP GAME EXPERIENCE: Played in NFC championship game after 1988-1990 seasons. . . . Played in Super Bowl XXIII after 1988 season and Super Bowl XXIV after 1989 season.
PRO STATISTICS: 1986—Recovered two fumbles. 1987—Recovered one fumble for seven yards. 1989—Recovered one fumble. 1990—Recovered two fumbles.

Year	Team	G	INTERCEPTIONS No.	Yds.	Avg.	TD	PUNT RETURNS No.	Yds.	Avg.	TD	KICKOFF RETURNS No.	Yds.	Avg.	TD	TOTAL TD	Pts.	F.
1986— San Francisco NFL		16	3	0	.0	0	38	377	9.9	1	5	97	19.4	0	1	6	3
1987— San Francisco NFL		12	5	1	.2	0	9	79	8.8	0	0	0		0	0	0	0

Year Team	G	INTERCEPTIONS No.	Yds.	Avg.	TD	PUNT RETURNS No.	Yds.	Avg.	TD	KICKOFF RETURNS No.	Yds.	Avg.	TD	TOTAL TD	Pts.	F.
1988— San Francisco NFL	10	0	0		0	4	28	7.0	0	0	0		0	0	0	0
1989— San Francisco NFL	16	2	6	3.0	0	1	9	9.0	0	0	0		0	0	0	0
1990— San Francisco NFL	16	3	32	10.7	0	16	105	6.6	0	1	15	15.0	0	0	0	1
Pro totals (5 years)	70	13	39	3.0	0	68	598	8.8	1	6	112	18.7	0	1	6	4

GRIFFIN, LARRY
S, STEELERS

PERSONAL: Born January 11, 1963, at Chesapeake, Va. . . . 6-0/200. . . . Full name: Larry Anthony Griffin.
HIGH SCHOOL: Great Bridge (Chesapeake, Va.).
COLLEGE: North Carolina.
TRANSACTIONS/CAREER NOTES: Selected by Baltimore Stars in 1986 USFL territorial draft. . . . Selected by Houston Oilers in eighth round (199th pick overall) of 1986 NFL draft. . . . Signed by Oilers (July 21, 1986). . . . Released by Oilers (August 25, 1986). . . . Re-signed by Oilers (October 1, 1986). . . . Released by Oilers (October 22, 1986). . . . Signed as free agent by Miami Dolphins (February 23, 1987). . . . Released by Dolphins (September 7, 1987). . . . Signed as free agent replacement player by Pittsburgh Steelers (September 28, 1987).
PRO STATISTICS: 1988—Recovered one fumble and fumbled once. 1989—Returned one kickoff for 21 yards and recovered one fumble. 1990—Returned two kickoffs for 16 yards and recovered one fumble and fumbled once for one yard.

Year Team	G	INTERCEPTIONS No.	Yds.	Avg.	TD
1986— Houston NFL	3	0	0		0
1987— Pittsburgh NFL	7	2	2	1.0	0
1988— Pittsburgh NFL	15	2	63	31.5	0
1989— Pittsburgh NFL	16	1	15	15.0	0
1990— Pittsburgh NFL	16	4	75	18.8	0
Pro totals (5 years)	57	9	155	17.2	0

GRIFFIN, LEONARD
DE, CHIEFS

PERSONAL: Born September 22, 1962, at Lake Providence, La. . . . 6-4/278. . . . Full name: Leonard James Griffin Jr. . . . Brother of Elinor Griffin, member of 1980 U.S. women's Olympic basketball team.
HIGH SCHOOL: Lake Providence (La.).
COLLEGE: Grambling State.
TRANSACTIONS/CAREER NOTES: Selected by Kansas City Chiefs in third round (63rd pick overall) of 1986 NFL draft. . . . Signed by Chiefs (July 26, 1986). . . . On injured reserve with ankle injury (September 2-October 25, 1986). . . . Granted free agency (February 1, 1990). . . . Re-signed by Chiefs (July 18, 1990).
PLAYING EXPERIENCE: Kansas City NFL, 1986-1990. . . . Games: 1986 (9), 1987 (12), 1988 (15), 1989 (16), 1990 (16). Total: 68.

GRIGGS, DAVID
LB, DOLPHINS

PERSONAL: Born February 5, 1967, at Camden, N.J. . . . 6-3/248. . . . Full name: David Wesley Griggs. . . . Brother of Billy Griggs, tight end with New York Jets, 1985-1989; and cousin of Anthony Griggs, linebacker with Philadelphia Eagles and Cleveland Browns, 1982-1988.
HIGH SCHOOL: Pennsauken (N.J.).
COLLEGE: Virginia.
TRANSACTIONS/CAREER NOTES: Selected by New Orleans Saints in seventh round (186th pick overall) of 1989 NFL draft. . . . Signed by Saints (July 20, 1989). . . . Released by Saints (August 30, 1989). . . . Re-signed by Saints (August 31, 1989). . . . Released by Saints (September 5, 1989). . . . Signed as free agent by Miami Dolphins to developmental squad (September 7, 1989). . . . On developmental squad (September 7-November 22, 1989). . . . Activated after clearing procedural waivers (November 24, 1989).
PLAYING EXPERIENCE: Miami NFL, 1989 and 1990. . . . Games: 1989 (5), 1990 (16). Total: 21.
PRO STATISTICS: 1990—Recovered one fumble.

GRIMES, RANDY
C, BUCCANEERS

PERSONAL: Born July 20, 1960, at Tyler, Tex. . . . 6-4/275. . . . Full name: Randall Collins Grimes.
HIGH SCHOOL: Robert E. Lee (Tyler, Tex.).
COLLEGE: Baylor.
TRANSACTIONS/CAREER NOTES: Selected by New Jersey Generals in sixth round (70th pick overall) of 1983 USFL draft. . . . Selected by Tampa Bay Buccaneers in second round (45th pick overall) of 1983 NFL draft. . . . Signed by Buccaneers (June 6, 1983).
PLAYING EXPERIENCE: Tampa Bay NFL, 1983-1990. . . . Games: 1983 (15), 1984 (10), 1985 (16), 1986 (16), 1987 (12), 1988 (16), 1989 (16), 1990 (15). Total: 116.
PRO STATISTICS: 1983—Recovered one fumble. 1990—Fumbled once for minus 14 yards.

GRIMM, RUSS
G, REDSKINS

PERSONAL: Born May 2, 1959, at Scottsdale, Pa. . . . 6-3/275.
HIGH SCHOOL: Southmoreland (Pa.).
COLLEGE: Pittsburgh.
TRANSACTIONS/CAREER NOTES: Selected by Washington Redskins in third round (69th pick overall) of 1981 NFL draft. . . . On injured reserve with knee injury (November 14-December 25, 1987). . . . On injured reserve with

knee injury (August 30-November 21, 1988).... On inactive list (December 9, 1990).
PLAYING EXPERIENCE: Washington NFL, 1981-1990.... Games: 1981 (14), 1982 (9), 1983 (16), 1984 (16), 1985 (16), 1986 (15), 1987 (6), 1988 (5), 1989 (12), 1990 (15). Total: 124.
CHAMPIONSHIP GAME EXPERIENCE: Played in NFC championship game after 1982, 1983, 1986 and 1987 seasons.... Played in Super Bowl XVII after 1982 season, Super Bowl XVIII after 1983 season and Super Bowl XXII after 1987 season.
RECORDS/HONORS: Played in Pro Bowl after 1983-1986 seasons.... Named to THE SPORTING NEWS NFL All-Pro team, 1985.
PRO STATISTICS: 1981—Recovered one fumble. 1982—Recovered one fumble. 1984—Recovered two fumbles. 1986—Recovered two fumbles. 1988—Recovered one fumble.

GRIMSLEY, JOHN
LB, DOLPHINS

PERSONAL: Born February 25, 1962, at Canton, O.... 6-2/238.... Full name: John Glenn Grimsley.
HIGH SCHOOL: McKinley (Canton, O.).
COLLEGE: Kentucky.
TRANSACTIONS/CAREER NOTES: Selected by Denver Gold in third round (59th pick overall) of 1984 USFL draft.... Selected by Houston Oilers in sixth round (141st pick overall) of 1984 NFL draft.... Signed by Oilers (July 7, 1984).... Granted free agency (February 1, 1990).... Re-signed by Oilers (September 11, 1990).... Granted roster exemption (September 11-September 15, 1990).... Traded by Oilers to Miami Dolphins for third-round pick in 1991 NFL draft (April 1, 1991).
PLAYING EXPERIENCE: Houston NFL, 1984-1990.... Games: 1984 (16), 1985 (15), 1986 (16), 1987 (12), 1988 (16), 1989 (16), 1990 (15). Total: 106.
RECORDS/HONORS: Played in Pro Bowl after 1988 season.
PRO STATISTICS: 1985—Recovered one fumble for five yards. 1986—Recovered two fumbles. 1987—Recovered one fumble. 1988—Intercepted one pass for nine yards and recovered one fumble. 1989—Recovered one fumble for three yards. 1990—Recovered three fumbles.

GROSSMAN, BURT
DE, CHARGERS

PERSONAL: Born April 10, 1967, at Philadelphia.... 6-4/255.... Full name: Burton L. Grossman.... Cousin of Randy Grossman, tight end with Pittsburgh Steelers, 1974-1981.
HIGH SCHOOL: Archbishop Carroll (Radnor, Pa.).
COLLEGE: Pittsburgh (bachelor's degree in economics, 1989).
TRANSACTIONS/CAREER NOTES: Selected by San Diego Chargers in first round (eighth pick overall) of 1989 NFL draft.... Signed by Chargers (August 26, 1989).... On injured reserve with rib injury (December 28, 1990-remainder of season).
PLAYING EXPERIENCE: San Diego NFL, 1989 and 1990.... Games: 1989 (16), 1990 (15). Total: 31.
PRO STATISTICS: 1990—Credited with a safety.

GRUBER, PAUL
OT, BUCCANEERS

PERSONAL: Born February 24, 1965, at Madison, Wis.... 6-5/290.... Full name: Paul Blake Gruber.
HIGH SCHOOL: Sauk Prairie (Prairie du Sac, Wis.).
COLLEGE: Wisconsin (degree in communication arts, 1988).
TRANSACTIONS/CAREER NOTES: Selected by Tampa Bay Buccaneers in first round (fourth pick overall) of 1988 NFL draft.... Signed by Buccaneers (August 7, 1988).
PLAYING EXPERIENCE: Tampa Bay NFL, 1988-1990.... Games: 1988 (16), 1989 (16), 1990 (16). Total: 48.
RECORDS/HONORS: Named as offensive tackle on THE SPORTING NEWS college All-America team, 1987.
PRO STATISTICS: 1988—Recovered two fumbles. 1990—Recovered one fumble.

GRUNHARD, TIM
C, CHIEFS

PERSONAL: Born May 17, 1968, at Chicago.... 6-2/299.... Full name: Timothy Gerard Grunhard.
HIGH SCHOOL: St. Laurence (Burbank, Ill.).
COLLEGE: Notre Dame (degree in political science).
TRANSACTIONS/CAREER NOTES: Selected by Kansas City Chiefs in second round (40th pick overall) of 1990 .. Signed by Chiefs (July 22, 1990).... On inactive list (November 18 and 25, 1990).
PLAYING EXPERIENCE: Kansas City NFL, 1990.... Games: 1990 (14).

GUYTON, MYRON
S, GIANTS

PERSONAL: Born August 26, 1967, at Metcalf, Ga.... 6-1/205.... Full name: Myron Mynard Guyton.... Related to William Andrews, running back with Atlanta Falcons, 1979-1983 and 1986.
HIGH SCHOOL: Central (Thomasville, Ga.).
COLLEGE: Eastern Kentucky.
TRANSACTIONS/CAREER NOTES: Selected by New York Giants in eighth round (218th pick overall) of 1989 NFL draft.... Signed by Giants (July 25, 1989).
CHAMPIONSHIP GAME EXPERIENCE: Played in NFC championship game after 1990 season.... Played in Super Bowl XXV after 1990 season.
PRO STATISTICS: 1989—Recovered three fumbles for four yards. 1990—Recovered two fumbles.

			—INTERCEPTIONS—			
Year Team	G	No.	Yds.	Avg.	TD
1989— N.Y. Giants NFL	16	2	27	13.5	0
1990— N.Y. Giants NFL	16	1	0	.0	0
Pro totals (2 years)	32	3	27	9.0	0

HABIB, BRIAN
OT, VIKINGS

PERSONAL: Born December 2, 1964, at Ellensburg, Wash.... 6-7/288.... Full name: Brian Richard Habib.
HIGH SCHOOL: Ellensburg (Wash.).
COLLEGE: Washington.
TRANSACTIONS/CAREER NOTES: Selected by Minnesota Vikings in 10th round (264th pick overall) of 1988 NFL draft.... Signed by Vikings (July 19, 1988).... On injured reserve with shoulder injury (September 3-December 24, 1988).
PLAYING EXPERIENCE: Minnesota NFL, 1989 and 1990.... Games: 1989 (16), 1990 (16). Total: 32.

HACKETT, DINO
LB, CHIEFS

PERSONAL: Born June 28, 1964, at Greensboro, N.C.... 6-3/230.... Full name: Barry Dean Hackett.... Brother of Joey Hackett, tight end with San Antonio Gunslingers (USFL), Denver Broncos and Green Bay Packers, 1984-1988.
HIGH SCHOOL: Southern Guilford (Greensboro, N.C.).
COLLEGE: Appalachian State (degree in criminal justice, 1986).
TRANSACTIONS/CAREER NOTES: Selected by Kansas City Chiefs in second round (35th pick overall) of 1986 NFL draft.... Signed by Chiefs (July 23, 1986).... On injured reserve with knee injury (November 29, 1988-remainder of season).
PLAYING EXPERIENCE: Kansas City NFL, 1986-1990.... Games: 1986 (16), 1987 (11), 1988 (13), 1989 (13), 1990 (16). Total: 69.
RECORDS/HONORS: Named to play in Pro Bowl after 1988 season; replaced due to injury by Matt Millen.
PRO STATISTICS: 1986—Intercepted one pass for no yards and recovered two fumbles. 1988—Credited with a safety and recovered one fumble. 1989—Recovered one fumble. 1990—Recovered two fumbles.

HADD, GARY
DE, LIONS

PERSONAL: Born October 19, 1965, at St. Paul, Minn.... 6-4/278.... Full name: Gary Allan Hadd.
HIGH SCHOOL: Burnsville (Minn.).
COLLEGE: Minnesota.
TRANSACTIONS/CAREER NOTES: Selected by Detroit Lions in eighth round (196th pick overall) of 1988 NFL draft.... Signed by Lions (July 15, 1988).... On injured reserve with broken foot (August 29-November 16, 1988).... Activated after clearing procedural waivers (November 18, 1988).... Granted unconditional free agency (February 1, 1989).... Signed by Phoenix Cardinals (March 13, 1989).... Released by Cardinals (September 3, 1990).... Signed by Detroit Lions (April 16, 1991).
PLAYING EXPERIENCE: Detroit NFL, 1988; Phoenix NFL, 1989.... Games: 1988 (5), 1989 (10). Total: 15.

HADDIX, MICHAEL
FB, PACKERS

PERSONAL: Born December 27, 1961, at Tippah County, Miss.... 6-1/239.... Cousin of Wayne Haddix, defensive back with Tampa Bay Buccaneers.
HIGH SCHOOL: Walnut (Miss.).
COLLEGE: Mississippi State.
TRANSACTIONS/CAREER NOTES: Selected by Denver Gold in second round (16th pick overall) of 1983 USFL draft.... Selected by Philadelphia Eagles in first round (eighth pick overall) of 1983 NFL draft.... Signed by Eagles (May 13, 1983).... Granted unconditional free agency (February 1, 1989).... Signed by Green Bay Packers (February 17, 1989).
PRO STATISTICS: 1983—Returned three kickoffs for 51 yards. 1986—Recovered one fumble. 1987—Returned two kickoffs for 16 yards. 1988—Recovered one fumble.

		RUSHING				RECEIVING				TOTAL		
Year Team	G	Att.	Yds.	Avg.	TD	No.	Yds.	Avg.	TD	TD	Pts.	F.
1983— Philadelphia NFL	14	91	220	2.4	2	23	254	11.0	0	2	12	4
1984— Philadelphia NFL	14	48	130	2.7	1	33	231	7.0	0	1	6	2
1985— Philadelphia NFL	16	67	213	3.2	0	43	330	7.7	0	0	0	2
1986— Philadelphia NFL	16	79	276	3.5	0	26	150	5.8	0	0	0	1
1987— Philadelphia NFL	12	59	165	2.8	0	7	58	8.3	0	0	0	1
1988— Philadelphia NFL	16	57	185	3.2	0	12	82	6.8	0	0	0	1
1989— Green Bay NFL	16	44	135	3.1	0	15	111	7.4	1	1	6	2
1990— Green Bay NFL	16	98	311	3.2	0	13	94	7.2	2	2	12	3
Pro totals (8 years)	120	543	1635	3.0	3	172	1310	7.6	3	6	36	16

HADDIX, WAYNE
DB, BUCCANEERS

PERSONAL: Born July 23, 1965, at Bolivar, Tenn.... 6-1/205... Cousin of Michael Haddix, fullback with Green Bay Packers.
HIGH SCHOOL: Middleton (Tenn.).
COLLEGE: Liberty (Va.).
TRANSACTIONS/CAREER NOTES: Signed as free agent by New York Giants (May 11, 1987).... On injured reserve with knee injury (September 7-November 7, 1987).... On injured reserve with bruised heel (September 7-November 12, 1988).... Released by Giants (September 5, 1989).... Signed as free agent by Tampa Bay Buccaneers (March 21, 1990).
RECORDS/HONORS: Played in Pro Bowl after 1990 season.
PRO STATISTICS: 1988—Returned six kickoffs for 123 yards and fumbled once. 1990—Fumbled once.

		INTERCEPTIONS			
Year Team	G	No.	Yds.	Avg.	TD
1987— N.Y. Giants NFL	5	0	0		0
1988— N.Y. Giants NFL	7	0	0		0
1990— Tampa Bay NFL	16	7	*231	33.0	*3
Pro totals (3 years)	28	7	231	33.0	3

HAGER, BRITT
LB, EAGLES

PERSONAL: Born February 20, 1966, at Odessa, Tex. . . . 6-1/225. . . . Full name: Britt Harley Hager. . . . Name pronounced HAY-ghurr.
HIGH SCHOOL: Permian (Odessa, Tex.).
COLLEGE: Texas.
TRANSACTIONS/CAREER NOTES: Selected by Philadelphia Eagles in third round (81st pick overall) of 1989 NFL draft. . . . Signed by Eagles (August 7, 1989).
PLAYING EXPERIENCE: Philadelphia NFL, 1989 and 1990. . . . Games: 1989 (16), 1990 (16). Total: 32.
PRO STATISTICS: 1989—Recovered two fumbles for nine yards. 1990—Returned one kickoff for no yards.

HAGY, JOHN
S, OILERS

PERSONAL: Born December 9, 1965, at Okinawa, Japan. . . . 6-0/190. . . . Full name: John Kevin Hagy. . . . Name pronounced HAGH-ee.
HIGH SCHOOL: John Marshall (San Antonio, Tex.).
COLLEGE: Texas.
TRANSACTIONS/CAREER NOTES: Selected by Buffalo Bills in eighth round (204th pick overall) of 1988 NFL draft. . . . Signed by Bills (June 17, 1988). . . . On injured reserve with knee injury (September 27, 1988-remainder of season). . . . On reserve/physically unable to perform list with knee injury (August 29-October 27, 1989). . . . Granted unconditional free agency (February 1, 1991). . . . Signed by Houston Oilers (March 29, 1991).
PLAYING EXPERIENCE: Buffalo NFL, 1988-1990. . . . Games: 1988 (3), 1989 (9), 1990 (16). Total: 28.
CHAMPIONSHIP GAME EXPERIENCE: Played in AFC championship game after 1990 season. . . . Played in Super Bowl XXV after 1990 season.
PRO STATISTICS: 1990—Intercepted two passes for 23 yards.

HAIGHT, MIKE
G, JETS

PERSONAL: Born October 6, 1962, at Manchester, Ia. . . . 6-4/291. . . . Full name: Michael Haight. . . . Name pronounced HATE.
HIGH SCHOOL: Beckman (Dyersville, Ia.).
COLLEGE: Iowa.
TRANSACTIONS/CAREER NOTES: Selected by New York Jets in first round (22nd pick overall) of 1986 NFL draft. . . . Selected by Orlando Renegades in first round (first pick overall) of 1986 USFL draft. . . . Signed by New York Jets (July 23, 1986). . . . On injured reserve with knee injury (September 2-October 4, 1986). . . . Granted free agency (February 1, 1990). . . . Re-signed by Jets (July 13, 1990). . . . On inactive list (November 25 and December 2, 1990).
PLAYING EXPERIENCE: New York Jets NFL, 1986-1990. . . . Games: 1986 (2), 1987 (6), 1988 (14), 1989 (13), 1990 (14). Total: 49.

HALE, CHRIS
CB, BILLS

PERSONAL: Born January 4, 1966, at Monrovia, Calif. . . . 5-7/161.
HIGH SCHOOL: Monrovia, Calif.
COLLEGE: Nebraska, Glendale Community College (Ariz.), then Southern California.
TRANSACTIONS/CAREER NOTES: Selected by Buffalo Bills in seventh round (193rd pick overall) of 1989 NFL draft. . . . Signed by Bills (July 17, 1989). . . . On injured reserve with torn Achilles tendon (November 7, 1990-remainder of 1990 season playoffs).
PRO STATISTICS: 1990—Recovered three fumbles.

			PUNT RETURNS		
Year	Team	G	No.	Yds.	Avg.	TD
1989—	Buffalo NFL	16	0	0		0
1990—	Buffalo NFL	8	10	76	7.6	0
	Pro totals (2 years)	24	10	76	7.6	0

HALEY, CHARLES
LB/DE, 49ERS

PERSONAL: Born January 6, 1964, at Gladys, Va. . . . 6-5/230. . . . Full name: Charles Lewis Haley.
HIGH SCHOOL: William Campbell (Naruna, Va.).
COLLEGE: James Madison.
TRANSACTIONS/CAREER NOTES: Selected by San Francisco 49ers in fourth round (96th pick overall) of 1986 NFL draft. . . . Signed by 49ers (May 27, 1986). . . . On reserve/did not report list (July 24-August 23, 1989). . . . Granted free agency (February 1, 1990). . . . Re-signed by 49ers (August 23, 1990).
PLAYING EXPERIENCE: San Francisco NFL, 1986-1990. . . . Games: 1986 (16), 1987 (12), 1988 (16), 1989 (16), 1990 (16). Total: 76.
CHAMPIONSHIP GAME EXPERIENCE: Played in NFC championship game after 1988-1990 seasons. . . . Played in Super Bowl XXIII after 1988 season and Super Bowl XXIV after 1989 season.
RECORDS/HONORS: Played in Pro Bowl after 1988 and 1990 seasons.
PRO STATISTICS: 1986—Intercepted one pass for eight yards, recovered two fumbles for three yards and fumbled once. 1988—Recovered two fumbles and credited with a safety. 1989—Recovered one fumble for three yards and a touchdown. 1990—Recovered one fumble.

HALIBURTON, RONNIE
LB, BRONCOS

PERSONAL: Born April 4, 1968, at New Orleans. . . . 6-4/230. . . . Full name: Ronnie Maurice Haliburton.
HIGH SCHOOL: Lincoln (Port Arthur, Tex.).
COLLEGE: Louisiana State.
TRANSACTIONS/CAREER NOTES: Selected by Denver Broncos in sixth round (164th pick overall) of 1990 NFL draft. . . . On injured reserve with knee injury (September 4-November 2, 1990).
PLAYING EXPERIENCE: Denver NFL, 1990. . . . Games: 1990 (9).

HALL, COURTNEY
C/G, CHARGERS

PERSONAL: Born August 26, 1968, at Los Angeles. . . . 6-1/269. . . . Full name: Courtney Caesar Hall.
HIGH SCHOOL: Wilmington-Phineas Banning (Wilmington, Calif.).
COLLEGE: Rice.
TRANSACTIONS/CAREER NOTES: Selected by San Diego Chargers in second round (37th pick overall) of 1989 NFL draft. . . . Signed by Chargers (July 24, 1989).
PLAYING EXPERIENCE: San Diego NFL, 1989 and 1990. . . . Games: 1989 (16), 1990 (16). Total: 32.
PRO STATISTICS: 1989—Fumbled once for minus 29 yards.

HALL, DELTON
CB, STEELERS

PERSONAL: Born January 16, 1965, at Greensboro, N.C. . . . 6-1/211. . . . Full name: Delton Dwayne Hall.
HIGH SCHOOL: Grimsley (Greensboro, N.C.).
COLLEGE: Clemson.
TRANSACTIONS/CAREER NOTES: Selected by Pittsburgh Steelers in second round (38th pick overall) of 1987 NFL draft. . . . Signed by Steelers (August 6, 1987). . . . On injured reserve with knee injury (September 11-October 12, 1990).
PRO STATISTICS: 1987—Recovered two fumbles for 50 yards and a touchdown and fumbled once. 1989—Recovered one fumble.

Year Team	G	— INTERCEPTIONS —		
		No.	Yds.	Avg.	TD
1987— Pittsburgh NFL	12	3	29	9.7	1
1988— Pittsburgh NFL	14	0	0		0
1989— Pittsburgh NFL	16	1	6	6.0	0
1990— Pittsburgh NFL	12	1	0	.0	0
Pro totals (4 years)	54	5	35	7.0	1

HALL, RON
TE, BUCCANEERS

PERSONAL: Born March 15, 1964, at Fort Huachuca, Ariz. . . . 6-4/245. . . . Full name: Ronald A. Hall.
HIGH SCHOOL: San Pasqual (Escondido, Calif.).
COLLEGE: California State Poly, then Hawaii.
TRANSACTIONS/CAREER NOTES: Selected by Tampa Bay Buccaneers in fourth round (87th pick overall) of 1987 NFL draft. . . . Signed by Buccaneers (July 18, 1987).
PRO STATISTICS: 1989—Recovered one fumble. 1990—Returned one kickoff for no yards.

Year Team	G	— RECEIVING —		
		No.	Yds.	Avg.	TD
1987— Tampa Bay NFL	11	16	169	10.6	1
1988— Tampa Bay NFL	15	39	555	14.2	0
1989— Tampa Bay NFL	16	30	331	11.0	2
1990— Tampa Bay NFL	16	31	464	15.0	2
Pro totals (4 years)	58	116	1519	13.1	5

HALLSTROM, RON
G, PACKERS

PERSONAL: Born June 11, 1959, at Holden, Mass. . . . 6-6/305. . . . Full name: Ronald David Hallstrom.
HIGH SCHOOL: Moline (Ill.).
COLLEGE: Iowa Central Junior College, then Iowa.
TRANSACTIONS/CAREER NOTES: Selected by Green Bay Packers in first round (22nd pick overall) of 1982 NFL draft. . . . On inactive list (September 12 and September 20, 1982). . . . Granted free agency (February 1, 1988). . . . Re-signed by Packers (August 22, 1988). . . . Granted free agency (February 1, 1990). . . . Re-signed by Packers (August 23, 1990).
PLAYING EXPERIENCE: Green Bay NFL, 1982-1990. . . . Games: 1982 (6), 1983 (16), 1984 (16), 1985 (16), 1986 (16), 1987 (12), 1988 (16), 1989 (16), 1990 (16). Total: 130.
PRO STATISTICS: 1984—Recovered two fumbles for one yard. 1985—Recovered one fumble. 1987—Recovered one fumble.

HAMEL, DEAN
DT, COWBOYS

PERSONAL: Born July 7, 1961, at Detroit. . . . 6-3/271.
HIGH SCHOOL: Mott (Warren, Mich.).
COLLEGE: Coffeyville Community College (Kan.), then Tulsa.
TRANSACTIONS/CAREER NOTES: Selected by Washington Redskins in 12th round (309th pick overall) in 1985 NFL draft. . . . Signed by Redskins (June 14, 1985). . . . Left Redskins camp voluntarily (August 7-August 28, 1989). . . . Traded by Redskins to Dallas Cowboys for fifth-round pick in 1990 draft (August 29, 1989). . . . On injured reserve with sprained knee (October 12-November 5, 1990).
PLAYING EXPERIENCE: Washington NFL, 1985-1988; Dallas NFL, 1989 and 1990. . . . Games: 1985 (16), 1986 (16), 1987 (12), 1988 (16), 1989 (16), 1990 (12). Total: 88.
CHAMPIONSHIP GAME EXPERIENCE: Played in NFC championship game after 1986 and 1987 seasons. . . . Played in Super Bowl XXII after 1987 season.
PRO STATISTICS: 1985—Returned one kickoff for 14 yards. 1990—Recovered one fumble.

HAMILTON, DARRELL
OT, BRONCOS

PERSONAL: Born May 11, 1965, at Washington, D.C. . . . 6-5/298. . . . Full name: Darrell Franklin Hamilton.
HIGH SCHOOL: Anacostia (Washington, D.C.).
COLLEGE: North Carolina (bachelor of arts and science degree in communications, 1989).

TRANSACTIONS/CAREER NOTES: Selected by Denver Broncos in third round (69th pick overall) of 1989 NFL draft. . . . Signed by Broncos (July 18, 1989). . . . Released by Broncos (November 6, 1989). . . . Re-signed by Broncos to developmental squad (November 7, 1989). . . . On developmental squad (November 7, 1989-January 28, 1990). . . . Active for three games for Broncos in 1989; did not play. . . . Released by Broncos (January 29, 1990). . . . Re-signed by Broncos (April 3, 1990).
PLAYING EXPERIENCE: Denver NFL, 1989 and 1990. . . . Games: 1989 (0), 1990 (15). Total: 15.

HAMILTON, HARRY
S, BUCCANEERS

PERSONAL: Born November 29, 1962, at Jamaica, N.Y. . . . 6-0/195. . . . Full name: Harry E. Hamilton.
HIGH SCHOOL: John S. Fine (Nanticoke, Pa.).
COLLEGE: Penn State (bachelor of arts degree in pre-law and liberal arts, 1984).
TRANSACTIONS/CAREER NOTES: Selected by Philadelphia Stars in 1984 USFL territorial draft. . . . Selected by New York Jets in seventh round (176th pick overall) of 1984 NFL draft. . . . Signed by Jets (May 29, 1984). . . . On injured reserve with knee injury (October 22, 1984-remainder of season). . . . On injured reserve with shoulder injury (October 14-November 16, 1985). . . . Granted free agency (February 1, 1988). . . . Rights released (August 8, 1988). . . . Signed as free agent by Tampa Bay Buccaneers (August 11, 1988).
RECORDS/HONORS: Named to THE SPORTING NEWS NFL All-Pro team, 1989.
PRO STATISTICS: 1985—Recovered one fumble. 1986—Recovered two fumbles for 28 yards. 1987—Recovered one fumble. 1988—Recovered two fumbles and fumbled once. 1989—Recovered one fumble. 1990—Recovered two fumbles and fumbled once.

		—— INTERCEPTIONS——			
Year Team	G	No.	Yds.	Avg.	TD
1984—N.Y. Jets NFL	8	0	0		0
1985—N.Y. Jets NFL	11	2	14	7.0	0
1986—N.Y. Jets NFL	15	1	29	29.0	0
1987—N.Y. Jets NFL	12	3	25	8.3	0
1988—Tampa Bay NFL	16	6	123	20.5	0
1989—Tampa Bay NFL	13	6	70	11.7	0
1990—Tampa Bay NFL	16	5	39	7.8	0
Pro totals (7 years)	91	23	300	13.0	0

HAMMERSTEIN, MIKE
DT, VIKINGS

PERSONAL: Born March 3, 1963, at Kokomo, Ind. . . . 6-4/272. . . . Full name: Michael Scott Hammerstein.
HIGH SCHOOL: Wapakoneta (O.).
COLLEGE: Michigan (degree, 1987).
TRANSACTIONS/CAREER NOTES: Selected by Baltimore Stars in 1986 USFL territorial draft. . . . Selected by Cincinnati Bengals in third round (65th pick overall) of 1986 NFL draft. . . . Signed by Bengals (July 26, 1986). . . . On physically unable to perform/active list with knee injury (July 11-July 30, 1988). . . . Transferred to reserve/physically unable to perform list with knee injury (August 1, 1988-entire season). . . . Granted unconditional free agency (February 1, 1991). . . . Signed by Minnesota Vikings (March 30, 1991).
PLAYING EXPERIENCE: Cincinnati NFL, 1986, 1987, 1989 and 1990. . . . Games: 1986 (15), 1987 (11), 1989 (15), 1990 (15). Total: 56.
PRO STATISTICS: 1989—Recovered one fumble.

HAMPTON, ALONZO
CB, VIKINGS

PERSONAL: Born January 19, 1967, at Butler, Ala. . . . 5-10/191.
HIGH SCHOOL: Jefferson (Edgewater, Colo.).
COLLEGE: Riverside City College (Calif.), then Pittsburgh.
TRANSACTIONS/CAREER NOTES: Selected by Minnesota Vikings in fourth round (104th pick overall) of 1990 NFL draft. . . . Signed by Vikings (August 1, 1990). . . . On inactive list (September 9, 16, 23, 30; and November 25, 1990).
PLAYING EXPERIENCE: Minnesota NFL, 1990. . . . Games: 1990 (10).

HAMPTON, RODNEY
RB, GIANTS

PERSONAL: Born April 3, 1969, at Houston. . . . 5-11/215.
HIGH SCHOOL: Kashmere Senior (Houston).
COLLEGE: Georgia.
TRANSACTIONS/CAREER NOTES: Selected by New York Giants in first round (24th pick overall) of 1990 NFL draft. . . . Signed by Giants (July 26, 1990). . . . On inactive list (October 14, 1990). . . . Deactivated for NFC championship game and Super Bowl XXV after 1990 season due to broken leg (January, 1991).

		—— RUSHING——				—— RECEIVING——				– KICKOFF RETURNS –				—— TOTAL——		
Year Team	G	Att.	Yds.	Avg.	TD	No.	Yds.	Avg.	TD	No.	Yds.	Avg.	TD	TD	Pts.	F.
1990—N.Y. Giants NFL	15	109	455	4.2	2	32	274	8.6	2	20	340	17.0	0	4	24	2
Pro totals (1 year)	15	109	455	4.2	2	32	274	8.6	2	20	340	17.0	0	4	24	2

HAND, JON
DE, COLTS

PERSONAL: Born November 13, 1963, at Sylacauga, Ala. . . . 6-7/301. . . . Full name: Jon Thomas Hand.
HIGH SCHOOL: Sylacauga (Ala.).
COLLEGE: Alabama.
TRANSACTIONS/CAREER NOTES: Selected by Birmingham Stallions in 1986 USFL territorial draft. . . . Selected by Indianapolis

Colts in first round (fourth pick overall) of 1986 NFL draft.... Signed by Colts (August 7, 1986).... Granted free agency (February 1, 1990).... Re-signed by Colts (September 12, 1990).... Activated (September 14, 1990).... On inactive list (December 2, 9 and 16, 1990).
PLAYING EXPERIENCE: Indianapolis NFL, 1986-1990.... Games: 1986 (15), 1987 (12), 1988 (15), 1989 (16), 1990 (12). Total: 70.
RECORDS/HONORS: Named as defensive lineman of THE SPORTING NEWS college All-America team, 1985.
PRO STATISTICS: 1986—Intercepted one pass for eight yards and recovered two fumbles. 1988—Recovered one fumble. 1989—Recovered two fumbles for seven yards. 1990—Recovered one fumble.

HANSEN, BRIAN
P, BROWNS

PERSONAL: Born October 26, 1960, at Hawarden, Ia.... 6-4/220.
HIGH SCHOOL: West Sioux Community (Hawarden, Ia.).
COLLEGE: Sioux Falls (S.D.).
TRANSACTIONS/CAREER NOTES: Selected by New Orleans Saints in ninth round (237th pick overall) of 1984 NFL draft.... Released by Saints (September 5, 1989).... Signed as free agent by New England Patriots (May 3, 1990).... Granted unconditional free agency (February 1, 1991).... Signed by Cleveland Browns (April 1, 1991).
RECORDS/HONORS: Led NFL in punting yards (3752), 1990.... Played in Pro Bowl after 1984 season.
PRO STATISTICS: 1984—Rushed twice for minus 27 yards. 1985—Attempted one pass with one completion for eight yards. 1986—Rushed once for no yards, recovered one fumble and fumbled once. 1987—Rushed twice for minus six yards. 1988—Rushed once for 10 yards. 1990—Rushed once for no yards and recovered two fumbles and fumbled once for minus 18 yards.

		—PUNTING—		
Year Team	G	No.	Avg.	Blk.
1984— New Orleans NFL	16	69	43.8	1
1985— New Orleans NFL	16	89	42.3	0
1986— New Orleans NFL	16	81	42.7	1
1987— New Orleans NFL	12	52	40.5	0
1988— New Orleans NFL	16	72	40.5	1
1990— New England NFL	16	*90	41.7	2
Pro totals (6 years)	92	453	41.9	5

HARBAUGH, JIM
QB, BEARS

PERSONAL: Born December 23, 1964, at Toledo, O.... 6-3/220.... Full name: James Joseph Harbaugh.... Son of Jack Harbaugh, head coach at Western Kentucky; and cousin of Mike Gottfried, former head coach at Murray State, Cincinnati, Kansas and Pittsburgh.
HIGH SCHOOL: Pioneer (Ann Arbor, Mich.) and Palo Alto (Calif.).
COLLEGE: Michigan (bachelor's degree in communications, 1987).
TRANSACTIONS/CAREER NOTES: Selected by Chicago Bears in first round (26th pick overall) of 1987 NFL draft.... Signed by Bears (August 3, 1987).... On injured reserve with separated shoulder (December 19, 1990-remainder of season).
CHAMPIONSHIP GAME EXPERIENCE: Member of Chicago Bears for NFC championship game after 1988 season; did not play.
PRO STATISTICS: Passer rating points: 1987 (86.2), 1988 (55.9), 1989 (70.5), 1990 (81.9). Career: 74.4.... 1988—Fumbled once for minus one yard. 1990—Recovered three fumbles and fumbled eight times for minus four yards.

		—————PASSING—————							——RUSHING——				—TOTAL—		
Year Team	G	Att.	Cmp.	Pct.	Yds.	TD	Int.	Avg.	Att.	Yds.	Avg.	TD	TD	Pts.	F.
1987— Chicago NFL	6	11	8	72.7	62	0	0	5.64	4	15	3.8	0	0	0	0
1988— Chicago NFL	10	97	47	48.5	514	0	2	5.30	19	110	5.8	1	1	6	1
1989— Chicago NFL	12	178	111	62.4	1204	5	9	6.76	45	276	6.1	3	3	18	2
1990— Chicago NFL	14	312	180	57.7	2178	10	6	6.98	51	321	6.3	4	4	24	8
Pro totals (4 years)	42	598	346	57.9	3958	15	17	6.62	119	722	6.1	8	8	48	11

HARBOUR, DAVID
C/TE, LIONS

PERSONAL: Born October 23, 1965, at Boston.... 6-3/268.... Full name: David Lynn Harbour.
HIGH SCHOOL: St. Charles (Ill.).
COLLEGE: Illinois (bachelor of science degree in communications, 1988).
TRANSACTIONS/CAREER NOTES: Signed as free agent by Washington Redskins (May 10, 1988).... Released by Redskins (August 24, 1988).... Re-signed by Redskins (September 9, 1988).... Released by Redskins (August 30, 1989).... Re-signed by Redskins (August 31, 1989).... Released by Redskins (August 28, 1990).... Signed by WLAF (January 3, 1991).... Selected by London Monarchs in second round (third tight end) of 1991 WLAF positional draft.... Signed by Detroit Lions (July 20, 1991).
PLAYING EXPERIENCE: Washington NFL, 1988 and 1989; London WLAF, 1991.... Games: 1988 (15), 1989 (16), 1991 (10). Total NFL: 31. Total Pro: 41.
PRO STATISTICS: NFL: 1988—Returned one kickoff for six yards. 1989—Recovered one fumble.... WLAF: 1991—Caught one pass for four yards.

HARDEN, BOBBY
S, DOLPHINS

PERSONAL: Born February 8, 1967, at Pahokee, Fla.... 6-0/192.... Full name: Bobby Lee Harden.
HIGH SCHOOL: Piper (Fort Lauderdale, Fla.).
COLLEGE: Miami, Fla. (degree in business management, 1990).
TRANSACTIONS/CAREER NOTES: Selected by Miami Dolphins in 12th round (315th pick overall) of 1990 NFL draft.... Signed by Dolphins (July 29, 1990).... On active/non-football injury list with shoulder injury (July 29-August 27, 1990).... On reserve/physically unable to perform list with shoulder injury (August 28-November 7, 1990).... On injured reserve with

hamstring injury (November 16, 1990-remainder of regular season and playoffs).
PLAYING EXPERIENCE: Miami NFL, 1990. . . . Games: 1990 (1).

HARMON, RONNIE
RB, CHARGERS

PERSONAL: Born May 7, 1964, at Queens, N.Y. . . . 5-11/200. . . . Full name: Ronnie Keith Harmon. . . . Brother of Derrick Harmon, running back with San Francisco 49ers, 1984-1986; and brother of Kevin Harmon, running back with Seattle Seahawks, 1988 and 1989.

HIGH SCHOOL: Bayside (Queens, N.Y.).
COLLEGE: Iowa.
TRANSACTIONS/CAREER NOTES: Selected by Buffalo Bills in first round (16th pick overall) of 1986 NFL draft. . . . Signed by Bills (August 13, 1986). . . . Granted roster exemption (August 13-August 25, 1986). . . . Granted unconditional free agency (February 1, 1990). . . . Signed by San Diego Chargers (March 23, 1990).
CHAMPIONSHIP GAME EXPERIENCE: Played in AFC championship game after 1988 season.

		RUSHING				RECEIVING				KICKOFF RETURNS				TOTAL		
Year Team	G	Att.	Yds.	Avg.	TD	No.	Yds.	Avg.	TD	No.	Yds.	Avg.	TD	TD	Pts.	F.
1986— Buffalo NFL	14	54	172	3.2	0	22	185	8.4	1	18	321	17.8	0	1	6	2
1987— Buffalo NFL	12	116	485	4.2	2	56	477	8.5	2	1	30	30.0	0	4	24	2
1988— Buffalo NFL	16	57	212	3.7	1	37	427	11.5	3	11	249	22.6	0	4	24	2
1989— Buffalo NFL	15	17	99	5.8	0	29	363	12.5	4	18	409	22.7	0	4	24	2
1990— San Diego NFL	16	66	363	5.5	0	46	511	11.1	2	0	0		0	2	12	1
Pro totals (5 years)	73	310	1331	4.3	3	190	1963	10.3	12	48	1009	21.0	0	15	90	9

HARPER, DWAYNE
CB, SEAHAWKS

PERSONAL: Born March 29, 1966, at Orangeburg, S.C. . . . 5-11/174. . . . Full name: Dwayne Anthony Harper.
HIGH SCHOOL: Orangeburg-Wilkinson (Orangeburg, S.C.).
COLLEGE: South Carolina State.
TRANSACTIONS/CAREER NOTES: Selected by Seattle Seahawks in 11th round (299th pick overall) of 1988 NFL draft. . . . Signed by Seahawks (July 16, 1988).
PRO STATISTICS: 1988—Recovered one fumble. 1989—Recovered one fumble.

		INTERCEPTIONS			
Year Team	G	No.	Yds.	Avg.	TD
1988— Seattle NFL	16	0	0		0
1989— Seattle NFL	16	2	15	7.5	0
1990— Seattle NFL	16	3	69	23.0	0
Pro totals (3 years)	48	5	84	16.8	0

HARPER, MARK
CB, BROWNS

PERSONAL: Born November 5, 1961, at Memphis, Tenn. . . . 5-9/185.
HIGH SCHOOL: Northside (Memphis, Tenn.).
COLLEGE: Alcorn State (received degree, 1982).
TRANSACTIONS/CAREER NOTES: Signed by Chicago Blitz of USFL (July 31, 1983). . . . Franchise transferred to Arizona (September 30, 1983). . . . Traded by Arizona Wranglers to Pittsburgh Maulers for draft choice (February 13, 1984). . . . On developmental squad for five games (February 24-March 29, 1984). . . . Pittsburgh franchise disbanded (October 25, 1984). . . . Selected by Jacksonville Bulls in USFL dispersal draft (December 6, 1984). . . . On developmental squad for seven games (April 25-June 14, 1985). . . . Released by Bulls (February 28, 1986). . . . Signed as free agent by Cleveland Browns (April 7, 1986). . . . On injured reserve with shoulder injury (September 4-November 24, 1990).
CHAMPIONSHIP GAME EXPERIENCE: Played in AFC championship game after 1986, 1987 and 1989 seasons.
PRO STATISTICS: USFL: 1984—Returned seven kickoffs for 130 yards and recovered three fumbles. . . . NFL: 1986—Recovered two fumbles. 1988—Recovered one fumble. 1989—Recovered one fumble.

		INTERCEPTIONS				PUNT RETURNS				TOTAL		
Year Team	G	No.	Yds.	Avg.	TD	No.	Yds.	Avg.	TD	TD	Pts.	F.
1984— Pittsburgh USFL	12	0	0		0	22	157	7.1	0	0	0	1
1985— Jacksonville USFL	11	1	10	10.0	0	0	0		0	0	0	0
1986— Cleveland NFL	16	1	31	31.0	0	0	0		0	0	0	0
1987— Cleveland NFL	12	2	16	8.0	0	0	0		0	0	0	0
1988— Cleveland NFL	13	2	13	6.5	0	0	0		0	0	0	0
1989— Cleveland NFL	16	3	8	2.7	0	0	0		0	0	0	0
1990— Cleveland NFL	5	0	0		0	0	0		0	0	0	0
USFL totals (2 years)	23	1	10	10.0	0	22	157	7.1	0	0	0	1
NFL totals (5 years)	62	8	68	8.5	0	0	0		0	0	0	0
Pro totals (7 years)	85	9	78	8.7	0	22	157	7.1	0	0	0	1

HARRIS, JACKIE
TE, PACKERS

PERSONAL: Born January 4, 1968, at Pine Bluff, Ark. . . . 6-3/243. . . . Full name: Jackie Bernard Harris.
HIGH SCHOOL: Pine Bluff (Ark.).
COLLEGE: Northeast Louisiana (degree in business).
TRANSACTIONS/CAREER NOTES: Selected by Green Bay Packers in fourth round (102nd pick overall) of 1990 NFL draft. . . . Signed by Packers (July 22, 1990).

Year	Team	G	No.	Yds.	Avg.	TD
				RECEIVING		
1990— Green Bay NFL...........		16	12	157	13.1	0
Pro totals (1 year)		16	12	157	13.1	0

HARRIS, LEONARD
WR, OILERS

PERSONAL: Born November 27, 1960, at McKinney, Tex. . . . 5-8/162. . . . Full name: Leonard Milton Harris. . . . Cousin of Judson Flint, defensive back with Cleveland Browns and Buffalo Bills, 1980-1983.
HIGH SCHOOL: McKinney (Tex.).
COLLEGE: Austin College (Tex.), then Texas Tech.
TRANSACTIONS/CAREER NOTES: Selected by Denver Gold in 1984 USFL territorial draft. . . . Signed by Gold (January 24, 1984). . . . Franchise merged with Jacksonville Bulls (February 19, 1986). . . . Granted free agency when USFL suspended operations (August 7, 1986). . . . Signed as free agent by Tampa Bay Buccaneers (August 12, 1986). . . . Granted roster exemption (August 12-August 22, 1986). . . . On injured reserve with hamstring injury (November 10, 1986-remainder of season). . . . Released by Buccaneers (June 11, 1987). . . . Signed as free agent by Washington Redskins (June 26, 1987). . . . Released by Redskins (August 31, 1987). . . . Signed as free agent replacement player by Houston Oilers (September 23, 1987). . . . On injured reserve with knee injury (October 24, 1987-remainder of season). . . . Granted free agency (February 1, 1990). . . . Re-signed by Oilers (September 11, 1990). . . . Activated (September 15, 1990).
PRO STATISTICS: USFL: 1984—Returned one punt for four yards and recovered two fumbles. 1985—Returned seven punts for 35 yards, rushed six times for one yard and recovered two fumbles. . . . NFL: 1986—Returned three punts for 16 yards. 1987—Rushed once for 17 yards.

Year	Team	G	No.	Yds.	Avg.	TD	No.	Yds.	Avg.	TD	TD	Pts.	F.
				RECEIVING				KICKOFF RETURNS				TOTAL	
1984— Denver USFL.....................................		18	35	657	18.8	4	43	1086	25.3	0	4	24	2
1985— Denver USFL.....................................		18	101	*1432	14.2	8	4	86	21.5	0	8	48	8
1986— Tampa Bay NFL.................................		6	3	52	17.3	0	4	63	15.8	0	0	0	1
1987— Houston NFL.....................................		3	10	164	16.4	0	3	87	29.0	0	0	0	0
1988— Houston NFL.....................................		16	10	136	13.6	0	34	678	19.9	0	0	0	1
1989— Houston NFL.....................................		11	13	202	15.5	2	14	331	23.6	0	2	12	1
1990— Houston NFL.....................................		14	13	172	13.2	3	0	0		0	3	18	0
USFL totals (2 years)		36	136	2089	15.4	12	47	1172	24.9	0	12	72	10
NFL totals (5 years)		50	49	726	14.8	5	55	1159	21.1	0	5	30	3
Pro totals (7 years)		86	185	2815	15.2	17	102	2331	22.9	0	17	102	13

HARRIS, ODIE
S, COWBOYS

PERSONAL: Born April 1, 1966, at Bryan, Tex. . . . 6-0/190. . . . Full name: Odie Lazar Harris Jr. . . . Cousin of Gerald Carter, wide receiver with New York Jets and Tampa Bay Buccaneers, 1980-1987.
HIGH SCHOOL: Bryan (Tex.).
COLLEGE: Sam Houston State.
TRANSACTIONS/CAREER NOTES: Signed as free agent by Tampa Bay Buccaneers (April 29, 1988). . . . Granted unconditional free agency (February 1, 1991). . . . Signed by Dallas Cowboys (March 20, 1991).
PRO STATISTICS: 1988—Recovered one fumble.

Year	Team	G	No.	Yds.	Avg.	TD
				INTERCEPTIONS		
1988— Tampa Bay NFL.........		16	2	26	13.0	0
1989— Tampa Bay NFL.........		16	1	19	19.0	0
1990— Tampa Bay NFL.........		16	0	0		0
Pro totals (3 years)		48	3	45	15.0	0

HARRIS, ROD
WR, EAGLES

PERSONAL: Born November 14, 1966, at Dallas. . . . 5-10/185. . . . Full name: Roderick World Harris.
HIGH SCHOOL: Carter (Dallas).
COLLEGE: Texas A&M.
TRANSACTIONS/CAREER NOTES: Selected by Houston Oilers in fourth round (104th pick overall) of 1989 NFL draft. . . . Signed by Oilers (July 27, 1989). . . . Released by Oilers (September 5, 1989). . . . Signed as free agent by New Orleans Saints to developmental squad (September 6, 1989). . . . On developmental squad (September 6-October 4, 1989). . . . Granted unconditional free agency (February 1, 1990). . . . Signed by Dallas Cowboys (February 28, 1990). . . . On injured reserve with groin injury (November 1-November 29, 1990). . . . Released by Cowboys (November 29, 1990). . . . Awarded on waivers to Philadelphia Eagles (November 30, 1990). . . . On inactive list (December 2, 1990).
PRO STATISTICS: 1989—Recovered one fumble. 1990—Recovered one fumble.

Year	Team	G	No.	Yds.	Avg.	TD	No.	Yds.	Avg.	TD	TD	Pts.	F.
				PUNT RETURNS				KICKOFF RETURNS				TOTAL	
1989— New Orleans NFL..............................		11	27	196	7.3	0	19	378	19.9	0	0	0	4
1990— Dal. (7) -Phil. (4) NFL......................		11	28	214	7.6	0	2	44	22.0	0	0	0	3
Pro totals (2 years)		22	55	410	7.5	0	21	422	20.1	0	0	0	7

HARRIS, TIM
LB, PACKERS

PERSONAL: Born September 10, 1964, at Birmingham, Ala. . . . 6-6/258. . . . Full name: Timothy David Harris.
HIGH SCHOOL: Woodlawn (Birmingham, Ala.) and Catholic (Memphis, Tenn.).
COLLEGE: Memphis State.
TRANSACTIONS/CAREER NOTES: Selected by Memphis Showboats in 1986 USFL territorial draft. . . . Selected by Green Bay Packers in fourth round (84th pick overall) of 1986 NFL draft. . . . Signed by Packers (May 17, 1986).
PLAYING EXPERIENCE: Green Bay NFL, 1986-1990. . . . Games: 1986 (16), 1987 (12), 1988 (16), 1989 (16), 1990 (16). Total: 76.
RECORDS/HONORS: Tied NFL record for most safeties, season (2), 1988. . . . Played in Pro Bowl after 1989 season. . . . Named to THE SPORTING NEWS NFL All-Pro team, 1989.
PRO STATISTICS: 1986—Recovered one fumble. 1988—Returned blocked punt 10 yards for a touchdown and credited with two safeties. 1989—Recovered three fumbles. 1990—Recovered two fumbles for 28 yards.

HARRIS, WILLIAM
TE, PACKERS

PERSONAL: Born February 10, 1965, at Houston. . . . 6-5/253. . . . Full name: William Milton Harris.
HIGH SCHOOL: M.B. Smiley (Houston).
COLLEGE: Texas, then Bishop College (Tex.).
TRANSACTIONS/CAREER NOTES: Selected by St. Louis Cardinals in seventh round (195th pick overall) of 1987 NFL draft. . . . Signed by Cardinals (July 18, 1987). . . . Released by Cardinals (September 1, 1987). . . . Re-signed as replacement player by Cardinals (September 25, 1987). . . . Franchise transferred to Phoenix (March 15, 1988). . . . Released by Phoenix Cardinals (August 24, 1988). . . . Signed as free agent by San Francisco 49ers for 1989 (November 8, 1988). . . . Released by 49ers (April 18, 1989). . . . Awarded on waivers to Tampa Bay Buccaneers (May 1, 1989). . . . Granted unconditional free agency (February 1, 1990). . . . Signed by Green Bay Packers (March 7, 1990). . . . Released by Packers (September 3, 1990). . . . Re-signed by Packers (October 26, 1990). . . . Released by Packers (November 20, 1990). . . . Re-signed by Packers (March 5, 1991).

			RECEIVING		
Year Team	G	No.	Yds.	Avg.	TD
1987— St. Louis NFL	10	1	8	8.0	0
1989— Tampa Bay NFL	16	11	102	9.3	1
1990— Green Bay NFL	4	0	0	0	0
Pro totals (3 years)	30	12	110	9.2	1

HARRISON, MARTIN
LB/DE, 49ERS

PERSONAL: Born September 20, 1967, at Livermore, Calif. . . . 6-5/240. . . . Full name: Martin Allen Harrison.
HIGH SCHOOL: Newport (Bellevue, Wash.).
COLLEGE: Washington (degree in sociology).
TRANSACTIONS/CAREER NOTES: Selected by San Francisco 49ers in 10th round (276th pick overall) of 1990 NFL draft. . . . Signed by 49ers (July 18, 1990). . . . On injured reserve with shoulder injury (September 18, 1990-remainder of season). . . . Released by 49ers (December 13, 1990). . . . Re-signed by 49ers (offseason, 1991).
PLAYING EXPERIENCE: San Francisco NFL, 1990. . . . Games: 1990 (2).

HARRY, CARL
WR, REDSKINS

PERSONAL: Born October 26, 1967, at Fountain Valley, Calif. . . . 5-9/170. . . . Brother of Emile Harry, wide receiver with Kansas City Chiefs.
HIGH SCHOOL: Fountain Valley (Calif).
COLLEGE: Utah.
TRANSACTIONS/CAREER NOTES: Signed as free agent by Washington Redskins (April 26, 1989). . . . Released by Redskins (September 5, 1989). . . . Re-signed by Redskins to developmental squad (September 6, 1989). . . . On developmental squad (September 6-December 17, 1989). . . . Activated after clearing procedural waivers (December 19, 1989). . . . Granted unconditional free agency (February 1, 1990). . . . Signed by Houston Oilers (March 23, 1990). . . . Released by Oilers (August 27, 1990). . . . Signed by Washington Redskins to practice squad (November 16, 1990). . . . Released by Redskins (January 4, 1991). . . . Re-signed by Redskins (May 6, 1991).
PLAYING EXPERIENCE: Washington NFL, 1989. . . . Games: 1989 (1).

HARRY, EMILE
WR, CHIEFS

PERSONAL: Born April 5, 1963, at Los Angeles. . . . 5-11/186. . . . Full name: Emile Michael Harry. . . . First name pronounced uh-MEEL. . . . Brother of Carl Harry, wide receiver with Washington Redskins.
HIGH SCHOOL: Fountain Valley (Calif.).
COLLEGE: Stanford (bachelor of arts degree in political science, 1985).
TRANSACTIONS/CAREER NOTES: Selected by Oakland Invaders in 1985 USFL territorial draft. . . . Selected by Atlanta Falcons in fourth round (89th pick overall) of 1985 NFL draft. . . . Signed by Falcons (July 19, 1985). . . . Released by Falcons (September 2, 1985). . . . Signed as free agent by Kansas City Chiefs (January 18, 1986). . . . Released by Chiefs (September 1, 1986). . . . Re-signed by Chiefs (September 30, 1986). . . . On injured reserve with shoulder injury (August 14, 1987-entire season).
PRO STATISTICS: 1986—Returned six kickoffs for 115 yards, returned six punts for 20 yards and fumbled once. 1989—Returned two punts for six yards, rushed once for nine yards and fumbled once. 1990—Returned one punt for two yards.

			RECEIVING		
Year Team	G	No.	Yds.	Avg.	TD
1986— Kansas City NFL	12	9	211	23.4	1
1988— Kansas City NFL	16	26	362	13.9	1
1989— Kansas City NFL	16	33	430	13.0	2
1990— Kansas City NFL	16	41	519	12.7	2
Pro totals (4 years)	60	109	1522	14.0	6

HART, ROY
DT, RAIDERS

PERSONAL: Born July 10, 1965, at Tifton, Ga. . . . 6-0/285. . . . Full name: Roy Hart Jr. **HIGH SCHOOL:** Tift County (Tifton, Ga.). **COLLEGE:** Northwest Mississippi Junior College, then South Carolina. **TRANSACTIONS/CAREER NOTES:** Selected by Seattle Seahawks in sixth round (158th pick overall) of 1988 NFL draft. . . . Signed by Seahawks (June 8, 1988). . . . On injured reserve with hamstring injury (September 9, 1988-remainder of season). . . . Active for one game with Seahawks in 1988; did not play. . . . Released by Seahawks (August 28, 1990). . . . Signed by WLAF (January 4, 1991). . . . Selected by London Monarchs in first round (third defensive lineman) of 1991 WLAF positional draft. . . . Signed by Los Angeles Raiders (June, 1991). **PLAYING EXPERIENCE:** Seattle NFL, 1988 and 1989; London WLAF, 1991. . . . Games: 1988 (0), 1989 (16), 1991 (10). Total NFL: 16. Total Pro: 26. **PRO STATISTICS:** WLAF: 1991—Recovered one fumble.

HARVEY, JOHN
RB, BUCCANEERS

PERSONAL: Born December 28, 1966, at New York. . . . 5-11/200. . . . Full name: John Lewis Harvey. **HIGH SCHOOL:** Spring Valley (N.Y.). **COLLEGE:** Texas-El Paso. **TRANSACTIONS/CAREER NOTES:** Signed as free agent by Tampa Bay Buccaneers (April 27, 1989). . . . Released by Buccaneers (September 5, 1989). . . . Signed by Buccaneers to developmental squad (September 6, 1989). . . . Released by Buccaneers (November 22, 1989). . . . Re-signed by Buccaneers (February 20, 1990). **PRO STATISTICS:** 1990—Recovered one fumble.

		—RUSHING—				—RECEIVING—				– KICKOFF RETURNS–				— TOTAL —		
Year Team	G	Att.	Yds.	Avg.	TD	No.	Yds.	Avg.	TD	No.	Yds.	Avg.	TD	TD	Pts.	F.
1990— Tampa Bay NFL.....	16	27	113	4.2	0	11	86	7.8	1	12	207	17.3	0	1	6	2
Pro totals (1 year).........	16	27	113	4.2	0	11	86	7.8	1	12	207	17.3	0	1	6	2

HARVEY, KEN
LB, CARDINALS

PERSONAL: Born May 6, 1965, at Austin, Tex. . . . 6-3/230. . . . Full name: Kenneth Ray Harvey. **HIGH SCHOOL:** Lanier (Austin, Tex.). **COLLEGE:** Laney College (Calif.), then California. **TRANSACTIONS/CAREER NOTES:** Selected by Phoenix Cardinals in first round (12th pick overall) of 1988 NFL draft. . . . Signed by Cardinals (June 17, 1988). **PLAYING EXPERIENCE:** Phoenix NFL, 1988-1990. . . . Games: 1988 (16), 1989 (16), 1990 (16). Total: 48. **PRO STATISTICS:** 1988—Credited with a safety. 1990—Recovered one fumble.

HARVEY, RICHARD
LB, PATRIOTS

PERSONAL: Born September 11, 1966, at Pascagoula, Miss. . . . 6-1/227. . . . Full name: Richard Clemont Harvey. **HIGH SCHOOL:** Pascagoula (Miss.). **COLLEGE:** Tulane. **TRANSACTIONS/CAREER NOTES:** Selected by Buffalo Bills in 11th round (305th pick overall) of 1989 NFL draft. . . . On injured reserve with shoulder injury (September 4-entire 1989 season). . . . Granted unconditional free agency (February 1, 1990). . . . Signed by New England Patriots (March 23, 1990). **PLAYING EXPERIENCE:** New England NFL, 1990. . . . Games: 1990 (16).

HARVEY, STACEY
LB, 49ERS

PERSONAL: Born March 8, 1965, at Pasadena, Calif. . . . 6-3/250. **HIGH SCHOOL:** Pasadena (Calif.). **COLLEGE:** Arizona State. **TRANSACTIONS/CAREER NOTES:** Signed as free agent by Los Angeles Raiders (April 28, 1988). . . . Released by Raiders (August 30, 1988). . . . Signed as free agent by New Orleans Saints (April 6, 1989). . . . Released by Saints (September 5, 1989). . . . Signed as free agent by Kansas City Chiefs to developmental squad (September 20, 1989). . . . On developmental squad (September 20-October 24, 1989). . . . Activated after clearing procedural waivers (October 26, 1989). . . . Granted unconditional free agency (February 1, 1990). . . . Signed by Miami Dolphins (March 29, 1990). . . . Released by Dolphins (September 3, 1990). . . . Signed by San Francisco 49ers (March 26, 1991). **PLAYING EXPERIENCE:** Kansas City NFL, 1989. . . . Games: 1989 (9).

HASELRIG, CARLTON
G, STEELERS

PERSONAL: Born January 22, 1966, at Johnstown, Pa. . . . 6-1/291. . . . Full name: Carlton Lee Haselrig. **HIGH SCHOOL:** Greater Johnstown (Johnstown, Pa.). **COLLEGE:** Pittsburgh-Johnstown, Pa. (bachelor of science degree in communications, 1989). **TRANSACTIONS/CAREER NOTES:** Selected by Pittsburgh Steelers in 12th round (312th pick overall) of 1989 NFL draft. . . . Released by Steelers (September 5, 1989). . . . Signed by Steelers to developmental squad (September 6, 1989). . . . Released by Steelers (January 29, 1990). . . . Re-signed by Steelers (February 23, 1990). **PLAYING EXPERIENCE:** Pittsburgh NFL, 1990. . . . Games: 1990 (16).

HASTY, JAMES
CB, JETS

PERSONAL: Born May 23, 1965, at Seattle. . . . 6-0/201. . . . Full name: James Edward Hasty. **HIGH SCHOOL:** Franklin (Seattle). **COLLEGE:** Central Washington, then Washington State (degree in liberal arts and business, 1988).

TRANSACTIONS/CAREER NOTES: Selected by New York Jets in third round (74th pick overall) of 1988 NFL draft.... Signed by Jets (July 12, 1988).
PRO STATISTICS: 1988—Recovered three fumbles for 35 yards. 1989—Recovered two fumbles for two yards and fumbled once. 1990—Returned one punt for no yards, recovered three fumbles and fumbled once.

| | | | — INTERCEPTIONS — | | |
Year Team	G	No.	Yds.	Avg.	TD
1988— N.Y. Jets NFL	15	5	20	4.0	0
1989— N.Y. Jets NFL	16	5	62	12.4	1
1990— N.Y. Jets NFL	16	2	0	.0	0
Pro totals (3 years)	47	12	82	6.8	1

HATCHER, DALE
P, RAMS

PERSONAL: Born April 5, 1963, at Cheraw, S.C. ... 6-2/220. ... Full name: Roger Dale Hatcher.
HIGH SCHOOL: Cheraw (S.C.).
COLLEGE: Clemson.
TRANSACTIONS/CAREER NOTES: Selected by Orlando Renegades in eighth round (114th pick overall) of 1985 USFL draft.... Selected by Los Angeles Rams in third round (77th pick overall) of 1985 NFL draft.... Signed by Rams (July 12, 1985).... Crossed picket line during players' strike (October 2, 1987).... On injured reserve with knee injury (August 31-November 4, 1988).... Granted unconditional free agency (February 1, 1990).... Signed by Green Bay Packers (March 16, 1990).... Released by Packers (September 4, 1990).... Re-signed by Los Angeles Rams (April 12, 1991).
CHAMPIONSHIP GAME EXPERIENCE: Played in NFC championship game after 1985 and 1989 seasons.
RECORDS/HONORS: Led NFL in net punting average (38.0), 1985.... Led NFL in punting yards (3,140), 1987.... Played in Pro Bowl after 1985 season.... Named to THE SPORTING NEWS NFL All-Pro team, 1985.
PRO STATISTICS: 1989—Rushed once for no yards.

| | | | — PUNTING — | |
Year Team	G	No.	Avg.	Blk.
1985— L.A. Rams NFL	16	87	43.2	1
1986— L.A. Rams NFL	16	97	38.6	1
1987— L.A. Rams NFL	15	76	41.3	1
1988— L.A. Rams NFL	7	36	39.6	0
1989— L.A. Rams NFL	16	73	38.8	1
Pro totals (5 years)	70	369	40.3	4

HAUCK, TIM
S, PACKERS

PERSONAL: Born December 20, 1966, at Butte, Mont. ... 5-11/181. ... Full name: Tim Christian Hauck.
HIGH SCHOOL: Sweet Grass County (Big Timber, Mont.).
COLLEGE: Pacific (Ore.), then Montana.
TRANSACTIONS/CAREER NOTES: Signed as free agent by New England Patriots (May 1, 1990).... Released by Patriots (August 26, 1990).... Signed by Patriots to practice squad (October 1, 1990).... Activated (October 27, 1990). Granted unconditional free agency (February 1, 1991).... Signed by Green Bay Packers (April 1, 1991).
PLAYING EXPERIENCE: New England NFL, 1990.... Games: 1990 (10).

HAVERDINK, KEVIN
OT, SAINTS

PERSONAL: Born October 20, 1965, at Holland, Mich. ... 6-5/285. ... Full name: Kevin Dean Haverdink.
HIGH SCHOOL: Hamilton (Mich.).
COLLEGE: Western Michigan (degree in marketing).
TRANSACTIONS/CAREER NOTES: Selected by New Orleans Saints in fifth round (133rd pick overall) of 1989 NFL draft.... Signed by Saints (July 27, 1989).... On inactive list (December 9, 1990).
PLAYING EXPERIENCE: New Orleans NFL, 1989 and 1990.... Games: 1989 (16), 1990 (15). Total: 31.

HAWKINS, BILL
DE, RAMS

PERSONAL: Born May 9, 1966, at Miami.... 6-6/266.... Full name: William E. Hawkins.
HIGH SCHOOL: South Broward (Hollywood, Fla.).
COLLEGE: Miami, Fla. (degree in business, 1988).
TRANSACTIONS/CAREER NOTES: Selected by Los Angeles Rams in first round (21st pick overall) of 1989 NFL draft.... Signed by Rams (August 17, 1989).... On injured reserve with knee injury (December 15, 1989-remainder of season).... On inactive list (November 11, 1990).
PLAYING EXPERIENCE: Los Angeles Rams NFL, 1989 and 1990.... Games: 1989 (13), 1990 (15). Total: 28.

HAYES, ERIC
DT, SEAHAWKS

PERSONAL: Born November 12, 1967, at Tampa, Fla.... 6-3/297.
HIGH SCHOOL: King (Tampa, Fla.).
COLLEGE: Florida State (degree in political science).
TRANSACTIONS/CAREER NOTES: Selected by Seattle Seahawks in fifth round (119th pick overall) of 1990 NFL draft.... Signed by Seahawks (April 22, 1990).
PLAYING EXPERIENCE: Seattle NFL, 1990.... Games: 1990 (16).

HAYES, JONATHAN
TE, CHIEFS

PERSONAL: Born August 11, 1962, at South Fayette, Pa. . . . 6-5/248. . . . Full name: Jonathan Michael Hayes. . . . Brother of Jay Hayes, defensive end with Michigan Panthers, San Antonio Gunslingers and Memphis Showboats of USFL, 1984 and 1985.

HIGH SCHOOL: South Fayette (McDonald, Pa.).
COLLEGE: Iowa (degree in criminology, 1986).
TRANSACTIONS/CAREER NOTES: Selected by Kansas City Chiefs in second round (41st pick overall) of 1985 NFL draft. . . . Signed by Chiefs (June 19, 1985). . . . On injured reserve with shoulder injury (September 4-October 6, 1990).
PRO STATISTICS: 1985—Returned one kickoff for no yards. 1987—Recovered one fumble. 1989—Fumbled once.

			RECEIVING		
Year Team	G	No.	Yds.	Avg.	TD
1985— Kansas City NFL........	16	5	39	7.8	1
1986— Kansas City NFL........	16	8	69	8.6	0
1987— Kansas City NFL........	12	21	272	13.0	2
1988— Kansas City NFL........	16	22	233	10.6	1
1989— Kansas City NFL........	16	18	229	12.7	2
1990— Kansas City NFL........	12	9	83	9.2	1
Pro totals (6 years)........	88	83	925	11.1	7

HAYNES, MICHAEL
WR, FALCONS

PERSONAL: Born December 24, 1965, at New Orleans. . . . 6-0/180. . . . Full name: Michael David Haynes.
HIGH SCHOOL: Joseph S. Clark (New Orleans).
COLLEGE: Eastern Arizona Junior College, then Northern Arizona.
TRANSACTIONS/CAREER NOTES: Selected by Atlanta Falcons in seventh round (166th pick overall) of 1988 NFL draft. . . . Signed by Falcons (July 18, 1988). . . . On inactive list (September 23, October 21 and November 4, 1990).
PRO STATISTICS: 1988—Returned six kickoffs for 113 yards and fumbled once. 1989—Rushed four times for 35 yards.

			RECEIVING		
Year Team	G	No.	Yds.	Avg.	TD
1988— Atlanta NFL	15	13	232	17.9	4
1989— Atlanta NFL	13	40	681	17.0	4
1990— Atlanta NFL	13	31	445	14.4	0
Pro totals (3 years)........	41	84	1358	16.2	8

HAYWORTH, TRACY
LB, LIONS

PERSONAL: Born December 18, 1967, at Winchester, Tenn. . . . 6-3/250. . . . Full name: Tracy Keith Hayworth.
HIGH SCHOOL: Franklin County (Winchester, Tenn.).
COLLEGE: Tennessee (degree in education).
TRANSACTIONS/CAREER NOTES: Selected by Detroit Lions in seventh round (174th pick overall) of 1990 NFL draft. . . . Signed by Lions (July 20, 1990).
PLAYING EXPERIENCE: Detroit NFL, 1990. . . . Games: 1990 (16).
PRO STATISTICS: 1990—Recovered one fumble.

HEBERT, BOBBY
QB, SAINTS

PERSONAL: Born August 19, 1960, at Baton Rouge, La. . . . 6-4/215. . . . Full name: Bobby Joseph Hebert Jr. . . . Name pronounced AY-bear. . . . Brother of Billy Bob Hebert, wide receiver with Calgary Stampeders (CFL), 1989.
HIGH SCHOOL: South Lafourche (Galliano, La.).
COLLEGE: Northwestern Louisiana State (degree in business administration, 1983).
TRANSACTIONS/CAREER NOTES: Selected by Michigan Panthers in third round (34th pick overall) of 1983 USFL draft. . . . Signed by Panthers (January 22, 1983). . . . On reserve/did not report list (January 23-February 16, 1984). . . . Protected in merger of Michigan Panthers and Oakland Invaders (December 6, 1984). . . . Granted free agency (July 15, 1985). . . . Signed by New Orleans Saints (August 7, 1985). . . . On injured reserve with broken foot (September 22-November 8, 1986). . . . On reserve/asked to resign list (February 1, 1990-June 3, 1991). . . . Re-signed by Saints (June 4, 1991).
CHAMPIONSHIP GAME EXPERIENCE: Played in USFL championship game after 1983 and 1985 seasons.
RECORDS/HONORS: Named THE SPORTING NEWS USFL Player of the Year, 1983. . . . Named as quarterback on THE SPORTING NEWS USFL All-Star team, 1983.
PRO STATISTICS: USFL Passer rating points: 1983 (86.7), 1984 (76.4), 1985 (86.1). Career: 83.1. . . . NFL Passer rating points: 1985 (74.6), 1986 (40.5), 1987 (82.9), 1988 (79.3), 1989 (82.7). Career: 77.8. . . . USFL: 1983—Credited with one 2-point conversion and recovered two fumbles. 1984—Recovered three fumbles. 1985—Recovered three fumbles and fumbled five times for minus two yards. . . . NFL: 1985—Caught one pass for seven yards and a touchdown and recovered one fumble. 1986—Caught one pass for one yard. 1987—Recovered two fumbles. 1988—Caught two passes for no yards and recovered one fumble.

				PASSING						RUSHING				TOTAL	
Year Team	G	Att.	Cmp.	Pct.	Yds.	TD	Int.	Avg.	Att.	Yds.	Avg.	TD	TD	Pts.	F.
1983— Michigan USFL	18	451	257	57.0	3568	*27	17	*7.91	28	35	1.3	3	3	20	8
1984— Michigan USFL	17	500	272	54.4	3758	24	22	7.52	18	76	4.2	1	1	6	8
1985— Oakland USFL.............	18	456	244	53.5	3811	30	19	8.36	12	31	2.6	1	1	6	5
1985— New Orleans NFL.......	6	181	97	53.6	1208	5	4	6.67	12	26	2.2	0	1	6	1
1986— New Orleans NFL.......	5	79	41	51.9	498	2	8	6.30	5	14	2.8	0	0	0	3
1987— New Orleans NFL.......	12	294	164	55.8	2119	15	9	7.21	13	95	7.3	0	0	0	4

Year	Team	G	— PASSING —							— RUSHING —				— TOTAL —		
			Att.	Cmp.	Pct.	Yds.	TD	Int.	Avg.	Att.	Yds.	Avg.	TD	TD	Pts.	F.
1988—	New Orleans NFL	16	478	280	58.6	3156	20	15	6.60	37	79	2.1	0	0	0	9
1989—	New Orleans NFL	14	353	222	62.9	2686	15	15	7.61	25	87	3.5	0	0	0	2
USFL totals (3 years)		53	1407	773	54.9	11137	81	58	7.92	58	142	2.4	5	5	32	21
NFL totals (5 years)		53	1385	804	58.1	9667	57	51	6.98	92	301	3.3	0	1	6	19
Pro totals (8 years)		106	2792	1577	56.5	20804	138	109	7.45	150	443	3.0	5	6	38	40

HECK, ANDY
OT, SEAHAWKS

PERSONAL: Born January 1, 1967, at Fargo, N.D. . . . 6-6/286. . . . Full name: Andrew Robert Heck. **HIGH SCHOOL:** W.T. Woodson (Fairfax, Va.). **COLLEGE:** Notre Dame (bachelor of arts degree in American studies, 1989). **TRANSACTIONS/CAREER NOTES:** Selected by Seattle Seahawks in first round (15th pick overall) of 1989 NFL draft. . . . Signed by Seahawks (July 31, 1989). **PLAYING EXPERIENCE:** Seattle NFL, 1989 and 1990. . . . Games: 1989 (16), 1990 (16). Total: 32. **RECORDS/HONORS:** Named as offensive tackle on THE SPORTING NEWS college All-America team, 1988. **PRO STATISTICS:** 1989—Recovered one fumble. 1990—Recovered one fumble.

HECTOR, JOHNNY
RB, JETS

PERSONAL: Born November 26, 1960, at Lafayette, La. . . . 5-11/214. . . . Full name: Johnny Lyndell Hector. **HIGH SCHOOL:** New Iberia (La.). **COLLEGE:** Texas A&M. **TRANSACTIONS/CAREER NOTES:** Selected by Chicago Blitz in second round (19th pick overall) of 1983 USFL draft. . . . Selected by New York Jets in second round (51st pick overall) of 1983 NFL draft. . . . Signed by Jets (June 9, 1983). . . . Granted free agency (February 1, 1989). . . . Re-signed by Jets (September 12, 1989). . . . Granted free agency (February 1, 1990). . . . Re-signed by Jets (July 19, 1990). . . . On inactive list (September 9, 1990). . . . Granted unconditional free agency (February 1, 1991). . . . Re-signed by Jets (April 10, 1991). **PRO STATISTICS:** 1985—Recovered one fumble. 1987—Recovered one fumble. 1988—Attempted one pass with no completions and recovered one fumble.

Year	Team	G	— RUSHING —				— RECEIVING —				— KICKOFF RETURNS —				— TOTAL —		
			Att.	Yds.	Avg.	TD	No.	Yds.	Avg.	TD	No.	Yds.	Avg.	TD	TD	Pts.	F.
1983—	N.Y. Jets NFL	10	16	85	5.3	0	5	61	12.2	1	14	274	19.6	0	1	6	2
1984—	N.Y. Jets NFL	13	124	531	4.3	1	20	182	9.1	0	0	0		0	1	6	2
1985—	N.Y. Jets NFL	14	145	572	3.9	6	17	164	9.6	0	11	274	24.9	0	6	36	2
1986—	N.Y. Jets NFL	13	164	605	3.7	8	33	302	9.2	0	0	0		0	8	48	2
1987—	N.Y. Jets NFL	11	111	435	3.9	*11	32	249	7.8	0	0	0		0	11	66	2
1988—	N.Y. Jets NFL	16	137	561	4.1	10	26	237	9.1	0	0	0		0	10	60	3
1989—	N.Y. Jets NFL	15	177	702	4.0	3	38	330	8.7	2	0	0		0	5	30	1
1990—	N.Y. Jets NFL	15	91	377	4.1	2	8	72	9.0	0	0	0		0	2	12	2
Pro totals (8 years)		107	965	3868	4.0	41	179	1597	8.9	3	25	548	21.9	0	44	264	16

HELLER, RON
TE, SEAHAWKS

PERSONAL: Born September 18, 1963, at Gross Valley, Calif. . . . 6-3/242. . . . Full name: Ronald Jeffery Heller. **HIGH SCHOOL:** Clark Fork (Idaho). **COLLEGE:** Oregon State. **TRANSACTIONS/CAREER NOTES:** Signed as free agent by Dallas Cowboys (May 1, 1986). . . . Released by Cowboys (July 24, 1986). . . . Signed as free agent by San Francisco 49ers (July 29, 1986). . . . On injured reserve with neck and head injuries (September 1, 1986-entire season). . . . Crossed picket line during players' strike (October 7, 1987). . . . Granted unconditional free agency (February 1, 1989). . . . Signed by Atlanta Falcons (March 8, 1989). . . . Granted unconditional free agency (February 1, 1990). . . . Signed by Seattle Seahawks (March 5, 1990). **CHAMPIONSHIP GAME EXPERIENCE:** Played in NFC championship game after 1988 season. . . . Played in Super Bowl XXIII after 1988 season. **PRO STATISTICS:** 1987—Fumbled once. 1989—Fumbled once.

Year	Team	G	— RECEIVING —			
			No.	Yds.	Avg.	TD
1987—	San Francisco NFL	13	12	165	13.8	3
1988—	San Francisco NFL	16	14	140	10.0	0
1989—	Atlanta NFL	15	33	324	9.8	1
1990—	Seattle NFL	16	13	157	12.1	1
Pro totals (4 years)		60	72	786	10.9	5

HELLER, RON
OT, EAGLES

PERSONAL: Born August 25, 1962, at East Meadow, N.Y. . . . 6-6/280. . . . Full name: Ronald Ramon Heller. **HIGH SCHOOL:** Farming Dale (N.Y.). **COLLEGE:** Penn State (bachelor of science degree in administration of justice, 1984). **TRANSACTIONS/CAREER NOTES:** Selected by Philadelphia Stars in 1984 USFL territorial draft. . . . Selected by Tampa Bay Buccaneers in fourth round (112th pick overall) of 1984 NFL draft. . . . Signed by Buccaneers (June 6, 1984). . . . Granted free agency (February 1, 1988). . . . Re-signed by Buccaneers and traded to Seattle Seahawks for defensive end Randy Edwards and sixth-round pick in 1989 draft (May 4, 1988). . . . Traded by Seahawks to Philadelphia Eagles for fourth-round pick in

1989 draft (August 22, 1988)....Granted free agency (February 1, 1990)....Re-signed by Eagles (August 18, 1990).
PLAYING EXPERIENCE: Tampa Bay NFL, 1984-1987; Philadelphia NFL, 1988-1990....Games: 1984 (14), 1985 (16), 1986 (16), 1987 (12), 1988 (15), 1989 (16), 1990 (16). Total: 105.
PRO STATISTICS: 1986—Caught one pass for one yard and a touchdown and recovered one fumble. 1988—Recovered two fumbles.

HELLESTRAE, DALE
G/C, COWBOYS

PERSONAL: Born July 11, 1962, at Phoenix....6-5/285....Full name: Dale Robert Hellestrae....Name pronounced hellus-TRAY.
HIGH SCHOOL: Saguaro (Scottsdale, Ariz.).
COLLEGE: Southern Methodist.
TRANSACTIONS/CAREER NOTES: Selected by Houston Gamblers in 1985 USFL territorial draft....Selected by Buffalo Bills in fourth round (112th pick overall) of 1985 NFL draft....Signed by Bills (July 19, 1985)....On injured reserve with broken thumb (October 4, 1985-remainder of season)....On injured reserve with broken wrist (September 17-November 15, 1986). ...On injured reserve with hip injury (September 1, 1987-entire season)....Granted unconditional free agency (February 1, 1989)....Signed by Los Angeles Raiders (February 24, 1989)....On injured reserve with broken leg (August 29, 1989-entire season)....Traded by Raiders to Dallas Cowboys for an undisclosed draft pick (August 20, 1990).
PLAYING EXPERIENCE: Buffalo NFL, 1985, 1986 and 1988; Dallas NFL, 1990....Games: 1985 (4), 1986 (8), 1988 (16), 1990 (16). Total: 44.
CHAMPIONSHIP GAME EXPERIENCE: Played in AFC championship game after 1988 season.
PRO STATISTICS: 1986—Fumbled once for minus 14 yards.

HELTON, BARRY
P, 49ERS

PERSONAL: Born January 2, 1965, at Colorado Springs, Colo....6-3/205....Full name: Barry Bret Helton.
HIGH SCHOOL: Simla (Colo.).
COLLEGE: Colorado (bachelor of science degree in business finance, 1988).
TRANSACTIONS/CAREER NOTES: Selected by San Francisco 49ers in fourth round (102nd pick overall) of 1988 NFL draft.... Signed by 49ers (July 16, 1988)....Released by 49ers (August 30, 1988)....Re-signed by 49ers (September 6, 1988).... Released by 49ers (September 3, 1990)....Re-signed by 49ers (September 4, 1990).
CHAMPIONSHIP GAME EXPERIENCE: Played in NFC championship game after 1988-1990 seasons....Played in Super Bowl XXIII after 1988 season and Super Bowl XXIV after 1989 season.
RECORDS/HONORS: Named as punter on THE SPORTING NEWS college All-America team, 1986.
PRO STATISTICS: 1988—Rushed once for no yards and recovered one fumble. 1989—Rushed once for no yards, recovered one fumble for minus 13 yards and fumbled once. 1990—Attempted one pass with one completion for no yards.

| | | —PUNTING— | | |
Year	Team	G	No.	Avg.	Blk.
1988— San Francisco NFL		15	78	39.3	1
1989— San Francisco NFL		16	55	40.5	1
1990— San Francisco NFL		16	69	36.8	1
Pro totals (3 years)		47	202	38.9	3

HENDERSON, KEITH
FB, 49ERS

PERSONAL: Born August 4, 1966, at Carterville, Ga....6-1/220....Full name: Keith Pernell Henderson.
HIGH SCHOOL: Cartersville (Ga.).
COLLEGE: Georgia.
TRANSACTIONS/CAREER NOTES: Selected by San Francisco 49ers in third round (84th pick overall) of 1989 NFL draft....Signed by 49ers (June 27, 1989)....On reserve/non-football injury list with steroids (August 29-September 25, 1989)....Reinstated and transferred to reserve/physically unable to perform list with knee injury (September 26-October 27, 1989)....On injured reserve with knee injury (September 4-November 21, 1990)....On practice squad (November 21-December 22, 1990).
CHAMPIONSHIP GAME EXPERIENCE: Played in NFC championship game after 1989 and 1990 seasons.
PRO STATISTICS: 1989—Returned two kickoffs for 21 yards and recovered one fumble.

| | | | RUSHING | | | | RECEIVING | | | | TOTAL | | |
Year	Team	G	Att.	Yds.	Avg.	TD	No.	Yds.	Avg.	TD	TD	Pts.	F.
1989— San Francisco NFL		6	7	30	4.3	1	3	130	43.3	0	1	6	1
1990— San Francisco NFL		2	6	14	2.3	0	4	35	8.8	0	0	0	0
Pro totals (2 years)		8	13	44	3.4	1	7	165	23.6	0	1	6	1

HENDERSON, WYMON
CB, BRONCOS

PERSONAL: Born December 15, 1961, at North Miami Beach, Fla....5-9/186.
HIGH SCHOOL: North (Miami Beach, Fla.).
COLLEGE: Hancock Junior College, then UNLV.
TRANSACTIONS/CAREER NOTES: Selected by Los Angeles Express in eighth round (96th pick overall) of 1983 USFL draft....Signed by Express (January 20, 1983)....Granted free agency (August 1, 1985). ...Signed by San Francisco 49ers (August 7, 1985)....Released by 49ers (August 20, 1985)....Re-signed by 49ers (February 3, 1986)....On injured reserve with foot injury (August 19, 1986-entire season)....Granted free agency with option not exercised (February 1, 1987)....Signed by Minnesota Vikings (April 20, 1987)....Granted unconditional free agency (February 1, 1989)....Signed by Denver Broncos (March 13, 1989)....On inactive list (October 21, 1990).
CHAMPIONSHIP GAME EXPERIENCE: Played in NFC championship game after 1987 season....Played in AFC championship game after 1989 season....Played in Super Bowl XXIV after 1989 season.
PRO STATISTICS: USFL: 1983—Recovered one fumble for 30 yards and one touchdown. 1984—Returned one punt for three yards and recovered two fumbles. 1985—Recovered one fumble and fumbled three times. 1989—Fumbled once....NFL: 1988—Recovered two fumbles. 1990—Recovered one fumble for minus two yards.

Year	Team	G	INTERCEPTIONS No.	Yds.	Avg.	TD
1983—	Los Angeles USFL	16	0	0		0
1984—	Los Angeles USFL	18	3	23	7.7	0
1985—	Los Angeles USFL	18	4	44	11.0	0
1987—	Minnesota NFL	12	4	33	8.3	0
1988—	Minnesota NFL	16	1	13	13.0	0
1989—	Denver NFL	16	3	58	19.3	0
1990—	Denver NFL	15	2	71	35.5	1
	USFL totals (3 years)	52	7	67	9.6	0
	NFL totals (4 years)	59	10	175	17.5	1
	Pro totals (7 years)	111	17	242	14.2	1

HENDRICKSON, STEVE
LB/RB, CHARGERS

PERSONAL: Born August 30, 1966, at Richmond, Calif. . . . 6-0/250. . . . Full name: Steven Daniel Hendrickson.
HIGH SCHOOL: Napa (Calif.).
COLLEGE: California.

TRANSACTIONS/CAREER NOTES: Selected by San Francisco 49ers in sixth round (167th pick overall) of 1989 NFL draft. . . . Signed by 49ers (July 19, 1989). . . . Released by 49ers (September 27, 1989). . . . Re-signed by 49ers (September 29, 1989). . . . Released by 49ers (October 2, 1989). . . . Awarded on waivers to Dallas Cowboys (October 3, 1989). . . . Released by Cowboys (November 1, 1989). . . . Signed as free agent by San Francisco 49ers to developmental squad (November 4, 1989). . . . Activated after clearing procedural waivers (November 10, 1989). . . . Released by 49ers (September 3, 1990). . . . Signed by San Diego Chargers (September 19, 1990).
PLAYING EXPERIENCE: San Francisco (11)-Dallas (4) NFL, 1989; San Diego NFL, 1990. . . . Games: 1989 (15), 1990 (14). Total: 29.
CHAMPIONSHIP GAME EXPERIENCE: Played in NFC championship game after 1989 season. . . . Played in Super Bowl XXIV after 1989 season.
PRO STATISTICS: 1990—Caught one pass for 12 yards.

HENDRIX, MANNY
CB, COWBOYS

PERSONAL: Born October 20, 1964, at Phoenix. . . . 5-10/185. . . . Full name: Manuel Hendrix.
HIGH SCHOOL: South Mountain (Phoenix).
COLLEGE: Utah.

TRANSACTIONS/CAREER NOTES: Signed as free agent by Dallas Cowboys (May 1, 1986). . . . Released by Cowboys (August 26, 1986). . . . Re-signed by Cowboys (September 23, 1986).
PLAYING EXPERIENCE: Dallas NFL, 1986-1990. . . . Games: 1986 (13), 1987 (12), 1988 (16), 1989 (16), 1990 (16). Total: 73.
PRO STATISTICS: 1986—Recovered one fumble. 1987—Recovered one fumble. 1988—Intercepted one pass for no yards. 1989—Recovered one fumble. 1990—Intercepted one pass and recovered one fumble.

HENLEY, DARRYL
CB, RAMS

PERSONAL: Born October 30, 1966, at Los Angeles. . . . 5-9/172. . . . Full name: Darryl Keith Henley.
HIGH SCHOOL: Damien (La Verne, Calif.).
COLLEGE: UCLA (bachelor of arts degree in history, 1989).

TRANSACTIONS/CAREER NOTES: Selected by Los Angeles Rams in second round (53rd pick overall) of 1989 NFL draft. . . . Signed by Rams (July 16, 1989). . . . On injured reserve with groin injury (September 4-November 3, 1990).
CHAMPIONSHIP GAME EXPERIENCE: Played in NFC championship game after 1989 season.
RECORDS/HONORS: Named as defensive back on THE SPORTING NEWS college All-America team, 1988.
PRO STATISTICS: 1989—Recovered one fumble.

Year	Team	G	INTERCEPTIONS No.	Yds.	Avg.	TD	PUNT RETURNS No.	Yds.	Avg.	TD	TOTAL TD	Pts.	F.
1989—	L.A. Rams NFL	15	1	10	10.0	0	28	266	9.5	0	0	0	1
1990—	L.A. Rams NFL	9	1	0	.0	0	19	195	10.3	0	0	0	0
	Pro totals (2 years)	24	2	10	5.0	0	47	461	9.8	0	0	0	1

HENRY, MAURICE
LB, CHIEFS

PERSONAL: Born March 12, 1967, at Starkville, Miss. . . . 5-11/234. . . . Full name: Maurice Eugene Henry.
HIGH SCHOOL: Salina Central (Salina, Kan.).
COLLEGE: Kansas State.

TRANSACTIONS/CAREER NOTES: Selected by Detroit Lions in sixth round (147th pick overall) of 1990 NFL draft. . . . Signed by Lions (July 19, 1990). . . . Released by Lions (August 23, 1990). . . . Signed by Philadelphia Eagles (August 26, 1990). . . . Released by Eagles (October 31, 1990). . . . Signed by Kansas City Chiefs (April 12, 1991).
PLAYING EXPERIENCE: Philadelphia NFL, 1990. . . . Games: 1990 (7).

HERRMANN, MARK
QB, COLTS

PERSONAL: Born January 8, 1959, at Cincinnati. . . . 6-4/220. . . . Full name: Mark Donald Herrmann.
HIGH SCHOOL: Carmel (Ind.).
COLLEGE: Purdue (bachelor of science degree in business management, 1981).

TRANSACTIONS/CAREER NOTES: Selected by Denver Broncos in fourth round (98th pick overall) of 1981 NFL draft.... Active for 16 games with Broncos in 1981; did not play.... On inactive list (September 19, 1982).... Traded by Broncos with rights to offensive tackle Chris Hinton and first-round pick in 1984 draft to Baltimore Colts for rights to quarterback John Elway (May 2, 1983).... On injured reserve with broken collarbone (August 30-October 28, 1983).... Colts franchise transferred to Indianapolis (March 31, 1984).... On injured reserve with broken thumb (August 28-October 20, 1984).... Granted free agency (February 1, 1985).... Re-signed by Colts and traded to San Diego Chargers for 10th-round pick in 1986 draft (March 27, 1985).... Traded by Chargers to Indianapolis Colts for future considerations (April 27, 1988).... Released by Colts (August 23, 1988).... Signed as free agent by Los Angeles Rams (August 31, 1988).... Released by Rams (September 3, 1990).... Awarded on waivers to Indianapolis Colts (September 5, 1990).... On inactive list (September 9, 1990).... On injured reserve with separated shoulder (September 25-November 20, 1990).

CHAMPIONSHIP GAME EXPERIENCE: Member of Los Angeles Rams for NFC championship game after 1989 season; did not play.

PRO STATISTICS: Passer rating points: 1982 (53.5), 1983 (38.7), 1984 (37.8), 1985 (84.5), 1986 (66.8), 1987 (55.1), 1988 (98.3), 1989 (76.3), 1990 (91.7). Career: 65.3.... 1983—Recovered one fumble. 1985—Recovered two fumbles and fumbled eight times for minus 26 yards. 1987—Recovered one fumble and fumbled once for minus five yards. 1989—Fumbled twice for minus two yards.

Year Team	G	Att.	Cmp.	Pct.	Yds.	TD	Int.	Avg.	Att.	Yds.	Avg.	TD	TD	Pts.	F.
				PASSING							**RUSHING**			**TOTAL**	
1982— Denver NFL	2	60	32	53.3	421	1	4	7.02	3	7	2.3	1	1	6	1
1983— Baltimore NFL	2	36	18	50.0	256	0	3	7.11	1	0	.0	0	0	0	2
1984— Indianapolis NFL	3	56	29	51.8	352	1	6	6.29	0	0		0	0	0	0
1985— San Diego NFL	9	201	132	65.7	1537	10	10	7.65	18	-8	-.4	0	0	0	8
1986— San Diego NFL	6	97	51	52.6	627	2	3	6.46	2	6	3.0	0	0	0	2
1987— San Diego NFL	3	57	37	64.9	405	1	5	7.11	4	-1	-.2	0	0	0	1
1988— L.A. Rams NFL	6	5	4	80.0	38	0	1	7.60	1	-1	-1.0	0	0	0	0
1989— L.A. Rams NFL	3	5	4	80.0	59	0	1	11.80	2	-1	-.5	0	0	0	2
1990— Indianapolis NFL	3	1	1	100.0	6	0	0	6.00	0	0		0	0	0	0
Pro totals (9 years)	37	518	308	59.5	3701	15	32	7.15	31	2	.1	1	1	6	16

HERROD, JEFF
LB, COLTS

PERSONAL: Born July 29, 1966, at Birmingham, Ala.... 6-0/246.... Full name: Jeff Sylvester Herrod.
HIGH SCHOOL: Banks (Birmingham, Ala.).
COLLEGE: Mississippi.
TRANSACTIONS/CAREER NOTES: Selected by Indianapolis Colts in ninth round (243rd pick overall) of 1988 NFL draft.... Signed by Colts (July 13, 1988).... Granted free agency (February 1, 1990).... Re-signed by Colts (September 12, 1990).... Activated (September 14, 1990).... On inactive list (September 30, 1990).
PLAYING EXPERIENCE: Indianapolis NFL, 1988-1990.... Games: 1988 (16), 1989 (15), 1990 (13). Total: 44.
PRO STATISTICS: 1990—Intercepted one pass for 12 yards.

HESTER, JESSIE
WR, COLTS

PERSONAL: Born January 21, 1963, at Belle Glade, Fla.... 5-11/172.... Full name: Jessie Lee Hester.
HIGH SCHOOL: Central (Belle Glade, Fla.).
COLLEGE: Florida State (degree in social science).
TRANSACTIONS/CAREER NOTES: Selected by Tampa Bay Bandits in 1985 USFL territorial draft.... Selected by Los Angeles Raiders in first round (23rd pick overall) of 1985 NFL draft.... Signed by Raiders (July 23, 1985).... Traded by Raiders to Atlanta Falcons for fifth-round pick in 1989 draft (August 22, 1988).... Released by Falcons (August 30, 1989).... Signed as free agent by Indianapolis Colts (March 23, 1990).
PRO STATISTICS: 1985—Recovered one fumble. 1990—Recovered two fumbles.

Year Team	G	Att.	Yds.	Avg.	TD	No.	Yds.	Avg.	TD	TD	Pts.	F.
		RUSHING				**RECEIVING**				**TOTAL**		
1985— L.A. Raiders NFL	16	1	13	13.0	1	32	665	20.8	4	5	30	0
1986— L.A. Raiders NFL	13	0	0		0	23	632	27.5	6	6	36	1
1987— L.A. Raiders NFL	10	0	0		0	1	30	30.0	0	0	0	0
1988— Atlanta NFL	16	1	3	3.0	0	12	176	14.7	0	0	0	1
1990— Indianapolis NFL	16	4	9	2.3	0	54	924	17.1	6	6	36	0
Pro totals (5 years)	71	6	25	4.2	1	122	2427	19.9	16	17	102	2

HEYWARD, CRAIG
FB, SAINTS

PERSONAL: Born September 26, 1966, at Passaic, N.J.... 5-11/260.... Full name: Craig W. Heyward.
HIGH SCHOOL: Passaic (N.J.).
COLLEGE: Pittsburgh.
TRANSACTIONS/CAREER NOTES: Selected by New Orleans Saints in first round (24th pick overall) of 1988 NFL draft.... Signed by Saints (July 8, 1988).
RECORDS/HONORS: Named as running back on THE SPORTING NEWS college All-America team, 1987.
PRO STATISTICS: 1988—Recovered one fumble. 1989—Recovered one fumble. 1990—Attempted one pass with no completions.

Year Team	G	Att.	Yds.	Avg.	TD	No.	Yds.	Avg.	TD	TD	Pts.	F.
		RUSHING				**RECEIVING**				**TOTAL**		
1988— New Orleans NFL	11	74	355	4.8	1	13	105	8.1	0	1	6	0
1989— New Orleans NFL	16	49	183	3.7	1	13	69	5.3	0	1	6	2
1990— New Orleans NFL	16	129	599	4.6	4	18	121	6.7	0	4	24	3
Pro totals (3 years)	43	252	1137	4.5	6	44	295	6.7	0	6	36	5

HICKS, CLIFFORD
CB, BILLS

PERSONAL: Born August 18, 1964, at San Diego. . . . 5-10/188. . . . Full name: Clifford Wendell Hicks Jr.
HIGH SCHOOL: Kearny (San Diego).
COLLEGE: San Diego Mesa College, then Oregon.
TRANSACTIONS/CAREER NOTES: Selected by Los Angeles Rams in third round (74th pick overall) of 1987 NFL draft. . . . Signed by Rams (July 23, 1987). . . . On injured reserve with broken leg (August 29-November 4, 1988). . . . On injured reserve with knee injury (December 29, 1989-remainder of 1989 season playoffs). . . . On reserve/physically unable to perform list (August 28-November 6, 1990). . . . On inactive list (November 18, 1990). . . . Released by Rams (November 23, 1990). . . . Signed by Buffalo Bills (December 4, 1990).
CHAMPIONSHIP GAME EXPERIENCE: Played in AFC championship game after 1990 season. . . . Played in Super Bowl XXV after 1990 season.
PRO STATISTICS: 1987—Returned four kickoffs for 119 yards (29.8 avg.).

| | | | INTERCEPTIONS | | | | PUNT RETURNS | | | | TOTAL | |
Year Team	G	No.	Yds.	Avg.	TD	No.	Yds.	Avg.	TD	TD	Pts.	F.
1987— L.A. Rams NFL	11	1	9	9.0	0	13	110	8.5	0	0	0	1
1988— L.A. Rams NFL	7	0	0		0	25	144	5.8	0	0	0	1
1989— L.A. Rams NFL	15	2	27	13.5	0	4	39	9.8	0	0	0	0
1990— Rams (1)-Buff. (4) NFL	5	1	0	.0	0	0	0		0	0	0	0
Pro totals (4 years)	38	4	36	9.0	0	42	293	7.0	0	0	0	2

HIGGS, MARK
RB, DOLPHINS

PERSONAL: Born April 11, 1966, at Chicago. . . . 5-7/195. . . . Full name: Mark Deyon Higgs.
HIGH SCHOOL: Owensboro (Ky.).
COLLEGE: Kentucky.
TRANSACTIONS/CAREER NOTES: Selected by Dallas Cowboys in eighth round (205th pick overall) of 1988 NFL draft. . . . Signed by Cowboys (July 6, 1988). . . . Granted unconditional free agency (February 1, 1989). . . . Signed by Philadelphia Eagles (March 2, 1989). . . . Granted unconditional free agency (February 1, 1990). . . . Signed by Miami Dolphins (April 1, 1990). . . . On injured reserve with hamstring injury (December 7, 1990-remainder of regular season and playoffs).
PRO STATISTICS: 1989—Recovered one fumble. 1990—Returned blocked punt 19 yards for a touchdown.

| | | RUSHING | | | | RECEIVING | | | | KICKOFF RETURNS | | | | TOTAL | |
Year Team	G	Att.	Yds.	Avg.	TD	No.	Yds.	Avg.	TD	No.	Yds.	Avg.	TD	TD	Pts.	F.
1988— Dallas NFL	5	0	0		0	0	0		0	2	31	15.5	0	0	0	0
1989— Philadelphia NFL	15	49	184	3.8	0	3	9	3.0	0	16	293	18.3	0	0	0	3
1990— Miami NFL	12	10	67	6.7	0	0	0		0	10	210	21.0	0	1	6	1
Pro totals (3 years)	32	59	251	4.3	0	3	9	3.0	0	28	534	19.1	0	1	6	4

HIGHSMITH, ALONZO
FB, COWBOYS

PERSONAL: Born February 26, 1965, at Bartow, Fla. . . . 6-1/237. . . . Full name: Alonzo Walter Highsmith. . . . Son of Walter Highsmith, offensive lineman with Charleston of Continental Football League, 1965-1967; Denver Broncos and Houston Oilers, 1968, 1969 and 1972; with Montreal Alouettes; and currently head coach at Texas Southern University.
HIGH SCHOOL: Christopher Columbus (Miami).
COLLEGE: Miami, Fla. (bachelor of science degree in business management, 1987).
TRANSACTIONS/CAREER NOTES: Selected by Houston Oilers in first round (third pick overall) of 1987 NFL draft. . . . On reserve/unsigned list (August 31-October 27, 1987). . . . Signed by Houston Oilers (October 28, 1987). . . . Granted roster exemption (October 28-November 7, 1987). . . . Traded by Oilers to Dallas Cowboys for second-round pick in 1991 NFL draft and fifth-round pick in 1992 draft (September 3, 1990). . . . On injured reserve with knee injury (November 7, 1990-remainder of season).
PRO STATISTICS: 1988—Recovered two fumbles. 1989—Recovered two fumbles.

| | | RUSHING | | | | RECEIVING | | | | TOTAL | |
Year Team	G	Att.	Yds.	Avg.	TD	No.	Yds.	Avg.	TD	TD	Pts.	F.
1987— Houston NFL	8	29	106	3.7	1	4	55	13.8	1	2	12	2
1988— Houston NFL	16	94	466	5.0	2	12	131	10.9	0	2	12	7
1989— Houston NFL	16	128	531	4.2	4	18	201	11.2	2	6	36	6
1990— Dallas NFL	7	19	48	2.5	0	3	13	4.3	0	0	0	1
Pro totals (4 years)	47	270	1151	4.3	7	37	400	10.8	3	10	60	16

HILGENBERG, JAY
C, BEARS

PERSONAL: Born March 21, 1959, at Iowa City, Ia. . . . 6-3/260. . . . Full name: Jay Walter Hilgenberg. . . . Brother of Joel Hilgenberg, center/guard with New Orleans Saints; and nephew of Wally Hilgenberg, linebacker with Detroit Lions and Minnesota Vikings, 1964-1979.
HIGH SCHOOL: City (Iowa City, Ia.).
COLLEGE: Iowa.
TRANSACTIONS/CAREER NOTES: Signed as free agent by Chicago Bears (May 8, 1981).
PLAYING EXPERIENCE: Chicago NFL, 1981-1990. Games: 1981 (16), 1982 (9), 1983 (16), 1984 (16), 1985 (16), 1986 (16), 1987 (12), 1988 (16), 1989 (16), 1990 (14). Total: 147.
CHAMPIONSHIP GAME EXPERIENCE: Played in NFC championship game after 1984, 1985 and 1988 seasons. . . . Played in Super Bowl XX after 1985 season.
RECORDS/HONORS: Played in Pro Bowl after 1985-1990 seasons. . . . Named to THE SPORTING NEWS NFL All-Pro team, 1987 and 1988.

PRO STATISTICS: 1982—Recovered one fumble for five yards. 1983—Recovered one fumble. 1985—Recovered one fumble. 1986—Fumbled once for minus 28 yards. 1988—Fumbled once for minus 18 yards and recovered one fumble.

HILGENBERG, JOEL
C/G, SAINTS

PERSONAL: Born July 10, 1962, at Iowa City, Ia. . . . 6-2/252. . . . Brother of Jay Hilgenberg, center with Chicago Bears; and nephew of Wally Hilgenberg, linebacker with Detroit Lions and Minnesota Vikings, 1964-1979.
HIGH SCHOOL: City (Iowa City, Ia.).

COLLEGE: Iowa.
TRANSACTIONS/CAREER NOTES: Selected by Washington Federals in sixth round (109th pick overall) of 1984 USFL draft. . . . USFL rights traded by Federals with first-round pick in 1985 draft to Birmingham Stallions for quarterback Reggie Collier (January 12, 1984). . . . Selected by New Orleans Saints in fourth round (97th pick overall) of 1984 NFL draft. . . . Signed by Saints (July 24, 1984). . . . On injured reserve with dislocated elbow (October 30-December 7, 1984).
PLAYING EXPERIENCE: New Orleans NFL, 1984-1990. . . . Games: 1984 (10), 1985 (15), 1986 (16), 1987 (12), 1988 (16), 1989 (16), 1990 (16). Total: 101.
PRO STATISTICS: 1985—Recovered one fumble. 1987—Recovered one fumble. 1989—Recovered one fumble and fumbled once for minus 37 yards. 1990—Caught one pass for nine yards and recovered one fumble.

HILGER, RUSTY
QB, COLTS

PERSONAL: Born May 9, 1962, at Oklahoma City. . . . 6-4/209. . . . Full name: Russell Todd Hilger.
HIGH SCHOOL: Southeast (Oklahoma City).
COLLEGE: Oklahoma State.

TRANSACTIONS/CAREER NOTES: Selected by Denver Gold in 1985 USFL territorial draft. . . . Selected by Los Angeles Raiders in sixth round (143rd pick overall) of 1985 NFL draft. . . . Signed by Raiders (July 21, 1985). . . . Crossed picket line during players' strike (October 14, 1987). . . . Released by Raiders (August 30, 1988). . . . Signed by Detroit Lions (October 4, 1988). . . . Released by Lions (September 4, 1989). . . . Signed by Seattle Seahawks (July 22, 1990). . . . Released by Seahawks (August 28, 1990). . . . Signed by Indianapolis Colts (October 31, 1990). . . . Active for nine games with Colts in 1990; did not play.
PRO STATISTICS: Passer rating points: 1985 (70.7), 1986 (70.7), 1987 (55.8), 1988 (48.9). Career: 52.9. . . . 1985—Recovered one fumble. 1986—Recovered one fumble and fumbled three times for minus seven yards. 1987—Recovered one fumble. 1988—Recovered five fumbles and fumbled seven times for minus 19 yards.

| | | | PASSING | | | | | | RUSHING | | | | TOTAL | | |
Year Team	G	Att.	Cmp.	Pct.	Yds.	TD	Int.	Avg.	Att.	Yds.	Avg.	TD	TD	Pts.	F.
1985— L.A. Raiders NFL	4	13	4	30.8	54	1	0	4.15	3	8	2.7	0	0	0	1
1986— L.A. Raiders NFL	2	38	19	50.0	266	1	1	7.00	6	48	8.0	0	0	0	3
1987— L.A. Raiders NFL	5	106	55	51.9	706	2	6	6.66	8	8	1.0	0	0	0	3
1988— Detroit NFL	11	306	126	41.2	1558	7	12	5.09	18	27	1.5	0	0	0	7
Pro totals (4 years)	22	463	204	44.1	2584	11	19	5.58	35	91	2.6	0	0	0	14

HILL, BRUCE
WR, BUCCANEERS

PERSONAL: Born February 29, 1964, at Fort Dix, N.J. . . . 6-0/180. . . . Full name: Bruce Edward Hill.
HIGH SCHOOL: Antelope Valley (Lancaster, Calif.).
COLLEGE: Arizona State.

TRANSACTIONS/CAREER NOTES: Selected by Tampa Bay Buccaneers in fourth round (106th pick overall) of 1987 NFL draft. . . . Signed by Buccaneers (July 20, 1987). . . . On injured reserve with knee injury (September 7-November 7, 1987). . . . Granted free agency (February 1, 1990). . . . Re-signed by Buccaneers (August 3, 1990). . . . On inactive list (October 21; and November 4 and 18, 1990).
PRO STATISTICS: 1987—Returned one kickoff for eight yards and recovered one fumble. 1988—Recovered one fumble.

| | | RUSHING | | | | RECEIVING | | | | TOTAL | | |
Year Team	G	Att.	Yds.	Avg.	TD	No.	Yds.	Avg.	TD	TD	Pts.	F.
1987— Tampa Bay NFL	8	3	3	1.0	0	23	402	17.5	2	2	12	1
1988— Tampa Bay NFL	14	2	-11	-5.5	0	58	1040	17.9	9	9	54	2
1989— Tampa Bay NFL	16	0	0		0	50	673	13.5	5	5	30	2
1990— Tampa Bay NFL	13	1	0	.0	0	42	641	15.3	5	5	30	0
Pro totals (4 years)	51	6	-8	-1.3	0	173	2756	15.9	21	21	126	5

HILL, DEREK
WR, CARDINALS

PERSONAL: Born November 4, 1967, at Detroit. . . . 6-2/210. . . . Full name: Derek Keith Hill.
HIGH SCHOOL: Carson (Los Angeles).
COLLEGE: Arizona.

TRANSACTIONS/CAREER NOTES: Selected by Pittsburgh Steelers in third round (61st pick overall) of 1989 NFL draft. . . . Signed by Steelers (July 22, 1989). . . . Granted unconditional free agency (February 1, 1991). . . . Signed by Phoenix Cardinals (March 12, 1991).
PRO STATISTICS: 1990—Recovered one fumble.

| | | RECEIVING | | | | PUNT RETURNS | | | | TOTAL | | |
Year Team	G	No.	Yds.	Avg.	TD	No.	Yds.	Avg.	TD	TD	Pts.	F.
1989— Pittsburgh NFL	16	28	455	16.3	1	5	22	4.4	0	1	6	2
1990— Pittsburgh NFL	16	25	391	15.6	0	1	0	.0	0	0	0	1
Pro totals (2 years)	32	53	846	16.0	1	6	22	3.7	0	1	6	3

HILL, DREW
WR, OILERS

PERSONAL: Born October 5, 1956, at Newman, Ga. . . . 5-9/172. . . . Full name: Andrew Hill.
HIGH SCHOOL: Newman (Ga.).
COLLEGE: Georgia Tech (bachelor of arts degree in industrial management, 1981).
TRANSACTIONS/CAREER NOTES: Selected by Los Angeles Rams in 12th round (328th pick overall) of 1979 NFL draft. . . . On injured reserve with back injury (August 24, 1983-entire season). . . . Traded by Rams to Houston Oilers for seventh-round pick in 1986 draft and fourth-round pick in 1987 draft (July 3, 1985). . . . On reserve/did not report list (July 31-September 5, 1989).
CHAMPIONSHIP GAME EXPERIENCE: Played in NFC championship game after 1979 season. . . . Played in Super Bowl XIV after 1979 season.
RECORDS/HONORS: Established NFL record for most kickoff returns, season (60), 1981. . . . Named to play in Pro Bowl after 1988 season; replaced due to injury by Andre Reed. . . . Played in Pro Bowl after 1990 season.
PRO STATISTICS: 1979—Returned one punt for no yards. 1980—Recovered one fumble and rushed once for four yards. 1981—Rushed once for 14 yards, returned two punts for 22 yards and recovered one fumble. 1987—Attempted one pass with no completions. 1989—Recovered one fumble for five yards.

			RECEIVING				KICKOFF RETURNS				TOTAL		
Year Team	G	No.	Yds.	Avg.	TD	No.	Yds.	Avg.	TD		TD	Pts.	F.
1979— L.A. Rams NFL	16	4	94	23.5	1	40	803	20.1	0		1	6	2
1980— L.A. Rams NFL	16	19	416	21.9	2	43	880	20.5	*1		3	18	2
1981— L.A. Rams NFL	16	16	355	22.2	3	*60	1170	19.5	0		3	18	1
1982— L.A. Rams NFL	9	7	92	13.1	0	2	42	21.0	0		0	0	0
1984— L.A. Rams NFL	16	14	390	27.9	4	26	543	20.9	0		4	24	0
1985— Houston NFL	16	64	1169	18.3	9	1	22	22.0	0		9	54	0
1986— Houston NFL	16	65	1112	17.1	5	0	0		0		5	30	0
1987— Houston NFL	12	49	989	20.2	6	0	0		0		6	36	1
1988— Houston NFL	16	72	1141	15.9	10	0	0		0		10	60	0
1989— Houston NFL	14	66	938	14.2	8	0	0		0		8	48	1
1990— Houston NFL	16	74	1019	13.8	5	0	0		0		5	30	0
Pro totals (11 years)	163	450	7715	17.1	53	172	3460	20.1	1		54	324	7

HILL, ERIC
LB, CARDINALS

PERSONAL: Born November 14, 1966, at Galveston, Tex. . . . 6-2/250.
HIGH SCHOOL: Ball (Galveston, Tex.).
COLLEGE: Louisiana State.
TRANSACTIONS/CAREER NOTES: Selected by Phoenix Cardinals in first round (10th pick overall) of 1989 NFL draft. . . . Signed by Cardinals (August 18, 1989).
PLAYING EXPERIENCE: Phoenix NFL, 1989 and 1990. . . . Games: 1989 (15), 1990 (16). Total: 31.
PRO STATISTICS: 1989—Recovered one fumble.

HILL, LONZELL
WR, SAINTS

PERSONAL: Born September 25, 1965, at Stockton, Calif. . . . 5-11/189. . . . Full name: Lonzell Ramon Hill. . . . Son of J.D. Hill Sr., wide receiver with Buffalo Bills and Detroit Lions, 1971-1977; and cousin of Paul Dunn, former wide receiver with Cincinnati Bengals, Washington Redskins and Philadelphia Bell (WFL).
HIGH SCHOOL: Amos Alonzo Stagg (Stockton, Calif.).
COLLEGE: Washington.
TRANSACTIONS/CAREER NOTES: Selected by New Orleans Saints in second round (40th pick overall) of 1987 NFL draft. . . . Signed by Saints (August 8, 1987). . . . Granted free agency (February 1, 1990). . . . Re-signed by Saints (July 29, 1990). . . . On inactive list (October 21, 1990).
PRO STATISTICS: 1987—Recovered one fumble. 1988—Attempted one pass with no completions. 1989—Returned one kickoff for 13 yards.

		RUSHING				RECEIVING				PUNT RETURNS				TOTAL		
Year Team	G	Att.	Yds.	Avg.	TD	No.	Yds.	Avg.	TD	No.	Yds.	Avg.	TD	TD	Pts.	F.
1987— New Orleans NFL	10	1	-9	-9.0	0	19	322	17.0	2	0	0		0	2	12	0
1988— New Orleans NFL	16	2	7	3.5	0	66	703	10.7	7	10	108	10.8	0	7	42	3
1989— New Orleans NFL	16	1	-7	-7.0	0	48	636	13.3	4	7	41	5.9	0	4	24	1
1990— New Orleans NFL	13	0	0		0	3	35	11.7	0	0	0		0	0	0	0
Pro totals (4 years)	55	4	-9	-2.2	0	136	1696	12.5	13	17	149	8.8	0	13	78	4

HILLIARD, DALTON
RB, SAINTS

PERSONAL: Born January 21, 1964, at Patterson, La. . . . 5-8/204. . . . Name pronounced HILL-yerd.
HIGH SCHOOL: Patterson (La.).
COLLEGE: Louisiana State.
TRANSACTIONS/CAREER NOTES: Selected by Tampa Bay Bandits in 1986 USFL territorial draft. . . . Selected by New Orleans Saints in second round (31st pick overall) of 1986 NFL draft. . . . Signed by Saints (July 21, 1986). . . . On inactive list (October 28; November 4, 11, 18, 25; and December 2, 16, 23 and 31, 1990).
RECORDS/HONORS: Played in Pro Bowl after 1989 season.
PRO STATISTICS: 1986—Attempted three passes with one completion for 29 yards and a touchdown. 1987—Attempted one pass with one completion for 23 yards and a touchdown. 1988—Attempted two passes with one completion for 27 yards and a touchdown. 1989—Attempted one pass with one completion for 35 yards and a touchdown and recovered two fumbles. 1990—Recovered one fumble.

		RUSHING				RECEIVING				KICKOFF RETURNS				TOTAL		
Year Team	G	Att.	Yds.	Avg.	TD	No.	Yds.	Avg.	TD	No.	Yds.	Avg.	TD	TD	Pts.	F.
1986— New Orleans NFL	16	121	425	3.5	5	17	107	6.3	0	0	0		0	5	30	3
1987— New Orleans NFL	12	123	508	4.1	7	23	264	11.5	1	10	248	24.8	0	8	48	4

Year — Team		RUSHING				RECEIVING				KICKOFF RETURNS				TOTAL		
	G	Att.	Yds.	Avg.	TD	No.	Yds.	Avg.	TD	No.	Yds.	Avg.	TD	TD	Pts.	F.
1988— New Orleans NFL...	16	204	823	4.0	5	34	335	9.9	1	6	111	18.5	0	6	36	3
1989— New Orleans NFL...	16	344	1262	3.7	13	52	514	9.9	5	1	20	20.0	0	*18	108	7
1990— New Orleans NFL...	6	90	284	3.2	0	14	125	8.9	1	0	0		0	1	6	2
Pro totals (5 years)	66	882	3302	3.7	30	140	1345	9.6	8	17	379	22.3	0	38	228	19

HILLIARD, RANDY
CB, BROWNS

PERSONAL: Born June 2, 1967, at Metairie, La. . . . 5-11/160.
HIGH SCHOOL: East Jefferson (Metairie, La.).
COLLEGE: Northwestern (La.) State.
TRANSACTIONS/CAREER NOTES: Selected by Cleveland Browns in sixth round (157th pick overall) of 1990 NFL draft. . . . Signed by Browns (July 22, 1990).
PLAYING EXPERIENCE: Cleveland NFL, 1990. . . . Games: 1990 (15).

HINKLE, BRYAN
LB, STEELERS

PERSONAL: Born June 4, 1959, at Long Beach, Calif. . . . 6-2/220. . . . Full name: Bryan Eric Hinkle.
HIGH SCHOOL: Central Kitsap (Silverdale, Wash.).
COLLEGE: Oregon (degree in business).
TRANSACTIONS/CAREER NOTES: Selected by Pittsburgh Steelers in sixth round (156th pick overall) of 1981 NFL draft. . . . On injured reserve with ankle injury and concussion (August 31, 1981-entire season). . . . On injured reserve with torn quadricep (January 7, 1983-remainder of 1982 season playoffs). . . . On injured reserve with dislocated toe (December 1, 1988-remainder of season).
CHAMPIONSHIP GAME EXPERIENCE: Played in AFC championship game after 1984 season.
PRO STATISTICS: 1983—Recovered two fumbles for four yards. 1984—Recovered two fumbles for 21 yards and a touchdown. 1986—Recovered one fumble. 1987—Recovered one fumble and fumbled once. 1988—Recovered one fumble for five yards. 1989—Recovered one fumble. 1990—Recovered two fumbles.

Year — Team		INTERCEPTIONS			
	G	No.	Yds.	Avg.	TD
1982— Pittsburgh NFL	9	0	0		0
1983— Pittsburgh NFL	16	1	14	14.0	1
1984— Pittsburgh NFL	15	3	77	25.7	0
1985— Pittsburgh NFL	14	0	0		0
1986— Pittsburgh NFL	16	3	7	2.3	0
1987— Pittsburgh NFL	12	3	15	5.0	0
1988— Pittsburgh NFL	13	1	1	1.0	0
1989— Pittsburgh NFL	13	1	4	4.0	0
1990— Pittsburgh NFL	16	1	19	19.0	0
Pro totals (9 years)	124	13	137	10.5	1

HINKLE, GEORGE
DE, CHARGERS

PERSONAL: Born March 17, 1965, at St. Louis. . . . 6-5/269. . . . Full name: George Allen Hinkle Jr.
HIGH SCHOOL: Pacific (Mo.).
COLLEGE: Arizona (received degree, 1988).
TRANSACTIONS/CAREER NOTES: Selected by San Diego Chargers in 11th round (293rd pick overall) of 1988 NFL draft. . . . Signed by Chargers (July 13, 1988). . . . On injured reserve with foot injury (August 29-December 3, 1988).
PLAYING EXPERIENCE: San Diego NFL, 1988-1990. . . . Games: 1988 (3), 1989 (14), 1990 (16). Total: 33.

HINTON, CHRIS
OT, FALCONS

PERSONAL: Born July 31, 1961, at Chicago. . . . 6-4/300. . . . Full name: Christopher Jerrod Hinton.
HIGH SCHOOL: Wendell Phillips (Chicago).
COLLEGE: Northwestern (degree in sociology).
TRANSACTIONS/CAREER NOTES: Selected by Chicago Blitz in 1983 USFL territorial draft. . . . Selected by Denver Broncos in first round (fourth pick overall) of 1983 NFL draft. . . . Rights traded by Broncos with quarterback Mark Herrmann and first-round pick in 1984 draft to Baltimore Colts for rights to quarterback John Elway (May 2, 1983). . . . Signed by Colts (May 12, 1983). . . . Franchise transferred to Indianapolis (March 31, 1984). . . . On injured reserve with fractured fibula (October 8, 1984-remainder of season). . . . Traded by Indianapolis Colts with wide receiver Andre Rison, fifth-round pick in 1990 NFL draft and first-round pick in 1991 draft to Atlanta Falcons for first- and fourth-round picks in 1990 draft (April 20, 1990). . . . On reserve/did not report list (July 27-August 28, 1990). . . . Granted roster exemption (August 28-August 30, 1990).
PLAYING EXPERIENCE: Baltimore NFL, 1983; Indianapolis NFL, 1984-1989; Atlanta 1990. . . . Games: 1983 (16), 1984 (6), 1985 (16), 1986 (16), 1987 (12), 1988 (14), 1989 (14), 1990 (15). Total: 109.
RECORDS/HONORS: Named as offensive tackle on THE SPORTING NEWS college All-America team, 1982. . . . Played in Pro Bowl after 1983 and 1985-1989 seasons. . . . Named to THE SPORTING NEWS NFL All-Pro team, 1987.
PRO STATISTICS: 1983—Recovered one fumble. 1986—Recovered two fumbles. 1987—Recovered one fumble. 1988—Caught one pass for one yard. 1989—Recovered two fumbles. 1990—Recovered one fumble.

HOAGE, TERRY
S, REDSKINS

PERSONAL: Born April 11, 1962, at Ames, Ia. . . . 6-2/201. . . . Full name: Terrell Lee Hoage.
HIGH SCHOOL: Huntsville (Tex.).
COLLEGE: Georgia (degree in genetics).
TRANSACTIONS/CAREER NOTES: Selected by Jacksonville Bulls in 1984 USFL territorial draft. . . .

Selected by New Orleans Saints in third round (68th pick overall) of 1984 NFL draft.... Signed by Saints (July 25, 1984)....
Released by Saints (August 26, 1986).... Signed as free agent by Philadelphia Eagles (September 3, 1986).... On injured reserve with calf injury (September 15-November 9, 1989).... Transferred to developmental squad (November 9-November 13, 1989).... Granted free agency (February 1, 1990).... Re-signed by Eagles (August 16, 1990).... Granted unconditional free agency (February 1, 1991).... Signed by Washington Redskins (March 28, 1991).
RECORDS/HONORS: Named as defensive back on THE SPORTING NEWS college All-America team, 1983.
PRO STATISTICS: 1984—Recovered one fumble. 1985—Recovered two fumbles. 1986—Recovered two fumbles. 1987—Recovered two fumbles. 1988—Rushed once for 38 yards and a touchdown.

			—— INTERCEPTIONS——		
Year Team	G	No.	Yds.	Avg.	TD
1984— New Orleans NFL	14	0	0		0
1985— New Orleans NFL	16	4	79	19.8	*1
1986— Philadelphia NFL	16	1	18	18.0	0
1987— Philadelphia NFL	11	2	3	1.5	0
1988— Philadelphia NFL	16	8	116	14.5	0
1989— Philadelphia NFL	6	0	0		0
1990— Philadelphia NFL	16	1	0	.0	0
Pro totals (7 years)	95	16	216	13.5	1

HOARD, LEROY
RB, BROWNS

PERSONAL: Born May 5, 1968, at New Orleans.... 5-11/230.
HIGH SCHOOL: St. Augustine (New Orleans).
COLLEGE: Michigan.
TRANSACTIONS/CAREER NOTES: Selected by Cleveland Browns in second round (45th pick overall) of 1990 NFL draft.... Signed by Browns (July 29, 1990).

		——RUSHING——				——RECEIVING——				– KICKOFF RETURNS –				——TOTAL——		
Year Team	G	Att.	Yds.	Avg.	TD	No.	Yds.	Avg.	TD	No.	Yds.	Avg.	TD	TD	Pts.	F.
1990— Cleveland NFL	14	58	149	2.6	3	10	73	7.3	0	2	18	9.0	0	3	18	6
Pro totals (1 year)	14	58	149	2.6	3	10	73	7.3	0	2	18	9.0	0	3	18	6

HOBBS, STEPHEN
WR, REDSKINS

PERSONAL: Born November 14, 1965, at Mendenhall, Miss.... 5-11/195.
HIGH SCHOOL: Mendenhall (Miss.).
COLLEGE: Copiah-Lincoln Junior College (Miss.), then North Alabama.
TRANSACTIONS/CAREER NOTES: Signed as free agent by Kansas City Chiefs (May, 1988).
... On injured reserve with knee injury (August 22, 1988-entire season).... Granted unconditional free agency (February 1, 1989).... Signed by Washington Redskins (March 7, 1989).... On injured reserve (September 6, 1989-entire season).... Released by Redskins (September 3, 1990).... Re-signed by Redskins (September 5, 1990).... On injured reserve with knee injury (September 5-November 16, 1990).

		——RECEIVING——				— KICKOFF RETURNS—				— TOTAL —		
Year Team	G	No.	Yds.	Avg.	TD	No.	Yds.	Avg.	TD	TD	Pts.	F.
1990— Washington NFL	7	1	18	18.0	1	6	92	15.3	0	1	6	0
Pro totals (1 year)	7	1	18	18.0	1	6	92	15.3	0	1	6	0

HOBBY, MARION
DE, PATRIOTS

PERSONAL: Born November 7, 1966, at Birmingham, Ala.... 6-4/277.... Full name: Marion Eugene Hobby Jr.
HIGH SCHOOL: Shades Valley (Birmingham, Ala.).
COLLEGE: Tennessee (degree in theraputic recreation).
TRANSACTIONS/CAREER NOTES: Selected by Minnesota Vikings in third round (74th pick overall) of 1990 NFL draft.... Signed by Vikings (July 30, 1990).... Released by Vikings (September 3, 1990).... Awarded on waivers to New England Patriots (September 4, 1990).
PLAYING EXPERIENCE: New England NFL, 1990.... Games: 1990 (16).

HOBLEY, LIFFORT
S, DOLPHINS

PERSONAL: Born May 12, 1962, at Shreveport, La. ... 6-0/202. ... Name pronounced LIFF-ert HOBB-lee.
HIGH SCHOOL: C.E. Byrd (Shreveport, La.).
COLLEGE: Louisiana State.
TRANSACTIONS/CAREER NOTES: Selected by Portland Breakers in 1985 USFL territorial draft.... Selected by Pittsburgh Steelers in third round (74th pick overall) of 1985 NFL draft.... Signed by Steelers (June 5, 1985).... Released by Steelers (August 25, 1985).... Signed as free agent by San Diego Chargers (August 28, 1985).... Released by Chargers after failing physical (August 29, 1985).... Signed as free agent by St. Louis Cardinals (September 11, 1985).... Released by Cardinals (October 15, 1985).... Signed as free agent by Miami Dolphins (March 6, 1986).... Released by Dolphins (August 19, 1986).... Re-signed by Dolphins (April 21, 1987).... Released by Dolphins (September 7, 1987).... Re-signed by Dolphins (September 8, 1987).... Crossed picket line during players' strike (October 7, 1987).... On injured reserve with knee injury (December 19, 1990-remainder of regular season and playoffs).
PRO STATISTICS: 1987—Recovered four fumbles for 55 yards and a touchdown. 1988—Recovered two fumbles for 19 yards and a touchdown. 1989—Recovered one fumble for 12 yards. 1990—Fumbled once.

Year	Team	G	No.	Yds.	Avg.	TD
			— INTERCEPTIONS —			
1985— St. Louis NFL		5	0	0		0
1987— Miami NFL		14	2	7	3.5	0
1988— Miami NFL		16	0	0		0
1989— Miami NFL		16	1	22	22.0	0
1990— Miami NFL		14	1	15	15.0	0
Pro totals (5 years)		65	4	44	11.0	0

HODGE, MILFORD
DE, 49ERS

PERSONAL: Born March 11, 1961, at Los Angeles. . . . 6-3/278.
HIGH SCHOOL: South (San Francisco).
COLLEGE: Washington State.
TRANSACTIONS/CAREER NOTES: Selected by New England Patriots in eighth round (224th pick overall) of 1985 NFL draft. . . . Signed by Patriots (July 19, 1985). . . . Released by Patriots (August 28, 1985). . . . Re-signed by Patriots (February 24, 1986). . . . On injured reserve with thumb injury (August 18-September 29, 1986). . . . Released by Patriots (September 30, 1986). . . . Signed as free agent by New Orleans Saints (October 10, 1986). . . . Released by Saints (October 14, 1986). . . . Signed as free agent by New England Patriots (November 14, 1986). . . . Released by Patriots (September 7, 1987). . . . Re-signed by Patriots (September 8, 1987). . . . Granted free agency with no qualifying offer (February 1, 1988). . . . Re-signed by Patriots (April 26, 1988). . . . Granted unconditional free agency (February 1, 1990). . . . Signed by Washington Redskins (March 15, 1990). . . . Released by Redskins (September 3, 1990). . . . Signed by San Francisco 49ers (May 3, 1991).
PLAYING EXPERIENCE: New Orleans (1)-New England (6) NFL, 1986; New England NFL, 1987-1989. . . . Games: 1986 (7), 1987 (12), 1988 (15), 1989 (16). Total: 50.
PRO STATISTICS: 1988—Recovered one fumble for two yards. 1989—Returned two kickoffs for 19 yards.

HODSON, TOM
QB, PATRIOTS

PERSONAL: Born January 28, 1967, at Mathews, La. . . . 6-3/195. . . . Full name: Thomas Paul Hodson.
HIGH SCHOOL: Central Lafourche (Mathews, La.).
COLLEGE: Louisiana State (degree in finance).
TRANSACTIONS/CAREER NOTES: Selected by New England Patriots in third round (59th pick overall) of 1990 NFL draft. . . . Signed by Patriots (July 19, 1990).
PRO STATISTICS: Passer rating points: 1990 (68.5).

Year	Team	G	Att.	Cmp.	Pct.	Yds.	TD	Int.	Avg.	Att.	Yds.	Avg.	TD	TD	Pts.	F.
				— PASSING —						— RUSHING —				— TOTAL —		
1990— New England NFL		7	156	85	54.5	968	4	5	6.21	12	79	6.6	0	0	0	5
Pro totals (1 year)		7	156	85	54.5	968	4	5	6.21	12	79	6.6	0	0	0	5

HOGE, MERRIL
RB, STEELERS

PERSONAL: Born January 26, 1965, at Pocatello, Idaho. . . . 6-2/229. . . . Full name: Merril D. Hoge. . . . Name pronounced HODGE.
HIGH SCHOOL: Highland (Pocatello, Idaho).
COLLEGE: Idaho State.
TRANSACTIONS/CAREER NOTES: Selected by Pittsburgh Steelers in 10th round (261st pick overall) of 1987 NFL draft. . . . Signed by Steelers (July 26, 1987). . . . Crossed picket line during players' strike (October 13, 1987).
PRO STATISTICS: 1987—Returned one kickoff for 13 yards. 1988—Recovered six fumbles. 1989—Recovered two fumbles.

Year	Team	G	Att.	Yds.	Avg.	TD	No.	Yds.	Avg.	TD	TD	Pts.	F.
			— RUSHING —				— RECEIVING —				— TOTAL —		
1987— Pittsburgh NFL		13	3	8	2.7	0	7	97	13.9	1	1	6	0
1988— Pittsburgh NFL		16	170	705	4.1	3	50	487	9.7	3	6	36	8
1989— Pittsburgh NFL		16	186	621	3.3	8	34	271	8.0	0	8	48	2
1990— Pittsburgh NFL		16	203	772	3.8	7	40	342	8.6	3	10	60	6
Pro totals (4 years)		61	562	2106	3.8	18	131	1197	9.1	7	25	150	16

HOLLAND, JAMIE
WR, RAIDERS

PERSONAL: Born February 1, 1964, at Raleigh, N.C. . . . 6-1/195. . . . Full name: Jamie Lorenza Holland.
HIGH SCHOOL: Rolesville (Wake Forest, N.C.).
COLLEGE: Butler County Community College (Kan.), then Ohio State (bachelor's degree in education, 1986).
TRANSACTIONS/CAREER NOTES: Selected by San Diego Chargers in seventh round (173rd pick overall) of 1987 NFL draft. . . . Signed by Chargers (July 25, 1987). . . . Granted free agency (February 1, 1990). . . . Re-signed by Chargers and traded to Los Angeles Raiders for conditional draft pick (May 4, 1990).
CHAMPIONSHIP GAME EXPERIENCE: Played in AFC championship game after 1990 season.

Year	Team	G	Att.	Yds.	Avg.	TD	No.	Yds.	Avg.	TD	No.	Yds.	Avg.	TD	TD	Pts.	F.
			— RUSHING —				— RECEIVING —				— KICKOFF RETURNS —				— TOTAL —		
1987— San Diego NFL		12	1	17	17.0	0	6	138	23.0	0	19	410	21.6	0	0	0	0
1988— San Diego NFL		16	3	19	6.3	0	39	536	13.7	1	31	810	26.1	*1	2	12	1
1989— San Diego NFL		16	6	46	7.7	0	26	336	12.9	0	29	510	17.6	0	0	0	0
1990— L.A. Raiders NFL		16	0	0		0	0	0		0	32	655	20.5	0	0	0	0
Pro totals (4 years)		60	10	82	8.2	0	71	1010	14.2	1	111	2385	21.5	1	2	12	1

HOLLAND, JOHNNY

LB, PACKERS

PERSONAL: Born March 11, 1965, at Bellville, Tex.... 6-2/232.... Full name: Johnny Ray Holland.
HIGH SCHOOL: Hempstead (Tex.).
COLLEGE: Texas A&M.

TRANSACTIONS/CAREER NOTES: Selected by Green Bay Packers in second round (41st pick overall) of 1987 NFL draft.... Signed by Packers (July 25, 1987).
PRO STATISTICS: 1987—Recovered one fumble. 1988—Recovered one fumble. 1989—Recovered three fumbles. 1990—Recovered one fumble.

Year Team	G	No.	Yds.	Avg.	TD
		INTERCEPTIONS			
1987— Green Bay NFL	12	2	4	2.0	0
1988— Green Bay NFL	13	0	0		0
1989— Green Bay NFL	16	1	26	26.0	0
1990— Green Bay NFL	16	1	32	32.0	0
Pro totals (4 years)	57	4	62	15.5	0

HOLLOWAY, CORNELL

DB, COLTS

PERSONAL: Born January 30, 1966, at Alliance, O.... 5-11/182.... Full name: Cornell Duane Holloway.
HIGH SCHOOL: Alliance (O.).
COLLEGE: Pittsburgh.

TRANSACTIONS/CAREER NOTES: Selected by Cincinnati Bengals in 10th round (256th pick overall) of 1989 NFL draft.... Released by Bengals (September 5, 1989).... Signed by Indianapolis Colts to developmental squad (September 7, 1989).... Released by Colts (December 26, 1989).... Re-signed as free agent by Colts (February 20, 1990).
PLAYING EXPERIENCE: Indianapolis NFL, 1990.... Games: 1990 (15).

HOLMAN, RODNEY

TE, BENGALS

PERSONAL: Born April 20, 1960, at Ypsilanti, Mich.... 6-3/238.... Full name: Rodney A. Holman.... Cousin of Preston Pearson, running back with Baltimore Colts, Pittsburgh Steelers and Dallas Cowboys, 1967-1980.
HIGH SCHOOL: Ypsilanti (Mich.).

COLLEGE: Tulane (undergraduate degree, 1981).
TRANSACTIONS/CAREER NOTES: Selected by Cincinnati Bengals in third round (82nd pick overall) of 1982 NFL draft.
CHAMPIONSHIP GAME EXPERIENCE: Played in AFC championship game after 1988 season.... Played in Super Bowl XXIII after 1988 season.
RECORDS/HONORS: Played in Pro Bowl after 1988-1990 seasons.
PRO STATISTICS: 1984—Fumbled once and recovered one fumble. 1985—Fumbled once and recovered one fumble. 1986—Returned one kickoff for 18 yards and fumbled once. 1987—Recovered one fumble. 1988—Fumbled twice and recovered one fumble. 1990—Fumbled once.

Year Team	G	No.	Yds.	Avg.	TD
		RECEIVING			
1982— Cincinnati NFL	9	3	18	6.0	1
1983— Cincinnati NFL	16	2	15	7.5	0
1984— Cincinnati NFL	16	21	239	11.4	1
1985— Cincinnati NFL	16	38	479	12.6	7
1986— Cincinnati NFL	16	40	570	14.3	2
1987— Cincinnati NFL	12	28	438	15.6	2
1988— Cincinnati NFL	16	39	527	13.5	3
1989— Cincinnati NFL	16	50	736	14.7	9
1990— Cincinnati NFL	16	40	596	14.9	5
Pro totals (9 years)	133	261	3618	13.9	30

HOLMES, BRUCE

LB, JETS

PERSONAL: Born October 24, 1965, at El Paso, Tex.... 6-2/241.
HIGH SCHOOL: Henry Ford (Detroit).
COLLEGE: Minnesota.
TRANSACTIONS/CAREER NOTES: Selected by Kansas City Chiefs in 12th round (325th pick overall) of 1987 NFL draft.... Signed by Chiefs (June, 1987).... Released by Chiefs (September, 1987).... Re-signed as replacement player by Chiefs (1987).... Released by Chiefs (1987).... Signed by Cleveland Browns (March, 1988).... Released by Browns (August, 1988).... Signed as free agent by Toronto Argonauts of CFL (September, 1988).... Traded by Argonauts to Ottawa Roughriders for future considerations (October 29, 1989).... Granted free agency (February, 1991).... Signed by New York Jets (March 11, 1991).
PLAYING EXPERIENCE: Kansas City NFL, 1987; Toronto CFL, 1988; Toronto (13)-Ottawa (4) CFL, 1989; Ottawa CFL, 1990.... Games: 1987 (3), 1988 (4), 1989 (17), 1990 (18). Total NFL: 3. Total Pro: 42.

HOLMES, DON

WR, CARDINALS

PERSONAL: Born April 1, 1961, at Miami.... 5-10/181.... Full name: Don Ira Holmes.
HIGH SCHOOL: Northwestern (Miami).
COLLEGE: Colorado, then Gavilan College (Calif.), then Mesa College (Colo.).
TRANSACTIONS/CAREER NOTES: Selected by Oakland Invaders in supplemental round (404th pick overall) of 1984 USFL draft.... Selected by Atlanta Falcons in 12th round (318th pick overall) of 1986 NFL draft.... Signed by Falcons (April 29, 1985).... Released by Falcons (August 23, 1985).... Signed as free agent by Indianapolis Colts for 1986 (December 6, 1985).... On injured reserve with toe injury (August 18-September 28, 1986).... Released after clearing proce-

dural waivers (September 29, 1986).... Awarded to St. Louis Cardinals (September 30, 1986).... Franchise transferred to Phoenix (March 15, 1988).... On injured reserve with ankle injury (October 24, 1990-remainder of season).
PRO STATISTICS: 1986—Returned one kickoff for two yards. 1987—Returned one kickoff for 25 yards.

			RECEIVING			
Year	Team	G	No.	Yds.	Avg.	TD
1986— St. Louis NFL		12	0	0		0
1987— St. Louis NFL		11	11	132	12.0	0
1988— Phoenix NFL		16	1	10	10.0	0
1989— Phoenix NFL		15	13	271	20.8	1
1990— Phoenix NFL		6	0	0		0
Pro totals (5 years)		60	25	413	16.5	1

HOLMES, JERRY
CB, PACKERS

PERSONAL: Born December 22, 1957, at Newport News, Va.... 6-2/178.
HIGH SCHOOL: Bethel (Hampton, Va.).
COLLEGE: Chowan Junior College (N.C.), then West Virginia (degree in personnel management).
TRANSACTIONS/CAREER NOTES: Signed as free agent by New York Jets (June 4, 1980).... On injured reserve with knee injury (October 21-November 22, 1980).... Signed by Pittsburgh Maulers of USFL (September 2, 1983) for contract to take effect after being granted free agency February 1, 1984.... Pittsburgh franchise disbanded (October 25, 1984).... Assigned to Baltimore Stars (November 1, 1984).... Assigned by USFL to New Jersey Generals (January 18, 1985).... On developmental squad for four games (February 23-March 23, 1985).... Granted free agency when USFL suspended operations (August 7, 1986).... Re-signed by New York Jets (August 30, 1986).... Granted roster exemption (August 30-September 10, 1986).... On injured reserve with broken rib (November 16-December 19, 1987).... Released by Jets (August 9, 1988).... Signed as free agent by Detroit Lions (August 17, 1988).... Granted unconditional free agency (February 1, 1990).... Signed by Green Bay Packers (March 27, 1990).
CHAMPIONSHIP GAME EXPERIENCE: Played in AFC championship game after 1982 season.
RECORDS/HONORS: Named as cornerback on THE SPORTING NEWS USFL All-Star team, 1984 and 1985.
PRO STATISTICS: 1981—Recovered one fumble. 1983—Ran back blocked field-goal attempt 57 yards for a touchdown and recovered one fumble for three yards. 1985—Recovered three fumbles and fumbled once. 1990—Recovered three fumbles for 44 yards.

			INTERCEPTIONS			
Year	Team	G	No.	Yds.	Avg.	TD
1980— N.Y. Jets NFL		12	0	0		0
1981— N.Y. Jets NFL		16	1	0	.0	0
1982— N.Y. Jets NFL		9	3	2	.7	0
1983— N.Y. Jets NFL		16	3	107	35.7	1
1984— Pittsburgh USFL		18	2	0	.0	0
1985— New Jersey USFL		14	3	27	9.0	0
1986— N.Y. Jets NFL		15	6	29	4.8	0
1987— N.Y. Jets NFL		8	1	20	20.0	0
1988— Detroit NFL		16	1	32	32.0	0
1989— Detroit NFL		16	6	77	12.8	1
1990— Green Bay NFL		16	3	39	13.0	0
NFL totals (9 years)		124	24	306	12.8	2
USFL totals (2 years)		32	5	27	5.4	0
Pro totals (11 years)		156	29	333	11.5	2

HOLMES, RON
DE, BRONCOS

PERSONAL: Born August 26, 1963, at Fort Benning, Ga. ... 6-4/265. ... Full name: Ronald Holmes.
HIGH SCHOOL: Timberline (Lacey, Wash.).
COLLEGE: Washington.
TRANSACTIONS/CAREER NOTES: Selected by Portland Breakers in 1985 USFL territorial draft.... USFL rights traded by Breakers with rights to linebacker Tim Meamber to Baltimore Stars for rights to defensive end Kenny Neil (February 13, 1985).... Selected by Tampa Bay Buccaneers in first round (eighth pick overall) of 1985 NFL draft.... Signed by Buccaneers (August 4, 1985).... On injured reserve with knee injury (November 18, 1988-remainder of season).... Granted free agency (February 1, 1989).... Re-signed by Buccaneers and traded to Denver Broncos for fourth-round pick in 1990 NFL draft (September 5, 1989).... Granted roster exemption (September 5-September 16, 1989).... On inactive list (September 30 and October 8, 1990).
PLAYING EXPERIENCE: Tampa Bay NFL, 1985-1988; Denver NFL, 1989 and 1990.... Games: 1985 (16), 1986 (14), 1987 (10), 1988 (10), 1989 (15), 1990 (14). Total: 79.
CHAMPIONSHIP GAME EXPERIENCE: Played in AFC championship game after 1989 season.... Played in Super Bowl XXIV after 1989 season.
PRO STATISTICS: 1985—Recovered two fumbles. 1986—Recovered one fumble. 1987—Recovered one fumble. 1990—Recovered one fumble for two yards.

HOLOHAN, PETE
TE, CHIEFS

PERSONAL: Born July 25, 1959, at Albany, N.Y. ... 6-4/247.... Full name: Peter Joseph Holohan.... Name pronounced HO-luh-han.
HIGH SCHOOL: Liverpool (N.Y.).
COLLEGE: Notre Dame.
TRANSACTIONS/CAREER NOTES: Selected by San Diego Chargers in seventh round (189th pick overall) of 1981 NFL draft.... Left

Chargers voluntarily and placed on reserve/left squad list (October 28, 1981).... Reinstated (April 30, 1982).... USFL rights traded by Chicago Blitz with wide receiver Neil Balholm, defensive end Bill Purifoy, tight end Mike Hirn and linebacker Orlando Flanagan to Denver Gold for center Glenn Hyde and defensive end Larry White (December 28, 1983).... Traded by San Diego Chargers to Los Angeles Rams for fourth-round pick in 1988 NFL draft (April 24, 1988).... Granted free agency (February 1, 1990).... Re-signed by Rams (July 25, 1990).... Granted unconditional free agency (February 1, 1991).... Signed by Kansas City Chiefs (April 2, 1991).

CHAMPIONSHIP GAME EXPERIENCE: Played in NFC championship game after 1989 season.

PRO STATISTICS: 1982—Recovered one fumble. 1983—Attempted one pass with no completions. 1984—Attempted two passes with one completion for 25 yards and a touchdown and recovered two fumbles for 19 yards. 1985—Returned one kickoff for no yards, attempted one pass with no completions and fumbled once. 1986—Attempted two passes with one completion for 21 yards. 1987—Recovered one fumble. 1988—Fumbled once. 1989—Rushed once for three yards and fumbled once. 1990—Fumbled twice.

			RECEIVING		
Year Team	G	No.	Yds.	Avg.	TD
1981— San Diego NFL	7	1	14	14.0	0
1982— San Diego NFL	9	0	0		0
1983— San Diego NFL	16	23	272	11.8	2
1984— San Diego NFL	15	56	734	13.1	1
1985— San Diego NFL	15	42	458	10.9	3
1986— San Diego NFL	16	29	356	12.3	1
1987— San Diego NFL	12	20	239	12.0	0
1988— L.A. Rams NFL	16	59	640	10.8	3
1989— L.A. Rams NFL	16	51	510	10.0	2
1990— L.A. Rams NFL	16	49	475	9.7	2
Pro totals (10 years)	138	330	3698	11.2	14

HOLT, ISSIAC
CB, COWBOYS

PERSONAL: Born October 4, 1962, at Birmingham, Ala.... 6-2/198.... Full name: Issiac Holt III.
HIGH SCHOOL: Carver (Birmingham, Ala.).
COLLEGE: Alcorn State.
TRANSACTIONS/CAREER NOTES: Selected by San Antonio Gunslingers in first round (third pick overall) of 1985 USFL draft.... Selected by Minnesota Vikings in second round (30th pick overall) of 1985 NFL draft.... Signed by Vikings (May 24, 1985).... Traded as part of a six-player, 12 draft-choice deal in which Dallas Cowboys sent running back Herschel Walker to Minnesota Vikings in exchange for Holt, linebackers David Howard and Jesse Solomon, running back Darrin Nelson, defensive end Alex Stewart, first-round pick in 1992 draft and conditional first-round picks in 1990 and 1991 drafts, conditional second-round picks in 1990, 1991 and 1992 drafts and conditional third-round pick in 1992 draft (October 12, 1989); Nelson refused to report to Cowboys and was traded to San Diego Chargers, with Minnesota giving Dallas a sixth-round pick in 1990 as well as the original conditional second-round pick in 1991 and San Diego sending a fifth-round pick in 1990 to Minnesota through Dallas (October 17, 1989); deal completed with Dallas retaining Howard, Solomon and Holt and all conditional picks and Cowboys sending third-round picks in 1990 and 1991 and 10th-round pick in 1990 to Minnesota (February 2, 1990).... On inactive list (September 23, 1990).

CHAMPIONSHIP GAME EXPERIENCE: Played in NFC championship game after 1987 season.

PRO STATISTICS: 1986—Recovered blocked punt in end zone for a touchdown and fumbled once. 1988—Credited with a safety.

			INTERCEPTIONS		
Year Team	G	No.	Yds.	Avg.	TD
1985— Minnesota NFL	15	1	0	.0	0
1986— Minnesota NFL	16	8	54	6.8	0
1987— Minnesota NFL	9	2	7	3.5	0
1988— Minnesota NFL	13	2	15	7.5	0
1990— Dallas NFL	15	3	72	24.0	1
1989— Min. (5)-Dal. (9) NFL.	14	1	90	90.0	1
Pro totals (6 years)	82	17	238	14.0	2

HOLT, PIERCE
DE, 49ERS

PERSONAL: Born January 1, 1962, at Marlin, Tex.... 6-4/280.
HIGH SCHOOL: Lamar (Rosenberg, Tex.).
COLLEGE: Angelo State, Tex. (degree in physical education and history).
TRANSACTIONS/CAREER NOTES: Selected by San Francisco 49ers in second round (39th pick overall) of 1988 NFL draft.... Signed by 49ers (July 17, 1988).... On injured reserve with toe injury (August 30-October 24, 1988).
PLAYING EXPERIENCE: San Francisco NFL, 1988-1990.... Games: 1988 (9), 1989 (16), 1990 (16). Total: 41.
CHAMPIONSHIP GAME EXPERIENCE: Played in NFC championship game after 1988-1990 seasons.... Played in Super Bowl XXIII after 1988 season and Super Bowl XXIV after 1989 season.
PRO STATISTICS: 1988—Recovered one fumble. 1989—Recovered one fumble. 1990—Recovered two fumbles.

HOOVER, HOUSTON
G, FALCONS

PERSONAL: Born June 2, 1965, at Yazoo City, Miss.... 6-2/295.... Full name: Houston Roosevelt Hoover.
HIGH SCHOOL: Yazoo City (Miss.).
COLLEGE: Jackson State (degree in business management, 1988).
TRANSACTIONS/CAREER NOTES: Selected by Atlanta Falcons in sixth round (140th pick overall) of 1988 NFL draft.... Signed by Falcons (June 8, 1988).... Granted free agency (February 1, 1990).... Re-signed by Falcons (August 21, 1990).
PLAYING EXPERIENCE: Atlanta NFL, 1988-1990.... Games: 1988 (15), 1989 (16), 1990 (16). Total: 47.
PRO STATISTICS: 1988—Recovered two fumbles.

HOPKINS, WES
S, EAGLES

PERSONAL: Born September 26, 1961, at Birmingham, Ala. . . . 6-1/215.
HIGH SCHOOL: John Carroll (Birmingham, Ala.).
COLLEGE: Southern Methodist.
TRANSACTIONS/CAREER NOTES: Selected by New Jersey Generals in fourth round (46th pick overall) of 1983 USFL draft. . . . Selected by Philadelphia Eagles in second round (35th pick overall) of 1983 NFL draft. . . . Signed by Eagles (May 26, 1983). . . . On injured reserve with knee injury (October 1, 1986-remainder of season). . . . On reserve/physically unable to perform list with knee injury (September 6, 1987-entire season). . . . Crossed picket line during players' strike (October 14, 1987). . . . Granted free agency (February 1, 1990). . . . Re-signed by Eagles (June 19, 1990).
RECORDS/HONORS: Played in Pro Bowl after 1985 season. . . . Named to THE SPORTING NEWS NFL All-Pro team, 1985.
PRO STATISTICS: 1984—Recovered three fumbles. 1985—Recovered two fumbles for 42 yards and fumbled once. 1986—Recovered one fumble for minus four yards. 1988—Recovered one fumble. 1989—Recovered three fumbles for 17 yards. 1990—Recovered one fumble.

			—INTERCEPTIONS—		
Year Team	G	No.	Yds.	Avg.	TD
1983—Philadelphia NFL	14	0	0		0
1984—Philadelphia NFL	16	5	107	21.4	0
1985—Philadelphia NFL	15	6	36	6.0	*1
1986—Philadelphia NFL	4	0	0		0
1988—Philadelphia NFL	16	5	21	4.2	0
1989—Philadelphia NFL	16	0	0		0
1990—Philadelphia NFL	15	5	45	9.0	0
Pro totals (7 years)	96	21	209	10.0	1

HOPPER, DARREL
WR, RAIDERS

PERSONAL: Born March 14, 1964, at Los Angeles. . . . 6-1/210.
HIGH SCHOOL: Carson (Calif.).
COLLEGE: Southern California.
TRANSACTIONS/CAREER NOTES: Signed as free agent by Seattle Seahawks (1985). . . . Released by Seahawks (August 20, 1985). . . . Signed by Los Angeles Raiders (May, 1986); released prior to season. . . . Signed by Edmonton Eskimos of CFL for 1987; released prior to season. . . . Signed by San Diego Chargers (preseason, 1987). . . . Released by Chargers (August, 1987). . . . Re-signed by Chargers for 1987. . . . Signed as free agent by Ottawa Rough Riders of CFL (June, 1989). . . . On practice roster (August 15-August 21, 1990). . . . Granted free agency (September 10, 1990). . . . Signed by Los Angeles Raiders (May, 1991).
PLAYING EXPERIENCE: San Diego NFL, 1987; Ottawa CFL, 1989 and 1990. . . . Games: 1987 (4), 1989 (10), 1990 (6). Total NFL: 4. Total Pro: 20.
MISCELLANEOUS: Played defensive back in CFL.
PRO STATISTICS: CFL: 1989—Recovered three fumbles for one yard and a touchdown. 1990—Intercepted one pass for 25 yards.

HORAN, MIKE
P, BRONCOS

PERSONAL: Born February 1, 1959, at Orange, Calif. . . . 5-11/190. . . . Full name: Michael William Horan. . . . Name pronounced hor-RAN.
HIGH SCHOOL: Sunny Hills (Fullerton, Calif.).
COLLEGE: Fullerton College (Calif.), then Long Beach State (degree in mechanical engineering).
TRANSACTIONS/CAREER NOTES: Selected by Atlanta Falcons in ninth round (235th pick overall) of 1982 NFL draft. . . . Released by Falcons (September 4, 1982). . . . Signed as free agent by Green Bay Packers (March 15, 1983). . . . Released by Packers after failing physical (May 6, 1983). . . . Signed as free agent by Buffalo Bills (May 25, 1983). . . . Released by Bills (August 22, 1983). . . . Signed as free agent by Philadelphia Eagles (May 7, 1984). . . . Released by Eagles (August 28, 1986). . . . Signed as free agent by Minnesota Vikings (October 31, 1986). . . . Released by Vikings (November 3, 1986). . . . Active for one game with Vikings in 1986; did not play. . . . Signed as free agent by Denver Broncos (November 25, 1986).
CHAMPIONSHIP GAME EXPERIENCE: Played in AFC championship game after 1986, 1987 and 1989 seasons. . . . Played in Super Bowl XXI after 1986 season, Super Bowl XXII after 1987 season and Super Bowl XXIV after 1989 season.
RECORDS/HONORS: Led NFL in net punting average (37.8), 1988. . . . Led NFL in net punting average (38.9), 1990. . . . Played in Pro Bowl after 1988 season. . . . Named to THE SPORTING NEWS NFL All-Pro team, 1988.
PRO STATISTICS: 1985—Rushed once for 12 yards. 1986—Rushed once for no yards and recovered one fumble and fumbled once for minus 12 yards.

		—PUNTING—		
Year Team	G	No.	Avg.	Blk.
1984—Philadelphia NFL	16	92	42.2	0
1985—Philadelphia NFL	16	91	41.5	0
1986—Minn. (0)-Den. (4) NFL........	4	21	41.1	0
1987—Denver NFL	12	44	41.1	*2
1988—Denver NFL	16	65	44.0	0
1989—Denver NFL	16	77	40.4	0
1990—Denver NFL	15	58	*44.4	1
Pro totals (7 years)	95	448	42.1	3

HORTON, ETHAN
TE, RAIDERS

PERSONAL: Born December 19, 1962, at Kannapolis, N.C. . . . 6-4/240. . . . Full name: Ethan Shane Horton.
HIGH SCHOOL: A.L. Brown (Kannapolis, N.C.).
COLLEGE: North Carolina.
TRANSACTIONS/CAREER NOTES: Selected by Baltimore Stars in 1985 USFL territorial draft. . . . Selected by Kansas City Chiefs in first round (15th pick overall) of 1985 NFL draft. . . . Signed by Chiefs (July 26, 1985). . . . Released by Chiefs (September 1, 1986). . . . Signed as free agent by Los Angeles Raiders (May 6, 1987). . . . Released by Raiders (September 7, 1987). . . . Re-

signed by Raiders (September 16, 1987).... Crossed picket line during players' strike (October 2, 1987).... Released by Los Angeles Raiders (November 3, 1987).... Re-signed by Raiders (April 27, 1988).... Released by Raiders (August 23, 1988). ... Re-signed by Raiders (February 24, 1989).

CHAMPIONSHIP GAME EXPERIENCE: Played in AFC championship game after 1990 season.

PRO STATISTICS: 1985—Attempted one pass with no completions.

		RUSHING				RECEIVING				TOTAL		
Year	Team	G	Att.	Yds.	Avg.	TD	No.	Yds.	Avg.	TD	TD	Pts.	F.
1985— Kansas City NFL	16	48	146	3.0	3	28	185	6.6	1	4	24	2
1987— L.A. Raiders NFL	4	31	95	3.1	0	3	44	14.7	1	1	6	2
1989— L.A. Raiders NFL	16	0	0		0	4	44	11.0	1	1	6	0
1990— L.A. Raiders NFL	16	0	0		0	33	404	12.2	3	3	18	1
Pro totals (4 years)	52	79	241	3.1	3	68	677	10.0	6	9	54	5

HORTON, RAY
S, COWBOYS

PERSONAL: Born April 12, 1960, at Tacoma, Wash.... 5-11/186.... Full name: Raymond Anthony Horton.
HIGH SCHOOL: Mt. Tahoma (Tacoma, Wash.).
COLLEGE: Washington (bachelor of arts degree in sociology, 1983).

TRANSACTIONS/CAREER NOTES: Selected by Los Angeles Express in third round (25th pick overall) of 1983 USFL draft.... Selected by Cincinnati Bengals in second round (53rd pick overall) of 1983 NFL draft.... Signed by Bengals (May 21, 1983).... Granted unconditional free agency (February 1, 1989).... Signed by Dallas Cowboys (March 15, 1989).... On inactive list (October 7, 1990).

CHAMPIONSHIP GAME EXPERIENCE: Played in AFC championship game after 1988 season.... Played in Super Bowl XXIII after 1988 season.

PRO STATISTICS: 1983—Returned five kickoffs for 128 yards (25.6 avg.) and recovered one fumble. 1984—Recovered one fumble. 1985—Recovered two fumbles. 1986—Fumbled twice. 1990—Recovered four fumbles for 11 yards.

		INTERCEPTIONS				PUNT RETURNS				TOTAL		
Year	Team	G	No.	Yds.	Avg.	TD	No.	Yds.	Avg.	TD	TD	Pts.	F.
1983— Cincinnati NFL	16	5	121	24.2	1	1	10	10.0	0	1	6	1
1984— Cincinnati NFL	15	3	48	16.0	1	2	-1	-.5	0	1	6	0
1985— Cincinnati NFL	16	2	3	1.5	0	0	0		0	0	0	1
1986— Cincinnati NFL	16	1	4	4.0	0	11	111	10.1	0	0	0	0
1987— Cincinnati NFL	12	0	0		0	1	0	.0	0	0	0	0
1988— Cincinnati NFL	14	3	13	4.3	0	0	0		0	0	0	0
1989— Dallas NFL	16	1	0	.0	0	0	0		0	0	0	0
1990— Dallas NFL	14	1	0	.0	0	0	0		0	0	0	0
Pro totals (8 years)	119	16	189	11.8	2	15	120	8.0	0	2	12	2

HOSTETLER, JEFF
QB, GIANTS

PERSONAL: Born April 22, 1961, at Hollsopple, Pa.... 6-3/212.... Full name: Jeff W. Hostetler.... Son-in-law of Don Nehlen, head coach at West Virginia.
HIGH SCHOOL: Conemaugh Valley (Johnstown, Pa.).
COLLEGE: West Virginia.

TRANSACTIONS/CAREER NOTES: Selected by Pittsburgh Maulers in 1984 USFL territorial draft.... Selected by New York Giants in third round (59th pick overall) of 1984 NFL draft.... USFL rights traded by Pittsburgh Maulers with rights to cornerback Dwayne Woodruff to Arizona Wranglers for draft choice (May 2, 1984).... Signed by New York Giants (June 12, 1984).... Active for 16 with Giants in 1984; did not play.... On injured reserve with pulled hamstring (December 14, 1985-remainder of season).... On injured reserve with leg injury (December 6, 1986-remainder of season).... On injured reserve with kidney injury (September 7-November 7, 1987).... Crossed picket line during players' strike (October 14, 1987).... Active for two games with Giants in 1987; did not play.

CHAMPIONSHIP GAME EXPERIENCE: Played in NFC championship game after 1990 season.... Played in Super Bowl XXV after 1990 season.

PRO STATISTICS: Passer rating points: 1988 (65.9), 1989 (80.5), 1990 (83.2). Career: 79.3.... 1988—Caught one pass for 10 yards and recovered one fumble. 1989—Recovered one fumble. 1990—Recovered five fumbles and fumbled four times for minus four yards.

		PASSING							RUSHING				TOTAL		
Year	Team	G	Att.	Cmp.	Pct.	Yds.	TD	Int.	Avg.	Att.	Yds.	Avg.	TD	TD	Pts.	F.
1985— N.Y. Giants NFL	5	0	0		0	0	0		0	0		0	0	0	0
1986— N.Y. Giants NFL	13	0	0		0	0	0		1	1	1.0	0	0	0	0
1988— N.Y. Giants NFL	16	29	16	55.2	244	1	2	8.41	5	-3	-.6	0	0	0	1
1989— N.Y. Giants NFL	16	39	20	51.3	294	3	2	7.54	11	71	6.5	2	2	12	2
1990— N.Y. Giants NFL	16	87	47	54.0	614	3	1	7.06	39	190	4.9	2	2	12	4
Pro totals (5 years)	66	155	83	53.5	1152	7	5	7.43	56	259	4.6	4	4	24	7

HOUSTON, BOBBY
LB, JETS

PERSONAL: Born October 26, 1967, at Washington, D.C.... 6-2/235.
HIGH SCHOOL: DeMatha Catholic (Hyattsville, Md.).
COLLEGE: North Carolina State (degree in accounting).
TRANSACTIONS/CAREER NOTES: Selected by Green Bay Packers in third round (75th pick overall) of 1990 NFL draft.... Signed by Packers (July 23, 1990).... On inactive list (September 16, 1990).... On reserve/non-football injury list with pneumonia (September 22-December 19, 1990).... Released by Packers (December 20, 1990). ... Awarded on waivers to Atlanta Falcons (December 21, 1990).... On inactive list (December 23 and 30, 1990).... Granted

unconditional free agency (February 1, 1991).... Signed by New York Jets (March 27, 1991).
PLAYING EXPERIENCE: Green Bay (1)-Atlanta (0) NFL, 1990.... Games: 1990 (1).

HOWARD, DAVID
LB, PATRIOTS

PERSONAL: Born December 8, 1961, at Enterprise, Ala.... 6-1/232.
HIGH SCHOOL: Poly (Long Beach, Calif.).
COLLEGE: Oregon State, then Long Beach State.
TRANSACTIONS/CAREER NOTES: Selected by Los Angeles Express in 1984 USFL territorial draft.... Signed by Express (February 10, 1984).... On developmental squad for two games (April 28-May 11, 1984).... Selected by Minnesota Vikings in third round (67th pick overall) of 1984 NFL supplemental draft.... Released by Los Angeles Express (August 22, 1985).... Signed by Minnesota Vikings (August 25, 1985).... Granted roster exemption (August 25-September 7, 1985).... Traded as part of a six-player, 12 draft-choice deal in which Dallas Cowboys sent running back Herschel Walker to Minnesota Vikings in exchange for Howard, cornerback Issiac Holt, linebacker Jesse Solomon, running back Darrin Nelson, defensive end Alex Stewart, first-round pick in 1992 draft and conditional first-round picks in 1990 and 1991 drafts, conditional second-round picks in 1990, 1991 and 1992 drafts and conditional third-round pick in 1992 draft (October 12, 1989); Nelson refused to report to Dallas and was traded to San Diego Chargers, with Minnesota giving Dallas a sixth-round pick in 1990 as well as the original conditional second-round pick in 1991 and San Diego sending a fifth-round pick in 1990 to Minnesota through Dallas (October 17, 1989); deal completed with Dallas retaining Howard, Solomon and Holt and all conditional picks and Cowboys sending third-round picks in 1990 and 1991 and 10th-round pick in 1990 to Minnesota (February 2, 1990).... Traded by Dallas Cowboys with linebacker Eugene Lockhart and defensive back Ron Francis to New England Patriots (April 22, 1991) to complete deal in which Dallas traded first- and second-round picks in 1991 draft to New England for first-round pick in 1991 draft (April 20, 1991).
PLAYING EXPERIENCE: Los Angeles USFL, 1984 and 1985; Minnesota NFL, 1985-1988; Minnesota (5)-Dallas (11) NFL, 1989; Dallas NFL, 1990.... Games: 1984 (15), 1985 USFL (18), 1985 NFL (16), 1986 (14), 1987 (10), 1988 (16), 1989 (16), 1990 (16). Total USFL: 33. Total NFL: 88. Total Pro: 121.
CHAMPIONSHIP GAME EXPERIENCE: Played in NFC championship game after 1987 season.
PRO STATISTICS: USFL: 1984—Intercepted two passes for 14 yards, credited with 4 ½ sacks for 39 yards, recovered three fumbles and fumbled once. 1985—Intercepted one pass for six yards, recovered four fumbles for 12 yards, credited with three sacks for 30 yards and returned two kickoffs for 10 yards.... NFL: 1987—Intercepted one pass for one yard. 1988—Intercepted three passes for 16 yards and recovered two fumbles for 33 yards.

HOWARD, ERIK
NT, GIANTS

PERSONAL: Born November 12, 1964, at Pittsfield, Mass.... 6-4/268.
HIGH SCHOOL: Bellarmine College Prep (San Jose, Calif.).
COLLEGE: Washington State.
TRANSACTIONS/CAREER NOTES: Selected by New York Giants in second round (46th pick overall) of 1986 NFL draft.... Selected by Baltimore Stars in first round (seventh pick overall) of 1986 USFL draft.... Signed by Giants (July 30, 1986).... On injured reserve with hand injury (October 9-December 6, 1986).... Granted free agency (February 1, 1990).... Re-signed by Giants (August 22, 1990).
PLAYING EXPERIENCE: New York Giants NFL, 1986-1990.... Games: 1986 (8), 1987 (12), 1988 (16), 1989 (16), 1990 (16). Total: 68.
CHAMPIONSHIP GAME EXPERIENCE: Played in NFC championship game after 1986 and 1990 seasons.... Played in Super Bowl XXI after 1986 season and Super Bowl XXV after 1990 season.
RECORDS/HONORS: Played in Pro Bowl after 1990 season.
PRO STATISTICS: 1987—Recovered one fumble. 1988—Recovered two fumbles. 1989—Recovered one fumble.

HULL, KENT
C, BILLS

PERSONAL: Born January 13, 1961, at Ponotoc, Miss.... 6-5/275.... Full name: James Kent Hull.
HIGH SCHOOL: Greenwood (Miss.).
COLLEGE: Mississippi State (bachelor of arts degree).
TRANSACTIONS/CAREER NOTES: Selected by New Jersey Generals in seventh round (75th pick overall) of 1983 USFL draft.... Signed by Generals (January 19, 1983).... Granted free agency when USFL suspended operations (August 7, 1986).... Signed as free agent by Buffalo Bills (August 18, 1986).... Granted roster exemption (August 18-August 22, 1986).
PLAYING EXPERIENCE: New Jersey USFL, 1983-1985; Buffalo NFL, 1986-1990.... Games: 1983 (18), 1984 (18), 1985 (18), 1986 (16), 1987 (12), 1988 (16), 1989 (16), 1990 (16). Total USFL: 54. Total NFL: 76. Total Pro: 130.
CHAMPIONSHIP GAME EXPERIENCE: Played in AFC championship game after 1988 and 1990 seasons.... Played in Super Bowl XXV after 1990 season.
RECORDS/HONORS: Named as center on THE SPORTING NEWS USFL All-Star team, 1985.... Played in Pro Bowl after 1988-1990 seasons.... Named to THE SPORTING NEWS NFL All-Pro team, 1989 and 1990.
PRO STATISTICS: 1989—Recovered two fumbles.

HUMPHERY, BOBBY
DB, CHARGERS

PERSONAL: Born August 23, 1961, at Lubbock, Tex.... 5-11/180.... Full name: Robert Charles Humphery.
HIGH SCHOOL: Estacado (Lubbock, Tex.).
COLLEGE: New Mexico State (degree in social work).
TRANSACTIONS/CAREER NOTES: Selected by New York Jets in ninth round (247th pick overall) of 1983 NFL draft.... On injured reserve with broken finger (August 1, 1983-entire season).... On injured reserve with fractured wrist (September 3-October 5, 1985).... Traded by Jets to Los Angeles Rams for fifth-round pick in 1990 NFL draft (April 22, 1990).... Granted unconditional free agency (February 1, 1991).... Signed by San Diego Chargers (March 15, 1991).
RECORDS/HONORS: Named as kick returner to THE SPORTING NEWS NFL All-Pro team, 1984.
PRO STATISTICS: 1984—Caught 14 passes for 206 yards (14.7 avg.) and one touchdown and recovered two fumbles. 1985—Returned one punt for no yards, rushed once for 10 yards and recovered one fumble. 1986—Credited with a safety. 1987—Recov-

ered two fumbles for 46 yards and a touchdown. 1988—Intercepted one pass for no yards and recovered two fumbles. 1989—Recovered four fumbles. 1990—Recovered two fumbles for five yards.

Year	Team	G	No.	Yds.	Avg.	TD	No.	Yds.	Avg.	TD	TD	Pts.	F.
			INTERCEPTIONS				KICKOFF RETURNS				TOTAL		
1984— N.Y. Jets NFL		16	0	0		0	22	675	*30.7	*1	2	12	1
1985— N.Y. Jets NFL		12	0	0		0	17	363	21.4	0	0	0	2
1986— N.Y. Jets NFL		16	0	0		0	28	655	23.4	*1	1	8	1
1987— N.Y. Jets NFL		12	0	0		0	18	357	19.8	0	1	6	1
1988— N.Y. Jets NFL		16	1	0	.0	0	21	510	24.3	0	0	0	0
1989— N.Y. Jets NFL		16	0	0		0	24	414	17.3	0	0	0	4
1990— L.A. Rams NFL		16	4	52	13.0	1	0	0		0	1	6	0
Pro totals (7 years)		104	5	52	10.4	1	130	2974	22.9	2	5	32	9

HUMPHREY, BOBBY
RB, BRONCOS

PERSONAL: Born October 11, 1966, at Birmingham, Ala.... 6-1/201. **HIGH SCHOOL:** Glenn (Birmingham, Ala.). **COLLEGE:** Alabama. **TRANSACTIONS/CAREER NOTES:** Selected by Denver Broncos in first round of 1989 NFL supplemental draft (July 7, 1989).... Signed by Broncos (August 17, 1989).... On inactive list (October 14, 1990). **CHAMPIONSHIP GAME EXPERIENCE:** Played in AFC championship game after 1989 season.... Played in Super Bowl XXIV after 1989 season. **RECORDS/HONORS:** Named as running back on THE SPORTING NEWS college All-America team, 1987.... Played in Pro Bowl after 1990 season. **PRO STATISTICS:** 1989—Attempted two passes with one completion for 17 yards and a touchdown, returned four kickoffs for 86 yards and recovered three fumbles. 1990—Attempted two passes with no completions and recovered two fumbles.

Year	Team	G	Att.	Yds.	Avg.	TD	No.	Yds.	Avg.	TD	TD	Pts.	F.
			RUSHING				RECEIVING				TOTAL		
1989— Denver NFL		16	294	1151	3.9	7	22	156	7.1	1	8	48	4
1990— Denver NFL		15	288	1202	4.2	7	24	152	6.3	0	7	42	8
Pro totals (2 years)		31	582	2353	4.0	14	46	308	6.7	1	15	90	12

HUMPHRIES, STAN
QB, REDSKINS

PERSONAL: Born April 14, 1965, at Shreveport, La.... 6-2/223. **HIGH SCHOOL:** Southwood (Shreveport, La.). **COLLEGE:** Louisiana State, then Northeast Louisiana. **TRANSACTIONS/CAREER NOTES:** Selected by Washington Redskins in sixth round (159th pick overall) of 1988 NFL draft.... Signed by Redskins (July 13, 1988).... On non-football injury list with blood disorder (September 3, 1988-entire season).... On injured reserve with sprained knee (November 17, 1990-January 11, 1991). **PRO STATISTICS:** Passer rating points: 1989 (75.4), 1990 (57.5). Career: 58.5.... 1989—Recovered one fumble.

Year	Team	G	Att.	Cmp.	Pct.	Yds.	TD	Int.	Avg.	Att.	Yds.	Avg.	TD	TD	Pts.	F.
			PASSING							RUSHING				TOTAL		
1989— Washington NFL		2	10	5	50.0	91	1	1	9.10	5	10	2.0	0	0	0	1
1990— Washington NFL		7	156	91	58.3	1015	3	10	6.51	23	106	4.6	2	2	12	0
Pro totals (2 years)		9	166	96	57.8	1106	4	11	6.66	28	116	4.1	2	2	12	1

HUNLEY, RICKY
LB, COLTS

PERSONAL: Born November 11, 1961, at Petersburg, Va.... 6-2/250.... Full name: Ricky Cardell Hunley.... Brother of LaMonte Hunley, linebacker with Indianapolis Colts, 1985 and 1986. **HIGH SCHOOL:** Petersburg (Va.).
COLLEGE: Arizona (degree in business, 1984).
TRANSACTIONS/CAREER NOTES: Selected by Arizona Wranglers in 1984 USFL territorial draft.... Selected by Cincinnati Bengals in first round (seventh pick overall) in 1984 NFL draft.... NFL rights traded by Bengals to Denver Broncos for first- and third-round picks in 1986 draft and fifth-round pick in 1987 draft (October 9, 1984).... Signed by Broncos (October 16, 1984).... Granted roster exemption (October 16-October 26, 1984).... Granted free agency (February 1, 1988).... Re-signed by Broncos and traded to Phoenix Cardinals for center Mike Ruether (July 19, 1988).... Released by Cardinals (September 5, 1989). ... Signed as free agent by Los Angeles Raiders (September 26, 1989).... Released by Raiders (September 3, 1990).... Re-signed by Raiders (October 10, 1990).... Released by Raiders (January 2, 1991).... Signed by Indianapolis Colts (July 17, 1990). **PLAYING EXPERIENCE:** Denver NFL, 1984-1987; Phoenix NFL, 1988; Los Angeles Raiders NFL, 1989 and 1990.... Games: 1984 (8), 1985 (16), 1986 (16), 1987 (12), 1988 (16), 1989 (12), 1990 (11). Total: 91. **CHAMPIONSHIP GAME EXPERIENCE:** Played in AFC championship game after 1986 and 1987 seasons.... Played in Super Bowl XXI after 1986 season and Super Bowl XXII after 1987 season. **MISCELLANEOUS:** Selected by Pittsburgh Pirates' organization in 26th round of free-agent baseball draft (June 3, 1980). **PRO STATISTICS:** 1986—Intercepted one pass for 22 yards, returned two kickoffs for 11 yards and recovered one fumble. 1987—Intercepted two passes for 64 yards and a touchdown. 1988—Returned one punt for three yards. 1989—Recovered one fumble.

HUNTER, IVY JOE
RB, PATRIOTS

PERSONAL: Born November 16, 1966, at Gainesville, Fla.... 6-1/248.... Full name: Ivy Joe Hunter. **HIGH SCHOOL:** Buchholz (Gainesville, Fla.). **COLLEGE:** Kentucky.

TRANSACTIONS/CAREER NOTES: Selected by Indianapolis Colts in seventh round (182nd pick overall) of 1989 NFL draft. . . . Signed by Colts (July 26, 1989). . . . Granted unconditional free agency (February 1, 1991). . . . Signed by New England Patriots (April 1, 1991).
PLAYING EXPERIENCE: Indianapolis NFL, 1989 and 1990. . . . Games: 1989 (16), 1990 (16). Total: 32.
PRO STATISTICS: 1989—Rushed 13 times for 47 yards and returned four kickoffs for 58 yards. 1990—Recovered one fumble.

HUNTER, JEFF
DE, LIONS

PERSONAL: Born April 12, 1966, at Hampton, Va. . . . 6-5/285. . . . Full name: Jeffrey Orlando Hunter.
HIGH SCHOOL: Hephzibah (Ga.).
COLLEGE: Albany State (Ga.).
TRANSACTIONS/CAREER NOTES: Selected by Phoenix Cardinals in 11th round (291st pick overall) of 1989 NFL draft. . . . Signed by Cardinals (July 21, 1989). . . . Released by Cardinals (August 29, 1989). . . . Signed by Buffalo Bills (February 8, 1990). . . . On inactive list (September 9, 16; and October 21 and 28, 1990). . . . Released by Bills (October 31, 1990). . . . Signed by Detroit Lions (November 2, 1990). . . . On inactive list (November 4, 1990).
PLAYING EXPERIENCE: Buffalo (3)-Detroit (7) NFL, 1990. . . . Games: 1990 (10).

HUNTER, JOHN
OT, FALCONS

PERSONAL: Born August 16, 1965, at Roseburg, Ore. . . . 6-8/300. . . . Full name: John Rosel Hunter.
HIGH SCHOOL: North Bend (Ore.).
COLLEGE: Brigham Young.
TRANSACTIONS/CAREER NOTES: Selected by Minnesota Vikings in third round (80th pick overall) of 1989 NFL draft. . . . Signed by Vikings (July 31, 1989). . . . Released by Vikings (September 4, 1989). . . . Awarded on waivers to Atlanta Falcons (September 5, 1989). . . . On injured reserve with back injury (September 26-November 6, 1989). . . . Transferred to developmental squad (November 7-November 23, 1989). . . . Activated (November 24, 1989). . . . On inactive list (October 7, 1990).
PLAYING EXPERIENCE: Atlanta NFL, 1989 and 1990. . . . Games: 1989 (4), 1990 (15). Total: 19.

HUNTER, PATRICK
CB, SEAHAWKS

PERSONAL: Born October 24, 1964, at San Francisco. . . . 5-11/186. . . . Full name: Patrick Edward Hunter. . . . Cousin of Louis Wright, cornerback with Denver Broncos, 1975-1986.
HIGH SCHOOL: South San Francisco (Calif.).
COLLEGE: Nevada-Reno.
TRANSACTIONS/CAREER NOTES: Selected by Seattle Seahawks in third round (68th pick overall) of 1986 NFL draft. . . . Signed by Seahawks (July 16, 1986). . . . On non-football injury list with lacerated kidney (November 1-December 10, 1988). . . . Granted free agency (February 1, 1990). . . . Re-signed by Seahawks (July 18, 1990).
PLAYING EXPERIENCE: Seattle NFL, 1986-1990. . . . Games: 1986 (16), 1987 (11), 1988 (10), 1989 (16), 1990 (16). Total: 69.
PRO STATISTICS: 1987—Intercepted one pass for three yards. 1988—Returned one punt for no yards and fumbled once. 1990—Intercepted one pass for no yards and recovered one fumble for 13 yards.

HURST, MAURICE
CB, PATRIOTS

PERSONAL: Born September 17, 1967, at New Orleans. . . . 5-10/185. . . . Full name: Maurice Roy Hurst.
HIGH SCHOOL: Fortier (New Orleans).
COLLEGE: Southern.
TRANSACTIONS/CAREER NOTES: Selected by New England Patriots in fourth round (96th pick overall) of 1989 NFL draft. . . . Signed by Patriots (July 19, 1989).
PRO STATISTICS: 1989—Returned one punt for six yards. 1990—Fumbled once.

			INTERCEPTIONS		
Year Team	G	No.	Yds.	Avg.	TD
1989— New England NFL	16	5	31	6.2	1
1990— New England NFL	16	4	61	15.3	0
Pro totals (2 years)	32	9	92	10.2	1

HUTSON, BRIAN
S, PACKERS

PERSONAL: Born February 20, 1965, at Jackson, Miss. . . . 6-1/195. . . . Full name: Brian S. Hutson.
HIGH SCHOOL: Brandon (Miss.).
COLLEGE: Mississippi State.
TRANSACTIONS/CAREER NOTES: Signed as free agent by Los Angeles Raiders (June 19, 1987). . . . On injured reserve with broken foot (August 27-entire 1987 season). . . . Released by Raiders (August 23, 1988). . . . Signed as free agent by New England Patriots (April 25, 1990). . . . Released by Patriots (September 3, 1990). . . . Re-signed by Patriots (October 1, 1990). . . . On injured reserve with ankle injury (October 24-December 4, 1990). . . . Released by Patriots (December 4, 1990). . . . Signed by Green Bay Packers (March 8, 1991).
PLAYING EXPERIENCE: New England NFL, 1990. . . . Games: 1990 (2).

HYCHE, STEVE
LB, CARDINALS

PERSONAL: Born June 12, 1963, at Jasper, Ala. . . . 6-2/226. . . . Full name: Steve Jay Hyche.
HIGH SCHOOL: Cordova (Ala.).
COLLEGE: Livingston University (Ala.).
TRANSACTIONS/CAREER NOTES: Signed as free agent by Chicago Bears (May 4, 1989). . . . Re-

leased by Bears (September 5, 1989).... Re-signed by Bears to developmental squad (September 6, 1989).... On developmental squad (September 6-September 27, 1989).... Activated after clearing procedural waivers (September 29, 1989).... On injured reserve with thumb injury (November 8, 1989-remainder of season).... Released by Bears (August 26, 1990).... Signed by WLAF (January 4, 1991).... Selected by Birmingham Fire in fourth round (35th linebacker) of 1991 WLAF positional draft.... Signed by Phoenix Cardinals (June 13, 1991).

PLAYING EXPERIENCE: Chicago NFL, 1989; Birmingham WLAF, 1991.... Games: 1989 (6), 1991 (10). Total NFL: 6. Total Pro: 16.

IGWEBUIKE, DONALD
PK, VIKINGS

PERSONAL: Born December 27, 1960, at Anambra, Nigeria.... 5-9/184.... Full name: Donald Amechi Igwebuike.... Name pronounced ig-way-BWEE-kay.
HIGH SCHOOL: Immaculate Conception (Anambra, Nigeria).
COLLEGE: Clemson.

TRANSACTIONS/CAREER NOTES: Selected by Tampa Bay Buccaneers in 10th round (260th pick overall) of 1985 NFL draft.... Signed by Buccaneers (June 6, 1985).... On injured reserve with pulled groin (November 22, 1988-remainder of season).... Released by Buccaneers (September 2, 1990).... Awarded on waivers to Minnesota Vikings (September 4, 1990).... Granted roster exemption (November 9, 1990-remainder of season).

			PLACE-KICKING			
Year Team	G	XPM	XPA	FGM	FGA	Pts.
1985— Tampa Bay NFL.........	16	30	32	22	32	96
1986— Tampa Bay NFL.........	16	26	27	17	24	77
1987— Tampa Bay NFL.........	12	24	26	14	18	66
1988— Tampa Bay NFL.........	12	21	21	19	25	78
1989— Tampa Bay NFL.........	16	33	35	22	28	99
1990— Minnesota NFL	8	19	19	14	16	61
Pro totals (6 years)	80	153	160	108	143	477

ILKIN, TUNCH
OT, STEELERS

PERSONAL: Born September 23, 1957, at Istanbul, Turkey.... 6-3/269.... Full name: Tunch Ali Ilkin.... Name pronounced TOONCH ILL-kin.
HIGH SCHOOL: Highland Park (Ill.).
COLLEGE: Indiana State (bachelor of science degree in broadcasting, 1980).

TRANSACTIONS/CAREER NOTES: Selected by Pittsburgh Steelers in sixth round (165th pick overall) of 1980 NFL draft.... Released by Steelers (August 25, 1980).... Re-signed by Steelers (October 15, 1983).... On injured reserve with shoulder injury (August 30-September 30, 1983).... On injured reserve with elbow injury (November 3-November 30, 1990).
PLAYING EXPERIENCE: Pittsburgh NFL, 1980-1990.... Games: 1980 (10), 1981 (16), 1982 (8), 1983 (11), 1984 (16), 1985 (16), 1986 (15), 1987 (11), 1988 (16), 1989 (16), 1990 (13). Total: 148.
CHAMPIONSHIP GAME EXPERIENCE: Played in AFC championship game after 1984 season.
RECORDS/HONORS: Played in Pro Bowl after 1988 and 1989 seasons.
PRO STATISTICS: 1981—Recovered one fumble. 1983—Recovered one fumble. 1985—Recovered one fumble. 1990—Recovered one fumble.

INGRAM, DARRYL
TE, 49ERS

PERSONAL: Born May 2, 1966, at Lubbock, Tex.... 6-3/240.
HIGH SCHOOL: Hart (New Hall, Calif.).
COLLEGE: California (bachelor of arts degree in political economy, 1989).
TRANSACTIONS/CAREER NOTES: Selected by Minnesota Vikings in fourth round (108th pick overall) of 1989 NFL draft.... Signed by Vikings (July 31, 1989).... Released by Vikings (September 3, 1990).... Signed by San Francisco 49ers (February 15, 1991).

			RECEIVING		
Year Team	G	No.	Yds.	Avg.	TD
1989— Minnesota NFL	16	5	47	9.4	1
Pro totals (1 year)	16	5	47	9.4	1

INGRAM, MARK
WR, GIANTS

PERSONAL: Born August 23, 1965, at Rockford, Ill.... 5-10/188.... Cousin of Steve Atwater, safety with Denver Broncos.
HIGH SCHOOL: Northwestern (Flint, Mich.).
COLLEGE: Michigan State.

TRANSACTIONS/CAREER NOTES: Selected by New York Giants in first round (28th pick overall) of 1987 NFL draft.... Signed by Giants (July 31, 1987).... On injured reserve with broken collarbone (September 26-December 3, 1988).
CHAMPIONSHIP GAME EXPERIENCE: Played in NFC championship game after 1990 season.... Played in Super Bowl XXV after 1990 season.
PRO STATISTICS: 1989—Rushed once for one yard and recovered two fumbles. 1990—Rushed once for four yards.

			RECEIVING				KICKOFF RETURNS				TOTAL		
Year Team	G	No.	Yds.	Avg.	TD	No.	Yds.	Avg.	TD	TD	Pts.	F.
1987— N.Y. Giants NFL	9	2	32	16.0	0	6	114	19.0	0	0	0	0
1988— N.Y. Giants NFL	7	13	158	12.2	1	8	129	16.1	0	1	6	0
1989— N.Y. Giants NFL	16	17	290	17.1	1	22	332	15.1	0	1	6	2
1990— N.Y. Giants NFL	16	26	499	19.2	5	3	42	14.0	0	5	30	1
Pro totals (4 years)	48	58	979	16.9	7	39	617	15.8	0	7	42	3

IRVIN, MICHAEL
WR, COWBOYS

PERSONAL: Born March 5, 1966, at Fort Lauderdale, Fla. . . . 6-2/199. . . . Full name: Michael Jerome Irvin.
HIGH SCHOOL: St. Thomas Aquinas (Fort Lauderdale, Fla.).
COLLEGE: Miami, Fla. (degree in business management, 1988).
TRANSACTIONS/CAREER NOTES: Selected by Dallas Cowboys in first round (11th pick overall) of 1988 NFL draft. . . . Signed by Cowboys (July 9, 1988). . . . On injured reserve with knee injury (October 17, 1989-remainder of season). . . . On injured reserve with knee injury (September 4-October 7, 1990).
PRO STATISTICS: 1989—Recovered one fumble.

		RUSHING				RECEIVING				TOTAL		
Year Team	G	Att.	Yds.	Avg.	TD	No.	Yds.	Avg.	TD	TD	Pts.	F.
1988— Dallas NFL	14	1	2	2.0	0	32	654	20.4	5	5	30	0
1989— Dallas NFL	6	1	6	6.0	0	26	378	14.5	2	2	12	0
1990— Dallas NFL	12	0	0		0	20	413	20.7	5	5	30	0
Pro totals (3 years)	32	2	8	4.0	0	78	1445	18.5	12	12	72	0

IRWIN, TIM
OT, VIKINGS

PERSONAL: Born December 13, 1958, at Knoxville, Tenn. . . . 6-7/295. . . . Full name: Timothy Edward Irwin.
HIGH SCHOOL: Central (Knoxville, Tenn.).
COLLEGE: Tennessee (degree in political science, 1981).
TRANSACTIONS/CAREER NOTES: Selected by Minnesota Vikings in third round (74th pick overall) of 1981 NFL draft.
PLAYING EXPERIENCE: Minnesota NFL, 1981-1990. . . . Games: 1981 (7), 1982 (9), 1983 (16), 1984 (16), 1985 (16), 1986 (16), 1987 (12), 1988 (16), 1989 (16), 1990 (16). Total: 140.
CHAMPIONSHIP GAME EXPERIENCE: Played in NFC championship game after 1987 season.
PRO STATISTICS: 1983—Recovered one fumble. 1984—Recovered one fumble for two yards. 1986—Returned one kickoff for no yards and recovered two fumbles. 1990—Recovered two fumbles and fumbled once for two yards.

JACKE, CHRIS
PK, PACKERS

PERSONAL: Born March 12, 1966, at Richmond, Va. . . . 6-0/197. . . . Full name: Christopher Lee Jacke. . . . Name pronounced JACK-ee.
HIGH SCHOOL: J.J. Pierce (Richardson, Tex.).
COLLEGE: Texas-El Paso (bachelor's degree in business, 1989).
TRANSACTIONS/CAREER NOTES: Selected by Green Bay Packers in sixth round (142nd pick overall) of 1989 NFL draft. . . . Signed by Packers (July 28, 1989).

		PLACE-KICKING				
Year Team	G	XPM	XPA	FGM	FGA	Pts.
1989— Green Bay NFL	16	42	42	22	28	108
1990— Green Bay NFL	16	28	29	23	30	97
Pro totals (2 years)	32	70	71	45	58	205

JACKSON, ALFRED
CB, RAMS

PERSONAL: Born July 10, 1967, at Tulare, Calif. . . . 6-0/180. . . . Full name: Alfred Melvin Jackson Jr.
HIGH SCHOOL: Tulare (Calif.).
COLLEGE: San Diego State.
TRANSACTIONS/CAREER NOTES: Selected by Los Angeles Rams in fifth round (135th pick overall) of 1989 NFL draft. . . . Signed by Rams (July 14, 1989). . . . On injured reserve with groin injury (October 18-December 1, 1989). . . . On inactive list (October 21 and 29, 1990). . . . Released by Rams (November 3, 1990). . . . Re-signed by Rams (February 27, 1991).
PLAYING EXPERIENCE: Los Angeles Rams NFL, 1989 and 1990. . . . Games: 1989 (7), 1990 (5). Total: 12.
CHAMPIONSHIP GAME EXPERIENCE: Played in NFC championship game after 1989 season.

JACKSON, BO
RB, RAIDERS

PERSONAL: Born November 30, 1962, at Bessemer, Ala. . . . 6-1/230. . . . Full name: Vincent Edward Jackson.
HIGH SCHOOL: McAdory (McCalla, Ala.).
COLLEGE: Auburn.
TRANSACTIONS/CAREER NOTES: Selected by Tampa Bay Buccaneers in first round (first pick overall) of 1986 NFL draft. . . . Selected by Birmingham Stallions in 1986 USFL territorial draft. . . . On reserve/did not sign list (entire 1986 season-April 27, 1987). . . . Selected by Los Angeles Raiders in seventh round (183rd pick overall) of 1987 NFL draft. . . . Signed by Raiders (July 17, 1987). . . . On reserve/did not report list (August 27-October 24, 1987). . . . On reserve/did not report list (August 22-October 12, 1988). . . . Activated from reserve/did not report list (October 15, 1988). . . . On reserve/did not report list (July 21-October 11, 1989). . . . On reserve/did not report list (July-October 21, 1990).
CHAMPIONSHIP GAME EXPERIENCE: Member of Los Angeles Raiders for AFC championship game after 1990 season; inactive.
RECORDS/HONORS: Heisman Trophy winner, 1985. . . . Named THE SPORTING NEWS College Football Player of the Year, 1985. . . . Named as running back on THE SPORTING NEWS college All-America team, 1985. . . . Named to play in Pro Bowl after 1990 season; replaced due to injury by John L. Williams.
PRO STATISTICS: 1987—Recovered one fumble. 1988—Recovered two fumbles.

		RUSHING				RECEIVING				TOTAL		
Year Team	G	Att.	Yds.	Avg.	TD	No.	Yds.	Avg.	TD	TD	Pts.	F.
1987— L.A. Raiders NFL	7	81	554	6.8	4	16	136	8.5	2	6	36	2
1988— L.A. Raiders NFL	10	136	580	4.3	3	9	79	8.8	0	3	18	5
1989— L.A. Raiders NFL	11	173	950	5.5	4	9	69	7.7	0	4	24	1
1990— L.A. Raiders NFL	10	125	698	5.6	5	6	68	11.3	0	5	30	3
Pro totals (4 years)	38	515	2782	5.4	16	40	352	8.8	2	18	108	11

BASEBALL TRANSACTIONS: Selected by New York Yankees' organization in second round of free-agent draft (June 7, 1982). . . . Selected by California Angels' organization in 20th round of free-agent draft (June 3, 1985). . . . Selected by Kansas City Royals' organization in fourth round of free-agent draft (June 2, 1986). . . . On temporary inactive list (June 20-June 30, 1986). . . . On disabled list (June 1-July 2, 1988). . . . On disabled list (July 25-August 9, 1989). . . . On disabled list (July 18-August 26, 1990).

BASEBALL RECORDS/HONORS/NOTES: Shares major league record for most consecutive home runs (4), with three on July 17 and one on August 26, 1990; most strikeouts, nine-inning game (5), April 18, 1987; most strikeouts, inning (2), April 8, 1987, in fourth inning. . . . Major League stolen bases: 1986 (3), 1987 (10), 1988 (27), 1989 (26), 1990 (15). Total: 81. . . . Led American League in strikeouts (172), 1989. . . . Shares All-Star game record for hitting home run in first at-bat, July 11, 1989. . . . Hit three home runs in a game, July 17, 1990.

BASEBALL RECORD AS PLAYER

Year	Team	League	Pos.	G	AB	R	H	2B	3B	HR	RBI	Avg.	PO	A	E	F.A.
1986—	Memphis	South.	OF	53	184	30	51	9	3	7	25	.277	116	8	7	.947
1986—	Kansas City	Amer.	OF	25	82	9	17	2	1	2	9	.207	29	2	4	.886
1987—	Kansas City	Amer.	OF	116	396	46	93	17	2	22	53	.235	180	9	9	.955
1988—	Kansas City	Amer.	OF	124	439	63	108	16	4	25	68	.246	246	11	7	.973
1989—	Kansas City	Amer.	OF	135	515	86	132	15	6	32	105	.256	224	11	8	.967
1990—	Kansas City	Amer.	OF	111	405	74	110	16	1	28	78	.272	230	8	12	.952
Major league totals (5 years)				511	1837	278	460	66	14	109	313	.250	909	41	40	.960

ALL-STAR GAME RECORD

Year	League	Pos.	AB	R	H	2B	3B	HR	RBI	Avg.	PO	A	E	F.A.
1989—	American	OF	4	1	2	0	0	1	2	.500	2	0	0	1.000

JACKSON, GREG
S, GIANTS

PERSONAL: Born August 20, 1966, at Hialeah, Fla. . . . 6-1/200. . . . Full name: Greg Allen Jackson.
HIGH SCHOOL: American (Miami).
COLLEGE: Louisiana State.
TRANSACTIONS/CAREER NOTES: Selected by New York Giants in third round (78th pick overall) of 1989 NFL draft. . . . Signed by Giants (July 24, 1989). . . . On inactive list (December 23 and 30, 1990).
CHAMPIONSHIP GAME EXPERIENCE: Played in NFC championship game after 1990 season. . . . Played in Super Bowl XXV after 1990 season.
PRO STATISTICS: 1989—Recovered one fumble.

			— INTERCEPTIONS —			
Year	Team	G	No.	Yds.	Avg.	TD
1989—	N.Y. Giants NFL	16	0	0		0
1990—	N.Y. Giants NFL	14	5	8	1.6	0
Pro totals (2 years)		30	5	8	1.6	0

JACKSON, JOHN
WR, CARDINALS

PERSONAL: Born January 1, 1967, at Brooklyn, N.Y. . . . 5-10/183.
HIGH SCHOOL: Bishop Amat (La Puente, Calif.).
COLLEGE: Southern California (bachelor's degree in business finance, 1990).
TRANSACTIONS/CAREER NOTES: Signed as free agent by Phoenix Cardinals (April 30, 1990). . . . Released by Cardinals (September 3, 1990). . . . Re-signed by Cardinals (September 4, 1990). . . . On inactive list (September 9, 16, 23, 30; and October 14, 1990). . . . Released by Cardinals and signed to practice squad (October 17, 1990). . . . Activated (November 3, 1990).
PLAYING EXPERIENCE: Phoenix NFL, 1990. . . . Games: 1990 (9).
PRO STATISTICS: 1990—Recovered one fumble.

JACKSON, JOHN
OT, STEELERS

PERSONAL: Born January 4, 1965, at Camp Kwe, Okinawa, Japan. . . . 6-6/285.
HIGH SCHOOL: Woodward (Cincinnati).
COLLEGE: Eastern Kentucky.
TRANSACTIONS/CAREER NOTES: Selected by Pittsburgh Steelers in 10th round (252nd pick overall) of 1988 NFL draft. . . . Signed by Steelers (May 17, 1988).
PLAYING EXPERIENCE: Pittsburgh NFL, 1988-1990. . . . Games: 1988 (16), 1989 (14), 1990 (16). Total: 46.
PRO STATISTICS: 1988—Returned one kickoff for 10 yards.

JACKSON, JOHNNY
S, 49ERS

PERSONAL: Born January 11, 1967, at Harlingen, Tex. . . . 6-1/204. . . . Full name: Johnny Bobby Jackson.
HIGH SCHOOL: Harlington (Tex.).
COLLEGE: Houston.
TRANSACTIONS/CAREER NOTES: Selected by San Francisco 49ers in fifth round (122nd pick overall) of 1989 NFL draft. . . . Signed by 49ers (July 20, 1989). . . . Released by 49ers (September 4, 1989). . . . Re-signed by 49ers (September 5, 1989).
PLAYING EXPERIENCE: San Francisco NFL, 1989 and 1990. . . . Games: 1989 (16), 1990 (16). Total: 32.
CHAMPIONSHIP GAME EXPERIENCE: Played in NFC championship game after 1989 and 1990 seasons. . . . Played in Super Bowl XXIV after 1989 season.
PRO STATISTICS: 1989—Returned blocked field goal 75 yards for a touchdown, returned one kickoff for no yards and recovered one fumble.

		INTERCEPTIONS			
Year	Team	G	No.	Yds.	Avg.	TD
1989— San Francisco NFL....	16	2	35	17.5	0
1990— San Francisco NFL....	16	0	0	0	0
Pro totals (2 years)	32	2	35	17.5	0

JACKSON, KEITH
TE, EAGLES

PERSONAL: Born April 19, 1965, at Little Rock, Ark. ... 6-2/250. ... Full name: Keith Jerome Jackson.
HIGH SCHOOL: Parkview (Little Rock, Ark.).
COLLEGE: Oklahoma (degree in communications, 1988).
TRANSACTIONS/CAREER NOTES: Selected by Philadelphia Eagles in first round (13th pick overall) of 1988 NFL draft.... Signed by Eagles (August 10, 1988).... On reserve/did not report list (August 28-September 21, 1990).
RECORDS/HONORS: Named as tight end on THE SPORTING NEWS college All-America team, 1986.... Played in Pro Bowl after 1988-1990 seasons.... Named THE SPORTING NEWS NFL Rookie of the Year, 1988.... Named to THE SPORTING NEWS NFL All-Pro team, 1988-1990.
PRO STATISTICS: 1988—Fumbled three times. 1989—Fumbled once. 1990—Fumbled once.

		RECEIVING			
Year	Team	G	No.	Yds.	Avg.	TD
1988— Philadelphia NFL	16	81	869	10.7	6
1989— Philadelphia NFL	14	63	648	10.3	3
1990— Philadelphia NFL	14	50	670	13.4	6
Pro totals (3 years)	44	194	2187	11.3	15

JACKSON, KENNY
WR, EAGLES

PERSONAL: Born February 15, 1962, at Neptune, N.J. ... 6-0/180. ... Cousin of Tony Collins, running back with New England Patriots and Miami Dolphins, 1981-1987 and 1990.
HIGH SCHOOL: South River (N.J.).
COLLEGE: Penn State (degree in finance).
TRANSACTIONS/CAREER NOTES: Selected by Philadelphia Stars in 1984 USFL territorial draft.... Selected by Philadelphia Eagles in first round (fourth pick overall) of 1984 NFL draft.... Signed by Eagles (May 1, 1984).... On injured reserve with separated shoulder (October 22-November 23, 1984).... Granted free agency (February 1, 1988).... Re-signed by Eagles (October 31, 1988).... Granted roster exemption (October 31-November 4, 1988).... Granted unconditional free agency (February 1, 1989).... Signed by Houston Oilers (April 1, 1989).... Released by Oilers (September 2, 1990).... Signed by Philadelphia Eagles (September 19, 1990).
PRO STATISTICS: 1986—Rushed once for six yards. 1987—Rushed six times for 27 yards, recovered one fumble and fumbled once. 1990—Returned six kickoffs for 125 yards.

		RECEIVING			
Year	Team	G	No.	Yds.	Avg.	TD
1984— Philadelphia NFL	11	26	398	15.3	1
1985— Philadelphia NFL	16	40	692	17.3	1
1986— Philadelphia NFL	16	30	506	16.9	6
1987— Philadelphia NFL	12	21	471	22.4	3
1988— Philadelphia NFL	7	0	0		0
1989— Houston NFL..............	10	4	31	7.8	0
1990— Philadelphia NFL	14	1	43	43.0	0
Pro totals (7 years)	86	122	2141	17.6	11

JACKSON, KIRBY
CB, BILLS

PERSONAL: Born February 2, 1965, at Sturgis, Miss. ... 5-10/180.
HIGH SCHOOL: Sturgis (Miss.).
COLLEGE: Mississippi State.
TRANSACTIONS/CAREER NOTES: Selected by New York Jets in fifth round (129th pick overall) of 1987 NFL draft.... Signed by Jets (July 24, 1987).... Released by Jets (September 6, 1987).... Signed as free agent replacement player by Los Angeles Rams (September 23, 1987).... Released by Rams (November 16, 1987).... Signed as free agent by Buffalo Bills (November 27, 1987).... On injured reserve with hamstring injury (August 17-October 29, 1988). ...On inactive list (November 18, 1990).... On injured reserve with hamstring injury (December 14, 1990-January 11, 1991).
CHAMPIONSHIP GAME EXPERIENCE: Played in AFC championship game after 1988 and 1990 seasons.... Played in Super Bowl XXV after 1990 season.
PRO STATISTICS: 1987—Recovered blocked punt in end zone for a touchdown. 1989—Returned one kickoff for no yards and recovered one fumble.

		INTERCEPTIONS			
Year	Team	G	No.	Yds.	Avg.	TD
1987— L.A. Rams NFL..........	5	1	36	36.0	0
1988— Buffalo NFL..............	8	0	0		0
1989— Buffalo NFL..............	14	2	43	21.5	1
1990— Buffalo NFL..............	12	3	16	5.3	0
Pro totals (4 years)	39	6	95	15.8	1

JACKSON, MARK
WR, BRONCOS

PERSONAL: Born July 23, 1963, at Chicago. . . . 5-9/180. . . . Full name: Mark Anthony Jackson.
HIGH SCHOOL: South Vigo (Terre Haute, Ind.).
COLLEGE: Purdue (bachelor's degree in public relations, 1986).
TRANSACTIONS/CAREER NOTES: Selected by Denver Broncos in sixth round (161st pick overall) of 1986 NFL draft. . . . Selected by New Jersey Generals in second round (11th pick overall) of 1986 USFL draft. . . . Signed by Denver Broncos (July 16, 1986). . . . On injured reserve with broken collarbone (September 12-October 10, 1988).
CHAMPIONSHIP GAME EXPERIENCE: Played in AFC championship game after 1986, 1987 and 1989 seasons. . . . Played in Super Bowl XXI after 1986 season, Super Bowl XXII after 1987 season and Super Bowl XXIV after 1989 season.
PRO STATISTICS: 1986—Returned two punts for seven yards and returned one kickoff for 16 yards. 1988—Recovered one fumble. 1989—Fumbled once for minus eight yards. 1990—Returned one kickoff for 18 yards.

		RUSHING				RECEIVING				TOTAL		
Year Team	G	Att.	Yds.	Avg.	TD	No.	Yds.	Avg.	TD	TD	Pts.	F.
1986— Denver NFL	16	2	6	3.0	0	38	738	19.4	1	1	6	3
1987— Denver NFL	12	0	0		0	26	436	16.8	2	2	12	0
1988— Denver NFL	12	1	5	5.0	0	46	852	18.5	6	6	30	1
1989— Denver NFL	16	5	13	2.6	0	28	446	15.9	2	2	12	1
1990— Denver NFL	16	5	28	5.6	1	57	926	16.3	4	5	30	1
Pro totals (5 years)	72	13	52	4.0	1	195	3398	17.4	15	16	90	6

JACKSON, RICKEY
LB, SAINTS

PERSONAL: Born March 20, 1958, at Pahokee, Fla. . . . 6-2/243. . . . Full name: Rickey Anderson Jackson.
HIGH SCHOOL: Pahokee (Fla.).
COLLEGE: Pittsburgh.
TRANSACTIONS/CAREER NOTES: Selected by New Orleans Saints in second round (51st pick overall) of 1981 NFL draft. . . . Granted free agency (February 1, 1990). . . . Re-signed by Saints (July 25, 1990).
PLAYING EXPERIENCE: New Orleans NFL, 1981-1990. . . . Games: 1981 (16), 1982 (9), 1983 (16), 1984 (16), 1985 (16), 1986 (16), 1987 (12), 1988 (16), 1989 (14), 1990 (16). Total: 147.
RECORDS/HONORS: Played in Pro Bowl after 1983-1986 seasons. . . . Named to THE SPORTING NEWS NFL All-Pro team, 1987.
PRO STATISTICS: 1981—Recovered one fumble. 1982—Intercepted one pass for 32 yards and recovered two fumbles. 1983—Intercepted one pass for no yards, recovered two fumbles for minus two yards and fumbled once. 1984—Recovered four fumbles for four yards, fumbled once and intercepted one pass for 14 yards. 1986—Intercepted one pass for one yard and recovered one fumble. 1987—Intercepted two passes for four yards. 1988—Intercepted one pass for 16 yards and credited with a safety. 1990—Recovered seven fumbles.

JACKSON, VESTEE
CB, DOLPHINS

PERSONAL: Born August 14, 1963, at Fresno, Calif. . . . 6-0/186. . . . Full name: Vestee Jackson II.
HIGH SCHOOL: McLane (Fresno, Calif.).
COLLEGE: Washington.
TRANSACTIONS/CAREER NOTES: Selected by Chicago Bears in second round (55th pick overall) of 1986 NFL draft. . . . Signed by Bears (July 24, 1986). . . . Granted free agency (February 1, 1990). . . . Re-signed by Bears (August 7, 1990). . . . Traded by Bears to Miami Dolphins for linebacker Eric Kumerow (January 31, 1991).
CHAMPIONSHIP GAME EXPERIENCE: Played in NFC championship game after 1988 season.
PRO STATISTICS: 1986—Recovered two fumbles for minus seven yards. 1989—Recovered one fumble.

		INTERCEPTIONS			
Year Team	G	No.	Yds.	Avg.	TD
1986— Chicago NFL	16	3	0	.0	0
1987— Chicago NFL	12	1	0	.0	0
1988— Chicago NFL	16	8	94	11.8	0
1989— Chicago NFL	16	2	16	8.0	0
1990— Chicago NFL	16	1	45	45.0	1
Pro totals (5 years)	76	15	155	10.3	1

JACOBY, JOE
OT, REDSKINS

PERSONAL: Born July 6, 1959, at Louisville, Ky. . . . 6-7/310.
HIGH SCHOOL: Western (Louisville, Ky.).
COLLEGE: Louisville.
TRANSACTIONS/CAREER NOTES: Signed as free agent by Washington Redskins (May 1, 1981). . . . On injured reserve with knee injury (November 16, 1989-remainder of season).
PLAYING EXPERIENCE: Washington NFL, 1981-1990. . . . Games: 1981 (14), 1982 (9), 1983 (16), 1984 (16), 1985 (11), 1986 (16), 1987 (12), 1988 (16), 1989 (10), 1990 (16). Total: 136.
CHAMPIONSHIP GAME EXPERIENCE: Played in NFC championship game after 1982, 1983, 1986 and 1987 seasons. . . . Played in Super Bowl XVII after 1982 season, Super Bowl XVIII after 1983 season and Super Bowl XXII after 1987 season.
RECORDS/HONORS: Played in Pro Bowl after 1983-1986 seasons. . . . Named to THE SPORTING NEWS NFL All-Pro team, 1983 and 1984.
PRO STATISTICS: 1981—Recovered one fumble. 1982—Recovered one fumble. 1984—Recovered one fumble in end zone for a touchdown. 1988—Recovered one fumble.

JAEGER, JEFF
PK, RAIDERS

PERSONAL: Born November 26, 1964, at Tacoma, Wash. . . . 5-11/195. . . . Full name: Jeff Todd Jaeger. . . . Name pronounced JAY-ger.
HIGH SCHOOL: Kent-Meridian (Kent, Wash.).
COLLEGE: Washington.

TRANSACTIONS/CAREER NOTES: Selected by Cleveland Browns in third round (82nd pick overall) of 1987 NFL draft.... Signed by Browns (July 26, 1987).... Crossed picket line during players' strike (October 14, 1987).... On injured reserve with foot injury (August 26, 1988-entire season).... Granted unconditional free agency (February 1, 1989).... Signed by Los Angeles Raiders (March 20, 1989).

CHAMPIONSHIP GAME EXPERIENCE: Played in AFC championship game after 1990 season.

PRO STATISTICS: 1987—Attempted one pass with no completions and recovered one fumble.

			PLACE-KICKING			
Year	Team	G	XPM	XPA	FGM	FGA	Pts.
1987— Cleveland NFL		10	33	33	14	22	75
1989— L.A. Raiders NFL		16	34	34	23	34	103
1990— L.A. Raiders NFL		16	40	42	15	20	85
Pro totals (3 years)		42	107	109	52	76	263

JAMES, LYNN
WR, BENGALS

PERSONAL: Born January 25, 1965, at Navasota, Tex.... 6-0/191.
HIGH SCHOOL: Navasota (Tex.).
COLLEGE: Arizona State.
TRANSACTIONS/CAREER NOTES: Selected by Cincinnati Bengals in fifth round (123rd pick overall) of 1990 NFL draft.... Signed by Bengals (July 17, 1990).... On injured reserve with ulcer (September 4-October 13, 1990).
PRO STATISTICS: 1990—Attempted one pass with no completions.

			RUSHING				RECEIVING				KICKOFF RETURNS				TOTAL		
Year	Team	G	Att.	Yds.	Avg.	TD	No.	Yds.	Avg.	TD	No.	Yds.	Avg.	TD	TD	Pts.	F.
1990— Cincinnati NFL		11	1	11	11.0	0	3	36	12.0	0	1	43	43.0	0	0	0	0
Pro totals (1 year)		11	1	11	11.0	0	3	36	12.0	0	1	43	43.0	0	0	0	0

JAMES, ROLAND
S, PATRIOTS

PERSONAL: Born February 18, 1958, at Xenia, O.... 6-2/191.... Full name: Roland Orlando James.
HIGH SCHOOL: Greenview (Jamestown, O.).
COLLEGE: Tennessee.
TRANSACTIONS/CAREER NOTES: Selected by New England Patriots in first round (14th pick overall) of 1980 NFL draft.... On injured reserve with knee injury (January 6, 1983-remainder of 1982 season playoffs).... On injured reserve with knee injury (September 8-October 23, 1987).... Granted free agency (February 1, 1990).... Re-signed by Patriots (May 8, 1990).... On inactive list (October 7, 18, 28; and November 4, 1990).
CHAMPIONSHIP GAME EXPERIENCE: Played in AFC championship game after 1985 season.... Played in Super Bowl XX after 1985 season.
RECORDS/HONORS: Named as cornerback on THE SPORTING NEWS college All-America team, 1979.
PRO STATISTICS: 1980—Recovered one fumble. 1981—Recovered one fumble. 1983—Recovered four fumbles. 1984—Credited with a safety. 1988—Recovered one fumble. 1989—Recovered one fumble for seven yards.

			INTERCEPTIONS				PUNT RETURNS				TOTAL		
Year	Team	G	No.	Yds.	Avg.	TD	No.	Yds.	Avg.	TD	TD	Pts.	F.
1980— New England NFL		16	4	32	8.0	0	33	331	10.0	1	1	6	2
1981— New England NFL		16	2	29	14.5	0	7	56	8.0	0	0	0	1
1982— New England NFL		7	3	12	4.0	0	0	0		0	0	0	1
1983— New England NFL		16	5	99	19.8	0	0	0		0	0	0	0
1984— New England NFL		15	2	14	7.0	0	0	0		0	0	0	0
1985— New England NFL		16	4	51	12.8	0	2	13	6.5	0	0	0	1
1986— New England NFL		15	2	39	19.5	0	0	0		0	0	0	0
1987— New England NFL		9	1	27	27.0	0	0	0		0	0	0	0
1988— New England NFL		15	4	30	7.5	0	0	0		0	0	0	0
1989— New England NFL		14	2	50	25.0	0	0	0		0	0	0	0
1990— New England NFL		6	0	0		0	0	0		0	0	0	0
Pro totals (11 years)		145	29	383	13.2	0	42	400	9.5	1	1	6	5

JAMISON, GEORGE
LB, LIONS

PERSONAL: Born September 30, 1962, at Bridgeton, N.J.... 6-1/228.... Full name: George R. Jamison.... Cousin of Anthony (Bubba) Green, defensive tackle with Baltimore Colts, 1981; and Larry Milbourne, infielder with Houston Astros, Seattle Mariners, New York Yankees, Minnesota Twins, Cleveland Indians and Philadelphia Phillies, 1975-1984.
HIGH SCHOOL: Bridgeton (N.J.).
COLLEGE: Cincinnati.
TRANSACTIONS/CAREER NOTES: Selected by Philadelphia Stars in second round (34th pick overall) of 1984 USFL draft.... Signed by Stars (January 17, 1984).... On developmental squad for two games (February 24-March 2, 1984; and June 21, 1984-remainder of season).... Selected by Detroit Lions in second round (47th pick overall) of 1984 NFL supplemental draft.... Philadelphia Stars franchise transferred to Baltimore (November 1, 1984).... On developmental squad for one game (May 3-May 10, 1985).... Granted free agency when USFL suspended operations (August 7, 1986).... Signed by Detroit Lions (August 17, 1986).... On injured reserve with achilles tendon injury (August 30, 1986-entire season).... On injured reserve with knee injury (December 21, 1989-remainder of season).... On inactive list (September 30 and October 7, 1990).
PLAYING EXPERIENCE: Philadelphia USFL, 1984; Baltimore USFL, 1985; Detroit NFL, 1987-1990.... Games: 1984 (15), 1985 (17), 1987 (12), 1988 (16), 1989 (10), 1990 (14).... Total USFL: 32. Total NFL: 52. Total Pro: 84.
CHAMPIONSHIP GAME EXPERIENCE: Played in USFL championship game after 1984 and 1985 seasons.

PRO STATISTICS: USFL: 1984—Credited with four sacks for 37 yards. 1985—Intercepted one pass for 16 yards and credited with five sacks for 40½ yards. . . . NFL: 1987—Credited with a safety. 1988—Intercepted three passes for 56 yards and a touchdown and recovered three fumbles for four yards and a touchdown. 1990—Recovered one fumble.

JAROSTCHUK, ILIA
LB, PATRIOTS

PERSONAL: Born August 1, 1964, at Utica, N.Y. . . . 6-3/245 . . . Name pronounced ILL-ee-uh jur-ROSS-chuk.
HIGH SCHOOL: Central (Whitesboro, N.Y.).
COLLEGE: New Hampshire (bachelor of science degree in civil engineering, 1987).
TRANSACTIONS/CAREER NOTES: Selected by St. Louis Cardinals in fifth round (127th pick overall) of 1987 NFL draft. . . . Signed by Cardinals (July 20, 1987). . . . Franchise transferred to Phoenix (March 15, 1988). . . . Released by Phoenix Cardinals (August 30, 1988). . . . Signed as free agent by San Francisco 49ers (September 13, 1988). . . . Released by 49ers (September 16, 1988). . . . Signed as free agent by Miami Dolphins (September 28, 1988). . . . Released by Dolphins (November 10, 1988). . . . Signed as free agent by Phoenix Cardinals (February 10, 1989). . . . Granted unconditional free agency (February 1, 1990). . . . Signed by New England Patriots (March 24, 1990). . . . Released by Patriots (September 3, 1990). . . . Re-signed by Patriots (September 27, 1990).
PLAYING EXPERIENCE: St. Louis NFL, 1987; Miami NFL, 1988; Phoenix NFL, 1989, New England NFL, 1990. . . . Games: 1987 (12), 1988 (6), 1989 (16), 1990 (12). Total: 46.

JAX, GARTH
LB, CARDINALS

PERSONAL: Born September 16, 1963, at Houston. . . . 6-3/230. . . . Full name: James Garth Jax.
HIGH SCHOOL: Strake Jesuit Preparatory (Houston).
COLLEGE: Florida State (bachelor of science degree in criminology, 1986).
TRANSACTIONS/CAREER NOTES: Selected by Tampa Bay Bandits in 1986 USFL territorial draft. . . . Selected by Dallas Cowboys in 11th round (296th pick overall) of 1986 NFL draft. . . . Signed by Cowboys (July 1, 1986). . . . Released by Cowboys (September 1, 1986). . . . Re-signed by Cowboys (September 8, 1986). . . . On injured reserve with fractured wrist (November 2, 1987-remainder of season). . . . Granted unconditional free agency (February 1, 1989). . . . Signed by Phoenix Cardinals (April 1, 1989).
PLAYING EXPERIENCE: Dallas NFL, 1986-1988; Phoenix NFL, 1989 and 1990. . . . Games: 1986 (16), 1987 (3), 1988 (16), 1989 (16), 1990 (16). Total: 67.
PRO STATISTICS: 1988—Recovered one fumble. 1990—Returned two kickoffs for 17 yards and intercepted two passes for five yards.

JEFFCOAT, JIM
DE, COWBOYS

PERSONAL: Born April 1, 1961, at Long Branch, N.J. . . . 6-5/270. . . . Full name: James Wilson Jeffcoat Jr.
HIGH SCHOOL: Regional (Matawan, N.J.).
COLLEGE: Arizona State (bachelor of arts degree in communications, 1983).
TRANSACTIONS/CAREER NOTES: Selected by Arizona Wranglers in 1983 USFL territorial draft. . . . Selected by Dallas Cowboys in first round (23rd pick overall) of 1983 NFL draft. . . . Signed by Cowboys (May 24, 1983).
PLAYING EXPERIENCE: Dallas NFL, 1983-1990. . . . Games: 1983 (16), 1984 (16), 1985 (16), 1986 (16), 1987 (12), 1988 (16), 1989 (16), 1990 (16). Total: 124.
PRO STATISTICS: 1984—Recovered fumble in end zone for a touchdown. 1985—Intercepted one pass for 65 yards and a touchdown and recovered two fumbles. 1986—Recovered two fumbles for eight yards. 1987—Intercepted one pass for 26 yards and a touchdown and recovered two fumbles for eight yards. 1989—Recovered three fumbles for 77 yards and a touchdown. 1990—Recovered one fumble for 28 yards.

JEFFERSON, BEN
OT, BROWNS

PERSONAL: Born January 15, 1966, at New Rochelle, N.Y. . . . 6-9/330.
HIGH SCHOOL: New Rochelle (N.Y.).
COLLEGE: Maryland.
TRANSACTIONS/CAREER NOTES: Signed as free agent by Indianapolis Colts (May, 1989). . . . Released by Colts (September 5, 1989). . . . Re-signed by Colts to developmental squad (September 6, 1989). . . . Released by Colts (October 19, 1989). . . . Signed by Cleveland Browns to developmental squad (November 8, 1989). . . . Released by Browns (January 29, 1990). . . . Re-signed by Browns (February 27, 1990). . . . On inactive list (October 8 and 14, 1990). . . . On injured reserve with back injury (October 22, 1990-remainder of season).
PLAYING EXPERIENCE: Cleveland NFL, 1990. . . . Games: 1990 (4).

JEFFERSON, JAMES
CB, SEAHAWKS

PERSONAL: Born November 18, 1963, at Portsmouth, Va. . . . 6-1/199. . . . Full name: James Andrew Jefferson III.
HIGH SCHOOL: H.M. King (Kingsville, Tex.).
COLLEGE: Texas A&I.
TRANSACTIONS/CAREER NOTES: Signed as free agent by Winnipeg Blue Bombers of CFL (March 10, 1986). . . . Granted free agency (March 1, 1989). . . . Signed by Seattle Seahawks (March 21, 1989).
CHAMPIONSHIP GAME EXPERIENCE: Played in Grey Cup (CFL championship game) after 1988 season.
PRO STATISTICS: CFL: 1986—Recovered one fumble for minus 17 yards. 1987—Recovered three fumbles for 26 yards and a touchdown. 1988—Recovered one fumble. . . . NFL: 1989—Recovered three fumbles. 1990—Recovered one fumble.

			— INTERCEPTIONS—				— PUNT RETURNS —				– KICKOFF RETURNS –				— TOTAL—		
Year	Team	G	No.	Yds.	Avg.	TD	No.	Yds.	Avg.	TD	No.	Yds.	Avg.	TD	TD	Pts.	F.
1986— Winnipeg CFL	....	14	2	38	19.0	0	44	415	9.4	1	4	91	22.8	0	1	6	1
1987— Winnipeg CFL	....	17	8	99	12.4	2	4	73	18.3	1	0	26		0	4	24	0
1988— Winnipeg CFL	....	18	2	56	28.0	0	71	650	9.2	1	28	666	23.8	1	2	12	5

Year Team	G	No.	Yds.	Avg.	TD	No.	Yds.	Avg.	TD	No.	Yds.	Avg.	TD	TD	Pts.	F.
		—INTERCEPTIONS—				—PUNT RETURNS—				—KICKOFF RETURNS—				—TOTAL—		
1989— Seattle NFL	16	0	0		0	12	87	7.3	0	22	511	23.2	*1	1	6	3
1990— Seattle NFL	15	1	0	.0	0	8	68	8.5	0	4	96	24.0	0	0	0	1
CFL totals (3 years)	49	12	193	16.1	2	119	1138	9.6	3	32	783	24.5	1	7	42	6
NFL totals (2 years)	31	1	0		0	20	155	7.8	0	26	607	23.4	1	1	6	4
Pro totals (5 years)	80	13	193	14.9	2	139	1293	9.3	3	58	1390	24.0	2	8	48	10

JEFFIRES, HAYWOOD
WR, OILERS

PERSONAL: Born December 12, 1964, at Greensboro (N.C.).... 6-2/201.... Full name: Haywood Franklin Jeffires.... Name pronounced JEFF-rees.
HIGH SCHOOL: Page (Greensboro, N.C.).
COLLEGE: North Carolina State (bachelor of arts degree in recreation administration, 1987).
TRANSACTIONS/CAREER NOTES: Selected by Houston Oilers in first round (20th pick overall) of 1987 NFL draft.... Signed by Oilers (July 22, 1987).... Crossed picket line during players' strike (October 14, 1987).... On injured reserve with ankle injury (August 29-December 10, 1988).

Year Team	G	No.	Yds.	Avg.	TD
		—RECEIVING—			
1987— Houston NFL	9	7	89	12.7	0
1988— Houston NFL	2	2	49	24.5	1
1989— Houston NFL	16	47	619	13.2	2
1990— Houston NFL	16	74	1048	14.2	8
Pro totals (4 years)	43	130	1805	13.9	11

JENKINS, A.J.
DE, STEELERS

PERSONAL: Born April 12, 1966, at Havelock, N.C.... 6-2/229.
HIGH SCHOOL: Havelock (N.C.).
COLLEGE: Merced College (Calif.), then Cal State Fullerton.
TRANSACTIONS/CAREER NOTES: Selected by Pittsburgh Steelers in ninth round (228th pick overall) of 1989 NFL draft.... Signed by Steelers (July 19, 1989).... On injured reserve with knee injury (January 5, 1990-remainder of 1989 season playoffs).... On injured reserve with knee injury (October 5-December 28, 1990).
PLAYING EXPERIENCE: Pittsburgh NFL, 1989 and 1990.... Games: 1989 (16), 1990 (5). Total: 21.

JENKINS, IZEL
CB, EAGLES

PERSONAL: Born May 27, 1964, at Wilson, N.C.... 5-10/190.... Full name: Izel Jenkins Jr.... First name pronounced EYE-ZELL.
HIGH SCHOOL: R.L. Fike (Wilson, N.C.).
COLLEGE: Taft College (Calif.), then North Carolina State.
TRANSACTIONS/CAREER NOTES: Selected by Philadelphia Eagles in 11th round (288th pick overall) of 1988 NFL draft.... Signed by Eagles (July 18, 1988).... Granted free agency (February 1, 1990).... Re-signed by Eagles (August 19, 1990).
PLAYING EXPERIENCE: Philadelphia NFL, 1988-1990.... Games: 1988 (16), 1989 (16), 1990 (15). Total: 47.
PRO STATISTICS: 1988—Credited with a safety and returned one kickoff for 20 yards. 1989—Intercepted four passes for 58 yards. 1990—Returned one kickoff for 14 yards.

JENKINS, MELVIN
CB, LIONS

PERSONAL: Born March 16, 1962, at Jackson, Miss.... 5-10/173.
HIGH SCHOOL: Wingfield (Jackson, Miss.).
COLLEGE: Cincinnati.
TRANSACTIONS/CAREER NOTES: Signed as free agent by Calgary Stampeders of CFL (April 17, 1984).... Granted free agency (March 1, 1987).... Signed as free agent by Seattle Seahawks (April 22, 1987).... Granted unconditional free agency (February 1, 1991).... Signed by Detroit Lions (March 30, 1991).
PRO STATISTICS: CFL: 1984—Recovered three fumbles. 1985—Recovered one fumble. 1986—Recovered one fumble.... NFL: 1988—Recovered one fumble for 50 yards. 1989—Recovered one fumble. 1990—Recovered two fumbles.

Year Team	G	No.	Yds.	Avg.	TD	No.	Yds.	Avg.	TD	No.	Yds.	Avg.	TD	TD	Pts.	F.
		—INTERCEPTIONS—				—PUNT RETURNS—				—KICKOFF RETURNS—				—TOTAL—		
1984— Calgary CFL	13	3	50	16.7	1	41	349	8.5	0	15	312	20.8	0	1	6	4
1985— Calgary CFL	9	1	-5	-5.0	0	7	74	10.6	0	6	110	18.3	0	0	0	1
1986— Calgary CFL	18	7	139	19.9	1	1	10	10.0	0	0	0		0	1	6	0
1987— Seattle NFL	12	3	46	15.3	0	0	0		0	0	0		0	0	0	1
1988— Seattle NFL	16	3	41	13.7	0	0	0		0	0	0		0	0	0	1
1989— Seattle NFL	16	0	0		0	0	0		0	0	0		0	0	0	0
1990— Seattle NFL	16	1	0	.0	0	0	0		0	0	0		0	0	0	0
CFL totals (3 years)	40	11	184	16.7	2	49	433	8.8	0	21	422	20.1	0	2	12	5
NFL totals (4 years)	60	7	87	12.4	0	0	0		0	0	0		0	0	0	2
Pro totals (7 years)	100	18	271	15.1	2	49	433	8.8	0	21	422	20.1	0	2	12	7

JENNINGS, KEITH
TE, BRONCOS

PERSONAL: Born May 19, 1966, at Summerville, S.C.... 6-4/250.... Full name: Keith O'Neal Jennings.... Brother of Stanford Jennings, running back with Cincinnati Bengals.
HIGH SCHOOL: Summerville (S.C.).

COLLEGE: Clemson.

TRANSACTIONS/CAREER NOTES: Selected by Dallas Cowboys in fifth round (113th pick overall) of 1989 NFL draft.... Signed by Cowboys (August 2, 1989).... Released by Cowboys (September 5, 1989).... Re-signed by Cowboys to developmental squad (September 6, 1989).... On developmental squad (September 6-October 16, 1989).... Activated after clearing procedural waivers (October 18, 1989).... Released by Cowboys (September 3, 1990).... Signed by WLAF (January 31, 1991).... Selected by Montreal Machine in first round (first tight end) of 1991 WLAF positional draft.... Signed by Denver Broncos (July 3, 1991).

			RECEIVING		
Year	Team	G	No.	Yds.	Avg.	TD
1989— Dallas NFL		10	6	47	7.8	0
1991— Montreal WLAF		4	4	54	13.5	1
NFL totals (1 year)		10	6	47	7.8	0
WLAF totals (1 year)		4	4	54	13.5	1
Pro totals (2 years)		14	10	101	10.1	1

JENNINGS, STANFORD
RB, BENGALS

PERSONAL: Born March 12, 1962, at Summerville, S.C.... 6-1/212.... Full name: Stanford Jamison Jennings.... Brother of Keith Jennings, tight end with Denver Broncos.
HIGH SCHOOL: Summerville (S.C.).

COLLEGE: Furman.

TRANSACTIONS/CAREER NOTES: Selected by Michigan Panthers in first round (17th pick overall) of 1984 USFL draft.... Selected by Cincinnati Bengals in third round (65th pick overall) of 1984 NFL draft.... Signed by Bengals (July 2, 1984).

CHAMPIONSHIP GAME EXPERIENCE: Played in AFC championship game after 1988 season.... Played in Super Bowl XXIII after 1988 season.

PRO STATISTICS: 1984—Recovered two fumbles. 1985—Recovered one fumble. 1987—Recovered one fumble.

			RUSHING				RECEIVING				KICKOFF RETURNS				TOTAL	
Year	Team	G	Att.	Yds.	Avg.	TD	No.	Yds.	Avg.	TD	No.	Yds.	Avg.	TD	TD	Pts.	F.
1984— Cincinnati NFL	15	79	379	4.8	2	35	346	9.9	3	22	452	20.6	0	5	30	3
1985— Cincinnati NFL	16	31	92	3.0	1	12	101	8.4	3	13	218	16.8	0	4	24	1
1986— Cincinnati NFL	16	16	54	3.4	1	6	86	14.3	0	12	257	21.4	0	1	6	0
1987— Cincinnati NFL	12	70	314	4.5	1	35	277	7.9	2	2	32	16.0	0	3	18	0
1988— Cincinnati NFL	16	17	47	2.8	1	5	75	15.0	0	32	684	21.4	*1	2	12	1
1989— Cincinnati NFL	16	83	293	3.5	2	10	119	11.9	1	26	525	20.2	0	3	18	1
1990— Cincinnati NFL	16	12	46	3.8	1	4	23	5.8	0	29	584	20.1	0	1	6	2
Pro totals (7 years)	107	308	1225	4.0	9	107	1027	9.6	9	136	2752	20.2	1	19	114	8

JENSEN, JIM
WR/RB, DOLPHINS

PERSONAL: Born November 14, 1958, at Abington, Pa.... 6-4/224.... Full name: James Christopher Jensen.
HIGH SCHOOL: Central Bucks (Doylestown, Pa.).
COLLEGE: Boston University (bachelor of science degree in special education, 1981).

TRANSACTIONS/CAREER NOTES: Selected by Miami Dolphins in 11th round (291st pick overall) of 1981 NFL draft.... On inactive list (September 12 and 19, 1982).... Granted free agency (February 1, 1985).... Re-signed by Dolphins (August 31, 1985). ... Granted roster exemption (August 31-September 7, 1985).... Granted free agency (February 1, 1990).... Re-signed by Dolphins (September 12, 1990).... Granted roster exemption (September 12-September 15, 1990).

CHAMPIONSHIP GAME EXPERIENCE: Played in AFC championship game after 1982, 1984 and 1985 seasons.... Played in Super Bowl XVII after 1982 season and Super Bowl XIX after 1984 season.

PRO STATISTICS: 1982—Attempted one pass with no completions. 1984—Attempted one pass with one completion for 35 yards and a touchdown. 1986—Attempted two passes with no completions. 1987—Recovered three fumbles for two yards. 1988—Recovered two fumbles. 1989—Attempted one pass with one completion for 19 yards and a touchdown. 1990—Attempted one pass with one completion for 31 yards.

			RUSHING				RECEIVING				TOTAL	
Year	Team	G	Att.	Yds.	Avg.	TD	No.	Yds.	Avg.	TD	TD	Pts.	F.
1981— Miami NFL	16	0	0		0	0	0	0	0	0	0	0
1982— Miami NFL	6	0	0		0	0	0	0	0	0	0	0
1983— Miami NFL	16	0	0		0	0	0	0	0	0	0	0
1984— Miami NFL	16	0	0		0	13	139	10.7	2	0	0	0
1985— Miami NFL	16	0	0		0	1	4	4.0	1	1	6	0
1986— Miami NFL	16	0	0		0	5	50	10.0	1	1	6	0
1987— Miami NFL	12	4	18	4.5	0	26	221	8.5	1	1	6	1
1988— Miami NFL	16	10	68	6.8	0	58	652	11.2	5	5	30	2
1989— Miami NFL	16	8	50	6.3	0	61	557	9.1	6	6	36	0
1990— Miami NFL	15	4	6	1.5	0	44	365	8.3	1	1	6	1
Pro totals (10 years)	145	26	142	5.5	0	208	1988	9.6	17	15	90	4

JETTON, PAUL
C/G, BENGALS

PERSONAL: Born October 6, 1964, at Houston.... 6-4/288.... Full name: Paul Ray Jetton.
HIGH SCHOOL: Jersey Village (Houston).
COLLEGE: Texas.
TRANSACTIONS/CAREER NOTES: Selected by Cincinnati Bengals in sixth round (141st pick overall) of 1988 NFL draft.... Signed by Bengals (June 30, 1988).... On injured reserve with dislocated finger (August 29, 1988-

entire season).... On injured reserve with knee injury (October 21-December 7, 1989); then transferred to developmental squad (December 8, 1989-remainder of season).
PLAYING EXPERIENCE: Cincinnati NFL, 1989 and 1990.... Games: 1989 (5), 1990 (15). Total: 20.

JIMERSON, A.J.
LB, RAIDERS
PERSONAL: Born May 12, 1968, at Erie, Pa.... 6-3/235.... Full name: Arthur Jimerson.
HIGH SCHOOL: Deep Creek (Chesapeake, Va.).
COLLEGE: Norfolk State (Va.).
TRANSACTIONS/CAREER NOTES: Selected by Los Angeles Raiders in eighth round (197th pick overall) of 1990 NFL draft.... On inactive list (September 9 and 16, 1990).... On injured reserve (October 21, 1990-remainder of season).
PLAYING EXPERIENCE: Los Angeles Raiders NFL, 1990.... Games: 1990 (4).
PRO STATISTICS: 1990—Intercepted one pass for no yards.

JOHNSON, A.J.
CB, REDSKINS
PERSONAL: Born June 22, 1967, at Lompoc, Calif.... 5-8/176.... Full name: Anthony Sean Johnson.
HIGH SCHOOL: Samuel Clemens (Schertz, Tex.).
COLLEGE: Southwest Texas State.
TRANSACTIONS/CAREER NOTES: Selected by Washington Redskins in sixth round (149th pick overall) of 1989 NFL draft.... Signed by Redskins (July 23, 1989).... On physically unable to perform list with knee injury (August 28-December 1, 1990).

| | | — INTERCEPTIONS — | | | | — KICKOFF RETURNS — | | | | — TOTAL — | | |
Year Team	G	No.	Yds.	Avg.	TD	No.	Yds.	Avg.	TD	TD	Pts.	F.
1989— Washington NFL	16	4	94	23.5	1	24	504	21.0	0	1	6	0
1990— Washington NFL	5	1	0	.0	0	0	0		0	0	0	0
Pro totals (2 years)	21	5	94	18.8	1	24	504	21.0	0	1	6	0

JOHNSON, ANTHONY
FB, COLTS
PERSONAL: Born October 25, 1967, at Indianapolis.... 6-0/222.... Full name: Anthony Scott Johnson.
HIGH SCHOOL: John Adams (South Bend, Ind.).
COLLEGE: Notre Dame.
TRANSACTIONS/CAREER NOTES: Selected by Indianapolis Colts in second round (36th pick overall) of 1990 NFL draft.... Signed by Colts (July 27, 1990).

| | | — RUSHING — | | | | — RECEIVING — | | | | — TOTAL — | | |
Year Team	G	Att.	Yds.	Avg.	TD	No.	Yds.	Avg.	TD	TD	Pts.	F.
1990— Indianapolis NFL	16	0	0		0	5	32	6.4	2	2	12	0
NFL totals (1 year)	16	0	0		0	5	32	6.4	2	2	12	0

JOHNSON, DAMONE
TE, RAMS
PERSONAL: Born March 2, 1962, at Los Angeles.... 6-4/250.
HIGH SCHOOL: Santa Monica (Calif.).
COLLEGE: California Poly State (SLO).
TRANSACTIONS/CAREER NOTES: Selected by Oakland Invaders in 1985 USFL territorial draft.... Selected by Los Angeles Rams in sixth round (162nd pick overall) of 1985 NFL draft.... Signed by Rams (July 9, 1985).... Released by Rams (August 10, 1985).... Re-signed by Rams (March 21, 1986).... On injured reserve with knee injury (September 2-November 21, 1986).... On reserve/did not report (July 24-August 31, 1989).... Granted free agency (February 1, 1990).... Re-signed by Rams (May 10, 1990).... Released by Rams (August 29, 1990).... Re-signed by Rams (September 12, 1990).... Activated (September 14, 1990).... On inactive list (December 2 and 23, 1990).
CHAMPIONSHIP GAME EXPERIENCE: Played in NFC championship game after 1989 season.

| | | — RECEIVING — | | | |
Year Team	G	No.	Yds.	Avg.	TD
1986— L.A. Rams NFL	5	0	0		0
1987— L.A. Rams NFL	12	21	198	9.4	2
1988— L.A. Rams NFL	16	42	350	8.3	6
1989— L.A. Rams NFL	16	25	148	5.9	5
1990— L.A. Rams NFL	13	12	66	5.5	3
Pro totals (5 years)	62	100	762	7.6	16

JOHNSON, DAVID
CB, STEELERS
PERSONAL: Born April 14, 1966, at Louisville, Ky.... 6-0/185.... Full name: David Allen Johnson.
HIGH SCHOOL: Male (Louisville, Ky.).
COLLEGE: Kentucky.
TRANSACTIONS/CAREER NOTES: Selected by Pittsburgh Steelers in seventh round (174th pick overall) of 1989 NFL draft.... Signed by Steelers (July 24, 1989).
PRO STATISTICS: 1990—Recovered one fumble for nine yards.

| | | — INTERCEPTIONS — | | | |
Year Team	G	No.	Yds.	Avg.	TD
1989— Pittsburgh NFL	16	1	0	.0	0
1990— Pittsburgh NFL	16	2	60	30.0	1
Pro totals (2 years)	32	3	60	20.0	1

JOHNSON, EDDIE
LB, BROWNS

PERSONAL: Born February 3, 1959, at Albany, Ga.... 6-1/235. **HIGH SCHOOL:** Daughtery (Albany, Ga.). **COLLEGE:** Louisville. **TRANSACTIONS/CAREER NOTES:** Selected by Cleveland Browns in seventh round (187th pick overall) of 1981 NFL draft.
PLAYING EXPERIENCE: Cleveland NFL, 1981-1990.... Games: 1981 (16), 1982 (9), 1983 (16), 1984 (16), 1985 (16), 1986 (16), 1987 (12), 1988 (15), 1989 (16), 1990 (16). Total: 148.
CHAMPIONSHIP GAME EXPERIENCE: Played in AFC championship game after 1986, 1987 and 1989 seasons.
PRO STATISTICS: 1981—Returned one kickoff for seven yards and recovered one fumble. 1984—Intercepted two passes for three yards. 1985—Intercepted one pass for six yards. 1987—Intercepted one pass for 11 yards and recovered one fumble. 1988—Intercepted two passes for no yards and recovered three fumbles. 1989—Returned one kickoff for eight yards. 1990—Returned two kickoffs for 17 yards.

JOHNSON, EZRA
DE, OILERS

PERSONAL: Born October 2, 1955, at Shreveport, La.... 6-4/257.... Full name: Ezra Ray Johnson. **HIGH SCHOOL:** Green Oaks (Shreveport, La.). **COLLEGE:** Morris Brown College (Ga.).
TRANSACTIONS/CAREER NOTES: Selected by Green Bay Packers in first round (28th pick overall) of 1977 NFL draft.... On injured reserve with knee injury (December 14, 1984-remainder of season).... On injured reserve with knee injury (September 11-November 7, 1987).... Granted free agency with no qualifying offer (February 1, 1988).... Signed by Indianapolis Colts (April 27, 1988).... Granted unconditional free agency (February 1, 1990).... Signed by Houston Oilers (March 30, 1990).
PLAYING EXPERIENCE: Green Bay NFL, 1977-1987; Indianapolis NFL, 1988 and 1989; Houston NFL, 1990.... Games: 1977 (14), 1978 (16), 1979 (11), 1980 (15), 1981 (16), 1982 (9), 1983 (16), 1984 (13), 1985 (16), 1986 (16), 1987 (6), 1988 (10), 1989 (16), 1990 (16). Total: 190.
RECORDS/HONORS: Played in Pro Bowl after 1978 season.
PRO STATISTICS: 1977—Recovered one fumble. 1978—Returned one kickoff for 14 yards and recovered two fumbles. 1983—Recovered two fumbles. 1985—Recovered two fumbles. 1989—Recovered one fumble.

JOHNSON, FLIP
WR, BROWNS

PERSONAL: Born July 13, 1963, at Cheek, Tex.... 5-9/181.... Full name: Fulton Johnson. **HIGH SCHOOL:** Hamshire Fannett (Hamshire, Tex.). **COLLEGE:** McNeese State. **TRANSACTIONS/CAREER NOTES:** Signed as free agent by Buffalo Bills (May 2, 1987).... On injured reserve with thigh injury (September 1, 1987-entire season).... On injured reserve with hamstring injury (August 30-October 1, 1988).... Granted unconditional free agency (February 1, 1990).... Signed by Green Bay Packers (March 21, 1990).... Released by Packers (September 3, 1990).... Signed by Cleveland Browns (April 1, 1991).
CHAMPIONSHIP GAME EXPERIENCE: Played in AFC championship game after 1988 season.

			RECEIVING				PUNT RETURNS				KICKOFF RETURNS				TOTAL	
Year	Team	G	No.	Yds.	Avg.	TD	No.	Yds.	Avg.	TD	No.	Yds.	Avg.	TD	TD	Pts.	F.
1988—Buffalo NFL		11	9	170	18.9	1	16	72	4.5	0	14	250	17.9	0	1	6	1
1989—Buffalo NFL		16	25	303	12.1	1	1	7	7.0	0	0	0		0	1	6	0
Pro totals (2 years)		27	34	473	13.9	2	17	79	4.7	0	14	250	17.9	0	2	12	1

JOHNSON, JASON
WR, SAINTS

PERSONAL: Born November 8, 1965, at Gary, Ind.... 5-10/178.... Full name: Jason Mansfield Johnson. **HIGH SCHOOL:** West Side (Gary, Ind.). **COLLEGE:** Illinois State.
TRANSACTIONS/CAREER NOTES: Signed as free agent by Denver Broncos (April 27, 1988).... On injured reserve with back injury (August 22-October 27, 1988).... Granted unconditional free agency (February 1, 1989).... Signed by Pittsburgh Steelers (March 16, 1989).... Granted unconditional free agency (February 1, 1990).... Signed by Denver Broncos (March 28, 1990).... Released by Broncos (September 3, 1990).... Signed by New Orleans Saints (July 17, 1991).
PRO STATISTICS: 1988—Returned one punt for five yards and rushed once for three yards and recovered one fumble. 1989—Returned two punts for 22 yards and recovered one fumble.

			RECEIVING				KICKOFF RETURNS				TOTAL	
Year	Team	G	No.	Yds.	Avg.	TD	No.	Yds.	Avg.	TD	TD	Pts.	F.
1988—Denver NFL		8	1	6	6.0	0	14	292	20.9	0	0	0	1
1989—Pittsburgh NFL		14	0	0		0	3	43	14.3	0	0	0	1
Pro totals (2 years)		22	1	6	6.0	0	17	335	19.7	0	0	0	2

JOHNSON, JIMMIE
TE, REDSKINS

PERSONAL: Born October 6, 1966, at Augusta, Ga.... 6-2/246. **HIGH SCHOOL:** T.W. Josey (Augusta, Ga.). **COLLEGE:** Howard (degree in consumer studies, 1989). **TRANSACTIONS/CAREER NOTES:** Selected by Washington Redskins in 12th round (316th pick overall) of 1989 NFL draft.... Signed by Redskins (July 23, 1989).
PRO STATISTICS: 1990—Fumbled once.

			RECEIVING			
Year	Team	G	No.	Yds.	Avg.	TD
1989—Washington NFL		16	4	84	21.0	0
1990—Washington NFL		16	15	218	14.5	2
Pro totals (2 years)		32	19	302	15.9	2

JOHNSON, JOE
WR, REDSKINS

PERSONAL: Born December 21, 1962, at Washington, D.C. . . . . 5-9/170. . . . Full name: Joseph Pernell Johnson. . . . Formerly known as Joe Howard.
HIGH SCHOOL: Archbishop Carroll (Washington, D.C.).
COLLEGE: Notre Dame (degree in sociology).
TRANSACTIONS/CAREER NOTES: Signed as free agent by Tampa Bay Buccaneers (May 9, 1985). . . . Released by Buccaneers (August 20, 1985). . . . Signed as free agent by Buffalo Bills (May 6, 1986). . . . Released by Bills (August 18, 1986). . . . Re-signed by Bills (March 10, 1987). . . . Released by Bills (August 31, 1987). . . . Re-signed as replacement player by Bills (September 24, 1987). . . . On injured reserve with knee injury (October 1, 1987-remainder of season). . . . On injured reserve with rib injury (August 22, 1988-entire season). . . . Released by Bills (August 17, 1989). . . . Awarded on waivers to Washington Redskins (August 18, 1989). . . . Released by Redskins (September 4, 1989). . . . Re-signed by Redskins (September 5, 1989). . . . On injured reserve with rib injury (December 19, 1989-remainder of season). . . . On inactive list (November 18, 1990).
PRO STATISTICS: 1990—Recovered one fumble.

			RECEIVING			PUNT RETURNS				KICKOFF RETURNS				TOTAL		
Year	Team	G	No.	Yds.	Avg.	TD	No.	Yds.	Avg.	TD	No.	Yds.	Avg.	TD	TD	Pts.	F.
1989— Washington NFL.		15	0	0		0	21	200	9.5	0	21	522	24.9	*1	1	6	2
1990— Washington NFL.		15	3	36	12.0	0	10	99	9.9	0	22	427	19.4	0	0	0	0
Pro totals (2 years)		30	3	36	12.0	0	31	299	9.7	0	43	949	22.1	1	1	6	2

JOHNSON, JOHNNY
RB, CARDINALS

PERSONAL: Born June 11, 1968, at Santa Clara, Calif. . . . 6-3/220.
HIGH SCHOOL: Santa Cruz (Calif.).
COLLEGE: San Jose State.
TRANSACTIONS/CAREER NOTES: Selected by Phoenix Cardinals in seventh round (169th pick overall) of 1990 NFL draft. . . . Signed by Cardinals (July 25, 1990). . . . On inactive list (November 25 and December 9, 1990).
RECORDS/HONORS: Played in Pro Bowl after 1990 season.
PRO STATISTICS: 1990—Attempted one pass with one interception and recovered one fumble.

			RUSHING				RECEIVING				TOTAL		
Year	Team	G	Att.	Yds.	Avg.	TD	No.	Yds.	Avg.	TD	TD	Pts.	F.
1990— Phoenix NFL		14	234	926	4.0	5	25	241	9.6	0	5	30	7
Pro totals (1 year)		14	234	926	4.0	5	25	241	9.6	0	5	30	7

JOHNSON, KENNETH
S, JETS

PERSONAL: Born September 14, 1966, at Thomaston, Ga. . . . 6-2/216. . . . Full name: Kenneth Lee Johnson.
HIGH SCHOOL: Robert E. Lee Institute (Thomaston, Ga.).
COLLEGE: Florida A&M.
TRANSACTIONS/CAREER NOTES: Signed as free agent by Minnesota Vikings (May 5, 1989). . . . Released by Vikings (September 5, 1989). . . . Re-signed by Vikings to developmental squad (September 6, 1989). . . . On developmental squad (September 6-September 12, 1989). . . . Activated after clearing procedural waivers (September 14, 1989). . . . Released by Vikings (September 18, 1989). . . . Re-signed by Vikings to developmental squad (September 19, 1989). . . . On developmental squad (September 19-October 11, 1989). . . . Activated after clearing procedural waivers (October 13, 1989). . . . Released by Vikings (October 25, 1989). . . . Re-signed by Vikings to developmental squad (November 1, 1989). . . . On developmental squad (November 1, 1989-January 7, 1990). . . . Released by Vikings (January 8, 1990). . . . Re-signed by Vikings (February 12, 1990). . . . Released by Vikings (October 6, 1990). . . . Signed by Vikings to practice squad (October 11, 1990). . . . Signed by New York Jets (November 6, 1990). . . . Released by Jets (November 25, 1990). . . . Re-signed by Jets (December, 1990).
PLAYING EXPERIENCE: Minnesota NFL, 1989; Minnesota (4)-New York Jets (4) NFL, 1990. . . . Games: 1989 (1), 1990 (8). Total: 9.

JOHNSON, LEE
P/PK, BENGALS

PERSONAL: Born November 27, 1961, at Dallas. . . . 6-2/200.
HIGH SCHOOL: McCullough (The Woodlands, Tex.).
COLLEGE: Brigham Young.
TRANSACTIONS/CAREER NOTES: Selected by Houston Gamblers in ninth round (125th pick overall) of 1985 USFL draft. . . . Selected by Houston Oilers in fifth round (138th pick overall) of 1985 NFL draft. . . . Signed by Oilers (June 25, 1985). . . . Crossed picket line during players' strike (October 14, 1987). . . . Released by Oilers (December 1, 1987). . . . Awarded on waivers to Buffalo Bills (December 2, 1987). . . . Released by Bills (December 9, 1987). . . . Awarded on waivers to Cleveland Browns (December 10, 1987). . . . Released by Browns (September 22, 1988). . . . Awarded on waivers to Cincinnati Bengals (September 23, 1988).
CHAMPIONSHIP GAME EXPERIENCE: Played in AFC championship game after 1987 and 1988 seasons. . . . Played in Super Bowl XXIII after 1988 season.
PRO STATISTICS: 1985—Rushed once for no yards, recovered one fumble for seven yards and fumbled twice. 1988—Made one of two field goal attempts. 1989—Rushed once for minus seven yards and missed only extra point attempt. 1990—Attempted one pass with one completion for four yards and a touchdown and missed only field goal attempt.

			PUNTING		
Year	Team	G	No.	Avg.	Blk.
1985— Houston NFL..........................		16	83	41.7	0
1986— Houston NFL..........................		16	88	41.2	0
1987— Hou. (9)-Cle. (3) NFL..........		12	50	39.4	0
1988— Cle. (3)-Cin. (12) NFL.........		15	31	39.9	0
1989— Cincinnati NFL......................		16	61	40.1	2
1990— Cincinnati NFL......................		16	64	42.3	0
Pro totals (6 years)		91	377	40.8	2

JOHNSON, MIKE
LB, BROWNS

PERSONAL: Born November 26, 1962, at Southport, N.C. . . . 6-1/230. . . . Full name: Michael Johnson.
HIGH SCHOOL: DeMatha (Hyattsville, Md.).
COLLEGE: Virginia Tech.

TRANSACTIONS/CAREER NOTES: Selected by Pittsburgh Maulers in 1984 USFL territorial draft. . . . USFL rights traded by Maulers with defensive end Mark Buben, rights to linebacker Al Chesley and draft choice to Philadelphia Stars for rights to linebacker Ron Crosby (February 1, 1984). . . . Signed by Stars (February 20, 1984). . . . Granted roster exemption (February 20-March 2, 1984). . . . Selected by Cleveland Browns in first round (18th pick overall) of 1984 NFL supplemental draft. . . . Philadelphia Stars franchise transferred to Baltimore (November 1, 1984). . . . Granted free agency when USFL suspended operations (August 7, 1986). . . . Signed by Cleveland Browns (August 12, 1986). . . . Granted roster exemption (August 12-August 22, 1986). . . . Granted free agency (February 1, 1990). . . . Re-signed by Browns (August 31, 1990). . . . Granted roster exemption (September 3-September 8, 1990).
CHAMPIONSHIP GAME EXPERIENCE: Played in USFL championship game after 1984 and 1985 seasons. . . . Played in AFC championship game after 1986, 1987 and 1989 seasons.
RECORDS/HONORS: Played in Pro Bowl after 1990 season.
PRO STATISTICS: USFL: 1984—Credited with two sacks for four yards and recovered one fumble for eight yards. 1985—Credited with 3½ sacks for 25½ yards and recovered two fumbles. . . . NFL: 1986—Recovered two fumbles. 1987—Recovered one fumble.

| | | | —— INTERCEPTIONS—— | | |
Year	Team	G	No.	Yds.	Avg.	TD
1984—	Philadelphia USFL	17	0	0		0
1985—	Baltimore USFL	18	0	0		0
1986—	Cleveland NFL	16	0	0		0
1987—	Cleveland NFL	11	1	3	3.0	0
1988—	Cleveland NFL	16	2	36	18.0	0
1989—	Cleveland NFL	16	3	43	14.3	0
1990—	Cleveland NFL	16	1	64	64.0	1
	USFL totals (2 years)	35	0	0		0
	NFL totals (5 years)	75	7	146	20.9	1
	Pro totals (7 years)	110	7	146	20.9	1

JOHNSON, NORM
PK, SEAHAWKS

PERSONAL: Born May 31, 1960, at Inglewood, Calif. . . . 6-2/203.
HIGH SCHOOL: Pacifica (Garden Grove, Calif.).
COLLEGE: UCLA.
TRANSACTIONS/CAREER NOTES: Signed as free agent by Seattle Seahawks (May 4, 1982). . . . Crossed picket line during players' strike (October 14, 1987).
CHAMPIONSHIP GAME EXPERIENCE: Played in AFC championship game after 1983 season.
RECORDS/HONORS: Tied NFL record for most field goals, 50 or more yards, game (2), against Los Angeles Raiders (December 8, 1986). . . . Played in Pro Bowl after 1984 season. . . . Named to THE SPORTING NEWS NFL All-Pro team, 1984.
PRO STATISTICS: 1982—Attempted one pass with one completion for 27 yards.

| | | | —— PLACE-KICKING —— | | | |
Year	Team	G	XPM	XPA	FGM	FGA	Pts.
1982—	Seattle NFL	9	13	14	10	14	43
1983—	Seattle NFL	16	49	50	18	25	103
1984—	Seattle NFL	16	50	51	20	24	110
1985—	Seattle NFL	16	40	41	14	25	82
1986—	Seattle NFL	16	42	42	22	35	108
1987—	Seattle NFL	13	40	40	15	20	85
1988—	Seattle NFL	16	39	39	22	28	105
1989—	Seattle NFL	16	27	27	15	25	72
1990—	Seattle NFL	16	33	34	23	32	102
	Pro totals (9 years)	134	333	338	159	228	810

JOHNSON, PEPPER
LB, GIANTS

PERSONAL: Born June 29, 1964, at Detroit. . . . 6-3/248. . . . Full name: Thomas Johnson.
HIGH SCHOOL: MacKenzie (Detroit).
COLLEGE: Ohio State.

TRANSACTIONS/CAREER NOTES: Selected by New Jersey Generals in 1986 USFL territorial draft. . . . Selected by New York Giants in second round (51st pick overall) of 1986 NFL draft. . . . Signed by Giants (July 30, 1986). . . . Granted free agency (February 1, 1989). . . . Re-signed by Giants (September 14, 1989). . . . Granted roster exemption (September 14-September 23, 1989).
CHAMPIONSHIP GAME EXPERIENCE: Played in NFC championship game after 1986 and 1990 seasons. . . . Played in Super Bowl XXI after 1986 season and Super Bowl XXV after 1990 season.
RECORDS/HONORS: Played in Pro Bowl after 1990 season. . . . Named to THE SPORTING NEWS NFL All-Pro team, 1990.
PRO STATISTICS: 1987—Recovered one fumble. 1988—Recovered one fumble. 1989—Recovered one fumble. 1990—Recovered one fumble.

| | | | —— INTERCEPTIONS—— | | |
Year	Team	G	No.	Yds.	Avg.	TD
1986—	N.Y. Giants NFL	16	1	13	13.0	0
1987—	N.Y. Giants NFL	12	0	0		0
1988—	N.Y. Giants NFL	16	1	33	33.0	1
1989—	N.Y. Giants NFL	14	3	60	20.0	1
1990—	N.Y. Giants NFL	16	1	0	.0	0
	Pro totals (5 years)	74	6	106	17.7	2

JOHNSON, RICHARD
CB, OILERS

PERSONAL: Born September 16, 1963, at Harvey, Ill. . . . 6-1/195.
HIGH SCHOOL: Thornton (Harvey, Ill.).
COLLEGE: Wisconsin.
TRANSACTIONS/CAREER NOTES: Selected by Jacksonville Bulls in 1985 USFL territorial draft. . . . Selected by Houston Oilers in first round (11th pick overall) of 1985 NFL draft. . . . Signed by Oilers (August 22, 1985). . . . Granted roster exemption (August 22-August 30, 1985). . . . On injured reserve with knee injury (November 14, 1987-remainder of season). . . . On post-season deactivation list (December 29, 1989-remainder of 1989 season playoffs).
RECORDS/HONORS: Named as defensive back on THE SPORTING NEWS college All-America team, 1984.
PRO STATISTICS: 1985—Recovered one fumble. 1988—Returned one kickoff for two yards.

		— INTERCEPTIONS—			
Year Team	G	No.	Yds.	Avg.	TD
1985— Houston NFL	16	0	0		0
1986— Houston NFL	16	2	6	3.0	0
1987— Houston NFL	5	1	0	.0	0
1988— Houston NFL	16	3	0	.0	0
1989— Houston NFL	14	1	0	.0	0
1990— Houston NFL	16	8	100	12.5	1
Pro totals (6 years)	83	15	106	7.1	1

JOHNSON, SIDNEY
CB, REDSKINS

PERSONAL: Born March 7, 1965, at Los Angeles. . . . 5-9/175.
HIGH SCHOOL: Cerritos (Calif.).
COLLEGE: Cerritos College (Calif.), then California.
TRANSACTIONS/CAREER NOTES: Signed as free agent by Kansas City Chiefs (May 14, 1987). . . . On injured reserve with knee injury (August 31, 1987-entire season). . . . Granted unconditional free agency (February 1, 1989). . . . Signed by Tampa Bay Buccaneers (March 20, 1989). . . . Released by Buccaneers (August 29, 1989). . . . Signed as free agent by Kansas City Chiefs (May 1, 1990). . . . Released by Chiefs (September 3, 1990). . . . Signed by Washington Redskins (October 17, 1990). . . . Released by Redskins (December 30, 1990). . . . Re-signed by Redskins (January 2, 1991).
PLAYING EXPERIENCE: Kansas City NFL, 1988; Washington NFL, 1990. . . . Games: 1988 (13), 1990 (10). Total: 23.

JOHNSON, TIM
DT, REDSKINS

PERSONAL: Born January 29, 1965, at Sarasota, Fla. . . . 6-3/261. . . . Full name: Timothy Johnson.
HIGH SCHOOL: Sarasota (Fla.).
COLLEGE: Penn State (bachelor of arts degree in hotel, restaurant and institutional management, 1987).
TRANSACTIONS/CAREER NOTES: Selected by Pittsburgh Steelers in sixth round (141st pick overall) of 1987 NFL draft. . . . Signed by Steelers (July 26, 1987). . . . Traded by Steelers to Washington Redskins for fourth-round pick in 1991 draft (August 23, 1990).
PLAYING EXPERIENCE: Pittsburgh NFL, 1987-1989; Washington NFL, 1990. . . . Games: 1987 (12), 1988 (15), 1989 (14), 1990 (16). Total: 57.
PRO STATISTICS: 1990—Recovered one fumble.

JOHNSON, TRACY
RB, FALCONS

PERSONAL: Born March 13, 1966, at Concord, N.C. . . . 6-0/230. . . . Full name: Tracy Illya Johnson.
HIGH SCHOOL: A.L. Brown (Kannapolis, N.C.).
COLLEGE: Clemson.
TRANSACTIONS/CAREER NOTES: Selected by Houston Oilers in 10th round (271st pick overall) of 1989 NFL draft. . . . Signed by Oilers (July 27, 1989). . . . Granted unconditional free agency (February 1, 1990). . . . Signed by Atlanta Falcons (March 30, 1990).

		—RUSHING—				—RECEIVING—				– KICKOFF RETURNS–				—TOTAL—		
Year Team	G	Att.	Yds.	Avg.	TD	No.	Yds.	Avg.	TD	No.	Yds.	Avg.	TD	TD	Pts.	F.
1989— Houston NFL	16	4	16	4.0	0	1	8	8.0	0	13	224	17.2	0	0	0	1
1990— Atlanta NFL	16	30	106	3.5	3	10	79	7.9	1	2	2	1.0	0	4	24	1
Pro totals (2 years)	32	34	122	3.6	3	11	87	7.9	1	15	226	15.1	0	4	24	2

JOHNSON, TROY
LB, JETS

PERSONAL: Born November 10, 1964, at Houston. . . . 6-0/236. . . . Full name: Troy Antwain Johnson. . . . Cousin of David Lewis, linebacker with Tampa Bay Buccaneers, San Diego Chargers and Los Angeles Rams, 1977-1983.
HIGH SCHOOL: Hastings (Alief, Tex.).
COLLEGE: Oklahoma.
TRANSACTIONS/CAREER NOTES: Selected by Chicago Bears in fifth round (133rd pick overall) of 1988 NFL draft. . . . Signed by Bears (July 21, 1988). . . . On injured reserve with shoulder injury (September 15-November 1, 1989). . . . Transferred to developmental squad (November 2-November 9, 1989). . . . Released by Bears (September 3, 1990). . . . Awarded on waivers to New York Jets (September 4, 1990).
PLAYING EXPERIENCE: Chicago NFL, 1988 and 1989; New York Jets NFL, 1990. . . . Games: 1988 (16), 1989 (7), 1990 (16). Total: 39.
CHAMPIONSHIP GAME EXPERIENCE: Played in NFC championship game after 1988 season.

JOHNSON, UNDRA

RB, COWBOYS

PERSONAL: Born January 8, 1966, at Valdosta, Ga. . . . 5-9/204. . . . Full name: Undra Jerome Johnson.
HIGH SCHOOL: Stranahan (Fort Lauderdale, Fla.).
COLLEGE: West Virginia.

TRANSACTIONS/CAREER NOTES: Selected by Atlanta Falcons in seventh round (172nd pick overall) of 1989 NFL draft. . . . Signed by Falcons (July 20, 1989). . . . Released by Falcons (September 5, 1989). . . . Re-signed by Falcons to developmental squad (September 6-October 12, 1989). . . . Awarded on procedural waivers to New Orleans Saints (October 13, 1989). . . . Released by Saints (November 29, 1989). . . . Signed as free agent by Dallas Cowboys for developmental squad (December 2, 1989). . . . On developmental squad (December 2-December 7, 1989). . . . Released by Cowboys (December 18, 1989). . . . Active for one game with Cowboys in 1989; did not play. . . . Awarded on waivers to Atlanta Falcons (December 19, 1989). . . . Released by Falcons (September 3, 1990). . . . Signed by WLAF (January 31, 1991). . . . Selected by San Antonio Riders in first round (fifth running back) of 1991 WLAF positional draft. . . . Signed by Dallas Cowboys (July 8, 1991).

		— RUSHING —				— RECEIVING —				– KICKOFF RETURNS –				— TOTAL —		
Year Team	G	Att.	Yds.	Avg.	TD	No.	Yds.	Avg.	TD	No.	Yds.	Avg.	TD	TD	Pts.	F.
1989— NO (5)-Dal (0)-Atl (1) NFL.	6	0	0		0	0	0		0	2	34	17.0	0	0	0	0
1991— San Antonio WLAF	10	76	258	3.4	2	10	55	5.5	0	14	305	21.8	0	2	12	—
NFL totals (1 year)	6	0	0		0	0	0		0	2	34	17.0	0	0	0	0
WLAF totals (1 year)	10	76	258	3.4	2	10	55	5.5	0	14	305	21.8	0	2	12	—
Pro totals (2 years)	16	76	258	3.4	2	10	55	5.5	0	16	339	21.2	0	2	12	0

JOHNSON, VANCE

WR, BRONCOS

PERSONAL: Born March 13, 1963, at Trenton, N.J. . . . 5-11/185. . . . Full name: Vance Edward Johnson.
HIGH SCHOOL: Cholla (Tucson, Ariz.).
COLLEGE: Arizona.

TRANSACTIONS/CAREER NOTES: Selected by Arizona Outlaws in 1985 USFL territorial draft. . . . Selected by Denver Broncos in second round (31st pick overall) of 1985 NFL draft. . . . Signed by Broncos (July 16, 1985). . . . On injured reserve with knee injury (September 9-October 10, 1986).
CHAMPIONSHIP GAME EXPERIENCE: Played in AFC championship game after 1986 and 1989 seasons. . . . Played in Super Bowl XXI after 1986 season, Super Bowl XXII after 1987 season and Super Bowl XXIV after 1989 season.
PRO STATISTICS: 1985—Attempted one pass with no completions and recovered two fumbles. 1986—Attempted one pass with no completions. 1987—Attempted one pass with no completions. 1989—Attempted one pass with no completions.

		— RUSHING —				— RECEIVING —				– PUNT RETURNS –				KICKOFF RETURNS				– TOTALS –		
Year Team	G	Att.	Yds.	Avg.	TD	No.	Yds.	Avg.	TD	No.	Yds.	Avg.	TD	No.	Yds.	Avg.	TD	TD	Pts.	F.
1985— Denver NFL	16	10	36	3.6	0	51	721	14.1	3	30	260	8.7	0	30	740	24.7	0	3	18	5
1986— Denver NFL	12	5	15	3.0	0	31	363	11.7	2	3	36	12.0	0	2	21	10.5	0	2	12	1
1987— Denver NFL	11	1	-8	-8.0	0	42	684	16.3	7	1	9	9.0	0	7	140	20.0	0	7	42	1
1988— Denver NFL	16	1	1	1.0	0	68	896	13.2	5	0	0		0	0	0		0	5	30	0
1989— Denver NFL	16	0	0		0	76	1095	14.4	7	12	118	9.8	0	0	0		0	7	42	0
1990— Denver NFL	16	0	0		0	54	747	13.8	3	11	92	8.4	0	6	126	21.0	0	3	18	1
Pro totals (6 years)	87	17	44	2.6	0	322	4506	14.0	27	57	515	9.0	0	45	1027	22.8	0	27	162	8

JOHNSON, VAUGHAN

LB, SAINTS

PERSONAL: Born March 24, 1962, at Morehead City, N.C. . . . 6-3/235. . . . Full name: Vaughan Monroe Johnson.
HIGH SCHOOL: West Carteret (Morehead City, N.C.).
COLLEGE: North Carolina State.

TRANSACTIONS/CAREER NOTES: Selected by Jacksonville Bulls in 1984 USFL territorial draft. . . . Signed by Bulls (January 17, 1984). . . . On developmental squad for one game (April 6-April 13, 1984). . . . Selected by New Orleans Saints in first round (15th pick overall) of 1984 NFL supplemental draft. . . . Granted free agency when USFL suspended operations (August 7, 1986). . . . Signed by Saints (August 12, 1986). . . . Granted roster exemption (August 12-August 25, 1986).
PLAYING EXPERIENCE: Jacksonville USFL, 1984 and 1985; New Orleans NFL, 1986-1990. . . . Games: 1984 (17), 1985 (18), 1986 (16), 1987 (12), 1988 (16), 1989 (16), 1990 (16). Total USFL: 35. Total NFL: 76. Total Pro: 111.
RECORDS/HONORS: Named as linebacker on THE SPORTING NEWS college All-America team, 1983. . . . Played in Pro Bowl after 1989 and 1990 seasons.
PRO STATISTICS: USFL: 1984—Credited with one sack for 13 yards, intercepted one pass for four yards and recovered blocked kick in end zone for a touchdown. 1985—Credited with three sacks for 18 yards and recovered one fumble for three yards. . . . NFL: 1986—Intercepted one pass for 15 yards and recovered one fumble. 1987—Intercepted one pass for no yards and recovered one fumble. 1988—Intercepted one pass for 34 yards and recovered one fumble. 1989—Recovered one fumble for minus one yard. 1990—Recovered one fumble.

JOHNSON, WALTER

LB, COLTS

PERSONAL: Born November 13, 1963, at Monroe, La. . . . 6-0/240. . . . Full name: Walter Ulysses Johnson.
HIGH SCHOOL: Ferriday (La.).
COLLEGE: Louisiana Tech.

TRANSACTIONS/CAREER NOTES: Selected by Houston Oilers in second round (46th pick overall) of 1987 NFL draft. . . . Signed by Oilers (July 31, 1987). . . . Crossed picket line during players' strike (October 14, 1987). . . . Granted unconditional free agency (February 1, 1989). . . . Signed by New Orleans Saints (March 28, 1989). . . . Granted unconditional free agency (February 1, 1990). . . . Signed by Dallas Cowboys (March 3, 1990). . . . Released by Cowboys (August 26, 1990). . . . Signed by Indianapolis Colts (February 1, 1991).
PLAYING EXPERIENCE: Houston NFL, 1987 and 1988; New Orleans NFL, 1989. . . . Games: 1987 (10), 1988 (16), 1989 (15). Total: 41.

JOHNSTON, DARYL
FB, COWBOYS

PERSONAL: Born February 10, 1966, at Youngstown, N.Y.... 6-2/238.
HIGH SCHOOL: Lewiston-Porter Central (Youngstown, N.Y.).
COLLEGE: Syracuse (degree in economics, 1989).
TRANSACTIONS/CAREER NOTES: Selected by Dallas Cowboys in second round (39th pick overall) of 1989 NFL draft.... Signed by Cowboys (July 24, 1989).
PRO STATISTICS: 1990—Recovered one fumble.

			RUSHING				RECEIVING				TOTAL	
Year Team	G	Att.	Yds.	Avg.	TD	No.	Yds.	Avg.	TD	TD	Pts.	F.
1989— Dallas NFL	16	67	212	3.2	0	16	133	8.3	3	3	18	3
1990— Dallas NFL	16	10	35	3.5	1	14	148	10.6	1	2	12	1
Pro totals (2 years)	32	77	247	3.2	1	30	281	9.4	4	5	30	4

JOINES, VERNON
WR, BROWNS

PERSONAL: Born June 20, 1965, at Charlotte, N.C.... 6-2/210.... Full name: Vernon Willis Joines.
HIGH SCHOOL: Southwestern (Baltimore).
COLLEGE: Maryland (degree in criminal justice, 1990).
TRANSACTIONS/CAREER NOTES: Selected by Cleveland Browns in fifth round (116th pick overall) of 1989 NFL draft.... Signed by Browns (June 23, 1989).... Released by Browns (October 3, 1989).... Re-signed by Browns (October 4, 1989).... Released by Browns (October 12, 1989).... Re-signed by Browns to developmental squad (October 18, 1989).... On developmental squad (October 18, 1989-remainder of season).... Released by Browns (January 29, 1990).... Re-signed by Browns (February 26, 1990).
PRO STATISTICS: 1989—Returned one kickoff for 12 yards. 1990—Recovered one fumble.

		RECEIVING		
Year Team	G	No.	Yds.	Avg.	TD
1989— Cleveland NFL	4	0	0		0
1990— Cleveland NFL	16	6	86	14.3	0
Pro totals (2 years)	20	6	86	14.3	0

JONES, AARON
DE, STEELERS

PERSONAL: Born December 18, 1966, at Orlando, Fla.... 6-5/268.... Full name: Aaron Delmas Jones II.
HIGH SCHOOL: Apopka (Fla.).
COLLEGE: Eastern Kentucky.
TRANSACTIONS/CAREER NOTES: Selected by Pittsburgh Steelers in first round (18th pick overall) of 1988 NFL draft.... Signed by Steelers (July 15, 1988).... On injured reserve with knee injury (December 16, 1988-remainder of season).... On injured reserve with foot injury (October 25, 1990-remainder of season).
PLAYING EXPERIENCE: Pittsburgh NFL, 1988-1990.... Games: 1988 (15), 1989 (16), 1990 (7). Total: 38.
PRO STATISTICS: 1990—Intercepted one pass for three yards and recovered one fumble.

JONES, BILL
RB, CHIEFS

PERSONAL: Born September 10, 1966, at Abilene, Tex.... 5-11/227.... Full name: William Jones Jr.
HIGH SCHOOL: Corsicana (Tex.).
COLLEGE: Southwest Texas State.
TRANSACTIONS/CAREER NOTES: Selected by Kansas City Chiefs in 12th round (311th pick overall) of 1989 NFL draft.... Signed by Chiefs (July 20, 1989).... Released by Chiefs (August 29, 1989).... Re-signed by Chiefs to practice squad (October 25, 1989).... Released by Chiefs (January 18, 1990).... Re-signed by Chiefs (February 6, 1990).

			RUSHING				RECEIVING				TOTAL	
Year Team	G	Att.	Yds.	Avg.	TD	No.	Yds.	Avg.	TD	TD	Pts.	F.
1990— Kansas City NFL	16	10	47	4.7	0	19	137	7.2	5	5	30	0
Pro totals (1 year)	16	10	47	4.7	0	19	137	7.2	5	5	30	0

JONES, BRENT
TE, 49ERS

PERSONAL: Born February 13, 1963, at Santa Clara, Calif.... 6-4/230.... Full name: Brent Michael Jones.... Son of Mike Jones, selected by Oakland Raiders in 21st round of 1961 AFL draft and by Pittsburgh Steelers in 20th round of 1961 NFL draft.
HIGH SCHOOL: Leland (San Jose, Calif.).
COLLEGE: Santa Clara (bachelor of science degree in economics, 1986).
TRANSACTIONS/CAREER NOTES: Selected by Pittsburgh Steelers in fifth round (135th pick overall) of 1986 NFL draft.... Signed by Steelers (July 30, 1986).... On injured reserve with neck injury (August 19-September 23, 1986).... Released by Steelers (September 24, 1986).... Signed as free agent by San Francisco 49ers for 1987 (December 24, 1986).... On injured reserve with neck injury (September 1-December 5, 1987).... Crossed picket line during players' strike (October 14, 1987).... On injured reserve with knee injury (August 29-October 5, 1988).... Re-signed by 49ers after clearing procedural waivers (October 7, 1988).... Granted unconditional free agency (February 1, 1989).... Re-signed by 49ers (April 28, 1989).
CHAMPIONSHIP GAME EXPERIENCE: Played in NFC championship game after 1988-1990 seasons.... Played in Super Bowl XXIII after 1988 season and Super Bowl XXIV after 1989 season.
PRO STATISTICS: 1990—Recovered two fumbles and fumbled twice.

		RECEIVING		
Year Team	G	No.	Yds.	Avg.	TD
1987— San Francisco NFL	4	2	35	17.5	0
1988— San Francisco NFL	11	8	57	7.1	2

		— RECEIVING —			
Year Team	G	No.	Yds.	Avg.	TD
1989— San Francisco NFL....	16	40	500	12.5	4
1990— San Francisco NFL....	16	56	747	13.3	5
Pro totals (4 years)........	47	106	1339	12.6	11

JONES, CEDRIC
WR, OILERS

PERSONAL: Born June 1, 1960, at Norfolk, Va.... 6-1/180.... Full name: Cedric Decorrus Jones.... First name pronounced SEED-rick.
HIGH SCHOOL: Weldon (N.C.).
COLLEGE: Duke (bachelor of arts degree in history and political science, 1982).
TRANSACTIONS/CAREER NOTES: Selected by New England Patriots in third round (56th pick overall) of 1982 NFL draft.... On inactive list (September 19, 1982).... Granted unconditional free agency (February 1, 1991).... Signed by Houston Oilers (April 1, 1991).
CHAMPIONSHIP GAME EXPERIENCE: Played in AFC championship game after 1985 season.... Played in Super Bowl XX after 1985 season.
PRO STATISTICS: 1984—Recovered fumble in end zone for a touchdown. 1985—Recovered one fumble for 15 yards and a touchdown. 1986—Rushed once for minus seven yards. 1987—Attempted one pass with no completions. 1989—Rushed once for three yards and recovered two fumbles for four yards.

		— RECEIVING —				— KICKOFF RETURNS —				— TOTAL —		
Year Team	G	No.	Yds.	Avg.	TD	No.	Yds.	Avg.	TD	TD	Pts.	F.
1982— New England NFL.............................	2	1	5	5.0	0	0	0		0	0	0	0
1983— New England NFL.............................	15	20	323	16.2	1	4	63	15.8	0	1	6	1
1984— New England NFL.............................	14	19	244	12.8	2	1	20	20.0	0	3	18	1
1985— New England NFL.............................	16	21	237	11.3	2	3	37	12.3	0	3	18	0
1986— New England NFL.............................	16	14	222	15.9	1	4	63	15.8	0	1	6	1
1987— New England NFL.............................	12	25	388	15.5	3	0	0		0	3	18	0
1988— New England NFL.............................	16	22	313	14.2	1	0	0		0	1	6	1
1989— New England NFL.............................	15	48	670	14.0	6	0	0		0	6	36	1
1990— New England NFL.............................	14	21	301	14.3	0	2	24	12.0	0	0	0	0
Pro totals (9 years).............................	120	191	2703	14.2	16	14	207	14.8	0	18	108	5

JONES, DANTE
LB, BEARS

PERSONAL: Born March 23, 1965, at Dallas.... 6-1/236.... Full name: Dante Delaneo Jones.
HIGH SCHOOL: Skyline (Dallas).
COLLEGE: Oklahoma (bachelor of science degree in political science, 1988).
TRANSACTIONS/CAREER NOTES: Selected by Chicago Bears in second round (51st pick overall) of 1988 NFL draft.... Signed by Bears (July 21, 1988).... On injured reserve with hamstring injury (September 29-November 8, 1989).... On injured reserve with knee injury (September 4-December 19, 1990).
PLAYING EXPERIENCE: Chicago NFL, 1988-1990.... Games: 1988 (15), 1989 (10), 1990 (2). Total: 27.
CHAMPIONSHIP GAME EXPERIENCE: Played in NFC championship game after 1988 season.

JONES, ERNIE
WR, CARDINALS

PERSONAL: Born December 15, 1964, at Elkhart, Ind.... 6-0/200.... Full name: Ernest Lee Jones.
HIGH SCHOOL: Memorial (Elkhart, Ind.).
COLLEGE: Indiana (degree in general studies, 1988).
TRANSACTIONS/CAREER NOTES: Selected by Phoenix Cardinals in seventh round (179th pick overall) of 1988 NFL draft.... Signed by Cardinals (July 11, 1988).
PRO STATISTICS: 1989—Returned one punt for 13 yards and recovered one fumble.

		— RUSHING —				— RECEIVING —				— KICKOFF RETURNS —				— TOTAL —		
Year Team	G	Att.	Yds.	Avg.	TD	No.	Yds.	Avg.	TD	No.	Yds.	Avg.	TD	TD	Pts.	F.
1988— Phoenix NFL	16	0	0		0	23	496	21.6	3	11	147	13.4	0	3	18	1
1989— Phoenix NFL	15	1	18	18.0	0	45	838	18.6	3	7	124	17.7	0	3	18	3
1990— Phoenix NFL	15	4	33	8.3	0	43	724	16.8	4	0	0		0	4	24	0
Pro totals (3 years)	46	5	51	10.2	0	111	2058	18.5	10	18	271	15.1	0	10	60	4

JONES, FRED
WR/KR, CHIEFS

PERSONAL: Born March 6, 1967, at Atlanta.... 5-9/182.... Full name: Frederick Cornelius Jones.
HIGH SCHOOL: Southwest Dekalb (Decatur, Ga.).
COLLEGE: Grambling State (degree in criminal justice).
TRANSACTIONS/CAREER NOTES: Selected by Kansas City Chiefs in fourth round (96th pick overall) of 1990 NFL draft.... Signed by Chiefs (July 26, 1990).... On injured reserve list with knee injury (September 4-November 10, 1990).... On inactive list (December 2 and 9, 1990).
PRO STATISTICS: 1990—Recovered one fumble.

		— RUSHING —				— RECEIVING —				— KICKOFF RETURNS —				— TOTAL —		
Year Team	G	Att.	Yds.	Avg.	TD	No.	Yds.	Avg.	TD	No.	Yds.	Avg.	TD	TD	Pts.	F.
1990— Kansas City NFL....	6	1	-1	-1.0	0	1	5	5.0	0	9	175	19.4	0	0	0	1
Pro totals (1 year).........	6	1	-1	-1.0	0	1	5	5.0	0	9	175	19.4	0	0	0	1

JONES, GARY
S, STEELERS

PERSONAL: Born November 30, 1967, at San Augustine, Tex. . . . 6-1/208. . . . Full name: Gary DeWayne Jones.
HIGH SCHOOL: John Tyler (Tyler, Tex.).
COLLEGE: Texas A&M.
TRANSACTIONS/CAREER NOTES: Selected by Pittsburgh Steelers in ninth round (239th pick overall) of 1990 NFL draft. . . . Signed by Steelers (July 18, 1990).
PLAYING EXPERIENCE: Pittsburgh NFL, 1990. . . . Games: 1990 (16).

JONES, HASSAN
WR, VIKINGS

PERSONAL: Born July 2, 1964, at Clearwater, Fla. . . . 6-0/195. . . . Full name: Hassan Ameer Jones.
HIGH SCHOOL: Clearwater (Fla.).
COLLEGE: Florida State.
TRANSACTIONS/CAREER NOTES: Selected by Tampa Bay Bandits in 1986 USFL territorial draft. . . . Selected by Minnesota Vikings in fifth round (120th pick overall) of 1986 NFL draft. . . . Signed by Vikings (July 9, 1986).
CHAMPIONSHIP GAME EXPERIENCE: Played in NFC championship game after 1987 season.

		— RUSHING —				— RECEIVING —				— TOTAL —		
Year Team	G	Att.	Yds.	Avg.	TD	No.	Yds.	Avg.	TD	TD	Pts.	F.
1986— Minnesota NFL	16	1	14	14.0	0	28	570	20.4	4	4	24	1
1987— Minnesota NFL	12	0	0		0	7	189	27.0	2	2	12	0
1988— Minnesota NFL	16	1	7	7.0	0	40	778	19.5	5	5	30	0
1989— Minnesota NFL	16	1	37	37.0	0	42	694	16.5	1	1	6	2
1990— Minnesota NFL	15	1	-7	-7.0	0	51	810	15.9	7	7	42	0
Pro totals (5 years)	75	4	51	12.8	0	168	3041	18.1	19	19	114	3

JONES, JAMES
FB, SEAHAWKS

PERSONAL: Born March 21, 1961, at Pompano Beach, Fla. . . . 6-2/232. . . . Full name: James Roosevelt Jones.
HIGH SCHOOL: Ely (Pompano Beach, Fla.).
COLLEGE: Florida.
TRANSACTIONS/CAREER NOTES: Selected by Tampa Bay Bandits in 1983 USFL territorial draft. . . . Selected by Detroit Lions in first round (13th pick overall) of 1983 NFL draft. . . . Signed by Lions (May 12, 1983). . . . Traded by Lions to Seattle Seahawks for cornerback Terry Taylor (August 31, 1989). . . . On injured reserve with dislocated wrist (November 1, 1989-remainder of season). . . . On inactive list (September 9, 1990).
PRO STATISTICS: 1983—Attempted two passes with no completions and recovered one fumble. 1984—Attempted five passes with three completions for 62 yards and a touchdown and recovered three fumbles. 1985—Attempted one pass with no completions and recovered one fumble. 1986—Recovered two fumbles. 1987—Attempted one pass with one interception. 1988—Attempted one pass with no completions. 1990—Returned two kickoffs for 21 yards.

		— RUSHING —				— RECEIVING —				— TOTAL —		
Year Team	G	Att.	Yds.	Avg.	TD	No.	Yds.	Avg.	TD	TD	Pts.	F.
1983— Detroit NFL	14	135	475	3.5	6	46	467	10.2	1	7	42	4
1984— Detroit NFL	16	137	532	3.9	3	77	662	8.6	5	8	48	6
1985— Detroit NFL	14	244	886	3.6	6	45	334	7.4	3	9	54	7
1986— Detroit NFL	16	252	903	3.6	8	54	334	6.2	1	9	54	6
1987— Detroit NFL	11	96	342	3.6	0	34	262	7.7	0	0	0	2
1988— Detroit NFL	14	96	314	3.3	0	29	259	8.9	0	0	0	2
1989— Seattle NFL	2	0	0		0	1	8	8.0	0	0	0	0
1990— Seattle NFL	16	5	20	4.0	0	1	22	22.0	0	0	0	0
Pro totals (8 years)	103	965	3472	3.6	23	287	2348	8.2	10	33	198	27

JONES, JIMMIE
DL, COWBOYS

PERSONAL: Born January 9, 1966, at Lakeland, Fla. . . . 6-4/280. . . . Full name: Jimmie Sims Jones.
HIGH SCHOOL: Okeechobee (Fla.).
COLLEGE: Miami (Fla.).
TRANSACTIONS/CAREER NOTES: Selected by Dallas Cowboys in third round (63rd pick overall) of 1990 NFL draft. . . . Signed by Cowboys (August 3, 1990).
PLAYING EXPERIENCE: Dallas NFL, 1990. . . . Games: 1990 (16).

JONES, JOCK
LB, BROWNS

PERSONAL: Born March 13, 1968, at Ashland, Va. . . . 6-2/230. . . . Full name: Jock Stacy Jones.
HIGH SCHOOL: Lee-Davis (Mechanicsville, Va.).
COLLEGE: Virginia Tech.
TRANSACTIONS/CAREER NOTES: Selected by Cleveland Browns in eighth round (212th pick overall) of 1990 NFL draft. . . . Signed by Browns (July 22, 1990). . . . On inactive list (September 9, 16, 23, 30; and October 8, 1990).
PLAYING EXPERIENCE: Cleveland NFL, 1990. . . . Games: 1990 (11).

JONES, KEITH
RB, FALCONS

PERSONAL: Born March 20, 1966, at Rock Hill, Mo. . . . 6-1/210.
HIGH SCHOOL: Webster Groves (Mo.).
COLLEGE: Illinois.
TRANSACTIONS/CAREER NOTES: Selected by Atlanta Falcons in third round (62nd pick overall) of

1989 NFL draft. . . . Signed by Falcons (July 24, 1989). . . . On inactive list (October 16, 1990).
PRO STATISTICS: 1989—Attempted one pass with no completion. 1990—Attempted one pass with one completion for 37 yards.

		RUSHING				RECEIVING				KICKOFF RETURNS				TOTAL	
Year	Team	G	Att.	Yds.	Avg.	TD	No.	Yds.	Avg.	TD	No.	Yds.	Avg.	TD	TD	Pts.	F.
1989— Atlanta NFL		14	52	202	3.9	6	41	396	9.7	0	23	440	19.1	0	6	36	0
1990— Atlanta NFL		15	49	185	3.8	0	13	103	7.9	0	8	236	29.5	1	1	6	2
Pro totals (2 years)		29	101	387	3.8	6	54	499	9.2	0	31	676	21.8	1	7	42	2

JONES, KEITH
RB, COWBOYS

PERSONAL: Born February 5, 1966, at Omaha, Neb. . . . 5-9/190.
HIGH SCHOOL: Central (Omaha, Neb.).
COLLEGE: Nebraska.
TRANSACTIONS/CAREER NOTES: Selected by Los Angeles Rams in sixth round (147th pick over-all) of 1988 NFL draft. . . . Signed by Rams (July 7, 1988). . . . On injured reserve with ankle injury (August 23-September 11, 1988). . . . Released by Rams (September 12, 1988). . . . Re-signed by Rams (September 13, 1988). . . . On injured reserve with ankle injury (September 30, 1988-remainder of season). . . . On inactive list for two games in 1988. . . . Granted unconditional free agency (February 1, 1989). . . . Signed by Cleveland Browns (February 13, 1989). . . . Granted unconditional free agency (February 1, 1990). . . . Signed by Dallas Cowboys (March 3, 1990). . . . On injured reserve with knee injury (August 26, 1990-entire season).
CHAMPIONSHIP GAME EXPERIENCE: Played in AFC championship game after 1989 season.
PRO STATISTICS: 1989—Returned four kickoffs for 42 yards and recovered one fumble.

		RUSHING				RECEIVING				TOTAL	
Year	Team	G	Att.	Yds.	Avg.	TD	No.	Yds.	Avg.	TD	TD	Pts.	F.
1989— Cleveland NFL		16	43	160	3.7	1	15	126	8.4	0	1	6	1
Pro totals (1 year)		16	43	160	3.7	1	15	126	8.4	0	1	6	1

JONES, MARLON
DL, BUCCANEERS

PERSONAL: Born July 1, 1964, at Baltimore. . . . 6-4/270.
HIGH SCHOOL: Milford Mill (Baltimore).
COLLEGE: Central State (O.).
TRANSACTIONS/CAREER NOTES: Signed as free agent by Toronto Argonauts of CFL (Febru-ary, 1986). . . . Released by Argonauts (October 19, 1987). . . . Signed by Cleveland Browns (November 19, 1987). . . . On in-jured reserve with back injury (December 21, 1988-remainder of 1988 season playoffs). . . . On injured reserve with broken thumb (November 27, 1989-remainder of season). . . . On injured reserve with foot injury (August 15, 1990-entire season). . . . Granted unconditional free agency (February 1, 1991). . . . Signed by Tampa Bay Buccaneers (March 25, 1991).
PLAYING EXPERIENCE: Toronto CFL, 1986 and 1987; Cleveland NFL, 1987-1989. . . . Games: 1986 (14), 1987 CFL (10), 1987 NFL (1), 1988 (16), 1989 (8). Total CFL: 24. Total NFL: 25. Total Pro: 49.
PRO STATISTICS: CFL: 1986—Intercepted one pass for 35 yards, recovered one fumble and credited with nine sacks. 1987—Credited with three sacks.

JONES, MIKE
TE, VIKINGS

PERSONAL: Born November 10, 1966, at Bridgeport, Conn. . . . 6-3/255. . . . Full name: Michael Le-nere Jones.
HIGH SCHOOL: Warren Harding (Bridgeport, Conn.).
COLLEGE: Texas A&M.
TRANSACTIONS/CAREER NOTES: Selected by Minnesota Vikings in third round (54th pick overall) of 1990 NFL draft. . . . Signed by Vikings (July 26, 1990). . . . On inactive list (December 2, 9, 16, 22 and 30, 1990).
PLAYING EXPERIENCE: Minnesota NFL, 1990. . . . Games: 1990 (11).

JONES, ROD
CB, BENGALS

PERSONAL: Born March 31, 1964, at Dallas. . . . 6-0/185. . . . Full name: Roderick Wayne Jones.
HIGH SCHOOL: South Oak Cliff (Dallas).
COLLEGE: Southern Methodist.
TRANSACTIONS/CAREER NOTES: Selected by Tampa Bay Buccaneers in first round (25th pick overall) of 1986 NFL draft. . . . Signed by Buccaneers (June 19, 1986). . . . Granted free agency (February 1, 1990). . . . Re-signed by Buccaneers (August 12, 1990). . . . Traded by Buccaneers to Cincinnati Bengals for defensive end Jim Skow (September 1, 1990).
PRO STATISTICS: 1986—Recovered one fumble. 1987—Recovered one fumble for eight yards. 1990—Recovered one fumble for one yard.

		INTERCEPTIONS			
Year	Team	G	No.	Yds.	Avg.	TD
1986— Tampa Bay NFL		16	1	0	.0	0
1987— Tampa Bay NFL		11	2	9	4.5	0
1988— Tampa Bay NFL		14	1	0	.0	0
1989— Tampa Bay NFL		16	0	0		0
1990— Cincinnati NFL		16	0	0		0
Pro totals (5 years)		73	4	9	2.3	0

JONES, SCOTT
OT, PACKERS

PERSONAL: Born March 20, 1966, at Portland, Ore. . . . 6-6/284. . . . Full name: Robert Scott Jones.
HIGH SCHOOL: Clallam Bay (Wash.) and Port Angeles (Wash.).
COLLEGE: Washington (degree in forestry, 1989).

TRANSACTIONS/CAREER NOTES: Selected by Cincinnati Bengals in 12th round (334th pick overall) of 1989 NFL draft.... Signed by Bengals (July 20, 1989).... Traded by Bengals with linebacker Joe Kelly to New York Jets in exchange for rights to wide receiver Reggie Rembert (August 27, 1990).... On injured reserve with foot injury (September 4-November 24, 1990).... On inactive list (December 30, 1990).... Granted unconditional free agency (February 1, 1991).... Signed by Green Bay Packers (April 1, 1991).
PLAYING EXPERIENCE: Cincinnati NFL, 1989; New York Jets NFL, 1990.... Games: 1989 (15), 1990 (3). Total: 18.

JONES, SEAN
DE, OILERS

PERSONAL: Born December 19, 1962, at Kingston, Jamaica.... 6-7/264.... Full name: Dwight Sean Jones.... Brother of Max Jones, linebacker with Birmingham Stallions (USFL), 1984.
HIGH SCHOOL: Kimberly Academy (Montclair, N.J.).
COLLEGE: Northeastern.
TRANSACTIONS/CAREER NOTES: Selected by Washington Federals in fifth round (91st pick overall) of 1984 USFL draft.... Selected by Los Angeles Raiders in second round (51st pick overall) of 1984 NFL draft.... Signed by Raiders (July 12, 1984).... Traded by Raiders with second- and third-round picks in 1988 NFL draft to Houston Oilers for first-, third- and fourth-round picks in draft (April 21, 1988).... Granted free agency (February 1, 1990).... Re-signed by Oilers (August 24, 1990).
PLAYING EXPERIENCE: Los Angeles Raiders NFL, 1984-1987; Houston NFL, 1988-1990.... Games: 1984 (16), 1985 (15), 1986 (16), 1987 (12), 1988 (16), 1989 (16), 1990 (16). Total: 107.
PRO STATISTICS: 1985—Recovered one fumble, 1987—Recovered two fumbles. 1989—Recovered two fumbles. 1990—Recovered one fumble.

JONES, TONY
WR, OILERS

PERSONAL: Born December 30, 1965, at Grapeland, Tex.... 5-7/139.... Full name: Anthony Bernard Jones.
HIGH SCHOOL: Grapeland (Tex.).
COLLEGE: Angelina Junior College (Tex.), then Texas.
TRANSACTIONS/CAREER NOTES: Selected by Houston Oilers in sixth round (153rd pick overall) of 1990 NFL draft.... Signed by Oilers (July 22, 1990).

Year Team	G		RUSHING				RECEIVING				TOTAL	
		Att.	Yds.	Avg.	TD	No.	Yds.	Avg.	TD	TD	Pts.	F.
1990— Houston NFL	15	1	-2	-2.0	0	30	409	13.6	6	6	36	0
Pro totals (1 year)	15	1	-2	-2.0	0	30	409	13.6	6	6	36	0

JONES, TONY
OT, BROWNS

PERSONAL: Born May 24, 1966, at Royston, Ga.... 6-5/290.... Full name: Tony Edward Jones.
HIGH SCHOOL: Franklin County (Carnesville, Ga.).
COLLEGE: Western Carolina (bachelor of science degree in management, 1989).
TRANSACTIONS/CAREER NOTES: Signed as free agent by Cleveland Browns (May 2, 1988).... On injured reserve with toe injury (August 29-October 22, 1988).... On injured reserve with toe injury (September 20-November 7, 1989).
PLAYING EXPERIENCE: Cleveland NFL, 1988-1990.... Games: 1988 (4), 1989 (9), 1990 (16). Total: 29.
CHAMPIONSHIP GAME EXPERIENCE: Played in AFC championship game after 1989 season.
PRO STATISTICS: 1989—Recovered one fumble.

JONES, VICTOR
RB, PATRIOTS

PERSONAL: Born December 5, 1967, at Zachary, La.... 5-8/212.
HIGH SCHOOL: Zachary (La.).
COLLEGE: Louisiana State.
TRANSACTIONS/CAREER NOTES: Signed as free agent by Houston Oilers (May 25, 1990).... Released by Oilers (September 2, 1990).... Re-signed by Oilers (October 2, 1990).... On inactive list (October 28 and November 4, 1990).... Granted unconditional free agency (February 1, 1991).... Signed by New England Patriots (April 1, 1991).
PRO STATISTICS: 1990—Fumbled once.

Year Team	G	RUSHING			
		Att.	Yds.	Avg.	TD
1990— Houston NFL	10	14	75	5.4	0
Pro totals (1 year)	10	14	75	5.4	0

JONES, VICTOR
LB, LIONS

PERSONAL: Born October 19, 1966, at Rockville, Md.... 6-2/240.... Full name: Victor Pernell Jones.
HIGH SCHOOL: Robert E. Peary (Rockville, Md.).
COLLEGE: Virginia Tech.
TRANSACTIONS/CAREER NOTES: Selected by Tampa Bay Buccaneers in 12th round (310th pick overall) of 1988 NFL draft.... Signed by Buccaneers (July 6, 1988).... On injured reserve with back injury (August 22-October 12, 1988).... Activated after clearing procedural waivers (October 14, 1988).... Granted unconditional free agency (February 1, 1989).... Signed by Detroit Lions (February 24, 1989).
PLAYING EXPERIENCE: Tampa Bay NFL, 1988; Detroit NFL, 1989 and 1990.... Games: 1988 (8), 1989 (11), 1990 (16). Total: 35.
PRO STATISTICS: 1989—Recovered two fumbles. 1990—Intercepted one pass for no yards.

JORDAN, BRIAN

S, FALCONS

PERSONAL: Born March 29, 1967, at Baltimore. . . . 6-1/205. . . . Full name: Brian O'Neil Jordan.
HIGH SCHOOL: Milford Mill (Baltimore).
COLLEGE: Richmond.
TRANSACTIONS/CAREER NOTES: Selected by Buffalo Bills in seventh round (173rd pick overall) of 1989 NFL draft. . . . Signed by Bills (July 17, 1989). . . . Released by Bills (September 4, 1989). . . . Awarded on waivers to Atlanta Falcons (September 5, 1989). . . . On injured reserve with ankle injury (September 9-October 22, 1989). . . . Transferred to developmental squad (October 23-December 2, 1989).
PRO STATISTICS: 1989—Recovered two fumbles. 1990—Recovered one fumble.

Year	Team	G	No.	Yds.	Avg.	TD	No.	Yds.	Avg.	TD	No.	Yds.	Avg.	TD	TD	Pts.	F.
			— INTERCEPTIONS—				— PUNT RETURNS —				– KICKOFF RETURNS –				— TOTAL —		
1989— Atlanta NFL		4	0	0		0	4	34	8.5	0	3	27	9.0	0	0	0	1
1990— Atlanta NFL		16	3	14	4.7	0	2	19	9.5	0	0	0		0	0	0	0
Pro totals (2 years)		20	3	14	4.7	0	6	53	8.8	0	3	27	9.0	0	0	0	1

BASEBALL TRANSACTIONS: Selected by Cleveland Indians' organization in 20th round of free-agent draft (June 3, 1985). . . . Selected by St. Louis Cardinals' organization in first round (29th pick overall) of free-agent draft (June 1, 1988).

BASEBALL RECORD AS PLAYER

Year	Team	League	Pos.	G	AB	R	H	2B	3B	HR	RBI	Avg.	PO	A	E	F.A.
1988— Hamilton	NYP	OF	19	71	12	22	3	1	4	12	.310	32	1	1	.971
1989— St. Pete.	Fla. St.	OF	11	43	7	15	4	1	2	11	.349	22	2	0	1.000
1990— Arkansas	Texas	OF	16	50	4	8	1	0	0	0	.160	28	0	2	.933
1990— St. Pete.	Fla. St.	OF	9	30	3	5	0	1	0	1	.167	23	0	0	1.000

JORDAN, BUFORD

FB, SAINTS

PERSONAL: Born June 26, 1962, at Lafayette, La. . . . 6-0/223. . . . Full name: Paul Buford Jordan.
HIGH SCHOOL: Iota (La.).
COLLEGE: McNeese State.
TRANSACTIONS/CAREER NOTES: Selected by New Orleans Breakers in first round (13th pick overall) of 1984 USFL draft. . . . Signed by Breakers (January 9, 1984). . . . Selected by Green Bay Packers in first round (12th pick overall) of 1984 NFL supplemental draft. . . . New Orleans Breakers franchise transferred to Portland (November 13, 1984). . . . On developmental squad for two games (April 6-April 21, 1985). . . . Released by Breakers (July 31, 1985). . . . Signed by Green Bay Packers (September 2, 1985). . . . Granted roster exemption (September 2-September 15, 1985). . . . Released by Packers (September 16, 1985). . . . Signed as free agent by New Orleans Saints (March 6, 1986). . . . On injured reserve with knee injury (August 23-September 12, 1988). . . . Released by Saints (September 13, 1988). . . . Re-signed by Saints (September 14, 1988). . . . Released by Saints (September 3, 1990). . . . Re-signed by Saints (November 19, 1990).
PRO STATISTICS: USFL: 1984—Recovered four fumbles. 1985—Credited with one 2-point conversion and recovered four fumbles. . . . NFL: 1987—Returned one punt for 13 yards and returned two kickoffs for 28 yards. 1988—Recovered one fumble for seven yards and a touchdown.

Year	Team	G	Att.	Yds.	Avg.	TD	No.	Yds.	Avg.	TD	TD	Pts.	F.
			— RUSHING —				— RECEIVING —				— TOTAL —		
1984— New Orleans USFL	18	214	1276	*6.0	8	45	427	9.5	4	12	72	9
1985— Portland USFL	15	165	817	5.0	5	12	192	16.0	1	6	38	11
1986— New Orleans NFL	16	68	207	3.0	1	11	127	11.5	0	1	6	2
1987— New Orleans NFL	12	12	36	3.0	2	2	13	6.5	0	2	12	0
1988— New Orleans NFL	14	19	115	6.1	0	5	70	14.0	0	1	6	1
1989— New Orleans NFL	11	38	179	4.7	3	4	53	13.3	0	3	18	0
1990— New Orleans NFL	6	0	0		0	0	0		0	0	0	0
USFL totals (2 years)	33	379	2093	5.5	13	57	619	10.9	5	18	110	20
NFL totals (5 years)	59	137	537	3.9	6	22	263	12.0	0	7	42	3
Pro totals (7 years)	92	516	2630	5.1	19	79	882	11.2	5	25	152	23

JORDAN, DARIN

LB, 49ERS

PERSONAL: Born December 4, 1964, at Boston. . . . 6-2/245. . . . Full name: Darin Godfrey Jordan.
HIGH SCHOOL: Stoughton (Mass.).
COLLEGE: Northeastern (bachelor of arts degree in speech communications, 1988).
TRANSACTIONS/CAREER NOTES: Selected by Pittsburgh Steelers in fifth round (121st pick overall) of 1988 NFL draft. . . . Signed by Steelers (September 5, 1989). . . . Signed as free agent by Los Angeles Raiders (September 19, 1989). . . . Released by Raiders (September 21, 1989). . . . Re-signed by Raiders (February 2, 1990). . . . Released by Raiders (September 3, 1990). . . . Did not play during 1990 regular season; played for Raiders for 1990 season playoffs (January 2, 1991). . . . Granted unconditional free agency (February 1, 1991). . . . Signed by San Francisco 49ers (April 1, 1991).
PLAYING EXPERIENCE: Pittsburgh NFL, 1988; Los Angeles Raiders NFL, 1990. . . . Games: 1988 (15), 1990 (0). Total: 15.
CHAMPIONSHIP GAME EXPERIENCE: Played in AFC championship game after 1990 season.
PRO STATISTICS: 1988—Intercepted one pass for 28 yards and a touchdown and recovered four fumbles.

JORDAN, STEVE

TE, VIKINGS

PERSONAL: Born January 10, 1961, at Phoenix. . . . 6-3/240. . . . Full name: Steven Russell Jordan.
HIGH SCHOOL: South Mountain (Phoenix).
COLLEGE: Brown (bachelor of science degree in civil engineering, 1982).

TRANSACTIONS/CAREER NOTES: Selected by Minnesota Vikings in seventh round (179th pick overall) of 1982 NFL draft.
CHAMPIONSHIP GAME EXPERIENCE: Played in NFC championship game after 1987 season.
RECORDS/HONORS: Played in Pro Bowl after 1986- 1990 seasons.
PRO STATISTICS: 1984—Rushed once for four yards and a touchdown and recovered one fumble. 1985—Fumbled twice. 1986—Recovered one fumble. 1987—Fumbled once. 1988—Fumbled twice. 1989—Fumbled once. 1990—Returned one kickoff for minus three yards and fumbled three times.

			RECEIVING			
Year	Team	G	No.	Yds.	Avg.	TD
1982— Minnesota NFL		9	3	42	14.0	0
1983— Minnesota NFL		13	15	212	14.1	2
1984— Minnesota NFL		14	38	414	10.9	2
1985— Minnesota NFL		16	68	795	11.7	0
1986— Minnesota NFL		16	58	859	14.8	6
1987— Minnesota NFL		12	35	490	14.0	2
1988— Minnesota NFL		16	57	756	13.3	5
1989— Minnesota NFL		16	35	506	14.5	3
1990— Minnesota NFL		16	45	636	14.1	3
Pro totals (9 years)		128	354	4710	13.3	23

JORDAN, TONY
RB, OILERS

PERSONAL: Born May 8, 1965, at Rochester, N.Y. . . . 6-2/220. . . . Full name: Anthony T. Jordan.
HIGH SCHOOL: East (Rochester, N.Y.).
COLLEGE: Kansas State (degree in social science, 1988).
TRANSACTIONS/CAREER NOTES: Selected by Phoenix Cardinals in fifth round (132nd pick overall) of 1988 NFL draft. . . . Signed by Cardinals (July 7, 1988). . . . On injured reserve with stress fracture in back (November 16, 1988-remainder of season). . . . Granted free agency (February 1, 1990). . . . Re-signed by Cardinals (August 3, 1990). . . . On injured reserve with shoulder (August 27-September 18, 1990). . . . Released by Cardinals (September 18, 1990). . . . Signed by Houston Oilers (April 1, 1991).

			RUSHING				RECEIVING				TOTAL		
Year	Team	G	Att.	Yds.	Avg.	TD	No.	Yds.	Avg.	TD	TD	Pts.	F.
1988— Phoenix NFL		9	61	160	2.6	3	4	24	6.0	0	3	18	1
1989— Phoenix NFL		13	83	211	2.5	2	6	20	3.3	0	2	12	4
Pro totals (2 years)		22	144	371	2.6	5	10	44	4.4	0	5	30	5

JORDEN, TIM
TE, CARDINALS

PERSONAL: Born October 30, 1966, at Lakewood, O. . . . 6-3/235. . . . Full name: Timothy Robert Jorden.
HIGH SCHOOL: Fenwick (Middletown, O.).
COLLEGE: Indiana (bachelor's degree in finance, 1989).
TRANSACTIONS/CAREER NOTES: Signed as free agent by Phoenix Cardinals (May 5, 1989). . . . Released by Cardinals (September 5, 1989). . . . Signed by Cardinals to developmental squad (September 6, 1989). . . . Released by Cardinals (January 3, 1990). . . . Re-signed by Cardinals (February 22, 1990).

			RECEIVING			
Year	Team	G	No.	Yds.	Avg.	TD
1990— Phoenix NFL		16	2	10	5.0	0
Pro totals (1 year)		16	2	10	5.0	0

JOYNER, SETH
LB, EAGLES

PERSONAL: Born November 18, 1964, at Spring Valley, N.Y. . . . 6-2/235.
HIGH SCHOOL: Spring Valley (N.Y.).
COLLEGE: Texas-El Paso.
TRANSACTIONS/CAREER NOTES: Selected by Philadelphia Eagles in eighth round (208th pick overall) of 1986 NFL draft. . . . Signed by Eagles (July 17, 1986). . . . Released by Eagles (September 1, 1986). . . . Re-signed by Eagles (September 17, 1986).
PRO STATISTICS: 1987—Recovered two fumbles for 18 yards and a touchdown. 1988—Recovered one fumble and fumbled once. 1990—Fumbled once.

			INTERCEPTIONS			
Year	Team	G	No.	Yds.	Avg.	TD
1986— Philadelphia NFL		14	1	4	4.0	0
1987— Philadelphia NFL		12	2	42	21.0	0
1988— Philadelphia NFL		16	4	96	24.0	0
1989— Philadelphia NFL		14	1	0	.0	0
1990— Philadelphia NFL		16	1	9	9.0	0
Pro totals (5 years)		72	9	151	16.8	0

JUNIOR, E.J.
LB, DOLPHINS

PERSONAL: Born December 8, 1959, at Sallsburg, N.C. . . . 6-3/242. . . . Full name: Ester James Junior III.
HIGH SCHOOL: Maplewood (Nashville, Tenn.).
COLLEGE: Alabama (degree in public relations).

TRANSACTIONS/CAREER NOTES: Selected by St. Louis Cardinals in first round (fifth pick overall) of 1981 NFL draft.... On suspended list for drug use (July 25-September 26, 1983).... Crossed picket line during players' strike (October 2, 1987).... St. Louis Cardinals franchise transferred to Phoenix (March 15, 1988).... Granted unconditional free agency (February 1, 1989). ... Signed by Miami Dolphins (February 24, 1989).

RECORDS/HONORS: Named as defensive end on THE SPORTING NEWS college All-America team, 1980.... Played in Pro Bowl after 1984 and 1985 seasons.

PRO STATISTICS: 1982—Recovered one fumble. 1983—Recovered one fumble for one yard. 1986—Recovered one fumble. 1987—Recovered two fumbles for five yards and fumbled once. 1988—Recovered one fumble for 36 yards and a touchdown.

			— INTERCEPTIONS —		
Year Team	G	No.	Yds.	Avg.	TD
1981— St. Louis NFL	16	1	5	5.0	0
1982— St. Louis NFL	9	0	0		0
1983— St. Louis NFL	12	3	27	9.0	0
1984— St. Louis NFL	16	1	18	18.0	0
1985— St. Louis NFL	16	5	109	21.8	0
1986— St. Louis NFL	13	0	0		0
1987— St. Louis NFL	13	1	25	25.0	0
1988— Phoenix NFL	16	1	2	2.0	0
1989— Miami NFL	16	0	0		0
1990— Miami NFL	16	0	0		0
Pro totals (10 years)	143	12	186	15.5	0

JUNKIN, TREY
TE, SEAHAWKS

PERSONAL: Born January 23, 1961, at Conway, Ark.... 6-2/240.... Full name: Abner Kirk Junkin.... Brother of Mike Junkin, linebacker with Cleveland Browns and Kansas City Chiefs, 1987-1989.
HIGH SCHOOL: Northeast (North Little Rock, Ark.).
COLLEGE: Louisiana Tech.
TRANSACTIONS/CAREER NOTES: Selected by Buffalo Bills in fourth round (93rd pick overall) of 1983 NFL draft.... Released by Bills (September 12, 1984).... Signed as free agent by Washington Redskins (September 25, 1984).... Granted free agency after not receiving qualifying offer (February 1, 1985).... Signed by Los Angeles Raiders (March 10, 1985).... On injured reserve with knee injury (September 24, 1986-remainder of season).... Released by Raiders (September 3, 1990).... Signed by Seattle Seahawks (October 3, 1990).
PRO STATISTICS: 1983—Recovered one fumble. 1984—Recovered one fumble. 1989—Returned one kickoff for no yards.

			— RECEIVING —		
Year Team	G	No.	Yds.	Avg.	TD
1983— Buffalo NFL	16	0	0		0
1984— Buf. (2)-Was. (12) NFL	14	0	0		0
1985— L.A. Raiders NFL	16	2	8	4.0	1
1986— L.A. Raiders NFL	3	2	38	19.0	0
1987— L.A. Raiders NFL	12	2	15	7.5	0
1988— L.A. Raiders NFL	16	4	25	6.3	2
1989— L.A. Raiders NFL	16	3	32	10.7	2
1990— Seattle NFL	12	0	0		0
Pro totals (8 years)	105	13	118	9.1	5

JURIGA, JIM
G/OT, BRONCOS

PERSONAL: Born September 12, 1964, at Fort Wayne, Ind.... 6-6/275.... Full name: James Allen Juriga.
HIGH SCHOOL: North (Wheaton, Ill.).
COLLEGE: Illinois.
TRANSACTIONS/CAREER NOTES: Selected by Orlando Renegades in 1986 USFL territorial draft.... Selected by Denver Broncos in fourth round (104th pick overall) of 1986 NFL draft.... Signed by Broncos (July 16, 1988).... On injured reserve with knee injury (September 1, 1986-entire season).... On injured reserve with knee injury (September 8, 1987-entire season).... On inactive list (December 2, 1990).... On injured reserve with back injury (December 19, 1990-remainder of season).
PLAYING EXPERIENCE: Denver NFL, 1988-1990.... Games: 1988 (16), 1989 (16), 1990 (12). Total: 44.
CHAMPIONSHIP GAME EXPERIENCE: Played in AFC championship game after 1989 season.... Played in Super Bowl XXIV after 1989 season.

KALIS, TODD
G, VIKINGS

PERSONAL: Born May 10, 1965, at Stillwater, Minn.... 6-5/286.... Full name: Todd Alexander Kalis.... Name pronounced KA-lis.
HIGH SCHOOL: Thunderbird (Phoenix).
COLLEGE: Arizona State.
TRANSACTIONS/CAREER NOTES: Selected by Minnesota Vikings in fourth round (108th pick overall) of 1988 NFL draft.... Signed by Vikings (July 21, 1988).... On inactive list (September 16, 1990).
PLAYING EXPERIENCE: Minnesota NFL, 1988-1990.... Games: 1988 (14), 1989 (16), 1990 (15). Total: 45.

KANE, TOMMY
WR, SEAHAWKS

PERSONAL: Born January 14, 1964, at Montreal, Que.... 5-11/176.... Full name: Tommy Henry Kane.
HIGH SCHOOL: Dawson (Montreal, Que.).
COLLEGE: Syracuse (bachelor of science degree in retailing, 1988).

TRANSACTIONS/CAREER NOTES: Selected by Seattle Seahawks in third round (75th pick overall) of 1988 NFL draft.... Signed by Seahawks (July 11, 1988).... On injured reserve with groin injury (November 5, 1988-remainder of season).... On injured reserve with knee injury (October 12, 1989-remainder of season).
PRO STATISTICS: 1990—Fumbled once.

| | | | RECEIVING | | |
Year	Team	G	No.	Yds.	Avg.	TD
1988— Seattle NFL		9	6	32	5.3	0
1989— Seattle NFL		5	7	94	13.4	0
1990— Seattle NFL		16	52	776	14.9	4
Pro totals (3 years)		30	65	902	13.9	4

KARLIS, RICH
PK, FALCONS

PERSONAL: Born May 23, 1959, at Salem, O.... 6-0/180.... Full name: Richard John Karlis.... Brother-in-law of Kirk Lowdermilk, center with Minnesota Vikings.
HIGH SCHOOL: Salem (O.).
COLLEGE: Cincinnati (degree in economics).
TRANSACTIONS/CAREER NOTES: Signed as free agent by Houston Oilers (June 5, 1981).... Released by Oilers (July 31, 1981). ... Signed as free agent by Denver Broncos (June 4, 1982).... Granted unconditional free agency (February 1, 1989).... Rights relinqushed (August 28, 1989).... Signed by Minnesota Vikings (September 26, 1989).... Rights relinquished (October 9, 1990).... Signed by Detroit Lions (October 12, 1990).... Released by Lions (November 30, 1990).... Signed by Atlanta Falcons (April 1, 1991).
CHAMPIONSHIP GAME EXPERIENCE: Played in AFC championship game after 1986 and 1987 seasons.... Played in Super Bowl XXI after 1986 season.... Played in Super Bowl XXII after 1987 season.
RECORDS/HONORS: Established NFL record for most field goals, no misses, game (7), against Los Angeles Rams (November 5, 1989). Tied NFL record for most field goals, game (7), against Los Angeles Rams (November 5, 1989).

| | | | PLACE-KICKING | | | | |
Year	Team	G	XPM	XPA	FGM	FGA	Pts.
1982— Denver NFL		9	15	16	11	13	48
1983— Denver NFL		16	33	34	21	25	96
1984— Denver NFL		16	38	41	21	28	101
1985— Denver NFL		16	41	44	23	38	110
1986— Denver NFL		16	44	45	20	28	104
1987— Denver NFL		12	37	37	18	25	91
1988— Denver NFL		16	36	37	23	36	105
1989— Minnesota NFL		13	27	28	*31	39	120
1990— Detroit NFL		6	12	12	4	7	24
Pro totals (9 years)		120	283	294	172	239	799

KARTZ, KEITH
C, BRONCOS

PERSONAL: Born May 5, 1963, at Las Vegas.... 6-4/270.... Full name: Keith Leonard Kartz.
HIGH SCHOOL: San Dieguito (Encinitas, Calif.).
COLLEGE: California (bachelor of science degree in social science, 1986).
TRANSACTIONS/CAREER NOTES: Signed as free agent by Seattle Seahawks (May 9, 1986).... Released by Seahawks (August 18, 1986).... Signed as free agent by Denver Broncos (May 1, 1987).... On injured reserve with back injury (September 7-September 30, 1987).... Crossed picket line during players' strike (September 30, 1987).
PLAYING EXPERIENCE: Denver NFL, 1987-1990.... Games: 1987 (12), 1988 (13), 1989 (16), 1990 (16). Total: 57.
CHAMPIONSHIP GAME EXPERIENCE: Played in AFC championship game after 1987 and 1989 seasons.... Played in Super Bowl XXII after 1987 season and Super Bowl XXIV after 1989 season.
PRO STATISTICS: 1990—Recovered one fumble and fumbled once.

KATTUS, ERIC
TE, BENGALS

PERSONAL: Born March 4, 1963, at Cincinnati.... 6-5/251.... Full name: John Eric Kattus.
HIGH SCHOOL: Colerain (Cincinnati).
COLLEGE: Michigan.
TRANSACTIONS/CAREER NOTES: Selected by Baltimore Stars in 1986 USFL territorial draft.... Selected by Cincinnati Bengals in fourth round (91st pick overall) of 1986 NFL draft.... Signed by Bengals (July 18, 1986).... On injured reserve with knee injury (October 1, 1988-remainder of season).
PRO STATISTICS: 1987—Returned two kickoffs for 22 yards. 1988—Fumbled once. 1990—Returned one kickoff for 10 yards.

| | | | RECEIVING | | |
Year	Team	G	No.	Yds.	Avg.	TD
1986— Cincinnati NFL		16	11	99	9.0	1
1987— Cincinnati NFL		11	18	217	12.1	2
1988— Cincinnati NFL		4	2	8	4.0	0
1989— Cincinnati NFL		16	12	93	7.8	0
1990— Cincinnati NFL		16	11	145	13.2	2
Pro totals (5 years)		63	54	562	10.4	5

KAUAHI, KANI
C, CARDINALS

PERSONAL: Born September 6, 1959, at Kekaha, Hawaii.... 6-3/275.... Full name: Daniel Kani Kauahi.... Name pronounced Ka-WAH-he.
HIGH SCHOOL: Kamehameha (Honolulu).
COLLEGE: Arizona State, then Hawaii.

TRANSACTIONS/CAREER NOTES: Signed as free agent by Seattle Seahawks (April 30, 1982).... Released by Seahawks (August 22, 1986).... Re-signed by Seahawks (September 3, 1986).... Released by Seahawks (September 1, 1987).... Signed as free agent by Green Bay Packers (June 24, 1988).... Granted unconditional free agency (February 1, 1989).... Signed by Phoenix Cardinals (March 31, 1989).
PLAYING EXPERIENCE: Seattle NFL, 1982-1986; Green Bay NFL, 1988; Phoenix NFL, 1989 and 1990.... Games: 1982 (2), 1983 (10), 1984 (16), 1985 (16), 1986 (16), 1988 (16), 1989 (16), 1990 (15). Total: 107.
CHAMPIONSHIP GAME EXPERIENCE: Member of Seattle Seahawks for AFC championship game after 1983 season; did not play.
PRO STATISTICS: 1984—Recovered two fumbles.

KAUFUSI, STEVE
DE, EAGLES

PERSONAL: Born October 17, 1963, at Nukualofa, Tonga. ... 6-4/257. ... Name pronounced kow-FOO-see. ... Cousin of Vai Sikahema, running back-kick returner with Green Bay Packers.
HIGH SCHOOL: South (Salt Lake City).
COLLEGE: Dixie College (Utah), then Brigham Young.
TRANSACTIONS/CAREER NOTES: Selected by Philadelphia Eagles in 12th round (319th pick overall) of 1988 NFL draft.... Signed by Eagles (May 18, 1988).... On injured reserve with ankle injury (August 29, 1988-entire season).... Granted free agency (February 1, 1990).... Re-signed by Eagles (August 7, 1990).
PLAYING EXPERIENCE: Philadelphia NFL, 1989 and 1990.... Games: 1989 (16), 1990 (16). Total: 32.

KAUMEYER, THOM
S, GIANTS

PERSONAL: Born March 17, 1967, at La Jolla, Calif.... 5-11/190.... Full name: Thomas E. Kaumeyer Jr.
HIGH SCHOOL: San Dieguito (Encinitas, Calif.).
COLLEGE: Palomar College (Calif.), then Oregon.
TRANSACTIONS/CAREER NOTES: Selected by Los Angeles Rams in sixth round (148th pick overall) of 1989 NFL draft.... Signed by Rams (July 12, 1989).... Released by Rams (September 5, 1989).... Signed as free agent by Seattle Seahawks to developmental squad (September 6, 1989).... Activated (December 22, 1989).... On inactive list (November 4, 11, 18 and 25, 1990).... On injured reserve with knee injury (December 2, 1990-remainder of season).... Granted unconditional free agency (February 1, 1991).... Signed by New York Giants (off-season, 1991).
PLAYING EXPERIENCE: Seattle NFL, 1989 and 1990.... Games: 1989 (1), 1990 (7). Total: 8.

KAURIC, JERRY
PK, LIONS

PERSONAL: Born June 28, 1963, at Windsor, Ontario, Canada.... 6-0/210.
HIGH SCHOOL: Kennedy Collegiate.
COLLEGE: None.
TRANSACTIONS/CAREER NOTES: Signed as free agent by Calgary Stampeders of CFL (May 10, 1987).... Released by Stampeders (June 20, 1987).... Signed as free agent by Edmonton Eskimos (July 10, 1987).... Granted free agency (March 1, 1990).... Signed by Cleveland Browns (May 1, 1990).... Granted unconditional free agency (February 1, 1991).... Rights relinquished by Browns (April 1, 1991).... Signed by Detroit Lions (May 14, 1991).
CHAMPIONSHIP GAME EXPERIENCE: Played in Grey Cup (CFL championship game) after 1987 season.
PRO STATISTICS: CFL: 1987—Scored 14 singles and fumbled twice. 1988—Scored 18 singles, rushed three times for 43 yards, caught one pass for minus 15 yards and attempted one pass with no completions and fumbled once. 1989—Scored 19 singles, rushed once for 16 yards and fumbled once.... NFL: 1990—Caught one pass for 21 yards.

		— PUNTING—			— PLACE-KICKING —				
Year Team	G	No.	Avg.	Blk.	XPM	XPA	FGM	FGA	Pts.
1987— Edmonton CFL	13	99	38.6	—	47	47	28	41	145
1988— Edmonton CFL	18	154	43.6	—	46	46	39	56	181
1989— Edmonton CFL	18	141	39.9	—	70	70	45	66	224
1990— Cleveland NFL	14	0	0	0	24	27	14	20	66
Total CFL (3 years)	49	394	41.0	—	163	163	112	163	550
Total NFL (1 year)	14	0	0	0	24	27	14	20	66
Pro totals (4 years)	63	394	41.0	0	187	190	126	183	616

KAY, CLARENCE
TE, BRONCOS

PERSONAL: Born July 30, 1961, at Seneca, S.C.... 6-2/237.... Full name: Clarence Hubert Kay.
HIGH SCHOOL: Seneca (S.C.).
COLLEGE: Georgia.
TRANSACTIONS/CAREER NOTES: Selected by Jacksonville Bulls in 1984 USFL territorial draft.... Selected by Denver Broncos in seventh round (186th pick overall) of 1984 NFL draft.... Signed by Broncos (May 17, 1984).... On suspended list (November 15-November 19, 1986).... On suspended list (December 12, 1986-January 10, 1987).
CHAMPIONSHIP GAME EXPERIENCE: Played in AFC championship game after 1986, 1987 and 1989 seasons.... Played in Super Bowl XXI after 1986 season, Super Bowl XXII after 1987 season and Super Bowl XXIV after 1989 season.
PRO STATISTICS: 1984—Fumbled once. 1985—Recovered one fumble and fumbled once. 1987—Fumbled three times. 1988—Fumbled once. 1989—Recovered one fumble. 1990—Returned one kickoff 10 yards and recovered one fumble.

		— RECEIVING —			
Year Team	G	No.	Yds.	Avg.	TD
1984— Denver NFL	16	16	136	8.5	3
1985— Denver NFL	16	29	339	11.7	3
1986— Denver NFL	13	15	195	13.0	1
1987— Denver NFL	12	31	440	14.2	0
1988— Denver NFL	14	34	352	10.4	4

Year	Team	G	No.	Yds.	Avg.	TD
			RECEIVING			
1989— Denver NFL		16	21	197	9.4	2
1990— Denver NFL		16	29	282	9.7	0
Pro totals (7 years)		103	175	1941	11.1	13

KELLY, JIM
QB, BILLS

PERSONAL: Born February 14, 1960, at Pittsburgh. . . . 6-3/218. . . . Full name: James Edward Kelly. . . . Brother of Pat Kelly, linebacker with Birmingham Vulcans (WFL), 1975.
HIGH SCHOOL: East Brady (Pa.).
COLLEGE: Miami, Fla. (bachelor of business management degree, 1982).
TRANSACTIONS/CAREER NOTES: Selected by Chicago Blitz in 14th round (163rd pick overall) of 1983 USFL draft. . . . Selected by Buffalo Bills in first round (14th pick overall) of 1983 NFL draft. . . . USFL rights traded by Chicago Blitz with running back Mark Rush to Houston Gamblers for 1st-, 3rd-, 8th- and 10th-round picks in 1984 draft (June 9, 1983). . . . Signed by Gamblers (June 9, 1983). . . . On developmental squad for four games (June 1-June 29, 1985). . . . Traded by Gamblers with defensive backs Luther Bradley, Will Lewis, Mike Mitchell and Durwood Roquemore, defensive end Pete Catan, quarterback Todd Dillon, defensive tackles Tony Fitzpatrick, Van Hughes and Hosea Taylor, running back Sam Harrell, linebackers Andy Hawkins and Ladell Wills, wide receivers Richard Johnson, Scott McGhee, Gerald McNeil, Ricky Sanders and Clarence Verdin, guard Rich Kehr, center Billy Kidd and offensive tackles Chris Riehm and Tommy Robison to New Jersey Generals for past considerations (March 7, 1986). . . . Granted free agency when USFL suspended operations (August 7, 1986). . . . Signed by Buffalo Bills (August 18, 1986). . . . Granted roster exemption (August 18-August 29, 1986). . . . On inactive list (December 23 and 30, 1990).
CHAMPIONSHIP GAME EXPERIENCE: Played in AFC championship game after 1988 and 1990 seasons. . . . Played in Super Bowl XXV after 1990 season.
RECORDS/HONORS: Led USFL quarterbacks in passing with 97.9 points, 1985. . . . Led NFL quarterbacks in passing with 101.2 points, 1990. . . . Named THE SPORTING NEWS USFL Rookie of the Year, 1984. . . . Named to THE SPORTING NEWS USFL All-Star team, 1985. . . . Played in Pro Bowl after 1987 and 1990 seasons. . . . Named to play in Pro Bowl after 1988 season; replaced due to injury by Dave Krieg.
PRO STATISTICS: USFL Passer rating points: 1984 (98.2), 1985 (97.9). Total: 98.1. . . . NFL Passer rating points: 1986 (83.3), 1987 (83.8), 1988 (78.2), 1989 (86.2), 1990 (101.2). Total: 85.8. . . . USFL: 1984—Credited with one 2-point conversion, caught one pass for minus 13 yards and recovered four fumbles. 1985—Caught one pass for three yards and recovered three fumbles. . . . NFL: 1986—Recovered two fumbles. 1987—Caught one pass for 35 yards and recovered two fumbles. 1988—Caught one pass for five yards. 1989—Recovered three fumbles and fumbled six times for minus six yards. 1990—Recovered two fumbles and fumbled four times for minus eight yards.

Year	Team	G	Att.	Cmp.	Pct.	Yds.	TD	Int.	Avg.	Att.	Yds.	Avg.	TD	TD	Pts.	F.
			PASSING							RUSHING				TOTAL		
1984— Houston USFL		18	*587	*370	63.0	*5219	*44	*26	8.89	85	493	5.8	5	5	32	9
1985— Houston USFL		14	*567	*360	63.5	*4623	*39	19	8.15	28	170	6.1	1	1	6	10
1986— Buffalo NFL		16	480	285	59.4	3593	22	17	7.49	41	199	4.9	0	0	0	7
1987— Buffalo NFL		12	419	250	59.7	2798	19	11	6.68	29	133	4.6	0	0	0	6
1988— Buffalo NFL		16	452	269	59.5	3380	15	17	7.48	35	154	4.4	0	0	0	5
1989— Buffalo NFL		13	391	228	58.3	3130	25	18	8.01	29	137	4.7	2	2	12	6
1990— Buffalo NFL		14	346	219	*63.3	2829	24	9	8.18	22	63	2.9	0	0	0	4
USFL totals (2 years)		32	1154	730	63.3	9842	83	45	8.53	113	663	5.9	6	6	38	19
NFL totals (5 years)		71	2088	1251	59.9	15730	105	72	7.53	156	686	4.4	2	2	12	28
Pro totals (7 years)		103	3242	1981	61.1	25572	188	117	7.89	269	1349	5.0	8	8	50	47

KELLY, JOE
LB, JETS

PERSONAL: Born December 11, 1964, at Sun Valley, Calif. . . . 6-2/235. . . . Full name: Joseph Winston Kelly. . . . Son of Joe Kelly Sr., former player with Ottawa Rough Riders (CFL), 1959-1961; and nephew of Bob Kelly, tackle with Houston Oilers, Kansas City Chiefs, Cincinnati Bengals and Atlanta Falcons, 1961-1964 and 1967-1969.
HIGH SCHOOL: Jefferson (Los Angeles).
COLLEGE: Washington (received degree, 1986).
TRANSACTIONS/CAREER NOTES: Selected by Cincinnati Bengals in first round (11th pick overall) of 1986 NFL draft. . . . Signed by Bengals (August 29, 1986). . . . Granted roster exemption (August 29-September 3, 1986). . . . Traded by Bengals with offensive tackle Scott Jones to New York Jets for rights to wide receiver Reggie Rembert (August 27, 1990). . . . On inactive list (December 2 and 16, 1990). . . . On injured reserve with knee injury (December 21, 1990-remainder of season).
PLAYING EXPERIENCE: Cincinnati NFL, 1986-1989; New York Jets NFL, 1990. . . . Games: 1986 (16), 1987 (10), 1988 (16), 1989 (16), 1990 (12). Total: 70.
CHAMPIONSHIP GAME EXPERIENCE: Played in AFC championship game after 1988 season. . . . Played in Super Bowl XXIII after 1988 season.
PRO STATISTICS: 1986—Intercepted one pass for six yards and recovered one fumble. 1989—Intercepted one pass for 25 yards and recovered three fumbles for 23 yards. 1990—Recovered one fumble.

KELLY, PAT
TE, JETS

PERSONAL: Born October 29, 1965, at Rochester, N.Y. . . . 6-6/252. . . . Full name: Patrick Joseph Kelly.
HIGH SCHOOL: R.L. Thomas (Webster, N.Y.).
COLLEGE: Syracuse (bachelor of science degree in speech communications and public relations, 1988).
TRANSACTIONS/CAREER NOTES: Selected by Denver Broncos in seventh round (174th pick overall) of 1988 NFL draft. . . . Signed by Broncos (June 17, 1988). . . . On injured reserve with knee injury (January 26, 1990-remainder of 1989 season playoffs). . . . Granted unconditional free agency (February 1, 1990). . . . Signed by New York Jets (March 30, 1990). . . . On reserve/

physically unable to perform list with knee injury (August 27-December 28, 1990).
CHAMPIONSHIP GAME EXPERIENCE: Played in AFC championship game after 1989 season.
PRO STATISTICS: 1988—Fumbled once.

			—— RECEIVING ——		
Year	Team	G	No.	Yds.	Avg.	TD
1988— Denver NFL	16	1	4	4.0	0
1989— Denver NFL	16	3	13	4.3	0
1990— N.Y. Jets NFL	1	0	0		0
Pro totals (3 years)	33	4	17	4.3	0

KELM, LARRY
LB, RAMS

PERSONAL: Born November 29, 1964, at Corpus Christi, Tex. . . . 6-4/240. . . . Full name: Larry Dean Kelm.
HIGH SCHOOL: Richard King (Corpus Christi, Tex.).
COLLEGE: Texas A&M.
TRANSACTIONS/CAREER NOTES: Selected by Los Angeles Rams in fourth round (108th pick overall) of 1987 NFL draft. . . . Signed by Rams (July 23, 1987). . . . On injured reserve with foot injury (September 29-November 10, 1989). . . . On injured reserve with knee injury (September 4-October 10, 1990). . . . Transferred to practice squad (October 10, 1990). . . . Activated (October 18, 1990).
PLAYING EXPERIENCE: Los Angeles Rams NFL, 1987-1990. . . . Games: 1987 (12), 1988 (16), 1989 (7), 1990 (11). Total: 46.
CHAMPIONSHIP GAME EXPERIENCE: Played in NFC championship game after 1989 season.
PRO STATISTICS: 1988—Intercepted two passes for 15 yards. 1989—Recovered one fumble.

KELSO, MARK
S, BILLS

PERSONAL: Born July 23, 1963, at Pittsburgh. . . . 5-11/185. . . . Full name: Mark Alan Kelso.
HIGH SCHOOL: North Hills (Pittsburgh).
COLLEGE: William & Mary.
TRANSACTIONS/CAREER NOTES: Selected by Baltimore Stars in sixth round (84th pick overall) of 1985 USFL draft. . . . Selected by Philadelphia Eagles in 10th round (261st pick overall) of 1985 NFL draft. . . . Signed by Eagles (July 19, 1985). . . . Released by Eagles (August 27, 1985). . . . Signed as free agent by Buffalo Bills (April 17, 1986). . . . On injured reserve with knee injury (September 22, 1986-remainder of season). . . . On injured reserve with ankle injury (October 10-December 14, 1990).
CHAMPIONSHIP GAME EXPERIENCE: Played in AFC championship game after 1988 and 1990 seasons. . . . Played in Super Bowl XXV after 1990 season.
PRO STATISTICS: 1987—Recovered two fumbles for 56 yards and a touchdown. 1989—Returned blocked field goal attempt 76 yards for a touchdown and recovered two fumbles.

			—— INTERCEPTIONS ——		
Year	Team	G	No.	Yds.	Avg.	TD
1986— Buffalo NFL	3	0	0		0
1987— Buffalo NFL	12	6	25	4.2	0
1988— Buffalo NFL	16	7	*180	25.7	1
1989— Buffalo NFL	16	6	101	16.8	0
1990— Buffalo NFL	6	2	0	.0	0
Pro totals (5 years)	53	21	306	14.6	1

KEMP, JEFF
QB, SEAHAWKS

PERSONAL: Born July 11, 1959, at Santa Ana, Calif. . . . 6-0/201. . . . Full name: Jeffrey Allan Kemp. . . . Son of Jack Kemp, quarterback with Pittsburgh Steelers, Los Angeles-San Diego Chargers and Buffalo Bills, 1957, 1960-1967 and 1969; former Republican congressman from New York and current Secretary of Housing and Urban Development.
HIGH SCHOOL: Winston Churchill (Potomac, Md.).
COLLEGE: Dartmouth (bachelor of arts degree in economics, 1981); attended Pepperdine (master's in business administration degree, 1986).
TRANSACTIONS/CAREER NOTES: Signed as free agent by Los Angeles Rams (May 11, 1981). . . . Released by Rams (August 31, 1981). . . . Re-signed by Rams (September 1, 1981). . . . On injured reserve with back injury (October 3-December 2, 1981). . . . On inactive list (September 12 and 19, 1982). . . . Active for seven games with Rams in 1982; did not play. . . . Granted free agency (February 1, 1986). . . . Re-signed by Rams and traded to San Francisco 49ers (May 26, 1986); this completed deal (April 29, 1986) in which 49ers traded third-round pick in 1986 draft to Rams for two fourth-round picks in 1986 draft. . . . Traded by 49ers to Seattle Seahawks for fifth-round pick in 1988 draft (May 19, 1987). . . . Crossed picket line during players' strike (October 14, 1987).
CHAMPIONSHIP GAME EXPERIENCE: Member of Los Angeles Rams for NFC championship game after 1985 season; did not play.
PRO STATISTICS: Passer rating points: 1981 (7.6), 1983 (77.9), 1984 (78.7), 1985 (49.7), 1986 (85.7), 1987 (137.1), 1988 (9.2). Career: 76.8. . . . 1984—Recovered three fumbles and fumbled eight times for minus 16 yards. 1986—Recovered one fumble and fumbled three times for minus three yards. 1987—Recovered one fumble and fumbled twice for minus eight yards. 1989—Fumbled once for minus three yards.

			——————— PASSING ———————							—— RUSHING ——				—— TOTAL ——		
Year	Team	G	Att.	Cmp.	Pct.	Yds.	TD	Int.	Avg.	Att.	Yds.	Avg.	TD	TD	Pts.	F.
1981— L.A. Rams NFL	1	6	2	33.3	25	0	1	4.17	2	9	4.5	0	0	0	0
1983— L.A. Rams NFL	4	25	12	48.0	135	1	0	5.40	3	-2	-.7	0	0	0	2
1984— L.A. Rams NFL	14	284	143	50.4	2021	13	7	7.12	34	153	4.5	1	1	6	8
1985— L.A. Rams NFL	5	38	16	42.1	214	0	1	5.63	5	0	.0	0	0	0	2
1986— San Francisco NFL	10	200	119	59.5	1554	11	8	7.77	15	49	3.3	0	0	0	3
1987— Seattle NFL	13	33	23	69.7	396	5	1	12.00	5	9	1.8	0	0	0	2

Year	Team					PASSING						RUSHING				TOTAL	
		G	Att.	Cmp.	Pct.	Yds.	TD	Int.	Avg.	Att.	Yds.	Avg.	TD	TD	Pts.	F.
1988— Seattle NFL		11	35	13	37.1	132	0	5	3.77	6	51	8.5	0	0	0	0
1989— Seattle NFL		9	0	0		0	0	0		1	0	.0	0	0	0	1
1990— Seattle NFL		15	0	0		0	0	0		0	0		0	0	0	0
Pro totals (9 years)		82	621	328	52.8	4477	30	23	7.21	71	269	3.8	1	1	6	18

KEMP, PERRY
WR, PACKERS

PERSONAL: Born December 31, 1961, at Canonsburg, Pa. . . . 5-11/163. . . . Full name: Perry Commodore Kemp.
HIGH SCHOOL: Fort Cherry (McDonald, Pa.).
COLLEGE: California (Pa.).
TRANSACTIONS/CAREER NOTES: Selected by Jacksonville Bulls in 11th round (208th pick overall) of 1984 USFL draft. . . . Signed by Bulls (January 21, 1984). . . . Released by Bulls (February 20, 1986). . . . Awarded on waivers to Memphis Showboats (February 21, 1986). . . . Granted free agency when USFL suspended operations (August 7, 1986). . . . Signed as free agent by Dallas Cowboys (August 12, 1986). . . . Granted roster exemption (August 12-August 23, 1986). . . . Released by Cowboys (August 26, 1986). . . . Signed as free agent by Cleveland Browns (April 22, 1987). . . . Released by Browns (August 25, 1987). . . . Signed as free-agent replacement player by Browns (October 1, 1987). . . . Released by Cleveland Browns (November 3, 1987). . . . Signed as free agent by Green Bay Packers (April 15, 1988).
PRO STATISTICS: USFL: 1984—Returned four kickoffs for 84 yards and recovered one fumble. 1985—Credited with one 2-point conversion, rushed once for minus one yard and recovered one fumble. . . . NFL: 1989—Rushed five times for 43 yards and recovered one fumble. 1990—Rushed once for minus one yard.

Year	Team		RECEIVING				PUNT RETURNS				TOTAL	
		G	No.	Yds.	Avg.	TD	No.	Yds.	Avg.	TD	TD	Pts.	F.
1984— Jacksonville USFL		18	44	730	16.6	2	3	7	2.3	0	2	12	1
1985— Jacksonville USFL		18	59	915	15.5	4	13	116	8.9	0	4	26	2
1987— Cleveland NFL		3	12	224	18.7	2	0	0		0	2	12	0
1988— Green Bay NFL		16	48	620	12.9	0	0	0		0	0	0	3
1989— Green Bay NFL		14	48	611	12.7	2	0	0		0	2	12	3
1990— Green Bay NFL		16	44	527	12.0	2	0	0		0	2	12	2
USFL totals (2 years)		36	103	1645	16.0	6	16	123	7.7	0	6	38	3
NFL totals (4 years)		49	152	1982	13.0	6	0	0		0	6	36	8
Pro totals (6 years)		85	255	3627	14.2	12	16	123	7.7	0	12	74	11

KENN, MIKE
OT, FALCONS

PERSONAL: Born February 9, 1956, at Evanston, Ill. . . . 6-7/280. . . . Full name: Michael Lee Kenn.
HIGH SCHOOL: Evanston (Ill.).
COLLEGE: Michigan (bachelor of arts degree in general studies, 1978).
TRANSACTIONS/CAREER NOTES: Selected by Atlanta Falcons in first round (13th pick overall) of 1978 NFL draft. . . . On injured reserve with knee injury (November 18, 1985-remainder of season).
PLAYING EXPERIENCE: Atlanta NFL, 1978-1990. . . . Games: 1978 (16), 1979 (16), 1980 (16), 1981 (16), 1982 (9), 1983 (16), 1984 (14), 1985 (11), 1986 (14), 1987 (12), 1988 (16), 1989 (15), 1990 (16). Total: 189.
RECORDS/HONORS: Played in Pro Bowl after 1980-1984 seasons. . . . Named to THE SPORTING NEWS NFL All-Pro team, 1980.
PRO STATISTICS: 1978—Recovered one fumble. 1979—Recovered two fumbles. 1980—Recovered three fumbles. 1981—Recovered one fumble. 1982—Recovered one fumble. 1983—Recovered one fumble. 1990—Recovered one fumble.

KENNARD, DEREK
G, CARDINALS

PERSONAL: Born September 9, 1962, at Stockton, Calif. . . . 6-3/300.
HIGH SCHOOL: Edison (Stockton, Calif.).
COLLEGE: Nevada-Reno.
TRANSACTIONS/CAREER NOTES: Selected by Los Angeles Express in third round (52nd pick overall) of 1984 USFL draft. . . . Signed by Express (March 22, 1984). . . . Granted roster exemption (March 22, 1984). . . . Activated (April 13, 1984). . . . On developmental squad for two games (April 13-April 28, 1984). . . . Selected by St. Louis Cardinals in second round (45th pick overall) of 1984 NFL supplemental draft. . . . On developmental squad for four games with Los Angeles Express (March 15-April 13, 1985). . . . Released by Express (August 1, 1985). . . . Re-signed by Express (August 2, 1985). . . . Released by Express (April 29, 1986). . . . Signed by St. Louis Cardinals (May 29, 1986). . . . Franchise transferred to Phoenix (March 15, 1988). . . . On non-football injury list with alcohol problem (October 19-October 30, 1989). . . . Reinstated (November 1, 1989).
PLAYING EXPERIENCE: Los Angeles USFL, 1984 and 1985; St. Louis NFL, 1986 and 1987; Phoenix NFL, 1988-1990. . . . Games: 1984 (6), 1985 (14), 1986 (15), 1987 (12), 1988 (16), 1989 (14), 1990 (16). Total USFL: 20. Total NFL: 73. Total Pro: 93.
PRO STATISTICS: USFL: 1985—Returned one kickoff for no yards and recovered one fumble. . . . NFL: 1987—Fumbled twice for minus four yards.

KENNEDY, CORTEZ
DT, SEAHAWKS

PERSONAL: Born August 23, 1968, at Osceola, Ark. . . . 6-3/293.
HIGH SCHOOL: Rivercrest (Wilson, Ark.).
COLLEGE: Northwest Mississippi Junior College, then Miami, Fla. (degree in criminal justice).
TRANSACTIONS/CAREER NOTES: Selected by Seattle Seahawks in first round (third pick overall) of 1990 NFL draft. . . . Signed by Seahawks (September 3, 1990). . . . Granted roster exemption (September 3-September 9, 1990).
PLAYING EXPERIENCE: Seattle NFL, 1990. . . . Games: 1990 (16).
RECORDS/HONORS: Named as defensive tackle on THE SPORTING NEWS college All-America team, 1989.
PRO STATISTICS: 1990—Recovered one fumble.

KER, CRAWFORD
G, BRONCOS

PERSONAL: Born May 5, 1962, at Philadelphia. . . . 6-3/285. . . . Full name: Crawford Francis Ker.
HIGH SCHOOL: Dunedin (Fla.).
COLLEGE: Arizona Western College, then Florida.
TRANSACTIONS/CAREER NOTES: Selected by Tampa Bay Bandits in 1985 USFL territorial draft. . . . Selected by Dallas Cowboys in third round (76th pick overall) of 1985 NFL draft. . . . Signed by Cowboys (July 12, 1985). . . . On injured reserve with back injury (October 23, 1985-remainder of season). . . . On inactive list (September 23, 1990). . . . Granted unconditional free agency (February 1, 1991). . . . Signed by Denver Broncos (March 28, 1991).
PLAYING EXPERIENCE: Dallas NFL, 1985-1990. . . . Games: 1985 (5), 1986 (16), 1987 (12), 1988 (16), 1989 (16), 1990 (15). Total: 80.
PRO STATISTICS: 1990—Recovered one fumble.

KIDD, JOHN
P, CHARGERS

PERSONAL: Born August 22, 1961, at Springfield, Ill. . . . 6-3/208. . . . Full name: Max John Kidd.
HIGH SCHOOL: Findlay (O.).
COLLEGE: Northwestern (bachelor of science degree in industrial engineering and management science, 1984).
TRANSACTIONS/CAREER NOTES: Selected by Chicago Blitz in 1984 USFL territorial draft. . . . Selected by Buffalo Bills in fifth round (128th pick overall) of 1984 NFL draft. . . . Signed by Bills (June 1, 1984). . . . Granted unconditional free agency (February 1, 1990). . . . Signed by San Diego Chargers (March 15, 1990).
CHAMPIONSHIP GAME EXPERIENCE: Played in AFC championship game after 1988 season.
PRO STATISTICS: 1986—Rushed once for no yards and recovered one fumble. 1987—Attempted one pass with no completions. 1990—Recovered one fumble and fumbled once.

			PUNTING		
Year	Team	G	No.	Avg.	Blk.
1984— Buffalo NFL		16	88	42.0	2
1985— Buffalo NFL		16	92	41.5	0
1986— Buffalo NFL		16	75	40.4	0
1987— Buffalo NFL		12	64	39.0	0
1988— Buffalo NFL		16	62	39.5	0
1989— Buffalo NFL		16	65	39.4	2
1990— San Diego NFL		16	61	40.0	1
Pro totals (7 years)		108	507	40.3	5

KIEL, BLAIR
QB, PACKERS

PERSONAL: Born November 29, 1961, at Columbus, Ind. . . . 6-0/209. . . . Full name: Blair Armstrong Kiel.
HIGH SCHOOL: East (Columbus, Ind.).
COLLEGE: Notre Dame (degree in marketing, 1984).
TRANSACTIONS/CAREER NOTES: Selected by Chicago Blitz in 1984 USFL territorial draft. . . . Selected by Tampa Bay Buccaneers in 11th round (281st pick overall) of 1984 NFL draft. . . . Signed by Buccaneers (June 5, 1984). . . . On reserve/non-football injury list with ulcerative colitis (November 13, 1984-remainder of season). . . . On non-football injury list with Crohn's disease (August 12-September 30, 1985). . . . Released by Buccaneers (October 1, 1985). . . . Signed as free agent by Indianapolis Colts (February 13, 1986). . . . Released by Colts (September 1, 1986). . . . Signed by Colts (September 16, 1986). . . . Crossed picket line during players' strike (October 7, 1987). . . . Released by Colts (November 24, 1987). . . . Signed as free agent by Green Bay Packers (May 10, 1988). . . . Released by Packers (September 5, 1989). . . . Re-signed by Packers (September 26, 1989). . . . Active for nine games with Green Bay Packers in 1989; did not play. . . . On inactive list (September 9, 16, 23, 30; October 7, 28; and November 4, 11, and 18, 1990).
PRO STATISTICS: Passer rating points: 1986 (104.8), 1987 (41.9), 1990 (74.8). Career: 72.5. . . . 1986—Punted five times for 38.0 average. 1987—Punted 12 times for 36.7 average. 1990—Recovered one fumble.

			PASSING						RUSHING				TOTAL		
Year	Team	G	Att.	Cmp.	Pct.	Yds.	TD	Int.	Avg.	Att.	Yds.	Avg.	TD	TD	Pts.	F.
1984— Tampa Bay NFL	10	0	0		0	0	0		0	0		0	0	0	0
1986— Indianapolis NFL	3	25	11	44.0	236	2	0	9.44	3	20	6.7	0	0	0	0
1987— Indianapolis NFL	4	33	17	51.5	195	1	3	5.91	4	30	7.5	0	0	0	0
1988— Green Bay NFL	1	0	0		0	0	0		0	0		0	0	0	0
1990— Green Bay NFL	3	85	51	60.0	504	2	2	5.93	5	9	1.8	1	1	6	2
Pro totals (5 years)	21	143	79	55.2	935	5	5	6.54	12	59	4.9	1	1	6	2

KINARD, TERRY
S, OILERS

PERSONAL: Born November 24, 1959, at Bitburg, West Germany. . . . 6-1/198. . . . Full name: Alfred Terance Kinard.
HIGH SCHOOL: Sumter (S.C.).
COLLEGE: Clemson.
TRANSACTIONS/CAREER NOTES: Selected by Washington Federals in 1983 USFL territorial draft. . . . Selected by New York Giants in first round (10th pick overall) of 1983 NFL draft. . . . Signed by Giants (May 17, 1983). . . . On injured reserve with knee injury (December 9, 1986-remainder of season). . . . Granted unconditional free agency (February 1, 1990). . . . Signed by Houston Oilers (April 1, 1990).
RECORDS/HONORS: Named as defensive back on THE SPORTING NEWS college All-America team, 1982. . . . Played in Pro Bowl after 1988 season.
PRO STATISTICS: 1983—Recovered one fumble for 10 yards. 1984—Returned one punt for no yards, recovered one fumble and fumbled once. 1985—Recovered one fumble. 1986—Recovered two fumbles. 1988—Returned one punt for eight yards. 1989—Recovered one fumble for four yards. 1990—Recovered one fumble for 72 yards and a touchdown.

Year — Team	G		INTERCEPTIONS		
		No.	Yds.	Avg.	TD
1983— N.Y. Giants NFL	16	3	49	16.3	0
1984— N.Y. Giants NFL	15	2	29	14.5	0
1985— N.Y. Giants NFL	16	5	100	20.0	0
1986— N.Y. Giants NFL	14	4	52	13.0	0
1987— N.Y. Giants NFL	12	5	163	32.6	1
1988— N.Y. Giants NFL	16	3	46	15.3	0
1989— N.Y. Giants NFL	16	5	135	27.0	1
1990— Houston NFL	16	4	75	18.8	0
Pro totals (8 years)	121	31	649	20.9	2

KINCHEN, BRIAN
TE, PACKERS

PERSONAL: Born August 6, 1965, at Baton Rouge, La. . . . 6-2/234. . . . Full name: Brian Douglas Kinchen.
HIGH SCHOOL: University (Baton Rouge, La.).
COLLEGE: Louisiana State.
TRANSACTIONS/CAREER NOTES: Selected by Miami Dolphins in 12th round (320th pick overall) of 1988 NFL draft. . . . Signed by Dolphins (June 6, 1988). . . . On injured reserve with hamstring injury (October 4, 1990-remainder of season). . . . Granted unconditional free agency (February 1, 1991). . . . Signed by Green Bay Packers (April 1, 1991).
PRO STATISTICS: 1989—Returned two kickoffs for 26 yards and fumbled twice for minus 35 yards. 1990—Returned one kickoff for 16 yards.

Year — Team	G		RECEIVING		
		No.	Yds.	Avg.	TD
1988— Miami NFL	16	1	3	3.0	0
1989— Miami NFL	16	1	12	12.0	0
1990— Miami NFL	4	0	0		0
Pro totals (3 years)	36	2	15	7.5	0

KING, EMANUEL
DE, RAIDERS

PERSONAL: Born August 15, 1963, at Leroy, Ala. . . . 6-4/270.
HIGH SCHOOL: Leroy (Ala.)
COLLEGE: Alabama.
TRANSACTIONS/CAREER NOTES: Selected by Birmingham Stallions in 1985 USFL territorial draft. . . . Selected by Cincinnati Bengals in first round (25th pick overall) of 1985 NFL draft. . . . Signed by Bengals (May 30, 1985). . . . On non-football injury list with substance abuse (September 1-September 28, 1988). . . . On injured reserve with back injury (October 1-November 5, 1988). . . . Granted unconditional free agency (February 1, 1989). . . . Signed by Los Angeles Raiders (March 23, 1989). . . . Released by Raiders (August 26, 1990). . . . Re-signed by Raiders (March 10, 1991).
PLAYING EXPERIENCE: Cincinnati NFL, 1985-1988; Los Angeles Raiders NFL, 1989. . . . Games: 1985 (16), 1986 (16), 1987 (12), 1988 (7), 1989 (16). Total: 67.
CHAMPIONSHIP GAME EXPERIENCE: Played in AFC championship game after 1988 season. . . . Played in Super Bowl XXIII after 1988 season.
PRO STATISTICS: 1985—Recovered one fumble. 1986—Recovered one fumble for one yard.

KIRK, RANDY
LB, BROWNS

PERSONAL: Born December 27, 1964, at San Jose, Calif. . . . 6-2/231. . . . Full name: Randall Scott Kirk.
HIGH SCHOOL: Bellarmine College Prep (San Jose, Calif.).
COLLEGE: De Anza College (Calif.), then San Diego State.
TRANSACTIONS/CAREER NOTES: Signed as free agent by New York Giants (May 10, 1987). . . . Released by Giants (August 31, 1987). . . . Signed as free-agent replacement player by San Diego Chargers (September 24, 1987). . . . Granted unconditional free agency (February 1, 1989). . . . Signed by Phoenix Cardinals (March 31, 1989). . . . On injured reserve with broken ankle (October 16, 1989-remainder of season). . . . On injured reserve with foot injury (August 27-September 18, 1990). . . . Released by Cardinals (September 18, 1990). . . . Signed by Washington Redskins (November 7, 1990). . . . Released by Redskins (November 13, 1990). . . . Signed by Cleveland Browns (July 27, 1991).
PLAYING EXPERIENCE: San Diego NFL, 1987 and 1988; Phoenix NFL, 1989; Washington NFL, 1990. . . . Games: 1987 (13), 1988 (16), 1989 (6), 1990 (1). Total: 36.
PRO STATISTICS: 1988—Recovered one fumble.

KIRKSEY, WILLIAM
LB, VIKINGS

PERSONAL: Born January 29, 1966, at Birmingham, Ala. . . . 6-2/221.
HIGH SCHOOL: Leeds (Ala.).
COLLEGE: Southern Mississippi.
TRANSACTIONS/CAREER NOTES: Signed as free agent by Minnesota Vikings (May 8, 1990). . . . On inactive list (November 11, 1990). . . . Released by Vikings (November 24, 1990). . . . Re-signed by Vikings to practice squad (November 26, 1990). . . . Signed by Atlanta Falcons to practice squad (December 12, 1990). . . . Contract expired (December 31, 1990). . . . Re-signed by Minnesota Vikings (March 31, 1991).
PLAYING EXPERIENCE: Minnesota NFL, 1990. . . . Games: 1990 (9).

KLINGBEIL, CHUCK
NT, DOLPHINS

PERSONAL: Born November 2, 1965, at Houghton, Mich. . . . 6-1/260. . . . Full name: Charles E. Klingbeil.
HIGH SCHOOL: Houghton (Mich.).
COLLEGE: Northern Michigan.

TRANSACTIONS/CAREER NOTES: Signed as free agent by Saskatchewan Roughriders of CFL (March, 1989). . . . Granted free agency (February, 1991). . . . Signed by Miami Dolphins (April 4, 1991).
PLAYING EXPERIENCE: Saskatchewan CFL, 1989 and 1990. . . . Games: 1989 (5), 1990 (18). Total CFL: 23.
CHAMPIONSHIP GAME EXPERIENCE: Played in Grey Cup (CFL championship game) after 1989 season.
PRO STATISTICS: CFL: 1990—Recovered one fumble.

KLOSTERMANN, BRUCE
LB, RAIDERS

PERSONAL: Born April 17, 1963, at Dubuque, Ia. . . . 6-4/235. . . . Full name: Bruce Donald Klostermann.
HIGH SCHOOL: Beckman (Dyersville, Ia.).
COLLEGE: Waldorf College (Ia.), then Iowa, then South Dakota State (bachelor of science degree in agricultural business, 1986).
TRANSACTIONS/CAREER NOTES: Selected by Denver Broncos in eighth round (217th pick overall) of 1986 NFL draft. . . . Signed by Broncos (July 14, 1986). . . . On injured reserve with knee injury (August 25, 1986-entire season). . . . On injured reserve with back injury (November 23, 1988-remainder of season). . . . Granted unconditional free agency (February 1, 1990). . . . Signed by Los Angeles Raiders (April 1, 1990). . . . Released by Raiders (August 27, 1990). . . . Re-signed by Raiders to practice squad (October 29, 1990). . . . Released by Raiders (November 4, 1990). . . . Signed by Los Angeles Rams (November 28, 1990). . . . Granted unconditional free agency (February 1, 1991). . . . Signed by Los Angeles Raiders (March, 1991).
PLAYING EXPERIENCE: Denver NFL, 1987-1989; Los Angeles Raiders (0)-Los Angeles Rams (5) NFL, 1990. . . . Games: 1987 (9), 1988 (12), 1989 (16), 1990 (5). Total: 42.
CHAMPIONSHIP GAME EXPERIENCE: Played in AFC championship game after 1987 and 1989 seasons. . . . Played in Super Bowl XXII after 1987 season and Super Bowl XXIV after 1989 season.

KNIGHT, LEANDER
S, OILERS

PERSONAL: Born February 16, 1963, at East Orange, N.J. . . . 6-1/193. . . . Full name: Leander Knight Jr.
HIGH SCHOOL: East Orange (N.J.).
COLLEGE: Hudson Valley Community College (N.Y.), then Ferrum College (Va.), then Montclair State (N.J.).
TRANSACTIONS/CAREER NOTES: Signed as free agent by New Jersey Generals of USFL (May 30, 1986). . . . Granted free agency when USFL suspended operations (August 7, 1986). . . . Played with Connecticut Giants of Continental International Football League (1986). . . . Signed by San Diego Chargers (May 8, 1987). . . . Released by Chargers (August 24, 1987). . . . Signed as free agent replacement player by Atlanta Falcons (September 24, 1987). . . . Released by Falcons (October 19, 1987). . . . Re-signed by Falcons for 1988 (November 13, 1987). . . . Released by Falcons (August 30, 1988). . . . Re-signed by Falcons (September 21, 1988). . . . Released by Falcons (September 28, 1988). . . . Re-signed by Falcons (October 14, 1988). . . . Released by Falcons (October 19, 1988). . . . Signed as free agent by New York Jets (April 10, 1989). . . . Released by Jets (September 5, 1989). . . . Re-signed by Jets to developmental squad (September 6, 1989). . . . On developmental squad (September 6-September 27, 1989). . . . Activated after clearing procedural waivers (September 29, 1989). . . . Granted unconditional free agency (February 1, 1990). . . . Signed by Houston Oilers (March 9, 1990).
PLAYING EXPERIENCE: Atlanta NFL, 1987 and 1988; New York Jets NFL, 1989; Houston NFL, 1990. . . . Games: 1987 (1), 1988 (2), 1989 (13), 1990 (16). Total: 32.
PRO STATISTICS: 1990—Intercepted one pass for no yards and recovered one fumble.

KOCH, MARKUS
DE, REDSKINS

PERSONAL: Born February 13, 1963, at Niedermarsberg, West Germany. . . . 6-5/275. . . . Name pronounce COOK.
HIGH SCHOOL: Eastwood Collegiate (Kitchener, Ont.).
COLLEGE: Boise State.
TRANSACTIONS/CAREER NOTES: Selected by Washington Redskins in second round (30th pick overall) of 1986 NFL draft. . . . Signed by Redskins (July 22, 1986). . . . On injured reserve with stress fracture in back (November 17, 1988-remainder of season). . . . On injured reserve with knee injury (November 22, 1989-remainder of season). . . . Granted free agency (February 1, 1990). . . . Re-signed by Redskins (August 8, 1990). . . . On inactive list (December 22 and 30, 1990).
PLAYING EXPERIENCE: Washington NFL, 1986-1990. . . . Games: 1986 (16), 1987 (12), 1988 (11), 1989 (10), 1990 (13). Total: 62.
CHAMPIONSHIP GAME EXPERIENCE: Played in NFC championship game after 1986 and 1987 seasons. . . . Played in Super Bowl XXII after 1987 season.
PRO STATISTICS: 1990—Recovered one fumble.

KOSAR, BERNIE
QB, BROWNS

PERSONAL: Born November 25, 1963, at Boardman, O. . . . 6-5/215.
HIGH SCHOOL: Boardman (O.).
COLLEGE: Miami, Fla. (degree in finance and economics, 1985).
TRANSACTIONS/CAREER NOTES: Selected by Cleveland Browns in first round of NFL supplemental draft (July 2, 1985). . . . Signed by Browns (July 2, 1985). . . . On injured reserve with elbow injury (September 10-October 21, 1988). . . . On inactive list (December 23 and 30, 1990).
CHAMPIONSHIP GAME EXPERIENCE: Played in AFC championship game after 1986, 1987 and 1989 seasons.
RECORDS/HONORS: Established NFL record for lowest percentage, passes had intercepted, career (2.62). . . . Played in Pro Bowl after 1987 season.
PRO STATISTICS: Passer rating points: 1985 (69.3), 1986 (83.8), 1987 (95.4), 1988 (84.3), 1989 (80.3), 1990 (65.7). Career: 80.3. . . . 1985—Recovered two fumbles and fumbled 14 times for minus 25 yards. 1986—Caught one pass for one yard and recovered three fumbles and fumbled seven times for minus 15 yards. 1987—Recovered one fumble and fumbled twice for minus three yards. 1988—Recovered two fumbles. 1989—Caught one pass for minus seven yards and recovered two fumbles and fumbled twice for minus one yard. 1990—Recovered one fumble and fumbled six times for minus nine yards.

Year	Team	G	Att.	Cmp.	Pct.	Yds.	TD	Int.	Avg.	Att.	Yds.	Avg.	TD	TD	Pts.	F.
1985— Cleveland NFL		12	248	124	50.0	1578	8	7	6.36	26	-12	-.5	1	1	6	14
1986— Cleveland NFL		16	531	310	58.4	3854	17	10	7.26	24	19	.8	0	0	0	7
1987— Cleveland NFL		12	389	241	62.0	3033	22	9	7.80	15	22	1.5	1	1	6	2
1988— Cleveland NFL		9	259	156	60.2	1890	10	7	7.30	12	-1	-.1	1	1	6	0
1989— Cleveland NFL		16	513	303	59.1	3533	18	14	6.89	30	70	2.3	1	1	6	2
1990— Cleveland NFL		13	423	230	54.4	2562	10	15	6.06	10	13	1.3	0	0	0	6
Pro totals (6 years)		78	2363	1364	57.7	16450	85	62	6.96	117	111	1.0	4	4	24	31

KOZAK, SCOTT
LB, OILERS

PERSONAL: Born November 28, 1965, at Hillsboro, Ore.... 6-3/226.... Full name: Scott Allen Kozak.... Son of Albert Kozak, minor league pitcher, 1959 and 1960.
HIGH SCHOOL: Colton (Ore.).
COLLEGE: Oregon (bachelor of science degree in physical education, 1989).
TRANSACTIONS/CAREER NOTES: Selected by Houston Oilers in second round (50th pick overall) of 1989 NFL draft.... Signed by Oilers (July 27, 1989).
PLAYING EXPERIENCE: Houston NFL, 1989 and 1990.... Games: 1989 (16), 1990 (16). Total: 32.
PRO STATISTICS: 1990—Recovered one fumble.

KOZERSKI, BRUCE
C, BENGALS

PERSONAL: Born April 2, 1962, at Plains, Pa.... 6-4/287.
HIGH SCHOOL: James M. Coughlin (Wilkes-Barre, Pa.).
COLLEGE: Holy Cross.
TRANSACTIONS/CAREER NOTES: Selected by Houston Gamblers in 12th round (245th pick overall) of 1984 USFL draft.... Selected by Cincinnati Bengals in ninth round (231st pick overall) of 1984 NFL draft.... Signed by Bengals (June 10, 1984).... On injured reserve with pinched neck (November 14-December 11, 1987).
PLAYING EXPERIENCE: Cincinnati NFL, 1984-1990.... Games: 1984 (16), 1985 (14), 1986 (16), 1987 (8), 1988 (16), 1989 (15), 1990 (16). Total: 101.
CHAMPIONSHIP GAME EXPERIENCE: Played in AFC championship game after 1988 season.... Played in Super Bowl XXIII after 1988 season.
PRO STATISTICS: 1987—Recovered one fumble. 1989—Recovered one fumble.

KOZLOWSKI, GLEN
WR, BEARS

PERSONAL: Born December 31, 1962, at Honolulu.... 6-1/205.... Full name: Glen Allen Kozlowski.... Brother of Mike Kozlowski, safety with Miami Dolphins, 1979 and 1981-1986.
HIGH SCHOOL: Carlsbad (N.M.).
COLLEGE: Brigham Young.
TRANSACTIONS/CAREER NOTES: Selected by Chicago Bears in 11th round (305th pick overall) of 1986 NFL draft.... Selected by Memphis Showboats in 10th round (73rd pick overall) of 1986 USFL draft.... Signed by Bears (July 15, 1986).... On non-football injury list with knee injury (August 14, 1986-entire season).... Released by Bears (September 7, 1987).... Re-signed as replacement player by Bears (October 3, 1987).... On injured reserve with broken ankle (October 19, 1987-remainder of season).... On injured reserve with groin injury (September 4-October 6, 1990).
CHAMPIONSHIP GAME EXPERIENCE: Played in NFC championship game after 1988 season.
PRO STATISTICS: 1988—Rushed once for three yards and returned one punt for no yards. 1989—Returned four punts for minus two yards.

			RECEIVING				KICKOFF RETURNS				TOTAL		
Year	Team	G	No.	Yds.	Avg.	TD	No.	Yds.	Avg.	TD	TD	Pts.	F.
1987— Chicago NFL		3	15	199	13.3	3	3	72	24.0	0	3	18	0
1988— Chicago NFL		16	3	92	30.7	0	2	37	18.5	0	0	0	1
1989— Chicago NFL		15	3	74	24.7	0	1	12	12.0	0	0	0	1
1990— Chicago NFL		12	7	83	11.9	0	0	0		0	0	0	0
Pro totals (4 years)		46	28	448	16.0	3	6	121	20.2	0	3	18	2

KRAGEN, GREG
NT, BRONCOS

PERSONAL: Born March 4, 1962, at Chicago.... 6-3/265.... Full name: Greg John Kragen.
HIGH SCHOOL: Amador (Pleasanton, Calif.).
COLLEGE: Utah State.
TRANSACTIONS/CAREER NOTES: Selected by Oklahoma Outlaws in 15th round (296th pick overall) of 1984 USFL draft.... Signed as free agent by Denver Broncos (May 2, 1984).... Released by Broncos (August 27, 1984).... Re-signed by Broncos (January 20, 1985).
PLAYING EXPERIENCE: Denver NFL, 1985-1990.... Games: 1985 (16), 1986 (16), 1987 (12), 1988 (16), 1989 (14), 1990 (16). Total: 90.
CHAMPIONSHIP GAME EXPERIENCE: Played in AFC championship game after 1986, 1987 and 1989 seasons.... Played in Super Bowl XXI after 1986 season, Super Bowl XXII after 1987 season and Super Bowl XXIV after 1989 season.
RECORDS/HONORS: Played in Pro Bowl after 1989 season.
PRO STATISTICS: 1986—Recovered three fumbles. 1987—Recovered one fumble. 1988—Recovered one fumble. 1989—Recovered four fumbles for 17 yards and a touchdown. 1990—Recovered two fumbles.

KRAMER, ERIK
QB, LIONS

PERSONAL: Born November 6, 1964, at Encino, Calif.... 6-1/195.
HIGH SCHOOL: Conoga Park (Calif.).
COLLEGE: Los Angeles Pierce Junior College, then North Carolina State.
TRANSACTIONS/CAREER NOTES: Signed as free agent by New Orleans Saints (May 6, 1987)....

Released by Saints (August 31, 1987).... Signed as free-agent replacement player by Atlanta Falcons (September 24, 1987). ... Released by Falcons (September 1, 1988).... Signed as free agent by Calgary Stampeders of CFL (September 28, 1988). ... Released by Stampeders (July 4, 1989).... Signed as free agent by Detroit Lions (March 21, 1990).... On injured reserve with shoulder injury (September 4-December 28, 1990).... Released by Lions (December 28, 1990).... Re-signed by Lions (March 6, 1991).

PRO STATISTICS: Passer rating points: 1987 (60.0).

				PASSING					RUSHING				TOTAL		
Year	Team	G	Att.	Cmp.	Pct.	Yds.	TD	Int.	Avg.	Att.	Yds.	Avg.	TD	TD	Pts.	F.
1987—	Atlanta NFL	3	92	45	48.9	559	4	5	6.08	2	10	5.0	0	0	0	0
1988—	Calgary CFL	6	153	62	40.5	964	5	13	6.30	12	17	1.4	1	1	6	7
NFL totals (1 year)		3	92	45	48.9	559	4	5	6.08	2	10	5.0	0	0	0	0
CFL totals (1 year)		6	153	62	40.5	964	5	13	6.30	12	17	1.4	1	1	6	7
Pro totals (2 years)		9	245	107	43.7	1523	9	18	6.22	14	27	1.9	1	1	6	7

KRATCH, BOB
G, GIANTS

PERSONAL: Born January 6, 1966, at Brooklyn, N.Y.... 6-3/288.... Full name: Robert A. Kratch. **HIGH SCHOOL:** Mahwah (N.J.). **COLLEGE:** Iowa (bachelor of arts degree in communications, 1989). **TRANSACTIONS/CAREER NOTES:** Selected by New York Giants in third round (64th pick overall) of 1989 NFL draft.... Signed by Giants (July 24, 1989).... On injured reserve with broken finger (September 5-October 17, 1989).... Transferred to developmental squad (October 18-October 21, 1989).
PLAYING EXPERIENCE: New York Giants NFL, 1989 and 1990.... Games: 1989 (4), 1990 (14). Total: 18.
CHAMPIONSHIP GAME EXPERIENCE: Played in NFC championship game after 1990 season.... Played in Super Bowl XXV after 1990 season.

KRAUSS, BARRY
LB, DOLPHINS

PERSONAL: Born March 17, 1957, at Pompano Beach, Fla.... 6-3/250.... Full name: Richard Barry Krauss. **HIGH SCHOOL:** Pompano Beach (Fla.). **COLLEGE:** Alabama (bachelor of science degree in education).
TRANSACTIONS/CAREER NOTES: Selected by Baltimore Colts in first round (sixth pick overall) of 1979 NFL draft.... Colts franchise transferred to Indianapolis (March 31, 1984).... On injured reserve with knee injury (September 29, 1986-remainder of season).... Granted unconditional free agency (February 1, 1989).... Signed by Cleveland Browns (March 8, 1989).... Released by Browns (September 4, 1989).... Awarded on waivers to Miami Dolphins (September 6, 1989).... On injured reserve with knee injury (September 4, 1990-January 11, 1991).... Active for one playoff game after 1990 season; did not play.
PLAYING EXPERIENCE: Baltimore NFL, 1979-1983; Indianapolis NFL, 1984-1988; Miami NFL, 1989 and 1990.... Games: 1979 (15), 1980 (16), 1981 (16), 1982 (9), 1983 (16), 1984 (16), 1985 (16), 1986 (4), 1987 (12), 1988 (16), 1989 (16), 1990 (0). Total: 152.
RECORDS/HONORS: Named as linebacker on THE SPORTING NEWS college All-America team, 1978.
PRO STATISTICS: 1979—Recovered two fumbles. 1980—Recovered one fumble. 1981—Intercepted one pass for 10 yards and recovered two fumbles. 1982—Caught one pass for five yards and a touchdown. 1983—Rushed once for minus one yard and recovered two fumbles. 1984—Intercepted three passes for 20 yards, recovered two fumbles for minus five yards and fumbled once. 1985—Intercepted one pass for no yards and recovered two fumbles. 1986—Recovered one fumble. 1987—Recovered two fumbles. 1988—Intercepted one pass for three yards and recovered two fumbles.

KRIEG, DAVE
QB, SEAHAWKS

PERSONAL: Born October 20, 1958, at Iola, Wis.... 6-1/192.... Full name: David M. Krieg.... Name pronounced CRAIG. **HIGH SCHOOL:** D.C. Everest (Schofield, Wis.). **COLLEGE:** Milton College (bachelor of science degree in marketing management, 1980).
TRANSACTIONS/CAREER NOTES: Signed as free agent by Seattle Seahawks (May 6, 1980).... On injured reserve with separated shoulder (September 19-November 12, 1988).
CHAMPIONSHIP GAME EXPERIENCE: Played in AFC championship game after 1983 season.
RECORDS/HONORS: Established NFL record for most own fumbles recovered, season (9), 1989. Tied NFL record for most fumbles, season (18), 1989; most fumbles recovered, own and opponents', season (9), 1989.... Played in Pro Bowl after 1984, 1988 and 1989 seasons.
PRO STATISTICS: Passer rating points: 1980 (39.6), 1981 (83.3), 1982 (79.0), 1983 (95.0), 1984 (83.3), 1985 (76.2), 1986 (91.0), 1987 (87.6), 1988 (94.6), 1989 (74.8), 1990 (73.6). Career: 82.3.... 1982—Recovered one fumble and fumbled twice for minus 14 yards. 1983—Caught one pass for 11 yards and recovered two fumbles. 1984—Recovered three fumbles and fumbled 11 times for minus 24 yards. 1985—Recovered three fumbles and fumbled 11 times for minus two yards. 1986—Recovered one fumble and fumbled 10 times for minus five yards. 1987—Recovered five fumbles and fumbled 11 times for minus two yards. 1989—Recovered nine fumbles and fumbled 18 times for minus 20 yards. 1990—Caught one pass for minus six yards and recovered two fumbles.

				PASSING					RUSHING				TOTAL		
Year	Team	G	Att.	Cmp.	Pct.	Yds.	TD	Int.	Avg.	Att.	Yds.	Avg.	TD	TD	Pts.	F.
1980—	Seattle NFL	1	2	0	.0	0	0	0	.00	0	0		0	0	0	0
1981—	Seattle NFL	7	112	64	57.1	843	7	5	7.53	11	56	5.1	0	1	6	4
1982—	Seattle NFL	3	78	49	62.8	501	2	2	6.42	6	-3	-.5	0	0	0	5
1983—	Seattle NFL	9	243	147	60.5	2139	18	11	8.80	16	55	3.4	2	2	12	10
1984—	Seattle NFL	16	480	276	57.5	3671	32	*24	7.65	46	186	4.0	3	3	18	11
1985—	Seattle NFL	16	532	285	53.6	3602	27	20	6.77	35	121	3.5	1	1	6	11
1986—	Seattle NFL	15	375	225	60.0	2921	21	11	7.79	35	122	3.5	1	1	6	10
1987—	Seattle NFL	12	294	178	60.5	2131	23	15	7.25	36	155	4.3	2	2	12	11
1988—	Seattle NFL	9	228	134	58.8	1741	18	8	7.64	24	64	2.7	0	0	0	6

Year — Team	G	Att.	Cmp.	Pct.	Yds.	TD	Int.	Avg.	Att.	Yds.	Avg.	TD	TD	Pts.	F.
				PASSING						RUSHING				TOTAL	
1989— Seattle NFL	15	499	286	57.3	3309	21	20	6.63	40	160	4.0	0	0	0	*18
1990— Seattle NFL	16	448	265	59.2	3194	15	20	7.13	32	115	3.6	0	0	0	16
Pro totals (11 years)	119	3291	1909	58.0	24052	184	136	7.31	281	1031	3.7	10	10	60	102

KRUMRIE, TIM
NT, BENGALS

PERSONAL: Born May 20, 1960, at Eau Claire, Wis. . . . 6-2/274. . . . Full name: Timothy A. Krumrie. . . . Name pronounced KRUM-rye.
HIGH SCHOOL: Mondovi (Wis.).
COLLEGE: Wisconsin.
TRANSACTIONS/CAREER NOTES: Selected by Tampa Bay Bandits in seventh round (84th pick overall) of 1983 USFL draft. . . . Selected by Cincinnati Bengals in 10th round (276th pick overall) of 1983 NFL draft. . . . Signed by Bengals (May 19, 1983).
PLAYING EXPERIENCE: Cincinnati NFL, 1983-1990. . . . Games: 1983 (16), 1984 (16), 1985 (16), 1986 (16), 1987 (12), 1988 (16), 1989 (16), 1990 (16). Total: 124.
CHAMPIONSHIP GAME EXPERIENCE: Played in AFC championship game after 1988 season. . . . Played in Super Bowl XXIII after 1988 season.
RECORDS/HONORS: Played in Pro Bowl after 1987 season. . . . Named to play in Pro Bowl after 1988 season; replaced due to injury by Brian Sochia. . . . Named to THE SPORTING NEWS NFL All-Pro team, 1988.
PRO STATISTICS: 1983—Recovered one fumble. 1984—Recovered one fumble for eight yards. 1985—Recovered two fumbles. 1986—Recovered two fumbles for 18 yards. 1988—Recovered three fumbles. 1989—Recovered one fumble for nine yards. 1990—Recovered one fumble.

KUBIAK, GARY
QB, BRONCOS

PERSONAL: Born August 15, 1961, at Houston. . . . 6-0/192. . . . Full name: Gary Wayne Kubiak.
HIGH SCHOOL: Saint Pius X (Houston).
COLLEGE: Texas A&M (degree in physical education).
TRANSACTIONS/CAREER NOTES: Selected by Denver Broncos in eighth round (197th pick overall) of 1983 NFL draft.
CHAMPIONSHIP GAME EXPERIENCE: Played in AFC championship game after 1986, 1987 and 1989 seasons. . . . Played in Super Bowl XXI after 1986 season, Super Bowl XXII after 1987 season and Super Bowl XXIV after 1989 season.
PRO STATISTICS: Passer rating points: 1983 (78.9), 1984 (87.6), 1985 (125.8), 1986 (55.7), 1987 (13.1), 1988 (90.1), 1989 (69.1), 1990 (31.6). Career: 70.4. . . . 1984—Caught one pass for 20 yards. 1988—Recovered three fumbles and fumbled three times for minus nine yards. 1989—Recovered one fumble and punted twice for 21.5 avg. 1990—Recovered two fumbles and fumbled twice for minus eight yards.

Year — Team	G	Att.	Cmp.	Pct.	Yds.	TD	Int.	Avg.	Att.	Yds.	Avg.	TD	TD	Pts.	F.
				PASSING						RUSHING				TOTAL	
1983— Denver NFL	4	22	12	54.5	186	1	1	8.45	4	17	4.3	1	1	6	0
1984— Denver NFL	7	75	44	58.7	440	4	1	5.87	9	27	3.0	1	1	6	1
1985— Denver NFL	16	5	2	40.0	61	1	0	12.20	1	6	6.0	0	0	0	0
1986— Denver NFL	16	38	23	60.5	249	1	3	6.55	6	22	3.7	0	0	0	0
1987— Denver NFL	12	7	3	42.9	25	0	2	3.57	1	3	3.0	0	0	0	3
1988— Denver NFL	16	69	43	62.3	497	5	3	7.20	17	65	3.8	0	0	0	3
1989— Denver NFL	16	55	32	58.2	284	2	2	5.16	15	35	2.3	0	0	0	2
1990— Denver NFL	16	22	11	50.0	145	0	4	6.59	9	52	5.8	0	0	0	2
Pro totals (8 years)	103	293	170	58.0	1887	14	16	6.44	62	227	3.7	2	2	12	8

KUMEROW, ERIC
DE, BEARS

PERSONAL: Born April 17, 1965, at Chicago. . . . 6-7/260. . . . Full name: Eric Palmer Kumerow. . . . Name pronounced KOOM-uh-row. . . . Son of Palmer Pyle, guard with Baltimore Colts, Minnesota Vikings and Oakland Raiders, 1960-1964 and 1966; and stepson of Ernie Kumerow, minor league pitcher, 1961 and 1962.
HIGH SCHOOL: River Forest (Oak Park, Ill.).
COLLEGE: Ohio State (bachelor of arts degree in education, 1988).
TRANSACTIONS/CAREER NOTES: Selected by Miami Dolphins in first round (16th pick overall) of 1988 NFL draft. . . . Signed by Dolphins (July 13, 1988). . . . On injured reserve with pulled groin (December 15, 1988-remainder of season). . . . Traded by Dolphins to Chicago Bears for cornerback Vestee Jackson (January 31, 1991).
PLAYING EXPERIENCE: Miami NFL, 1988-1990. . . . Games: 1988 (14), 1989 (12), 1990 (16). Total: 42.
PRO STATISTICS: 1990—Intercepted one pass for five yards.

KYLES, TROY
WR, CHARGERS

PERSONAL: Born August 13, 1968, at Loreign, O. . . . 6-1/188. . . . Full name: Troy Thomas Kyles.
HIGH SCHOOL: St. Martin DePorres (Detroit).
COLLEGE: Howard (degree in radiologic technology).
TRANSACTIONS/CAREER NOTES: Signed as free agent by New York Giants (April 26, 1990). . . . Released by Giants (September 3, 1990). . . . Signed by Giants to practice squad (October 1, 1990). . . . Activated (November 11, 1990). . . . Granted unconditional free agency (February 1, 1991). . . . Signed by San Diego Chargers (March 26, 1991).
CHAMPIONSHIP GAME EXPERIENCE: Member of New York Giants for NFC championship game after 1990 season; did not play. . . . Played in Super Bowl XXV after 1990 season.

Year — Team	G	No.	Yds.	Avg.	TD
		RECEIVING			
1990— N.Y. Giants NFL	9	4	77	19.3	0
Pro totals (1 year)	9	4	77	19.3	0

LACHEY, JIM
OT, REDSKINS

PERSONAL: Born June 4, 1963, at St. Henry, O. . . . 6-6/290. . . . Full name: James Michael Lachey. . . . Name pronounced luh-SHAY.
HIGH SCHOOL: St. Henry (O.).
COLLEGE: Ohio State (degree in marketing, 1985).
TRANSACTIONS/CAREER NOTES: Selected by New Jersey Generals in 1985 USFL territorial draft. . . . Selected by San Diego Chargers in first round (12th pick overall) of 1985 NFL draft. . . . Signed by Chargers (July 28, 1985). . . . Traded by Chargers to Los Angeles Raiders for offensive tackle John Clay, third-round pick in 1989 draft and conditional pick in 1990 draft (July 30, 1988). . . . Traded by Raiders with second-, fourth- and fifth-round picks in 1989 draft and fourth- and fifth-round picks in 1990 draft to Washington Redskins for quarterback Jay Schroeder and second-round pick in 1989 draft (September 7, 1988).
PLAYING EXPERIENCE: San Diego NFL, 1985-1987; Los Angeles Raiders (1)-Washington (15) NFL, 1988; Washington NFL, 1989 and 1990. . . . Games: 1985 (16), 1986 (16), 1987 (12), 1988 (16), 1989 (14), 1990 (16). Total: 90.
RECORDS/HONORS: Played in Pro Bowl after 1987 and 1990 seasons. . . . Named to THE SPORTING NEWS NFL All-Pro team, 1989 and 1990.
PRO STATISTICS: 1988—Recovered one fumble. 1989—Recovered one fumble. 1990—Recovered one fumble.

LAGEMAN, JEFF
DE, JETS

PERSONAL: Born July 18, 1967, at Fairfax, Va. . . . 6-5/265. . . . Full name: Jeffrey David Lageman. . . . Name pronounced LOG-a-man.
HIGH SCHOOL: Park View (Sterling, Va.).
COLLEGE: Virginia (degree in economics, 1989).
TRANSACTIONS/CAREER NOTES: Selected by New York Jets in first round (14th pick overall) of 1989 NFL draft. . . . Signed by Jets (August 24, 1989).
PLAYING EXPERIENCE: New York Jets NFL, 1989 and 1990. . . . Games: 1989 (16), 1990 (16). Total: 32.
PRO STATISTICS: 1989—Rushed once for minus five yards.

LAKE, CARNELL
S, STEELERS

PERSONAL: Born July 15, 1967, at Salt Lake City. . . . 6-1/206. . . . Full name: Carnell Augustino Lake.
HIGH SCHOOL: Culver City (Calif.).
COLLEGE: UCLA.
TRANSACTIONS/CAREER NOTES: Selected by Pittsburgh Steelers in second round (34th pick overall) of 1989 NFL draft. . . . Signed by Steelers (July 23, 1989).
PRO STATISTICS: 1989—Recovered six fumbles for two yards. 1990—Recovered one fumble.

| | | — INTERCEPTIONS — | | | |
Year Team	G	No.	Yds.	Avg.	TD
1989— Pittsburgh NFL	15	1	0	.0	0
1990— Pittsburgh NFL	16	1	0	.0	0
Pro totals (2 years)	31	2	0	.0	0

LAND, DAN
S, RAIDERS

PERSONAL: Born July 3, 1965, at Donalsonville, Ga. . . . 6-0/195.
HIGH SCHOOL: Seminole County (Donalsonville, Ga.).
COLLEGE: Albany State (Ga.).
TRANSACTIONS/CAREER NOTES: Signed as free agent by Tampa Bay Buccaneers (May 4, 1987). . . . Released by Buccaneers (September 7, 1987). . . . Re-signed as replacement player by Buccaneers (September 24, 1987). . . . Released by Buccaneers (October 19, 1987). . . . Signed as free agent by Atlanta Falcons for 1988 (December 5, 1987). . . . Released by Falcons (August 30, 1988). . . . Signed as free agent by Los Angeles Raiders (January 10, 1989). . . . Released by Raiders (September 5, 1989). . . . Re-signed by Raiders (October 4, 1989).
PLAYING EXPERIENCE: Tampa Bay NFL, 1987; Los Angeles Raiders NFL, 1989 and 1990. . . . Games: 1987 (3), 1989 (10), 1990 (16). Total: 29.
CHAMPIONSHIP GAME EXPERIENCE: Played in AFC championship game after 1990 season.
PRO STATISTICS: 1987—Rushed nine times for 20 yards.

LANDETA, SEAN
P, GIANTS

PERSONAL: Born January 6, 1962, at Baltimore. . . . 6-0/200. . . . Full name: Sean Edward Landeta.
HIGH SCHOOL: Loch Raven (Baltimore).
COLLEGE: Towson State.
TRANSACTIONS/CAREER NOTES: Selected by Philadelphia Stars in 14th round (161st pick overall) of 1983 USFL draft. . . . Signed by Stars (January 24, 1983). . . . Franchise transferred to Baltimore (November 1, 1984). . . . Granted free agency (August 1, 1985). . . . Signed by New York Giants (August 5, 1985). . . . On injured reserve with back injury (September 7, 1988-remainder of season). . . . Granted free agency (February 1, 1990). . . . Re-signed by Giants (July 23, 1990).
CHAMPIONSHIP GAME EXPERIENCE: Played in USFL championship game after 1983-1985 seasons. . . . Played in NFC championship game after 1986 and 1990 seasons. . . . Played in Super Bowl XXI after 1986 season and Super Bowl XXV after 1990 season.
RECORDS/HONORS: Led USFL in net punting average (38.1), 1984. . . . Led NFL in net punting average (37.8), 1989. . . . Named as punter on THE SPORTING NEWS USFL All-Star team, 1983 and 1984. . . . Played in Pro Bowl after 1986 and 1990 seasons. . . . Named to THE SPORTING NEWS NFL All-Pro team, 1986, 1989 and 1990.
PRO STATISTICS: USFL: 1983—Rushed once for minus five yards, recovered one fumble and fumbled once. 1984—Recovered one fumble. . . . NFL: 1985—Attempted one pass with no completions.

| | | — PUNTING — | | |
Year Team	G	No.	Avg.	Blk.
1983— Philadelphia USFL	18	86	41.9	0
1984— Philadelphia USFL	18	53	41.0	0

Year Team	G	No.	Avg.	Blk.
1985— Baltimore USFL	18	65	41.8	0
1985— N.Y. Giants NFL	16	81	42.9	0
1986— N.Y. Giants NFL	16	79	44.8	0
1987— N.Y. Giants NFL	12	65	42.7	1
1988— N.Y. Giants NFL	1	6	37.0	0
1989— N.Y. Giants NFL	16	70	43.1	0
1990— N.Y. Giants NFL	16	75	44.1	0
USFL totals (3 years)	54	204	41.6	0
NFL totals (6 years)	77	376	42.4	1
Pro totals (9 years)	131	580	42.1	1

— PUNTING— (header above No./Avg./Blk.)

LANG, LE-LO
DB, BRONCOS

PERSONAL: Born January 23, 1967, at Los Angeles. . . . 5-11/185. . . . Name pronounced LEE-lo. **HIGH SCHOOL:** Jordan (Los Angeles). **COLLEGE:** Washington. **TRANSACTIONS/CAREER NOTES:** Selected by Denver Broncos in fifth round (136th pick overall) of 1990 NFL draft. . . . On reserve/non-football injury list with foot injury (August 28-November 20, 1990).

Year Team	G	No.	Yds.	Avg.	TD
1990— Denver NFL	6	1	5	5.0	0
Pro totals (1 year)	6	1	5	5.0	0

— INTERCEPTIONS—

LANGHORNE, REGGIE
WR, BROWNS

PERSONAL: Born April 7, 1963, at Suffolk, Va. . . . 6-2/205. . . . Full name: Reginald Devan Langhorne. **HIGH SCHOOL:** Smithfield, Va. **COLLEGE:** Elizabeth City State (N.C.). **TRANSACTIONS/CAREER NOTES:** Selected by Oakland Invaders in fourth round (52nd pick overall) of 1985 USFL draft. . . . Selected by Cleveland Browns in seventh round (175th pick overall) of 1985 NFL draft. . . . Signed by Browns (July 15, 1985). . . . On injured reserve with rib injury (October 16-November 17, 1990). . . . On inactive list (December 30, 1990). **CHAMPIONSHIP GAME EXPERIENCE:** Played in AFC championship game after 1986, 1987 and 1989 seasons. **PRO STATISTICS:** 1985—Recovered one fumble. 1988—Recovered one fumble. 1990—Recovered one fumble.

Year Team	G	RUSHING Att.	Yds.	Avg.	TD	RECEIVING No.	Yds.	Avg.	TD	KICKOFF RETURNS No.	Yds.	Avg.	TD	TOTAL TD	Pts.	F.
1985— Cleveland NFL	16	0	0		0	1	12	12.0	0	3	46	15.3	0	0	0	1
1986— Cleveland NFL	16	1	11	11.0	0	39	678	17.4	1	4	57	14.3	0	1	6	2
1987— Cleveland NFL	12	0	0		0	20	288	14.4	1	1	8	8.0	0	1	6	0
1988— Cleveland NFL	16	2	26	13.0	1	57	780	13.7	7	0	0		0	8	48	3
1989— Cleveland NFL	16	5	19	3.8	0	60	749	12.5	2	0	0		0	2	12	3
1990— Cleveland NFL	12	0	0		0	45	585	13.0	2	0	0		0	2	12	2
Pro totals (6 years)	88	8	56	7.0	1	222	3092	13.9	13	8	111	13.9	0	14	84	11

LANIER, KEN
OT, BRONCOS

PERSONAL: Born July 8, 1959, at Columbus, O. . . . 6-3/290. . . . Full name: Kenneth Wayne Lanier. **HIGH SCHOOL:** Marion Franklin (Columbus, O.). **COLLEGE:** Florida State (degree in industrial arts, 1981). **TRANSACTIONS/CAREER NOTES:** Selected by Denver Broncos in fifth round (125th pick overall) of 1981 NFL draft. **PLAYING EXPERIENCE:** Denver NFL, 1981-1990. . . . Games: 1981 (8), 1982 (9), 1983 (16), 1984 (16), 1985 (16), 1986 (16), 1987 (12), 1988 (16), 1989 (16), 1990 (16). Total: 141. **CHAMPIONSHIP GAME EXPERIENCE:** Played in AFC championship game after 1986, 1987 and 1989 seasons. . . . Played in Super Bowl XXI after 1986 season, Super Bowl XXII after 1987 season and Super Bowl XXIV after 1989 season. **PRO STATISTICS:** 1982—Recovered one fumble. 1984—Recovered one fumble. 1990—Caught one pass for minus four yards and recovered one fumble.

LANKFORD, PAUL
CB, DOLPHINS

PERSONAL: Born June 15, 1958, at New York. . . . 6-1/191. . . . Full name: Paul Jay Lankford. **HIGH SCHOOL:** Farmingdale (N.Y.). **COLLEGE:** Penn State (bachelor of science degree in health planning and administration, 1982). **TRANSACTIONS/CAREER NOTES:** Selected by Miami Dolphins in third round (80th pick overall) of 1982 NFL draft. . . . On inactive list (September 12 and 19, 1982). . . . On injured reserve with cracked tibia (November 28, 1986-remainder of season). . . . On injured reserve with knee injury (September 7-November 8, 1990). **CHAMPIONSHIP GAME EXPERIENCE:** Played in AFC championship game after 1982, 1984 and 1985 seasons. . . . Played in Super Bowl XVII after 1982 season and Super Bowl XIX after 1984 season. **PRO STATISTICS:** 1984—Recovered one fumble. 1986—Recovered one fumble. 1987—Recovered one fumble for four yards.

Year Team	G	No.	Yds.	Avg.	TD
1982— Miami NFL	7	0	0		0
1983— Miami NFL	16	1	10	10.0	0

— INTERCEPTIONS—

Year	Team	G	No.	Yds.	Avg.	TD
				INTERCEPTIONS		
1984— Miami NFL	16	3	25	8.3	0
1985— Miami NFL	16	4	10	2.5	0
1986— Miami NFL	12	0	0		0
1987— Miami NFL	12	3	44	14.7	0
1988— Miami NFL	13	1	0	.0	0
1989— Miami NFL	16	1	0	.0	0
1990— Miami NFL	7	0	0		0
Pro totals (9 years)	115	13	89	6.8	0

LANZA, CHUCK
C, STEELERS

PERSONAL: Born September 20, 1964, at Coraopolis, Pa. . . . 6-2/270. . . . Full name: Charles Louis Lanza.
HIGH SCHOOL: Christian Brothers (Memphis, Tenn.).
COLLEGE: Notre Dame (bachelor of arts degree in sociology, 1988).
TRANSACTIONS/CAREER NOTES: Selected by Pittsburgh Steelers in third round (70th pick overall) of 1988 NFL draft. . . . Signed by Steelers (July 28, 1988). . . . On injured reserve with arm injury (August 27, 1990-entire season).
PLAYING EXPERIENCE: Pittsburgh NFL, 1988 and 1989. . . . Games: 1988 (16), 1989 (11). Total: 27.

LARSON, KURT
LB, PACKERS

PERSONAL: Born February 25, 1966, at Waukesha, Wis. . . . 6-4/241. . . . Full name: Kurt A. Larson.
HIGH SCHOOL: North (Waukesha, Wis.).
COLLEGE: Michigan State (degree in general business administration, 1989).
TRANSACTIONS/CAREER NOTES: Selected by Indianapolis Colts in eighth round (212th pick overall) of 1989 NFL draft. . . . Signed by Colts (July 22, 1989). . . . Granted unconditional free agency (February 1, 1991). . . . Signed by Green Bay Packers (March 29, 1991).
PLAYING EXPERIENCE: Indianapolis NFL, 1989 and 1990. . . . Games: 1989 (13), 1990 (16). Total: 29.
PRO STATISTICS: 1990—Recovered two fumbles.

LATHON, LAMAR
LB, OILERS

PERSONAL: Born December 23, 1967, at Wharton, Tex. . . . 6-3/244. . . . Full name: Lamar Lavantha Lathon. . . . Name pronounced LAY-thin.
HIGH SCHOOL: Wharton (Tex.).
COLLEGE: Houston.
TRANSACTIONS/CAREER NOTES: Selected by Houston Oilers in first round (15th pick overall) of 1990 NFL draft. . . . Signed by Oilers (July 18, 1990). . . . On inactive list (September 9, 1990). . . . On injured reserve with shoulder injury (September 19-October 19, 1990).
PLAYING EXPERIENCE: Houston NFL, 1990. . . . Games: 1990 (11).
PRO STATISTICS: 1990—Recovered one fumble.

LAWSON, JAMIE
FB, BUCCANEERS

PERSONAL: Born October 2, 1965, at New Orleans. . . . 5-10/250. . . . Full name: Jamie Lee Lawson.
HIGH SCHOOL: Central Lafourche (Raceland, La.).
COLLEGE: Nicholls State.
TRANSACTIONS/CAREER NOTES: Selected by Tampa Bay Buccaneers in fifth round (117th pick overall) of 1989 NFL draft. . . . Signed by Buccaneers (July 15, 1989). . . . On injured reserve with broken collarbone (October 17-November 28, 1989). . . . Transferred to developmental squad (November 29, 1989-remainder of season). . . . On inactive list (September 16 and October 28, 1990). . . . Released by Buccaneers (November 2, 1990). . . . Signed by New England Patriots (November 26, 1990). . . . On inactive list (December 2, 9 and 15, 1990). . . . Granted unconditional free agency (February 1, 1991). . . . Signed by Tampa Bay Buccaneers (March 26, 1991).
PLAYING EXPERIENCE: Tampa Bay NFL, 1989; Tampa Bay (6)-New England (1) NFL, 1990. . . . Games: 1989 (5), 1990 (7). Total: 12.

LEAHY, PAT
PK, JETS

PERSONAL: Born March 19, 1951, at St. Louis. . . . 6-0/200. . . . Full name: Patrick Joseph Leahy.
HIGH SCHOOL: Augustinian Academy (St. Louis).
COLLEGE: Did not play college football; attended St. Louis (degree in marketing and business administration).
TRANSACTIONS/CAREER NOTES: Signed as free agent by St. Louis Cardinals (1974). . . . Released by Cardinals and signed as free agent by New York Jets (November 8, 1974). . . . On injured reserve with knee injury (October 13, 1979-remainder of season).
CHAMPIONSHIP GAME EXPERIENCE: Played in AFC championship game after 1982 season.
RECORDS/HONORS: Tied NFL record for most field goals, 50 or more yards, game (2), against New England Patriots (October 20, 1985). . . . Named to THE SPORTING NEWS AFC All-Star team, 1978.
PRO STATISTICS: 1975—Recovered one fumble. 1988—Rushed once for 10 yards. 1990—Punted once for 12 yards.

Year	Team	G	XPM	XPA	FGM	FGA	Pts.
				PLACE-KICKING			
1974— N.Y. Jets NFL	6	18	19	6	11	36
1975— N.Y. Jets NFL	14	27	30	13	21	66
1976— N.Y. Jets NFL	14	16	20	11	16	49
1977— N.Y. Jets NFL	14	18	21	15	25	63
1978— N.Y. Jets NFL	16	41	42	22	30	107

Year	Team	G	PLACE-KICKING				
			XPM	XPA	FGM	FGA	Pts.
1979— N.Y. Jets NFL		6	12	15	8	13	36
1980— N.Y. Jets NFL		16	36	36	14	22	78
1981— N.Y. Jets NFL		16	38	39	25	36	113
1982— N.Y. Jets NFL		9	26	31	11	17	59
1983— N.Y. Jets NFL		16	36	37	16	24	84
1984— N.Y. Jets NFL		16	38	39	17	24	89
1985— N.Y. Jets NFL		16	43	45	26	34	121
1986— N.Y. Jets NFL		16	44	44	16	19	92
1987— N.Y. Jets NFL		12	31	31	18	22	85
1988— N.Y. Jets NFL		16	43	43	23	28	112
1989— N.Y. Jets NFL		16	29	30	14	21	71
1990— N.Y. Jets NFL		16	32	32	23	26	101
Pro totals (17 years)		235	528	554	278	389	1362

LE BEL, HARPER
TE, FALCONS

PERSONAL: Born July 14, 1963, at Granada Hills, Calif. . . . 6-4/245. . . . Full name: Brian Harper Le Bel.
HIGH SCHOOL: Notre Dame (Sherman Oaks, Calif.).
COLLEGE: Colorado State.
TRANSACTIONS/CAREER NOTES: Selected by Kansas City Chiefs in 12th round (321st pick overall) of 1985 NFL draft. . . . Signed by Chiefs (July 18, 1985). . . . Released by Chiefs (August 12, 1985). . . . Signed as free agent by San Francisco 49ers for 1986 (December 20, 1985). . . . Released by 49ers after failing physical (April 7, 1986). . . . Signed as free agent replacement player by San Diego Chargers (September 29, 1987). . . . Released by Chargers (October 20, 1987). . . . Signed as free agent by Dallas Cowboys (April 27, 1988). . . . Released by Cowboys (August 2, 1988). . . . Signed as free agent by Tampa Bay Buccaneers (August 15, 1988). . . . Released by Buccaneers (August 23, 1988). . . . Signed as free agent by Seattle Seahawks (August 8, 1989). . . . Granted unconditional free agency (February 1, 1990). . . . Signed by Philadelphia Eagles (March 30, 1990). . . . Granted unconditional free agency (February 1, 1991). . . . Signed by Atlanta Falcons (April 1, 1991).
PLAYING EXPERIENCE: Seattle NFL, 1989; Philadelphia NFL, 1990. . . . Games: 1989 (16), 1990 (16). Total: 32.
PRO STATISTICS: 1989—Fumbled once for minus 25 yards. 1990—Caught one pass for nine yards and fumbled once.

LEE, CARL
CB, VIKINGS

PERSONAL: Born April 6, 1961, at South Charleston, W.Va. . . . 5-11/184. . . . Full name: Carl Lee III.
HIGH SCHOOL: South Charleston (W.Va.).
COLLEGE: Marshall.
TRANSACTIONS/CAREER NOTES: Selected by Minnesota Vikings in seventh round (186th pick overall) of 1983 NFL draft. . . . Released by Vikings (August 27, 1985). . . . Re-signed by Vikings (September 2, 1985).
CHAMPIONSHIP GAME EXPERIENCE: Played in NFC championship game after 1987 season.
RECORDS/HONORS: Played in Pro Bowl after 1988-1990 seasons. . . . Named to THE SPORTING NEWS NFL All-Pro team, 1988.
PRO STATISTICS: 1984—Recovered one fumble. 1988—Recovered one fumble.

Year	Team	G	INTERCEPTIONS			
			No.	Yds.	Avg.	TD
1983— Minnesota NFL		16	1	31	31.0	0
1984— Minnesota NFL		16	1	0	.0	0
1985— Minnesota NFL		15	3	68	22.7	0
1986— Minnesota NFL		16	3	10	3.3	0
1987— Minnesota NFL		12	3	53	17.7	0
1988— Minnesota NFL		16	8	118	14.8	*2
1989— Minnesota NFL		16	2	0	.0	0
1990— Minnesota NFL		16	2	29	14.5	0
Pro totals (8 years)		123	23	309	13.4	2

LEE, MARK
CB, PACKERS

PERSONAL: Born March 20, 1958, at Hanford, Calif. . . . 6-0/197. . . . Full name: Mark Anthony Lee.
HIGH SCHOOL: Hanford (Calif.).
COLLEGE: Washington.
TRANSACTIONS/CAREER NOTES: Selected by Green Bay Packers in second round (34th pick overall) of 1980 NFL draft.
PRO STATISTICS: 1981—Recovered one fumble. 1983—Recovered one fumble for 15 yards. 1984—Recovered two fumbles. 1986—Recovered one fumble. 1988—Recovered one fumble.

Year	Team	G	INTERCEPTIONS				PUNT RETURNS				KICKOFF RETURNS				TOTAL		
			No.	Yds.	Avg.	TD	No.	Yds.	Avg.	TD	No.	Yds.	Avg.	TD	TD	Pts.	F.
1980— Green Bay NFL		15	0	0		0	5	32	6.4	0	30	589	19.6	0	0	0	1
1981— Green Bay NFL		16	6	50	8.3	0	20	187	9.4	1	14	270	19.3	0	1	6	0
1982— Green Bay NFL		9	1	40	40.0	0	0	0		0	0	0		0	0	0	0
1983— Green Bay NFL		16	4	23	5.8	0	1	-4	-4.0	0	1	0	.0	0	0	0	1
1984— Green Bay NFL		16	3	33	11.0	0	0	0		0	0	0		0	0	0	0
1985— Green Bay NFL		14	1	23	23.0	0	0	0		0	0	0		0	0	0	0
1986— Green Bay NFL		16	9	33	3.7	0	0	0		0	0	0		0	0	0	0
1987— Green Bay NFL		12	1	0	.0	0	0	0		0	0	0		0	0	0	0
1988— Green Bay NFL		15	3	37	12.3	0	0	0		0	0	0		0	0	0	0
1989— Green Bay NFL		12	2	10	5.0	0	0	0		0	0	0		0	0	0	0
1990— Green Bay NFL		16	1	0	.0	0	0	0		0	0	0		0	0	0	0
Pro totals (11 years)		157	31	249	8.0	0	26	215	8.3	1	45	859	19.1	0	1	6	2

LEE, RONNIE

OT, SEAHAWKS

PERSONAL: Born December 24, 1956, at Pine Bluff, Ark. . . . 6-3/275. . . . Full name: Ronald Van Lee. **HIGH SCHOOL:** Tyler (Tex.). **COLLEGE:** Baylor.
TRANSACTIONS/CAREER NOTES: Selected by Miami Dolphins in third round (65th pick overall) of 1979 NFL draft. . . . Released by Dolphins (August 29, 1983). . . . Signed as free agent by Atlanta Falcons (September 14, 1983). . . . Traded by Falcons with sixth-round pick in 1985 draft to Miami Dolphins for cornerback Gerald Small (August 26, 1984). . . . On injured reserve with groin injury (October 18-November 24, 1986). . . . Granted unconditional free agency (February 1, 1990). . . . Signed by Atlanta Falcons (March 1, 1990). . . . Traded by Falcons to Seattle Seahawks for conditional draft pick (August 28, 1990).
CHAMPIONSHIP GAME EXPERIENCE: Played in AFC championship game after 1982, 1984 and 1985 seasons. . . . Played in Super Bowl XVII after 1982 season and Super Bowl XIX after 1984 season.
MISCELLANEOUS: Switched positions from tight end to offensive lineman, 1983.
PRO STATISTICS: 1990—Recovered two fumbles.

| | | | —— RECEIVING —— | | | |
Year	Team	G	No.	Yds.	Avg.	TD
1979—	Miami NFL	16	2	14	7.0	0
1980—	Miami NFL	16	7	83	11.9	2
1981—	Miami NFL	16	14	64	4.6	1
1982—	Miami NFL	9	2	6	3.0	0
1983—	Atlanta NFL	14	0	0		0
1984—	Miami NFL	16	0	0		0
1985—	Miami NFL	15	0	0		0
1986—	Miami NFL	10	0	0		0
1987—	Miami NFL	9	0	0		0
1988—	Miami NFL	16	0	0		0
1989—	Miami NFL	15	0	0		0
1990—	Seattle NFL	15	0	0		0
	Pro totals (12 years)	167	25	167	6.7	3

LEE, SHAWN

NT, DOLPHINS

PERSONAL: Born October 24, 1966, at Brooklyn, N.Y. . . . 6-2/285. . . . Full name: Shawn Swaboda Lee. **HIGH SCHOOL:** Erasmus Hall (Brooklyn, N.Y.). **COLLEGE:** North Alabama.
TRANSACTIONS/CAREER NOTES: Selected by Tampa Bay Buccaneers in sixth round (163rd pick overall) of 1988 NFL draft. . . . Signed by Buccaneers (July 10, 1988). . . . Granted unconditional free agency (February 1, 1990). . . . Re-signed by Buccaneers (July 20, 1990). . . . Released by Buccaneers (August 28, 1990). . . . Awarded on waivers to Atlanta Falcons (August 29, 1990). . . . Traded by Falcons to Miami Dolphins for conditional pick in 1991 NFL draft (September 3, 1990). . . . On injured reserve with ankle injury (September 29-October 27, 1990).
PLAYING EXPERIENCE: Tampa Bay NFL, 1988 and 1989; Miami NFL, 1990. . . . Games: 1988 (15), 1989 (15), 1990 (13). Total: 43.

LEE, ZEPH

S, RAIDERS

PERSONAL: Born June 17, 1963, at San Francisco. . . . 6-3/215. . . . Full name: Zephrini Lee. . . . First name pronounced ZEF-ren-EYE. . . . Cousin of Ricky Bell, running back with Tampa Bay Buccaneers and San Diego Chargers, 1977-1982. **HIGH SCHOOL:** Abraham Lincoln (San Francisco).
COLLEGE: Southern California (bachelor of science degree in exercise science, 1986).
TRANSACTIONS/CAREER NOTES: Selected by New Jersey Generals in 1986 USFL territorial draft. . . . Selected by Los Angeles Raiders in ninth round (246th pick overall) of 1986 NFL draft. . . . Signed by Raiders (July 14, 1986). . . . On injured reserve with groin injury (August 26-entire 1986 season). . . . Released by Raiders (September 1, 1987). . . . Signed as free agent replacement player by Denver Broncos (September 25, 1987). . . . Released by Broncos (October 6, 1987). . . . Signed as free agent replacement player by Los Angeles Raiders (October 10, 1987). . . . Released by Raiders (November 3, 1987). . . . Re-signed by Raiders (November 9, 1987). . . . On injured reserve with groin injury (November 9-December 18, 1987). . . . On injured reserve with neck injury (October 29, 1988-remainder of season). . . . Released by Raiders prior to 1990 season. . . . Re-signed by Raiders (January 27, 1991). . . . Assigned to London Monarchs in 1991 WLAF enhancement allocation program (March 4, 1991).
PLAYING EXPERIENCE: Denver (1)-Los Angeles Raiders (2) NFL, 1987; Los Angeles Raiders NFL, 1988 and 1989. . . . Games: 1987 (3), 1988 (8), 1989 (13). Total: 24.
PRO STATISTICS: 1988—Intercepted one pass for 30 yards and returned one kickoff for no yards. 1989—Returned one kickoff for no yards and fumbled once.

LEWIS, ALBERT

CB, CHIEFS

PERSONAL: Born October 6, 1960, at Mansfield, La. . . . 6-2/195. . . . Full name: Albert Ray Lewis. **HIGH SCHOOL:** DeSoto (Mansfield, La.). **COLLEGE:** Grambling State (degree in political science, 1983).
TRANSACTIONS/CAREER NOTES: Selected by Philadelphia Stars in 15th round (175th pick overall) of 1983 USFL draft. . . . Selected by Kansas City Chiefs in third round (61st pick overall) of 1983 NFL draft. . . . Signed by Chiefs (May 19, 1983). . . . On injured reserve with knee injury (December 10, 1984-remainder of season). . . . On reserve/did not report list (July 24-September 17, 1990).
RECORDS/HONORS: Played in Pro Bowl after 1987, 1989 and 1990 seasons. . . . Named to play in Pro Bowl after 1988 season; replaced due to injury by Eric Thomas. . . . Named to THE SPORTING NEWS NFL All-Pro team, 1989 and 1990.
PRO STATISTICS: 1983—Recovered two fumbles. 1985—Recovered one fumble in end zone for a touchdown. 1986—Recovered

two fumbles. 1987—Recovered one fumble. 1988—Credited with a safety and recovered one fumble. 1990—Recovered three fumbles for one yard.

Year	Team	G	No.	Yds.	Avg.	TD
				— INTERCEPTIONS —		
1983—	Kansas City NFL	16	4	42	10.5	0
1984—	Kansas City NFL	15	4	57	14.3	0
1985—	Kansas City NFL	16	8	59	7.4	0
1986—	Kansas City NFL	15	4	18	4.5	0
1987—	Kansas City NFL	12	1	0	.0	0
1988—	Kansas City NFL	14	1	19	19.0	0
1989—	Kansas City NFL	16	4	37	9.3	0
1990—	Kansas City NFL	15	2	15	7.5	0
	Pro totals (8 years)	119	28	247	8.8	0

LEWIS, BILL
C, CARDINALS

PERSONAL: Born July 12, 1963, at Sioux City, Ia. . . . 6-6/290. . . . Full name: William Glenn Lewis. **HIGH SCHOOL:** East (Sioux City, Ia.). **COLLEGE:** Nebraska. **TRANSACTIONS/CAREER NOTES:** Selected by Memphis Showboats in 1986 USFL territorial draft. . . . Selected by Los Angeles Raiders in seventh round (191st pick overall) of 1986 NFL draft. . . . Signed by Raiders (July 14, 1986). . . . On non-football injury list with appendectomy (September 22-October 24, 1987). . . . On reserve/did not report list (July 25-September 5, 1989). . . . Reinstated and granted roster exemption (September 6-September 16, 1989). . . . Active for eight games with Raiders in 1989; did not play. . . . Granted unconditional free agency (February 1, 1990). . . . Signed by Phoenix Cardinals (March 23, 1990). **PLAYING EXPERIENCE:** Los Angeles Raiders NFL, 1986-1989; Phoenix NFL, 1990. . . . Games: 1986 (4), 1987 (8), 1988 (14), 1990 (16). Total: 42.

LEWIS, GARRY
CB, RAIDERS

PERSONAL: Born August 25, 1967, at New Orleans. . . . 5-11/185. **HIGH SCHOOL:** Walter Cohen (New Orleans). **COLLEGE:** Alcorn State. **TRANSACTIONS/CAREER NOTES:** Selected by Los Angeles Raiders in seventh round (173rd pick overall) of 1990 NFL draft. . . . Signed by Raiders (June 9, 1990). . . . On injured reserve (September 24-October 24, 1990). . . . Transferred to practice squad (October 24, 1990). . . . Activated (November 4, 1990). **PLAYING EXPERIENCE:** Los Angeles Raiders NFL, 1990. . . . Games: 1990 (12). **CHAMPIONSHIP GAME EXPERIENCE:** Played in AFC championship game after 1990 season.

LEWIS, KEVIN
CB, 49ERS

PERSONAL: Born November 14, 1966, at New Orleans. . . . 5-11/173. **HIGH SCHOOL:** Alcee Fortier (New Orleans). **COLLEGE:** Northwestern (La.) State (degree in business management). **TRANSACTIONS/CAREER NOTES:** Signed as free agent by Phoenix Cardinals (May 4, 1989). . . . Released by Cardinals (July 28, 1989). . . . Signed by San Francisco 49ers (April 30, 1990). . . . Released by 49ers (September 3, 1990). . . . Re-signed by 49ers (September 27, 1990). . . . Released by 49ers (November 3, 1990). . . . Signed by 49ers to practice squad (November 5, 1990). . . . Activated (November 23, 1990). **CHAMPIONSHIP GAME EXPERIENCE:** Played in NFC championship game after 1990 season.

Year	Team	G	No.	Yds.	Avg.	TD
				— INTERCEPTIONS —		
1990—	San Francisco NFL	10	1	28	28.0	0
	Pro totals (1 year)	10	1	28	28.0	0

LEWIS, LEO
WR, VIKINGS

PERSONAL: Born September 17, 1956, at Columbia, Mo. . . . 5-8/166. . . . Full name: Leo E. Lewis III. . . . Son of Leo Lewis, member of CFL Hall of Fame and running back with Winnipeg Blue Bombers, 1955-1966; brother of Marc Lewis, wide receiver with Oakland Invaders and Denver Gold of USFL, 1983-1985; and related to Mickey Pruitt, linebacker with Chicago Bears.
HIGH SCHOOL: Hickman (Columbia, Mo.).
COLLEGE: Missouri (degree in education); Tennessee (master's degree).
TRANSACTIONS/CAREER NOTES: Signed as free agent by St. Louis Cardinals (May 21, 1979). . . . On injured reserve with ankle injury (August 21-November 15, 1979). . . . Released by Cardinals (November 16, 1979). . . . Signed as free agent by Calgary Stampeders of CFL (March, 1980). . . . Released by Stampeders (August 7, 1980). . . . Signed as free agent by Hamilton Tiger-Cats of CFL (August 13, 1980). . . . Released by Tiger-Cats (August 20, 1980). . . . Signed as free agent by Minnesota Vikings (May 10, 1981). . . . Released by Vikings (August 25, 1981). . . . Re-signed after clearing procedural waivers (November 11, 1981). . . . Granted free agency (February 1, 1989). . . . Rights relinquished (July 31, 1989). . . . Re-signed by Vikings (August 7, 1989). . . . Released by Vikings (September 3, 1990). . . . Awarded on waivers to Cleveland Browns (September 4, 1990). . . . Released by Browns (September 26, 1990). . . . Re-signed by Minnesota Vikings (October 2, 1990).
CHAMPIONSHIP GAME EXPERIENCE: Played in NFC championship game after 1987 season.
RECORDS/HONORS: Established NFL record for most fair catches, season (27), 1989.
PRO STATISTICS: 1984—Recovered three fumbles. 1985—Recovered one fumble. 1986—Recovered one fumble. 1987—Recovered two fumbles. 1989—Recovered two fumbles.

Year	Team	G	Att.	Yds.	Avg.	TD	No.	Yds.	Avg.	TD	No.	Yds.	Avg.	TD	No.	Yds.	Avg.	TD	TD	Pts.	F.
			— RUSHING —				— RECEIVING —				— PUNT RETURNS —				KICKOFF RETURNS				– TOTALS –		
1980—	Cal. (5)-Ham. (1) CFL	6	1	62	62.0	1	8	91	11.4	1	22	163	7.4	0	15	345	23.0	0	2	12	0
1981—	Minnesota NFL	4	1	16	16.0	0	2	58	29.0	0	0	0	0	0	0	0	0	0	0	0	0

Year	Team	G	RUSHING				RECEIVING				PUNT RETURNS				KICKOFF RETURNS				TOTALS		
			Att.	Yds.	Avg.	TD	No.	Yds.	Avg.	TD	No.	Yds.	Avg.	TD	No.	Yds.	Avg.	TD	TD	Pts.	F.
1982— Minnesota NFL ...		9	0	0		0	8	150	18.8	3	0	0		0	0	0		0	3	18	0
1983— Minnesota NFL ...		14	1	2	2.0	0	12	127	10.6	0	3	52	17.3	0	1	25	25.0	0	0	0	0
1984— Minnesota NFL ...		16	2	11	5.5	0	47	830	17.7	4	4	31	7.8	0	1	31	31.0	0	4	24	1
1985— Minnesota NFL ...		10	1	2	2.0	0	29	442	15.2	3	0	0		0	0	0		0	3	18	1
1986— Minnesota NFL ...		16	3	-16	-5.3	0	32	600	18.8	2	7	53	7.6	0	0	0		0	2	12	3
1987— Minnesota NFL ...		12	5	-7	-1.4	0	24	383	16.0	2	22	275	12.5	1	0	0		0	3	18	1
1988— Minnesota NFL ...		16	0	0		0	11	141	12.8	1	*58	550	9.5	0	1	12	12.0	0	1	6	2
1989— Minnesota NFL ...		16	1	11	11.0	0	12	148	12.3	1	44	446	10.1	0	2	30	15.0	0	1	6	4
1990— Cle. (3)-Min. (11) NFL		14	0	0		0	1	9	9.0	0	33	236	7.2	0	3	39	13.0	0	0	0	1
CFL totals (1 year)		6	1	62	62.0	1	8	91	11.4	1	22	163	7.4	0	15	345	23.0	0	2	12	0
NFL totals (10 years)		127	14	19	1.4	0	178	2888	16.2	16	171	1643	9.6	1	8	137	17.1	0	17	102	13
Pro totals (11 years)		133	15	81	5.4	1	186	2979	16.0	17	193	1806	9.4	1	23	482	21.0	0	19	114	13

LEWIS, NATE
WR, CHARGERS

PERSONAL: Born October 19, 1966, at Moultrie, Ga.... 5-11/189.... Full name: Nathaniel Lewis.
HIGH SCHOOL: Colquitt County (Moultrie, Ga.).
COLLEGE: Oregon Tech.
TRANSACTIONS/CAREER NOTES: Selected by San Diego Chargers in seventh round (187th pick overall) of 1990 NFL draft.... Signed by Chargers (July 11, 1990).... On inactive list (October 7, 14; and December 16, 1990).
PRO STATISTICS: 1990—Recovered two fumbles.

Year	Team	G	RUSHING				RECEIVING				PUNT RETURNS				KICKOFF RETURNS				TOTALS		
			Att.	Yds.	Avg.	TD	No.	Yds.	Avg.	TD	No.	Yds.	Avg.	TD	No.	Yds.	Avg.	TD	TD	Pts.	F.
1990— San Diego NFL		12	4	25	6.3	1	14	192	13.7	1	13	117	9.0	*1	17	383	22.5	0	3	18	3
Pro totals (1 year)		12	4	25	6.3	1	14	192	13.7	1	13	117	9.0	1	17	383	22.5	0	3	18	3

LEWIS, RONALD
WR, 49ERS

PERSONAL: Born March 25, 1968, at Jacksonville, Fla.... 5-11/173.... Full name: Ronald Alexander Lewis.
HIGH SCHOOL: Raines (Jacksonville, Fla.).
COLLEGE: Florida State.
TRANSACTIONS/CAREER NOTES: Selected by San Francisco 49ers in third round (68th pick overall) of 1990 NFL draft.... Signed by 49ers (July 31, 1990).... On injured reserve with back injury (September 3-November 7, 1990).... On inactive list (January 12, 1991).... Deactivated for remainder of 1990 season playoffs (January 19, 1991).

Year	Team	G	RECEIVING			
			No.	Yds.	Avg.	TD
1990— San Francisco NFL		8	5	44	8.8	0
Pro totals (1 year)		8	5	44	8.8	0

BASEBALL TRANSACTIONS: Selected by Toronto Blue Jays' organization in 13th round of 1986 free-agent draft (June 2, 1986).... Selected by California Angels' organization in 10th round of 1989 free-agent draft (June 5, 1989).

				BASEBALL RECORD AS PLAYER												
Year	Team	League	Pos.	G	AB	R	H	2B	3B	HR	RBI	Avg.	PO	A	E	F.A.
1989— Mesa Angels	Arizona		OF	8	24	3	6	1	0	0	4	.250	5	0	0	1.000
1989— Bend	Northwest		OF	5	14	2	2	0	0	0	0	.143	10	0	0	1.000

LILLY, SAMMY
CB, RAMS

PERSONAL: Born February 12, 1965, at Anchorage, Alaska.... 5-9/178.... Full name: Samuel Julius Lilly IV.
HIGH SCHOOL: George P. Butler (Augusta, Ga.).
COLLEGE: Georgia Tech (bachelor of science degree in industrial management, 1988).
TRANSACTIONS/CAREER NOTES: Selected by New York Giants in eighth round (202nd pick overall) of 1988 NFL draft.... Signed by Giants (July 18, 1988).... On injured reserve with hamstring injury (August 29, 1988-entire season).... Granted unconditional free agency (February 1, 1989).... Signed by Philadelphia Eagles (March 13, 1989).... On inactive list (November 4, 12 and 18, 1990).... Released by Eagles (November 26, 1990).... Signed by San Diego Chargers (December 5, 1990).... Granted unconditional free agency (February 1, 1991).... Signed by Los Angeles Rams (April 1, 1991).
PLAYING EXPERIENCE: Philadelphia NFL, 1989; Philadelphia (8)-San Diego (2) NFL, 1990.... Games: 1989 (15), 1990 (10). Total: 25.

LIMBRICK, GARRETT
FB, DOLPHINS

PERSONAL: Born November 16, 1965, at Houston.... 6-2/240.... Full name: Garrett Limbrick IV.
HIGH SCHOOL: Northbrook (Houston).
COLLEGE: Oklahoma State.
TRANSACTIONS/CAREER NOTES: Signed as free agent by Chicago Bears (May 16, 1989).... Released by Bears (August 28, 1989).... Signed by Philadelphia Eagles to developmental squad (September 6, 1989).... Released by Eagles (September 22, 1989).... Signed as free agent by Miami Dolphins (February 22, 1990).... Released by Dolphins (September 3, 1990).... Signed by Dolphins to practice squad (October 1, 1990).... Activated (November 19, 1990).
PRO STATISTICS: 1990—Recovered one fumble.

Year Team	G	RUSHING Att.	Yds.	Avg.	TD	RECEIVING No.	Yds.	Avg.	TD	TOTAL TD	Pts.	F.
1990— Miami NFL	7	5	14	2.8	0	4	23	5.8	0	0	0	1
Pro totals (1 year)	7	5	14	2.8	0	4	23	5.8	0	0	0	1

LINGNER, ADAM
C, BILLS

PERSONAL: Born November 2, 1960, at Indianapolis. . . . 6-4/268. . . . Full name: Adam James Lingner.
HIGH SCHOOL: Alleman (Rock Island, Ill.).
COLLEGE: Illinois.
TRANSACTIONS/CAREER NOTES: Selected by Chicago Blitz in 1983 USFL territorial draft. . . . Selected by Kansas City Chiefs in ninth round (231st pick overall) of 1983 NFL draft. . . . Signed by Chiefs (June 1, 1983). . . . Released by Chiefs (November 24, 1986). . . . Signed as free agent by New England Patriots (November 28, 1986). . . . Active for one game with Patriots in 1986; did not play. . . . Released by Patriots (December 2, 1986). . . . Signed as free agent by Denver Broncos (May 1, 1987). . . . Released by Broncos (August 26, 1987). . . . Awarded on waivers to Buffalo Bills (August 27, 1987). . . . Released by Bills (August 22, 1988). . . . Awarded on waivers to Kansas City Chiefs (August 23, 1988). . . . Granted unconditional free agency (February 1, 1989). . . . Signed as free agent by Buffalo Bills (March 16, 1989).
PLAYING EXPERIENCE: Kansas City NFL, 1983-1985 and 1988; Kansas City (12)-New England (0) NFL, 1986; Buffalo NFL, 1987, 1989 and 1990. . . . Games: 1983 (16), 1984 (16), 1985 (16), 1986 (12), 1987 (12), 1988 (16), 1989 (16), 1990 (16). Total: 120.
CHAMPIONSHIP GAME EXPERIENCE: Played in AFC championship game after 1990 season. . . . Played in Super Bowl XXV after 1990 season.
PRO STATISTICS: 1987—Recovered one fumble.

LIPPETT, RONNIE
CB, PATRIOTS

PERSONAL: Born December 10, 1960, at Melborne, Fla. . . . 5-11/180. . . . Full name: Ronnie Leon Lippett. . . . Name pronounced lip-PET.
HIGH SCHOOL: Sebring (Fla.).
COLLEGE: Miami (Fla.).
TRANSACTIONS/CAREER NOTES: Selected by New England Patriots in eighth round (214th pick overall) of 1983 NFL draft. . . . On injured reserve with ruptured Achilles tendon (September 4-entire 1989 season).
CHAMPIONSHIP GAME EXPERIENCE: Played in AFC championship game after 1985 season. . . . Played in Super Bowl XX after 1985 season.
PRO STATISTICS: 1983—Recovered one fumble. 1984—Recovered one fumble and fumbled once. 1988—Recovered one fumble. 1990—Recovered four fumbles for 16 yards.

Year Team	G	INTERCEPTIONS No.	Yds.	Avg.	TD
1983— New England NFL	16	0	0		0
1984— New England NFL	16	3	23	7.7	0
1985— New England NFL	16	3	93	31.0	0
1986— New England NFL	15	8	76	9.5	0
1987— New England NFL	12	3	103	34.3	*2
1988— New England NFL	15	1	4	4.0	0
1990— New England NFL	16	4	94	23.5	0
Pro totals (7 years)	106	22	393	17.9	2

LIPPS, LOUIS
WR, STEELERS

PERSONAL: Born August 9, 1962, at New Orleans. . . . 5-10/186. . . . Full name: Louis Adam Lipps. . . . Cousin of Garry James, running back with Detroit Lions, 1986-1988.
HIGH SCHOOL: East St. John's (Reserve, La.).
COLLEGE: Southern Mississippi.
TRANSACTIONS/CAREER NOTES: Selected by Arizona Wranglers in eighth round (155th pick overall) of 1984 USFL draft. . . . Selected by Pittsburgh Steelers in first round (23rd pick overall) of 1984 NFL draft. . . . Signed by Steelers (May 19, 1984). . . . On injured reserve with hamstring injury (November 21-December 19, 1987). . . . On inactive list (December 9 and 16, 1990).
CHAMPIONSHIP GAME EXPERIENCE: Played in AFC championship game after 1984 season.
RECORDS/HONORS: Established NFL record for most yards gained, punt returning, rookie season (656), 1984. . . . Played in Pro Bowl after 1984 and 1985 seasons. . . . Named THE SPORTING NEWS NFL Rookie of the Year, 1984.
PRO STATISTICS: 1984—Recovered two fumbles. 1985—Recovered four fumbles for three yards. 1986—Recovered one fumble. 1988—Attempted two passes with one completion for 13 yards and a touchdown and one interception. 1989—Recovered one fumble.

Year Team	G	RUSHING Att.	Yds.	Avg.	TD	RECEIVING No.	Yds.	Avg.	TD	PUNT RETURNS No.	Yds.	Avg.	TD	KICKOFF RETURNS No.	Yds.	Avg.	TD	TOTALS TD	Pts.	F.
1984— Pittsburgh NFL	14	3	71	23.7	1	45	860	19.1	9	53	*656	12.4	1	0	0		0	11	66	8
1985— Pittsburgh NFL	16	2	16	8.0	1	59	1134	19.2	12	36	437	12.1	*2	13	237	18.2	0	15	90	5
1986— Pittsburgh NFL	13	4	-3	-.8	0	38	590	15.5	3	3	16	5.3	0	0	0		0	3	18	2
1987— Pittsburgh NFL	4	0	0		0	11	164	14.9	0	7	46	6.6	0	0	0		0	0	0	0
1988— Pittsburgh NFL	16	6	129	21.5	1	50	973	19.5	5	4	30	7.5	0	0	0		0	6	36	2
1989— Pittsburgh NFL	16	13	180	13.8	1	50	944	18.9	5	4	27	6.8	0	0	0		0	6	36	2
1990— Pittsburgh NFL	14	1	-5	-5.0	0	50	682	13.6	3	0	0		0	1	9	9.0	0	3	18	1
Pro totals (7 years)	93	29	388	13.4	4	303	5347	17.7	37	107	1212	11.3	3	14	246	17.6	0	44	264	20

LITTLE, DAVID
LB, STEELERS

PERSONAL: Born January 3, 1959, at Miami. . . . 6-1/236. . . . Full name: David Lamar Little. . . . Brother of Larry Little, guard with San Diego Chargers and Miami Dolphins, 1967-1980; and currently head coach at Bethune-Cookman College.
HIGH SCHOOL: Jackson (Miami).
COLLEGE: Florida (degree in sociology).
TRANSACTIONS/CAREER NOTES: Selected by Pittsburgh Steelers in seventh round (183rd pick overall) of 1981 NFL draft.
PLAYING EXPERIENCE: Pittsburgh NFL, 1981-1990. . . . Games: 1981 (16), 1982 (9), 1983 (16), 1984 (16), 1985 (16), 1986 (16), 1987 (12), 1988 (16), 1989 (16), 1990 (16). Total: 149.
CHAMPIONSHIP GAME EXPERIENCE: Played in AFC championship game after 1984 season.
RECORDS/HONORS: Played in Pro Bowl after 1990 season.
PRO STATISTICS: 1981—Recovered one fumble. 1982—Recovered one fumble for two yards. 1985—Intercepted two passes for no yards and recovered two fumbles for 11 yards. 1987—Recovered one fumble. 1988—Intercepted one pass for no yards and recovered two fumbles for two yards. 1989—Intercepted three passes for 23 yards and recovered two fumbles. 1990—Intercepted one pass for 35 yards and recovered two fumbles for six yards.

LLOYD, GREG
LB, STEELERS

PERSONAL: Born May 26, 1965, at Miami. . . . 6-2/221. . . . Full name: Gregory Lenard Lloyd.
HIGH SCHOOL: Peach County (Ga.).
COLLEGE: Fort Valley State College (Ga.).
TRANSACTIONS/CAREER NOTES: Selected by Pittsburgh Steelers in sixth round (150th pick overall) of 1987 NFL draft. . . . Signed by Steelers (May 19, 1987). . . . On injured reserve with knee injury (August 31, 1987-entire season). . . . On injured reserve with knee injury (August 30-October 22, 1988). . . . On inactive list (December 23, 1990).
PLAYING EXPERIENCE: Pittsburgh NFL, 1988-1990. . . . Games: 1988 (9), 1989 (16), 1990 (15). Total: 40.
PRO STATISTICS: 1988—Recovered one fumble. 1989—Intercepted three passes for 49 yards, recovered three fumbles and fumbled once. 1990—Intercepted one pass for nine yards.

LOCKHART, EUGENE
LB, PATRIOTS

PERSONAL: Born March 8, 1961, at Crockett, Tex. . . . 6-2/233. . . . Full name: Eugene Lockhart Jr.
HIGH SCHOOL: Crockett (Tex.).
COLLEGE: Houston (bachelor of arts degree in marketing, 1983).
TRANSACTIONS/CAREER NOTES: Selected by Houston Gamblers in 1984 USFL territorial draft. . . . Selected by Dallas Cowboys in sixth round (152nd pick overall) of 1984 NFL draft. . . . Signed by Cowboys (May 8, 1984). . . . On injured reserve with broken leg (December 8, 1987-remainder of season). . . . Traded by Cowboys with linebacker David Howard and defensive back Ron Francis to New England Patriots (April 22, 1991), to complete deal in which Dallas traded first- and second-round picks in 1991 draft to New England for first-round pick in 1991 draft (April 20, 1991).
RECORDS/HONORS: Named to THE SPORTING NEWS NFL All-Pro team, 1989.
PRO STATISTICS: 1984—Recovered one fumble. 1985—Recovered four fumbles for 17 yards. 1986—Recovered one fumble. 1987—Recovered one fumble. 1989—Recovered two fumbles for 40 yards and a touchdown. 1990—Recovered one fumble.

| | | | —— INTERCEPTIONS —— | | |
Year Team	G	No.	Yds.	Avg.	TD
1984— Dallas NFL	15	1	32	32.0	0
1985— Dallas NFL	16	1	19	19.0	1
1986— Dallas NFL	16	1	5	5.0	0
1987— Dallas NFL	9	1	13	13.0	0
1988— Dallas NFL	16	0	0		0
1989— Dallas NFL	16	2	14	7.0	0
1990— Dallas NFL	16	0	0		0
Pro totals (7 years)	104	6	83	13.8	1

LODISH, MIKE
NT, BILLS

PERSONAL: Born August 11, 1967, at Detroit. . . . 6-3/260. . . . Full name: Michael Timothy Lodish.
HIGH SCHOOL: Brother Rice (Birmingham, Mich.).
COLLEGE: UCLA (degree in history and business administration, 1990).
TRANSACTIONS/CAREER NOTES: Selected by Buffalo Bills in 10th round (265th pick overall) of 1990 draft. . . . Signed by Bills (July 26, 1990). . . . On inactive list (November 26, 1990).
PLAYING EXPERIENCE: Buffalo NFL, 1990. . . . Games: 1990 (12).
CHAMPIONSHIP GAME EXPERIENCE: Played in AFC championship game after 1990 season. . . . Played in Super Bowl XXV after 1990 season.

LOFTON, JAMES
WR, BILLS

PERSONAL: Born July 5, 1956, at Fort Ord, Calif. . . . 6-3/190. . . . Full name: James David Lofton. . . . Cousin of Kevin Bass, outfielder with San Francisco Giants.
HIGH SCHOOL: Washington (Los Angeles).
COLLEGE: Stanford (bachelor of science degree in industrial engineering, 1978).
TRANSACTIONS/CAREER NOTES: Selected by Green Bay Packers in first round (sixth pick overall) of 1978 NFL draft. . . . On suspended list (December 18, 1986-remainder of season). . . . Traded by Packers to Los Angeles Raiders for third-round pick in 1987 draft and fourth-round pick in 1988 draft (April 13, 1987). . . . Released by Raiders (August 30, 1989). . . . Signed as free agent by Buffalo Bills (September 26, 1989).
CHAMPIONSHIP GAME EXPERIENCE: Played in AFC championship game after 1990 season. . . . Played in Super Bowl XXV after 1990 season.
RECORDS/HONORS: Played in Pro Bowl after 1978 and 1980-1985 seasons. . . . Named to THE SPORTING NEWS NFL All-Pro team, 1980 and 1981.

PRO STATISTICS: 1978—Returned one kickoff for no yards and attempted two passes with no completions. 1979—Attempted one pass with no completions. 1981—Recovered one fumble. 1982—Attempted one pass with one completion for 43 yards. 1986—Attempted one pass with no completions and recovered two fumbles for eight yards. 1988—Recovered one fumble for 19 yards. 1990—Recovered one fumble.

			RUSHING				RECEIVING				TOTAL	
Year	Team	G	Att.	Yds.	Avg.	TD	No.	Yds.	Avg.	TD	TD	Pts.	F.
1978— Green Bay NFL	16	3	13	4.3	0	46	818	17.8	6	6	36	2
1979— Green Bay NFL	15	1	-1	-1.0	0	54	968	17.9	4	4	24	5
1980— Green Bay NFL	16	0	0		0	71	1226	17.3	4	4	24	0
1981— Green Bay NFL	16	0	0		0	71	1294	18.2	8	8	48	0
1982— Green Bay NFL	9	4	101	25.3	1	35	696	19.9	4	5	30	0
1983— Green Bay NFL	16	9	36	4.0	0	58	1300	*22.4	8	8	48	0
1984— Green Bay NFL	16	10	82	8.2	0	62	1361	*22.0	7	7	42	1
1985— Green Bay NFL	16	4	14	3.5	0	69	1153	16.7	4	4	24	3
1986— Green Bay NFL	15	0	0		0	64	840	13.1	4	4	24	3
1987— L.A. Raiders NFL	12	1	1	1.0	0	41	880	21.5	5	5	30	0
1988— L.A. Raiders NFL	16	0	0		0	28	549	19.6	0	0	0	0
1989— Buffalo NFL	12	0	0		0	8	166	20.8	3	3	18	0
1990— Buffalo NFL	16	0	0		0	35	712	20.3	4	4	24	0
Pro totals (13 years)	191	32	246	7.7	1	642	11963	18.6	61	62	372	14

LOGAN, MARC
FB, DOLPHINS

PERSONAL: Born May 9, 1965, at Lexington, Ky. . . . 5-11/222. . . . Full name: Marc Anthony Logan. . . . Cousin of Dermontti Dawson, center with Pittsburgh Steelers.
HIGH SCHOOL: Bryan Station (Lexington, Ky.).
COLLEGE: Kentucky (bachelor of arts degree in political science, 1987).
TRANSACTIONS/CAREER NOTES: Selected by Cincinnati Bengals in fifth round (130th pick overall) of 1987 NFL draft. . . . Signed by Bengals (July 7, 1987). . . . Released by Bengals (September 7, 1987). . . . Re-signed as replacement player by Bengals (September 25, 1987). . . . Released by Bengals (October 19, 1987). . . . Awarded on waivers to Cleveland Browns (October 20, 1987). . . . Released by Browns (November 5, 1987). . . . Re-signed by Browns for 1988 (November 7, 1987). . . . Released by Browns (August 24, 1988). . . . Signed as free agent by Cincinnati Bengals (October 4, 1988). . . . Granted unconditional free agency (February 1, 1989). . . . Signed by Miami Dolphins (February 16, 1989). . . . On injured reserve with knee injury (October 25-December 6, 1989).
CHAMPIONSHIP GAME EXPERIENCE: Member of Cincinnati Bengals for AFC championship game after 1988 season; inactive. . . . Played in Super Bowl XXIII after 1988 season.
PRO STATISTICS: 1989—Returned blocked punt two yards for a touchdown and recovered two fumbles for minus one yard. 1990—Recovered one fumble.

			RUSHING				RECEIVING				KICKOFF RETURNS				TOTAL	
Year	Team	G	Att.	Yds.	Avg.	TD	No.	Yds.	Avg.	TD	No.	Yds.	Avg.	TD	TD	Pts.	F.
1987— Cincinnati NFL	3	37	203	5.5	1	3	14	4.7	0	3	31	10.3	0	1	6	0
1988— Cincinnati NFL	9	2	10	5.0	0	2	20	10.0	0	4	80	20.0	0	0	0	1
1989— Miami NFL	10	57	201	3.5	0	5	34	6.8	0	24	613	25.5	*1	2	12	1
1990— Miami NFL	16	79	317	4.0	2	7	54	7.7	0	20	367	18.4	0	2	12	4
Pro totals (4 years)	38	175	731	4.2	3	17	122	7.2	0	51	1091	21.4	1	5	30	6

LOHMILLER, CHIP
PK, REDSKINS

PERSONAL: Born July 16, 1966, at Woodbury, Minn. . . . 6-3/213. . . . Full name: John M. Lohmiller.
HIGH SCHOOL: Woodbury (Minn.).
COLLEGE: Minnesota.
TRANSACTIONS/CAREER NOTES: Selected by Washington Redskins in second round (55th pick overall) of 1988 NFL draft. . . . Signed by Redskins (July 17, 1988).
RECORDS/HONORS: Tied NFL record for most field goals, 50 or more yards, game (2), against Indianapolis Colts (December 22, 1990).
PRO STATISTICS: 1988—Punted six times for a 34.7 avg.

			PLACE-KICKING			
Year	Team	G	XPM	XPA	FGM	FGA	Pts.
1988— Washington NFL	16	40	41	19	26	97
1989— Washington NFL	16	41	41	29	*40	128
1990— Washington NFL	16	41	41	30	*40	131
Pro totals (3 years)	48	122	123	78	106	356

LOMACK, TONY
WR, CARDINALS

PERSONAL: Born April 27, 1968, at Tallahassee, Fla. . . . 5-10/190. . . . Full name: Tony J. Lomack.
HIGH SCHOOL: Leon (Tallahassee, Fla.).
COLLEGE: Florida.
TRANSACTIONS/CAREER NOTES: Selected by Los Angeles Rams in ninth round (245th pick overall) of 1990 NFL draft. . . . Signed by Rams (July 11, 1990). . . . On injured reserve with hamstring injury (September 7-October 1, 1990). . . . On practice squad (October 1-November 23, 1990). . . . On inactive list (December 17, 1990). . . . Released by Rams (December 24, 1990). . . . Re-signed by Rams to practice squad (December 27, 1990). . . . Signed by Phoenix Cardinals (March 12, 1991).
PLAYING EXPERIENCE: Los Angeles Rams NFL, 1990. . . . Games: 1990 (3).

LONG, CHUCK
QB, RAMS

PERSONAL: Born February 18, 1963, at Norman, Okla. . . . 6-4/221. . . . Full name: Charles Franklin Long II.
HIGH SCHOOL: North (Wheaton, Ill.).
COLLEGE: Iowa (degree in marketing, 1985).
TRANSACTIONS/CAREER NOTES: Selected by Detroit Lions in first round (12th pick overall) of 1986 NFL draft. . . . Selected by Baltimore Stars in 10th round (75th pick overall) of 1986 USFL draft. . . . Signed by Detroit Lions (August 18, 1986). . . . Granted roster exemption (August 18-August 30, 1986). . . . On injured reserve with knee injury (October 11-November 19, 1988). . . . On injured reserve with elbow injury (September 5-November 7, 1989). . . . Re-signed by Lions and traded to Los Angeles Rams for future draft pick (May 2, 1990).
RECORDS/HONORS: Named as quarterback on THE SPORTING NEWS college All-America team, 1985.
PRO STATISTICS: Passer rating points: 1986 (67.4), 1987 (63.4), 1988 (68.2), 1989 (70.4), 1990 (39.6). Career: 64.5. . . . 1987—Recovered three fumbles and fumbled eight times for minus eight yards. 1988—Recovered two fumbles and fumbled four times for minus three yards.

					PASSING					RUSHING				TOTAL	
Year	Team	G	Att.	Cmp.	Pct.	Yds.	TD	Int.	Avg.	Att.	Yds.	Avg.	TD	TD	Pts.	F.
1986— Detroit NFL		3	40	21	52.5	247	2	2	6.18	2	0	.0	0	0	0	1
1987— Detroit NFL		12	416	232	55.8	2598	11	*20	6.25	22	64	2.9	0	0	0	8
1988— Detroit NFL		7	141	75	53.2	856	6	6	6.07	7	22	3.1	0	0	0	4
1989— Detroit NFL		1	5	2	40.0	42	0	0	8.40	3	2	.7	0	0	0	0
1990— L.A. Rams NFL		4	5	1	20.0	4	0	0	.80	0	0		0	0	0	0
Pro totals (5 years)		27	607	331	54.5	3747	19	28	6.17	34	88	2.6	0	0	0	13

LONG, HOWIE
DE, RAIDERS

PERSONAL: Born January 6, 1960, at Somerville, Mass. . . . 6-5/270. . . . Full name: Howard M. Long.
HIGH SCHOOL: Milford (Mass.).
COLLEGE: Villanova (bachelor of arts degree in communications, 1981).
TRANSACTIONS/CAREER NOTES: Selected by Oakland Raiders in second round (48th pick overall) of 1981 NFL draft. . . . Franchise transferred to Los Angeles (May 7, 1982). . . . Left Los Angeles Raiders camp voluntarily (July 30-August 3, 1984). . . . Crossed picket line during players' strike (October 6, 1987). . . . On injured reserve with broken toe and dislocated toe (September 17-October 21, 1990).
PLAYING EXPERIENCE: Oakland NFL, 1981; Los Angeles Raiders NFL, 1982-1990. . . . Games: 1981 (16), 1982 (9), 1983 (16), 1984 (16), 1985 (16), 1986 (13), 1987 (14), 1988 (7), 1989 (14), 1990 (12). Total: 133.
CHAMPIONSHIP GAME EXPERIENCE: Played in AFC championship game after 1983 and 1990 seasons. . . . Played in Super Bowl XVIII after 1983 season.
RECORDS/HONORS: Played in Pro Bowl after 1983-1987 and 1989 seasons. . . . Named to THE SPORTING NEWS NFL All-Pro team, 1983.
PRO STATISTICS: 1983—Recovered two fumbles. 1984—Recovered two fumbles for four yards. 1986—Recovered two fumbles. 1987—Recovered two fumbles. 1988—Intercepted one pass for 73 yards. 1989—Recovered one fumble. 1990—Recovered one fumble for one yard.

LONG, TERRY
G, STEELERS

PERSONAL: Born July 21, 1959, at Columbia, S.C. . . . 5-11/284. . . . Full name: Terry Luther Long.
HIGH SCHOOL: Eau Claire (Columbia, S.C.).
COLLEGE: East Carolina (spent two years in Army before entering college).
TRANSACTIONS/CAREER NOTES: Selected by Washington Federals in fourth round (76th pick overall) of 1984 USFL draft. . . . Selected by Pittsburgh Steelers in fourth round (111th pick overall) of 1984 NFL draft. . . . Signed by Steelers (July 10, 1984). . . . Crossed picket line during players' strike (October 14, 1987).
PLAYING EXPERIENCE: Pittsburgh NFL, 1984-1990. . . . Games: 1984 (12), 1985 (15), 1986 (16), 1987 (13), 1988 (12), 1989 (13), 1990 (16). Total: 97.
CHAMPIONSHIP GAME EXPERIENCE: Played in AFC championship game after 1984 season.
PRO STATISTICS: 1984—Returned one punt for no yards and fumbled once. 1986—Recovered one fumble. 1988—Recovered one fumble.

LOTT, RONNIE
S, RAIDERS

PERSONAL: Born May 8, 1959, at Albuquerque, N.M. . . . 6-0/200. . . . Full name: Ronald Mandel Lott.
HIGH SCHOOL: Eisenhower (Rialto, Calif.).
COLLEGE: Southern California (bachelor of science degree in public administration, 1981).
TRANSACTIONS/CAREER NOTES: Selected by San Francisco 49ers in first round (eighth pick overall) of 1981 NFL draft. . . . On inactive list (December 9, 17, 23 and 30, 1990). . . . Granted unconditional free agency (February 1, 1991). . . . Signed by Los Angeles Raiders (March 25, 1991).
CHAMPIONSHIP GAME EXPERIENCE: Played in NFC championship game after 1981, 1983, 1984 and 1988-1990 seasons. . . . Played in Super Bowl XVI after 1981 season, Super Bowl XIX after 1984 season, Super Bowl XXIII after 1988 season and Super Bowl XXIV after 1989 season.
RECORDS/HONORS: Tied NFL record for most touchdowns scored by interception, rookie, season (3), 1981. . . . Named as defensive back on THE SPORTING NEWS college All-America team, 1980. . . . Played in Pro Bowl after 1981-1984 and 1986-1990 seasons. . . . Named to THE SPORTING NEWS NFL All-Pro team, 1981, 1987 and 1990.
PRO STATISTICS: 1981—Returned seven kickoffs for 111 yards, recovered two fumbles and fumbled once. 1983—Recovered one fumble. 1985—Returned one kickoff for two yards and recovered two fumbles. 1987—Recovered two fumbles for 33 yards. 1988—Recovered four fumbles for three yards. 1990—Recovered one fumble for three yards.

			INTERCEPTIONS		
Year	Team	G	No.	Yds.	Avg.	TD
1981— San Francisco NFL	16	7	117	16.7	*3
1982— San Francisco NFL	9	2	95	47.5	*1

Year	Team	G	No.	Yds.	Avg.	TD
			INTERCEPTIONS			
1983— San Francisco NFL....		15	4	22	5.5	0
1984— San Francisco NFL....		12	4	26	6.5	0
1985— San Francisco NFL....		16	6	68	11.3	0
1986— San Francisco NFL....		14	*10	134	13.4	1
1987— San Francisco NFL....		12	5	62	12.4	0
1988— San Francisco NFL....		13	5	59	11.8	0
1989— San Francisco NFL....		11	5	34	6.8	0
1990— San Francisco NFL....		11	3	26	8.7	0
Pro totals (10 years)		129	51	643	12.6	5

LOVE, DUVAL
G, RAMS

PERSONAL: Born June 24, 1963, at Los Angeles.... 6-3/287.... Full name: Duval Lee Love.
HIGH SCHOOL: Fountain Valley (Calif.).
COLLEGE: UCLA.
TRANSACTIONS/CAREER NOTES: Selected by Memphis Showboats in 1985 USFL territorial draft.... Selected by Los Angeles Rams in 10th round (274th pick overall) of 1985 NFL draft.... Signed by Rams (July 16, 1985).... On injured reserve with shoulder injury (September 2-October 4, 1985).... On injured reserve with pinched nerve in neck (November 15, 1985-remainder of season).... On injured reserve with knee injury (September 8-October 24, 1987).
PLAYING EXPERIENCE: Los Angeles Rams NFL, 1985-1990.... Games: 1985 (6), 1986 (16), 1987 (10), 1988 (15), 1989 (15), 1990 (16). Total: 78.
CHAMPIONSHIP GAME EXPERIENCE: Played in NFC championship game after 1989 season.
PRO STATISTICS: 1986—Returned one kickoff for minus six yards and fumbled once. 1988—Recovered one fumble. 1990—Recovered two fumbles.

LOVILLE, DEREK
RB, SEAHAWKS

PERSONAL: Born July 4, 1968, at San Francisco.... 5-9/196.... Full name: Derek Kevin Loville.... Named pronounced luh-VILL.
HIGH SCHOOL: Riordan (San Francisco).
COLLEGE: Oregon (degree in American studies).
TRANSACTIONS/CAREER NOTES: Signed as free agent by Seattle Seahawks (May 9, 1990).... On inactive list (December 2, 9, 16, 23 and 30, 1990).

Year	Team	G	No.	Yds.	Avg.	TD	No.	Yds.	Avg.	TD	TD	Pts.	F.
			RUSHING				KICKOFF RETURNS				TOTAL		
1990— Seattle NFL		11	7	12	1.7	0	18	359	19.9	0	0	0	1
Pro totals (1 year)		11	7	12	1.7	0	18	359	19.9	0	0	0	1

LOWDERMILK, KIRK
C, VIKINGS

PERSONAL: Born April 10, 1963, at Canton, O.... 6-3/263.... Full name: Robert Kirk Lowdermilk.... Brother-in-law of Rich Karlis, place-kicker with Atlanta Falcons.
HIGH SCHOOL: Salem (O.).
COLLEGE: Ohio State.
TRANSACTIONS/CAREER NOTES: Selected by New Jersey Generals in 1985 USFL territorial draft.... Selected by Minnesota Vikings in third round (59th pick overall) of 1985 NFL draft.... Signed by Vikings (August 12, 1985).... On injured reserve with knee injury (September 2-October 11, 1986).... Granted free agency (February 1, 1988).... Re-signed by Vikings (August 23, 1988).... On injured reserve with fractured thumb (September 27-October 29, 1988).... Granted free agency (February 1, 1990).... Re-signed by Vikings (September 12, 1990).... Granted roster exemption (September 12-September 15, 1990).
PLAYING EXPERIENCE: Minnesota NFL, 1985-1990.... Games: 1985 (16), 1986 (11), 1987 (12), 1988 (12), 1989 (16), 1990 (15). Total: 82.
CHAMPIONSHIP GAME EXPERIENCE: Played in NFC championship game after 1987 season.
PRO STATISTICS: 1989—Recovered one fumble. 1990—Recovered one fumble.

LOWERY, NICK
PK, CHIEFS

PERSONAL: Born May 27, 1956, at Munich, Germany.... 6-4/205.... Full name: Dominic Gerald Lowery.
HIGH SCHOOL: Albans (Washington, D.C.).
COLLEGE: Dartmouth (bachelor of arts degree in government, 1978).
TRANSACTIONS/CAREER NOTES: Signed as free agent by New York Jets (May 17, 1978).... Released by Jets (August 21, 1978). ... Signed as free agent by New England Patriots (September 19, 1978).... Released by Patriots (October 6, 1978).... Signed as free agent by Cincinnati Bengals (July 2, 1979).... Released by Bengals (August 13, 1979).... Signed as free agent by Washington Redskins (August 18, 1979).... Released by Redskins (August 20, 1979).... Re-signed by Redskins (August 25, 1979).... Released by Redskins (August 27, 1979).... Signed as free agent by Kansas City Chiefs (February 16, 1980).
RECORDS/HONORS: Established NFL record for highest field-goal percentage, career (78.96); most field goals, 50 or more yards, career (18); and most seasons, 100 or more points (8). Tied NFL record with most field goals, 50 or more yards, game (2): against Seattle Seahawks (January 4, 1980), New Orleans Saints (September 8, 1985) and Detroit Lions (November 26, 1987).... Played in Pro Bowl after 1981 and 1990 seasons.... Named to The Sporting News NFL All-Pro team, 1990.
PRO STATISTICS: 1981—Recovered one fumble.

Year	Team	G	XPM	XPA	FGM	FGA	Pts.
			PLACE-KICKING				
1978— New England NFL		2	7	7	0	1	7
1980— Kansas City NFL		16	37	37	20	26	97

Year	Team	G	— PLACE-KICKING —				
			XPM	XPA	FGM	FGA	Pts.
1981—	Kansas City NFL	16	37	38	26	36	115
1982—	Kansas City NFL	9	17	17	19	*24	74
1983—	Kansas City NFL	16	44	45	24	30	116
1984—	Kansas City NFL	16	35	35	23	33	104
1985—	Kansas City NFL	16	35	35	24	27	107
1986—	Kansas City NFL	16	43	43	19	26	100
1987—	Kansas City NFL	12	26	26	19	23	83
1988—	Kansas City NFL	16	23	23	27	32	104
1989—	Kansas City NFL	16	34	35	24	33	106
1990—	Kansas City NFL	16	37	38	*34	37	*139
Pro totals (12 years)		167	375	379	259	328	1152

LUCAS, TIM
LB, BRONCOS

PERSONAL: Born April 3, 1961, at Stockton, Calif. . . . 6-3/230. . . . Full name: Timothy Brian Lucas.
HIGH SCHOOL: Rio Vista (Calif.).
COLLEGE: California (bachelor of arts degree in economics).
TRANSACTIONS/CAREER NOTES: Selected by Oakland Invaders in 1983 USFL territorial draft. . . . Selected by St. Louis Cardinals in 10th round (269th pick overall) of 1983 NFL draft. . . . Signed by Oakland Invaders (May 6, 1983). . . . On developmental squad for three games (May 6-May 29, 1983). . . . Protected in merger of Oakland Invaders and Michigan Panthers (December 6, 1984). . . . On developmental squad for 12 games (April 6, 1985-remainder of season). . . . Granted free agency (August 1, 1985). . . . Signed by St. Louis Cardinals (July 22, 1986). . . . Left St. Louis Cardinals camp and placed on reserve/left camp list (July 10, 1986). . . . Traded by Cardinals to San Diego Chargers for draft pick (July 18, 1987). . . . Released by Chargers (August 29, 1987). . . . Signed as free agent replacement player by Denver Broncos (September 25, 1987). . . . Released by Broncos (August 29, 1988). . . . Re-signed by Broncos (August 30, 1988). . . . On injured reserve with foot injury (September 4-October 11, 1990). . . . Released by Broncos (October 11, 1990). . . . Re-signed by Broncos (October 12, 1990).
PLAYING EXPERIENCE: Oakland USFL, 1983-1985; Denver NFL, 1987-1990. . . . Games: 1983 (6), 1984 (18), 1985 (6), 1987 (11), 1988 (16), 1989 (16), 1990 (11). Total USFL: 30. Total NFL: 54. Total Pro: 84.
CHAMPIONSHIP GAME EXPERIENCE: On developmental squad for USFL championship game after 1985 season. . . . Played in AFC championship game after 1987 and 1989 seasons. . . . Played in Super Bowl XXII after 1987 season and Super Bowl XXIV after 1989 season.
PRO STATISTICS: USFL: 1984—Credited with 5½ sacks for 47½ yards. 1985—Intercepted one pass for 18 yards and credited with two sacks for six yards. . . . NFL: 1987—Intercepted one pass for 11 yards and recovered one fumble. 1990—Recovered one fumble.

LUTZ, DAVE
G, CHIEFS

PERSONAL: Born December 30, 1959, at Monroe, N.C. . . . 6-6/305. . . . Full name: David Graham Lutz. . . . Name pronounced LOOTS.
HIGH SCHOOL: Bowman (Wadesboro, N.C.).
COLLEGE: Georgia Tech.
TRANSACTIONS/CAREER NOTES: Selected by Oakland Invaders in third round (31st pick overall) of 1983 USFL draft. . . . Selected by Kansas City Chiefs in second round (34th pick overall) of 1983 NFL draft. . . . Signed by Chiefs (June 1, 1983). . . . On injured reserve with knee injury (September 4-November 9, 1984). . . . On injured reserve with knee injury (October 7-November 28, 1986). . . . Granted free agency (February 1, 1990). . . . Re-signed by Chiefs (August 15, 1990).
PLAYING EXPERIENCE: Kansas City NFL, 1983-1990. . . . Games: 1983 (16), 1984 (7), 1985 (16), 1986 (9), 1987 (12), 1988 (15), 1989 (16), 1990 (16). Total: 107.
PRO STATISTICS: 1985—Recovered one fumble. 1989—Recovered one fumble.

LYLES, ROBERT
LB, FALCONS

PERSONAL: Born March 21, 1961, at Los Angeles. . . . 6-1/230.
HIGH SCHOOL: Belmont (Los Angeles).
COLLEGE: Texas Christian.
TRANSACTIONS/CAREER NOTES: Selected by Houston Oilers in fifth round (114th pick overall) of 1984 NFL draft. . . . On injured reserve with knee injury (September 25-December 7, 1984). . . . Released by Oilers (October 16, 1990). . . . Awarded on waivers to Atlanta Falcons (October 18, 1990).
PRO STATISTICS: 1986—Recovered one fumble for 93 yards and a touchdown. 1987—Recovered three fumbles for 55 yards and a touchdown. 1988—Recovered two fumbles for five yards. 1989—Returned one kickoff for no yards. 1990—Recovered one fumble.

Year	Team	G	— INTERCEPTIONS —			
			No.	Yds.	Avg.	TD
1984—	Houston NFL	6	0	0		0
1985—	Houston NFL	16	0	0		0
1986—	Houston NFL	16	2	0	.0	0
1987—	Houston NFL	12	2	42	21.0	0
1988—	Houston NFL	16	2	3	1.5	0
1989—	Houston NFL	13	4	66	16.5	0
1990—	Hou. (3)-Atl. (11) NFL	14	0	0		0
Pro totals (7 years)		93	10	111	11.1	0

LYNCH, LORENZO
CB, CARDINALS

PERSONAL: Born April 6, 1963, at Oakland, Calif. . . . 5-10/200.
HIGH SCHOOL: Oakland (Calif.).
COLLEGE: Cal State Sacramento.
TRANSACTIONS/CAREER NOTES: Signed as free agent by Dallas Cowboys (April 30, 1987).

... Released by Cowboys (July 27, 1987).... Signed as free agent by Chicago Bears (July 31, 1987).... Released by Bears (September 1, 1987).... Re-signed as replacement player by Bears (September 24, 1987).... On injured reserve with dislocated shoulder (October 16, 1987-remainder of season).... On injured reserve with hamstring injury (August 29-October 12, 1988).... Activated after clearing procedural waivers (October 14, 1988).... Granted unconditional free agency (February 1, 1990).... Signed by Phoenix Cardinals (March 30, 1990).
PLAYING EXPERIENCE: Chicago NFL, 1987-1989; Phoenix NFL, 1990.... Games: 1987 (2), 1988 (9), 1989 (16), 1990 (16). Total: 43.
CHAMPIONSHIP GAME EXPERIENCE: Played in NFC championship game after 1988 season.
PRO STATISTICS: 1989—Intercepted three passes for 55 yards.

LYONS, ROBERT
S, BROWNS

PERSONAL: Born May 16, 1966, at Wheeling, W.Va.... 6-2/200.... Full name: Robert Louis Lyons Jr.
HIGH SCHOOL: St. Clairesville (O.).
COLLEGE: Akron (bachelor of fine arts degree in graphic design, 1989).
TRANSACTIONS/CAREER NOTES: Signed as free agent by Cleveland Browns (July 19, 1989).... Released by Browns (September 5, 1989).... Re-signed by Browns to developmental squad (September 6, 1989).... On developmental squad (September 6-October 27, 1989).... Granted unconditional free agency (February 1, 1990).... Signed by Minnesota Vikings (March 16, 1990).... Released by Vikings (September 3, 1990).... Signed by Cleveland Browns (March 12, 1991).
CHAMPIONSHIP GAME EXPERIENCE: Played in AFC championship game after 1989 season.

| | | | — INTERCEPTIONS — | | |
Year Team	G	No.	Yds.	Avg.	TD
1989— Cleveland NFL	9	1	0	.0	0
Pro totals (1 year)	9	1	0	.0	0

MAAS, BILL
DE, CHIEFS

PERSONAL: Born March 2, 1962, at Newton Square, Pa.... 6-5/275.... Full name: William Thomas Maas.... Brother-in-law of Dan Marino, quarterback with Miami Dolphins.
HIGH SCHOOL: Marple Newtown (Newton Square, Pa.).
COLLEGE: Pittsburgh.
TRANSACTIONS/CAREER NOTES: Selected by Pittsburgh Maulers in 1984 USFL territorial draft.... Selected by Kansas City Chiefs in first round (fifth pick overall) of 1984 NFL draft.... Signed by Chiefs (July 13, 1984).... On injured reserve with knee injury (October 28, 1988-remainder of season).... On injured reserve with broken arm (November 15, 1989-remainder of season).
PLAYING EXPERIENCE: Kansas City NFL, 1984-1990.... Games: 1984 (14), 1985 (16), 1986 (16), 1987 (11), 1988 (8), 1989 (10), 1990 (16). Total: 91.
RECORDS/HONORS: Played in Pro Bowl after 1986 and 1987 seasons.
PRO STATISTICS: 1985—Recovered one fumble. 1986—Recovered two fumbles. 1987—Recovered one fumble for six yards and a touchdown. 1988—Credited with a safety. 1989—Recovered two fumbles for four yards and a touchdown. 1990—Credited with a safety and recovered one fumble.

MACK, CEDRIC
CB, CARDINALS

PERSONAL: Born September 14, 1960, at Freeport, Tex.... 5-11/190.... Full name: Cedric Manuel Mack.... Cousin of Phillip Epps, wide receiver with Green Bay Packers and New York Jets, 1982-1989; and cousin of Milton Mack, cornerback with New Orleans Saints.
HIGH SCHOOL: Brazosport (Freeport, Tex.).
COLLEGE: Baylor.
TRANSACTIONS/CAREER NOTES: Selected by Oakland Invaders in 12th round (138th pick overall) of 1983 USFL draft.... Selected by St. Louis Cardinals in second round (44th pick overall) of 1983 NFL draft.... Signed by Cardinals (July 11, 1983). ... On injured reserve with dislocated shoulder (September 28-October 26, 1984).... Franchise transferred to Phoenix (March 15, 1988).... Granted free agency (February 1, 1990).... Re-signed by Phoenix Cardinals (July 30, 1990).
MISCELLANEOUS: Selected by New York Yankees' organization in 22nd round of free-agent baseball draft (June 5, 1979).
PRO STATISTICS: 1984—Caught five passes for 61 yards. 1985—Caught one pass for 16 yards and recovered two fumbles. 1986—Recovered one fumble. 1987—Recovered two fumbles. 1988—Recovered one fumble for 45 yards and a touchdown. 1990—Recovered one fumble for 17 yards.

| | | | — INTERCEPTIONS — | | |
Year Team	G	No.	Yds.	Avg.	TD
1983— St. Louis NFL	16	3	25	8.3	0
1984— St. Louis NFL	12	0	0		0
1985— St. Louis NFL	16	2	10	5.0	0
1986— St. Louis NFL	15	4	42	10.5	0
1987— St. Louis NFL	10	2	0	.0	0
1988— Phoenix NFL	16	3	33	11.0	0
1989— Phoenix NFL	16	4	15	3.8	0
1990— Phoenix NFL	16	2	53	26.5	0
Pro totals (8 years)	117	20	178	8.9	0

MACK, KEVIN
FB, BROWNS

PERSONAL: Born August 9, 1962, at Kings Mountain, N.C.... 6-0/230.
HIGH SCHOOL: Kings Mountain (N.C.).
COLLEGE: Clemson.
TRANSACTIONS/CAREER NOTES: Selected by Washington Federals in 1984 USFL territorial draft.
... Rights traded by Federals with rights to defensive tackle James Robinson to Los Angeles Express for draft choices (March

16, 1984).... Signed by Express (March 16, 1984).... Granted roster exemption (March 16-March 23, 1984).... On developmental squad for three games (March 30-April 7 and April 28-May 11, 1984).... Selected by Cleveland Browns in first round (11th pick overall) of 1984 NFL supplemental draft.... Released by Los Angeles Express (January 31, 1985).... Signed by Cleveland Browns (February 1, 1985).... On reserve/non-football injury with cocaine problem (September 1-October 2, 1989).... Granted roster exemption (October 4-November 20, 1989); included prison term on drug charges (October 4-November 5, 1989).... On inactive list (September 16 and 23, 1990).

CHAMPIONSHIP GAME EXPERIENCE: Played in AFC championship game after 1986, 1987 and 1989 seasons.

RECORDS/HONORS: Played in Pro Bowl after 1985 and 1987 seasons.

PRO STATISTICS: USFL: 1984—Returned three kickoffs for 20 yards and recovered four fumbles.... NFL: 1985—Recovered three fumbles. 1986—Recovered one fumble. 1987—Recovered one fumble. 1988—Recovered one fumble. 1990—Recovered five fumbles and fumbled six times for one yard.

		RUSHING				RECEIVING				TOTAL		
Year Team	G	Att.	Yds.	Avg.	TD	No.	Yds.	Avg.	TD	TD	Pts.	F.
1984— Los Angeles USFL	12	73	330	4.5	4	6	38	6.3	0	4	24	3
1985— Cleveland NFL	16	222	1104	5.0	7	29	297	10.2	3	10	60	4
1986— Cleveland NFL	12	174	665	3.8	10	28	292	10.4	0	10	60	6
1987— Cleveland NFL	12	201	735	3.7	5	32	223	7.0	1	6	36	6
1988— Cleveland NFL	11	123	485	3.9	3	11	87	7.9	0	3	18	5
1989— Cleveland NFL	4	37	130	3.5	1	2	7	3.5	0	1	6	1
1990— Cleveland NFL	14	158	702	4.4	5	42	360	8.6	2	7	42	6
USFL totals (1 year)	12	73	330	4.5	4	6	38	6.3	0	4	24	3
NFL totals (6 years)	69	915	3821	4.2	31	144	1266	8.8	6	37	222	28
Pro totals (7 years)	81	988	4151	4.2	35	150	1304	8.7	6	41	246	31

MACK, MILTON
CB, SAINTS

PERSONAL: Born September 20, 1963, at Jackson, Miss.... 5-11/182.... Full name: Milton Jerome Mack.... Cousin of Cedric Mack, cornerback with Phoenix Cardinals.
HIGH SCHOOL: Callaway (Jackson, Miss.).
COLLEGE: Alcorn State.

TRANSACTIONS/CAREER NOTES: Selected by New Orleans Saints in fifth round (123rd pick overall) of 1987 NFL draft.... Signed by Saints (July 24, 1987).... Crossed picket line during players' strike (October 14, 1987).... On injured reserve with hamstring injury (January 2, 1991-remainder of 1990 season playoffs).

PRO STATISTICS: 1990—Returned one kickoff for 17 yards.

		INTERCEPTIONS			
Year Team	G	No.	Yds.	Avg.	TD
1987— New Orleans NFL	13	4	32	8.0	0
1988— New Orleans NFL	14	1	19	19.0	0
1989— New Orleans NFL	16	2	0	.0	0
1990— New Orleans NFL	16	0	0		0
Pro totals (4 years)	59	7	51	7.3	0

MAGGS, DON
OT/G, OILERS

PERSONAL: Born November 1, 1961, at Youngstown, O.... 6-5/290.... Full name: Donald James Maggs.
HIGH SCHOOL: Cardinal Mooney (Youngstown, O.).
COLLEGE: Tulane.

TRANSACTIONS/CAREER NOTES: Selected by Pittsburgh Maulers in second round (28th pick overall) of 1984 USFL draft.... Signed by Maulers (January 10, 1984).... On developmental squad for two games (March 3-March 18, 1984).... Selected by Houston Oilers in second round (29th pick overall) of 1984 NFL supplemental draft.... Pittsburgh Maulers franchise disbanded (October 25, 1984).... Selected by New Jersey Generals in USFL dispersal draft (December 6, 1984).... Granted free agency when USFL suspended operations (August 7, 1986).... Signed by Houston Oilers (August 13, 1986).... Granted roster exemption (August 13-August 25, 1986).... On injured reserve with knee injury (August 31-December 19, 1987).... Active for one game with Houston Oilers in 1987; did not play.

PLAYING EXPERIENCE: Pittsburgh USFL, 1984; New Jersey USFL, 1985; Houston NFL, 1986-1990.... Games: 1984 (16), 1985 (18), 1986 (14), 1988 (16), 1989 (16), 1990 (16). Total USFL: 34. Total NFL: 62. Total Pro: 96.

PRO STATISTICS: 1984—Recovered one fumble. 1989—Recovered three fumbles.

MAJKOWSKI, DON
QB, PACKERS

PERSONAL: Born February 25, 1964, at Buffalo, N.Y.... 6-2/206.... Full name: Donald Vincent Majkowski.... Name pronounced muh-KOW-skee.... Grandson of Edward Majkowski, minor league pitcher, 1931 and 1940.
HIGH SCHOOL: Depew (N.Y.) and Fork Union Military Academy (Fork Union, Va.).
COLLEGE: Virginia (degree in sports management, 1987).

TRANSACTIONS/CAREER NOTES: Selected by Green Bay Packers in 10th round (255th pick overall) of 1987 NFL draft.... Signed by Packers (July 25, 1987).... Granted free agency (February 1, 1990).... Re-signed by Packers (September 4, 1990).... Activated (September 8, 1990).... On inactive list (November 25; and December 2 and 9, 1990).... On injured reserve with shoulder injury (December 14, 1990-remainder of season).

RECORDS/HONORS: Named to play in Pro Bowl after 1989 season; replaced due to injury by Jim Everett.

PRO STATISTICS: Passer rating points: 1987 (70.2), 1988 (67.8), 1989 (82.3), 1990 (73.5). Career: 75.7.... 1988—Recovered three fumbles. 1989—Recovered six fumbles and fumbled 15 times for minus 13 yards. 1990—Recovered three fumbles and fumbled six times for minus 10 yards.

Year Team	G	Att.	Cmp.	Pct.	Yds.	TD	Int.	Avg.	Att.	Yds.	Avg.	TD	TD	Pts.	F.
				PASSING						**RUSHING**				**TOTAL**	
1987— Green Bay NFL	7	127	55	43.3	875	5	3	6.89	15	127	8.5	0	0	0	5
1988— Green Bay NFL	13	336	178	53.0	2119	9	11	6.31	47	225	4.8	1	1	6	8
1989— Green Bay NFL	16	*599	*353	58.9	*4318	27	20	7.21	75	358	4.8	5	5	30	15
1990— Green Bay NFL	9	264	150	56.8	1925	10	12	7.29	29	186	6.4	1	1	6	6
Pro totals (4 years)	45	1326	736	55.5	9237	51	46	6.97	166	896	5.4	7	7	42	34

MANDARICH, TONY
OT, PACKERS

PERSONAL: Born September 23, 1966, at Oakville, Ont. . . . 6-5/298. . . . Full name: Tony Joseph Mandarich. . . . Brother of John Mandarich, defensive tackle with Ottawa Rough Riders (CFL).
HIGH SCHOOL: White Oaks (Ont.) and Roosevelt (Kent, O.).
COLLEGE: Michigan State (degree in telecommunications, 1990).
TRANSACTIONS/CAREER NOTES: Selected by Green Bay Packers in first round (second pick overall) of 1989 NFL draft. . . . Signed by Packers (September 5, 1989). . . . Granted roster exemption (September 5-September 18, 1989).
PLAYING EXPERIENCE: Green Bay NFL, 1989 and 1990. . . . Games: 1989 (14), 1990 (16). Total: 30.
RECORDS/HONORS: Named as offensive tackle on THE SPORTING NEWS college All-America team, 1988.
PRO STATISTICS: 1989—Returned one kickoff for no yards. 1990—Recovered one fumble.

MANDLEY, PETE
WR, 49ERS

PERSONAL: Born July 29, 1961, at Mesa, Ariz. . . . 5-10/192. . . . Full name: William H. Mandley.
HIGH SCHOOL: Westwood (Mesa, Ariz.).
COLLEGE: Northern Arizona.
TRANSACTIONS/CAREER NOTES: Selected by Arizona Wranglers in 1984 USFL territorial draft. . . . Selected by Detroit Lions in second round (47th pick overall) of 1984 NFL draft. . . . Signed by Lions (July 10, 1984). . . . Released by Lions (September 5, 1989). . . . Signed as free agent by Kansas City Chiefs (September 13, 1989). . . . Granted free agency (February 1, 1990). . . . Re-signed by Chiefs (August 16, 1990). . . . Released by Chiefs (October 10, 1990). . . . Signed by San Francisco 49ers (May 3, 1991).
PRO STATISTICS: 1984—Recovered two fumbles. 1985—Recovered two fumbles. 1986—Recovered one fumble. 1987—Rushed once for three yards and recovered one fumble. 1988—Rushed six times for 44 yards and a touchdown and recovered one fumble for minus two yards. 1989—Rushed twice for one yard.

Year Team	G	No.	Yds.	Avg.	TD	No.	Yds.	Avg.	TD	No.	Yds.	Avg.	TD	TD	Pts.	F.
			RECEIVING				**PUNT RETURNS**				**KICKOFF RETURNS**				**TOTAL**	
1984— Detroit NFL	15	3	38	12.7	0	2	0	.0	0	22	390	17.7	0	0	0	2
1985— Detroit NFL	16	18	316	17.6	0	38	403	10.6	1	6	152	25.3	0	1	6	3
1986— Detroit NFL	16	7	106	15.1	0	43	420	9.8	1	2	37	18.5	0	1	6	3
1987— Detroit NFL	12	58	720	12.4	7	23	250	10.9	0	0	0		0	7	42	0
1988— Detroit NFL	15	44	617	14.0	4	37	287	7.8	0	0	0		0	5	30	3
1989— Kansas City NFL	13	35	476	13.6	1	19	151	8.0	0	1	0	.0	0	1	6	1
1990— Kansas City NFL	5	7	97	13.9	0	0	0		0	4	51	12.8	0	0	0	1
Pro totals (7 years)	92	172	2370	13.8	12	162	1511	9.3	2	35	630	18.0	0	15	90	13

MANGUM, JOHN
CB, BEARS

PERSONAL: Born March 16, 1967, at Magee, Miss. . . . 5-10/173. . . . Son of John Mangum, defensive tackle with Boston Patriots (AFL), 1966 and 1967.
HIGH SCHOOL: Magee (Miss.).
COLLEGE: Alabama (bachelor of arts degree in finance).
TRANSACTIONS/CAREER NOTES: Selected by Chicago Bears in sixth round (144th pick overall) of 1990 NFL draft. . . . Signed by Bears (July 24, 1990). . . . Released by Bears (September 3, 1990). . . . Signed by Tampa Bay Buccaneers to practice squad (October 1, 1990). . . . Signed by Chicago Bears off Buccaneers' practice squad (October 23, 1990).
PLAYING EXPERIENCE: Chicago NFL, 1990. . . . Games: 1990 (10).
PRO STATISTICS: 1990—Recovered one fumble.

MANLEY, DEXTER
DE, CARDINALS

PERSONAL: Born February 2, 1959, at Houston. . . . 6-4/270. . . . Cousin of Eric Dickerson, running back with Indianapolis Colts.
HIGH SCHOOL: Yates (Houston).
COLLEGE: Oklahoma State.
TRANSACTIONS/CAREER NOTES: Selected by Washington Redskins in fifth round (119th pick overall) of 1981 NFL draft. . . . Granted free agency (February 1, 1986). . . . Re-signed by Redskins (August 27, 1986). . . . Granted roster exemption (August 27-September 5, 1986). . . . On reserve/non-football injury list with drug problem (July 28-August 29, 1988). . . . Suspended for life due to substance abuse (November 18, 1989). . . . Reinstated (November 19, 1990). . . . Released by Redskins (November 19, 1990). . . . Awarded on waivers to Phoenix Cardinals (November 21, 1990). . . . Received roster exemption (November 21-December 3, 1990).
PLAYING EXPERIENCE: Washington NFL, 1981-1989; Phoenix NFL, 1990. . . . Games: 1981 (16), 1982 (9), 1983 (16), 1984 (15), 1985 (16), 1986 (16), 1987 (11), 1988 (16), 1989 (10), 1990 (4). Total: 129.
CHAMPIONSHIP GAME EXPERIENCE: Played in NFC championship game after 1982, 1983, 1986 and 1987 seasons. . . . Played in Super Bowl XVII after 1982 season, Super Bowl XVIII after 1983 season and Super Bowl XXII after 1987 season.
RECORDS/HONORS: Played in Pro Bowl after 1986 season. . . . Named to THE SPORTING NEWS NFL All-Pro team, 1986.
PRO STATISTICS: 1982—Intercepted one pass for minus two yards and recovered three fumbles for three yards. 1983—Intercepted one pass for one yard. 1984—Recovered one fumble. 1986—Recovered one fumble for 26 yards and a touchdown. 1989—Credited with a safety.

MANN, CHARLES
DE, REDSKINS

PERSONAL: Born April 12, 1961, at Sacramento, Calif. . . . 6-6/270.
HIGH SCHOOL: Valley (Sacramento, Calif.).
COLLEGE: Nevada-Reno.
TRANSACTIONS/CAREER NOTES: Selected by Oakland Invaders in 18th round (210th pick overall) of 1983 USFL draft. . . . Selected by Washington Redskins in third round (84th pick overall) of 1983 NFL draft. . . . Signed by Redskins (May 9, 1983).
PLAYING EXPERIENCE: Washington NFL, 1983-1990. . . . Games: 1983 (16), 1984 (16), 1985 (16), 1986 (15), 1987 (12), 1988 (14), 1989 (16), 1990 (15). Total: 120.
CHAMPIONSHIP GAME EXPERIENCE: Played in NFC championship game after 1983, 1986 and 1987 seasons. . . . Played in Super Bowl XVIII after 1983 season and Super Bowl XXII after 1987 season.
RECORDS/HONORS: Played in Pro Bowl after 1987-1989 seasons.
PRO STATISTICS: 1983—Credited with one safety. 1984—Recovered one fumble. 1985—Recovered one fumble. 1987—Recovered one fumble. 1989—Recovered two fumbles.

MANOA, TIM
FB, SAINTS

PERSONAL: Born September 9, 1964, at Tonga. . . . 6-1/245.
HIGH SCHOOL: Kahuka (Hawaii), then North Alleghany (Wexford, Pa.).
COLLEGE: Penn State.
TRANSACTIONS/CAREER NOTES: Selected by Cleveland Browns in third round (80th pick overall) of 1987 NFL draft. . . . Signed by Browns (July 26, 1987). . . . On injured reserve with elbow injury (August 28, 1990-entire season). . . . Granted unconditional free agency (February 1, 1991). . . . Signed by New Orleans Saints (April 1, 1991).
CHAMPIONSHIP GAME EXPERIENCE: Played in AFC championship game after 1987 and 1989 seasons.
PRO STATISTICS: 1987—Returned two kickoffs for 14 yards and recovered one fumble.

			RUSHING				RECEIVING				TOTAL	
Year Team	G	Att.	Yds.	Avg.	TD	No.	Yds.	Avg.	TD	TD	Pts.	F.
1987— Cleveland NFL	12	23	116	5.0	0	1	8	8.0	0	0	0	1
1988— Cleveland NFL	16	99	389	3.9	2	10	54	5.4	0	2	12	4
1989— Cleveland NFL	16	87	289	3.3	3	27	241	8.9	2	5	30	2
Pro totals (3 years)	44	209	794	3.8	5	38	303	8.0	2	7	42	7

MANUSKY, GREG
LB, VIKINGS

PERSONAL: Born August 12, 1966, at Wilkes-Barre, Pa. . . . 6-1/242. . . . Full name: Gregory Manusky.
HIGH SCHOOL: Dallas (Pa.).
COLLEGE: Colgate (bachelor of arts degree in education, 1988).
TRANSACTIONS/CAREER NOTES: Signed as free agent by Washington Redskins (May 3, 1988). . . . On injured reserve with thigh injury (August 29-November 2, 1988). . . . Activated after clearing procedural waivers (November 4, 1988). . . . Granted unconditional free agency (February 1, 1991). . . . Signed by Minnesota Vikings (March 27, 1991).
PLAYING EXPERIENCE: Washington NFL, 1988-1990. . . . Games: 1988 (7), 1989 (16), 1990 (16). Total: 39.
PRO STATISTICS: 1989—Recovered one fumble.

MARINO, DAN
QB, DOLPHINS

PERSONAL: Born September 15, 1961, at Pittsburgh. . . . 6-4/224. . . . Full name: Daniel Constantine Marino Jr. . . . Brother-in-law of Bill Maas, defensive end with Kansas City Chiefs.
HIGH SCHOOL: Central Catholic (Pittsburgh).
COLLEGE: Pittsburgh (bachelor of arts degree in communications).
TRANSACTIONS/CAREER NOTES: Selected by Los Angeles Express in first round (first pick overall) of 1983 USFL draft. . . . Selected by Miami Dolphins in first round (27th pick overall) of 1983 NFL draft. . . . Signed by Dolphins (July 9, 1983). . . . Left Dolphins camp voluntarily (July 25-August 31, 1985). . . . Reported and granted roster exemption (September 1-September 5, 1985).
CHAMPIONSHIP GAME EXPERIENCE: Played in AFC championship game after 1984 and 1985 seasons. . . . Played in Super Bowl XIX after 1984 season.
RECORDS/HONORS: Established NFL record for completion percentage, rookie, season (58.45), 1983; highest pass rating, rookie, season (96.0), 1983; lowest percentage, passes had intercepted, rookie, season (2.03), 1983; most touchdowns passing, season (48), 1984; most games, four or more touchdown passes, season (6), 1984; most consecutive games, four or more touchdown passes, season (4), 1984; most passing yards gained, season (5,084), 1984; most passes completed, season (378), 1984; most games, 400 or more yards passing, season (4), 1984; most passes attempted, season (623), 1986; most games, 400 or more yards passing, career (10); most 4,000-yard seasons (4); most consecutive seasons, 20 or more touchdown passes (8), 1983-1990; most consecutive seasons, 3,000 yards passing (7), 1984-1990. Tied NFL record for most consecutive games, 400 yards passing (2), 1984; most consecutive seasons leading league in completions (3), 1984-1986; most games, 300 yards passing, season (9), 1984; most seasons, 20 or more touchdown passes (8); most seasons, 3,000 or more yards passing (7). . . . Led NFL quarterbacks in passing with 108.9 points in 1984. . . . Named as quarterback on THE SPORTING NEWS college All-America team, 1981. . . . Named to play in Pro Bowl after 1983 season; replaced due to injury by Bill Kenney. . . . Played in Pro Bowl after 1984 season. . . . Named to play in Pro Bowl after 1985 season; replaced due to injury by Ken O'Brien. . . . Named to play in Pro Bowl after 1986 season; replaced due to injury by Boomer Esiason. . . . Named to play in Pro Bowl after 1987 season; replaced due to injury by Jim Kelly. . . . Named THE SPORTING NEWS NFL Rookie of the Year, 1983. . . . Named THE SPORTING NEWS NFL Player of the Year, 1984. . . . Named to THE SPORTING NEWS NFL All-Pro team, 1984-1986.
MISCELLANEOUS: Selected by Kansas City Royals' organization in fourth round of free-agent baseball draft (June 5, 1979).
PRO STATISTICS: Passer rating points: 1983 (96.0), 1984 (108.9), 1985 (84.1), 1986 (92.5), 1987 (89.2), 1988 (80.8), 1989 (76.9), 1990 (82.6). Career: 88.5. . . . 1983—Recovered two fumbles. 1984—Recovered two fumbles and fumbled six times for minus three yards. 1985—Recovered two fumbles and fumbled nine times for minus four yards. 1986—Recovered four fumbles and fumbled eight times for minus 12 yards. 1987—Recovered four fumbles and fumbled five times for minus 25 yards. 1988—Recovered eight fumbles and fumbled 10 times for minus 31 yards. 1989—Fumbled seven times for minus four yards. 1990—Recovered two fumbles.

Year	Team	G	Att.	Cmp.	Pct.	Yds.	TD	Int.	Avg.	Att.	Yds.	Avg.	TD	TD	Pts.	F.
					PASSING						**RUSHING**				**TOTAL**	
1983—	Miami NFL	11	296	173	58.5	2210	20	6	7.47	28	45	1.6	2	2	12	5
1984—	Miami NFL	16	*564	*362	64.2	*5084	*48	17	*9.01	28	-7	-.2	0	0	0	6
1985—	Miami NFL	16	567	*336	59.3	*4137	*30	21	7.30	26	-24	-.9	0	0	0	9
1986—	Miami NFL	16	*623	*378	60.7	*4746	*44	23	7.62	12	-3	-.2	0	0	0	8
1987—	Miami NFL	12	444	263	59.2	3245	26	13	7.31	12	-5	-.4	1	1	6	5
1988—	Miami NFL	16	*606	*354	58.4	*4434	28	23	7.32	20	-17	-.8	0	0	0	10
1989—	Miami NFL	16	550	308	56.0	3997	24	22	7.27	14	-7	-.5	2	2	12	7
1990—	Miami NFL	16	531	306	57.6	3563	21	11	6.71	16	29	1.8	0	0	0	3
Pro totals (8 years)		119	4181	2480	59.3	31416	241	136	7.51	156	11	.1	5	5	30	53

MARION, FRED
S, PATRIOTS

PERSONAL: Born January 2, 1959, at Gainesville, Fla. . . . 6-2/191. . . . Full name: Fred D. Marion. . . . Brother of Frank Marion, linebacker with Memphis Southmen (WFL) and New York Giants, 1975 and 1977-1983.
HIGH SCHOOL: Buchholz (Gainesville, Fla.).
COLLEGE: Miami (Fla.).
TRANSACTIONS/CAREER NOTES: Selected by New England Patriots in fifth round (112th pick overall) of 1982 NFL draft.
CHAMPIONSHIP GAME EXPERIENCE: Played in AFC championship game after 1985 season. . . . Played in Super Bowl XX after 1985 season.
RECORDS/HONORS: Played in Pro Bowl after 1985 season.
PRO STATISTICS: 1982—Recovered one fumble. 1984—Recovered one fumble. 1985—Recovered three fumbles for nine yards. 1986—Returned one punt for 12 yards. 1987—Returned one punt for no yards and recovered one fumble. 1988—Recovered two fumbles for 16 yards. 1989—Recovered one fumble. 1990—Recovered four fumbles.

				INTERCEPTIONS		
Year	Team	G	No.	Yds.	Avg.	TD
1982—	New England NFL	9	0	0		0
1983—	New England NFL	16	2	4	2.0	0
1984—	New England NFL	16	2	39	19.5	0
1985—	New England NFL	16	7	*189	27.0	0
1986—	New England NFL	16	2	56	28.0	1
1987—	New England NFL	12	4	53	13.3	0
1988—	New England NFL	16	4	47	11.8	0
1989—	New England NFL	16	2	19	9.5	0
1990—	New England NFL	16	4	17	4.3	0
Pro totals (9 years)		133	27	424	15.7	1

MARK, GREG
DE, BROWNS

PERSONAL: Born July 7, 1967, at Pennsauken, N.J. . . . 6-3/260.
HIGH SCHOOL: Pennsauken (N.J.).
COLLEGE: Miami (Fla.).
TRANSACTIONS/CAREER NOTES: Selected by New York Giants in third round (79th pick overall) of 1990 NFL draft. . . . Signed by New York Giants (July 23, 1990). . . . Released by Giants (September 3, 1990). . . . Signed by Miami Dolphins (September 5, 1990). . . . Released by Dolphins (October 6, 1990). . . . Awarded on waivers to Philadelphia Eagles (October 8, 1990). . . . On inactive list (October 15, 1990). . . . On injured reserve with shoulder injury (October 31-December 18, 1990). . . . Released by Eagles (December 18, 1990). . . . Signed by Los Angeles Raiders (April 24, 1991). . . . Released by Raiders (July 24, 1991). . . . Signed by Cleveland Browns (July 25, 1991).
PLAYING EXPERIENCE: Miami (4)-Philadelphia (2) NFL, 1990. . . . Games: 1990 (6).
RECORDS/HONORS: Named as defensive end to THE SPORTING NEWS college All-America team, 1989.

MARRONE, DOUG
C, STEELERS

PERSONAL: Born July 25, 1964, at Bronx, N.Y. . . . 6-4/302. . . . Full name: Douglas Charles Marrone.
HIGH SCHOOL: Herbert H. Lehman (Bronx, N.Y.).
COLLEGE: Syracuse.
TRANSACTIONS/CAREER NOTES: Selected by New Jersey Generals in 1986 USFL territorial draft. . . . Selected by Los Angeles Raiders in sixth round (164th pick overall) of 1986 NFL draft. . . . Signed by Raiders (July 14, 1986). . . . Released by Raiders (August 19, 1986). . . . Signed as free agent by Miami Dolphins for 1987 (October 16, 1986). . . . Released by Dolphins (September 7, 1987). . . . Re-signed by Dolphins (September 8, 1987). . . . On injured reserve with thigh injury (September 19-December 12, 1987). . . . Left Dolphins camp voluntarily (August 16, 1988). . . . Released by Dolphins (August 24, 1988). . . . Signed as free agent by Dallas Cowboys (February 3, 1989). . . . Released by Cowboys (July 25, 1989). . . . Signed as free agent by New Orleans Saints (July 26, 1989). . . . Released by Saints (September 5, 1989). . . . Re-signed by Saints (December 7, 1989). . . . Granted unconditional free agency (February 1, 1990). . . . Signed by Minnesota Vikings (March 6, 1990). . . . Released by Vikings (August 23, 1990). . . . Selected by London Monarchs in third round (30th offensive lineman) of 1991 WLAF positional draft. . . . Signed by Pittsburgh Steelers (June 24, 1991).
PLAYING EXPERIENCE: Miami NFL, 1987; New Orleans NFL, 1989; London WLAF, 1991. . . . Games: 1987 (4), 1989 (1), 1991 (10). Total NFL: 5. Total Pro: 15.

MARSHALL, LEONARD
DE, GIANTS

PERSONAL: Born October 22, 1961, at Franklin, La. . . . 6-3/285. . . . Full name: Leonard Allen Marshall. . . . Related to Eddie Robinson, head coach at Grambling State; Ernie Ladd, defensive lineman with San Diego Chargers, Houston Oilers and Kansas City Chiefs, 1961-1968; and Warren Wells, wide receiver

with Detroit Lions and Oakland Raiders, 1964 and 1967-1970.
HIGH SCHOOL: Franklin (La.).
COLLEGE: Louisiana State.
TRANSACTIONS/CAREER NOTES: Selected by Tampa Bay Bandits in 10th round (109th pick overall) of 1983 USFL draft.... Selected by New York Giants in second round (37th pick overall) of 1983 NFL draft.... Signed by Giants (June 13, 1983).... On injured reserve with dislocated wrist (December 15, 1987-remainder of season).
PLAYING EXPERIENCE: New York Giants NFL, 1983-1990.... Games: 1983 (14), 1984 (16), 1985 (16), 1986 (16), 1987 (10), 1988 (15), 1989 (16), 1990 (16). Total: 119.
CHAMPIONSHIP GAME EXPERIENCE: Played in NFC championship game after 1986 and 1990 seasons.... Played in Super Bowl XXI after 1986 season and Super Bowl XXV after 1990 season.
RECORDS/HONORS: Played in Pro Bowl after 1985 and 1986 seasons.
PRO STATISTICS: 1983—Credited with one safety. 1985—Intercepted one pass for three yards. 1986—Intercepted one pass for no yards and recovered three fumbles. 1989—Credited with one safety.

MARSHALL, WILBER
LB, REDSKINS

PERSONAL: Born April 18, 1962, at Titusville, Fla.... 6-1/230.... Full name: Wilber Buddyhia Marshall.
HIGH SCHOOL: Astronaut (Titusville, Fla.).
COLLEGE: Florida.
TRANSACTIONS/CAREER NOTES: Selected by Tampa Bay Bandits in 1984 USFL territorial draft.... Selected by Chicago Bears in first round (11th pick overall) of 1984 NFL draft.... Signed by Bears (June 19, 1984).... Granted free agency (February 1, 1988).... Signed by Washington Redskins (March 15, 1988) after Bears elected not to match offer; Bears received first-round picks in 1988 and 1989 NFL drafts in compensation.
CHAMPIONSHIP GAME EXPERIENCE: Played in NFC championship game after 1984 and 1985 seasons.... Played in Super Bowl XX after 1985 season.
RECORDS/HONORS: Played in Pro Bowl after 1986 and 1987 seasons.... Named to THE SPORTING NEWS NFL All-Pro team, 1986.
PRO STATISTICS: 1985—Ran two yards with lateral on kickoff return and recovered one fumble for eight yards. 1986—Recovered three fumbles for 12 yards and a touchdown. 1987—Ran once for one yard and recovered one fumble. 1989—Recovered two fumbles for six yards. 1990—Recovered one fumble for four yards.

		— INTERCEPTIONS—			
Year Team	G	No.	Yds.	Avg.	TD
1984— Chicago NFL	15	0	0		0
1985— Chicago NFL	16	4	23	5.8	0
1986— Chicago NFL	16	5	68	13.6	1
1987— Chicago NFL	12	0	0		0
1988— Washington NFL	16	3	61	20.3	0
1989— Washington NFL	16	1	18	18.0	0
1990— Washington NFL	16	1	6	6.0	0
Pro totals (7 years)	107	14	176	12.6	1

MARTIN, CHRIS
LB, CHIEFS

PERSONAL: Born December 19, 1960, at Huntsville, Ala.... 6-2/241.... Full name: Christopher Martin.
HIGH SCHOOL: J.O. Johnson (Huntsville, Ala.).
COLLEGE: Auburn (degree in human resource management, 1983).
TRANSACTIONS/CAREER NOTES: Selected by Birmingham Stallions in 1983 USFL territorial draft.... Signed as free agent by New Orleans Saints (May 5, 1983).... On injured reserve with ankle injury (December 17, 1983-remainder of season).... Released by Saints (August 27, 1984).... Awarded on waivers to Minnesota Vikings (August 28, 1984).... Released by Vikings (November 2, 1988).... Signed as free agent by Kansas City Chiefs (November 9, 1988).
PLAYING EXPERIENCE: New Orleans NFL, 1983; Minnesota NFL, 1984-1987; Minnesota (9)-Kansas City (6) NFL, 1988; Kansas City NFL, 1989 and 1990.... Games: 1983 (15), 1984 (16), 1985 (12), 1986 (16), 1987 (12), 1988 (15), 1989 (16), 1990 (16). Total: 118.
CHAMPIONSHIP GAME EXPERIENCE: Played in NFC championship game after 1987 season.
PRO STATISTICS: 1984—Recovered one fumble for eight yards and a touchdown. 1986—Recovered one fumble. 1987—Recovered one fumble. 1988—Recovered one fumble in end zone for a touchdown. 1989—Recovered three fumbles. 1990—Returned blocked punt 31 yards for touchdown and recovered four fumbles for three yards.

MARTIN, ERIC
WR, SAINTS

PERSONAL: Born November 8, 1961, at Van Vleck, Tex.... 6-1/207.
HIGH SCHOOL: Van Vleck (Tex.).
COLLEGE: Louisiana State.
TRANSACTIONS/CAREER NOTES: Selected by Portland Breakers in 1985 USFL territorial draft.... Selected by New Orleans Saints in seventh round (179th pick overall) of 1985 NFL draft.... Signed by Saints (June 21, 1985).... Crossed picket line during players' strike (September 30, 1987).
RECORDS/HONORS: Named as wide receiver on THE SPORTING NEWS college All-America team, 1983.... Played in Pro Bowl after 1988 season.
PRO STATISTICS: 1985—Rushed twice for minus one yard. 1987—Recovered one fumble. 1988—Rushed twice for 12 yards. 1989—Recovered one fumble. 1990—Recovered two fumbles.

		— RECEIVING—				— PUNT RETURNS —				— KICKOFF RETURNS—				— TOTAL—		
Year Team	G	No.	Yds.	Avg.	TD	No.	Yds.	Avg.	TD	No.	Yds.	Avg.	TD	TD	Pts.	F.
1985— New Orleans NFL	16	35	522	14.9	4	8	53	6.6	0	15	384	25.6	0	4	24	1
1986— New Orleans NFL	16	37	675	18.2	5	24	227	9.5	0	3	64	21.3	0	5	30	5
1987— New Orleans NFL	15	44	778	17.7	7	14	88	6.3	0	1	15	15.0	0	7	42	3

Year	Team	G	No.	RECEIVING Yds.	Avg.	TD	No.	PUNT RETURNS Yds.	Avg.	TD	No.	KICKOFF RETURNS Yds.	Avg.	TD	TD	TOTAL Pts.	F.
1988— New Orleans NFL		16	85	1083	12.7	7	0	0		0	3	32	10.7	0	7	42	2
1989— New Orleans NFL		16	68	1090	16.0	8	0	0		0	0	0		0	8	48	1
1990— New Orleans NFL		16	63	912	14.5	5	0	0		0	0	0		0	5	30	3
Pro totals (6 years)		95	332	5060	15.2	36	46	368	8.0	0	22	495	22.5	0	36	216	15

MARTIN, KELVIN
WR, COWBOYS

PERSONAL: Born May 14, 1965, at San Diego. . . . 5-9/170. . . . Full name: Kelvin Brian Martin.
HIGH SCHOOL: Ribault (Jacksonville, Fla.).
COLLEGE: Boston College (bachelor of arts degree in speech communication, 1987).
TRANSACTIONS/CAREER NOTES: Selected by Dallas Cowboys in fourth round (95th pick overall) of 1987 NFL draft. . . . Signed by Cowboys (July 13, 1987). . . . On injured reserve with leg injury (September 15-November 14, 1987). . . . Crossed picket line during players' strike (October 14, 1987). . . . On injured reserve with knee injury (November 21, 1989-remainder of season).
RECORDS/HONORS: Named as wide receiver on THE SPORTING NEWS college All-America team, 1985.
PRO STATISTICS: 1990—Recovered one fumble.

Year	Team	G	Att.	RUSHING Yds.	Avg.	TD	No.	RECEIVING Yds.	Avg.	TD	No.	PUNT RETURNS Yds.	Avg.	TD	No.	KICKOFF RETURNS Yds.	Avg.	TD	TD	TOTALS Pts.	F.
1987— Dallas NFL		7	0	0		0	5	103	20.6	0	22	216	9.8	0	12	237	19.8	0	0	0	1
1988— Dallas NFL		16	4	-4	-1.0	0	49	622	12.7	3	44	360	8.2	0	12	210	17.5	0	3	18	2
1989— Dallas NFL		11	0	0		0	46	644	14.0	2	4	32	8.0	0	0	0		0	2	12	0
1990— Dallas NFL		16	4	-2	-.5	0	64	732	11.4	0	5	46	9.2		0	0		0	0	0	2
Pro totals (4 years)		50	8	-6	-.7	0	164	2101	12.8	5	75	654	8.7	0	24	447	18.6	0	5	30	5

MARTIN, SAMMY
WR, PATRIOTS

PERSONAL: Born August 21, 1965, at Gretna, La. . . . 5-11/175.
HIGH SCHOOL: De La Salle (New Orleans).
COLLEGE: Louisiana State.
TRANSACTIONS/CAREER NOTES: Selected by New England Patriots in fourth round (97th pick overall) of 1988 NFL draft. . . . Signed by Patriots (July 17, 1988). . . . On non-football injury/active with hamstring injury (July 18-July 31, 1988). . . . Passed physical (August 1, 1988). . . . On injured reserve with foot injury (November 15, 1989-remainder of season). . . . On inactive list (November 25, 1990). . . . On injured reserve with knee injury (December 1, 1990-remainder of season).
PRO STATISTICS: 1989—Rushed twice for 20 yards.

Year	Team	G	No.	RECEIVING Yds.	Avg.	TD	No.	PUNT RETURNS Yds.	Avg.	TD	No.	KICKOFF RETURNS Yds.	Avg.	TD	TD	TOTAL Pts.	F.
1988— New Eng. NFL		16	4	51	12.8	0	0	0		0	31	735	23.7	*1	1	6	0
1989— New Eng. NFL		10	13	229	17.6	0	19	164	8.6	0	24	584	24.3	0	0	0	1
1990— New Eng. NFL		10	4	65	16.3	1	1	1	1.0	0	25	515	20.6	0	1	6	0
Pro totals (3 years)		36	21	345	16.4	1	20	165	8.3	0	80	1834	22.9	1	2	12	1

MARTIN, TONY
WR, DOLPHINS

PERSONAL: Born September 5, 1965, at Miami. . . . 6-0/180. . . . Full name: Tony Derrick Martin.
HIGH SCHOOL: Miami Northwestern (Miami).
COLLEGE: Bishop (Tex.), then Mesa State (Colo.).
TRANSACTIONS/CAREER NOTES: Selected by New York Jets in fifth round (126th pick overall) of 1989 NFL draft. . . . Released by Jets (September 4, 1989). . . . Signed by Miami Dolphins to developmental squad (September 5, 1989). . . . Activated (December 23, 1989). . . . Inactive for one game in 1989.
PRO STATISTICS: 1990—Recovered two fumbles.

Year	Team	G	Att.	RUSHING Yds.	Avg.	TD	No.	RECEIVING Yds.	Avg.	TD	No.	PUNT RETURNS Yds.	Avg.	TD	TD	TOTAL Pts.	F.
1990— Miami NFL..............		16	1	8	8.0	0	29	388	13.4	2	26	140	5.4	0	2	12	4
Pro totals (1 year)		16	1	8	8.0	0	29	388	13.4	2	26	140	5.4	0	2	12	4

MARTIN, TRACY
WR, PACKERS

PERSONAL: Born December 4, 1964, at Minneapolis. . . . 6-3/208. . . . Son of Bill Lordan, former drummer for Sly and the Family Stone, Jimi Hendrix and James Brown.
HIGH SCHOOL: Brooklyn Center (Minn.).
COLLEGE: North Dakota.
TRANSACTIONS/CAREER NOTES: Selected by New York Jets in sixth round (161st pick overall) of 1987 NFL draft. . . . Signed by Jets (July 24, 1987). . . . On injured reserve with quadricep injury (August 22, 1988-entire season). . . . Granted unconditional free agency (February 1, 1989). . . . Signed by Pittsburgh Steelers (March 31, 1989). . . . Released by Steelers (August 30, 1989). . . . Signed as free agent by Green Bay Packers (April 9, 1990). . . . Released by Packers (August 27, 1990). . . . Re-signed by Packers (May 2, 1991).

Year	Team	G	No.	KICKOFF RETURNS Yds.	Avg.	TD
1987— N.Y. Jets NFL.............		12	8	180	22.5	0
Pro totals (1 year)		12	8	180	22.5	0

MARTIN, WAYNE
DE, SAINTS

PERSONAL: Born October 26, 1965, at Forrest City, Ark. . . . 6-5/275. . . . Full name: Jerald Wayne Martin.
HIGH SCHOOL: Cross Country (Cherry Valley, Ark.).
COLLEGE: Arkansas (degree in criminal justice, 1990).
TRANSACTIONS/CAREER NOTES: Selected by New Orleans Saints in first round (19th pick overall) of 1989 NFL draft. . . . Signed by Saints (August 10, 1989). . . . On inactive list (November 4, 11 and 18, 1990). . . . On injured reserve with knee injury (December 19, 1990-remainder of 1990 season playoffs).
PLAYING EXPERIENCE: New Orleans NFL, 1989 and 1990. . . . Games: 1989 (16), 1990 (11). Total: 27.
RECORDS/HONORS: Named as defensive lineman on THE SPORTING NEWS college All-America team, 1988.
PRO STATISTICS: 1989—Recovered two fumbles.

MARVE, EUGENE
LB, BUCCANEERS

PERSONAL: Born August 14, 1960, at Flint, Mich. . . . 6-2/240. . . . Full name: Eugene Raymond Marve.
HIGH SCHOOL: Northern (Flint, Mich.).
COLLEGE: Saginaw Valley State (Mich.).
TRANSACTIONS/CAREER NOTES: Selected by Buffalo Bills in third round (59th pick overall) of 1982 NFL draft. . . . On injured reserve with dislocated elbow (November 14, 1987-remainder of season). . . . Traded by Bills to Tampa Bay Buccaneers for seventh-round pick in 1989 draft (June 13, 1988). . . . Granted free agency (February 1, 1990). . . . Re-signed by Buccaneers (July 19, 1990).
PLAYING EXPERIENCE: Buffalo NFL, 1982-1987; Tampa Bay NFL, 1988-1990. . . . Games: 1982 (9), 1983 (16), 1984 (16), 1985 (14), 1986 (16), 1987 (5), 1988 (16), 1989 (16), 1990 (16). Total: 124.
PRO STATISTICS: 1982—Intercepted one pass for no yards and recovered one fumble. 1984—Recovered three fumbles. 1985—Recovered one fumble. 1988—Intercepted one pass for 29 yards. 1989—Recovered one fumble.

MASSEY, ROBERT
CB, SAINTS

PERSONAL: Born February 17, 1967, at Rock Hill, S.C. . . . 5-10/182. . . . Full name: Robert Lee Massey.
HIGH SCHOOL: Garinger (Charlotte, N.C.).
COLLEGE: North Carolina Central (degree in history, 1990).
TRANSACTIONS/CAREER NOTES: Selected by New Orleans Saints in second round (46th pick overall) of 1989 NFL draft. . . . Signed by Saints (July 30, 1989).
PRO STATISTICS: 1989—Ran 54 yards with a lateral on punt return. 1990—Recovered two fumbles.

			— INTERCEPTIONS —		
Year	Team	G	No.	Yds.	Avg.	TD
1989— New Orleans NFL	16	5	26	5.2	0
1990— New Orleans NFL	16	0	0		0
Pro totals (2 years)	32	5	26	5.2	0

MATHIS, TERANCE
WR/KR, JETS

PERSONAL: Born June 7, 1967, at Detroit. . . . 5-10/170.
HIGH SCHOOL: Redan (Stone Mountain, Ga.).
COLLEGE: New Mexico.
TRANSACTIONS/CAREER NOTES: Selected by New York Jets in sixth round (140th pick overall) of 1990 NFL draft. . . . Signed by Jets (July 12, 1990).
RECORDS/HONORS: Tied NFL record for longest punt return (98 yards), against Dallas Cowboys (November 4, 1990). . . . Named as wide receiver on THE SPORTING NEWS college All-America team, 1989.

		— RUSHING—				—RECEIVING—				—PUNT RETURNS—				KICKOFF RETURNS				– TOTALS –		
Year	Team	G	Att.	Yds.	Avg.	TD	No.	Yds.	Avg.	TD	No.	Yds.	Avg.	TD	No.	Yds.	Avg.	TD	TD	Pts.	F.
1990— N.Y. Jets NFL	16	2	9	4.5	0	19	245	12.9	0	11	165	15.0	*1	43	787	18.3	0	1	6	1
Pro totals (1 year)	16	2	9	4.5	0	19	245	12.9	0	11	165	15.0	1	43	787	18.3	0	1	6	1

MATICH, TREVOR
OL, JETS

PERSONAL: Born October 9, 1961, at Sacramento, Calif. . . . 6-4/297. . . . Full name: Trevor Anthony Matich.
HIGH SCHOOL: Rio Americano (Sacramento, Calif.).
COLLEGE: Brigham Young.
TRANSACTIONS/CAREER NOTES: Selected by Houston Gamblers in 10th round (139th pick overall) of 1985 USFL draft. . . . Selected by New England Patriots in first round (28th pick overall) of 1985 NFL draft. . . . Signed by Patriots (July 30, 1985). . . . On injured reserve with ankle injury (October 12, 1985-remainder of season). . . . On injured reserve with broken foot (September 7-November 7, 1987). . . . Released by Patriots (September 7, 1989). . . . Signed as free agent by Detroit Lions (September 14, 1989). . . . Granted unconditional free agency (February 1, 1990). . . . Signed by New York Jets (March 19, 1990).
PLAYING EXPERIENCE: New England NFL, 1985-1988; Detroit NFL, 1989; New York Jets NFL, 1990. . . . Games: 1985 (1), 1986 (11), 1987 (6), 1988 (8), 1989 (11), 1990 (16). Total: 53.
PRO STATISTICS: 1990—Recovered one fumble.

MATTES, RON
OT, JETS

PERSONAL: Born August 8, 1963, at Shenandoah, Pa. . . . 6-6/302. . . . Full name: Ronald Anthony Mattes.
HIGH SCHOOL: North Schuylkill (Ashland, Pa.).
COLLEGE: Virginia.
TRANSACTIONS/CAREER NOTES: Selected by Orlando Renegades in 1985 USFL territorial draft. . . . Selected by Seattle Seahawks

in seventh round (193rd pick overall) of 1985 NFL draft. . . . Signed by Seahawks (July 19, 1985). . . . On injured reserve with back injury (August 27, 1985-entire season). . . . On inactive list (October 1, 1990). . . . Traded by Seahawks to New York Jets for undisclosed draft pick (January 31, 1991).
PLAYING EXPERIENCE: Seattle NFL, 1986-1990. . . . Games: 1986 (16), 1987 (12), 1988 (16), 1989 (16), 1990 (15). Total: 75.

MATTHEWS, AUBREY
WR, LIONS

PERSONAL: Born September 15, 1962, at Pasaquola, Miss. . . . 5-7/165. . . . Full name: Aubrey Derron Matthews.
HIGH SCHOOL: Moss Point (Miss.).
COLLEGE: Gulf Coast Junior College (Fla.), then Delta State (Miss.).
TRANSACTIONS/CAREER NOTES: Signed by Jacksonville Bulls of USFL (January 10, 1984). . . . On developmental squad for two games (April 10-April 25, 1984). . . . On developmental squad for one game (June 10-June 15, 1985). . . . Granted free agency when USFL suspended operations (August 7, 1986). . . . Signed as free agent by Atlanta Falcons (August 18, 1986). . . . Granted roster exemption (August 18-August 22, 1986). . . . On injured reserve with hamstring injury (August 26-November 26, 1986). . . . Activated after clearing procedural waivers (November 28, 1986). . . . Released by Falcons (September 29, 1988). . . . Signed as free agent by Green Bay Packers (November 2, 1988). . . . Granted unconditional free agency (February 1, 1990). . . . Signed by Detroit Lions (March 2, 1990).
PRO STATISTICS: USFL: 1984—Rushed three times for five yards and recovered four fumbles. 1985—Recovered two fumbles. . . . NFL: 1986—Rushed once for 12 yards. 1987—Rushed once for minus four yards and recovered one fumble. 1988—Returned six punts for 26 yards and rushed three times for three yards.

		RECEIVING				KICKOFF RETURNS				TOTAL	
Year Team	G	No.	Yds.	Avg.	TD	No.	Yds.	Avg.	TD	TD	Pts.	F.
1984— Jacksonville USFL	16	27	406	15.0	1	29	623	21.5	0	1	6	5
1985— Jacksonville USFL	16	25	271	10.8	5	19	366	19.3	0	5	30	2
1986— Atlanta NFL	4	1	25	25.0	0	3	42	14.0	0	0	0	0
1987— Atlanta NFL	12	32	537	16.8	3	0	0		0	3	18	2
1988— Atl. (4)-G.B. (7) NFL	11	20	231	11.6	2	0	0		0	2	12	2
1989— Green Bay NFL	13	18	200	11.1	0	0	0		0	0	0	0
1990— Detroit NFL	13	30	349	11.6	1	0	0		0	1	6	2
USFL totals (2 years)	32	52	677	13.0	6	48	989	20.6	0	6	36	7
NFL totals (5 years)	53	101	1342	13.3	6	3	42	14.0	0	6	36	6
Pro totals (7 years)	85	153	2019	13.2	12	51	1031	20.2	0	12	72	13

MATTHEWS, BRUCE
G/C, OILERS

PERSONAL: Born August 8, 1961, at Arcadia, Calif. . . . 6-5/291. . . . Son of Clay Matthews Sr., end with San Francisco 49ers, 1950 and 1953-1955; and brother of Clay Matthews Jr., linebacker with Cleveland Browns.
HIGH SCHOOL: Arcadia (Calif.).
COLLEGE: Southern California (degree in industrial engineering, 1983).
TRANSACTIONS/CAREER NOTES: Selected by Los Angeles Express in 1983 USFL territorial draft. . . . Selected by Houston Oilers in first round (ninth pick overall) of 1983 NFL draft. . . . Signed by Oilers (July 24, 1983). . . . Granted free agency (February 1, 1987). . . . Placed on reserve/unsigned list (August 31-November 3, 1987). . . . Re-signed by Oilers (November 4, 1987). . . . Granted roster exemption (November 4-November 7, 1987).
PLAYING EXPERIENCE: Houston NFL, 1983-1990. . . . Games: 1983 (16); 1984 (16), 1985 (16), 1986 (16), 1987 (8), 1988 (16), 1989 (16), 1990 (16). Total: 120.
RECORDS/HONORS: Named as guard on THE SPORTING NEWS college All-America team, 1982. . . . Played in Pro Bowl after 1988-1990 seasons. . . . Named to THE SPORTING NEWS NFL All-Pro team, 1988-1990.
PRO STATISTICS: 1985—Recovered three fumbles. 1986—Recovered one fumble for seven yards. 1989—Recovered one fumble and fumbled twice for minus 29 yards. 1990—Recovered one fumble.

MATTHEWS, CLAY
LB, BROWNS

PERSONAL: Born March 15, 1956, at Palo Alto, Calif. . . . 6-2/245. . . . Full name: William Clay Matthews Jr. . . . Son of Clay Matthews Sr., end with San Francisco 49ers, 1950 and 1953-1955; brother of Bruce Matthews, guard/center with Houston Oilers.
HIGH SCHOOL: Arcadia (Calif.) and New Trier East (Winnetka, Ill.).
COLLEGE: Southern California (bachelor of science degree in business administration, 1978).
TRANSACTIONS/CAREER NOTES: Selected by Cleveland Browns in first round (12th pick overall) of 1978 NFL draft. . . . On injured reserve with broken ankle (September 16-December 31, 1982). . . . Granted free agency (February 1, 1990). . . . Re-signed by Browns (August 30, 1990). . . . Granted roster exemption (September 3-September 8, 1990).
CHAMPIONSHIP GAME EXPERIENCE: Played in AFC championship game after 1986, 1987 and 1989 seasons.
RECORDS/HONORS: Named as linebacker to THE SPORTING NEWS college All-America team, 1977. . . . Named to THE SPORTING NEWS NFL All-Pro team, 1984. . . . Played in Pro Bowl after 1985 and 1987-1989 seasons.
PRO STATISTICS: 1979—Recovered two fumbles. 1980—Recovered one fumble. 1981—Recovered two fumbles for 16 yards. 1984—Recovered one fumble. 1985—Recovered one fumble for 15 yards. 1987—Recovered two fumbles. 1988—Recovered two fumbles. 1989—Recovered two fumbles for minus two yards and a touchdown and fumbled once.

		INTERCEPTIONS			
Year Team	G	No.	Yds.	Avg.	TD
1978— Cleveland NFL	15	1	5	5.0	0
1979— Cleveland NFL	16	1	30	30.0	0
1980— Cleveland NFL	14	1	6	6.0	0
1981— Cleveland NFL	16	2	14	7.0	0
1982— Cleveland NFL	2	0	0		0
1983— Cleveland NFL	16	0	0		0

Year	Team	G	No.	Yds.	Avg.	TD
			|—— INTERCEPTIONS ——|			
1984— Cleveland NFL		16	0	0		0
1985— Cleveland NFL		14	0	0		0
1986— Cleveland NFL		16	2	12	6.0	0
1987— Cleveland NFL		12	3	62	20.7	1
1988— Cleveland NFL		16	0	0		0
1989— Cleveland NFL		16	1	25	25.0	0
1990— Cleveland NFL		16	0	0		0
Pro totals (13 years)		185	11	154	14.0	1

MAXIE, BRETT
S, SAINTS

PERSONAL: Born January 13, 1962, at Dallas.... 6-2/194.... Full name: Brett Derrell Maxie.
HIGH SCHOOL: James Madison (Dallas).
COLLEGE: Texas Southern.
TRANSACTIONS/CAREER NOTES: Signed as free agent by New Orleans Saints (June 21, 1985)....
Released by Saints (September 2, 1985).... Re-signed by Saints (September 3, 1985).... Granted free agency (February 1, 1990).... Re-signed by Saints (August 13, 1990).
PRO STATISTICS: 1985—Recovered one fumble. 1986—Recovered one fumble. 1987—Returned one punt for 12 yards and credited with a safety. 1989—Recovered one fumble.

Year	Team	G	No.	Yds.	Avg.	TD
			|—— INTERCEPTIONS ——|			
1985— New Orleans NFL		16	0	0		0
1986— New Orleans NFL		15	2	15	7.5	0
1987— New Orleans NFL		12	3	17	5.7	0
1988— New Orleans NFL		16	0	0		0
1989— New Orleans NFL		16	3	41	13.7	1
1990— New Orleans NFL		16	2	88	44.0	1
Pro totals (6 years)		91	10	161	16.1	2

MAXWELL, VERNON
LB, RAMS

PERSONAL: Born October 25, 1961, at Birmingham, Ala.... 6-2/230.... Full name: Vernon Leroy Maxwell.
HIGH SCHOOL: Verbum Dei (Los Angeles).
COLLEGE: Arizona State.
TRANSACTIONS/CAREER NOTES: Selected by Arizona Wranglers in 1983 USFL territorial draft.... Selected by Baltimore Colts in second round (29th pick overall) of 1983 NFL draft.... Signed by Colts (July 21, 1983).... Franchise transferred to Indianapolis (March 31, 1984).... Traded by Indianapolis Colts to San Diego Chargers for fifth-round pick in 1986 NFL draft (August 1, 1985).... Released by Chargers (August 27, 1985).... Signed as free agent by Detroit Lions (October 25, 1985).... Released by Lions (August 29, 1988).... Signed as free agent by Seattle Seahawks (June 26, 1989).... Released by Seahawks (November 13, 1989).... Signed as free agent by Phoenix Cardinals (May 1, 1990).... Released by Cardinals (September 3, 1990).... Signed by Los Angeles Rams (June 11, 1991).
PLAYING EXPERIENCE: Baltimore NFL, 1983; Indianapolis NFL, 1984; Detroit NFL, 1985-1987; Seattle NFL, 1989.... Games: 1983 (16), 1984 (16), 1985 (9), 1986 (15), 1987 (12), 1989 (9). Total: 77.
RECORDS/HONORS: Named as linebacker on THE SPORTING NEWS college All-America team, 1982.
PRO STATISTICS: 1983—Intercepted one pass for 31 yards and recovered two fumbles. 1984—Recovered two fumbles. 1986—Recovered four fumbles.

MAY, MARK
G/OT, CHARGERS

PERSONAL: Born November 2, 1959, at Oneonta, N.Y.... 6-6/290.
HIGH SCHOOL: Oneonta (N.Y.).
COLLEGE: Pittsburgh.
TRANSACTIONS/CAREER NOTES: Selected by Washington Redskins in first round (20th pick overall) of 1981 NFL draft.... On injured reserve with knee injury (September 8-October 24, 1987).... On injured reserve with knee injury (November 8, 1989-remainder of season).... On physically unable to perform list with knee injury (August 28, 1990-entire season).... Granted unconditional free agency (February 1, 1991).... Signed by San Diego Chargers (March 4, 1991).
PLAYING EXPERIENCE: Washington NFL, 1981-1989.... Games: 1981 (16), 1982 (9), 1983 (15), 1984 (16), 1985 (16), 1986 (16), 1987 (10), 1988 (16), 1989 (9). Total: 123.
CHAMPIONSHIP GAME EXPERIENCE: Played in NFC championship game after 1982, 1983, 1986 and 1987 seasons.... Played in Super Bowl XVII after 1982 season, Super Bowl XVIII after 1983 season and Super Bowl XXII after 1987 season.
RECORDS/HONORS: Outland Trophy winner, 1980.... Named as offensive tackle on THE SPORTING NEWS college All-America team, 1980.... Played in Pro Bowl after 1988 season.
PRO STATISTICS: 1983—Recovered one fumble. 1985—Recovered one fumble. 1986—Recovered one fumble. 1987—Recovered one fumble. 1989—Recovered two fumbles.

MAYBERRY, TONY
C, BUCCANEERS

PERSONAL: Born December 8, 1967, at Wurzburg, West Germany.... 6-4/285.... Full name: Eino Anthony Mayberry.
HIGH SCHOOL: Hayfield (Alexandria, Va.).
COLLEGE: Wake Forest (bachelor's degree in sociology).
TRANSACTIONS/CAREER NOTES: Selected by Tampa Bay Buccaneers in fourth round (108th pick overall) of 1990 NFL draft.... Signed by Buccaneers (July 19, 1990).
PLAYING EXPERIENCE: Tampa Bay NFL, 1990.... Games: 1990 (16).

MAYES, MIKE
CB, JETS

PERSONAL: Born August 17, 1966, at DeRidder, La.... 5-10/179.... Full name: Michael Mayes. **HIGH SCHOOL:** DeRidder (La.).
COLLEGE: Louisiana State.
TRANSACTIONS/CAREER NOTES: Selected by New Orleans Saints in fourth round (106th pick overall) of 1989 NFL draft.... Signed by Saints (July 22, 1989).... Released by Saints (September 25, 1989).... Signed as free agent by Kansas City Chiefs to developmental squad (November 11, 1989).... On developmental squad (November 11, 1989-remainder of season).... Released by Chiefs (January 18, 1990).... Signed as free agent by New York Jets (March 28, 1990).
PLAYING EXPERIENCE: New Orleans NFL, 1989; New York Jets NFL, 1990.... Games: 1989 (2), 1990 (16). Total: 18.
PRO STATISTICS: 1990—Intercepted one pass for no yards and recovered one fumble for three yards.

MAYHEW, MARTIN
CB, REDSKINS

PERSONAL: Born October 8, 1965, at Daytona Beach, Fla.... 5-8/172.... Full name: Martin R. Mayhew.
HIGH SCHOOL: Florida (Tallahassee, Fla.).
COLLEGE: Florida State (bachelor of science degree in management, 1987).
TRANSACTIONS/CAREER NOTES: Selected by Buffalo Bills in 10th round (262nd pick overall) of 1988 NFL draft.... Signed by Bills (July 15, 1988).... On injured reserve with broken hand (August 17, 1988-entire season).... Granted unconditional free agency (February 1, 1989).... Signed by Washington Redskins (March 7, 1989).
PRO STATISTICS: 1989—Returned one punt for no yards and fumbled once.

			INTERCEPTIONS		
Year Team	G	No.	Yds.	Avg.	TD
1989— Washington NFL........	16	0	0		0
1990— Washington NFL........	16	7	20	2.9	0
Pro totals (2 years)........	32	7	20	2.9	0

MAYS, ALVOID
CB, REDSKINS

PERSONAL: Born August 10, 1966, at Palmetto, Fla.... 5-9/180.... Full name: Alvoid W. Mays.
HIGH SCHOOL: Manatee (Bradenton, Fla.).
COLLEGE: West Virginia.
TRANSACTIONS/CAREER NOTES: Selected by Houston Oilers in eighth round (217th pick overall) of 1989 NFL draft.... Released by Oilers (August 30, 1989).... Signed by Washington Redskins (May 17, 1990).... Released by Redskins (September 3, 1990).... Re-signed by Redskins (September 5, 1990).... On inactive list (September 23, 1990).
PLAYING EXPERIENCE: Washington NFL, 1990.... Games: 1990 (15).
PRO STATISTICS: 1990—Recovered one fumble.

McCALLUM, NAPOLEON
RB, RAIDERS

PERSONAL: Born October 6, 1963, at Milford, O.... 6-2/225.... Full name: Napoleon Ardel McCallum.
HIGH SCHOOL: Milford (O.).
COLLEGE: Navy.
TRANSACTIONS/CAREER NOTES: Selected by Los Angeles Raiders in fourth round (108th pick overall) of 1986 NFL draft.... Selected by Baltimore Stars in third round (21st pick overall) of 1986 USFL draft.... Signed by Los Angeles Raiders (June 29, 1986).... On reserve/military list (August 27, 1987-entire 1987, 1988 and 1989 seasons).... Traded by Los Angeles Raiders to San Diego Chargers for third-round pick in 1989 NFL draft and fourth-round pick in 1990 NFL draft (October 11, 1988).... Traded by Chargers to Los Angeles Raiders for conditional draft pick in 1991 NFL draft (April 27, 1990).... Reinstated from reserve/military list (May 8, 1990).
CHAMPIONSHIP GAME EXPERIENCE: Played in AFC championship game after 1990 season.
PRO STATISTICS: 1986—Returned eight kickoffs for 183 yards (22.9 avg.), returned seven punts for 44 yards and recovered one fumble. 1990—Returned one kickoff for no yards.

		RUSHING				RECEIVING				TOTAL		
Year Team	G	Att.	Yds.	Avg.	TD	No.	Yds.	Avg.	TD	TD	Pts.	F.
1986— L.A. Raiders NFL	15	142	536	3.8	1	13	103	7.9	0	1	6	5
1990— L.A. Raiders NFL	16	10	25	2.5	0	0	0		0	0	0	0
Pro totals (2 years)	31	152	561	3.7	1	13	103	7.9	0	1	6	5

McCANTS, KEITH
DL, BUCCANEERS

PERSONAL: Born April 19, 1968, at Mobile, Ala.... 6-3/265.
HIGH SCHOOL: Murphy (Mobile, Ala.).
COLLEGE: Alabama.
TRANSACTIONS/CAREER NOTES: Selected by Tampa Bay Buccaneers in first round (fourth pick overall) of 1990 NFL draft.... Signed by Buccaneers (July 11, 1990).... On inactive list (November 18, 1990).
PLAYING EXPERIENCE: Tampa Bay NFL, 1990.... Games: 1990 (15).
RECORDS/HONORS: Named as linebacker on THE SPORTING NEWS college All-America team, 1989.
PRO STATISTICS: 1990—Recovered one fumble.

McCLENDON, SKIP
DE, BENGALS

PERSONAL: Born April 9, 1964, at Detroit.... 6-7/287.... Full name: Kenneth Christopher McClendon.
HIGH SCHOOL: Redford (Detroit).
COLLEGE: Northwestern, then Butler County Community College (Pa.), then Arizona State.

TRANSACTIONS/CAREER NOTES: Selected by Cincinnati Bengals in third round (77th pick overall) of 1987 NFL draft. . . . Signed by Bengals (May 29, 1987). . . . On inactive list (October 14, 1990).
PLAYING EXPERIENCE: Cincinnati NFL, 1987-1990. . . . Games: 1987 (12), 1988 (16), 1989 (16), 1990 (15). Total: 59.
CHAMPIONSHIP GAME EXPERIENCE: Played in AFC championship game after 1988 season. . . . Played in Super Bowl XXIII after 1988 season.
PRO STATISTICS: 1989—Recovered one fumble.

McCULLOUGH, RICHARD
DE, COLTS

PERSONAL: Born July 22, 1965, at Loris, S.C. . . . 6-5/270. . . . Full name: Richard Charles McCullough.
HIGH SCHOOL: Loris (S.C.).
COLLEGE: Clemson.
TRANSACTIONS/CAREER NOTES: Selected by Denver Broncos in fourth round (97th pick overall) of 1989 NFL draft. . . . Signed by Broncos (July 26, 1989). . . . On injured reserve with hip injury (December 14, 1989-remainder of season). . . . Released by Broncos (October 19, 1990). . . . Signed by Indianapolis Colts (March 4, 1991).
PLAYING EXPERIENCE: Denver NFL, 1989 and 1990. . . . Games: 1989 (10), 1990 (6). Total: 16.

McDANIEL, RANDALL
G, VIKINGS

PERSONAL: Born December 19, 1964, at Phoenix. . . . 6-3/270. . . . Full name: Randall Cornell McDaniel.
HIGH SCHOOL: Agua Fria Union (Avondale, Ariz.).
COLLEGE: Arizona State (degree in physical education, 1988).
TRANSACTIONS/CAREER NOTES: Selected by Minnesota Vikings in first round (19th pick overall) of 1988 NFL draft. . . . Signed by Vikings (July 22, 1988).
PLAYING EXPERIENCE: Minnesota NFL, 1988-1990. . . . Games: 1988 (16), 1989 (14), 1990 (16). Total: 46.
RECORDS/HONORS: Played in Pro Bowl after 1989 and 1990 seasons.

McDANIEL, TERRY
CB, RAIDERS

PERSONAL: Born February 8, 1965, at Saginaw, Mich. . . . 5-10/180. . . . Full name: Terence Lee McDaniel.
HIGH SCHOOL: Saginaw (Mich.).
COLLEGE: Tennessee.
TRANSACTIONS/CAREER NOTES: Selected by Los Angeles Raiders in first round (ninth pick overall) of 1988 NFL draft. . . . Signed by Raiders (July 13, 1988). . . . On injured reserve with broken leg (September 14, 1988-remainder of season).
CHAMPIONSHIP GAME EXPERIENCE: Played in AFC championship game after 1990 season.
PRO STATISTICS: 1990—Recovered two fumbles for 44 yards (including one for 42 yards and a touchdown).

			INTERCEPTIONS		
Year	Team	G	No.	Yds.	Avg.	TD
1988—L.A. Raiders NFL	2	0	0		0
1989—L.A. Raiders NFL	16	3	21	7.0	0
1990—L.A. Raiders NFL	16	3	20	6.7	0
Pro totals (3 years)	34	6	41	6.8	0

McDONALD, QUINTUS
LB, COLTS

PERSONAL: Born December 14, 1966, at Rockingham, N.C. . . . 6-3/263. . . . Full name: Quintus Alonzo McDonald.
HIGH SCHOOL: Montclair (N.J.).
COLLEGE: Penn State.
TRANSACTIONS/CAREER NOTES: Selected by Indianapolis Colts in sixth round (155th pick overall) of 1989 NFL draft. . . . Signed by Colts (July 25, 1989). . . . On non-football illness/injury list (October 19-November 23, 1990). . . . On inactive list (December 2, 1990).
PLAYING EXPERIENCE: Indianapolis NFL, 1989 and 1990. . . . Games: 1989 (15), 1990 (9). Total: 24.

McDONALD, TIM
S, CARDINALS

PERSONAL: Born January 6, 1965, at Fresno, Calif. . . . 6-2/215.
HIGH SCHOOL: Edison (Calif.).
COLLEGE: Southern California.
TRANSACTIONS/CAREER NOTES: Selected by St. Louis Cardinals in second round (34th pick overall) of 1987 NFL draft. . . . Signed by Cardinals (August 2, 1987). . . . On injured reserve with broken ankle (September 1-December 12, 1987). . . . Franchise transferred to Phoenix (March 15, 1988). . . . Granted free agency (February 1, 1990). . . . Re-signed by Phoenix Cardinals (August 21, 1990).
RECORDS/HONORS: Named as defensive back on THE SPORTING NEWS college All-America team, 1985. . . . Played in Pro Bowl after 1989 season.
PRO STATISTICS: 1988—Recovered one fumble for nine yards. 1989—Recovered one fumble for one yard. 1990—Recovered one fumble.

			INTERCEPTIONS		
Year	Team	G	No.	Yds.	Avg.	TD
1987—St. Louis NFL	3	0	0		0
1988—Phoenix NFL	16	2	11	5.5	0
1989—Phoenix NFL	16	7	140	20.0	1
1990—Phoenix NFL	16	4	63	15.8	0
Pro totals (4 years)	51	13	214	16.5	1

McDOWELL, BUBBA
S, OILERS

PERSONAL: Born November 4, 1966, at Fort Gaines, Ga. . . . 6-1/198. . . . Full name: Leonard McDowell.
HIGH SCHOOL: Merritt Island (Fla.).
COLLEGE: Miami, Fla. (bachelor of science degree in business management, 1989).
TRANSACTIONS/CAREER NOTES: Selected by Houston Oilers in third round (77th pick overall) of 1989 NFL draft. . . . Signed by Oilers (July 28, 1989). . . . On inactive list (December 23, 1990).
PRO STATISTICS: 1989—Credited with a safety, recovered one fumble and fumbled once. 1990—Recovered one fumble.

				INTERCEPTIONS		
Year	Team	G	No.	Yds.	Avg.	TD
1989—Houston NFL		16	4	65	16.3	0
1990—Houston NFL		15	2	11	5.5	0
Pro totals (2 years)		31	6	76	12.7	0

McELROY, REGGIE
OT, RAIDERS

PERSONAL: Born March 4, 1960, at Beaumont, Tex. . . . 6-6/285. . . . Full name: Reginald Lee McElroy.
HIGH SCHOOL: Charlton Pollard (Beaumont, Tex.).
COLLEGE: West Texas State (degree in physical education).
TRANSACTIONS/CAREER NOTES: Selected by New York Jets in second round (51st pick overall) of 1982 NFL draft. . . . On injured reserve with knee injury (August 24, 1982-entire season). . . . Granted free agency (February 1, 1985). . . . Re-signed by Jets (September 10, 1985). . . . Granted roster exemption (September 10-September 14, 1985). . . . On injured reserve with knee injury (October 22-December 12, 1986). . . . On injured reserve with knee injury (December 17, 1986-remainder of season). . . . On reserve/physically unable to perform list with knee injury (September 6-November 9, 1987). . . . On injured reserve with knee injury (December 19, 1989-remainder of season). . . . Released by Jets (June 21, 1990). . . . Signed by Los Angeles Raiders (March 20, 1991).
PLAYING EXPERIENCE: New York Jets NFL, 1983-1989. . . . Games: 1983 (16), 1984 (16), 1985 (13), 1986 (8), 1987 (8), 1988 (16), 1989 (15). Total: 92.
PRO STATISTICS: 1983—Returned one kickoff for seven yards. 1986—Recovered one fumble for minus two yards. 1988—Recovered one fumble.

McELROY, VANN
S, SEAHAWKS

PERSONAL: Born January 13, 1960, at Birmingham, Ala. . . . 6-2/190. . . . Full name: Vann William McElroy.
HIGH SCHOOL: Uvalde (Tex.).
COLLEGE: Baylor (bachelor of business administration degree in marketing management, 1983).
TRANSACTIONS/CAREER NOTES: Selected by Los Angeles Raiders in third round (64th pick overall) of 1982 NFL draft. . . . On inactive list (September 12 and 19, 1982). . . . On injured reserve with knee injury (September 8-October 8, 1988). . . . On injured reserve with hamstring injury (October 4-December 5, 1989). . . . Transferred to developmental squad (December 6-December 9, 1989). . . . Granted free agency (February 1, 1990). . . . Re-signed by Raiders (September 10, 1990). . . . Activated (September 24, 1990). . . . Traded by Raiders to Seattle Seahawks for undisclosed draft pick (October 16, 1990).
CHAMPIONSHIP GAME EXPERIENCE: Played in AFC championship game after 1983 season. . . . Played in Super Bowl XVIII after 1983 season.
RECORDS/HONORS: Played in Pro Bowl after 1983 and 1984 seasons.
PRO STATISTICS: 1982—Intercepted one pass for no yards. 1983—Recovered three fumbles for five yards. 1984—Recovered four fumbles for 12 yards. 1985—Recovered one fumble. 1988—Recovered one fumble.

				INTERCEPTIONS		
Year	Team	G	No.	Yds.	Avg.	TD
1982—L.A. Raiders NFL		7	0	0		0
1983—L.A. Raiders NFL		16	8	68	8.5	0
1984—L.A. Raiders NFL		16	4	42	10.5	0
1985—L.A. Raiders NFL		12	2	23	11.5	0
1986—L.A. Raiders NFL		16	7	105	15.0	0
1987—L.A. Raiders NFL		12	4	41	10.3	1
1988—L.A. Raiders NFL		12	3	17	5.7	0
1989—L.A. Raiders NFL		7	2	0	.0	0
1990—Raiders (3)-Sea. (10) NFL		13	0	0		0
Pro totals (9 years)		111	30	296	9.9	1

McEWEN, CRAIG
RB, CHARGERS

PERSONAL: Born December 16, 1965, at Northport, N.Y. . . . 6-1/220. . . . Name pronounced mick-YOU-en.
HIGH SCHOOL: Northport (N.Y.).
COLLEGE: Utah.
TRANSACTIONS/CAREER NOTES: Signed as free agent by Washington Redskins (May 4, 1987). . . . Released by Redskins (September 7, 1987). . . . Re-signed as replacement player by Redskins (September 23, 1987). . . . On injured reserve with back injury (November 3, 1987-remainder of season). . . . Released by Redskins (September 5, 1989). . . . Signed as free agent by San Diego Chargers (November 29, 1989).
PRO STATISTICS: 1990—Fumbled once.

				RECEIVING		
Year	Team	G	No.	Yds.	Avg.	TD
1987—Washington NFL		4	12	164	13.7	0
1988—Washington NFL		14	23	323	14.0	0

Year	Team	G	RECEIVING No.	RECEIVING Yds.	RECEIVING Avg.	RECEIVING TD
1989— San Diego NFL		4	7	99	14.1	0
1990— San Diego NFL		16	29	325	11.2	3
Pro totals (4 years)		38	71	911	12.8	3

McGEE, BUFORD
FB, RAMS

PERSONAL: Born August 16, 1960, at Durant, Miss. . . . 6-0/210. . . . Full name: Buford Lamar McGee.
HIGH SCHOOL: Durant (Miss.).
COLLEGE: Mississippi (bachelor of science degree in business, 1984).
TRANSACTIONS/CAREER NOTES: Selected by Birmingham Stallions in 1984 USFL territorial draft. . . . Selected by San Diego Chargers in 11th round (286th pick overall) of 1984 NFL draft. . . . Signed by Chargers (June 2, 1984). . . . On injured reserve with hamstring injury (September 3-October 5, 1985). . . . On injured reserve with knee injury (November 8, 1986-remainder of season). . . . Granted free agency (February 1, 1987). . . . Re-signed by Chargers and traded with second-round pick in 1988 draft and sixth-round pick in 1989 draft to Los Angeles Rams for running back Barry Redden (June 9, 1987). . . . On injured reserve with ruptured Achilles tendon (October 28, 1987-remainder of season).
CHAMPIONSHIP GAME EXPERIENCE: Played in NFC championship game after 1989 season.
PRO STATISTICS: 1984—Recovered one fumble. 1985—Recovered two fumbles. 1986—Attempted one pass with one completion for one yard. 1990—Attempted two passes with two completions for 23 yards and one touchdown and recovered one fumble.

Year	Team	G	RUSHING Att.	RUSHING Yds.	RUSHING Avg.	RUSHING TD	RECEIVING No.	RECEIVING Yds.	RECEIVING Avg.	RECEIVING TD	KICKOFF RETURNS No.	KICKOFF RETURNS Yds.	KICKOFF RETURNS Avg.	KICKOFF RETURNS TD	TOTAL TD	TOTAL Pts.	F.
1984— San Diego NFL		16	67	226	3.4	4	9	76	8.4	2	14	315	22.5	0	6	36	1
1985— San Diego NFL		11	42	181	4.3	3	3	15	5.0	0	7	135	19.3	0	3	18	4
1986— San Diego NFL		9	63	187	3.0	7	10	105	10.5	0	1	15	15.0	0	7	42	4
1987— L.A. Rams NFL		3	3	6	2.0	1	7	40	5.7	0	0	0		0	1	6	0
1988— L.A. Rams NFL		16	22	69	3.1	0	16	117	7.3	3	1	0	.0	0	3	18	0
1989— L.A. Rams NFL		16	21	99	4.7	1	37	303	8.2	4	0	0		0	5	30	2
1990— L.A. Rams NFL		16	44	234	5.3	1	47	388	8.3	4	0	0		0	5	30	0
Pro totals (7 years)		87	262	1002	3.8	17	129	1044	8.1	13	23	465	20.2	0	30	180	11

McGEE, TIM
WR, BENGALS

PERSONAL: Born August 7, 1964, at Cleveland. . . . 5-10/183. . . . Full name: Timothy Dwanye McGee.
HIGH SCHOOL: John Jay (Cleveland).
COLLEGE: Tennessee.
TRANSACTIONS/CAREER NOTES: Selected by Memphis Showboats in 1986 USFL territorial draft. . . . Selected by Cincinnati Bengals in first round (21st pick overall) of 1986 NFL draft. . . . USFL rights traded by Memphis Showboats to Jacksonville Bulls for rights to center Leonard Burton and offensive tackle Doug Williams (May 6, 1986). . . . Signed by Cincinnati Bengals (July 26, 1986). . . . On injured reserve with hamstring injury (September 19-October 21, 1987).
CHAMPIONSHIP GAME EXPERIENCE: Played in AFC championship game after 1988 season. . . . Played in Super Bowl XXIII after 1988 season.
PRO STATISTICS: 1986—Returned three punts for 21 yards and recovered one fumble. 1988—Recovered one fumble.

Year	Team	G	RUSHING Att.	RUSHING Yds.	RUSHING Avg.	RUSHING TD	RECEIVING No.	RECEIVING Yds.	RECEIVING Avg.	RECEIVING TD	KICKOFF RETURNS No.	KICKOFF RETURNS Yds.	KICKOFF RETURNS Avg.	KICKOFF RETURNS TD	TOTAL TD	TOTAL Pts.	F.
1986— Cincinnati NFL		16	4	10	2.5	0	16	276	17.3	1	43*	1007	23.4	0	1	6	0
1987— Cincinnati NFL		11	1	-10	-10.0	0	23	408	17.7	1	15	242	16.1	0	1	6	0
1988— Cincinnati NFL		16	0	0		0	36	686	19.1	6	0	0		0	6	36	0
1989— Cincinnati NFL		16	2	36	18.0	0	65	1211	18.6	8	0	0		0	8	48	0
1990— Cincinnati NFL		16	0	0		0	43	737	17.1	1	0	0		0	1	6	1
Pro totals (5 years)		75	7	36	5.1	0	183	3318	18.1	17	58	1249	21.5	0	17	102	1

McGOVERN, ROB
LB, STEELERS

PERSONAL: Born October 1, 1966, at Teaneck, N.J. . . . 6-2/220. . . . Full name: Robert Patrick McGovern. . . . Brother of Jim McGovern, professional golfer; and brother of Bill McGovern, assistant football coach at Holy Cross.
HIGH SCHOOL: Bergen Catholic (Oradell, N.J.).
COLLEGE: Holy Cross (degree in history, 1989).
TRANSACTIONS/CAREER NOTES: Selected by Kansas City Chiefs in 10th round (255th pick overall) of 1989 NFL draft. . . . Signed by Chiefs (July 17, 1989). . . . Released by Chiefs (October 6, 1990). . . . Re-signed by Chiefs (October 18, 1990). . . . On inactive list (November 4, 1990). . . . Released by Chiefs (November 10, 1990). . . . Re-signed by Chiefs (November 21, 1990). . . . Granted unconditional free agency (February 1, 1991). . . . Signed by Pittsburgh Steelers (March 26, 1991).
PLAYING EXPERIENCE: Kansas City NFL, 1989 and 1990. . . . Games: 1989 (16). 1990 (11). Total: 27.
PRO STATISTICS: 1989—Credited with a safety.

McGREW, LARRY
LB, GIANTS

PERSONAL: Born July 23, 1957, at Berkeley, Calif. . . . 6-6/250. . . . Full name: Lawrence McGrew.
HIGH SCHOOL: Berkeley (Calif.).
COLLEGE: Contra Costa Junior College (Calif.), then Southern California (degree in speech communications, 1980).
TRANSACTIONS/CAREER NOTES: Selected by New England Patriots in second round (45th pick overall) of 1980 NFL draft. . . . On injured reserve with knee and elbow injuries (December 19, 1980-remainder of season). . . . On injured reserve with knee injury

(August 31, 1981-entire season).... Granted unconditional free agency (February 1, 1990).... Signed by Cleveland Browns (March 28, 1990).... Released by Browns (September 3, 1990).... Signed by New York Giants (October 17, 1990).
PLAYING EXPERIENCE: New England NFL, 1980 and 1982-1989; New York Giants NFL, 1990. ... Games: 1980 (11), 1982 (8), 1983 (16), 1984 (16), 1985 (13), 1986 (14), 1987 (12), 1988 (16), 1989 (16), 1990 (11). Total: 133.
CHAMPIONSHIP GAME EXPERIENCE: Played in AFC championship game after 1985 season.... Played in NFC championship game after 1990 season.... Played in Super Bowl XX after 1985 season and Super Bowl XXV after 1990 season.
PRO STATISTICS: 1983—Intercepted one pass for three yards and recovered one fumble. 1985—Intercepted one pass for no yards and recovered two fumbles. 1986—Intercepted two passes for 44 yards. 1987—Recovered one fumble. 1988—Intercepted one pass for six yards. 1989—Intercepted one pass for minus four yards and recovered one fumble.

McGRUDER, MIKE
CB, DOLPHINS

PERSONAL: Born May 6, 1962, at Cleveland Heights, O. ... 5-11/190. ... Full name: Michael J.P. McGruder.
HIGH SCHOOL: Cleveland Heights (O.).
COLLEGE: Kent (degree in business management).
TRANSACTIONS/CAREER NOTES: Signed as free agent by Ottawa Rough Riders of CFL (May, 1985).... Released by Rough Riders (July, 1985).... Signed as free agent by Saskatchewan Roughriders of CFL (April, 1986).... Granted free agency (March 1, 1989).... Signed as free agent by Green Bay Packers (April 26, 1989).... Released by Packers (September 19, 1989).... Re-signed by Packers to developmental squad (September 22, 1989).... On developmental squad (September 22, 1989-remainder of season).... Released by Packers (January 29, 1990).... Signed as free agent by Miami Dolphins (April 3, 1990).... On injured reserve with shoulder injury (September 14, 1990-remainder of regular season and playoffs).
PRO STATISTICS: CFL: 1986—Recovered one fumble and lost four yards on lateral of punt return. 1987—Recovered four fumbles for 26 yards. 1988—Recovered two fumbles for 20 yards and a touchdown.... NFL: 1989—Recovered one fumble.

		—— INTERCEPTIONS ——			
Year	Team	G	No.	Yds.	Avg.	TD
1986— Saskatchewan CFL ...		14	5	35	7.0	0
1987— Saskatchewan CFL ...		14	5	26	5.2	0
1988— Saskatchewan CFL ...		18	7	89	12.7	0
1989— Green Bay NFL..........		2	0	0		0
1990— Miami NFL..............		1	0	0		0
CFL totals (3 years)		46	17	150	8.8	0
NFL totals (2 years)		3	0	0		0
Pro totals (5 years)		49	17	150	8.8	0

McHALE, TOM
G, BUCCANEERS

PERSONAL: Born February 25, 1963, at Gaithersburg, Md. ... 6-4/280. ... Full name: Thomas McHale.
HIGH SCHOOL: Gaithersburg (Md.).
COLLEGE: Cornell.
TRANSACTIONS/CAREER NOTES: Signed as free agent by Tampa Bay Buccaneers (May 4, 1987).... On injured reserve with back injury (September 7-November 28, 1987).... On injured reserve (September 24-November 23, 1990).
PLAYING EXPERIENCE: Tampa Bay NFL, 1987-1990.... Games: 1987 (3), 1988 (10), 1989 (15), 1990 (7). Total: 35.
PRO STATISTICS: 1987—Recovered one fumble. 1988—Fumbled once for minus four yards.

McINTYRE, GUY
G, 49ERS

PERSONAL: Born February 17, 1961, at Thomasville, Ga. ... 6-3/265. ... Full name: Guy Maurice McIntyre.... Cousin of Lomas Brown, offensive tackle with Detroit Lions.
HIGH SCHOOL: Thomasville (Ga.).
COLLEGE: Georgia.
TRANSACTIONS/CAREER NOTES: Selected by Jacksonville Bulls in 1984 USFL territorial draft.... Selected by San Francisco 49ers in third round (73rd pick overall) of 1984 NFL draft.... Signed by 49ers (May 8, 1984).... On injured reserve with foot injury (October 31, 1987-remainder of season).... On reserve/did not report list (July 30-August 27, 1990).
PLAYING EXPERIENCE: San Francisco NFL, 1984-1990.... Games: 1984 (15), 1985 (15), 1986 (16), 1987 (3), 1988 (16), 1989 (16), 1990 (16). Total: 97.
CHAMPIONSHIP GAME EXPERIENCE: Played in NFC championship game after 1984 and 1988-1990 seasons.... Played in Super Bowl XIX after 1984 season, Super Bowl XXIII after 1988 season and Super Bowl XXIV after 1989 season.
RECORDS/HONORS: Played in Pro Bowl after 1989 and 1990 seasons.
PRO STATISTICS: 1984—Returned one kickoff for no yards. 1985—Recovered one fumble in end zone for a touchdown. 1988—Caught one pass for 17 yards and a touchdown.

McKELLER, KEITH
TE, BILLS

PERSONAL: Born July 9, 1964, at Fairfield, Ala.... 6-4/245.
HIGH SCHOOL: Fairfield (Ala.).
COLLEGE: Jacksonville State.
TRANSACTIONS/CAREER NOTES: Selected by Buffalo Bills in ninth round (227th pick overall) of 1987 NFL draft.... Signed by Bills (July 16, 1987).... On injured reserve with back injury (September 1, 1987-entire season).
CHAMPIONSHIP GAME EXPERIENCE: Member of Buffalo Bills for AFC championship game after 1988 season; inactive.... Played in AFC championship game after 1990 season.... Played in Super Bowl XXV after 1990 season.
PRO STATISTICS: 1989—Fumbled once. 1990—Fumbled once.

		—— RECEIVING ——			
Year	Team	G	No.	Yds.	Avg.	TD
1988— Buffalo NFL...............		12	0	0		0

Year	Team	G	No.	Yds.	Avg.	TD
			RECEIVING			
1989— Buffalo NFL		16	20	341	17.1	2
1990— Buffalo NFL		16	34	464	13.6	5
Pro totals (3 years)		44	54	805	14.9	7

McKENZIE, RALEIGH
C/G, REDSKINS

PERSONAL: Born February 8, 1963, at Knoxville, Tenn. ... 6-2/270. ... Twin brother of Reggie McKenzie, linebacker with Los Angeles Raiders and Phoenix Cardinals, 1985-1988 and 1990.
HIGH SCHOOL: Austin-East (Knoxville, Tenn.).
COLLEGE: Tennessee.
TRANSACTIONS/CAREER NOTES: Selected by Washington Redskins in 11th round (290th pick overall) of 1985 NFL draft. ... Signed by Redskins (June 20, 1985).
PLAYING EXPERIENCE: Washington NFL, 1985-1990. ... Games: 1985 (6), 1986 (15), 1987 (12), 1988 (16), 1989 (15), 1990 (16). Total: 80.
CHAMPIONSHIP GAME EXPERIENCE: Played in NFC championship game after 1986 and 1987 seasons. ... Played in Super Bowl XXII after 1987 season.

McKNIGHT, DENNIS
C/G, EAGLES

PERSONAL: Born September 12, 1959, at Dallas. ... 6-3/280. ... Full name: Dennis N. McKnight.
HIGH SCHOOL: Wagner (Staten Island, N.Y.).
COLLEGE: Drake (received degree, 1981).
TRANSACTIONS/CAREER NOTES: Signed as free agent by Cleveland Browns (May 3, 1981). ... Released by Browns (August 18, 1981). ... Signed as free agent by San Diego Chargers (March 30, 1982). ... On inactive list (September 12 and 19, 1982). ... On injured reserve with knee injury (September 4, 1989-entire season). ... Released by Chargers (September 3, 1990). ... Awarded on waivers to Detroit Lions (September 5, 1990). ... Granted unconditional free agency (February 1, 1991). ... Signed by Philadelphia Eagles (March 20, 1991).
PLAYING EXPERIENCE: San Diego NFL, 1982-1988; Detroit NFL, 1990. ... Games: 1982 (7), 1983 (16), 1984 (16), 1985 (16), 1986 (16), 1987 (12), 1988 (16), 1990 (14). Total: 113.
PRO STATISTICS: 1983—Recovered two fumbles. 1984—Recovered two fumbles. 1990—Returned one kickoff for no yards.

McKYER, TIM
CB, FALCONS

PERSONAL: Born September 5, 1963, at Orlando, Fla. ... 6-0/174. ... Full name: Tim B. McKyer.
HIGH SCHOOL: Lincoln (Port Arthur, Tex.).
COLLEGE: Texas-Arlington.
TRANSACTIONS/CAREER NOTES: Selected by San Francisco 49ers in third round (64th pick overall) of 1986 NFL draft. ... Signed by 49ers (July 20, 1986). ... On suspended list (October 7-October 24, 1989). ... Traded by 49ers to Miami Dolphins for 11th-round pick in 1990 NFL draft and second-round pick in 1991 draft (April 22, 1990). ... Traded by Dolphins to Atlanta Falcons for third- and 12th-round picks in 1991 NFL draft (April 22, 1991).
CHAMPIONSHIP GAME EXPERIENCE: Played in NFC championship game after 1988 and 1989 seasons. ... Played in Super Bowl XXIII after 1988 season. ... Played in Super Bowl XXIV after 1989 season.
PRO STATISTICS: 1986—Returned one kickoff for 15 yards and returned one punt for five yards.

Year	Team	G	No.	Yds.	Avg.	TD
			INTERCEPTIONS			
1986— San Francisco NFL		16	6	33	5.5	1
1987— San Francisco NFL		12	2	0	.0	0
1988— San Francisco NFL		16	7	11	1.6	0
1989— San Francisco NFL		7	1	18	18.0	0
1990— Miami NFL		16	4	40	10.0	0
Pro totals (5 years)		67	20	102	5.1	1

McLEMORE, CHRIS
FB, SEAHAWKS

PERSONAL: Born December 31, 1963, at Las Vegas. ... 6-1/230.
HIGH SCHOOL: Valley (Las Vegas).
COLLEGE: Colorado, then Arizona.
TRANSACTIONS/CAREER NOTES: Selected by Los Angeles Raiders in 11th round (288th pick overall) of 1987 NFL draft. ... Signed by Raiders (July 10, 1987). ... Released by Raiders (September 7, 1987). ... Signed as free agent replacement player by Indianapolis Colts (September 23, 1987). ... Released by Colts (October 27, 1987). ... Signed as free agent by Los Angeles Raiders (November 11, 1987). ... On injured reserve with elbow injury (December 26, 1987-remainder of season). ... On injured reserve with elbow injury (August 29-October 25, 1988). ... Re-signed by Raiders after clearing procedural waivers (October 27, 1988). ... On injured reserve with elbow injury (December 17, 1988-remainder of season). ... Granted unconditional free agency (February 1, 1989). ... Signed by Seattle Seahawks (March 21, 1989). ... On reserve/retired list (July 28, 1989-entire season). ... Reinstated from reserve/retired list (March 20, 1990). ... Released by Seahawks (September 3, 1990). ... Re-signed by Seahawks (April 23, 1991).

Year	Team	G	Att.	Yds.	Avg.	TD	No.	Yds.	Avg.	TD	TD	Pts.	F.
			RUSHING				RECEIVING				TOTAL		
1987— Ind. (2)-Raiders (3) NFL		5	17	58	3.4	0	2	9	4.5	0	0	0	1
1988— L.A. Raiders NFL		7	0	0		0	0	0		0	0	0	0
Pro totals (2 years)		12	17	58	3.4	0	2	9	4.5	0	0	0	1

McMAHON, JIM
QB, EAGLES

PERSONAL: Born August 21, 1959, at Jersey City, N.J. . . . 6-1/195. . . . Full name: James Robert McMahon.
HIGH SCHOOL: Roy (Utah).
COLLEGE: Brigham Young.

TRANSACTIONS/CAREER NOTES: Selected by Chicago Bears in first round (fifth pick overall) of 1982 NFL draft. . . . On injured reserve with lacerated kidney (November 9, 1984-remainder of season). . . . On injured reserve with shoulder injury (November 28, 1986-remainder of season). . . . On injured reserve with shoulder injury (September 7-October 22, 1987). . . . On injured reserve with knee injury (November 5-December 9, 1988). . . . Traded by Bears to San Diego Chargers for second-round pick in 1990 NFL draft (August 18, 1989). . . . Granted free agency (February 1, 1990). . . . Rights relinquished by Chargers (April 26, 1990). . . . Signed by Philadelphia Eagles (July 10, 1990).
CHAMPIONSHIP GAME EXPERIENCE: Played in NFC championship game after 1985 and 1988 seasons. . . . Played in Super Bowl XX after 1985 season.
RECORDS/HONORS: Played in Pro Bowl after 1985 season.
PRO STATISTICS: Passer rating points: 1982 (80.1), 1983 (77.6), 1984 (97.8), 1985 (82.6), 1986 (61.4), 1987 (87.4), 1988 (76.0), 1989 (73.5), 1990 (86.8). Career: 79.3. . . . 1982—Punted once for 59 yards. 1983—Caught one pass for 18 yards and a touchdown, punted once for 36 yards and recovered three fumbles. 1984—Caught one pass for 42 yards. 1985—Caught one pass for 13 yards and a touchdown. 1988—Recovered three fumbles. 1989—Caught one pass for four yards and recovered one fumble.

			PASSING						RUSHING				TOTAL		
Year Team	G	Att.	Cmp.	Pct.	Yds.	TD	Int.	Avg.	Att.	Yds.	Avg.	TD	TD	Pts.	F.
1982—Chicago NFL	8	210	120	57.1	1501	9	7	7.15	24	105	4.4	1	1	6	1
1983—Chicago NFL	14	295	175	59.3	2184	12	13	7.40	55	307	5.6	2	3	18	4
1984—Chicago NFL	9	143	85	59.4	1146	8	2	8.01	39	276	7.1	2	2	12	1
1985—Chicago NFL	13	313	178	56.9	2392	15	11	7.64	47	252	5.4	3	4	24	4
1986—Chicago NFL	6	150	77	51.3	995	5	8	6.63	22	152	6.9	1	1	6	1
1987—Chicago NFL	7	210	125	59.5	1639	12	8	7.81	22	88	4.0	2	2	12	2
1988—Chicago NFL	9	192	114	59.4	1346	6	7	7.01	26	104	4.0	4	4	24	6
1989—San Diego NFL	12	318	176	55.4	2132	10	10	6.70	29	141	4.9	0	0	0	3
1990—Philadelphia NFL	5	9	6	66.7	63	0	0	7.00	3	1	.3	0	0	0	0
Pro totals (9 years)	83	1840	1056	57.4	13398	77	66	7.28	267	1426	5.3	15	17	102	22

McMICHAEL, STEVE
DT, BEARS

PERSONAL: Born October 17, 1957, at Houston. . . . 6-2/268. . . . Full name: Steve Douglas McMichael.
HIGH SCHOOL: Freer (Tex.).
COLLEGE: Texas.

TRANSACTIONS/CAREER NOTES: Selected by New England Patriots in third round (73rd pick overall) of 1980 NFL draft. . . . On injured reserve with back injury (November 3, 1980-remainder of season). . . . Released by Patriots (August 24, 1981). . . . Signed as free agent by Chicago Bears (October 15, 1981). . . . Granted roster exemption (September 3-September 9, 1990).
PLAYING EXPERIENCE: New England NFL, 1980; Chicago NFL, 1981-1990. . . . Games: 1980 (6), 1981 (10), 1982 (9), 1983 (16), 1984 (16), 1985 (16), 1986 (16), 1987 (12), 1988 (16), 1989 (16), 1990 (16). Total: 149.
CHAMPIONSHIP GAME EXPERIENCE: Played in NFC championship game after 1984, 1985 and 1988 seasons. . . . Played in Super Bowl XX after 1985 season.
RECORDS/HONORS: Played in Pro Bowl after 1986 and 1987 seasons. . . . Named to THE SPORTING NEWS NFL All-Pro team, 1986 and 1987.
PRO STATISTICS: 1981—Recovered one fumble. 1982—Recovered one fumble for 64 yards. 1983—Recovered two fumbles. 1985—Credited with one safety and recovered one fumble. 1986—Credited with one safety, intercepted one pass for five yards and recovered two fumbles. 1988—Credited with one safety and recovered two fumbles for one yard. 1989—Recovered one fumble.

McMILLAN, ERIK
S, JETS

PERSONAL: Born May 3, 1965, at St. Louis. . . . 6-2/200. . . . Full name: Erik Charles McMillan. . . . Son of Ernie McMillan, offensive tackle with St. Louis Cardinals and Green Bay Packers, 1961-1975; assistant coach with Green Bay Packers, 1979-1983; and assistant coach with Dallas Cowboys and Seattle Seahawks, 1981-1987.
HIGH SCHOOL: John F. Kennedy (Silver Springs, Md.).
COLLEGE: Missouri (degree in business management, 1988); attended Fordham (master's degree in education administration, 1991).
TRANSACTIONS/CAREER NOTES: Selected by New York Jets in third round (63rd pick overall) of 1988 NFL draft. . . . Signed by Jets (July 6, 1988). . . . On injured reserve with sprained arch (December 17, 1988-remainder of season).
RECORDS/HONORS: Tied NFL record for most touchdowns scored by fumble recovery, season (2), 1989; most touchdowns scored by recovery of opponents' fumbles, season (2), 1989. . . . Played in Pro Bowl after 1988 and 1989 seasons.
PRO STATISTICS: 1988—Fumbled once. 1989—Recovered two fumbles for 119 yards and two touchdowns. 1990—Recovered one fumble and fumbled three times for one yard.

		INTERCEPTIONS			
Year Team	G	No.	Yds.	Avg.	TD
1988—N.Y. Jets NFL	13	8	168	21.0	*2
1989—N.Y. Jets NFL	16	6	180	30.0	1
1990—N.Y. Jets NFL	16	5	92	18.4	0
Pro totals (3 years)	45	19	440	23.2	3

McMILLIAN, AUDREY
CB, VIKINGS

PERSONAL: Born August 13, 1962, at Carthage, Tex. . . . 6-0/189. . . . Full name: Audrey Glenn McMillian.
HIGH SCHOOL: Carthage (Tex.).
COLLEGE: Purdue (bachelor of science degree in industrial distribution, 1985).
TRANSACTIONS/CAREER NOTES: Selected by Houston Gamblers in 1985 USFL territorial draft. . . . Selected by New England Patriots in third round (84th pick overall) of 1985 NFL draft. . . . Signed by Patriots (July 1, 1985). . . . Released by Patriots (September 2, 1985). . . . Awarded on waivers to Houston Oilers (September 3, 1985). . . . Released by Oilers (September 22, 1986). . . . Re-signed by Oilers (September 24, 1986). . . . On injured reserve with knee injury (August 29, 1988-entire season). . . . Granted unconditional free agency (February 1, 1989). . . . Signed by Minnesota Vikings (March 16, 1989). . . . On inactive list (October 15, 1990).
PLAYING EXPERIENCE: Houston NFL, 1985-1987; Minnesota NFL, 1989 and 1990. . . . Games: 1985 (16), 1986 (16), 1987 (12), 1989 (16), 1990 (15). Total: 75.
PRO STATISTICS: 1986—Recovered two fumbles for four yards. 1990—Intercepted three passes for 20 yards.

McMURTRY, GREG
WR, PATRIOTS

PERSONAL: Born October 15, 1967, at Brockton, Mass. . . . 6-2/207. . . . Full name: Greg Wendell McMurtry.
HIGH SCHOOL: Brockton (Mass.).
COLLEGE: Michigan (degree in general studies).
TRANSACTIONS/CAREER NOTES: Selected by New England Patriots in third round (80th pick overall) of 1990 NFL draft.
PRO STATISTICS: 1990—Fumbled once.

| | | | RECEIVING | | |
Year Team	G	No.	Yds.	Avg.	TD
1990— New England NFL......	13	22	240	10.9	0
Pro totals (1 year)	13	22	240	10.9	0

McNAIR, TODD
RB/KR, CHIEFS

PERSONAL: Born August 16, 1965, at Camden, N.J. . . . 6-1/191. . . . Full name: Todd Darren McNair.
HIGH SCHOOL: Pennsauken (N.J.).
COLLEGE: Temple.
TRANSACTIONS/CAREER NOTES: Selected by Kansas City Chiefs in eighth round (220th pick overall) of 1989 NFL draft. . . . Signed by Chiefs (July 12, 1989). . . . Released by Chiefs (September 5, 1989). . . . Re-signed by Chiefs to developmental squad (September 6, 1989). . . . On developmental squad (September 6-September 20, 1989). . . . Activated after clearing procedural waivers (September 22, 1989). . . . On inactive list (September 23, 1990).
PRO STATISTICS: 1990—Recovered one fumble.

| | | RUSHING | | | | RECEIVING | | | | KICKOFF RETURNS | | | | TOTAL | | |
Year Team	G	Att.	Yds.	Avg.	TD	No.	Yds.	Avg.	TD	No.	Yds.	Avg.	TD	TD	Pts.	F.
1989— Kansas City NFL....	14	23	121	5.3	0	34	372	10.9	1	13	257	19.8	0	1	6	1
1990— Kansas City NFL....	15	14	61	4.4	0	40	507	12.7	2	14	227	16.2	0	2	12	1
Pro totals (2 years)	29	37	182	4.9	0	74	879	11.9	3	27	484	17.9	0	3	18	2

McNEAL, TRAVIS
TE, SEAHAWKS

PERSONAL: Born January 10, 1967, at Birmingham, Ala. . . . 6-3/244. . . . Full name: Travis S. McNeal.
HIGH SCHOOL: West End (Birmingham, Ala.).
COLLEGE: Tennessee-Chattanooga.
TRANSACTIONS/CAREER NOTES: Selected by Seattle Seahawks in fourth round (101st pick overall) of 1989 NFL draft. . . . Signed by Seahawks (July 23, 1989).
PRO STATISTICS: 1989—Returned one kickoff for 17 yards. 1990—Rushed once for two yards and returned two kickoffs for 29 yards.

| | | | RECEIVING | | |
Year Team	G	No.	Yds.	Avg.	TD
1989— Seattle NFL	16	9	147	16.3	0
1990— Seattle NFL	16	10	143	14.3	0
Pro totals (2 years)	32	19	290	15.3	0

McNEIL, EMANUEL
DT, JETS

PERSONAL: Born June 9, 1967, at Richmond, Va. . . . 6-3/277.
HIGH SCHOOL: Highland Springs (Va.).
COLLEGE: Tennessee-Martin.
TRANSACTIONS/CAREER NOTES: Selected by New England Patriots in 10th round (267th pick overall) of 1989 NFL draft. . . . Signed by Patriots (May 15, 1989). . . . Released by Patriots (September 5, 1989). . . . Re-signed by Patriots to developmental squad (September 6, 1989). . . . On developmental squad (September 6-December 19, 1989). . . . Activated after clearing procedural waivers (December 21, 1989). . . . Granted unconditional free agency (February 1, 1990). . . . Signed by New York Jets (February 20, 1990). . . . On inactive list (September 9, 16, 23, 30; October 14, 28; and November 4, 1990). . . . On injured reserve with knee injury (November 6, 1990-remainder of season).
PLAYING EXPERIENCE: New England NFL, 1989; New York Jets NFL, 1990. . . . Games: 1989 (1), 1990 (2). Total: 3.

McNEIL, FREEMAN
RB, JETS

PERSONAL: Born April 22, 1959, at Jackson, Miss. . . . 5-11/208.
HIGH SCHOOL: Banning (Wilmington, Calif.).
COLLEGE: UCLA.
TRANSACTIONS/CAREER NOTES: Selected by New York Jets in first round (third pick

overall) of 1981 NFL draft.... On injured reserve with foot injury (October 10-November 14, 1981).... On injured reserve with separated shoulder (September 27-November 11, 1983).... On injured reserve with broken ribs (December 6, 1984-remainder of season).... On injured reserve with dislocated elbow (September 14-October 20, 1986).... Granted free agency (February 1, 1990).... Re-signed by Jets (June 6, 1990).

CHAMPIONSHIP GAME EXPERIENCE: Played in AFC championship game after 1982 season.

RECORDS/HONORS: Played in Pro Bowl after 1982 and 1985 seasons.... Named to play in Pro Bowl after 1984 season; replaced due to injury by Greg Bell.

PRO STATISTICS: 1983—Attempted one pass with one completion for five yards and a touchdown and recovered one fumble. 1984—Recovered one fumble.

			—— RUSHING ——				—— RECEIVING ——				— TOTAL —		
Year	Team	G	Att.	Yds.	Avg.	TD	No.	Yds.	Avg.	TD	TD	Pts.	F.
1981— N.Y. Jets NFL		11	137	623	4.6	2	18	171	9.5	1	3	18	5
1982— N.Y. Jets NFL		9	151	*786	*5.2	6	16	187	11.7	1	7	42	7
1983— N.Y. Jets NFL		9	160	654	4.1	1	21	172	8.2	3	4	24	4
1984— N.Y. Jets NFL		12	229	1070	4.7	5	25	294	11.8	1	6	36	4
1985— N.Y. Jets NFL		14	294	1331	4.5	3	38	427	11.2	2	5	30	9
1986— N.Y. Jets NFL		12	214	856	4.0	5	49	410	8.4	1	6	36	8
1987— N.Y. Jets NFL		9	121	530	4.4	0	24	262	10.9	1	1	6	1
1988— N.Y. Jets NFL		16	219	944	4.3	6	34	288	8.5	1	7	42	3
1989— N.Y. Jets NFL		11	80	352	4.4	2	31	310	10.0	1	3	18	1
1990— N.Y. Jets NFL		16	99	458	4.6	6	16	230	14.4	0	6	36	1
Pro totals (10 years)		119	1704	7604	4.5	36	272	2751	10.1	12	48	288	43

McNEIL, GERALD
WR/KR, OILERS

PERSONAL: Born March 27, 1962, at Frankfurt, West Germany.... 5-8/142.... Full name: Gerald Lynn McNeil.
HIGH SCHOOL: Killeen (Tex.).
COLLEGE: Baylor.

TRANSACTIONS/CAREER NOTES: Selected by San Antonio Gunslingers in 1984 USFL territorial draft.... Signed by Houston Gamblers (February 16, 1984).... USFL rights traded by San Antonio Gunslingers to Houston Gamblers for second-round pick in 1985 draft (February 23, 1984).... On developmental squad for three games (March 23-April 14, 1984).... Selected by Cleveland Browns in second round (44th pick overall) of 1984 NFL supplemental draft.... Traded by Houston Gamblers with defensive backs Luther Bradley, Will Lewis, Mike Mitchell and Durwood Roquemore, defensive end Pete Catan, quarterbacks Jim Kelly and Todd Dillon, defensive tackles Tony Fitzpatrick, Van Hughes and Hosea Taylor, running back Sam Harrell, linebackers Andy Hawkins and Ladell Wills, wide receivers Richard Johnson, Scott McGhee, Ricky Sanders and Clarence Verdin, guard Rich Kehr, center Billy Kidd and offensive tackles Chris Riehm and Tommy Robison to New Jersey Generals for past considerations (March 7, 1986).... Granted free agency when USFL suspended operations (August 7, 1986).... Signed by Cleveland Browns (August 12, 1986).... Granted roster exemption (August 12-August 22, 1986).... Granted unconditional free agency (February 1, 1990).... Signed by Houston Oilers (March 21, 1990).

CHAMPIONSHIP GAME EXPERIENCE: Played in AFC championship game after 1986, 1987 and 1989 seasons.

RECORDS/HONORS: Named as punt returner on THE SPORTING NEWS USFL All-Star team, 1985.... Played in Pro Bowl after 1987 season.

PRO STATISTICS: USFL: 1984—Rushed once for 11 yards and recovered two fumbles. 1985—Recovered one fumble.... NFL: 1986—Rushed once for 12 yards. 1987—Rushed once for 17 yards. 1988—Recovered one fumble. 1989—Rushed twice for 32 yards.

			—— RECEIVING ——				— PUNT RETURNS —				– KICKOFF RETURNS –				—— TOTAL——		
Year	Team	G	No.	Yds.	Avg.	TD	No.	Yds.	Avg.	TD	No.	Yds.	Avg.	TD	TD	Pts.	F.
1984— Houston USFL		15	33	501	15.2	1	31	323	10.4	*1	0	0		0	2	12	4
1985— Houston USFL		18	58	1017	17.5	6	39	*505	*13.0	*2	2	62	31.0	0	8	48	4
1986— Cleveland NFL		12	1	9	9.0	0	40	348	8.7	1	47	997	21.2	*1	2	12	3
1987— Cleveland NFL		12	8	120	15.0	2	34	386	11.4	0	11	205	18.6	0	2	12	2
1988— Cleveland NFL		16	5	74	14.8	0	38	315	8.3	0	2	38	19.0	0	0	0	3
1989— Cleveland NFL		16	10	114	11.4	0	*49	496	10.1	0	4	61	15.3	0	0	0	0
1990— Houston NFL		16	5	63	12.6	0	30	172	5.7	0	27	551	20.4	0	0	0	4
USFL totals (2 years)		33	91	1518	16.7	7	70	828	11.8	3	2	62	31.0	0	10	60	8
NFL totals (5 years)		76	29	380	13.1	2	191	1717	9.0	1	91	1852	20.4	1	4	24	12
Pro totals (7 years)		109	120	1898	15.8	9	261	2545	9.8	4	93	1914	20.6	1	14	84	20

McPHERSON, DON
QB, EAGLES

PERSONAL: Born April 2, 1965, at Brooklyn, N.Y.... 6-1/190.... Full name: Donald Glenn McPherson.... Brother of Miles McPherson, safety with San Diego Chargers, 1982-1985.
HIGH SCHOOL: Hempstead (N.Y.).

COLLEGE: Syracuse (degree in psychology, 1988).

TRANSACTIONS/CAREER NOTES: Selected by Philadelphia Eagles in sixth round (149th pick overall) of 1988 NFL draft.... Signed by Eagles (July 27, 1988).... Active for two games with Eagles in 1988; did not play.... Active for one game with Eagles in 1989; did not play.... Traded by Eagles to Houston Oilers for conditional pick in 1991 NFL draft (August 3, 1990).... Released by Oilers (September 2, 1990).... Re-signed by Oilers (September 5, 1990).... Released by Oilers (September 7, 1990).... Re-signed by Oilers (September 12, 1990).... Released by Oilers (September 15, 1990).... Re-signed by Oilers (September 20, 1990).... On inactive list (September 23 and 30, 1990).... Released by Oilers (October 2, 1990).... Signed by Philadelphia Eagles (March 5, 1991).

PLAYING EXPERIENCE: Philadelphia NFL, 1988 and 1989.... Games: none.

RECORDS/HONORS: Named as quarterback on THE SPORTING NEWS college All-America team, 1987.

MEADS, JOHNNY
LB, OILERS

PERSONAL: Born June 25, 1961, at Labadieville, La. . . . 6-2/226.
HIGH SCHOOL: Assumption (Napoleonville, La.).
COLLEGE: Nicholls State.
TRANSACTIONS/CAREER NOTES: Selected by New Orleans Breakers in third round (55th pick overall) of 1984 USFL draft. . . . Selected by Houston Oilers in third round (58th pick overall) of 1984 NFL draft. . . . Signed by Oilers (July 17, 1984). . . . On injured reserve with knee injury (October 8, 1985-remainder of season).
PLAYING EXPERIENCE: Houston NFL, 1984-1990. . . . Games: 1984 (16), 1985 (5), 1986 (16), 1987 (12), 1988 (16), 1989 (16), 1990 (16). Total: 97.
PRO STATISTICS: 1986—Recovered one fumble. 1990—Intercepted one pass for 32 yards.

MECKLENBURG, KARL
LB, BRONCOS

PERSONAL: Born September 1, 1960, at Seattle. . . . 6-3/240. . . . Full name: Karl Bernard Mecklenburg.
HIGH SCHOOL: West (Edina, Minn.).
COLLEGE: Augustana College (S.D.) and Minnesota (bachelor of science degree in biology, 1983).
TRANSACTIONS/CAREER NOTES: Selected by Chicago Blitz in 21st round (246th pick overall) of 1983 USFL draft. . . . Selected by Denver Broncos in 12th round (310th pick overall) of 1983 NFL draft. . . . Signed by Broncos (May 14, 1983). . . . On injured reserve with broken thumb (October 28-December 10, 1988).
PLAYING EXPERIENCE: Denver NFL, 1983-1990. . . . Games: 1983 (16), 1984 (16), 1985 (16), 1986 (16), 1987 (12), 1988 (9), 1989 (15), 1990 (16). Total: 116.
CHAMPIONSHIP GAME EXPERIENCE: Played in AFC championship game after 1986, 1987 and 1989 seasons. . . . Played in Super Bowl XXI after 1986 season, Super Bowl XXII after 1987 season and Super Bowl XXIV after 1989 season.
RECORDS/HONORS: Played in Pro Bowl after 1985-1987 seasons. . . . Named to play in Pro Bowl after 1989 season; replaced due to injury by Johnny Rembert. . . . Named to THE SPORTING NEWS NFL All-Pro team, 1986.
PRO STATISTICS: 1984—Intercepted two passes for 105 yards and recovered one fumble. 1985—Recovered one fumble. 1986—Recovered one fumble. 1987—Intercepted three passes for 23 yards and recovered one fumble. 1989—Recovered four fumbles for 23 yards and a touchdown. 1990—Recovered two fumbles for 24 yards and a touchdown and credited with a safety.

MEGGETT, DAVE
RB, GIANTS

PERSONAL: Born April 30, 1966, at Charleston, S.C. . . . 5-7/180. . . . Full name: David Lee Meggett.
HIGH SCHOOL: Bonds-Wilson (North Charleston, S.C.).
COLLEGE: Morgan State, then Towson State.
TRANSACTIONS/CAREER NOTES: Selected by New York Giants in fifth round (132nd pick overall) of 1989 NFL draft. . . . Signed by Giants (July 24, 1989).
CHAMPIONSHIP GAME EXPERIENCE: Played in NFC championship game after 1990 season. . . . Played in Super Bowl XXV after 1990 season.
RECORDS/HONORS: Played in Pro Bowl after 1989 season. . . . Named as punt returner to THE SPORTING NEWS NFL All-Pro team, 1990.
PRO STATISTICS: 1989—Recovered three fumbles. 1990—Recovered two fumbles.

			RUSHING				RECEIVING				PUNT RETURNS			KICKOFF RETURNS				TOTALS		
Year Team	G	Att.	Yds.	Avg.	TD	No.	Yds.	Avg.	TD	No.	Yds.	Avg.	TD	No.	Yds.	Avg.	TD	TD	Pts.	F.
1989— N.Y. Giants NFL ..	16	28	117	4.2	0	34	531	15.6	4	46	*582	12.7	*1	27	577	21.4	0	5	30	8
1990— N.Y. Giants NFL ..	16	22	164	7.5	0	39	410	10.5	1	*43	*467	10.9	*1	21	492	23.4	0	2	12	3
Pro totals (2 years)	32	50	281	5.6	0	73	941	12.9	5	89	1049	11.8	2	48	1069	22.3	0	7	42	11

MERRIWEATHER, MIKE
LB, VIKINGS

PERSONAL: Born November 26, 1960, at Albans, N.Y. . . . 6-2/222. . . . Full name: Michael Lamar Merriweather.
HIGH SCHOOL: Vallejo (Calif.).
COLLEGE: Pacific (bachelor of arts degree in history, 1982).
TRANSACTIONS/CAREER NOTES: Selected by Pittsburgh Steelers in third round (70th pick overall) of 1982 NFL draft. . . . On reserve/did not report list (August 29, 1988-entire season). . . . Traded by Steelers to Minnesota Vikings for first-round pick in 1989 NFL draft (April 23, 1989).
CHAMPIONSHIP GAME EXPERIENCE: Played in AFC championship game after 1984 season.
RECORDS/HONORS: Played in Pro Bowl after 1984-1986 seasons.
PRO STATISTICS: 1982—Returned one punt for three yards. 1983—Recovered two fumbles. 1984—Recovered one fumble. 1985—Fumbled once. 1986—Returned one kickoff for 27 yards and recovered two fumbles for 18 yards. 1987—Recovered four fumbles for four yards. 1989—Credited with a safety and recovered one fumble. 1990—Recovered four fumbles for 44 yards and a touchdown.

		INTERCEPTIONS			
Year Team	G	No.	Yds.	Avg.	TD
1982— Pittsburgh NFL	9	0	0		0
1983— Pittsburgh NFL	16	3	55	18.3	1
1984— Pittsburgh NFL	16	2	9	4.5	0
1985— Pittsburgh NFL	16	2	36	18.0	*1
1986— Pittsburgh NFL	16	2	14	7.0	0
1987— Pittsburgh NFL	12	2	26	13.0	0
1989— Minnesota NFL	15	3	29	9.7	1
1990— Minnesota NFL	16	3	108	36.0	0
Pro totals (8 years)	116	17	277	16.3	3

MERSEREAU, SCOTT
DT, JETS

PERSONAL: Born April 8, 1965, at Riverhead, N.Y. . . . 6-3/277. . . . Full name: Scott Robert Mersereau. . . . Name pronounced MER-ser-oh.
HIGH SCHOOL: Riverhead (N.Y.).
COLLEGE: Southern Connecticut State (bachelor of science degree in marketing).
TRANSACTIONS/CAREER NOTES: Selected by Los Angeles Rams in fifth round (136th pick overall) of 1987 NFL draft. . . . Signed by Rams (July 25, 1987). . . . Released by Rams (September 7, 1987). . . . Signed as replacement player by New York Jets (September 24, 1987).
PLAYING EXPERIENCE: New York Jets NFL, 1987-1990. . . . Games: 1987 (13), 1988 (16), 1989 (16), 1990 (16). Total: 61.
PRO STATISTICS: 1987—Recovered one fumble. 1988—Recovered one fumble. 1989—Intercepted one pass for four yards.

METCALF, ERIC
RB, BROWNS

PERSONAL: Born January 23, 1968, at Seattle. . . . 5-10/190. . . . Full name: Eric Quinn Metcalf. . . . Son of Terry Metcalf, running back with St. Louis Cardinals, Toronto Argonauts (CFL) and Washington Redskins (1973-1981).
HIGH SCHOOL: Bishop Dennis J. O'Connell (Arlington, Va.).
COLLEGE: Texas (degree in liberal arts, 1990).
TRANSACTIONS/CAREER NOTES: Selected by Cleveland Browns in first round (13th pick overall) of 1989 NFL draft. . . . Signed by Browns (August 20, 1989).
CHAMPIONSHIP GAME EXPERIENCE: Played in AFC championship game after 1989 season.
PRO STATISTICS: 1989—Attempted two passes with one completion for 32 yards and a touchdown. 1990—Recovered one fumble.

			RUSHING				RECEIVING				KICKOFF RETURNS				TOTAL		
Year	Team	G	Att.	Yds.	Avg.	TD	No.	Yds.	Avg.	TD	No.	Yds.	Avg.	TD	TD	Pts.	F.
1989— Cleveland NFL		16	187	633	3.4	6	54	397	7.4	4	31	718	23.2	0	10	60	5
1990— Cleveland NFL		16	80	248	3.1	1	57	452	7.9	1	*52	*1052	20.2	*2	4	24	8
Pro totals (2 years)		32	267	881	3.3	7	111	849	7.7	5	83	1770	21.3	2	14	84	13

METZELAARS, PETE
TE, BILLS

PERSONAL: Born May 24, 1960, at Three Rivers, Mich. . . . 6-7/250. . . . Full name: Peter Henry Metzelaars.
HIGH SCHOOL: Central (Portage, Mich.).
COLLEGE: Wabash, Ind. (bachelor of science degree in economics, 1982).
TRANSACTIONS/CAREER NOTES: Selected by Seattle Seahawks in third round (75th pick overall) of 1982 NFL draft. . . . On injured reserve with knee injury (October 17-December 1, 1984). . . . Traded by Seahawks to Buffalo Bills for wide receiver Byron Franklin (August 20, 1985).
CHAMPIONSHIP GAME EXPERIENCE: Played in AFC championship game after 1983, 1988 and 1990 seasons. . . . Played in Super Bowl XXV after 1990 season.
PRO STATISTICS: 1982—Recovered one fumble and fumbled twice. 1983—Returned one kickoff for no yards. 1984—Fumbled once. 1985—Recovered one fumble for two yards. 1986—Recovered one fumble in end zone for a touchdown and fumbled twice. 1987—Recovered one fumble and fumbled three times. 1988—Recovered one fumble. 1990—Fumbled once.

			RECEIVING		
Year	Team	G	No.	Yds.	Avg.	TD
1982— Seattle NFL		9	15	152	10.1	0
1983— Seattle NFL		16	7	72	10.3	1
1984— Seattle NFL		9	5	80	16.0	0
1985— Buffalo NFL		16	12	80	6.7	1
1986— Buffalo NFL		16	49	485	9.9	3
1987— Buffalo NFL		12	28	290	10.4	0
1988— Buffalo NFL		16	33	438	13.3	1
1989— Buffalo NFL		16	18	179	9.9	2
1990— Buffalo NFL		16	10	60	6.0	1
Pro totals (9 years)		126	177	1836	10.4	9

MIANO, RICH
S, EAGLES

PERSONAL: Born September 3, 1962, at Newton, Mass. . . . 6-1/200. . . . Full name: Richard James Miano. . . . Name pronounced mee-ON-oh.
HIGH SCHOOL: Kaiser (Honolulu).
COLLEGE: Hawaii.
TRANSACTIONS/CAREER NOTES: Selected by Denver Gold in ninth round (132nd pick overall) of 1985 USFL draft. . . . Selected by New York Jets in sixth round (166th pick overall) of 1985 NFL draft. . . . Signed by Jets (July 16, 1985). . . . Released by Jets (September 2, 1985). . . . Re-signed by Jets (September 3, 1985). . . . On injured reserve with knee injury (September 19, 1989-remainder of season). . . . On reserve/physically unable to perform list (August 27, 1990-November 14, 1990). . . . Released by Jets (November 14, 1990). . . . Signed by Philadelphia Eagles (May 22, 1991).
PRO STATISTICS: 1987—Returned blocked field goal attempt 67 yards for a touchdown.

			INTERCEPTIONS		
Year	Team	G	No.	Yds.	Avg.	TD
1985— N.Y. Jets NFL		16	2	9	4.5	0
1986— N.Y. Jets NFL		14	0	0		0
1987— N.Y. Jets NFL		12	3	24	8.0	0
1988— N.Y. Jets NFL		16	2	0	.0	0
1989— N.Y. Jets NFL		2	0	0		0
Pro totals (5 years)		60	7	33	4.7	0

MIDDLETON, RON
TE, REDSKINS

PERSONAL: Born July 17, 1965, at Atmore, Ala.... 6-2/255.... Full name: Ronald Allen Middleton.
HIGH SCHOOL: Escambia County (Atmore, Ala.).
COLLEGE: Auburn.
TRANSACTIONS/CAREER NOTES: Selected by Birmingham Stallions in 1986 USFL territorial draft.... Signed as free agent by Atlanta Falcons (May 3, 1986).... Released by Falcons (August 30, 1988).... Signed as free agent by Washington Redskins (September 13, 1988).... Released by Redskins (October 3, 1988).... Re-signed by Redskins (November 14, 1988).... Released by Redskins (December 12, 1988).... Re-signed by Redskins (December 13, 1988).... Released by Redskins (August 29, 1989).... Awarded on waivers to Tampa Bay Buccaneers (August 30, 1989).... Released by Buccaneers (September 4, 1989).... Re-signed by Buccaneers (September 5, 1989).... Released by Buccaneers (September 12, 1989).... Inactive for one game with Buccaneers in 1989.... Signed as free agent by Cleveland Browns (October 11, 1989).... Released by Browns (November 21, 1989).... Re-signed by Browns (November 27, 1989).... Granted unconditional free agency (February 1, 1990).... Signed by Washington Redskins (March 15, 1990).
CHAMPIONSHIP GAME EXPERIENCE: Played in AFC championship game after 1989 season.
PRO STATISTICS: 1990—Returned one kickoff for seven yards.

			RECEIVING		
Year Team	G	No.	Yds.	Avg.	TD
1986— Atlanta NFL	16	6	31	5.2	0
1987— Atlanta NFL	12	1	1	1.0	0
1988— Washington NFL........	2	0	0		0
1989— T.B. (0)-Cle. (9) NFL....	9	1	5	5.0	1
1990— Washington NFL........	16	0	0		0
Pro totals (5 years)	55	8	37	4.6	1

MILES, EDDIE
LB, FALCONS

PERSONAL: Born September 13, 1968, at Miami.... 6-1/233.
HIGH SCHOOL: Miami Springs (Miami).
COLLEGE: Minnesota.
TRANSACTIONS/CAREER NOTES: Selected by Pittsburgh Steelers in 10th round (266th pick overall) of 1990 NFL draft.... Signed by Steelers (July 10, 1990).... Released by Steelers (September 4, 1990).... Signed by Steelers to practice squad (October 1, 1990).... Activated (October 5, 1990).... Released by Steelers (October 12, 1990).... Re-signed by Steelers to practice squad (October 15, 1990).... On practice squad (October 15, 1990-remainder of season).... Signed by Atlanta Falcons (March 5, 1991).
PLAYING EXPERIENCE: Pittsburgh NFL, 1990.... Games: 1990 (1).

MILINICHIK, JOE
G, RAMS

PERSONAL: Born March 30, 1963, at Allentown, Pa.... 6-5/275.... Full name: Joseph Michael Milinichik.... Name pronounced mil-IN-i-chik.
HIGH SCHOOL: Emmaus (Pa.).
COLLEGE: North Carolina State (bachelor of science degree in vocational industrial education, 1985).
TRANSACTIONS/CAREER NOTES: Selected by Jacksonville Bulls in 1986 USFL territorial draft.... Selected by Detroit Lions in third round (69th pick overall) of 1986 NFL draft.... Signed by Lions (July 15, 1986).... On injured reserve with dislocated elbow (September 2, 1986-entire season).... Granted unconditional free agency (February 1, 1990).... Signed by Los Angeles Rams (March 9, 1990).... On inactive list (September 9, 16, 23; October 7; November 18, 25; and December 9 and 17, 1990).
PLAYING EXPERIENCE: Detroit NFL, 1987-1989; Los Angeles Rams NFL, 1990.... Games: 1987 (11), 1988 (15), 1989 (15), 1990 (8). Total: 49.

MILLARD, BRYAN
G, SEAHAWKS

PERSONAL: Born December 2, 1960, at Sioux City, Ia.... 6-5/277.... Name pronounced MILL-ard.
HIGH SCHOOL: Dumas (Tex.).
COLLEGE: Texas.
TRANSACTIONS/CAREER NOTES: Selected by New Jersey Generals in 12th round (142nd pick overall) of 1983 USFL draft.... Signed by Generals (February 4, 1983).... On injured reserve with knee injury (April 18, 1983-remainder of season).... On developmental squad for one game (May 6-May 11, 1984).... Granted free agency (July 15, 1984).... Signed as free agent by Seattle Seahawks (July 31, 1984).... On injured reserve with knee injury (December 8, 1984-remainder of season).
PLAYING EXPERIENCE: New Jersey USFL, 1983 and 1984; Seattle NFL, 1984-1990.... Games: 1983 (7), 1984 USFL (17), 1984 NFL (14), 1985 (16), 1986 (16), 1987 (12), 1988 (15), 1989 (16), 1990 (16). Total USFL: 24. Total NFL: 105. Total Pro: 129.
PRO STATISTICS: 1986—Recovered one fumble. 1987—Caught one pass for minus five yards and recovered two fumbles. 1989—Recovered one fumble for four yards. 1990—Recovered one fumble.

MILLARD, KEITH
DT, VIKINGS

PERSONAL: Born March 18, 1962, at Pleasanton, Calif.... 6-5/263.... Name pronounced mill-ARD.
HIGH SCHOOL: Foothill (Pleasanton, Calif.).
COLLEGE: Washington State.
TRANSACTIONS/CAREER NOTES: Selected by Arizona Wranglers in first round (fifth pick overall) of 1984 USFL draft.... Selected by Minnesota Vikings in first round (13th pick overall) of 1984 NFL draft.... USFL rights traded by Arizona Wranglers to Jacksonville Bulls for first-round pick in 1985 USFL draft (July 5, 1984).... Signed by Bulls (July 5, 1984).... On developmental squad for one game with Bulls (March 2-March 9, 1985).... On suspended list (May 23-May 30, 1985).... Released by Bulls (August 5, 1985).... Signed by Minnesota Vikings (August 6, 1985).... On injured reserve with knee injury (October 2, 1990-remainder of season).

PLAYING EXPERIENCE: Jacksonville USFL, 1985; Minnesota NFL, 1985- 1990. . . . Games: 1985 USFL (17), 1985 NFL (16), 1986 (15), 1987 (9), 1988 (15), 1989 (16), 1990 (4). Total NFL: 75. Total Pro: 92.
CHAMPIONSHIP GAME EXPERIENCE: Played in NFC championship game after 1987 season.
RECORDS/HONORS: Played in Pro Bowl after 1988 and 1989 seasons. . . . Named to THE SPORTING NEWS NFL All-Pro team, 1988 and 1989.
PRO STATISTICS: USFL: 1985—Credited with 12 sacks for 86 ½ yards and recovered one fumble. . . . NFL: 1985—Recovered one fumble. 1986—Intercepted one pass for 17 yards and recovered one fumble for three yards. 1987—Recovered two fumbles for eight yards. 1988—Recovered two fumbles for five yards. 1989—Intercepted one pass for 48 yards and recovered one fumble for 31 yards and a touchdown.

MILLEN, HUGH
QB, PATRIOTS

PERSONAL: Born November 22, 1963, at Des Moines, Ia. . . . 6-5/216.
HIGH SCHOOL: Roosevelt (Seattle).
COLLEGE: Santa Rosa Junior College (Calif.), then Washington.
TRANSACTIONS/CAREER NOTES: Selected by Los Angeles Rams in third round (71st pick overall) of 1986 NFL draft. . . . Signed by Rams (July 17, 1986). . . . On injured reserve with broken ankle (August 19, 1986-entire season). . . . On injured reserve with knee injury (September 7-December 4, 1987). . . . Released by Rams (August 29, 1988). . . . Awarded on waivers to Atlanta Falcons (August 30, 1988). . . . Granted free agency (February 1, 1990). . . . Re-signed by Falcons (July 27, 1990). . . . On inactive list (September 9, 1990). . . . Released by Falcons (September 11, 1990). . . . Re-signed by Falcons (October 17, 1990). . . . On inactive list (November 4, 11, 25; and December 2, 1990). . . . Granted unconditional free agency (February 1, 1991). . . . Signed by New England Patriots (April 1, 1991).
PRO STATISTICS: Passer rating points: 1987 (79.2), 1988 (49.8), 1989 (79.8), 1990 (80.6). Career: 73.8. . . . 1989—Recovered one fumble and fumbled twice for minus 11 yards.

		PASSING								RUSHING				TOTAL		
Year Team	G	Att.	Cmp.	Pct.	Yds.	TD	Int.	Avg.	Att.	Yds.	Avg.	TD	TD	Pts.	F.
1987— L.A. Rams NFL	1	1	1	100.0	0	0	0	.00	0	0		0	0	0	0
1988— Atlanta NFL	3	31	17	54.8	215	0	2	6.94	1	7	7.0	0	0	0	1
1989— Atlanta NFL	5	50	31	62.0	432	1	2	8.64	1	0	.0	0	0	0	2
1990— Atlanta NFL	3	63	34	54.0	427	1	0	6.78	7	-12	-1.7	0	0	0	3
Pro totals (4 years)	12	145	83	57.2	1074	2	4	7.41	9	-5	-.6	0	0	0	6

MILLEN, MATT
LB, REDSKINS

PERSONAL: Born March 12, 1958, at Hokendauqua, Pa. . . . 6-2/245. . . . Full name: Matt G. Millen. . . . Nephew of Andy Tomasic, back with Pittsburgh Steelers, 1942 and 1946 and pitcher with New York Giants, 1949.
HIGH SCHOOL: Whitehall (Pa.).
COLLEGE: Penn State (bachelor of business administration degree in marketing, 1980).
TRANSACTIONS/CAREER NOTES: Selected by Oakland Raiders in second round (43rd pick overall) of 1980 NFL draft. . . . Franchise transferred to Los Angeles (May 7, 1982). . . . Granted free agency (February 1, 1988). . . . Re-signed by Raiders (August 23, 1988). . . . Released by Los Angeles Raiders (September 5, 1989). . . . Signed as free agent by San Francisco 49ers (September 15, 1989). . . . Granted unconditional free agency (February 1, 1991). . . . Signed by Washington Redskins (April 1, 1991).
CHAMPIONSHIP GAME EXPERIENCE: Played in AFC championship game after 1980 and 1983 seasons. . . . Played in NFC championship game after 1989 and 1990 seasons. . . . Played in Super Bowl XV after 1980 season, Super Bowl XVIII after 1983 season and Super Bowl XXIV after 1989 season.
RECORDS/HONORS: Played in Pro Bowl after 1988 season.
PRO STATISTICS: 1981—Recovered one fumble. 1982—Returned one kickoff for 13 yards and recovered two fumbles. 1983—Returned two kickoffs for 19 yards. 1986—Returned three kickoffs for 40 yards. 1987—Returned one kickoff for no yards and fumbled once. 1988—Recovered one fumble. 1989—Recovered three fumbles for two yards. 1990—Recovered one fumble.

		INTERCEPTIONS			
Year Team	G	No.	Yds.	Avg.	TD
1980— Oakland NFL	16	2	17	8.5	0
1981— Oakland NFL	16	0	0		0
1982— L.A. Raiders NFL	9	3	77	25.7	0
1983— L.A. Raiders NFL	16	1	14	14.0	0
1984— L.A. Raiders NFL	16	0	0		0
1985— L.A. Raiders NFL	16	0	0		0
1986— L.A. Raiders NFL	16	0	0		0
1987— L.A. Raiders NFL	12	1	6	6.0	0
1988— L.A. Raiders NFL	16	0	0		0
1989— San Francisco NFL	15	1	10	10.0	0
1990— San Francisco NFL	16	1	8	8.0	0
Pro totals (11 years)	164	9	132	14.7	0

MILLER, ANTHONY
WR, CHARGERS

PERSONAL: Born April 15, 1965, at Los Angeles. . . . 5-11/185. . . . Full name: Lawrence Anthony Miller.
HIGH SCHOOL: John Muir (Pasadena, Calif.).
COLLEGE: San Diego State, then Pasadena City College (Calif.), then Tennessee.
TRANSACTIONS/CAREER NOTES: Selected by San Diego Chargers in first round (15th pick overall) of 1988 NFL draft. . . . Signed by Chargers (July 12, 1988).
RECORDS/HONORS: Played in Pro Bowl after 1989 and 1990 seasons.
PRO STATISTICS: 1990—Recovered one fumble.

Year	Team	G	Att.	Yds.	Avg.	TD	No.	Yds.	Avg.	TD	No.	Yds.	Avg.	TD	TD	Pts.	F.
			RUSHING				RECEIVING				KICKOFF RETURNS				TOTAL		
1988— San Diego NFL		16	7	45	6.4	0	36	526	14.6	3	25	648	25.9	*1	4	24	1
1989— San Diego NFL		16	4	21	5.3	0	75	1252	16.7	10	21	533	25.4	*1	11	66	1
1990— San Diego NFL		16	3	13	4.3	0	63	933	14.8	7	1	13	13.0	0	7	42	2
Pro totals (3 years)		48	14	79	5.6	0	174	2711	15.6	20	47	1194	25.4	2	22	132	4

MILLER, BRETT
OT, JETS

PERSONAL: Born October 2, 1958, at Lynwood, Calif.... 6-7/286.
HIGH SCHOOL: Glendale (Calif.).
COLLEGE: Glendale Community College (Calif.), then Iowa.
TRANSACTIONS/CAREER NOTES: Selected by Washington Federals in fifth round (57th pick overall) of 1983 USFL draft.... Selected by Atlanta Falcons in fifth round (129th pick overall) of 1983 NFL draft.... Signed by Falcons (May 25, 1983).... On injured reserve with sprained ankle (November 12-December 10, 1985).... On injured reserve with knee injury (October 16-November 15, 1986).... On injured reserve with knee injury (November 28, 1986-remainder of season).... On injured reserve with injured arch in foot (September 8-October 31, 1987).... Granted unconditional free agency (February 1, 1989).... Signed by San Diego Chargers (March 13, 1989).... Granted unconditional free agency (February 1, 1990).... Signed by New York Jets (February 23, 1990).
PLAYING EXPERIENCE: Atlanta NFL, 1983-1988; San Diego NFL, 1989; New York Jets NFL, 1990.... Games: 1983 (16), 1984 (15), 1985 (12), 1986 (8), 1987 (2), 1988 (15), 1989 (14), 1990 (16). Total: 98.
PRO STATISTICS: 1986—Recovered one fumble.

MILLER, CHRIS
QB, FALCONS

PERSONAL: Born August 9, 1965, at Pomona, Calif.... 6-2/205.... Full name: Christopher James Miller.
HIGH SCHOOL: Sheldon (Eugene, Ore.).
COLLEGE: Oregon.
TRANSACTIONS/CAREER NOTES: Selected by Atlanta Falcons in first round (13th pick overall) of 1987 NFL draft.... Signed by Falcons (October 30, 1987).... Granted roster exemption (October 30-November 9, 1987).... On injured reserve with broken collarbone (December 4, 1990-remainder of season).
PRO STATISTICS: Passer rating points: 1987 (26.4), 1988 (67.3), 1989 (76.1), 1990 (78.7). Career: 71.1.... 1988—Recovered one fumble. 1989—Successful on only field goal attempt, recovered five fumbles and fumbled 13 times for minus three yards. 1990—Recovered four fumbles and fumbled 11 times for minus nine yards.

Year	Team	G	Att.	Cmp.	Pct.	Yds.	TD	Int.	Avg.	Att.	Yds.	Avg.	TD	TD	Pts.	F.
			PASSING							RUSHING				TOTAL		
1987— Atlanta NFL		3	92	39	42.4	552	1	9	6.00	4	21	5.3	0	0	0	0
1988— Atlanta NFL		13	351	184	52.4	2133	11	12	6.08	31	138	4.5	1	1	6	2
1989— Atlanta NFL		15	526	280	53.2	3459	16	10	6.58	10	20	2.0	0	0	0	13
1990— Atlanta NFL		12	388	222	57.2	2735	17	14	7.05	26	99	3.8	1	1	6	11
Pro totals (4 years)		43	1357	725	53.4	8879	45	45	6.54	71	278	3.9	2	2	12	26

MILLER, DONALD
LB, SEAHAWKS

PERSONAL: Born April 6, 1964, at Chicago.... 6-2/223.
HIGH SCHOOL: Fenger of Chicago (Chicago).
COLLEGE: College of Eastern Utah, then Utah State, then Idaho State (degree in sociology).
TRANSACTIONS/CAREER NOTES: Signed as free agent by Seattle Seahawks (May 27, 1990).... Released by Seahawks (August 27, 1990).... Re-signed by Seahawks (November 14, 1990).... Released by Seahawks (November 19, 1990).... Re-signed by Seahawks (December 5, 1990).
PLAYING EXPERIENCE: Seattle NFL, 1990.... Games: 1990 (7).

MILLER, LES
DE, SAINTS

PERSONAL: Born March 1, 1965, at Arkansas City, Kan.... 6-7/285.... Full name: Les P. Miller.
HIGH SCHOOL: Arkansas City (Kan.).
COLLEGE: Fort Hays State (Kan.).
TRANSACTIONS/CAREER NOTES: Signed as free agent by New Orleans Saints (May 11, 1987).... Released by Saints (September 7, 1987).... Signed as free agent replacement player by San Diego Chargers (September 24, 1987).... On injured reserve with back injury (December 22, 1990-remainder of season).... Granted unconditional free agency (February 1, 1991).... Signed by New Orleans Saints (April 1, 1991).
PLAYING EXPERIENCE: San Diego NFL, 1987-1990.... Games: 1987 (9), 1988 (13), 1989 (14), 1990 (14). Total: 50.
RECORDS/HONORS: Tied NFL record for most touchdowns scored by fumble recovery, season (2), 1990; most touchdowns scored by recovery of opponents' fumbles, season (2), 1990; most touchdowns scored by recovery of opponents' fumbles, career (3).
PRO STATISTICS: 1987—Recovered two fumbles (including one in end zone for a touchdown). 1989—Recovered one fumble. 1990—Recovered three fumbles for one yard (including two in end zone for two touchdowns).

MILLING, JAMES
WR, GIANTS

PERSONAL: Born February 14, 1965, at Winnsboro, S.C.... 5-9/156.... Full name: James Thomas Milling Jr.
HIGH SCHOOL: Potomac (Oxon Hill, Md.).
COLLEGE: Maryland.
TRANSACTIONS/CAREER NOTES: Selected by Atlanta Falcons in 11th round (278th pick overall) of 1988 NFL draft.... Signed by Falcons (July 16, 1988).... On injured reserve with ankle injury (September 1-October 29, 1988).... Released by Falcons

(September 5, 1989).... Re-signed by Falcons (April 16, 1990).... On inactive list (December 16, 1990).... On injured reserve with ankle injury (December 19, 1990-remainder of season).... Granted unconditional free agency (February 1, 1991). ... Signed by New York Giants (April 1, 1991).

			RECEIVING		
Year Team	G	No.	Yds.	Avg.	TD
1988— Atlanta NFL	6	5	66	13.2	0
1990— Atlanta NFL	13	18	161	8.9	1
Pro totals (2 years)	19	23	227	9.9	1

MILLS, JEFF
LB, BRONCOS

PERSONAL: Born October 8, 1968, at Montclair, N.J.... 6-3/238.... Full name: Jeff Jonathan Mills. **HIGH SCHOOL:** Montclair (N.J.). **COLLEGE:** Nebraska.
TRANSACTIONS/CAREER NOTES: Selected by San Diego Chargers in third round (57th pick overall) of 1990 NFL draft.... Signed by Chargers (June 28, 1990).... On injured reserve with hamstring injury (October 27-November 28, 1990).... On reserve/suspended list (November 19-November 28, 1990).... Released by Chargers (December 20, 1990). ... Awarded on waivers to Denver Broncos (December 21, 1990).
PLAYING EXPERIENCE: San Diego (5)-Denver (2) NFL, 1990.... Games: 1990 (7).

MILLS, SAM
LB, SAINTS

PERSONAL: Born June 3, 1959, at Neptune, N.J.... 5-9/225.... Full name: Samuel Davis Mills Jr. **HIGH SCHOOL:** Long Branch (N.J.). **COLLEGE:** Montclair State (N.J.).
TRANSACTIONS/CAREER NOTES: Signed as free agent by Cleveland Browns (May 3, 1981).... Released by Browns (August 24, 1981).... Signed as free agent by Toronto Argonauts of CFL (March, 1982).... Released by Argonauts (June 30, 1982).... Signed by Philadelphia Stars of USFL (October 21, 1982).... Stars franchise transferred to Baltimore (November 1, 1984).... Granted free agency (August 1, 1985).... Re-signed by Stars (August 7, 1985).... Granted free agency when USFL suspended operations (August 7, 1986).... Signed as free agent by New Orleans Saints (August 12, 1986).... Granted roster exemption (August 12-August 22, 1986).
PLAYING EXPERIENCE: Philadelphia USFL, 1983 and 1984; Baltimore USFL, 1985; New Orleans NFL, 1986-1990.... Games: 1983 (18), 1984 (18), 1985 (18), 1986 (16), 1987 (12), 1988 (16), 1989 (16), 1990 (16). Total USFL: 54. Total NFL: 76. Total Pro: 130.
CHAMPIONSHIP GAME EXPERIENCE: Played in USFL championship game after 1983-1985 seasons.
RECORDS/HONORS: Named as inside linebacker on THE SPORTING NEWS USFL All-Star Team, 1983 and 1985.... Played in Pro Bowl after 1987 and 1988 seasons.
PRO STATISTICS: USFL: 1983—Intercepted three passes for 13 yards, credited with 3½ sacks for 37 yards and recovered five fumbles for eight yards. 1984—Intercepted three passes for 24 yards, credited with five sacks for 39 yards and recovered three fumbles for two yards. 1985—Intercepted three passes for 32 yards and a touchdown, credited with 5½ sacks for 41 yards and recovered two fumbles.... NFL: 1986—Recovered one fumble. 1987—Recovered three fumbles. 1988—Recovered four fumbles. 1989—Recovered one fumble. 1990—Recovered one fumble.

MINNIFIELD, FRANK
CB, BROWNS

PERSONAL: Born January 1, 1960, at Lexington, Ky.... 5-9/180.... Full name: Franky LyDale Minnifield. ... Cousin of Dirk Minniefield, guard with Cleveland Cavaliers, Houston Rockets, Golden State Warriors and Boston Celtics, 1985-86 through 1987-88.
HIGH SCHOOL: Henry Clay (Lexington, Ky.).
COLLEGE: Louisville.
TRANSACTIONS/CAREER NOTES: Selected by Chicago Blitz in third round (30th pick overall) of 1983 USFL draft.... Signed by Blitz (January 28, 1983).... On injured reserve with knee injury (March 8, 1983-remainder of season).... Franchise transferred to Arizona (September 30, 1983).... On developmental squad (March 4-March 22 and April 27-May 7, 1984).... Signed by Cleveland Browns (May 20, 1984).... Released by Arizona Wranglers (August 23, 1984).... Cleveland Browns contract approved by NFL (August 25, 1984).... Granted roster exemption (August 25-August 31, 1984).... Granted free agency (February 1, 1990).... Re-signed by Browns (October 1, 1990).... Activated (October 7, 1990).... On inactive list (December 2, 1990).
CHAMPIONSHIP GAME EXPERIENCE: Played in USFL championship game after 1984 season.... Played in AFC championship game after 1986, 1987 and 1989 seasons.
RECORDS/HONORS: Played in Pro Bowl after 1986-1989 seasons.... Named to THE SPORTING NEWS NFL All-Pro team, 1987 and 1988.
PRO STATISTICS: USFL: 1984—Recovered two fumbles for minus six yards.... NFL: 1984—Recovered two fumbles for 10 yards. 1985—Recovered one fumble for six yards. 1986—Recovered blocked punt in end zone for a touchdown and recovered two fumbles. 1988—Returned blocked punt 11 yards for a touchdown. 1989—Recovered one fumble.

			INTERCEPTIONS		
Year Team	G	No.	Yds.	Avg.	TD
1983— Chicago USFL	1	0	0		0
1984— Arizona USFL	15	4	74	18.5	1
1984— Cleveland NFL	15	1	26	26.0	0
1985— Cleveland NFL	16	1	3	3.0	0
1986— Cleveland NFL	15	3	20	6.7	0
1987— Cleveland NFL	12	4	24	6.0	0
1988— Cleveland NFL	15	4	16	4.0	0

Year	Team	G	No.	Yds.	Avg.	TD
					INTERCEPTIONS	
1989 — Cleveland NFL		16	3	29	9.7	0
1990 — Cleveland NFL		9	2	0	.0	0
USFL totals (2 years)		16	4	74	18.5	1
NFL totals (7 years)		98	18	118	10.7	0
Pro totals (9 years)		114	22	192	8.7	1

MITCHELL, BRIAN
RB, REDSKINS

PERSONAL: Born August 18, 1968, at Fort Polk, La. . . . 5-10/195. . . . Full name: Brian Keith Mitchell.
HIGH SCHOOL: Plaquemine (La.).
COLLEGE: Southwestern Louisiana.
TRANSACTIONS/CAREER NOTES: Selected by Washington Redskins in fifth round (130th pick overall) of 1990 NFL draft. . . . Signed by Redskins (July 22, 1990).
PRO STATISTICS: 1990—Attempted six passes with three completions for 40 yards.

			RUSHING				RECEIVING				PUNT RETURNS				KICKOFF RETURNS				TOTALS		
Year	Team	G	Att.	Yds.	Avg.	TD	No.	Yds.	Avg.	TD	No.	Yds.	Avg.	TD	No.	Yds.	Avg.	TD	TD	Pts.	F.
1990 — Washington NFL.		15	15	81	5.4	1	2	5	2.5	0	12	107	8.9	0	18	365	20.3	0	1	6	2
Pro totals (1 year)		15	15	81	5.4	1	2	5	2.5	0	12	107	8.9	0	18	365	20.3	0	1	6	2

MITCHELL, ROLAND
CB, PACKERS

PERSONAL: Born March 15, 1964, at Columbus, Tex. . . . 5-11/198. . . . Full name: Roland Earl Mitchell.
HIGH SCHOOL: Bay City (Tex.).
COLLEGE: Texas Tech.
TRANSACTIONS/CAREER NOTES: Selected by Buffalo Bills in second round (33rd pick overall) of 1987 NFL draft. . . . Signed by Bills (July 24, 1987). . . . Traded by Bills with sixth-round pick in 1989 draft to Phoenix Cardinals for safety Leonard Smith (September 21, 1988). . . . Released by Cardinals (September 4, 1989). . . . Re-signed by Cardinals (September 21, 1988). . . . Released by Cardinals (September 4, 1989). . . . Re-signed by Cardinals (September 5, 1989). . . . Released by Cardinals (September 27, 1989). . . . Signed as free agent by Atlanta Falcons (March 6, 1990). . . . On injured reserve (December 15, 1990-remainder of season). . . . Granted unconditional free agency (February 1, 1991). . . . Signed by Green Bay Packers (March 25, 1991).
PLAYING EXPERIENCE: Buffalo NFL, 1987; Buffalo (3)-Phoenix (11) NFL, 1988; Phoenix NFL, 1989; Atlanta NFL, 1990. . . . Games: 1987 (11), 1988 (14), 1989 (3), 1990 (13). Total: 41.
PRO STATISTICS: 1988—Intercepted one pass for no yards. 1990—Intercepted two passes for 16 yards, returned one punt for no yards, recovered two fumbles and fumbled once.

MITCHELL, SCOTT
QB, DOLPHINS

PERSONAL: Born January 2, 1968, at Salt Lake City. . . . 6-6/236.
HIGH SCHOOL: Springville (Utah).
COLLEGE: Utah.
TRANSACTIONS/CAREER NOTES: Selected by Miami Dolphins in fourth round (93rd pick overall) of 1990 NFL draft. . . . Signed by Dolphins (July 20, 1990). . . . On inactive list for all 16 games, 1990.
PLAYING EXPERIENCE: Miami NFL, 1990. . . . Games: none.

MITCHELL, STUMP
RB, CHIEFS

PERSONAL: Born March 15, 1959, at St. Mary's, Ga. . . . 5-9/200. . . . Full name: Lyvonia Albert Mitchell.
HIGH SCHOOL: Camden County (St. Mary's, Ga.).
COLLEGE: The Citadel.
TRANSACTIONS/CAREER NOTES: Selected by St. Louis Cardinals in ninth round (226th pick overall) of 1981 NFL draft. . . . Franchise transferred to Phoenix (March 15, 1988). . . . On injured reserve with knee injury (September 29, 1989-remainder of season). . . . Released by Cardinals (August 7, 1990). . . . Signed by Kansas City Chiefs (April 4, 1991).
RECORDS/HONORS: Established NFL record for most yards, combined kick returns, season (1,737), 1981; most kickoff returns, rookie season (55), 1981; most combined kick returns, game (13), against Atlanta Falcons (October 10, 1981).
PRO STATISTICS: 1982—Recovered one fumble. 1983—Recovered one fumble. 1984—Attempted one pass with one completion for 20 yards and recovered two fumbles. 1985—Attempted two passes with one completion for 31 yards and recovered two fumbles. 1986—Attempted three passes with one completion for 15 yards and a touchdown and recovered one fumble. 1987—Attempted three passes with one completion for 17 yards and recovered one fumble. 1988—Recovered three fumbles for minus three yards.

			RUSHING				RECEIVING				PUNT RETURNS				KICKOFF RETURNS				TOTALS		
Year	Team	G	Att.	Yds.	Avg.	TD	No.	Yds.	Avg.	TD	No.	Yds.	Avg.	TD	No.	Yds.	Avg.	TD	TD	Pts.	F.
1981 — St. Louis NFL		16	31	175	5.6	0	6	35	5.8	1	42	445	10.6	1	55	*1292	23.5	0	2	12	3
1982 — St. Louis NFL		9	39	189	4.8	1	11	149	13.5	0	27	165	6.1	0	16	364	22.8	0	1	6	3
1983 — St. Louis NFL		15	68	373	5.5	3	7	54	7.7	0	38	337	8.9	0	36	778	21.6	0	3	18	5
1984 — St. Louis NFL		16	81	434	5.4	9	26	318	12.2	2	38	333	8.8	0	35	804	23.0	0	11	66	6
1985 — St. Louis NFL		16	183	1006	*5.5	7	47	502	10.7	3	11	97	8.8	0	19	345	18.2	0	10	60	6
1986 — St. Louis NFL		15	174	800	4.6	5	41	276	6.7	0	0	0		0	6	203	33.8	0	5	30	4
1987 — St. Louis NFL		12	203	781	3.9	3	45	397	8.8	2	0	0		0	0	0		0	5	30	3
1988 — Phoenix NFL		14	164	726	4.4	4	25	214	8.6	1	0	0		0	10	221	22.1	0	5	30	6
1989 — Phoenix NFL		3	43	165	3.8	0	1	10	10.0	0	0	0		0	0	0		0	0	0	0
Pro totals (9 years)		116	986	4649	4.7	32	209	1955	9.4	9	156	1377	8.8	1	177	4007	22.6	0	42	252	36

MITZ, ALONZO

DE, 49ERS

PERSONAL: Born June 5, 1963, at Henderson, N.C. . . . 6-4/278. . . . Full name: Alanza Loqwone Mitz.
HIGH SCHOOL: Central (Fort Pierce, Fla.).
COLLEGE: Florida.
TRANSACTIONS/CAREER NOTES: Selected by Tampa Bay Bandits in 1986 USFL territorial draft. . . . Selected by Seattle Seahawks in eighth round (211th pick overall) of 1986 NFL draft. . . . Signed by Seahawks (June 15, 1986). . . . On injured reserve with shoulder injury (September 1-November 14, 1986). . . . On injured reserve with elbow injury (September 7-October 24, 1987). . . . Released by Seahawks (December 4, 1989). . . . Signed as free agent by Washington Redskins (April 4, 1990). . . . Released by Redskins (September 3, 1990). . . . Signed by San Francisco 49ers (April 8, 1991).
PLAYING EXPERIENCE: Seattle NFL, 1986-1989. . . . Games: 1986 (6), 1987 (6), 1988 (16), 1989 (12). Total: 40.

MOBLEY, ORSON

TE, COLTS

PERSONAL: Born March 4, 1963, at Brookeville, Fla. . . . 6-5/259. . . . Full name: Orson Odell Mobley.
HIGH SCHOOL: Palmetto (Miami).
COLLEGE: Florida State, then Salem College (W.Va.).
TRANSACTIONS/CAREER NOTES: Selected by Denver Broncos in sixth round (151st pick overall) of 1986 NFL draft. . . . Signed by Broncos (July 17, 1986). . . . On reserve/non-football injury list with alcohol problem (August 29-September 26, 1989). . . . Reinstated and granted roster exemption (September 27-October 2, 1989). . . . On inactive list (November 22; and December 2 and 9, 1990). . . . Released by Broncos (December 14, 1990). . . . Awarded on waivers to Indianapolis Colts (December 17, 1990). . . . Granted unconditional free agency (February 1, 1991). . . . Re-signed by Colts (April 27, 1991).
CHAMPIONSHIP GAME EXPERIENCE: Played in AFC championship game after 1986, 1987 and 1989 seasons. . . . Played in Super Bowl XXI after 1986 season, Super Bowl XXII after 1987 season and Super Bowl XXIV after 1989 season.
PRO STATISTICS: 1986—Rushed once for minus one yard and fumbled once. 1987—Fumbled once. 1988—Recovered one fumble and fumbled once. 1990—Returned one kickoff for nine yards, recovered one fumble and fumbled once.

| | | —— RECEIVING —— | | | |
Year	Team	G	No.	Yds.	Avg.	TD
1986— Denver NFL		14	22	332	15.1	1
1987— Denver NFL		10	16	228	14.3	1
1988— Denver NFL		16	21	218	10.4	2
1989— Denver NFL		12	17	200	11.8	0
1990— Denver NFL		9	8	41	5.1	0
Pro totals (5 years)		61	84	1019	12.1	4

MOHR, CHRIS

P, BILLS

PERSONAL: Born May 11, 1966, at Atlanta. . . . 6-5/215. . . . Full name: Christopher Mohr. . . . Name pronounced MORE.
HIGH SCHOOL: Briarwood Academy (Thomson, Ga.).
COLLEGE: Alabama.
TRANSACTIONS/CAREER NOTES: Selected by Tampa Bay Buccaneers in sixth round (146th pick overall) of 1989 NFL draft. . . . Signed by Buccaneers (July 15, 1989). . . . Released by Buccaneers (September 2, 1990). . . . Signed by WLAF (January 31, 1991). . . . Selected by Montreal Machine in first round (eighth punter) of 1991 WLAF positional draft. . . . Signed by Buffalo Bills (June 12, 1991).
PRO STATISTICS: NFL: 1989—Scored an extra point. . . . WLAF: 1991—Attempted one pass with one interception and rushed three times for minus four yards.

| | | — PUNTING— | | | |
Year	Team	G	No.	Avg.	Blk.
1989— Tampa Bay NFL		16	84	39.4	2
1991— Montreal WLAF		10	57	42.7	2
NFL totals (1 year)		16	84	39.4	2
WLAF totals (1 year)		10	57	42.7	2
Pro totals (2 years)		26	141	41.1	4

MOJSIEJENKO, RALF

P, 49ERS

PERSONAL: Born January 28, 1963, at Salzgitter Lebenstadt, West Germany. . . . 6-3/212. . . . Name pronounced mose-YEN-ko.
HIGH SCHOOL: Bridgman (Mich.).
COLLEGE: Michigan State.
TRANSACTIONS/CAREER NOTES: Selected by Jacksonville Bulls in ninth round (118th pick overall) of 1985 USFL draft. . . . Selected by San Diego Chargers in fourth round (96th pick overall) of 1985 NFL draft. . . . Signed by Chargers (July 23, 1985). . . . Traded by Chargers to Washington Redskins for seventh-round pick in 1990 NFL draft (August 30, 1989). . . . Released by Redskins (December 4, 1990). . . . Signed by San Francisco 49ers (May 3, 1991).
RECORDS/HONORS: Named as punter on THE SPORTING NEWS college All-America team, 1983. . . . Played in Pro Bowl after 1987 season.
PRO STATISTICS: 1985—Rushed once for no yards and fumbled once for minus 13 yards. 1989—Recovered one fumble. 1990—Rushed once for no yards.

| | | — PUNTING— | | | |
Year	Team	G	No.	Avg.	Blk.
1985— San Diego NFL		16	68	42.4	0
1986— San Diego NFL		16	72	42.0	2
1987— San Diego NFL		12	67	42.9	0
1988— San Diego NFL		16	85	44.1	1
1989— Washington NFL		16	62	43.0	1
1990— Washington NFL		12	43	39.2	1
Pro totals (6 years)		88	397	42.3	5

MONGER, MATT
LB, BILLS

PERSONAL: Born November 15, 1961, at Denver. . . . 6-1/235. . . . Full name: Matthew L. Monger.
HIGH SCHOOL: Miami (Okla.).
COLLEGE: Oklahoma State (bachelor of science degree in marketing, 1985).
TRANSACTIONS/CAREER NOTES: Selected by New York Jets in eighth round (208th pick overall) of 1985 NFL draft. . . . Signed by Jets (July 23, 1985). . . . On injured reserve with broken arm (August 15, 1988-entire season). . . . Granted unconditional free agency (February 1, 1989). . . . Signed by Houston Oilers (March 28, 1989). . . . Released by Oilers (August 30, 1989). . . . Signed as free agent by Buffalo Bills (September 21, 1989). . . . Released by Bills (September 4, 1990). . . . Re-signed by Bills (September 26, 1990). . . . On injured reserve with back injury (November 3, 1990-January 26, 1991).
PLAYING EXPERIENCE: New York Jets NFL, 1985-1987; Buffalo NFL, 1989 and 1990. . . . Games: 1985 (15), 1986 (16), 1987 (12), 1989 (9), 1990 (4). Total: 56.
CHAMPIONSHIP GAME EXPERIENCE: Member of Buffalo Bills for Super Bowl XXV after 1990 season; inactive.
PRO STATISTICS: 1985—Recovered two fumbles. 1986—Recovered one fumble.

MONK, ART
WR, REDSKINS

PERSONAL: Born December 5, 1957, at White Plains, N.Y. . . . 6-3/209.
HIGH SCHOOL: White Plains (N.Y.).
COLLEGE: Syracuse.
TRANSACTIONS/CAREER NOTES: Selected by Washington Redskins in first round (18th pick overall) of 1980 NFL draft. . . . On injured reserve with broken foot (January 7, 1983-remainder of 1982 season playoffs). . . . On injured reserve with knee injury (September 2-September 30, 1983). . . . On injured reserve with knee injury (December 9, 1987-January 30, 1988).
CHAMPIONSHIP GAME EXPERIENCE: Played in NFC championship game after 1983 and 1986 seasons. . . . Played in Super Bowl XVIII after 1983 season and Super Bowl XXII after 1987 season.
RECORDS/HONORS: Established NFL record for most pass receptions, season (106), 1984. . . . Played in Pro Bowl after 1984-1986 seasons. . . . Named to THE SPORTING NEWS NFL All-Pro team, 1984 and 1985.
PRO STATISTICS: 1980—Returned one kickoff for 10 yards. 1983—Attempted one pass with one completion for 46 yards. 1986—Recovered two fumbles. 1988—Attempted one pass with no completions and recovered one fumble. 1990—Recovered one fumble.

			RUSHING				RECEIVING				TOTAL		
Year Team	G	Att.	Yds.	Avg.	TD	No.	Yds.	Avg.	TD		TD	Pts.	F.
1980— Washington NFL	16	0	0		0	58	797	13.7	3		3	18	0
1981— Washington NFL	16	1	-5	-5.0	0	56	894	16.0	6		6	36	0
1982— Washington NFL	9	7	21	3.0	0	35	447	12.8	1		1	6	3
1983— Washington NFL	12	3	-19	-6.3	0	47	746	15.9	5		5	30	0
1984— Washington NFL	16	2	18	9.0	0	*106	1372	12.9	7		7	42	1
1985— Washington NFL	15	7	51	7.3	0	91	1226	13.5	2		2	12	2
1986— Washington NFL	16	4	27	6.8	0	73	1068	14.6	4		4	24	2
1987— Washington NFL	9	6	63	10.5	0	38	483	12.7	6		6	36	0
1988— Washington NFL	16	7	46	6.6	0	72	946	13.1	5		5	30	0
1989— Washington NFL	16	3	8	2.7	0	86	1186	13.8	8		8	48	2
1990— Washington NFL	16	7	59	8.4	0	68	770	11.3	5		5	30	0
Pro totals (11 years)	157	47	269	5.7	0	730	9935	13.6	52		52	312	10

MONTANA, JOE
QB, 49ERS

PERSONAL: Born June 11, 1956, at Monongahela, Pa. . . . 6-2/195. . . . Full name: Joseph C. Montana.
HIGH SCHOOL: Ringgold (Monongahela, Pa.).
COLLEGE: Notre Dame (bachelor of business administration degree in marketing, 1978).
TRANSACTIONS/CAREER NOTES: Selected by San Francisco 49ers in third round (82nd pick overall) of 1979 NFL draft. . . . On injured reserve with back injury (September 15-November 6, 1986). . . . Crossed picket line during players' strike (October 7, 1987).
CHAMPIONSHIP GAME EXPERIENCE: Played in NFC championship game after 1981, 1983, 1984 and 1988-1990 seasons. . . . Played in Super Bowl XVI after 1981 season, Super Bowl XIX after 1984 season, Super Bowl XXIII after 1988 season and Super Bowl XXIV after 1989 season.
RECORDS/HONORS: Established NFL record for most consecutive games, 300 or more yards passing, season (5), 1982; most consecutive passes completed (22), with five against Cleveland Browns (November 29, 1987) and 17 against Green Bay Packers (December 6, 1987); highest quarterback rating, season (112.4), 1989; highest completion percentage, career (63.64); highest quarterback rating, career (93.4). Tied NFL record for most seasons, 3,000 or more yards passing (7). Led NFL quarterbacks in passing with 102.1 points in 1987 and 112.4 in 1989. . . . Played in Pro Bowl after 1981, 1983, 1984 and 1987 seasons. . . . Named to play in Pro Bowl after 1985 season; replaced due to injury by Jim McMahon. . . . Named to play in Pro Bowl after 1989 season; replaced due to injury by Mark Rypien. . . . Named to play in Pro Bowl after 1990 season; replaced due to injury by Jim Everett. . . . Named THE SPORTING NEWS Man of the Year, 1989. . . . Named THE SPORTING NEWS NFL Player of the Year, 1989. . . . Named to THE SPORTING NEWS NFL All-Pro team, 1989.
PRO STATISTICS: Passer rating points: 1979 (80.9), 1980 (87.8), 1981 (88.2), 1982 (87.9), 1983 (94.6), 1984 (102.9), 1985 (91.3), 1986 (80.7), 1987 (102.1), 1988 (87.9), 1989 (112.4), 1990 (89.0). Career: 93.4. . . . 1979—Recovered one fumble. 1980—Recovered one fumble. 1982—Recovered two fumbles and fumbled four times for minus two yards. 1984—Recovered two fumbles and fumbled four times for minus three yards. 1985—Recovered three fumbles and fumbled five times for minus 11 yards. 1987—Recovered two fumbles and fumbled three times for minus five yards. 1988—Recovered one fumble and fumbled three times for minus three yards. 1989—Recovered three fumbles and fumbled nine times for minus three yards.

				PASSING					RUSHING				TOTAL		
Year Team	G	Att.	Cmp.	Pct.	Yds.	TD	Int.	Avg.	Att.	Yds.	Avg.	TD	TD	Pts.	F.
1979— San Francisco NFL....	16	23	13	56.5	96	1	0	4.17	3	22	7.3	0	0	0	1
1980— San Francisco NFL....	15	273	176	*64.5	1795	15	9	6.58	32	77	2.4	2	2	12	4
1981— San Francisco NFL....	16	488	311	*63.7	3565	19	12	7.31	25	95	3.8	2	2	12	2

			PASSING						RUSHING				TOTAL		
Year Team	G	Att.	Cmp.	Pct.	Yds.	TD	Int.	Avg.	Att.	Yds.	Avg.	TD	TD	Pts.	F.
1982— San Francisco NFL....	9	*346	213	61.6	2613	*17	11	7.55	30	118	3.9	1	1	6	4
1983— San Francisco NFL....	16	515	332	64.5	3910	26	12	7.59	61	284	4.7	2	2	12	3
1984— San Francisco NFL....	16	432	279	64.6	3630	28	10	8.40	39	118	3.0	2	2	12	4
1985— San Francisco NFL....	15	494	303	*61.3	3653	27	13	7.40	42	153	3.6	3	3	18	5
1986— San Francisco NFL....	8	307	191	62.2	2236	8	9	7.28	17	38	2.2	0	0	0	3
1987— San Francisco NFL....	13	398	266	*66.8	3054	*31	13	7.67	35	141	4.0	1	1	6	3
1988— San Francisco NFL....	14	397	238	60.0	2981	18	10	7.51	38	132	3.5	3	3	18	3
1989— San Francisco NFL....	13	386	271	*70.2	3521	26	8	*9.12	49	227	4.6	3	3	18	9
1990— San Francisco NFL....	15	520	321	61.7	3944	26	16	7.59	40	162	4.1	1	1	6	4
Pro totals (12 years)............	166	4579	2914	63.6	34998	242	123	7.64	411	1567	3.8	20	20	120	45

MONTGOMERY, ALTON
DB, BRONCOS

PERSONAL: Born June 16, 1968, at Griffin, Ga.... 6-0/195.
HIGH SCHOOL: Griffin (Ga.).
COLLEGE: Northwest Mississippi Junior College, then Houston.
TRANSACTIONS/CAREER NOTES: Selected by Denver Broncos in second round (52nd pick overall) of 1990 NFL draft.... Signed by Broncos (July, 1990).
PRO STATISTICS: 1990—Recovered two fumbles.

		INTERCEPTIONS			KICKOFF RETURNS			TOTAL		
Year Team	G	No.	Yds.	Avg.	TD	No.	Yds.	Avg.	TD	TD	Pts.	F.
1990— Denver NFL...	15	2	43	21.5	0	14	286	20.4	0	0	0	1
Pro totals (1 year)	15	2	43	21.5	0	14	286	20.4	0	0	0	1

MONTGOMERY, GLENN
DT, OILERS

PERSONAL: Born March 31, 1967, at New Orleans.... 6-0/268.... Full name: Glenn Steven Montgomery.
HIGH SCHOOL: West Jefferson (Harvey, La.).
COLLEGE: Houston.
TRANSACTIONS/CAREER NOTES: Selected by Houston Oilers in fifth round (131st pick overall) of 1989 NFL draft.... Signed by Oilers (July 27, 1989).... On inactive list (October 28, 1990).
PLAYING EXPERIENCE: Houston NFL, 1989 and 1990.... Games: 1989 (15), 1990 (15). Total: 30.
PRO STATISTICS: 1989—Returned one kickoff for no yards.

MONTGOMERY, GREG
P, OILERS

PERSONAL: Born October 29, 1964, at Morristown, N.J. ... 6-4/245. ... Full name: Gregory Hugh Montgomery Jr.
HIGH SCHOOL: Red Bank Regional (Little Silver, N.J.).
COLLEGE: Penn State, then Michigan State (received bachelor of arts degree in communications/sales, 1988).
TRANSACTIONS/CAREER NOTES: Selected by Houston Oilers in third round (72nd pick overall) of 1988 NFL draft.... Signed by Oilers (August 3, 1988).
PRO STATISTICS: 1989—Rushed three times for 17 yards and fumbled once.

		PUNTING		
Year Team	G	No.	Avg.	Blk.
1988— Houston NFL.........................	16	65	38.8	0
1989— Houston NFL.........................	16	56	43.3	2
1990— Houston NFL.........................	16	34	45.0	0
Pro totals (3 years)	48	155	42.4	2

MONTOYA, MAX
G, RAIDERS

PERSONAL: Born May 12, 1956, at Montebello, Calif.... 6-5/290.... Full name: Max Montoya Jr.
HIGH SCHOOL: La Puente (Calif.).
COLLEGE: Mt. San Jacinto Junior College (Calif.), then UCLA.
TRANSACTIONS/CAREER NOTES: Selected by Cincinnati Bengals in seventh round (168th pick overall) of 1979 NFL draft.... Granted unconditional free agency (February 1, 1990).... Signed by Los Angeles Raiders (February 27, 1990).
PLAYING EXPERIENCE: Cincinnati NFL, 1979-1989; Los Angeles Raiders NFL, 1990.... Games: 1979 (11), 1980 (16), 1981 (16), 1982 (9), 1983 (16), 1984 (16), 1985 (16), 1986 (16), 1987 (10), 1988 (15), 1989 (16), 1990 (16). Total: 173.
CHAMPIONSHIP GAME EXPERIENCE: Played in AFC championship game after 1981, 1988 and 1990 seasons. Played in Super Bowl XVI after 1981 season and Super Bowl XXIII after 1988 season.
RECORDS/HONORS: Played in Pro Bowl after 1986, 1988 and 1989 seasons.
PRO STATISTICS: 1981—Recovered one fumble. 1986—Recovered one fumble. 1990—Recovered one fumble.

MOON, WARREN
QB, OILERS

PERSONAL: Born November 18, 1956, at Los Angeles.... 6-3/212.
HIGH SCHOOL: Hamilton (Los Angeles).
COLLEGE: Washington.
TRANSACTIONS/CAREER NOTES: Signed as free agent by Edmonton Eskimos of CFL (March, 1978).... USFL rights traded by Memphis Showboats to Los Angeles Express for future draft pick (August 30, 1983)....

Granted free agency (March 1, 1984).... Signed by Houston Oilers (March 1, 1984).... On injured reserve with fractured scapula (September 5-October 15, 1988).... On inactive list (December 30, 1990).

CHAMPIONSHIP GAME EXPERIENCE: Played in Grey Cup (CFL championship game) after 1978-1982 seasons.

RECORDS/HONORS: Established NFL record for most times sacked, game (12) against Dallas Cowboys (September 29, 1985). Tied NFL record for most games, 300 or more yards passing, season (9), 1990; most fumbles, season (18), 1990.... Played in Pro Bowl after 1988-1990 seasons.... Named to THE SPORTING NEWS NFL All-Pro team, 1990.

PRO STATISTICS: Passer rating points: 1984 (76.9), 1985 (68.5), 1986 (62.3), 1987 (74.2), 1988 (88.4), 1989 (88.9), 1990 (96.8). Career: 79.9.... CFL: 1982—Recovered one fumble.... NFL: 1984—Recovered seven fumbles and fumbled 17 times for minus one yard. 1985—Recovered five fumbles and fumbled 12 times for minus eight yards. 1986—Recovered three fumbles and fumbled 11 times for minus four yards. 1987—Recovered six fumbles and fumbled eight times for minus seven yards. 1988—Recovered four fumbles and fumbled eight times for minus 12 yards. 1989—Recovered six fumbles and fumbled 11 times for minus 13 yards. 1990—Recovered four fumbles.

			PASSING						RUSHING				TOTAL		
Year Team	G	Att.	Cmp.	Pct.	Yds.	TD	Int.	Avg.	Att.	Yds.	Avg.	TD	TD	Pts.	F.
1978— Edmonton CFL	15	173	89	51.5	1112	5	7	6.43	30	114	3.8	1	1	6	1
1979— Edmonton CFL	16	274	149	54.4	2382	20	12	8.69	56	150	2.7	2	2	12	1
1980— Edmonton CFL	16	331	181	54.7	3127	25	11	9.45	55	352	6.4	3	3	18	0
1981— Edmonton CFL	15	378	237	62.7	3959	27	12	10.47	50	298	6.0	3	3	18	1
1982— Edmonton CFL	16	562	333	59.3	5000	36	16	8.90	54	259	4.8	4	4	24	1
1983— Edmonton CFL	16	664	380	57.2	5648	31	19	8.51	85	527	6.2	3	3	18	7
1984— Houston NFL	16	450	259	57.6	3338	12	14	7.42	58	211	3.6	1	1	6	*17
1985— Houston NFL	14	377	200	53.1	2709	15	19	7.19	39	130	3.3	0	0	0	12
1986— Houston NFL	15	488	256	52.5	3489	13	*26	7.15	42	157	3.7	2	2	12	11
1987— Houston NFL	12	368	184	50.0	2806	21	18	7.63	34	112	3.3	3	3	18	8
1988— Houston NFL	11	294	160	54.4	2327	17	8	7.92	33	88	2.7	5	5	30	8
1989— Houston NFL	16	464	280	60.3	3631	23	14	7.83	70	268	3.8	4	4	24	11
1990— Houston NFL	15	*584	*362	62.0	*4689	*33	13	8.03	55	215	3.9	2	2	12	*18
CFL totals (6 years)	94	2382	1369	57.5	21228	144	77	8.91	330	1700	5.2	16	16	96	11
NFL totals (7 years)	99	3025	1701	56.2	22989	134	112	7.60	331	1181	3.6	17	17	102	85
Pro totals (13 years)	193	5407	3070	56.8	44217	278	189	8.18	661	2881	4.4	33	33	198	96

MOORE, ERIC
OT, GIANTS

PERSONAL: Born January 21, 1965, at Berkeley, Mo.... 6-5/290.... Full name: Eric Patrick Moore.... Cousin of Dwight Scales, wide receiver with Los Angeles Rams, New York Giants, San Diego Chargers and Seattle Seahawks, 1976-1979 and 1981-1984.

HIGH SCHOOL: Berkeley (Mo.).

COLLEGE: Northeastern Oklahoma A&M, then Indiana (degree in general studies and criminal justice, 1988).

TRANSACTIONS/CAREER NOTES: Selected by New York Giants in first round (10th pick overall) of 1988 NFL draft.... Signed by Giants (August 1, 1988).... On inactive list (December 9, 1990).

PLAYING EXPERIENCE: New York Giants NFL, 1988-1990.... Games: 1988 (11), 1989 (16), 1990 (15). Total: 42.

CHAMPIONSHIP GAME EXPERIENCE: Played in NFC championship game after 1990 season.... Played in Super Bowl XXV after 1990 season.

PRO STATISTICS: 1989—Recovered three fumbles.

MOORE, ROB
WR, JETS

PERSONAL: Born September 27, 1968, at New York.... 6-3/205.... Full name: Robert S. Moore.

HIGH SCHOOL: Hemstead (N.Y.).

COLLEGE: Syracuse (bachelor of arts degree in psychology, 1990).

TRANSACTIONS/CAREER NOTES: Selected by New York Jets in first round of 1990 NFL supplemental draft.... Signed by Jets (July 22, 1990).

RECORDS/HONORS: Named as wide receiver on THE SPORTING NEWS college All-America team, 1989.

		RUSHING				RECEIVING				TOTAL		
Year Team	G	Att.	Yds.	Avg.	TD	No.	Yds.	Avg.	TD	TD	Pts.	F.
1990— N.Y. Jets NFL	15	2	-4	-2.0	0	44	692	15.7	6	6	36	1
Pro totals (1 year)	15	2	-4	-2.0	0	44	692	15.7	6	6	36	1

MOORE, STEVON
S, DOLPHINS

PERSONAL: Born February 9, 1967, at Wiggins, Miss.... 5-11/204.... Full name: Stevon N. Moore.

HIGH SCHOOL: Stone County (Wiggins, Miss.).

COLLEGE: Mississippi.

TRANSACTIONS/CAREER NOTES: Selected by New York Jets in seventh round (181st pick overall) of 1989 NFL draft.... Signed by Jets (July 22, 1989).... On injured reserve with knee injury (August 28, 1989-entire season).... Granted unconditional free agency (February 1, 1990).... Signed by Miami Dolphins (March 30, 1990).... On active/physically unable to perform list with knee injury (July 21-August 27, 1990).... On reserve/physically unable to perform list with knee injury (August 28-October 18, 1990).... On injured reserve with hamstring injury (November 8-December 8, 1990).

PLAYING EXPERIENCE: Miami NFL, 1990.... Games: 1990 (7).

PRO STATISTICS: 1990—Recovered one fumble.

MORAN, RICH
G, PACKERS

PERSONAL: Born March 19, 1962, at Boise, Idaho.... 6-3/280.... Full name: Richard James Moran.... Son of Jim Moran, defensive tackle with New York Giants, 1964-1967; and brother of Eric Moran, offensive tackle-guard with Los Angeles Express (USFL) and Houston Oilers, 1983-1986.

HIGH SCHOOL: Foothill (Pleasanton, Calif.).
COLLEGE: San Diego State (degree in marketing, 1985).
TRANSACTIONS/CAREER NOTES: Selected by Arizona Outlaws in fourth round (57th pick overall) of 1985 USFL draft.... Selected by Green Bay Packers in third round (71st pick overall) of 1985 NFL draft.... Signed by Packers (July 24, 1985).... On injured reserve with knee injury (September 10-November 26, 1986).
PLAYING EXPERIENCE: Green Bay NFL, 1985-1990.... Games: 1985 (16), 1986 (5), 1987 (12), 1988 (16), 1989 (16), 1990, (16). Total: 81.
PRO STATISTICS: 1987—Recovered one fumble and fumbled once for three yards. 1989—Recovered one fumble.

MORGAN, STANLEY
WR, COLTS

PERSONAL: Born February 17, 1955, at Easley, S.C.... 5-11/185.... Full name: Stanley Douglas Morgan.
HIGH SCHOOL: Easley (S.C.).
COLLEGE: Tennessee (bachelor of science degree in education, 1979).
TRANSACTIONS/CAREER NOTES: Selected by New England Patriots in first round (25th pick overall) of 1977 NFL draft.... On injured reserve with fractured fibula (November 16, 1989-remainder of season).... Granted unconditional free agency (February 1, 1990).... Rights relinquished (May 18, 1990).... Signed by Indianapolis Colts (July 23, 1990).
CHAMPIONSHIP GAME EXPERIENCE: Played in AFC championship game after 1985 season.... Played in Super Bowl XX after 1985 season.
RECORDS/HONORS: Played in Pro Bowl after 1979, 1980, 1986 and 1987 seasons.... Named to THE SPORTING NEWS NFL All-Pro team, 1986.
PRO STATISTICS: 1978—Returned one kickoff for 17 yards. 1979—Returned one kickoff for 12 yards. 1980—Recovered one fumble for three yards. 1981—Recovered two fumbles. 1983—Recovered two fumbles. 1988—Recovered one fumble.

		RUSHING				RECEIVING				PUNT RETURNS				TOTAL		
Year Team	G	Att.	Yds.	Avg.	TD	No.	Yds.	Avg.	TD	No.	Yds.	Avg.	TD	TD	Pts.	F.
1977— New England NFL..	14	1	10	10.0	0	21	443	*21.1	3	16	220	13.8	0	3	18	0
1978— New England NFL..	16	2	11	5.5	0	34	820	24.1	5	32	335	10.5	0	5	30	6
1979— New England NFL..	16	7	39	5.6	0	44	1002	*22.8	*12	29	289	10.0	1	13	78	1
1980— New England NFL..	16	4	36	9.0	0	45	991	*22.0	6	0	0		0	6	36	0
1981— New England NFL..	13	2	21	10.5	0	44	1029	*23.4	6	15	116	7.7	0	6	36	2
1982— New England NFL..	9	2	3	1.5	0	28	584	20.9	3	0	0		0	3	18	0
1983— New England NFL..	16	1	13	13.0	0	58	863	14.9	2	0	0		0	2	12	5
1984— New England NFL..	13	0	0		0	38	709	18.7	5	0	0		0	5	30	0
1985— New England NFL..	15	1	0	.0	0	39	760	19.5	5	0	0		0	5	30	1
1986— New England NFL..	16	0	0		0	84	1491	17.8	10	0	0		0	10	60	0
1987— New England NFL..	10	0	0		0	40	672	16.8	3	0	0		0	3	18	0
1988— New England NFL..	16	1	-6	-6.0	0	31	502	16.2	4	0	0		0	4	24	1
1989— New England NFL..	10	0	0		0	28	486	17.4	3	0	0		0	3	18	0
1990— Indianapolis NFL ...	16	0	0		0	23	364	15.8	5	0	0		0	5	30	1
Pro totals (14 years)	196	21	127	6.1	0	557	10716	19.2	72	92	960	10.4	1	73	438	17

MORRIS, JOE
RB, BROWNS

PERSONAL: Born September 15, 1960, at Fort Bragg, N.C.... 5-7/195.... Full name: Joseph Morris.... Brother of Jamie Morris, running back with Hamilton Tiger-Cats of CFL.
HIGH SCHOOL: Southern Pines (N.C.) and Ayer (Mass.).
COLLEGE: Syracuse.
TRANSACTIONS/CAREER NOTES: Selected by New York Giants in second round (45th pick overall) of 1982 NFL draft.... Granted roster exemption (August 26-August 29, 1986).... On injured reserve with broken foot (September 4, 1989-entire season). ... Released by Giants (September 3, 1990).... Signed by Cleveland Browns (April 1, 1991).
CHAMPIONSHIP GAME EXPERIENCE: Played in NFC championship game after 1986 season.... Played in Super Bowl XXI after 1986 season.
RECORDS/HONORS: Played in Pro Bowl after 1985 and 1986 seasons.... Named to THE SPORTING NEWS All-Pro team, 1986.
PRO STATISTICS: 1982—Recovered one fumble. 1983—Recovered one fumble. 1985—Recovered two fumbles. 1986—Recovered two fumbles. 1988—Recovered one fumble.

		RUSHING				RECEIVING				KICKOFF RETURNS				TOTAL		
Year Team	G	Att.	Yds.	Avg.	TD	No.	Yds.	Avg.	TD	No.	Yds.	Avg.	TD	TD	Pts.	F.
1982— N.Y. Giants NFL	5	15	48	3.2	1	8	34	4.3	0	0	0		0	1	6	1
1983— N.Y. Giants NFL	15	35	145	4.1	0	2	1	.5	1	14	255	18.2	0	1	6	2
1984— N.Y. Giants NFL	16	133	510	3.8	4	12	124	10.3	0	6	69	11.5	0	4	24	1
1985— N.Y. Giants NFL	16	294	1336	4.5	*21	22	212	9.6	0	2	25	12.5	0	*21	126	6
1986— N.Y. Giants NFL	15	341	1516	4.5	14	21	233	11.1	1	0	0		0	15	90	6
1987— N.Y. Giants NFL	11	193	658	3.4	3	11	114	10.4	0	0	0		0	3	18	2
1988— N.Y. Giants NFL	16	307	1083	3.5	5	22	166	7.6	0	0	0		0	5	30	7
Pro totals (7 years)	94	1318	5296	4.0	48	98	884	9.0	2	22	349	15.9	0	50	300	25

MORRIS, MIKE
C, BROWNS

PERSONAL: Born February 22, 1961, at Centerville, Ia.... 6-5/285.... Full name: Michael Stephen Morris.
HIGH SCHOOL: Centerville (Ia.).
COLLEGE: Northeast Missouri State (degree in psychology and physical education).
TRANSACTIONS/CAREER NOTES: Signed as free agent by Arizona Outlaws of USFL (November 1, 1984).... Released by Outlaws (February 11, 1985).... Signed as free agent by Denver Broncos (May 8, 1986).... Released by Broncos (July 21, 1986).... Signed as free agent by St. Louis Cardinals (May 20, 1987).... Crossed picket line during players' strike (October 7, 1987). ... Franchise transferred to Phoenix (March 15, 1988).... On injured reserve with knee injury (August 23, 1988-entire sea-

son).... Granted unconditional free agency (February 1, 1989).... Signed by Washington Redskins (March 20, 1989).... Released by Redskins (August 29, 1989).... Awarded on waivers to Kansas City Chiefs (August 30, 1989).... Released by Chiefs (October 11, 1989).... Signed as free agent by New England Patriots (October 13, 1989).... Granted unconditional free agency (February 1, 1990).... Signed by Kansas City Chiefs (April 1, 1990).... Released by Chiefs (July 28, 1990).... Signed by Seattle Seahawks (preseason, 1990).... Released by Seattle (October 4, 1990).... Signed by Cleveland Browns (October 16, 1990).

PLAYING EXPERIENCE: St. Louis NFL, 1987; Kansas City (5)-New England (11) NFL, 1989; Seattle (4)-Cleveland (10) NFL, 1990.... Games: 1987 (14), 1989 (16), 1990 (14). Total: 44.

PRO STATISTICS: 1990—Fumbled once for minus 23 yards.

MORRIS, RON
WR, BEARS

PERSONAL: Born November 14, 1964, at Cooper, Tex.... 6-1/195.... Full name: Ronald Wayne Morris.
HIGH SCHOOL: Cooper (Tex.).
COLLEGE: Southern Methodist.
TRANSACTIONS/CAREER NOTES: Selected by Chicago Bears in second round (54th pick overall) of 1987 NFL draft.... Signed by Bears (July 31, 1987).... On inactive list (December 9, 1990).
CHAMPIONSHIP GAME EXPERIENCE: Played in NFC championship game after 1988 season.

		— RUSHING —				— RECEIVING —				— TOTAL —		
Year Team	G	Att.	Yds.	Avg.	TD	No.	Yds.	Avg.	TD	TD	Pts.	F.
1987—Chicago NFL	12	0	0		0	20	379	19.0	1	1	6	0
1988—Chicago NFL	16	3	40	13.3	0	28	498	17.8	4	4	24	0
1989—Chicago NFL	16	1	-14	-14.0	0	30	486	16.2	1	1	6	1
1990—Chicago NFL	15	2	26	13.0	0	31	437	14.1	3	3	18	0
Pro totals (4 years)	59	6	52	8.7	0	109	1800	16.5	9	9	54	1

MORRISSEY, JIM
LB, BEARS

PERSONAL: Born December 24, 1962, at Flint, Mich.... 6-3/227.... Full name: James Morrissey.
HIGH SCHOOL: Powers (Flint, Mich.).
COLLEGE: Michigan State.
TRANSACTIONS/CAREER NOTES: Selected by Baltimore Stars in eighth round (106th pick overall) of 1985 USFL draft.... Selected by Chicago Bears in 11th round (302nd pick overall) of 1985 NFL draft.... Signed by Bears (June 26, 1985).... Released by Bears (September 2, 1985).... Re-signed by Bears (September 10, 1985).... On injured reserve with knee injury (September 30-November 5, 1988).... On injured reserve with lacerated kidney (October 17, 1989-remainder of season).
CHAMPIONSHIP GAME EXPERIENCE: Played in NFC championship game after 1985 and 1988 seasons.... Played in Super Bowl XX after 1985 season.
PRO STATISTICS: 1988—Recovered one fumble. 1990—Recovered three fumbles.

		— INTERCEPTIONS —			
Year Team	G	No.	Yds.	Avg.	TD
1985—Chicago NFL	15	0	0		0
1986—Chicago NFL	16	0	0		0
1987—Chicago NFL	10	0	0		0
1988—Chicago NFL	11	3	13	4.3	0
1989—Chicago NFL	6	2	0	.0	0
1990—Chicago NFL	16	2	12	6.0	0
Pro totals (6 years)	74	7	25	3.6	0

MORSE, BOBBY
FB, SAINTS

PERSONAL: Born October 3, 1965, at Muskegon, Mich.... 5-10/213.
HIGH SCHOOL: Catholic Central (Muskegon, Mich.).
COLLEGE: Michigan State (degree in advertising, 1987).
TRANSACTIONS/CAREER NOTES: Selected by Philadelphia Eagles in 12th round (316th pick overall) of 1987 NFL draft.... Signed by Eagles (August 6, 1987).... Left Eagles camp voluntarily (July 28-August 21, 1988).... Transferred to reserve/left camp list (August 22, 1988-entire season).... Traded by Eagles to New Orleans Saints for conditional 11th-round pick in 1990 draft (April 24, 1989).... Released by Saints (September 5, 1989).... Re-signed by Saints (September 22, 1989).... Released by Saints (November 10, 1989).... Signed as free agent by San Francisco 49ers (November 22, 1989).... Released by 49ers (November 27, 1989).... Signed as free agent by New Orleans Saints (November 30, 1989).... On injured reserve with broken forearm (November 19, 1990-remainder of season).
PRO STATISTICS: 1987—Recovered one fumble. 1989—Recovered one fumble.

		— RUSHING —				— RECEIVING —				— PUNT RETURNS —				KICKOFF RETURNS				— TOTALS —		
Year Team	G	Att.	Yds.	Avg.	TD	No.	Yds.	Avg.	TD	No.	Yds.	Avg.	TD	No.	Yds.	Avg.	TD	TD	Pts.	F.
1987—Philadelphia NFL	11	6	14	2.3	0	1	8	8.0	0	20	121	6.1	0	24	386	16.1	0	0	0	1
1989—New Orleans NFL	11	2	43	21.5	0	0	0		0	10	29	2.9	0	10	278	27.8	*1	1	6	0
1990—New Orleans NFL	10	0	0		0	0	0		0	8	95	11.9	0	4	56	14.0	0	0	0	1
Pro totals (3 years)	32	8	57	7.1	0	1	8	8.0	0	38	245	6.5	0	38	720	19.0	1	1	6	2

MOSEBAR, DON
C, RAIDERS

PERSONAL: Born September 11, 1961, at Yakima, Calif.... 6-6/280.... Full name: Donald Howard Mosebar.
HIGH SCHOOL: Mount Whitney (Visalia, Calif.).
COLLEGE: Southern California.

TRANSACTIONS/CAREER NOTES: Selected by Los Angeles Express in 1983 USFL territorial draft. . . . Selected by Los Angeles Raiders in first round (26th pick overall) of 1983 NFL draft. . . . Signed by Raiders (August 29, 1983). . . . Granted roster exemption (August 29-September 9, 1983). . . . On injured reserve with back injury (November 8, 1984-remainder of season).
PLAYING EXPERIENCE: Los Angeles Raiders NFL, 1983-1990. . . . Games: 1983 (14), 1984 (10), 1985 (16), 1986 (16), 1987 (12), 1988 (13), 1989 (12), 1990 (16). Total: 109.
CHAMPIONSHIP GAME EXPERIENCE: Played in AFC championship game after 1983 and 1990 seasons. . . . Played in Super Bowl XVIII after 1983 season.
RECORDS/HONORS: Played in Pro Bowl after 1990 season.
PRO STATISTICS: 1986—Recovered one fumble and fumbled once. 1990—Recovered one fumble.

MOSS, WINSTON
LB, RAIDERS

PERSONAL: Born December 24, 1965, at Miami. . . . 6-3/245. . . . Full name: Winston N. Moss.
HIGH SCHOOL: Southridge (Miami).
COLLEGE: Miami (Fla.).
TRANSACTIONS/CAREER NOTES: Selected by Tampa Bay Buccaneers in second round (50th pick overall) of 1987 NFL draft. . . . Signed by Buccaneers (July 18, 1987). . . . Granted free agency (February 1, 1990). . . . Re-signed by Buccaneers (July 27, 1990). . . . Traded by Buccaneers to Los Angeles Raiders for third- and fifth-round picks in 1991 NFL draft (April 22, 1991).
PLAYING EXPERIENCE: Tampa Bay NFL, 1987-1990. . . . Games: 1987 (12), 1988 (16), 1989 (16), 1990 (16). Total: 60.
PRO STATISTICS: 1987—Recovered one fumble in end zone for a touchdown. 1990—Intercepted one pass for 31 yards and recovered one fumble.

MOSS, ZEFROSS
OL, COLTS

PERSONAL: Born August 17, 1966, at Holt, Ala. . . . 6-6/338.
HIGH SCHOOL: Holt (Ala.).
COLLEGE: Alabama State.
TRANSACTIONS/CAREER NOTES: Signed as free agent by Dallas Cowboys (April 29, 1988). . . . Released by Cowboys (August 24, 1988). . . . Re-signed by Cowboys for 1989 (December 8, 1988). . . . Traded by Cowboys to Indianapolis Colts for 10th-round pick in 1990 NFL draft (August 22, 1989).
PLAYING EXPERIENCE: Indianapolis NFL, 1989 and 1990. . . . Games: 1989 (16), 1990 (16). Total: 32.

MOTT, JOE
LB, JETS

PERSONAL: Born October 6, 1965, at Endicott, N.Y. . . . 6-4/234. . . . Full name: John Christopher Mott.
HIGH SCHOOL: Union Endicott Central (Endicott, N.Y.).
COLLEGE: Iowa (bachelor of general studies degree, 1989).
TRANSACTIONS/CAREER NOTES: Selected by New York Jets in third round (70th pick overall) of 1989 NFL draft. . . . Signed by Jets (July 21, 1989).
PLAYING EXPERIENCE: New York Jets NFL, 1989 and 1990. . . . Games: 1989 (16), 1990 (16). Total: 32.
PRO STATISTICS: 1990—Recovered one fumble.

MOWATT, ZEKE
TE, GIANTS

PERSONAL: Born March 5, 1961, at Wauchula, Fla. . . . 6-3/240.
HIGH SCHOOL: Hardee County (Wauchula, Fla.).
COLLEGE: Florida State.
TRANSACTIONS/CAREER NOTES: Selected by Tampa Bay Bandits in 1983 USFL territorial draft. . . . Signed as free agent by New York Giants (June 1, 1983). . . . On injured reserve with knee injury (August 31, 1985-entire season). . . . Granted unconditional free agency (February 1, 1990). . . . Signed by New England Patriots (March 23, 1990). . . . On injured reserve with hand injury (September 4-October 26, 1990). . . . Released by Patriots (July 9, 1990). . . . Signed by New York Giants (July 14, 1990).
CHAMPIONSHIP GAME EXPERIENCE: Played in NFC championship game after 1986 season. . . . Played in Super Bowl XXI after 1986 season.
PRO STATISTICS: 1986—Recovered one fumble and fumbled once. 1988—Fumbled twice. 1989—Recovered one fumble and fumbled once. 1990—Fumbled once.

			RECEIVING		
Year Team	G	No.	Yds.	Avg.	TD
1983— N.Y. Giants NFL	16	21	280	13.3	1
1984— N.Y. Giants NFL	16	48	698	14.5	6
1986— N.Y. Giants NFL	16	10	119	11.9	2
1987— N.Y. Giants NFL	12	3	39	13.0	1
1988— N.Y. Giants NFL	16	15	196	13.1	1
1989— N.Y. Giants NFL	16	27	288	10.7	0
1990— New England NFL	10	6	67	11.2	0
Pro totals (7 years)	102	130	1687	13.0	11

MOYER, KEN
G, BENGALS

PERSONAL: Born November 19, 1966, at Canoga Park, Calif. . . . 6-7/297. . . . Full name: Kenneth Wayne Moyer.
HIGH SCHOOL: Bedford (Temperance, Mich.).
COLLEGE: Toledo.
TRANSACTIONS/CAREER NOTES: Signed as free agent by Cincinnati Bengals (April 27, 1989). . . . Released by Bengals (September 5, 1989). . . . Re-signed by Bengals to developmental squad (September 6, 1989). . . . On developmental squad (September 6-October 11, 1989). . . . Activated after clearing procedural waivers (October 13, 1989).
PLAYING EXPERIENCE: Cincinnati NFL, 1989 and 1990. . . . Games: 1989 (8), 1990 (16). Total: 24.

MRAZ, MARK
DE, CHARGERS

PERSONAL: Born February 9, 1965, at Glendale, Calif. . . . 6-4/260. . . . Full name: Mark David Mraz.
HIGH SCHOOL: Glendora (Calif.).
COLLEGE: Utah State.
TRANSACTIONS/CAREER NOTES: Selected by Atlanta Falcons in fifth round (125th pick overall) of 1987 NFL draft. . . . Signed by Falcons (July 26, 1987). . . . Released by Falcons (August 31, 1988). . . . Signed as free agent by Los Angeles Raiders (April 4, 1989). . . . On reserve/non-football injury with steroids (August 29-September 25, 1989). . . . Reinstated and granted roster exemption (September 26-October 2, 1989). . . . Granted unconditional free agency (February 1, 1990). . . . Signed by Denver Broncos (March 19, 1990). . . . Released by Broncos (August 22, 1990). . . . Signed by WLAF (January 7, 1991). . . . Selected by Frankfurt Galaxy in second round (14th defensive lineman) of 1991 WLAF positional draft. . . . Signed by San Diego Chargers (June 14, 1991).
PLAYING EXPERIENCE: Atlanta NFL, 1987; Los Angeles Raiders NFL, 1989; Frankfurt WLAF, 1991. . . . Games: 1987 (11), 1989 (11), 1991 (9). Total NFL: 22. Total Pro: 31.
PRO STATISTICS: WLAF: 1991—Recovered one fumble.

MROSKO, BOB
TE, GIANTS

PERSONAL: Born November 13, 1965, at Cleveland. . . . 6-5/270. . . . Full name: Robert Allen Mrosko.
HIGH SCHOOL: Wickliffe (O.).
COLLEGE: Penn State (bachelor of science degree in exercise and sport science, 1989).
TRANSACTIONS/CAREER NOTES: Selected by Houston Oilers in ninth round (244th pick overall) of 1989 NFL draft. . . . Signed by Oilers (July 11, 1989). . . . Granted unconditional free agency (February 1, 1990). . . . Signed by New York Giants (February 27, 1990).
CHAMPIONSHIP GAME EXPERIENCE: Played in NFC championship game after 1990 season. . . . Played in Super Bowl XXV after 1990 season.
PRO STATISTICS: 1989—Returned three kickoffs for 46 yards. 1990—Recovered one fumble.

			RECEIVING		
Year	Team	G	No.	Yds.	Avg.	TD
1989— Houston NFL		15	3	28	9.3	0
1990— N.Y. Giants NFL		16	3	27	9.0	1
Pro totals (2 years)		31	6	55	9.2	1

MUECKE, TOM
QB, OILERS

PERSONAL: Born August 20, 1963, at Galveston, Tex. . . . 6-1/195. . . . Name pronounced MICK-EY.
HIGH SCHOOL: Angleton (Tex.).
COLLEGE: Baylor.
TRANSACTIONS/CAREER NOTES: Signed as free agent by Winnipeg Blue Bombers of CFL (August, 1986). . . . Retired prior to 1989 season. . . . Signed by Houston Oilers to practice squad (October 24, 1990). . . . Released by Oilers (November 22, 1990). . . . Re-signed by Oilers (June 3, 1991).
PRO STATISTICS: 1988—Credited with one 2-point conversion and recovered one fumble.

			PASSING							RUSHING				TOTAL		
Year	Team	G	Att.	Cmp.	Pct.	Yds.	TD	Int.	Avg.	Att.	Yds.	Avg.	TD	TD	Pts.	F.
1986— Winnipeg CFL		10	2	1	50.0	14	0	0	7.00	1	0	.0	0	0	0	0
1987— Winnipeg CFL		18	37	20	54.1	212	3	3	5.73	2	0	.0	0	0	0	2
1988— Winnipeg CFL		15	250	124	49.6	1892	11	11	7.57	25	79	3.2	1	1	8	7
Pro totals (3 years)		43	289	145	50.2	2118	14	14	7.33	28	79	2.8	1	1	8	9

MUELLER, JAMIE
FB, BILLS

PERSONAL: Born October 4, 1964, at Cleveland. . . . 6-1/230. . . . Full name: Jamie F. Mueller. . . . Name pronounced MYOO-ler.
HIGH SCHOOL: Fairview (Fairview Park, O.).
COLLEGE: Bendictine College (Kan.).
TRANSACTIONS/CAREER NOTES: Selected by Buffalo Bills in third round (78th pick overall) of 1987 NFL draft. . . . Signed by Bills (July 25, 1987).
CHAMPIONSHIP GAME EXPERIENCE: Played in AFC championship game after 1988 and 1990 seasons. . . . Played in Super Bowl XXV after 1990 season.
PRO STATISTICS: 1987—Returned five kickoffs for 74 yards and recovered one fumble. 1988—Recovered one fumble. 1989—Returned one kickoff for 19 yards.

			RUSHING				RECEIVING				TOTAL		
Year	Team	G	Att.	Yds.	Avg.	TD	No.	Yds.	Avg.	TD	TD	Pts.	F.
1987— Buffalo NFL		12	82	354	4.3	2	3	13	4.3	0	2	12	5
1988— Buffalo NFL		15	81	296	3.7	0	8	42	5.3	0	0	0	2
1989— Buffalo NFL		14	16	44	2.8	0	1	8	8.0	0	0	0	1
1990— Buffalo NFL		16	59	207	3.5	2	16	106	6.6	1	3	18	1
Pro totals (4 years)		57	238	901	3.8	4	28	169	6.0	1	5	30	9

MUELLER, VANCE
RB, RAIDERS

PERSONAL: Born May 5, 1964, at Tucson, Ariz. . . . 6-0/220. . . . Full name: Vance Alan Mueller. . . . Name pronounced MYOO-ler.
HIGH SCHOOL: Jackson (Calif.).
COLLEGE: Occidental (bachelor of science degree in psychology and physiology, 1986).

TRANSACTIONS/CAREER NOTES: Selected by Los Angeles Raiders in fourth round (103rd pick overall) of 1986 NFL draft. . . . Signed by Raiders (July 15, 1986).
CHAMPIONSHIP GAME EXPERIENCE: Played in AFC championship game after 1990 season.
PRO STATISTICS: 1987—Recovered one fumble. 1988—Recovered one fumble. 1989—Recovered one fumble. 1990—Recovered one fumble.

Year Team	G	RUSHING Att.	Yds.	Avg.	TD	RECEIVING No.	Yds.	Avg.	TD	KICKOFF RETURNS No.	Yds.	Avg.	TD	TOTAL TD	Pts.	F.
1986— L.A. Raiders NFL ...	15	13	30	2.3	0	6	54	9.0	0	2	73	36.5	0	0	0	1
1987— L.A. Raiders NFL ...	12	37	175	4.7	1	11	95	8.6	0	27	588	21.8	0	1	6	3
1988— L.A. Raiders NFL ...	14	17	60	3.5	0	5	63	12.6	0	5	97	19.4	0	0	0	1
1989— L.A. Raiders NFL ...	16	48	161	3.4	2	18	240	13.3	2	5	120	24.0	0	4	24	0
1990— L.A. Raiders NFL ...	16	13	43	3.3	0	0	0		0	0	0		0	0	0	0
Pro totals (5 years)	73	128	469	3.7	3	40	452	11.3	2	39	878	22.5	0	5	30	5

MULARKEY, MIKE
TE, STEELERS

PERSONAL: Born November 19, 1961, at Miami. . . . 6-4/238. . . . Full name: Michael Rene Mularkey.
HIGH SCHOOL: Northeast (Fort Lauderdale, Fla.).
COLLEGE: Florida.
TRANSACTIONS/CAREER NOTES: Selected by Tampa Bay Bandits in 1983 USFL territorial draft. . . . Selected by San Francisco 49ers in ninth round (229th pick overall) of 1983 NFL draft. . . . Signed by 49ers (June 1, 1983). . . . Released by 49ers (August 29, 1983). . . . Awarded on waivers to Minnesota Vikings (August 30, 1983). . . . On injured reserve with ankle injury (September 30, 1983-remainder of season). . . . On injured reserve with knee injury (September 8-October 31, 1987). . . . Crossed picket line during players' strike (October 7, 1987). . . . Returned to picket line (October 12, 1987). . . . Granted unconditional free agency (February 1, 1989). . . . Signed by Pittsburgh Steelers (March 31, 1989).
PRO STATISTICS: 1984—Recovered one fumble and fumbled once. 1985—Ran nine yards with lateral on kickoff return. 1987—Returned one kickoff for 16 yards. 1988—Rushed once for minus six yards. 1990—Fumbled once.

Year Team	G	RECEIVING No.	Yds.	Avg.	TD
1983— Minnesota NFL	3	0	0		0
1984— Minnesota NFL	16	14	134	9.6	2
1985— Minnesota NFL	15	13	196	15.1	1
1986— Minnesota NFL	16	11	89	8.1	2
1987— Minnesota NFL	9	1	6	6.0	0
1988— Minnesota NFL	16	3	39	13.0	0
1989— Pittsburgh NFL	14	22	326	14.8	1
1990— Pittsburgh NFL	16	32	365	11.4	3
Pro totals (8 years)	105	96	1155	12.0	9

MUNCHAK, MIKE
G, OILERS

PERSONAL: Born March 5, 1960, at Scranton, Pa. . . . 6-3/284.
HIGH SCHOOL: Central (Scranton, Pa.).
COLLEGE: Penn State (bachelor of business administration degree, 1982).
TRANSACTIONS/CAREER NOTES: Selected by Houston Oilers in first round (eighth pick overall) of 1982 NFL draft. . . . On injured reserve with broken ankle (November 24-December 24, 1982). . . . On injured reserve with knee injury (October 14, 1986-remainder of season).
PLAYING EXPERIENCE: Houston NFL, 1982-1990. . . . Games: 1982 (4), 1983 (16), 1984 (16), 1985 (16), 1986 (6), 1987 (12), 1988 (16), 1989 (16), 1990 (16). Total: 118.
RECORDS/HONORS: Played in Pro Bowl after 1984, 1985 and 1987-1990 seasons. . . . Named to THE SPORTING NEWS NFL All-Pro team, 1987.
PRO STATISTICS: 1985—Recovered two fumbles for three yards. 1986—Recovered one fumble in end zone for a touchdown. 1987—Recovered one fumble. 1988—Recovered one fumble.

MUNFORD, MARC
LB, CHIEFS

PERSONAL: Born February 14, 1965, at Lincoln, Neb. . . . 6-2/231. . . . Full name: Marc Christopher Munford.
HIGH SCHOOL: Heritage (Littleton, Colo.).
COLLEGE: Nebraska.
TRANSACTIONS/CAREER NOTES: Selected by Denver Broncos in fourth round (111th pick overall) of 1987 NFL draft. . . . Signed by Broncos (July 19, 1987). . . . On injured reserve with back injury (January 9, 1988-remainder of 1987 season playoffs). . . . Released by Broncos (August 30, 1988). . . . Re-signed by Broncos (September 21, 1988). . . . On injured reserve with knee injury (October 10-November 21, 1988). . . . Re-signed by Broncos after clearing procedural waivers (November 23, 1988). . . . Granted free agency (February 1, 1990). . . . Re-signed by Broncos (July 22, 1990). . . . On inactive list (October 21, 1990). . . . On injured reserve with elbow injury (December 21, 1990-remainder of season). . . . Granted unconditional free agency (February 1, 1991). . . . Signed by Kansas City Chiefs (April 2, 1991).
PLAYING EXPERIENCE: Denver NFL, 1987-1990. . . . Games: 1987 (12), 1988 (7), 1989 (16), 1990 (13). Total: 48.
CHAMPIONSHIP GAME EXPERIENCE: Played in AFC championship game after 1989 season. . . . Played in Super Bowl XXIV after 1989 season.
PRO STATISTICS: 1987—Recovered two fumbles. 1989—Intercepted two passes for 16 yards and recovered one fumble.

MUNOZ, ANTHONY
OT, BENGALS

PERSONAL: Born August 19, 1958, at Ontario, Calif. . . . 6-6/284. . . . Full name: Michael Anthony Munoz.
HIGH SCHOOL: Chaffey (Ontario, Calif.).
COLLEGE: Southern California (bachelor of science degree in public administration, 1980).

TRANSACTIONS/CAREER NOTES: Selected by Cincinnati Bengals in first round (third pick overall) of 1980 NFL draft.... Granted free agency (February 1, 1987).... Re-signed by Bengals (September 12, 1987).... Granted roster exemption (September 12-September 19, 1987).... Granted free agency (February 1, 1990).... Re-signed by Bengals (July 20, 1990).
PLAYING EXPERIENCE: Cincinnati NFL, 1980-1990.... Games: 1980 (16), 1981 (16), 1982 (9), 1983 (16), 1984 (16), 1985 (16), 1986 (16), 1987 (11), 1988 (16), 1989 (16), 1990 (16). Total: 164.
CHAMPIONSHIP GAME EXPERIENCE: Played in AFC championship game after 1981 and 1988 seasons.... Played in Super Bowl XVI after 1981 season.... Played in Super Bowl XXIII after 1988 season.
RECORDS/HONORS: Played in Pro Bowl after 1981, 1983-1986, 1988 and 1989 seasons.... Named to play in Pro Bowl after 1987 season; replaced due to injury by Jim Lachey.... Named to play in Pro Bowl after 1990 season; replaced due to injury by Will Wolford.... Named to THE SPORTING NEWS NFL All-Pro team, 1981, 1984-1986, 1988 and 1989 seasons.
PRO STATISTICS: 1980—Caught one pass for minus six yards. 1984—Caught one pass for one yard and a touchdown and recovered one fumble. 1985—Caught one pass for one yard. 1986—Caught two passes for seven yards and two touchdowns. 1987—Caught two passes for 15 yards and a touchdown. 1988—Recovered two fumbles. 1989—Recovered two fumbles.

MURPHY, KEVIN
LB, BUCCANEERS

PERSONAL: Born September 8, 1963, at Plano, Tex.... 6-2/235.... Full name: Kevin Dion Murphy.
HIGH SCHOOL: L.V. Berkner (Richardson, Tex.).
COLLEGE: Oklahoma (degree in marketing, 1986).

TRANSACTIONS/CAREER NOTES: Selected by Los Angeles Express in 11th round (154th pick overall) of 1985 USFL draft (elected to return to college for final year of eligibility).... Selected by Tampa Bay Buccaneers in second round (40th pick overall) of 1986 NFL draft.... Signed by Buccaneers (July 22, 1986).... Granted free agency (February 1, 1990).... Re-signed by Buccaneers (August 14, 1990).... On inactive list (September 23, 1990).
PLAYING EXPERIENCE: Tampa Bay NFL, 1986-1990.... Games: 1986 (16), 1987 (9), 1988 (16), 1989 (16), 1990 (15). Total: 72.
RECORDS/HONORS: Named as linebacker on THE SPORTING NEWS college All-America team, 1985.
PRO STATISTICS: 1986—Recovered one fumble. 1988—Intercepted one pass for 35 yards and a touchdown and recovered one fumble for four yards. 1989—Recovered two fumbles.

MURPHY, MARK
S, PACKERS

PERSONAL: Born April 22, 1958, at Canton, O.... 6-2/209.... Full name: Mark Steven Murphy.
HIGH SCHOOL: Glen Oaks (Canton, O.).
COLLEGE: West Liberty State, W.Va. (bachelor of science degree in business administration).

TRANSACTIONS/CAREER NOTES: Signed as free agent by Green Bay Packers (April 25, 1980).... On injured reserve with broken hand (August 14-December 17, 1980).... Activated after clearing procedural waivers (December 19, 1980).... On injured reserve with ankle injury (September 2, 1986-entire season).
PRO STATISTICS: 1981—Recovered two fumbles. 1983—Recovered one fumble. 1984—Recovered one fumble for two yards and fumbled once. 1985—Returned one punt for four yards and recovered one fumble. 1987—Recovered two fumbles. 1988—Recovered four fumbles. 1989—Recovered one fumble.

			— INTERCEPTIONS —		
Year Team	G	No.	Yds.	Avg.	TD
1980— Green Bay NFL	1	0	0		0
1981— Green Bay NFL	16	3	57	19.0	0
1982— Green Bay NFL	9	0	0		0
1983— Green Bay NFL	16	0	0		0
1984— Green Bay NFL	16	1	4	4.0	0
1985— Green Bay NFL	15	2	50	25.0	*1
1987— Green Bay NFL	12	0	0		0
1988— Green Bay NFL	14	5	19	3.8	0
1989— Green Bay NFL	16	3	31	10.3	0
1990— Green Bay NFL	16	3	6	2.0	0
Pro totals (10 years)	131	17	167	9.8	1

MURRAY, EDDIE
PK, LIONS

PERSONAL: Born August 29, 1956, at Halifax, Nova Scotia.... 5-10/180.... Full name: Edward Peter Murray.... Cousin of Mike Rogers, center with Edmonton Oilers, New England-Hartford Whalers and New York Rangers, 1974-75 through 1985-86.
HIGH SCHOOL: Spectrum (Victoria, B.C.).
COLLEGE: Tulane (bachelor of science degree in education, 1980).
TRANSACTIONS/CAREER NOTES: Selected by Detroit Lions in seventh round (166th pick overall) of 1980 NFL draft.... On suspended list (September 10-November 20, 1982).... On injured reserve with hip injury (October 12-November 20, 1990).
RECORDS/HONORS: Tied NFL record for highest field-goal percentage, season (95.24), 1988 and 1989.... Played in Pro Bowl after 1980 and 1989 seasons.
PRO STATISTICS: 1986—Punted once for 37 yards. 1987—Punted four times for a 38.8 average.

		— PLACE-KICKING —				
Year Team	G	XPM	XPA	FGM	FGA	Pts.
1980— Detroit NFL	16	35	36	*27	*42	116
1981— Detroit NFL	16	46	46	25	35	*121
1982— Detroit NFL	7	16	16	11	12	49
1983— Detroit NFL	16	38	38	25	32	113
1984— Detroit NFL	16	31	31	20	27	91
1985— Detroit NFL	16	31	33	26	31	109

Year	Team	G	XPM	XPA	FGM	FGA	Pts.
				PLACE-KICKING			
1986— Detroit NFL		16	31	32	18	25	85
1987— Detroit NFL		12	21	21	20	32	81
1988— Detroit NFL		16	22	23	20	21	82
1989— Detroit NFL		16	36	36	20	21	96
1990— Detroit NFL		11	34	34	13	19	73
Pro totals (11 years)		158	341	346	225	297	1016

MUSTER, BRAD
FB, BEARS

PERSONAL: Born April 11, 1965, at Novato, Calif. . . . 6-3/231. . . . Full name: Brad William Muster.
HIGH SCHOOL: San Marin (Novato, Calif.).
COLLEGE: Stanford (bachelor of arts degree in economics, 1988).
TRANSACTIONS/CAREER NOTES: Selected by Chicago Bears in first round (23rd pick overall) of 1988 NFL draft. . . . Signed by Bears (July 20, 1988).
CHAMPIONSHIP GAME EXPERIENCE: Played in NFC championship game after 1988 season.
PRO STATISTICS: 1988—Returned three kickoffs for 33 yards and recovered one fumble. 1990—Recovered one fumble.

Year	Team	G	Att.	Yds.	Avg.	TD	No.	Yds.	Avg.	TD	TD	Pts.	F.
				RUSHING				RECEIVING				TOTAL	
1988— Chicago NFL		16	44	197	4.5	0	21	236	11.2	1	1	6	1
1989— Chicago NFL		16	82	327	4.0	5	32	259	8.1	3	8	48	2
1990— Chicago NFL		16	141	664	4.7	6	47	452	9.6	0	6	36	3
Pro totals (3 years)		48	267	1188	4.5	11	100	947	9.5	4	15	90	6

NAPOSKI, ERIC
LB, REDSKINS

PERSONAL: Born December 10, 1966, at Manhattan, N.Y. . . . 6-2/245. . . . Full name: Eric Andrew Naposki.
HIGH SCHOOL: Eastchester (N.Y.).
COLLEGE: Connecticut.
TRANSACTIONS/CAREER NOTES: Signed as free agent by New England Patriots (April 29, 1988); signing later voided. . . . Signed as free agent by Patriots (July 13, 1988). . . . Released by Patriots (August 29, 1988). . . . Re-signed by Patriots (August 30, 1988). . . . On injured reserve with broken ribs (September 29, 1988-remainder of season). . . . Granted unconditional free agency (February 1, 1989). . . . Signed by Dallas Cowboys (March 1, 1989). . . . Released by Cowboys (August 15, 1989). . . . Awarded on waivers to Indianapolis Colts (August 16, 1989). . . . Released by Colts (August 30, 1989). . . . Signed as free agent by New England Patriots (September 6, 1989). . . . Released by Patriots (September 13, 1989). . . . Signed as free agent by Indianapolis Colts (October 6, 1989). . . . Released by Colts (October 11, 1989). . . . Signed as free agent by New York Jets (March 26, 1990). . . . Released by Jets prior to 1990 season. . . . Signed by WLAF (January 17, 1991). . . . Selected by Barcelona Dragons in fourth round (31st linebacker) of 1991 WLAF positional draft. . . . Signed by Washington Redskins (July 9, 1991).
PLAYING EXPERIENCE: New England NFL, 1988; New England (1)-Indianapolis (1) NFL, 1989; Barcelona WLAF, 1991. . . . Games: 1988 (3), 1989 (2), 1991 (10). Total NFL: 5. Total Pro: 15.
PRO STATISTICS: WLAF: 1991—Intercepted one pass for 27 yards and a touchdown.

NASH, JOE
NT, SEAHAWKS

PERSONAL: Born October 11, 1960, at Boston. . . . 6-3/278. . . . Full name: Joseph Andrew Nash.
HIGH SCHOOL: Boston College High (Dorchester, Mass.).
COLLEGE: Boston College (bachelor of arts degree in sociology, 1982).
TRANSACTIONS/CAREER NOTES: Signed as free agent by Seattle Seahawks (April 30, 1982). . . . On inactive list (September 12 and 19, 1982).
PLAYING EXPERIENCE: Seattle NFL, 1982-1990. . . . Games: 1982 (7), 1983 (16), 1984 (16), 1985 (16), 1986 (16), 1987 (12), 1988 (15), 1989 (16), 1990 (16). Total: 130.
CHAMPIONSHIP GAME EXPERIENCE: Played in AFC championship game after 1983 season.
RECORDS/HONORS: Played in Pro Bowl after 1984 season.
PRO STATISTICS: 1984—Recovered three fumbles (including one in end zone for a touchdown). 1986—Recovered two fumbles. 1988—Recovered one fumble. 1990—Recovered one fumble.

NATTIEL, RICKY
WR, BRONCOS

PERSONAL: Born January 25, 1966, at Gainesville, Fla. . . . 5-9/180. . . . Full name: Ricky Rennard Nattiel. . . . Name pronounced na-TEEL.
HIGH SCHOOL: Newberry, Fla.
COLLEGE: Florida (degree in rehabilitation counseling, 1987).
TRANSACTIONS/CAREER NOTES: Selected by Denver Broncos in first round (27th pick overall) of 1987 NFL draft. . . . Signed by Broncos (July 23, 1987). . . . On injured reserve with cracked knee cap (September 23-November 4, 1989). . . . On injured reserve with shoulder injury (December 29, 1990-remainder of season).
CHAMPIONSHIP GAME EXPERIENCE: Played in AFC championship after 1987 and 1989 seasons. . . . Played in Super Bowl XXII after 1987 season and Super Bowl XXIV after 1989 season.
PRO STATISTICS: 1987—Rushed twice for 13 yards and recovered one fumble. 1988—Attempted one pass with no completions and rushed five times for 51 yards and recovered one fumble.

Year	Team	G	No.	Yds.	Avg.	TD	No.	Yds.	Avg.	TD	No.	Yds.	Avg.	TD	TD	Pts.	F.
				RECEIVING				PUNT RETURNS				KICKOFF RETURNS				TOTAL	
1987— Denver NFL		12	31	630	20.3	2	12	73	6.1	0	4	78	19.5	0	2	12	2
1988— Denver NFL		15	46	574	12.5	1	23	223	9.7	0	6	124	20.7	0	1	6	3

Year	Team	G	RECEIVING No.	Yds.	Avg.	TD	PUNT RETURNS No.	Yds.	Avg.	TD	KICKOFF RETURNS No.	Yds.	Avg.	TD	TOTAL TD	Pts.	F.
1989— Denver NFL		8	10	183	18.3	1	9	77	8.6	0	0	0		0	1	6	2
1990— Denver NFL		15	18	297	16.5	2	1	5	5.0	0	1	0	.0	0	2	12	0
Pro totals (4 years)		50	105	1684	16.0	6	45	378	8.4	0	11	202	18.4	0	6	36	7

NELSON, BOB
NT, PACKERS

PERSONAL: Born March 3, 1959, at Baltimore.... 6-4/283.... Full name: Robert William Nelson.
HIGH SCHOOL: Patapsco (Baltimore).
COLLEGE: Miami (Fla.).
TRANSACTIONS/CAREER NOTES: Selected by Miami Dolphins in fifth round (120th pick overall) of 1982 NFL draft.... Released by Dolphins (September 6, 1982).... Signed by Chicago Blitz of USFL (November 30, 1983).... Traded by Blitz with running back Kevin McLee and 12th-round picks in 1984 and 1985 drafts to Arizona Wranglers for rights to guard Bruce Branch (January 13, 1983).... Franchise transferred to Chicago (September 30, 1983).... Traded by Chicago Blitz to Oklahoma Outlaws for guard Terry Crouch (January 19, 1984).... Not protected in merger of Oklahoma Outlaws and Arizona Wranglers.... Selected by Jacksonville Bulls in USFL dispersal draft (December 6, 1984).... Granted free agency (August 1, 1985).... Signed by Tampa Bay Buccaneers (August 6, 1985).... Released by Buccaneers (September 2, 1985). ... Re-signed by Buccaneers (March 21, 1986).... Released by Buccaneers (September 7, 1987).... Signed as free agent by Green Bay Packers (May 5, 1988).... Released by Packers (August 30, 1988).... Re-signed by Packers (September 13, 1988).... Granted free agency (February 1, 1990).... Re-signed by Packers (August 6, 1990).
PLAYING EXPERIENCE: Arizona USFL, 1983; Oklahoma USFL, 1984; Jacksonville USFL, 1985; Tampa Bay NFL, 1986; Green Bay NFL, 1988-1990.... Games: 1983 (18), 1984 (18), 1985 (18), 1986 (16), 1988 (14), 1989 (16), 1990 (16). Total USFL: 54. Total NFL: 62. Total Pro: 116.
PRO STATISTICS: USFL: 1983—Credited with six sacks for 44 yards. 1984—Recovered two fumbles and credited with 6 ½ sacks for 43 yards. 1985—Credited with 5 ½ sacks for 37 yards.... NFL: 1986—Recovered one fumble. 1989—Recovered one fumble.

NELSON, DARRIN
RB, VIKINGS

PERSONAL: Born January 2, 1959, at Sacramento, Calif.... 5-9/185.... Full name: Darrin Milo Nelson. ... Brother of Kevin Nelson, running back with Los Angeles Express, 1984 and 1985; cousin of Ozzie Newsome, tight end with Cleveland Browns, 1978-1990; cousin of Carlos Carson, wide receiver with Kansas City Chiefs and Philadelphia Eagles, 1980-1989; and cousin of Charles Alexander, running back with Cincinnati Bengals, 1979-1985.
HIGH SCHOOL: Pius X (Downey, Calif.).
COLLEGE: Stanford (bachelor of science degree in urban and enviromental planning, 1981).
TRANSACTIONS/CAREER NOTES: Selected by Minnesota Vikings in first round (seventh pick overall) of 1982 NFL draft.... Traded as part of a six-player, 12 draft-choice deal in which Dallas Cowboys sent running back Herschel Walker to Minnesota Vikings in exchange for Nelson, defensive back Issiac Holt, linebackers David Howard and Jesse Solomon, defensive end Alex Stewart, first-round pick in 1992 draft and conditional first-round picks in 1990 and 1991 drafts, conditional second-round picks in 1990, 1991 and 1992 drafts and conditional third-round pick in 1992 draft (October 12, 1989); Nelson refused to report to Dallas and was traded to San Diego Chargers, with Minnesota giving Dallas a sixth-round pick in 1990 as well as the original conditional second-round pick in 1991 and San Diego sending a fifth-round pick in 1990 to Minnesota through Dallas (October 17, 1989); deal completed with Dallas retaining Howard, Solomon and Holt and all conditional picks and Cowboys sending third-round picks in 1990 and 1991 and 10th-round pick in 1990 to Minnesota (February 2, 1990).... Active for one game with Dallas Cowboys in 1989; did not play.... Released by San Diego Chargers (September 3, 1990).... Re-signed by Chargers (September 12, 1990).... Granted unconditional free agency (February 1, 1991).... Signed by Minnesota Vikings (July 15, 1991).
CHAMPIONSHIP GAME EXPERIENCE: Played in NFC championship game after 1987 season.
PRO STATISTICS: 1983—Recovered one fumble. 1984—Recovered three fumbles. 1985—Recovered two fumbles for 16 yards. 1988—Recovered two fumbles.

Year	Team	G	RUSHING Att.	Yds.	Avg.	TD	RECEIVING No.	Yds.	Avg.	TD	PUNT RETURNS No.	Yds.	Avg.	TD	KICKOFF RETURNS No.	Yds.	Avg.	TD	TOTALS TD	Pts.	F.
1982— Minnesota NFL ...		7	44	136	3.1	0	9	100	11.1	0	0	0		0	6	132	22.0	0	0	0	2
1983— Minnesota NFL ...		15	154	642	4.2	1	51	618	12.1	0	0	0		0	18	445	24.7	0	1	6	5
1984— Minnesota NFL ...		15	80	406	5.1	3	27	162	6.0	1	23	180	7.8	0	39	891	22.9	0	4	24	4
1985— Minnesota NFL ...		16	200	893	4.5	5	43	301	7.0	1	16	133	8.3	0	3	51	17.0	0	6	36	7
1986— Minnesota NFL ...		16	191	793	4.2	4	53	593	11.2	3	0	0		0	3	105	35.0	0	7	42	3
1987— Minnesota NFL ...		13	131	642	*4.9	2	26	129	5.0	0	0	0		0	7	164	23.4	0	2	12	2
1988— Minnesota NFL ...		13	112	380	3.4	1	16	105	6.6	0	0	0		0	9	210	23.3	0	1	6	3
1989— M'n(5)-D'l(0)-SD(9) NFL ..		14	67	321	4.8	0	38	380	10.0	0	0	0		0	14	317	22.6	0	0	0	1
1990— San Diego NFL		14	3	14	4.7	0	4	29	7.3	0	3	44	14.7	0	4	36	9.0	0	0	0	1
Pro totals (9 years)		120	982	4227	4.3	16	267	2417	9.1	5	42	357	8.5	0	103	2351	22.8	0	21	126	28

NEUBERT, KEITH
TE, PACKERS

PERSONAL: Born September 13, 1964, at Fort Atkinson, Wis.... 6-6/249.... Full name: Keith Robert Neubert.
HIGH SCHOOL: Fort Atkinson (Wis.).
COLLEGE: Nebraska (degree in speech communications, 1988).
TRANSACTIONS/CAREER NOTES: Selected by New York Jets in eighth round (203rd pick overall) of 1988 NFL draft.... Signed by Jets (June 2, 1988).... On injured reserve with rib injury (August 29-December 16, 1988).... Released by Jets (September 5, 1990).... Signed by Green Bay Packers (March 25, 1991).
PRO STATISTICS: 1989—Recovered one fumble and fumbled twice.

Year Team	G	No.	RECEIVING Yds.	Avg.	TD
1988— N.Y. Jets NFL	1	0	0		0
1989— N.Y. Jets NFL	16	28	302	10.8	1
Pro totals (2 years)	17	28	302	10.8	1

NEVILLE, TOM
G, 49ERS

PERSONAL: Born September 4, 1961, at Great Falls, Mont. . . . 6-5/298. . . . Full name: Thomas Lee Neville.
HIGH SCHOOL: Ben Eielson AFB (Fairbanks, Ala.).
COLLEGE: Weber State, then Fresno State.
TRANSACTIONS/CAREER NOTES: Selected by Oakland Invaders in 1985 USFL territorial draft. . . . Signed as free agent by Seattle Seahawks (May 7, 1985). . . . Released by Seahawks (August 12, 1985). . . . Signed as free agent by Green Bay Packers (March 28, 1986). . . . Released by Packers (September 14, 1988). . . . Signed as free agent by Detroit Lions (July 20, 1989). . . . On injured reserve with thumb injury (August 29-October 30, 1989). . . . Released by Lions (October 31, 1989). . . . Signed as free agent by Kansas City Chiefs (March 12, 1990). . . . Released by Chiefs (August 14, 1990). . . . Signed by San Francisco 49ers (August 18, 1990). . . . Released by 49ers (August 28, 1990). . . . Re-signed by 49ers (offseason, 1991).
PLAYING EXPERIENCE: Green Bay NFL, 1986-1988. . . . Games: 1986 (16), 1987 (12), 1988 (2). Total: 30.
PRO STATISTICS: 1987—Recovered one fumble.

NEWBERRY, TOM
C/G, RAMS

PERSONAL: Born December 20, 1962, at Onalaska, Wis. . . . 6-2/285. . . . Full name: Tom G. Newberry.
HIGH SCHOOL: Onalaska (Wis.).
COLLEGE: Wisconsin at La Crosse (degree in geography, 1986).
TRANSACTIONS/CAREER NOTES: Selected by Los Angeles Rams in second round (50th pick overall) of 1986 NFL draft. . . . Signed by Rams (July 18, 1986). . . . On reserve/did not report list (August 22, 1988). . . . Reported (August 23, 1988).
PLAYING EXPERIENCE: Los Angeles Rams NFL, 1986-1990. . . . Games: 1986 (16), 1987 (12), 1988 (16), 1989 (16), 1990 (15). Total: 75.
CHAMPIONSHIP GAME EXPERIENCE: Played in NFC championship game after 1989 season.
RECORDS/HONORS: Played in Pro Bowl after 1988 season. . . . Named to THE SPORTING NEWS NFL All-Pro team, 1988 and 1989.
PRO STATISTICS: 1986—Recovered one fumble in end zone for a touchdown.

NEWBILL, RICHARD
LB, SEAHAWKS

PERSONAL: Born February 8, 1968, at Camden, N.J. . . . 6-1/240. . . . Full name: Richard Arthur Newbill.
HIGH SCHOOL: Clearview Regional (Mullica Hill, N.J.).
COLLEGE: Bakersfield Community College (Calif.), then Miami, Fla. (degree in law enforcement).
TRANSACTIONS/CAREER NOTES: Selected by Houston Oilers in fifth round (126th pick overall) of 1990 NFL draft. . . . Signed by Oilers (July 22, 1990). . . . Released by Oilers (September 2, 1990). . . . Signed by Minnesota Vikings to practice squad (November 13, 1990). . . . Activated (November 24, 1990). . . . Released by Vikings (December 4, 1990). . . . Re-signed by Vikings to practice squad (December 5, 1990). . . . Signed by Seattle Seahawks off Vikings' practice squad (December 26, 1990).
PLAYING EXPERIENCE: Minnesota (2)-Seattle (1) NFL, 1990. . . . Games: 1990 (3).

NEWMAN, ANTHONY
S, RAMS

PERSONAL: Born November 21, 1965, at Bellingham, Wash. . . . 6-0/199. . . . Full name: Anthony Q. Newman.
HIGH SCHOOL: Beaverton (Ore.).
COLLEGE: Oregon.
TRANSACTIONS/CAREER NOTES: Selected by Los Angeles Rams in second round (35th pick overall) of 1988 NFL draft. . . . Signed by Rams (July 11, 1988). . . . On injured reserve with fractured elbow (December 21, 1989-remainder of season).
MISCELLANEOUS: Selected by Toronto Blue Jays' organization in 26th round of free-agent baseball draft (June 4, 1984). . . . Selected by Cleveland Indians' organization in secondary phase of free-agent baseball draft (January 9, 1985). . . . Selected by Texas Rangers' organization in secondary phase of free-agent baseball draft (June 3, 1985).
PRO STATISTICS: 1988—Recovered one fumble. 1990—Recovered one fumble.

Year Team	G	No.	INTERCEPTIONS Yds.	Avg.	TD
1988— L.A. Rams NFL	16	2	27	13.5	0
1989— L.A. Rams NFL	15	0	0		0
1990— L.A. Rams NFL	16	2	0	.0	0
Pro totals (3 years)	47	4	27	6.8	0

NEWSOME, HARRY
P, VIKINGS

PERSONAL: Born January 25, 1963, at Cheraw, S.C. . . . 6-0/188. . . . Full name: Harry Kent Newsome Jr.
HIGH SCHOOL: Cheraw (S.C.).
COLLEGE: Wake Forest.
TRANSACTIONS/CAREER NOTES: Selected by New Jersey Generals in 15th round (213th pick overall) of 1985 USFL draft. . . . Selected by Pittsburgh Steelers in eighth round (214th pick overall) of 1985 NFL draft. . . . Signed by Steelers (July 26, 1985). . . . Granted unconditional free agency (February 1, 1990). . . . Signed by Minnesota Vikings (March 22, 1990).

RECORDS/HONORS: Established NFL record for having most punts blocked, season (6), 1988.
PRO STATISTICS: 1986—Attempted two passes with one completion for 12 yards and a touchdown. 1987—Rushed twice for 16 yards and recovered one fumble and fumbled once for minus 17 yards. 1988—Rushed twice for no yards and recovered one fumble. 1989—Rushed twice for minus eight yards and recovered one fumble and fumbled once for minus 13 yards. 1990—Rushed twice for minus two yards and recovered one fumble and fumbled once for minus 13 yards.

| | | | — PUNTING— | | |
Year	Team	G	No.	Avg.	Blk.
1985— Pittsburgh NFL		16	78	39.6	1
1986— Pittsburgh NFL		16	86	40.1	*3
1987— Pittsburgh NFL		12	64	41.8	1
1988— Pittsburgh NFL		16	65	*45.4	*6
1989— Pittsburgh NFL		16	82	41.1	1
1990— Minnesota NFL		16	78	42.3	1
Pro totals (6 years)		92	453	41.7	13

NEWSOME, VINCE
S, BROWNS

PERSONAL: Born January 22, 1961, at Braintree, Wash.... 6-1/185.... Full name: Vincent Karl Newsome.
HIGH SCHOOL: Vacaville (Calif.).
COLLEGE: Washington.
TRANSACTIONS/CAREER NOTES: Selected by Oakland Invaders in fourth round (42nd pick overall) of 1983 USFL draft.... Selected by Los Angeles Rams in fourth round (97th pick overall) of 1983 NFL draft.... Signed by Rams (May 22, 1983).... On injured reserve with knee injury (December 8, 1987-remainder of season).... On injured reserve with herniated disc (October 20, 1987-remainder of season).... Granted unconditional free agency (February 1, 1991).... Signed by Cleveland Browns (March 29, 1991).
CHAMPIONSHIP GAME EXPERIENCE: Played in NFC championship game after 1985 season.... Member of Los Angeles Rams for NFC championship game after 1989 season; did not play.
PRO STATISTICS: 1985—Recovered one fumble. 1986—Recovered one fumble. 1987—Recovered one fumble for seven yards. 1988—Recovered one fumble. 1989—Recovered one fumble. 1990—Recovered one fumble.

| | | | — INTERCEPTIONS— | | | |
Year	Team	G	No.	Yds.	Avg.	TD
1983— L.A. Rams NFL		16	0	0		0
1984— L.A. Rams NFL		16	1	31	31.0	0
1985— L.A. Rams NFL		16	3	20	6.7	0
1986— L.A. Rams NFL		16	3	45	15.0	0
1987— L.A. Rams NFL		8	0	0		0
1988— L.A. Rams NFL		6	0	3		0
1989— L.A. Rams NFL		16	1	81	81.0	0
1990— L.A. Rams NFL		16	4	47	11.8	0
Pro totals (8 years)		110	12	227	18.9	0

NEWTON, NATE
G/OT, COWBOYS

PERSONAL: Born December 20, 1961, at Orlando, Fla.... 6-3/322.... Full name: Nathaniel Newton Jr.... Brother of Tim Newton, defensive lineman with Tampa Bay Buccaneers.
HIGH SCHOOL: Jones (Orlando, Fla.).
COLLEGE: Florida A&M.
TRANSACTIONS/CAREER NOTES: Selected by Tampa Bay Bandits in 1983 USFL territorial draft.... Signed as free agent by Washington Redskins (May 5, 1983).... Released by Redskins (August 29, 1983).... Signed by Tampa Bay Bandits of USFL (November 6, 1983).... Granted free agency when USFL suspended operations (August 7, 1986).... Signed as free agent by Dallas Cowboys (August 14, 1986).... Granted roster exemption (August 14-August 21, 1986).... Crossed picket line during players' strike (October 24, 1987).
PLAYING EXPERIENCE: Tampa Bay USFL, 1984 and 1985; Dallas NFL, 1986-1990.... Games: 1984 (18), 1985 (18), 1986 (11), 1987 (11), 1988 (15), 1989 (16), 1990 (16). Total USFL: 36. Total NFL: 69. Total Pro: 105.
PRO STATISTICS: 1988—Caught one pass for two yards. 1990—Recovered two fumbles.

NEWTON, TIM
DL, BUCCANEERS

PERSONAL: Born March 23, 1963, at Orlando, Fla.... 6-0/275.... Full name: Timothy Reginald Newton.... Brother of Nate Newton, guard/tackle with Dallas Cowboys.
HIGH SCHOOL: Jones (Orlando, Fla.).
COLLEGE: Florida.
TRANSACTIONS/CAREER NOTES: Selected by Tampa Bay Bandits in 1985 USFL territorial draft.... Selected by Minnesota Vikings in sixth round (164th pick overall) of 1985 NFL draft.... Signed by Vikings (June 17, 1985).... On injured reserve with knee injury (December 24, 1988-remainder of 1988 season playoffs).... Released by Vikings (December 26, 1989).... Signed as free agent by Tampa Bay Buccaneers (February 27, 1990).... On injured reserve with broken leg (December 17, 1990-remainder of season).
PLAYING EXPERIENCE: Minnesota NFL, 1985-1989; Tampa Bay NFL, 1990.... Games: 1985 (16), 1986 (14), 1987 (9), 1988 (14), 1989 (9), 1990 (14). Total: 76.
CHAMPIONSHIP GAME EXPERIENCE: Played in NFC championship game after 1987 season.
PRO STATISTICS: 1985—Intercepted two passes for 63 yards, recovered one fumble and fumbled once. 1986—Recovered one fumble. 1988—Recovered one fumble. 1989—Recovered one fumble for five yards and a touchdown.

NICHOLS, GERALD

DT/DE, JETS

PERSONAL: Born February 10, 1964, at St. Louis. . . . 6-2/260. . . . Full name: Gerald W. Nichols.
HIGH SCHOOL: Hazelwood East (St. Louis).
COLLEGE: Florida State (degree in psychology, 1987).
TRANSACTIONS/CAREER NOTES: Selected by New York Jets in seventh round (187th pick overall) of 1987 NFL draft. . . . Signed by Jets (July 20, 1987). . . . Crossed picket line during players' strike (October 12, 1987). . . . Granted free agency (February 1, 1990). . . . Re-signed by Jets (June 27, 1990). . . . On inactive list (October 21, 1990).
PLAYING EXPERIENCE: New York Jets NFL, 1987-1990. . . . Games: 1987 (13), 1988 (16), 1989 (16), 1990 (15). Total: 60.
PRO STATISTICS: 1989—Returned two kickoffs for nine yards. 1990—Returned two kickoffs for three yards and recovered one fumble.

NICHOLSON, CALVIN

CB, SAINTS

PERSONAL: Born July 9, 1967, at Los Angeles. . . . 5-9/183. . . . Full name: Calvin T. Nicholson. . . . Nephew of Paul Silas, assistant coach with New York Knicks.
HIGH SCHOOL: El Camino Real (Los Angeles).
COLLEGE: West Los Angeles College (Calif.), then Oregon State.
TRANSACTIONS/CAREER NOTES: Selected by New Orleans Saints in 11th round (300th pick overall) of 1989 NFL draft. . . . Signed by Saints (July 22, 1989). . . . Released by Saints (September 5, 1989). . . . Re-signed by Saints to developmental squad (September 6, 1989). . . . On developmental squad (September 6-December 13, 1989). . . . Activated after clearing procedural waivers (December 15, 1989). . . . Released by Saints (September 3, 1990). . . . Signed by Saints to practice squad (January 3, 1991). . . . Signed by Saints for 1991 (February 15, 1991). . . . Assigned to Raleigh-Durham Skyhawks in 1991 WLAF enhancement allocation program. . . . Assigned to Team Dallas (March 17, 1991). . . . Signed by San Antonio Riders (March 29, 1991).
PLAYING EXPERIENCE: New Orleans NFL, 1989; San Antonio WLAF, 1991. . . . Games: 1989 (1), 1991 (9). Total NFL: 1. Total Pro: 10.
PRO STATISTICS: WLAF: 1991—Intercepted three passes for 23 yards and recovered two fumbles.

NICKERSON, HARDY

LB, STEELERS

PERSONAL: Born September 1, 1965, at Los Angeles. . . . 6-2/225. . . . Full name: Hardy Otto Nickerson.
HIGH SCHOOL: Verbum Dei (Los Angeles).
COLLEGE: California.
TRANSACTIONS/CAREER NOTES: Selected by Pittsburgh Steelers in fifth round (122nd pick overall) of 1987 NFL draft. . . . Signed by Steelers (July 26, 1987). . . . On injured reserve with ankle and knee injuries (November 3-December 16, 1989).
PLAYING EXPERIENCE: Pittsburgh NFL, 1987-1990. . . . Games: 1987 (12), 1988 (15), 1989 (10), 1990 (16). Total: 53.
PRO STATISTICS: 1987—Recovered one fumble. 1988—Intercepted one pass for no yards and recovered one fumble.

NITTMO, BJORN

PK, BILLS

PERSONAL: Born July 26, 1966, at Lund, Sweden. . . . 5-11/185. . . . Full name: Bjorn Arne Nittmo.
HIGH SCHOOL: Enterprise (Ala.).
COLLEGE: Appalachian State.
TRANSACTIONS/CAREER NOTES: Signed as free agent by New York Giants (May 12, 1989). . . . Released by Giants (September 5, 1989). . . . Re-signed by Giants to developmental squad (September 6, 1989). . . . On developmental squad (September 6-November 14, 1989). . . . Released by Giants (November 15, 1989). . . . Re-signed by Giants to developmental squad (November 16, 1989). . . . Activated (November 18, 1989). . . . Deactivated for playoffs (January 6, 1990). . . . Granted unconditional free agency (February 1, 1990). . . . Signed by Kansas City Chiefs (April 1, 1990). . . . Released by Chiefs (August 28, 1990). . . . Signed by WLAF (January 10, 1991). . . . Selected by Montreal Machine in first round (fifth kicker) of 1991 WLAF positional draft. . . . Signed by Buffalo Bills (June 12, 1991).

———— PLACE-KICKING ————

Year Team	G	XPM	XPA	FGM	FGA	Pts.
1989— N.Y. Giants NFL	6	12	13	9	12	39
1991— Montreal WLAF	10	12	13	13	18	51
NFL totals (1 year)	6	12	13	9	12	39
WLAF totals (1 year)	10	12	13	13	18	51
Pro totals (2 years)	16	24	26	22	30	90

NOBLE, BRIAN

LB, PACKERS

PERSONAL: Born September 6, 1962, at Anaheim, Calif. . . . 6-4/250. . . . Full name: Brian David Noble.
HIGH SCHOOL: Anaheim (Calif.).
COLLEGE: Fullerton College (Calif.), then Arizona State.
TRANSACTIONS/CAREER NOTES: Selected by Arizona Outlaws in 1985 USFL territorial draft. . . . Selected by Green Bay Packers in fifth round (125th pick overall) of 1985 NFL draft. . . . Signed by Packers (July 19, 1985). . . . Granted free agency (February 1, 1988). . . . Re-signed by Packers (September 27, 1988). . . . Granted free agency (February 1, 1990). . . . Re-signed by Packers (August 7, 1990). . . . On inactive list (December 22, 1990). . . . On injured reserve with knee injury (December 29, 1990-remainder of season).
PLAYING EXPERIENCE: Green Bay NFL, 1985-1990. . . . Games: 1985 (16), 1986 (16), 1987 (12), 1988 (12), 1989 (16), 1990 (14). Total: 86.
PRO STATISTICS: 1986—Returned one kickoff for one yard. 1987—Intercepted one pass for 10 yards and recovered five fumbles. 1988—Recovered one fumble. 1989—Intercepted two passes for 10 yards and recovered one fumble.

NOGA, AL

DE, VIKINGS

PERSONAL: Born September 16, 1965, at American Samoa. . . . 6-1/248. . . . Full name: Alapati Noga. . . . Brother of Niko Noga, linebacker with Detroit Lions; and Pete Noga, linebacker with St. Louis Cardinals, 1987.
HIGH SCHOOL: Farrington (Honolulu).

COLLEGE: Hawaii.
TRANSACTIONS/CAREER NOTES: Selected by Minnesota Vikings in third round (71st pick overall) of 1988 NFL draft.... Signed by Vikings (July 29, 1988).... On suspended list (September 10-September 13, 1988).... On non-football injury list with viral infection (October 5-November 19, 1988).
PLAYING EXPERIENCE: Minnesota NFL, 1988-1990.... Games: 1988 (9), 1989 (16), 1990 (16). Total: 41.
PRO STATISTICS: 1989—Recovered one fumble. 1990—Intercepted one pass for 26 yards and a touchdown and recovered one fumble in the end zone for a touchdown.

NOGA, NIKO
LB, LIONS

PERSONAL: Born March 2, 1962, at American Samoa.... 6-1/235.... Full name: Falaniko Noga.... First name pronounced Fah-lah-NEE-koh.... Brother of Pete Noga, linebacker with St. Louis Cardinals, 1987; and Al Noga, defensive end with Minnesota Vikings.
HIGH SCHOOL: Farrington (Honolulu, Hawaii).
COLLEGE: Hawaii.
TRANSACTIONS/CAREER NOTES: Selected by Oakland Invaders in 10th round (192nd pick overall) of 1984 USFL draft.... Selected by St. Louis Cardinals in eighth round (201st pick overall) of 1984 NFL draft.... Signed by Cardinals (July 16, 1984).... Franchise transferred to Phoenix (March 15, 1988).... Released by Phoenix Cardinals (August 29, 1989).... Signed as free agent by Detroit Lions (September 20, 1989).
PLAYING EXPERIENCE: St. Louis NFL, 1984-1987; Phoenix NFL, 1988; Detroit NFL, 1989 and 1990.... Games: 1984 (16), 1985 (16), 1986 (16), 1987 (12), 1988 (16), 1989 (14), 1990 (16). Total: 106.
PRO STATISTICS: 1984—Recovered one fumble. 1985—Recovered two fumbles. 1986—Recovered two fumbles. 1987—Recovered one fumble for 23 yards and a touchdown. 1989—Intercepted one pass for no yards.

NOONAN, DANNY
DT, COWBOYS

PERSONAL: Born July 14, 1965, at Lincoln, Neb.... 6-4/275.... Full name: Daniel Nicholas Noonan.
HIGH SCHOOL: Northeast (Lincoln, Neb.).
COLLEGE: Nebraska.
TRANSACTIONS/CAREER NOTES: Selected by Dallas Cowboys in first round (12th pick overall) of 1987 NFL draft.... Signed by Cowboys (August 30, 1987).... Granted roster exemption (August 30-September 14, 1987).... On injured reserve with groin injury (October 6-November 17, 1989).
PLAYING EXPERIENCE: Dallas NFL, 1987-1990.... Games: 1987 (11), 1988 (16), 1989 (7), 1990 (16). Total: 50.
PRO STATISTICS: 1988—Intercepted one pass for 17 yards and a touchdown and credited with a safety.

NORGARD, ERIK
C/G, OILERS

PERSONAL: Born November 4, 1965, at Bellevue, Wash.... 6-1/278.... Full name: Erik Christian Norgard.
HIGH SCHOOL: Arlington (Wash.).
COLLEGE: Colorado (bachelor of arts degree in communications).
TRANSACTIONS/CAREER NOTES: Signed as free agent by Houston Oilers (May 12, 1989).... Released by Oilers (August 30, 1989).... Re-signed by Oilers to developmental squad (September 6, 1989).... Released by Oilers (January 2, 1990).... Re-signed by Oilers (March 8, 1990).
PLAYING EXPERIENCE: Houston NFL, 1990.... Games: 1990 (16).
PRO STATISTICS: 1990—Returned two kickoffs for no yards.

NORSETH, MIKE
QB, OILERS

PERSONAL: Born August 22, 1964, at Hollywood, Calif.... 6-2/200.... Full name: Michael Adam Norseth.
HIGH SCHOOL: Valley (LaCrescenta, Calif.).
COLLEGE: Snow College (Utah), then Kansas.
TRANSACTIONS/CAREER NOTES: Selected by Cleveland Browns in seventh round (174th pick overall) of 1986 NFL draft.... Signed by Browns (July 18, 1986).... On injured reserve with stomach injury (August 28, 1986-entire season).... Released by Browns (September 7, 1987).... Awarded on waivers to Cincinnati Bengals (September 8, 1987).... Active for three games with Bengals in 1987; did not play.... Granted unconditional free agency (February 1, 1989).... Signed by Cleveland Browns (February 24, 1989).... Released by Browns (September 5, 1989).... Signed as free agent by Green Bay Packers (March 20, 1990).... Released by Packers (September 3, 1990).... Re-signed by Packers (November 21, 1990).... On inactive list (November 25, 1990).... Released by Packers (December 1, 1990).... Re-signed by Packers (December 15, 1990). ... On inactive list (December 16, 1990).... Active for two games in 1990; did not play.... Granted unconditional free agency (February 1, 1991).... Rights relinquished by Packers (May 2, 1991).... Signed by Houston Oilers (July 16, 1991).
PLAYING EXPERIENCE: Cincinnati NFL, 1987 and 1988; Green Bay NFL, 1990.... Games: 1987 (0), 1988 (1), 1990 (0). Total: 1.
CHAMPIONSHIP GAME EXPERIENCE: Member of Cincinnati Bengals for AFC championship game and Super Bowl XXIII after 1988 season; did not play.
PRO STATISTICS: 1988—Rushed once for five yards.

NORTON, KEN
LB, COWBOYS

PERSONAL: Born September 29, 1966, at Jacksonville, Ill.... 6-2/237.... Full name: Kenneth Howard Norton Jr.... Son of Ken Norton Sr., former world heavyweight boxing champion.
HIGH SCHOOL: Westchester (Los Angeles).
COLLEGE: UCLA.
TRANSACTIONS/CAREER NOTES: Selected by Dallas Cowboys in second round (41st pick overall) of 1988 NFL draft.... Signed by Cowboys (July 13, 1988).... On injured reserve with broken arm (August 23-December 3, 1988).... On injured reserve with knee injury (December 24, 1990-remainder of season).
PLAYING EXPERIENCE: Dallas NFL, 1988-1990.... Games: 1988 (3), 1989 (13), 1990 (15). Total: 31.
RECORDS/HONORS: Named as linebacker on THE SPORTING NEWS college All-America team, 1987.
PRO STATISTICS: 1988—Recovered one fumble. 1990—Recovered two fumbles.

NORWOOD, SCOTT
PK, BILLS

PERSONAL: Born July 17, 1960, at Alexandria, Va. . . . 6-0/207. . . . Full name: Scott Allan Norwood.
HIGH SCHOOL: Thomas Jefferson (Alexandria, Va.).
COLLEGE: James Madison (bachelor of business administration degree in management).
TRANSACTIONS/CAREER NOTES: Signed as free agent by Atlanta Falcons (May 5, 1982). . . . Released by Falcons (August 30, 1982). . . . Signed by Birmingham Stallions of USFL (January 4, 1983). . . . On developmental squad for two games (March 15-March 25, 1984). . . . On injured reserve with knee injury (March 26, 1984-remainder of season). . . . Released by Stallions (February 18, 1985). . . . Signed as free agent by Buffalo Bills (March 22, 1985). . . . Released by Bills (September 1, 1986). . . . Re-signed by Bills (September 2, 1986).
CHAMPIONSHIP GAME EXPERIENCE: Played in AFC championship game after 1988 and 1990 seasons. . . . Played in Super Bowl XXV after 1990 season.
RECORDS/HONORS: Played in Pro Bowl after 1988 season.
PRO STATISTICS: 1983—Caught one pass for no yards and recovered one fumble.

| | | | —— PLACE-KICKING —— | | | |
Year	Team	G	XPM	XPA	FGM	FGA	Pts.
1983— Birmingham USFL		18	34	35	25	34	109
1984— Birmingham USFL		3	4	4	3	4	13
1985— Buffalo NFL		16	23	23	13	17	62
1986— Buffalo NFL		16	32	34	17	27	83
1987— Buffalo NFL		12	31	31	10	15	61
1988— Buffalo NFL		16	33	33	*32	37	*129
1989— Buffalo NFL		16	46	47	23	30	115
1990— Buffalo NFL		16	*50	52	20	29	110
USFL totals (2 years)		21	38	39	28	38	122
NFL totals (6 years)		92	215	220	115	155	560
Pro totals (8 years)		113	253	259	143	193	682

NOVACEK, JAY
TE, COWBOYS

PERSONAL: Born October 24, 1962, at Martin, S.D. . . . 6-4/230. . . . Full name: Jay McKinley Novacek.
HIGH SCHOOL: Gothenburg (Neb.).
COLLEGE: Wyoming (bachelor of science degree in industrial education, 1986).
TRANSACTIONS/CAREER NOTES: Selected by Houston Gamblers in fifth round (69th pick overall) of 1985 USFL draft. . . . Selected by St. Louis Cardinals in sixth round (158th pick overall) of 1985 NFL draft. . . . Signed by Cardinals (July 21, 1985). . . . On injured reserve with broken thumb (August 19-October 17, 1986). . . . On injured reserve with knee injury (December 10, 1986-remainder of season). . . . On injured reserve with broken bone in elbow (November 3-December 5, 1987). . . . Franchise transferred to Phoenix (March 15, 1988). . . . Granted unconditional free agency (February 1, 1990). . . . Signed by Dallas Cowboys (March 5, 1990).
PRO STATISTICS: 1985—Returned one kickoff for 20 yards. 1987—Fumbled once. 1988—Rushed once for 10 yards and recovered one fumble. 1989—Recovered one fumble. 1990—Fumbled once.

| | | | —— RECEIVING —— | | | |
Year	Team	G	No.	Yds.	Avg.	TD
1985— St. Louis NFL		16	1	4	4.0	0
1986— St. Louis NFL		8	1	2	2.0	0
1987— St. Louis NFL		7	20	254	12.7	3
1988— Phoenix NFL		16	38	569	15.0	4
1989— Phoenix NFL		16	23	225	9.8	1
1990— Dallas NFL		16	59	657	11.1	4
Pro totals (6 years)		79	142	1711	12.1	12

NOVOSELSKY, BRENT
TE, VIKINGS

PERSONAL: Born January 8, 1966, at Skokie, Ill. . . . 6-2/238. . . . Full name: Brent Howard Novoselsky.
HIGH SCHOOL: Niles North (Skokie, Ill.).
COLLEGE: Pennsylvania (bachelor of science degree in economics, 1988).
TRANSACTIONS/CAREER NOTES: Signed as free agent by Chicago Bears (May 16, 1988). . . . Released by Bears (August 24, 1988). . . . Re-signed by Bears (September 20, 1988). . . . On injured reserve with ankle injury (November 11-December 8, 1988). . . . Released by Bears (December 9, 1988). . . . Re-signed by Bears (December 14, 1988). . . . Granted unconditional free agency (February 1, 1989). . . . Signed by Green Bay Packers (March 15, 1989). . . . Released by Packers (August 29, 1989). . . . Signed as free agent by Minnesota Vikings (September 13, 1989).
CHAMPIONSHIP GAME EXPERIENCE: Played in NFC championship game after 1988 season.
PRO STATISTICS: 1990—Recovered one fumble.

| | | | —— RECEIVING —— | | | |
Year	Team	G	No.	Yds.	Avg.	TD
1988— Chicago NFL		8	0	0		0
1989— Minnesota NFL		15	4	11	2.8	2
1990— Minnesota NFL		16	0	0		0
Pro totals (3 years)		39	4	11	2.8	2

NUNN, FREDDIE JOE
LB, CARDINALS

PERSONAL: Born April 9, 1962, at Noxubee County, Miss. . . . 6-4/250. . . . Full name: Freddie Joe Nunn.
HIGH SCHOOL: Nanih Waiya (Louisville, Miss.).
COLLEGE: Mississippi.

TRANSACTIONS/CAREER NOTES: Selected by Birmingham Stallions in 1985 USFL territorial draft. . . . Selected by St. Louis Cardinals in first round (18th pick overall) of 1985 NFL draft. . . . Signed by Cardinals (August 5, 1985). . . . Franchise transferred to Phoenix (March 15, 1988). . . . On non-football injury list with substance abuse (September 26-October 23, 1989). . . . Reinstated and granted roster exemption (October 24-October 27, 1989). . . . Granted free agency (February 1, 1990). . . . Re-signed by Phoenix Cardinals (July 30, 1990).
PLAYING EXPERIENCE: St. Louis NFL, 1985-1987; Phoenix NFL, 1988-1990. . . . Games: 1985 (16), 1986 (16), 1987 (12), 1988 (16), 1989 (12), 1990 (16). Total: 88.
PRO STATISTICS: 1985—Recovered two fumbles. 1986—Recovered one fumble. 1988—Recovered two fumbles for eight yards. 1989—Recovered one fumble. 1990—Recovered one fumble.

OATES, BART
C, GIANTS

PERSONAL: Born December 16, 1958, at Mesa, Ariz. . . . 6-3/265. . . . Full name: Bart Steven Oates. . . . Brother of Brad Oates, offensive tackle with St. Louis Cardinals, Detroit Lions, Kansas City Chiefs, Cincinnati Bengals, Green Bay Packers and Philadelphia Stars (USFL), 1976-1981, 1983 and 1984.
HIGH SCHOOL: Albany (Ga.).
COLLEGE: Brigham Young (bachelor's degree in accounting).
TRANSACTIONS/CAREER NOTES: Selected by Philadelphia Stars in second round (17th pick overall) of 1983 USFL draft. . . . Signed by Stars (January 24, 1983). . . . On developmental squad for one game (April 28-May 6, 1983). . . . Franchise transferred to Baltimore (November 1, 1984). . . . Released by Baltimore Stars (August 27, 1985). . . . Signed as free agent by New York Giants (August 28, 1985).
PLAYING EXPERIENCE: Philadelphia USFL, 1983 and 1984; Baltimore USFL, 1985; New York Giants NFL, 1985-1990. . . . Games: 1983 (17), 1984 (17), 1985 USFL (18), 1985 NFL (16), 1986 (16), 1987 (12), 1988 (16), 1989 (16), 1990 (16). Total USFL: 52. Total NFL: 92. Total Pro: 144.
CHAMPIONSHIP GAME EXPERIENCE: Played in USFL championship game after 1983-1985 seasons. . . . Played in NFC championship game after 1986 and 1990 seasons. . . . Played in Super Bowl XXI after 1986 season and Super Bowl XXV after 1990 season.
RECORDS/HONORS: Named as center on THE SPORTING NEWS USFL All-Star team, 1983. . . . Played in Pro Bowl after 1990 season.
PRO STATISTICS: USFL: 1984—Rushed once for five yards and recovered two fumbles. 1985—Recovered one fumble for four yards. . . . NFL: 1985—Recovered two fumbles. 1986—Fumbled once for minus four yards. 1987—Recovered one fumble. 1988—Fumbled once for minus 10 yards. 1989—Fumbled once. 1990—Fumbled once for minus 19 yards.

O'BRIEN, KEN
QB, JETS

PERSONAL: Born November 27, 1960, at Long Island, N.Y. . . . 6-4/212. . . . Full name: Kenneth John O'Brien Jr.
HIGH SCHOOL: Jesuit (Sacramento, Calif.).
COLLEGE: Cal State Sacramento; then Cal Davis (degree in political science, 1983).
TRANSACTIONS/CAREER NOTES: Selected by Oakland Invaders in sixth round (66th pick overall) of 1983 USFL draft. . . . Selected by New York Jets in first round (24th pick overall) of 1983 NFL draft. . . . Signed by Jets (July 21, 1983). . . . Active for 16 games with Jets in 1983; did not play.
RECORDS/HONORS: Led NFL quarterbacks in passing with 96.2 points, 1985. . . . Played in Pro Bowl after 1985 season.
PRO STATISTICS: Passer rating points: 1984 (74.0), 1985 (96.2), 1986 (85.8), 1987 (82.8), 1988 (78.6), 1989 (74.3), 1990 (77.3). Career: 82.2. . . . 1984—Recovered two fumbles. 1985—Recovered four fumbles. 1986—Recovered five fumbles and fumbled 10 times for minus three yards. 1987—Recovered one fumble and fumbled eight times for minus 10 yards. 1988—Recovered five fumbles and fumbled 11 times for minus 14 yards. 1989—Recovered four fumbles and fumbled 10 times for minus 13 yards. 1990—Punted once for 23 yards and recovered four fumbles and fumbled five times for minus four yards.

			PASSING						RUSHING				TOTAL		
Year Team	G	Att.	Cmp.	Pct.	Yds.	TD	Int.	Avg.	Att.	Yds.	Avg.	TD	TD	Pts.	F.
1984— N.Y. Jets NFL	10	203	116	57.1	1402	6	7	6.91	16	29	1.8	0	0	0	4
1985— N.Y. Jets NFL	16	488	297	60.9	3888	25	8	7.97	25	58	2.3	0	0	0	14
1986— N.Y. Jets NFL	15	482	300	62.2	3690	25	20	7.66	17	46	2.7	0	0	0	10
1987— N.Y. Jets NFL	12	393	234	59.5	2696	13	8	6.86	30	61	2.0	0	0	0	8
1988— N.Y. Jets NFL	14	424	236	55.7	2567	15	7	6.05	21	25	1.2	0	0	0	11
1989— N.Y. Jets NFL	15	477	288	60.4	3346	12	18	7.01	9	18	2.0	0	0	0	10
1990— N.Y. Jets NFL	16	411	226	55.0	2855	13	10	6.95	21	72	3.4	0	0	0	5
Pro totals (7 years)	98	2878	1697	59.0	20444	109	78	7.10	139	309	2.2	0	0	0	62

ODEGARD, DON
CB/KR, JETS

PERSONAL: Born November 22, 1966, at Seattle. . . . 6-0/180. . . . Full name: Donald Lee Odegard.
HIGH SCHOOL: Kennewick (Wash.).
COLLEGE: Oregon State, then UNLV (bachelor of arts degree in political science).
TRANSACTIONS/CAREER NOTES: Selected by Cincinnati Bengals in sixth round (150th pick overall) of 1990 NFL draft. . . . Signed by Bengals (July 17, 1990). . . . Released by Bengals (September 3, 1990). . . . Signed by New York Jets (September 11, 1990). . . . On inactive list (September 16, 1990).

		PUNT RETURNS				KICKOFF RETURNS				TOTAL		
Year Team	G	No.	Yds.	Avg.	TD	No.	Yds.	Avg.	TD	TD	Pts.	F.
1990— N.Y. Jets NFL	14	1	0	.0	0	5	89	17.8	0	0	0	0
Pro totals (1 year)	14	1	0	.0	0	5	89	17.8	0	0	0	0

ODOM, CLIFF

LB, DOLPHINS

PERSONAL: Born August 15, 1958, at Beaumont, Tex. . . . 6-2/243. . . . Full name: Clifton Louis Odom.
HIGH SCHOOL: French (Beaumont, Tex.).
COLLEGE: Texas-Arlington.

TRANSACTIONS/CAREER NOTES: Selected by Cleveland Browns in third round (72nd pick overall) of 1980 NFL draft. . . . On injured reserve with knee injury (November 3, 1980-remainder of season). . . . Released by Cleveland Browns (August 18, 1981). . . . Signed as free agent by Oakland Raiders (March 1, 1982). . . . Raiders franchise transferred to Los Angeles (May 7, 1982). . . . Released by Los Angeles Raiders (August 10, 1982). . . . Signed as free agent by Baltimore Colts (August 12, 1982). . . . Released by Colts (September 6, 1982). . . . Re-signed by Colts (September 7, 1982). . . . Colts franchise transferred to Indianapolis (March 31, 1984). . . . Granted free agency (February 1, 1986). . . . Re-signed by Colts (August 17, 1986). . . . Granted roster exemption (August 17-August 22, 1986). . . . Granted unconditional free agency (February 1, 1990). . . . Signed by Miami Dolphins (March 27, 1990).
PLAYING EXPERIENCE: Cleveland NFL, 1980; Baltimore NFL, 1982 and 1983; Indianapolis NFL, 1984-1989; Miami NFL, 1990. . . . Games: 1980 (8), 1982 (8), 1983 (15), 1984 (16), 1985 (16), 1986 (16), 1987 (12), 1988 (13), 1989 (16), 1990 (16). Total: 136.
PRO STATISTICS: 1984—Recovered one fumble. 1985—Recovered two fumbles. 1986—Recovered two fumbles. 1987—Recovered three fumbles for eight yards. 1988—Recovered one fumble. 1990—Recovered one fumble for one yard and a touchdown.

ODOMES, NATE

CB, BILLS

PERSONAL: Born August 25, 1965, at Columbus, Ga. . . . 5-10/188. . . . Full name: Nathaniel Bernard Odomes. . . . Name pronounced O-dums.
HIGH SCHOOL: Carver (Columbus, Ga.).
COLLEGE: Wisconsin.

TRANSACTIONS/CAREER NOTES: Selected by Buffalo Bills in second round (29th pick overall) of 1987 NFL draft. . . . Signed by Bills (July 22, 1987).
CHAMPIONSHIP GAME EXPERIENCE: Played in AFC championship game after 1988 and 1990 seasons. . . . Played in Super Bowl XXV after 1990 season.
PRO STATISTICS: 1987—Recovered two fumbles. 1990—Returned one punt for nine yards and recovered three fumbles for 49 yards and a touchdown.

			INTERCEPTIONS		
Year Team	G	No.	Yds.	Avg.	TD
1987— Buffalo NFL	12	0	0		0
1988— Buffalo NFL	16	1	0	.0	0
1989— Buffalo NFL	16	5	20	4.0	0
1990— Buffalo NFL	16	1	0	.0	0
Pro totals (4 years)	60	7	20	2.9	0

O'DONNELL, NEIL

QB, STEELERS

PERSONAL: Born July 3, 1966, at Morristown, N.J. . . . 6-3/221. . . . Full name: Neil Kennedy O'Donnell.
HIGH SCHOOL: Madison-Boro (Madison, N.J.).
COLLEGE: Maryland (bachelor's degree in economics, 1990).

TRANSACTIONS/CAREER NOTES: Selected by Pittsburgh Steelers in third round (70th pick overall) of 1990 NFL draft. . . . Signed by Steelers (August 8, 1990). . . . On inactive list (September 9, 16, 23, 30; October 7, 28; November 4, 18, 25; and December 2, 9, 16 and 30, 1990). . . . Active for three games in 1990; did not play.
PLAYING EXPERIENCE: Pittsburgh NFL, 1990. . . . Games: none.

OFFERDAHL, JOHN

LB, DOLPHINS

PERSONAL: Born August 17, 1964, at Wisconsin Rapids, Wis. . . . 6-3/238. . . . Full name: John Arnold Offerdahl. . . . Name pronounced OFF-er-doll.
HIGH SCHOOL: Fort Atkinson (Wis.).
COLLEGE: Western Michigan.

TRANSACTIONS/CAREER NOTES: Selected by Miami Dolphins in second round (52nd pick overall) of 1986 NFL draft. . . . Signed by Dolphins (July 29, 1986). . . . On injured reserve with torn bicep (September 8-October 31, 1987). . . . On reserve/did not report list (July 28-October 15, 1989). . . . Reinstated and granted roster exemption (October 16-October 21, 1989). . . . On inactive list (January 12, 1991).
PLAYING EXPERIENCE: Miami NFL, 1986-1990. . . . Games: 1986 (15), 1987 (9), 1988 (16), 1989 (10), 1990 (16). Total: 66.
RECORDS/HONORS: Played in Pro Bowl after 1986, 1987 and 1989 seasons. . . . Named to play in Pro Bowl after 1988 season; replaced due to injury by Johnny Rembert. . . . Named to play in Pro Bowl after 1990 season; replaced due to injury by Mike Johnson. . . . Named to THE SPORTING NEWS NFL All-Pro team, 1990.
PRO STATISTICS: 1986—Intercepted one pass for 14 yards. 1988—Intercepted two passes for two yards and recovered one fumble. 1990—Intercepted one pass for 28 yards.

OGLESBY, ALFRED

NT/DE, DOLPHINS

PERSONAL: Born January 27, 1967, at Weimar, Tex. . . . 6-3/278. . . . Full name: Alfred Lee Oglesby.
HIGH SCHOOL: Weimar (Tex.).
COLLEGE: Houston.

TRANSACTIONS/CAREER NOTES: Selected by Miami Dolphins in third round (66th pick overall) of 1990 NFL draft. . . . On inactive list (October 28 and December 30, 1990).
PLAYING EXPERIENCE: Miami NFL, 1990. . . . Games: 1990 (13).
PRO STATISTICS: 1990—Recovered one fumble.

OGLETREE, CRAIG
LB, BENGALS

PERSONAL: Born April 2, 1968, at Barnesville, Ga. . . . 6-2/236. . . . Full name: Craig Algernon Ogletree.
HIGH SCHOOL: Lamar County (Barnesville, Ga.).
COLLEGE: Auburn.
TRANSACTIONS/CAREER NOTES: Selected by Cincinnati Bengals in seventh round (177th pick overall) of 1990 NFL draft. . . . Signed by Bengals (July 16, 1990). . . . On inactive list (September 9; October 28; and December 9, 23 and 30, 1990).
PLAYING EXPERIENCE: Cincinnati NFL, 1990. . . . Games: 1990 (11).
RECORDS/HONORS: Named as linebacker on THE SPORTING NEWS college All-America team, 1989.

OKOYE, CHRISTIAN
RB, CHIEFS

PERSONAL: Born August 16, 1961, at Enugu, Nigeria. . . . 6-1/260. . . . Full name: Christian Emeka Okoye. . . . Name pronounced oh-KOY-yeah.
HIGH SCHOOL: Uwani Secondary School (Enugu, Nigeria).
COLLEGE: Azusa Pacific, Calif. (degree in physical education, 1987).
TRANSACTIONS/CAREER NOTES: Selected by Kansas City Chiefs in second round (35th pick overall) of 1987 NFL draft. . . . Signed by Chiefs (July 21, 1987). . . . On injured reserve with broken thumb (August 30-October 1, 1988). . . . On injured reserve with broken hand (December 14, 1988-remainder of season). . . . On inactive list (December 16 and 23, 1990).
RECORDS/HONORS: Played in Pro Bowl after 1989 season. . . . Named to THE SPORTING NEWS NFL All-Pro team, 1989.
PRO STATISTICS: 1990—Recovered one fumble.

		RUSHING				RECEIVING				TOTAL		
Year Team	G	Att.	Yds.	Avg.	TD	No.	Yds.	Avg.	TD	TD	Pts.	F.
1987— Kansas City NFL	12	157	660	4.2	3	24	169	7.0	0	3	18	5
1988— Kansas City NFL	9	105	473	4.5	3	8	51	6.4	0	3	18	1
1989— Kansas City NFL	15	*370	*1480	4.0	12	2	12	6.0	0	12	72	8
1990— Kansas City NFL	14	245	805	3.3	7	4	23	5.8	0	7	42	6
Pro totals (4 years)	50	877	3418	3.9	25	38	255	6.7	0	25	150	20

OLDHAM, CHRIS
CB, LIONS

PERSONAL: Born October 26, 1968, at Sacramento, Calif. . . . 5-9/183. . . . Full name: Christopher Martin Oldham.
HIGH SCHOOL: O. Perry Walker (New Orleans).
COLLEGE: Oregon (degree in communications).
TRANSACTIONS/CAREER NOTES: Selected by Detroit Lions in fourth round (105th pick overall) of 1990 NFL draft. . . . Signed by Lions (July 19, 1990).

		INTERCEPTIONS				KICKOFF RETURNS				TOTAL		
Year Team	G	No.	Yds.	Avg.	TD	No.	Yds.	Avg.	TD	TD	Pts.	F.
1990— Detroit NFL	16	1	28	28.0	0	13	234	18.0	0	0	0	2
Pro totals (1 year)	16	1	28	28.0	0	13	234	18.0	0	0	0	2

OLIPHANT, MIKE
WR/KR, BROWNS

PERSONAL: Born May 19, 1963, at Jacksonville, Fla. . . . 5-9/171. . . . Full name: Michael Nathaniel Oliphant.
HIGH SCHOOL: Federal Way (Wash.).
COLLEGE: Puget Sound (degree in physical education, 1988).
TRANSACTIONS/CAREER NOTES: Played semi-pro football for Auburn (Wash.) Panthers before attending Puget Sound. . . . Selected by Washington Redskins in third round (66th pick overall) of 1988 NFL draft. . . . Signed by Redskins (July 18, 1988). . . . On injured reserve with hamstring injury (September 30-November 21, 1988). . . . Traded by Redskins to Cleveland Browns for running back Earnest Byner (April 23, 1989). . . . On injured reserve with hamstring injury (September 8, 1990-entire season).
CHAMPIONSHIP GAME EXPERIENCE: Played in AFC championship game after 1989 season.
PRO STATISTICS: 1988—Recovered one fumble.

		RUSHING				RECEIVING				PUNT RETURNS				KICKOFF RETURNS				TOTALS		
Year Team	G	Att.	Yds.	Avg.	TD	No.	Yds.	Avg.	TD	No.	Yds.	Avg.	TD	No.	Yds.	Avg.	TD	TD	Pts.	F.
1988— Washington NFL.	8	8	30	3.8	0	15	111	7.4	0	7	24	3.4	0	7	127	18.1	0	0	0	2
1989— Cleveland NFL	14	15	97	6.5	1	3	22	7.3	0	0	0		0	5	69	13.8	0	1	6	3
Pro totals (2 years)	22	23	127	5.5	1	18	133	7.4	0	7	24	3.4	0	12	196	16.3	0	1	6	5

OLIVER, LOUIS
S, DOLPHINS

PERSONAL: Born March 9, 1966, at Belle Glade, Fla. . . . 6-2/226. . . . Full name: Louis Oliver III.
HIGH SCHOOL: Glades Central (Belle Glade, Fla.).
COLLEGE: Florida (bachelor of science degree in criminology and law, 1989).
TRANSACTIONS/CAREER NOTES: Selected by Miami Dolphins in first round (25th pick overall) of 1989 NFL draft. . . . Signed by Dolphins (August 9, 1989).
RECORDS/HONORS: Named as defensive back on THE SPORTING NEWS college All-America team, 1987.

		INTERCEPTIONS		
Year Team	G	No.	Yds.	Avg.	TD
1989— Miami NFL	15	4	32	8.0	0
1990— Miami NFL	16	5	87	17.4	0
Pro totals (2 years)	31	9	119	13.2	0

OLSAVSKY, JERRY
LB, STEELERS

PERSONAL: Born March 29, 1967, at Youngstown, O. . . . 6-1/218. . . . Full name: Jerome Donald Olsavsky. . . . Name pronounced ol-SAV-skee.
HIGH SCHOOL: Chaney (Youngstown, O.).
COLLEGE: Pittsburgh (bachelor of science degree in information science).
TRANSACTIONS/CAREER NOTES: Selected by Pittsburgh Steelers in 10th round (258th pick overall) of 1989 NFL draft. . . . Signed by Steelers (July 18, 1989). . . . On inactive list (September 23, 1990).
PLAYING EXPERIENCE: Pittsburgh NFL, 1989 and 1990. . . . Games: 1989 (16), 1990 (15). Total: 31.

O'NEAL, LESLIE
LB, CHARGERS

PERSONAL: Born May 7, 1964, at Pulaski County, Ark. . . . 6-4/259. . . . Full name: Leslie Cornelius O'Neal.
HIGH SCHOOL: Hall (Little Rock, Ark.).
COLLEGE: Oklahoma State.
TRANSACTIONS/CAREER NOTES: Selected by New Jersey Generals in 1986 USFL territorial draft. . . . Selected by San Diego Chargers in first round (eighth pick overall) of 1986 NFL draft. . . . Signed by Chargers (August 5, 1986). . . . On injured reserve with knee injury (December 4, 1986-remainder of season). . . . On reserve/physically unable to perform list with knee injury (August 30, 1987-entire season). . . . On physically unable to perform/active list with knee injury (July 23-August 21, 1988). . . . Transferred to reserve/physically unable to perform list with knee injury (August 22-October 15, 1988). . . . Granted free agency (February 1, 1990). . . . Re-signed by Chargers (August 21, 1990).
PLAYING EXPERIENCE: San Diego NFL, 1986, 1988-1990. . . . Games: 1986 (13), 1988 (9), 1989 (16), 1990 (16). Total: 54.
RECORDS/HONORS: Named as defensive lineman on THE SPORTING NEWS college All-America Team, 1984 and 1985. . . . Played in Pro Bowl after 1989 and 1990 seasons.
PRO STATISTICS: 1986—Intercepted two passes for 22 yards and a touchdown and recovered two fumbles. 1989—Recovered two fumbles for 10 yards. 1990—Recovered two fumbles and fumbled once for 10 yards.

ORLANDO, BO
S, OILERS

PERSONAL: Born April 3, 1968, at Berwick, Pa. . . . 5-10/180. . . . Full name: Joseph John Orlando.
HIGH SCHOOL: Berwick Area Senior (Berwick, Pa.).
COLLEGE: West Virginia.
TRANSACTIONS/CAREER NOTES: Selected by Houston Oilers in sixth round (157th pick overall) of 1989 NFL draft. . . . Signed by Oilers (July 26, 1989). . . . Released by Oilers (September 5, 1989). . . . Re-signed by Oilers to developmental squad (September 8, 1989). . . . Released by Oilers (January 2, 1990). . . . Re-signed by Oilers (April 17, 1990).
PLAYING EXPERIENCE: Houston NFL, 1990. . . . Games: 1990 (16).

ORR, TERRY
RB, CHARGERS

PERSONAL: Born September 27, 1961, at Savannah, Ga. . . . 6-2/235.
HIGH SCHOOL: Cooper (Abilene, Tex.).
COLLEGE: Texas (bachelor of science degree in speech communications, 1985).
TRANSACTIONS/CAREER NOTES: Selected by San Antonio Gunslingers in 1985 USFL territorial draft. . . . Selected by Washington Redskins in 10th round (263rd pick overall) of 1985 NFL draft. . . . Signed by Redskins (July 18, 1985). . . . On injured reserve with ankle injury (August 20, 1985-entire season). . . . On injured reserve with shoulder injury (September 7-October 24, 1987). . . . Released by Redskins (August 29, 1988). . . . Re-signed by Redskins (August 30, 1988). . . . Granted unconditional free agency (February 1, 1989). . . . Re-signed by Redskins (May 11, 1989). . . . Released by Redskins (September 3, 1990). . . . Re-signed by Redskins (September 5, 1990). . . . On inactive list (September 9 and 30, 1990). . . . Released by Redskins (October 15, 1990). . . . Signed by San Diego Chargers (October 26, 1990).
CHAMPIONSHIP GAME EXPERIENCE: Played in NFC championship game after 1986 and 1987 seasons. . . . Played in Super Bowl XXII after 1987 season.
PRO STATISTICS: 1988—Returned two punts for 10 yards and recovered two fumbles. 1990—Recovered one fumble.

		RECEIVING				KICKOFF RETURNS				TOTAL		
Year Team	G	No.	Yds.	Avg.	TD	No.	Yds.	Avg.	TD	TD	Pts.	F.
1986— Washington NFL	16	3	45	15.0	1	2	31	15.5	0	1	6	0
1987— Washington NFL	10	3	35	11.7	0	4	62	15.5	0	0	0	0
1988— Washington NFL	16	11	222	20.2	2	1	6	6.0	0	2	12	0
1989— Washington NFL	16	3	80	26.7	0	1	0	.0	0	0	0	0
1990— Wash. (2)-S.D. (9) NFL	11	0	0		0	1	13	13.0	0	0	0	0
Pro totals (5 years)	69	20	382	19.1	3	9	112	12.4	0	3	18	0

O'SHEA, TERRY
TE, STEELERS

PERSONAL: Born December 3, 1966, at Pittsburgh. . . . 6-4/238. . . . Full name: Terence William O'Shea.
HIGH SCHOOL: Seton-LaSalle (Pittsburgh).
COLLEGE: Indiana, Pa. (degree in marketing, 1990).
TRANSACTIONS/CAREER NOTES: Signed as free agent by Pittsburgh Steelers (April 26, 1989).

		RECEIVING		
Year Team	G	No.	Yds.	Avg.	TD
1989— Pittsburgh NFL	16	1	8	8.0	0
1990— Pittsburgh NFL	16	1	13	13.0	0
Pro totals (2 years)	32	2	21	10.5	0

OVERTON, DON
RB, LIONS

PERSONAL: Born September 24, 1967, at Columbus, O. . . . 6-0/221. . . . Full name: Donald Eugene Overton.
HIGH SCHOOL: Whitehall (O.).
COLLEGE: Fairmont State, W.Va. (bachelor of science degree).

TRANSACTIONS/CAREER NOTES: Signed as free agent by New England Patriots (May 17, 1990).... Released by Patriots (October 29, 1990).... Signed by Detroit Lions (April 15, 1991).

Year Team	G	Att.	Yds.	Avg.	TD	No.	Yds.	Avg.	TD	No.	Yds.	Avg.	TD	TD	Pts.	F.
1990— New England NFL	7	5	8	1.6	0	2	19	9.5	0	10	188	18.8	0	0	0	0
Pro totals (1 year)	7	5	8	1.6	0	2	19	9.5	0	10	188	18.8	0	0	0	0

OWENS, DAN
DE, LIONS

PERSONAL: Born March 16, 1967, at Whittier, Calif.... 6-3/268.... Full name: Daniel William Owens.
HIGH SCHOOL: La Habra (Calif.).
COLLEGE: Southern California (bachelor of arts degree).
TRANSACTIONS/CAREER NOTES: Selected by Detroit Lions in second round (35th pick overall) of 1990 NFL draft.... Signed by Lions (July 26, 1990).
PLAYING EXPERIENCE: Detroit NFL, 1990.... Games: 1990 (16).

PAGEL, MIKE
QB, RAMS

PERSONAL: Born September 13, 1960, at Douglas, Ariz.... 6-2/220.... Full name: Michael Jonathan Pagel.... Brother of Karl Pagel, outfielder-first baseman with Chicago Cubs and Cleveland Indians, 1978, 1979 and 1981-1983; and minor league coach, Cleveland Indians' organization, 1984.
HIGH SCHOOL: Washington (Phoenix).
COLLEGE: Arizona State.
TRANSACTIONS/CAREER NOTES: Selected by Baltimore Colts in fourth round (84th pick overall) of 1982 NFL draft.... Franchise transferred to Indianapolis (March 31, 1984).... Granted free agency (February 1, 1986).... Re-signed by Colts and traded to Cleveland Browns for ninth-round pick in 1987 draft (May 22, 1986).... On injured reserve with separated shoulder (October 14-December 23, 1988).... Released by Browns (April 26, 1991).... Signed by Los Angeles Rams (May 20, 1991).
CHAMPIONSHIP GAME EXPERIENCE: Member of Cleveland Browns for AFC championship game after 1986 season; did not play.... Played in AFC championship game after 1987 and 1989 seasons.
PRO STATISTICS: Passer rating points: 1982 (62.4), 1983 (64.0), 1984 (71.8), 1985 (65.8), 1986 (109.7), 1988 (64.1), 1989 (43.8), 1990 (48.2). Career: 63.7.... 1982—Recovered three fumbles and fumbled nine times for minus four yards. 1984—Recovered one fumble. 1985—Recovered two fumbles and caught one pass for six yards. 1986—Recovered one fumble and fumbled twice for minus four yards. 1988—Recovered one fumble. 1990—Recovered one fumble.

Year Team	G	Att.	Cmp.	Pct.	Yds.	TD	Int.	Avg.	Att.	Yds.	Avg.	TD	TD	Pts.	F.
1982— Baltimore NFL	9	221	111	50.2	1281	5	7	5.80	19	82	4.3	1	1	6	9
1983— Baltimore NFL	15	328	163	49.7	2353	12	17	7.17	54	441	8.2	0	0	0	4
1984— Indianapolis NFL	11	212	114	53.8	1426	8	8	6.73	26	149	5.7	1	1	6	4
1985— Indianapolis NFL	16	393	199	50.6	2414	14	15	6.14	25	160	6.4	2	2	12	6
1986— Cleveland NFL	1	3	2	66.7	53	0	0	17.67	2	0	.0	0	0	0	2
1987— Cleveland NFL	4	0	0		0	0	0		0	0		0	0	0	0
1988— Cleveland NFL	5	134	71	53.0	736	3	4	5.49	4	1	.3	0	0	0	0
1989— Cleveland NFL	16	14	5	35.7	60	1	1	4.29	2	-1	-.5	0	0	0	0
1990— Cleveland NFL	16	148	69	46.6	819	3	8	5.53	3	-1	-.3	0	0	0	3
Pro totals (9 years)	93	1453	734	50.5	9142	46	60	6.29	135	831	6.2	4	4	24	28

PAIGE, STEPHONE
WR, CHIEFS

PERSONAL: Born October 15, 1961, at Long Beach, Calif.... 6-2/188.... First name pronounced STEFF-on.
HIGH SCHOOL: Polytechnic (Long Beach, Calif.).
COLLEGE: Saddleback College (Calif.), then Fresno State.
TRANSACTIONS/CAREER NOTES: Selected by Oakland Invaders in 1983 USFL territorial draft.... Signed as free agent by Kansas City Chiefs (May 9, 1983).... Granted free agency (February 1, 1989).... Re-signed by Chiefs (September 2, 1989).... Granted roster exemption (September 2-September 18, 1989).
PRO STATISTICS: 1983—Recovered one fumble. 1984—Rushed three times for 19 yards. 1985—Rushed once for 15 yards. 1986—Rushed twice for minus two yards. 1988—Recovered two fumbles. 1989—Recovered one fumble. 1990—Recovered one fumble.

Year Team	G	No.	Yds.	Avg.	TD	No.	Yds.	Avg.	TD	TD	Pts.	F.
1983— Kansas City NFL	16	30	528	17.6	6	0	0		0	6	36	1
1984— Kansas City NFL	16	30	541	18.0	4	27	544	20.2	0	4	24	0
1985— Kansas City NFL	16	43	943	*21.9	10	2	36	18.0	0	10	60	0
1986— Kansas City NFL	16	52	829	15.9	11	0	0		0	11	66	0
1987— Kansas City NFL	12	43	707	16.4	4	0	0		0	4	24	0
1988— Kansas City NFL	16	61	902	14.8	7	0	0		0	7	42	2
1989— Kansas City NFL	14	44	759	17.3	2	0	0		0	2	12	3
1990— Kansas City NFL	16	65	1021	15.7	5	0	0		0	5	30	3
Pro totals (8 years)	122	368	6230	16.9	49	29	580	20.0	0	49	294	9

PAIGE, TONY
FB, DOLPHINS

PERSONAL: Born October 14, 1962, at Washington, D.C.... 5-10/235.... Full name: Anthony R. Paige.
HIGH SCHOOL: DeMatha Catholic (Hyattsville, Md.).
COLLEGE: Virginia Tech (degree in broadcasting).

TRANSACTIONS/CAREER NOTES: Selected by Pittsburgh Maulers in 1984 USFL territorial draft. . . . Selected by New York Jets in sixth round (149th pick overall) of 1984 NFL draft. . . . Signed by Jets (May 29, 1984). . . . Granted free agency (February 1, 1987). . . . Withdrew qualifying offer (August 25, 1987). . . . Signed by Detroit Lions (November 19, 1987). . . . Released by Lions (August 29, 1988). . . . Re-signed by Lions (August 30, 1988). . . . Granted unconditional free agency (February 1, 1990). . . . Signed by Miami Dolphins (March 13, 1990). . . . On inactive list (November 19, 25; and December 16, 1990).
PRO STATISTICS: 1984—Returned three kickoffs for seven yards. 1985—Recovered one fumble. 1987—Recovered one fumble. 1989—Recovered one fumble. 1990—Returned one kickoff for 18 yards and recovered two fumbles.

Year	Team	G	RUSHING Att.	RUSHING Yds.	RUSHING Avg.	RUSHING TD	RECEIVING No.	RECEIVING Yds.	RECEIVING Avg.	RECEIVING TD	TOTAL TD	TOTAL Pts.	F.
1984	N.Y. Jets NFL	16	35	130	3.7	7	6	31	5.2	1	8	48	1
1985	N.Y. Jets NFL	16	55	158	2.9	8	18	120	6.7	2	10	60	1
1986	N.Y. Jets NFL	16	47	109	2.3	2	18	121	6.7	0	2	12	2
1987	Detroit NFL	5	4	13	3.3	0	2	1	.5	0	0	0	0
1988	Detroit NFL	16	52	207	4.0	0	11	100	9.1	0	0	0	1
1989	Detroit NFL	16	30	105	3.5	0	2	27	13.5	0	0	0	1
1990	Miami NFL	13	32	95	3.0	2	35	247	7.1	4	6	36	1
	Pro totals (7 years)	98	255	817	3.2	19	92	647	7.0	7	26	156	7

PANKEY, IRV
OT, RAMS

PERSONAL: Born February 15, 1958, at Aberdeen, Md. . . . 6-5/292. . . . Full name: Irvin Lee Pankey.
HIGH SCHOOL: Aberdeen (Md.).
COLLEGE: Penn State.
TRANSACTIONS/CAREER NOTES: Selected by Los Angeles Rams in second round (50th pick overall) of 1980 NFL draft. . . . On injured reserve with torn Achilles tendon (August 16, 1983-entire season).
PLAYING EXPERIENCE: Los Angeles Rams NFL, 1980-1990. . . . Games: 1980 (16), 1981 (13), 1982 (9), 1984 (16), 1985 (16), 1986 (16), 1987 (12), 1988 (16), 1989 (14), 1990 (16). Total: 144.
CHAMPIONSHIP GAME EXPERIENCE: Played in NFC championship game after 1985 and 1989 seasons.
PRO STATISTICS: 1981—Recovered two fumbles and returned one kickoff for no yards. 1985—Recovered one fumble. 1986—Recovered one fumble. 1988—Recovered one fumble. 1989—Recovered one fumble.

PARIS, BUBBA
OT, 49ERS

PERSONAL: Born October 6, 1960, at Louisville, Ky. . . . 6-6/299. . . . Full name: William Paris.
HIGH SCHOOL: DeSales (Louisville, Ky.).
COLLEGE: Michigan (received degree, 1982).
TRANSACTIONS/CAREER NOTES: Selected by San Francisco 49ers in second round (29th pick overall) of 1982 NFL draft. . . . On injured reserve with knee injury (September 6, 1982-entire season).
PLAYING EXPERIENCE: San Francisco NFL, 1983-1990. . . . Games: 1983 (16), 1984 (16), 1985 (16), 1986 (10), 1987 (11), 1988 (16), 1989 (16), 1990 (16). Total: 117.
CHAMPIONSHIP GAME EXPERIENCE: Played in NFC championship game after 1983, 1984 and 1988-1990 seasons. . . . Played in Super Bowl XIX after 1984 season, Super Bowl XXIII after 1988 season and Super Bowl XXIV after 1989 season.
PRO STATISTICS: 1984—Recovered one fumble. 1986—Recovered one fumble. 1989—Recovered one fumble.

PARKER, ANTHONY
CB, CARDINALS

PERSONAL: Born February 11, 1966, at Sylacauga, Ala. . . . 5-10/180. . . . Full name: Will Anthony Parker.
HIGH SCHOOL: McClintock (Tempe, Ariz.).
COLLEGE: Arizona State (bachelor of science degree in physical education, 1989).
TRANSACTIONS/CAREER NOTES: Signed as free agent by Indianapolis Colts (April 21, 1989). . . . On injured reserve with hamstring injury (September 5-November 17, 1989). . . . Granted unconditional free agency (February 1, 1990). . . . Signed by New York Jets (March 31, 1990). . . . Released by Jets (September 4, 1990). . . . Signed by WLAF (January 31, 1991). . . . Selected by New York/New Jersey Knights in first round (second defensive back) of 1991 WLAF positional draft. . . . Signed by Phoenix Cardinals (July 9, 1991).

Year	Team	G	INTERCEPTIONS No.	Yds.	Avg.	TD
1989	Indianapolis NFL	1	0	0		0
1991	N.Y./N.J. WLAF	10	11	270	24.6	2
	NFL totals (1 year)	1	0	0		0
	WLAF totals (1 year)	10	11	270	24.6	2
	Pro totals (2 years)	11	11	270	24.6	2

PARKER, CARL
WR, STEELERS

PERSONAL: Born February 5, 1965, at Columbus, Ga. . . . 6-2/210.
HIGH SCHOOL: Lowndes County (Valdosta, Ga.).
COLLEGE: Vanderbilt.
TRANSACTIONS/CAREER NOTES: Selected by Cincinnati Bengals in 12th round (307th pick overall) of 1988 NFL draft. . . . Signed by Bengals (June 6, 1988). . . . On injured reserve with foot injury (August 29-November 26, 1988). . . . Released by Bengals (October 13, 1989). . . . Awarded on waivers to New York Jets (October 16, 1989). . . . Released by Jets (October 18, 1989). . . . Re-signed by Jets (March 9, 1990). . . . Released by Jets (August 16, 1990). . . . Signed by Hamilton Tiger-Cats of CFL (September 8, 1990). . . . Released by Tiger-Cats (October, 1990). . . . Signed by WLAF (January 31, 1991). . . . Selected by Sacramento Surge in fourth round (36th wide receiver) of 1991 WLAF positional draft. . . . Signed by Pittsburgh Steelers (June 24, 1991).

CHAMPIONSHIP GAME EXPERIENCE: Played in AFC championship game after 1988 season. . . . Played in Super Bowl XXIII after 1988 season.
PRO STATISTICS: CFL: 1990—Recovered one fumble. . . . WLAF: 1991—Credited with one 2-point conversion.

Year Team	G	No.	Yds.	Avg.	TD	No.	Yds.	Avg.	TD	No.	Yds.	Avg.	TD	TD	Pts.	F.
			RECEIVING				PUNT RETURNS				KICKOFF RETURNS				TOTAL	
1988— Cincinnati NFL....	3	0	0		0	0	0		0	0	0		0	0	0	0
1989— Cincinnati NFL....	3	1	45	45.0	0	0	0		0	0	0		0	0	0	0
1990— Hamilton CFL......	2	5	55	11.0	1	5	24	4.8	0	2	37	18.5	0	1	6	1
1991— Sacra. WLAF	10	52	801	15.4	8	15	127	8.5	0	0	0		0	8	50	—
NFL totals (2 years) ...	6	1	45	45.0	0	0	0		0	0	0		0	0	0	0
CFL totals (1 year)	2	5	55	11.0	1	5	24	4.8	0	2	37	18.5	0	1	6	1
WLAF totals (1 year) ..	10	52	801	15.4	8	15	127	8.5	0	0	0		0	8	50	—
Pro totals (4 years)	18	58	901	15.5	9	20	151	7.6	0	2	37	18.5	0	9	56	1

PARKER, GLENN
G, BILLS

PERSONAL: Born April 22, 1966, at Westminster, Calif. . . . 6-5/301. . . . Full name: Glenn Andrew Parker.
HIGH SCHOOL: Edison (Huntington Beach, Calif.).
COLLEGE: Arizona.
TRANSACTIONS/CAREER NOTES: Selected by Buffalo Bills in third round (69th pick overall) of 1990 NFL draft. . . . Signed by Bills (July 26, 1990).
PLAYING EXPERIENCE: Buffalo NFL, 1990. . . . Games: 1990 (16).
CHAMPIONSHIP GAME EXPERIENCE: Played in AFC championship game after 1990 season. . . . Played in Super Bowl XXV after 1990 season.

PATTEN, JOEL
OT, RAIDERS

PERSONAL: Born February 7, 1958, at Augsburg, West Germany. . . . 6-7/305.
HIGH SCHOOL: Robinson (Fairfax, Va.).
COLLEGE: Duke (bachelor of arts degree in history education).
TRANSACTIONS/CAREER NOTES: Signed as free agent by Cleveland Browns (May 7, 1980). . . . On injured reserve with groin injury (September 6-November 7, 1980). . . . On injured reserve with knee injury (August 24, 1981-entire season). . . . Released by Browns (September 8, 1982). . . . USFL rights traded by Michigan Panthers to Washington Federals for past consideration (February 8, 1983). . . . Signed by Federals (February 8, 1983). . . . On developmental squad for four games (May 4-June 3, 1984). . . . Washington Federals' franchise transferred to Orlando (October 12, 1984). . . . Released by Orlando Renegades (August 26, 1985). . . . Signed as free agent by Dallas Cowboys (March 21, 1986). . . . Released by Cowboys (August 21, 1986). . . . Signed as free agent by Indianapolis Colts (May 11, 1987). . . . Granted unconditional free agency (February 1, 1989). . . . Signed by San Diego Chargers (February 15, 1989). . . . On injured reserve with knee injury (September 4-October 4, 1990). . . . Transferred to practice squad (October 4, 1990). . . . Activated (October 27, 1990). . . . On injured reserve with neck injury (December 29, 1990-remainder of season). . . . Granted unconditional free agency (February 1, 1991). . . . Signed by Los Angeles Raiders (offseason, 1991).
PLAYING EXPERIENCE: Cleveland NFL, 1980; Washington USFL, 1983 and 1984; Orlando USFL, 1985; Indianapolis NFL, 1987 and 1988; San Diego NFL, 1989 and 1990. . . . Games: 1980 (16), 1983 (18), 1984 (14), 1985 (18), 1987 (12), 1988 (15), 1989 (14), 1990 (8). Total NFL: 65. Total USFL: 50. Total Pro: 115.
PRO STATISTICS: 1983—Recovered two fumbles.

PATTERSON, ELVIS
CB, RAIDERS

PERSONAL: Born October 21, 1960, at Bryan, Tex. . . . 5-11/ 195. . . . Full name: Elvis Vernell Patterson.
HIGH SCHOOL: Jack Yates (Houston).
COLLEGE: Kansas.
TRANSACTIONS/CAREER NOTES: Selected by Jacksonville Bulls in 10th round (207th pick overall) of 1984 USFL draft. . . . Signed as free agent by New York Giants (May 3, 1984). . . . Released by Giants (September 16, 1987). . . . Signed as free-agent replacement player by San Diego Chargers (September 24, 1987). . . . Granted unconditional free agency (February 1, 1990). . . . Signed by Los Angeles Raiders (April 1, 1990). . . . Released by Raiders (September 3, 1990). . . . Re-signed by Raiders (September 4, 1990).
CHAMPIONSHIP GAME EXPERIENCE: Played in NFC championship game after 1986 season. . . . Played in Super Bowl XXI after 1986 season. . . . Played in AFC championship game after 1990 season.
PRO STATISTICS: 1985—Recovered one fumble. 1987—Recovered one fumble. 1988—Recovered one fumble. 1989—Recovered one fumble. 1990—Recovered one fumble.

Year Team	G	No.	Yds.	Avg.	TD
		INTERCEPTIONS			
1984— N.Y. Giants NFL	15	0	0		0
1985— N.Y. Giants NFL	16	6	88	14.7	*1
1986— N.Y. Giants NFL	15	2	26	13.0	0
1987— NYG (1)-S.D. (13) NFL .	14	1	75	75.0	1
1988— San Diego NFL	14	1	0	.0	0
1989— San Diego NFL	16	2	44	22.0	0
1990— L.A. Raiders NFL	16	0	0		0
Pro totals (7 years)	106	12	233	19.4	2

PATTERSON, SHAWN
DE, PACKERS

PERSONAL: Born June 13, 1964, at Tempe, Ariz. . . . 6-5/273. . . . Full name: Kenneth Shawn Patterson.
HIGH SCHOOL: McClintock (Tempe, Ariz.).
COLLEGE: Arizona State.

TRANSACTIONS/CAREER NOTES: Selected by Green Bay Packers in second round (34th pick overall) of 1988 NFL draft.... Signed by Packers (July 17, 1988).... On injured reserve with knee injury (October 17, 1989-remainder of season).... On injured reserve with hamstring injury (September 5-October 6, 1990).... On inactive list (October 14, 1990).
PLAYING EXPERIENCE: Green Bay NFL, 1988-1990.... Games: 1988 (15), 1989 (6), 1990 (11). Total: 32.
PRO STATISTICS: 1988—Recovered one fumble. 1990—Intercepted one pass for nine yards and a touchdown.

PATTON, MARVCUS
LB, BILLS
PERSONAL: Born May 1, 1967, at Los Angeles.... 6-2/225.... Full name: Marvcus Raymond Patton.
HIGH SCHOOL: Leuzinger (Lawndale, Calif.).
COLLEGE: UCLA (degree in political science, 1990).
TRANSACTIONS/CAREER NOTES: Selected by Buffalo Bills in eighth round (208th pick overall) of 1990 NFL draft.... Signed by Bills (July 27, 1990).... On injured reserve with broken leg (January 26, 1991-remainder of 1990 season playoffs).
PLAYING EXPERIENCE: Buffalo NFL, 1990.... Games: 1990 (16).

PAUL, MARKUS
S, BEARS
PERSONAL: Born April 1, 1966, at Orlando, Fla.... 6-2/199.... Full name: Markus Dwayne Paul.
HIGH SCHOOL: Osceola (Kissimmee, Fla.).
COLLEGE: Syracuse (bachelor of arts degree in retailing, 1989).
TRANSACTIONS/CAREER NOTES: Selected by Chicago Bears in fourth round (95th pick overall) of 1989 NFL draft.... Signed by Bears (July 27, 1989).
RECORDS/HONORS: Named as defensive back on THE SPORTING NEWS college All-America team, 1988.
PRO STATISTICS: 1990—Fumbled once.

			—— INTERCEPTIONS——			
Year	Team	G	No.	Yds.	Avg.	TD
1989— Chicago NFL		16	1	20	20.0	0
1990— Chicago NFL		16	2	49	24.5	0
Pro totals (2 years)		32	3	69	23.0	0

PAUP, BRYCE
LB, PACKERS
PERSONAL: Born February 29, 1968, at Scranton, Ia.... 6-5/247.... Full name: Bryce Eric Paup.
HIGH SCHOOL: Scranton (Ia.).
COLLEGE: Northern Iowa (degree in business).
TRANSACTIONS/CAREER NOTES: Selected by Green Bay Packers in sixth round (159th pick overall) of 1990 NFL draft.... Signed by Packers (July 22, 1990).... On injured reserve with hand injury (September 4-November 17, 1990).... On inactive list (November 18 and December 2, 1990).
PLAYING EXPERIENCE: Green Bay NFL, 1990.... Games: 1990 (5).

PEARSON, JAYICE
CB, CHIEFS
PERSONAL: Born August 17, 1963, at Japan.... 5-11/186.... First name pronounced JAY-SEE.
HIGH SCHOOL: El Camino (Oceanside, Calif.).
COLLEGE: California State Poly, then Fullerton (Calif.) College, then Washington.
TRANSACTIONS/CAREER NOTES: Signed as free agent by Washington Redskins (May 13, 1985).... Released by Redskins (August 27, 1985).... Signed as free agent by Kansas City Chiefs (April 14, 1986).... On injured reserve with sprained ankle (August 18-October 29, 1986).... Activated after clearing procedural waivers (October 31, 1986).
PLAYING EXPERIENCE: Kansas City NFL, 1986-1990.... Games: 1986 (8), 1987 (12), 1988 (16), 1989 (16), 1990 (16). Total: 68.
PRO STATISTICS: 1988—Intercepted two passes for eight yards. 1989—Ran one yard with blocked punt for a touchdown. 1990—Intercepted one pass for 10 yards and recovered one fumble.

PEAT, TODD
G, RAIDERS
PERSONAL: Born May 20, 1964, at Champaign, Ill.... 6-2/315.... Full name: Marion Todd Peat.
HIGH SCHOOL: Central (Champaign, Ill.).
COLLEGE: Northern Illinois (degree in criminal justice, 1987).
TRANSACTIONS/CAREER NOTES: Selected by St. Louis Cardinals in 11th round (285th pick overall) of 1987 NFL draft.... Signed by Cardinals (July 14, 1987).... Franchise transferred to Phoenix (March 15, 1988).... Left Phoenix Cardinals camp voluntarily (October 4, 1989).... Released by Cardinals (October 6, 1989).... Awarded on waivers to Buffalo Bills (October 9, 1989).... Released by Bills (October 11, 1989).... Signed as free agent by Los Angeles Raiders (March 8, 1990).
PLAYING EXPERIENCE: St. Louis NFL, 1987; Phoenix NFL, 1988 and 1989; Los Angeles Raiders NFL, 1990.... Games: 1987 (12), 1988 (15), 1989 (4), 1990 (16). Total: 47.
CHAMPIONSHIP GAME EXPERIENCE: Played in AFC championship game after 1990 season.

PEEBLES, DANNY
WR, BUCCANEERS
PERSONAL: Born April 30, 1966, at Raleigh, N.C.... 5-11/180.... Full name: Daniel Percy Peebles III.
HIGH SCHOOL: Needham Broughton (Raleigh, N.C.).
COLLEGE: North Carolina State (degrees in accounting and business management).
TRANSACTIONS/CAREER NOTES: Selected by Tampa Bay Buccaneers in second round (33rd pick overall) of 1989 NFL draft....

Signed by Buccaneers (July 15, 1989). . . . On injured reserve with knee injury (November 14, 1990-remainder of season).
PRO STATISTICS: 1989—Rushed twice for minus six yards and recovered one fumble. 1990—Recovered one fumble and fumbled once for three yards.

			RECEIVING				KICKOFF RETURNS				TOTAL		
Year	Team	G	No.	Yds.	Avg.	TD	No.	Yds.	Avg.	TD	TD	Pts.	F.
1989— Tampa Bay NFL		13	11	180	16.4	0	0	0	0	0	0	0	1
1990— Tampa Bay NFL		10	6	50	8.3	1	18	369	20.5	0	1	6	1
Pro totals (2 years)		23	17	230	13.5	1	18	369	20.5	0	1	6	2

PEETE, RODNEY
QB, LIONS

PERSONAL: Born March 16, 1966, at Mesa, Ariz. . . . 6-0/ 193 . . . Son of Willie Peete, assistant coach at University of Arizona, 1971- 1982; assistant coach with Kansas City Chiefs, 1983- 1986; and assistant coach with Green Bay Packers since 1987; and cousin of Calvin Peete, professional golfer.
HIGH SCHOOL: Sahuaro (Tucson, Ariz.) and South (Shawnee Mission, Kan.).
COLLEGE: Southern California (bachelor of science degree in communications, 1989).
TRANSACTIONS/CAREER NOTES: Selected by Detroit Lions in sixth round (141st pick overall) of 1989 NFL draft. . . . Signed by Lions (July 13, 1989). . . . On inactive list (November 11, 18 and 22, 1990).
MISCELLANEOUS: Selected by Toronto Blue Jays' organization in 30th round of free-agent baseball draft (June 4, 1984). . . . Selected by Oakland Athletics' organization in 14th round of free-agent baseball draft (June 1, 1988). . . . Selected by Oakland Athletics' organization in 13th round of free-agent baseball draft (June 5, 1989).
PRO STATISTICS: Passer rating points: 1989 (67.0), 1990 (79.8). Career: 74.4. . . . 1989—Recovered three fumbles. 1990—Recovered one fumble.

			PASSING							RUSHING				TOTAL		
Year	Team	G	Att.	Cmp.	Pct.	Yds.	TD	Int.	Avg.	Att.	Yds.	Avg.	TD	TD	Pts.	F.
1989— Detroit NFL		8	195	103	52.8	1479	5	9	7.58	33	148	4.5	4	4	24	9
1990— Detroit NFL		11	271	142	52.4	1974	13	8	7.28	47	363	7.7	6	6	36	9
Pro totals (2 years)		19	466	245	52.6	3453	18	17	7.41	80	511	6.4	10	10	60	18

PEGUESE, WILLIS
DE, OILERS

PERSONAL: Born December 18, 1966, at Miami. . . . 6-4/267. . . . Name pronounced pe-GEESE.
HIGH SCHOOL: Miami Southridge Senior (Miami).
COLLEGE: Miami (Fla.).
TRANSACTIONS/CAREER NOTES: Selected by Houston Oilers in third round (72nd pick overall) of 1990 NFL draft. . . . Signed by Oilers (July 22, 1990). . . . On inactive list (September 16, 23, 30; October 8, 14, 21; November 4, 18; and December 9, 16 and 23, 1990). . . . On injured reserve with back injury (December 28, 1990-remainder of 1990 season playoffs).
PLAYING EXPERIENCE: Houston NFL, 1990. . . . Games: 1990 (2).

PELLUER, STEVE
QB, CHIEFS

PERSONAL: Born July 29, 1962, at Yakima, Wash. . . . 6-4/209. . . . Full name: Steven Carl Pelluer. . . . Name pronounced puh-LURE. . . . Brother of Scott Pelluer, linebacker with New Orleans Saints, 1981- 1985.
HIGH SCHOOL: Interlake (Bellevue, Wash.).
COLLEGE: Washington (degree in building construction, 1984).
TRANSACTIONS/CAREER NOTES: Selected by Oakland Invaders in sixth round (110th pick overall) of 1984 USFL draft. . . . Selected by Dallas Cowboys in fifth round (113th pick overall) of 1984 NFL draft. . . . Signed by Cowboys (July 7, 1984). . . . Granted free agency (February 1, 1989). . . . Re-signed by Cowboys and traded to Kansas City Chiefs for third-round pick in 1990 NFL draft and conditional pick in 1991 NFL draft (October 17, 1989). . . . Granted roster exemption (October 17-October 21, 1989).
PRO STATISTICS: Passer rating points: 1985 (78.6), 1986 (67.9), 1987 (75.6), 1988 (73.9), 1989 (82.0), 1990 (8.3). Career: 71.6. . . . 1986—Recovered three fumbles. 1988—Recovered two fumbles and fumbled six times for minus 18 yards. 1989—Recovered one fumble and fumbled twice for minus eight yards.

			PASSING							RUSHING				TOTAL		
Year	Team	G	Att.	Cmp.	Pct.	Yds.	TD	Int.	Avg.	Att.	Yds.	Avg.	TD	TD	Pts.	F.
1984— Dallas NFL		1	0			0	0	0		0	0		0	0	0	0
1985— Dallas NFL		2	8	5	62.5	47	0	0	5.88	3	-2	-.7	0	0	0	0
1986— Dallas NFL		16	378	215	56.9	2727	8	17	7.21	41	255	6.2	1	1	6	9
1987— Dallas NFL		12	101	55	54.5	642	3	2	6.36	25	142	5.7	1	1	6	0
1988— Dallas NFL		16	435	245	56.3	3139	17	19	7.22	51	314	6.2	2	2	12	6
1989— Kansas City NFL		5	47	26	55.3	301	1	0	6.40	17	143	8.4	2	2	12	2
1990— Kansas City NFL		13	5	2	40.0	14	0	1	2.80	5	6	1.2	0	0	0	0
Pro totals (7 years)		65	974	548	56.3	6870	29	39	7.05	142	858	6.0	6	6	36	17

PENNISON, JAY
C, FALCONS

PERSONAL: Born September 9, 1961, at Houma, La. . . . 6-1/282. . . . Full name: Jay Leslie Pennison.
HIGH SCHOOL: Terrebonne (Houma, La.).
COLLEGE: Nicholls State.
TRANSACTIONS/CAREER NOTES: Selected by Jacksonville Bulls in 13th round (267th pick overall) of 1984 USFL draft. . . . Signed by Bulls (January 19, 1984). . . . Released by Bulls (February 20, 1984). . . . Signed as free agent by Washington Redskins (May 2, 1984). . . . Released by Redskins (August 21, 1984). . . . Re-signed by Jacksonville Bulls (October 9, 1984). . . . Re-

leased by Bulls (August 7, 1986).... Signed as free agent by Houston Oilers (August 12, 1986).... Granted unconditional free agency (February 1, 1991).... Rights relinquished by Oilers and signed by Atlanta Falcons (July 29, 1991).
PLAYING EXPERIENCE: Jacksonville USFL, 1985; Houston NFL, 1986-1990.... Games: 1985 (18), 1986 (16), 1987 (12), 1988 (16), 1989 (12), 1990 (15). Total NFL: 71. Total Pro: 89.
PRO STATISTICS: USFL: 1985—Recovered two fumbles.... NFL: 1986—Fumbled once. 1987—Recovered one fumble and fumbled once for minus 12 yards. 1988—Recovered one fumble and fumbled once. 1989—Recovered one fumble and fumbled twice for minus 17 yards.

PERKINS, BRUCE
FB, BUCCANEERS

PERSONAL: Born August 14, 1967, at Waterloo, Ia.... 6-2/230.... Full name: Bruce Kerry Perkins.
HIGH SCHOOL: Waterloo Central (Waterloo, Ia.).
COLLEGE: Butler Community College (Kan.), then Arizona State.
TRANSACTIONS/CAREER NOTES: Signed as free agent by Tampa Bay Buccaneers (April 26, 1990).
PRO STATISTICS: 1990—Recovered one fumble.

		RUSHING				RECEIVING				TOTAL	
Year Team	G	Att.	Yds.	Avg.	TD	No.	Yds.	Avg.	TD	TD	Pts.	F.
1990— Tampa Bay NFL	16	13	36	2.8	0	8	85	10.6	2	2	12	0
Pro totals (1 year)	16	13	36	2.8	0	8	85	10.6	2	2	12	0

PERRIMAN, BRETT
WR, SAINTS

PERSONAL: Born October 10, 1965, at Miami.... 5-9/180.
HIGH SCHOOL: Northwestern (Miami).
COLLEGE: Miami (Fla.).
TRANSACTIONS/CAREER NOTES: Selected by New Orleans Saints in second round (52nd pick overall) of 1988 NFL draft.... Signed by Saints (May 19, 1988).
PRO STATISTICS: 1988—Rushed three times for 17 yards and fumbled once. 1989—Returned one punt for 10 yards and rushed once for minus 10 yards. 1990—Recovered one fumble and fumbled twice.

		RECEIVING		
Year Team	G	No.	Yds.	Avg.	TD
1988— New Orleans NFL	16	16	215	13.4	2
1989— New Orleans NFL	14	20	356	17.8	0
1990— New Orleans NFL	16	36	382	10.6	2
Pro totals (3 years)	46	72	953	13.2	4

PERRY, GERALD
OT, RAMS

PERSONAL: Born November 12, 1964, at Columbia, S.C.... 6-6/305.
HIGH SCHOOL: Dreher (Columbia, S.C.).
COLLEGE: Northwest Mississippi Junior College, then Southern A&M.
TRANSACTIONS/CAREER NOTES: Selected by Denver Broncos in second round (45th pick overall) of 1988 NFL draft.... Signed by Broncos (July 15, 1988).... On inactive list (November 22, 1990).... On reserve/left squad list (December 6, 1990-remainder of season).... Traded by Broncos with 12th-round pick in 1991 NFL draft to Los Angeles Rams for running back Gaston Green and fourth-round pick in 1991 draft (April 22, 1991).
PLAYING EXPERIENCE: Denver NFL, 1988-1990.... Games: 1988 (16), 1989 (16), 1990 (8). Total: 40.
CHAMPIONSHIP GAME EXPERIENCE: Played in AFC championship game after 1989 season.... Played in Super Bowl XXIV after 1989 season.
PRO STATISTICS: 1989—Recovered one fumble.

PERRY, MICHAEL DEAN
DT, BROWNS

PERSONAL: Born August 27, 1965, at Aiken, S.C.... 6-1/285.... Full name: Michael Dean Perry.... Brother of William Perry, defensive tackle with Chicago Bears.
HIGH SCHOOL: South Aiken (Aiken, S.C.).
COLLEGE: Clemson.
TRANSACTIONS/CAREER NOTES: Selected by Cleveland Browns in second round (50th pick overall) of 1988 NFL draft.... Signed by Browns (July 23, 1988).
PLAYING EXPERIENCE: Cleveland NFL, 1988-1990.... Games: 1988 (16), 1989 (16), 1990 (16). Total: 48.
CHAMPIONSHIP GAME EXPERIENCE: Played in AFC championship game after 1989 season.
RECORDS/HONORS: Played in Pro Bowl after 1989 and 1990 seasons.... Named to THE SPORTING NEWS NFL All-Pro team, 1989 and 1990.
PRO STATISTICS: 1988—Returned one kickoff for 13 yards and recovered two fumbles for 10 yards and a touchdown. 1989—Recovered two fumbles. 1990—Recovered one fumble.

PERRY, WILLIAM
DT, BEARS

PERSONAL: Born December 16, 1962, at Aiken, S.C.... 6-2/325.... Brother of Michael Dean Perry, defensive tackle with Cleveland Browns.
HIGH SCHOOL: Aiken (S.C.).
COLLEGE: Clemson.
TRANSACTIONS/CAREER NOTES: Selected by Orlando Renegades in 1985 USFL territorial draft.... Selected by Chicago Bears in first round (22nd pick overall) of 1985 NFL draft.... Signed by Bears (August 5, 1985).... On non-football injury list with eating disorder (July 23-August 23, 1988).... On injured reserve with broken arm (September 20, 1988-remainder of season).... On injured reserve with knee injury (December 7, 1989-remainder of season).

PLAYING EXPERIENCE: Chicago NFL, 1985-1990. . . . Games: 1985 (16), 1986 (16), 1987 (12), 1988 (3), 1989 (13), 1990 (16). Total: 76.
CHAMPIONSHIP GAME EXPERIENCE: Played in NFC championship game after 1985 season. . . . Played in Super Bowl XX after 1985 season.
PRO STATISTICS: 1985—Rushed five times for seven yards and two touchdowns, caught one pass for four yards and a touchdown and recovered two fumbles for 66 yards. 1986—Rushed once for minus one yard and fumbled once. 1987—Rushed once for no yards and fumbled once. 1989—Recovered two fumbles for five yards. 1990—Rushed once for minus one yard.

PERRYMAN, ROBERT
RB, BRONCOS

PERSONAL: Born October 16, 1964, at Raleigh, N.C. . . . 6-2/233.
HIGH SCHOOL: Bourne (Mass.).
COLLEGE: Michigan (undergraduate degree, 1987).
TRANSACTIONS/CAREER NOTES: Selected by New England Patriots in third round (79th pick overall) of 1987 NFL draft. . . . Signed by Patriots (July 26, 1987). . . . Released by Patriots (November 5, 1990). . . . Signed by Dallas Cowboys (November 9, 1990). . . . On inactive list (December 2, 16, 23 and 30, 1990). . . . Active for three games with Cowboys in 1990; did not play. . . . Granted unconditional free agency (February 1, 1991). . . . Signed by Denver Broncos (April 1, 1991).
PRO STATISTICS: 1987—Returned three kickoffs for 43 yards and recovered two fumbles. 1989—Recovered one fumble.

		RUSHING				RECEIVING				TOTAL		
Year Team	G	Att.	Yds.	Avg.	TD	No.	Yds.	Avg.	TD	TD	Pts.	F.
1987— New England NFL	9	41	187	4.6	0	3	13	4.3	0	0	0	1
1988— New England NFL	16	146	448	3.1	6	17	134	7.9	0	6	36	4
1989— New England NFL	16	150	562	3.7	2	29	195	6.7	0	2	12	2
1990— N.E. (8)-Dal. (0) NFL	8	32	97	3.0	1	15	88	5.9	0	1	6	2
Pro totals (4 years)	49	369	1294	3.5	9	64	430	6.7	0	9	54	9

PETE, LAWRENCE
NT, LIONS

PERSONAL: Born January 18, 1966, at Wichita, Kan. . . . 6-0/282.
HIGH SCHOOL: South (Wichita, Kan.).
COLLEGE: Nebraska.
TRANSACTIONS/CAREER NOTES: Selected by Detroit Lions in fifth round (115th pick overall) of 1989 NFL draft. . . . Signed by Lions (July 23, 1989). . . . On injured reserve with pinched nerve in shoulder (September 4-November 16, 1990).
PLAYING EXPERIENCE: Detroit NFL, 1989 and 1990. . . . Games: 1989 (16), 1990 (6). Total: 22.

PETRY, STAN
CB, CHIEFS

PERSONAL: Born August 14, 1966, at Alvin, Tex. . . . 5-11/180. . . . Full name: Stanley Edward Petry.
HIGH SCHOOL: Willowridge (Fort Bend, Tex.).
COLLEGE: Texas Christian.
TRANSACTIONS/CAREER NOTES: Selected by Kansas City Chiefs in fourth round (88th pick overall) of 1989 NFL draft. . . . Signed by Chiefs (July 25, 1989).

		INTERCEPTIONS			
Year Team	G	No.	Yds.	Avg.	TD
1989— Kansas City NFL	16	0	0		0
1990— Kansas City NFL	16	3	33	11.0	1
Pro totals (2 years)	32	3	33	11.0	1

PHILCOX, TODD
QB, BROWNS

PERSONAL: Born September 25, 1966, at Norwalk, Conn. . . . 6-4/225. . . . Full name: Todd Stuart Philcox.
HIGH SCHOOL: Norwalk (Conn.).
COLLEGE: Syracuse (bachelor's degree in finance, 1988).
TRANSACTIONS/CAREER NOTES: Signed as free agent by Cincinnati Bengals (May, 1989). . . . Released by Bengals (September 5, 1989). . . . Re-signed by Bengals to developmental squad (September 6, 1989). . . . Released by Bengals (January 29, 1990). . . . Re-signed by Bengals (May, 1990). . . . On inactive list (September 16; October 1; and December 23 and 30, 1990). . . . Granted unconditional free agency (February 1, 1991). . . . Signed by Cleveland Browns (April 1, 1991).
PRO STATISTICS: Passer rating points: 1990 (0.0).

		PASSING							RUSHING				TOTAL		
Year Team	G	Att.	Cmp.	Pct.	Yds.	TD	Int.	Avg.	Att.	Yds.	Avg.	TD	TD	Pts.	F.
1990— Cincinnati NFL	2	2	0	.0	0	0	1	.0	0	0		0	0	0	0
Pro totals (1 year)	2	2	0	.0	0	0	1	.0	0	0		0	0	0	0

PHILLIPS, JASON
WR, FALCONS

PERSONAL: Born October 11, 1966, at Crowley, La. . . . 5-7/168. . . . Full name: Jason H. Phillips.
HIGH SCHOOL: Sterling (Houston).
COLLEGE: Taft (Calif.) College and Houston.
TRANSACTIONS/CAREER NOTES: Selected by Detroit Lions in 10th round (253rd pick overall) of 1989 NFL draft. . . . Signed by Lions (July 14, 1989). . . . On inactive list (November 22, 1990). . . . Granted unconditional free agency (February 1, 1991). . . .

Signed by Atlanta Falcons (April 1, 1991).
PRO STATISTICS: 1989—Recovered one fumble and fumbled once. 1990—Returned two kickoffs for 43 yards.

| | | | —— RECEIVING —— | | | |
Year	Team	G	No.	Yds.	Avg.	TD
1989— Detroit NFL		16	30	352	11.7	1
1990— Detroit NFL		13	8	112	14.0	0
Pro totals (2 years)		29	38	464	12.2	1

PHILLIPS, JOE
NT, CHARGERS

PERSONAL: Born July 15, 1963, at Portland, Ore. . . . 6-5/315. . . . Full name: Joseph Gordon Phillips.
HIGH SCHOOL: Columbia River (Vancouver, Wash.).
COLLEGE: Oregon State, then Chemeketa Community College (Ore.), then Southern Methodist (bachelor of arts degree in economics, 1986).
TRANSACTIONS/CAREER NOTES: Selected by Minnesota Vikings in fourth round (93rd pick overall) of 1986 NFL draft. . . . Signed by Vikings (July 28, 1986). . . . Released by Vikings (September 7, 1987). . . . Signed as free-agent replacement player by San Diego Chargers (September 24, 1987). . . . Granted free agency (February 1, 1988). . . . Re-signed by Chargers (August 29, 1988). . . . On reserve/non-football injury list with head injuries (September 26, 1990-remainder of season).
PLAYING EXPERIENCE: Minnesota NFL, 1986; San Diego NFL, 1987-1990. . . . Games: 1986 (16), 1987 (13), 1988 (16), 1989 (16), 1990 (3). Total: 64.
PRO STATISTICS: 1986—Recovered one fumble.

PICKEL, BILL
DT, JETS

PERSONAL: Born November 5, 1959, at Queens, N.Y. . . . 6-5/265. . . . Name pronounced pick-ELL.
HIGH SCHOOL: Milford (Conn.) and St. Francis (Brooklyn, N.Y.).
COLLEGE: Rutgers.
TRANSACTIONS/CAREER NOTES: Selected by New Jersey Generals in 1983 USFL territorial draft. . . . Selected by Los Angeles Raiders in second round (54th pick overall) of 1983 NFL draft. . . . Signed by Raiders (May 26, 1983). . . . Crossed picket line during players' strike (October 6, 1987). . . . On inactive list (November 11 and 19, 1990). . . . Granted unconditional free agency (February 1, 1991). . . . Signed by New York Jets (March 19, 1991).
PLAYING EXPERIENCE: Los Angeles Raiders NFL, 1983-1990. . . . Games: 1983 (16), 1984 (16), 1985 (16), 1986 (15), 1987 (12), 1988 (16), 1989 (16), 1990 (14). Total: 121.
CHAMPIONSHIP GAME EXPERIENCE: Played in AFC championship game after 1983 and 1990 seasons. . . . Played in Super Bowl XVIII after 1983 season.
RECORDS/HONORS: Named to THE SPORTING NEWS NFL All-Pro team, 1986.
PRO STATISTICS: 1983—Recovered one fumble. 1986—Recovered two fumbles. 1987—Recovered two fumbles. 1988—Recovered one fumble. 1990—Recovered one fumble.

PIEL, MIKE
DT, RAMS

PERSONAL: Born September 21, 1965, at Carmel, Calif. . . . 6-4/270. . . . Full name: Mike Lloyd Piel. . . . Name pronounced PEEL.
HIGH SCHOOL: El Toro (Calif.).
COLLEGE: Saddleback Community College (Calif.), then Illinois (degree in speech communications, 1988).
TRANSACTIONS/CAREER NOTES: Selected by Los Angeles Rams in third round (82nd pick overall) of 1988 NFL draft. . . . Signed by Rams (July 22, 1988). . . . On injured reserve with neck injury (August 23, 1988-entire season).
PLAYING EXPERIENCE: Los Angeles Rams NFL, 1989 and 1990. . . . Games: 1989 (13), 1990 (16). Total: 29.
CHAMPIONSHIP GAME EXPERIENCE: Played in NFC championship game after 1989 season.
PRO STATISTICS: 1989—Recovered one fumble. 1990—Recovered two fumbles.

PIKE, MARK
DE, BILLS

PERSONAL: Born December 27, 1963, at Elizabethtown, Ky. . . . 6-4/272. . . . Full name: Mark Harold Pike.
HIGH SCHOOL: Dixie Heights (Edgewood, Ky.).
COLLEGE: Georgia Tech.
TRANSACTIONS/CAREER NOTES: Selected by Jacksonville Bulls in 1986 USFL territorial draft. . . . Selected by Buffalo Bills in seventh round (178th pick overall) of 1986 NFL draft. . . . Signed by Bills (July 20, 1986). . . . On injured reserve with shoulder injury (August 26, 1986-entire season). . . . On injured reserve with leg injury (September 16-November 14, 1987). . . . On injured reserve with foot injury (December 8, 1987-remainder of season).
PLAYING EXPERIENCE: Buffalo NFL, 1987-1990. . . . Games: 1987 (3), 1988 (16), 1989 (16), 1990 (16). Total: 51.
CHAMPIONSHIP GAME EXPERIENCE: Played in AFC championship game after 1988 and 1990 seasons. . . . Played in Super Bowl XXV after 1990 season.
PRO STATISTICS: 1988—Returned one kickoff for five yards. 1989—Recovered one fumble.

PILLOW, FRANK
WR, LIONS

PERSONAL: Born March 11, 1965, at Nashville, Tenn. . . . 5-11/170. . . . Full name: William Frank Pillow Jr.
HIGH SCHOOL: Whites Creek (Nashville, Tenn.).
COLLEGE: Tennessee State.
TRANSACTIONS/CAREER NOTES: Selected by Tampa Bay Buccaneers in 11th round (279th pick overall) of 1988 NFL draft. . . . Signed by Buccaneers (July 10, 1988). . . . On injured reserve with broken foot (September 5-November 8, 1989). . . . Granted free agency (February 1, 1990). . . . Re-signed by Buccaneers (July 10, 1990). . . . Granted unconditional free agency (Febru-

ary 1, 1991).... Signed by Detroit Lions (March 22, 1991).
PRO STATISTICS: 1990—Returned three kickoffs for 38 yards. 1989—Returned one kickoff for 17 yards. 1990—Recovered one fumble.

			—— RECEIVING ——		
Year	Team	G	No.	Yds.	Avg.	TD
1988— Tampa Bay NFL.........		15	15	206	13.7	1
1989— Tampa Bay NFL.........		3	0	0		0
1990— Tampa Bay NFL.........		16	8	118	14.8	0
Pro totals (3 years)........		34	23	324	14.1	1

PINKETT, ALLEN
RB, OILERS

PERSONAL: Born January 25, 1964, at Washington, D.C.... 5-9/196.... Full name: Allen Jerome Pinkett.... Cousin of Eric Dorsey, defensive end with New York Giants.
HIGH SCHOOL: Parkview (South Hill, Va.).
COLLEGE: Notre Dame (bachelor of business administration degree in marketing, 1986).
TRANSACTIONS/CAREER NOTES: Selected by Orlando Renegades in 1986 USFL territorial draft.... Selected by Houston Oilers in third round (61st pick overall) of 1986 NFL draft.... Signed by Oilers (July 31, 1986).... On injured reserve with shoulder injury (October 27-November 28, 1987).... Granted free agency (February 1, 1990).... Re-signed by Oilers (July 24, 1990). ... On inactive list (December 9, 1990).
PRO STATISTICS: 1986—Returned one punt for minus one yard and recovered one fumble. 1990—Recovered two fumbles.

			—— RUSHING——				—— RECEIVING——				– KICKOFF RETURNS–				—— TOTAL——		
Year	Team	G	Att.	Yds.	Avg.	TD	No.	Yds.	Avg.	TD	No.	Yds.	Avg.	TD	TD	Pts.	F.
1986— Houston NFL..........		16	77	225	2.9	2	35	248	7.1	1	26	519	20.0	0	3	18	2
1987— Houston NFL..........		8	31	149	4.8	2	1	7	7.0	0	17	322	18.9	0	2	12	1
1988— Houston NFL..........		16	122	513	4.2	7	12	114	9.5	2	7	137	19.6	0	9	54	2
1989— Houston NFL..........		16	94	449	4.8	1	31	239	7.7	1	0	0		0	2	12	1
1990— Houston NFL..........		15	66	268	4.1	0	11	85	7.7	0	4	91	22.8	0	0	0	0
Pro totals (5 years).......		71	390	1604	4.1	12	90	693	7.7	4	54	1069	19.8	0	16	96	6

PITTS, MIKE
DT, EAGLES

PERSONAL: Born September 25, 1960, at Baltimore.... 6-5/280.... Cousin of Rick Porter, running back with Detroit Lions, Baltimore Colts and Memphis Showboats (USFL), 1982, 1983 and 1985.
HIGH SCHOOL: Polytechnic (Baltimore).
COLLEGE: Alabama.
TRANSACTIONS/CAREER NOTES: Selected by Birmingham Stallions in 1983 USFL territorial draft.... Selected by Atlanta Falcons in first round (16th pick overall) of 1983 NFL draft.... Signed by Falcons (July 16, 1983).... On injured reserve with knee injury (December 6, 1984-remainder of season).... Granted free agency (February 1, 1987).... Re-signed by Falcons and traded to Philadelphia Eagles for defensive end Greg Brown (September 7, 1987).... Granted roster exemption (September 7-September 11, 1987).... On injured reserve with knee injury (September 19-December 21, 1990).
PLAYING EXPERIENCE: Atlanta NFL, 1983-1986; Philadelphia NFL, 1987-1990.... Games: 1983 (16), 1984 (14), 1985 (16), 1986 (16), 1987 (12), 1988 (16), 1989 (16), 1990 (4). Total: 110.
RECORDS/HONORS: Named as defensive end on THE SPORTING NEWS college All-America team, 1982.
PRO STATISTICS: 1983—Recovered one fumble for 26 yards. 1984—Recovered two fumbles. 1985—Intercepted one pass for one yard, recovered one fumble for six yards and fumbled once. 1986—Recovered two fumbles for 22 yards and a touchdown. 1987—Recovered four fumbles for 21 yards. 1989—Recovered two fumbles.

PITTS, RON
CB, PACKERS

PERSONAL: Born October 14, 1962, at Detroit.... 5-10/185.... Full name: Ronald Dwayne Pitts.... Son of Elijah Pitts, running back with Green Bay Packers, Los Angeles Rams and New Orleans Saints, 1961-1971; scout, Green Bay Packers, 1972; and assistant coach with Los Angeles Rams, 1973-1977; Houston Oilers, 1981-1983; Hamilton Tiger-Cats (CFL), 1984 and Buffalo Bills, 1978-1980 and since 1985.
HIGH SCHOOL: Orchard Park (N.Y.).
COLLEGE: UCLA (degree in communications, 1985).
TRANSACTIONS/CAREER NOTES: Selected by Buffalo Bills in seventh round (169th pick overall) of 1985 NFL draft.... Signed by Bills (July 30, 1985).... On injured reserve with foot injury (August 19, 1985-entire season).... On injured reserve with foot injury (September 2-October 18, 1986).... Released by Bills (August 30, 1988).... Signed as free agent by Green Bay Packers (September 15, 1988).... Granted free agency (February 1, 1990).... Re-signed by Packers (August 6, 1990).
PRO STATISTICS: 1986—Returned one kickoff for seven yards and recovered two fumbles. 1987—Recovered one fumble. 1988—Returned one kickoff for 17 yards and recovered four fumbles. 1990—Recovered one fumble.

			—— INTERCEPTIONS——				—— PUNT RETURNS ——				—— TOTAL ——		
Year	Team	G	No.	Yds.	Avg.	TD	No.	Yds.	Avg.	TD	TD	Pts.	F.
1986— Buffalo NFL..............................		10	0	0		0	18	194	10.8	1	1	6	2
1987— Buffalo NFL..............................		12	3	19	6.3	0	23	149	6.5	0	0	0	3
1988— Green Bay NFL........................		14	2	56	28.0	0	9	93	10.3	1	1	6	1
1989— Green Bay NFL........................		14	1	37	37.0	0	0	0		0	0	0	0
1990— Green Bay NFL........................		16	1	0	.0	0	0	0		0	0	0	0
Pro totals (5 years)..............................		66	7	112	16.0	0	50	436	8.7	2	2	12	6

PLEASANT, ANTHONY
DE, BROWNS

PERSONAL: Born January 27, 1967, at Century, Fla.... 6-5/258.
HIGH SCHOOL: Century (Ullin, Fla.).
COLLEGE: Tennessee State.
TRANSACTIONS/CAREER NOTES: Selected by Cleveland Browns in third round

(73rd pick overall) of 1990 NFL draft.... Signed by Browns (July 22, 1990).
PLAYING EXPERIENCE: Cleveland NFL, 1990.... Games: 1990 (16).

PLUMMER, BRUCE
S, 49ERS

PERSONAL: Born September 1, 1964, at Bogalusa, La.... 6-0/198.... Full name: Bruce Elliott Plummer.
HIGH SCHOOL: Bogalusa (La.).
COLLEGE: Mississippi State.

TRANSACTIONS/CAREER NOTES: Selected by Denver Broncos in ninth round (250th pick overall) of 1987 NFL draft.... Signed by Broncos (July 19, 1987).... Released by Broncos (November 26, 1988).... Awarded on waivers to Miami Dolphins (November 28, 1988).... Granted unconditional free agency (February 1, 1989).... Signed by Indianapolis Colts (March 8, 1989).... Granted unconditional free agency (February 1, 1990).... Signed by San Diego Chargers (February 21, 1990).... Released by Chargers (September 3, 1990).... Signed by Denver Broncos (September 25, 1990).... On inactive list (November 4, 1990). ... Released by Broncos (November 30, 1990).... Signed by San Francisco 49ers (December 13, 1990).... Released by 49ers (December 24, 1990).... Re-signed by 49ers (February 25, 1991).
PLAYING EXPERIENCE: Dallas NFL, 1987; Denver (8)-Miami (3) NFL, 1988; Indianapolis NFL, 1989; Denver (7)-San Francisco (1) NFL, 1990..... Games: 1987 (11), 1988 (11), 1989 (16), 1990 (8). Total: 46.
CHAMPIONSHIP GAME EXPERIENCE: Played in AFC championship game after 1987 season.... Played in Super Bowl XXII after 1987 season.
PRO STATISTICS: 1989—Intercepted one pass for 18 yards and recovered one fumble. 1990—Intercepted one pass for 16 yards.

PLUMMER, GARY
LB, CHARGERS

PERSONAL: Born January 26, 1960, at Fremont, Calif. ... 6-2/240.... Full name: Gary Lee Plummer.
HIGH SCHOOL: Mission San Jose (Calif.).
COLLEGE: Ohlone Junior College (Calif.), then California.

TRANSACTIONS/CAREER NOTES: Selected by Oakland Invaders in 1983 USFL territorial draft.... Signed by Invaders (January 26, 1983).... On developmental squad for one game (March 30-April 6, 1984).... Protected in merger of Oakland Invaders and Michigan Panthers (December 6, 1984).... Released by Invaders (August 2, 1985).... Awarded on waivers to Tampa Bay Bandits (August 3, 1985).... Granted free agency when USFL suspended operations (August 7, 1986).... Signed as free agent by San Diego Chargers (August 18, 1986).... Granted roster exemption (August 18-August 22, 1986).... On injured reserve with broken wrist (October 27-November 28, 1987).
PLAYING EXPERIENCE: Oakland USFL, 1983-1985; San Diego NFL, 1986-1990. ... Games: 1983 (18), 1984 (17), 1985 (18), 1986 (15), 1987 (8), 1988 (16), 1989 (16), 1990 (16). Total USFL: 53. Total NFL: 71. Total Pro: 124.
CHAMPIONSHIP GAME EXPERIENCE: Played in USFL championship game after 1985 season.
PRO STATISTICS: USFL: 1983—Intercepted three passes for 20 yards and recovered one fumble. 1984—Credited with one sack for eight yards, intercepted two passes for 11 yards and recovered one fumble. 1985—Credited with one sack for seven yards, intercepted one pass for 46 yards, returned three kickoffs for 31 yards and recovered one fumble. ... NFL: 1986—Returned one kickoff for no yards and recovered two fumbles. 1987—Intercepted one pass for two yards. 1989—Rushed once for six yards and recovered one fumble. 1990—Caught one pass for two yards and a touchdown and rushed twice for three yards and a touchdown.

POLLACK, FRANK
OT/G, 49ERS

PERSONAL: Born November 5, 1967, at Camp Springs, Md. ... 6-5/285.... Full name: Frank Steven Pollack.
HIGH SCHOOL: Greenway (Phoenix).
COLLEGE: Northern Arizona (bachelor's degree in advertising, 1990).

TRANSACTIONS/CAREER NOTES: Selected by San Francisco 49ers in sixth round (165th pick overall) of 1990 NFL draft. ... Signed by 49ers (July 18, 1990).
PLAYING EXPERIENCE: San Francisco NFL, 1990.... Games: (15).
CHAMPIONSHIP GAME EXPERIENCE: Played in NFC championship game after 1990 season.

POLLARD, DARRYL
CB, 49ERS

PERSONAL: Born May 11, 1964, at Ellsworth, Me. ... 5-11/187.... Full name: Cedric Darryl Pollard.
HIGH SCHOOL: General William Mitchell (Colorado Springs, Colo.).
COLLEGE: Weber State.

TRANSACTIONS/CAREER NOTES: Signed as free agent by Seattle Seahawks (May 3, 1986).... Released by Seahawks (August 19, 1986).... Signed as free agent by San Francisco 49ers (April 10, 1987).... Released by 49ers (August 31, 1987).... Re-signed as replacement player by 49ers (September 24, 1987).... Released by 49ers (October 24, 1987).... Re-signed by 49ers (August 3, 1988).... Released by 49ers (August 23, 1988).... Re-signed by 49ers (August 25, 1988).... Released by 49ers (August 30, 1988).... Re-signed by 49ers (September 15, 1988).
PLAYING EXPERIENCE: San Francisco NFL, 1987-1990.... Games: 1987 (3), 1988 (14), 1989 (16), 1990 (16). Total: 49.
CHAMPIONSHIP GAME EXPERIENCE: Played in NFC championship game after 1988-1990 seasons.... Played in Super Bowl XXIII after 1988 season and Super Bowl XXIV after 1989 season.
PRO STATISTICS: 1987—Returned one punt for no yards. 1989—Intercepted one pass for 12 yards. 1990—Intercepted one pass and recovered one fumble.

POOL, DAVID
CB, BILLS

PERSONAL: Born December 20, 1966, at Cincinnati.... 5-9/188.... Full name: David Allen Pool.
HIGH SCHOOL: Cincinnati Academy of Physical Education (Cincinnati).
COLLEGE: Tennessee, then Carson-Newman (Tenn.).
TRANSACTIONS/CAREER NOTES: Selected by San Diego Chargers in sixth round (145th pick overall)

of 1990 NFL draft. . . . On injured reserve with hamstring injury (August 27-September 19, 1990). . . . Released by Chargers (September 19, 1990). . . . Signed by Buffalo Bills (October 1, 1990). . . . On inactive list (December 2 and 9, 1990).
CHAMPIONSHIP GAME EXPERIENCE: Member of Buffalo Bills for AFC championship game and Super Bowl XXV after 1990 season; inactive.

| | | | — INTERCEPTIONS— | | | |
Year	Team	G	No.	Yds.	Avg.	TD
1990—	Buffalo NFL...............	9	1	0	.0	0
	Pro totals (1 year)	9	1	0	.0	0

PORTER, KEVIN
S, CHIEFS

PERSONAL: Born April 11, 1966, at Bronx, N.Y. . . . 5-10/214. . . . Full name: Kevin James Porter. . . . Cousin of James Brooks, running back with Cincinnati Bengals.
HIGH SCHOOL: Warner Robins (Ga.).
COLLEGE: Auburn.
TRANSACTIONS/CAREER NOTES: Selected by Kansas City Chiefs in third round (59th pick overall) of 1988 NFL draft. . . . Signed by Chiefs (May 25, 1988).
PLAYING EXPERIENCE: Kansas City NFL, 1988-1990. . . . Games: 1988 (15), 1989 (16), 1990 (16). Total: 47.
PRO STATISTICS: 1988—Returned one kickoff for 16 yards, recovered two fumbles and fumbled once. 1990—Intercepted one pass for 13 yards and fumbled once.

PORTER, RUFUS
LB, SEAHAWKS

PERSONAL: Born May 18, 1965, at Amite, La. . . . 6-1/226.
HIGH SCHOOL: Capitol (Baton Rouge, La.).
COLLEGE: Southern.
TRANSACTIONS/CAREER NOTES: Signed as free agent by Seattle Seahawks (May 11, 1988). . . . On injured reserve with groin injury (December 5, 1990-remainder of season).
PLAYING EXPERIENCE: Seattle NFL, 1988-1990. . . . Games: 1988 (16), 1989 (16), 1990 (12). Total: 44.
RECORDS/HONORS: Played in Pro Bowl after following 1988 and 1989 seasons.
PRO STATISTICS: 1988—Recovered one fumble. 1990—Recovered four fumbles for 11 yards.

POWERS, WARREN
DE, BRONCOS

PERSONAL: Born February 4, 1965, at Baltimore. . . . 6-6/287.
HIGH SCHOOL: Edmondson (Baltimore).
COLLEGE: Maryland.
TRANSACTIONS/CAREER NOTES: Selected by Denver Broncos in second round (47th pick overall) of 1989 NFL draft. . . . Signed by Broncos (July 17, 1989).
PLAYING EXPERIENCE: Denver NFL, 1989 and 1990. . . . Games: 1989 (15), 1990 (16). Total: 31.
CHAMPIONSHIP GAME EXPERIENCE: Played in AFC championship game after 1989 season. . . . Played in Super Bowl XXIV after 1989 season.

POZDERAC, PHIL
OT, COLTS

PERSONAL: Born December 19, 1959, at Cleveland. . . . 6-9/292. . . . Full name: Philip Maurice Pozderac.
HIGH SCHOOL: Garfield Heights (O.).
COLLEGE: Notre Dame (received bachelor of business administration degree in finance, 1982).
TRANSACTIONS/CAREER NOTES: Selected by Dallas Cowboys in fifth round (137th pick overall) of 1982 NFL draft. . . . Retired (October 22, 1987). . . . Signed by Indianapolis Colts (April 26, 1991).
PLAYING EXPERIENCE: Dallas NFL, 1982-1987. . . . Games: 1982 (7), 1983 (16), 1984 (15), 1985 (14), 1986 (16), 1987 (2). Total: 70.
CHAMPIONSHIP GAME EXPERIENCE: Member of Dallas Cowboys for NFC championship game after 1982 season; did not play.
PRO STATISTICS: 1984—Caught one pass for one yard.

PRICE, DENNIS
CB, JETS

PERSONAL: Born June 14, 1965, at Los Angeles. . . . 6-1/175. . . . Full name: Dennis Sean Price.
HIGH SCHOOL: Polytechnic (Long Beach, Calif.).
COLLEGE: UCLA (degree in economics, 1988).
TRANSACTIONS/CAREER NOTES: Selected by Los Angeles Raiders in fifth round (131st pick overall) of 1988 USFL draft. . . . Signed by Raiders (July 13, 1988). . . . On injured reserve with knee injury (September 16-October 31, 1989). . . . Transferred to developmental squad (November 1-December 2, 1989). . . . On injured reserve with shoulder injury (September 5-October 15, 1990). . . . Traded by Raiders to New York Jets for linebacker Alex Gordon (October 15, 1990). . . . On injured reserve with knee injury (October 31, 1990-remainder of season).
PLAYING EXPERIENCE: Los Angeles Raiders NFL, 1988 and 1989. . . . Games: 1988 (12), 1989 (5). Total: 17.
PRO STATISTICS: 1988—Intercepted two passes for 18 yards.

PRICE, MITCHELL
CB, BENGALS

PERSONAL: Born May 10, 1967, at Jacksonville, Tex. . . . 5-9/181.
HIGH SCHOOL: James Madison (San Antonio, Tex.).
COLLEGE: Southern Methodist, then Tulane.
TRANSACTIONS/CAREER NOTES: Selected by Cincinnati Bengals in ninth round (234th pick overall) of 1990 NFL draft. . . . Signed by Bengals (July 20, 1990).
PRO STATISTICS: 1990—Recovered two fumbles.

Year Team	G	No.	Yds.	Avg.	TD	No.	Yds.	Avg.	TD	No.	Yds.	Avg.	TD	TD	Pts.	F.
		— INTERCEPTIONS —				— PUNT RETURNS —				– KICKOFF RETURNS –				— TOTAL —		
1990— Cincinnati NFL	16	1	0	.0	0	29	251	8.7	*1	10	191	19.1	0	1	6	2
Pro totals (1 year)	16	1	0	.0	0	29	251	8.7	1	10	191	19.1	0	1	6	2

PRICE, TERRY
DE, DOLPHINS

PERSONAL: Born April 5, 1968, at Atlanta. . . . 6-4/272. . . . Full name: Terrence Todd Price.
HIGH SCHOOL: Plano Senior (Plano, Tex.).
COLLEGE: Texas A&M.
TRANSACTIONS/CAREER NOTES: Selected by Chicago Bears in 10th round (255th pick overall) of 1990 NFL draft. . . . Signed by Bears (July 24, 1990). . . . On injured reserve with elbow injury (September 9-October 3, 1990). . . . On developmental squad (October 3-December 21, 1990). . . . Granted unconditional free agency (February 1, 1991). . . . Signed by Miami Dolphins (March 11, 1991).
PLAYING EXPERIENCE: Chicago NFL, 1990. . . . Games: 1990 (2).

PRINGLE, MIKE
RB, FALCONS

PERSONAL: Born October 1, 1967, at Los Angeles. . . . 5-8/186. . . . Full name: Michael A. Pringle.
HIGH SCHOOL: John F. Kennedy (Granada Hills, Calif.).
COLLEGE: Washington State, then Cal State Fullerton.
TRANSACTIONS/CAREER NOTES: Selected by Atlanta Falcons in sixth round (139th pick overall) of 1990 NFL draft. . . . Signed by Falcons (July 26, 1990). . . . On injured reserve with rib injury (September 4-October 2, 1990). . . . On practice squad (October 2-December 5, 1990). . . . On inactive list (December 9, 1990).

Year Team	G	No.	Yds.	Avg.	TD	No.	Yds.	Avg.	TD	TD	Pts.	F.
		— RUSHING —				– KICKOFF RETURNS —				— TOTAL —		
1990— Atlanta NFL	3	2	9	4.5	0	1	14	14.0	0	0	0	0
Pro totals (1 year)	3	2	9	4.5	0	1	14	14.0	0	0	0	0

PRIOR, MIKE
DB, COLTS

PERSONAL: Born November 14, 1963, at Chicago Heights, Ill. . . . 6-0/210. . . . Full name: Michael Robert Prior.
HIGH SCHOOL: Marian Catholic (Chicago Heights, Ill.).
COLLEGE: Illinois State (bachelor of science degree in business administration, 1985).
TRANSACTIONS/CAREER NOTES: Selected by Memphis Showboats in fourth round (60th pick overall) of 1985 USFL draft. . . . Selected by Tampa Bay Buccaneers in seventh round (176th pick overall) of 1985 NFL draft. . . . Signed by Buccaneers (June 10, 1985). . . . On injured reserve with fractured wrist (August 25-September 28, 1986). . . . Released by Buccaneers (September 29, 1986). . . . Signed as free agent by Indianapolis Colts (May 11, 1987). . . . Released by Colts (August 31, 1987). . . . Re-signed as replacement player by Colts (September 23, 1987).
MISCELLANEOUS: Selected by Baltimore Orioles' organization in 18th round of free-agent baseball draft (June 4, 1984). . . . Selected by Los Angeles Dodgers' organization in fourth round of free-agent baseball draft (June 3, 1985).
PRO STATISTICS: 1985—Recovered three fumbles. 1987—Recovered three fumbles. 1988—Recovered one fumble for 12 yards. 1989—Recovered one fumble for 10 yards. 1990—Caught one pass for 40 yards and recovered two fumbles and fumbled once for six yards.

Year Team	G	No.	Yds.	Avg.	TD	No.	Yds.	Avg.	TD	No.	Yds.	Avg.	TD	TD	Pts.	F.
		— INTERCEPTIONS —				— PUNT RETURNS —				– KICKOFF RETURNS –				— TOTAL —		
1985— Tampa Bay NFL	16	0	0		0	13	105	8.1	0	10	131	13.1	0	0	0	4
1987— Indianapolis NFL	13	6	57	9.5	0	0	0		0	3	47	15.7	0	0	0	0
1988— Indianapolis NFL	16	3	46	15.3	0	1	0	.0	0	0	0		0	0	0	1
1989— Indianapolis NFL	16	6	88	14.7	1	0	0		0	0	0		0	1	6	0
1990— Indianapolis NFL	16	3	66	22.0	0	2	0	.0	0	0	0		0	0	0	1
Pro totals (5 years)	77	18	257	14.3	1	16	105	6.6	0	13	178	13.7	0	1	6	6

PROEHL, RICKY
WR, CARDINALS

PERSONAL: Born March 7, 1968, at Belle Mead, N.J. . . . 6-0/190. . . . Full name: Richard Scott Proehl.
HIGH SCHOOL: Hillsborough (N.J.).
COLLEGE: Wake Forest.
TRANSACTIONS/CAREER NOTES: Selected by Phoenix Cardinals in third round (58th pick overall) of 1990 NFL draft. . . . Signed by Cardinals (July 23, 1990).

Year Team	G	Att.	Yds.	Avg.	TD	No.	Yds.	Avg.	TD	No.	Yds.	Avg.	TD	No.	Yds.	Avg.	TD	TD	Pts.	F.
		— RUSHING —				— RECEIVING —				– PUNT RETURNS –				KICKOFF RETURNS				– TOTALS –		
1990— Phoenix NFL	16	1	4	4.0	0	56	802	14.3	4	1	2	2.0	0	4	53	13.3	0	4	24	0
Pro totals (1 year)	16	1	4	4.0	0	56	802	14.3	4	1	2	2.0	0	4	53	13.3	0	4	24	0

PROKOP, JOE
P, JETS

PERSONAL: Born July 7, 1960, at St. Paul, Minn. . . . 6-2/225.
HIGH SCHOOL: White Bear Lake (Minn.).
COLLEGE: Cal Poly-Pomona.
TRANSACTIONS/CAREER NOTES: Signed as free agent by Los Angeles Rams (June 20, 1984). . . . Released by Rams (July 16, 1984). . . . USFL rights traded by Los Angeles Express to Houston Gamblers for past considerations (November 12, 1984). . . . Signed by Gamblers (November 12, 1984). . . . Released by Gamblers (January 28, 1985). . . .

Signed as free agent by San Antonio Gunslingers of USFL (February 5, 1985). . . . Released by Gunslingers (February 12, 1985). . . . Signed as free agent by New York Giants (June 21, 1985). . . . Released by Giants (August 26, 1985). . . . Signed as free agent by Green Bay Packers (September 4, 1985). . . . Released by Packers (November 5, 1985). . . . Signed as free agent by New York Jets (March 25, 1986). . . . Released by Jets (August 25, 1986). . . . Signed as free agent by San Diego Chargers (April 13, 1987). . . . On injured reserve with quadricep injury (September 1-September 14, 1987). . . . Released by Chargers (September 15, 1987). . . . Re-signed as replacement player by Chargers (September 24, 1987). . . . Released by Chargers (October 21, 1987). . . . Signed as free agent by New York Jets (April 8, 1988).
PRO STATISTICS: 1989—Rushed once for 17 yards and a touchdown. 1990—Rushed three times for two yards and fumbled once for minus 17 yards.

			PUNTING	
Year Team	G	No.	Avg.	Blk.
1985— Green Bay NFL	9	56	39.5	0
1987— San Diego NFL	3	17	38.5	0
1988— N.Y. Jets NFL	16	85	38.9	0
1989— N.Y. Jets NFL	16	87	39.4	0
1990— N.Y. Jets NFL	16	59	40.1	0
Pro totals (5 years)	60	304	39.3	0

PRUITT, JAMES
WR, VIKINGS

PERSONAL: Born January 29, 1964, at Los Angeles. . . . 6-3/201. . . . Full name: James Bouvias Pruitt.
HIGH SCHOOL: Thomas Jefferson (Los Angeles).
COLLEGE: Cal State Fullerton.
TRANSACTIONS/CAREER NOTES: Selected by Miami Dolphins in fourth round (107th pick overall) of 1986 NFL draft. . . . Selected by New Jersey Generals in first round (fifth pick overall) of 1986 USFL draft. . . . Signed by Dolphins (July 24, 1986). . . . Released by Dolphins (November 19, 1988). . . . Awarded on waivers to Indianapolis Colts (November 21, 1988). . . . Granted free agency (February 1, 1990). . . . Re-signed by Colts (September 5, 1990). . . . Received two-game roster exemption (September, 1990). . . . Released by Colts (September 17, 1990). . . . Re-signed by Miami Dolphins (November 16, 1990). . . . Granted unconditional free agency (February 1, 1991). . . . Signed by Minnesota Vikings (March 31, 1991).
PRO STATISTICS: 1986—Recovered two fumbles.

		RECEIVING				PUNT RETURNS				KICKOFF RETURNS				TOTAL		
Year Team	G	No.	Yds.	Avg.	TD	No.	Yds.	Avg.	TD	No.	Yds.	Avg.	TD	TD	Pts.	F.
1986— Miami NFL	16	15	235	15.7	2	11	150	13.6	1	0	0		0	3	18	4
1987— Miami NFL	12	26	404	15.5	3	0	0		0	0	0		0	3	18	1
1988— Mia.(11)-Ind.(1) NFL	12	2	38	19.0	0	0	0		0	0	0		0	0	0	1
1989— Indianapolis NFL	16	5	71	14.2	1	0	0		0	12	257	21.4	0	1	6	2
1990— Miami NFL	6	13	235	18.1	3	0	0		0	0	0		0	3	18	0
Pro totals (5 years)	62	61	983	16.1	9	11	150	13.6	1	12	257	21.4	0	10	60	8

PRUITT, MICKEY
LB, BEARS

PERSONAL: Born January 10, 1965, at Bamberg, S.C. . . . 6-1/215. . . . Full name: Mickey Aaron Pruitt. . . . Related to Leo Lewis, wide receiver with Minnesota Vikings.
HIGH SCHOOL: Paul Robeson (Chicago).
COLLEGE: Colorado (bachelor of arts degree in communications, 1988).
TRANSACTIONS/CAREER NOTES: Signed as free agent by Chicago Bears (May 4, 1988).
PLAYING EXPERIENCE: Chicago NFL, 1988-1990. . . . Games: 1988 (14), 1989 (14), 1990 (16). Total: 44.
CHAMPIONSHIP GAME EXPERIENCE: Played in NFC championship game after 1988 season.
RECORDS/HONORS: Named as defensive back on THE SPORTING NEWS college All-America team, 1987.
PRO STATISTICS: 1989—Returned two kickoffs for 17 yards. 1990—Recovered one fumble.

PUTZIER, ROLLIN
NT, BRONCOS

PERSONAL: Born December 10, 1965, at Coeur d'Alene, Idaho. . . . 6-4/303. . . . Full name: Rollin W. Putzier.
HIGH SCHOOL: Post Falls (Idaho).
COLLEGE: Oregon.
TRANSACTIONS/CAREER NOTES: Selected by Green Bay Packers in fourth round (88th pick overall) of 1988 NFL draft. . . . Signed by Packers (July 17, 1988). . . . Released by Packers (August 30, 1988). . . . Signed as free agent by Pittsburgh Steelers (September 7, 1988). . . . Released by Steelers after failing physical (September 9, 1988). . . . Re-signed by Steelers (November 2, 1988). . . . Released by Steelers (August 1, 1989). . . . Signed as free agent by San Francisco 49ers (August 9, 1989). . . . On reserve/non-football injury list with steroid use (August 29-September 25, 1989). . . . Reinstated and granted roster exemption (September 26-October 2, 1989). . . . On postseason deactivation list (January 5, 1990-remainder of 1989 season playoffs). . . . Released by 49ers (September 3, 1990). . . . Signed by WLAF (January 31, 1991). . . . Selected by Montreal Machine in third round (26th defensive lineman) of 1991 WLAF positional draft. . . . Signed by Denver Broncos (July, 1991).
PLAYING EXPERIENCE: Pittsburgh NFL, 1988; San Francisco NFL, 1989; Montreal WLAF, 1991. . . . Games: 1988 (5), 1989 (11), 1991 (10). Total NFL: 16. Total Pro: 26.

QUERY, JEFF
WR, PACKERS

PERSONAL: Born March 7, 1967, at Decatur, Ill. . . . 6-0/165. . . . Full name: Jeff Lee Query.
HIGH SCHOOL: Maroa-Forsyth (Maroa, Ill.).
COLLEGE: Millikin (degree in physical education).
TRANSACTIONS/CAREER NOTES: Selected by Green Bay Packers in fifth round (124th pick overall) of 1989 NFL draft. . . . Signed by Packers (July 19, 1989).
PRO STATISTICS: 1989—Returned six kickoffs for 125 yards and recovered one fumble. 1990—Rushed three times for 39 yards and recovered three fumbles for one touchdown.

Year	Team	G	No.	RECEIVING Yds.	Avg.	TD	No.	PUNT RETURNS Yds.	Avg.	TD	TD	TOTAL Pts.	F.
1989— Green Bay NFL		16	23	350	15.2	2	30	247	8.2	0	2	12	1
1990— Green Bay NFL		16	34	458	13.5	2	32	308	9.6	0	3	18	3
Pro totals (2 years)		32	57	808	14.2	4	62	555	9.0	0	5	30	4

RADACHOWSKY, GEORGE
S, CHARGERS

PERSONAL: Born September 7, 1962, at Danbury, Conn.... 6-0/195.... Full name: George Joseph Radachowsky Jr.... Name pronounced RAD-uh-CHOW-skee.
HIGH SCHOOL: Danbury (Conn.).
COLLEGE: Boston College.
TRANSACTIONS/CAREER NOTES: Selected by Philadelphia Stars in fifth round (84th pick overall) of 1984 USFL draft.... Selected by Los Angeles Rams in seventh round (188th pick overall) of 1984 NFL draft.... Signed by Rams (July 9, 1984).... Traded by Rams to Indianapolis Colts for 11th-round pick in 1985 draft (August 27, 1984).... Released by Colts (September 30, 1985).... Re-signed by Colts (April 1, 1986).... Released by Colts (August 18, 1986).... Signed as free agent by New York Jets (May 10, 1987).... Released by New York Jets (August 31, 1987).... Re-signed as replacement player by Jets (September 24, 1987).... Released by Jets (October 26, 1987).... Re-signed by Jets (October 28, 1987).... Released by Jets (November 3, 1987).... Re-signed by Jets (November 27, 1987).... On injured reserve with knee injury (August 22-October 19, 1988).... Activated after clearing procedural waivers (October 21, 1988).... Released by Jets (September 4, 1989).... Re-signed by Jets (September 5, 1989).... Released by Jets (August 27, 1990).... Signed by San Diego Chargers (February 19, 1991).
PLAYING EXPERIENCE: Indianapolis NFL, 1984 and 1985; New York Jets NFL, 1987-1989.... Games: 1984 (16), 1985 (3), 1987 (8), 1988 (9), 1989 (16). Total: 52.
PRO STATISTICS: 1984—Returned one kickoff for no yards and fumbled once. 1987—Intercepted two passes for 45 yards. 1989—Returned blocked field goal attempt 78 yards for a touchdown.

RADE, JOHN
LB, FALCONS

PERSONAL: Born August 31, 1960, at Ceres, Calif.... 6-1/240.... Name pronounced RAY-dee.
HIGH SCHOOL: Buena (Sierra Vista, Ariz.).
COLLEGE: Modesto Junior College (Calif.), then Boise State.
TRANSACTIONS/CAREER NOTES: Signed as free agent by Boston Breakers of USFL (February 10, 1983).... Released by Breakers (February 12, 1983).... Selected by Atlanta Falcons in eighth round (215th pick overall) of 1983 NFL draft.... Signed by Falcons (May 16, 1983).... On injured reserve with pinched nerve in neck (October 24, 1984-remainder of season).... On injured reserve with ankle injury (December 18, 1986-remainder of season).... Granted free agency (February 1, 1988).... Re-signed by Falcons (August 29, 1988).... On injured reserve with knee injury (December 14, 1988-remainder of season).... Granted free agency (February 1, 1990).... Re-signed by Falcons (July 18, 1990).
PLAYING EXPERIENCE: Atlanta NFL, 1983-1990.... Games: 1983 (16), 1984 (7), 1985 (16), 1986 (15), 1987 (11), 1988 (15), 1989 (15), 1990 (16). Total: 111.
PRO STATISTICS: 1983—Recovered two fumbles for 16 yards and a touchdown. 1984—Recovered one fumble. 1985—Intercepted two passes for 42 yards and a touchdown. 1986—Intercepted one pass for six yards. 1989—Recovered two fumbles for 14 yards and fumbled once. 1990—Recovered one fumble.

RADECIC, SCOTT
LB, COLTS

PERSONAL: Born June 14, 1962, at Pittsburgh.... 6-3/236.... Full name: J. Scott Radecic.... Name pronounced RAD-ah-seck.... Brother of Keith Radecic, center with St. Louis Cardinals, 1987.
HIGH SCHOOL: Brentwood (Pittsburgh).
COLLEGE: Penn State.
TRANSACTIONS/CAREER NOTES: Selected by Philadelphia Stars in 1984 USFL territorial draft.... Selected by Kansas City Chiefs in second round (34th pick overall) of 1984 NFL draft.... Signed by Chiefs (July 12, 1984).... Released by Chiefs (September 7, 1987).... Awarded on waivers to Buffalo Bills (September 8, 1987).... Released by Bills (September 4, 1990).... Awarded on waivers to Indianapolis Colts (September 5, 1990).
CHAMPIONSHIP GAME EXPERIENCE: Played in AFC championship game after 1988 season.
PRO STATISTICS: 1985—Recovered one fumble. 1986—Recovered one fumble. 1987—Returned one kickoff for 14 yards and recovered two fumbles. 1988—Recovered two fumbles.

Year	Team	G	INTERCEPTIONS No.	Yds.	Avg.	TD
1984— Kansas City NFL		16	2	54	27.0	1
1985— Kansas City NFL		16	1	21	21.0	0
1986— Kansas City NFL		16	1	20	20.0	0
1987— Buffalo NFL		12	2	4	2.0	0
1988— Buffalo NFL		16	0	0		0
1989— Buffalo NFL		16	0	0		0
1990— Indianapolis NFL		15	0	0		0
Pro totals (7 years)		107	6	99	16.5	1

DID YOU KNOW. . .

...that defensive end Dan Hampton and quarterback Sid Luckman are the only Chicago Bears to play for the team in three different decades?

RAKOCZY, GREGG
G/C, BROWNS

PERSONAL: Born May 18, 1965, at Medford Lakes, N.J. . . . 6-5/295. . . . Full name: Gregg Adam Rakoczy. . . . Name pronounced ruh-KOZE-ee.
HIGH SCHOOL: Shawnee (Medford, N.J.).
COLLEGE: Miami (Fla.).
TRANSACTIONS/CAREER NOTES: Selected by Cleveland Browns in second round (32nd pick overall) of 1987 NFL draft. . . . Signed by Browns (July 29, 1987).
PLAYING EXPERIENCE: Cleveland NFL, 1987-1990. . . . Games: 1987 (12), 1988 (16), 1989 (16), 1990 (16). Total: 60.
CHAMPIONSHIP GAME EXPERIENCE: Played in AFC championship game after 1987 and 1989 seasons.
PRO STATISTICS: 1988—Fumbled twice for minus 16 yards.

RANDLE, ERVIN
LB, BUCCANEERS

PERSONAL: Born October 12, 1962, at Hearne, Tex. . . . 6-1/250. . . . Brother of John Randle, defensive end with Minnesota Vikings.
HIGH SCHOOL: Hearne (Tex.).
COLLEGE: Baylor.
TRANSACTIONS/CAREER NOTES: Selected by San Antonio Gunslingers in 1985 USFL territorial draft. . . . Selected by Tampa Bay Buccaneers in third round (64th pick overall) of 1985 NFL draft. . . . Signed by Buccaneers (July 18, 1985). . . . On injured reserve with shoulder injury (September 30-November 4, 1988).
PLAYING EXPERIENCE: Tampa Bay NFL, 1985-1990. . . . Games: 1985 (16), 1986 (16), 1987 (12), 1988 (9), 1989 (16), 1990 (16). Total: 85.
PRO STATISTICS: 1985—Intercepted one pass for no yards and recovered two fumbles. 1987—Recovered one fumble.

RANDLE, JOHN
DE, VIKINGS

PERSONAL: Born December 12, 1967, at Hearne, Tex. . . . 6-1/248. . . . Brother of Ervin Randle, linebacker with Tampa Bay Buccaneers.
HIGH SCHOOL: Hearne (Tex.).
COLLEGE: Trinity Valley Community College (Tex.), then Texas A&I.
TRANSACTIONS/CAREER NOTES: Signed as free agent by Minnesota Vikings (May 4, 1990).
PLAYING EXPERIENCE: Minnesota NFL, 1990. . . . Games: 1990 (16).

RATHMAN, TOM
FB, 49ERS

PERSONAL: Born October 7, 1962, at Grand Island, Neb. . . . 6-1/232. . . . Full name: Thomas Dean Rathman.
HIGH SCHOOL: Grand Island (Neb.).
COLLEGE: Nebraska.
TRANSACTIONS/CAREER NOTES: Selected by Memphis Showboats in 1986 USFL territorial draft. . . . Selected by San Francisco 49ers in third round (56th pick overall) of 1986 NFL draft. . . . Signed by 49ers (July 16, 1986).
CHAMPIONSHIP GAME EXPERIENCE: Played in NFC championship game after 1988-1990 seasons. . . . Played in Super Bowl XXIII after 1988 season and Super Bowl XXIV after 1989 season.
PRO STATISTICS: 1986—Returned three kickoffs for 66 yards. 1987—Returned two kickoffs for 37 yards. 1988—Recovered one fumble. 1989—Recovered two fumbles for 12 yards. 1990—Recovered one fumble.

		RUSHING				RECEIVING				TOTAL		
Year Team	G	Att.	Yds.	Avg.	TD	No.	Yds.	Avg.	TD	TD	Pts.	F.
1986— San Francisco NFL	16	33	138	4.2	1	13	121	9.3	0	1	6	0
1987— San Francisco NFL	12	62	257	4.2	1	30	329	11.0	3	4	24	1
1988— San Francisco NFL	16	102	427	4.2	2	42	382	9.1	0	2	12	0
1989— San Francisco NFL	16	79	305	3.9	1	73	616	8.4	1	2	12	1
1990— San Francisco NFL	16	101	318	3.2	7	48	327	6.8	0	7	42	2
Pro totals (5 years)	76	377	1445	3.8	12	206	1775	8.6	4	16	96	4

REASONS, GARY
LB, GIANTS

PERSONAL: Born February 18, 1962, at Crowley, Tex. . . . 6-4/234. . . . Full name: Gary Phillip Reasons.
HIGH SCHOOL: Crowley (Tex.).
COLLEGE: Northwestern State (bachelor of science degree in business administration).
TRANSACTIONS/CAREER NOTES: Selected by New Jersey Generals in second round (26th pick overall) of 1984 USFL draft. . . . USFL rights traded by Generals to Tampa Bay Bandits for rights to linebacker Jim LeClair (January 30, 1984). . . . Selected by New York Giants in fourth round (105th pick overall) of 1984 NFL draft. . . . Signed by Giants (July 12, 1984). . . . Granted free agency (February 1, 1987). . . . Re-signed by Giants (September 10, 1987). . . . Granted roster exemption (September 10-September 21, 1987). . . . Granted free agency (February 1, 1990). . . . Re-signed by Giants (August 12, 1990).
CHAMPIONSHIP GAME EXPERIENCE: Played in NFC championship game after 1986 and 1990 seasons. . . . Played in Super Bowl XXI after 1986 season and Super Bowl XXV after 1990 season.
PRO STATISTICS: 1984—Recovered three fumbles. 1988—Recovered two fumbles for five yards. 1989—Credited with a safety and rushed once for two yards. 1990—Recovered three fumbles.

		INTERCEPTIONS			
Year Team	G	No.	Yds.	Avg.	TD
1984— N.Y. Giants NFL	16	2	26	13.0	0
1985— N.Y. Giants NFL	16	1	10	10.0	0
1986— N.Y. Giants NFL	16	2	28	14.0	0
1987— N.Y. Giants NFL	10	0	0		0
1988— N.Y. Giants NFL	16	1	20	20.0	0
1989— N.Y. Giants NFL	16	1	40	40.0	0
1990— N.Y. Giants NFL	16	3	13	4.3	0
Pro totals (7 years)	106	10	137	13.7	0

REED, ANDRE
WR, BILLS

PERSONAL: Born January 29, 1964, at Allentown, Pa. . . . 6-1/190. . . . Full name: Andre Darnell Reed.
HIGH SCHOOL: Louis E. Dieruff (Allentown, Pa.).
COLLEGE: Kutztown State.
TRANSACTIONS/CAREER NOTES: Selected by Orlando Renegades in third round (39th pick overall) of 1985 USFL draft. . . . Selected by Buffalo Bills in fourth round (86th pick overall) of 1985 NFL draft. . . . Signed by Bills (July 19, 1985).
CHAMPIONSHIP GAME EXPERIENCE: Played in AFC championship game after 1988 and 1990 seasons. . . . Played in Super Bowl XXV after 1990 season.
RECORDS/HONORS: Played in Pro Bowl after 1988-1990 seasons.
PRO STATISTICS: 1985—Returned five punts for 12 yards and recovered two fumbles. 1986—Recovered two fumbles for two yards. 1990—Recovered one fumble.

			RUSHING				RECEIVING				TOTAL	
Year Team	G	Att.	Yds.	Avg.	TD	No.	Yds.	Avg.	TD	TD	Pts.	F.
1985— Buffalo NFL	16	3	-1	-.3	1	48	637	13.3	4	5	30	1
1986— Buffalo NFL	15	3	-8	-2.7	0	53	739	13.9	7	7	42	2
1987— Buffalo NFL	12	1	1	1.0	0	57	752	13.2	5	5	30	0
1988— Buffalo NFL	15	6	64	10.7	0	71	968	13.6	6	6	36	1
1989— Buffalo NFL	16	2	31	15.5	0	88	1312	14.9	9	9	54	4
1990— Buffalo NFL	16	3	23	7.7	0	71	945	13.3	8	8	48	1
Pro totals (6 years)	90	18	110	6.1	1	388	5353	13.8	39	40	240	9

REED, DOUG
DT, RAMS

PERSONAL: Born July 16, 1960, at San Diego. . . . 6-3/265.
HIGH SCHOOL: Abraham Lincoln (San Diego).
COLLEGE: San Diego City College, then San Diego State.
TRANSACTIONS/CAREER NOTES: Selected by Los Angeles Express in 17th round (193rd pick overall) of 1983 USFL draft. . . . Selected by Los Angeles Rams in fourth round (111th pick overall) of 1983 NFL draft. . . . Signed by Rams (June 3, 1983). . . . On injured reserve with leg injury (August 29, 1983-entire season). . . . On injured reserve with sprained ankle (December 6, 1989-remainder of season). . . . Granted free agency (February 1, 1990). . . . Re-signed by Rams (September 4, 1990). . . . Activated (September 7, 1990).
PLAYING EXPERIENCE: Los Angeles Rams NFL, 1984-1990. . . . Games: 1984 (9), 1985 (16), 1986 (16), 1987 (12), 1988 (16), 1989 (11), 1990 (16). Total: 96.
CHAMPIONSHIP GAME EXPERIENCE: Played in NFC championship game after 1985 season.
PRO STATISTICS: 1984—Recovered one fumble for two yards. 1988—Recovered one fumble. 1989—Recovered one fumble.

REEVES, KEN
OL, BROWNS

PERSONAL: Born October 4, 1961, at Pittsburg, Tex. . . . 6-5/277.
HIGH SCHOOL: Pittsburg (Tex.).
COLLEGE: Texas A&M.
TRANSACTIONS/CAREER NOTES: Selected by Houston Gamblers in 1985 USFL territorial draft. . . . Selected by Philadelphia Eagles in sixth round (156th pick overall) of 1985 NFL draft. . . . Signed by Eagles (July 23, 1985). . . . Traded by Eagles to Cleveland Browns for an undisclosed draft pick (August 7, 1990).
PLAYING EXPERIENCE: Philadelphia NFL, 1985-1989; Cleveland NFL, 1990. . . . Games: 1985 (15), 1986 (15), 1987 (10), 1988 (15), 1989 (14), 1990 (16). Total: 85.
PRO STATISTICS: 1985—Recovered one fumble. 1986—Recovered one fumble. 1987—Ran one yard with lateral on kickoff return. 1989—Recovered one fumble.

REEVES, WALTER
TE, CARDINALS

PERSONAL: Born December 15, 1965, at Eufaula, Ala. . . . 6-3/266. . . . Full name: Walter James Reeves.
HIGH SCHOOL: Eufaula (Ala.).
COLLEGE: Auburn.
TRANSACTIONS/CAREER NOTES: Selected by Phoenix Cardinals in second round (40th pick overall) of 1989 NFL draft. . . . Signed by Cardinals (July 25, 1989).
RECORDS/HONORS: Named as tight end on THE SPORTING NEWS college All-America team, 1988.
PRO STATISTICS: 1989—Returned one kickoff for five yards and recovered one fumble for two yards. 1990—Recovered one fumble and fumbled once.

		RECEIVING			
Year Team	G	No.	Yds.	Avg.	TD
1989— Phoenix NFL	16	1	5	5.0	0
1990— Phoenix NFL	16	18	126	7.0	0
Pro totals (2 years)	32	19	131	6.9	0

REHDER, TOM
G/OT, GIANTS

PERSONAL: Born January 27, 1965, at Sacramento, Calif. . . . 6-7/290. . . . Full name: Thomas Bernard Rehder II. . . . Name pronounced RAY-der.
HIGH SCHOOL: St. Joseph (Santa Maria, Calif.).
COLLEGE: Notre Dame (degree in economics, 1987).
TRANSACTIONS/CAREER NOTES: Selected by New England Patriots in third round (69th pick overall) of 1988 NFL draft. . . . Signed by Patriots (July 15, 1988). . . . Granted unconditional free agency (February 1, 1990). . . . Signed by New York Jets (February 26, 1990). . . . Released by Jets (August 28, 1990). . . . Awarded on waivers to New York Giants (August 30, 1990). . . . On inactive list (September 9, 16, 23, 30; and December 15 and 23, 1990).
PLAYING EXPERIENCE: New England NFL, 1988 and 1989; New York Giants NFL, 1990. . . . Games: 1988 (16), 1989 (16), 1990

(8). Total: 40.
CHAMPIONSHIP GAME EXPERIENCE: Member of New York Giants for NFC championship game and Super Bowl XXV after 1990 season; inactive.
PRO STATISTICS: 1989—Returned one kickoff for 14 yards.

REICH, FRANK
QB, BILLS

PERSONAL: Born December 4, 1961, at Freeport, N.Y. . . . 6-4/210. . . . Full name: Frank Michael Reich. . . . Name pronounced RIKE.
HIGH SCHOOL: Cedar Crest (Lebanon, Pa.).
COLLEGE: Maryland (bachelor of science degree in finance, 1984).
TRANSACTIONS/CAREER NOTES: Selected by Tampa Bay Bandits in 1985 USFL territorial draft. . . . Selected by Buffalo Bills in third round (57th pick overall) of 1985 NFL draft. . . . Signed by Bills (August 1, 1985). . . . On injured reserve with Achilles' heel injury (September 3-December 6, 1985). . . . Active for 12 games with Bills in 1987; did not play.
CHAMPIONSHIP GAME EXPERIENCE: Member of Buffalo Bills for AFC championship game after 1988 season; did not play. . . . Played in AFC championship game after 1990 season. . . . Played in Super Bowl XXV after 1990 season.
PRO STATISTICS: Passer rating points: 1985 (118.8), 1986 (24.8), 1989 (103.7), 1990 (91.3). Career: 90.1

Year Team	G	Att.	Cmp.	Pct.	Yds.	TD	Int.	Avg.	Att.	Yds.	Avg.	TD	TD	Pts.	F.
1985— Buffalo NFL	1	1	1	100.0	19	0	0	19.00	0	0		0	0	0	0
1986— Buffalo NFL	3	19	9	47.4	104	0	2	5.47	1	0	.0	0	0	0	1
1988— Buffalo NFL	3	0	0		0	0	0		3	-3	-1.0	0	0	0	0
1989— Buffalo NFL	7	87	53	60.9	701	7	2	8.06	9	30	3.3	0	0	0	2
1990— Buffalo NFL	16	63	36	57.1	469	2	0	7.44	15	24	1.6	0	0	0	1
Pro totals (5 years)	30	170	99	58.2	1293	9	4	7.61	28	51	1.8	0	0	0	4

REICHENBACH, MIKE
LB, DOLPHINS

PERSONAL: Born September 14, 1961, at Fort Meade, Md. . . . 6-2/240. . . . Name pronounced RYE-ken-bock.
HIGH SCHOOL: Liberty (Bethlehem, Pa.).
COLLEGE: East Stroudsburg (Pa.).
TRANSACTIONS/CAREER NOTES: Signed as free agent by Philadelphia Eagles (June 18, 1984). . . . Released by Eagles (August 27, 1984). . . . Re-signed by Eagles (September 25, 1984). . . . Granted unconditional free agency (February 1, 1990). . . . Signed by Miami Dolphins (March 30, 1990).
PLAYING EXPERIENCE: Philadelphia NFL, 1984-1989; Miami NFL, 1990. . . . Games: 1984 (12), 1985 (16), 1986 (16), 1987 (11), 1988 (16), 1989 (16), 1990 (16). Total: 103.
PRO STATISTICS: 1984—Recovered two fumbles. 1985—Intercepted one pass for 10 yards. 1989—Rushed once for 30 yards and recovered one fumble.

REID, MICHAEL
LB, FALCONS

PERSONAL: Born June 25, 1964, at Albany, Ga. . . . 6-2/235. . . . Full name: Michael Edward Reid.
HIGH SCHOOL: Dougherty (Albany, Ga.).
COLLEGE: Wisconsin.
TRANSACTIONS/CAREER NOTES: Selected by Atlanta Falcons in seventh round (181st pick overall) of 1987 NFL draft. . . . Signed by Falcons (July 26, 1987). . . . On injured reserve with knee injury (October 23, 1990-remainder of season).
PLAYING EXPERIENCE: Atlanta NFL, 1987-1990. . . . Games: 1987 (11), 1988 (16), 1989 (16), 1990 (6). Total: 49.
PRO STATISTICS: 1990—Returned one punt for no yards and fumbled once.

REIMERS, BRUCE
G, BENGALS

PERSONAL: Born September 18, 1960, at Algona, Ia. . . . 6-7/298. . . . Full name: Bruce Michael Reimers.
HIGH SCHOOL: Humboldt (Ia.).
COLLEGE: Iowa State.
TRANSACTIONS/CAREER NOTES: Selected by Los Angeles Express in seventh round (136th pick overall) of 1984 USFL draft. . . . Selected by Cincinnati Bengals in eighth round (204th pick overall) of 1984 NFL draft. . . . Signed by Bengals (June 20, 1984). . . . On injured reserve with fractured foot (September 4-October 5, 1990).
PLAYING EXPERIENCE: Cincinnati NFL, 1984-1990. . . . Games: 1984 (15), 1985 (14), 1986 (16), 1987 (10), 1988 (16), 1989 (15), 1990 (12). Total: 98.
CHAMPIONSHIP GAME EXPERIENCE: Played in AFC championship game after 1988 season. . . . Played in Super Bowl XXIII after 1988 season.
PRO STATISTICS: 1987—Recovered one fumble.

REMBERT, JOHNNY
LB, PATRIOTS

PERSONAL: Born January 19, 1961, at Hollandale, Miss. . . . 6-3/234.
HIGH SCHOOL: DeSoto (Arcadia, Fla.).
COLLEGE: Cowley County Community College (Kan.), then Clemson.
TRANSACTIONS/CAREER NOTES: Selected by Washington Federals in 1983 USFL territorial draft. . . . Selected by New England Patriots in fourth round (101st pick overall) of 1983 NFL draft. . . . Signed by Patriots (May 16, 1983). . . . On injured reserve with knee injury (August 28-November 3, 1984). . . . On inactive list (October 18, 28; and November 4, 11 and 18, 1990). . . . On injured reserve with knee injury (November 21, 1990-remainder of season).

CHAMPIONSHIP GAME EXPERIENCE: Played in AFC championship game after 1985 season. . . . Played in Super Bowl XX after 1985 season.
RECORDS/HONORS: Played in Pro Bowl after 1988 and 1989 seasons.
PRO STATISTICS: 1983—Recovered one fumble. 1985—Recovered three fumbles for nine yards (including one in end zone for a touchdown). 1986—Recovered three fumbles (including one in end zone for a touchdown) and returned three kickoffs for 27 yards. 1988—Recovered three fumbles for 10 yards. 1989—Recovered one fumble for 27 yards.

			INTERCEPTIONS			
Year	Team	G	No.	Yds.	Avg.	TD
1983— New England NFL......		15	0	0		0
1984— New England NFL......		7	0	0		0
1985— New England NFL......		16	0	0		0
1986— New England NFL......		16	1	37	37.0	0
1987— New England NFL......		11	1	1	1.0	0
1988— New England NFL......		16	2	10	5.0	0
1989— New England NFL......		16	1	0	.0	0
1990— New England NFL......		5	2	22	11.0	0
Pro totals (8 years)		102	7	70	10.0	0

RENFROE, GILBERT
QB, FALCONS

PERSONAL: Born February 18, 1963, at Tuskegee, Ala. . . . 6-1/195.
HIGH SCHOOL: Tuskegee Institute (Tuskegee, Ala.).
COLLEGE: Tennessee State.
TRANSACTIONS/CAREER NOTES: Signed as free agent by Ottawa Rough Riders of CFL (May 15, 1986). . . . Traded by Rough Riders to Toronto Argonauts for running back Cedric Minter (June 18, 1987). . . . Granted free agency (February 1, 1990). . . . Signed by Atlanta Falcons (February 26, 1990). . . . Released by Falcons (September 4, 1990). . . . Re-signed by Falcons (September 11, 1990). . . . Released by Falcons (September 14, 1990). . . . Re-signed by Falcons (September 18, 1990). . . . Released by Falcons (September 20, 1990). . . . Signed by Minnesota Vikings (September 26, 1990). . . . On inactive list (October 7, 15, 28; November 4, 11, 18, 1990). . . . Active for one game with Vikings in 1990; did not play. . . . Released by Vikings (November 20, 1990). . . . Signed by Falcons to practice squad (December 12, 1990). . . . Activated (December 19, 1990). . . . Active for one game with Falcons in 1990; did not play.
CHAMPIONSHIP GAME EXPERIENCE: Played in Grey Cup (CFL championship game) after 1987 season.
PRO STATISTICS: CFL: 1987—Credited with one 2-point conversion.

			PASSING							RUSHING				TOTAL		
Year	Team	G	Att.	Cmp.	Pct.	Yds.	TD	Int.	Avg.	Att.	Yds.	Avg.	TD	TD	Pts.	F.
1986— Ottawa CFL..............		18	139	72	51.8	1051	7	9	7.56	22	174	7.9	1	1	6	5
1987— Toronto CFL.............		9	232	111	47.8	1686	9	4	7.27	27	164	6.1	1	1	8	1
1988— Toronto CFL.............		18	*527	*290	55.0	*4113	26	24	7.80	36	95	2.6	1	1	6	9
1989— Toronto CFL.............		8	249	119	47.8	1335	1	13	5.36	19	78	4.1	1	1	6	1
Pro totals (4 years)		53	1147	592	51.6	8185	43	50	7.14	104	511	4.9	4	4	26	16

RENTIE, CAESAR
G/OT, LIONS

PERSONAL: Born November 10, 1964, at Hartshorne, Okla. . . . 6-2/290. . . . Full name: Caesar Harris Rentie. . . . Name pronounced RENT-ay.
HIGH SCHOOL: Hartshorne, Okla.
COLLEGE: Oklahoma (bachelor of science degree in communications, 1988).
TRANSACTIONS/CAREER NOTES: Selected by Chicago Bears in seventh round (189th pick overall) of 1988 NFL draft. . . . Signed by Bears (July 20, 1988). . . . Granted unconditional free agency (February 1, 1989). . . . Signed by Buffalo Bills (March 2, 1989). . . . Released by Bills (September 5, 1989). . . . Signed as free agent by Indianapolis Colts (March 9, 1990). . . . Released by Colts (August 24, 1990). . . . Signed by WLAF (January 11, 1991). . . . Selected by New York/New Jersey Knights in first round (first offensive lineman) of 1991 WLAF positional draft. . . . Signed by Detroit Lions (July 17, 1991).
PLAYING EXPERIENCE: Chicago NFL, 1988; New York/New Jersey WLAF, 1991. . . . Games: 1988 (5), 1991 (10). Total NFL: 5. Total Pro: 15.
CHAMPIONSHIP GAME EXPERIENCE: Member of Chicago Bears for NFC championship game after 1988 season; inactive.

REVEIZ, FUAD
PK, VIKINGS

PERSONAL: Born February 24, 1963, at Bogota, Colombia. . . . 5-11/216.
HIGH SCHOOL: Sunset (Miami).
COLLEGE: Tennessee.
TRANSACTIONS/CAREER NOTES: Selected by Memphis Showboats in 1985 USFL territorial draft. . . . Selected by Miami Dolphins in seventh round (195th pick overall) of 1985 NFL draft. . . . Signed by Dolphins (July 20, 1985). . . . On injured reserve with pulled thigh (October 19-November 26, 1988). . . . On injured reserve with groin injury (September 4-October 24, 1989). . . . Released by Dolphins (October 25, 1989). . . . Signed as free agent by San Diego Chargers (April 3, 1990). . . . Released by Chargers (October 1, 1990). . . . Signed by Minnesota Vikings (November 3, 1990).
CHAMPIONSHIP GAME EXPERIENCE: Played in AFC championship game after 1985 season.

			PLACE-KICKING				
Year	Team	G	XPM	XPA	FGM	FGA	Pts.
1985— Miami NFL................		16	50	52	22	27	116
1986— Miami NFL................		16	*52	55	14	22	94
1987— Miami NFL................		11	28	30	9	11	55
1988— Miami NFL................		11	31	32	8	12	55
1990— SD (4)-Min. (9) NFL		13	26	27	13	19	65
Pro totals (5 years)		67	187	196	66	91	385

REYNOLDS, ED
LB, PATRIOTS

PERSONAL: Born September 23, 1961, at Stuttgart, West Germany. . . . 6-5/242. . . . Full name: Edward Rannell Reynolds.
HIGH SCHOOL: Drewry Mason (Ridgeway, Va.).
COLLEGE: Virginia (bachelor of science degree in elementary education, 1983).
TRANSACTIONS/CAREER NOTES: Signed as free agent by New England Patriots (May 10, 1983). . . . Released by Patriots (August 29, 1983). . . . Re-signed by Patriots (September 28, 1983). . . . Released by Patriots (August 27, 1984). . . . Re-signed by Patriots (August 28, 1984). . . . On injured reserve with knee injury (September 11-October 12, 1985). . . . On inactive list (September 16, 1990). . . . On injured reserve with knee injury (December 22, 1990-remainder of season).
PLAYING EXPERIENCE: New England NFL, 1983-1990. . . . Games: 1983 (12), 1984 (16), 1985 (12), 1986 (16), 1987 (12), 1988 (14), 1989 (16), 1990 (12). Total: 110.
CHAMPIONSHIP GAME EXPERIENCE: Played in AFC championship game after 1985 season. . . . Played in Super Bowl XX after 1985 season.
PRO STATISTICS: 1983—Recovered two fumbles. 1986—Recovered one fumble. 1989—Recovered one fumble.

REYNOLDS, RICKY
DB, BUCCANEERS

PERSONAL: Born January 19, 1965, at Sacramento, Calif. . . . 5-11/190. . . . Full name: Derrick Scott Reynolds. . . . Cousin of Jerry Royster, infielder with Los Angeles Dodgers, Atlanta Braves, San Diego Padres, Chicago White Sox and New York Yankees, 1973-1988.
HIGH SCHOOL: Luther Burbank (Sacramento, Calif.).
COLLEGE: Washington State.
TRANSACTIONS/CAREER NOTES: Selected by Tampa Bay Buccaneers in second round (36th pick overall) of 1987 NFL draft. . . . Signed by Buccaneers (July 18, 1987). . . . Granted roster exemption (beginning of 1990 season-September 14, 1990).
PRO STATISTICS: 1988—Recovered two fumbles. 1989—Returned blocked punt 33 yards for a touchdown and recovered two fumbles. 1990—Recovered two fumbles.

			— INTERCEPTIONS —		
Year Team	G	No.	Yds.	Avg.	TD
1987— Tampa Bay NFL.........	12	0	0		0
1988— Tampa Bay NFL.........	16	4	7	1.8	0
1989— Tampa Bay NFL.........	16	5	87	17.4	1
1990— Tampa Bay NFL.........	15	3	70	23.3	0
Pro totals (4 years)........	59	12	164	13.7	1

RICE, ALLEN
RB, PACKERS

PERSONAL: Born April 5, 1962, at Houston. . . . 5-10/206. . . . Full name: Allen Troy Rice.
HIGH SCHOOL: Klein (Houston).
COLLEGE: Wharton County Junior College (Tex.), then Ranger Junior College (Tex.), then Baylor.
TRANSACTIONS/CAREER NOTES: Selected by Houston Gamblers in 1984 USFL territorial draft. . . . Selected by Minnesota Vikings in fifth round (140th pick overall) of 1984 NFL draft. . . . Signed by Vikings (July 20, 1984). . . . On injured reserve with knee injury (November 9, 1989-remainder of season). . . . On injured reserve with knee injury (December 28, 1990-remainder of season). . . . Granted unconditional free agency (February 1, 1991). . . . Signed by Green Bay Packers (March 29, 1991).
CHAMPIONSHIP GAME EXPERIENCE: Played in NFC championship game after 1987 season.
PRO STATISTICS: 1984—Recovered two fumbles. 1985—Recovered one fumble. 1986—Returned one punt for no yards, attempted one pass with no completions and recovered two fumbles. 1987—Recovered one fumble. 1988—Recovered one fumble. 1989—Recovered one fumble. 1990—Recovered one fumble.

		— RUSHING —				— RECEIVING —				— KICKOFF RETURNS —				— TOTAL —		
Year Team	G	Att.	Yds.	Avg.	TD	No.	Yds.	Avg.	TD	No.	Yds.	Avg.	TD	TD	Pts.	F.
1984— Minnesota NFL......	14	14	58	4.1	1	4	59	14.8	1	3	34	11.3	0	2	12	1
1985— Minnesota NFL......	14	31	104	3.4	3	9	61	6.8	1	4	70	17.5	0	4	24	0
1986— Minnesota NFL......	14	73	220	3.0	2	30	391	13.0	3	5	88	17.6	0	5	30	5
1987— Minnesota NFL......	12	51	131	2.6	1	19	201	10.6	1	2	29	14.5	0	2	12	1
1988— Minnesota NFL......	16	110	322	2.9	6	30	279	9.3	0	1	0	.0	0	6	36	1
1989— Minnesota NFL......	4	6	25	4.2	0	4	29	7.3	0	1	13	13.0	0	0	0	0
1990— Minnesota NFL......	15	22	74	3.4	0	4	46	11.5	0	12	176	14.7	0	0	0	1
Pro totals (7 years).......	89	307	934	3.0	13	100	1066	10.7	6	28	410	14.6	0	19	114	9

RICE, JERRY
WR, 49ERS

PERSONAL: Born October 13, 1962, at Starkville, Miss. . . . 6-2/200. . . . Full name: Jerry Lee Rice.
HIGH SCHOOL: B.L. Moor (Crawford, Miss.).
COLLEGE: Mississippi Valley State.
TRANSACTIONS/CAREER NOTES: Selected by Birmingham Stallions in first round (first pick overall) of 1985 USFL draft. . . . Selected by San Francisco 49ers in first round (16th pick overall) of 1985 NFL draft. . . . Signed by 49ers (July 23, 1985).
CHAMPIONSHIP GAME EXPERIENCE: Played in NFC championship game after 1988-1990 seasons. . . . Played in Super Bowl XXIII after 1988 season and Super Bowl XXIV after 1989 season.
RECORDS/HONORS: Established NFL record for most consecutive games, touchdown receptions (13), 1986-1987; most touchdown receptions, season (22), 1987. Tied NFL record for most touchdown receptions, game (5), against Atlanta Falcons (October 14, 1990). . . . Named as wide receiver on THE SPORTING NEWS college All-America team, 1984. . . . Played in Pro Bowl after 1986, 1987, 1989 and 1990 seasons. . . . Named to play in Pro Bowl after 1988 season; replaced due to injury by J.T. Smith. . . . Named to THE SPORTING NEWS NFL All-Pro team, 1986-1990. . . . Named THE SPORTING NEWS NFL Player of the Year, 1987 and 1990.

PRO STATISTICS: 1985—Returned one kickoff for six yards. 1986—Attempted two passes with one completion for 16 yards and recovered three fumbles. 1987—Recovered one fumble. 1988—Attempted three passes with one completion for 14 yards and one interception and recovered one fumble.

Year	Team	G	Att.	Yds.	Avg.	TD	No.	Yds.	Avg.	TD	TD	Pts.	F.
1985—	San Francisco NFL	16	6	26	4.3	1	49	927	18.9	3	4	24	1
1986—	San Francisco NFL	16	10	72	7.2	1	86	*1570	18.3	*15	16	96	2
1987—	San Francisco NFL	12	8	51	6.4	1	65	1078	16.6	*22	*23	*138	2
1988—	San Francisco NFL	16	13	107	8.2	1	64	1306	20.4	9	10	60	2
1989—	San Francisco NFL	16	5	33	6.6	0	82	*1483	18.1	*17	17	102	0
1990—	San Francisco NFL	16	2	0	.0	0	*100	*1502	15.0	*13	13	78	1
Pro totals (6 years)		92	44	289	6.6	4	446	7866	17.6	79	83	498	8

RICHARDS, DAVID
G/OT, CHARGERS

PERSONAL: Born April 11, 1966, at Staten Island, N.Y.... 6-4/310.... Full name: David Reed Richards.
HIGH SCHOOL: Highland Park (Dallas).
COLLEGE: Southern Methodist, then UCLA.
TRANSACTIONS/CAREER NOTES: Selected by San Diego Chargers in fourth round (98th pick overall) of 1988 NFL draft.... Signed by Chargers (July 13, 1988).... Granted free agency (February 1, 1990).... Re-signed by Chargers (August 2, 1990).
PLAYING EXPERIENCE: San Diego NFL, 1988-1990.... Games: 1988 (16), 1989 (16), 1990 (16). Total: 48.
PRO STATISTICS: 1988—Recovered one fumble.

RICKETTS, TOM
OT/G, STEELERS

PERSONAL: Born November 21, 1965, at Pittsburgh.... 6-5/296.... Full name: Thomas Gordon Ricketts Jr.
HIGH SCHOOL: Franklin Regional (Murrysville, Pa.).
COLLEGE: Pittsburgh (degree in communications, 1989).
TRANSACTIONS/CAREER NOTES: Selected by Pittsburgh Steelers in first round (24th pick overall) of 1989 NFL draft.... Signed by Steelers (July 19, 1989).
PLAYING EXPERIENCE: Pittsburgh NFL, 1989 and 1990.... Games: 1989 (12), 1990 (16). Total: 28.

RIDGLE, ELSTON
DE, PACKERS

PERSONAL: Born August 24, 1963, at Los Angeles.... 6-5/277.... Full name: Elston Albert Ridgle.
HIGH SCHOOL: El Camino Real (Los Angeles).
COLLEGE: Northern Arizona, then Nevada-Reno (bachelor of science degree in criminal law).
TRANSACTIONS/CAREER NOTES: Signed as free agent by Los Angeles Rams (May 9, 1986).... Released by Rams (August 7, 1986).... Signed as free agent by San Francisco 49ers (December 22, 1986).... Released by 49ers (August 28, 1987).... Re-signed as replacement player by 49ers (September 24, 1987).... Released by 49ers (October 20, 1987).... Signed as free agent by Buffalo Bills (March 8, 1988).... On injured reserve with ankle injury (August 29, 1988-entire season).... Released by Bills (October 27, 1989).... Signed as free agent by Seattle Seahawks (November 11, 1989).... Released by Seahawks (August 28, 1990).... Awarded on waivers to Phoenix Cardinals (August 29, 1990).... Released by Cardinals (November 20, 1990).... Signed by Green Bay Packers (April 23, 1991).
PLAYING EXPERIENCE: San Francisco NFL, 1987; Buffalo (1)-Seattle (2) NFL, 1989; Phoenix NFL, 1990.... Games: 1987 (3), 1989 (3), 1990 (10). Total: 16.

RIENSTRA, JOHN
G, BROWNS

PERSONAL: Born March 22, 1963, at Grand Rapids, Mich.... 6-5/275.... Full name: John William Rienstra.... Name pronounced REEN-struh.
HIGH SCHOOL: Academy of the New Church (Bryn Athyn, Pa.).
COLLEGE: Temple.
TRANSACTIONS/CAREER NOTES: Selected by Baltimore Stars in 1986 USFL territorial draft.... Selected by Pittsburgh Steelers in first round (ninth pick overall) of 1986 NFL draft.... Signed by Steelers (August 12, 1986).... On injured reserve with broken foot (October 9, 1986-remainder of season).... On non-football injury/active with ulcer (July 22-July 31, 1988).... Passed physical (August 1, 1988).... On injured reserve with broken fibula (September 20-November 12, 1988).... On injured reserve with shoulder injury (November 26, 1988-remainder of season).... On inactive list (September 30; October 7, 14, 21; November 18, 25; and December 2 and 30, 1990).... Granted unconditional free agency (February 1, 1991).... Signed by Cleveland Browns (March 26, 1991).
PLAYING EXPERIENCE: Pittsburgh NFL, 1986-1990.... Games: 1986 (4), 1987 (12), 1988 (5), 1989 (15), 1990 (6). Total: 42.
PRO STATISTICS: 1988—Recovered one fumble. 1989—Recovered one fumble.

RIESENBERG, DOUG
OT, GIANTS

PERSONAL: Born July 22, 1965, at Moscow, Idaho.... 6-5/275.
HIGH SCHOOL: Moscow (Idaho).
COLLEGE: California.
TRANSACTIONS/CAREER NOTES: Selected by New York Giants in sixth round (168th pick overall) of 1987 NFL draft.... Signed by Giants (July 27, 1987).
PLAYING EXPERIENCE: New York Giants NFL, 1987-1990.... Games: 1987 (8), 1988 (16), 1989 (16), 1990 (16). Total: 56.
CHAMPIONSHIP GAME EXPERIENCE: Played in NFC championship game after 1990 season.... Played in Super Bowl XXV after 1990 season.
PRO STATISTICS: 1988—Recovered one fumble. 1989—Recovered two fumbles.

RIGGS, GERALD
RB, REDSKINS

PERSONAL: Born November 6, 1960, at Tullos, La. . . . 6-1/232. . . . Full name: Gerald Antonio Riggs.
HIGH SCHOOL: Bonanza (Las Vegas).
COLLEGE: Arizona State.
TRANSACTIONS/CAREER NOTES: Selected by Atlanta Falcons in first round (ninth pick overall) of 1982 NFL draft. . . . On did not report list (August 19-September 1, 1986). . . . Granted roster exemption (September 2-September 6, 1986). . . . Traded by Falcons with fifth-round pick in 1990 draft to Washington Redskins for second-round pick in 1989 draft and first-round pick in 1990 draft (April 23, 1989). . . . Granted free agency (February 1, 1990). . . . Re-signed by Redskins (August 1, 1990). . . . On injured reserve with arch injury (November 14-December 30, 1990).
RECORDS/HONORS: Played in Pro Bowl after 1985-1987 season.
PRO STATISTICS: 1983—Returned 17 kickoffs for 330 yards (19.4 avg.) and recovered one fumble. 1984—Recovered two fumbles. 1986—Attempted one pass with no completions and recovered one fumble. 1987—Recovered one fumble. 1990—Recovered one fumble.

		RUSHING				RECEIVING				TOTAL		
Year Team	G	Att.	Yds.	Avg.	TD	No.	Yds.	Avg.	TD	TD	Pts.	F.
1982—Atlanta NFL	9	78	299	3.8	5	23	185	8.0	0	5	30	1
1983—Atlanta NFL	14	100	437	4.4	8	17	149	8.8	0	8	48	7
1984—Atlanta NFL	15	353	1486	4.2	13	42	277	6.6	0	13	78	11
1985—Atlanta NFL	16	*397	1719	4.3	10	33	267	8.1	0	10	60	0
1986—Atlanta NFL	16	343	1327	3.9	9	24	136	5.7	0	9	54	6
1987—Atlanta NFL	12	203	875	4.3	2	25	199	8.0	0	2	12	4
1988—Atlanta NFL	9	113	488	4.3	1	22	171	7.8	0	1	6	3
1989—Washington NFL	12	201	834	4.2	4	7	67	9.6	0	4	24	3
1990—Washington NFL	10	123	475	3.9	6	7	60	8.6	0	6	36	2
Pro totals (9 years)	113	1911	7940	4.2	58	200	1511	7.6	0	58	348	37

RIGGS, JIM
TE, BENGALS

PERSONAL: Born September 29, 1963, at Fort Knox, Ky. . . . 6-5/245. . . . Full name: Jim Thomas Riggs.
HIGH SCHOOL: Scotland (Laurinburg, N.C.).
COLLEGE: Clemson (bachelor of science degree in economics and marketing, 1987).
TRANSACTIONS/CAREER NOTES: Selected by Cincinnati Bengals in fourth round (103rd pick overall) of 1987 NFL draft. . . . Signed by Bengals (July 26, 1987). . . . On injured reserve with torn hamstring injury (September 8-October 19, 1989). . . . Transferred to developmental squad (October 20, 1989). . . . Activated (October 21, 1989). . . . Granted free agency (February 1, 1990). . . . Re-signed by Bengals (July 20, 1990).
CHAMPIONSHIP GAME EXPERIENCE: Played in AFC championship game after 1988 season. . . . Played in Super Bowl XXIII after 1988 season.
PRO STATISTICS: 1988—Recovered one fumble and fumbled twice. 1990—Returned one kickoff for seven yards and recovered one fumble.

		RECEIVING			
Year Team	G	No.	Yds.	Avg.	TD
1987—Cincinnati NFL	9	0	0		0
1988—Cincinnati NFL	16	9	82	9.1	0
1989—Cincinnati NFL	10	5	29	5.8	0
1990—Cincinnati NFL	16	8	79	9.9	0
Pro totals (4 years)	51	22	190	8.6	0

RILEY, EUGENE
TE, LIONS

PERSONAL: Born October 9, 1966, at Cincinnati. . . . 6-3/238. . . . Full name: M. Eugene Riley.
HIGH SCHOOL: Mount Healthy (O.).
COLLEGE: Ball State.
TRANSACTIONS/CAREER NOTES: Signed as free agent by Indianapolis Colts (April 30, 1990). . . . On injured reserve with sprained ankle (September 14-October 16, 1990). . . . On practice squad (October 16, 1990-remainder of season). . . . Granted unconditional free agency (February 1, 1991). . . . Signed by Detroit Lions (March 22, 1991).
PLAYING EXPERIENCE: Indianapolis NFL, 1990. . . . Games: 1990 (1).

RISON, ANDRE
WR, FALCONS

PERSONAL: Born March 18, 1967, at Flint, Mich. . . . 6-0/188. . . . Full name: Andre Previn Rison.
HIGH SCHOOL: Northwestern (Flint, Mich.).
COLLEGE: Michigan State.
TRANSACTIONS/CAREER NOTES: Selected by Indianapolis Colts in first round (22nd pick overall) of 1989 NFL draft. . . . Signed by Colts (May 2, 1989). . . . Traded by Colts with offensive tackle Chris Hinton, fifth-round pick in 1990 NFL draft and first-round pick in 1991 draft to Atlanta Falcons for first- and fourth-round picks in 1990 draft (April 20, 1990).
RECORDS/HONORS: Played in Pro Bowl after 1990 season. . . . Named to THE SPORTING NEWS NFL All-Pro team, 1990.
PRO STATISTICS: 1989—Rushed three times for 18 yards.

		RECEIVING				PUNT RETURNS				KICKOFF RETURNS				TOTAL		
Year Team	G	No.	Yds.	Avg.	TD	No.	Yds.	Avg.	TD	No.	Yds.	Avg.	TD	TD	Pts.	F.
1989—Indianapolis NFL	16	52	820	15.8	4	2	20	10.0	0	8	150	18.8	0	4	24	1
1990—Atlanta NFL	16	82	1208	14.7	10	2	10	5.0	0					10	60	2
Pro totals (2 years)	32	134	2028	15.1	14	4	30	7.5	0	8	150	18.8	0	14	84	3

RITCHER, JIM
G, BILLS

PERSONAL: Born May 21, 1958, at Berea, O. . . . 6-3/273. . . . Full name: James Alexander Ritcher. . . . Name pronounced RICH-er.
HIGH SCHOOL: Highland (Granger, O.).
COLLEGE: North Carolina State.
TRANSACTIONS/CAREER NOTES: Selected by Buffalo Bills in first round (16th pick overall) of 1980 NFL draft.
PLAYING EXPERIENCE: Buffalo NFL, 1980-1990. . . . Games: 1980, (14), 1981 (14), 1982 (9), 1983 (16), 1984 (14), 1985 (16), 1986 (16), 1987 (12), 1988 (16), 1989 (16), 1990 (16). Total: 159.
CHAMPIONSHIP GAME EXPERIENCE: Played in AFC championship game after 1988 and 1990 seasons. . . . Played in Super Bowl XXV after 1990 season.
RECORDS/HONORS: Outland Trophy winner, 1979. . . . Named as center on THE SPORTING NEWS college All-America team, 1979.
PRO STATISTICS: 1986—Recovered one fumble. 1990—Recovered one fumble.

RIVERA, RON
LB, BEARS

PERSONAL: Born January 7, 1962, at Fort Ord, Calif. . . . 6-3/240. . . . Full name: Ronald Eugene Rivera.
HIGH SCHOOL: Seaside (Calif.).
COLLEGE: California.
TRANSACTIONS/CAREER NOTES: Selected by Oakland Invaders in 1984 USFL territorial draft. . . . Selected by Chicago Bears in second round (44th pick overall) of 1984 NFL draft. . . . Signed by Bears (July 2, 1984). . . . On inactive list (December 23 and 29, 1990).
CHAMPIONSHIP GAME EXPERIENCE: Played in NFC championship game after 1984, 1985 and 1988 seasons. . . . Played in Super Bowl XX after 1990 season.
RECORDS/HONORS: Named as linebacker on THE SPORTING NEWS college All-America team, 1983.
PRO STATISTICS: 1985—Recovered one fumble for five yards and a touchdown. 1988—Fumbled once. 1989—Recovered two fumbles. 1990—Recovered two fumbles.

			INTERCEPTIONS			
Year	Team	G	No.	Yds.	Avg.	TD
1984— Chicago NFL		15	0	0		0
1985— Chicago NFL		16	1	4	4.0	0
1986— Chicago NFL		16	0	0		0
1987— Chicago NFL		12	2	19	9.5	0
1988— Chicago NFL		16	2	0	.0	0
1989— Chicago NFL		16	2	1	.5	0
1990— Chicago NFL		14	2	13	6.5	0
Pro totals (7 years)		105	9	37	4.1	0

ROBBINS, KEVIN
OL, BROWNS

PERSONAL: Born December 12, 1966, at Washington, D.C. . . . 6-6/295. . . . Full name: Kevin Avery Robbins.
HIGH SCHOOL: Howard D. Woodson (Washington, D.C.).
COLLEGE: Wichita State, then Michigan State.
TRANSACTIONS/CAREER NOTES: Selected by Los Angeles Rams in third round (75th pick overall) of 1989 NFL draft. . . . Signed by Rams (July 13, 1989). . . . Released by Rams (September 4, 1989). . . . Awarded on waivers to Dallas Cowboys (September 5, 1989). . . . Inactive for one game with Cowboys . . . Released by Dallas Cowboys (September 15, 1989). . . . Signed as free agent by Cleveland Browns to developmental squad (September 21, 1989). . . . On developmental squad (September 21-December 12, 1989). . . . On inactive list (October 21, 28; November 4 and 18, 1990). . . . On injured reserve with knee injury (November 24, 1990-remainder of season).
PLAYING EXPERIENCE: Cleveland NFL, 1989 and 1990. . . . Games: 1989 (1), 1990 (6). Total: 7.
CHAMPIONSHIP GAME EXPERIENCE: Member of Cleveland Browns for AFC championship game after 1989 season; inactive.
PRO STATISTICS: 1990—Recovered one fumble.

ROBBINS, RANDY
S, BRONCOS

PERSONAL: Born September 14, 1962, at Casa Grande, Ariz. . . . 6-2/189.
HIGH SCHOOL: Union (Casa Grande, Ariz.).
COLLEGE: Arizona.
TRANSACTIONS/CAREER NOTES: Selected by Arizona Wranglers in 1984 USFL territorial draft. . . . Selected by Denver Broncos in fourth round (89th pick overall) of 1984 NFL draft. . . . Signed by Broncos (July 6, 1984). . . . On injured reserve with fractured forearm (August 20-October 16, 1985). . . . On injured reserve with knee injury (December 18, 1987-January 16, 1988).
CHAMPIONSHIP GAME EXPERIENCE: Played in AFC championship game after 1986 and 1989 seasons. . . . Played in Super Bowl XXI after 1986 season, Super Bowl XXII after 1987 season and Super Bowl XXIV after 1989 season.
PRO STATISTICS: 1984—Recovered one fumble. 1986—Recovered two fumbles. 1988—Recovered two fumbles and fumbled once. 1989—Recovered one fumble. 1990—Recovered two fumbles for 26 yards.

			INTERCEPTIONS			
Year	Team	G	No.	Yds.	Avg.	TD
1984— Denver NFL		16	2	62	31.0	1
1985— Denver NFL		10	1	3	3.0	0
1986— Denver NFL		16	0	0		0
1987— Denver NFL		10	3	9	3.0	0
1988— Denver NFL		16	2	66	33.0	0
1989— Denver NFL		16	2	18	9.0	1
1990— Denver NFL		16	0	0		0
Pro totals (7 years)		100	10	158	15.8	2

ROBBINS, TOOTIE
OT, CARDINALS

PERSONAL: Born June 2, 1958, at Windsor, N.C. . . . 6-5/310. . . . Full name: James Elbert Robbins.
HIGH SCHOOL: Bertie County (N.C.).
COLLEGE: East Carolina.
TRANSACTIONS/CAREER NOTES: Selected by St. Louis Cardinals in fourth round (90th pick overall) of 1982 NFL draft. . . . Granted free agency (February 1, 1986). . . . Re-signed by Cardinals (September 4, 1986). . . . Granted roster exemption (September 4-September 12, 1986). . . . Crossed picket line during players' strike (October 7, 1987). . . . Franchise transferred to Phoenix (March 15, 1988). . . . On injured reserve with groin and shoulder injuries (December 16, 1988-remainder of season). . . . On injured reserve with knee injury (September 15-October 28, 1989).
PLAYING EXPERIENCE: St. Louis NFL, 1982-1987; Phoenix NFL, 1988-1990. . . . Games: 1982 (9), 1983 (13), 1984 (16), 1985 (12), 1986 (12), 1987 (14), 1988 (15), 1989 (9), 1990 (16). Total: 116.
PRO STATISTICS: 1983—Recovered one fumble. 1985—Recovered one fumble. 1990—Recovered one fumble.

ROBERTS, ALFREDO
TE, COWBOYS

PERSONAL: Born March 1, 1965, at Fort Lauderdale, Fla. . . . 6-3/246.
HIGH SCHOOL: South Plantation (Plantation, Fla.).
COLLEGE: Miami, Fla. (degree in criminal justice, 1988).
TRANSACTIONS/CAREER NOTES: Selected by Kansas City Chiefs in eighth round (197th pick overall) of 1988 NFL draft. . . . Signed by Chiefs (July 16, 1988). . . . Granted unconditional free agency (February 1, 1991). . . . Signed by Dallas Cowboys (March 20, 1991).
PRO STATISTICS: 1990—Returned one kickoff for no yards.

			RECEIVING		
Year Team	G	No.	Yds.	Avg.	TD
1988— Kansas City NFL........	16	10	104	10.4	0
1989— Kansas City NFL........	16	8	55	6.9	1
1990— Kansas City NFL........	16	11	119	10.8	0
Pro totals (3 years)........	48	29	278	9.6	1

ROBERTS, LARRY
DE, 49ERS

PERSONAL: Born June 2, 1963, at Dothan, Ala. . . . 6-3/275.
HIGH SCHOOL: Northview (Dothan, Ala.).
COLLEGE: Alabama.
TRANSACTIONS/CAREER NOTES: Selected by Birmingham Stallions in 1986 USFL territorial draft. . . . Selected by San Francisco 49ers in second round (39th pick overall) of 1986 NFL draft. . . . Signed by 49ers (August 5, 1986). . . . On injured reserve with shoulder injury (September 7-October 25, 1990). . . . On inactive list (November 11, 18 and 25, 1990).
PLAYING EXPERIENCE: San Francisco NFL, 1986-1990. . . . Games: 1986 (16), 1987 (11), 1988 (16), 1989 (15), 1990 (6). Total: 64.
CHAMPIONSHIP GAME EXPERIENCE: Played in NFC championship game after 1988-1990 seasons. . . . Played in Super Bowl XXIII after 1988 season and Super Bowl XXIV after 1989 season.
PRO STATISTICS: 1986—Recovered one fumble. 1989—Recovered one fumble.

ROBERTS, WILLIAM
OT, GIANTS

PERSONAL: Born August 5, 1962, at Miami. . . . 6-5/280. . . . Full name: William Harold Roberts. . . . Cousin of Reggie Sandilands, wide receiver with Memphis Showboats (USFL), 1984.
HIGH SCHOOL: Carol City (Miami).
COLLEGE: Ohio State.
TRANSACTIONS/CAREER NOTES: Selected by New Jersey Generals in 1984 USFL territorial draft. . . . Selected by New York Giants in first round (27th pick overall) of 1984 NFL draft. . . . Signed by Giants (June 4, 1984). . . . On injured reserve with knee injury (July 20, 1985-entire season).
PLAYING EXPERIENCE: New York Giants NFL, 1984 and 1986-1990. . . . Games: 1984 (11), 1986 (16), 1987 (12), 1988 (16), 1989 (16), 1990 (16). Total: 87.
CHAMPIONSHIP GAME EXPERIENCE: Played in NFC championship game after 1986 and 1990 seasons. . . . Played in Super Bowl XXI after 1986 season and Super Bowl XXV after 1990 season.
RECORDS/HONORS: Played in Pro Bowl after 1990 season.
PRO STATISTICS: 1984—Recovered one fumble. 1988—Recovered two fumbles.

ROBINSON, EUGENE
S, SEAHAWKS

PERSONAL: Born May 28, 1963, at Hartford, Conn. . . . 6-0/190.
HIGH SCHOOL: Weaver (Hartford, Conn.).
COLLEGE: Colgate.
TRANSACTIONS/CAREER NOTES: Selected by New Jersey Generals in 1985 USFL territorial draft. . . . Signed as free agent by Seattle Seahawks (May 15, 1985).
PRO STATISTICS: 1985—Returned one kickoff for 10 yards. 1986—Recovered three fumbles for six yards. 1987—Returned blocked punt eight yards for a touchdown and recovered one fumble. 1989—Recovered one fumble and fumbled once. 1990—Recovered four fumbles for 16 yards and a touchdown.

			INTERCEPTIONS		
Year Team	G	No.	Yds.	Avg.	TD
1985— Seattle NFL	16	2	47	23.5	0
1986— Seattle NFL	16	3	39	13.0	0
1987— Seattle NFL	12	3	75	25.0	0
1988— Seattle NFL	16	1	0	.0	0
1989— Seattle NFL	16	5	24	4.8	0
1990— Seattle NFL	16	3	89	29.7	0
Pro totals (6 years)........	92	17	274	16.1	0

ROBINSON, GERALD
DE, RAMS

PERSONAL: Born May 4, 1963, at Tuskegee, Ala. . . . 6-3/262.
HIGH SCHOOL: Notasulga (Ala.).
COLLEGE: Auburn.
TRANSACTIONS/CAREER NOTES: Selected by Birmingham Stallions in 1986 USFL ter-
ritorial draft. . . . Selected by Minnesota Vikings in first round (14th pick overall) of 1986 NFL draft. . . . Signed by Vikings (July 27, 1986). . . . On injured reserve with broken leg (November 1, 1986-November 28, 1986). . . . On injured reserve with knee in-
jury (October 20-November 25, 1987). . . . Released by Vikings (August 30, 1988). . . . Awarded on waivers to Chicago Bears (August 31, 1988). . . . Released by Bears after not reporting (September 2, 1988). . . . Signed as free agent by San Diego Chargers (June 27, 1989). . . . On injured reserve with knee injury (September 13-November 7, 1989). . . . On developmental squad (November 8-December 16, 1989). . . . Released by Chargers (September 3, 1990). . . . Re-signed by Chargers (September 4, 1990). . . . On injured reserve with knee injury (September 12-October 12, 1990). . . . On inactive list (October 14, 1990). . . . Granted unconditional free agency (February 1, 1991). . . . Signed by Los Angeles Rams (April 1, 1991).
PLAYING EXPERIENCE: Minnesota NFL, 1986 and 1987; San Diego NFL, 1989 and 1990. . . . Games: 1986 (12), 1987 (4), 1989 (2), 1990 (11). Total: 29.

ROBINSON, JERRY
LB, RAIDERS

PERSONAL: Born December 18, 1956, at San Francisco. . . . 6-2/230. . . . Full name: Jerry Dewayne Robinson.
HIGH SCHOOL: Cardinal Newman (Santa Rosa, Calif.).
COLLEGE: UCLA.
TRANSACTIONS/CAREER NOTES: Selected by Philadelphia Eagles in first round (21st pick overall) of 1979 NFL draft. . . . On re-
serve/did not report list (August 20-September 25, 1985). . . . Reported and granted roster exemption (September 26-October 8, 1985). . . . Traded by Eagles to Los Angeles Raiders for second-round pick in 1986 draft (September 30, 1985). . . . Crossed picket line during players' strike (October 14, 1987).
CHAMPIONSHIP GAME EXPERIENCE: Played in NFC championship game after 1980 season. . . . Played in Super Bowl XV after 1980 season. . . . Played in AFC championship game after 1990 season.
RECORDS/HONORS: Named as linebacker on THE SPORTING NEWS college All-America team, 1978. . . . Played in Pro Bowl after 1981 season.
PRO STATISTICS: 1979—Recovered two fumbles. 1980—Recovered four fumbles for 59 yards and a touchdown and fumbled once. 1981—Recovered two fumbles. 1983—Recovered two fumbles. 1984—Recovered one fumble. 1986—Returned blocked punt two yards for a touchdown and recovered two fumbles. 1988—Recovered one fumble. 1989—Fumbled once.

			INTERCEPTIONS		
Year	Team	G	No.	Yds.	Avg.	TD
1979— Philadelphia NFL		16	0	0		0
1980— Philadelphia NFL		16	2	13	6.5	0
1981— Philadelphia NFL		15	1	3	3.0	0
1982— Philadelphia NFL		9	3	19	6.3	0
1983— Philadelphia NFL		16	0	0		0
1984— Philadelphia NFL		15	0	0		0
1985— L.A. Raiders NFL		11	0	0		0
1986— L.A. Raiders NFL		16	4	42	10.5	1
1987— L.A. Raiders NFL		12	0	0		0
1988— L.A. Raiders NFL		15	0	0		0
1989— L.A. Raiders NFL		11	1	25	25.0	0
1990— L.A. Raiders NFL		16	1	5	5.0	1
Pro totals (12 years)		168	12	107	8.9	2

ROBINSON, JUNIOR
CB, PATRIOTS

PERSONAL: Born February 3, 1968, at High Point, N.C. . . . 5-9/181. . . . Full name: David Lee Robinson Jr.
HIGH SCHOOL: T.W. Andrews (High Point, N.C.).
COLLEGE: East Carolina (bachelor of arts degree in education).
TRANSACTIONS/CAREER NOTES: Selected by New England Patriots in fifth round (110th pick overall) of 1990 NFL draft. . . . Signed by Patriots (July 19, 1990).
PRO STATISTICS: 1990—Fumbled twice.

			KICKOFF RETURNS		
Year	Team	G	No.	Yds.	Avg.	TD
1990— New England NFL		16	11	211	19.2	0
Pro totals (1 year)		16	11	211	19.2	0

ROBINSON, MARK
S, BUCCANEERS

PERSONAL: Born September 13, 1962, at Washington, D.C. . . . 5-11/200. . . . Full name: Mark Leon Robinson. . . . Brother of Eric Robinson, running back with Washington Fed-
erals, 1983 and 1984.
HIGH SCHOOL: John F. Kennedy (Silver Spring, Md.).
COLLEGE: Penn State (degree in business administration, 1988).
TRANSACTIONS/CAREER NOTES: Selected by Philadelphia Stars in 1984 USFL territorial draft. . . . Selected by Kansas City Chiefs in fourth round (90th pick overall) of 1984 NFL draft. . . . Signed by Chiefs (July 12, 1984). . . . On injured reserve with sprained ankle (September 3-October 12, 1985). . . . On injured reserve with thigh injury (October 24-December 5, 1986). . . . Traded by Chiefs with fourth- and eighth-round picks in 1988 draft to Tampa Bay Buccaneers for quarterback Steve DeBerg (March 30, 1988). . . . On injured reserve with groin injury (October 28-November 25, 1988).
PRO STATISTICS: 1985—Recovered one fumble. 1987—Returned five kickoffs for 97 yards and recovered two fumbles. 1989—Recovered three fumbles.

				— INTERCEPTIONS —			
Year	Team	G	No.	Yds.	Avg.	TD
1984— Kansas City NFL	16	0	0		0
1985— Kansas City NFL	11	1	20	20.0	0
1986— Kansas City NFL	9	0	0		0
1987— Kansas City NFL	12	2	42	21.0	0
1988— Tampa Bay NFL	9	2	28	14.0	0
1989— Tampa Bay NFL	15	6	44	7.3	0
1990— Tampa Bay NFL	16	4	81	20.3	0
Pro totals (7 years)	88	15	215	14.3	0

ROBY, REGGIE
P, DOLPHINS

PERSONAL: Born July 30, 1961, at Waterloo, Ia.... 6-2/246.... Full name: Reginald Henry Roby. ... Brother of Mike Roby, first baseman-outfielder in San Francisco Giants' organization, 1967 and 1968.
HIGH SCHOOL: East (Waterloo, Ia.).
COLLEGE: Iowa.
TRANSACTIONS/CAREER NOTES: Selected by Chicago Blitz in 16th round (187th pick overall) of 1983 USFL draft.... Selected by Miami Dolphins in sixth round (167th pick overall) of 1983 NFL draft.... Signed by Dolphins (July 9, 1983).... On injured reserve with knee, ankle and groin injuries (September 16-October 31, 1987).... Crossed picket line during players' strike (October 14, 1987).
CHAMPIONSHIP GAME EXPERIENCE: Played in AFC championship game after 1984 and 1985 seasons.... Played in Super Bowl XIX after 1984 season.
RECORDS/HONORS: Led NFL in net punting average with 38.1 in 1984 and 37.4 in 1986.... Played in Pro Bowl after 1984 and 1989 seasons.... Named to The Sporting News NFL All-Pro team, 1984.
PRO STATISTICS: 1986—Rushed twice for minus eight yards and recovered two fumbles and fumbled twice for minus 11 yards. 1987—Rushed once for no yards and recovered one fumble. 1989—Rushed twice for no yards and recovered two fumbles.

			— PUNTING —		
Year	Team	G	No.	Avg.	Blk.
1983— Miami NFL	16	74	43.1	1
1984— Miami NFL	16	51	44.7	0
1985— Miami NFL	16	59	43.7	0
1986— Miami NFL	15	56	44.2	0
1987— Miami NFL	10	32	42.8	0
1988— Miami NFL	15	64	43.0	0
1989— Miami NFL	16	58	42.4	1
1990— Miami NFL	16	72	42.0	0
Pro totals (8 years)	120	466	43.2	2

ROCKER, TRACY
DT, REDSKINS

PERSONAL: Born April 9, 1966, at Atlanta.... 6-3/288.... Full name: Tracy Quinton Rocker.
HIGH SCHOOL: Fulton (Atlanta).
COLLEGE: Auburn.
TRANSACTIONS/CAREER NOTES: Selected by Washington Redskins in third round (66th pick overall) of 1989 NFL draft.... Signed by Redskins (July 23, 1989).... On injured reserve with knee injury (November 3-December 30, 1990).
PLAYING EXPERIENCE: Washington NFL, 1989 and 1990.... Games: 1989 (16), 1990 (8). Total: 24.
RECORDS/HONORS: Outland Trophy winner, 1988.... Named as defensive lineman on The Sporting News college All-America team, 1988.
PRO STATISTICS: 1989—Recovered one fumble.

RODENHAUSER, MARK
C, CHARGERS

PERSONAL: Born June 1, 1961, at Elmhurst, Ill.... 6-5/263.... Full name: Mark Todd Rodenhauser.... Name pronounced RO-den-how-ser.
HIGH SCHOOL: Addison Trail (Addison, Ill.).
COLLEGE: Illinois State (bachelor of science degree in industrial technology).
TRANSACTIONS/CAREER NOTES: Signed as free agent by Michigan Panthers of USFL (January 15, 1984).... Released by Panthers (February 13, 1984).... Signed as free agent by Memphis Showboats of USFL (December 3, 1984).... Released by Showboats (January 22, 1985).... Signed as free agent by Chicago Bruisers of Arena Football League (June 29, 1987).... Granted free agency (August 15, 1987).... Signed as replacement player by Chicago Bears (September 24, 1987).... Left Bears camp voluntarily (August 16, 1988).... Released by Bears (August 17, 1988).... Signed as free agent by Minnesota Vikings (March 16, 1989).... Granted unconditional free agency (February 1, 1990).... Signed by San Diego Chargers (March 1, 1990).
PLAYING EXPERIENCE: Chicago Bruisers Arena Football, 1987; Chicago NFL, 1987; Minnesota NFL, 1989; San Diego NFL, 1990. ... Games: 1987 Chicago Arena Football (4), 1987 NFL (9), 1989 (16), 1990 (16). Total NFL: 41. Total Pro: 45.

RODRIGUEZ, RUBEN
P, CHARGERS

PERSONAL: Born March 3, 1965, at Visalia, Calif.... 6-2/224.... Full name: Ruben Angel Rodriguez.
HIGH SCHOOL: Woodlake (Calif.).
COLLEGE: College of the Sequoias (Calif.), then Arizona.
TRANSACTIONS/CAREER NOTES: Selected by Seattle Seahawks in fifth round (131st pick overall) of 1987 NFL draft.... Signed by Seahawks (July 21, 1987).... Released by Seahawks (September 7, 1987).... Re-signed by Seahawks (September 8, 1987). ... Released by Seahawks (September 3, 1990).... Signed by San Diego Chargers (June 5, 1991).

PRO STATISTICS: 1987—Rushed once for no yards. 1988—Rushed once for no yards, recovered one fumble and fumbled once. 1989—Rushed once for no yards, attempted one pass with one completion for four yards and recovered one fumble.

Year Team	G	No.	Avg.	Blk.
		— PUNTING —		
1987—Seattle NFL	12	47	40.0	0
1988—Seattle NFL	16	70	40.8	0
1989—Seattle NFL	16	75	39.9	1
Pro totals (3 years)	44	192	40.2	1

ROGERS, REGGIE
DE, BILLS

PERSONAL: Born January 21, 1964, at Sacramento, Calif. . . . 6-6/280. . . . Full name: Reginald O'Keith Rogers. . . . Brother of Don Rogers, safety with Cleveland Browns, 1984 and 1985.
HIGH SCHOOL: Norte Del Rio (Sacramento, Calif.).
COLLEGE: Washington.
TRANSACTIONS/CAREER NOTES: Selected by Detroit Lions in first round (seventh pick overall) of 1987 NFL draft. . . . On non-football injury list (November 6-December 7, 1987). . . . On injured reserve with ankle injury (October 8, 1988-remainder of season). . . . Granted unconditional free agency (February 1, 1989). . . . Signed by Buffalo Bills (February 26, 1991).
PLAYING EXPERIENCE: Detroit NFL, 1987 and 1988. . . . Games: 1987 (6), 1988 (5). Total: 11.

ROGERS, TRACY
LB, CHIEFS

PERSONAL: Born August 13, 1967, at Taft, Calif. . . . 6-2/241. . . . Full name: Tracy Darin Rogers.
HIGH SCHOOL: Taft Union (Taft, Calif.).
COLLEGE: Fresno State.
TRANSACTIONS/CAREER NOTES: Selected by Houston Oilers in seventh round (190th pick overall) of 1989 NFL draft. . . . Released by Oilers (September 5, 1989). . . . Re-signed by Oilers to developmental squad (September 8, 1989). . . . Released by Oilers (January 2, 1990). . . . Signed by Kansas City Chiefs (March 20, 1990). . . . On injured reserve with knee injury (November 21, 1990-remainder of season).
PLAYING EXPERIENCE: Kansas City NFL, 1990. . . . Games: 1990 (10).

ROLAND, BENJI
NT, FALCONS

PERSONAL: Born April 4, 1967, at Eastman, Ga. . . . 6-3/260. . . . Full name: Mitchell Benjamin Roland.
HIGH SCHOOL: Dodge (Eastman, Ga.).
COLLEGE: Auburn.
TRANSACTIONS/CAREER NOTES: Selected by Minnesota Vikings in seventh round (191st pick overall) of 1989 NFL draft. . . . Signed by Vikings (July 20, 1989). . . . Released by Vikings (September 5, 1989). . . . Signed by Atlanta Falcons to developmental squad (September 6, 1989). . . . Released by Falcons (January 9, 1990). . . . Signed by Tampa Bay Buccaneers (March 16, 1990). . . . Released by Buccaneers (August 27, 1990). . . . Re-signed by Buccaneers (November 14, 1990). . . . Granted unconditional free agency (February 1, 1991). . . . Signed by Atlanta Falcons (April 1, 1991).
PLAYING EXPERIENCE: Tampa Bay NFL, 1990. . . . Games: 1990 (3).
RECORDS/HONORS: Named as nose tackle on THE SPORTING NEWS college All-America team, 1988.

ROLLE, BUTCH
TE, BILLS

PERSONAL: Born August 19, 1964, at Miami. . . . 6-4/245. . . . Full name: Donald Demetrius Rolle. . . . Name pronounced ROLL.
HIGH SCHOOL: Hallandale (Fla.).
COLLEGE: Michigan State.
TRANSACTIONS/CAREER NOTES: Selected by Buffalo Bills in seventh round (180th pick overall) of 1986 NFL draft. . . . Signed by Bills (July 23, 1986).
CHAMPIONSHIP GAME EXPERIENCE: Played in AFC championship game after 1988 and 1990 seasons. . . . Played in Super Bowl XXV after 1990 season.
PRO STATISTICS: 1987—Returned one kickoff for six yards. 1988—Returned one kickoff for 12 yards. 1989—Returned two kickoffs for 20 yards. 1990—Returned two kickoffs for 22 yards.

Year Team	G	No.	Yds.	Avg.	TD
		— RECEIVING —			
1986—Buffalo NFL	16	4	56	14.0	0
1987—Buffalo NFL	12	2	6	3.0	2
1988—Buffalo NFL	16	2	3	1.5	2
1989—Buffalo NFL	16	1	1	1.0	1
1990—Buffalo NFL	16	3	6	2.0	3
Pro totals (5 years)	76	12	72	6.0	8

ROLLING, HENRY
LB, CHARGERS

PERSONAL: Born September 8, 1965, at Fort Eustis, Va. . . . 6-2/225. . . . Full name: Henry Lee Rolling.
HIGH SCHOOL: Basic (Henderson, Nev.).
COLLEGE: Nevada-Reno (degree in electrical engineering, 1987).
TRANSACTIONS/CAREER NOTES: Selected by Tampa Bay Buccaneers in fifth round (135th pick overall) of 1987 NFL draft. . . . Signed by Buccaneers (July 18, 1987). . . . On injured reserve with hamstring injury (August 10, 1987-entire season). . . . Released by Buccaneers (October 25, 1989). . . . Signed as free agent by San Diego Chargers (April 16, 1990).

PLAYING EXPERIENCE: Tampa Bay NFL, 1988 and 1989; San Diego NFL, 1990. . . . Games: 1988 (15), 1989 (6), 1990 (16). Total: 37.
PRO STATISTICS: 1988—Recovered two fumbles. 1989—Recovered one fumble. 1990—Intercepted one pass for 67 yards and recovered one fumble.

ROMANOWSKI, BILL
LB, 49ERS

PERSONAL: Born April 2, 1966, at Vernon, Conn. . . . 6-4/231. . . . Full name: William Thomas Romanowski.
HIGH SCHOOL: Rockville (Vernon, Conn.).
COLLEGE: Boston College (received degree, 1988).
TRANSACTIONS/CAREER NOTES: Selected by San Francisco 49ers in third round (80th pick overall) of 1988 NFL draft. . . . Signed by 49ers (July 15, 1988).
PLAYING EXPERIENCE: San Francisco NFL, 1988- 1990. . . . Games: 1988 (16), 1989 (16), 1990 (16). Total: 48.
CHAMPIONSHIP GAME EXPERIENCE: Played in NFC championship game after 1988- 1990 seasons. . . . Played in Super Bowl XXIII after 1988 season and Super Bowl XXIV after 1989 season.
PRO STATISTICS: 1988—Recovered one fumble. 1989—Intercepted one pass for 13 yards, returned one punt for no yards, recovered two fumbles and fumbled once.

ROPER, JOHN
LB, BEARS

PERSONAL: Born October 4, 1965, at Houston. . . . 6-1/228. . . . Full name: John Alfred Roper.
HIGH SCHOOL: Jack Yates (Houston).
COLLEGE: Texas A&M.
TRANSACTIONS/CAREER NOTES: Selected by Chicago Bears in second round (36th pick overall) of 1989 NFL draft. . . . Signed by Bears (July 21, 1989).
PLAYING EXPERIENCE: Chicago NFL, 1989 and 1990. . . . Games: 1989 (16), 1990 (14). Total: 30.
PRO STATISTICS: 1989—Intercepted two passes for 46 yards and fumbled once. 1990—Returned one kickoff for no yards.

ROSE, KEN
LB, EAGLES

PERSONAL: Born June 9, 1962, at Sacramento, Calif. . . . 6-1/215. . . . Full name: Kenny Frank Rose.
HIGH SCHOOL: Christian Brothers (Sacramento, Calif.).
COLLEGE: UNLV.
TRANSACTIONS/CAREER NOTES: Signed as free agent by Saskatchewan Roughriders of CFL (May 5, 1985). . . . Released by Roughriders (June 16, 1985). . . . Re-signed by Roughriders (June 23, 1985). . . . Released by Roughriders (July 3, 1985). . . . Signed as free agent by Los Angeles Raiders (July 10, 1985). . . . Released by Raiders (August 13, 1985). . . . Re-signed by Raiders (August 16, 1985). . . . Released by Raiders (August 20, 1985). . . . USFL rights traded by Oakland Invaders to Tampa Bay Bandits for past considerations (September 6, 1985). . . . Signed by Bandits (May 21, 1986). . . . Granted free agency when USFL suspended operations (August 7, 1986). . . . Signed as free agent by New York Jets (April 8, 1987). . . . Released by Jets (September 6, 1987). . . . Re-signed as replacement player by Jets (September 24, 1987). . . . On injured reserve with dislocated elbow (August 30-October 1, 1988). . . . Released by Jets (September 5, 1989). . . . Re-signed by Jets (September 12, 1989). . . . Granted unconditional free agency (February 1, 1990). . . . Signed by Cleveland Browns (March 29, 1990). . . . Released by Browns (October 16, 1990). . . . Re-signed by Browns (October 31, 1990). . . . Released by Browns (November 6, 1990). . . . Signed by Philadelphia Eagles (November 7, 1990).
PLAYING EXPERIENCE: New York Jets NFL, 1987- 1989; Cleveland (7)-Philadelphia (8) NFL, 1990. . . . Games: 1987 (10), 1988 (12), 1989 (15), 1990 (15). Total: 52.
PRO STATISTICS: 1987—Intercepted one pass for one yard. 1988—Returned one kickoff for no yards and recovered one fumble.

ROSENBACH, TIMM
QB, CARDINALS

PERSONAL: Born October 27, 1966, at Everett, Wash. . . . 6-1/210. . . . Name pronounced ROW-zen-ba.
HIGH SCHOOL: Hellgate (Missoula, Mont.) and Pullman (Wash.).
COLLEGE: Washington State.
TRANSACTIONS/CAREER NOTES: Selected by Phoenix Cardinals in first round of 1989 NFL supplemental draft (July 7, 1989). . . . Signed by Cardinals (August 18, 1989).
PRO STATISTICS: Passer rating points: 1989 (35.2), 1990 (72.8). Career: 71.0. . . . 1989—Recovered one fumble. 1990—Recovered four fumbles.

Year Team	G		PASSING								RUSHING				TOTAL	
		Att.	Cmp.	Pct.	Yds.	TD	Int.	Avg.	Att.	Yds.	Avg.	TD	TD	Pts.	F.
1989— Phoenix NFL	2	22	9	40.9	95	0	1	4.32	6	26	4.3	0	0	0	2
1990— Phoenix NFL	16	437	237	54.2	3098	16	17	7.09	86	470	5.5	3	3	18	10
Pro totals (2 years)	18	459	246	53.6	3193	16	18	6.96	92	496	5.4	3	3	18	12

ROSS, KEVIN
CB, CHIEFS

PERSONAL: Born January 16, 1962, at Camden, N.J. . . . 5-9/ 182. . . . Full name: Kevin Lesley Ross.
HIGH SCHOOL: Paulsboro (N.J.).
COLLEGE: Temple.
TRANSACTIONS/CAREER NOTES: Selected by Philadelphia Stars in 1984 USFL territorial draft. . . . Selected by Kansas City Chiefs in seventh round (173rd pick overall) of 1984 NFL draft. . . . Signed by Chiefs (June 21, 1984). . . . Crossed picket line during players' strike (October 14, 1987). . . . Granted roster exemption (September 3-September 8, 1990).
RECORDS/HONORS: Played in Pro Bowl after 1989 and 1990 seasons.
PRO STATISTICS: 1984—Recovered one fumble. 1985—Recovered one fumble. 1986—Recovered three fumbles for 33 yards and a touchdown. 1987—Returned blocked field-goal attempt 65 yards for a touchdown. 1989—Returned two punts for no yards and fumbled once. 1990—Returned blocked punt four yards for a touchdown and recovered three fumbles.

Year Team	G	No.	Yds.	Avg.	TD
		—— INTERCEPTIONS——			
1984— Kansas City NFL........	16	6	124	20.7	1
1985— Kansas City NFL........	16	3	47	15.7	0
1986— Kansas City NFL........	16	4	66	16.5	0
1987— Kansas City NFL........	12	3	40	13.3	0
1988— Kansas City NFL........	15	1	0	.0	0
1989— Kansas City NFL........	15	4	29	7.3	0
1990— Kansas City NFL........	16	5	97	19.4	0
Pro totals (7 years)........	106	26	403	15.5	1

ROTHER, TIM
DT, RAIDERS

PERSONAL: Born September 28, 1965, at St. Paul, Neb.... 6-7/280.
HIGH SCHOOL: East (Bellevue, Neb.).
COLLEGE: Nebraska.
TRANSACTIONS/CAREER NOTES: Selected by Los Angeles Raiders in fourth round (90th pick over-all) of 1988 NFL draft.... Signed by Raiders (July 14, 1988).... On injured reserve with wrist injury (August 22, 1988-entire season).... On inactive list (September 9, 16, and 23, 1990).... On injured reserve with foot injury (October 29, 1990-remainder of season).
PLAYING EXPERIENCE: Los Angeles Raiders NFL, 1989 and 1990.... Games: 1989 (16), 1990 (4). Total: 20.

ROUSE, JAMES
FB, BEARS

PERSONAL: Born December 18, 1966, at Little Rock, Ark.... 6-0/220.... Full name: James David Rouse.
HIGH SCHOOL: Parkview (Little Rock, Ark.).
COLLEGE: Arkansas.
TRANSACTIONS/CAREER NOTES: Selected by Chicago Bears in eighth round (200th pick overall) of 1990 NFL draft.... Signed by Bears (July 25, 1990).

Year Team	G	No.	Yds.	Avg.	TD	No.	Yds.	Avg.	TD	TD	Pts.	F.
		——RUSHING——				**— KICKOFF RETURNS—**				**— TOTAL —**		
1990— Chicago NFL	16	16	56	3.5	0	3	17	5.7	0	0	0	0
Pro totals (1 year)..	16	16	56	3.5	0	3	17	5.7	0	0	0	0

ROUSON, LEE
RB, BROWNS

PERSONAL: Born October 18, 1962, at Elizabeth City, N.C.... 6-1/222.... Cousin of Johnny Walton, quarterback with San Antonio Wings (WFL), Philadelphia Eagles and Boston-New Orleans Breakers (USFL), 1975, 1976, 1978, 1979, 1983 and 1984; and head coach at Elizabeth City State University, 1980-1982.
HIGH SCHOOL: Page (Greensboro, N.C.).
COLLEGE: Colorado.
TRANSACTIONS/CAREER NOTES: Selected by New Jersey Generals in first round (11th pick overall) of 1985 USFL draft.... Selected by New York Giants in eighth round (213th pick overall) of 1985 NFL draft.... Signed by Giants (July 2, 1985).... On injured reserve with hamstring injury (September 2-December 14, 1985).... Granted unconditional free agency (February 1, 1991).... Signed by Cleveland Browns (April 1, 1991).
CHAMPIONSHIP GAME EXPERIENCE: Played in NFC championship game after 1986 and 1990 seasons.... Played in Super Bowl XXI after 1986 season and Super Bowl XXV after 1990 season.
PRO STATISTICS: 1987—Recovered one fumble. 1988—Recovered two fumbles. 1989—Recovered one fumble.

Year Team	G	Att.	Yds.	Avg.	TD	No.	Yds.	Avg.	TD	No.	Yds.	Avg.	TD	TD	Pts.	F.
		——RUSHING——				**——RECEIVING——**				**— KICKOFF RETURNS—**				**— TOTAL—**		
1985— N.Y. Giants NFL	2	1	1	1.0	0	0	0		0	2	35	17.5	0	0	0	0
1986— N.Y. Giants NFL	14	54	179	3.3	2	8	121	15.1	1	2	21	10.5	0	3	18	0
1987— N.Y. Giants NFL	12	41	155	3.8	0	11	129	11.7	1	22	497	22.6	0	1	6	3
1988— N.Y. Giants NFL	16	1	1	1.0	0	4	61	15.3	0	8	130	16.3	0	0	0	2
1989— N.Y. Giants NFL	16	11	51	4.6	0	7	121	17.3	0	1	17	17.0	0	0	0	0
1990— N.Y. Giants NFL	16	3	14	4.7	0	1	12	12.0	0	0	0		0	0	0	0
Pro totals (6 years)........	76	111	401	3.6	2	31	444	14.3	2	35	700	20.0	0	4	24	5

ROWELL, EUGENE
WR, BROWNS

PERSONAL: Born June 12, 1968, at New York.... 6-1/180.
HIGH SCHOOL: Auburn (Ala.).
COLLEGE: Southern Mississippi.
TRANSACTIONS/CAREER NOTES: Selected by Cleveland Browns in ninth round (240th pick overall) of 1990 NFL draft.... Signed by Browns (July 22, 1990).... Released by Browns (September 3, 1990).... Re-signed by Browns (September 26, 1990).... On inactive list (September 30, 1990).... Released by Browns (October 7, 1990).... Signed by Browns to practice squad (October 10, 1990).... Activated (October 17, 1990).... Released by Browns (October 31, 1990).... Re-signed by Browns (November 6, 1990).... On injured reserve with back injury (November 17-December 24, 1990).
PLAYING EXPERIENCE: Cleveland NFL, 1990.... Games: 1990 (3).

ROYALS, MARK
P, BUCCANEERS

PERSONAL: Born June 22, 1964, at Hampton, Va. . . . 6-5/215. . . . Full name: Mark Alan Royals.
HIGH SCHOOL: Mathews (Va.).
COLLEGE: Chowan (N.C.), then William & Mary (bachelor of arts degree in political science).
TRANSACTIONS/CAREER NOTES: Signed as free agent by Dallas Cowboys (June 6, 1986). . . . Released by Cowboys (August 8, 1986). . . . Signed as replacement player by St. Louis Cardinals (September 30, 1987). . . . Released by Cardinals (October 7, 1987). . . . Signed as replacement player by Philadelphia Eagles (October 14, 1987). . . . Released by Eagles (November, 1987). . . . Signed by St. Louis Cardinals for 1988 (December 12, 1987). . . . Released by Cardinals (July 27, 1988). . . . Signed by Miami Dolphins (May 2, 1989). . . . Released by Dolphins (August 28, 1989). . . . Signed by Tampa Bay Buccaneers (April 24, 1990).

		— PUNTING—		
Year Team	G	No.	Avg.	Blk.
1987 — St.L. (1)-Phil. (1) NFL..........	2	11	39.2	0
1990 — Tampa Bay NFL....................	16	72	40.3	0
Pro totals (2 years)	18	83	39.8	0

ROZIER, MIKE
RB, FALCONS

PERSONAL: Born March 1, 1961, at Camden, N.J. . . . 5-10/213. . . . Name pronounced ro-ZEER.
HIGH SCHOOL: Wilson (Camden, N.J.).
COLLEGE: Coffeyville Community College (Kan.), then Nebraska.
TRANSACTIONS/CAREER NOTES: Selected by Pittsburgh Maulers in first round (first pick overall) of 1984 USFL draft. . . . Signed by Maulers (January 3, 1984). . . . On developmental squad for four games (May 18-June 16, 1984). . . . Selected by Houston Oilers in first round (second pick overall) of 1984 NFL supplemental draft. . . . Pittsburgh Maulers franchise disbanded (October 25, 1984). . . . Personal-services contract assigned to Baltimore Stars of USFL (November 1, 1984). . . . Signed as free agent with Jacksonville Bulls of USFL (February 1, 1985). . . . Granted roster exemption (February 1-February 14, 1985). . . . Granted free agency (July 1, 1985). . . . Signed by Houston Oilers (July 1, 1985). . . . On injured reserve with knee injury (December 2, 1986-remainder of season). . . . Granted free agency (February 1, 1989). . . . Re-signed by Oilers and granted roster exemption (September 6-September 15, 1989). . . . Released by Oilers (October 2, 1990). . . . Awarded on waivers to Atlanta Falcons (October 4, 1990).
RECORDS/HONORS: Heisman Trophy winner, 1983. . . . Named THE SPORTING NEWS College Football Player of the Year, 1983. . . . Named as running back on THE SPORTING NEWS college All-America team, 1983. . . . Played in Pro Bowl after 1987 and 1988 seasons.
PRO STATISTICS: USFL: 1984—Recovered eight fumbles. 1985—Recovered four fumbles. . . . NFL: 1985—Recovered three fumbles. 1986—Recovered two fumbles and attempted one pass with one completion for 13 yards. 1987—Recovered two fumbles. 1988—Recovered three fumbles. 1990—Recovered three fumbles.

		— RUSHING —				— RECEIVING —				— TOTAL —		
Year Team	G	Att.	Yds.	Avg.	TD	No.	Yds.	Avg.	TD	TD	Pts.	F.
1984— Pittsburgh USFL.............................	14	223	792	3.6	3	32	259	8.1	0	3	18	8
1985— Jacksonville USFL........................	18	320	1361	4.3	12	50	366	7.3	3	15	90	10
1985— Houston NFL................................	14	133	462	3.5	8	9	96	10.7	0	8	48	3
1986— Houston NFL................................	13	199	662	3.3	4	24	180	7.5	0	4	24	6
1987— Houston NFL................................	11	229	957	4.2	3	27	192	7.1	0	3	18	5
1988— Houston NFL................................	15	251	1002	4.0	10	11	99	9.0	1	11	66	7
1989— Houston NFL................................	12	88	301	3.4	2	4	28	7.0	0	2	12	4
1990— Hou. (3)-Atl. (13) NFL	16	163	717	4.4	3	13	105	8.1	0	3	18	6
USFL totals (2 years)	32	543	2153	4.0	15	82	625	7.6	3	18	108	18
NFL totals (6 years)	81	1063	4101	3.9	30	88	700	8.0	1	31	186	31
Pro totals (8 years)	113	1606	6254	3.9	45	170	1325	7.8	4	49	294	49

RUETHER, MIKE
C, FALCONS

PERSONAL: Born September 20, 1962, at Inglewood, Calif. . . . 6-4/286. . . . Full name: Mike Alan Ruether.
HIGH SCHOOL: Bishop Miege (Shawnee Mission, Kan.).
COLLEGE: Texas.
TRANSACTIONS/CAREER NOTES: Selected by Houston Gamblers in 1984 USFL territorial draft. . . . USFL rights traded by Gamblers with rights to offensive tackle Mark Adickes to Los Angeles Express for second-round pick in 1985 and 1986 USFL drafts (February 13, 1984). . . . Signed by Express (February 13, 1984). . . . Granted roster exemption (February 13-February 24, 1984). . . . Selected by St. Louis Cardinals in first round (17th pick overall) of 1984 NFL supplemental draft. . . . On developmental squad with Express for two games (February 21-March 8, 1985). . . . Granted free agency when USFL suspended operations (August 7, 1986). . . . Signed by St. Louis Cardinals (September 30, 1986). . . . Granted roster exemption (September 30-October 10, 1986). . . . Franchise transferred to Phoenix (March 15, 1988). . . . Traded by Phoenix Cardinals to Denver Broncos for linebacker Ricky Hunley (July 19, 1988). . . . Released by Broncos (September 18, 1989). . . . Re-signed by Broncos (October 25, 1989). . . . Granted unconditional free agency (February 1, 1990). . . . Signed by Atlanta Falcons (March 15, 1990).
PLAYING EXPERIENCE: Los Angeles USFL, 1984 and 1985; St. Louis NFL, 1986 and 1987; Denver NFL, 1988 and 1989; Atlanta NFL, 1990. . . . Games: 1984 (17), 1985 (17), 1986 (10), 1987 (12), 1988 (14), 1989 (3), 1990 (16). Total USFL: 34. Total NFL: 55. Total Pro: 89.
CHAMPIONSHIP GAME EXPERIENCE: Member of Denver Broncos for AFC championship game and Super Bowl XXIV after 1989 season; inactive.
PRO STATISTICS: 1984—Recovered two fumbles.

RUETTGERS, KEN

OT, PACKERS

PERSONAL: Born August 20, 1962, at Bakersfield, Calif.... 6-6/286.... Full name: Kenneth F. Ruettgers.... Name pronounced RUTT-gers.
HIGH SCHOOL: Garces Memorial (Bakersfield, Calif.).
COLLEGE: Southern California (bachelor of business administration degree, 1985).
TRANSACTIONS/CAREER NOTES: Selected by Green Bay Packers in first round (seventh pick overall) of 1985 NFL draft.... Signed by Packers (August 12, 1985).... Granted free agency (February 1, 1990).... Re-signed by Packers (August 15, 1990).... On injured reserve with knee injury (October 22-December 1, 1990).
PLAYING EXPERIENCE: Green Bay NFL, 1985-1990.... Games: 1985 (15), 1986 (16), 1987 (12), 1988 (15), 1989 (16), 1990 (11). Total: 85.
PRO STATISTICS: 1986—Recovered one fumble. 1988—Recovered one fumble. 1989—Recovered two fumbles. 1990—Recovered one fumble.

RUTLAND, REGGIE

CB, VIKINGS

PERSONAL: Born June 20, 1964, at East Point, Ga.... 6-1/192.... Full name: Reginald Bernard Rutland.
HIGH SCHOOL: Russell (East Point, Ga.).
COLLEGE: Georgia Tech.
TRANSACTIONS/CAREER NOTES: Selected by Minnesota Vikings in fourth round (100th pick overall) of 1987 NFL draft.... Signed by Vikings (July 17, 1987).... On injured reserve with ankle injury (November 18-December 25, 1987).... Granted free agency (February 1, 1990).... Re-signed by Vikings (August 1, 1990).
CHAMPIONSHIP GAME EXPERIENCE: Played in NFC championship game after 1987 season.
PRO STATISTICS: 1988—Recovered two fumbles for 17 yards and fumbled once. 1989—Recovered two fumbles for 27 yards and a touchdown.

Year Team	G	No.	Yds.	Avg.	TD
		INTERCEPTIONS			
1987— Minnesota NFL	7	0	0		0
1988— Minnesota NFL	16	3	63	21.0	0
1989— Minnesota NFL	16	2	7	3.5	0
1990— Minnesota NFL	16	2	21	10.5	0
Pro totals (4 years)	55	7	91	13.0	0

RUTLEDGE, JEFF

QB, REDSKINS

PERSONAL: Born January 22, 1957, at Birmingham, Ala.... 6-1/195.... Full name: Jeffrey Ronald Rutledge.... Son of Paul E. (Jack) Rutledge, minor league infielder, 1950-1952.
HIGH SCHOOL: Banks (Birmingham, Ala.).
COLLEGE: Alabama (degree in business education).
TRANSACTIONS/CAREER NOTES: Selected by Los Angeles Rams in ninth round (246th pick overall) of 1979 NFL draft.... On injured reserve with mononucleosis (October 22, 1980-remainder of season).... On injured reserve with broken thumb (November 2, 1981-remainder of season).... Traded by Rams to New York Giants for fourth-round pick in 1983 draft (September 5, 1982).... Active for nine games with Giants in 1982; did not play.... Crossed picket line during players' strike (October 14, 1987).... On injured reserve with knee injury (August 29-November 26, 1988).... Granted unconditional free agency (February 1, 1989).... Did not receive qualifying offer (April 15, 1989).... Re-signed by New York Giants (May 1, 1989).... Granted unconditional free agency (February 1, 1990).... Signed by Washington Redskins (April 1, 1990).... On injured reserve with shoulder injury (September 5-October 13, 1990).
CHAMPIONSHIP GAME EXPERIENCE: Member of Los Angeles Rams for NFC championship game and Super Bowl XIV after 1979 season; did not play.... Played in NFC championship game after 1986 season.... Played in Super Bowl XXI after 1986 season.
PRO STATISTICS: Passer rating points: 1979 (23.0), 1980 (54.2), 1981 (75.6), 1983 (59.3), 1984 (104.2), 1986 (87.5), 1987 (53.9), 1988 (59.2), 1990 (82.7). Career: 59.9.... 1987—Recovered three fumbles and fumbled seven times for minus three yards.

Year Team	G	Att.	Cmp.	Pct.	Yds.	TD	Int.	Avg.	Att.	Yds.	Avg.	TD	TD	Pts.	F.
		PASSING							RUSHING				TOTAL		
1979— L.A. Rams NFL	3	32	13	40.6	125	1	4	3.91	5	27	5.4	0	0	0	0
1980— L.A. Rams NFL	1	4	1	25.0	26	0	0	6.50	0	0		0	0	0	0
1981— L.A. Rams NFL	4	50	30	60.0	442	3	4	8.84	5	-3	-.6	0	0	0	0
1983— N.Y. Giants NFL	4	174	87	50.0	1208	3	8	6.94	7	27	3.9	0	0	0	6
1984— N.Y. Giants NFL	16	1	1	100.0	9	0	0	9.00	0	0		0	0	0	0
1985— N.Y. Giants NFL	16	0	0		0	0	0		2	-6	-3.0	0	0	0	1
1986— N.Y. Giants NFL	16	3	1	33.3	13	1	0	4.33	3	19	6.3	0	0	0	0
1987— N.Y. Giants NFL	13	155	79	51.0	1048	5	11	6.76	15	31	2.1	0	0	0	7
1988— N.Y. Giants NFL	1	17	11	64.7	113	0	1	6.65	3	-1	-.3	0	0	0	2
1989— N.Y. Giants NFL	1	0	0		0	0	0		0	0		0	0	0	0
1990— Washington NFL	10	68	40	58.8	455	2	1	6.69	4	12	3.0	1	1	6	1
Pro totals (11 years)	85	504	263	52.2	3439	15	29	6.82	44	106	2.4	1	1	6	17

RUZEK, ROGER

PK, EAGLES

PERSONAL: Born December 17, 1960, at San Francisco.... 6-1/200.... Full name: Roger Brian Ruzek.
HIGH SCHOOL: El Camino (San Francisco).
COLLEGE: Weber State (received degree).
TRANSACTIONS/CAREER NOTES: Signed as free agent by Cleveland Browns (May 5, 1983).... Released by Browns (August 16, 1983).... Signed by Pittsburgh Maulers of USFL (October 10, 1983).... Released by Maulers (December 16, 1983).... Signed as free agent by New Jersey Generals of USFL (January 7, 1984).... Released by Generals (July 31, 1985).... Awarded on waivers to Memphis Showboats (August 1, 1985).... Granted free agency when USFL suspended operations (August 7, 1986).... Signed as free agent by Dallas Cowboys (April 10, 1987).... Released by Cowboys (August 6, 1987).... Re-signed

by Cowboys (August 20, 1987).... On reserve/did not report list (August 23-August 29, 1988).... Granted roster exemption (August 29-September 13, 1988).... Released by Cowboys (November 8, 1989).... Signed as free agent by Philadelphia Eagles (November 22, 1989).... Granted free agency (February 1, 1990).... Re-signed by Eagles (August 10, 1990).
RECORDS/HONORS: Tied NFL record for most field goals, one quarter (4), against New York Giants (November 2, 1987) in fourth quarter.
PRO STATISTICS: 1985—Punted once for 36 yards. 1989—Attempted one pass with one completion for 22 yards and a touchdown, caught one pass for four yards, punted once for 28.0 avg. and recovered one fumble.

			——— PLACE-KICKING ———				
Year	Team	G	XPM	XPA	FGM	FGA	Pts.
1984— New Jersey USFL		18	51	53	17	23	102
1985— New Jersey USFL		18	49	52	17	25	100
1987— Dallas NFL		12	26	26	22	25	92
1988— Dallas NFL		14	27	27	12	22	63
1989— Dal. (9)-Phi. (5) NFL.....		14	28	29	13	22	67
1990— Philadelphia NFL		16	45	48	21	29	108
USFL totals (2 years)		36	100	105	34	48	202
NFL totals (4 years)		56	126	130	68	98	330
Pro totals (6 years)		92	226	235	102	146	532

RYAN, TIM
DT, BEARS
PERSONAL: Born September 8, 1967, at Memphis, Tenn.... 6-4/268.... Full name: Timothy Edward Ryan.
HIGH SCHOOL: Oak Grove (San Jose, Calif.).
COLLEGE: Southern California.
TRANSACTIONS/CAREER NOTES: Selected by Chicago Bears in third round (61st pick overall) of 1990 NFL draft.... Signed by Bears (May 15, 1990).
PLAYING EXPERIENCE: Chicago NFL, 1990.... Games: 1990 (15).
PRO STATISTICS: 1990—Returned one kickoff for minus one yard.

RYPIEN, MARK
QB, REDSKINS
PERSONAL: Born October 2, 1962, at Calgary, Alberta.... 6-4/234.... Full name: Mark Robert Rypien.... Name pronounced RIP-in.... Brother of Tim Rypien, catcher in Toronto Blue Jays' organization, 1984-1986; and cousin of Shane Churla, forward with Minnesota North Stars.
HIGH SCHOOL: Shadle Park (Spokane, Wash.).
COLLEGE: Washington State.
TRANSACTIONS/CAREER NOTES: Selected by Washington Redskins in sixth round (146th pick overall) of 1986 NFL draft.... Signed by Redskins (July 18, 1986).... On injured reserve with knee injury (September 5, 1986-entire season).... On injured reserve with back injury (September 7-November 28, 1987).... Active for one game with Redskins in 1987; did not play.... On injured reserve with knee injury (September 26-November 17, 1990).
CHAMPIONSHIP GAME EXPERIENCE: Member of Washington Redskins for Super Bowl XXII after 1987 season; inactive.
RECORDS/HONORS: Played in Pro Bowl after 1989 season.
PRO STATISTICS: Passer rating points: 1988 (85.2), 1989 (88.1), 1990 (78.4). Career: 84.5.... 1989—Recovered two fumbles.

			——————— PASSING ———————							———— RUSHING ————				——— TOTAL ———		
Year	Team	G	Att.	Cmp.	Pct.	Yds.	TD	Int.	Avg.	Att.	Yds.	Avg.	TD	TD	Pts.	F.
1988— Washington NFL........		9	208	114	54.8	1730	18	13	8.32	9	31	3.4	1	1	6	6
1989— Washington NFL........		14	476	280	58.8	3768	22	13	7.92	26	56	2.2	1	1	6	14
1990— Washington NFL........		10	304	166	54.6	2070	16	11	6.81	15	4	.3	0	0	0	2
Pro totals (3 years)		33	988	560	56.7	7568	56	37	7.66	50	91	1.8	2	2	12	22

SADDLER, ROD
DL, CARDINALS
PERSONAL: Born September 26, 1965, at Atlanta.... 6-5/280.... Full name: Roderick Saddler. ... Cousin of Clark Gaines, running back with New York Jets and Kansas City Chiefs, 1976-1982.
HIGH SCHOOL: Columbus (Decatur, Ga.).
COLLEGE: Texas A&M.
TRANSACTIONS/CAREER NOTES: Selected by St. Louis Cardinals in fourth round (90th pick overall) of 1987 NFL draft.... Signed by Cardinals (July 21, 1987).... Franchise transferred to Phoenix (March 15, 1988).... Granted free agency (February 1, 1990).... Re-signed by Phoenix Cardinals (July 29, 1990).
PLAYING EXPERIENCE: St. Louis NFL, 1987; Phoenix NFL, 1988-1990.... Games: 1987 (12), 1988 (16), 1989 (15), 1990 (16). Total: 59.
PRO STATISTICS: 1987—Intercepted one pass for no yards. 1988—Recovered one fumble for 16 yards and a touchdown. 1990—Recovered two fumbles.

SADOWSKI, TROY
TE, CHIEFS
PERSONAL: Born December 8, 1965, at Atlanta.... 6-5/258.... Full name: Troy Robert Sadowski.
HIGH SCHOOL: Chamblee (Ga.).
COLLEGE: Georgia.
TRANSACTIONS/CAREER NOTES: Selected by Atlanta Falcons in sixth round (145th pick overall) of 1989 NFL draft.... Released by Falcons (August 30, 1989).... Re-signed by Falcons to developmental squad (December 6, 1989).... Released by Falcons (January 9, 1990).... Re-signed by Falcons (February 20, 1990).... Released by Falcons (September 3, 1990).... Re-

signed by Falcons (September 4, 1990).... On inactive list (September 16 and 23, 1990).... Granted unconditional free agency (February 1, 1991).... Signed by Kansas City Chiefs (April 2, 1991).
PLAYING EXPERIENCE: Atlanta NFL, 1990.... Games: 1990 (13).

SALEAUMUA, DAN
NT, CHIEFS

PERSONAL: Born November 25, 1965, at San Diego.... 6-0/295.... Full name: Raymond Daniel Saleaumua.... Name pronounced SOL-ee-uh-MOO-uh.
HIGH SCHOOL: Sweetwater (National City, Calif.).
COLLEGE: Arizona State.
TRANSACTIONS/CAREER NOTES: Selected by Detroit Lions in seventh round (175th pick overall) of 1987 NFL draft.... Signed by Lions (July 25, 1987).... On injured reserve with hamstring injury (September 7-October 31, 1987).... Granted unconditional free agency (February 1, 1989).... Signed by Kansas City Chiefs (March 20, 1989).
PLAYING EXPERIENCE: Detroit NFL, 1987 and 1988; Kansas City NFL, 1989 and 1990.... Games: 1987 (9), 1988 (16), 1989 (16), 1990 (16). Total: 57.
PRO STATISTICS: 1987—Returned three kickoffs for 57 yards. 1988—Returned one kickoff for no yards and fumbled once. 1989—Intercepted one pass for 21 yards, returned one kickoff for eight yards and recovered five fumbles for two yards. 1990—Recovered six fumbles (including one for a touchdown).

SALEM, HARVEY
OT/G, LIONS

PERSONAL: Born January 15, 1961, at Berkeley, Calif.... 6-6/289.
HIGH SCHOOL: El Cerrito, Calif.
COLLEGE: California (undergraduate degree).
TRANSACTIONS/CAREER NOTES: Selected by Oakland Invaders in 1983 USFL territorial draft. ... Selected by Houston Oilers in second round (30th pick overall) of 1983 NFL draft.... Signed by Oilers (July 14, 1983).... On reserve/did not report list (August 19-September 7, 1986).... Granted roster exemption (September 8-September 19, 1986).... Traded by Oilers to Detroit Lions for second-round pick in 1987 draft (September 23, 1986).... Granted free agency (February 1, 1987).... Re-signed by Lions (September 12, 1987).... Granted roster exemption (September 12-September 19, 1987).... On injured reserve with shoulder injury (November 15, 1989-remainder of season).
PLAYING EXPERIENCE: Houston NFL, 1983-1985; Houston (1)-Detroit (13) NFL, 1986; Detroit NFL, 1987-1990.... Games: 1983 (16), 1984 (16), 1985 (16), 1986 (14), 1987 (11), 1988 (16), 1989 (10), 1990 (15). Total: 112.
RECORDS/HONORS: Named as offensive tackle on THE SPORTING NEWS college All-America team, 1982.
PRO STATISTICS: 1988—Recovered one fumble.

SALISBURY, SEAN
QB, VIKINGS

PERSONAL: Born March 9, 1963, at Escondido, Calif.... 6-5/210.... Full name: Richard Sean Salisbury.
HIGH SCHOOL: Orange Glen (Escondido, Calif.).
COLLEGE: Southern California (bachelor's degree in broadcasting, 1986).
TRANSACTIONS/CAREER NOTES: Selected by New Jersey Generals in 1986 USFL territorial draft.... Signed as free agent by Seattle Seahawks (May 12, 1986).... On injured reserve with shoulder injury (October 22, 1986-remainder of season).... Active for seven games with Seahawks in 1986; did not play.... Released by Seahawks (September 1, 1987).... Signed as free agent replacement player by Indianapolis Colts (October 14, 1987).... Released by Colts (July 23, 1988).... Signed as free agent by Winnipeg Blue Bombers of CFL (September 13, 1988).... Released by Blue Bombers (November 2, 1989).... Signed as free agent by Minnesota Vikings (March 19, 1990).... On inactive list (December 9 and 16, 1990).... Active for 14 games with Vikings in 1990; did not play.
CHAMPIONSHIP GAME EXPERIENCE: Played in Grey Cup (CFL championship game) after 1988 season.
PRO STATISTICS: Passer rating points: 1987 (41.7).... CFL: 1988—Recovered one fumble. 1989—Caught one pass for 13 yards and recovered three fumbles.

				PASSING						RUSHING			TOTAL		
Year Team	G	Att.	Cmp.	Pct.	Yds.	TD	Int.	Avg.	Att.	Yds.	Avg.	TD	TD	Pts.	F.
1987— Indianapolis NFL	2	12	8	66.7	68	0	2	5.67	0	0	0.	0	0	0	1
1988— Winnipeg CFL	7	202	100	49.5	1566	11	5	7.75	3	9	3.0	0	0	0	1
1989— Winnipeg CFL	17	595	293	49.2	4049	26	26	6.81	24	54	2.3	0	0	0	9
NFL totals (1 year)	2	12	8	66.7	68	0	2	5.67	0	0	0	0	0	0	1
CFL totals (2 years)	24	797	393	49.3	5615	37	31	7.05	27	63	2.3	0	0	0	10
Pro totals (3 years)	26	809	401	49.6	5683	37	33	7.03	27	63	2.3	0	0	0	11

SANDERS, BARRY
RB, LIONS

PERSONAL: Born July 16, 1968, at Wichita, Kan.... 5-8/203.
HIGH SCHOOL: North (Wichita, Kan.).
COLLEGE: Oklahoma State.
TRANSACTIONS/CAREER NOTES: Selected by Detroit Lions in first round (third pick overall) of 1989 NFL draft.... Signed by Lions (September 7, 1989).
RECORDS/HONORS: Named as kick returner on THE SPORTING NEWS college All-America team, 1987.... Heisman Trophy winner, 1988.... Named THE SPORTING NEWS College Football Player of the Year, 1988.... Named as running back on THE SPORTING NEWS college All-America team, 1988.... Named THE SPORTING NEWS NFL Rookie of the Year, 1989.... Named to THE SPORTING NEWS NFL All-Pro team, 1989 and 1990.... Played in Pro Bowl after 1989 and 1990 seasons.
PRO STATISTICS: 1989—Returned five kickoffs for 118 yards (23.6 avg.). 1990—Recovered two fumbles.

		RUSHING				RECEIVING				TOTAL		
Year Team	G	Att.	Yds.	Avg.	TD	No.	Yds.	Avg.	TD	TD	Pts.	F.
1989— Detroit NFL	15	280	1470	5.3	14	24	282	11.8	0	14	84	10
1990— Detroit NFL	16	255	*1304	5.1	13	36	480	13.3	3	*16	96	4
Pro totals (2 years)	31	535	2774	5.2	27	60	762	12.7	3	30	180	14

SANDERS, DEION
CB, FALCONS

PERSONAL: Born August 8, 1967, at Fort Myers, Fla. . . . 6-0/185. . . . Full name: Deion Luwynn Sanders.
HIGH SCHOOL: North Fort Myers (Fla.).
COLLEGE: Florida State.
TRANSACTIONS/CAREER NOTES: Selected by Atlanta Falcons in first round (fifth pick overall) of 1989 NFL draft. . . . Signed by Falcons (September 7, 1989). . . . On reserve/did not report list (July 27-August 13, 1990).
RECORDS/HONORS: Named as defensive back on THE SPORTING NEWS college All-America team, 1986-1988.
PRO STATISTICS: 1989—Recovered one fumble and caught one pass for minus eight yards. 1990—Recovered two fumbles.

		— INTERCEPTIONS—				— PUNT RETURNS —				– KICKOFF RETURNS–				— TOTAL—		
Year	Team	G	No.	Yds.	Avg.	TD	No.	Yds.	Avg.	TD	No.	Yds.	Avg.	TD	TD	Pts.	F.
1989— Atlanta NFL		15	5	52	10.4	0	28	307	11.0	*1	35	725	20.7	0	1	6	2
1990— Atlanta NFL		16	3	153	51.0	2	29	250	8.6	*1	39	851	21.8	0	3	18	4
Pro totals (2 years)		31	8	205	25.6	2	57	557	9.8	2	74	1576	21.3	0	4	24	6

BASEBALL TRANSACTIONS: Selected by Kansas City Royals' organization in sixth round of free-agent draft (June 3, 1985). . . . Selected by New York Yankees' organization in 30th round of free-agent draft (June 1, 1988). . . . On disqualified list (August 1-September 24, 1990). . . . Released (September 24, 1990).
BASEBALL RECORDS/HONORS/NOTES: Major League stolen bases: 1989 (1), 1990 (8). Total: 9.

BASEBALL RECORD AS PLAYER

Year	Team	League	Pos.	G	AB	R	H	2B	3B	HR	RBI	Avg.	PO	A	E	F.A.
1988— Sarasota Yanks	Gulf C.	OF	17	75	7	21	4	2	0	6	.280	33	1	2	.944
1988— Fort Lauderdale	Fla. St.	OF	6	21	5	9	2	0	0	2	.429	22	2	0	1.000
1988— Columbus	Int.	OF	5	20	3	3	1	0	0	0	.150	13	0	0	1.000
1989— Albany	East.	OF	33	119	28	34	2	2	1	6	.286	79	3	0	1.000
1989— New York	Amer.	OF	14	47	7	11	2	0	2	7	.234	30	1	1	.969
1989— Columbus	Int.	OF	70	259	38	72	12	7	5	30	.278	165	0	4	.976
1990— New York	Amer.	OF	57	133	24	21	2	2	3	9	.158	69	2	2	.973
1990— Columbus	Int.	OF	22	84	21	27	7	1	2	10	.321	49	1	0	1.000
Major league totals (2 Years)			71	180	31	32	4	2	5	16	.178	99	3	3	.971

SANDERS, ERIC
OT/G, LIONS

PERSONAL: Born October 22, 1958, at Reno, Nev. . . . 6-7/286. . . . Full name: Eric Downer Sanders.
HIGH SCHOOL: Wooster (Reno, Nev.).
COLLEGE: Nevada-Reno.
TRANSACTIONS/CAREER NOTES: Selected by Atlanta Falcons in fifth round (136th pick overall) of 1981 NFL draft. . . . On injured reserve with knee injury (November 10, 1984-remainder of season). . . . On injured reserve with back injury (October 31-November 26, 1986). . . . Awarded on procedural waivers to Detroit Lions (November 28, 1986).
PLAYING EXPERIENCE: Atlanta NFL, 1981-1985; Atlanta (8)-Detroit (3) NFL, 1986; Detroit NFL, 1987-1990. . . . Games: 1981 (16), 1982 (9), 1983 (15), 1984 (10), 1985 (16), 1986 (11), 1987 (12), 1988 (16), 1989 (16), 1990 (16). Total: 137.
PRO STATISTICS: 1982—Recovered one fumble. 1985—Recovered one fumble for minus 23 yards. 1988—Recovered one fumble and fumbled once for minus 17 yards.

SANDERS, GLENELL
LB, RAMS

PERSONAL: Born November 4, 1966, at New Orleans. . . . 6-0/224.
HIGH SCHOOL: Clinton (La.).
COLLEGE: Louisiana Tech.
TRANSACTIONS/CAREER NOTES: Signed as free agent by Chicago Bears (April 28, 1990). . . . Released by Bears (September 3, 1990). . . . Re-signed by Bears to practice squad (December 19, 1990). . . . Activated (December 21, 1990). . . . Granted unconditional free agency (February 1, 1991). . . . Signed by Los Angeles Rams (March 29, 1991).
PLAYING EXPERIENCE: Chicago NFL, 1990. . . . Games: 1990 (2).

SANDERS, RICKY
WR, REDSKINS

PERSONAL: Born August 30, 1962, at Temple, Tex. . . . 5-11/180. . . . Full name: Ricky Wayne Sanders.
HIGH SCHOOL: Belton (Tex.).
COLLEGE: Southwest Texas State.
TRANSACTIONS/CAREER NOTES: Selected by Houston Gamblers in 1984 USFL territorial draft. . . . Signed by Gamblers (January 26, 1984). . . . Selected by New England Patriots in first round (16th pick overall) of 1984 NFL supplemental draft. . . . On developmental squad for eight games with Houston Gamblers (March 7-May 6, 1985). . . . Traded by Gamblers with defensive backs Luther Bradley, Will Lewis, Mike Mitchell and Durwood Roquemore, defensive end Pete Catan, quarterbacks Jim Kelly and Todd Dillon, defensive tackles Tony Fitzpatrick, Van Hughes and Hosea Taylor, running back Sam Harrell, linebackers Andy Hawkins and Ladell Wills, wide receivers Richard Johnson, Scott McGhee, Gerald McNeil and Clarence Verdin, guard Rich Kehr, center Billy Kidd and offensive tackles Chris Riehm and Tommy Robison to New Jersey Generals for past considerations (March 7, 1986). . . . Granted free agency when USFL suspended operations (August 7, 1986). . . . NFL rights traded by New England Patriots to Washington Redskins for third-round pick in 1987 draft (August 11, 1986). . . . Signed by Redskins (August 13, 1986). . . . Granted roster exemption (August 13-August 25, 1986). . . . On injured reserve with pulled calf and hamstring (September 2-October 11, 1986).
CHAMPIONSHIP GAME EXPERIENCE: Played in NFC championship game after 1986 and 1987 seasons. . . . Played in Super Bowl XXII after 1987 season.
PRO STATISTICS: USFL:1984—Recovered two fumbles. 1985—Credited with one 2-point conversion and attempted one pass with no completions. . . . NFL: 1989—Attempted one pass with one completion for 32 yards.

Year Team	G	RUSHING				RECEIVING				PUNT RETURNS				KICKOFF RETURNS				TOTALS		
		Att.	Yds.	Avg.	TD	No.	Yds.	Avg.	TD	No.	Yds.	Avg.	TD	No.	Yds.	Avg.	TD	TD	Pts.	F.
1984— Houston USFL	18	10	58	5.8	0	101	1378	13.6	11	19	148	7.8	0	2	28	14.0	0	11	66	3
1985— Houston USFL	10	5	32	6.4	0	48	538	11.2	7	0	0		0	0	0		0	7	44	0
1986— Washington NFL	10	0	0		0	14	286	20.4	2	0	0		0	0	0		0	2	12	0
1987— Washington NFL	12	1	-4	-4.0	0	37	630	17.0	3	0	0		4	4	118	29.5	0	3	18	0
1988— Washington NFL	16	2	14	7.0	0	73	1148	15.7	12	0	0		0	19	362	19.1	0	12	72	0
1989— Washington NFL	16	4	19	4.8	0	80	1138	14.2	4	2	12	6.0	0	9	134	14.9	0	4	24	0
1990— Washington NFL	16	4	17	4.3	0	56	727	13.0	3	1	22	22.0	0	0	0		0	3	18	0
USFL totals (2 years)	28	15	90	6.0	0	149	1916	12.9	18	19	148	7.8	0	2	28	14.0	0	18	110	3
NFL totals (5 years)	70	11	46	4.2	0	260	3929	15.1	24	3	34	11.3	0	32	614	19.2	0	24	144	0
Pro totals (7 years)	98	26	136	5.2	0	409	5845	14.3	42	22	182	8.3	0	34	642	18.9	0	42	254	3

SANDERS, THOMAS
RB, EAGLES

PERSONAL: Born January 4, 1962, at Giddings, Tex....5-11/202. **HIGH SCHOOL:** Giddings (Tex.).
COLLEGE: Texas A&M.
TRANSACTIONS/CAREER NOTES: Selected by Houston Gamblers in 1985 USFL territorial draft.... Selected by Chicago Bears in ninth round (250th pick overall) of 1985 NFL draft.... Signed by Bears (July 10, 1985).... Granted unconditional free agency (February 1, 1990).... Signed by San Diego Chargers (March 14, 1990).... Released by Chargers (September 3, 1990).... Signed by Philadelphia Eagles (October 25, 1990).
CHAMPIONSHIP GAME EXPERIENCE: Played in NFC championship game after 1985 and 1988 seasons.... Played in Super Bowl XX after 1985 season.

Year Team	G	RUSHING				RECEIVING				KICKOFF RETURNS				TOTAL		
		Att.	Yds.	Avg.	TD	No.	Yds.	Avg.	TD	No.	Yds.	Avg.	TD	TD	Pts.	F.
1985— Chicago NFL	15	25	104	4.2	1	1	9	9.0	0	1	10	10.0	0	1	6	1
1986— Chicago NFL	16	27	224	8.3	5	2	18	9.0	0	22	399	18.1	0	5	30	2
1987— Chicago NFL	12	23	122	5.3	1	3	53	17.7	0	20	349	17.5	0	1	6	1
1988— Chicago NFL	16	95	332	3.5	3	9	94	10.4	0	13	248	19.1	0	3	18	5
1989— Chicago NFL	16	41	127	3.1	0	3	28	9.3	1	23	491	21.4	*1	2	12	2
1990— Philadelphia NFL	10	56	208	3.7	1	2	20	10.0	0	15	299	19.9	0	1	6	0
Pro totals (6 years)	85	267	1117	4.2	11	20	222	11.1	1	94	1796	19.1	1	13	78	11

SAPOLU, JESSE
C, 49ERS

PERSONAL: Born March 10, 1961, at Laie, Western Samoa.... 6-4/260.... Name pronounced SA-pole-low. **HIGH SCHOOL:** Farrington (Honolulu). **COLLEGE:** Hawaii.
TRANSACTIONS/CAREER NOTES: Selected by Oakland Invaders in 17th round (199th pick overall) of 1983 USFL draft.... Selected by San Francisco 49ers in 11th round (289th pick overall) of 1983 NFL draft.... Signed by 49ers (July 10, 1983).... On physically unable to perform/active list with fractured foot (July 19-August 12, 1984).... On reserve/physically unable to perform list with fractured foot (August 13-November 8, 1984).... On injured reserve with fractured foot (November 16, 1984-remainder of season).... On injured reserve with broken foot (August 12, 1985-entire season).... On injured reserve with broken leg (July 30, 1986-entire season).... On reserve/did not report list (July 30-August 27, 1990).
PLAYING EXPERIENCE: San Francisco NFL, 1983, 1984 and 1987-1990.... Games: 1983 (16), 1984 (1), 1987 (12), 1988 (16), 1989 (16), 1990 (16). Total: 77.
CHAMPIONSHIP GAME EXPERIENCE: Played in NFC championship game after 1983 and 1988-1990 seasons.... Played in Super Bowl XXIII after 1988 season and Super Bowl XXIV after 1989 season.

SAVAGE, TONY
NT, CHARGERS

PERSONAL: Born July 7, 1967, at San Francisco.... 6-3/300.... Full name: Anthony John Savage. **HIGH SCHOOL:** Riordan (San Francisco). **COLLEGE:** Washington State.
TRANSACTIONS/CAREER NOTES: Selected by New York Jets in fifth round (112th pick overall) of 1990 NFL draft.... Signed by Jets (July 12, 1990).... Released by Jets (September 3, 1990).... Signed by San Diego Chargers (October 3, 1990).... On inactive list (October 21, 28; November 4, 11, 18, 25; and December 2, 1990).... On injured reserve with knee injury (December 12, 1990-remainder of season).
PLAYING EXPERIENCE: San Diego NFL, 1990.... Games: 1990 (2).

SAXON, JAMES
RB, CHIEFS

PERSONAL: Born March 23, 1966, at Buford, S.C.... 5-11/234.... Full name: James Elijah Saxon. **HIGH SCHOOL:** Battery Creek (Burton, S.C.). **COLLEGE:** American River College (Calif.), then San Jose State.
TRANSACTIONS/CAREER NOTES: Selected by Kansas City Chiefs in sixth round (139th pick overall) of 1988 NFL draft.... Signed by Chiefs (July 19, 1988).... On injured reserve with ankle injury (September 8-November 24, 1990).
PRO STATISTICS: 1988—Recovered one fumble. 1989—Had only pass attempt intercepted.

Year Team	G	RUSHING				RECEIVING				KICKOFF RETURNS				TOTAL		
		Att.	Yds.	Avg.	TD	No.	Yds.	Avg.	TD	No.	Yds.	Avg.	TD	TD	Pts.	F.
1988— Kansas City NFL	16	60	236	3.9	2	19	177	9.3	0	2	40	20.0	0	2	12	0
1989— Kansas City NFL	16	58	233	4.0	3	11	86	7.8	0	3	16	5.3	0	3	18	2
1990— Kansas City NFL	6	3	15	5.0	0	1	5	5.0	0	5	81	16.2	0	0	0	1
Pro totals (3 years)	38	121	484	4.0	5	31	268	8.7	0	10	137	13.7	0	5	30	3

SAXON, MIKE
P, COWBOYS

PERSONAL: Born July 10, 1962, at Arcadia, Calif.... 6-3/200.
HIGH SCHOOL: Arcadia (Calif.).
COLLEGE: Pasadena City College (Calif.), then San Diego State.
TRANSACTIONS/CAREER NOTES: Selected by Arizona Wranglers in 13th round (265th pick overall) of 1984 USFL draft.... Selected by Detroit Lions in 11th round (300th pick overall) of 1984 NFL draft.... Signed by Lions (May 29, 1984).... Released by Lions (August 27, 1984).... Signed by Arizona Wranglers (November 7, 1984).... Released by Wranglers (February 11, 1985).... Signed as free agent by Dallas Cowboys (March 27, 1985).
PRO STATISTICS: 1989—Rushed once for one yard and attempted one pass for four yards. 1990—Rushed once for 20 yards.

			— PUNTING—		
Year	Team	G	No.	Avg.	Blk.
1985— Dallas NFL		16	81	41.9	1
1986— Dallas NFL		16	86	40.7	1
1987— Dallas NFL		12	68	39.5	0
1988— Dallas NFL		16	80	40.9	0
1989— Dallas NFL		16	79	40.9	2
1990— Dallas NFL		16	79	43.2	0
Pro totals (6 years)		92	473	41.2	4

SCALES, GREG
TE, SAINTS

PERSONAL: Born May 9, 1966, at Winston-Salem, N.C.... 6-4/253.
HIGH SCHOOL: East Forsyth (Winston-Salem, N.C.).
COLLEGE: Wake Forest.
TRANSACTIONS/CAREER NOTES: Selected by New Orleans Saints in fifth round (112th pick overall) of 1988 NFL draft.... Signed by Saints (July 17, 1988).... On injured reserve with hamstring injury (December 15, 1989-remainder of season).
PRO STATISTICS: 1989—Returned one kickoff for no yards.

			— RECEIVING —			
Year	Team	G	No.	Yds.	Avg.	TD
1988— New Orleans NFL		12	2	20	10.0	1
1989— New Orleans NFL		14	8	89	11.1	0
1990— New Orleans NFL		16	8	64	8.0	1
Pro totals (3 years)		42	18	173	9.6	2

SCHAD, MIKE
G, EAGLES

PERSONAL: Born October 2, 1963, at Trenton, Ont.... 6-5/290.... Name pronounced SHAD.
HIGH SCHOOL: Moira Secondary (Bellville, Ont.).
COLLEGE: Queens College, Canada (degrees in geography and physiology, 1986).
TRANSACTIONS/CAREER NOTES: Selected by Los Angeles Rams in first round (23rd pick overall) of 1986 NFL draft.... Signed by Rams (August 4, 1986).... On injured reserve with back injury (September 4, 1986-entire season).... On injured reserve with pinched nerve in neck (September 7-December 4, 1987).... Granted unconditional free agency (February 1, 1989).... Signed by Philadelphia Eagles (March 28, 1989).... On inactive list (December 29, 1990).
PLAYING EXPERIENCE: Los Angeles Rams NFL, 1987 and 1988; Philadelphia NFL, 1989 and 1990.... Games: 1987 (1), 1988 (6), 1989 (16), 1990 (12). Total: 35.
PRO STATISTICS: 1990—Recovered one fumble.

SCHLERETH, MARK
G, REDSKINS

PERSONAL: Born January 25, 1966, at Anchorage, Alaska.... 6-3/285.
HIGH SCHOOL: Robert Service (Anchorage, Alaska).
COLLEGE: Idaho.
TRANSACTIONS/CAREER NOTES: Selected by Washington Redskins in 10th round (263rd pick overall) of 1989 NFL draft.... Signed by Redskins (July 23, 1989).... On injured reserve with knee injury (September 5-November 11, 1989).... On inactive list (November 12, 18, 22; and December 2, 1990).
PLAYING EXPERIENCE: Washington NFL, 1989 and 1990.... Games: 1989 (6), 1990 (12). Total: 18.
PRO STATISTICS: 1989—Recovered one fumble.

SCHONERT, TURK
QB, JETS

PERSONAL: Born January 15, 1957, at Torrance, Calif.... 6-1/200.... Full name: Turk Leroy Schonert.
HIGH SCHOOL: Servite (Anaheim, Calif.).
COLLEGE: Stanford.
TRANSACTIONS/CAREER NOTES: Selected by Chicago Bears in ninth round (242nd pick overall) of 1980 NFL draft.... Released by Bears (August 25, 1980).... Awarded on waivers to Cincinnati Bengals (August 26, 1980).... Active for 16 games with Bengals in 1980; did not play.... USFL rights traded by Oakland Invaders to Jacksonville Bulls for rights to running back Ted McKnight, linebacker Mark Jerue and first- and fifth-round picks in 1984 draft (October 24, 1983).... On injured reserve with separated shoulder (December 5, 1984-remainder of season).... Granted free agency (February 1, 1985).... Re-signed by Bengals (April 4, 1985).... Traded by Bengals to Atlanta Falcons for third-round pick in 1986 draft (April 4, 1986).... Released by Falcons (September 8, 1987).... Signed as free agent by Cincinnati Bengals (September 10, 1987).... On injured reserve with broken hand (October 27, 1989-remainder of season).... Released by Bengals (May 15, 1990).... Signed by New York Jets (April 10, 1991).
CHAMPIONSHIP GAME EXPERIENCE: Member of Cincinnati Bengals for AFC championship game and Super Bowl XVI after 1981 season; did not play.... Played in AFC championship game after 1988 season.... Played in Super Bowl XXIII after 1988 season.

PRO STATISTICS: Passer rating points: 1981 (82.3), 1982 (91.7), 1983 (73.1), 1984 (77.8), 1985 (100.1), 1986 (68.4), 1988 (64.6), 1989 (39.6). Career: 75.5. . . . 1982—Recovered one fumble. 1983—Recovered four fumbles. 1985—Recovered two fumbles and fumbled three times for minus two yards. 1986—Recovered one fumble and fumbled five times for minus two yards.

				——PASSING——						——RUSHING——				——TOTAL——	
Year Team	G	Att.	Cmp.	Pct.	Yds.	TD	Int.	Avg.	Att.	Yds.	Avg.	TD	TD	Pts.	F.
1981— Cincinnati NFL..........	4	19	10	52.6	166	0	0	8.74	7	41	5.9	0	0	0	1
1982— Cincinnati NFL..........	2	1	1	100.0	6	0	0	6.00	3	-8	-2.7	0	0	0	1
1983— Cincinnati NFL..........	9	156	92	59.0	1159	2	5	7.43	29	117	4.0	2	2	12	6
1984— Cincinnati NFL..........	8	117	78	66.7	945	4	7	8.08	13	77	5.9	1	1	6	2
1985— Cincinnati NFL..........	7	51	33	64.7	460	1	0	9.02	8	39	4.9	0	0	0	3
1986— Atlanta NFL	8	154	95	61.7	1032	4	8	6.70	11	12	1.1	0	1	6	5
1987— Cincinnati NFL..........	11	0	0		0	0	0		0	0		0	0	0	0
1988— Cincinnati NFL..........	16	4	2	50.0	20	0	0	5.00	2	10	5.0	0	0	0	0
1989— Cincinnati NFL..........	7	2	0	.0	0	0	0	.00	0	0		0	0	0	0
Pro totals (9 years)	72	504	311	61.7	3788	11	20	7.52	73	288	4.0	4	4	24	18

SCHREIBER, ADAM
C/G, VIKINGS

PERSONAL: Born February 20, 1962, at Galveston, Tex. . . . 6-4/288. . . . Full name: Adam Blayne Schreiber.
HIGH SCHOOL: Butler (Huntsville, Ala.).
COLLEGE: Texas.

TRANSACTIONS/CAREER NOTES: Selected by Houston Gamblers in 1984 USFL territorial draft. . . . Selected by Seattle Seahawks in ninth round (243rd pick overall) of 1984 NFL draft. . . . Signed by Seahawks (June 20, 1984). . . . Released by Seahawks (August 27, 1984). . . . Re-signed by Seahawks (October 10, 1984). . . . Released by Seahawks (August 29, 1985). . . . Signed as free agent by New Orleans Saints (November 20, 1985). . . . Released by Saints (September 1, 1986). . . . Signed as free agent by Philadelphia Eagles (October 16, 1986). . . . Released by Eagles (October 18, 1988). . . . Awarded on waivers to New York Jets (October 19, 1988). . . . Granted unconditional free agency (February 1, 1990). . . . Signed by Minnesota Vikings (March 21, 1990).
PLAYING EXPERIENCE: Seattle NFL, 1984; New Orleans NFL, 1985; Philadelphia NFL, 1986 and 1987; Philadelphia (6)-New York Jets (7) NFL, 1988; New York Jets NFL, 1989; Minnesota NFL, 1990. . . . Games: 1984 (6), 1985 (1), 1986 (9), 1987 (12), 1988 (13), 1989 (16), 1990 (16). Total: 73.
PRO STATISTICS: 1990—Returned one kickoff for five yards.

SCHROEDER, JAY
QB, RAIDERS

PERSONAL: Born June 28, 1961, at Milwaukee. . . . 6-4/215. . . . Full name: Jay Brian Schroeder. . . . Name pronounced SHRAY-der.
HIGH SCHOOL: Pacific Palisades (Calif.).
COLLEGE: UCLA.

TRANSACTIONS/CAREER NOTES: Selected by Washington Redskins in third round (83rd pick overall) of 1984 NFL draft. . . . Active for 16 games with Redskins in 1984; did not play. . . . Inactive for one game with Redskins in 1988. . . . Traded by Redskins with second-round pick in 1989 draft to Los Angeles Raiders for offensive tackle Jim Lachey, second-, fourth- and fifth-round picks in 1989 draft and fourth and fifth-round picks in 1990 draft (September 7, 1988).
CHAMPIONSHIP GAME EXPERIENCE: Played in NFC championship game after 1986 and 1987 seasons. . . . Played in Super Bowl XXII after 1987 season. . . . Played in AFC championship game after 1990 season.
RECORDS/HONORS: Played in Pro Bowl after 1986 season.
PRO STATISTICS: Passer rating points: 1985 (73.8), 1986 (72.9), 1987 (71.0), 1988 (64.6), 1989 (60.3), 1990 (90.8). Career: 73.5. . . . 1985—Punted four times for 33.0 average, recovered one fumble and fumbled five times for minus three yards. 1986—Recovered five fumbles and fumbled nine times for minus 19 yards. 1988—Recovered three fumbles and fumbled six times for minus four yards. 1989—Recovered two fumbles. 1990—Recovered two fumbles and fumbled 11 times for minus 19 yards.

				——PASSING——						——RUSHING——				——TOTAL——	
Year Team	G	Att.	Cmp.	Pct.	Yds.	TD	Int.	Avg.	Att.	Yds.	Avg.	TD	TD	Pts.	F.
1985— Washington NFL........	9	209	112	53.6	1458	5	5	6.98	17	30	1.8	0	0	0	5
1986— Washington NFL........	16	541	276	51.0	4109	22	22	7.60	36	47	1.3	1	1	6	9
1987— Washington NFL........	11	267	129	48.3	1878	12	10	7.03	26	120	4.6	3	3	18	5
1988— Was. (0)-Rai. (9) NFL	9	256	113	44.1	1839	13	13	7.18	29	109	3.8	1	1	6	6
1989— L.A. Raiders NFL	11	194	91	46.9	1550	8	13	7.99	15	38	2.5	0	0	0	6
1990— L.A. Raiders NFL	16	334	182	54.5	2849	19	9	*8.53	37	81	2.2	0	0	0	11
Pro totals (6 years)	72	1801	903	50.1	13683	79	72	7.60	160	425	2.7	5	5	30	42

BASEBALL TRANSACTIONS: Selected by Toronto Blue Jays' organization in first round (third pick overall) of free-agent draft (June 5, 1979). . . . On temporary inactive list (June 30, 1979-remainder of season). . . . On temporary inactive list (August 14-September 3, 1980). . . . Released (February 28, 1984).
BASEBALL RECORDS/HONORS/NOTES: Led Carolina League batters in strikeouts (172), 1982. . . . Led South Atlantic League batters in strikeouts (142), 1981.

BASEBALL RECORD AS PLAYER

Year Team	League	Pos.	G	AB	R	H	2B	3B	HR	RBI	Avg.	PO	A	E	F.A.
1979— Utica..........................	NYP							Did not play							
1980— Medicine Hat............	Pion.	OF	52	171	27	40	6	2	2	21	.234	93	6	5	.952
1981— Florence	S. Atl.	3B/OF	131	417	51	85	17	1	10	47	.204	112	101	28	.884
1982— Kinston....................	Carol.	OF	132	435	59	95	17	1	15	55	.218	178	17	15	.929
1983— Kinston....................	Carol.	C/1B/OF	92	281	30	58	9	2	9	43	.206	519	53	20	.966

SCHULTZ, WILLIAM
OT, COLTS

PERSONAL: Born May 1, 1967, at Granada Hills, Calif. . . . 6-5/305.
HIGH SCHOOL: John F. Kennedy (Granada Hills, Calif.).
COLLEGE: Glendale Junior College (Calif.), then Southern California.
TRANSACTIONS/CAREER NOTES: Selected by Indianapolis Colts in fourth round (94th pick overall) of 1990 NFL draft. . . . Signed by Colts (July 23, 1990).
PLAYING EXPERIENCE: Indianapolis NFL, 1990. . . . Games: 1990 (12).

SCRAFFORD, KIRK
OT, BENGALS

PERSONAL: Born March 16, 1967, at Billings, Mont. . . . 6-6/255.
HIGH SCHOOL: Billings West (Billings, Mont.).
COLLEGE: Montana.
TRANSACTIONS/CAREER NOTES: Signed as free agent by Cincinnati Bengals (May, 1990). . . . On injured reserve with knee injury (September 4-November 23, 1990). . . . On practice squad (November 23-December 22, 1990).
PLAYING EXPERIENCE: Cincinnati NFL, 1990. . . . Games: 1990 (2).

SCULLY, JOHN
G, FALCONS

PERSONAL: Born August 2, 1958, at Huntington, N.Y. . . . 6-6/275. . . . Brother-in-law of Tom Thayer, guard with Chicago Bears.
HIGH SCHOOL: Holy Family (Huntington, N.Y.).
COLLEGE: Notre Dame (bachelor of arts degree in sociology, 1980).
TRANSACTIONS/CAREER NOTES: Selected by Atlanta Falcons in fourth round (109th pick overall) of 1981 NFL draft. . . . On injured reserve with broken leg (October 29, 1985-remainder of season). . . . On injured reserve with broken leg (December 13, 1986-remainder of season). . . . On injured reserve with hamstring injury (September 12-October 15, 1988). . . . Granted free agency (February 1, 1989). . . . On reserve/unsigned list (entire 1989 season). . . . Re-signed by Falcons (May 9, 1990). . . . On injured reserve with foot injury (October 18-November 20, 1990).
PLAYING EXPERIENCE: Atlanta NFL, 1981-1988 and 1990. . . . Games: 1981 (16), 1982 (9), 1983 (16), 1984 (16), 1985 (8), 1986 (14), 1987 (12), 1988 (11), 1990 (10). Total: 112.
RECORDS/HONORS: Named as center on THE SPORTING NEWS college All-America team, 1980.
PRO STATISTICS: 1982—Returned one kickoff for no yards. 1984—Recovered one fumble. 1986—Recovered two fumbles.

SEALE, EUGENE
LB, OILERS

PERSONAL: Born June 3, 1964, at Jasper, Tex. . . . 5-10/253.
HIGH SCHOOL: Jasper (Tex.).
COLLEGE: Lamar.
TRANSACTIONS/CAREER NOTES: Selected by New Jersey Generals in fifth round (34th pick overall) of 1986 USFL draft. . . . Signed by Generals (May 28, 1986). . . . Granted free agency when USFL suspended operations (August 7, 1986). . . . Signed as replacement player by Houston Oilers (September 23, 1987). . . . Released by Oilers (November 3, 1987). . . . Re-signed by Oilers (November 24, 1987). . . . On inactive list (November 18, 1990).
PLAYING EXPERIENCE: Houston NFL, 1987-1990. . . . Games: 1987 (9), 1988 (16), 1989 (15), 1990 (15). Total: 55.
PRO STATISTICS: 1987—Intercepted one pass for 73 yards and a touchdown. 1988—Intercepted one pass for 46 yards and credited with a safety. 1989—Recovered blocked punt in end zone for a touchdown.

SEALE, SAM
CB, CHARGERS

PERSONAL: Born October 6, 1962, at Barbados, West Indies. . . . 5-9/185. . . . Full name: Samuel Ricardo Seale.
HIGH SCHOOL: Orange (N.J.).
COLLEGE: Western State College (Colo).
TRANSACTIONS/CAREER NOTES: Selected by Memphis Showboats in 15th round (309th pick overall) of 1984 USFL draft. . . . Selected by Los Angeles Raiders in eighth round (224th pick overall) of 1984 NFL draft. . . . Signed by Raiders (June 6, 1984). . . . Released by Raiders (September 2, 1988). . . . Signed as free agent by San Diego Chargers (September 14, 1988). . . . On injured reserve with hamstring injury (December 16, 1989-remainder of season). . . . Granted free agency (February 1, 1990). . . . Re-signed by Chargers (August 6, 1990).
PRO STATISTICS: 1986—Recovered one fumble. 1987—Recovered one fumble for minus nine yards. 1988—Recovered two fumbles and ran 50 yards with a lateral from a fumble for a touchdown. 1990—Recovered one fumble.

			—INTERCEPTIONS—			—KICKOFF RETURNS—				—TOTAL—		
Year Team	G	No.	Yds.	Avg.	TD	No.	Yds.	Avg.	TD	TD	Pts.	F.
1984—L.A. Raiders NFL	12	0	0		0	0	0		0	0	0	0
1985—L.A. Raiders NFL	16	1	38	38.0	1	23	482	21.0	0	1	6	0
1986—L.A. Raiders NFL	16	4	2	.5	0	0	0		0	0	0	0
1987—L.A. Raiders NFL	12	0	0		0	0	0		0	0	0	0
1988—San Diego NFL	14	0	0		0	0	0		0	1	6	0
1989—San Diego NFL	13	4	47	11.8	0	0	0		0	0	0	0
1990—San Diego NFL	16	2	14	7.0	0	0	0		0	0	0	0
Pro totals (7 years)	99	11	101	9.2	1	23	482	21.0	0	2	12	0

DID YOU KNOW. . .

. . .that the New England Patriots' 181 points scored in 1990 were the fewest by any NFL team since the league expanded to a 16-game schedule in 1978?

SEALS, LEON
DE, BILLS

PERSONAL: Born January 30, 1964, at New Orleans. . . . 6-5/267.
HIGH SCHOOL: Scotlandville (Baton Rouge, La.).
COLLEGE: Jackson State.
TRANSACTIONS/CAREER NOTES: Selected by Buffalo Bills in fourth round (109th pick overall) of 1987 NFL draft. . . . Signed by Bills (July 26, 1987). . . . Crossed picket line during players' strike (October 14, 1987).
PLAYING EXPERIENCE: Buffalo NFL, 1987-1990. . . . Games: 1987 (13), 1988 (16), 1989 (16), 1990 (16). Total: 61.
CHAMPIONSHIP GAME EXPERIENCE: Played in AFC championship game after 1988 and 1990 seasons. . . . Played in Super Bowl XXV after 1990 season.
PRO STATISTICS: 1988—Recovered three fumbles for seven yards and a touchdown. 1989—Recovered one fumble. 1990—Intercepted one pass for no yards and recovered two fumbles for eight yards.

SEALS, RAY
DL, BUCCANEERS

PERSONAL: Born June 17, 1965, at Syracuse, N.Y. . . . 6-3/270. . . . Full name: Raymond Seals.
HIGH SCHOOL: Henninger (Syracuse, N.Y.).
COLLEGE: None.
TRANSACTIONS/CAREER NOTES: Played semi-pro football for Syracuse Express of Eastern Football League (1986 and 1987). . . . Signed as free agent by Tampa Bay Buccaneers for 1988 (November 18, 1987). . . . On injured reserve with back injury (August 8, 1988-entire season). . . . On injured reserve with broken bone in foot (September 20, 1989-remainder of season). . . . Released by Buccaneers (November 2, 1990). . . . Signed by Detroit Lions (November 8, 1990). . . . On inactive list (November 11 and 18, 1990). . . . Released by Lions (November 20, 1990). . . . Signed by Indianapolis Colts (November 27, 1990). . . . Active for one game for Colts in 1990; did not play. . . . Released by Colts (December 5, 1990). . . . Signed by Tampa Bay Buccaneers (March 6, 1991).
PLAYING EXPERIENCE: Tampa Bay NFL, 1989; Tampa Bay (8)-Detroit (0)-Indianapolis (0) NFL, 1990. . . . Games: 1989 (2), 1990 (8). Total: 10.

SEAU, JUNIOR
LB, CHARGERS

PERSONAL: Born January 19, 1969, at Samoa. . . . 6-3/250. . . . Full name: Tiaina Seau Jr. . . . Name pronounced SAY-ow.
HIGH SCHOOL: Oceanside (Calif.).
COLLEGE: Southern California.
TRANSACTIONS/CAREER NOTES: Selected by San Diego Chargers in first round (fifth pick overall) of 1990 NFL draft. . . . Signed by Chargers (August 27, 1990).
PLAYING EXPERIENCE: San Diego NFL, 1990. . . . Games: 1990 (16).
RECORDS/HONORS: Named as linebacker on The Sporting News college All-America team, 1989.

SECULES, SCOTT
QB, DOLPHINS

PERSONAL: Born November 8, 1964, at Newport News, Va. . . . 6-3/220. . . . Full name: Thomas Wescott Secules. . . . Name pronounced SEE-kyools.
HIGH SCHOOL: Chantilly (Va.).
COLLEGE: Virginia (degree in economics, 1988).
TRANSACTIONS/CAREER NOTES: Selected by Dallas Cowboys in sixth round (151st pick overall) of 1988 NFL draft. . . . Signed by Cowboys (July 8, 1988). . . . Active for 13 games with Cowboys in 1988; did not play. . . . Traded by Cowboys to Miami Dolphins for fifth-round pick in 1990 NFL draft (August 6, 1989).
PRO STATISTICS: Passer rating points: 1989 (44.3), 1990 (10.7). Career: 37.4.

				PASSING						RUSHING				TOTAL	
Year Team	G	Att.	Cmp.	Pct.	Yds.	TD	Int.	Avg.	Att.	Yds.	Avg.	TD	TD	Pts.	F.
1989— Miami NFL	15	50	22	44.0	286	1	3	5.72	4	39	9.8	0	0	0	0
1990— Miami NFL	16	7	3	42.9	17	0	1	2.43	8	34	4.3	0	0	0	0
Pro totals (2 years)	31	57	25	43.9	303	1	4	5.32	12	73	6.1	0	0	0	0

SETTLE, JOHN
RB, REDSKINS

PERSONAL: Born June 2, 1965, at Reidsville, N.C. . . . 5-9/210. . . . Full name: John R. Settle.
HIGH SCHOOL: Rockingham County (Ruffin, N.C.).
COLLEGE: Appalachian State.
TRANSACTIONS/CAREER NOTES: Signed as free agent by Atlanta Falcons (May 1, 1987). . . . On inactive list (September 9, 16; October 28; November 25; and December 9, 1990). . . . Granted unconditional free agency (February 1, 1991). . . . Signed by Washington Redskins (April 1, 1991).
RECORDS/HONORS: Played in Pro Bowl after 1988 season.
PRO STATISTICS: 1987—Returned 10 kickoffs for 158 yards and recovered one fumble. 1988—Recovered one fumble. 1989—Recovered one fumble.

		RUSHING				RECEIVING				TOTAL	
Year Team	G	Att.	Yds.	Avg.	TD	No.	Yds.	Avg.	TD	TD	Pts.	F.
1987— Atlanta NFL	9	19	72	3.8	0	11	153	13.9	0	0	0	2
1988— Atlanta NFL	16	232	1024	4.4	7	68	570	8.4	1	8	48	3
1989— Atlanta NFL	15	179	689	3.9	3	39	316	8.1	2	5	30	1
1990— Atlanta NFL	6	9	16	1.8	0	0	0		0	0	0	0
Pro totals (4 years)	46	439	1801	4.1	10	118	1039	8.8	3	13	78	6

SEWELL, STEVE
RB, BRONCOS

PERSONAL: Born April 2, 1963, at San Francisco.... 6-3/210.... Full name: Steven Edward Sewell.
HIGH SCHOOL: Riordan (San Francisco).
COLLEGE: Oklahoma.
TRANSACTIONS/CAREER NOTES: Selected by Los Angeles Express in first round (16th pick overall) of 1985 USFL draft.... Selected by Denver Broncos in first round (26th pick overall) of 1985 NFL draft.... Signed by Broncos (July 22, 1985).... On injured reserve with separated shoulder (November 14-December 17, 1986).... On injured reserve with broken jaw (November 24, 1987-January 9, 1988).... On injured reserve with shoulder injury (November 9-December 11, 1990).
CHAMPIONSHIP GAME EXPERIENCE: Played in AFC championship game after 1986, 1987 and 1989 seasons.... Played in Super Bowl XXI after 1986 season, Super Bowl XXII after 1987 season and Super Bowl XXIV after 1989 season.
PRO STATISTICS: 1985—Attempted one pass with no completions, returned one kickoff for 29 yards and recovered one fumble. 1986—Attempted one pass with one completion for 23 yards and a touchdown. 1988—Attempted one pass with no completions and recovered three fumbles for four yards. 1990—Attempted one pass with no completions.

| | | RUSHING | | | | RECEIVING | | | | TOTAL | | |
Year Team	G	Att.	Yds.	Avg.	TD	No.	Yds.	Avg.	TD	TD	Pts.	F.
1985— Denver NFL	16	81	275	3.4	4	24	224	9.3	1	5	30	0
1986— Denver NFL	11	23	123	5.4	1	23	294	12.8	1	2	12	0
1987— Denver NFL	7	19	83	4.4	2	13	209	16.1	1	3	18	1
1988— Denver NFL	16	32	135	4.2	1	38	507	13.3	5	6	36	2
1989— Denver NFL	16	7	44	6.3	0	25	416	16.6	3	3	18	0
1990— Denver NFL	12	17	46	2.7	3	26	268	10.3	0	3	18	0
Pro totals (6 years)	78	179	706	3.9	11	149	1918	12.9	11	22	132	3

SHANNON, JOHN
DT, 49ERS

PERSONAL: Born January 18, 1965, at Lexington, Ky.... 6-4/250.... Full name: John Byron Shannon.
HIGH SCHOOL: Boone County (Florence, Ky.).
COLLEGE: Kentucky (bachelor of science degree in communications, 1988).
TRANSACTIONS/CAREER NOTES: Signed as free agent by Chicago Bears (May 17, 1988).... Released by Bears (August 30, 1988).... Re-signed by Bears (September 8, 1988).... Released by Bears (September 5, 1989).... Re-signed by Bears (October 4, 1989).... Granted unconditional free agency (February 1, 1990).... Signed by San Francisco 49ers (March 29, 1990).... Released by 49ers (September 3, 1990).... Selected by London Monarchs in second round (18th defensive lineman) of 1991 WLAF positional draft.... Signed by San Francisco 49ers (July 26, 1991).
PLAYING EXPERIENCE: Chicago NFL, 1988 and 1989; London WLAF, 1991.... Games: 1988 (13), 1989 (12), 1991 (10). Total NFL: 25. Total Pro: 35.
CHAMPIONSHIP GAME EXPERIENCE: Played in NFC championship game after 1988 season.
PRO STATISTICS: WLAF: 1991—Recovered one fumble.

SHARPE, LUIS
OT, CARDINALS

PERSONAL: Born June 16, 1960, at Havana, Cuba.... 6-5/295.... Full name: Luis Ernesto Sharpe Jr.
HIGH SCHOOL: Southwestern (Detroit).
COLLEGE: UCLA.
TRANSACTIONS/CAREER NOTES: Selected by St. Louis Cardinals in first round (16th pick overall) of 1982 NFL draft.... Granted free agency (February 1, 1985).... USFL rights traded by Houston Gamblers to Memphis Showboats for draft picks (April 18, 1985).... Signed by Showboats (April 18, 1985).... Released by Showboats (August 25, 1985).... Re-signed by St. Louis Cardinals (August 31, 1985).... Granted roster exemption (August 31-September 3, 1985).... Franchise transferred to Phoenix (March 15, 1988).
PLAYING EXPERIENCE: St. Louis NFL, 1982-1987; Memphis USFL, 1985; Phoenix NFL, 1988-1990.... Games: 1982 (9), 1983 (16), 1984 (16), 1985 USFL (10), 1985 NFL (16), 1986 (16), 1987 (12), 1988 (16), 1989 (14), 1990 (16). Total NFL: 131. Total Pro: 141.
RECORDS/HONORS: Named as offensive tackle on THE SPORTING NEWS college All-America team, 1981.... Played in Pro Bowl after 1987-1989 seasons.
PRO STATISTICS: 1982—Recovered one fumble. 1983—Rushed once for 11 yards and recovered two fumbles. 1984—Recovered one fumble. 1987—Recovered one fumble. 1989—Recovered one fumble for three yards. 1990—Caught one pass for one yard and a touchdown.

SHARPE, SHANNON
WR, BRONCOS

PERSONAL: Born June 26, 1968, at Chicago.... 6-2/225.... Brother of Sterling Sharpe, wide receiver with Green Bay Packers.
HIGH SCHOOL: Glennville (Ga.).
COLLEGE: Savannah State (Ga.).
TRANSACTIONS/CAREER NOTES: Selected by Denver Broncos in seventh round (192nd pick overall) of 1990 NFL draft.... Signed by Broncos (July, 1990).
PRO STATISTICS: 1990—Fumbled once.

| | | RECEIVING | | | |
Year Team	G	No.	Yds.	Avg.	TD
1990— Denver NFL	16	7	99	14.1	1
Pro totals (1 year)	16	7	99	14.1	1

SHARPE, STERLING
WR, PACKERS

PERSONAL: Born April 6, 1965, at Chicago. . . . 6-1/205. . . . Brother of Shannon Sharpe, wide receiver with Denver Broncos.
HIGH SCHOOL: Glennville (Ga.).
COLLEGE: South Carolina (bachelor's degree in interdisciplinary studies, 1987).
TRANSACTIONS/CAREER NOTES: Selected by Green Bay Packers in first round (seventh pick overall) of 1988 NFL draft. . . . Signed by Packers (July 31, 1988).
RECORDS/HONORS: Named as wide receiver on THE SPORTING NEWS college All-America team, 1987. . . . Played in Pro Bowl after 1989 and 1990 seasons. . . . Named to THE SPORTING NEWS NFL All-Pro team, 1989.
PRO STATISTICS: 1988—Returned nine punts for 48 yards, returned one kickoff for 17 yards and recovered one fumble. 1989—Recovered one fumble for five yards and a touchdown.

		— RUSHING —				— RECEIVING —				— TOTAL —		
Year Team	G	Att.	Yds.	Avg.	TD	No.	Yds.	Avg.	TD	TD	Pts.	F.
1988— Green Bay NFL	16	4	-2	-.5	0	55	791	14.4	1	1	6	3
1989— Green Bay NFL	16	2	25	12.5	0	*90	1423	15.8	12	13	78	1
1990— Green Bay NFL	16	2	14	7.0	0	67	1105	16.5	6	6	36	0
Pro totals (3 years)	48	8	37	4.6	0	212	3319	15.7	19	20	120	4

SHAW, RICKY
LB, CHIEFS

PERSONAL: Born July 28, 1965, at Westchester, N.Y. . . . 6-4/248. . . . Full name: Ricky Andrew Shaw. . . . Nephew of Aundray Bruce, linebacker with Atlanta Falcons.
HIGH SCHOOL: Douglas Byrd (Fayetteville, N.C.).
COLLEGE: Oklahoma State.
TRANSACTIONS/CAREER NOTES: Selected by New York Giants in fourth round (92nd pick overall) of 1988 NFL draft. . . . Signed by Giants (July 18, 1988). . . . Released by Giants (October 25, 1989). . . . Signed as free agent by Philadelphia Eagles (October 28, 1989). . . . On injured reserve with hamstring injury (November 6, 1990-December 21, 1990). . . . Transferred to practice squad (December 21, 1990-remainder of season). . . . Granted unconditional free agency (February 1, 1991). . . . Signed by Kansas City Chiefs (April 2, 1991).
PLAYING EXPERIENCE: New York Giants NFL, 1988; New York Giants (7)-Philadelphia (8) NFL, 1989; Philadelphia NFL, 1990. . . . Games: 1988 (14), 1989 (15), 1990 (8). Total: 37.
PRO STATISTICS: 1988—Recovered one fumble.

SHELLEY, ELBERT
S, FALCONS

PERSONAL: Born December 24, 1964, at Tyronza, Ark. . . . 5-11/185. . . . Full name: Elbert Vernell Shelley.
HIGH SCHOOL: Trumann (Ark.).
COLLEGE: Arkansas State.
TRANSACTIONS/CAREER NOTES: Selected by Atlanta Falcons in 11th round (292nd pick overall) of 1987 NFL draft. . . . Signed by Falcons (July 27, 1987). . . . On injured reserve with neck injury (September 2-November 28, 1987). . . . On injured reserve with wrist injury (September 15-October 12, 1988). . . . Activated after clearing procedural waivers (October 14, 1988). . . . On injured reserve with hamstring injury (December 2, 1989-remainder of season). . . . Granted free agency (February 1, 1990). . . . Re-signed by Falcons (July 17, 1990). . . . Released by Falcons (September 3, 1990). . . . Re-signed by Falcons (September 4, 1990). . . . On injured reserve with hamstring injury (October 17-November 15, 1990).
PLAYING EXPERIENCE: Atlanta NFL, 1987-1990. . . . Games: 1987 (4), 1988 (12), 1989 (10), 1990 (12). Total: 38.
PRO STATISTICS: 1988—Returned two kickoffs for five yards and fumbled once. 1989—Intercepted one pass for 31 yards. 1990—Recovered one fumble.

SHELTON, ANTHONY
CB, CHARGERS

PERSONAL: Born September 4, 1967, at Fayetteville, Tenn. . . . 6-1/195. . . . Full name: Anthony Levala Shelton.
HIGH SCHOOL: Lincoln County (Fayetteville, Tenn.).
COLLEGE: Tennessee State.
TRANSACTIONS/CAREER NOTES: Selected by San Francisco 49ers in 11th round (289th pick overall) of 1990 NFL draft. . . . Signed by 49ers (July 26, 1990). . . . Released by 49ers (September 3, 1990). . . . Awarded on waivers to San Diego Chargers (September 4, 1990). . . . On inactive list (September 9 and 16, 1990).
PLAYING EXPERIENCE: San Diego NFL, 1990. . . . Games: 1990 (14).

SHELTON, RICHARD
CB, STEELERS

PERSONAL: Born January 2, 1966, at Marietta, Ga. . . . 5-9/200. . . . Full name: Richard Eddie Shelton.
HIGH SCHOOL: Marietta (Ga.).
COLLEGE: Liberty (degree in psychology, 1989).
TRANSACTIONS/CAREER NOTES: Selected by Denver Broncos in 11th round (292nd pick overall) of 1989 NFL draft. . . . Signed by Broncos (July 16, 1989). . . . Released by Broncos (October 25, 1989). . . . Signed as free agent by Seattle Seahawks to developmental squad (November 1, 1989). . . . On developmental squad (November 1, 1989-January 7, 1990). . . . Released by Broncos (January 29, 1990). . . . Signed as free agent by Pittsburgh Steelers (March 19, 1990). . . . Released by Steelers (September 4, 1990). . . . Re-signed by Steelers (September 11, 1990). . . . Released by Steelers (September 24, 1990). . . . Signed by WLAF (January 2, 1991). . . . Selected by Montreal Machine in second round (17th defensive back) of 1991 WLAF positional draft. . . . Signed by Pittsburgh Steelers (June 18, 1991).
PRO STATISTICS: WLAF: 1991—Returned one fumble recovery 25 yards for a touchdown.

Year	Team	G	INTERCEPTIONS No.	Yds.	Avg.	TD	PUNT RETURNS No.	Yds.	Avg.	TD	KICKOFF RETURNS No.	Yds.	Avg.	TD	TOTAL TD	Pts.	F.
1989— Denver NFL............		3	0	0		0	0	0		0	0	0		0	0	0	0
1990— Pittsburgh NFL......		2	0	0		0	0	0		0	0	0		0	0	0	0
1991— Montreal WLAF		10	3	65	21.7	1	25	228	9.1	1	2	108	54.0	1	4	24	—
NFL totals (2 years)......		5	0	0		0	0	0		0	0	0		0	0	0	0
WLAF totals (1 year).....		10	3	65	21.7	1	25	228	9.1	1	2	108	54.0	1	4	24	—
Pro totals (3 years).......		15	3	65	21.7	1	25	228	9.1	1	2	108	54.0	1	4	24	0

SHEPARD, DERRICK
WR, COWBOYS

PERSONAL: Born January 22, 1964, at Odessa, Tex. ... 5-10/181. ... Full name: Derrick Lathell Shepard.
HIGH SCHOOL: Odessa (Tex.).
COLLEGE: Oklahoma.
TRANSACTIONS/CAREER NOTES: Signed as free agent by Washington Redskins (May 4, 1987).... Released by Redskins (August 17, 1987).... Re-signed as replacement player by Redskins (September 23, 1987).... Released by Redskins (November 28, 1987).... Re-signed by Redskins (April 15, 1988).... On injured reserve with hip injury (August 29-September 30, 1988).... Activated after clearing procedural waivers (October 1, 1988).... On injured reserve with concussion (November 4-December 8, 1988).... Activated after clearing procedural waivers (December 9, 1988).... Granted unconditional free agency (February 1, 1989).... Signed by New Orleans Saints (March 8, 1989).... Released by Saints (October 3, 1989).... Awarded on waivers to Dallas Cowboys (October 4, 1989). ... Released by Cowboys (September 3, 1990).... Re-signed by Cowboys (September 6, 1990).... On injured reserve with hamstring injury (September 9-November 1, 1990).
PRO STATISTICS: 1989—Rushed three times for 12 yards. 1990—Recovered one fumble.

Year	Team	G	RECEIVING No.	Yds.	Avg.	TD	PUNT RETURNS No.	Yds.	Avg.	TD	KICKOFF RETURNS No.	Yds.	Avg.	TD	TOTAL TD	Pts.	F.
1987— Washington NFL.		2	0	0		0	6	146	24.3	0	1	20	20.0	0	0	0	0
1988— Washington NFL.		5	0	0		0	12	104	8.7	0	16	329	20.6	0	0	0	3
1989— N.O.(4)-Dal.(11) NFL		15	20	304	15.2	1	31	251	8.1	*1	27	529	19.6	0	2	12	2
1990— Dallas NFL..........		8	0	0		0	20	121	6.1	0	4	75	18.8	0	0	0	1
Pro totals (4 years)....		30	20	304	15.2	1	69	622	9.0	1	48	953	19.9	0	2	12	6

SHERMAN, HEATH
RB, EAGLES

PERSONAL: Born March 27, 1967, at Wharton, Tex. ... 6-0/205.
HIGH SCHOOL: El Campo (Tex.).
COLLEGE: Texas A&I.
TRANSACTIONS/CAREER NOTES: Selected by Philadelphia Eagles in sixth round (162nd pick overall) of 1989 NFL draft.... Signed by Eagles (July 25, 1989).... On inactive list (September 9 and December 16, 1990).
PRO STATISTICS: 1989—Recovered three fumbles. 1990—Recovered three fumbles.

Year	Team	G	RUSHING Att.	Yds.	Avg.	TD	RECEIVING No.	Yds.	Avg.	TD	KICKOFF RETURNS No.	Yds.	Avg.	TD	TOTAL TD	Pts.	F.
1989— Philadelphia NFL ...		15	40	177	4.4	2	8	85	10.6	0	13	222	17.1	0	2	12	4
1990— Philadelphia NFL ...		14	164	685	4.2	1	23	167	7.3	3	0	0		0	4	24	4
Pro totals (2 years).......		29	204	862	4.2	3	31	252	8.1	3	13	222	17.1	0	6	36	8

SHERRARD, MIKE
WR, 49ERS

PERSONAL: Born June 21, 1963, at Oakland, Calif. ... 6-2/187. ... Full name: Michael Watson Sherrard. ... Son of Cherrie Sherrard, sprinter in 100-meter hurdles for 1964 U.S. Olympic team.
HIGH SCHOOL: Chino (Calif.).
COLLEGE: UCLA (bachelor of arts degree in history, 1986).
TRANSACTIONS/CAREER NOTES: Selected by Arizona Outlaws in 1986 USFL territorial draft.... Selected by Dallas Cowboys in first round (18th pick overall) of 1986 NFL draft.... Signed by Cowboys (August 7, 1986).... On injured reserve with broken leg (September 1, 1987-entire season).... On reserve/physically unable to perform list with leg injury (July 25, 1988-entire season).... Granted unconditional free agency (February 1, 1989).... Signed by San Francisco 49ers (March 30, 1989).... On reserve/physically unable to perform list with leg injury (August 29, 1989-January 4, 1990).... On injured reserve with broken leg (October 29, 1990-January 11, 1991).
CHAMPIONSHIP GAME EXPERIENCE: Played in NFC championship game after 1989 and 1990 seasons.... Played in Super Bowl XXIV after 1989 season.
PRO STATISTICS: 1986—Rushed twice for 11 yards.

Year	Team	G	RECEIVING No.	Yds.	Avg.	TD
1986— Dallas NFL		16	41	744	18.1	5
1990— San Francisco NFL....		7	17	264	15.5	2
Pro totals (2 years)		23	58	1008	17.4	7

DID YOU KNOW. . .

...that at the end of the 1990 season, the San Francisco 49ers had won their last 19 road games while the Atlanta Falcons had lost 18 straight away from home?

SHULER, MICKEY
TE, EAGLES

PERSONAL: Born August 21, 1956, at Harrisburg, Pa. . . . 6-3/230. . . . Full name: Mickey Charles Shuler.
HIGH SCHOOL: East Pennsboro (Enola, Pa.).
COLLEGE: Penn State (degree in health and physical education).
TRANSACTIONS/CAREER NOTES: Selected by New York Jets in third round (61st pick overall) of 1978 NFL draft. . . . On injured reserve with shoulder separation (September 1-November 14, 1981). . . . On injured reserve with knee injury (October 30, 1989-remainder of season). . . . Released by Jets (September 3, 1990). . . . Signed by Philadelphia Eagles (September 5, 1990).
CHAMPIONSHIP GAME EXPERIENCE: Played in AFC championship game after 1982 season.
RECORDS/HONORS: Played in Pro Bowl after 1986 and 1988 seasons.
PRO STATISTICS: 1978—Returned one kickoff for 12 yards and fumbled once. 1979—Returned one kickoff for 15 yards and fumbled once. 1980—Returned two kickoffs for 25 yards and fumbled once. 1983—Returned one kickoff for three yards. 1984—Returned one kickoff for no yards and fumbled once. 1985—Recovered one fumble and fumbled once. 1986—Returned two kickoffs for minus three yards and recovered one fumble. 1987—Fumbled twice. 1988—Recovered two fumbles and fumbled once. 1990—Fumbled once.

| | | | RECEIVING | | |
Year Team	G	No.	Yds.	Avg.	TD
1978— N.Y. Jets NFL	16	11	67	6.1	3
1979— N.Y. Jets NFL	16	16	225	14.1	3
1980— N.Y. Jets NFL	16	22	226	10.3	2
1981— N.Y. Jets NFL	6	0	0		0
1982— N.Y. Jets NFL	9	8	132	16.5	3
1983— N.Y. Jets NFL	16	26	272	10.5	1
1984— N.Y. Jets NFL	16	68	782	11.5	6
1985— N.Y. Jets NFL	16	76	879	11.6	7
1986— N.Y. Jets NFL	16	69	675	9.8	4
1987— N.Y. Jets NFL	11	43	434	10.1	3
1988— N.Y. Jets NFL	15	70	805	11.5	5
1989— N.Y. Jets NFL	7	29	322	11.1	0
1990— Philadelphia NFL	16	18	190	10.6	0
Pro totals (13 years)	176	456	5009	11.0	37

SIEVERS, ERIC
TE, DOLPHINS

PERSONAL: Born November 9, 1957, at Urbana, Ill. . . . 6-4/238. . . . Full name: Eric Scott Sievers.
HIGH SCHOOL: Washington & Lee (Arlington, Va.).
COLLEGE: Maryland.
TRANSACTIONS/CAREER NOTES: Selected by San Diego Chargers in fourth round (107th pick overall) of 1981 NFL draft. . . . On injured reserve with knee injury (November 19, 1986-remainder of season). . . . On injured reserve with neck injury (October 13-December 6, 1988). . . . Lost through procedural waivers to Los Angeles Rams (December 7, 1988). . . . Granted unconditional free agency (February 1, 1989). . . . Signed by New England Patriots (April 1, 1989). . . . On injured reserve with knee injury (November 6, 1990-remainder of season). . . . Granted unconditional free agency (February 1, 1991). . . . Signed by Miami Dolphins (March 18, 1991).
CHAMPIONSHIP GAME EXPERIENCE: Played in AFC championship game after 1981 season.
PRO STATISTICS: 1981—Returned two kickoffs for four yards and recovered one fumble and fumbled once. 1982—Returned one kickoff for 17 yards. 1983—Returned one kickoff for six yards and rushed once for minus seven yards. 1984—Fumbled once. 1985—Returned one kickoff for three yards. 1989—Fumbled once. 1990—Fumbled once.

| | | | RECEIVING | | |
Year Team	G	No.	Yds.	Avg.	TD
1981— San Diego NFL	16	22	276	12.5	3
1982— San Diego NFL	9	12	173	14.4	1
1983— San Diego NFL	16	33	452	13.7	3
1984— San Diego NFL	14	41	438	10.7	3
1985— San Diego NFL	16	41	438	10.7	6
1986— San Diego NFL	9	2	14	7.0	0
1987— San Diego NFL	12	0	0		0
1988— S.D. (5)-Ram. (2) NFL	7	1	2	2.0	0
1989— New England NFL	16	54	615	11.4	0
1990— New England NFL	8	8	77	9.6	0
Pro totals (10 years)	123	214	2485	11.6	16

SIGLAR, RICKY
G/OT, 49ERS

PERSONAL: Born June 14, 1966, at Albuquerque, N.M. . . . 6-7/296. . . . Full name: Ricky Allan Siglar.
HIGH SCHOOL: Manzano (Albuquerque, N.M.).
COLLEGE: Arizona Western Junior College, then San Jose State.
TRANSACTIONS/CAREER NOTES: Signed as free agent by Dallas Cowboys (March 24, 1989). . . . Released by Cowboys (September 5, 1989). . . . Signed by San Francisco 49ers to developmental squad (September 20, 1989). . . . Released by 49ers (January 29, 1990). . . . Re-signed by 49ers (February 5, 1990).
PLAYING EXPERIENCE: San Francisco NFL, 1990. . . . Games: 1990 (15).
CHAMPIONSHIP GAME EXPERIENCE: Played in NFC championship game after 1990 season.

SIKAHEMA, VAI
RB/KR, PACKERS

PERSONAL: Born August 29, 1962, at Nuku'Alofa, Tonga. . . . 5-9/196. . . . Cousin of Steve Kaufusi, defensive end with Philadelphia Eagles.
HIGH SCHOOL: Mesa (Ariz.).
COLLEGE: Brigham Young.
TRANSACTIONS/CAREER NOTES: Selected by St. Louis Cardinals in 10th round (254th pick overall) of 1986 NFL draft. . . . Selected by Arizona Outlaws in seventh round (47th pick overall) of 1986 USFL draft. . . . Signed by St. Louis Cardinals (July 11, 1986). . . . Crossed picket line during players' strike (October 2, 1987). . . . Franchise transferred to Phoenix (March 15, 1988). . . . On injured reserve with knee injury (November 1-December 2, 1988). . . . Granted free agency (February 1, 1990). . . . Re-signed by Cardinals (July 30, 1990). . . . Granted unconditional free agency (February 1, 1991). . . . Signed by Green Bay Packers (April 1, 1991).
RECORDS/HONORS: Tied NFL record for most touchdowns, punt returns, game (2), against Tampa Bay Buccaneers (December 21, 1986); most touchdowns by combined kick return, game (2), against Tampa Bay Buccaneers (December 21, 1986). . . . Played in Pro Bowl after 1986 and 1987 seasons.
PRO STATISTICS: 1988—Recovered one fumble. 1989—Attempted one pass with no completions and recovered three fumbles. 1990—Recovered one fumble.

Year Team	G	RUSHING				RECEIVING				PUNT RETURNS				KICKOFF RETURNS				TOTALS		
		Att.	Yds.	Avg.	TD	No.	Yds.	Avg.	TD	No.	Yds.	Avg.	TD	No.	Yds.	Avg.	TD	TD	Pts.	F.
1986— St. Louis NFL	16	16	62	3.9	0	10	99	9.9	1	43	*522	12.1	*2	37	847	22.9	0	3	18	2
1987— St. Louis NFL	15	0	0		0	0	0		0	*44	*550	12.5	1	34	761	22.4	0	1	6	0
1988— Phoenix NFL	12	0	0		0	0	0		0	33	341	10.3	0	23	475	20.7	0	0	0	2
1989— Phoenix NFL	16	38	145	3.8	0	23	245	10.7	0	37	433	11.7	0	43	874	20.3	0	0	0	2
1990— Phoenix NFL	16	3	8	2.7	0	7	51	7.3	0	36	306	8.5	0	27	544	20.2	0	0	0	2
Pro totals (5 years)	75	57	215	3.8	0	40	395	9.9	1	193	2152	11.2	3	164	3501	21.4	0	4	24	8

SIMIEN, TRACY
LB, CHIEFS

PERSONAL: Born May 21, 1967, at Bay City, Tex. . . . 6-1/245. . . . Full name: Tracy Anthony Simien. . . . Related to Elmo Wright, wide receiver with Kansas City Chiefs, Houston Oilers and New England Patriots, 1971-1975.
HIGH SCHOOL: Sweeny (Tex.).
COLLEGE: Texas Christian.
TRANSACTIONS/CAREER NOTES: Signed as free agent by Pittsburgh Steelers (May 3, 1989). . . . Released by Steelers (September 5, 1989). . . . Re-signed by Steelers to developmental squad (September 6, 1989). . . . On developmental squad (September 6, 1989-January 5, 1990). . . . Played in one playoff game with Steelers after 1989 season. . . . Granted unconditional free agency (February 1, 1990). . . . Signed by New Orleans Saints (March 30, 1990). . . . Released by Saints (September 3, 1990). . . . Signed by Kansas City Chiefs to practice squad (November 30, 1990). . . . Re-signed by Chiefs after contract expired (February 2, 1991). . . . Assigned to Montreal Machine in 1991 WLAF enhancement allocation program (March 4, 1991).
PLAYING EXPERIENCE: Pittsburgh NFL, 1989; Montreal WLAF, 1991. . . . Games: 1989 (0), 1991 (10). Total Pro: 10.
PRO STATISTICS: WLAF: 1991—Recovered one fumble.

SIMMONDS, MIKE
G, CHARGERS

PERSONAL: Born August 12, 1964, at Belleville, Ill. . . . 6-4/295. . . . Full name: Michael Todd Simmonds.
HIGH SCHOOL: West (Belleville, Ill.).
COLLEGE: Indiana State (degree in general studies, 1989).
TRANSACTIONS/CAREER NOTES: Selected by Tampa Bay Buccaneers in 10th round (252nd pick overall) of 1987 NFL draft. . . . Signed by Buccaneers (July 18, 1989). . . . On injured reserve with broken leg (August 31, 1987-entire season). . . . On injured reserve with knee injury (August 22, 1988-entire season). . . . On injured reserve with knee injury (October 24, 1989-remainder of season). . . . Granted free agency (February 1, 1990). . . . Signed by San Diego Chargers (March 31, 1990). . . . On injured reserve with knee injury (August 27, 1990-entire season).
PLAYING EXPERIENCE: Tampa Bay NFL, 1989. . . . Games: 1989 (5).
PRO STATISTICS: 1990—Recovered one fumble.

SIMMONS, CLYDE
DE, EAGLES

PERSONAL: Born August 4, 1964, at Lanes, S.C. . . . 6-6/280.
HIGH SCHOOL: New Hanover (Wilmington, N.C.).
COLLEGE: Western Carolina.
TRANSACTIONS/CAREER NOTES: Selected by Philadelphia Eagles in ninth round (233rd pick overall) of 1986 NFL draft. . . . Signed by Eagles (July 3, 1986).
PLAYING EXPERIENCE: Philadelphia NFL, 1986-1990. . . . Games: 1986 (16), 1987 (12), 1988 (16), 1989 (16), 1990 (16). Total: 76.
PRO STATISTICS: 1986—Returned one kickoff for no yards. 1987—Recovered one fumble. 1988—Ran 15 yards with blocked field goal attempt, credited with a safety and recovered three fumbles. 1989—Intercepted one pass for 60 yards and a touchdown. 1990—Recovered two fumbles for 28 yards and a touchdown.

SIMMONS, ED
OT, REDSKINS

PERSONAL: Born December 31, 1963, at Seattle. . . . 6-5/300.
HIGH SCHOOL: Nathan Hale (Seattle).
COLLEGE: Eastern Washington.
TRANSACTIONS/CAREER NOTES: Selected by Washington Redskins in sixth round (164th pick overall) of 1987 NFL draft. . . . Signed by Redskins (July 24, 1987). . . . On injured reserve with knee injury (November 23, 1987-remainder of season). . . . On injured reserve with knee injury (December 11, 1990-remainder of season).
PLAYING EXPERIENCE: Washington NFL, 1987-1990. . . . Games: 1987 (5), 1988 (16), 1989 (16), 1990 (13). Total: 50.

SIMMONS, MICHAEL

DE, SAINTS

PERSONAL: Born November 14, 1965, at Eupora, Miss. . . . 6-4/269. . . . Full name: Michael G. Simmons.
HIGH SCHOOL: Eupora (Miss.).
COLLEGE: Mississippi State.
TRANSACTIONS/CAREER NOTES: Signed as free agent by Phoenix Cardinals (May 24, 1988). . . . Released by Cardinals (August 30, 1988). . . . Signed as free agent by New Orleans Saints for 1989 (October 12, 1988). . . . Released by Saints (September 5, 1989). . . . Re-signed by Saints to developmental squad (September 6, 1989). . . . On developmental squad (September 6-December 20, 1989). . . . Activated after clearing procedural waivers (December 22, 1989).
PLAYING EXPERIENCE: New Orleans NFL, 1989 and 1990. . . . Games: 1989 (1), 1990 (16). Total: 17.

SIMMONS, STACEY

WR, COLTS

PERSONAL: Born August 5, 1968, at Clearwater, Fla. . . . 5-9/183. . . . Full name: Stacey Andrew Simmons.
HIGH SCHOOL: Dunedin (Fla.).
COLLEGE: Florida (degree in exercise sports and sciences, 1990).
TRANSACTIONS/CAREER NOTES: Selected by Indianapolis Colts in fourth round (83rd pick overall) of 1990 NFL draft. . . . Signed by Colts (July 20, 1990).
PRO STATISTICS: 1990—Recovered one fumble.

Year Team	G	No.	Yds.	Avg.	TD	No.	Yds.	Avg.	TD	TD	Pts.	F.
			RECEIVING				KICKOFF RETURNS				TOTAL	
1990— Indianapolis NFL	14	4	33	8.3	0	19	348	18.3	0	0	0	1
Pro totals (1 year)	14	4	33	8.3	0	19	348	18.3	0	0	0	1

SIMMS, PHIL

QB, GIANTS

PERSONAL: Born November 3, 1956, at Lebanon, Ky. . . . 6-3/214. . . . Full name: Phillip Simms.
HIGH SCHOOL: Southern (Louisville, Ky.).
COLLEGE: Morehead State.
TRANSACTIONS/CAREER NOTES: Selected by New York Giants in first round (seventh pick overall) of 1979 NFL draft. . . . On injured reserve with separated shoulder (November 18-December 26, 1981). . . . On injured reserve with knee injury (August 30, 1982-entire season). . . . On injured reserve with dislocated thumb (October 13, 1983-remainder of season). . . . On injured reserve with foot injury (December 18, 1990-remainder of 1990 season playoffs).
CHAMPIONSHIP GAME EXPERIENCE: Played in NFC championship game after 1986 season. . . . Played in Super Bowl XXI after 1986 season.
RECORDS/HONORS: Tied NFL record for most consecutive games, 400 or more yards passing (2), 1985. . . . Played in Pro Bowl after 1985 season.
PRO STATISTICS: Passer rating points: 1979 (65.9), 1980 (58.9), 1981 (74.2), 1983 (56.6), 1984 (78.1), 1985 (78.6), 1986 (74.6), 1987 (90.0), 1988 (82.1), 1989 (77.6), 1990 (92.7). Career: 77.0. . . . 1979—Fumbled nine times for minus two yards. 1980—Fumbled six times for minus five yards and recovered two fumbles. 1981—Fumbled seven times for minus 15 yards and recovered two fumbles. 1984—Caught one pass for 13 yards and recovered four fumbles and fumbled eight times for minus five yards. 1985—Recovered five fumbles and fumbled 16 times for minus 22 yards. 1986—Recovered three fumbles and fumbled nine times for minus two yards. 1987—Recovered one fumble. 1988—Recovered one fumble. 1989—Recovered three fumbles and fumbled nine times for minus one yard. 1990—Recovered two fumbles and fumbled seven times for minus five yards.

Year Team	G	Att.	Cmp.	Pct.	Yds.	TD	Int.	Avg.	Att.	Yds.	Avg.	TD	TD	Pts.	F.
				PASSING						RUSHING				TOTAL	
1979— N.Y. Giants NFL	12	265	134	50.6	1743	13	14	6.58	29	166	5.7	1	1	6	9
1980— N.Y. Giants NFL	13	402	193	48.0	2321	15	19	5.77	36	190	5.3	1	1	6	6
1981— N.Y. Giants NFL	10	316	172	54.4	2031	11	9	6.43	19	42	2.2	0	0	0	7
1983— N.Y. Giants NFL	2	13	7	53.8	130	0	1	10.00	0	0		0	0	0	0
1984— N.Y. Giants NFL	16	533	286	53.7	4044	22	18	7.59	42	162	3.9	0	0	0	*8
1985— N.Y. Giants NFL	16	495	275	55.6	3829	22	20	7.74	37	132	3.6	0	0	0	*16
1986— N.Y. Giants NFL	16	468	259	55.3	3487	21	22	7.45	43	72	1.7	1	1	6	9
1987— N.Y. Giants NFL	9	282	163	57.8	2230	17	9	7.91	14	44	3.1	0	0	0	4
1988— N.Y. Giants NFL	15	479	263	54.9	3359	21	11	7.01	33	152	4.6	0	0	0	7
1989— N.Y. Giants NFL	15	405	228	56.3	3061	14	14	7.56	32	141	4.4	1	1	6	9
1990— N.Y. Giants NFL	14	311	184	59.2	2284	15	4	7.34	21	61	2.9	1	1	6	7
Pro totals (11 years)	138	3969	2164	54.5	28519	171	141	7.19	306	1162	3.8	5	5	30	82

SIMS, DARRYL

DE, BROWNS

PERSONAL: Born July 23, 1961, at Winston-Salem, N.C. . . . 6-3/275. . . . Full name: Darryl Leon Sims.
HIGH SCHOOL: Bassick (Bridgeport, Conn.).
COLLEGE: Wisconsin.
TRANSACTIONS/CAREER NOTES: Selected by Jacksonville Bulls in 1985 USFL territorial draft. . . . Selected by Pittsburgh Steelers in first round (20th pick overall) of 1985 NFL draft. . . . . Signed by Steelers (July 18, 1985). . . . Released by Steelers (September 7, 1987). . . . Signed as free-agent replacement player by Cleveland Browns (September 23, 1987). . . . On injured reserve (August 8, 1989-entire season). . . . Released by Browns (May 1, 1990). . . . Re-signed by Browns (July 17, 1990). . . . Released by Browns (September 3, 1990). . . . Re-signed by Browns (April 15, 1991).
PLAYING EXPERIENCE: Pittsburgh NFL, 1985 and 1986; Cleveland NFL, 1987 and 1988. . . . Games: 1985 (16), 1986 (16), 1987 (10), 1988 (16). Total: 58.
CHAMPIONSHIP GAME EXPERIENCE: Played in AFC championship game after 1987 season.
PRO STATISTICS: 1986—Recovered one fumble for two yards.

SIMS, KEITH
G, DOLPHINS

PERSONAL: Born June 17, 1967, at Baltimore. . . . 6-2/305. . . . Full name: Keith A. Sims.
HIGH SCHOOL: Watchung Hills Reg. (Warren, N.J.).
COLLEGE: Iowa State (bachelor of science degree in industrial technology).
TRANSACTIONS/CAREER NOTES: Selected by Miami Dolphins in second round (39th pick overall) of 1990 NFL draft. . . . Signed by Dolphins (July 30, 1990). . . . On inactive list (October 7 and 18, 1990).
PLAYING EXPERIENCE: Miami NFL, 1990. . . . Games: 1990 (14).
PRO STATISTICS: 1990—Returned one kickoff for nine yards and recovered one fumble.

SINGER, CURT
OT, SEAHAWKS

PERSONAL: Born November 4, 1961, at Aliquippa, Pa. . . . 6-5/292. . . . Full name: Curt Edward Singer.
HIGH SCHOOL: Hopewell (Aliquippa, Pa.).
COLLEGE: Tennessee.
TRANSACTIONS/CAREER NOTES: Selected by Memphis Showboats in 1984 USFL territorial draft. . . . Selected by Washington Redskins in sixth round (167th pick overall) of 1984 NFL draft. . . . Signed by Redskins (June 26, 1984). . . . Released by Redskins (August 27, 1984). . . . Re-signed by Redskins (August 28, 1984). . . . On injured reserve with back injury (August 30, 1984-entire season). . . . Released by Redskins (August 20, 1985). . . . Signed as free agent by Seattle Seahawks (April 15, 1986). . . . On injured reserve with ankle injury (September 8, 1987-entire season). . . . Released by Seahawks (August 30, 1988). . . . Signed as free agent by Detroit Lions (September 15, 1988). . . . Traded by Lions to Seattle Seahawks for conditional draft pick (July 28, 1989). . . . Released by Seahawks (September 5, 1989). . . . Signed as free agent by New York Jets (November 6, 1989). . . . Granted free agency (February 1, 1990). . . . Re-signed by Jets (July 20, 1990). . . . Released by Jets (September 3, 1990). . . . Signed by Seattle Seahawks (September 26, 1990). . . . On inactive list (October 7 and 14, 1990). . . . Active for one game in 1990; did not play.
PLAYING EXPERIENCE: Seattle NFL, 1986; Detroit NFL, 1988; New York Jets NFL, 1989; Seattle NFL, 1990. . . . Games: 1986 (11), 1988 (3), 1989 (6), 1990 (0). Total: 20.

SINGLETARY, MIKE
LB, BEARS

PERSONAL: Born October 9, 1958, at Houston. . . . 6-0/230. . . . Full name: Michael Singletary. . . . Uncle of Broderick Thomas, linebacker with Tampa Bay Buccaneers.
HIGH SCHOOL: Evan E. Worthing (Houston).
COLLEGE: Baylor (bachelor of arts degree in management).
TRANSACTIONS/CAREER NOTES: Selected by Chicago Bears in second round (38th pick overall) of 1981 NFL draft. . . . Placed on did-not-report list (August 19 and August 20, 1985). . . . Granted roster exemption (August 21-August 26, 1985).
CHAMPIONSHIP GAME EXPERIENCE: Played in NFC championship game after 1984, 1985 and 1988 seasons. . . . Played in Super Bowl XX after 1985 season.
RECORDS/HONORS: Named as linebacker on THE SPORTING NEWS college All-America team, 1980. . . . Played in Pro Bowl after 1983-1990 seasons. . . . Named to THE SPORTING NEWS NFL All-Pro team, 1984-1989.
PRO STATISTICS: 1982—Recovered one fumble. 1983—Recovered four fumbles for 15 yards. 1984—Recovered one fumble. 1985—Recovered three fumbles for 11 yards. 1987—Recovered one fumble. 1988—Recovered one fumble for four yards. 1990—Recovered one fumble.

			INTERCEPTIONS			
Year	Team	G	No.	Yds.	Avg.	TD
1981—	Chicago NFL	16	1	-3	-3.0	0
1982—	Chicago NFL	9	0	0		0
1983—	Chicago NFL	16	1	0	.0	0
1984—	Chicago NFL	16	1	4	4.0	0
1985—	Chicago NFL	16	1	23	23.0	0
1986—	Chicago NFL	14	1	3	3.0	0
1987—	Chicago NFL	12	0	0		0
1988—	Chicago NFL	16	1	13	13.0	0
1989—	Chicago NFL	16	0	0		0
1990—	Chicago NFL	16	0	0		0
	Pro totals (10 years)	147	6	40	6.7	0

SINGLETARY, REGGIE
OT, EAGLES

PERSONAL: Born January 17, 1964, at Whiteville, N.C. . . . 6-3/285.
HIGH SCHOOL: West Columbus (Cerro Gordo, N.C.).
COLLEGE: North Carolina State.
TRANSACTIONS/CAREER NOTES: Selected by Jacksonville Bulls in 1986 USFL territorial draft. . . . Selected by Philadelphia Eagles in 12th round (315th pick overall) of 1986 NFL draft. . . . Signed by Eagles (May 27, 1986). . . . Released by Eagles (September 5, 1989). . . . Re-signed by Eagles (December 21, 1989).
PLAYING EXPERIENCE: Philadelphia NFL, 1986-1990. . . . Games: 1986 (16), 1987 (12), 1988 (16), 1989 (1), 1990 (16). Total: 61.
PRO STATISTICS: 1986—Recovered one fumble. 1987—Caught one pass for minus 11 yards.

SINGLETON, CHRIS
LB, PATRIOTS

PERSONAL: Born February 20, 1967, at Parsippany, N.J. . . . 6-2/247.
HIGH SCHOOL: Parsippany Hills (Parsippany, N.J.).
COLLEGE: Arizona.
TRANSACTIONS/CAREER NOTES: Selected by New England Patriots in first round (eighth pick overall) of 1990 NFL draft. . . . Signed by Patriots (September 3, 1990). . . . Activated (September 17, 1990). . . . On inactive list (December 30, 1990).
PLAYING EXPERIENCE: New England NFL, 1990. . . . Games: 1990 (13).

SIRAGUSA, TONY

NT, COLTS

PERSONAL: Born May 14, 1967, at Kenilworth, N.J. . . . 6-3/303. . . . Full name: Anthony Siragusa.
HIGH SCHOOL: David Brearly Reg. (Kenilworth, N.J.).
COLLEGE: Pittsburgh.
TRANSACTIONS/CAREER NOTES: Signed as free agent by Indianapolis Colts (April 30, 1990). . . . On inactive list (October 21 and 28, 1990).
PLAYING EXPERIENCE: Indianapolis NFL, 1990. . . . Games: 1990 (13).
PRO STATISTICS: 1990—Recovered one fumble.

SKANSI, PAUL

WR, SEAHAWKS

PERSONAL: Born January 11, 1961, at Tacoma, Wash. . . . 5-11/187. . . . Full name: Paul Anthony Skansi.
HIGH SCHOOL: Peninsula (Gig Harbor, Wash.).
COLLEGE: Washington.
TRANSACTIONS/CAREER NOTES: Selected by Michigan Panthers in fourth round (39th pick overall) of 1983 USFL draft. . . . Selected by Pittsburgh Steelers in fifth round (133rd pick overall) of 1983 NFL draft. . . . Signed by Steelers (June 5, 1983). . . . Released by Steelers (August 27, 1984). . . . Signed as free agent by Seattle Seahawks (October 25, 1984). . . . Released by Seahawks (September 2, 1985). . . . Re-signed by Seahawks (October 2, 1985).
PRO STATISTICS: 1983—Recovered two fumbles. 1985—Recovered one fumble.

| | | RECEIVING | | | | PUNT RETURNS | | | | KICKOFF RETURNS | | | | TOTAL | | |
Year Team	G	No.	Yds.	Avg.	TD	No.	Yds.	Avg.	TD	No.	Yds.	Avg.	TD	TD	Pts.	F.
1983— Pittsburgh NFL ...	15	3	39	13.0	0	43	363	8.4	0	0	0		0	0	0	5
1984— Seattle NFL	7	7	85	12.1	0	16	145	9.1	0	0	0		0	0	0	0
1985— Seattle NFL	12	21	269	12.8	1	31	312	10.1	0	19	358	18.8	0	1	6	1
1986— Seattle NFL	16	22	271	12.3	0	5	38	7.6	0	1	21	21.0	0	0	0	1
1987— Seattle NFL	12	19	207	10.9	1	0	0		0	0	0		0	1	6	1
1988— Seattle NFL	16	24	238	9.9	1	0	0		0	0	0		0	1	6	0
1989— Seattle NFL	16	39	488	12.5	5	0	0		0	0	0		0	5	30	0
1990— Seattle NFL	16	22	257	11.7	2	0	0		0	0	0		0	2	12	0
Pro totals (8 years)	110	157	1854	11.8	10	95	858	9.0	0	20	379	19.0	0	10	60	8

SKOW, JIM

DL, BUCCANEERS

PERSONAL: Born June 29, 1963, at Omaha, Neb. . . . 6-3/250. . . . Full name: James Jeffrey Skow.
HIGH SCHOOL: Roncalli (Omaha, Neb.).
COLLEGE: Nebraska (received degree, 1987).
TRANSACTIONS/CAREER NOTES: Selected by Cincinnati Bengals in third round (58th pick overall) of 1986 NFL draft. . . . Signed by Bengals (August 9, 1986). . . . Traded by Bengals to Tampa Bay Buccaneers for defensive back Rod Jones (September 1, 1990). . . . On injured reserve with elbow injury (November 14-December 17, 1990).
PLAYING EXPERIENCE: Cincinnati NFL, 1986- 1989; Tampa Bay NFL, 1990. . . . Games: 1986 (16), 1987 (12), 1988 (16), 1989 (11), 1990 (12). Total: 67.
CHAMPIONSHIP GAME EXPERIENCE: Played in AFC championship game after 1988 season. . . . Played in Super Bowl XXIII after 1988 season.
PRO STATISTICS: 1990—Recovered one fumble.

SLACK, REGGIE

QB, OILERS

PERSONAL: Born May 2, 1968, at Milton, Fla. . . . 6-1/221. . . . Full name: Reginald Bernard Slack.
HIGH SCHOOL: Milton (Fla.).
COLLEGE: Auburn.
TRANSACTIONS/CAREER NOTES: Selected by Houston Oilers in 12th round (321st pick overall) of 1990 NFL draft. . . . Signed by Oilers (July 23, 1990). . . . Released by Oilers (August 27, 1990). . . . Re-signed by Oilers to practice squad (October 17, 1990). . . . Activated (December 28, 1990). . . . Active for one game in 1990; did not play.

SLATER, JACKIE

OT, RAMS

PERSONAL: Born May 27, 1954, at Jackson, Miss. . . . 6-4/287. . . . Full name: Jackie Ray Slater.
HIGH SCHOOL: Wingfield (Jackson, Miss.).
COLLEGE: Jackson State (bachelor of arts degree).
TRANSACTIONS/CAREER NOTES: Selected by Los Angeles Rams in third round (86th pick overall) of 1976 NFL draft. . . . On injured reserve with knee injury (October 17, 1984-remainder of season). . . . Crossed picket line during players' strike (October 14, 1987). . . . On inactive list (September 9, 1990).
PLAYING EXPERIENCE: Los Angeles Rams NFL, 1976- 1990. . . . Games: 1976 (14), 1977 (14), 1978 (16), 1979 (16), 1980 (15), 1981 (11), 1982 (9), 1983 (16), 1984 (7), 1985 (16), 1986 (16), 1987 (12), 1988 (16), 1989 (16), 1990 (15). Total: 209.
CHAMPIONSHIP GAME EXPERIENCE: Played in NFC championship game after 1976, 1978, 1979, 1985 and 1989 seasons. . . . Played in Super Bowl XIV after 1979 season.
RECORDS/HONORS: Played in Pro Bowl after 1983 and 1985- 1990 seasons.
PRO STATISTICS: 1978—Recovered one fumble. 1980—Recovered one fumble. 1983—Recovered one fumble for 13 yards. 1985—Recovered one fumble.

SLAUGHTER, WEBSTER

WR, BROWNS

PERSONAL: Born October 19, 1964, at Stockton, Calif. . . . 6-1/170. . . . Full name: Webster M. Slaughter.
HIGH SCHOOL: Franklin (Stockton, Calif.).
COLLEGE: San Diego State.
TRANSACTIONS/CAREER NOTES: Selected by Cleveland Browns in second round (43rd pick overall) of 1986 NFL draft. . . . Signed by Browns (July 24, 1986). . . . On injured reserve with broken arm (October 21-December 12, 1988).
CHAMPIONSHIP GAME EXPERIENCE: Played in AFC championship game after 1986, 1987 and 1989 seasons.
RECORDS/HONORS: Played in Pro Bowl after 1989 season.
PRO STATISTICS: 1986—Rushed once for one yard, returned one punt for two yards, recovered fumble in end zone for a touchdown and fumbled once. 1987—Fumbled once. 1988—Fumbled once. 1989—Fumbled twice. 1990—Rushed five times for 29 yards and fumbled twice.

			RECEIVING			
Year	Team	G	No.	Yds.	Avg.	TD
1986— Cleveland NFL		16	40	577	14.4	4
1987— Cleveland NFL		12	47	806	17.2	7
1988— Cleveland NFL		8	30	462	15.4	3
1989— Cleveland NFL		16	65	1236	19.0	6
1990— Cleveland NFL		16	59	847	14.4	4
Pro totals (5 years)		68	241	3928	16.3	24

SMAGALA, STAN

S, COWBOYS

PERSONAL: Born April 6, 1968, at Chicago. . . . 5-10/184. . . . Full name: Stanley Adam Smagala.
HIGH SCHOOL: St. Laurence (Burbank, Ill.).
COLLEGE: Notre Dame.
TRANSACTIONS/CAREER NOTES: Selected by Los Angeles Raiders in fifth round (122nd pick overall) of 1990 NFL draft. . . . Rights traded by Raiders to Dallas Cowboys for 6th-, 8th-, 9th-, 10th- and 11th-round picks of 1990 NFL draft (April 22, 1990). . . . Signed by Cowboys (July 19, 1990). . . . On injured reserve with forearm injury (September 25, 1990-remainder of season).
PLAYING EXPERIENCE: Dallas NFL, 1990. . . . Games: 1990 (3).

SMALL, JESSIE

LB, EAGLES

PERSONAL: Born November 30, 1966, at Boston, Ga. . . . 6-3/240.
HIGH SCHOOL: Central (Thomasville, Ga.).
COLLEGE: Eastern Kentucky.
TRANSACTIONS/CAREER NOTES: Selected by Philadelphia Eagles in second round (49th pick overall) of 1989 NFL draft. . . . Signed by Eagles (July 28, 1989). . . . On inactive list (October 28, 1990).
PLAYING EXPERIENCE: Philadelphia NFL, 1989 and 1990. . . . Games: 1989 (16), 1990 (15). Total: 31.

SMEENGE, JOEL

DE, SAINTS

PERSONAL: Born April 1, 1968, at Holland, Mich. . . . 6-5/255. . . . Full name: Joel Andrew Smeenge. . . . Name pronounced SMEN-ghee.
HIGH SCHOOL: Hudsonville (Mich.).
COLLEGE: Western Michigan.
TRANSACTIONS/CAREER NOTES: Selected by New Orleans Saints in third round (70th pick overall) of 1990 NFL draft. . . . Signed by Saints (July 17, 1990).
PLAYING EXPERIENCE: New Orleans NFL, 1990. . . . Games: 1990 (15).

SMERLAS, FRED

NT, PATRIOTS

PERSONAL: Born April 8, 1957, at Waltham, Mass. . . . 6-3/288. . . . Full name: Frederick C. Smerlas.
HIGH SCHOOL: Waltham (Mass.).
COLLEGE: Boston College.
TRANSACTIONS/CAREER NOTES: Selected by Buffalo Bills in second round (32nd pick overall) of 1979 NFL draft. . . . On injured reserve with knee injury (November 29, 1979-remainder of season). . . . Granted unconditional free agency (February 1, 1990). . . . Signed by San Francisco 49ers (March 28, 1990). . . . On injured reserve with back injury (October 25-December 5, 1990). . . . On practice squad (December 5, 1990-remainder of season and playoffs). . . . Granted unconditional free agency (February 1, 1991). . . . Rights relinquished by 49ers; signed by New England Patriots (July 18, 1991).
PLAYING EXPERIENCE: Buffalo NFL, 1979-1989; San Francisco NFL, 1990. . . . Games: 1979 (13), 1980 (16), 1981 (16), 1982 (9), 1983 (16), 1984 (16), 1985 (16), 1986 (16), 1987 (12), 1988 (16), 1989 (16), 1990 (6). Total: 168.
CHAMPIONSHIP GAME EXPERIENCE: Played in AFC championship game after 1988 season.
RECORDS/HONORS: Played in Pro Bowl after 1980-1983 and 1988 seasons.
PRO STATISTICS: 1979—Recovered three fumbles for 23 yards and one touchdown. 1981—Recovered one fumble for 17 yards. 1982—Recovered two fumbles. 1984—Intercepted one pass for 25 yards and recovered two fumbles. 1985—Recovered one fumble. 1986—Intercepted one pass for three yards. 1988—Recovered one fumble for four yards.

SMITH, AL

LB, OILERS

PERSONAL: Born November 26, 1964, at Los Angeles. . . . 6-1/244. . . . Full name: Al Fredrick Smith. . . . Brother of Aaron Smith, linebacker with Denver Broncos, 1984.
HIGH SCHOOL: St. Bernard (Playa Del Rey, Calif.).
COLLEGE: California State Poly, then Utah State (bachelor of science degree in sociology, 1987).
TRANSACTIONS/CAREER NOTES: Selected by Houston Oilers in sixth round (147th pick overall) of 1987 NFL draft. . . . Signed by

Oilers (July 31, 1987).... On inactive list (December 30, 1990).
PLAYING EXPERIENCE: Houston NFL, 1987-1990.... Games: 1987 (12), 1988 (16), 1989 (15), 1990 (15). Total: 58.
PRO STATISTICS: 1988—Recovered one fumble. 1989—Recovered one fumble. 1990—Recovered one fumble.

SMITH, BEN
DB, EAGLES

PERSONAL: Born May 14, 1967, at Warner Robins, Ga. ... 5-11/185. ... Full name: Benjamin J. Smith.
HIGH SCHOOL: Warner Robins (Ga.).
COLLEGE: Georgia.
TRANSACTIONS/CAREER NOTES: Selected by Philadelphia Eagles in first round (22nd pick overall) of 1990 NFL draft.... Signed by Eagles (August 15, 1990).

			—— INTERCEPTIONS ——			
Year	Team	G	No.	Yds.	Avg.	TD
1990— Philadelphia NFL		16	3	1	.3	0
Pro totals (1 year)		16	3	1	.3	0

SMITH, BILLY RAY
LB, CHARGERS

PERSONAL: Born August 10, 1961, at Fayetteville, Ark. ... 6-3/236. ... Full name: Billy Ray Smith Jr. ... Son of Billy Ray Smith Sr., defensive tackle with Los Angeles Rams, Pittsburgh Steelers and Baltimore Colts, 1957-1962 and 1964-1970.
HIGH SCHOOL: Plano (Tex.).
COLLEGE: Arkansas.
TRANSACTIONS/CAREER NOTES: Selected by Oakland Invaders in first round (seventh pick overall) of 1983 USFL draft.... Selected by San Diego Chargers in first round (fifth pick overall) of 1983 NFL draft.... Signed by Chargers (May 19, 1983).... On injured reserve with back injury (December 20, 1985-remainder of season).... On injured reserve with broken leg (November 23, 1988-remainder of season).... On injured reserve with strained stomach muscle (September 19-October 27, 1990).
RECORDS/HONORS: Named as defensive end on THE SPORTING NEWS college All-America team, 1981 and 1982.
PRO STATISTICS: 1983—Returned one kickoff for 10 yards and recovered one fumble. 1984—Recovered three fumbles. 1985—Recovered three fumbles. 1986—Recovered one fumble. 1987—Had only pass attempt intercepted and recovered three fumbles. 1989—Recovered two fumbles for 23 yards and a touchdown.

			—— INTERCEPTIONS ——			
Year	Team	G	No.	Yds.	Avg.	TD
1983— San Diego NFL		16	0	0		0
1984— San Diego NFL		16	3	41	13.7	0
1985— San Diego NFL		15	1	0	.0	0
1986— San Diego NFL		16	0	0		0
1987— San Diego NFL		12	5	28	5.6	0
1988— San Diego NFL		9	1	9	9.0	0
1989— San Diego NFL		16	1	9	9.0	0
1990— San Diego NFL		11	2	12	6.0	0
Pro totals (8 years)		111	13	99	7.6	0

SMITH, BRIAN
DT, RAMS

PERSONAL: Born April 23, 1966, at Brooklyn, N.Y. ... 6-6/268. ... Full name: Brian Mark Smith. ... Brother of Daryl Smith, cornerback with Cincinnati Bengals and Minnesota Vikings, 1987-1989.
HIGH SCHOOL: Opelika (Ala.).
COLLEGE: Auburn.
TRANSACTIONS/CAREER NOTES: Selected by Los Angeles Rams in second round (48th pick overall) of 1989 NFL draft.... Signed by Rams (July 16, 1989).... On injured reserve with wrist injury (September 5-November 15, 1989).... On developmental squad (November 16-December 6, 1989).
PLAYING EXPERIENCE: Los Angeles Rams NFL, 1989 and 1990.... Games: 1989 (3), 1990 (16). Total: 19.
CHAMPIONSHIP GAME EXPERIENCE: Member of Los Angeles Rams for NFC championship game after 1989 season; inactive.

SMITH, BRUCE
DE, BILLS

PERSONAL: Born June 18, 1963, at Norfolk, Va. ... 6-4/280. ... Full name: Bruce Bernard Smith.
HIGH SCHOOL: Booker T. Washington (Norfolk, Va.).
COLLEGE: Virginia Tech.
TRANSACTIONS/CAREER NOTES: Selected by Baltimore Stars in 1985 USFL territorial draft.... Signed by Buffalo Bills (February 28, 1985).... Selected officially by Bills in first round (first pick overall) of 1985 NFL draft.... On non-football injury list with substance abuse (September 2-September 28, 1988).... Granted free agency (February 1, 1989).... Tendered offer sheet by Denver Broncos (March 23, 1989); matched by Buffalo Bills (March 29, 1989).
PLAYING EXPERIENCE: Buffalo NFL, 1985-1990.... Games: 1985 (16), 1986 (16), 1987 (12), 1988 (12), 1989 (16), 1990 (16). Total: 88.
CHAMPIONSHIP GAME EXPERIENCE: Played in AFC championship game after 1988 and 1990 seasons. ... Played in Super Bowl XXV after 1990 season.
RECORDS/HONORS: Outland Trophy winner, 1984. ... Played in Pro Bowl after 1987-1990 seasons. ... Named to THE SPORTING NEWS NFL All-Pro team, 1987, 1988 and 1990.
PRO STATISTICS: 1985—Rushed once for no yards and recovered four fumbles. 1987—Recovered two fumbles for 15 yards and a touchdown. 1988—Credited with a safety.

SMITH, CEDRIC
RB, VIKINGS

PERSONAL: Born May 27, 1968, at Enterprise, Ala. . . . 5-10/223. . . . Full name: Cedric Delon Smith.
HIGH SCHOOL: Enterprise (Ala.).
COLLEGE: Florida (bachelor of science degree in rehabilitative counseling).
TRANSACTIONS/CAREER NOTES: Selected by Minnesota Vikings in fifth round (131st pick overall) of 1990 NFL draft. . . . Signed by Vikings (July 27, 1990). . . . On inactive list (December 22, 1990).

			RUSHING				KICKOFF RETURNS				TOTAL	
Year Team	G	No.	Yds.	Avg.	TD	No.	Yds.	Avg.	TD	TD	Pts.	F.
1990— Minnesota NFL	15	9	19	2.1	0	1	16	16.0	0	0	0	0
Pro totals (1 year)	15	9	19	2.1	0	1	16	16.0	0	0	0	0

SMITH, DARYLE
OT, EAGLES

PERSONAL: Born January 18, 1964, at Knoxville, Tenn. . . . 6-5/276. . . . Full name: Daryle Ray Smith.
HIGH SCHOOL: Powell (Tenn.).
COLLEGE: Tennessee.
TRANSACTIONS/CAREER NOTES: Signed as free agent by Seattle Seahawks (May 5, 1987). . . . Released by Seahawks (September 7, 1987). . . . Signed as free agent replacement player by Dallas Cowboys (September 23, 1987). . . . Traded by Cowboys to Seattle Seahawks for a ninth-round pick in 1990 NFL draft (July 24, 1989). . . . Released by Seahawks (August 23, 1989). . . . Signed by Cleveland Browns (September 20, 1989). . . . Released by Browns (October 31, 1989). . . . Signed by Philadelphia Eagles (May 10, 1990). . . . Released by Eagles (September 11, 1990). . . . Re-signed by Eagles (October 23, 1990).
PLAYING EXPERIENCE: Dallas NFL, 1987 and 1988; Cleveland NFL, 1989; Philadelphia NFL, 1990. . . . Games: 1987 (9), 1988 (14), 1989 (4), 1990 (3). Total: 30.
PRO STATISTICS: 1988—Returned two kickoffs for 24 yards.

SMITH, DENNIS
S, BRONCOS

PERSONAL: Born February 3, 1959, at Santa Monica, Calif. . . . 6-3/200.
HIGH SCHOOL: Santa Monica (Calif.).
COLLEGE: Southern California.
TRANSACTIONS/CAREER NOTES: Selected by Denver Broncos in first round (15th pick overall) of 1981 NFL draft. . . . On injured reserve with broken arm (November 24, 1987-January 16, 1988). . . . On injured reserve with hamstring injury (September 28-October 31, 1988). . . . On inactive list (September 23, 1990).
CHAMPIONSHIP GAME EXPERIENCE: Played in AFC championship game after 1986, 1987 and 1989 seasons. . . . Played in Super Bowl XXI after 1986 season, Super Bowl XXII after 1987 season and Super Bowl XXIV after 1989 season.
RECORDS/HONORS: Played in Pro Bowl after 1985, 1986, 1989 and 1990 seasons.
PRO STATISTICS: 1981—Recovered two fumbles. 1984—Recovered one fumble for 64 yards and a touchdown. 1986—Recovered one fumble. 1987—Recovered two fumbles. 1988—Recovered two fumbles. 1989—Recovered three fumbles. 1990—Recovered two fumbles.

			INTERCEPTIONS		
Year Team	G	No.	Yds.	Avg.	TD
1981— Denver NFL	16	1	65	65.0	0
1982— Denver NFL	8	1	29	29.0	0
1983— Denver NFL	14	4	39	9.8	0
1984— Denver NFL	15	3	13	4.3	0
1985— Denver NFL	13	3	46	15.3	0
1986— Denver NFL	14	1	0	.0	0
1987— Denver NFL	6	2	21	10.5	0
1988— Denver NFL	11	0	0		0
1989— Denver NFL	14	2	78	39.0	0
1990— Denver NFL	15	1	13	13.0	0
Pro totals (10 years)	126	18	304	16.9	0

SMITH, DOUG
C, RAMS

PERSONAL: Born November 25, 1956, at Columbus, O. . . . 6-3/275. . . . Full name: Carl Douglas Smith.
HIGH SCHOOL: Northland (Columbus, O.).
COLLEGE: Bowling Green State (bachelor of science degree in education, 1978).
TRANSACTIONS/CAREER NOTES: Signed as free agent by Los Angeles Rams (May 16, 1978). . . . On injured reserve with knee injury (September 28, 1979-remainder of season). . . . On injured reserve with knee injury (October 30, 1980-remainder of season). . . . On injured reserve with concussion (December 14, 1985-remainder of season).
PLAYING EXPERIENCE: Los Angeles Rams NFL, 1978-1990. . . . Games: 1978 (16), 1979 (4), 1980 (8), 1981 (16), 1982 (9), 1983 (14), 1984 (16), 1985 (13), 1986 (16), 1987 (12), 1988 (16), 1989 (16), 1990 (16). Total: 172.
CHAMPIONSHIP GAME EXPERIENCE: Played in NFC championship game after 1978 and 1989 seasons.
RECORDS/HONORS: Played in Pro Bowl after 1984 and 1986-1989 seasons. . . . Named to play in Pro Bowl after 1985 season; replaced due to injury by Fred Quillan.
PRO STATISTICS: 1978—Returned one kickoff for eight yards and recovered one fumble. 1981—Fumbled once. 1982—Recovered two fumbles. 1983—Fumbled once. 1985—Recovered one fumble. 1990—Recovered two fumbles.

DID YOU KNOW. . .

. . .that the Washington Redskins are 27-5 in their last 32 games against the St. Louis/Phoenix Cardinals?

SMITH, DOUG
DT, OILERS

PERSONAL: Born June 13, 1959, at Mesic, N.C. . . . 6-6/314. . . . Full name: Douglas Arthur Smith.
HIGH SCHOOL: Pamlico Central (Bayboro, N.C.).
COLLEGE: Auburn.
TRANSACTIONS/CAREER NOTES: Selected by Birmingham Stallions in 1984 USFL territorial draft.
. . . Selected by Houston Oilers in second round (29th pick overall) of 1984 NFL draft. . . . Signed by Birmingham Stallions (August 2, 1984). . . . On developmental squad for one game (March 2-March 8, 1985). . . . Released by Stallions (October 7, 1985). . . . Signed by Houston Oilers (October 10, 1985). . . . Granted roster exemption (October 10, 1985). . . . On injured reserve with hamstring injury (December 16, 1986-remainder of season). . . . Crossed picket line during players' strike (September 29, 1987). . . . On reserve/non-football injury list with substance abuse (November 10-December 7, 1988). . . . Granted free agency (February 1, 1990). . . . Re-signed by Oilers (July 16, 1990). . . . On inactive list (November 26 and December 2, 1990).
PLAYING EXPERIENCE: Birmingham USFL, 1985; Houston NFL, 1985-1990. . . . Games: 1985 USFL (17), 1985 NFL (11), 1986 (13), 1987 (14), 1988 (12), 1989 (15), 1990 (14). Total NFL: 79. Total Pro: 96.
RECORDS/HONORS: Named as defensive tackle on THE SPORTING NEWS USFL All-Star team, 1985.
PRO STATISTICS: USFL: 1985—Credited with five sacks and recovered one fumble. . . . NFL: 1988—Intercepted one pass for 20 yards and recovered two fumbles for three yards. 1990—Recovered one fumble.

SMITH, EMMITT
RB, COWBOYS

PERSONAL: Born May 15, 1969, at Pensacola, Fla. . . . 5-9/203. . . . Full name: Emmitt J. Smith III.
HIGH SCHOOL: Escambia (Pensacola, Fla.).
COLLEGE: Florida.
TRANSACTIONS/CAREER NOTES: Selected by Dallas Cowboys in first round (17th pick overall) of 1990 NFL draft. . . . Signed by Cowboys (September 4, 1990). . . . Granted roster exemption (September 4-September 8, 1990).
RECORDS/HONORS: Named to THE SPORTING NEWS college All-America team, 1989. . . . Played in Pro Bowl after 1990 season.

			RUSHING				RECEIVING				TOTAL	
Year Team	G	Att.	Yds.	Avg.	TD	No.	Yds.	Avg.	TD	TD	Pts.	F.
1990— Dallas NFL	16	241	937	3.9	11	24	228	9.5	0	11	66	7
Pro totals (1 year)	16	241	937	3.9	11	24	228	9.5	0	11	66	7

SMITH, KENDAL
WR, BENGALS

PERSONAL: Born November 23, 1965, at San Mateo, Calif. . . . 5-9/189. . . . Full name: Kendal Carson Smith.
HIGH SCHOOL: Mountain View (Calif.).
COLLEGE: Utah State.
TRANSACTIONS/CAREER NOTES: Selected by Cincinnati Bengals in seventh round (194th pick overall) of 1989 NFL draft. . . . Signed by Bengals (July 22, 1989). . . . Released by Bengals (September 3, 1990). . . . Re-signed by Bengals (September 4, 1990). . . . On inactive list (November 18, 1990). . . . On injured reserve with hamstring injury (November 23, 1990-remainder of season).

		RECEIVING				PUNT RETURNS				KICKOFF RETURNS				TOTAL	
Year Team	G	No.	Yds.	Avg.	TD	No.	Yds.	Avg.	TD	No.	Yds.	Avg.	TD	TD	Pts.	F.
1989— Cincinnati NFL....	11	10	140	14.0	1	12	54	4.5	0	5	65	13.0	0	1	6	1
1990— Cincinnati NFL....	9	7	45	6.4	0	1	4	4.0	0	2	35	17.5	0	0	0	0
Pro totals (2 years)	20	17	185	10.9	1	13	58	4.5	0	7	100	14.3	0	1	6	1

SMITH, LANCE
G, CARDINALS

PERSONAL: Born November 1, 1963, at Kannapolis, N.C. . . . 6-3/290.
HIGH SCHOOL: A.L. Brown (Kannapolis, N.C.).
COLLEGE: Louisiana State.
TRANSACTIONS/CAREER NOTES: Selected by Portland Breakers in 1985 USFL territorial draft.
. . . Selected by St. Louis Cardinals in third round (72nd pick overall) of 1985 NFL draft. . . . Signed by Cardinals (July 21, 1985). . . . Crossed picket line during players' strike (October 2, 1987). . . . Franchise transferred to Phoenix (March 15, 1988).
PLAYING EXPERIENCE: St. Louis NFL, 1985-1987; Phoenix NFL, 1988-1990. . . . Games: 1985 (14), 1986 (15), 1987 (15), 1988 (16), 1989 (16), 1990 (16). Total: 92.
PRO STATISTICS: 1985—Recovered one fumble. 1989—Recovered one fumble.

SMITH, LEONARD
S, BILLS

PERSONAL: Born September 2, 1960, at New Orleans. . . . 5-11/202. . . . Full name: Leonard Phillip Smith.
HIGH SCHOOL: Robert E. Lee (Baton Rouge, La.).
COLLEGE: McNeese State.
TRANSACTIONS/CAREER NOTES: Selected by Boston Breakers in second round (14th pick overall) of 1983 USFL draft. . . . Selected by St. Louis Cardinals in first round (17th pick overall) of 1983 NFL draft. . . . Signed by Cardinals (May 3, 1983). . . . Crossed picket line during players' strike (September 23, 1987). . . . Franchise transferred to Phoenix (March 15, 1988). . . . Traded by Phoenix Cardinals to Buffalo Bills for cornerback Roland Mitchell and sixth-round pick in 1989 draft (September 21, 1988).
CHAMPIONSHIP GAME EXPERIENCE: Played in AFC championship game after 1988 and 1990 seasons. . . . Played in Super Bowl XXV after 1990 season.
PRO STATISTICS: 1983—Returned one kickoff for 19 yards. 1984—Recovered one fumble. 1985—Returned five kickoffs for 68 yards and recovered three fumbles and fumbled once. 1987—Recovered one fumble for 29 yards and a touchdown. 1989—Recovered two fumbles for 14 yards. 1990—Recovered one fumble.

Year	Team	G	No.	Yds.	Avg.	TD
				INTERCEPTIONS		
1983— St. Louis NFL		16	0	0		0
1984— St. Louis NFL		12	2	31	15.5	1
1985— St. Louis NFL		16	2	73	36.5	0
1986— St. Louis NFL		16	1	13	13.0	0
1987— St. Louis NFL		15	0	0		0
1988— Pho.(3)-Buf.(13) NFL		16	2	29	14.5	0
1989— Buffalo NFL		15	2	46	23.0	0
1990— Buffalo NFL		16	2	39	19.5	1
Pro totals (8 years)		122	11	231	21.0	2

SMITH, MONTE
G, BRONCOS

PERSONAL: Born April 24, 1967, at Madison, Wis. . . . 6-5/270. . . . Full name: Monte Gene Smith.
HIGH SCHOOL: Oregon (Wis.).
COLLEGE: North Dakota.
TRANSACTIONS/CAREER NOTES: Selected by Denver Broncos in ninth round (236th pick overall) of 1989 NFL draft. . . . Signed by Broncos (July 19, 1989). . . . On reserve/non-football injury list with foot injury (August 28, 1990-entire season).
PLAYING EXPERIENCE: Denver NFL, 1989. . . . Games: 1989 (14).
CHAMPIONSHIP GAME EXPERIENCE: Played in AFC championship game after 1989 season. . . . Played in Super Bowl XXIV after 1989 season.

SMITH, NEIL
DE, CHIEFS

PERSONAL: Born April 10, 1966, at New Orleans. . . . 6-4/275.
HIGH SCHOOL: McDonogh 35 (New Orleans).
COLLEGE: Nebraska.
TRANSACTIONS/CAREER NOTES: Selected by Kansas City Chiefs in first round (second pick overall) of 1988 NFL draft. . . . Signed by Chiefs (July 19, 1988).
PLAYING EXPERIENCE: Kansas City NFL, 1988-1990. . . . Games: 1988 (13), 1989 (15), 1990 (16). Total: 44.
RECORDS/HONORS: Named as defensive lineman on THE SPORTING NEWS college All-America team, 1987.
PRO STATISTICS: 1989—Recovered two fumbles for three yards and a touchdown. 1990—Recovered one fumble.

SMITH, QUINTIN
WR, BEARS

PERSONAL: Born August 17, 1968, at Houston. . . . 5-10/172.
HIGH SCHOOL: Jack Yates (Houston).
COLLEGE: Kansas.
TRANSACTIONS/CAREER NOTES: Signed as free agent by Chicago Bears (April 25, 1990). . . . Released by Bears (September 3, 1990). . . . Re-signed by Bears (September 4, 1990). . . . Released by Bears (October 6, 1990). . . . Re-signed by Bears to practice squad (October 8, 1990-remainder of season).

Year	Team	G	No.	Yds.	Avg.	TD
				RECEIVING		
1990— Chicago NFL		4	2	20	10.0	0
Pro totals (1 year)		4	2	20	10.0	0

SMITH, SAMMIE
RB, DOLPHINS

PERSONAL: Born May 16, 1967, at Orlando, Fla. . . . 6-2/230. . . . Full name: Sammie Lee Smith.
HIGH SCHOOL: Apopka (Fla.).
COLLEGE: Florida State.
TRANSACTIONS/CAREER NOTES: Selected by Miami Dolphins in first round (ninth pick overall) of 1989 NFL draft. . . . Signed by Dolphins (September 11, 1989).
PRO STATISTICS: 1990—Recovered two fumbles.

Year	Team	G	Att.	Yds.	Avg.	TD	No.	Yds.	Avg.	TD	TD	Pts.	F.
			RUSHING				RECEIVING				TOTAL		
1989— Miami NFL		13	200	659	3.3	6	7	81	11.6	0	6	36	6
1990— Miami NFL		16	226	831	3.7	8	11	134	12.2	1	9	54	8
Pro totals (2 years)		29	426	1490	3.5	14	18	215	11.9	1	15	90	14

SMITH, SEAN
DE, PATRIOTS

PERSONAL: Born May 29, 1967, at Cincinnati. . . . 6-7/280. . . . Full name: Sean Warfield Smith.
HIGH SCHOOL: Wyoming (O.).
COLLEGE: Georgia Tech.
TRANSACTIONS/CAREER NOTES: Selected by New England Patriots in 11th round (280th pick overall) of 1990 NFL draft. . . . Signed by Patriots (July 18, 1990).
PLAYING EXPERIENCE: New England NFL, 1990. . . . Games: 1990 (15).

SMITH, STEVE
RB, RAIDERS

PERSONAL: Born August 30, 1964, at Washington, D.C. . . . 6-1/240. . . . Full name: Steven Anthony Smith.
HIGH SCHOOL: DeMatha Catholic (Hyattsville, Md.).
COLLEGE: Penn State (degree in hotel, restaurant and institutional management, 1987).
TRANSACTIONS/CAREER NOTES: Selected by Los Angeles Raiders in third round (81st pick overall) of 1987 NFL draft. . . . Signed by Raiders (July 22, 1987). . . . On injured reserve with knee injury (September 16-October 24, 1987). . . . On injured reserve with knee and ankle injuries (December 3, 1987-remainder of season). . . . Granted free agency (February 1, 1990). . . . Re-signed by Raiders (August 14, 1990).
CHAMPIONSHIP GAME EXPERIENCE: Played in AFC championship game after 1990 season.
PRO STATISTICS: 1987—Recovered one fumble. 1988—Returned three kickoffs for 46 yards and recovered one fumble. 1989—Returned two kickoffs for 19 yards and recovered one fumble. 1990—Recovered one fumble.

		RUSHING				RECEIVING				TOTAL		
Year Team	G	Att.	Yds.	Avg.	TD	No.	Yds.	Avg.	TD	TD	Pts.	F.
1987— L.A. Raiders NFL	7	5	18	3.6	0	3	46	15.3	0	0	0	0
1988— L.A. Raiders NFL	16	38	162	4.3	3	26	299	11.5	6	9	54	1
1989— L.A. Raiders NFL	16	117	471	4.0	1	19	140	7.4	0	1	6	2
1990— L.A. Raiders NFL	16	81	327	4.0	2	4	30	7.5	3	5	30	3
Pro totals (4 years)	55	241	978	4.1	6	52	515	9.9	9	15	90	6

SMITH, VERNICE
G/OT, CARDINALS

PERSONAL: Born October 24, 1964, at Orlando, Fla. . . . 6-3/298. . . . Full name: Vernice C. Smith.
HIGH SCHOOL: Oak Ridge (Orlando, Fla.).
COLLEGE: Florida A&M.
TRANSACTIONS/CAREER NOTES: Signed as free agent by Miami Dolphins (May 22, 1987). . . . Released by Dolphins (September 7, 1987). . . . Signed as free agent by Dallas Cowboys (March 8, 1988). . . . Released by Cowboys (August 30, 1988). . . . Signed as free agent by Cleveland Browns (March 24, 1989). . . . Released by Browns (August 30, 1989). . . . Signed by Phoenix Cardinals to developmental squad (September 14, 1989). . . . Released by Cardinals (November 1, 1989). . . . Re-signed by Cardinals to developmental squad (November 8, 1989). . . . Released by Cardinals (January 3, 1990). . . . Re-signed by Cardinals (off-season, 1990).
PLAYING EXPERIENCE: Phoenix NFL, 1990. . . . Games: 1990 (11).

SMITH, VINSON
LB, COWBOYS

PERSONAL: Born July 3, 1965, at Statesville, N.C. . . . 6-2/225. . . . Full name: Vinson Robert Smith.
HIGH SCHOOL: Statesville, N.C.
COLLEGE: East Carolina (received degree, 1989).
TRANSACTIONS/CAREER NOTES: Signed as free agent by Atlanta Falcons (May 2, 1988). . . . On injured reserve with elbow injury (August 29-November 2, 1988). . . . Activated after clearing procedural waivers (November 4, 1988). . . . On injured reserve with knee injury (December 10, 1988-remainder of season). . . . Granted unconditional free agency (February 1, 1989). . . . Signed by Pittsburgh Steelers (February 28, 1989). . . . On injured reserve with broken foot (August 29, 1989-entire season). . . . Granted unconditional free agency (February 1, 1990). . . . Signed by Dallas Cowboys (March 3, 1990).
PLAYING EXPERIENCE: Atlanta NFL, 1988; Dallas NFL, 1990. . . . Games: 1988 (3), 1990 (16). Total: 19.
PRO STATISTICS: 1990—Recovered two fumbles.

SNOW, PERCY
LB, CHIEFS

PERSONAL: Born November 5, 1967, at Canton, O. . . . 6-2/250. . . . Full name: Percy Lee Snow.
HIGH SCHOOL: McKinley (Canton, O.).
COLLEGE: Michigan State.
TRANSACTIONS/CAREER NOTES: Selected by Kansas City Chiefs in first round (13th pick overall) of 1990 NFL draft. . . . Signed by Chiefs (August 21, 1990). . . . On inactive list (December 30, 1990).
PLAYING EXPERIENCE: Kansas City NFL, 1990. . . . Games: 1990 (15).
RECORDS/HONORS: Named as linebacker to THE SPORTING NEWS college All-America team, 1988 and 1989.
PRO STATISTICS: 1990—Intercepted one pass for no yards.

SOCHIA, BRIAN
NT/DE, DOLPHINS

PERSONAL: Born July 21, 1961, at Massena, N.Y. . . . 6-3/278. . . . Name pronounced so-SHAY.
HIGH SCHOOL: St. Lawrence Central (Brasher Falls, N.Y.).
COLLEGE: Northwestern Oklahoma State.
TRANSACTIONS/CAREER NOTES: Signed as free agent by Houston Oilers (June 2, 1983). . . . On injured reserve with knee and ankle injuries (August 29-September 27, 1983). . . . Activated after clearing procedural waivers (September 27, 1983). . . . Granted free agency (February 1, 1986). . . . Re-signed by Oilers (October 21, 1986). . . . Granted roster exemption (October 21-November 2, 1986). . . . Released by Oilers (November 3, 1986). . . . Signed as free agent by Miami Dolphins (November 12, 1986). . . . On reserve/non-football illness list for steroid use (August 23-September 29, 1990). . . . On injured reserve with groin injury (October 12-December 8, 1990).
PLAYING EXPERIENCE: Houston NFL, 1983-1985; Miami NFL, 1986-1990. . . . Games: 1983 (12), 1984 (16), 1985 (16), 1986 (6), 1987 (12), 1988 (16), 1989 (16), 1990 (5). Total: 99.
RECORDS/HONORS: Played in Pro Bowl after 1988 season.
PRO STATISTICS: 1988—Recovered two fumbles. 1990—Recovered one fumble for 13 yards and a touchdown.

SOLOMON, JESSE
LB, COWBOYS

PERSONAL: Born November 4, 1963, at Madison, Fla. . . . 6-0/235. . . . Full name: Jesse William Solomon.
HIGH SCHOOL: Madison (Fla.).
COLLEGE: North Florida Junior College, then Florida State (bachelor of science degree in political science, 1986).
TRANSACTIONS/CAREER NOTES: Selected by Tampa Bay Bandits in 1986 USFL territorial draft. . . . Selected by Minnesota Vikings in 12th round (318th pick overall) of 1986 NFL draft. . . . Signed by Vikings (July 27, 1986). . . . Granted free agency (February 1, 1989). . . . Re-signed by Vikings and granted roster exemption (September 6-September 15, 1989). . . . Traded as part of a six-player, 12 draft-choice deal in which Dallas Cowboys sent running back Herschel Walker to Minnesota Vikings in exchange for Solomon, cornerback Issiac Holt, linebacker David Howard, running back Darrin Nelson, defensive end Alex Stewart, first-round pick in 1992 draft and conditional first-round picks in 1990 and 1991 drafts, conditional second-round picks in 1990, 1991 and 1992 drafts and conditional third-round pick in 1992 draft (October 12, 1989); Nelson refused to report to Dallas and was traded to San Diego Chargers, with Minnesota giving Dallas a sixth-round pick in 1990 as well as the original conditional second-round pick in 1991 and San Diego sending a fifth-round pick in 1990 to Minnesota through Dallas (October 17, 1989); deal completed with Dallas retaining Howard, Solomon and Holt and all conditional picks and Cowboys sending third-round picks in 1990 and 1991 and 10th-round pick in 1990 to Minnesota (February 2, 1990). . . . Granted free agency (February 1, 1990). . . . Re-signed by Cowboys (October 18, 1990). . . . On inactive list (October 21, 1990). . . . Activated (October 27, 1990).
CHAMPIONSHIP GAME EXPERIENCE: Played in NFC championship game after 1987 season.
PRO STATISTICS: 1986—Recovered two fumbles. 1987—Recovered one fumble for 33 yards. 1988—Recovered two fumbles for three yards.

				INTERCEPTIONS		
Year	Team	G	No.	Yds.	Avg.	TD
1986— Minnesota NFL		13	2	34	17.0	0
1987— Minnesota NFL		12	1	30	30.0	0
1988— Minnesota NFL		16	4	84	21.0	1
1989— Min.(4)-Dal.(11) NFL...		15	0	0		0
1990— Dallas NFL		9	0	0		0
Pro totals (5 years)		65	7	148	21.1	1

SOLT, RON
G, EAGLES

PERSONAL: Born May 19, 1962, at Bainebridge, Md. . . . 6-3/275. . . . Full name: Ronald Matthew Solt.
HIGH SCHOOL: James M. Coughlin (Wilkes-Barre, Pa.).
COLLEGE: Maryland.
TRANSACTIONS/CAREER NOTES: Selected by Washington Federals in 1984 USFL territorial draft. . . . Selected by Indianapolis Colts in first round (19th pick overall) of 1984 NFL draft. . . . Signed by Colts (August 11, 1984). . . . On injured reserve with knee injury (December 17, 1985-remainder of season). . . . Granted free agency (February 1, 1988). . . . Re-signed by Colts (September 28, 1988). . . . Traded by Colts to Philadelphia Eagles for first-round pick in 1989 draft and fourth-round pick in 1990 draft (October 5, 1988). . . . On injured reserve with knee injury (November 12, 1988-remainder of season). . . . On reserve/non-football injury list with steroid use (August 29-September 25, 1989). . . . Reinstated and granted roster exemption (September 26-October 2, 1989).
PLAYING EXPERIENCE: Indianapolis NFL, 1984-1987; Indianapolis (1)-Philadelphia (1) NFL, 1988; Philadelphia NFL, 1989 and 1990. . . . Games: 1984 (16), 1985 (15), 1986 (16), 1987 (12), 1988 (2), 1989 (13), 1990 (15). Total: 89.
RECORDS/HONORS: Played in Pro Bowl after 1987 season.
PRO STATISTICS: 1984—Recovered one fumble.

SPEARS, ERNEST
S, SAINTS

PERSONAL: Born November 6, 1967, at Oceanside, Calif. . . . 5-11/192.
HIGH SCHOOL: El Camino (Oceanside, Calif.).
COLLEGE: Southern California (degree in communications).
TRANSACTIONS/CAREER NOTES: Selected by New Orleans Saints in 10th round (267th pick overall) of 1990 NFL draft. . . . Signed by Saints (July 16, 1990).
PLAYING EXPERIENCE: New Orleans NFL, 1990. . . . Games: 1990 (16).

SPIELMAN, CHRIS
LB, LIONS

PERSONAL: Born October 11, 1965, at Canton, O. . . . 6-0/247.
HIGH SCHOOL: Washington (Massillon, O.).
COLLEGE: Ohio State.
TRANSACTIONS/CAREER NOTES: Selected by Detroit Lions in second round (29th pick overall) of 1988 NFL draft. . . . Signed by Lions (July 15, 1988). . . . On injured reserve with separated shoulder (September 19-October 26, 1990).
PLAYING EXPERIENCE: Detroit NFL, 1988-1990. . . . Games: 1988 (16), 1989 (16), 1990 (12). Total: 44.
RECORDS/HONORS: Named as linebacker on THE SPORTING NEWS college All-America team, 1986 and 1987. . . . Played in Pro Bowl after 1989 and 1990 seasons.
PRO STATISTICS: 1988—Recovered one fumble. 1989—Recovered two fumbles for 31 yards. 1990—Intercepted one pass for 12 yards and recovered two fumbles.

SPINDLER, MARC
DL, LIONS

PERSONAL: Born November 28, 1969, at West Scranton, Pa. . . . 6-5/277. . . . Full name: Marc Rudolph Spindler.
HIGH SCHOOL: West Scranton (Scranton, Pa.).
COLLEGE: Pittsburgh.
TRANSACTIONS/CAREER NOTES: Selected by Detroit Lions in third round (62nd pick overall) of 1990 NFL draft. . . . Signed by

Lions (July 24, 1990).... On injured reserve with knee injury (September 27, 1990-remainder of season).
PLAYING EXPERIENCE: Detroit NFL, 1990.... Games: 1990 (3).
RECORDS/HONORS: Named as defensive tackle on THE SPORTING NEWS college All-America team, 1989.

STALLWORTH, RON
DE, CHIEFS

PERSONAL: Born February 25, 1966, at Pensacola, Fla.... 6-5/260.... Full name: Ronald Tobias Stallworth.
HIGH SCHOOL: W.J. Woodham (Pensacola, Fla.).
COLLEGE: Auburn (degree in business management, 1989).
TRANSACTIONS/CAREER NOTES: Selected by New York Jets in fourth round (98th pick overall) of 1989 NFL draft.... Signed by Jets (July 21, 1989).... Traded by Jets to Kansas City Chiefs for offensive lineman Irv Eatman (February 1, 1991).
PLAYING EXPERIENCE: New York Jets NFL, 1989 and 1990.... Games: 1989 (16), 1990 (16). Total: 32.
PRO STATISTICS: 1990—Recovered one fumble.

STALLWORTH, TIM
WR, BRONCOS

PERSONAL: Born August 26, 1966, at Pacoima, Calif.... 5-10/185.... Cousin of John Stallworth, wide receiver with Pittsburgh Steelers, 1974-1987.
HIGH SCHOOL: Montclair Prep (Van Nuys, Calif.).
COLLEGE: Washington State.
TRANSACTIONS/CAREER NOTES: Selected by Los Angeles Rams in sixth round (161st pick overall) of 1990 NFL draft.... Signed by Rams (July 9, 1990).... Released by Rams (September 3, 1990).... Signed by Detroit Lions to practice squad (October 1, 1990).... Signed by Denver Broncos (December 29, 1990).
PLAYING EXPERIENCE: Denver NFL, 1990.... Games: 1990 (1).

STAMS, FRANK
LB, RAMS

PERSONAL: Born July 17, 1965, at Akron, O.... 6-2/240.... Full name: Frank Michael Stams.... Nephew of Steve Stonebreaker, linebacker with Minnesota Vikings, Baltimore Colts and New Orleans Saints, 1962-1968; and cousin of Mike Stonebreaker, rookie linebacker with Chicago Bears.
HIGH SCHOOL: St. Vincent St. Mary (Akron, O.).
COLLEGE: Notre Dame (bachelor of arts degree, 1989).
TRANSACTIONS/CAREER NOTES: Selected by Los Angeles Rams in second round (45th pick overall) of 1989 NFL draft.... Signed by Rams (July 26, 1989).... On inactive list (December 23 and 31, 1990).
PLAYING EXPERIENCE: Los Angeles Rams NFL, 1989 and 1990.... Games: 1989 (16), 1990 (14). Total: 30.
CHAMPIONSHIP GAME EXPERIENCE: Played in NFC championship game after 1989 season.
PRO STATISTICS: 1989—Intercepted one pass for 20 yards.

STANLEY, WALTER
WR, REDSKINS

PERSONAL: Born November 5, 1962, at Chicago.... 5-9/180.
HIGH SCHOOL: South Shore (Chicago).
COLLEGE: Colorado, then Mesa College (Colo.).
TRANSACTIONS/CAREER NOTES: Selected by Memphis Showboats in fourth round (54th pick overall) of 1985 USFL draft.... Selected by Green Bay Packers in fourth round (98th pick overall) of 1985 NFL draft.... Signed by Packers (July 19, 1985).... On injured reserve with separated shoulder (October 18, 1988-remainder of season).... Released by Packers (September 4, 1989).... Awarded on waivers to Detroit Lions (September 6, 1989).... Released by Lions (September 11, 1989).... Re-signed by Lions (September 12, 1989).... Granted unconditional free agency (February 1, 1990).... Signed by Washington Redskins (March 22, 1990).... On injured reserve with knee injury (November 14, 1990-remainder of season).
RECORDS/HONORS: Named as punt returner on THE SPORTING NEWS NFL All-Pro team, 1989.
PRO STATISTICS: 1986—Rushed once for 19 yards. 1987—Rushed four times for 38 yards and recovered three fumbles. 1988—Rushed once for one yard and recovered one fumble. 1989—Recovered one fumble.

		—RECEIVING—				—PUNT RETURNS—				–KICKOFF RETURNS–				—TOTAL—		
Year	Team	G	No.	Yds.	Avg.	TD	No.	Yds.	Avg.	TD	No.	Yds.	Avg.	TD	TD	Pts.	F.
1985— Green Bay NFL....		13	0	0		0	14	179	12.8	0	9	212	23.6	0	0	0	2
1986— Green Bay NFL....		16	35	723	20.7	2	33	316	9.6	1	28	559	20.0	0	3	18	1
1987— Green Bay NFL....		12	38	672	17.7	3	28	173	6.2	0	3	47	15.7	0	3	18	5
1988— Green Bay NFL....		7	28	436	15.6	0	12	52	4.3	0	2	39	19.5	0	0	0	3
1989— Detroit NFL		14	24	304	12.7	0	36	496	*13.8	0	9	95	10.6	0	0	0	5
1990— Washington NFL.		9	2	15	7.5	0	24	176	7.3	0	9	177	19.7	0	0	0	3
Pro totals (6 years)....		71	127	2150	16.9	5	147	1392	9.5	1	60	1129	18.8	0	6	36	19

STARGELL, TONY
CB, JETS

PERSONAL: Born August 7, 1966, at LaGrange, Ga.... 5-11/180.
HIGH SCHOOL: LaGrange (Ga.).
COLLEGE: Tennessee State (degree in health and physical education).
TRANSACTIONS/CAREER NOTES: Selected by New York Jets in third round (56th pick overall) of 1990 NFL draft.... Signed by Jets (July 22, 1990).
PRO STATISTICS: 1990—Recovered one fumble.

			—INTERCEPTIONS—			
Year	Team	G	No.	Yds.	Avg.	TD
1990— N.Y. Jets NFL..............		16	2	-3	-1.5	0
Pro totals (1 year)		16	2	-3	-1.5	0

STARK, ROHN
P, COLTS

PERSONAL: Born May 4, 1959, at Minneapolis. . . . 6-3/203. . . . Full name: Rohn Taylor Stark. . . . First name pronounced RON.
HIGH SCHOOL: Pine River (Minn.).
COLLEGE: United States Air Force Academy Prep School, then Florida State (degree in finance).
TRANSACTIONS/CAREER NOTES: Selected by Baltimore Colts in second round (34th pick overall) of 1982 NFL draft. . . . Franchise transferred to Indianapolis (March 31, 1984).
RECORDS/HONORS: Led NFL in punting yards with 4,124 in 1983. . . . Named as punter on THE SPORTING NEWS college All-America team, 1981. . . . Played in Pro Bowl after 1985, 1986 and 1990 seasons.
PRO STATISTICS: 1982—Attempted one pass with no completions, rushed once for eight yards and fumbled once. 1983—Attempted one pass with no completions and rushed once for eight yards. 1984—Attempted one pass with one interception, rushed twice for no yards and recovered one fumble. 1985—Attempted one pass with no completions and recovered one fumble. 1986—Recovered one fumble and fumbled once. 1989—Rushed once for minus 11 yards. 1990—Attempted one pass with one completion for 40 yards.

			— PUNTING—		
Year	Team	G	No.	Avg.	Blk.
1982— Baltimore NFL		9	46	44.4	0
1983— Baltimore NFL		16	91	*45.3	0
1984— Indianapolis NFL		16	*98	44.7	0
1985— Indianapolis NFL		16	78	*45.9	*2
1986— Indianapolis NFL		16	76	*45.2	0
1987— Indianapolis NFL		12	61	40.0	*2
1988— Indianapolis NFL		16	64	43.5	0
1989— Indianapolis NFL		16	79	42.9	1
1990— Indianapolis NFL		16	71	43.4	1
Pro totals (9 years)		133	664	43.9	6

STAUROVSKY, JASON
PK, PATRIOTS

PERSONAL: Born March 23, 1963, at Tulsa, Okla. . . . 5-9/170. . . . Full name: Jason Charles Staurovsky. . . . Name pronounced star-OFF-skee.
HIGH SCHOOL: Bishop Kelley (Tulsa, Okla.).
COLLEGE: Tulsa (bachelor of science degree in finance).
TRANSACTIONS/CAREER NOTES: Signed as free agent by Buffalo Bills (May 6, 1986). . . . Released by Bills (August 18, 1986). . . . Signed as free agent by New Orleans Saints (June 26, 1987). . . . Released by Saints (August 9, 1987). . . . Signed as free agent by St. Louis Cardinals (September 4, 1987). . . . Released by Cardinals (September 7, 1987). . . . Re-signed as replacement player by Cardinals (September 25, 1987). . . . Released by Cardinals (October 20, 1987). . . . Signed as free agent by New England Patriots (April 20, 1988). . . . Released by Patriots (August 17, 1988). . . . Re-signed by Patriots (October 27, 1988). . . . Granted unconditional free agency (February 1, 1989). . . . Did not receive qualifying offer (April 15, 1989). . . . Re-signed by Patriots (May 25, 1989). . . . Released by Patriots (August 30, 1989). . . . Re-signed by Patriots (November 8, 1989).

			— PLACE-KICKING—				
Year	Team	G	XPM	XPA	FGM	FGA	Pts.
1987— St. Louis NFL		2	6	6	1	3	9
1988— New England NFL		8	14	15	7	11	35
1989— New England NFL		7	14	14	14	17	56
1990— New England NFL		16	19	19	16	22	67
Pro totals (4 years)		33	53	54	38	53	167

STEINKUHLER, DEAN
OT, OILERS

PERSONAL: Born January 27, 1961, at Burr, Neb. . . . 6-3/287. . . . Name pronounced STINE-COOLER.
HIGH SCHOOL: Sterling (Neb.).
COLLEGE: Nebraska.
TRANSACTIONS/CAREER NOTES: Selected by Arizona Wranglers in sixth round (116th pick overall) of 1984 USFL draft. . . . Signed by Houston Oilers (April 30, 1984). . . . Selected officially by Oilers in first round (second pick overall) of 1984 NFL draft. . . . On injured reserve with knee injury (November 5, 1984-remainder of season). . . . On injured reserve with knee injury (October 11-December 20, 1985). . . . Active for six games with Oilers in 1985; did not play.
PLAYING EXPERIENCE: Houston NFL, 1984-1990. . . . Games: 1984 (10), 1986 (16), 1987 (11), 1988 (16), 1989 (16), 1990 (15). Total: 84.
RECORDS/HONORS: Outland Trophy winner, 1983. . . . Named as guard on THE SPORTING NEWS college All-America team, 1983.
PRO STATISTICS: 1986—Recovered two fumbles. 1988—Recovered two fumbles.

STEPHEN, SCOTT
LB, PACKERS

PERSONAL: Born June 18, 1964, at Los Angeles. . . . 6-2/243.
HIGH SCHOOL: Manual Arts (Los Angeles).
COLLEGE: Arizona State.
TRANSACTIONS/CAREER NOTES: Selected by Green Bay Packers in third round (69th pick overall) of 1987 NFL draft. . . . Signed by Packers (July 29, 1987).
PLAYING EXPERIENCE: Green Bay NFL, 1987-1990. . . . Games: 1987 (8), 1988 (16), 1989 (16), 1990 (16). Total: 56.
PRO STATISTICS: 1989—Intercepted two passes for 16 yards and recovered one fumble for 76 yards. 1990—Intercepted two passes for 26 yards, recovered two fumbles for 15 yards and fumbled once.

STEPHENS, JOHN
RB, PATRIOTS

PERSONAL: Born February 23, 1966, at Shreveport, La. . . . 6-1/215. . . . Full name: John Milton Stephens.
HIGH SCHOOL: Springhill (La.).
COLLEGE: Northwestern (La.) State.
TRANSACTIONS/CAREER NOTES: Selected by New England Patriots in first round (17th pick overall) of 1988 NFL draft. . . . Signed by Patriots (July 29, 1988).
RECORDS/HONORS: Played in Pro Bowl after 1988 season.
PRO STATISTICS: 1988—Recovered three fumbles for four yards (including one in end zone for a touchdown). 1989—Recovered one fumble. 1990—Attempted one pass with one interception and recovered three fumbles.

Year Team	G	RUSHING				RECEIVING				TOTAL		
		Att.	Yds.	Avg.	TD	No.	Yds.	Avg.	TD	TD	Pts.	F.
1988— New England NFL	16	297	1168	3.9	4	14	98	7.0	0	5	30	3
1989— New England NFL	14	244	833	3.4	7	21	207	9.9	0	7	42	3
1990— New England NFL	16	212	808	3.8	2	28	196	7.0	1	3	18	5
Pro totals (3 years)	46	753	2809	3.7	13	63	501	8.0	1	15	90	11

STEPHENS, ROD
LB, SEAHAWKS

PERSONAL: Born June 14, 1966, at Atlanta. . . . 6-1/237. . . . Full name: Rodrequis La'Vant Stephens.
HIGH SCHOOL: North Fulton (Atlanta).
COLLEGE: Georgia Tech.
TRANSACTIONS/CAREER NOTES: Signed as free agent by Seattle Seahawks (April 26, 1989). . . . Released by Seahawks (September 5, 1989). . . . Re-signed by Seahawks to developmental squad (September 6, 1989). . . . On developmental squad (September 6-September 20, 1989). . . . Activated after clearing procedural waivers (September 22, 1989). . . . Released by Seahawks (November 13, 1989). . . . Re-signed by Seahawks to developmental squad (November 14, 1989). . . . On developmental squad (November 14-November 29, 1989). . . . Activated after clearing procedural waivers (December 1, 1989). . . . Granted unconditional free agency (February 1, 1990). . . . Signed by Denver Broncos (April 1, 1990). . . . Released by Broncos (August 22, 1990). . . . Signed by Seattle Seahawks (December 5, 1990).
PLAYING EXPERIENCE: Seattle NFL, 1989 and 1990. . . . Games: 1989 (10), 1990 (4). Total: 14.

STEPNOSKI, MARK
C, COWBOYS

PERSONAL: Born January 20, 1967, at Erie, Pa. . . . 6-2/271. . . . Full name: Mark Matthew Stepnoski.
HIGH SCHOOL: Cathedral Prep (Erie, Pa.).
COLLEGE: Pittsburgh.
TRANSACTIONS/CAREER NOTES: Selected by Dallas Cowboys in third round (57th pick overall) of 1989 NFL draft. . . . Signed by Cowboys (July 23, 1989).
PLAYING EXPERIENCE: Dallas NFL, 1989 and 1990. . . . Games: 1989 (16), 1990 (16). Total: 32.
RECORDS/HONORS: Named as guard on THE SPORTING NEWS college All-America team, 1988.
PRO STATISTICS: 1989—Recovered three fumbles. 1990—Returned one kickoff 15 yards.

STEWART, ANDREW
DE, BENGALS

PERSONAL: Born November 20, 1965, at Jamaica. . . . 6-5/265.
HIGH SCHOOL: West Hempstead (N.Y.).
COLLEGE: Fresno City College (Calif.), then Cincinnati.
TRANSACTIONS/CAREER NOTES: Selected by Cleveland in fourth round (107th pick overall) of 1989 NFL draft. . . . Signed by Cleveland Browns (July 18, 1989). . . . On injured reserve with foot injury (September 3-November 28, 1990). . . . Released by Browns (November 28, 1990). . . . Signed by Cincinnati Bengals (March 12, 1991).
PLAYING EXPERIENCE: Cleveland NFL, 1989. . . . Games: 1989 (16).
CHAMPIONSHIP GAME EXPERIENCE: Played in AFC championship game after 1989 season.

STEWART, MICHAEL
S, RAMS

PERSONAL: Born July 12, 1965, at Atascadero, Calif. . . . 6-0/199.
HIGH SCHOOL: Bakersfield (Calif.).
COLLEGE: Bakersfield College (Calif.), then Fresno State.
TRANSACTIONS/CAREER NOTES: Selected by Los Angeles Rams in eighth round (213th pick overall) of 1987 NFL draft. . . . Signed by Rams (July 6, 1987). . . . Granted free agency (February 1, 1990). . . . Re-signed by Rams (September 3, 1990). . . . Activated (September 7, 1990).
PLAYING EXPERIENCE: Los Angeles Rams NFL, 1987-1990. . . . Games: 1987 (12), 1988 (16), 1989 (16), 1990 (16). Total: 60.
CHAMPIONSHIP GAME EXPERIENCE: Played in NFC championship game after 1989 season.
MISCELLANEOUS: Selected by Milwaukee Brewers' organization in 29th round of free-agent baseball draft (June 4, 1984). . . . Selected by Minnesota Twins' organization in 26th round of free-agent baseball draft (June 2, 1986). . . . Selected by Toronto Blue Jays' organization in 49th round of free-agent baseball draft (June 2, 1987).
PRO STATISTICS: 1987—Credited with a safety. 1988—Intercepted two passes for 61 yards, returned one kickoff for no yards and recovered two fumbles for 24 yards. 1989—Intercepted two passes for 76 yards and a touchdown, recovered three fumbles for four yards and fumbled once. 1990—Recovered two fumbles.

DID YOU KNOW. . .

. . .that the first round of the 1991 NFL draft took 4 hours, 55 minutes to complete, making it the longest since the first NFL-AFL combined draft in 1967?

STILLS, KEN
S, VIKINGS

PERSONAL: Born September 6, 1963, at Oceanside, Calif. . . . 5-10/186. . . . Full name: Kenneth Lee Stills.
HIGH SCHOOL: El Camino (Oceanside, Calif.).
COLLEGE: El Camino College (Calif.), then Wisconsin.
TRANSACTIONS/CAREER NOTES: Selected by Jacksonville Bulls in 1985 USFL territorial draft. . . . Selected by Green Bay Packers in eighth round (209th pick overall) of 1985 NFL draft. . . . Signed by Packers (July 19, 1985). . . . Released by Packers (September 2, 1985). . . . Re-signed by Packers (October 30, 1985). . . . On injured reserve with bruised thigh (December 10, 1988-remainder of season). . . . Granted unconditional free agency (February 1, 1990). . . . Signed by Minnesota Vikings (March 19, 1990). . . . On injured reserve with pulled calf muscle (September 4-October 6, 1990).
PRO STATISTICS: 1985—Returned one kickoff for 14 yards. 1986—Returned 10 kickoffs for 209 yards (20.9 avg.) and fumbled once. 1987—Recovered one fumble. 1988—Recovered three fumbles for four yards and returned one kickoff for four yards.

			— INTERCEPTIONS —			
Year	Team	G	No.	Yds.	Avg.	TD
1985— Green Bay NFL		8	0	0		0
1986— Green Bay NFL		16	1	58	58.0	1
1987— Green Bay NFL		11	0	0		0
1988— Green Bay NFL		14	3	29	9.7	0
1989— Green Bay NFL		16	3	20	6.7	0
1990— Minnesota NFL		12	0	0		0
Pro totals (6 years)		77	7	107	15.3	1

STINSON, LEMUEL
CB, BEARS

PERSONAL: Born May 10, 1966, at Houston. . . . 5-9/159. . . . Full name: Lemuel Dale Stinson.
HIGH SCHOOL: Evan E. Worthing (Houston).
COLLEGE: Texas Tech.
TRANSACTIONS/CAREER NOTES: Selected by Chicago Bears in sixth round (161st pick overall) of 1988 NFL draft. . . . Signed by Bears (June 30, 1988). . . . On injured reserve with knee injury (December 7, 1989-remainder of season). . . . On injured reserve with knee injury (November 24, 1990-remainder of season).
CHAMPIONSHIP GAME EXPERIENCE: Played in NFC championship game after 1988 season.

			— INTERCEPTIONS —			
Year	Team	G	No.	Yds.	Avg.	TD
1988— Chicago NFL		15	0	0		0
1989— Chicago NFL		12	4	59	14.8	1
1990— Chicago NFL		10	6	66	11.0	0
Pro totals (3 years)		37	10	125	12.5	1

STOCK, MARK
WR, PACKERS

PERSONAL: Born April 27, 1966, at Canton, O. . . . 5-11/187. . . . Full name: Mark Anthony Stock.
HIGH SCHOOL: Marist (Atlanta).
COLLEGE: Virginia Military Institute (bachelor of arts degree in economics, 1989).
TRANSACTIONS/CAREER NOTES: Selected by Pittsburgh Steelers in sixth round (144th pick overall) of 1989 NFL draft. . . . Signed by Steelers (July 20, 1989). . . . Released by Steelers (September 5, 1989). . . . Re-signed by Steelers to developmental squad (September 6, 1989). . . . On developmental squad (September 6-November 3, 1989). . . . Released by Steelers (September 4, 1990). . . . Signed by Green Bay Packers (April 23, 1991).

			— RECEIVING —			
Year	Team	G	No.	Yds.	Avg.	TD
1989— Pittsburgh NFL		8	4	74	18.5	0
Pro totals (1 year)		8	4	74	18.5	0

STOKES, FRED
DE, REDSKINS

PERSONAL: Born March 14, 1964, at Vidalia, Ga. . . . 6-3/262. . . . Full name: Louis Fred Stokes.
HIGH SCHOOL: Vidalia (Ga.).
COLLEGE: Georgia Southern.
TRANSACTIONS/CAREER NOTES: Selected by Los Angeles Rams in 12th round (332nd pick overall) of 1987 NFL draft. . . . Signed by Rams (July 18, 1987). . . . On injured reserve with shoulder injury (September 7-November 7, 1987). . . . On injured reserve with ankle injury (October 8, 1988-remainder of season). . . . Granted unconditional free agency (February 1, 1989). . . . Signed by Washington Redskins (March 20, 1989).
PLAYING EXPERIENCE: Los Angeles Rams NFL, 1987 and 1988; Washington NFL, 1989 and 1990. . . . Games: 1987 (8), 1988 (5), 1989 (16), 1990 (16). Total: 45.
PRO STATISTICS: 1988—Recovered two fumbles. 1989—Credited with a safety and recovered two fumbles for six yards. 1990—Recovered four fumbles for five yards.

STONE, DWIGHT
WR/RB, STEELERS

PERSONAL: Born January 28, 1964, at Florala, Ala. . . . 6-0/190.
HIGH SCHOOL: Florala (Ala.) and Marion Military Institute (Marion, Ala.).
COLLEGE: Middle Tennessee State.
TRANSACTIONS/CAREER NOTES: Signed as free agent by Pittsburgh Steelers (May 19, 1987). . . . Crossed picket line during players' strike (October 7, 1987).
PRO STATISTICS: 1987—Recovered one fumble. 1989—Recovered one fumble. 1990—Recovered two fumbles.

Year — Team	G	RUSHING Att.	Yds.	Avg.	TD	RECEIVING No.	Yds.	Avg.	TD	KICKOFF RETURNS No.	Yds.	Avg.	TD	TOTAL TD	Pts.	F.
1987— Pittsburgh NFL	14	17	135	7.9	0	1	22	22.0	0	28	568	20.3	0	0	0	0
1988— Pittsburgh NFL	16	40	127	3.2	0	11	196	17.8	1	29	610	21.0	*1	2	12	5
1989— Pittsburgh NFL	16	10	53	5.3	0	7	92	13.1	0	7	173	24.7	0	0	0	2
1990— Pittsburgh NFL	16	2	-6	-3.0	0	19	332	17.5	1	5	91	18.2	0	1	6	1
Pro totals (4 years)	62	69	309	4.5	0	38	642	16.9	2	69	1442	20.9	1	3	18	8

STOUDT, CLIFF
QB, COWBOYS

PERSONAL: Born March 27, 1955, at Oberlin, O. . . . 6-4/222. . . . Full name: Clifford Lewis Stoudt.
HIGH SCHOOL: Oberlin (O.).
COLLEGE: Youngstown State.
TRANSACTIONS/CAREER NOTES: Selected by Pittsburgh Steelers in fifth round (121st pick overall) of 1977 NFL draft. . . . Active for 11 games with Steelers in 1977; did not play. . . . Active for 16 games with Steelers in 1978 and 1979; did not play. . . . On injured reserve with broken arm (November 12, 1981-remainder of season). . . . On inactive list (September 13, 1982). . . . Signed by Birmingham Stallions of USFL with contract to take effect after being granted free agency February 1, 1984 (January 10, 1984). . . . Granted free agency when USFL suspended operations (August 7, 1986). . . . Re-signed by Pittsburgh Steelers and traded to St. Louis Cardinals for fifth-round pick in 1988 draft (September 2, 1986). . . . Franchise transferred to Phoenix (March 15, 1988). . . . Granted free agency (February 1, 1989). . . . Rights released (March 14, 1989). . . . Signed by Miami Dolphins (April 14, 1989). . . . Released by Miami Dolphins (September 5, 1989). . . . Re-signed by Dolphins (September 7, 1989). . . . Released by Dolphins (August 28, 1990). . . . Signed by Dallas Cowboys (December 23, 1990). . . . Active for one game with Cowboys in 1990; did not play.
CHAMPIONSHIP GAME EXPERIENCE: Member of Pittsburgh Steelers for AFC championship game after 1978 and 1979 seasons; did not play. . . . Member of Steelers for Super Bowl XIII after 1978 season and Super Bowl XIV after 1979 season; did not play.
PRO STATISTICS: NFL Passer rating points: 1980 (78.0), 1981 (53.5), 1982 (14.2), 1983 (60.6), 1986 (53.5), 1987 (39.6), 1988 (64.3). Total: 58.3. . . . USFL Passer rating points: 1984 (101.6), 1985 (91.2). Total: 95.9. . . . NFL: 1980—Recovered one fumble and fumbled once for minus two yards. 1983—Recovered two fumbles. 1988—Recovered two fumbles. . . . USFL: 1984—Credited with one 2-point conversion. 1985—Recovered two fumbles.

Year — Team	G	PASSING Att.	Cmp.	Pct.	Yds.	TD	Int.	Avg.	RUSHING Att.	Yds.	Avg.	TD	TOTAL TD	Pts.	F.
1980— Pittsburgh NFL	6	60	32	53.3	493	2	2	8.22	9	35	3.9	0	0	0	1
1981— Pittsburgh NFL	2	3	1	33.3	17	0	0	5.67	3	11	3.7	0	0	0	0
1982— Pittsburgh NFL	6	35	14	40.0	154	0	5	4.40	11	28	2.6	0	0	0	1
1983— Pittsburgh NFL	16	381	197	51.7	2553	12	21	6.70	77	479	6.2	4	4	24	10
1984— Birmingham USFL	17	366	212	57.9	3121	26	7	8.53	68	440	6.5	9	9	56	1
1985— Birmingham USFL	18	444	266	59.9	3358	34	19	7.56	80	437	5.5	5	5	30	9
1986— St. Louis NFL	5	91	52	57.1	542	3	7	5.96	7	53	7.6	0	0	0	1
1987— St. Louis NFL	12	1	0	.0	0	0	0	.00	1	-2	-2.0	0	0	0	0
1988— Phoenix NFL	16	113	63	55.8	747	6	8	6.61	14	57	4.1	0	0	0	4
1989— Miami NFL	3	0	0		0	0	0		0	0		0	0	0	0
NFL totals (8 years)	66	684	359	52.5	4506	23	43	6.59	122	661	5.4	4	4	24	17
USFL totals (2 years)	35	810	478	59.0	6479	60	26	8.00	148	877	5.9	14	14	86	10
Pro totals (10 years)	101	1494	837	56.0	10985	83	69	7.35	270	1538	5.7	18	18	110	27

STOUFFER, KELLY
QB, SEAHAWKS

PERSONAL: Born July 6, 1964, at Scottsbluff, Neb. . . . 6-3/207. . . . Full name: Kelly Wayne Stouffer. . . . Name pronounced STOFF-er.
HIGH SCHOOL: Rushville (Neb.).
COLLEGE: Garden City Community College (Kan.), then Colorado State (bachelor of science degree in biology).
TRANSACTIONS/CAREER NOTES: Selected by St. Louis Cardinals in first round (sixth pick overall) of 1987 NFL draft. . . . On reserve/unsigned list (entire 1987 season). . . . Franchise transferred to Phoenix (March 15, 1988). . . . Rights traded by Phoenix Cardinals to Seattle Seahawks for fifth-round pick in 1988 draft and first- and fifth-round picks in 1989 draft (April 22, 1988). . . . Signed by Seattle Seahawks (April 22, 1988). . . . On inactive list (September 9, 16, 23; October 1, 7, 14; November 4, 11, 18, 25; and December 2, 9, 16, 23 and 30, 1990). . . . Active for one game in 1990; did not play.
PRO STATISTICS: Passer rating points: 1988 (69.2), 1989 (40.9). Career: 62.0. . . . 1988—Recovered one fumble and fumbled five times for minus 17 yards. 1989—Recovered one fumble.

Year — Team	G	PASSING Att.	Cmp.	Pct.	Yds.	TD	Int.	Avg.	RUSHING Att.	Yds.	Avg.	TD	TOTAL TD	Pts.	F.
1988— Seattle NFL	8	173	98	56.7	1106	4	6	6.39	19	27	1.4	0	0	0	5
1989— Seattle NFL	3	59	29	49.2	270	0	3	4.58	2	11	5.5	0	0	0	3
Pro totals (2 years)	11	232	127	54.7	1376	4	9	5.93	21	38	1.8	0	0	0	8

STOWE, TYRONNE
LB, CARDINALS

PERSONAL: Born May 30, 1965, at Passaic, N.J. . . . 6-1/249. . . . Full name: Tyronne Kevin Stowe.
HIGH SCHOOL: Passaic (N.J.).
COLLEGE: Rutgers.
TRANSACTIONS/CAREER NOTES: Signed as free agent by San Diego Chargers (April 30, 1987). . . . Released by Chargers (September 7, 1987). . . . Signed as replacement player by Pittsburgh Steelers (September 24, 1987). . . . Released by Steelers (October 22, 1988). . . . Re-signed by Steelers (December 1, 1988). . . . Granted unconditional free agency (February 1, 1991). . . . Signed by Phoenix Cardinals (February 25, 1991).

PLAYING EXPERIENCE: Pittsburgh NFL, 1987-1990. . . . Games: 1987 (13), 1988 (10), 1989 (16), 1990 (16). Total: 55.
PRO STATISTICS: 1990—Credited with safety on blocked punt out of the end zone and recovered one fumble.

STOYANOVICH, PETE
PK, DOLPHINS

PERSONAL: Born April 28, 1967, at Dearborn, Mich. . . . 5-10/185. . . . Full name: Peter Stoyanovich. . . . Named pronounced sto-YAWN-o-vich.
HIGH SCHOOL: Crestwood (Dearborn Heights, Mich.).
COLLEGE: Indiana (bachelor of arts degree in public affairs, 1989).
TRANSACTIONS/CAREER NOTES: Selected by Miami Dolphins in eighth round (203rd pick overall) of 1989 NFL draft. . . . Signed by Dolphins (July 27, 1989).

				— PLACE-KICKING —		
Year Team	G	XPM	XPA	FGM	FGA	Pts.
1989— Miami NFL.................	16	38	39	19	26	95
1990— Miami NFL.................	16	37	37	21	25	100
Pro totals (2 years)	32	75	76	40	51	195

STRACHAN, STEVE
RB, PATRIOTS

PERSONAL: Born March 22, 1963, at Everett, Mass. . . . 6-1/225. . . . Full name: Stephen Michael Strachan.
HIGH SCHOOL: Burlington (Mass.).
COLLEGE: Boston College (bachelor of science degree in finance, 1985).
TRANSACTIONS/CAREER NOTES: Selected by Los Angeles Raiders in 11th round (303rd pick overall) of 1985 NFL draft. . . . Signed by Raiders (June 28, 1985). . . . Released by Raiders (August 27, 1985). . . . Re-signed by Raiders (September 23, 1985). . . . On injured reserve with hamstring injury (October 23, 1985-remainder of season). . . . Crossed picket line during players' strike (October 14, 1987). . . . Released by Raiders (August 22, 1990). . . . Signed by New England Patriots (April 12, 1991).
PRO STATISTICS: 1988—Recovered three fumbles.

		— RUSHING —				— RECEIVING —				— TOTAL —		
Year Team	G	Att.	Yds.	Avg.	TD	No.	Yds.	Avg.	TD	TD	Pts.	F.
1985— L.A. Raiders NFL	4	2	1	.5	0	0	0	0	0	0	0	0
1986— L.A. Raiders NFL	16	18	53	2.9	0	0	0	0	0	0	0	0
1987— L.A. Raiders NFL	11	28	108	3.9	0	4	42	10.5	0	0	0	1
1988— L.A. Raiders NFL	16	4	12	3.0	0	3	19	6.3	1	1	6	2
1989— L.A. Raiders NFL	16	0	0	0	0	0	0	0	0	0	0	0
Pro totals (5 years)	63	52	174	3.4	0	7	61	8.7	1	1	6	3

STRADFORD, TROY
RB, CHIEFS

PERSONAL: Born September 11, 1964, at Elizabeth, N.J. . . . 5-9/194. . . . Full name: Troy Edwin Stradford.
HIGH SCHOOL: Linden (N.J.).
COLLEGE: Boston College (bachelor of arts degree in communications, 1987).
TRANSACTIONS/CAREER NOTES: Selected by Miami Dolphins in fourth round (99th pick overall) of 1987 NFL draft. . . . Signed by Dolphins (July 24, 1987). . . . On injured reserve with knee injury (October 24, 1989-remainder of season). . . . Granted free agency (February 1, 1990). . . . Re-signed by Dolphins (September 10, 1990). . . . Granted roster exemption (September 10-September 15, 1990). . . . On injured reserve with hamstring injury (December 26, 1990-remainder of 1990 season playoffs). . . . Granted unconditional free agency (February 1, 1991). . . . Signed by Kansas City Chiefs (April 1, 1991).
PRO STATISTICS: 1987—Attempted one pass with one completion for six yards and recovered two fumbles. 1988—Attempted one pass with no completions. 1989—Recovered one fumble.

		— RUSHING —				— RECEIVING —				— PUNT RETURNS —				KICKOFF RETURNS				— TOTALS —		
Year Team	G	Att.	Yds.	Avg.	TD	No.	Yds.	Avg.	TD	No.	Yds.	Avg.	TD	No.	Yds.	Avg.	TD	TD	Pts.	F.
1987— Miami NFL..........	12	145	619	4.3	6	48	457	9.5	1	0	0		0	14	258	18.4	0	7	42	6
1988— Miami NFL..........	15	95	335	3.5	2	56	426	7.6	0	0	0		0	0	0		0	3	18	2
1989— Miami NFL..........	7	66	240	3.6	1	25	233	9.3	0	14	129	9.2	0	0	0		0	1	6	4
1990— Miami NFL..........	14	37	138	3.7	1	30	257	8.6	0	3	4	1.3	0	3	56	18.7	0	1	6	5
Pro totals (4 years)	48	343	1332	3.9	10	159	1373	8.6	2	17	133	7.8	0	17	314	18.5	0	12	72	17

STRAUTHERS, THOMAS
DE, VIKINGS

PERSONAL: Born April 6, 1961, at Wesson, Miss. . . . 6-4/262. . . . Full name: Thomas Bryan Strauthers.
HIGH SCHOOL: Brookhaven (Miss.).
COLLEGE: Jackson State.
TRANSACTIONS/CAREER NOTES: Selected by Oakland Invaders in 21st round (247th pick overall) of 1983 USFL draft. . . . Selected by Philadelphia Eagles in 10th round (258th pick overall) of 1983 NFL draft. . . . Signed by Eagles (June 15, 1983). . . . On injured reserve with broken hand (August 16-November 23, 1983). . . . Activated after clearing procedural waivers (November 25, 1983). . . . Granted free agency (February 1, 1984). . . . Re-signed by Eagles (August 11, 1987). . . . Released by Eagles after failing physical (August 12, 1987). . . . Signed as free agent by Miami Dolphins (August 21, 1987). . . . Released by Dolphins (September 7, 1987). . . . Signed as free agent by Atlanta Falcons (February 22, 1988). . . . Released by Falcons (September 2, 1988). . . . Signed as free agent by Detroit Lions (October 5, 1988). . . . Granted unconditional free agency (February 1, 1989). . . . Signed by Minnesota Vikings (March 16, 1989). . . . On injured reserve with foot injury (December 21-December 29, 1990). . . . On inactive list (December 30, 1990).
PLAYING EXPERIENCE: Philadelphia NFL, 1983-1986; Detroit NFL, 1988; Minnesota NFL, 1989 and 1990. . . . Games: 1983 (4), 1984 (16), 1985 (16), 1986 (11), 1988 (10), 1989 (12), 1990 (13). Total: 82.
PRO STATISTICS: 1984—Returned one kickoff for 12 yards. 1990—Recovered one fumble.

STREETER, GEORGE
DB, COLTS

PERSONAL: Born August 28, 1967, at Chicago. . . . 6-2/215. . . . Full name: George Leon Streeter.
HIGH SCHOOL: Percy L. Julian (Chicago).
COLLEGE: Notre Dame.
TRANSACTIONS/CAREER NOTES: Selected by Chicago Bears in 11th round (304th pick overall) of 1989 NFL draft. . . . Signed by Bears (May 18, 1989). . . . Released by Bears (August 29, 1989). . . . Re-signed by Bears to developmental squad (September 20, 1989). . . . On developmental squad (September 20 and 21, 1989). . . . Activated after clearing procedural waivers (September 22, 1989). . . . Released by Bears (October 3, 1989). . . . Re-signed by Bears to developmental squad (October 4, 1989). . . . On developmental squad (October 4-December 7, 1989). . . . Granted unconditional free agency (February 1, 1990). . . . Signed by Los Angeles Raiders (February 13, 1990). . . . Released by Raiders (August 27, 1990). . . . Signed by Atlanta Falcons (August 30, 1990). . . . Released by Falcons (September 4, 1990). . . . Signed by Indianapolis Colts (November 28, 1990). . . . Released by Colts (December 24, 1990). . . . Re-signed by Colts (February 11, 1991).
PLAYING EXPERIENCE: Chicago NFL, 1989; Indianapolis NFL, 1990. . . . Games: 1989 (4), 1990 (4). Total: 8.
PRO STATISTICS: 1989—Recovered one fumble.

STRICKLAND, FRED
LB, RAMS

PERSONAL: Born August 15, 1966, at Ringwood, N.J. . . . 6-2/250. . . . Full name: Fredrick William Strickland Jr.
HIGH SCHOOL: Lakeland Regional (Wanaque, N.J.).
COLLEGE: Purdue.
TRANSACTIONS/CAREER NOTES: Selected by Los Angeles Rams in second round (47th pick overall) of 1988 NFL draft. . . . Signed by Rams (July 10, 1988). . . . On injured reserve with foot injury (October 16, 1990-remainder of season).
PLAYING EXPERIENCE: Los Angeles Rams NFL, 1988-1990. . . . Games: 1988 (16), 1989 (12), 1990 (5). Total: 33.
CHAMPIONSHIP GAME EXPERIENCE: Played in NFC championship game after 1989 season.
PRO STATISTICS: 1988—Recovered two fumbles. 1989—Intercepted two passes for 56 yards and recovered one fumble for minus three yards.

STROM, RICK
QB, STEELERS

PERSONAL: Born March 11, 1965, at Pittsburgh. . . . 6-2/201. . . . Full name: Richard James Strom.
HIGH SCHOOL: Fox Chapel (Pittsburgh).
COLLEGE: Georgia Tech (bachelor of science degree in management).
TRANSACTIONS/CAREER NOTES: Signed as free agent by Pittsburgh Steelers (April 26, 1988). . . . Released by Steelers (August 24, 1988). . . . Re-signed by Steelers (February 24, 1989). . . . Released by Steelers (September 5, 1989). . . . Re-signed by Steelers to developmental squad (September 6, 1989). . . . On developmental squad (September 6-October 14, 1989).
PRO STATISTICS: Passer rating points: 1989 (39.6), 1990 (69.9). Career: 66.9. . . . 1989—Fumbled once for minus 18 yards.

| | | | PASSING | | | | | | | RUSHING | | | | TOTAL | | |
Year Team	G	Att.	Cmp.	Pct.	Yds.	TD	Int.	Avg.	Att.	Yds.	Avg.	TD	TD	Pts.	F.
1989— Pittsburgh NFL	3	1	0	.0	0	0	0	.00	4	-3	-.7	0	0	0	1
1990— Pittsburgh NFL	6	21	14	66.7	162	0	1	7.71	4	10	2.5	0	0	0	1
Pro totals (2 years)	9	22	14	63.6	162	0	1	7.36	8	7	.9	0	0	0	2

STRYZINSKI, DAN
P, STEELERS

PERSONAL: Born May 15, 1965, at Indianapolis. . . . 6-1/193. . . . Full name: Daniel Thomas Stryzinski. . . . Name pronounced stri-ZIN-skee.
HIGH SCHOOL: Lincoln (Vincennes, Ind.).
COLLEGE: Indiana (bachelor of science degree in public finance and management, 1988).
TRANSACTIONS/CAREER NOTES: Signed as free agent by Indianapolis Colts (July, 1988). . . . Released by Colts (August 23, 1988). . . . Signed as free agent by Cleveland Browns (August 25, 1988). . . . Released by Browns (August 30, 1988). . . . Re-signed by Browns (off-season, 1989). . . . Released by Browns (August 30, 1989). . . . Signed by New Orleans Saints to developmental squad (October 11, 1989). . . . On developmental squad (October 11, 1989-remainder of season). . . . Signed as free agent by Pittsburgh Steelers (March 14, 1990).
PRO STATISTICS: 1990—Rushed three times for 17 yards and recovered one fumble.

| | | PUNTING | | |
Year Team	G	No.	Avg.	Blk.
1990— Pittsburgh NFL	16	65	37.8	1
Pro totals (1 year)	16	65	37.8	1

STRZELCZYK, JUSTIN
OT/G, STEELERS

PERSONAL: Born August 18, 1968, at Seneca, N.Y. . . . 6-5/302. . . . Full name: Justin Conrad Strzelczyk. . . . Named pronounced STREL-zik.
HIGH SCHOOL: West Seneca West (West Seneca, N.Y.).
COLLEGE: Maine.
TRANSACTIONS/CAREER NOTES: Selected by Pittsburgh Steelers in 11th round (293rd pick overall) of 1990 NFL draft. . . . Signed by Steelers (July 18, 1990).
PLAYING EXPERIENCE: Pittsburgh NFL, 1990. . . . Games: 1990 (16).

STUBBS, DANIEL
DE, COWBOYS

PERSONAL: Born January 3, 1965, at Long Branch, N.J. . . . 6-4/264. . . . Full name: Daniel Stubbs II.
HIGH SCHOOL: Red Bank Regional (Little Silver, N.J.).
COLLEGE: Miami, Fla. (degree in criminal justice, 1988).
TRANSACTIONS/CAREER NOTES: Selected by San Francisco 49ers in second round (33rd pick overall) of 1988 NFL draft. . . .

Signed by 49ers (July 19, 1988).... Traded by 49ers with running back Terrence Flagler, 3rd- and 11th-round picks in 1990 NFL draft to Dallas Cowboys for 2nd- and 3rd-round picks in 1990 NFL draft (April 19, 1990).
PLAYING EXPERIENCE: San Francisco NFL, 1988 and 1989; Dallas NFL, 1990.... Games: 1988 (16), 1989 (16), 1990 (16). Total: 48.
CHAMPIONSHIP GAME EXPERIENCE: Played in NFC championship game after 1988 season.... Played in Super Bowl XXIII after 1988 season.
RECORDS/HONORS: Named as defensive lineman on THE SPORTING NEWS college All-America team, 1987.
PRO STATISTICS: 1988—Recovered one fumble. 1990—Recovered two fumbles.

SWAYNE, HARRY
OT, CHARGERS

PERSONAL: Born February 2, 1965, at Philadelphia.... 6-3/290.
HIGH SCHOOL: Cardinal Dougherty (Philadelphia).
COLLEGE: Rutgers.
TRANSACTIONS/CAREER NOTES: Selected by Tampa Bay Buccaneers in seventh round (190th pick overall) of 1987 NFL draft.... Signed by Buccaneers (July 18, 1987).... On injured reserve with fractured hand (September 8-October 31, 1987).... On injured reserve with neck injury (November 18, 1988-remainder of season).... Granted free agency (February 1, 1990).... Re-signed by Buccaneers (July 19, 1990).... On inactive list (September 9, 30; and October 7, 1990).... Granted unconditional free agency (February 1, 1991).... Signed by San Diego Chargers (April 1, 1991).
PLAYING EXPERIENCE: Tampa Bay NFL, 1987-1990.... Games: 1987 (8), 1988 (10), 1989 (16), 1990 (10). Total: 44.

SWEENEY, JIM
C/G, JETS

PERSONAL: Born August 8, 1962, at Pittsburgh.... 6-4/286.... Full name: James Joseph Sweeney.
HIGH SCHOOL: Seton LaSalle (Pittsburgh).
COLLEGE: Pittsburgh.
TRANSACTIONS/CAREER NOTES: Selected by Pittsburgh Maulers in 1984 USFL territorial draft.... Selected by New York Jets in second round (37th pick overall) of 1984 NFL draft.... Signed by Jets (July 12, 1984).... Granted free agency (February 1, 1990).... Re-signed by Jets (August 27, 1990).
PLAYING EXPERIENCE: New York Jets NFL, 1984-1990.... Games: 1984 (10), 1985 (16), 1986 (16), 1987 (12), 1988 (16), 1989 (16), 1990 (16). Total: 102.
PRO STATISTICS: 1990—Recovered one fumble.

SWILLING, PAT
LB, SAINTS

PERSONAL: Born October 25, 1964, at Toccoa, Ga.... 6-3/242.
HIGH SCHOOL: Stephens County (Toccoa, Ga.).
COLLEGE: Georgia Tech.
TRANSACTIONS/CAREER NOTES: Selected by Jacksonville Bulls in 1986 USFL territorial draft.... Selected by New Orleans Saints in third round (60th pick overall) of 1986 NFL draft.... Signed by Saints (July 21, 1986).... Granted free agency (February 1, 1990).... Re-signed by Saints (September 1, 1990).
PLAYING EXPERIENCE: New Orleans NFL, 1986-1990.... Games: 1986 (16), 1987 (12), 1988 (15), 1989 (16), 1990 (16). Total: 75.
RECORDS/HONORS: Played in Pro Bowl after 1990 season.
PRO STATISTICS: 1987—Intercepted one pass for 10 yards and recovered three fumbles for one yard. 1988—Recovered one fumble. 1989—Intercepted one pass for 14 yards and recovered one fumble.

SWOOPES, PATRICK
NT, CHIEFS

PERSONAL: Born March 4, 1964, at Florence, Ala.... 6-3/277.... Full name: Patrick Roaman Swoopes.
HIGH SCHOOL: Bradshaw (Florence, Ala.).
COLLEGE: Mississippi State.
TRANSACTIONS/CAREER NOTES: Selected by New Jersey Generals in 1986 USFL territorial draft.... Selected by New Orleans Saints in 11th round (284th pick overall) of 1986 NFL draft.... Signed by Saints (July 14, 1986).... Released by Saints (August 18, 1986).... Re-signed as replacement player by Saints (September 23, 1987).... Released by Saints (August 30, 1988).... Signed as free agent by Hamilton Tiger-Cats of CFL (September 26, 1988).... Released by Tiger-Cats (October 22, 1988).... Re-signed by New Orleans Saints (March 16, 1989).... Granted unconditional free agency (February 1, 1990).... Signed by Washington Redskins (March 28, 1990).... Awarded on waivers to New Orleans Saints (September 4, 1990).... Released by Saints (September 9, 1990).... Signed by Kansas City Chiefs (May 1, 1991).
PLAYING EXPERIENCE: New Orleans NFL, 1987; Hamilton CFL, 1988; New Orleans NFL, 1989.... Games: 1987 (9), 1988 (4), 1989 (15). Total NFL: 24. Total Pro: 28.

SYDNEY, HARRY
FB, 49ERS

PERSONAL: Born June 26, 1959, at Petersburg, Va.... 6-0/217.... Full name: Harry Flanroy Sydney III.
HIGH SCHOOL: 71st (Fayetteville, N.C.).
COLLEGE: Kansas (bachelor of general studies degree in criminal justice, 1982).
TRANSACTIONS/CAREER NOTES: Signed as free agent by Seattle Seahawks (April 30, 1981).... Released by Seahawks (August 25, 1981).... Signed as free agent by Cincinnati Bengals (February 2, 1982).... Released by Bengals (September 6, 1982).... Signed by Denver Gold of USFL (November 23, 1982).... Traded by Gold with fourth-round pick in 1985 draft to Memphis Showboats for right of first refusal to free agent defensive back Terry Love and first-round pick in 1985 draft (January 3, 1985).... On developmental squad for six games (April 14-April 19, 1985; May 18-June 1, 1985; and June 7, 1985-remainder of season).... Granted free agency when USFL suspended operations (August 7, 1986).... Signed as free agent by Montreal Alouettes of CFL (August 19, 1986).... Released by Alouettes (September 16, 1986).... Signed as free agent by San Fran-

cisco 49ers (April 8, 1987).... Crossed picket line during players' strike (October 7, 1987).... On injured reserve with broken arm (October 24, 1989-January 18, 1990).... Transferred to developmental squad (January 19-January 27, 1990).
CHAMPIONSHIP GAME EXPERIENCE: Played in NFC championship game after 1988 and 1990 seasons.... Played in Super Bowl XXIII after 1988 season and Super Bowl XXIV after 1989 season.
PRO STATISTICS: USFL: 1983—Attempted three passes with one completion for 46 yards and one interception and recovered two fumbles. 1984—Attempted four passes with no completions and one interception and recovered two fumbles. 1985—Recovered two fumbles.... CFL: 1986—Credited with one 2-point conversion.... NFL: 1987—Attempted one pass with one completion for 50 yards and a touchdown. 1988—Attempted one pass with no completions.

		RUSHING				RECEIVING				KICKOFF RETURNS				TOTAL		
Year Team	G	Att.	Yds.	Avg.	TD	No.	Yds.	Avg.	TD	No.	Yds.	Avg.	TD	TD	Pts.	F.
1983— Denver USFL..........	18	176	801	4.6	9	31	306	9.9	2	1	13	13.0	0	11	66	9
1984— Denver USFL..........	18	230	961	4.2	10	44	354	8.1	2	3	24	8.0	0	12	72	5
1985— Memphis USFL........	13	76	341	4.5	4	10	79	7.9	0	3	25	8.3	0	4	24	2
1986— Montreal CFL........	4	38	115	3.0	2	18	162	9.0	0	0	0		0	2	14	1
1987— San Francisco NFL	14	29	125	4.3	0	1	3	3.0	0	12	243	20.3	0	0	0	2
1988— San Francisco NFL	16	9	50	5.6	0	2	18	9.0	0	1	8	8.0	0	0	0	0
1989— San Francisco NFL	7	9	56	6.2	0	9	71	7.9	0	3	16	5.3	0	0	0	1
1990— San Francisco NFL	16	35	166	4.7	2	10	116	11.6	1	2	33	16.5	0	3	18	1
USFL totals (3 years)	49	482	2103	4.4	23	85	739	8.7	4	7	62	8.9	0	27	162	16
CFL totals (1 year)	4	38	115	3.0	2	18	162	9.0	0	0	0		0	2	14	1
NFL totals (4 years)	53	82	397	4.8	2	22	208	9.5	1	18	300	16.7	0	3	18	4
Pro totals (8 years)	106	602	2615	4.3	27	125	1109	8.9	5	25	362	14.5	0	32	194	21

SZOTT, DAVID
G, CHIEFS
PERSONAL: Born December 12, 1967, at Passaic, N.J.... 6-4/275.... Full name: David Andrew Szott.... Name pronounced ZOT.
HIGH SCHOOL: Clifton (N.J.).
COLLEGE: Penn State (degree in political science).
TRANSACTIONS/CAREER NOTES: Selected by Kansas City Chiefs in seventh round (180th pick overall) of 1990 NFL draft.... Signed by Chiefs (July 25, 1990).
PLAYING EXPERIENCE: Kansas City NFL, 1990.... Games: 1990 (16).
PRO STATISTICS: 1990—Recovered one fumble.

SZYMANSKI, JIM
DE, BRONCOS
PERSONAL: Born September 7, 1967, at Sterling Heights, Mich.... 6-5/268.... Full name: James Szymanski.... Name pronounced SHU-man-ski.
HIGH SCHOOL: Stevenson (Sterling Heights, Mich.).
COLLEGE: Michigan State.
TRANSACTIONS/CAREER NOTES: Selected by Denver Broncos in 10th round (259th pick overall) of 1990 NFL draft.... Signed by Broncos (July 13, 1990).... On injured reserve with broken leg (October 16, 1990-remainder of season).
PLAYING EXPERIENCE: Denver NFL, 1990.... Games: 1990 (6).

TALLEY, DARRYL
LB, BILLS
PERSONAL: Born July 10, 1960, at Cleveland.... 6-4/235.... Full name: Darryl Victor Talley.... Brother of John Talley, tight end with Cleveland Browns.
HIGH SCHOOL: Shaw (East Cleveland, O.).
COLLEGE: West Virginia (degree in physical education).
TRANSACTIONS/CAREER NOTES: Selected by New Jersey Generals in second round (24th pick overall) of 1983 USFL draft.... Selected by Buffalo Bills in second round (39th pick overall) of 1983 NFL draft.... Signed by Bills (June 14, 1983).
PLAYING EXPERIENCE: Buffalo NFL, 1983-1990.... Games: 1983 (16), 1984 (16), 1985 (16), 1986 (16), 1987 (12), 1988 (16), 1989 (16), 1990 (16). Total: 124.
CHAMPIONSHIP GAME EXPERIENCE: Played in AFC championship game after 1988 and 1990 seasons.... Played in Super Bowl XXV after 1990 season.
RECORDS/HONORS: Named as linebacker on THE SPORTING NEWS college All-America team, 1982.... Played in Pro Bowl after 1990 season.... Named to THE SPORTING NEWS NFL All-Pro team, 1990.
PRO STATISTICS: 1983—Returned two kickoffs for nine yards and recovered two fumbles for six yards. 1984—Intercepted one pass for no yards and recovered one fumble. 1986—Recovered one fumble for 47 yards. 1987—Recovered one fumble for one yard. 1988—Recovered one fumble. 1990—Intercepted two passes for 60 yards and a touchdown and recovered one fumble for four yards.

TALLEY, JOHN
TE, BROWNS
PERSONAL: Born December 19, 1964, at Cleveland.... 6-5/245.... Full name: John Thomas Eugene Talley Jr.... Brother of Darryl Talley, linebacker with Buffalo Bills.
HIGH SCHOOL: Shaw (East Cleveland, O.).
COLLEGE: West Virginia.
TRANSACTIONS/CAREER NOTES: Signed as free agent by Phoenix Cardinals (July, 1988).... Released by Cardinals (August 20, 1988).... Signed by Cleveland Browns (February, 1989).... Released by Browns (September 4, 1989).... Signed by Browns to developmental squad (September 5, 1989).... Released by Browns (September 21, 1989).... Signed by Miami Dolphins to developmental squad (September 28, 1989).... Released by Dolphins (October 19, 1989)... Signed by Philadelphia Eagles to developmental squad (October 25, 1989).... Released by Eagles (January 9, 1990).... Signed by Cleveland Browns (February 27, 1990).... On inactive list (December 16 and 23, 1990).

Year	Team	G	RECEIVING				KICKOFF RETURNS				TOTAL		
			No.	Yds.	Avg.	TD	No.	Yds.	Avg.	TD	TD	Pts.	F.
1990—	Cleveland NFL	14	2	28	14.0	0	1	6	6.0	0	0	0	0
	Pro totals (1 year)	14	2	28	14.0	0	1	6	6.0	0	0	0	0

TAMBURELLO, BEN
C/G, EAGLES

PERSONAL: Born September 9, 1964, at Birmingham, Ala. . . . 6-3/270. . . . Full name: Ben Allen Tamburello Jr. . . . Name pronounced TAM-bur-RELL-o.
HIGH SCHOOL: Shades Valley (Birmingham, Ala.) and Tennessee Military Institute (Sweetwater, Tenn.).
COLLEGE: Auburn.
TRANSACTIONS/CAREER NOTES: Selected by Philadelphia Eagles in third round (65th pick overall) of 1987 NFL draft. . . . Signed by Eagles (August 6, 1987). . . . On injured reserve with broken wrist (August 25-December 17, 1987). . . . Granted free agency (February 1, 1990). . . . Re-signed by Eagles (July 18, 1990).
PLAYING EXPERIENCE: Philadelphia NFL, 1987-1990. . . . Games: 1987 (2), 1988 (16), 1989 (16), 1990 (16). Total: 50.
RECORDS/HONORS: Named as center on THE SPORTING NEWS college All-America team, 1986.
PRO STATISTICS: 1987—Recovered one fumble.

TAMM, RALPH
G/C, BROWNS

PERSONAL: Born March 11, 1966, at Philadelphia. . . . 6-4/280. . . . Full name: Ralph Earl Tamm.
HIGH SCHOOL: Bensalem (Pa.).
COLLEGE: West Chester, Pa.
TRANSACTIONS/CAREER NOTES: Selected by New York Jets in ninth round (230th pick overall) of 1988 NFL draft. . . . On injured reserve (August 29, 1988-entire season). . . . Granted unconditional free agency (February 1, 1989). . . . Signed by Washington Redskins (off-season, 1989). . . . On injured reserve with shoulder injury (September 1989-entire season). . . . Granted unconditional free agency (February 1, 1990). . . . Signed by Cleveland Browns (March 21, 1990).
PLAYING EXPERIENCE: Cleveland NFL, 1990. . . . Games: 1990 (16).

TARDITS, RICHARD
LB, PATRIOTS

PERSONAL: Born July 30, 1965, at Biarritz, France. . . . 6-2/235.
HIGH SCHOOL: Lycee Rene-Cassin (Biarritz, France).
COLLEGE: Georgia (bachelor of business administration in international business/MIS and master of business administration in finance/MIS).
TRANSACTIONS/CAREER NOTES: Selected by Phoenix Cardinals in first round (123rd pick overall) of 1989 NFL draft. . . . Released by Cardinals (September 5, 1989). . . . Signed by Cardinals to developmental squad (September 6, 1989). . . . Released by Cardinals (November 8, 1989). . . . Re-signed by Cardinals to developmental squad (November 10, 1989). . . . Released by Cardinals (January 3, 1990). . . . Signed by New England Patriots (March 23, 1990). . . . On inactive list (September 23, 1990). . . . On injured reserve with ankle injury (September 27, 1990-remainder of season).
PLAYING EXPERIENCE: New England NFL, 1990. . . . Games: 1990 (2).

TASKER, STEVE
WR, BILLS

PERSONAL: Born April 10, 1962, at Leoti, Kan. . . . 5-9/185.
HIGH SCHOOL: Wichita County (Leoti, Kan.).
COLLEGE: Dodge City Community College (Kan.), then Northwestern.
TRANSACTIONS/CAREER NOTES: Selected by Houston Oilers in ninth round (226th pick overall) of 1985 NFL draft. . . . Signed by Oilers (June 14, 1985). . . . On injured reserve with knee injury (October 23, 1985-remainder of season). . . . On injured reserve with knee injury (September 15-November 5, 1986). . . . Released by Oilers (November 6, 1986). . . . Awarded on waivers to Buffalo Bills (November 7, 1986).
CHAMPIONSHIP GAME EXPERIENCE: Played in AFC championship game after 1988 and 1990 seasons. . . . Played in Super Bowl XXV after 1990 season.
RECORDS/HONORS: Played in Pro Bowl after 1987 and 1990 seasons.
PRO STATISTICS: 1985—Rushed twice for 16 yards and caught two passes for 19 yards. 1987—Credited with a safety and fumbled twice. 1990—Caught two passes for 44 yards and two touchdowns and recovered two fumbles for five yards.

Year	Team	G	KICKOFF RETURNS			
			No.	Yds.	Avg.	TD
1985—	Houston NFL	7	17	447	26.3	0
1986—	Hou. (2)-Buf. (7) NFL	9	12	213	17.8	0
1987—	Buffalo NFL	12	11	197	17.9	0
1988—	Buffalo NFL	14	0	0		0
1989—	Buffalo NFL	16	2	39	19.5	0
1990—	Buffalo NFL	16	0	0		0
	Pro totals (6 years)	74	42	896	21.3	0

TATE, DAVID
S, BEARS

PERSONAL: Born November 22, 1964, at Denver. . . . 6-0/177.
HIGH SCHOOL: Mullen (Denver).
COLLEGE: Colorado.
TRANSACTIONS/CAREER NOTES: Selected by Chicago Bears in eighth round (208th pick overall) of 1988 NFL draft. . . . Signed by Bears (July 6, 1988). . . . On injured reserve with knee injury (December 31, 1990-remainder of 1990 season playoffs).

CHAMPIONSHIP GAME EXPERIENCE: Played in NFC championship game after 1988 season.
PRO STATISTICS: 1989—Returned one kickoff for 12 yards.

Year	Team	G	INTERCEPTIONS No.	Yds.	Avg.	TD
1988— Chicago NFL		16	4	35	8.8	0
1989— Chicago NFL		14	1	0	.0	0
1990— Chicago NFL		16	0	0		0
Pro totals (3 years)		46	5	35	7.0	0

TATUPU, MOSI
FB, RAMS

PERSONAL: Born April 26, 1955, at Pago Pago, American Samoa. . . . 6-0/227. . . . Full name: Mosiula Tatupu. . . . Name pronounced mo-SEE ta-TOO-poo. . . . Son of Mosi Tatupu, former Samoan boxing champion; and cousin of Terry Tautolo, linebacker with Philadelphia Eagles, San Francisco 49ers, Detroit Lions and Miami Dolphins, 1976-1984; and John Tautolo, guard with New York Giants, Portland Breakers (USFL) and Los Angeles Raiders, 1982, 1983, 1985 and 1987.
HIGH SCHOOL: Punahou (Honolulu).
COLLEGE: Southern California.
TRANSACTIONS/CAREER NOTES: Selected by New England Patriots in eighth round (215th pick overall) of 1978 NFL draft. . . . Granted unconditional free agency (February 1, 1991). . . . Signed by Los Angeles Rams (March 31, 1991).
CHAMPIONSHIP GAME EXPERIENCE: Played in AFC championship game after 1985 season. . . . Played in Super Bowl XX after 1985 season.
RECORDS/HONORS: Played in Pro Bowl after 1986 season.
PRO STATISTICS: 1978—Returned one kickoff for 17 yards. 1979—Returned three kickoffs for 15 yards. 1981—Recovered three fumbles. 1983—Recovered one fumble. 1984—Returned one kickoff for nine yards and recovered one fumble. 1985—Recovered one fumble. 1986—Returned blocked punt 17 yards for a touchdown. 1987—Attempted one pass with one completion for 15 yards and a touchdown. 1988—Returned one kickoff for 13 yards. 1989—Returned one kickoff for two yards and attempted one pass with one completion for 15 yards.

Year	Team	G	RUSHING Att.	Yds.	Avg.	TD	RECEIVING No.	Yds.	Avg.	TD	TOTAL TD	Pts.	F.
1978— New England NFL		16	3	6	2.0	0	0	0		0	0	0	0
1979— New England NFL		16	23	71	3.1	0	2	9	4.5	0	0	0	0
1980— New England NFL		16	33	97	2.9	3	4	27	6.8	0	3	18	0
1981— New England NFL		16	38	201	5.3	2	12	132	11.0	1	3	18	2
1982— New England NFL		9	30	168	5.6	0	0	0		0	0	0	0
1983— New England NFL		16	106	578	*5.5	4	10	97	9.7	1	5	30	1
1984— New England NFL		16	133	553	4.2	4	16	159	9.9	0	4	24	4
1985— New England NFL		16	47	152	3.2	2	2	16	8.0	0	2	12	1
1986— New England NFL		16	71	172	2.4	1	15	145	9.7	0	2	12	1
1987— New England NFL		12	79	248	3.1	0	15	136	9.1	0	0	0	1
1988— New England NFL		16	22	75	3.4	2	8	58	7.3	0	2	12	0
1989— New England NFL		14	11	38	3.5	0	10	54	5.4	0	0	0	0
1990— New England NFL		15	16	56	3.5	0	2	10	5.0	0	0	0	0
Pro totals (13 years)		194	612	2415	4.0	18	96	843	8.8	2	21	126	10

TAYLOR, BRIAN
CB, BILLS

PERSONAL: Born October 1, 1967, at New Orleans. . . . 5-10/195. . . . Son of Roosevelt Taylor, defensive back with Chicago Bears and San Francisco 49ers, 1961-1972.
HIGH SCHOOL: St. Augustine (New Orleans).
COLLEGE: Laney College (Calif.), then Oregon State.
TRANSACTIONS/CAREER NOTES: Signed as free agent by Chicago Bears (June 21, 1989). . . . Released by Bears (September 5, 1989). . . . Re-signed by Bears to developmental squad (September 6, 1989). . . . On developmental squad (September 6-November 1, 1989). . . . Activated after clearing procedural waivers (November 3, 1989). . . . Released by Bears (August 26, 1990). . . . Signed by Buffalo Bills (April 1, 1991).
PLAYING EXPERIENCE: Chicago NFL, 1989. . . . Games: 1989 (5).
PRO STATISTICS: 1989—Rushed twice for seven yards.

TAYLOR, CRAIG
RB, BENGALS

PERSONAL: Born January 3, 1966, at Elizabeth, N.J. . . . 6-0/228.
HIGH SCHOOL: Linden (N.J.).
COLLEGE: West Virginia.
TRANSACTIONS/CAREER NOTES: Selected by Cincinnati Bengals in sixth round (166th pick overall) of 1989 NFL draft. . . . Signed by Bengals (July 21, 1989). . . . Released by Bengals (September 5, 1989). . . . Re-signed by Bengals to developmental squad (September 6, 1989). . . . On developmental squad (September 6-September 23, 1989). . . . On inactive list (November 4 and December 16, 1990). . . . On injured reserve with ankle injury (December 22, 1990-remainder of season).

Year	Team	G	RUSHING Att.	Yds.	Avg.	TD	RECEIVING No.	Yds.	Avg.	TD	KICKOFF RETURNS No.	Yds.	Avg.	TD	TOTAL TD	Pts.	F.
1989— Cincinnati NFL		12	30	111	3.7	3	4	44	11.0	2	1	5	5.0	0	5	30	0
1990— Cincinnati NFL		12	51	216	4.2	2	3	22	7.3	1	1	16	16.0	0	3	18	0
Pro totals (2 years)		24	81	327	4.0	5	7	66	9.4	3	2	21	10.5	0	8	48	0

TAYLOR, GENE
WR, PATRIOTS

PERSONAL: Born November 12, 1962, at Oakland, Calif. . . . 6-2/190. . . . Full name: Eugene Taylor.
HIGH SCHOOL: Salesian (Richmond, Calif.).
COLLEGE: Contra Costa College (Calif.), then Fresno State.
TRANSACTIONS/CAREER NOTES: Selected by New England Patriots in sixth round (163rd pick overall) of 1987 NFL draft. . . . Signed by Patriots (July 26, 1987). . . . Released by Patriots (August 31, 1987). . . . Awarded on waivers to Tampa Bay Buccaneers (September 1, 1987). . . . Released by Buccaneers (September 7, 1987). . . . Re-signed by Buccaneers (September 8, 1987). . . . Released by Buccaneers (September 14, 1988). . . . Re-signed by Buccaneers (October 18, 1988). . . . Released by Buccaneers (November 9, 1988). . . . Signed as free agent by San Francisco 49ers (February 27, 1989). . . . Released by 49ers (August 30, 1989). . . . Signed as free agent by Saskatchewan Roughriders of CFL (September 12, 1989). . . . Released by Roughriders (October 3, 1989). . . . Signed as free agent by Los Angeles Rams (April 11, 1990). . . . Released by Rams (August 17, 1990). . . . Signed by WLAF (January 7, 1991). . . . Selected by Barcelona Dragons in first round (second wide receiver) of 1991 WLAF positional draft. . . . Signed by New England Patriots (July 9, 1991).
PRO STATISTICS: CFL: 1989—Returned three kickoffs for 70 yards and fumbled once. . . . WLAF: 1991—Rushed once for minus four yards.

			RECEIVING		
Year Team	G	No.	Yds.	Avg.	TD
1987— Tampa Bay NFL	7	2	21	10.5	0
1988— Tampa Bay NFL	4	5	53	10.6	0
1989— Saskatchewan CFL	3	2	20	10.0	1
1991— Barcelona WLAF	9	35	745	21.3	6
NFL totals (2 years)	11	7	74	10.6	0
CFL totals (1 year)	3	2	20	10.0	1
WLAF totals (1 year)	9	35	745	21.3	6
Pro totals (4 years)	23	44	839	19.1	7

TAYLOR, JAY
CB, CARDINALS

PERSONAL: Born November 8, 1967, at San Diego. . . . 5-10/175.
HIGH SCHOOL: St. Augustine (San Diego).
COLLEGE: Grossmont College (Calif.), then San Jose State.
TRANSACTIONS/CAREER NOTES: Selected by Phoenix Cardinals in sixth round (150th pick overall) of 1989 NFL draft. . . . Signed by Cardinals (July 20, 1989).
PRO STATISTICS: 1989—Recovered one fumble for one yard.

			INTERCEPTIONS		
Year Team	G	No.	Yds.	Avg.	TD
1989— Phoenix NFL	16	0	0		0
1990— Phoenix NFL	16	3	50	16.7	0
Pro totals (2 years)	32	3	50	16.7	0

TAYLOR, JOHN
WR, 49ERS

PERSONAL: Born March 31, 1962, at Pennsauken, N.J. . . . 6-1/185. . . . Full name: John Gregory Taylor. . . . Brother of Keith Taylor, defensive back with Indianapolis Colts.
HIGH SCHOOL: Pennsauken (N.J.).
COLLEGE: Delaware State.
TRANSACTIONS/CAREER NOTES: Selected by San Francisco 49ers in third round (76th pick overall) of 1986 NFL draft. . . . Selected by Baltimore Stars in second round (13th pick overall) of 1986 USFL draft. . . . Signed by San Francisco 49ers (July 21, 1986). . . . On injured reserve with back injury (August 26, 1986-entire season). . . . On non-football injury list with substance abuse (September 2-September 28, 1988). . . . On inactive list (September 23, 1990).
CHAMPIONSHIP GAME EXPERIENCE: Played in NFC championship game after 1988-1990 seasons. . . . Played in Super Bowl XXIII after 1988 season and Super Bowl XXIV after 1989 season.
RECORDS/HONORS: Played in Pro Bowl after 1988 season. . . . Named to play in Pro Bowl after 1989 season; replaced due to injury by Mark Carrier. . . . Named as punt returner to THE SPORTING NEWS NFL All-Pro team, 1988.
PRO STATISTICS: 1987—Recovered one fumble for 26 yards and a touchdown. 1988—Recovered two fumbles. 1989—Rushed once for six yards.

		RECEIVING				PUNT RETURNS				KICKOFF RETURNS				TOTAL		
Year Team	G	No.	Yds.	Avg.	TD	No.	Yds.	Avg.	TD	No.	Yds.	Avg.	TD	TD	Pts.	F.
1987— San Fran. NFL	12	9	151	16.8	0	1	9	9.0	0	0	0		0	0	0	0
1988— San Fran. NFL	12	14	325	23.2	2	44	*556	*12.6	*2	12	225	18.8	0	4	24	6
1989— San Fran. NFL	15	60	1077	18.0	10	36	417	11.6	0	2	51	25.5	0	10	60	3
1990— San Fran. NFL	14	49	748	15.3	7	26	212	8.2	0	0	0		0	7	42	2
Pro totals (4 years)	53	132	2301	17.4	19	107	1194	11.2	2	14	276	19.7	0	21	126	11

TAYLOR, KEITH
DB, COLTS

PERSONAL: Born December 21, 1964, at Pennsauken, N.J. . . . 5-11/206. . . . Full name: Keith Gerard Taylor. . . . Brother of John Taylor, wide receiver with San Francisco 49ers.
HIGH SCHOOL: Pennsauken (N.J.).
COLLEGE: Illinois.
TRANSACTIONS/CAREER NOTES: Selected by New Orleans Saints in fifth round (134th pick overall) of 1988 NFL draft. . . . Signed by Saints (June 24, 1988). . . . Released by Saints (August 30, 1988). . . . Signed as free agent by Indianapolis Colts (November 30, 1988).
PRO STATISTICS: 1990—Recovered one fumble.

Year	Team	G	INTERCEPTIONS No.	Yds.	Avg.	TD
1988— Indianapolis NFL		3	0	0		0
1989— Indianapolis NFL		16	7	225	32.1	1
1990— Indianapolis NFL		16	2	51	25.5	0
Pro totals (3 years)		35	9	276	30.7	1

TAYLOR, KITRICK
WR, CHARGERS

PERSONAL: Born July 22, 1964, at Los Angeles. . . . 5-11/191. . . . Full name: Kitrick Lavell Taylor. . . . First name pronounced KIT-trick.
HIGH SCHOOL: Pomona (Calif.).
COLLEGE: Washington State (degree in social welfare, 1987).
TRANSACTIONS/CAREER NOTES: Selected by Kansas City Chiefs in fifth round (128th pick overall) of 1987 NFL draft. . . . Signed by Chiefs (July 19, 1987). . . . On injured reserve with pulled groin (September 7, 1987-entire season). . . . Granted unconditional free agency (February 1, 1989). . . . Signed by Atlanta Falcons (March 28, 1989). . . . Released by Falcons (September 5, 1989). . . . Signed as free agent by New England Patriots (November 16, 1989). . . . On injured reserve with knee injury (December 15, 1989-remainder of season). . . . Released by Patriots (September 3, 1990). . . . Signed by San Diego Chargers (December 12, 1990).
PRO STATISTICS: 1988—Rushed once for two yards.

Year	Team	G	RECEIVING No.	Yds.	Avg.	TD	PUNT RETURNS No.	Yds.	Avg.	TD	KICKOFF RETURNS No.	Yds.	Avg.	TD	TOTAL TD	Pts.	F.
1988— Kansas City NFL.		16	9	105	11.7	0	29	187	6.5	0	5	80	16.0	0	0	0	1
1989— New Eng. NFL		4	0	0		0	0	0		0	3	52	17.3	0	0	0	0
1990— San Diego NFL		3	0	0		0	6	112	18.7	*1	0	0		0	1	6	0
Pro totals (3 years)		23	9	105	11.7	0	35	299	8.5	1	8	132	16.5	0	1	6	1

TAYLOR, LAWRENCE
LB, GIANTS

PERSONAL: Born February 4, 1959, at Williamsburg, Va. . . . 6-3/243.
HIGH SCHOOL: Lafayette (Williamsburg, Va.).
COLLEGE: North Carolina.
TRANSACTIONS/CAREER NOTES: Selected by New York Giants in first round (second pick overall) of 1981 NFL draft. . . . Crossed picket line during players' strike (October 14, 1987). . . . On non-football injury list with substance abuse (August 29-September 28, 1988). . . . Granted roster exemption (September 5-September 9, 1990).
CHAMPIONSHIP GAME EXPERIENCE: Played in NFC championship game after 1986 and 1990 seasons. . . . Played in Super Bowl XXI after 1986 season and Super Bowl XXV after 1990 season.
RECORDS/HONORS: Named as linebacker on THE SPORTING NEWS college All-America team, 1980. . . . Played in Pro Bowl after 1981-1990 seasons. . . . Named to THE SPORTING NEWS NFL All-Pro team, 1981, 1983-1986 and 1988. . . . Named THE SPORTING NEWS NFL Player of the Year, 1986.
PRO STATISTICS: 1981—Recovered one fumble for four yards and fumbled once. 1983—Recovered two fumbles for three yards and fumbled once. 1985—Recovered two fumbles for 25 yards. 1988—Recovered one fumble. 1990—Recovered one fumble.

Year	Team	G	INTERCEPTIONS No.	Yds.	Avg.	TD
1981— N.Y. Giants NFL		16	1	1	1.0	0
1982— N.Y. Giants NFL		9	1	97	97.0	*1
1983— N.Y. Giants NFL		16	2	10	5.0	0
1984— N.Y. Giants NFL		16	1	-1	-1.0	0
1985— N.Y. Giants NFL		16	0	0		0
1986— N.Y. Giants NFL		16	0	0		0
1987— N.Y. Giants NFL		12	3	16	5.3	0
1988— N.Y. Giants NFL		12	0	0		0
1989— N.Y. Giants NFL		16	0	0		0
1990— N.Y. Giants NFL		16	1	11	11.0	1
Pro totals (10 years)		145	9	134	14.9	2

TAYLOR, ROB
OT, BUCCANEERS

PERSONAL: Born November 14, 1960, at St. Charles, Ill. . . . 6-6/290. . . . Full name: Robert Earl Taylor.
HIGH SCHOOL: Fairmonst East (Kettering, O.).
COLLEGE: Northwestern (degree in electrical engineering).
TRANSACTIONS/CAREER NOTES: Selected by Philadelphia Eagles in 12th round (328th pick overall) of 1982 NFL draft. . . . Released by Eagles (August 23, 1982). . . . Awarded on waivers to Baltimore Colts (August 25, 1982). . . . Released by Colts (September 6, 1982). . . . Signed as free agent by Chicago Blitz of USFL (October 4, 1982). . . . Franchise transferred to Arizona (September 30, 1983). . . . Protected in merger of Arizona Wranglers and Oklahoma Outlaws (December 6, 1984). . . . Granted free agency (November 30, 1984). . . . Signed by Birmingham Stallions (January 23, 1985); Arizona did not exercise right of first refusal. . . . Traded by Stallions to Houston Gamblers for defensive end Malcolm Taylor (February 12, 1985). . . . On developmental squad for one game (February 21-March 3, 1985). . . . Released by Gamblers (July 31, 1985). . . . Awarded on waivers to Baltimore Stars (August 1, 1985). . . . Released by Stars (August 2, 1985). . . . Signed as free agent by Tampa Bay Buccaneers (March 26, 1986). . . . On injured reserve with knee injury (November 11, 1987-remainder of season). . . . Granted free agency (February 1, 1990). . . . Re-signed by Buccaneers (July 17, 1990).
PLAYING EXPERIENCE: Chicago USFL, 1983 and 1984; Houston USFL, 1985; Tampa Bay NFL, 1986-1990. . . . Games: 1983 (18), 1984 (18), 1985 (16), 1986 (16), 1987 (5), 1988 (16), 1989 (16), 1990 (16). Total USFL: 52. Total NFL: 69. Total Pro: 121.
CHAMPIONSHIP GAME EXPERIENCE: Played in USFL championship game after 1984 season.
PRO STATISTICS: 1983—Recovered one fumble. 1990—Recovered one fumble for minus one yard.

TAYLOR, TROY

QB, JETS

PERSONAL: Born April 5, 1968, at Downey, Calif. . . . 6-4/200. . . . Full name: Troy Scott Taylor.
HIGH SCHOOL: Cordova Senior (Rancho Cordova, Calif.).
COLLEGE: California (bachelor's degree in sociology, 1990).
TRANSACTIONS/CAREER NOTES: Selected by New York Jets in fourth round (84th pick overall) of 1990 NFL draft. . . . Signed by Jets (July 22, 1990). . . . On inactive list (September 24, 30; and October 7, 1990).
PRO STATISTICS: Passer rating points: 1990 (114.2).

				PASSING					RUSHING				TOTAL		
Year Team	G	Att.	Cmp.	Pct.	Yds.	TD	Int.	Avg.	Att.	Yds.	Avg.	TD	TD	Pts.	F.
1990— N.Y. Jets NFL	2	10	7	70.0	49	1	0	4.90	2	20	10.0	1	1	6	0
Pro totals (1 year)	2	10	7	70.0	49	1	0	4.90	2	20	10.0	1	1	6	0

TENNELL, DEREK

TE, LIONS

PERSONAL: Born February 12, 1964, at Los Angeles. . . . 6-5/250. . . . Full name: Derek Wayne Tennell. . . . Name pronounced te-NELL.
HIGH SCHOOL: West Covina (Calif.).
COLLEGE: UCLA.
TRANSACTIONS/CAREER NOTES: Selected by Seattle Seahawks in seventh round (185th pick overall) of 1987 NFL draft. . . . Signed by Seahawks (July 21, 1987). . . . Released by Seahawks (September 7, 1987). . . . Signed as free-agent replacement player by Cleveland Browns (September 24, 1987). . . . Released by Browns (December 13, 1989). . . . Signed as free agent by San Francisco 49ers (March 8, 1990). . . . Released by 49ers (August 27, 1990). . . . Signed by Detroit Lions (April 26, 1991).
CHAMPIONSHIP GAME EXPERIENCE: Played in AFC championship game after 1987 season.
PRO STATISTICS: 1988—Returned one kickoff for 11 yards.

		RECEIVING			
Year Team	G	No.	Yds.	Avg.	TD
1987— Cleveland NFL	11	9	102	11.3	3
1988— Cleveland NFL	16	9	88	9.8	1
1989— Cleveland NFL	14	1	4	4.0	1
Pro totals (3 years)	41	19	194	10.2	5

TERRELL, PAT

S, RAMS

PERSONAL: Born March 18, 1968, at Memphis, Tenn. . . . 6-0/195. . . . Full name: Patrick Christopher Terrell. . . . Name pronounced TAIR-el.
HIGH SCHOOL: Lakewood Senior (St. Petersburg, Fla.).
COLLEGE: Notre Dame (degree in business administration with emphasis in marketing).
TRANSACTIONS/CAREER NOTES: Selected by Los Angeles Rams in second round (49th pick overall) of 1990 NFL draft. . . . Signed by Rams (August 1, 1990). . . . On inactive list (September 23, 1990).
PRO STATISTICS: 1990—Recovered one fumble.

		INTERCEPTIONS			
Year Team	G	No.	Yds.	Avg.	TD
1990— L.A. Rams NFL	15	1	6	6.0	0
Pro totals (1 year)	15	1	6	6.0	0

TESTAVERDE, VINNY

QB, BUCCANEERS

PERSONAL: Born November 13, 1963, at Brooklyn, N.Y. . . . 6-5/215. . . . Full name: Vincent Frank Testaverde. . . . Name pronounced tess-tuh-VER-dee.
HIGH SCHOOL: Sewanhaka (Floral Park, N.Y.) and Fork Union Military Academy (Fork Union, Va.).
COLLEGE: Miami (Fla.).
TRANSACTIONS/CAREER NOTES: Signed by Tampa Bay Buccaneers (April 3, 1987). . . . Selected officially by Buccaneers in first round (first pick overall) of 1987 NFL draft. . . . On injured reserve with ankle injury (December 20, 1989-remainder of season). . . . On inactive list (October 28, 1990).
RECORDS/HONORS: Heisman Trophy winner, 1986. . . . Named THE SPORTING NEWS College Football Player of the Year, 1986. . . . Named as quarterback on THE SPORTING NEWS college All-America team, 1986.
PRO STATISTICS: Passer rating points: 1987 (60.2), 1988 (48.8), 1989 (68.9), 1990 (75.6). Career: 63.2. . . . 1987—Recovered four fumbles and fumbled seven times for minus three yards. 1988—Recovered two fumbles. 1989—Recovered two fumbles. 1990—Caught one pass for three yards and recovered three fumbles.

				PASSING					RUSHING				TOTAL		
Year Team	G	Att.	Cmp.	Pct.	Yds.	TD	Int.	Avg.	Att.	Yds.	Avg.	TD	TD	Pts.	F.
1987— Tampa Bay NFL	6	165	71	43.0	1081	5	6	6.55	13	50	3.9	1	1	6	7
1988— Tampa Bay NFL	15	466	222	47.6	3240	13	*35	6.95	28	138	4.9	1	1	6	8
1989— Tampa Bay NFL	14	480	258	53.8	3133	20	22	6.53	25	139	5.6	0	0	0	4
1990— Tampa Bay NFL	14	365	203	55.6	2818	17	18	7.72	38	280	7.4	1	1	6	10
Pro totals (4 years)	49	1476	754	51.1	10272	55	81	6.96	104	607	5.8	3	3	18	29

THAXTON, GALAND

LB, CHARGERS

PERSONAL: Born October 23, 1964, at Mildinhall, England. . . . 6-1/240. . . . Full name: Galand W. Thaxton.
HIGH SCHOOL: South (Denver).
COLLEGE: Wyoming.
TRANSACTIONS/CAREER NOTES: Signed as free agent by New York Giants (May 2, 1988). . . . Released by Giants (August 30, 1988). . . . Signed as free agent by Atlanta Falcons (January 20, 1989). . . . On injured reserve with ankle injury (August 28,

1990-entire season).... Granted unconditional free agency (February 1, 1991).... Signed by San Diego Chargers (March 26, 1991).
PLAYING EXPERIENCE: Atlanta NFL, 1989.... Games: 1989 (16).

THAYER, TOM
G, BEARS

PERSONAL: Born August 16, 1961, at Joliet, Ill.... 6-4/270.... Full name: Thomas Allen Thayer. ... Brother-in-law of John Scully, guard with Atlanta Falcons.
HIGH SCHOOL: Catholic (Joliet, Ill.).
COLLEGE: Notre Dame (bachelor of arts degree in communications and public relations).
TRANSACTIONS/CAREER NOTES: Selected by Chicago Blitz in 1983 USFL territorial draft.... Signed by Blitz (April 26, 1983).... Selected by Chicago Bears in fourth round (91st pick overall) of 1983 NFL draft.... Chicago Blitz franchise transferred to Arizona (September 30, 1983).... Protected in merger of Arizona Wranglers and Oklahoma Outlaws (December 6, 1984).... On developmental squad for one game (March 3-March 11, 1985).... Granted free agency (July 15, 1985).... Signed by Chicago Bears (July 19, 1985).
PLAYING EXPERIENCE: Chicago USFL, 1983 and 1984; Arizona USFL, 1985; Chicago NFL, 1985-1990.... Games 1983 (10), 1984 (18), 1985 USFL (17), 1985 NFL (16), 1986 (16), 1987 (11), 1988 (16), 1989 (16), 1990 (16). Total USFL: 45. Total NFL: 91. Total Pro: 136.
CHAMPIONSHIP GAME EXPERIENCE: Played in USFL championship game after 1984 season.... Played in NFC championship game after 1985 and 1988 seasons.... Played in Super Bowl XX after 1985 season.
PRO STATISTICS: USFL: 1985—Recovered two fumbles.... NFL: 1990—Recovered one fumble.

THOMAS, BEN
DE, RAMS

PERSONAL: Born July 2, 1961, at Ashburn, Ga.... 6-3/275.... Full name: Benjamin Thomas Jr.
HIGH SCHOOL: Turner County (Ashburn, Ga.).
COLLEGE: Auburn.
TRANSACTIONS/CAREER NOTES: Selected by Birmingham Stallions in 1985 USFL territorial draft. ... Selected by New England Patriots in second round (56th pick overall) of 1985 NFL draft.... Signed by Patriots (July 24, 1985).... Released by Patriots (October 17, 1986).... Awarded on waivers to Green Bay Packers (October 20, 1986).... On injured reserve with knee injury (September 1, 1987-entire season).... Crossed picket line during players' strike (October 14, 1987).... Released by Packers (August 9, 1988).... Signed as free agent by Pittsburgh Steelers (August 11, 1988).... Released by Steelers (November 2, 1988).... Signed as free agent by Atlanta Falcons (May 2, 1989).... Released by Falcons (September 3, 1990).... Signed by Los Angeles Rams (March 27, 1991).
PLAYING EXPERIENCE: New England NFL, 1985; New England (4)-Green Bay (9) NFL, 1986; Pittsburgh NFL, 1988; Atlanta NFL, 1989.... Games: 1985 (15), 1986 (13), 1988 (8), 1989 (16). Total: 52.
CHAMPIONSHIP GAME EXPERIENCE: Played in AFC championship game after 1985 season.... Played in Super Bowl XX after 1985 season.
PRO STATISTICS: 1989—Recovered one fumble for nine yards.

THOMAS, BLAIR
RB, JETS

PERSONAL: Born October 7, 1967, at Philadelphia.... 5-10/195.... Full name: Blair L. Thomas.
HIGH SCHOOL: Frankford (Pa.).
COLLEGE: Penn State (bachelor of arts degree in recreation and parks, 1990).
TRANSACTIONS/CAREER NOTES: Selected by New York Jets in first round (second pick overall) of 1990 NFL draft.... Signed by Jets (August 26, 1990).... On inactive list (November 25, 1990).

		RUSHING				RECEIVING				TOTAL		
Year Team	G	Att.	Yds.	Avg.	TD	No.	Yds.	Avg.	TD	TD	Pts.	F.
1990—N.Y. Jets NFL	15	123	620	5.0	1	20	204	10.2	1	2	12	3
Pro totals (1 year)	15	123	620	5.0	1	20	204	10.2	1	2	12	3

THOMAS, BRODERICK
LB, BUCCANEERS

PERSONAL: Born February 20, 1967, at Houston.... 6-4/245.... Nephew of Mike Singletary, linebacker with Chicago Bears.
HIGH SCHOOL: James Madison (Houston).
COLLEGE: Nebraska.
TRANSACTIONS/CAREER NOTES: Selected by Tampa Bay Buccaneers in first round (sixth pick overall) of 1989 NFL draft.... Signed by Buccaneers (August 29, 1989).
PLAYING EXPERIENCE: Tampa Bay NFL, 1989 and 1990.... Games: 1989 (16), 1990 (16). Total: 32.
PRO STATISTICS: 1990—Recovered two fumbles.

THOMAS, CHUCK
C, 49ERS

PERSONAL: Born December 24, 1960, at Houston.... 6-3/280.
HIGH SCHOOL: Stratford (Houston).
COLLEGE: Oklahoma.
TRANSACTIONS/CAREER NOTES: Selected by San Antonio Gunslingers in 1985 USFL territorial draft.... Selected by Houston Oilers in eighth round (199th pick overall) of 1985 NFL draft.... Signed by Oilers (July 13, 1985).... Released by Oilers (September 2, 1985).... Signed as free agent by Atlanta Falcons (November 22, 1985).... Released by Falcons (August 12, 1986).... Signed as free agent by San Francisco 49ers (December 22, 1986).... On injured reserve with thigh injury (August 28-September 6, 1987).... Released by 49ers (September 7, 1987).... Re-signed as replacement player by 49ers (September 24, 1987).... Granted free agency (February 1, 1990).... Re-signed by 49ers (July 29, 1990).
PLAYING EXPERIENCE: Atlanta NFL, 1985; San Francisco NFL, 1987-1990.... Games: 1985 (4), 1987 (7), 1988 (16), 1989 (16), 1990 (15). Total: 58.

CHAMPIONSHIP GAME EXPERIENCE: Played in NFC championship game after 1988-1990 seasons. . . . Played in Super Bowl XXIII after 1988 season and Super Bowl XXIV after 1989 season.
PRO STATISTICS: 1988—Returned one kickoff for five yards and fumbled once for minus 12 yards.

THOMAS, DEE
CB, OILERS

PERSONAL: Born November 7, 1967, at Morgan City, La. . . . 5-10/176. . . . Full name: Derward Heith Thomas.
HIGH SCHOOL: Central Catholic (Morgan City, La.).
COLLEGE: Nicholls State.
TRANSACTIONS/CAREER NOTES: Selected by Houston Oilers in 10th round (264th pick overall) of 1990 NFL draft. . . . Signed by Oilers (July 16, 1990). . . . On injured reserve with elbow injury (September 5-October 18, 1990). . . . On inactive list (October 21; November 26; and December 2 and 16, 1990).
PLAYING EXPERIENCE: Houston NFL, 1990. . . . Games: 1990 (6).

THOMAS, DERRICK
LB, CHIEFS

PERSONAL: Born January 1, 1967, at Miami. . . . 6-3/236. . . . Full name: Derrick Vincent Thomas.
HIGH SCHOOL: South (Miami).
COLLEGE: Alabama.
TRANSACTIONS/CAREER NOTES: Selected by Kansas City Chiefs in first round (fourth pick overall) of 1989 NFL draft. . . . Signed by Chiefs (August 24, 1989).
PLAYING EXPERIENCE: Kansas City NFL, 1989 and 1990. . . . Games: 1989 (16), 1990 (15). Total: 31.
RECORDS/HONORS: Established NFL record for most sacks, game (7), against Seattle Seahawks (November 11, 1990). . . . Named as linebacker on THE SPORTING NEWS college All-America team, 1988. . . . Played in Pro Bowl after 1989 and 1990 seasons. . . . Named to THE SPORTING NEWS NFL All-Pro team, 1990.
PRO STATISTICS: 1989—Recovered one fumble. 1990—Recovered two fumbles for 14 yards.

THOMAS, ED
TE, BUCCANEERS

PERSONAL: Born May 4, 1966, at New Orleans. . . . 6-3/245. . . . Full name: Edward Lee Thomas.
HIGH SCHOOL: Booker T. Washington (New Orleans).
COLLEGE: Houston.
TRANSACTIONS/CAREER NOTES: Signed as free agenct by Tampa Bay Buccaneers (August 2, 1990). . . . Released by Buccaneers (August 27, 1990). . . . Signed by Buccaneers to practice squad (October 1, 1990). . . . Activated (October 26, 1990). . . . Released by Buccaneers (December 21, 1990). . . . Re-signed by Buccaneers (March 6, 1991).
PLAYING EXPERIENCE: Tampa Bay NFL, 1990. . . . Games: 1990 (7).

THOMAS, ERIC
CB, BENGALS

PERSONAL: Born September 11, 1964, at Tucson, Ariz. . . . 5-11/181. . . . Full name: Eric Jason Thomas.
HIGH SCHOOL: Norte Del Rio (Sacramento, Calif.).
COLLEGE: Pasadena City College (Calif.), then Tulane.
TRANSACTIONS/CAREER NOTES: Selected by Cincinnati Bengals in second round (49th pick overall) of 1987 NFL draft. . . . Signed by Bengals (July 27, 1987). . . . On reserve/non-football injury list (September 3-November 6, 1990). . . . On inactive list (November 18, 25 and December 2, 1990).
CHAMPIONSHIP GAME EXPERIENCE: Played in AFC championship game after 1988 season. . . . Played in Super Bowl XXIII after 1988 season.
RECORDS/HONORS: Played in Pro Bowl after 1988 season.
PRO STATISTICS: 1989—Recovered one fumble.

			INTERCEPTIONS		
Year Team	G	No.	Yds.	Avg.	TD
1987— Cincinnati NFL	12	1	3	3.0	0
1988— Cincinnati NFL	16	7	61	8.7	0
1989— Cincinnati NFL	16	4	18	4.5	1
1990— Cincinnati NFL	4	0	0		0
Pro totals (4 years)	48	12	82	6.8	1

THOMAS, GEORGE
WR, FALCONS

PERSONAL: Born July 11, 1964, at Riverside, Calif. . . . 5-9/169. . . . Full name: George Ray Thomas Jr.
HIGH SCHOOL: Indio (Calif.).
COLLEGE: UNLV.
TRANSACTIONS/CAREER NOTES: Selected by Atlanta Falcons in sixth round (138th pick overall) of 1988 NFL draft. . . . Signed by Falcons (July 15, 1988). . . . On physically unable to perform/active list with stress fracture in leg (July 16-August 9, 1988). . . . Passed physical (August 10, 1988). . . . On injured reserve with foot injury (August 29, 1988-entire season). . . . On injured reserve (September 4-October 2, 1990). . . . On practice squad (October 2-October 6, 1990).

		RECEIVING				KICKOFF RETURNS				TOTAL		
Year Team	G	No.	Yds.	Avg.	TD	No.	Yds.	Avg.	TD	TD	Pts.	F.
1989— Atlanta NFL	16	4	46	11.5	0	7	142	20.3	0	0	0	0
1990— Atlanta NFL	13	18	383	21.3	1	0	0		0	1	6	0
Pro totals (2 years)	29	22	429	19.5	1	7	142	20.3	0	1	6	0

THOMAS, HENRY
NT, VIKINGS

PERSONAL: Born January 12, 1965, at Houston. . . . 6-2/268. . . . Full name: Henry Lee Thomas Jr.
HIGH SCHOOL: Dwight D. Eisenhower (Houston).
COLLEGE: Louisiana State.
TRANSACTIONS/CAREER NOTES: Selected by Minnesota Vikings in third round (72nd pick overall) of 1987 NFL draft. . . . Signed by Vikings (July 14, 1987).
PLAYING EXPERIENCE: Minnesota NFL, 1987-1990. . . . Games: 1987 (12), 1988 (15), 1989 (14), 1990 (16). Total: 57.
CHAMPIONSHIP GAME EXPERIENCE: Played in NFC championship game after 1987 season.
PRO STATISTICS: 1987—Intercepted one pass for no yards and recovered one fumble. 1988—Intercepted one pass for seven yards and recovered one fumble for two yards and a touchdown. 1989—Recovered three fumbles for 37 yards and a touchdown. 1990—Recovered one fumble.

THOMAS, ROBB
WR, CHIEFS

PERSONAL: Born March 29, 1966, at Portland, Ore. . . . 5-11/175. . . . Full name: Robb Douglas Thomas. . . . Son of Aaron Thomas, wide receiver with San Francisco 49ers and New York Giants, 1961-1970.
HIGH SCHOOL: Corvallis (Ore.).
COLLEGE: Oregon State.
TRANSACTIONS/CAREER NOTES: Selected by Kansas City Chiefs in sixth round (143rd pick overall) of 1989 NFL draft. . . . Signed by Chiefs (May 30, 1989). . . . On injured reserve with dislocated shoulder (October 24-December 4, 1989). . . . Transferred to developmental squad (December 5-December 23, 1989).
PRO STATISTICS: 1989—Fumbled once.

			RECEIVING		
Year Team	G	No.	Yds.	Avg.	TD
1989— Kansas City NFL........	8	8	58	7.3	2
1990— Kansas City NFL........	16	41	545	13.3	4
Pro totals (2 years)........	24	49	603	12.3	6

THOMAS, RODNEY
CB, RAMS

PERSONAL: Born December 21, 1965, at Los Angeles. . . . 5-10/190. . . . Full name: Rodney Lamar Thomas.
HIGH SCHOOL: Chaffey (Ontario, Calif.).
COLLEGE: Brigham Young.
TRANSACTIONS/CAREER NOTES: Selected by Miami Dolphins in fifth round (126th pick overall) of 1988 NFL draft. . . . Signed by Dolphins (July 12, 1988). . . . On injured reserve with knee injury (November 26, 1988-remainder of season). . . . Granted unconditional free agency (February 1, 1991). . . . Signed by Los Angeles Rams (March 21, 1991).
PRO STATISTICS: 1989—Recovered two fumbles for 46 yards.

			INTERCEPTIONS		
Year Team	G	No.	Yds.	Avg.	TD
1988— Miami NFL.................	12	1	48	48.0	0
1989— Miami NFL.................	16	2	4	2.0	0
1990— Miami NFL.................	15	0	0		0
Pro totals (3 years)........	43	3	52	17.3	0

THOMAS, THURMAN
RB, BILLS

PERSONAL: Born May 16, 1966, at Houston. . . . 5-10/198. . . . Full name: Thurman L. Thomas.
HIGH SCHOOL: Willow Ridge (Missouri City, Tex.).
COLLEGE: Oklahoma State.
TRANSACTIONS/CAREER NOTES: Selected by Buffalo Bills in second round (40th pick overall) of 1988 NFL draft. . . . Signed by Bills (July 14, 1988).
CHAMPIONSHIP GAME EXPERIENCE: Played in AFC championship game after 1988 and 1990 seasons. . . . Played in Super Bowl XXV after 1990 season.
RECORDS/HONORS: Played in Pro Bowl after 1989 and 1990 seasons. . . . Named to THE SPORTING NEWS NFL All-Pro team, 1990.
PRO STATISTICS: 1988—Recovered one fumble. 1989—Recovered two fumbles. 1990—Recovered two fumbles.

		RUSHING				RECEIVING				TOTAL		
Year Team	G	Att.	Yds.	Avg.	TD	No.	Yds.	Avg.	TD	TD	Pts.	F.
1988— Buffalo NFL......................................	15	207	881	4.3	2	18	208	11.6	0	2	12	9
1989— Buffalo NFL......................................	16	298	1244	4.2	6	60	669	11.2	6	12	72	7
1990— Buffalo NFL......................................	16	271	1297	4.8	11	49	532	10.9	2	13	78	6
Pro totals (3 years)................................	47	776	3422	4.4	19	127	1409	11.1	8	27	162	22

THOMPSON, ANTHONY
LB, BRONCOS

PERSONAL: Born June 19, 1967, at Stantonsburg, N.C. . . . 6-1/227.
HIGH SCHOOL: Ralph L. Fike (Wilson, N.C.).
COLLEGE: East Carolina.
TRANSACTIONS/CAREER NOTES: Selected by Denver Broncos in 10th round (275th pick overall) of 1990 NFL draft. . . . Released by Broncos (September 3, 1990). . . . Re-Signed by Broncos (September 4, 1990). . . . On inactive list (September 17, 1990). . . . On injured reserve with ankle injury (October 11-November 20, 1990).
PLAYING EXPERIENCE: Denver NFL, 1990. . . . Games: 1990 (10).

THOMPSON, ANTHONY
RB, CARDINALS

PERSONAL: Born April 8, 1967, at Terre Haute, Ind. . . . 6-0/210. . . . Full name: Anthony Q. Thompson.
HIGH SCHOOL: North (Terre Haute, Ind.).
COLLEGE: Indiana.

TRANSACTIONS/CAREER NOTES: Selected by Phoenix Cardinals in second round (31st pick overall) of 1990 NFL draft. . . . Signed by Cardinals (August 22, 1990).
RECORDS/HONORS: Named as running back to THE SPORTING NEWS college All-America team, 1988 and 1989.

Year Team	G	RUSHING Att.	Yds.	Avg.	TD	RECEIVING No.	Yds.	Avg.	TD	TOTAL TD	Pts.	F.
1990—Phoenix NFL	13	106	390	3.7	4	2	11	5.5	0	4	24	1
Pro totals (1 year)	13	106	390	3.7	4	2	11	5.5	0	4	24	1

THOMPSON, BENNIE
S, SAINTS

PERSONAL: Born February 10, 1963, at New Orleans. . . . 6-0/200.
HIGH SCHOOL: John McDonough (New Orleans).
COLLEGE: Grambling State.
TRANSACTIONS/CAREER NOTES: Signed as free agent by Kansas City Chiefs (May 9, 1985). . . . Released by Chiefs (August 5, 1985). . . . Signed by Winnipeg Blue Bombers of CFL (April 21, 1986). . . . Granted free agency (March 1, 1989). . . . Signed by New Orleans Saints (April 12, 1989). . . . Released by Saints (September 5, 1989). . . . Re-signed by Saints to developmental squad (September 6, 1989). . . . On developmental squad (September 6-December 13, 1989). . . . Activated after clearing procedural waivers (December 15, 1989).
PRO STATISTICS: 1987—Recovered one fumble. 1988—Recovered two fumbles for two yards and fumbled once.

Year Team	G	INTERCEPTIONS No.	Yds.	Avg.	TD
1986—Winnipeg CFL	9	2	49	24.5	0
1987—Winnipeg CFL	8	1	0	.0	0
1988—Winnipeg CFL	18	4	58	14.5	0
1989—New Orleans NFL	2	0	0		0
1990—New Orleans NFL	16	2	0	.0	0
CFL totals (3 years)	35	7	107	15.3	0
NFL totals (2 years)	18	2	0		0
Pro totals (5 years)	53	9	107	11.9	0

THOMPSON, BRODERICK
G/OT, CHARGERS

PERSONAL: Born August 14, 1960, at Birmingham, Ala. . . . 6-4/295.
HIGH SCHOOL: Richard Gahr (Cerritos, Calif.).
COLLEGE: Cerritos College (Calif.), then Kansas.
TRANSACTIONS/CAREER NOTES: Signed as free agent by Dallas Cowboys (April 28, 1983). . . . Released by Cowboys (August 2, 1983). . . . Signed as free agent by San Antonio Gunslingers of USFL (November 12, 1983). . . . Traded by Gunslingers with first-round pick in 1984 draft to Chicago Blitz for rights to quarterback Bob Gagliano (January 3, 1984). . . . Released by Blitz (January 31, 1984). . . . Signed as free agent by Los Angeles Express (February 10, 1984). . . . Released by Express (February 13, 1984). . . . Signed as free agent by Los Angeles Rams (May 4, 1984). . . . Released by Rams (August 21, 1984). . . . Signed as free agent by Portland Breakers of USFL (January 23, 1985). . . . Released by Breakers (July 31, 1985). . . . Awarded on waivers to Memphis Showboats (August 1, 1985). . . . Released by Showboats (August 2, 1985). . . . Signed as free agent by Dallas Cowboys (August 3, 1985). . . . Released by Cowboys (August 26, 1986). . . . Signed as free agent by San Diego Chargers (April 13, 1987). . . . Released by Chargers (September 7, 1987). . . . Re-signed by Chargers (September 8, 1987).
PLAYING EXPERIENCE: Portland USFL, 1985; Dallas NFL, 1985; San Diego NFL, 1987-1990. . . . Games: 1985 USFL (18), 1985 NFL (11), 1987 (8), 1988 (16), 1989 (16), 1990 (16). Total NFL: 67. Total Pro: 85.

THOMPSON, DARRELL
FB, PACKERS

PERSONAL: Born November 23, 1967, at Rochester, Minn. . . . 6-0/227. . . . Full name: Darrell Alexander Thompson.
HIGH SCHOOL: John Marshall (Rochester, Minn.).
COLLEGE: Minnesota (degree in business).

TRANSACTIONS/CAREER NOTES: Selected by Green Bay Packers in first round (19th pick overall) of 1990 NFL draft. . . . Signed by Packers (July 22, 1990).

Year Team	G	RUSHING Att.	Yds.	Avg.	TD	RECEIVING No.	Yds.	Avg.	TD	KICKOFF RETURNS No.	Yds.	Avg.	TD	TOTAL TD	Pts.	F.
1990—Green Bay NFL	16	76	264	3.5	1	3	1	.3	0	3	103	34.3	1	2	12	1
Pro totals (1 year)	16	76	264	3.5	1	3	1	.3	0	3	103	34.3	1	2	12	1

THOMPSON, DONNELL
DE, COLTS

PERSONAL: Born October 27, 1958, at Lumberton, N.C. . . . 6-4/280. . . . Full name: Lawrence Donnell Thompson.
HIGH SCHOOL: Lumberton (N.C.).
COLLEGE: North Carolina (bachelor of arts and science degree).

TRANSACTIONS/CAREER NOTES: Selected by Baltimore Colts in first round (18th pick overall) of 1981 NFL draft. . . . On physically unable to perform/active list with shoulder injury (July 24-August 23, 1982). . . . Franchise transferred to Indianapolis (March 31, 1984). . . . On suspended list (August 12-September 11, 1984). . . . On non-football injury list with shoulder and back injuries (September 12-October 12, 1984). . . . On inactive list (November 5, 11, 18 and 25, 1990).
PLAYING EXPERIENCE: Baltimore NFL, 1981-1983; Indianapolis NFL, 1984-1990. . . . Games: 1981 (13), 1982 (9), 1983 (14),

1984 (10), 1985 (15), 1986 (16), 1987 (12), 1988 (16), 1989 (16), 1990 (12). Total: 133.
PRO STATISTICS: 1981—Recovered one fumble. 1983—Credited with one safety. 1985—Recovered one fumble for nine yards. 1987—Recovered one fumble for 28 yards and a touchdown. 1988—Recovered two fumbles. 1989—Recovered two fumbles.

THOMPSON, REYNA
CB, GIANTS

PERSONAL: Born August 28, 1963, at Dallas. . . . 6-0/193. . . . Full name: Reyna Onald Thompson. . . . First name pronounced ruh-NAY.
HIGH SCHOOL: Thomas Jefferson (Dallas).
COLLEGE: Baylor (bachelor of arts degree in communications, 1986).
TRANSACTIONS/CAREER NOTES: Selected by Miami Dolphins in ninth round (247th pick overall) of 1986 NFL draft. . . . Signed by Dolphins (July 17, 1986). . . . Released by Dolphins (August 17, 1986). . . . Re-signed by Dolphins (August 18, 1986). . . . On injured reserve with shoulder injury (September 8-October 24, 1987). . . . Granted unconditional free agency (February 1, 1989). . . . Signed by New York Giants (March 31, 1989).
PLAYING EXPERIENCE: Miami NFL, 1986-1988; New York Giants NFL, 1989 and 1990. . . . Games: 1986 (16), 1987 (9), 1988 (16), 1989 (16), 1990 (16). Total: 73.
CHAMPIONSHIP GAME EXPERIENCE: Played in NFC championship game after 1990 season. . . . Played in Super Bowl XXV after 1990 season.
RECORDS/HONORS: Played in Pro Bowl after 1990 season.
PRO STATISTICS: 1986—Returned one punt for no yards and fumbled once. 1990—Recovered one fumble.

THORNTON, JAMES
TE, BEARS

PERSONAL: Born February 8, 1965, at Santa Rosa, Calif. . . . 6-2/242. . . . Full name: James Michael Thornton.
HIGH SCHOOL: Analy (Sebastopol, Calif.).
COLLEGE: Cal State Fullerton.
TRANSACTIONS/CAREER NOTES: Selected by Chicago Bears in fourth round (105th pick overall) of 1988 NFL draft. . . . Signed by Bears (July 21, 1988).
CHAMPIONSHIP GAME EXPERIENCE: Played in NFC championship game after 1988 season.
PRO STATISTICS: 1988—Fumbled once. 1989—Rushed once for four yards and fumbled twice. 1990—Fumbled once.

Year	Team	G	RECEIVING No.	Yds.	Avg.	TD
1988— Chicago NFL		16	15	135	9.0	0
1989— Chicago NFL		16	24	392	16.3	3
1990— Chicago NFL		16	19	254	13.4	1
Pro totals (3 years)		48	58	781	13.5	4

TICE, JOHN
TE, SAINTS

PERSONAL: Born June 22, 1960, at Bayshore, N.Y. . . . 6-5/249. . . . Brother of Mike Tice, tight end with Seattle Seahawks.
HIGH SCHOOL: Central Islip (N.Y.).
COLLEGE: Maryland.
TRANSACTIONS/CAREER NOTES: Selected by Washington Federals in 1983 USFL territorial draft. . . . Selected by New Orleans Saints in third round (65th pick overall) of 1983 NFL draft. . . . Signed by Saints (July 6, 1983). . . . On injured reserve with ankle injury (November 19, 1984-remainder of season).
PRO STATISTICS: 1983—Recovered two fumbles. 1985—Recovered one fumble. 1986—Recovered one fumble and fumbled once. 1989—Recovered one fumble. 1990—Recovered one fumble and fumbled once.

Year	Team	G	RECEIVING No.	Yds.	Avg.	TD
1983— New Orleans NFL		16	7	33	4.7	1
1984— New Orleans NFL		10	6	55	9.2	1
1985— New Orleans NFL		16	24	266	11.1	2
1986— New Orleans NFL		16	37	330	8.9	3
1987— New Orleans NFL		12	16	181	11.3	6
1988— New Orleans NFL		15	26	297	11.4	1
1989— New Orleans NFL		15	9	98	10.9	1
1990— New Orleans NFL		16	11	113	10.3	0
Pro totals (8 years)		116	136	1373	10.1	15

TICE, MIKE
TE, SEAHAWKS

PERSONAL: Born February 2, 1959, at Bayshore, N.Y. . . . 6-7/247. . . . Full name: Michael Peter Tice. . . . Brother of John Tice, tight end with New Orleans Saints.
HIGH SCHOOL: Central Islip (N.Y.).
COLLEGE: Maryland.
TRANSACTIONS/CAREER NOTES: Signed as free agent by Seattle Seahawks (April 30, 1981). . . . On injured reserve with fractured ankle (October 15-December 7, 1985). . . . Granted unconditional free agency (February 1, 1989). . . . Signed by Washington Redskins (February 20, 1989). . . . Released by Redskins (September 4, 1990). . . . Signed by Seattle Seahawks (November 28, 1990).
CHAMPIONSHIP GAME EXPERIENCE: Played in AFC championship game after 1983 season.
PRO STATISTICS: 1982—Recovered one fumble. 1983—Returned two kickoffs for 28 yards and recovered one fumble. 1985—Returned one kickoff for 17 yards. 1986—Returned one kickoff for 17 yards and recovered one fumble. 1988—Returned one kickoff for 17 yards and fumbled once.

Year	Team	G	No.	Yds.	Avg.	TD
1981— Seattle NFL		16	5	47	9.4	0
1982— Seattle NFL		9	9	46	5.1	0
1983— Seattle NFL		15	0	0		0
1984— Seattle NFL		16	8	90	11.3	3
1985— Seattle NFL		9	2	13	6.5	0
1986— Seattle NFL		16	15	150	10.0	0
1987— Seattle NFL		12	14	106	7.6	2
1988— Seattle NFL		16	29	244	8.4	0
1989— Washington NFL		16	1	2	2.0	0
1990— Seattle NFL		5	0	0		0
Pro totals (10 years)		130	83	698	8.4	5

TILLMAN, LAWYER
WR, BROWNS

PERSONAL: Born May 20, 1966, at Mobile, Ala. . . . 6-5/230. . . . Full name: Lawyer James Tillman Jr.
HIGH SCHOOL: John L. LeFlore (Mobile, Ala.).
COLLEGE: Auburn.
TRANSACTIONS/CAREER NOTES: Selected by Cleveland Browns in second round (31st pick overall) of 1989 NFL draft. . . . Signed by Browns (September 8, 1989). . . . Granted roster exemption (September 8-September 18, 1989). . . . On injured reserve with leg injury (September 4, 1990-entire season).
CHAMPIONSHIP GAME EXPERIENCE: Played in AFC championship game after 1989 season.
PRO STATISTICS: 1989—Recovered blocked punt in end zone for a touchdown.

Year	Team	G	No.	Yds.	Avg.	TD
1989— Cleveland NFL		14	6	70	11.7	2
Pro totals (1 year)		14	6	70	11.7	2

TILLMAN, LEWIS
RB, GIANTS

PERSONAL: Born April 16, 1966, at Oklahoma City. . . . 6-0/195. . . . Full name: Lewis D. Tillman.
HIGH SCHOOL: Hazlehurst (Miss.).
COLLEGE: Jackson State (bachelor of science degree in business management, 1989).
TRANSACTIONS/CAREER NOTES: Selected by New York Giants in fourth round (93rd pick overall) of 1989 NFL draft. . . . Signed by Giants (July 24, 1989).
CHAMPIONSHIP GAME EXPERIENCE: Played in NFC championship game after 1990 season. . . . Played in Super Bowl XXV after 1990 season.

Year	Team	G		RUSHING				RECEIVING				TOTAL	
			Att.	Yds.	Avg.	TD	No.	Yds.	Avg.	TD	TD	Pts.	F.
1989— N.Y. Giants NFL		16	79	290	3.7	0	1	9	9.0	0	0	0	1
1990— N.Y. Giants NFL		16	84	231	2.8	1	8	18	2.3	0	1	6	0
Pro totals (2 years)		32	163	521	3.2	1	9	27	3.0	0	1	6	1

TILLMAN, SPENCER
RB, 49ERS

PERSONAL: Born April 21, 1964, at Tulsa, Okla. . . . 5-11/206. . . . Full name: Spencer Allen Tillman.
HIGH SCHOOL: Thomas Edison (Tulsa, Okla.).
COLLEGE: Oklahoma (bachelor of science degree in radio and television communications, 1987).
TRANSACTIONS/CAREER NOTES: Selected by Houston Oilers in fifth round (133rd pick overall) of 1987 NFL draft. . . . Signed by Oilers (July 28, 1987). . . . Granted unconditional free agency (February 1, 1989). . . . Signed by San Francisco 49ers (March 27, 1989).
CHAMPIONSHIP GAME EXPERIENCE: Played in NFC championship game after 1989 and 1990 seasons. . . . Played in Super Bowl XXIV after 1989 season.
PRO STATISTICS: 1987—Fumbled once. 1989—Recovered one fumble.

Year	Team	G		RUSHING				KICKOFF RETURNS				TOTAL	
			No.	Yds.	Avg.	TD	No.	Yds.	Avg.	TD	TD	Pts.	F.
1987— Houston NFL		5	12	29	2.4	1	1	0	.0	0	1	6	1
1988— Houston NFL		16	3	5	1.7	0	1	13	13.0	0	0	0	0
1989— San Francisco NFL		15	0	0		0	10	206	20.6	0	0	0	0
1990— San Francisco NFL		16	0	0		0	6	111	18.5	0	0	0	0
Pro totals (4 years)		52	15	34	2.3	1	18	330	18.3	0	1	6	1

DID YOU KNOW. . .

. . .that the New Orleans Saints had beaten AFC opponents in 13 consecutive games until a 23-10 loss at Houston on October 21, 1990?

TIMPSON, MICHAEL
WR, PATRIOTS

PERSONAL: Born June 6, 1967, at Baxley, Ga. . . . 5-10/175. . . . Full name: Michael Dwain Timpson.
HIGH SCHOOL: Miami Lakes (Hialeah, Fla.).
COLLEGE: Penn State.
TRANSACTIONS/CAREER NOTES: Selected by New England Patriots in fourth round (100th pick overall) of 1989 NFL draft. . . . Signed by Patriots (July 18, 1989). . . . On injured reserve with hamstring injury (September 9-October 26, 1989). . . . Transferred to developmental squad (October 27-November 3, 1989). . . . On injured reserve with knee injury (November 16. 1989-remainder of season). . . . On injured reserve with finger injury (September 4-December 1, 1990).

		— RECEIVING —				— KICKOFF RETURNS —				— TOTAL —		
Year Team	G	No.	Yds.	Avg.	TD	No.	Yds.	Avg.	TD	TD	Pts.	F.
1989— New England NFL	2	0	0		0	2	13	6.5	0	0	0	1
1990— New England NFL	5	5	91	18.2	0	3	62	20.7	0	0	0	0
Pro totals (2 years)	7	5	91	18.2	0	5	75	15.0	0	0	0	1

TIPPETT, ANDRE
LB, PATRIOTS

PERSONAL: Born December 27, 1959, at Birmingham, Ala. . . . 6-3/241. . . . Full name: Andre Bernard Tippett.
HIGH SCHOOL: Barringer (Newark, N.J.).
COLLEGE: Ellsworth Junior College (Ia.), then Iowa (bachelor of liberal arts degree, 1983).
TRANSACTIONS/CAREER NOTES: Selected by New England Patriots in second round (41st pick overall) of 1982 NFL draft. . . . Crossed picket line during players' strike (October 14, 1987). . . . On injured reserve with shoulder injury (September 4, 1989-entire season). . . . On inactive list (September 23, 30; and October 7, 1990).
PLAYING EXPERIENCE: New England NFL, 1982-1988 and 1990. . . . Games: 1982 (9), 1983 (15), 1984 (16), 1985 (16), 1986 (11), 1987 (13), 1988 (12), 1990 (13). Total: 105.
CHAMPIONSHIP GAME EXPERIENCE: Played in AFC championship game after 1985 season. . . . Played in Super Bowl XX after 1985 season.
RECORDS/HONORS: Played in Pro Bowl after 1984-1988 seasons. . . . Named to THE SPORTING NEWS NFL All-Pro team, 1985.
PRO STATISTICS: 1982—Recovered one fumble. 1983—Recovered one fumble. 1985—Recovered four fumbles for 25 yards and a touchdown. 1986—Ran 32 yards with lateral from interception and recovered one fumble. 1987—Recovered three fumbles for 29 yards and a touchdown. 1990—Recovered two fumbles for seven yards.

TIPPINS, KEN
LB, FALCONS

PERSONAL: Born July 22, 1966, at Adel, Ga. . . . 6-1/230.
HIGH SCHOOL: Cook (Adel, Ga.).
COLLEGE: Middle Tennessee State.
TRANSACTIONS/CAREER NOTES: Signed as free agent by Dallas Cowboys (April 27, 1989). . . . Released by Cowboys (September 5, 1989). . . . Re-signed by Cowboys to developmental squad (September 11, 1989). . . . On developmental squad (September 11-September 13, 1989). . . . Activated after clearing procedural waivers (September 15, 1989). . . . Released by Cowboys (October 24, 1989). . . . Re-signed by Cowboys to developmental squad (November 21, 1989). . . . On developmental squad (November 21, 1989-remainder of season). . . . Released by Cowboys (January 5, 1990). . . . Signed as free agent by Atlanta Falcons (May 9, 1990).
PLAYING EXPERIENCE: Dallas NFL, 1989; Atlanta NFL, 1990. . . . Games: 1989 (6), 1990 (16). Total: 22.

TOFFLEMIRE, JOE
C, SEAHAWKS

PERSONAL: Born July 7, 1965, at Los Angeles. . . . 6-2/273. . . . Full name: Joseph Salvatore Tofflemire.
HIGH SCHOOL: Post Falls (Idaho).
COLLEGE: Arizona (degree in real estate, 1989).
TRANSACTIONS/CAREER NOTES: Selected by Seattle Seahawks in second round (44th pick overall) of 1989 NFL draft. . . . Signed by Seahawks (July 22, 1989). . . . Active for 16 games with Seattle Seahawks in 1989; did not play.
PLAYING EXPERIENCE: Seattle NFL, 1989 and 1990. . . . Games: 1989 (0), 1990 (16). Total: 16.

TOLBERT, TONY
DE, COWBOYS

PERSONAL: Born December 29, 1967, at Tuskeegee, Ala. . . . 6-6/270. . . . Full name: Tony Lewis Tolbert.
HIGH SCHOOL: Dwight Morrow (Englewood, N.J.).
COLLEGE: Texas-El Paso.
TRANSACTIONS/CAREER NOTES: Selected by Dallas Cowboys in fourth round (85th pick overall) of 1989 NFL draft. . . . Signed by Cowboys (July 23, 1989).
PLAYING EXPERIENCE: Dallas NFL, 1989 and 1990. . . . Games: 1989 (16), 1990 (16). Total: 32.

TOLLIVER, BILLY JOE
QB, CHARGERS

PERSONAL: Born February 7, 1966, at Dallas. . . . 6-1/218. . . . Full name: Billy Joe Tolliver.
HIGH SCHOOL: Boyd (Tex.).
COLLEGE: Texas Tech.
TRANSACTIONS/CAREER NOTES: Selected by San Diego Chargers in second round (51st pick overall) of 1989 NFL draft. . . . Signed by Chargers (July 30, 1989). . . . On injured reserve with broken collarbone (September 5-October 18, 1989). . . . Transferred to developmental squad (October 19 and October 20, 1989). . . . Activated (October 21, 1989).
PRO STATISTICS: Passer rating points: 1989 (57.9), 1990 (68.9). Career: 65.5. . . . 1989—Recovered one fumble and fumbled four times for minus six yards. 1990—Recovered two fumbles.

Year Team	G	Att.	Cmp.	Pct.	Yds.	TD	Int.	Avg.	Att.	Yds.	Avg.	TD	TD	Pts.	F.
1989— San Diego NFL	5	185	89	48.1	1097	5	8	5.93	7	0	.0	0	0	0	4
1990— San Diego NFL	15	410	216	52.7	2574	16	16	6.28	14	22	1.6	0	0	0	6
Pro totals (2 years)	20	595	305	51.3	3671	21	24	6.17	21	22	1.1	0	0	0	10

TOMBERLIN, PAT
OT, COLTS

PERSONAL: Born January 29, 1966, at Jacksonville, Fla. . . . 6-2/310. . . . Full name: Howard Patrick Tomberlin.
HIGH SCHOOL: Middleburg (Fla.).
COLLEGE: Florida State.
TRANSACTIONS/CAREER NOTES: Selected by Indianapolis Colts in fourth round (99th pick overall) of 1989 NFL draft. . . . Signed by Colts (August 7, 1989). . . . Active for one game with Colts in 1989; did not play.
PLAYING EXPERIENCE: Indianapolis NFL, 1989 and 1990. . . . Games: 1989 (0), 1990 (16). Total: 16.

TOMCZAK, MIKE
QB, PACKERS

PERSONAL: Born October 23, 1962, at Calumet City, Ill. . . . 6-1/204. . . . Name pronounced TOM-zak.
HIGH SCHOOL: Thornton Fractional North (Calumet City, Ill.).
COLLEGE: Ohio State.
TRANSACTIONS/CAREER NOTES: Selected by New Jersey Generals in 1985 USFL territorial draft. . . . Signed as free agent by Chicago Bears (May 9, 1985). . . . Granted free agency (February 1, 1990). . . . Re-signed by Bears (July 25, 1990). . . . Granted unconditional free agency (February 1, 1991). . . . Signed by Green Bay Packers (March 30, 1991).
CHAMPIONSHIP GAME EXPERIENCE: Member of Chicago Bears for NFC championship game after 1985 season; did not play. . . . Played in Super Bowl XX after 1985 season. . . . Played in NFC championship game after 1988 season.
PRO STATISTICS: Passer rating points: 1985 (52.8), 1986 (50.2), 1987 (62.0), 1988 (75.4), 1989 (68.2), 1990 (43.8). Career: 62.5. . . . 1985—Recovered one fumble and fumbled once for minus 13 yards. 1987—Recovered one fumble. 1988—Fumbled once for minus three yards. 1990—Caught one pass for five yards and fumbled twice for minus two yards.

Year Team	G	Att.	Cmp.	Pct.	Yds.	TD	Int.	Avg.	Att.	Yds.	Avg.	TD	TD	Pts.	F.
1985— Chicago NFL	6	6	2	33.3	33	0	0	5.50	2	3	1.5	0	0	0	1
1986— Chicago NFL	13	151	74	49.0	1105	2	10	7.32	23	117	5.1	3	3	18	2
1987— Chicago NFL	12	178	97	54.5	1220	5	10	6.85	18	54	3.0	1	1	6	6
1988— Chicago NFL	14	170	86	50.6	1310	7	6	7.71	13	40	3.1	1	1	6	1
1989— Chicago NFL	16	306	156	51.0	2058	16	16	6.73	24	71	3.0	1	1	6	2
1990— Chicago NFL	16	104	39	37.5	521	3	5	5.01	12	41	3.4	2	2	12	2
Pro totals (6 years)	77	915	454	49.6	6247	33	47	6.83	92	326	3.5	8	8	48	14

TONEY, ANTHONY
RB, EAGLES

PERSONAL: Born September 23, 1962, at Salinas, Calif. . . . 6-0/230. . . . Cousin of Del Rodgers, running back with Green Bay Packers and San Francisco 49ers, 1982, 1984, 1987 and 1988.
HIGH SCHOOL: North Salinas (Salinas, Calif.).
COLLEGE: Hartnell Community College (Calif.), then Texas A&M.
TRANSACTIONS/CAREER NOTES: Selected by Jacksonville Bulls in 1986 USFL territorial draft. . . . Selected by Philadelphia Eagles in second round (37th pick overall) of 1986 NFL draft. . . . Signed by Eagles (July 25, 1986). . . . On injured reserve with sprained ankle (September 2-October 1, 1986). . . . Granted roster exemption (September 4-September 8, 1990). . . . On inactive list (November 4, 1990).
PRO STATISTICS: 1987—Attempted one pass with no completions and recovered three fumbles. 1989—Recovered three fumbles for minus three yards. 1990—Recovered three fumbles.

		— RUSHING —				— RECEIVING —				— TOTAL —		
Year Team	G	Att.	Yds.	Avg.	TD	No.	Yds.	Avg.	TD	TD	Pts.	F.
1986— Philadelphia NFL	12	69	285	4.1	1	13	177	13.6	0	1	6	0
1987— Philadelphia NFL	11	127	473	3.7	5	39	341	8.7	1	6	36	5
1988— Philadelphia NFL	15	139	502	3.6	4	34	256	7.5	1	5	30	2
1989— Philadelphia NFL	14	172	582	3.4	3	19	124	6.5	0	3	18	4
1990— Philadelphia NFL	15	132	452	3.4	1	17	133	7.8	3	4	24	3
Pro totals (5 years)	67	639	2294	3.6	14	122	1031	8.5	5	19	114	14

TOON, AL
WR, JETS

PERSONAL: Born April 30, 1963, at Newport News, Va. . . . 6-4/205. . . . Full name: Al Lee Toon Jr.
HIGH SCHOOL: Menchville (Newport News, Va.).
COLLEGE: Wisconsin.
TRANSACTIONS/CAREER NOTES: Selected by Jacksonville Bulls in 1985 USFL territorial draft. . . . Selected by New York Jets in first round (10th pick overall) of 1985 NFL draft. . . . Signed by Jets (September 11, 1985). . . . Granted roster exemption (September 11-September 14, 1985). . . . On inactive list (December 22, 1990). . . . On injured reserve with groin injury (December 28, 1990-remainder of season).
RECORDS/HONORS: Played in Pro Bowl after 1986-1988 seasons.
PRO STATISTICS: 1985—Rushed once for five yards. 1986—Rushed twice for minus three yards, recovered one fumble and fumbled three times. 1988—Rushed once for five yards and fumbled twice. 1990—Attempted two passes with no completions.

Year	Team	G	No.	Yds.	Avg.	TD
			RECEIVING			
1985— N.Y. Jets NFL		15	46	662	14.4	3
1986— N.Y. Jets NFL		16	85	1176	13.8	8
1987— N.Y. Jets NFL		12	68	976	14.4	5
1988— N.Y. Jets NFL		15	*93	1067	11.5	5
1989— N.Y. Jets NFL		11	63	693	11.0	2
1990— N.Y. Jets NFL		14	57	757	13.3	6
Pro totals (6 years)		83	412	5331	12.9	29

TOWNSELL, JOJO
WR/KR, JETS

PERSONAL: Born November 4, 1960, at Reno, Nev. . . . 5-9/182. . . . Full name: Joseph Ray Townsell.
HIGH SCHOOL: Hug (Reno, Nev.).
COLLEGE: UCLA (degree in sociology, 1982).
TRANSACTIONS/CAREER NOTES: Selected by Los Angeles Express in sixth round (72nd pick overall) of 1983 USFL draft. . . . Selected by New York Jets in third round (78th pick overall) of 1983 NFL draft. . . . Signed by Los Angeles Express (June 3, 1983). . . . Released by Express (August 1, 1985). . . . Signed by New York Jets (August 5, 1985). . . . On inactive list (October 14, 21, 28; November 4, 11, 18; and December 16, 1990).
PRO STATISTICS: USFL: 1984—Rushed eight times for 19 yards. 1985—Rushed twice for nine yards and recovered one fumble. . . . NFL: 1985—Recovered one fumble. 1986—Rushed once for two yards. 1987—Rushed once for minus two yards and recovered two fumbles. 1989—Recovered three fumbles.

Year	Team	G	No.	Yds.	Avg.	TD	No.	Yds.	Avg.	TD	No.	Yds.	Avg.	TD	TD	Pts.	F.
			RECEIVING				PUNT RETURNS				KICKOFF RETURNS				TOTAL		
1983— Los Ang. USFL		5	21	326	15.5	3	0	0		0	1	8	8.0	0	3	18	0
1984— Los Ang. USFL		18	58	889	15.3	7	0	0		0	0	0		0	7	42	2
1985— Los Ang. USFL		16	47	777	16.5	6	8	33	4.1	0	0	0		0	6	36	2
1985— N.Y. Jets NFL		16	12	187	15.6	0	6	65	10.8	0	2	42	21.0	0	0	0	1
1986— N.Y. Jets NFL		14	1	11	11.0	0	4	52	13.0	0	13	322	24.8	*1	1	6	0
1987— N.Y. Jets NFL		12	4	37	9.3	0	32	381	11.9	1	11	272	24.7	0	1	6	3
1988— N.Y. Jets NFL		16	4	40	10.0	0	35	409	11.7	1	31	601	19.4	0	1	6	3
1989— N.Y. Jets NFL		16	45	787	17.5	5	33	299	9.1	0	34	653	19.2	0	5	30	4
1990— N.Y. Jets NFL		9	4	57	14.3	0	17	154	9.1	0	7	158	22.6	0	0	0	2
USFL totals (3 years)		39	126	1992	15.8	16	8	33	4.1	0	1	8	8.0	0	16	96	4
NFL totals (6 years)		83	70	1119	16.0	5	127	1360	10.7	2	98	2048	20.9	1	8	48	13
Pro totals (9 years)		122	196	3111	15.9	21	135	1393	10.3	2	99	2056	20.8	1	24	144	17

TOWNSEND, ANDRE
DE/NT, BRONCOS

PERSONAL: Born October 8, 1962, at Chicago. . . . 6-3/265.
HIGH SCHOOL: Aberdeen (Miss.).
COLLEGE: Mississippi.
TRANSACTIONS/CAREER NOTES: Selected by Birmingham Stallions in 1984 USFL territorial draft. . . . Selected by Denver Broncos in second round (46th pick overall) of 1984 NFL draft. . . . Signed by Broncos (June 18, 1984). . . . On inactive list (September 9, 1990).
PLAYING EXPERIENCE: Denver NFL, 1984-1990. . . . Games: 1984 (16), 1985 (16), 1986 (16), 1987 (12), 1988 (16), 1989 (13), 1990 (15). Total: 104.
CHAMPIONSHIP GAME EXPERIENCE: Played in AFC championship game after 1986, 1987 and 1989 seasons. . . . Played in Super Bowl XXI after 1986 season, Super Bowl XXII after 1987 season and Super Bowl XXIV after 1989 season.
PRO STATISTICS: 1984—Recovered one fumble. 1985—Recovered one fumble. 1986—Recovered one fumble for seven yards and a touchdown. 1988—Recovered one fumble. 1989—Recovered two fumbles.

TOWNSEND, GREG
DE, RAIDERS

PERSONAL: Born November 3, 1961, at Los Angeles. . . . 6-3/270.
HIGH SCHOOL: Dominguez (Compton, Calif.).
COLLEGE: Long Beach City College (Calif.), then Texas Christian.
TRANSACTIONS/CAREER NOTES: Selected by Oakland Invaders in seventh round (79th pick overall) of 1983 USFL draft. . . . Selected by Los Angeles Raiders in fourth round (110th pick overall) of 1983 NFL draft. . . . Signed by Raiders (July 7, 1983). . . . On suspended list (October 9, 1986). . . . Reinstated (October 10, 1986). . . . On suspended list (October 13-October 20, 1986). . . . Crossed picket line during players' strike (October 14, 1987). . . . On non-football injury list with substance abuse (August 5-August 31, 1988).
PLAYING EXPERIENCE: Los Angeles Raiders NFL, 1983-1990. . . . Games: 1983 (16), 1984 (16), 1985 (16), 1986 (15), 1987 (13), 1988 (16), 1989 (16), 1990 (16). Total: 124.
CHAMPIONSHIP GAME EXPERIENCE: Played in AFC championship game after 1983 and 1990 seasons. . . . Played in Super Bowl XVIII after 1983 season.
RECORDS/HONORS: Tied NFL record for most touchdowns scored by recovery of opponents' fumbles, career (3). . . . Played in Pro Bowl after 1990 season. . . . Named to THE SPORTING NEWS NFL All-Pro team, 1990.
PRO STATISTICS: 1983—Recovered one fumble for 66 yards and a touchdown. 1985—Recovered one fumble. 1986—Credited with a safety. 1988—Intercepted one pass for 86 yards and a touchdown and recovered one fumble in end zone for a touchdown. 1989—Recovered one fumble. 1990—Recovered one fumble for one yard and a touchdown and intercepted one pass.

TRAPILO, STEVE
G, SAINTS

PERSONAL: Born September 20, 1964, at Boston. . . . 6-5/281. . . . Full name: Stephen Paul Trapilo. . . . Name pronounced tru-PILL-o.
HIGH SCHOOL: Boston College (Boston).
COLLEGE: Boston College (degree in sociology, 1986).
TRANSACTIONS/CAREER NOTES: Selected by New Orleans Saints in fourth round (96th pick overall) of 1987 NFL draft. . . . Signed by Saints (July 27, 1987). . . . On injured reserve with sprained arch (September 5-October 29, 1988). . . . Granted free agency (February 1, 1990). . . . Re-signed by Saints (August 21, 1990).
PLAYING EXPERIENCE: New Orleans NFL, 1987-1990. . . . Games: 1987 (11), 1988 (9), 1989 (16), 1990 (16). Total: 52.
PRO STATISTICS: 1990—Recovered one fumble.

TREADWELL, DAVID
PK, BRONCOS

PERSONAL: Born February 27, 1967, at Columbia, S.C. . . . 6-1/175. . . . Full name: David Mark Treadwell.
HIGH SCHOOL: The Bolles (Jacksonville, Fla.).
COLLEGE: Clemson (bachelor of science degree in electrical engineering, 1989).
TRANSACTIONS/CAREER NOTES: Signed as free agent by Denver Broncos (April 27, 1988). . . . Released by Broncos (August 23, 1988). . . . Signed as free agent by Phoenix Cardinals (January 4, 1989). . . . Traded by Cardinals to Denver Broncos for 12th-round pick in 1990 NFL draft (May 30, 1989).
CHAMPIONSHIP GAME EXPERIENCE: Played in AFC championship game after 1989 season. . . . Played in Super Bowl XXIV after 1989 season.
RECORDS/HONORS: Named as place-kicker on THE SPORTING NEWS college All-America team, 1987. . . . Played in Pro Bowl after 1989 season.

| | | ——— PLACE-KICKING ——— | | | | |
Year Team	G	XPM	XPA	FGM	FGA	Pts.
1989—Denver NFL	16	39	40	27	33	120
1990—Denver NFL	16	34	36	25	34	109
Pro totals (2 years)	32	73	76	52	67	229

TRUDEAU, JACK
QB, COLTS

PERSONAL: Born September 9, 1962, at Forest Lake, Minn. . . . 6-3/219. . . . Full name: Jack Francis Trudeau.
HIGH SCHOOL: Granada (Livermore, Calif.).
COLLEGE: Illinois (degree in political science, 1986).
TRANSACTIONS/CAREER NOTES: Selected by Orlando Renegades in 1986 USFL territorial draft. . . . Selected by Indianapolis Colts in second round (47th pick overall) of 1986 NFL draft. . . . Signed by Colts (July 31, 1986). . . . On injured reserve with knee injury (October 11, 1988-remainder of season). . . . On injured reserve with knee injury (October 31, 1990-remainder of season).
PRO STATISTICS: Passer rating points: 1986 (53.5), 1987 (75.4), 1988 (19.0), 1989 (71.3), 1990 (78.4). Career: 65.2. . . . 1986—Recovered six fumbles and fumbled 13 times for minus 15 yards. 1987—Recovered two fumbles and fumbled 10 times for minus 28 yards. 1989—Recovered seven fumbles and fumbled 10 times for minus five yards. 1990—Recovered four fumbles.

| | | ———————PASSING——————— | | | | | | | ——RUSHING—— | | | | ——TOTAL—— | |
Year Team	G	Att.	Cmp.	Pct.	Yds.	TD	Int.	Avg.	Att.	Yds.	Avg.	TD	TD	Pts.	F.
1986—Indianapolis NFL	12	417	204	48.9	2225	8	18	5.34	13	21	1.6	1	1	6	*13
1987—Indianapolis NFL	10	229	128	55.9	1587	6	6	6.93	15	7	.5	0	0	0	10
1988—Indianapolis NFL	2	34	14	41.2	158	0	3	4.65	0	0		0	0	0	0
1989—Indianapolis NFL	13	362	190	52.5	2317	15	13	6.40	35	91	2.6	2	2	12	10
1990—Indianapolis NFL	6	144	84	58.3	1078	6	6	7.49	10	28	2.8	0	0	0	11
Pro totals (5 years)	43	1186	620	52.3	7365	35	46	6.21	73	147	2.0	3	3	18	44

TUATAGALOA, NATU
DE, BENGALS

PERSONAL: Born May 25, 1966, at San Francisco. . . . 6-4/274. . . . Full name: Gerardus Mauritius Natuitasina Tuatagaloa. . . . Nickname and last name pronounced NA-too TOO-un-TAG-uh-LOW-uh.
HIGH SCHOOL: San Rafael (Calif.).
COLLEGE: California (bachelor of science degree in history, 1989).
TRANSACTIONS/CAREER NOTES: Selected by Cincinnati Bengals in fifth round (138th pick overall) of 1989 NFL draft. . . . Signed by Bengals (July 22, 1989).
PLAYING EXPERIENCE: Cincinnati NFL, 1989 and 1990. . . . Games: 1989 (14), 1990 (16). Total: 30.
PRO STATISTICS: 1990—Recovered two fumbles.

TUGGLE, JESSIE
LB, FALCONS

PERSONAL: Born February 14, 1965, at Spalding County, Ga. . . . 5-11/230. . . . Full name: Jessie Lloyd Tuggle.
HIGH SCHOOL: Griffin (Ga.).
COLLEGE: Valdosta State (Ga.).
TRANSACTIONS/CAREER NOTES: Signed as free agent by Atlanta Falcons (May 2, 1987).
PLAYING EXPERIENCE: Atlanta NFL, 1987-1990. . . . Games: 1987 (12), 1988 (16), 1989 (16), 1990 (16). Total: 60.
PRO STATISTICS: 1988—Recovered one fumble for two yards and a touchdown. 1989—Recovered one fumble. 1990—Recovered two fumbles for 65 yards and a touchdown.

TUINEI, MARK
OT, COWBOYS

PERSONAL: Born March 31, 1960, at Nanakuli, Oahu, Hawaii. . . . 6-5/293. . . . Full name: Mark Pulemau Tuinei. . . . Name pronounced TWO-ee-nay. . . . Brother of Tom Tuinei, defensive end with Edmonton Eskimos (CFL), 1982-1987.
HIGH SCHOOL: Punahou (Honolulu, Hawaii).
COLLEGE: UCLA, then Hawaii.
TRANSACTIONS/CAREER NOTES: Selected by Boston Breakers in 19th round (227th pick overall) of 1983 USFL draft. . . . Signed as free agent by Dallas Cowboys (April 28, 1983). . . . On injured reserve with knee injury (December 2, 1987-remainder of season). . . . On injured reserve with knee injury (October 19, 1988-remainder of season). . . . Granted free agency (February 1, 1990). . . . Re-signed by Cowboys (May 21, 1990). . . . On inactive list (November 11 and 18, 1990).
PLAYING EXPERIENCE: Dallas NFL, 1983-1990. . . . Games: 1983 (10), 1984 (16), 1985 (16), 1986 (16), 1987 (8), 1988 (5), 1989 (16), 1990 (13). Total: 100.
PRO STATISTICS: 1986—Returned one kickoff for no yards, recovered three fumbles and fumbled once. 1987—Recovered one fumble.

TUPA, TOM
QB/P, CARDINALS

PERSONAL: Born February 6, 1966, at Cleveland. . . . 6-5/215. . . . Full name: Thomas Joseph Tupa.
HIGH SCHOOL: Brecksville (Broadview Heights, O.).
COLLEGE: Ohio State.
TRANSACTIONS/CAREER NOTES: Selected by Phoenix Cardinals in third round (68th pick overall) of 1988 NFL draft. . . . Signed by Cardinals (July 12, 1988).
PRO STATISTICS: Passer rating points: 1988 (91.7), 1989 (52.2). Career: 53.9. . . . 1989—Punted six times for 46.7 avg. and recovered one fumble and fumbled twice for minus six yards. 1990—Fumbled once for minus seven yards.

Year Team	G	Att.	Cmp.	Pct.	Yds.	TD	Int.	Avg.	Att.	Yds.	Avg.	TD	TD	Pts.	F.
					PASSING					RUSHING				TOTAL	
1988—Phoenix NFL	2	6	4	66.7	49	0	0	8.17	0	0		0	0	0	0
1989—Phoenix NFL	14	134	65	48.5	973	0	9	7.26	15	75	5.0	0	0	0	2
1990—Phoenix NFL	15	0	0		0	0	0		1	0	.0	0	0	0	1
Pro totals (3 years)	31	140	69	49.3	1022	3	9	7.30	16	75	4.7	0	0	0	3

TURK, DAN
C, RAIDERS

PERSONAL: Born June 25, 1962, at Milwaukee. . . . 6-4/275. . . . Full name: Daniel Anthony Turk.
HIGH SCHOOL: James Madison (Milwaukee).
COLLEGE: Drake, then Wisconsin.
TRANSACTIONS/CAREER NOTES: Selected by Jacksonville Bulls in 1985 USFL territorial draft. . . . USFL rights traded by Bulls with rights to running back Marck Harrison and tight end Ken Whisenhunt to Tampa Bay Bandits for rights to running back Cedric Jones, kicker Bobby Raymond and defensive back Eric Riley (January 3, 1985). . . . Selected by Pittsburgh Steelers in fourth round (101st pick overall) of 1985 NFL draft. . . . Signed by Steelers (July 19, 1985). . . . On injured reserve with broken wrist (September 16, 1985-remainder of season). . . . Traded by Steelers to Tampa Bay Buccaneers for sixth-round pick in 1987 draft (April 13, 1987). . . . Crossed picket line during players' strike (October 14, 1987). . . . On injured reserve with knee injury (October 18-November 18, 1988). . . . Granted free agency (February 1, 1989). . . . Rights relinquished (June 6, 1989). . . . Signed by Los Angeles Raiders (June 21, 1989).
PLAYING EXPERIENCE: Pittsburgh NFL, 1985 and 1986; Tampa Bay NFL, 1987 and 1988; Los Angeles Raiders NFL, 1989 and 1990. . . . Games: 1985 (1), 1986 (16), 1987 (13), 1988 (12), 1989 (16), 1990 (16). Total: 74.
CHAMPIONSHIP GAME EXPERIENCE: Played in AFC championship game after 1990 season.
PRO STATISTICS: 1988—Recovered one fumble and fumbled once for minus 19 yards. 1989—Returned one kickoff for two yards and fumbled once for minus eight yards. 1990—Returned one kickoff for seven yards.

TURNBULL, RENALDO
DE, SAINTS

PERSONAL: Born January 5, 1966, at St. Thomas, Virgin Islands. . . . 6-4/255. . . . Full name: Renaldo Antonio Turnbull.
HIGH SCHOOL: Charlotte Amalie (St. Thomas, Virgin Islands).
COLLEGE: West Virginia (degree in communications).
TRANSACTIONS/CAREER NOTES: Selected by New Orleans Saints in first round (14th pick overall) of 1990 NFL draft. . . . Signed by Saints (July 15, 1990).
PLAYING EXPERIENCE: New Orleans NFL, 1990. . . . Games: 1990 (16).
PRO STATISTICS: 1990—Recovered one fumble.

TURNER, FLOYD
WR, SAINTS

PERSONAL: Born May 29, 1966, at Shreveport, La. . . . 5-11/188. . . . Full name: Floyd Turner Jr.
HIGH SCHOOL: Mansfield (La.).
COLLEGE: Northwestern (La.) State (degree in education).
TRANSACTIONS/CAREER NOTES: Selected by New Orleans Saints in sixth round (159th pick overall) of 1989 NFL draft. . . . Signed by Saints (July 22, 1989). . . . On injured reserve with broken arm (December 6, 1989-remainder of season).
PRO STATISTICS: 1989—Rushed twice for eight yards, returned one punt for seven yards, recovered three fumbles and fumbled once.

		RECEIVING			
Year Team	G	No.	Yds.	Avg.	TD
1989—New Orleans NFL	13	22	279	12.7	1
1990—New Orleans NFL	16	21	396	18.9	4
Pro totals (2 years)	29	43	675	15.7	5

TURNER, MARCUS
DB, CARDINALS

PERSONAL: Born January 13, 1966, at Harbor City, Calif. . . . 6-1/190. . . . Full name: Marcus Jared Turner.
HIGH SCHOOL: David Starr Jordan (Long Beach, Calif.).
COLLEGE: UCLA.
TRANSACTIONS/CAREER NOTES: Selected by Kansas City Chiefs in 11th round (283rd pick overall) of 1989 NFL draft. . . . Signed by Chiefs (July 21, 1989). . . . Released by Chiefs (September 5, 1989). . . . Signed as free agent by Phoenix Cardinals to developmental squad (September 6, 1989). . . . On developmental squad (September 6-September 29, 1989).
PLAYING EXPERIENCE: Phoenix NFL, 1989 and 1990. . . . Games: 1989 (13), 1990 (16). Total: 29.
PRO STATISTICS: 1989—Recovered one fumble. 1990—Intercepted one pass for 47 yards and a touchdown, ran 23 yards for a touchdown with lateral from interception and recovered one fumble.

TURNER, T.J.
DE, DOLPHINS

PERSONAL: Born May 16, 1963, at Lufkin, Tex. . . . 6-4/280. . . . Full name: Thomas James Turner.
HIGH SCHOOL: Lufkin (Tex.).
COLLEGE: Houston.
TRANSACTIONS/CAREER NOTES: Selected by Miami Dolphins in third round (81st pick overall) of 1986 NFL draft. . . . Signed by Dolphins (July 23, 1986).
PLAYING EXPERIENCE: Miami NFL, 1986-1990. . . . Games: 1986 (16), 1987 (12), 1988 (16), 1989 (14), 1990 (14). Total: 72.
PRO STATISTICS: 1987—Recovered one fumble. 1988—Recovered one fumble. 1989—Recovered two fumbles.

TURNER, VERNON
WR, BILLS

PERSONAL: Born January 6, 1967, at Brooklyn, N.Y. . . . 5-8/185. . . . Full name: Vernon Maurice Turner.
HIGH SCHOOL: Curtis (Staten Island, N.Y.).
COLLEGE: Carson-Newman (Tenn.).
TRANSACTIONS/CAREER NOTES: Signed as free agent by Denver Broncos (May, 1990). . . . Released by Broncos (September 3, 1990). . . . Signed by Buffalo Bills to practice squad (October 5, 1990). . . . Activated (December 29, 1990). . . . Deactivated for playoffs (January 11, 1991).
PLAYING EXPERIENCE: Buffalo NFL, 1990. . . . Games: 1990 (1).

TUTEN, RICK
P, BILLS

PERSONAL: Born January 5, 1965, at Perry, Fla. . . . 6-2/218. . . . Full name: Richard Lamar Tuten. . . . Name pronounced TOOT-en.
HIGH SCHOOL: Forest (Ocala, Fla.).
COLLEGE: Miami (Fla.), then Florida State (bachelor of science degree in economics, 1986).
TRANSACTIONS/CAREER NOTES: Signed as free agent by San Diego Chargers (May 10, 1988). . . . Released by Chargers (August 23, 1988). . . . Signed as free agent by Washington Redskins (June 2, 1989). . . . Released by Redskins (August 27, 1989). . . . Signed as free agent by Philadelphia Eagles (December 13, 1989). . . . Granted unconditional free agency (February 1, 1990). . . . Signed by Buffalo Bills (March 28, 1990). . . . Released by Bills (August 15, 1990). . . . Re-signed by Bills (September 19, 1990).
CHAMPIONSHIP GAME EXPERIENCE: Played in AFC championship game after 1990 season. . . . Played in Super Bowl XXV after 1990 season.

| | | | —PUNTING— | |
Year Team	G	No.	Avg.	Blk.
1989— Philadelphia NFL	2	7	36.6	0
1990— Buffalo NFL	14	53	39.8	0
Pro totals (2 years)	16	60	38.2	0

TYLER, ROB
TE, RAIDERS

PERSONAL: Born October 12, 1965, at Savannah, Ga. . . . 6-5/255. . . . Full name: Robert Tyler.
HIGH SCHOOL: Wagener-Salley (Wagener, S.C.).
COLLEGE: South Carolina State.
TRANSACTIONS/CAREER NOTES: Selected by Seattle Seahawks in eighth round (215th pick overall) of 1988 NFL draft. . . . Signed by Seahawks (July 16, 1988). . . . On injured reserve with calf injury (August 29, 1988-entire season). . . . On injured reserve with ankle injury (November 8, 1989-remainder of season). . . . Released by Seahawks (September 3, 1990). . . . Signed by Los Angeles Raiders (March 20, 1991).

| | | | —RECEIVING— | | |
Year Team	G	No.	Yds.	Avg.	TD
1989— Seattle NFL	9	14	148	10.6	0
Pro totals (1 year)	9	14	148	10.6	0

UECKER, KEITH
G/OT, PACKERS

PERSONAL: Born June 29, 1960, at Hollywood, Fla. . . . 6-6/299. . . . Full name: Richard Keith Uecker.
HIGH SCHOOL: Hollywood Hills (Hollywood, Fla.).
COLLEGE: Auburn.
TRANSACTIONS/CAREER NOTES: Selected by Denver Broncos in ninth round (243rd pick overall) of 1982 NFL draft. . . . On injured reserve with Achilles tendon injury (August 14-October 21, 1984). . . . Awarded on procedural waivers to Green Bay Packers (October 23, 1984). . . . On injured reserve with knee injury (November 2, 1985-remainder of season). . . . On injured reserve with knee injury (August 22, 1986-entire season). . . . Crossed picket line during players' strike (October 14, 1987). . . . On injured reserve with knee injury (October 31-December 5, 1987). . . . On reserve/non-football injury list with steroid use (August 20-September 25, 1989). . . . Transferred to injured reserve with knee injury (September 26, 1989-entire season).

PLAYING EXPERIENCE: Denver NFL, 1982 and 1983; Green Bay NFL, 1984, 1985, 1987, 1988 and 1990.... Games: 1982 (5), 1983 (16), 1984 (6), 1985 (7), 1987 (8), 1988 (16), 1990 (13). Total: 71.
PRO STATISTICS: 1982—Returned one kickoff for 12 yards and fumbled once. 1985—Recovered one fumble. 1988—Recovered two fumbles.

UHLENHAKE, JEFF
C, DOLPHINS

PERSONAL: Born January 28, 1966, at Indianapolis.... 6-3/284.... Full name: Jeffrey Alan Uhlenhake.... Named pronounced you-lun-HAKE.
HIGH SCHOOL: Newark Catholic (Newark, O.).
COLLEGE: Ohio State.
TRANSACTIONS/CAREER NOTES: Selected by Miami Dolphins in fifth round (121st pick overall) of 1989 NFL draft.... Signed by Dolphins (July 21, 1989).
PLAYING EXPERIENCE: Miami NFL, 1989 and 1990.... Games: 1989 (16), 1990 (16). Total: 32.
RECORDS/HONORS: Named as center on THE SPORTING NEWS college All-America team, 1988.
PRO STATISTICS: 1989—Fumbled once for minus 19 yards.

UTLEY, MIKE
G/OT, LIONS

PERSONAL: Born December 20, 1965, at Seattle.... 6-6/279.
HIGH SCHOOL: John F. Kennedy Memorial (Seattle).
COLLEGE: Washington State.
TRANSACTIONS/CAREER NOTES: Selected by Detroit Lions in third round (59th pick overall) of 1989 NFL draft.... Signed by Lions (July 18, 1989).... On injured reserve with knee injury (October 11, 1989-remainder of season).
PLAYING EXPERIENCE: Detroit NFL, 1989 and 1990.... Games: 1989 (5), 1990 (16). Total: 21.

VANDERBEEK, MATT
LB, VIKINGS

PERSONAL: Born August 16, 1967, at Saugatuck, Mich.... 6-3/246.... Full name: Matthew James Vanderbeek.
HIGH SCHOOL: West Ottawa (Holland, Mich.).
COLLEGE: Michigan State.
TRANSACTIONS/CAREER NOTES: Signed as free agent by Indianapolis Colts (April 30, 1990).... Granted unconditional free agency (February 1, 1991).... Signed by Minnesota Vikings (March 18, 1991).
PLAYING EXPERIENCE: Indianapolis NFL, 1990.... Games: 1990 (16).

VAN HORNE, KEITH
OT, BEARS

PERSONAL: Born November 6, 1957, at Mt. Lebanon, Pa.... 6-6/283.... Brother of Pete Van Horne, first baseman in Chicago Cubs organization, 1977.
HIGH SCHOOL: Fullerton (Calif.).
COLLEGE: Southern California (bachelor of arts degree in broadcast journalism).
TRANSACTIONS/CAREER NOTES: Selected by Chicago Bears in first round (11th pick overall) of 1981 NFL draft.
PLAYING EXPERIENCE: Chicago NFL, 1981-1990.... Games: 1981 (14), 1982 (9), 1983 (14), 1984 (14), 1985 (16), 1986 (16), 1987 (12), 1988 (15), 1989 (15), 1990 (16). Total: 141.
CHAMPIONSHIP GAME EXPERIENCE: Played in NFC championship game after 1984, 1985 and 1988 seasons.... Played in Super Bowl XX after 1985 season.
RECORDS/HONORS: Named as offensive tackle on THE SPORTING NEWS college All-America team, 1980.
PRO STATISTICS: 1981—Recovered one fumble. 1982—Recovered one fumble. 1986—Recovered one fumble. 1988—Recovered one fumble. 1989—Recovered one fumble.

VAUGHN, CLARENCE
S, REDSKINS

PERSONAL: Born July 17, 1964, at Chicago.... 6-0/202.
HIGH SCHOOL: Gage Park (Chicago).
COLLEGE: Northern Illinois.
TRANSACTIONS/CAREER NOTES: Selected by Washington Redskins in eighth round (219th pick overall) of 1987 NFL draft.... Signed by Redskins (July 24, 1987).... On injured reserve with ankle injury (December 5, 1987-January 9, 1988).... Released by Redskins (September 3, 1990).... Re-signed by Redskins (September 5, 1990).... On injured reserve with knee injury (September 20, 1990-remainder of season).
PLAYING EXPERIENCE: Washington NFL, 1987-1990.... Games: 1987 (5), 1988 (14), 1989 (16), 1990 (1). Total: 36.
CHAMPIONSHIP GAME EXPERIENCE: Played in NFC championship game after 1987 season.... Played in Super Bowl XXII after 1987 season.
PRO STATISTICS: 1989—Recovered one fumble.

VEASEY, CRAIG
DL, STEELERS

PERSONAL: Born December 25, 1965, at Clear Lake City, Tex.... 6-2/294.... Full name: Anthony Craig Veasey.
HIGH SCHOOL: Clear Lake (Houston).
COLLEGE: Houston.
TRANSACTIONS/CAREER NOTES: Selected by Pittsburgh Steelers in third round (81st pick overall) of 1990 NFL draft.... Signed by Steelers (August 13, 1990).... On injured reserve with eye injury (September 5-October 13, 1990).
PLAYING EXPERIENCE: Pittsburgh NFL, 1990.... Games: 1990 (10).
RECORDS/HONORS: Named as defensive end on THE SPORTING NEWS college All-America team, 1989.
PRO STATISTICS: 1990—Recovered one fumble.

VEINGRAD, ALAN
OT, COWBOYS

PERSONAL: Born July 24, 1963, at Brooklyn, N.Y. . . . 6-5/277. . . . Full name: Alan Stuart Veingrad.
HIGH SCHOOL: Sunset (Miami).
COLLEGE: East Texas State (bachelor of science degree in physical education and health, 1985).
TRANSACTIONS/CAREER NOTES: Selected by San Antonio Gunslingers in 11th round (163rd pick overall) of 1985 USFL draft. . . . Signed as free agent by Tampa Bay Buccaneers (June 26, 1985). . . . Released by Buccaneers (July 30, 1985). . . . Awarded on waivers to Houston Oilers (August 1, 1985). . . . Released by Oilers (August 20, 1985). . . . Signed as free agent by Green Bay Packers (March 28, 1986). . . . On injured reserve with hip injury (August 23, 1988-entire season). . . . Granted unconditional free agency (February 1, 1991). . . . Signed by Dallas Cowboys (April 1, 1991).
PLAYING EXPERIENCE: Green Bay NFL, 1986, 1987, 1989 and 1990. . . . Games: 1986 (16), 1987 (11), 1989 (16), 1990 (16). Total: 59.
PRO STATISTICS: 1986—Recovered one fumble.

VERDIN, CLARENCE
WR, COLTS

PERSONAL: Born June 14, 1963, at New Orleans. . . . 5-8/162.
HIGH SCHOOL: South Terrebonne (Bourg, La.).
COLLEGE: Southwestern Louisiana (bachelor of science degree in business).
TRANSACTIONS/CAREER NOTES: Selected by Houston Gamblers in 17th round (353rd pick overall) of 1984 USFL draft. . . . Signed by Gamblers (January 19, 1984). . . . On developmental squad for four games (February 24-March 23, 1984). . . . Selected by Washington Redskins in third round (83rd pick overall) of 1984 NFL supplemental draft. . . . Traded by Houston Gamblers with defensive backs Luther Bradley, Will Lewis, Mike Mitchell and Durwood Roquemore, defensive end Pete Catan, quarterbacks Jim Kelly and Todd Dillon, defensive tackles Tony Fitzpatrick, Van Hughes and Hosea Taylor, running back Sam Harrell, linebackers Andy Hawkins and Ladell Wills, wide receivers Richard Johnson, Scott McGhee, Gerald McNeil and Ricky Sanders, guard Rich Kehr, center Billy Kidd and offensive tackles Chris Riehm and Tommy Robison to New Jersey Generals for past considerations (March 7, 1986). . . . Granted free agency when USFL suspended operations (August 7, 1986). . . . Signed by Washington Redskins (August 13, 1986). . . . Granted roster exemption (August 13-August 25, 1986). . . . On injured reserve with hamstring injury (September 1-October 18, 1986). . . . On injured reserve with ribs and shoulder injuries (December 9, 1986-remainder of season). . . . On injured reserve with leg injury (September 7-December 12, 1987). . . . Traded by Redskins to Indianapolis Colts for sixth-round pick in 1988 draft (March 29, 1988).
CHAMPIONSHIP GAME EXPERIENCE: Member of Washington Redskins for Super Bowl XXII after 1987 season; inactive.
RECORDS/HONORS: Named as kick returner on THE SPORTING NEWS USFL All-Star team, 1985. . . . Played in Pro Bowl after 1990 season.
PRO STATISTICS: 1984—Recovered four fumbles. 1989—Recovered two fumbles for minus five yards.

			—RUSHING—				—RECEIVING—				—PUNT RETURNS—				KICKOFF RETURNS				—TOTALS—		
Year	Team	G	Att.	Yds.	Avg.	TD	No.	Yds.	Avg.	TD	No.	Yds.	Avg.	TD	No.	Yds.	Avg.	TD	TD	Pts.	F.
1984— Houston USFL.....		14	1	-2	-2.0	0	16	315	19.7	3	0	0		0	25	643	25.7	*1	4	24	2
1985— Houston USFL.....		18	7	20	2.9	0	84	1004	12.0	9	0	0		0	28	746	*26.6	*3	12	72	0
1986— Washington NFL....		8	0	0		0	0	0		0	0	0		0	12	240	20.0	0	0	0	0
1987— Washington NFL.		3	1	14	14.0	0	2	62	31.0	0	0	0		0	12	244	20.3	0	0	0	0
1988— Indianapolis NFL		16	8	77	9.6	0	20	437	21.9	4	22	239	10.9	1	7	145	20.7	0	5	30	0
1989— Indianapolis NFL		16	4	39	9.8	0	20	381	19.1	1	23	296	12.9	*1	19	371	19.5	0	2	12	1
1990— Indianapolis NFL		15	0	0		0	14	178	12.7	1	31	396	12.8	0	18	350	19.4	0	1	6	1
USFL totals (2 years)	....	32	8	18	2.3	0	100	1319	13.2	12	0	0		0	53	1389	26.2	4	16	96	2
NFL totals (5 years)	......	58	13	130	10.0	0	56	1058	18.9	6	76	931	12.3	2	68	1350	19.9	0	8	48	2
Pro totals (7 years)	....	90	21	148	7.1	0	156	2377	15.2	18	76	931	12.3	2	121	2739	22.6	4	24	144	4

VERHULST, CHRIS
TE, BRONCOS

PERSONAL: Born May 16, 1966, at Sacramento, Calif. . . . 6-3/249. . . . Full name: Christopher Sean Verhulst.
HIGH SCHOOL: California (San Ramon, Calif.).
COLLEGE: Cal State Chico.
TRANSACTIONS/CAREER NOTES: Selected by Houston Oilers in fifth round (130th pick overall) of 1988 NFL draft. . . . Signed by Oilers (July 15, 1988). . . . Granted unconditional free agency (February 1, 1990). . . . Signed by Denver Broncos (March 19, 1990). . . . On injured reserve with groin injury (September 25-November 9, 1990).
PRO STATISTICS: 1989—Returned one kickoff for no yards.

			—RECEIVING—			
Year	Team	G	No.	Yds.	Avg.	TD
1988— Houston NFL..............		1	0	0		0
1989— Houston NFL..............		16	4	48	12.0	0
1990— Denver NFL................		11	3	13	4.3	0
Pro totals (3 years)	....	28	7	61	8.7	0

VERIS, GARIN
DE, PATRIOTS

PERSONAL: Born February 27, 1963, at Chillicothe, O. . . . 6-4/255. . . . Full name: Garin Lee Veris. . . . Name pronounced GARR-in VAIR-is.
HIGH SCHOOL: Chillicothe (O.).
COLLEGE: Stanford.
TRANSACTIONS/CAREER NOTES: Selected by Oakland Invaders in 1985 USFL territorial draft. . . . Selected by New England Patriots in second round (48th pick overall) of 1985 NFL draft. . . . Signed by Patriots (July 25, 1985). . . . On injured reserve with knee injury (October 27-December 3, 1988). . . . On injured reserve with knee injury (September 4, 1989-entire season). . . . On inactive list (November 11, 18 and 25, 1990). . . . On injured reserve with knee injury (December 1, 1990-remainder of season).

PLAYING EXPERIENCE: New England NFL, 1985-1988 and 1990.... Games: 1985 (16), 1986 (16), 1987 (12), 1988 (11), 1990 (7). Total: 62.
CHAMPIONSHIP GAME EXPERIENCE: Played in AFC championship game after 1985 season.... Played in Super Bowl XX after 1985 season.
PRO STATISTICS: 1985—Recovered two fumbles. 1986—Recovered two fumbles. 1988—Recovered one fumble.

VIAENE, DAVID
OT, PATRIOTS

PERSONAL: Born July 14, 1965, at Appleton, Wis.... 6-5/300.... Full name: David Ronald Viaene.... Name pronounced vee-EN.
HIGH SCHOOL: Kaukauna (Wis.).
COLLEGE: Minnesota-Duluth.
TRANSACTIONS/CAREER NOTES: Selected by Houston Oilers in eighth round (214th pick overall) of 1988 NFL draft.... Signed by Oilers (July 18, 1988).... On injured reserve with back injury (August 29, 1988-entire season).... Granted unconditional free agency (February 1, 1989).... Signed by New England Patriots (March 30, 1989).... On inactive list (September 9, 1990). ... On injured reserve with knee injury (September 12-December 1, 1990).
PLAYING EXPERIENCE: New England NFL, 1989 and 1990.... Games: 1989 (16), 1990 (4). Total: 20.

VICK, ROGER
RB, EAGLES

PERSONAL: Born August 11, 1964, at Conroe, Tex.... 6-3/235.
HIGH SCHOOL: Tomball (Tex.).
COLLEGE: Texas A&M.
TRANSACTIONS/CAREER NOTES: Selected by New York Jets in first round (21st pick overall) of 1987 NFL draft.... Signed by Jets (July 21, 1987).... Traded by Jets to Philadelphia Eagles for undisclosed draft pick (September 3, 1990).... On inactive list (September 23 and October 21, 1990).
PRO STATISTICS: 1989—Recovered one fumble. 1990—Returned two kickoffs for 22 yards.

		RUSHING				RECEIVING				TOTAL		
Year Team	G	Att.	Yds.	Avg.	TD	No.	Yds.	Avg.	TD	TD	Pts.	F.
1987—N.Y. Jets NFL	12	77	257	3.3	1	13	108	8.3	0	1	6	3
1988—N.Y. Jets NFL	16	128	540	4.2	3	19	120	6.3	0	3	18	5
1989—N.Y. Jets NFL	16	112	434	3.9	5	34	241	7.1	2	7	42	4
1990—Philadelphia NFL	14	16	58	3.6	1	0	0		0	1	6	0
Pro totals (4 years)	58	333	1289	3.9	10	66	469	7.1	2	12	72	12

VILLA, DANNY
C/OT, PATRIOTS

PERSONAL: Born September 21, 1964, at Nogales, Ariz.... 6-5/305.... Name pronounced VEE-uh.
HIGH SCHOOL: Nogales (Ariz.).
COLLEGE: Arizona State.
TRANSACTIONS/CAREER NOTES: Selected by New England Patriots in fifth round (113th pick overall) of 1987 NFL draft.... Signed by Patriots (July 25, 1987).
PLAYING EXPERIENCE: New England NFL, 1987-1990.... Games: 1987 (11), 1988 (16), 1989 (15), 1990 (16). Total: 58.
PRO STATISTICS: 1987—Fumbled once for minus 13 yards. 1988—Fumbled once for minus 39 yards. 1990—Recovered one fumble.

VLASIC, MARK
QB, CHIEFS

PERSONAL: Born October 25, 1963, at Rochester, Pa.... 6-3/205.... Full name: Mark Richard Vlasic.
HIGH SCHOOL: Center (Monaca, Pa.).
COLLEGE: Iowa (degree in finance, 1987).
TRANSACTIONS/CAREER NOTES: Selected by San Diego Chargers in fourth round (88th pick overall) of 1987 NFL draft.... Signed by Chargers (July 26, 1987).... On injured reserve with knee injury (November 23, 1988-remainder of season).... On reserve/physically unable to perform list with knee injury (August 29, 1989-entire season).... Granted unconditional free agency (February 1, 1991).... Signed by Kansas City Chiefs (April 2, 1991).
PRO STATISTICS: Passer rating points: 1987 (16.7), 1988 (54.2), 1990 (46.7). Career: 46.6.... 1987—Recovered one fumble. 1988—Recovered one fumble and fumbled once for minus 10 yards. 1990—Fumbled once for minus one yard.

		PASSING							RUSHING				TOTAL		
Year Team	G	Att.	Cmp.	Pct.	Yds.	TD	Int.	Avg.	Att.	Yds.	Avg.	TD	TD	Pts.	F.
1987—San Diego NFL	1	6	3	50.0	8	0	1	1.33	0	0	0	0	0	0	1
1988—San Diego NFL	2	52	25	48.1	270	1	2	5.19	2	0	.0	0	0	0	1
1990—San Diego NFL	6	40	19	47.5	168	1	2	4.20	1	0	.0	0	0	0	1
Pro totals (3 years)	9	98	47	48.0	446	2	5	4.55	3	0	.0	0	0	0	3

WADDLE, TOM
WR, BEARS

PERSONAL: Born February 20, 1967, at Cincinnati.... 6-0/181.... Full name: Gregory Thomas Waddle.
HIGH SCHOOL: Moeller (Cincinnati).
COLLEGE: Boston College (degree in finance, 1989).
TRANSACTIONS/CAREER NOTES: Signed as free agent by Chicago Bears (May 8, 1989).... Released by Bears (September 5, 1989).... Re-signed by Bears to developmental squad (September 6, 1989).... On developmental squad (September 6-September 15, 1989).... Released by Bears (September 25, 1989).... Re-signed by Bears to developmental squad (September 26, 1989).... On developmental squad (September 26-December 6, 1989).... Activated after clearing procedural waivers (December 8, 1989).... Released by Bears (September 3, 1990).... Re-signed by Bears (September 4, 1990).... On inactive list (September 9, 16, 23; October 14, 28; November 4, 11, 18, 25; and December 16, 1990).

Year Team		G	No.	RECEIVING Yds.	Avg.	TD	No.	PUNT RETURNS Yds.	Avg.	TD	TD	TOTAL Pts.	F.
1989— Chicago NFL		3	1	8	8.0	0	1	2	2.0	0	0	0	0
1990— Chicago NFL		5	2	32	16.0	0	0	0		0	0	0	0
Pro totals (2 years)		8	3	40	13.3	0	1	2	2.0	0	0	0	0

WAGNER, BRYAN
P, PATRIOTS

PERSONAL: Born March 28, 1962, at Escondido, Calif.... 6-2/200.... Full name: Bryan J. Wagner.
HIGH SCHOOL: Hilltop (Chula Vista, Calif.).
COLLEGE: California Lutheran College, then Cal State Northridge.
TRANSACTIONS/CAREER NOTES: Selected by Baltimore Stars in 15th round (216th pick overall) of 1985 USFL draft.... Signed as free agent by Dallas Cowboys (May 2, 1985).... Released by Cowboys (August 27, 1985).... Signed as free agent by New York Giants (May 10, 1986).... Released by Giants (August 11, 1986).... Signed as free agent by St. Louis Cardinals (August 19, 1986).... Released by Cardinals (August 26, 1986).... Signed as free agent by Denver Broncos (May 1, 1987).... Traded by Broncos with draft pick to Chicago Bears for guard Stefan Humphries (August 25, 1987).... On injured reserve with back injury (December 16, 1987-remainder of season).... Granted unconditional free agency (February 1, 1989).... Signed by Cleveland Browns (March 30, 1989).... Granted unconditional free agency (February 1, 1991).... Rights relinquished by Browns (April 1, 1991).... Signed by New England Patriots (May 23, 1991).
CHAMPIONSHIP GAME EXPERIENCE: Played in NFC championship game after 1988 season.... Played in AFC championship game after 1989 season.
PRO STATISTICS: 1988—Attempted one pass with one completion for three yards, rushed twice for no yards and recovered one fumble and fumbled once for minus nine yards.

Year Team		G	No.	PUNTING Avg.	Blk.
1987— Chicago NFL		10	36	40.6	1
1988— Chicago NFL		16	79	41.5	0
1989— Cleveland NFL		16	*97	39.4	0
1990— Cleveland NFL		16	74	38.9	*4
Pro totals (4 years)		58	286	40.1	5

WAHLER, JIM
NT, CARDINALS

PERSONAL: Born July 29, 1966, at San Jose, Calif. ... 6-4/275. ... Full name: James Joseph Wahler.
HIGH SCHOOL: Bellamine College Prep (San Jose, Calif.).
COLLEGE: UCLA.
TRANSACTIONS/CAREER NOTES: Selected by Phoenix Cardinals in fourth round (94th pick overall) of 1989 NFL draft.... Signed by Cardinals (July 22, 1989).
PLAYING EXPERIENCE: Phoenix NFL, 1989 and 1990.... Games: 1989 (13), 1990 (16). Total: 29.
PRO STATISTICS: 1989—Intercepted one pass for five yards and recovered one fumble.

WAITERS, VAN
LB, BROWNS

PERSONAL: Born February 27, 1965, at Coral Gables, Fla.... 6-4/250.... Full name: Van Allen Waiters.
HIGH SCHOOL: Coral Gables (Fla.).
COLLEGE: Indiana.
TRANSACTIONS/CAREER NOTES: Selected by Cleveland Browns in third round (77th pick overall) of 1988 NFL draft.... Signed by Browns (July 23, 1988).
PLAYING EXPERIENCE: Cleveland NFL, 1988-1990.... Games: 1988 (16), 1989 (16), 1990 (16). Total: 48.
CHAMPIONSHIP GAME EXPERIENCE: Played in AFC championship game after 1989 season.
PRO STATISTICS: 1989—Caught one pass for 14 yards and a touchdown. 1990—Intercepted one pass for 15 yards and returned one punt for no yards.

WALKER, DERRICK
TE, CHARGERS

PERSONAL: Born June 23, 1967, at Glenwood, Ill.... 6-5/244.... Full name: Derrick N. Walker.
HIGH SCHOOL: Bloom (Chicago Heights, Ill.).
COLLEGE: Michigan (degree in communications).
TRANSACTIONS/CAREER NOTES: Selected by San Diego Chargers in sixth round (163rd pick overall) of 1990 NFL draft.... Signed by Chargers (July 21, 1990).
PRO STATISTICS: 1990—Fumbled once.

Year Team		G	No.	RECEIVING Yds.	Avg.	TD
1990— San Diego NFL		16	23	240	10.4	1
Pro totals (1 year)		16	23	240	10.4	1

DID YOU KNOW...

...that Seattle quarterback Dave Krieg was the only player last season to account for all his club's passing yardage?

WALKER, HERSCHEL

RB, VIKINGS

PERSONAL: Born March 3, 1962, at Wrightsville, Ga. . . . 6-1/226.
HIGH SCHOOL: Johnson County (Wrightsville, Ga.).
COLLEGE: Georgia (degree in criminal justice, 1984).
TRANSACTIONS/CAREER NOTES: Signed by New Jersey Generals of USFL (February 22, 1983); Generals forfeited first-round pick in 1984 draft. . . . On developmental squad for one game with Generals (April 8-April 14, 1984). . . . Selected by Dallas Cowboys in fifth round (114th pick overall) of 1985 NFL draft. . . . Granted free agency when USFL suspended operations (August 7, 1986). . . . Signed by Dallas Cowboys (August 13, 1986). . . . Granted roster exemption (August 13-August 23, 1986). . . . Traded as part of a six-player, 12 draft-choice deal in which Cowboys sent Walker to Minnesota Vikings in exchange for defensive back Issiac Holt, linebackers David Howard and Jesse Solomon, running back Darrin Nelson, defensive end Alex Stewart, first-round pick in 1992 draft and conditional first-round picks in 1990 and 1991 drafts, conditional second-round picks in 1990, 1991 and 1992 drafts and conditional third-round pick in 1992 draft (October 12, 1989); Nelson refused to report to Dallas and was traded to San Diego Chargers, with Minnesota giving Dallas a sixth-round pick in 1990 as well as the original conditional second-round pick in 1991 and San Diego sending a fifth-round pick in 1990 to Minnesota through Dallas (October 17, 1989); deal completed with Dallas retaining Howard, Solomon and Holt and all conditional picks and Cowboys sending third-round picks in 1990 and 1991 and 10th-round pick in 1990 to Minnesota (February 2, 1990).
RECORDS/HONORS: Named as running back on THE SPORTING NEWS college All-America team, 1980-1982. . . . Heisman Trophy winner, 1982. . . . Named THE SPORTING NEWS College Football Player of the Year, 1982. . . . Named as running back on THE SPORTING NEWS USFL All-Star team, 1983 and 1985. . . . Named THE SPORTING NEWS USFL Player of the Year, 1985. . . . Played in Pro Bowl after 1987 and 1988 seasons.
PRO STATISTICS: USFL: 1983—Credited with one 2-point conversion and recovered four fumbles. 1984—Credited with one 2-point conversion and recovered two fumbles. 1985—Recovered three fumbles. . . . NFL: 1986—Recovered two fumbles. 1987—Recovered one fumble. 1988—Recovered three fumbles. 1990—Attempted two passes with one completion for 12 yards.

			RUSHING				RECEIVING				KICKOFF RETURNS				TOTAL		
Year	Team	G	Att.	Yds.	Avg.	TD	No.	Yds.	Avg.	TD	No.	Yds.	Avg.	TD	TD	Pts.	F.
1983— New Jersey USFL ..		18	*412	*1812	4.4	*17	53	489	9.2	1	3	69	23.0	0	*18	*110	12
1984— New Jersey USFL ..		17	293	1339	4.6	16	40	528	13.2	5	0	0		0	*21	128	6
1985— New Jersey USFL ..		18	*438	*2411	5.5	*21	37	467	12.6	1	0	0		0	*22	*132	9
1986— Dallas NFL		16	151	737	4.9	12	76	837	11.0	2	0	0		0	14	84	5
1987— Dallas NFL		12	209	891	4.3	7	60	715	11.9	1	0	0		0	8	48	4
1988— Dallas NFL		16	361	1514	4.2	5	53	505	9.5	2	0	0		0	7	42	6
1989— Dal. (5)-Min. (11) NFL		16	250	915	3.7	7	40	423	10.6	2	13	374	28.8	1	10	60	7
1990— Minnesota NFL		16	184	770	4.2	5	35	315	9.0	4	44	966	22.0	0	9	54	4
USFL totals (3 years)		53	1143	5562	4.9	54	130	1484	11.4	7	3	69	23.0	0	61	370	27
NFL totals (5 years)		76	1155	4827	4.2	36	264	2795	10.6	11	57	1340	23.5	1	48	288	26
Pro totals (8 years)		129	2298	10389	4.5	90	394	4279	10.9	18	60	1409	23.5	1	109	658	53

WALKER, JEFF

G/OT, CARDINALS

PERSONAL: Born January 22, 1963, at Jonesboro, Ark. . . . 6-4/286. . . . Full name: Jeffrey Lynn Walker.
HIGH SCHOOL: Olive Branch (Miss.).
COLLEGE: Memphis State.
TRANSACTIONS/CAREER NOTES: Selected by Memphis Showboats in 1986 USFL territorial draft. . . . Selected by San Diego Chargers in third round (70th pick overall) of 1986 NFL draft. . . . Signed by Chargers (July 23, 1986). . . . On injured reserve with knee injury (September 7, 1987). . . . Traded by Chargers to Los Angeles Rams for 11th-round pick in 1988 draft (September 8, 1987). . . . On injured reserve with knee injury (September 8-October 24, 1987; and October 27, 1987-remainder of season). . . . Inactive for one game with Rams in 1987. . . . On injured reserve with fractured fibula (August 23-October 17, 1988). . . . Released by Rams (October 18, 1988). . . . Signed as free agent by New Orleans Saints (November 1, 1988). . . . On injured reserve with leg injury (November 11, 1988-remainder of season). . . . Granted unconditional free agency (February 1, 1990). . . . Signed by Phoenix Cardinals (March 23, 1990). . . . On injured reserve with knee injury (August 27, 1990-entire season).
PLAYING EXPERIENCE: San Diego NFL, 1986; Los Angeles Rams NFL, 1987; New Orleans NFL, 1988 and 1989. . . . Games: 1986 (16), 1988 (1), 1989 (13). Total: 30.

WALKER, KEVIN

LB, BENGALS

PERSONAL: Born December 24, 1965, at Denville, N.J. . . . 6-3/244. . . . Full name: Kevin P. Walker.
HIGH SCHOOL: West Milford (N.J.).
COLLEGE: Maryland.
TRANSACTIONS/CAREER NOTES: Selected by Cincinnati Bengals in third round (57th pick overall) of 1988 NFL draft. . . . Signed by Bengals (May 23, 1988). . . . On injured reserve with knee injury (October 10, 1988-remainder of season).
PLAYING EXPERIENCE: Cincinnati NFL, 1988-1990. . . . Games: 1988 (3), 1989 (16), 1990 (16). Total: 35.
PRO STATISTICS: 1989—Recovered one fumble.

WALKER, TONY

LB, COLTS

PERSONAL: Born April 2, 1968, at Birmingham, Ala. . . . 6-3/235. . . . Full name: Tony Maurice Walker.
HIGH SCHOOL: Phillips (Birmingham, Ala.).
COLLEGE: Southeast Missouri State.
TRANSACTIONS/CAREER NOTES: Selected by Indianapolis Colts in sixth round (148th pick overall) of 1990 NFL draft. . . . Signed by Colts (July 26, 1990). . . . On inactive list (September 16 and 23, 1990).
PLAYING EXPERIENCE: Indianapolis NFL, 1990. . . . Games: 1990 (14).
PRO STATISTICS: 1990—Recovered one fumble.

WALKER, WAYNE
WR, VIKINGS

PERSONAL: Born December 27, 1966, at Waco, Tex. . . . 5-8/162. . . . Full name: Ronald Wayne Walker.
HIGH SCHOOL: Jefferson-Moore (Waco, Tex.).
COLLEGE: Texas Tech.
TRANSACTIONS/CAREER NOTES: Signed as free agent by San Diego Chargers (May 2, 1989). . . . On injured reserve with knee injury (August 27, 1990-entire season). . . . Granted unconditional free agency (February 1, 1991). . . . Signed by Minnesota Vikings (March 26, 1991).
PRO STATISTICS: 1989—Returned six punts for 31 yards, rushed once for nine yards and fumbled twice.

			RECEIVING		
Year Team	G	No.	Yds.	Avg.	TD
1989— San Diego NFL	13	24	395	16.5	1
Pro totals (1 year)	13	24	395	16.5	1

WALLACE, AARON
LB, RAIDERS

PERSONAL: Born April 17, 1967, at Paris, Tex. . . . 6-3/235.
HIGH SCHOOL: Franklin D. Roosevelt (Dallas).
COLLEGE: Texas A&M.
TRANSACTIONS/CAREER NOTES: Selected by Los Angeles Raiders in second round (37th pick overall) of 1990 NFL draft. . . . Signed by Raiders (July 16, 1990).
PLAYING EXPERIENCE: Los Angeles Raiders NFL, 1990. . . . Games: 1990 (16).
CHAMPIONSHIP GAME EXPERIENCE: Played in AFC championship game after 1990 season.

WALLACE, DARRELL
RB/WR, LIONS

PERSONAL: Born September 27, 1965, at St. Louis. . . . 5-9/180.
HIGH SCHOOL: Fort Campbell (Ky.).
COLLEGE: Missouri.
TRANSACTIONS/CAREER NOTES: Signed as free agent by B.C. Lions of CFL (December, 1988). . . . Released by Lions (August, 1990). . . . Signed by Calgary Stampeders of CFL (August, 1990). . . . Released by Stampeders (October 18, 1990). . . . Signed as free agent by Detroit Lions (February 25, 1991).

		RUSHING				RECEIVING				PUNT RETURNS				KICKOFF RETURNS				TOTALS		
Year Team	G	Att.	Yds.	Avg.	TD	No.	Yds.	Avg.	TD	No.	Yds.	Avg.	TD	No.	Yds.	Avg.	TD	TD	Pts.	F.
1989— B.C. CFL	17	75	382	5.1	2	18	115	6.4	1	83	780	9.4	1	57	1255	22.0	1	5	30	3
1990— B.C.(5)-Cal.(5) CFL.	10	60	303	5.1	2	18	108	6.0	1	23	90	3.9	0	14	247	17.6	0	3	18	3
Pro totals (2 years)	27	135	685	5.1	4	36	223	6.2	2	106	870	8.2	1	71	1502	21.2	1	8	48	6

WALLACE, STEVE
OT, 49ERS

PERSONAL: Born December 27, 1964, at Atlanta. . . . 6-5/276. . . . Full name: Barron Steven Wallace.
HIGH SCHOOL: Chamblee (Atlanta).
COLLEGE: Auburn.
TRANSACTIONS/CAREER NOTES: Selected by Birmingham Stallions in 1986 USFL territorial draft. . . . Selected by San Francisco 49ers in fourth round (101st pick overall) of 1986 NFL draft. . . . Signed by 49ers (July 18, 1986).
PLAYING EXPERIENCE: San Francisco NFL, 1986-1990. . . . Games: 1986 (16), 1987 (11), 1988 (16), 1989 (16), 1990 (16). Total: 75.
CHAMPIONSHIP GAME EXPERIENCE: Played in NFC championship game after 1988-1990 seasons. . . . Played in Super Bowl XXIII after 1988 season and Super Bowl XXIV after 1989 season.

WALLS, EVERSON
CB, GIANTS

PERSONAL: Born December 28, 1959, at Dallas. . . . 6-1/194. . . . Full name: Everson Collins Walls. . . . Cousin of Ralph Anderson, back with Pittsburgh Steelers and New England Patriots, 1971-1973; and Herkie Walls, wide receiver-kick returner with Houston Oilers and Tampa Bay Buccaneers, 1983-1985 and 1987.
HIGH SCHOOL: L.V. Berkner (Dallas).
COLLEGE: Grambling State (bachelor of arts degree in accounting, 1981).
TRANSACTIONS/CAREER NOTES: Signed as free agent by Dallas Cowboys (May, 1981). . . . Granted unconditional free agency (February 1, 1990). . . . Rights relinquished (April 13, 1990). . . . Signed by New York Giants (April 30, 1990).
CHAMPIONSHIP GAME EXPERIENCE: Played in NFC championship game after 1981, 1982 and 1990 seasons. . . . Played in Super Bowl XXV after 1990 season.
RECORDS/HONORS: Established NFL record for most seasons leading league in interceptions (3). . . . Played in Pro Bowl after 1981-1983 and 1985 seasons.
PRO STATISTICS: 1981—Recovered one fumble. 1982—Fumbled once. 1985—Recovered one fumble for four yards. 1988—Returned one punt for no yards, recovered one fumble for four yards and fumbled once.

			INTERCEPTIONS		
Year Team	G	No.	Yds.	Avg.	TD
1981— Dallas NFL	16	*11	133	12.1	0
1982— Dallas NFL	9	*7	61	8.7	0
1983— Dallas NFL	16	4	70	17.5	0
1984— Dallas NFL	16	3	12	4.0	0
1985— Dallas NFL	16	*9	31	3.4	0
1986— Dallas NFL	16	3	46	15.3	0
1987— Dallas NFL	12	5	38	7.6	0
1988— Dallas NFL	16	2	0	.0	0
1989— Dallas NFL	16	0	0		0
1990— N.Y. Giants NFL	16	6	80	13.3	1
Pro totals (10 years)	149	50	471	9.4	1

WALLS, WESLEY
TE, 49ERS

PERSONAL: Born February 26, 1966, at Batesville, Miss. . . . 6-5/246. . . . Full name: Charles Wesley Walls.
HIGH SCHOOL: Pontotoc (Miss.).
COLLEGE: Mississippi.
TRANSACTIONS/CAREER NOTES: Selected by San Francisco 49ers in second round (56th pick overall) of 1989 NFL draft. . . . Signed by 49ers (July 26, 1989).
CHAMPIONSHIP GAME EXPERIENCE: Played in NFC championship game after 1989 and 1990 seasons. . . . Played in Super Bowl XXIV after 1989 season.
PRO STATISTICS: 1989—Recovered one fumble and fumbled once. 1990—Returned one kickoff for 16 yards.

			RECEIVING			
Year	Team	G	No.	Yds.	Avg.	TD
1989—	San Francisco NFL....	16	4	16	4.0	1
1990—	San Francisco NFL....	16	5	27	5.4	0
	Pro totals (2 years)	32	9	43	4.8	1

WALSH, STEVE
QB, SAINTS

PERSONAL: Born December 1, 1966, at St. Paul, Minn. . . . 6-2/200.
HIGH SCHOOL: Cretin (St. Paul, Minn.).
COLLEGE: Miami (Fla.).
TRANSACTIONS/CAREER NOTES: Selected by Dallas Cowboys in first round of 1989 NFL supplemental draft (July 7, 1989). . . . Signed by Cowboys (July 29, 1989). . . . Traded by Cowboys to New Orleans Saints for first- and third-round picks in 1991 NFL draft and conditional pick in 1992 draft (September 25, 1990).
PRO STATISTICS: Passer rating points: 1989 (60.5), 1990 (67.2). Career: 64.6. . . . 1989—Recovered two fumbles and fumbled three times for minus 14 yards. 1990—Recovered two fumbles.

			PASSING							RUSHING				TOTAL		
Year	Team	G	Att.	Cmp.	Pct.	Yds.	TD	Int.	Avg.	Att.	Yds.	Avg.	TD	TD	Pts.	F.
1989—	Dallas NFL	8	219	110	50.2	1371	5	9	6.26	6	16	2.7	0	0	0	3
1990—	Dal.(1)-N.O.(12) NFL	13	336	179	53.3	2010	12	13	5.98	20	25	1.3	0	0	0	6
	Pro totals (2 years)	21	555	289	52.1	3381	17	22	6.09	26	41	1.6	0	0	0	9

WALTER, JOE
OT, BENGALS

PERSONAL: Born June 18, 1963, at Dallas. . . . 6-7/292. . . . Full name: Joseph Follmann Walter Jr.
HIGH SCHOOL: North (Garland, Tex.).
COLLEGE: Texas Tech.
TRANSACTIONS/CAREER NOTES: Selected by Denver Gold in 1985 USFL territorial draft. . . . Selected by Cincinnati Bengals in seventh round (181st pick overall) of 1985 NFL draft. . . . Signed by Bengals (July 15, 1985). . . . On injured reserve with knee injury (December 30, 1988-remainder of 1988 season playoffs). . . . On reserve/physically unable to perform list with knee injury (September 4-October 21, 1989).
PLAYING EXPERIENCE: Cincinnati NFL, 1985-1990. . . . Games: 1985 (14), 1986 (15), 1987 (12), 1988 (16), 1989 (10), 1990 (16). Total: 83.
PRO STATISTICS: 1987—Recovered two fumbles.

WALTER, MIKE
LB, 49ERS

PERSONAL: Born November 30, 1960, at Salem, Ore. . . . 6-3/238. . . . Full name: Michael David Walter.
HIGH SCHOOL: Sheldon (Eugene, Ore.).
COLLEGE: Oregon.
TRANSACTIONS/CAREER NOTES: Selected by Los Angeles Express in 20th round (240th pick overall) of 1983 USFL draft. . . . Selected by Dallas Cowboys in second round (50th pick overall) of 1983 NFL draft. . . . Signed by Cowboys (July 7, 1983). . . . Released by Cowboys (August 27, 1984). . . . Awarded on waivers to San Francisco 49ers (August 28, 1984). . . . On inactive list (September 23, 1990). . . . On injured reserve with finger injury (October 1-November 2, 1990). . . . On injured reserve with neck injury (November 10-December 19, 1990). . . . On practice squad (December 19, 1990-January 19, 1991).
PLAYING EXPERIENCE: Dallas NFL, 1983; San Francisco NFL, 1984-1990. . . . Games: 1983 (15), 1984 (16), 1985 (14), 1986 (16), 1987 (12), 1988 (16), 1989 (16), 1990 (3). Total: 108.
CHAMPIONSHIP GAME EXPERIENCE: Played in NFC championship game after 1984 and 1988-1990 seasons. . . . Played in Super Bowl XIX after 1984 season, Super Bowl XXIII after 1988 season and Super Bowl XXIV after 1989 season.
PRO STATISTICS: 1985—Intercepted one pass for no yards. 1986—Recovered one fumble. 1987—Intercepted one pass for 16 yards and recovered one fumble. 1988—Recovered two fumbles. 1989—Recovered one fumble.

WALTON, ALVIN
S, REDSKINS

PERSONAL: Born March 14, 1964, at Riverside, Calif. . . . 6-0/180. . . . Full name: Alvin Earl Walton.
HIGH SCHOOL: Banning (Calif.).
COLLEGE: Mt. San Jacinto Junior College (Calif.), then Kansas.
TRANSACTIONS/CAREER NOTES: Selected by Washington Redskins in third round (75th pick overall) of 1986 NFL draft. . . . Signed by Redskins (July 18, 1986).
CHAMPIONSHIP GAME EXPERIENCE: Played in NFC championship game after 1986 and 1987 seasons. . . . Played in Super Bowl XXII after 1987 season.
PRO STATISTICS: 1989—Recovered one fumble and fumbled once.

Year	Team	G	No.	Yds.	Avg.	TD
				INTERCEPTIONS		
1986— Washington NFL		16	0	0		0
1987— Washington NFL		12	3	28	9.3	0
1988— Washington NFL		16	3	54	18.0	0
1989— Washington NFL		13	4	58	14.5	1
1990— Washington NFL		16	2	118	59.0	1
Pro totals (5 years)		73	12	258	21.5	2

WARE, ANDRE
QB, LIONS

PERSONAL: Born July 31, 1968, at Galveston, Tex. . . . 6-2/205. . . . Full name: Andre T. Ware.
HIGH SCHOOL: Dickinson (Tex.).
COLLEGE: Houston (bachelor of arts degree).
TRANSACTIONS/CAREER NOTES: Selected by Detroit Lions in first round (seventh pick overall) of 1990 NFL draft. . . . Signed by Lions (August 27, 1990). . . . On inactive list (September 9 and November 11, 1990).
RECORDS/HONORS: Heisman Trophy winner, 1989.
PRO STATISTICS: Passer rating points: 1990 (44.3).

Year	Team	G	Att.	Cmp.	Pct.	Yds.	TD	Int.	Avg.	Att.	Yds.	Avg.	TD	TD	Pts.	F.
					PASSING						RUSHING				TOTAL	
1990— Detroit NFL		4	30	13	43.3	164	1	2	5.47	7	64	9.1	0	0	0	0
Pro totals (1 year)		4	30	13	43.3	164	1	2	5.47	7	64	9.1	0	0	0	0

WARREN, CHRIS
RB, SEAHAWKS

PERSONAL: Born January 24, 1967, at Silver Spring, Md. . . . 6-2/225. . . . Full name: Christopher Collins Warren Jr.
HIGH SCHOOL: Robinson Secondary (Fairfax, Va.).
COLLEGE: Ferrum, Va. (degree in psychology).
TRANSACTIONS/CAREER NOTES: Selected by Seattle Seahawks in fourth round (89th pick overall) of 1990 NFL draft. . . . Signed by Seahawks (July 24, 1990).
PRO STATISTICS: 1990—Recovered one fumble.

Year	Team	G	Att.	Yds.	Avg.	TD	No.	Yds.	Avg.	TD	No.	Yds.	Avg.	TD	TD	Pts.	F.
			RUSHING				PUNT RETURNS				KICKOFF RETURNS				TOTAL		
1990— Seattle NFL		16	6	11	1.8	1	28	269	9.6	0	23	478	20.8	0	1	6	3
NFL totals (1 year)		16	6	11	1.8	1	28	269	9.6	0	23	478	20.8	0	1	6	3

WARREN, DON
TE, REDSKINS

PERSONAL: Born May 5, 1956, at Bellingham, Wash. . . . 6-4/242.
HIGH SCHOOL: Royal Oak (Covina, Calif.).
COLLEGE: Mt. San Antonio Junior College (Calif.), then San Diego State.
TRANSACTIONS/CAREER NOTES: Selected by Washington Redskins in fourth round (103rd pick overall) of 1979 NFL draft.
CHAMPIONSHIP GAME EXPERIENCE: Played in NFC championship game after 1982, 1983, 1986 and 1987 seasons. . . . Played in Super Bowl XVII after 1982 season, Super Bowl XVIII after 1983 season and Super Bowl XXII after 1987 season.
PRO STATISTICS: 1979—Recovered one fumble. 1980—Fumbled once. 1985—Rushed once for five yards and recovered one fumble. 1986—Recovered one fumble and fumbled once. 1988—Recovered one fumble and fumbled once. 1989—Recovered one fumble.

Year	Team	G	No.	Yds.	Avg.	TD
				RECEIVING		
1979— Washington NFL		16	26	303	11.7	0
1980— Washington NFL		13	31	323	10.4	0
1981— Washington NFL		16	29	335	11.6	1
1982— Washington NFL		9	27	310	11.5	0
1983— Washington NFL		13	20	225	11.3	2
1984— Washington NFL		16	18	192	10.7	0
1985— Washington NFL		16	15	163	10.9	1
1986— Washington NFL		16	20	164	8.2	1
1987— Washington NFL		12	7	43	6.1	0
1988— Washington NFL		14	12	112	9.3	0
1989— Washington NFL		15	15	167	11.1	1
1990— Washington NFL		16	15	123	8.2	1
Pro totals (12 years)		172	235	2460	10.5	7

WARREN, FRANK
DE, SAINTS

PERSONAL: Born September 14, 1959, at Birmingham, Ala. . . . 6-4/290. . . . Full name: Frank William Warren III.
HIGH SCHOOL: Phillips (Birmingham, Ala.).
COLLEGE: Auburn.
TRANSACTIONS/CAREER NOTES: Selected by New Orleans Saints in third round (57th pick overall) of 1981 NFL draft. . . . On reserve/non-football injury list with substance abuse (May 1, 1990-entire 1990 season). . . . Reinstated (July 10, 1991). . . . Re-signed by Saints (July 12, 1991).

PLAYING EXPERIENCE: New Orleans NFL, 1981-1989. . . . Games: 1981 (16), 1982 (9), 1983 (16), 1984 (16), 1985 (16), 1986 (16), 1987 (12), 1988 (16), 1989 (16). Total: 133.
PRO STATISTICS: 1981—Recovered one fumble. 1983—Intercepted one pass for six yards and recovered one fumble. 1985—Recovered one fumble for 50 yards and a touchdown and returned blocked field goal attempt 42 yards for a touchdown. 1986—Recovered three fumbles. 1988—Recovered one fumble. 1989—Credited with a safety and recovered one fumble.

WASHINGTON, BRIAN
S, JETS

PERSONAL: Born September 10, 1965, at Richmond, Va. . . . 6-0/212. . . . Full name: Brian Wayne Washington.
HIGH SCHOOL: Highland Springs (Va.).
COLLEGE: Nebraska.
TRANSACTIONS/CAREER NOTES: Selected by Cleveland Browns in 10th round (272nd pick overall) of 1988 NFL draft. . . . Signed by Browns (July 13, 1988). . . . On injured reserve with broken nose and elbow (September 4-September 6, 1989). . . . Released by Browns (September 7, 1989). . . . Signed as free agent by New York Jets (September 12, 1989). . . . On retired list (September 14-September 19, 1989). . . . Transferred to retired/left camp list (September 20, 1989-entire season). . . . Reinstated (February 12, 1990). . . . On inactive list (November 11 and 18, 1990).
PRO STATISTICS: 1990—Recovered one fumble.

Year Team	G	No.	Yds.	Avg.	TD
		INTERCEPTIONS			
1988— Cleveland NFL	16	3	104	34.7	1
1990— N.Y. Jets NFL	14	3	22	7.3	0
Pro totals (2 years)	30	6	126	21.0	1

WASHINGTON, CHARLES
S, CHIEFS

PERSONAL: Born October 8, 1966, at Shreveport, La. . . . 6-1/217. . . . Full name: Charles Edwin Washington.
HIGH SCHOOL: H. Grady Spruce (Dallas).
COLLEGE: Texas, then Cameron (Okla.).
TRANSACTIONS/CAREER NOTES: Selected by Indianapolis Colts in seventh round (185th pick overall) of 1989 NFL draft. . . . Signed by Colts (July 26, 1989). . . . Released by Colts (September 4, 1989). . . . Re-signed by Colts (September 5, 1989). . . . Granted unconditional free agency (February 1, 1990). . . . Signed by Kansas City Chiefs (April 1, 1990). . . . On injured reserve with ankle injury (October 18, 1990-January 4, 1991).
PLAYING EXPERIENCE: Indianapolis NFL, 1989; Kansas City NFL, 1990. . . . Games: 1989 (16), 1990 (6). Total: 22.
PRO STATISTICS: 1989—Returned one punt for six yards.

WASHINGTON, CHRIS
LB, 49ERS

PERSONAL: Born March 6, 1962, at Jackson, Miss. . . . 6-4/240.
HIGH SCHOOL: Percy L. Julian (Chicago).
COLLEGE: Iowa State.
TRANSACTIONS/CAREER NOTES: Selected by Washington Federals in third round (49th pick overall) of 1984 USFL draft. . . . Selected by Tampa Bay Buccaneers in sixth round (142nd pick overall) of 1984 NFL draft. . . . Signed by Buccaneers (June 5, 1984). . . . Granted unconditional free agency (February 1, 1989). . . . Signed by San Francisco 49ers (March 7, 1989). . . . On injured reserve with broken leg (August 29, 1989-entire season). . . . Released by 49ers (August 31, 1990). . . . Signed by Phoenix Cardinals (October 23, 1990). . . . On inactive list (November 4 and 11, 1990). . . . Granted unconditional free agency (February 1, 1991). . . . Signed by San Francisco 49ers (April 1, 1991).
PLAYING EXPERIENCE: Tampa Bay NFL, 1984-1988; Phoenix NFL, 1990. . . . Games: 1984 (16), 1985 (16), 1986 (16), 1987 (12), 1988 (16), 1990 (8). Total: 84.
PRO STATISTICS: 1985—Recovered one fumble. 1986—Intercepted one pass for 12 yards and recovered two fumbles. 1988—Recovered one fumble.

WASHINGTON, JAMES
S, COWBOYS

PERSONAL: Born January 10, 1965, at Los Angeles. . . . 6-1/ 195. . . . Full name: James McArthur Washington.
HIGH SCHOOL: Jordan (Los Angeles).
COLLEGE: UCLA.
TRANSACTIONS/CAREER NOTES: Selected by Los Angeles Rams in fifth round (137th pick overall) of 1988 NFL draft. . . . Signed by Rams (July 12, 1988). . . . On injured reserve with thigh injury (November 10-December 27, 1989). . . . Transferred to developmental squad (December 28, 1989). . . . Granted unconditional free agency (February 1, 1990). . . . Signed by Dallas Cowboys (March 3, 1990).
CHAMPIONSHIP GAME EXPERIENCE: Played in NFC championship game after 1989 season.
PRO STATISTICS: 1989—Recovered one fumble. 1990—Recovered three fumbles.

Year Team	G	No.	Yds.	Avg.	TD
		INTERCEPTIONS			
1988— L.A. Rams NFL	16	1	7	7.0	0
1989— L.A. Rams NFL	9	0	0		0
1990— Dallas NFL	15	3	24	8.0	0
Pro totals (3 years)	40	4	31	7.8	0

WASHINGTON, JOHN
DE, GIANTS

PERSONAL: Born February 20, 1963, at Houston. . . . 6-4/275.
HIGH SCHOOL: Sterling (Houston).
COLLEGE: Oklahoma State.
TRANSACTIONS/CAREER NOTES: Selected by New Jersey Generals in 1986 USFL territorial draft. . . . Selected by New York Giants in third round (73rd pick overall) of 1986 NFL draft. . . . Signed by Giants (July 17, 1986). . . . On injured reserve with back injury (January 3, 1987-remainder of 1986 season playoffs).
PLAYING EXPERIENCE: New York Giants NFL, 1986-1990. . . . Games: 1986 (16), 1987 (12), 1988 (16), 1989 (16), 1990 (16). Total: 76.
CHAMPIONSHIP GAME EXPERIENCE: Played in NFC championship game after 1990 season. . . . Played in Super Bowl XXV after 1990 season.
PRO STATISTICS: 1989—Recovered two fumbles.

WASHINGTON, LIONEL
CB, RAIDERS

PERSONAL: Born October 21, 1960, at New Orleans. . . . 6-0/185.
HIGH SCHOOL: Lutcher (La.).
COLLEGE: Tulane (degree in sports administration).
TRANSACTIONS/CAREER NOTES: Selected by Tampa Bay Bandits in 20th round (229th pick overall) of 1983 USFL draft. . . . Selected by St. Louis Cardinals in fourth round (103rd pick overall) of 1983 NFL draft. . . . Signed by Cardinals (May 6, 1983). . . . On injured reserve with broken fibula (September 16, 1985-November 22, 1985). . . . Granted free agency (February 1, 1987). . . . Re-signed by Cardinals and traded to Los Angeles Raiders for fifth-round pick in 1987 draft (March 18, 1987).
CHAMPIONSHIP GAME EXPERIENCE: Played in AFC championship game after 1990 season.
PRO STATISTICS: 1983—Recovered one fumble. 1984—Recovered one fumble. 1986—Recovered one fumble. 1989—Recovered three fumbles for 44 yards and a touchdown.

			INTERCEPTIONS		
Year Team	G	No.	Yds.	Avg.	TD
1983— St. Louis NFL	16	8	92	11.5	0
1984— St. Louis NFL	15	5	42	8.4	0
1985— St. Louis NFL	5	1	48	48.0	*1
1986— St. Louis NFL	16	2	19	9.5	0
1987— L.A. Raiders NFL	11	0	0		0
1988— L.A. Raiders NFL	12	1	0	.0	0
1989— L.A. Raiders NFL	16	3	46	15.3	1
1990— L.A. Raiders NFL	16	1	2	2.0	0
Pro totals (8 years)	107	21	249	11.9	2

WASHINGTON, MARVIN
DE, JETS

PERSONAL: Born October 22, 1965, at Denver. . . . 6-6/276. . . . Full name: Marvin Andrew Washington. . . . Cousin of Andrew Lang, center with Phoenix Suns.
HIGH SCHOOL: Justin F. Kimball (Dallas).
COLLEGE: Texas-El Paso, then Hinds Junior College (Miss.), then Idaho.
TRANSACTIONS/CAREER NOTES: Selected by New York Jets in sixth round (151st pick overall) of 1989 NFL draft. . . . Signed by Jets (July 21, 1989).
PLAYING EXPERIENCE: New York Jets NFL, 1989 and 1990. . . . Games: 1989 (16), 1990 (16). Total: 32.
PRO STATISTICS: 1989—Returned one kickoff for 11 yards and recovered one fumble.

WASHINGTON, MICKEY
CB, PATRIOTS

PERSONAL: Born July 8, 1968, at Galveston, Tex. . . . 5-9/187. . . . Full name: Mickey Lynn Washington. . . . Cousin of Joe Washington, running back with San Diego Chargers, Baltimore Colts, Washington Redskins and Atlanta Falcons, 1977-1985.
HIGH SCHOOL: West Brook Sr. (Beaumont, Tex.).
COLLEGE: Texas A&M (degree in sociology).
TRANSACTIONS/CAREER NOTES: Selected by Phoenix Cardinals in eighth round (199th pick overall) of 1990 NFL draft. . . . Signed by Cardinals (July 23, 1990). . . . Released by Cardinals (September 3, 1990). . . . Signed by Indianapolis Colts to practice squad (October 1, 1990). . . . Signed by New England Patriots off Colts' practice squad (October 30, 1990).
PLAYING EXPERIENCE: New England NFL, 1990. . . . Games: 1990 (9).

WATERS, ANDRE
S, EAGLES

PERSONAL: Born March 10, 1962, at Belle Glade, Fla. . . . 5-11/200.
HIGH SCHOOL: Pahokee (Fla.).
COLLEGE: Cheyney (degree in business administration).
TRANSACTIONS/CAREER NOTES: Signed as free agent by Philadelphia Eagles (June 20, 1984).
PRO STATISTICS: 1984—Recovered one fumble. 1985—Returned one punt for 23 yards and recovered one fumble. 1986—Recovered two fumbles for 81 yards. 1987—Recovered two fumbles for 11 yards. 1989—Recovered three fumbles for 21 yards and a touchdown.

		INTERCEPTIONS				KICKOFF RETURNS				TOTAL		
Year Team	G	No.	Yds.	Avg.	TD	No.	Yds.	Avg.	TD	TD	Pts.	F.
1984— Philadelphia NFL	16	0	0		0	13	319	24.5	*1	1	6	1
1985— Philadelphia NFL	16	0	0		0	4	74	18.5	0	0	0	1
1986— Philadelphia NFL	16	6	39	6.5	0	0	0		0	0	0	0

— 333 —

Year Team	G	INTERCEPTIONS				KICKOFF RETURNS				TOTAL		
		No.	Yds.	Avg.	TD	No.	Yds.	Avg.	TD	TD	Pts.	F.
1987— Philadelphia NFL	12	3	63	21.0	0	0	0		0	0	0	0
1988— Philadelphia NFL	16	3	19	6.3	0	0	0		0	0	0	0
1989— Philadelphia NFL	16	1	20	20.0	0	0	0		0	1	6	0
1990— Philadelphia NFL	14	0	0		0	0	0		0	0	0	0
Pro totals (7 years)	106	13	141	10.9	0	17	393	23.1	1	2	12	2

WAYMER, DAVE
S, 49ERS

PERSONAL: Born July 1, 1958, at Brooklyn, N.Y. . . . 6-1/188. . . . Full name: David Benjamin Waymer Jr.
HIGH SCHOOL: West (Charlotte, N.C.).
COLLEGE: Notre Dame (bachelor of arts degree in economics, 1980).
TRANSACTIONS/CAREER NOTES: Selected by New Orleans Saints in second round (41st pick overall) of 1980 NFL draft. . . . Granted unconditional free agency (February 1, 1990). . . . Signed by San Francisco 49ers (February 20, 1990).
CHAMPIONSHIP GAME EXPERIENCE: Played in NFC championship game after 1990 season.
RECORDS/HONORS: Played in Pro Bowl after 1987 season.
PRO STATISTICS: 1980—Returned three punts for 29 yards, recovered two fumbles and fumbled once. 1981—Recovered two fumbles. 1982—Recovered two fumbles. 1983—Recovered three fumbles. 1985—Fumbled once. 1986—Caught one pass for 13 yards and recovered one fumble. 1987—Recovered three fumbles for two yards. 1988—Returned two kickoffs for 39 yards, returned blocked field-goal attempt 58 yards for a touchdown, recovered one fumble and fumbled once. 1989—Recovered one fumble. 1990—Recovered one fumble.

Year Team	G	INTERCEPTIONS			
		No.	Yds.	Avg.	TD
1980— New Orleans NFL	16	0	0		0
1981— New Orleans NFL	16	4	54	13.5	0
1982— New Orleans NFL	9	0	0		0
1983— New Orleans NFL	16	0	0		0
1984— New Orleans NFL	16	4	9	2.3	0
1985— New Orleans NFL	16	6	49	8.2	0
1986— New Orleans NFL	16	9	48	5.3	0
1987— New Orleans NFL	12	5	78	15.6	0
1988— New Orleans NFL	16	3	91	30.3	0
1989— New Orleans NFL	16	6	66	11.0	0
1990— San Francisco NFL	16	7	64	9.1	0
Pro totals (11 years)	165	44	459	10.4	0

WEATHERS, CLARENCE
WR, PACKERS

PERSONAL: Born January 10, 1962, at Green's Pond, S.C. . . . 5-9/169. . . . Brother of Robert Weathers, running back with New England Patriots, 1982-1986.
HIGH SCHOOL: Fort Pierce (Fla.).
COLLEGE: Delaware State.
TRANSACTIONS/CAREER NOTES: Signed as free agent by New England Patriots (July 20, 1983). . . . On injured reserve with broken foot (August 28-October 20, 1984). . . . Released by Patriots (September 2, 1985). . . . Awarded on waivers to Cleveland Browns (September 3, 1985). . . . Granted unconditional free agency (February 1, 1989). . . . Signed by Indianapolis Colts (March 30, 1989). . . . Released by Colts (October 5, 1989). . . . Signed as free agent by Kansas City Chiefs (October 10, 1989). . . . Granted unconditional free agency (February 1, 1990). . . . Signed by Green Bay Packers (April 1, 1990). . . . On inactive list (December 22 and 30, 1990).
CHAMPIONSHIP GAME EXPERIENCE: Played in AFC championship game after 1986 and 1987 seasons.
PRO STATISTICS: 1983—Returned three kickoffs for 58 yards, rushed once for 28 yards and recovered one fumble. 1985—Returned one kickoff for 17 yards, rushed once for 18 yards and recovered one fumble. 1989—Recovered one fumble for two yards.

Year Team	G	RECEIVING				PUNT RETURNS				TOTAL		
		No.	Yds.	Avg.	TD	No.	Yds.	Avg.	TD	TD	Pts.	F.
1983— New England NFL	16	19	379	19.9	3	4	1	.3	0	3	18	2
1984— New England NFL	9	8	115	14.4	2	1	7	7.0	0	2	12	0
1985— Cleveland NFL	13	16	449	28.1	3	28	218	7.8	0	3	18	3
1986— Cleveland NFL	16	9	100	11.1	0	0	0		0	0	0	0
1987— Cleveland NFL	12	11	153	13.9	2	0	0		0	2	12	0
1988— Cleveland NFL	16	29	436	15.0	1	2	10	5.0	0	1	6	2
1989— Ind. (4)-KC (11) NFL	15	23	254	11.0	0	0	0		0	0	0	1
1990— Green Bay NFL	14	33	390	11.8	1	0	0		0	1	6	0
Pro totals (8 years)	111	148	2276	15.4	12	35	236	6.7	0	12	72	8

WEBB, RICHMOND
OT, DOLPHINS

PERSONAL: Born January 11, 1967, at Dallas. . . . 6-6/298. . . . Full name: Richmond Jewel Webb.
HIGH SCHOOL: Franklin D. Roosevelt (Dallas).
COLLEGE: Texas A&M (bachelor of arts degree in industrial distribution).
TRANSACTIONS/CAREER NOTES: Selected by Miami Dolphins in first round (ninth pick overall) of 1990 NFL draft. . . . Signed by Dolphins (July 27, 1990).

PLAYING EXPERIENCE: Miami NFL, 1990. . . . Games: 1990 (16).
RECORDS/HONORS: Played in Pro Bowl after 1990 season. . . . Named THE SPORTING NEWS NFL Rookie of the Year, 1990.

WEIDNER, BERT
G/C, DOLPHINS

PERSONAL: Born January 20, 1966, at Eden, N.Y. . . . 6-3/284. . . . Name pronounced WIDE-ner.
HIGH SCHOOL: Eden Jr. Sr. (Eden, N.Y).
COLLEGE: Kent.
TRANSACTIONS/CAREER NOTES: Selected by Miami Dolphins in 11th round (288th pick overall) of 1989 NFL draft. . . . Signed by Dolphins (July 18, 1989). . . . Released by Dolphins (September 4, 1989). . . . Re-signed by Dolphins to developmental squad (September 5, 1989). . . . Released by Dolphins (January 29, 1990). . . . Re-signed by Dolphins (February 22, 1990). . . . On in-active list (September 16, 23, 30; November 11; and December 2 and 9, 1990).
PLAYING EXPERIENCE: Miami NFL, 1990. . . . Games: 1990 (8).

WEIR, ROBERT
DL, COLTS

PERSONAL: Born February 4, 1961, at Birmingham, England. . . . 6-3/270. . . . Last name pro-nounced WEAR.
COLLEGE: Southern Methodist.
TRANSACTIONS/CAREER NOTES: Signed as free agent by Miami Dolphins (May 3, 1985). . . . On injured reserve with fractured foot (August 19-October 1, 1985). . . . Released by Dolphins (October 2, 1985). . . . Signed as free agent by San Francisco 49ers (June 17, 1986). . . . Released by 49ers (August 8, 1986). . . . Re-signed by 49ers (April 6, 1987). . . . Released by 49ers (May 12, 1987). . . . Signed as free agent by Winnipeg Blue Bombers of CFL (May 22, 1987). . . . Released by Blue Bombers (June 17, 1987). . . . Signed as free agent by Ottawa Rough Riders of CFL (August, 1987). . . . Granted free agency (March 1, 1990). . . . Re-signed by San Francisco 49ers (April 12, 1990). . . . Released by 49ers (August 27, 1990). . . . Signed by Hamilton Tiger-Cats of CFL (September, 1990). . . . Signed by Indianapolis Colts (February 11, 1991).
PLAYING EXPERIENCE: Ottawa CFL, 1987-1989; Hamilton CFL, 1990. . . . Games: 1987 (12), 1988 (10), 1989 (18), 1990 (8). Total: 48.
MISCELLANEOUS: Participated in hammer-throw during 1984 Olympics representing Great Britain.

WELCH, HERB
S, LIONS

PERSONAL: Born January 12, 1961, at Los Angeles. . . . 5-11/180. . . . Full name: Herb Doyan Welch.
HIGH SCHOOL: Warren (Downey, Calif.).
COLLEGE: Cerritos College (Calif.), then UCLA.
TRANSACTIONS/CAREER NOTES: Selected by Portland Breakers in 10th round (135th pick overall) of 1985 USFL draft. . . . Se-lected by New York Giants in 12th round (326th pick overall) of 1985 NFL draft. . . . Signed by Giants (July 9, 1985). . . . On in-jured reserve with knee injury (July 25, 1988-entire season). . . . Released by Giants (August 29, 1989). . . . Signed as free agent by Washington Redskins (October 24, 1989). . . . Granted unconditional free agency (February 1, 1990). . . . Signed by Detroit Lions (March 26, 1990). . . . Released by Lions (September 3, 1990). . . . Re-signed by Lions (September 4, 1990).
CHAMPIONSHIP GAME EXPERIENCE: Played in NFC championship game after 1986 season. . . . Played in Super Bowl XXI after 1986 season.
PRO STATISTICS: 1986—Recovered one fumble for seven yards. 1990—Recovered one fumble.

			INTERCEPTIONS		
Year Team	G	No.	Yds.	Avg.	TD
1985— N.Y. Giants NFL	16	2	8	4.0	0
1986— N.Y. Giants NFL	16	2	22	11.0	0
1987— N.Y. Giants NFL	12	2	7	3.5	0
1989— Washington NFL	9	0	0		0
1990— Detroit NFL	16	1	16	16.0	0
Pro totals (5 years)	69	7	53	7.6	0

WELLS, KENT
NT, 49ERS

PERSONAL: Born July 25, 1967, at Lincoln, Neb. . . . 6-4/295. . . . Full name: Kent E. Wells.
HIGH SCHOOL: Lincoln East (Lincoln, Neb.).
COLLEGE: Nebraska.
TRANSACTIONS/CAREER NOTES: Selected by Washington Redskins in sixth round (160th pick overall) of 1990 NFL draft. . . . Released by Redskins (August 27, 1990). . . . Awarded on waivers to New York Giants (August 30, 1990). . . . On inactive list (October 28; and November 5, 18 and 25, 1990). . . . Released by Giants (December 3, 1990). . . . Signed by San Francisco 49ers (April 12, 1991).
PLAYING EXPERIENCE: New York Giants NFL, 1990. . . . Games: 1990 (6).

WELLSANDT, DOUG
TE, JETS

PERSONAL: Born February 9, 1967, at Moses Lake, Wash. . . . 6-3/248. . . . Full name: Douglas D. Wellsandt.
HIGH SCHOOL: Ritzville (Wash.).
COLLEGE: Washington State (degree in physical education).
TRANSACTIONS/CAREER NOTES: Selected by Cincinnati Bengals in eighth round (204th pick overall) of 1990 NFL draft. . . . Signed by Bengals (July 17, 1990). . . . Released by Bengals (September 3, 1990). . . . Awarded on waivers to New York Jets (September 4, 1990).
PRO STATISTICS: 1990—Rushed once for minus three yards.

			RECEIVING		
Year Team	G	No.	Yds.	Avg.	TD
1990— N.Y. Jets NFL	16	5	57	11.4	0
Pro totals (1 year)	16	5	57	11.4	0

WEST, ED

TE, PACKERS

PERSONAL: Born August 2, 1961, at Colbert County, Ala.... 6-1/244.... Full name: Edward Lee West III. **HIGH SCHOOL:** Colbert County (Leighton, Ala.).
COLLEGE: Auburn.
TRANSACTIONS/CAREER NOTES: Selected by Birmingham Stallions in 1984 USFL territorial draft.... Signed as free agent by Green Bay Packers (May 3, 1984).... Released by Packers (August 27, 1984).... Re-signed by Packers (August 30, 1984).
PRO STATISTICS: 1984—Rushed once for two yards and a touchdown and recovered one fumble. 1985—Rushed once for no yards and fumbled once. 1986—Recovered one fumble. 1988—Fumbled once. 1990—Fumbled three times and returned one kickoff for no yards.

			RECEIVING			
Year Team	G	No.	Yds.	Avg.	TD	
1984— Green Bay NFL..........	16	6	54	9.0	4	
1985— Green Bay NFL..........	16	8	95	11.9	1	
1986— Green Bay NFL..........	16	15	199	13.3	1	
1987— Green Bay NFL..........	12	19	261	13.7	1	
1988— Green Bay NFL..........	16	30	276	9.2	3	
1989— Green Bay NFL..........	13	22	269	12.2	5	
1990— Green Bay NFL..........	16	27	356	13.2	5	
Pro totals (7 years)........	105	127	1510	11.9	20	

WESTON, RHONDY

DL, BROWNS

PERSONAL: Born June 7, 1966, at Belle Glade, Fla.... 6-5/280.
HIGH SCHOOL: Glades Central (Belle Glade, Fla.).
COLLEGE: Florida.
TRANSACTIONS/CAREER NOTES: Selected by Dallas Cowboys in third round (68th pick overall) of 1989 NFL draft.... Signed by Cowboys (July 24, 1989).... Released by Cowboys (August 29, 1989).... Awarded on waivers to Tampa Bay Buccaneers (August 30, 1989).... Released by Buccaneers (September 5, 1989).... Re-signed by Buccaneers to developmental squad (September 6, 1989).... On developmental squad (September 6-September 20, 1989).... Granted unconditional free agency (February 1, 1990).... Signed by Cleveland Browns (March 8, 1990).... On injured reserve with knee injury (September 8, 1990-entire season).
PLAYING EXPERIENCE: Tampa Bay NFL, 1989.... Games: 1989 (12).
PRO STATISTICS: 1989—Recovered one fumble.

WHEAT, WARREN

G, SEAHAWKS

PERSONAL: Born May 13, 1967, at Phoenix.... 6-6/274.
HIGH SCHOOL: Camelback (Phoenix).
COLLEGE: Brigham Young.
TRANSACTIONS/CAREER NOTES: Selected by Los Angeles Rams in eighth round (215th pick overall) of 1989 NFL draft.... Signed by Rams (July 14, 1989).... Released by Rams (September 4, 1989).... Awarded on waivers to Seattle Seahawks (September 5, 1989).... On injured reserve with knee injury (September 21, 1989-remainder of season).... On injured reserve with back injury (September 4-December 2, 1990).... Active for five games in 1990; did not play.
PLAYING EXPERIENCE: Seattle NFL, 1989 and 1990.... Games: 1989 (2), 1990 (0). Total: 2.

WHISENHUNT, KEN

TE, REDSKINS

PERSONAL: Born February 28, 1962, at Atlanta.... 6-3/240.... Full name: Kenneth Moore Whisenhunt.
HIGH SCHOOL: Richmond (Augusta, Ga.).
COLLEGE: Georgia Tech.
TRANSACTIONS/CAREER NOTES: Selected by Jacksonville Bulls in 1985 USFL territorial draft.... USFL rights traded by Bulls with rights to running back Marck Harrison and center Dan Turk to Tampa Bay Bandits for rights to kicker Bobby Raymond, running back Cedric Jones and defensive back Eric Riley (January 3, 1985).... Selected by Atlanta Falcons in 12th round (313th pick overall) of 1985 NFL draft.... Signed by Falcons (July 18, 1985).... On injured reserve with separated shoulder (December 2, 1987-remainder of season).... Granted unconditional free agency (February 1, 1989).... Signed by Washington Redskins (March 8, 1989).... On reserve/physically unable to perform list with shin injury (August 29, 1989-entire season).... Released by Redskins (September 4, 1990).... Signed by Los Angeles Raiders (October 24, 1990).... Released by Raiders (October 29, 1990).... Re-signed by Washington Redskins (December 18, 1990).
PRO STATISTICS: 1985—Rushed once for three yards, returned four kickoffs for 33 yards and recovered one fumble. 1986—Rushed once for 20 yards. 1987—Recovered one fumble and fumbled once. 1988—Recovered one fumble and fumbled once.

			RECEIVING			
Year Team	G	No.	Yds.	Avg.	TD	
1985— Atlanta NFL	16	3	48	16.0	0	
1986— Atlanta NFL	16	20	184	9.2	3	
1987— Atlanta NFL	7	17	145	8.5	1	
1988— Atlanta NFL	16	16	174	10.9	1	
1990— Washington NFL........	2	0	0		0	
Pro totals (5 years)........	57	56	551	9.8	5	

WHITAKER, DANTA
TE, CHIEFS

PERSONAL: Born March 14, 1964, at Atlanta. . . . 6-4/248. . . . Full name: Danta Antonio Whitaker.
HIGH SCHOOL: W.F. George (Atlanta).
COLLEGE: Mississippi Valley State.
TRANSACTIONS/CAREER NOTES: Selected by New York Giants in seventh round (186th pick overall) of 1988 NFL draft. . . . On injured reserve with ankle injury (August 23, 1988-entire season). . . . Granted unconditional free agency (February 1, 1989). . . . Signed as free agent by Atlanta Falcons (March 29, 1989). . . . Released by Falcons (September 5, 1989). . . . Signed by Kansas City Chiefs to developmental squad (November 1, 1989). . . . Released by Chiefs (January 18, 1990). . . . Re-signed by Chiefs (April 3, 1990).
PRO STATISTICS: 1990—Returned one punt for no yards and fumbled once.

			RECEIVING		
Year Team	G	No.	Yds.	Avg.	TD
1990— Kansas City NFL	16	2	17	8.5	1
Pro totals (1 year)	16	2	17	8.5	1

WHITE, ADRIAN
S, GIANTS

PERSONAL: Born April 6, 1964, at Orange Park, Fla. . . . 6-0/200. . . . Full name: Adrian Darnell White.
HIGH SCHOOL: Orange Park (Fla.).
COLLEGE: Southern Illinois, then Florida.
TRANSACTIONS/CAREER NOTES: Selected by New York Giants in second round (55th pick overall) of 1987 NFL draft. . . . Signed by Giants (July 27, 1987). . . . On injured reserve with knee injury (August 22-October 14, 1987). . . . Crossed picket line during players' strike (October 14, 1987). . . . Granted free agency (February 1, 1990). . . . Re-signed by Giants (July 23, 1990). . . . On injured reserve with knee injury (September 3, 1990-entire regular season and playoffs).
PLAYING EXPERIENCE: New York Giants NFL, 1987-1989. . . . Games: 1987 (6), 1988 (16), 1989 (15). Total: 37.
PRO STATISTICS: 1988—Intercepted one pass for 29 yards. 1989—Intercepted two passes for eight yards.

WHITE, DWAYNE
G, JETS

PERSONAL: Born February 10, 1967, at Philadelphia. . . . 6-2/312. . . . Full name: Dwayne Allen White.
HIGH SCHOOL: South Philadelphia (Philadelphia).
COLLEGE: Alcorn State (bachelor of arts degree in political science, 1990).
TRANSACTIONS/CAREER NOTES: Selected by New York Jets in seventh round (167th pick overall) of 1990 NFL draft. . . . Signed by Jets (July 12, 1990). . . . On injured reserve with back injury (September 4-October 13, 1990).
PLAYING EXPERIENCE: New York Jets NFL, 1990. . . . Games: 1990 (11).

WHITE, LEON
LB, BENGALS

PERSONAL: Born October 4, 1963, at San Diego. . . . 6-3/242. . . . Full name: Thomas Leon White.
HIGH SCHOOL: Helix (La Mesa, Calif.).
COLLEGE: Brigham Young.
TRANSACTIONS/CAREER NOTES: Selected by Cincinnati Bengals in fifth round (123rd pick overall) of 1986 NFL draft. . . . Signed by Bengals (July 20, 1986).
PLAYING EXPERIENCE: Cincinnati NFL, 1986-1990. . . . Games: 1986 (16), 1987 (12), 1988 (16), 1989 (16), 1990 (16). Total: 76.
CHAMPIONSHIP GAME EXPERIENCE: Played in AFC championship game after 1988 season. . . . Played in Super Bowl XXIII after 1988 season.
PRO STATISTICS: 1986—Credited with a safety. 1988—Recovered one fumble. 1989—Intercepted one pass for 22 yards and recovered two fumbles for 22 yards and a touchdown.

WHITE, LORENZO
RB, OILERS

PERSONAL: Born April 12, 1966, at Hollywood, Fla. . . . 5-11/222. . . . Full name: Lorenzo Maurice White.
HIGH SCHOOL: Dillard (Fort Lauderdale, Fla.).
COLLEGE: Michigan State.
TRANSACTIONS/CAREER NOTES: Selected by Houston Oilers in first round (22nd pick overall) of 1988 NFL draft. . . . Signed by Oilers (July 23, 1988).
RECORDS/HONORS: Named as running back on THE SPORTING NEWS college All-America team, 1985.
PRO STATISTICS: 1989—Recovered one fumble. 1990—Recovered three fumbles.

		RUSHING				RECEIVING				KICKOFF RETURNS				TOTAL		
Year Team	G	Att.	Yds.	Avg.	TD	No.	Yds.	Avg.	TD	No.	Yds.	Avg.	TD	TD	Pts.	F.
1988— Houston NFL	11	31	115	3.7	0	0	0	0		8	196	24.5	*1	1	6	0
1989— Houston NFL	16	104	349	3.4	5	6	37	6.2	0	17	303	17.8	0	5	30	2
1990— Houston NFL	16	168	702	4.2	8	39	368	9.4	4	0	0		0	12	72	7
Pro totals (3 years)	43	303	1166	3.9	13	45	405	9.0	4	25	499	20.0	1	18	108	9

WHITE, REGGIE
DE, EAGLES

PERSONAL: Born December 19, 1961, at Chattanooga, Tenn. . . . 6-5/285. . . . Full name: Reginald Howard White.
HIGH SCHOOL: Howard (Chattanooga, Tenn.).
COLLEGE: Tennessee.
TRANSACTIONS/CAREER NOTES: Selected by Memphis Showboats in 1984 USFL territorial draft. . . . Signed by Showboats (January 15, 1984). . . . On developmental squad for two games (March 9-March 24, 1984). . . . Selected by Philadelphia Eagles in

first round (fourth pick overall) of 1984 NFL supplemental draft. . . . Released by Memphis Showboats (September 19, 1985). . . . Signed by Philadelphia Eagles (September 21, 1985). . . . Granted roster exemption (September 21-September 27, 1985). . . . On reserve/did not report list (July 28-August 23, 1989).
PLAYING EXPERIENCE: Memphis USFL, 1984 and 1985; Philadelphia NFL, 1985-1990. . . . Games: 1984 (16), 1985 USFL (18), 1985 NFL (13), 1986 (16), 1987 (12), 1988 (16), 1989 (16), 1990 (16). Total USFL: 34. Total NFL: 89. Total Pro: 123.
RECORDS/HONORS: Named as defensive end on THE SPORTING NEWS college All-America team, 1983. . . . Named as defensive end on THE SPORTING NEWS USFL All-Star team, 1985. . . . Played in Pro Bowl after 1986-1990 seasons. . . . Named to THE SPORTING NEWS NFL All-Pro team, 1987 and 1988.
PRO STATISTICS: USFL: 1984—Credited with 12 sacks for 84 yards and recovered one fumble. 1985—Credited with 11½ sacks for 93½ yards, credited with one safety and recovered one fumble for 20 yards and a touchdown. . . . NFL: 1985—Recovered two fumbles. 1987—Recovered one fumble for 70 yards and a touchdown. 1988—Recovered two fumbles. 1989—Recovered one fumble for 10 yards. 1990—Intercepted one pass for 33 yards and recovered one fumble.

WHITE, ROBB
DL, BUCCANEERS

PERSONAL: Born May 26, 1965, at Aberdeen, S.D. . . . 6-5/280.
HIGH SCHOOL: Central (Aberdeen, S.D.).
COLLEGE: South Dakota.
TRANSACTIONS/CAREER NOTES: Signed as free agent by Washington Redskins (May 12, 1988). . . . On injured reserve with back injury (August 29-November 16, 1988). . . . Released by Redskins (November 17, 1988). . . . Awarded on waivers to New York Giants (November 18, 1988). . . . On injured reserve with back injury (December 17, 1988-remainder of season). . . . Granted unconditional free agency (February 1, 1990). . . . Signed by Denver Broncos (March 28, 1990). . . . Released by Broncos (August 22, 1990). . . . Signed by New York Giants for 1990. . . . Released by Giants (September 5, 1990). . . . Signed by Tampa Bay Buccaneers (November 7, 1990).
PLAYING EXPERIENCE: New York Giants NFL, 1988 and 1989; Tampa Bay NFL, 1990. . . . Games: 1988 (1), 1989 (15), 1990 (7). Total: 23.

WHITE, SHELDON
CB, LIONS

PERSONAL: Born March 1, 1965, at Dayton, O. . . . 5-11/188. . . . Full name: Sheldon Darnell White.
HIGH SCHOOL: Meadowdale (Dayton, O.).
COLLEGE: Miami of Ohio.
TRANSACTIONS/CAREER NOTES: Selected by New York Giants in third round (62nd pick overall) of 1988 NFL draft. . . . Signed by Giants (July 18, 1988). . . . Released by Giants (September 3, 1990). . . . Awarded on waivers to Detroit Lions (September 4, 1990). . . . On injured reserve with ankle injury (September 8-December 14, 1990).
PRO STATISTICS: 1988—Returned three kickoffs for 62 yards (20.7 avg.).

			INTERCEPTIONS		
Year	Team	G	No.	Yds.	Avg.	TD
1988—N.Y. Giants NFL		16	4	70	17.5	0
1989—N.Y. Giants NFL		16	2	18	9.0	0
1990—Detroit NFL		3	0	0		0
Pro totals (3 years)		35	6	88	14.7	0

WHITE, WILLIAM
DB, LIONS

PERSONAL: Born February 19, 1966, at Lima, O. . . . 5-10/191. . . . Full name: William Eugene White.
HIGH SCHOOL: Lima (O.).
COLLEGE: Ohio State.
TRANSACTIONS/CAREER NOTES: Selected by Detroit Lions in fourth round (85th pick overall) of 1988 NFL draft. . . . Signed by Lions (July 11, 1988).
PRO STATISTICS: 1988—Recovered one fumble. 1989—Recovered one fumble for 20 yards and a touchdown.

			INTERCEPTIONS		
Year	Team	G	No.	Yds.	Avg.	TD
1988—Detroit NFL		16	0	0		0
1989—Detroit NFL		15	1	0	.0	0
1990—Detroit NFL		16	5	120	24.0	1
Pro totals (3 years)		47	6	120	20.0	1

WHITMORE, DAVID
S, 49ERS

PERSONAL: Born July 6, 1967, at Daingerfield, Tex. . . . 6-0/235. . . . Full name: David L. Whitmore.
HIGH SCHOOL: Daingerfield (Tex.).
COLLEGE: Stephen F. Austin State.
TRANSACTIONS/CAREER NOTES: Selected by New York Giants in fourth round (107th pick overall) of 1990 NFL draft. . . . Signed by Giants (July 23, 1990). . . . Granted unconditional free agency (February 1, 1991). . . . Signed by San Francisco 49ers (March 13, 1991).
PLAYING EXPERIENCE: New York Giants NFL, 1990. . . . Games: 1990 (16).
CHAMPIONSHIP GAME EXPERIENCE: Played in NFC championship game after 1990 season. . . . Played in Super Bowl XXV after 1990 season.
PRO STATISTICS: 1990—Returned one kickoff for no yards and fumbled once.

WIDELL, DAVE
OT, BRONCOS

PERSONAL: Born May 14, 1965, at Hartford, Conn. . . . 6-6/292. . . . Full name: David Harold Widell. . . . Name pronounced wi-DEL. . . . Brother of Doug Widell, center with Denver Broncos.
HIGH SCHOOL: South Catholic (Hartford, Conn.).
COLLEGE: Boston College (degree in finance, 1988).
TRANSACTIONS/CAREER NOTES: Selected by Dallas Cowboys in fourth round (94th pick overall) of 1988 NFL draft. . . . Signed by Cowboys (July 12, 1988). . . . Traded by Cowboys to Denver Broncos for seventh-round pick in 1991 NFL draft and a conditional pick in 1992 draft (August 24, 1990).
PLAYING EXPERIENCE: Dallas NFL, 1988 and 1989; Denver NFL, 1990. . . . Games: 1988 (14), 1989 (15), 1990 (16). Total: 45.
PRO STATISTICS: 1988—Recovered one fumble.

WIDELL, DOUG
C, BRONCOS

PERSONAL: Born September 23, 1966, at Hartford, Conn. . . . 6-4/287. . . . Full name: Douglas Joseph Widell. . . . Name pronounced wi-DEL. . . . Brother of Dave Widell, offensive tackle with Denver Broncos.
HIGH SCHOOL: South Catholic (Hartford, Conn.).
COLLEGE: Boston College (bachelor of science degree in marketing, 1989).
TRANSACTIONS/CAREER NOTES: Selected by Denver Broncos in second round (41st pick overall) of 1989 NFL draft. . . . Signed by Broncos (July 23, 1989).
PLAYING EXPERIENCE: Denver NFL, 1989 and 1990. . . . Games: 1989 (16), 1990 (16). Total: 32.
CHAMPIONSHIP GAME EXPERIENCE: Played in AFC championship game after 1989 season. . . . Played in Super Bowl XXIV after 1989 season.
PRO STATISTICS: 1990—Recovered one fumble.

WILCHER, MIKE
LB, RAMS

PERSONAL: Born March 20, 1960, at Washington, D.C. . . . 6-3/245.
HIGH SCHOOL: Eastern (Washington, D.C.).
COLLEGE: North Carolina.
TRANSACTIONS/CAREER NOTES: Selected by Philadelphia Stars in 1983 USFL territorial draft. . . . Selected by Los Angeles Rams in second round (36th pick overall) of 1983 NFL draft. . . . Signed by Rams (June 16, 1983).
PLAYING EXPERIENCE: Los Angeles Rams NFL, 1983-1990. . . . Games: 1983 (15), 1984 (15), 1985 (16), 1986 (16), 1987 (12), 1988 (16), 1989 (16), 1990 (16). Total: 122.
CHAMPIONSHIP GAME EXPERIENCE: Played in NFC championship game after 1985 and 1989 seasons.
PRO STATISTICS: 1985—Intercepted one pass for no yards. 1986—Intercepted one pass for no yards. 1987—Intercepted one pass for 11 yards and recovered one fumble for 35 yards and a touchdown. 1988—Recovered one fumble for eight yards. 1989—Intercepted one pass for four yards and fumbled once. 1990—Recovered four fumbles for two yards.

WILCOTS, SOLOMON
S, VIKINGS

PERSONAL: Born October 3, 1964, at Los Angeles. . . . 5-11/195.
HIGH SCHOOL: Rubidoux (Riverside, Calif.).
COLLEGE: Colorado.
TRANSACTIONS/CAREER NOTES: Selected by Cincinnati Bengals in eighth round (215th pick overall) of 1987 NFL draft. . . . Signed by Bengals (July 22, 1987). . . . Granted unconditional free agency (February 1, 1991). . . . Signed by Minnesota Vikings (March 27, 1991).
PLAYING EXPERIENCE: Cincinnati NFL, 1987-1990. . . . Games: 1987 (12), 1988 (16), 1989 (16), 1990 (16). Total: 60.
CHAMPIONSHIP GAME EXPERIENCE: Played in AFC championship game after 1988 season. . . . Played in Super Bowl XXIII after 1988 season.
PRO STATISTICS: 1987—Intercepted one pass for 37 yards. 1988—Intercepted one pass for six yards and recovered two fumbles. 1990—Recovered one fumble for three yards.

WILDER, JAMES
RB, LIONS

PERSONAL: Born May 12, 1958, at Sikeston, Mo. . . . 6-3/225. . . . Full name: James Curtis Wilder.
HIGH SCHOOL: Sikeston (Mo.).
COLLEGE: Northeastern Oklahoma A&M, then Missouri.
TRANSACTIONS/CAREER NOTES: Selected by Tampa Bay Buccaneers in second round (34th pick overall) of 1981 NFL draft. . . . On injured reserve with broken ribs (November 15, 1983-remainder of season). . . . On injured reserve with ankle injury (December 19, 1986-remainder of season). . . . On injured reserve with knee injury (November 4, 1988-remainder of season). . . . Granted unconditional free agency (February 1, 1990). . . . Signed by Washington Redskins (March 6, 1990). . . . Traded by Redskins with fourth-round pick in 1991 draft to Detroit Lions for defensive lineman Eric Williams (September 11, 1990).
RECORDS/HONORS: Established NFL records for most rushing attempts, season (407), 1984; most combined attempts, season (496), 1984; most combined attempts, game (48), against Pittsburgh Steelers (October 30, 1983). . . . Played in Pro Bowl after 1984 season.
PRO STATISTICS: 1981—Returned one kickoff for 19 yards and recovered one fumble. 1982—Recovered one fumble for three yards. 1984—Attempted one pass with one completion for 16 yards and a touchdown and recovered four fumbles. 1985—Recovered one fumble. 1986—Recovered three fumbles. 1987—Recovered two fumbles. 1989—Returned two kickoffs for 42 yards and recovered one fumble.

| | | RUSHING | | | | RECEIVING | | | | TOTAL | | |
Year Team	G	Att.	Yds.	Avg.	TD	No.	Yds.	Avg.	TD	TD	Pts.	F.
1981— Tampa Bay NFL	16	107	370	3.5	4	48	507	10.6	1	5	30	3
1982— Tampa Bay NFL	9	83	324	3.9	3	53	466	8.8	1	4	24	5
1983— Tampa Bay NFL	10	161	640	4.0	4	57	380	6.7	2	6	36	1
1984— Tampa Bay NFL	16	*407	1544	3.8	13	85	685	8.1	0	13	78	10
1985— Tampa Bay NFL	16	365	1300	3.6	10	53	341	6.4	0	10	60	9
1986— Tampa Bay NFL	12	190	704	3.7	2	43	326	7.6	1	3	18	10

Year	Team		G	Att.	RUSHING Yds.	Avg.	TD	No.	RECEIVING Yds.	Avg.	TD	TD	TOTAL Pts.	F.
1987	— Tampa Bay NFL		12	106	488	4.6	0	40	328	8.2	1	1	6	3
1988	— Tampa Bay NFL		7	86	343	4.0	1	15	124	8.3	0	1	6	1
1989	— Tampa Bay NFL		15	70	244	3.5	0	36	335	9.3	3	3	18	2
1990	— Was. (1)-Det. (15) NFL		16	11	51	4.6	0	1	8	8.0	1	1	6	0
	Pro totals (10 years)		129	1586	6008	3.8	37	431	3500	8.1	10	47	282	44

WILHELM, ERIK
QB, BENGALS

PERSONAL: Born November 19, 1965, at Dayton, O. . . . 6-3/217. . . . Full name: Erik Bradley Wilhelm.
HIGH SCHOOL: Gladstone (Ore.) and Lakeridge (Lake Oswego, Ore.).
COLLEGE: Oregon State.
TRANSACTIONS/CAREER NOTES: Selected by Cincinnati Bengals in third round (83rd pick overall) of 1989 NFL draft. . . . Signed by Bengals (July 22, 1989). . . . On inactive list (September 9 and 23, 1990).
PRO STATISTICS: Passer rating points: 1989 (87.3), 1990 (80.4). Career: 85.5. . . . 1989—Recovered one fumble. 1990—Recovered one fumble.

Year	Team		G	Att.	Cmp.	PASSING Pct.	Yds.	TD	Int.	Avg.	Att.	RUSHING Yds.	Avg.	TD	TD	TOTAL Pts.	F.
1989	— Cincinnati NFL		6	56	30	53.6	425	4	2	7.59	6	30	5.0	0	0	0	2
1990	— Cincinnati NFL		7	19	12	63.2	117	0	0	6.16	6	6	1.0	0	0	0	1
	Pro totals (2 years)		13	75	42	56.0	542	4	2	7.23	12	36	3.0	0	0	0	3

WILKERSON, BRUCE
OT, RAIDERS

PERSONAL: Born July 28, 1964, at Loudon, Tenn. . . . 6-5/295. . . . Full name: Bruce Alan Wilkerson.
HIGH SCHOOL: Loudon (Tenn.).
COLLEGE: Tennessee.
TRANSACTIONS/CAREER NOTES: Selected by Los Angeles Raiders in second round (52nd pick overall) of 1987 NFL draft. . . . Signed by Raiders (July 10, 1987). . . . Crossed picket line during players' strike (October 2, 1987). . . . On injured reserve with knee injury (September 4-November 4, 1990).
PLAYING EXPERIENCE: Los Angeles Raiders NFL, 1987-1990. . . . Games: 1987 (11), 1988 (16), 1989 (16), 1990 (8). Total: 51.
CHAMPIONSHIP GAME EXPERIENCE: Played in AFC championship game after 1990 season.
PRO STATISTICS: 1989—Recovered two fumbles.

WILKINS, GARY
TE, FALCONS

PERSONAL: Born November 23, 1963, at West Palm Beach, Fla. . . . 6-2/248. . . . Full name: Gary Clifton Wilkins.
HIGH SCHOOL: Twin Lakes (West Palm Beach, Fla.).
COLLEGE: Georgia Tech.
TRANSACTIONS/CAREER NOTES: Selected by Jacksonville Bulls in 1985 USFL territorial draft. . . . Signed as free agent by Dallas Cowboys (May 3, 1985). . . . Released by Cowboys (August 16, 1985). . . . Signed as free agent by Buffalo Bills (July 19, 1986). . . . Released by Bills (September 1, 1986). . . . Re-signed by Bills (September 2, 1986). . . . Released by Bills (August 31, 1987). . . . Re-signed as replacement player by Bills (October 17, 1987). . . . Released by Bills (November 3, 1987). . . . Signed as free agent by Atlanta Falcons for 1988 (December 10, 1987). . . . Granted unconditional free agency (February 1, 1989). . . . Signed by Green Bay Packers (March 9, 1989). . . . Released by Packers (July 28, 1989). . . . Signed as free agent by Atlanta Falcons (August 14, 1989). . . . Released by Falcons (September 6, 1989). . . . Re-signed by Falcons (September 26, 1989).
PRO STATISTICS: 1986—Rushed three times for 18 yards. 1989—Recovered one fumble. 1990—Returned one kickoff for seven yards.

Year	Team		G	No.	RECEIVING Yds.	Avg.	TD
1986	— Buffalo NFL		16	8	74	9.3	0
1987	— Buffalo NFL		1	0	0		0
1988	— Atlanta NFL		14	11	134	12.2	0
1989	— Atlanta NFL		13	8	179	22.4	3
1990	— Atlanta NFL		16	12	175	14.6	2
	Pro totals (5 years)		60	39	562	14.4	5

WILKS, JIM
DE/NT, SAINTS

PERSONAL: Born March 12, 1958, at Los Angeles. . . . 6-5/275. . . . Full name: Jimmy Ray Wilks.
HIGH SCHOOL: Pasadena (Calif.).
COLLEGE: Pasadena Community College (Calif.), then San Diego State.
TRANSACTIONS/CAREER NOTES: Selected by New Orleans Saints in 12th round (305th pick overall) of 1981 NFL draft. . . . On inactive list (September 19, 1982). . . . On inactive list (December 23, 1990).
PLAYING EXPERIENCE: New Orleans NFL, 1981-1990. . . . Games: 1981 (16), 1982 (8), 1983 (16), 1984 (16), 1985 (16), 1986 (16), 1987 (12), 1988 (16), 1989 (16), 1990 (15). Total: 147.
PRO STATISTICS: 1981—Recovered two fumbles. 1983—Recovered one fumble. 1984—Recovered one fumble. 1987—Recovered one fumble for 10 yards. 1988—Recovered one fumble.

WILLIAMS, BRENT
DE, PATRIOTS

PERSONAL: Born October 23, 1964, at Flint, Mich. . . . 6-4/275. . . . Full name: Brent Dione Williams.
HIGH SCHOOL: Northern (Flint, Mich.).
COLLEGE: Toledo (degree in marketing, 1986).
TRANSACTIONS/CAREER NOTES: Selected by New England Patriots in seventh round (192nd pick overall) of 1986 NFL draft. . . . Signed by Patriots (July 16, 1986).
PLAYING EXPERIENCE: New England NFL, 1986-1990. . . . Games: 1986 (16), 1987 (12), 1988 (16), 1989 (16), 1990 (16). Total: 76.
PRO STATISTICS: 1986—Recovered four fumbles for 54 yards and a touchdown. 1988—Recovered one fumble. 1989—Recovered two fumbles for two yards. 1990—Recovered two fumbles for 45 yards and a touchdown.

WILLIAMS, BRIAN
C/G, GIANTS

PERSONAL: Born June 8, 1966, at Mount Lebanon, Pa. . . . 6-5/300. . . . Full name: Brian Scott Williams.
HIGH SCHOOL: Mount Lebanon (Pittsburgh).
COLLEGE: Minnesota.
TRANSACTIONS/CAREER NOTES: Selected by New York Giants in first round (18th pick overall) of 1989 NFL draft. . . . Signed by Giants (August 14, 1989). . . . On injured reserve with knee injury (January 6, 1990-remainder of 1989 season playoffs).
PLAYING EXPERIENCE: New York Giants NFL, 1989 and 1990. . . . Games: 1989 (14), 1990 (16). Total: 30.
CHAMPIONSHIP GAME EXPERIENCE: Played in NFC championship game after 1990 season. . . . Played in Super Bowl XXV after 1990 season.

WILLIAMS, CALVIN
WR, EAGLES

PERSONAL: Born March 3, 1967, at Baltimore. . . . 5-11/190. . . . Full name: Calvin John Williams Jr.
HIGH SCHOOL: Dunbar (Baltimore).
COLLEGE: Purdue (degree in hotel/restaurant management).
TRANSACTIONS/CAREER NOTES: Selected by Philadelphia Eagles in fifth round (133rd pick overall) of 1990 NFL draft. . . . Signed by Eagles (August 8, 1990).
PRO STATISTICS: 1990—Recovered two fumbles.

		RUSHING				RECEIVING				PUNT RETURNS				TOTAL		
Year Team	G	Att.	Yds.	Avg.	TD	No.	Yds.	Avg.	TD	No.	Yds.	Avg.	TD	TD	Pts.	F.
1990— Philadelphia NFL ...	16	2	20	10.0	0	37	602	16.3	9	2	-1	-.5	0	9	54	2
Pro totals (1 year)	16	2	20	10.0	0	37	602	16.3	9	2	-1	-.5	0	9	54	2

WILLIAMS, DAVID
OT, OILERS

PERSONAL: Born June 21, 1966, at Mulberry, Fla. . . . 6-5/292. . . . Full name: David Wayne Williams.
HIGH SCHOOL: Lakeland (Fla.).
COLLEGE: Florida.
TRANSACTIONS/CAREER NOTES: Selected by Houston Oilers in first round (23rd pick overall) of 1989 NFL draft. . . . Signed by Oilers (July 29, 1989).
PLAYING EXPERIENCE: Houston NFL 1989 and 1990. . . . Games: 1989 (14), 1990 (15). Total: 29.
PRO STATISTICS: 1989—Returned two kickoffs for eight yards. 1990—Recovered one fumble.

WILLIAMS, ERIC
DT, REDSKINS

PERSONAL: Born February 24, 1962, at Stockton, Calif. . . . 6-4/286. . . . Full name: Eric Michael Williams. . . . Son of Roy Williams, second-round selection of Detroit Lions in 1962 NFL draft.
HIGH SCHOOL: St. Mary's (Stockton, Calif.).
COLLEGE: Washington State.
TRANSACTIONS/CAREER NOTES: Selected by New Jersey Generals in first round (19th pick overall) of 1984 USFL draft. . . . Selected by Detroit Lions in third round (62nd pick overall) of 1984 NFL draft. . . . Signed by Lions (July 21, 1984). . . . On injured reserve with cracked cervical disc (December 4, 1985-remainder of season). . . . Granted free agency (February 1, 1990). . . . Re-signed by Lions (September 6, 1990). . . . Traded by Lions to Washington Redskins for running back James Wilder and a fourth-round pick in 1991 draft (September 13, 1990). . . . On inactive list (September 16 and December 30, 1990). . . . On injured reserve with foot injury (January 2, 1991-remainder of 1990 season playoffs).
PLAYING EXPERIENCE: Detroit NFL, 1984-1989; Washington NFL, 1990. . . . Games: 1984 (12), 1985 (12), 1986 (16), 1987 (11), 1988 (16), 1989 (16), 1990 (13). Total: 96.
PRO STATISTICS: 1985—Recovered one fumble. 1986—Intercepted one pass for two yards and recovered one fumble.

WILLIAMS, GERALD
NT, STEELERS

PERSONAL: Born September 3, 1963, at Waycross, Ga. . . . 6-3/291.
HIGH SCHOOL: Valley (Ala.).
COLLEGE: Auburn.
TRANSACTIONS/CAREER NOTES: Selected by Birmingham Stallions in 1986 USFL territorial draft. . . . Selected by Pittsburgh Steelers in second round (36th pick overall) of 1986 NFL draft. . . . Signed by Steelers (July 25, 1986). . . . Crossed picket line during players' strike (October 13, 1987). . . . Granted free agency (February 1, 1990). . . . Re-signed by Steelers (July 18, 1990).
PLAYING EXPERIENCE: Pittsburgh NFL, 1986-1990. . . . Games: 1986 (16), 1987 (9), 1988 (16), 1989 (16), 1990 (16). Total: 73.
PRO STATISTICS: 1987—Recovered one fumble. 1988—Recovered one fumble for one yard. 1989—Recovered one fumble.

WILLIAMS, JAMES

CB, BILLS

PERSONAL: Born March 30, 1967, at Osceola, Ark. . . . 5-10/172. . . . Full name: James Earl Williams.
HIGH SCHOOL: Coalinga (Calif.).
COLLEGE: Fresno State (degree in physical education, 1990).
TRANSACTIONS/CAREER NOTES: Selected by Buffalo Bills in first round (16th pick overall) of 1990 NFL draft. . . . Signed by Bills (July 27, 1990).
CHAMPIONSHIP GAME EXPERIENCE: Played in AFC championship game after 1990 season. . . . Played in Super Bowl XXV after 1990 season.
PRO STATISTICS: 1990—Returned blocked punt 38 yards for a touchdown.

| | | | — INTERCEPTIONS — | | | |
Year Team	G	No.	Yds.	Avg.	TD	
1990—Buffalo NFL	16	2	0	.0	0	
Pro totals (1 year)	16	2	0	.0	0	

WILLIAMS, JAMES

LB, SAINTS

PERSONAL: Born October 10, 1968, at Natchez, Miss. . . . 6-0/230. . . . Full name: James Edward Williams.
HIGH SCHOOL: Natchez (Miss.).
COLLEGE: Mississippi State.
TRANSACTIONS/CAREER NOTES: Selected by New Orleans Saints in sixth round (158th pick overall) of 1990 NFL draft. . . . Signed by Saints (May 9, 1990). . . . On inactive list (November 25 and December 2, 1990).
PLAYING EXPERIENCE: New Orleans NFL, 1990. . . . Games: 1990 (14).

WILLIAMS, JAMIE

TE, 49ERS

PERSONAL: Born February 25, 1960, at Vero Beach, Fla. . . . 6-4/245.
HIGH SCHOOL: Central (Davenport, Ia.).
COLLEGE: Nebraska.
TRANSACTIONS/CAREER NOTES: Selected by Boston Breakers in 1983 USFL territorial draft. . . . Selected by New York Giants in third round (63rd pick overall) of 1983 NFL draft. . . . Signed by Giants (June 30, 1983). . . . Released by Giants (August 29, 1983). . . . Signed as free agent by St. Louis Cardinals (September 13, 1983). . . . Released by Cardinals (October 5, 1983). . . . Signed as free agent by Tampa Bay Buccaneers (January 25, 1984). . . . USFL rights traded by New Orleans Breakers to New Jersey Generals for past consideration (March 26, 1984). . . . Released by Tampa Bay Buccaneers (May 8, 1984). . . . Awarded on waivers to Houston Oilers (May 21, 1984). . . . Granted unconditional free agency (February 1, 1989). . . . Signed by San Francisco 49ers (March 14, 1989). . . . On injured reserve with broken finger (September 5-December 11, 1989).
CHAMPIONSHIP GAME EXPERIENCE: Played in NFC championship game after 1989 and 1990 seasons. . . . Played in Super Bowl XXIV after 1989 season.
PRO STATISTICS: 1984—Returned one kickoff for no yards, recovered one fumble and fumbled twice. 1985—Returned two kickoffs for 21 yards and fumbled once. 1986—Recovered one fumble. 1987—Recovered one fumble. 1990—Returned two kickoffs for seven yards.

| | | | — RECEIVING — | | |
Year Team	G	No.	Yds.	Avg.	TD
1983—St. Louis NFL	1	0	0		0
1984—Houston NFL	16	41	545	13.3	3
1985—Houston NFL	16	39	444	11.4	1
1986—Houston NFL	16	22	227	10.3	1
1987—Houston NFL	12	13	158	12.2	3
1988—Houston NFL	16	6	46	7.7	0
1989—San Francisco NFL	3	3	38	12.7	0
1990—San Francisco NFL	16	9	54	6.0	0
Pro totals (8 years)	96	133	1512	11.4	8

WILLIAMS, JARVIS

S, DOLPHINS

PERSONAL: Born May 16, 1965, at Palatka, Fla. . . . 5-11/200. . . . Full name: Jarvis Eric Williams.
HIGH SCHOOL: Palatka (Fla.).
COLLEGE: Florida.
TRANSACTIONS/CAREER NOTES: Selected by Miami Dolphins in second round (42nd pick overall) of 1988 NFL draft. . . . Signed by Dolphins (July 19, 1988).
PRO STATISTICS: 1988—Returned three punts for 29 yards and recovered three fumbles for 26 yards. 1990—Returned one punt for no yards and recovered one fumble.

| | | — INTERCEPTIONS — | | | — KICKOFF RETURNS — | | | | — TOTAL — | | |
Year Team	G	No.	Yds.	Avg.	TD	No.	Yds.	Avg.	TD	TD	Pts.	F.
1988—Miami NFL	16	4	62	15.5	0	8	159	19.9	0	0	0	0
1989—Miami NFL	16	2	43	21.5	0	1	21	21.0	0	0	0	0
1990—Miami NFL	16	5	82	16.4	1	0	0		0	1	6	0
Pro totals (3 years)	48	11	187	17.0	1	9	180	20.0	0	1	6	0

WILLIAMS, JERROL
LB, STEELERS

PERSONAL: Born July 5, 1967, at Las Vegas.... 6-5/244.... Full name: Jerrol Lynn Williams.
HIGH SCHOOL: Chaparral (Las Vegas).
COLLEGE: Purdue.
TRANSACTIONS/CAREER NOTES: Selected by Pittsburgh Steelers in fourth round (91st pick overall) of 1989 NFL draft.... Signed by Steelers (July 19, 1989).
PLAYING EXPERIENCE: Pittsburgh NFL, 1989 and 1990.... Games: 1989 (16), 1990 (16). Total: 32.
PRO STATISTICS: 1989—Returned four kickoffs for 31 yards. 1990—Returned three kickoffs for 31 yards and recovered two fumbles and fumbled once for one yard.

WILLIAMS, JIMMY
LB, VIKINGS

PERSONAL: Born November 15, 1960, at Washington, D.C.... 6-3/225.... Full name: James Henry Williams.... Brother of Toby Williams, nose tackle with New England Patriots, 1983-1988.
HIGH SCHOOL: Woodrow Wilson (Washington, D.C.).
COLLEGE: Nebraska.
TRANSACTIONS/CAREER NOTES: Selected by Detroit Lions in first round (15th pick overall) of 1982 NFL draft.... On injured reserve with broken foot (December 20, 1982-remainder of season).... Granted roster exemption (August 18-August 22, 1986). ... On injured reserve with knee injury (November 11, 1986-remainder of season).... On injured reserve with knee injury (October 15, 1988-remainder of season).... Granted free agency (February 1, 1990).... Re-signed by Lions (August 29, 1990). ... Activated (September 10, 1990).... On inactive list (September 16, 1990).... Released by Lions (December 3, 1990).... Awarded on waivers to Minnesota Vikings (December 4, 1990).
PRO STATISTICS: 1983—Recovered one fumble. 1984—Recovered one fumble. 1985—Recovered one fumble. 1986—Recovered one fumble. 1987—Recovered two fumbles. 1988—Recovered one fumble. 1989—Recovered one fumble. 1990—Recovered three fumbles for 53 yards and a touchdown.

		INTERCEPTIONS			
Year Team	G	No.	Yds.	Avg.	TD
1982— Detroit NFL	6	1	4	4.0	0
1983— Detroit NFL	16	0	0		0
1984— Detroit NFL	16	0	0		0
1985— Detroit NFL	16	0	0		0
1986— Detroit NFL	10	2	12	6.0	0
1987— Detroit NFL	12	2	51	25.5	0
1988— Detroit NFL	5	1	5	5.0	0
1989— Detroit NFL	16	5	15	3.0	0
1990— Det.(10)-Min.(4)NFL	14	0	0		0
Pro totals (9 years)	111	11	87	7.9	0

WILLIAMS, JOHN L.
FB, SEAHAWKS

PERSONAL: Born November 23, 1964, at Palatka, Fla.... 5-11/231.... Full name: John L. Williams.
HIGH SCHOOL: Palatka (Fla.).
COLLEGE: Florida.
TRANSACTIONS/CAREER NOTES: Selected by Tampa Bay Bandits in 1986 USFL territorial draft.... Selected by Seattle Seahawks in first round (15th pick overall) of 1986 NFL draft.... Signed by Seahawks (July 23, 1986).
RECORDS/HONORS: Played in Pro Bowl after 1990 season.
PRO STATISTICS: 1987—Recovered one fumble. 1988—Recovered two fumbles for minus two yards. 1989—Recovered one fumble. 1990—Recovered two fumbles.

		RUSHING				RECEIVING				TOTAL		
Year Team	G	Att.	Yds.	Avg.	TD	No.	Yds.	Avg.	TD	TD	Pts.	F.
1986— Seattle NFL	16	129	538	4.2	0	33	219	6.6	0	0	0	1
1987— Seattle NFL	12	113	500	4.4	1	38	420	11.1	3	4	24	2
1988— Seattle NFL	16	189	877	4.6	4	58	651	11.2	3	7	42	0
1989— Seattle NFL	15	146	499	3.4	1	76	657	8.6	6	7	42	2
1990— Seattle NFL	16	187	714	3.8	3	73	699	9.6	0	3	18	5
Pro totals (5 years)	75	764	3128	4.1	9	278	2646	9.5	12	21	126	10

WILLIAMS, LARRY
G, CHIEFS

PERSONAL: Born July 3, 1963, at Orange, Calif.... 6-5/294.... Full name: Lawrence Richard Williams II.
HIGH SCHOOL: Mater Dei (Santa Ana, Calif.).
COLLEGE: Notre Dame (bachelor of arts degree in American studies (journalism) and business, 1985).
TRANSACTIONS/CAREER NOTES: Selected by Portland Breakers in 10th round (136th pick overall) of 1985 USFL draft.... Selected by Cleveland Browns in 10th round (259th pick overall) of 1985 NFL draft.... Signed by Browns (July 15, 1985).... On injured reserve with wrist injury (August 20, 1985-entire season).... Granted unconditional free agency (February 1, 1989). ... Signed by San Diego Chargers (March 7, 1989).... On reserve/physically unable to perform list with shoulder injury (August 29, 1989-entire season).... Released by Chargers (September 3, 1990).... Signed by Kansas City Chiefs (March 13, 1991).
PLAYING EXPERIENCE: Cleveland NFL, 1986-1988.... Games: 1986 (16), 1987 (12), 1988 (14). Total: 42.
CHAMPIONSHIP GAME EXPERIENCE: Played in AFC championship game after 1986 and 1987 seasons.
PRO STATISTICS: 1988—Recovered one fumble.

WILLIAMS, LEE
DE, CHARGERS

PERSONAL: Born October 15, 1962, at Fort Lauderdale, Fla. . . . 6-5/271. . . . Full name: Lee Eric Williams.
HIGH SCHOOL: Stranahan (Fort Lauderdale, Fla.).
COLLEGE: Bethune-Cookman (degree in business administration).
TRANSACTIONS/CAREER NOTES: Selected by Tampa Bay Bandits in 1984 USFL territorial draft. . . . USFL rights traded by Bandits with rights to defensive tackle Dewey Forte to Los Angeles Express for draft choice (March 2, 1984). . . . Signed by Express (March 6, 1984). . . . Granted roster exemption (March 6-March 16, 1984). . . . Selected by San Diego Chargers in first round (sixth pick overall) of 1984 NFL supplemental draft. . . . Released by Los Angeles Express (October 20, 1984). . . . Signed by San Diego Chargers (October 22, 1984). . . . Granted roster exemption (October 22-October 29, 1984).
PLAYING EXPERIENCE: Los Angeles USFL, 1984; San Diego NFL, 1984-1990. . . . Games: 1984 USFL (14), 1984 NFL (8), 1985 (16), 1986 (16), 1987 (12), 1988 (16), 1989 (16), 1990 (16). Total NFL: 100. Total Pro: 114.
RECORDS/HONORS: Played in Pro Bowl after 1988 and 1989 seasons. . . . Named to THE SPORTING NEWS NFL All-Pro team, 1989.
PRO STATISTICS: USFL: 1984—Credited with 13 sacks for 92 yards. . . . NFL: 1984—Intercepted one pass for 66 yards and a touchdown. 1985—Intercepted one pass for 17 yards and recovered one fumble for two yards. 1986—Recovered one fumble for six yards. 1987—Credited with a safety. 1988—Recovered one fumble.

WILLIAMS, MIKE
WR, FALCONS

PERSONAL: Born October 9, 1966, at Mt. Kisco, N.Y. . . . 5-10/177. . . . Full name: Michael J. Williams.
HIGH SCHOOL: John Jay (Katonah, N.Y.).
COLLEGE: Northeastern.
TRANSACTIONS/CAREER NOTES: Selected by Los Angeles Rams in 10th round (269th pick overall) of 1989 NFL draft. . . . Signed by Rams (July 15, 1989). . . . On injured reserve with knee injury (September 2-September 25, 1989). . . . Released by Rams (September 26, 1989). . . . Signed as free agent by Detroit Lions to developmental squad (October 11, 1989). . . . On developmental squad (October 11-December 21, 1989). . . . Granted unconditional free agency (February 1, 1990). . . . Signed by Dallas Cowboys (March 3, 1990). . . . Released by Cowboys (September 3, 1990). . . . Signed by Atlanta Falcons (April 1, 1991).
PLAYING EXPERIENCE: Detroit NFL, 1989. . . . Games: 1989 (1).

WILLIAMS, PERRY
CB, GIANTS

PERSONAL: Born May 12, 1961, at Hamlet, N.C. . . . 6-2/203. . . . Full name: Perry Lamar Williams.
HIGH SCHOOL: Richmond County (Hamlet, N.C.).
COLLEGE: North Carolina State.
TRANSACTIONS/CAREER NOTES: Selected by Washington Federals in seventh round (76th pick overall) of 1983 USFL draft. . . . Selected by New York Giants in seventh round (178th pick overall) of 1983 NFL draft. . . . Signed by Giants (June 13, 1983). . . . On injured reserve with foot injury (August 17, 1983-entire season). . . . On injured reserve with pinched nerve (September 7-October 24, 1987).
CHAMPIONSHIP GAME EXPERIENCE: Played in NFC championship game after 1986 and 1990 seasons. . . . Played in Super Bowl XXI after 1986 season and Super Bowl XXV after 1990 season.
PRO STATISTICS: 1984—Recovered one fumble. 1985—Recovered one fumble. 1987—Recovered two fumbles for one yard. 1988—Recovered three fumbles for six yards. 1989—Fumbled once.

| | | | INTERCEPTIONS | | | |
Year	Team	G	No.	Yds.	Avg.	TD
1984—	N.Y. Giants NFL	16	3	7	2.3	0
1985—	N.Y. Giants NFL	16	2	28	14.0	0
1986—	N.Y. Giants NFL	16	4	31	7.8	0
1987—	N.Y. Giants NFL	10	1	-5	-5.0	0
1988—	N.Y. Giants NFL	16	1	0	.0	0
1989—	N.Y. Giants NFL	16	3	14	4.7	0
1990—	N.Y. Giants NFL	16	3	4	1.3	0
Pro totals (7 years)		106	17	79	4.7	0

WILLIAMS, ROBERT
CB, COWBOYS

PERSONAL: Born October 2, 1962, at Galveston, Tex. . . . 5-10/186. . . . Full name: Robert Cole Williams.
HIGH SCHOOL: Ball (Galveston, Tex.).
COLLEGE: Baylor.
TRANSACTIONS/CAREER NOTES: Signed as free agent by Washington Redskins (May 1, 1986). . . . Released by Redskins (August 4, 1986). . . . Signed as free agent by Dallas Cowboys (April 10, 1987). . . . Released by Cowboys (September 7, 1987). . . . Re-signed as replacement player by Cowboys (September 23, 1987).
PLAYING EXPERIENCE: Dallas NFL, 1987-1990. . . . Games: 1987 (11), 1988 (16), 1989 (13), 1990 (16). Total: 56.
PRO STATISTICS: 1987—Recovered one fumble. 1988—Intercepted two passes for 18 yards and recovered one fumble. 1990—Intercepted one pass.

WILLIAMS, WARREN
RB, STEELERS

PERSONAL: Born July 29, 1965, at Fort Myers, Fla. . . . 6-0/201. . . . Full name: Warren Williams Jr.
HIGH SCHOOL: North Fort Myers (Fla.).
COLLEGE: Miami (Fla.).
TRANSACTIONS/CAREER NOTES: Selected by Pittsburgh Steelers in sixth round (155th pick overall) of 1988 NFL draft. . . . Signed by Steelers (July 15, 1988). . . . On injured reserve with foot injury (December 16, 1989-remainder of season).
PRO STATISTICS: 1988—Returned one kickoff for 10 yards. 1989—Recovered one fumble.

Year Team	G	RUSHING Att.	Yds.	Avg.	TD	RECEIVING No.	Yds.	Avg.	TD	TOTAL TD	Pts.	F.
1988— Pittsburgh NFL	15	87	409	4.7	0	11	66	6.0	1	1	6	3
1989— Pittsburgh NFL	5	37	131	3.5	1	6	48	8.0	0	1	6	0
1990— Pittsburgh NFL	14	68	389	5.7	3	5	42	8.4	1	4	24	5
Pro totals (3 years)	34	192	929	4.8	4	22	156	7.1	2	6	36	8

WILLIS, KEITH
DE, STEELERS

PERSONAL: Born July 29, 1959, at Newark, N.J. . . . 6-1/263.
HIGH SCHOOL: Malcolm X. Shabazz (Newark, N.J.).
COLLEGE: Northwestern.
TRANSACTIONS/CAREER NOTES: Signed as free agent by Pittsburgh Steelers (April 30, 1982).
. . . On injured reserve with herniated disc (August 15, 1988-entire season).
PLAYING EXPERIENCE: Pittsburgh NFL, 1982-1987, 1989 and 1990. . . . Games: 1982 (9), 1983 (14), 1984 (12), 1985 (16), 1986 (16), 1987 (11), 1989 (16), 1990 (16). Total: 110.
CHAMPIONSHIP GAME EXPERIENCE: Played in AFC championship game after 1984 season.
PRO STATISTICS: 1983—Recovered one fumble. 1984—Recovered one fumble. 1990—Intercepted one pass for five yards and re-covered one fumble.

WILLIS, KEN
PK, COWBOYS

PERSONAL: Born October 6, 1966, at Owensboro, Ky. . . . 5-11/189. . . . Full name: Robert Kenneth Willis II.
HIGH SCHOOL: Owensboro (Ky.).
COLLEGE: Kentucky (degree in math education).
TRANSACTIONS/CAREER NOTES: Signed as free agent by Dallas Cowboys (April 25, 1990). . . . Released by Cowboys (September 3, 1990). . . . Re-signed by Cowboys (September 4, 1990).

Year Team	G	PLACE-KICKING XPM	XPA	FGM	FGA	Pts.
1990— Dallas NFL	16	26	26	18	25	80
Pro totals (1 year)	16	26	26	18	25	80

WILLIS, PETER TOM
QB, BEARS

PERSONAL: Born January 4, 1967, at Morris, Ala. . . . 6-2/188. . . . Full name: Peter Tom Willis.
HIGH SCHOOL: Mortimer Jordan (Morris, Ala.).
COLLEGE: Florida State (bachelor of science degree in communications).
TRANSACTIONS/CAREER NOTES: Selected by Chicago Bears in third round (64th pick overall) of 1990 NFL draft. . . . Signed by Bears (August 8, 1990). . . . On inactive list (September 9, 16, 23, 30; and October 7 and 28, 1990).
PRO STATISTICS: Passer rating points: 1990 (87.3).

Year Team	G	PASSING Att.	Cmp.	Pct.	Yds.	TD	Int.	Avg.	RUSHING Att.	Yds.	Avg.	TD	TOTAL TD	Pts.	F.
1990— Chicago NFL	3	13	9	69.2	106	1	1	8.15	0	0		0	0	0	0
NFL totals (1 year)	3	13	9	69.2	106	1	1	8.15	0	0		0	0	0	0

WILSON, CHARLES
WR, PACKERS

PERSONAL: Born July 1, 1968, at Tallahassee, Fla. . . . 5-9/178. . . . Full name: Charles Joseph Wilson.
HIGH SCHOOL: Godby (Tallahassee, Fla.).
COLLEGE: Memphis State (degree in general studies).
TRANSACTIONS/CAREER NOTES: Selected by Green Bay Packers in fifth round (132nd pick overall) of 1990 NFL draft. . . . Signed by Packers (June 25, 1990). . . . On inactive list (September 23, 1990).

Year Team	G	RECEIVING No.	Yds.	Avg.	TD	KICKOFF RETURNS No.	Yds.	Avg.	TD	TOTAL TD	Pts.	F.
1990— Green Bay NFL	15	7	84	12.0	0	35	798	22.8	0	0	0	0
Pro totals (1 year)	15	7	84	12.0	0	35	798	22.8	0	0	0	0

WILSON, KARL
DE, RAMS

PERSONAL: Born March 10, 1964, at Amite, La. . . . 6-4/275. . . . Full name: Karl Wendell Wilson.
HIGH SCHOOL: Baker (La.).
COLLEGE: Louisiana State (degree in general studies, 1987).
TRANSACTIONS/CAREER NOTES: Selected by San Diego Chargers in third round (59th pick overall) of 1987 NFL draft. . . . Signed by Chargers (July 29, 1987). . . . On injured reserve with hamstring injury (November 3-December 5, 1987). . . . Released by Chargers (September 5, 1989). . . . Signed as free agent by Phoenix Cardinals (September 15, 1989). . . . Granted unconditional free agency (February 1, 1990). . . . Signed by Miami Dolphins (March 26, 1990). . . . Granted unconditional free agency (February 1, 1991). . . . Signed by Los Angeles Rams (March 5, 1991).
PLAYING EXPERIENCE: San Diego NFL, 1987 and 1988; Phoenix NFL, 1989; Miami NFL, 1990. . . . Games: 1987 (7), 1988 (13), 1989 (15), 1990 (16). Total: 51.
PRO STATISTICS: 1989—Credited with a safety.

WILSON, WADE
QB, VIKINGS

PERSONAL: Born February 1, 1959, at Greenville, Tex. . . . 6-3/210. . . . Full name: Charles Wade Wilson.
HIGH SCHOOL: Commerce (Tex.).
COLLEGE: East Texas State.
TRANSACTIONS/CAREER NOTES: Selected by Minnesota Vikings in eighth round (210th pick overall) of 1981 NFL draft. . . . On inactive list (September 12, 1982). . . . On commissioner's exempt list (November 20-December 8, 1982). . . . Active for four games with Vikings in 1982; did not play. . . . On injured reserve with broken thumb (September 26-November 24, 1990). . . . On injured reserve with separated shoulder (December 26, 1990-remainder of season).
CHAMPIONSHIP GAME EXPERIENCE: Played in NFC championship game after 1987 season.
RECORDS/HONORS: Played in Pro Bowl after 1988 season.
PRO STATISTICS: Passer rating points: 1981 (16.4), 1983 (50.3), 1984 (52.5), 1985 (71.8), 1986 (84.4), 1987 (76.7), 1988 (91.5), 1989 (70.5), 1990 (79.6). Career: 75.0. . . . 1981—Recovered one fumble. 1986—Punted twice for 38.0 average with one blocked and recovered one fumble and fumbled three times for minus two yards. 1987—Fumbled three times for minus three yards. 1988—Recovered four fumbles and fumbled four times for minus nine yards. 1989—Recovered two fumbles and fumbled five times for minus seven yards. 1990—Recovered one fumble and fumbled three times for minus two yards.

Year Team	G	PASSING							RUSHING				TOTAL		
		Att.	Cmp.	Pct.	Yds.	TD	Int.	Avg.	Att.	Yds.	Avg.	TD	TD	Pts.	F.
1981— Minnesota NFL	3	13	6	46.2	48	0	2	3.69	0	0			0	0	2
1983— Minnesota NFL	1	28	16	57.1	124	1	2	4.43	3	-3	-1.0	0	0	0	1
1984— Minnesota NFL	8	195	102	52.3	1019	5	11	5.23	9	30	3.3	0	0	0	2
1985— Minnesota NFL	4	60	33	55.0	404	3	3	6.73	0	0			0	0	0
1986— Minnesota NFL	9	143	80	55.9	1165	7	5	8.15	13	9	.7	1	1	6	3
1987— Minnesota NFL	12	264	140	53.0	2106	14	13	*7.98	41	263	6.4	5	5	30	3
1988— Minnesota NFL	14	332	204	*61.4	2746	15	9	8.27	36	136	3.8	2	2	12	4
1989— Minnesota NFL	14	362	194	53.6	2543	9	12	7.03	32	132	4.1	1	1	6	5
1990— Minnesota NFL	6	146	82	56.2	1155	9	8	7.91	12	79	6.6	0	0	0	3
Pro totals (9 years)	71	1543	857	55.5	11310	63	65	7.33	146	646	4.4	9	9	54	23

WILSON, WALTER
WR, CHARGERS

PERSONAL: Born October 6, 1966, at Baltimore. . . . 5-10/185. . . . Full name: Walter James Wilson.
HIGH SCHOOL: Southern (Baltimore).
COLLEGE: East Carolina (degree in criminal justice).
TRANSACTIONS/CAREER NOTES: Selected by San Diego Chargers in third round (67th pick overall) of 1990 NFL draft. . . . Signed by Chargers (July 11, 1990). . . . On inactive list (December 16 and 23, 1990).

Year Team	G	RUSHING				RECEIVING				TOTAL		
		Att.	Yds.	Avg.	TD	No.	Yds.	Avg.	TD	TD	Pts.	F.
1990— San Diego NFL	14	1	0	.0	0	10	87	8.7	0	0	0	0
Pro totals (1 year)	14	1	0	.0	0	10	87	8.7	0	0	0	0

WINSTON, DeMOND
LB, SAINTS

PERSONAL: Born September 14, 1968, at Birmingham, Ala. . . . 6-2/239. . . . Full name: Edward DeMond Winston.
HIGH SCHOOL: Catholic Central (Lansing, Mich.).
COLLEGE: Vanderbilt (degree in electrical engineering).
TRANSACTIONS/CAREER NOTES: Selected by New Orleans Saints in fourth round (98th pick overall) of 1990 NFL draft. . . . Signed by Saints (July 17, 1990).
PLAYING EXPERIENCE: New Orleans NFL, 1990. . . . Games: 1990 (16).

WINTERS, FRANK
G/C, CHIEFS

PERSONAL: Born January 23, 1964, at Hoboken, N.J. . . . 6-3/285. . . . Full name: Frank Mitchell Winters.
HIGH SCHOOL: Emerson (Union City, N.J.).
COLLEGE: College of Eastern Utah, then Western Illinois (degree in political science administration, 1987).
TRANSACTIONS/CAREER NOTES: Selected by Cleveland Browns in 10th round (276th pick overall) of 1987 NFL draft. . . . Signed by Browns (July 25, 1987). . . . Granted unconditional free agency (February 1, 1989). . . . Signed by New York Giants (March 17, 1989). . . . Granted unconditional free agency (February 1, 1990). . . . Signed by Kansas City Chiefs (March 26, 1990).
PLAYING EXPERIENCE: Cleveland NFL, 1987 and 1988; New York Giants NFL, 1989; Kansas City NFL, 1990. . . . Games: 1987 (12), 1988 (16), 1989 (15), 1990 (16). Total: 59.
CHAMPIONSHIP GAME EXPERIENCE: Played in AFC championship game after 1987 season.
PRO STATISTICS: 1987—Fumbled once. 1990—Recovered two fumbles.

WISE, MIKE
DE, RAIDERS

PERSONAL: Born June 5, 1964, at Greenbrae, Calif. . . . 6-7/270.
HIGH SCHOOL: Novato (Calif.).
COLLEGE: California at Davis.
TRANSACTIONS/CAREER NOTES: Selected by Los Angeles Raiders in fourth round (85th pick overall) of 1986 NFL draft. . . . Signed by Raiders (July 11, 1986). . . . On injured reserve with elbow injury (August 26-November 1, 1986). . . . On injured reserve with elbow injury (December 11, 1986-remainder of season). . . . On non-football injury list with virus (September 7-December 5, 1987). . . . Active for one game with Raiders in 1987; did not play. . . . On inactive list (October 7, 14 and 21, 1990).

PLAYING EXPERIENCE: Los Angeles Raiders NFL, 1986-1990. . . . Games: 1986 (6), 1988 (16), 1989 (16), 1990 (12). Total: 50.
CHAMPIONSHIP GAME EXPERIENCE: Played in AFC championship game after 1990 season.
PRO STATISTICS: 1988—Recovered two fumbles. 1989—Recovered two fumbles.

WISNIEWSKI, STEVE
G, RAIDERS

PERSONAL: Born April 7, 1967, at Rutland, Vt. . . . 6-4/280. . . . Full name: Stephen Adam Wisniewski. . . . Brother of Leo Wisniewski, nose tackle with Baltimore-Indianapolis Colts, 1982-1984.
HIGH SCHOOL: Westfield (Houston).
COLLEGE: Penn State.
TRANSACTIONS/CAREER NOTES: Selected by Dallas Cowboys in second round (29th pick overall) of 1989 NFL draft. . . . Rights traded by Cowboys with sixth-round pick in 1989 NFL draft to Los Angeles Raiders for second-, third- and fifth-round picks in 1989 NFL draft (April 23, 1989). . . . Signed by Raiders (July 22, 1989).
PLAYING EXPERIENCE: Los Angeles Raiders NFL, 1989 and 1990. . . . Games: 1989 (15), 1990 (16). Total: 31.
CHAMPIONSHIP GAME EXPERIENCE: Played in AFC championship game after 1990 season.
RECORDS/HONORS: Named as guard on THE SPORTING NEWS college All-America team, 1987 and 1988. . . . Played in Pro Bowl after 1990 season. . . . Named to THE SPORTING NEWS NFL All-Pro team, 1990.
PRO STATISTICS: 1989—Recovered three fumbles.

WITHYCOMBE, MIKE
OT, CHARGERS

PERSONAL: Born November 18, 1964, at Meridan, Miss. . . . 6-5/312. . . . Name pronounced WITH-ee-come.
HIGH SCHOOL: Lemoore (Calif.).
COLLEGE: West Hills College (Calif.), then Fresno State.
TRANSACTIONS/CAREER NOTES: Selected by New York Jets in fifth round (119th pick overall) of 1988 NFL draft. . . . Signed by Jets (July 12, 1988). . . . On injured reserve with knee injury (October 13-November 23, 1989). . . . Transferred to developmental squad (November 24, 1989-remainder of season). . . . Released by Jets (September 3, 1990). . . . Signed by San Diego Chargers (September 11, 1990). . . . On inactive list (September 16, 23 and 30, 1990). . . . Released by Chargers (October 3, 1990). . . . Signed by WLAF (January 31, 1991). . . . Selected by Orlando Thunder in first round (seventh offensive lineman) of 1991 WLAF positional draft. . . . Re-signed by San Diego Chargers (June 5, 1991).
PLAYING EXPERIENCE: New York Jets NFL, 1988 and 1989; San Diego NFL, 1990; Orlando WLAF, 1991. . . . Games: 1988 (6), 1989 (5), 1990 (0), 1991 (10). Total NFL: 11. Total Pro: 21.

WOJCIECHOWSKI, JOHN
G, BEARS

PERSONAL: Born July 30, 1963, at Detroit. . . . 6-4/270. . . . Full name: John Stanley Wojciechowski. . . . Name pronounced WO-ja-COW-skee.
HIGH SCHOOL: Fitzgerald (Warren, Mich.).
COLLEGE: Michigan State (bachelor of science degree in education, 1986).
TRANSACTIONS/CAREER NOTES: Selected by Birmingham Stallions in 1986 USFL territorial draft. . . . Signed as free agent by Buffalo Bills (May 6, 1986). . . . Released by Bills (August 18, 1986). . . . Signed as free agent by Chicago Bears (March 10, 1987). . . . Released by Bears (September 7, 1987). . . . Re-signed as replacement player by Bears (September 28, 1987). . . . Granted free agency (February 1, 1990). . . . Re-signed by Bears (July 23, 1990).
PLAYING EXPERIENCE: Chicago NFL, 1987-1990. . . . Games: 1987 (4), 1988 (16), 1989 (13), 1990 (13). Total: 46.
CHAMPIONSHIP GAME EXPERIENCE: Member of Chicago Bears for NFC championship game after 1988 season; did not play.
PRO STATISTICS: 1987—Recovered one fumble.

WOLF, JOE
G/OT, CARDINALS

PERSONAL: Born December 28, 1966, at Allentown, Pa. . . . 6-5/279. . . . Full name: Joseph Francis Wolf Jr.
HIGH SCHOOL: William Allen (Allentown, Pa.).
COLLEGE: Boston College (bachelor of arts degree in communications, 1988).
TRANSACTIONS/CAREER NOTES: Selected by Phoenix Cardinals in first round (17th pick overall) of 1989 NFL draft. . . . Signed by Cardinals (August 15, 1989).
PLAYING EXPERIENCE: Phoenix NFL, 1989 and 1990. . . . Games: 1989 (16), 1990 (15). Total: 31.

WOLFLEY, CRAIG
G, VIKINGS

PERSONAL: Born May 19, 1958, at Buffalo, N.Y. . . . 6-1/277. . . . Full name: Craig Alan Wolfley. . . . Brother of Ron Wolfley, running back with Phoenix Cardinals.
HIGH SCHOOL: Orchard Park (N.Y.)
COLLEGE: Syracuse (bachelor of science degree in speech communication, 1980).
TRANSACTIONS/CAREER NOTES: Selected by Pittsburgh Steelers in fifth round (138th pick overall) of 1980 NFL draft. . . . On injured reserve with pulled hamstring (October 5-November 19, 1984). . . . On injured reserve with knee injury (August 19-October 25, 1986). . . . Granted unconditional free agency (February 1, 1990). . . . Signed by Minnesota Vikings (March 6, 1990). . . . On injured reserve with ankle injury (September 27-October 25, 1990).
PLAYING EXPERIENCE: Pittsburgh NFL, 1980-1989; Minnesota NFL, 1990. . . . Games: 1980 (16), 1981 (16), 1982 (9), 1983 (14), 1984 (9), 1985 (13), 1986 (9), 1987 (12), 1988 (16), 1989 (15), 1990 (8). Total: 137.
CHAMPIONSHIP GAME EXPERIENCE: Played in AFC championship game after 1984 season.
PRO STATISTICS: 1982—Recovered two fumbles. 1983—Recovered one fumble. 1985—Recovered one fumble. 1986—Recovered one fumble. 1987—Recovered one fumble. 1990—Recovered one fumble.

WOLFLEY, RON

RB, CARDINALS

PERSONAL: Born October 14, 1962, at Blasdel, N.Y. . . . 6-0/230. . . . Full name: Ronald Paul Wolfley. . . . Brother of Craig Wolfley, guard with Minnesota Vikings.
HIGH SCHOOL: Frontier Central (Hamburg, N.Y.).
COLLEGE: West Virginia.
TRANSACTIONS/CAREER NOTES: Selected by Birmingham Stallions in 1985 USFL territorial draft. . . . Selected by St. Louis Cardinals in fourth round (104th pick overall) of 1985 NFL draft. . . . Signed by Cardinals (July 21, 1985). . . . Franchise transferred to Phoenix (March 15, 1988). . . . Granted free agency (February 1, 1990). . . . Re-signed by Cardinals (August 1, 1990). . . . On injured reserve with shoulder injury (September 27-October 24, 1990).
RECORDS/HONORS: Played in Pro Bowl after 1986-1989 seasons.
PRO STATISTICS: 1985—Returned 13 kickoffs for 234 yards. 1986—Lost six yards on lateral from kickoff return. 1988—Recovered one fumble.

			RUSHING				RECEIVING				TOTAL	
Year Team	G	Att.	Yds.	Avg.	TD	No.	Yds.	Avg.	TD	TD	Pts.	F.
1985— St. Louis NFL	16	24	64	2.7	0	2	18	9.0	0	0	0	1
1986— St. Louis NFL	16	8	19	2.4	0	2	32	16.0	0	0	0	0
1987— St. Louis NFL	12	26	87	3.4	1	8	68	8.5	0	1	6	0
1988— Phoenix NFL	16	9	43	4.8	0	2	11	5.5	0	0	0	0
1989— Phoenix NFL	16	13	36	2.8	1	5	38	7.6	0	1	6	0
1990— Phoenix NFL	13	2	3	1.5	0	0	0		0	0	0	0
Pro totals (6 years)	89	82	252	3.1	2	19	167	8.8	0	2	12	1

WOLFOLK, KEVIN

LB, REDSKINS

PERSONAL: Born June 2, 1967, at Cocoa Beach, Fla. . . . 6-1/231. . . . Full name: Kevin Jay Wolfolk.
HIGH SCHOOL: Winston Churchill (Eugene, Ore.).
COLLEGE: Portland State.
TRANSACTIONS/CAREER NOTES: Signed as free agent by Toronto Argonauts of CFL (April 10, 1989). . . . Released by Argonauts (August 28, 1989). . . . Signed as free agent by Washington Redskins (April 26, 1990). . . . Released by Redskins (July 30, 1990). . . . Signed by WLAF (December 17, 1990). . . . Selected by Frankfurt Galaxy in third round (28th linebacker) of 1991 WLAF positional draft. . . . Signed by Washington Redskins (July 16, 1991).
PLAYING EXPERIENCE: Toronto CFL, 1989; Frankfurt WLAF, 1991. . . . Games: 1989 (3), 1991 (9). Total Pro: 12.

WOLFORD, WILL

OT, BILLS

PERSONAL: Born May 18, 1964, at Louisville, Ky. . . . 6-5/290. . . . Full name: William Charles Wolford. . . . Name pronounced WOOL-ford.
HIGH SCHOOL: St. Xavier (Louisville, Ky.).
COLLEGE: Vanderbilt.
TRANSACTIONS/CAREER NOTES: Selected by Memphis Showboats in 1986 USFL territorial draft. . . . Selected by Buffalo Bills in first round (20th pick overall) of 1986 NFL draft. . . . Signed by Bills (August 12, 1986). . . . Granted roster exemption (August 12-August 22, 1986). . . . Granted free agency (February 1, 1990). . . . Re-signed by Bills (August 28, 1990). . . . Granted roster exemption (September 9, 1990).
PLAYING EXPERIENCE: Buffalo NFL, 1986-1990. . . . Games: 1986 (16), 1987 (9), 1988 (16), 1989 (16), 1990 (14). Total: 71.
CHAMPIONSHIP GAME EXPERIENCE: Played in AFC championship game after 1988 and 1990 seasons. . . . Played in Super Bowl XXV after 1990 season.
RECORDS/HONORS: Played in Pro Bowl after 1990 season.
PRO STATISTICS: 1988—Recovered one fumble.

WOODEN, TERRY

LB, SEAHAWKS

PERSONAL: Born January 14, 1967, at Hartford, Conn. . . . 6-3/232. . . . Full name: Terrence Tylon Wooden.
HIGH SCHOOL: Farmington (Conn.).
COLLEGE: Syracuse (bachelor of arts degree in sociology).
TRANSACTIONS/CAREER NOTES: Selected by Seattle Seahawks in second round (29th pick overall) of 1990 NFL draft. . . . Signed by Seahawks (July 27, 1990). . . . On injured reserve with knee injury (November 10, 1990-remainder of season).
PLAYING EXPERIENCE: Seattle NFL, 1990. . . . Games: 1990 (8).

WOODS, ICKEY

RB, BENGALS

PERSONAL: Born February 28, 1966, at Fresno, Calif. . . . 6-2/232. . . . Full name: Elbert Woods.
HIGH SCHOOL: Edison (Calif.).
COLLEGE: UNLV.
TRANSACTIONS/CAREER NOTES: Selected by Cincinnati Bengals in second round (31st pick overall) of 1988 NFL draft. . . . Signed by Bengals (June 13, 1988). . . . On injured reserve with knee injury (September 23, 1989-remainder of season). . . . On physically unable to perform list with knee injury (September 3-October 22, 1990).
CHAMPIONSHIP GAME EXPERIENCE: Played in AFC championship game after 1988 season. . . . Played in Super Bowl XXIII after 1988 season.
PRO STATISTICS: 1988—Recovered one fumble.

			RUSHING				RECEIVING				TOTAL	
Year Team	G	Att.	Yds.	Avg.	TD	No.	Yds.	Avg.	TD	TD	Pts.	F.
1988— Cincinnati NFL	16	203	1066	*5.3	15	21	199	9.5	0	15	90	8
1989— Cincinnati NFL	2	29	94	3.2	2	0	0		0	2	12	1
1990— Cincinnati NFL	10	64	268	4.2	6	20	162	8.1	0	3	36	1
Pro totals (3 years)	28	296	1428	4.8	23	41	361	8.8	0	20	138	10

WOODS, JERRY
S, PACKERS

PERSONAL: Born February 13, 1966, at Dyersburg, Tenn. . . . 5-10/196. . . . Full name: Jerry Lee Woods.
HIGH SCHOOL: Washington Park (Racine, Wis.).
COLLEGE: Northern Michigan (degree in industrial technology).
TRANSACTIONS/CAREER NOTES: Selected by Detroit Lions in seventh round (170th pick overall) of 1989 NFL draft. . . . Signed by Lions (July 13, 1989). . . . Released by Lions (September 25, 1989). . . . Re-signed by Lions to developmental squad (September 26, 1989). . . . On developmental squad (September 26-December 21, 1989). . . . Released by Lions (December 22, 1989). . . . Signed as free agent by Green Bay Packers (February 26, 1990).
PLAYING EXPERIENCE: Detroit NFL, 1989; Green Bay NFL, 1990. . . . Games: 1989 (2), 1990 (16). Total: 18.
PRO STATISTICS: 1989—Returned two kickoffs for 28 yards and fumbled once.

WOODS, TONY
DT, COWBOYS

PERSONAL: Born March 14, 1966, at Fort Lee, Va. . . . 6-4/274. . . . Full name: Clinton Anthony Woods.
HIGH SCHOOL: Harrison (Colorado Springs, Colo.).
COLLEGE: Rose State College (Okla.), then Oklahoma.
TRANSACTIONS/CAREER NOTES: Selected by Chicago Bears in eighth round (216th pick overall) of 1989 NFL draft. . . . Signed by Bears (July 27, 1989). . . . Granted unconditional free agency (February 1, 1990). . . . Signed by New Orleans Saints (April 1, 1990). . . . Released by Saints (September 3, 1990). . . . Signed by WLAF (December 27, 1990). . . . Selected by New York/New Jersey Knights in first round (fourth defensive lineman) of 1991 WLAF positional draft. . . . Signed by Dallas Cowboys (July 3, 1991).
PLAYING EXPERIENCE: Chicago NFL, 1989; New York/New Jersey WLAF, 1991. . . . Games: 1989 (15), 1991 (10). Total NFL: 15. Total Pro: 25.
PRO STATISTICS: WLAF: 1991—Recovered one fumble.

WOODS, TONY
DE, SEAHAWKS

PERSONAL: Born September 11, 1965, at Newark, N.J. . . . 6-4/269. . . . Full name: Stanley Anthony Woods.
HIGH SCHOOL: Seton Hall Prep (South Orange, N.J.).
COLLEGE: Pittsburgh.
TRANSACTIONS/CAREER NOTES: Selected by Seattle Seahawks in first round (18th pick overall) of 1987 NFL draft. . . . Signed by Seahawks (July 20, 1987).
PLAYING EXPERIENCE: Seattle NFL, 1987-1990. . . . Games: 1987 (12), 1988 (16), 1989 (16), 1990 (16). Total: 60.
RECORDS/HONORS: Named as defensive lineman on THE SPORTING NEWS college All-America team, 1986.
PRO STATISTICS: 1987—Recovered one fumble. 1988—Recovered one fumble. 1989—Returned one kickoff for 13 yards and fumbled once.

WOODSIDE, KEITH
RB, PACKERS

PERSONAL: Born July 29, 1964, at Natchez, Miss. . . . 6-0/217. . . . Full name: Keith A. Woodside.
HIGH SCHOOL: Vidalia (La.).
COLLEGE: Texas A&M.
TRANSACTIONS/CAREER NOTES: Selected by Green Bay Packers in third round (61st pick overall) of 1988 NFL draft. . . . Signed by Packers (July 18, 1988). . . . Granted free agency (February 1, 1990). . . . Re-signed by Packers (August 2, 1990).
PRO STATISTICS: 1988—Recovered one fumble. 1989—Recovered one fumble.

		RUSHING				RECEIVING				KICKOFF RETURNS				TOTAL		
Year Team	G	Att.	Yds.	Avg.	TD	No.	Yds.	Avg.	TD	No.	Yds.	Avg.	TD	TD	Pts.	F.
1988— Green Bay NFL	16	83	195	2.4	3	39	352	9.0	2	19	343	18.1	0	5	30	3
1989— Green Bay NFL	16	46	273	5.9	1	59	527	8.9	0	2	38	19.0	0	1	6	4
1990— Green Bay NFL	16	46	182	4.0	1	24	184	7.7	0	0	0		0	1	6	2
Pro totals (3 years)	48	175	650	3.7	5	122	1063	8.7	2	21	381	18.1	0	7	42	9

WOODSON, ROD
CB/KR, STEELERS

PERSONAL: Born March 10, 1965, at Fort Wayne, Ind. . . . 6-0/197. . . . Full name: Roderick Kevin Woodson.
HIGH SCHOOL: R. Nelson Snider (Fort Wayne, Ind.).
COLLEGE: Purdue.
TRANSACTIONS/CAREER NOTES: Selected by Pittsburgh Steelers in first round (10th pick overall) of 1987 NFL draft. . . . Placed on reserve/unsigned list (August 31-October 27, 1987). . . . Signed by Steelers (October 28, 1987). . . . Granted roster exemption (October 28-November 7, 1987).
RECORDS/HONORS: Named as kick returner on THE SPORTING NEWS college All-America team, 1986. . . . Played in Pro Bowl after 1989 and 1990 seasons. . . . Named as kick returner on THE SPORTING NEWS NFL All-Pro team, 1989. . . . Named to THE SPORTING NEWS NFL All-Pro team, 1990.
PRO STATISTICS: 1987—Recovered two fumbles. 1988—Recovered three fumbles for two yards. 1989—Recovered four fumbles for one yard. 1990—Recovered three fumbles.

		INTERCEPTIONS				PUNT RETURNS				KICKOFF RETURNS				TOTAL		
Year Team	G	No.	Yds.	Avg.	TD	No.	Yds.	Avg.	TD	No.	Yds.	Avg.	TD	TD	Pts.	F.
1987— Pittsburgh NFL	8	1	45	45.0	1	16	135	8.4	0	13	290	22.3	0	1	6	3
1988— Pittsburgh NFL	16	4	98	24.5	0	33	281	8.5	0	37	850	23.0	*1	1	6	3
1989— Pittsburgh NFL	15	3	39	13.0	0	29	207	7.1	0	36	982	*27.3	*1	1	6	3
1990— Pittsburgh NFL	16	5	67	13.4	0	38	398	10.5	*1	35	764	21.8	0	1	6	3
Pro totals (4 years)	55	13	249	19.2	1	116	1021	8.8	1	121	2886	23.9	2	4	24	12

WOOLFORD, DONNELL
CB, BEARS

PERSONAL: Born January 6, 1966, at Baltimore. . . . 5-9/187.
HIGH SCHOOL: Douglass Byrd (Fayetteville, N.C.).
COLLEGE: Clemson.
TRANSACTIONS/CAREER NOTES: Selected by Chicago Bears in first round (11th pick overall) of 1989 NFL draft. . . . Signed by Bears (August 16, 1989). . . . On inactive list (November 4, 11 and 18, 1990).
RECORDS/HONORS: Named as defensive back on THE SPORTING NEWS college All-America team, 1988.
PRO STATISTICS: 1989—Returned one punt for 12 yards.

			INTERCEPTIONS		
Year Team	G	No.	Yds.	Avg.	TD
1989— Chicago NFL	11	3	0	.0	0
1990— Chicago NFL	13	3	18	6.0	0
Pro totals (2 years)	24	6	18	3.0	0

WORD, BARRY
RB, CHIEFS

PERSONAL: Born July 17, 1964, at Long Island, Va. . . . 6-2/242. . . . Full name: Barry Quentin Word.
HIGH SCHOOL: Halifax County (South Boston, Va.).
COLLEGE: Virginia.
TRANSACTIONS/CAREER NOTES: Selected by Jacksonville Bulls in 1986 USFL territorial draft. . . . Selected by New Orleans Saints in third round (62nd pick overall) of 1986 NFL draft. . . . Missed 1986 season due to time spent in prison on drug charges (November 1986-March 1987). . . . Signed by Saints (April 14, 1987). . . . On reserve/retired list (September 14, 1988-remainder of season). . . . Released by Saints (June 27, 1989). . . . Signed as free agent by Kansas City Chiefs (May 7, 1990).
PRO STATISTICS: 1987—Returned three kickoffs for 100 yards (33.3 avg.) and recovered one fumble. 1990—Returned one kickoff for 10 yards and recovered one fumble.

		RUSHING				RECEIVING				TOTAL		
Year Team	G	Att.	Yds.	Avg.	TD	No.	Yds.	Avg.	TD	TD	Pts.	F.
1987— New Orleans NFL	12	36	133	3.7	2	6	54	9.0	0	2	12	1
1988— New Orleans NFL	2	0	0		0	0	0		0	0	0	0
1990— Kansas City NFL	16	204	1015	5.0	4	4	28	7.0	0	4	24	4
Pro totals (3 years)	30	240	1148	4.8	6	10	82	8.2	0	6	36	5

WORKMAN, VINCE
RB, PACKERS

PERSONAL: Born May 9, 1968, at Buffalo, N.Y. . . . 5-10/193. . . . Full name: Vincent Workman Jr.
HIGH SCHOOL: Dublin (O.).
COLLEGE: Ohio State.
TRANSACTIONS/CAREER NOTES: Selected by Green Bay Packers in fifth round (127th pick overall) of 1989 NFL draft. . . . Signed by Packers (July 23, 1989). . . . On inactive list (September 30, 1990).
PRO STATISTICS: 1989—Recovered one fumble.

		RUSHING				RECEIVING				KICKOFF RETURNS				TOTAL		
Year Team	G	Att.	Yds.	Avg.	TD	No.	Yds.	Avg.	TD	No.	Yds.	Avg.	TD	TD	Pts.	F.
1989— Green Bay NFL	15	4	8	2.0	1	0	0		0	33	547	16.6	0	1	6	1
1990— Green Bay NFL	15	8	51	6.4	0	4	30	7.5	1	14	210	15.0	0	1	6	0
Pro totals (2 years)	30	12	59	4.9	1	4	30	7.5	1	47	757	16.1	0	2	12	1

WORLEY, TIM
RB, STEELERS

PERSONAL: Born September 24, 1966, at Lumberton, N.C. . . . 6-2/221. . . . Full name: Timothy Ashley Worley.
HIGH SCHOOL: Lumberton (N.C.).
COLLEGE: Georgia.
TRANSACTIONS/CAREER NOTES: Selected by Pittsburgh Steelers in first round (seventh pick overall) of 1989 NFL draft. . . . Signed by Steelers (August 20, 1989). . . . On inactive list (October 14, 21, 28; and December 23, 1990).
PRO STATISTICS: 1989—Recovered one fumble.

		RUSHING				RECEIVING				TOTAL		
Year Team	G	Att.	Yds.	Avg.	TD	No.	Yds.	Avg.	TD	TD	Pts.	F.
1989— Pittsburgh NFL	15	195	770	4.0	5	15	113	7.5	0	5	30	9
1990— Pittsburgh NFL	11	109	418	3.8	0	8	70	8.8	0	0	0	6
Pro totals (2 years)	26	304	1188	3.9	5	23	183	8.0	0	5	30	15

WORTHEN, NAZ
WR, FALCONS

PERSONAL: Born March 27, 1966, at Jacksonville, Fla. . . . 5-8/177. . . . Full name: Nasrallah Onea Worthen.
HIGH SCHOOL: Jean Ribault (Jacksonville, Fla.).
COLLEGE: North Carolina State (degree in sociology, 1989).
TRANSACTIONS/CAREER NOTES: Selected by Kansas City Chiefs in third round (60th pick overall) of 1989 NFL draft. . . . Signed by Chiefs (July 25, 1989). . . . On injured reserve with cracked ribs (September 28-November 11, 1989). . . . On injured reserve with ankle injury (November 24, 1990-remainder of season). . . . Granted unconditional free agency (February 1, 1991). . . . Signed by Atlanta Falcons (April 1, 1991).
PRO STATISTICS: 1990—Recovered one fumble.

Year	Team	G	— RECEIVING —				— PUNT RETURNS —				— KICKOFF RETURNS —				— TOTAL —		
			No.	Yds.	Avg.	TD	No.	Yds.	Avg.	TD	No.	Yds.	Avg.	TD	TD	Pts.	F.
1989— Kansas City NFL.		10	5	69	13.8	0	19	133	7.0	0	5	113	22.6	0	0	0	1
1990— Kansas City NFL.		9	0	0		0	25	180	7.2	0	11	226	20.6	0	0	0	1
Pro totals (2 years)		19	5	69	13.8	0	44	313	7.1	0	16	339	21.2	0	0	0	2

WRIGHT, ALEXANDER
WR, COWBOYS

PERSONAL: Born July 19, 1967, at Albany, Ga.... 6-0/189.
HIGH SCHOOL: Albany (Ga.).
COLLEGE: Auburn (degree in adult education).
TRANSACTIONS/CAREER NOTES: Selected by Dallas Cowboys in second round (26th pick overall) of 1990 NFL draft.... Signed by Cowboys (August 25, 1990).... On inactive list (November 22, 1990).
PRO STATISTICS: 1990—Recovered one fumble.

Year	Team	G	— RUSHING —				— RECEIVING —				— KICKOFF RETURNS —				— TOTAL —		
			Att.	Yds.	Avg.	TD	No.	Yds.	Avg.	TD	No.	Yds.	Avg.	TD	TD	Pts.	F.
1990— Dallas NFL		15	3	26	8.7	0	11	104	9.5	0	12	276	23.0	1	1	6	1
Pro totals (1 year)		15	3	26	8.7	0	11	104	9.5	0	12	276	23.0	1	1	6	1

WRIGHT, ALVIN
DT, RAMS

PERSONAL: Born February 5, 1961, at Wedowee, Ala.... 6-2/285.
HIGH SCHOOL: Randolph County (Wedowee, Ala.).
COLLEGE: Jacksonville State.
TRANSACTIONS/CAREER NOTES: Selected by Birmingham Stallions in 14th round (199th pick overall) of 1985 USFL draft.... Signed as free agent by Los Angeles Rams (June 22, 1985).... On injured reserve with neck injury (August 27-September 3, 1985).... Released by Rams (September 4, 1985).... Re-signed by Rams (March 9, 1986). ... On injured reserve with knee injury (September 2-October 31, 1986).... Crossed picket line during players' strike (September 30, 1987).... Granted free agency (February 1, 1990).... Re-signed by Rams (July 27, 1990).
PLAYING EXPERIENCE: Los Angeles Rams NFL, 1986-1990.... Games: 1986 (4), 1987 (15), 1988 (16), 1989 (16), 1990 (16). Total: 67.
CHAMPIONSHIP GAME EXPERIENCE: Played in NFC championship game after 1989 season.
PRO STATISTICS: 1990—Recovered one fumble.

WRIGHT, FELIX
S, VIKINGS

PERSONAL: Born June 22, 1959, at Carthage, Mo. ... 6-2/195. ... Full name: Felix Carl Wright.... Brother of Charles Wright, former defensive back with St. Louis Cardinals, Dallas Cowboys and Tampa Bay Buccaneers, 1987 and 1988.
HIGH SCHOOL: Carthage (Mo.).
COLLEGE: Drake (bachelor of science degree in physical education and history, 1981).
TRANSACTIONS/CAREER NOTES: Signed as free agent by Houston Oilers (May 17, 1982).... Released by Oilers (August 23, 1982).... Signed as free agent by Hamilton Tiger-Cats of CFL (October 24, 1982).... Granted free agency (March 1, 1985). ... Signed by Cleveland Browns (May 6, 1985).... Granted free agency (February 1, 1990).... Re-signed by Browns (September 4, 1990).... Activated (September 8, 1990).... Granted unconditional free agency (February 1, 1991).... Signed by Minnesota Vikings (March 31, 1991).
CHAMPIONSHIP GAME EXPERIENCE: Played in AFC championship game after 1986, 1987 and 1989 seasons.
PRO STATISTICS: CFL: 1982—Returned one punt for three yards. 1983—Returned seven punts for 36 yards, recovered three fumbles for 10 yards and fumbled twice. 1984—Recovered two fumbles.... NFL: 1985—Recovered two fumbles. 1986—Returned blocked punt 30 yards for a touchdown and recovered one fumble. 1987—Recovered one fumble. 1988—Recovered one fumble and fumbled once. 1990—Recovered one fumble.

Year	Team	G	— INTERCEPTIONS —			
			No.	Yds.	Avg.	TD
1982— Hamilton CFL		2	2	32	16.0	0
1983— Hamilton CFL		12	6	140	23.3	1
1984— Hamilton CFL		16	7	100	14.3	1
1985— Cleveland NFL		16	2	11	5.5	0
1986— Cleveland NFL		16	3	33	11.0	0
1987— Cleveland NFL		12	4	152	38.0	1
1988— Cleveland NFL		16	5	126	25.2	0
1989— Cleveland NFL		16	*9	91	10.1	1
1990— Cleveland NFL		16	3	56	18.7	0
CFL totals (3 years)		30	15	272	18.1	2
NFL totals (6 years)		92	26	469	18.0	2
Pro totals (9 years)		122	41	741	18.1	4

WRIGHT, JEFF
NT, BILLS

PERSONAL: Born June 13, 1963, at San Bernardino, Calif.... 6-2/270.... Full name: Jeff Dee Wright.
HIGH SCHOOL: Lawrence (Kan.).
COLLEGE: Tulsa, then Coffeyville Community College (Kan.), then Central Missouri State.
TRANSACTIONS/CAREER NOTES: Selected by Buffalo Bills in eighth round (213th pick overall) of 1988 NFL draft.... Signed by Bills (May 27, 1988).
PLAYING EXPERIENCE: Buffalo NFL, 1988-1990.... Games: 1988 (15), 1989 (15), 1990 (16). Total: 46.

CHAMPIONSHIP GAME EXPERIENCE: Played in AFC championship game after 1988 and 1990 seasons. . . . Played in Super Bowl XXV after 1990 season.
PRO STATISTICS: 1988—Recovered one fumble. 1989—Intercepted one pass for no yards and recovered two fumbles.

WRIGHT, KEITH
WR, RAIDERS

PERSONAL: Born February 10, 1964, at New York. . . . 6-0/185.
HIGH SCHOOL: Verbum Dei (Los Angeles).
COLLEGE: Cal State Northridge.
TRANSACTIONS/CAREER NOTES: Signed as free agent by Edmonton Eskimos of CFL (1988).
. . . Granted free agency (February, 1991). . . . Signed by Los Angeles Raiders (May, 1991).
CHAMPIONSHIP GAME EXPERIENCE: Played in Grey Cup (CFL championship game) after 1990 season.
PRO STATISTICS: CFL: 1989—Recovered one fumble.

			RECEIVING			PUNT RETURNS				KICKOFF RETURNS				TOTAL		
Year	Team	G	No.	Yds.	Avg.	TD	No.	Yds.	Avg.	TD	No.	Yds.	Avg.	TD	TD	Pts.	F.
1989— Edmonton CFL....		15	44	697	15.8	6	3	27	9.0	0	26	485	18.7	0	6	36	1
1990— Edmonton CFL....		17	54	900	16.7	9	0	0		0	2	27	13.5	0	9	54	1
Pro totals (2 years)		32	98	1597	16.3	15	3	27	9.0	0	28	512	18.3	0	15	90	2

WRIGHT, STEVE
OT, RAIDERS

PERSONAL: Born April 8, 1959, at St. Louis. . . . 6-6/280. . . . Full name: Stephen Hough Wright.
HIGH SCHOOL: Wayzata (Minn.).
COLLEGE: Northern Iowa.
TRANSACTIONS/CAREER NOTES: Signed as free agent by Dallas Cowboys (May, 1981). . . . Traded by Cowboys to Baltimore Colts for seventh-round pick in 1985 draft (August 27, 1983). . . . Franchise transferred to Indianapolis (March 31, 1984). . . . Signed by Oakland Invaders of USFL (December 1, 1984) for contract to take effect after being granted free agency, February 1, 1984. . . . Released by Invaders (May 28, 1986). . . . Re-signed by Indianapolis Colts (July 16, 1986). . . . Released by Colts (August 18, 1986). . . . Signed as free agent by Los Angeles Raiders (May 2, 1987). . . . Released by Raiders (September 7, 1987). . . . Re-signed as replacement player by Raiders (September 29, 1987). . . . On injured reserve with knee injury (December 26, 1987-remainder of season). . . . Released by Raiders (September 2, 1988). . . . Re-signed by Raiders (September 7, 1988).
PLAYING EXPERIENCE: Dallas NFL, 1981 and 1982; Baltimore NFL, 1983; Indianapolis NFL, 1984; Oakland USFL, 1985; Los Angeles Raiders NFL, 1987-1990. . . . Games: 1981 (16), 1982 (9), 1983 (13), 1984 (12), 1985 (18), 1987 (9), 1988 (15), 1989 (16), 1990 (16). Total NFL: 106. Total Pro: 124.
CHAMPIONSHIP GAME EXPERIENCE: Played in NFC championship game after 1981 and 1982 seasons. . . . Played in USFL championship game after 1985 season. . . . Played in AFC championship game after 1990 season.
PRO STATISTICS: USFL: 1985—Caught one pass for two yards and a touchdown. . . . NFL: 1990—Recovered two fumbles.

WYATT, WILLIE
NT, STEELERS

PERSONAL: Born September 27, 1967, at Birmingham, Ala. . . . 6-0/280. . . . Full name: Willie Porter Wyatt.
HIGH SCHOOL: Gardendale (Ala.).
COLLEGE: Alabama.
TRANSACTIONS/CAREER NOTES: Signed as free agent by Tampa Bay Buccaneers (May 14, 1990). . . . Released by Buccaneers (September 2, 1990). . . . Signed by Buccaneers to practice squad (October 1, 1990). . . . Activated (November 1, 1990). . . . Granted unconditional free agency (February 1, 1991). . . . Signed by Pittsburgh Steelers (March 29, 1991).
PLAYING EXPERIENCE: Tampa Bay NFL, 1990. . . . Games: 1990 (7).
PRO STATISTICS: 1990—Recovered one fumble.

WYMAN, DAVID
LB, SEAHAWKS

PERSONAL: Born March 31, 1964, at San Diego. . . . 6-2/250. . . . Full name: David Matthew Wyman.
HIGH SCHOOL: Earl Wooster (Reno, Nev.).
COLLEGE: Stanford.
TRANSACTIONS/CAREER NOTES: Selected by Seattle Seahawks in second round (45th pick overall) of 1987 NFL draft. . . . Signed by Seahawks (July 21, 1987). . . . Traded by Seahawks with draft choice to San Francisco 49ers for draft choice (November 3, 1987). . . . Trade voided after failing physical (November 4, 1987). . . . On injured reserve with ankle injury (December 30, 1987-remainder of season). . . . Granted free agency (February 1, 1990). . . . Re-signed by Seahawks (July 18, 1990). . . . On injured reserve with knee injury (September 4-November 10, 1990).
PLAYING EXPERIENCE: Seattle NFL, 1987-1990. . . . Games: 1987 (4), 1988 (16), 1989 (16), 1990 (8). Total: 44.
RECORDS/HONORS: Named as linebacker on THE SPORTING NEWS college All-America team, 1986.
PRO STATISTICS: 1988—Recovered two fumbles. 1990—Intercepted two passes for 24 yards and recovered one fumble.

YOUNG, LONNIE
DB, JETS

PERSONAL: Born July 18, 1963, at Flint, Mich. . . . 6-1/192.
HIGH SCHOOL: Beecher (Flint, Mich.).
COLLEGE: Michigan State (degree in communications, 1985).
TRANSACTIONS/CAREER NOTES: Selected by New Jersey Generals in eighth round (112th pick overall) of 1985 USFL draft. . . . Selected by St. Louis Cardinals in 12th round (325th pick overall) of 1985 NFL draft. . . . Signed by Cardinals (July 15, 1985). . . . Franchise transferred to Phoenix (March 15, 1988). . . . On injured reserve with torn ligaments in elbow (November 22, 1988-remainder of season). . . . On injured reserve with fractured shoulder (September 15-October 28, 1989). . . . Traded by Phoenix Cardinals to New York Jets for undisclosed draft pick (June 12, 1991).

PRO STATISTICS: 1985—Recovered one fumble. 1987—Recovered three fumbles. 1988—Recovered two fumbles. 1990—Recovered two fumbles.

		INTERCEPTIONS			
Year	Team	G	No.	Yds.	Avg.	TD
1985— St. Louis NFL	16	3	0	.0	0
1986— St. Louis NFL	13	0	0		0
1987— St. Louis NFL	12	1	0	.0	0
1988— Phoenix NFL	12	1	2	2.0	0
1989— Phoenix NFL	10	1	32	32.0	0
1990— Phoenix NFL	16	2	8	4.0	0
Pro totals (6 years)	79	8	42	5.3	0

YOUNG, MIKE
WR, BRONCOS

PERSONAL: Born February 21, 1962, at Hanford, Calif. . . . 6-1/183. . . . Full name: Michael David Young.
HIGH SCHOOL: Mount Whitney (Visalia, Calif.).
COLLEGE: UCLA.
TRANSACTIONS/CAREER NOTES: Selected by Memphis Showboats in 1985 USFL territorial draft. . . . Selected by Los Angeles Rams in sixth round (161st pick overall) of 1985 NFL draft. . . . Signed by Rams (July 23, 1985). . . . On injured reserve with back injury (November 4, 1988-remainder of season). . . . Granted unconditional free agency (February 1, 1989). . . . Signed by Denver Broncos (March 20, 1989).
CHAMPIONSHIP GAME EXPERIENCE: Played in NFC championship game after 1985 season. . . . Played in AFC championship game after 1989 season. . . . Played in Super Bowl XXIV after 1989 season.
PRO STATISTICS: 1985—Fumbled once. 1986—Fumbled twice.

		RECEIVING			
Year	Team	G	No.	Yds.	Avg.	TD
1985— L.A. Rams NFL	15	14	157	11.2	0
1986— L.A. Rams NFL	16	15	181	12.1	3
1987— L.A. Rams NFL	12	4	56	14.0	1
1988— L.A. Rams NFL	8	2	27	13.5	0
1989— Denver NFL	16	22	402	18.3	2
1990— Denver NFL	16	28	385	13.8	4
Pro totals (6 years)	83	85	1208	14.2	10

YOUNG, STEVE
QB, 49ERS

PERSONAL: Born October 11, 1961, at Salt Lake City. . . . 6-2/200.
HIGH SCHOOL: Greenwich (Conn.).
COLLEGE: Brigham Young.
TRANSACTIONS/CAREER NOTES: Selected by Los Angeles Express in first round (10th pick overall) of 1984 USFL draft. . . . Signed by Express (March 5, 1984). . . . Granted roster exemption (March 5, 1984). . . . Activated (March 30, 1984). . . . Selected by Tampa Bay Buccaneers in first round (first pick overall) of 1984 NFL supplemental draft. . . . On developmental squad for three games with Los Angeles Express (March 31-April 16, 1985). . . . Released by Express (September 9, 1985). . . . Signed by Tampa Bay Buccaneers (September 10, 1985). . . . Granted roster exemption (September 10-September 23, 1985). . . . Traded by Buccaneers to San Francisco 49ers for second- and fourth-round picks in 1987 draft and cash (April 24, 1987).
CHAMPIONSHIP GAME EXPERIENCE: Played in NFC championship game after 1988-1990 seasons. . . . Member of San Francisco 49ers for Super Bowl XXIII after 1988 season; did not play. . . . Played in Super Bowl XXIV after 1989 season.
RECORDS/HONORS: Named as quarterback on THE SPORTING NEWS college All-America team, 1983.
PRO STATISTICS: USFL Passer rating points: 1984 (80.6), 1985 (63.1). Total USFL: 73.1. . . . NFL Passer rating points: 1985 (56.9), 1986 (65.5), 1987 (120.8), 1988 (72.2), 1989 (120.8), 1990 (92.6). Total NFL: 78.4. . . . USFL: 1984—Credited with three 2-point conversions and recovered four fumbles. 1985—Recovered one fumble and fumbled seven times for minus 11 yards. . . . NFL: 1985—Recovered one fumble and fumbled four times for minus one yard. 1986—Recovered four fumbles and fumbled 11 times for minus 24 yards. 1988—Recovered two fumbles and fumbled five times for minus 10 yards. 1989—Recovered one fumble.

			PASSING						RUSHING				TOTAL		
Year	Team	G	Att.	Cmp.	Pct.	Yds.	TD	Int.	Avg.	Att.	Yds.	Avg.	TD	TD	Pts.	F.
1984— Los Angeles USFL	12	310	179	57.7	2361	10	9	7.62	79	515	6.5	7	7	48	7
1985— Los Angeles USFL	13	250	137	54.8	1741	6	13	6.96	56	368	6.6	2	2	12	7
1985— Tampa Bay NFL	5	138	72	52.2	935	3	8	6.78	40	233	5.8	1	1	6	4
1986— Tampa Bay NFL	14	363	195	53.7	2282	8	13	6.29	74	425	5.7	5	5	30	11
1987— San Francisco NFL	8	69	37	53.6	570	10	0	8.26	26	190	7.3	1	1	6	0
1988— San Francisco NFL	11	101	54	53.5	680	3	3	6.73	27	184	6.8	1	1	6	5
1989— San Francisco NFL	10	92	64	69.6	1001	8	3	10.88	38	126	3.3	2	2	12	2
1990— San Francisco NFL	6	62	38	61.3	427	2	0	6.89	15	159	10.6	0	0	0	1
USFL totals (2 years)	25	560	316	56.4	4102	16	22	7.33	135	883	6.5	9	9	60	14
NFL totals (6 years)	54	825	460	55.8	5895	34	27	7.15	220	1317	6.0	10	10	60	23
Pro totals (8 years)	79	1385	776	56.0	9997	50	49	7.22	355	2200	6.2	19	19	120	37

ZACKERY, TONY

S, PATRIOTS

COLLEGE: Washington.

PERSONAL: Born November 20, 1966, at Seattle. . . . 6-2/195. . . . Full name: Anthony Eugene Zackery. . . . Step-nephew of Otis Armstrong, running back with Denver Broncos, 1973-1980.
HIGH SCHOOL: Franklin (Seattle).

TRANSACTIONS/CAREER NOTES: Selected by New England Patriots in eighth round (223rd pick overall) of 1989 NFL draft. . . . Signed by Patriots (July 22, 1989). . . . Released by Patriots (August 30, 1989). . . . Signed as free agent by Atlanta Falcons to developmental squad (September 6, 1989). . . . On developmental squad (September 6-December 23, 1989). . . . Granted unconditional free agency (February 1, 1990). . . . Signed by New England Patriots (March 29, 1990). . . . On injured reserve with shoulder injury (September 17, 1990-remainder of season).
PLAYING EXPERIENCE: Atlanta NFL, 1989; New England NFL, 1990. . . . Games: 1989 (1), 1990 (2). Total: 3.
PRO STATISTICS: 1989—Intercepted one pass for three yards and recovered one fumble.

ZANDER, CARL

LB, BENGALS

PERSONAL: Born March 23, 1963, at Mendham, N.J. . . . 6-2/235. . . . Full name: Carl August Zander Jr.
HIGH SCHOOL: West Morris (Mendham, N.J.).
COLLEGE: Tennessee.

TRANSACTIONS/CAREER NOTES: Selected by Memphis Showboats in 1985 USFL territorial draft. . . . Selected by Cincinnati Bengals in second round (43rd pick overall) of 1985 NFL draft. . . . Signed by Bengals (July 21, 1985).
PLAYING EXPERIENCE: Cincinnati NFL, 1985-1990. . . . Games: 1985 (16), 1986 (16), 1987 (12), 1988 (16), 1989 (16), 1990 (16). Total: 92.
CHAMPIONSHIP GAME EXPERIENCE: Played in AFC championship game after 1988 season. . . . Played in Super Bowl XXIII after 1988 season.
PRO STATISTICS: 1985—Returned one kickoff for 19 yards and recovered one fumble for 34 yards. 1986—Intercepted one pass for 18 yards and recovered one fumble. 1988—Intercepted one pass for three yards and recovered one fumble. 1989—Recovered one fumble for 25 yards. 1990—Intercepted one pass for 12 yards and recovered two fumbles for 40 yards.

ZANDOFSKY, MIKE

G, CHARGERS

PERSONAL: Born November 30, 1965, at Corvallis, Ore. . . . 6-2/285. . . . Full name: Michael Leslie Zandofsky. . . . Name pronounced zan-DOFF-skee.
HIGH SCHOOL: Corvallis (Ore.).
COLLEGE: Washington.

TRANSACTIONS/CAREER NOTES: Selected by Phoenix Cardinals in third round (67th pick overall) of 1989 NFL draft. . . . Signed by Cardinals (July 22, 1989). . . . Traded by Cardinals to San Diego Chargers for undisclosed draft pick (August 29, 1990). . . . On inactive list (November 18, 1990).
PLAYING EXPERIENCE: Phoenix NFL, 1989; San Diego NFL, 1990. . . . Games: 1989 (15), 1990 (13). Total: 28.

ZAWATSON, DAVE

G/OT, JETS

PERSONAL: Born April 13, 1966, at Cleveland. . . . 6-5/287. . . . Full name: David F. Zawatson.
HIGH SCHOOL: Fairview (Fairview Park, O.) and Ygnacio Valley (Concord, Calif.).
COLLEGE: California.

TRANSACTIONS/CAREER NOTES: Selected by Chicago Bears in second round (54th pick overall) of 1989 NFL draft. . . . Signed by Bears (July 24, 1989). . . . Granted unconditional free agency (February 1, 1990). . . . Signed by New York Jets (March 12, 1990).
PLAYING EXPERIENCE: Chicago NFL, 1989; New York Jets NFL, 1990. . . . Games: 1989 (4), 1990 (16). Total: 20.

ZENDEJAS, TONY

PK, RAMS

PERSONAL: Born May 15, 1960, at Curimeo Michucan, Mexico. . . . 5-8/165. . . . Name pronounced zen-DAY-haas. . . . Cousin of Joaquin Zendejas, placekicker with New England Patriots, 1983; cousin of Max Zendejas, placekicker with Washington Redskins and Green Bay Packers, 1986-1988; and cousin of Luis Zendejas, placekicker with Arizona (USFL), Dallas Cowboys and Philadelphia Eagles, 1985 and 1987-1989.
HIGH SCHOOL: Chino (Calif.).
COLLEGE: Nevada-Reno.

TRANSACTIONS/CAREER NOTES: Selected by Los Angeles Express in fifth round (90th pick overall) of 1984 USFL draft. . . . Signed by Express (February 21, 1984). . . . Selected by Washington Redskins in first round (27th pick overall) of 1984 NFL supplemental draft. . . . Granted free agency (July 1, 1985). . . . Signed by Redskins (July 3, 1985). . . . Traded by Redskins to Houston Oilers for fifth-round pick in 1987 draft (August 27, 1985). . . . Crossed picket line during players' strike (October 14, 1987). . . . On injured reserve with leg injury (October 24, 1990-remainder of season). . . . Granted unconditional free agency (February 1, 1991). . . . Signed by Los Angeles Rams (March 12, 1991).
RECORDS/HONORS: Tied NFL record for most field goals, 50 or more yards, game (2), against San Diego Chargers (November 24, 1985). . . . Named as kicker on THE SPORTING NEWS USFL All-Star team, 1984 and 1985.
PRO STATISTICS: NFL: 1985—Attempted one pass with one completion for minus seven yards and recovered one fumble. 1986—Punted once for 36 yards. 1989—Had only pass attempt intercepted and recovered one fumble.

				PLACE-KICKING		
Year Team	G	XPM	XPA	FGM	FGA	Pts.
1984— Los Angeles USFL	18	33	33	21	30	96
1985— Los Angeles USFL	18	22	23	*26	*34	100
1985— Houston NFL..............	14	29	31	21	27	92
1986— Houston NFL..............	15	28	29	22	27	94
1987— Houston NFL..............	13	32	33	20	26	92
1988— Houston NFL..............	16	48	50	22	34	114

Year	Team	G	PLACE-KICKING				
			XPM	XPA	FGM	FGA	Pts.
1989— Houston NFL		16	40	40	25	37	115
1990— Houston NFL		7	20	21	7	12	41
USFL totals (2 years)		36	55	56	47	64	196
NFL totals (6 years)		81	197	204	117	163	548
Pro totals (8 years)		117	252	260	164	227	744

ZIMMERMAN, GARY
OT, VIKINGS

PERSONAL: Born December 13, 1961, at Fullerton, Calif. . . . 6-6/283. . . . Full name: Gary Wayne Zimmerman.
HIGH SCHOOL: Walnut (Calif.).
COLLEGE: Oregon.
TRANSACTIONS/CAREER NOTES: Selected by Los Angeles Express in second round (36th pick overall) of 1984 USFL draft. . . . Signed by Express (February 13, 1984). . . . Granted roster exemption (February 13-February 24, 1984). . . . Selected by New York Giants in first round (third pick overall) of 1984 NFL supplemental draft. . . . NFL rights traded by Giants to Minnesota Vikings for two second-round picks in 1986 draft (April 29, 1986). . . . Released by Los Angeles Express (May 19, 1986). . . . Signed by Minnesota Vikings (May 21, 1986). . . . Granted free agency (February 1, 1988). . . . Re-signed by Vikings (August 29, 1988).
PLAYING EXPERIENCE: Los Angeles USFL, 1984 and 1985; Minnesota NFL, 1986-1990. . . . Games: 1984 (17), 1985 (17), 1986 (16), 1987 (12), 1988 (16), 1989 (16), 1990 (16). Total USFL: 34. Total NFL: 76. Total Pro: 110.
CHAMPIONSHIP GAME EXPERIENCE: Played in NFC championship game after 1987 season.
RECORDS/HONORS: Named as offensive tackle on THE SPORTING NEWS USFL All-Star team, 1984 and 1985. . . . Played in Pro Bowl after 1987-1989 seasons. . . . Named to THE SPORTING NEWS NFL All-Pro team, 1987.
PRO STATISTICS: USFL: 1984—Returned one kickoff for no yards, recovered two fumbles and fumbled once. . . . NFL: 1986—Recovered two fumbles. 1987—Recovered one fumble for four yards.

ZORDICH, MICHAEL
S, CARDINALS

PERSONAL: Born October 12, 1963, at Youngstown, O. . . . 6-1/200. . . . Full name: Michael Edward Zordich.
HIGH SCHOOL: Chaney (Youngstown, O.).
COLLEGE: Penn State (bachelor of science degree in hotel, restaurant and institutional management, 1986).
TRANSACTIONS/CAREER NOTES: Selected by Baltimore Stars in 1986 USFL territorial draft. . . . Selected by San Diego Chargers in ninth round (235th pick overall) of 1986 NFL draft. . . . Signed by Chargers (June 24, 1986). . . . Released by Chargers (August 22, 1986). . . . Signed as free agent by New York Jets (April 9, 1987). . . . Released by Jets (September 6, 1987). . . . Re-signed by Jets (September 14, 1987). . . . Granted unconditional free agency (February 1, 1989). . . . Signed by Phoenix Cardinals (March 2, 1989).
PRO STATISTICS: 1990—Recovered one fumble.

Year	Team	G	INTERCEPTIONS			
			No.	Yds.	Avg.	TD
1987— N.Y. Jets NFL		10	0	0		0
1988— N.Y. Jets NFL		16	1	35	35.0	1
1989— Phoenix NFL		16	1	16	16.0	1
1990— Phoenix NFL		16	1	25	25.0	0
Pro totals (4 years)		58	3	76	25.3	2

ADDITIONAL PLAYERS

ALLEGRE, RAUL
PK

PERSONAL: Born June 15, 1959, at Torreon, Coahuila, Mex. . . . 5-10/167. . . . Full name: Raul Enrique Allegre.
HIGH SCHOOL: Shelton (Wash.).
COLLEGE: Montana, then Texas (degree in civil engineering).
TRANSACTIONS/CAREER NOTES: Signed as free agent by Dallas Cowboys (April 28, 1983). . . . Traded by Cowboys to Baltimore Colts for ninth-round pick in 1984 draft (August 29, 1983). . . . Franchise transferred to Indianapolis (March 31, 1984). . . . Released by Indianapolis Colts (September 1, 1986). . . . Signed as free agent by New York Giants (September 25, 1986). . . . On injured reserve with groin injury (November 26, 1988-remainder of season). . . . On injured reserve with quadricep injury (November 18, 1989-January 6, 1990). . . . On injured reserve with groin injury (September 28, 1990-remainder of 1990 season playoffs). . . . Granted unconditional free agency (February 1, 1991). . . . Rights relinquished (May 22, 1991).
CHAMPIONSHIP GAME EXPERIENCE: Played in NFC championship game after 1986 season. . . . Played in Super Bowl XXI after 1986 season.
RECORDS/HONORS: Tied NFL record for most field goals, 50 or more yards, game (2), against Philadelphia Eagles (November 15, 1987).

			PLACE-KICKING			
Year	Team	G	XPM	XPA	FGM	FGA	Pts.
1983— Baltimore NFL		16	22	24	30	35	112
1984— Indianapolis NFL		12	14	14	11	18	47
1985— Indianapolis NFL		16	36	39	16	26	84
1986— N.Y. Giants NFL		13	33	33	24	32	105
1987— N.Y. Giants NFL		12	25	26	17	27	76
1988— N.Y. Giants NFL		6	14	14	10	11	44
1989— N.Y. Giants NFL		10	23	24	20	26	83
1990— N.Y. Giants NFL		3	9	9	4	5	21
Pro totals (8 years)		88	176	183	132	180	572

ARMSTRONG, HARVEY
NT

PERSONAL: Born December 29, 1959, at Houston. . . . 6-3/282. . . . Full name: Harvey Lee Armstrong.
HIGH SCHOOL: Kashmere (Houston).
COLLEGE: Southern Methodist (degree in business management).
TRANSACTIONS/CAREER NOTES: Selected by Philadelphia Eagles in seventh round (190th pick overall) of 1982 NFL draft. . . . Released by Eagles (August 20, 1985). . . . Signed as free agent by Indianapolis Colts (May 21, 1986). . . . On injured reserve (November 7-December 5, 1990). . . . Released by Colts after failing physical (July 20, 1991).
PLAYING EXPERIENCE: Philadelphia NFL, 1982-1984; Indianapolis NFL, 1986-1990. . . . Games: 1982 (8), 1983 (16), 1984 (16), 1986 (16), 1987 (11), 1988 (16), 1989 (16), 1990 (12). Total: 111.
PRO STATISTICS: 1983—Recovered two fumbles. 1986—Intercepted one pass for four yards and recovered three fumbles. 1987—Recovered two fumbles. 1988—Recovered two fumbles.

ASHLEY, WALKER LEE
LB

PERSONAL: Born July 28, 1960, at Bayonne, N.J. . . . 6-0/232. . . . Full name: Walker Lee Ashley.
HIGH SCHOOL: Snyder (Jersey City, N.J.).
COLLEGE: Penn State (degree in community development).
TRANSACTIONS/CAREER NOTES: Selected by Philadelphia Stars in 1983 USFL territorial draft. . . . Selected by Minnesota Vikings in third round (73rd pick overall) of 1983 NFL draft. . . . Signed by Vikings (June 16, 1983). . . . On injured reserve with ruptured Achilles tendon (August 20, 1985-entire season). . . . Granted unconditional free agency (February 1, 1989). . . . Signed by Kansas City Chiefs (March 2, 1989). . . . Released by Chiefs (September 3, 1990). . . . Re-signed by Minnesota Vikings (September 21, 1990). . . . On inactive list (October 7, 1990). . . . Released by Vikings (October 15, 1990). . . . Re-signed by Vikings (October 23, 1990). . . . On inactive list (October 28 and November 4, 1990). . . . Released by Vikings (November 19, 1990).
PLAYING EXPERIENCE: Minnesota NFL, 1983, 1984, 1986-1988 and 1990; Kansas City NFL, 1989. . . . Games: 1983 (15), 1984 (15), 1986 (16), 1987 (12), 1988 (16), 1989 (16), 1990 (4). Total: 94.
CHAMPIONSHIP GAME EXPERIENCE: Played in NFC championship game after 1987 season.
PRO STATISTICS: 1986—Recovered one fumble. 1988—Intercepted one pass for 94 yards and a touchdown. 1989—Intercepted one pass for no yards.

BAVARO, MARK
TE

PERSONAL: Born April 28, 1963, at Winthrop, Mass. . . . 6-4/245. . . . Brother of David Bavaro, linebacker with Buffalo Bills.
HIGH SCHOOL: Danvers (Mass.).
COLLEGE: Notre Dame (bachelor of arts degree in history, 1985).
TRANSACTIONS/CAREER NOTES: Selected by Orlando Renegades in 15th round (212th pick overall) of 1985 USFL draft. . . . Selected by New York Giants in fourth round (100th pick overall) of 1985 NFL draft. . . . Signed by Giants (July 7, 1985). . . . Granted free agency (February 1, 1988). . . . Re-signed by Giants (August 23, 1988). . . . On injured reserve with knee injury (November 18, 1989-remainder of season). . . . Released by Giants after failing physical (July 15, 1991).
CHAMPIONSHIP GAME EXPERIENCE: Played in NFC championship game after 1986 and 1990 seasons. . . . Played in Super Bowl XXI after 1986 season and Super Bowl XXV after 1990 season.
RECORDS/HONORS: Played in Pro Bowl after 1986 season. . . . Named to play in Pro Bowl after 1987 season; replaced due to injury by Hoby Brenner. . . . Named to THE SPORTING NEWS NFL All-Pro team, 1986 and 1987.

PRO STATISTICS: 1986—Recovered two fumbles and fumbled three times. 1987—Returned one kickoff for 16 yards and fumbled twice. 1988—Fumbled once.

			RECEIVING		
Year Team	G	No.	Yds.	Avg.	TD
1985—N.Y. Giants NFL	16	37	511	13.8	4
1986—N.Y. Giants NFL	16	66	1001	15.2	4
1987—N.Y. Giants NFL	12	55	867	15.8	8
1988—N.Y. Giants NFL	16	53	672	12.7	4
1989—N.Y. Giants NFL	7	22	278	12.6	3
1990—N.Y. Giants NFL	15	33	393	11.9	5
Pro totals (6 years)	82	266	3722	14.0	28

BRINKLEY, LESTER
DE

PERSONAL: Born May 16, 1965, at Ruleville, Miss. . . . 6-6/255. . . . Full name: Lester L. Brinkley.
HIGH SCHOOL: Drew (Miss.).
COLLEGE: Mississippi.
TRANSACTIONS/CAREER NOTES: Signed as free agent by Pittsburgh Steelers (May 5, 1989). . . . Released by Steelers (September 5, 1989). . . . Re-signed by Steelers to developmental squad (September 7, 1989). . . . Released by Steelers (January 9, 1990). . . . Signed by Dallas Cowboys (March 9, 1990). . . . On inactive list (September 16, 1990). . . . Released by Cowboys (November 5, 1990). . . . Signed by Atlanta Falcons (March 1, 1991). . . . Released by Falcons (August 7, 1991).
PLAYING EXPERIENCE: Dallas NFL, 1990. . . . Games: 1990 (6).

BROOKS, CHET
S

PERSONAL: Born January 1, 1966, at Midland, Tex. . . . 5-11/191. . . . Full name: Terrance Donnell Brooks.
HIGH SCHOOL: David W. Carter (Dallas).
COLLEGE: Texas A&M.
TRANSACTIONS/CAREER NOTES: Selected by San Francisco 49ers in 11th round (303rd pick overall) of 1988 NFL draft. . . . Signed by 49ers (July 16, 1988). . . . On injured reserve with knee injury (November 12, 1988-remainder of season). . . . Granted free agency (February 1, 1990). . . . Re-signed by 49ers (August 15, 1990). . . . On inactive list (November 11, 18, 23; and December 3, 1990). . . . On injured reserve with knee injury (December 13, 1990-remainder of 1990 season playoffs). . . . Granted unconditional free agency (February 1, 1991). . . . Released by 49ers after failing physical (May 3, 1991).
PLAYING EXPERIENCE: San Francisco NFL, 1988-1990. . . . Games: 1988 (10), 1989 (15), 1990 (8). Total: 33.
CHAMPIONSHIP GAME EXPERIENCE: Played in NFC championship game after 1989 season. . . . Played in Super Bowl XXIV after 1989 season.
PRO STATISTICS: 1989—Intercepted three passes for 31 yards and recovered one fumble. 1990—Recovered one fumble.

BRYANT, KELVIN
RB

PERSONAL: Born September 26, 1960, at Tarboro, N.C. . . . 6-2/195. . . . Full name: Kelvin Leroy Bryant. . . . Cousin of Donald Frank, cornerback with San Diego Chargers.
HIGH SCHOOL: Tarboro (N.C.).
COLLEGE: North Carolina.
TRANSACTIONS/CAREER NOTES: Selected by Philadelphia Stars in 1983 USFL territorial draft. . . . Signed by Stars (February 8, 1983). . . . Selected by Washington Redskins in seventh round (196th pick overall) of 1983 NFL draft. . . . On developmental squad for one game (July 1-July 5, 1983). . . . On developmental squad for three games (April 8-April 26, 1984). . . . Franchise transferred to Baltimore (November 1, 1984). . . . On developmental squad for two games (March 31-April 13, 1985). . . . Granted free agency when USFL suspended operations (August 7, 1986). . . . Signed by Washington Redskins (August 13, 1986). . . . Granted roster exemption (August 13-August 23, 1986). . . . On injured reserve with knee and ankle injuries (September 16-November 1, 1986). . . . On injured reserve with knee injury (December 9, 1988-remainder of season). . . . On reserve/non-football injury list with back injury (August 29, 1989-entire season). . . . Granted unconditional free agency (February 1, 1990). . . . On injured reserve with knee injury (December 30, 1990-remainder of season). . . . Granted unconditional free agency (February 1, 1991).
CHAMPIONSHIP GAME EXPERIENCE: Played in USFL championship game after 1983-1985 seasons. . . . Played in NFC championship game after 1986 and 1987 seasons. . . . Played in Super Bowl XXII after 1987 season.
RECORDS/HONORS: Named as running back on THE SPORTING NEWS USFL All-Star team, 1983 and 1984.
PRO STATISTICS: USFL: 1983—Recovered two fumbles. 1984—Recovered three fumbles for 38 yards and a touchdown. 1985—Recovered one fumble and attempted one pass with no completions. . . . NFL: 1986—Recovered one fumble. 1987—Attempted one pass with no completions and recovered one fumble. 1988—Recovered one fumble.

		RUSHING				RECEIVING				TOTAL		
Year Team	G	Att.	Yds.	Avg.	TD	No.	Yds.	Avg.	TD	TD	Pts.	F.
1983—Philadelphia USFL	17	318	1442	4.5	16	53	410	7.7	1	17	102	4
1984—Philadelphia USFL	15	*297	1406	4.7	13	48	453	9.4	1	15	90	8
1985—Baltimore USFL	15	238	1207	5.1	12	40	407	10.2	4	16	96	3
1986—Washington NFL	10	69	258	3.7	4	43	449	10.4	3	7	42	2
1987—Washington NFL	11	77	406	5.3	1	43	490	11.4	5	6	36	4
1988—Washington NFL	10	108	498	4.6	1	42	447	10.6	5	6	36	3
1990—Washington NFL	15	6	24	4.0	0	26	248	9.5	1	1	6	0
USFL totals (3 years)	47	853	4055	4.8	41	141	1270	9.0	6	48	288	15
NFL totals (4 years)	46	260	1186	4.6	6	154	1634	10.6	14	20	120	9
Pro totals (7 years)	93	1113	5241	4.7	47	295	2904	9.8	20	68	408	24

BURT, JIM
NT

PERSONAL: Born June 7, 1959, at Buffalo, N.Y.... 6-1/260.... Full name: James P. Burt.
HIGH SCHOOL: Orchard Park (N.Y.).
COLLEGE: Miami (Fla.).
TRANSACTIONS/CAREER NOTES: Signed as free agent by New York Giants (May 4, 1981).... On injured reserve with back injury (December 24, 1982-remainder of season).... On injured reserve with back injury (November 2, 1983-remainder of season).... On injured reserve with back injury (December 7, 1987-remainder of season).... Granted unconditional free agency (February 1, 1989).... Re-signed by Giants (June 20, 1989).... Released by Giants (July 24, 1989). ... Signed as free agent by San Francisco 49ers (November 1, 1989).... Granted unconditional free agency (February 1, 1990).... Re-signed by 49ers (August 2, 1990).... Granted unconditional free agency (February 1, 1991).
PLAYING EXPERIENCE: New York Giants NFL, 1981-1988; San Francisco NFL, 1989 and 1990.... Games: 1981 (13), 1982 (4), 1983 (7), 1984 (16), 1985 (16), 1986 (13), 1987 (8), 1988 (16), 1989 (8), 1990 (11). Total: 112.
CHAMPIONSHIP GAME EXPERIENCE: Played in NFC championship game after 1986, 1989 and 1990 seasons.... Played in Super Bowl XXI after 1986 season and Super Bowl XXIV after 1989 season.
RECORDS/HONORS: Played in Pro Bowl after 1986 season.
PRO STATISTICS: 1983—Recovered one fumble. 1984—Recovered two fumbles. 1985—Recovered two fumbles. 1986—Recovered three fumbles for one yard. 1988—Recovered two fumbles for 39 yards and a touchdown.

CARAVELLO, JOE
RB/TE

PERSONAL: Born June 6, 1963, at Santa Monica, Calif.... 6-3/262.... Full name: Joseph J. Caravello.
HIGH SCHOOL: El Segundo (Calif.).
COLLEGE: Tulane.
TRANSACTIONS/CAREER NOTES: Signed as free agent by Atlanta Falcons (May 2, 1986).... Released by Falcons (September 1, 1986).... Re-signed by Falcons (March 13, 1987).... Released by Falcons (September 7, 1987).... Signed as free-agent replacement player by Washington Redskins (September 24, 1987).... On injured reserve with back injury (August 30-October 1, 1988).... Granted unconditional free agency (February 1, 1989).... Signed by San Diego Chargers (February 27, 1989).... On injured reserve with knee injury (December 6, 1989-remainder of season).... On injured reserve with hamstring injury (October 26, 1990-remainder of season).... Granted unconditional free agency (February 1, 1991).... Released by Chargers (July 11, 1991).
CHAMPIONSHIP GAME EXPERIENCE: Member of Washington Redskins for Super Bowl XXII after 1987 season; inactive.
PRO STATISTICS: 1987—Recovered one fumble. 1988—Recovered one fumble. 1989—Rushed once for no yards and recovered one fumble.

				RECEIVING		
Year	Team	G	No.	Yds.	Avg.	TD
1987— Washington NFL		11	2	29	14.5	0
1988— Washington NFL		12	2	15	7.5	0
1989— San Diego NFL		12	10	95	9.5	0
1990— San Diego NFL		7	2	21	10.5	1
Pro totals (4 years)		42	16	160	10.0	1

COLEMAN, ERIC
CB

PERSONAL: Born December 27, 1966, at Denver.... 6-0/190.... Full name: Eric Gerard Coleman.
HIGH SCHOOL: Thomas Jefferson (Denver).
COLLEGE: Wyoming.
TRANSACTIONS/CAREER NOTES: Selected by New England Patriots in second round (43rd pick overall) of 1989 NFL draft.... Signed by Patriots (July 19, 1989).... On injured reserve with foot injury (November 10, 1989-remainder of season).... On injured reserve with knee injury (October 29, 1990-remainder of season).... Released by Patriots after failing physical (July 22, 1991).
PLAYING EXPERIENCE: New England NFL, 1989 and 1990.... Games: 1989 (8), 1990 (7). Total: 15.
PRO STATISTICS: 1989—Intercepted one pass for one yard.

DAWSON, LIN
TE

PERSONAL: Born June 24, 1959, at Norfolk, Va.... 6-3/240.... Full name: James Linwood Dawson.
HIGH SCHOOL: Kinston (N.C.).
COLLEGE: North Carolina State.
TRANSACTIONS/CAREER NOTES: Selected by New England Patriots in eighth round (212th pick overall) of 1981 NFL draft.... On inactive list (September 19, 1982).... On injured reserve with knee injury (August 19, 1986-entire season).... On injured reserve with shoulder injury (August 30-September 30, 1988).... On injured reserve with fractured ankle (November 11, 1988-remainder of season).... Released by Patriots (September 3, 1990).... Re-signed by Patriots (September 4, 1990).... On inactive list (September 30, 1990).... On injured reserve with ankle injury (October 30-December 4, 1990).... Released by Patriots (December 4, 1990).... Signed by Detroit Lions (June 10, 1991).... Released by Lions (August 6, 1991).
CHAMPIONSHIP GAME EXPERIENCE: Played in AFC championship game after 1985 season.... Played in Super Bowl XX after 1985 season.
PRO STATISTICS: 1984—Recovered one fumble. 1985—Recovered one fumble and fumbled once.

DID YOU KNOW. . .

...that Philadelphia Eagles running back Keith Byars attempted four passes in 1990—and completed each one for a touchdown?

Year	Team	G	No.	Yds.	Avg.	TD
			—— RECEIVING ——			
1981— New England NFL......		15	7	126	18.0	0
1982— New England NFL......		8	13	160	12.3	1
1983— New England NFL......		13	9	84	9.3	1
1984— New England NFL......		16	39	427	11.0	4
1985— New England NFL......		16	17	148	8.7	0
1987— New England NFL......		12	12	81	6.8	0
1988— New England NFL......		6	8	106	13.3	2
1989— New England NFL......		16	12	101	8.4	0
1990— New England NFL......		3	0	0		0
Pro totals (9 years)		105	117	1233	10.5	8

DOUGLAS, DAVID
C

PERSONAL: Born March 20, 1963, at Spring City, Tenn.... 6-4/280.... Full name: David Glenn Douglas.
HIGH SCHOOL: Rhea County (Evansville, Tenn.).
COLLEGE: Tennessee.
TRANSACTIONS/CAREER NOTES: Selected by Memphis Showboats in 1986 USFL territorial draft.... Selected by Cincinnati Bengals in eighth round (204th pick overall) of 1986 NFL draft.... Signed by Bengals (July 10, 1986).... Granted unconditional free agency (February 1, 1989).... Signed by New England Patriots (March 18, 1989).... Released by Patriots (September 5, 1989).... Re-signed by Patriots (September 13, 1989).... Released by Patriots (October 2, 1989).... Re-signed by Patriots (October 18, 1989).... Released by Patriots (September 3, 1990).... Re-signed by Patriots (September 4, 1990).... On injured reserve with knee injury (October 25-November 9, 1990).... Released by Patriots (November 9, 1990).... Re-signed by Patriots (November 14, 1990).... Granted unconditional free agency (February 1, 1991).
PLAYING EXPERIENCE: Cincinnati NFL, 1986-1988; New England NFL, 1989 and 1990.... Games: 1986 (14), 1987 (12), 1988 (14), 1989 (5), 1990 (11). Total: 56.
CHAMPIONSHIP GAME EXPERIENCE: Played in AFC championship game after 1988 season.... Played in Super Bowl XXIII after 1988 season.

EASON, TONY
QB

PERSONAL: Born October 8, 1959, at Blythe, Calif.... 6-4/212.... Full name: Charles Carroll Eason IV.... Brother of Bo Eason, safety with Houston Oilers, 1984-1987.
HIGH SCHOOL: Delta (Clarksburg, Calif.).
COLLEGE: American River College (Calif.), then Illinois (bachelor of science degree in physical education, 1983).
TRANSACTIONS/CAREER NOTES: Selected by Chicago Blitz in 1983 USFL territorial draft.... USFL rights traded by Blitz with running back Calvin Murray and first-round pick in 1983 draft to Arizona Wranglers for rights to place-kicker Frank Corral and first-round pick in 1983 draft (January 4, 1983).... Selected by New England Patriots in first round (15th pick overall) of 1983 NFL draft.... Signed by Patriots (June 2, 1983).... On injured reserve with separated shoulder (November 3, 1987-remainder of season).... On injured reserve with nerve damage in elbow (August 30-December 5, 1988).... Released by Patriots (October 31, 1989).... Awarded on waivers to New York Jets (November 1, 1989).... Granted roster exemption (November 1-November 8, 1989).... Granted free agency (May 16, 1991).
CHAMPIONSHIP GAME EXPERIENCE: Played in AFC championship game after 1985 season.... Played in Super Bowl XX after 1985 season.
PRO STATISTICS: Passer rating points: 1983 (48.4), 1984 (93.4), 1985 (67.5), 1986 (89.2), 1987 (72.4), 1988 (61.1), 1989 (70.5), 1990 (49.0). Career: 79.7.... 1983—Recovered one fumble. 1984—Recovered two fumbles and fumbled seven times for minus five yards. 1985—Recovered one fumble and fumbled four times for minus 19 yards. 1986—Recovered three fumbles. 1988—Recovered one fumble for two yards. 1990—Recovered one fumble.

| | | | | —— PASSING —— | | | | | —— RUSHING —— | | | | —— TOTAL —— | | |
Year Team	G	Att.	Cmp.	Pct.	Yds.	TD	Int.	Avg.	Att.	Yds.	Avg.	TD	TD	Pts.	F.
1983— New England NFL......	16	95	46	48.4	557	1	5	5.86	19	39	2.1	0	0	0	5
1984— New England NFL......	16	431	259	60.1	3228	23	8	7.49	40	154	3.9	5	5	30	7
1985— New England NFL......	16	299	168	56.2	2156	11	17	7.21	22	70	3.2	1	1	6	4
1986— New England NFL......	15	448	276	61.6	3328	19	10	7.42	35	170	4.9	0	0	0	4
1987— New England NFL......	4	79	42	53.2	453	3	2	5.73	3	25	8.3	0	0	0	1
1988— New England NFL......	2	43	28	65.1	249	0	2	5.79	5	18	3.6	0	0	0	0
1989— NE (3)-NYJ (2) NFL	5	141	79	56.0	1016	4	6	7.21	3	-2	-.7	0	0	0	3
1990— N.Y. Jets NFL.............	16	28	13	46.4	155	0	1	5.54	7	29	4.1	0	0	0	2
Pro totals (8 years)	90	1564	911	58.3	11142	61	51	7.12	134	503	3.8	6	6	36	26

FERGUSON, KEITH
DE

PERSONAL: Born April 3, 1959, at Miami.... 6-5/276.... Full name: Keith Tyrone Ferguson.
HIGH SCHOOL: Edison (Miami).
COLLEGE: Ohio State.
TRANSACTIONS/CAREER NOTES: Selected by San Diego Chargers in fifth round (131st pick overall) of 1981 NFL draft.... Released by Chargers (November 20, 1985).... Awarded on waivers to Detroit Lions (November 21, 1985).... On injured reserve with ankle injury (September 15-November 15, 1989).... Transferred to developmental squad (November 16-November 22, 1989).... Granted unconditional free agency (February 1, 1991).... Rights relinquished by Lions (July 22, 1991).
PLAYING EXPERIENCE: San Diego NFL, 1981-1984; San Diego (10)-Detroit (5) NFL, 1985; Detroit NFL, 1986-1990.... Games: 1981 (16), 1982 (9), 1983 (16), 1984 (16), 1985 (15), 1986 (16), 1987 (12), 1988 (14), 1989 (4), 1990 (16). Total: 134.
CHAMPIONSHIP GAME EXPERIENCE: Played in AFC championship game after 1981 season.

PRO STATISTICS: 1982—Recovered one fumble. 1983—Recovered two fumbles. 1984—Recovered one fumble. 1985—Recovered one fumble. 1986—Intercepted one pass for seven yards, recovered one fumble and fumbled once. 1987—Recovered one fumble.

FOURCADE, JOHN
QB

PERSONAL: Born October 11, 1960, at Gretna, La. . . . 6-1/215. . . . Full name: John Charles Fourcade.
HIGH SCHOOL: Archbishop Shaw (Marrero, La.).
COLLEGE: Mississippi (bachelor of science degree in education and sports marketing).
TRANSACTIONS/CAREER NOTES: Signed as free agent by Toronto Argonauts of CFL (May 5, 1982). . . . Traded by Argonauts to B.C. Lions (May 20, 1982). . . . Released by Lions (July 4, 1982). . . . Re-signed by Lions (July 8, 1982). . . . Released by Lions (June 30, 1983). . . . Signed by Birmingham Stallions of USFL (October 10, 1983). . . . Released by Stallions (February 13, 1984). . . . Signed as free agent by Memphis Showboats of USFL (May 31, 1984). . . . On developmental squad for four games (May 31, 1984-remainder of season). . . . Released by Showboats (January 23, 1985). . . . Signed as free agent by New York Giants (May 3, 1985). . . . Released by Giants (July 22, 1985). . . . Signed as free agent by New Orleans Saints (May 13, 1986). . . . Released by Saints (August 19, 1986). . . . Signed as free agent by Denver Dynamite of Arena Football League (July 15, 1987). . . . Granted free agency (August 15, 1987). . . . Re-signed as replacement player by New Orleans Saints (September 24, 1987). . . . Released by Saints (July 30, 1991).
PRO STATISTICS: NFL Passer rating points: 1987 (75.9), 1988 (39.6), 1989 (92.0), 1990 (46.1). Career: 70.1. . . . 1989—Recovered two fumbles. 1990—Recovered one fumble.

Year Team	G	Att.	Cmp.	Pct.	Yds.	TD	Int.	Avg.	Att.	Yds.	Avg.	TD	TD	Pts.	F.
				PASSING						RUSHING				TOTAL	
1982— B.C. CFL	4	14	5	35.7	55	0	3	3.93	2	37	18.5	0	0	0	0
1987— New Orleans NFL	3	89	48	53.9	597	4	3	6.71	19	134	7.1	0	0	0	1
1988— New Orleans NFL	1	1	0	.0	0	0	0	.00	0	0		0	0	0	0
1989— New Orleans NFL	13	107	61	57.0	930	7	4	8.69	14	91	6.5	1	1	6	2
1990— New Orleans NFL	7	116	50	43.1	785	3	8	6.77	15	77	5.1	1	1	6	4
CFL totals (1 year)	4	14	5	35.7	55	0	3	3.93	2	37	18.5	0	0	0	0
NFL totals (4 years)	24	313	159	50.8	2312	14	15	7.39	48	302	6.3	2	2	12	7
Pro totals (5 years)	28	327	164	50.2	2367	14	18	7.24	50	339	6.8	2	2	12	7

GREER, TERRY
WR

PERSONAL: Born September 27, 1957, at Memphis, Tenn. . . . 6-1/192. . . . Full name: Terry Lee Greer.
HIGH SCHOOL: Messick (Memphis, Tenn.).
COLLEGE: Alabama State (bachelor of science degree in business administration, 1980).
TRANSACTIONS/CAREER NOTES: Signed as free agent by Toronto Argonauts of CFL (March 21, 1980). . . . Selected by Los Angeles Rams in 11th round (304th pick overall) of 1980 NFL draft. . . . On injured reserve (August 10, 1981-remainder of season). . . . Granted free agency (March 1, 1986). . . . Los Angeles Rams matched Cleveland Browns offer sheet and traded him to Browns for fourth-round pick in 1986 draft (April 18, 1986). . . . On injured reserve with knee injury (October 10-November 10, 1986). . . . On injured reserve with bruised thumb (December 23, 1986-remainder of 1986 season playoffs). . . . Released by Browns (September 7, 1987). . . . Signed as free-agent replacement player by San Francisco 49ers (September 30, 1987). . . . Released by 49ers (November 3, 1987). . . . Re-signed by 49ers (April 5, 1988). . . . On injured reserve with shoulder injury (August 29-October 12, 1988). . . . Activated after clearing procedural waivers (October 14, 1988). . . . Granted unconditional free agency (February 1, 1989). . . . Re-signed by 49ers (April 28, 1989). . . . Released by 49ers (September 4, 1989). . . . Re-signed by 49ers (September 5, 1989). . . . On injured reserve with knee injury (November 22, 1989-remainder of season). . . . Granted unconditional free agency (February 1, 1990). . . . Signed by Detroit Lions (March 31, 1990). . . . Granted unconditional free agency (February 1, 1991). . . . Rights relinquished by Lions (July 22, 1991).
CHAMPIONSHIP GAME EXPERIENCE: Played in Grey Cup (CFL championship game) after 1982 and 1983 seasons. . . . Played in NFC championship game after 1988 season. . . . Played in Super Bowl XXIII after 1988 season.
PRO STATISTICS: CFL: 1982—Credited with one 2-point conversion and attempted one pass with one completion for 39 yards and a touchdown. 1983—Attempted two passes with one completion for 39 yards with one touchdown and one interception. 1984—Attempted three passes with one completion for 42 yards and a touchdown. 1985—Attempted two passes with one completion for minus one yard and recovered one fumble for two yards. . . . NFL: 1989—Returned one punt for three yards. 1990—Recovered one fumble.

Year Team	G	Att.	Yds.	Avg.	TD	No.	Yds.	Avg.	TD	No.	Yds.	Avg.	TD	TD	Pts.	F.
		RUSHING				RECEIVING				KICKOFF RETURNS				TOTAL		
1980— Toronto CFL	14	2	38	19.0	1	37	552	14.9	2	23	533	23.2	0	3	18	0
1981— Toronto CFL	6	1	22	22.0	0	21	284	13.5	3	11	418	38.0	1	4	24	1
1982— Toronto CFL	15	7	52	7.4	1	85	1466	17.3	11	12	285	23.8	0	12	74	1
1983— Toronto CFL	16	2	15	7.5	0	*113	*2003	17.7	8	1	0	.0	0	8	48	1
1984— Toronto CFL	15	2	13	6.5	0	70	1189	17.0	14	3	31	10.3	0	14	84	1
1985— Toronto CFL	16	3	45	15.0	0	78	1323	17.0	9	0	0	0	0	9	54	0
1986— Cleveland NFL	11	3	51	17.0	0	3	51	17.0	0	0	0	0	0	0	0	0
1987— San Francisco NFL	3	0	0		0	6	111	18.5	1	0	0		0	1	6	0
1988— San Francisco NFL	10	0	0		0	8	120	15.0	0	0	0		0	0	0	0
1989— San Francisco NFL	11	0	0		0	1	26	26.0	0	1	17	17.0	0	0	0	1
1990— Detroit NFL	15	0	0		0	20	332	16.6	3	0	0		0	3	18	0
CFL totals (6 years)	82	17	185	10.9	2	404	6817	16.9	47	50	1267	25.3	1	50	302	4
NFL totals (5 years)	50	3	51	17.0	0	38	640	16.8	4	1	17	17.0	0	4	24	1
Pro totals (11 years)	132	20	236	11.8	2	442	7457	16.9	51	51	1284	25.2	1	54	326	5

HARPER, DAVID
LB

PERSONAL: Born May 5, 1966, at Eureka, Calif. . . . 6-1/230. . . . Full name: David Douglas Harper.
HIGH SCHOOL: Eureka (Calif.).
COLLEGE: Humboldt State (Calif.).
TRANSACTIONS/CAREER NOTES: Selected by Dallas Cowboys in 11th round (277th pick overall) of 1990 NFL draft. . . . Signed by Cowboys (July 17, 1990). . . . Released by Cowboys (August 26, 1990). . . . Signed by Cowboys to practice squad (October 1, 1990). . . . Activated (November 14, 1990). . . . Granted unconditional free agency (February 1, 1991). . . . Released by Cowboys (July 24, 1991).
PLAYING EXPERIENCE: Dallas NFL, 1990. . . . Games: 1990 (6).

HARRIS, AL
LB

PERSONAL: Born December 31, 1956, at Bangor, Me. . . . 6-5/265. . . . Full name: Alfred Carl Harris. . . . Cousin of Ricky Bell, running back with Tampa Bay Buccaneers and San Diego Chargers, 1977-1982.
HIGH SCHOOL: Leilehua (Wahiawa, Hawaii).
COLLEGE: Arizona State (bachelor of science degree in communications).
TRANSACTIONS/CAREER NOTES: Selected by Chicago Bears in first round (ninth pick overall) of 1979 NFL draft. . . . On injured reserve with knee injury (August 28-October 26, 1979). . . . On inactive list (September 19, 1982). . . . Granted free agency (February 1, 1985). . . . On reserve/unsigned free agency list (August 20, 1985-entire season). . . . Re-signed by Bears (July 16, 1986). . . . Granted unconditional free agency (February 1, 1989). . . . Signed by Philadelphia Eagles (March 30, 1989). . . . Granted unconditional free agency (February 1, 1991). . . . Rights relinquished by Eagles (April 2, 1991).
PLAYING EXPERIENCE: Chicago NFL, 1979-1984 and 1986-1988; Philadelphia NFL, 1989 and 1990. . . . Games: 1979 (4), 1980 (16), 1981 (16), 1982 (8), 1983 (13), 1984 (16), 1986 (16), 1987 (12), 1988 (16), 1989 (16), 1990 (16). Total: 149.
CHAMPIONSHIP GAME EXPERIENCE: Played in NFC championship game after 1984 and 1988 seasons.
RECORDS/HONORS: Named as defensive lineman on THE SPORTING NEWS college All-America team, 1978.
PRO STATISTICS: 1981—Caught one pass for 18 yards, intercepted one pass for 44 yards and a touchdown and recovered three fumbles for five yards. 1983—Recovered two fumbles. 1984—Intercepted one pass for 34 yards. 1988—Recovered three fumbles. 1989—Intercepted two passes for 18 yards, credited with a safety and recovered two fumbles.

HARRIS, MICHAEL
G

PERSONAL: Born August 30, 1966, at Shreveport, La. . . . 6-4/306. . . . Full name: Anthony Michael Harris.
HIGH SCHOOL: Booker T. Washington (Shreveport, La.).
COLLEGE: Grambling State.
TRANSACTIONS/CAREER NOTES: Signed as free agent by Kansas City Chiefs (May 3, 1989). . . . Released by Chiefs (September 5, 1989). . . . Re-signed by Chiefs to developmental squad (September 6, 1989). . . . On developmental squad (September 6-October 25, 1989). . . . Activated after clearing procedural waivers (October 27, 1989). . . . Released by Chiefs (September 3, 1990). . . . Signed by WLAF (January 2, 1991). . . . Selected by Montreal Machine in fourth round (38th offensive lineman) of 1991 WLAF positional draft. . . . Released by Machine (May 13, 1991). . . . Re-signed by Kansas City Chiefs (June 4, 1991). . . . Released by Chiefs (August 12, 1991).
PLAYING EXPERIENCE: Kansas City NFL, 1989; Montreal WLAF, 1991. . . . Games: 1989 (3), 1991 (7). Total NFL: 3. Total Pro: 10.

HOGEBOOM, GARY
QB

PERSONAL: Born August 21, 1958, at Grand Rapids, Mich. . . . 6-4/207. . . . Full name: Gary Keith Hogeboom. . . . Name pronounced HOAG-ih-boom.
HIGH SCHOOL: Northview (Grand Rapids, Mich.).
COLLEGE: Central Michigan.
TRANSACTIONS/CAREER NOTES: Selected by Dallas Cowboys in fifth round (133rd pick overall) of 1980 NFL draft. . . . Traded by Cowboys with second-round pick in 1986 draft to Indianapolis Colts for second-round pick in 1986 draft and conditional 1987 pick (April 28, 1986). . . . On injured reserve with separated shoulder (September 16-December 5, 1986). . . . Crossed picket line during players' strike (September 23, 1987). . . . Granted unconditional free agency (February 1, 1989). . . . Signed by Phoenix Cardinals (March 3, 1989). . . . Released by Cardinals (September 3, 1990). . . . Signed by Washington Redskins (September 26, 1990). . . . On inactive list (October 14, 21, 28; November 4, 12, 22; and December 2, 9, 15, and 22, 1990). . . . Active for three games with Redskins in 1990; did not play. . . . Released by Redskins (January 11, 1991).
CHAMPIONSHIP GAME EXPERIENCE: Member of Dallas Cowboys for NFC championship game after 1980 and 1981 seasons; did not play. . . . Played in NFC championship game after 1982 season.
PRO STATISTICS: Passer rating points: 1982 (17.2), 1983 (90.6), 1984 (63.7), 1985 (70.8), 1986 (81.2), 1987 (85.0), 1988 (77.7), 1989 (69.5). Career: 71.9. . . . 1984—Recovered four fumbles and fumbled eight times for minus three yards. 1986—Recovered two fumbles and fumbled three times for 50 yards. 1987—Recovered one fumble and fumbled once for minus one yard. 1989—Recovered one fumble and fumbled five times for minus four yards.

			PASSING						RUSHING				TOTAL		
Year Team	G	Att.	Cmp.	Pct.	Yds.	TD	Int.	Avg.	Att.	Yds.	Avg.	TD	TD	Pts.	F.
1980—Dallas NFL	2	0	0		0	0	0		0	0		0	0	0	0
1981—Dallas NFL	1	0	0		0	0	0		0	0		0	0	0	0
1982—Dallas NFL	4	8	3	37.5	45	0	1	5.63	3	0	.0	0	0	0	2
1983—Dallas NFL	6	17	11	64.7	161	1	1	9.47	6	-10	-1.7	0	0	0	0
1984—Dallas NFL	16	367	195	53.1	2366	7	14	6.45	15	19	1.3	0	0	0	8
1985—Dallas NFL	16	126	70	55.6	978	5	7	7.76	8	48	6.0	1	1	6	0
1986—Indianapolis NFL	5	144	85	59.0	1154	6	6	8.01	10	20	2.0	1	1	6	3
1987—Indianapolis NFL	6	168	99	58.9	1145	9	5	6.82	3	3	1.0	0	0	0	1
1988—Indianapolis NFL	9	131	76	58.0	996	7	7	7.60	11	-8	-.7	1	1	6	2
1989—Phoenix NFL	14	364	204	56.0	2591	14	19	7.12	27	89	3.3	1	1	6	5
Pro totals (10 years)	79	1325	743	56.1	9436	49	60	7.12	83	161	1.9	4	4	24	21

IRVIN, LEROY

DB

PERSONAL: Born September 15, 1957, at Fort Dix, N.J. . . . 5-11/184. . . . Full name: Leroy Irvin Jr.
HIGH SCHOOL: Glenn Hills (Augusta, Ga.).
COLLEGE: Kansas.
TRANSACTIONS/CAREER NOTES: Selected by Los Angeles Rams in third round (70th pick overall) of 1980 NFL draft. . . . On suspended list (November 4-November 10, 1987). . . . On reserve/non-football injury list with drugs (August 29-September 25, 1989). . . . Granted roster exemption (September 26-September 29, 1989). . . . Granted unconditional free agency (February 1, 1990). . . . Released by Rams (April 17, 1990). . . . Signed by Detroit Lions (August 2, 1990). . . . Granted unconditional free agency (February 1, 1991).
CHAMPIONSHIP GAME EXPERIENCE: Played in NFC championship game after 1985 and 1989 seasons.
RECORDS/HONORS: Established NFL record for most punt return yards, game (207), against Atlanta Falcons (October 11, 1981). Tied NFL record for most touchdowns, punt returns, game (2), against Atlanta Falcons (October 11, 1981); most touchdowns by combined kick returns, game (2) against Atlanta Falcons (October 11, 1981). . . . Named as punt returner to THE SPORTING NEWS NFL All-Pro team, 1981. . . . Played in Pro Bowl after 1985 and 1986 seasons. . . . Named to THE SPORTING NEWS NFL All-Pro team, 1986.
PRO STATISTICS: 1980—Returned one kickoff for five yards and recovered three fumbles. 1981—Recovered three fumbles for 14 yards. 1982—Recovered two fumbles. 1983—Returned one kickoff for 22 yards and recovered two fumbles. 1984—Returned two kickoffs for 33 yards. 1986—Returned blocked field goal 65 yards for a touchdown and recovered three fumbles for 55 yards and a touchdown.

Year Team	G	— INTERCEPTIONS —				— PUNT RETURNS —				— TOTAL —		
		No.	Yds.	Avg.	TD	No.	Yds.	Avg.	TD	TD	Pts.	F.
1980—L.A. Rams NFL	16	2	80	40.0	0	42	296	7.1	0	0	0	5
1981—L.A. Rams NFL	16	3	18	6.0	0	46	*615	*13.4	*3	3	18	3
1982—L.A. Rams NFL	9	0	0		0	22	242	11.0	1	1	6	4
1983—L.A. Rams NFL	15	4	42	10.5	0	25	212	8.5	0	0	0	4
1984—L.A. Rams NFL	16	5	166	33.2	*2	9	83	9.2	0	2	12	0
1985—L.A. Rams NFL	16	6	83	13.8	*1	0	0		0	1	6	0
1986—L.A. Rams NFL	16	6	150	25.0	1	0	0		0	3	18	1
1987—L.A. Rams NFL	10	2	47	23.5	1	1	0	.0	0	1	6	0
1988—L.A. Rams NFL	16	3	25	8.3	0	1	2	2.0	0	0	0	1
1989—L.A. Rams NFL	13	3	43	14.3	0	1	7	7.0	0	0	0	0
1990—Detroit NFL	16	1	22	22.0	0	0	0		0	0	0	0
Pro totals (11 years)	159	35	676	19.3	5	147	1457	9.9	4	11	66	18

JOHNSON, RICHARD L.

WR

PERSONAL: Born October 19, 1961, at Los Angeles. . . . 5-6/184. . . . Full name: Richard Lavon Johnson.
HIGH SCHOOL: San Pedro (Calif.).
COLLEGE: Los Angeles Harbor Junior College (Calif.), then Colorado (bachelor of arts degree).
TRANSACTIONS/CAREER NOTES: Selected by Denver Gold in 1983 USFL territorial draft. . . . Signed by Gold (January 28, 1983). . . . Released by Gold (February 14, 1983). . . . Re-signed by Gold (April 27, 1983). . . . On developmental squad for eight games (April 27-May 10, 1983; May 20-May 27, 1983; and June 3, 1983-remainder of season). . . . Selected by Houston Gamblers in 10th round (59th pick overall) of USFL expansion draft (September 6, 1983). . . . Traded by Gamblers with defensive backs Luther Bradley, Will Lewis, Mike Mitchell and Durwood Roquemore, defensive end Pete Catan, quarterbacks Jim Kelly and Todd Dillon, defensive tackles Tony Fitzpatrick, Van Hughes and Hosea Taylor, running back Sam Harrell, linebackers Andy Hawkins and Ladell Wills, wide receivers Scott McGhee, Gerald McNeil, Ricky Sanders and Clarence Verdin, guard Rich Kehr, center Billy Kidd and offensive tackles Chris Riehm and Tommy Robison to New Jersey Generals for past considerations (March 7, 1986). . . . Granted free agency when USFL suspended operations (August 7, 1986). . . . Signed as free agent by New York Jets (April 19, 1987). . . . Released by Jets (August 10, 1987). . . . Signed as free-agent replacement player by Washington Redskins (September 23, 1987). . . . Released by Redskins (October 6, 1987). . . . Signed as free agent by Buffalo Bills (October 9, 1987). . . . Released by Bills (October 19, 1987). . . . Signed as free agent by Detroit Lions (March 15, 1989). . . . Granted unconditional free agency (February 1, 1991). . . . Signed by Houston Oilers (March 29, 1991). . . . Released by Oilers (June 21, 1991).
RECORDS/HONORS: Named as wide receiver on THE SPORTING NEWS USFL All-Star team, 1985.
PRO STATISTICS: 1983—Recovered one fumble. 1984—Returned six kickoffs for 109 yards and recovered one fumble. 1985—Recovered two fumbles. 1990—Recovered one fumble.

Year Team	G	— RUSHING —				— RECEIVING —				— TOTAL —		
		Att.	Yds.	Avg.	TD	No.	Yds.	Avg.	TD	TD	Pts.	F.
1983—Denver USFL	1	0	0		0	0	0		0	0	0	0
1984—Houston USFL	18	4	19	4.8	0	*115	1455	12.7	*15	15	90	3
1985—Houston USFL	17	2	15	7.5	0	*103	1384	13.4	14	14	84	2
1987—Washington NFL	1	0	0		0	1	5	5.0	0	0	0	0
1989—Detroit NFL	16	12	38	3.2	0	70	1091	15.6	8	8	48	3
1990—Detroit NFL	16	0	0		0	64	727	11.4	6	6	36	2
USFL totals (3 years)	36	6	34	5.7	0	218	2839	13.0	29	29	174	5
NFL totals (3 years)	33	12	38	3.2	0	135	1823	13.5	14	14	84	5
Pro totals (6 years)	69	18	72	4.0	0	353	4662	13.2	43	43	258	10

KNIGHT, SHAWN

DE

PERSONAL: Born June 4, 1964, at Provo, Utah. . . . 6-6/292. . . . Full name: Shawn Matt Knight.
HIGH SCHOOL: Edward C. Reed (Sparks, Nev.).
COLLEGE: Brigham Young.
TRANSACTIONS/CAREER NOTES: Selected by New Orleans Saints in first round (11th pick overall) of 1987 NFL draft. . . . Signed by Saints (August 31, 1987). . . . Granted roster exemption (August 31-September 2, 1987). . . . On injured reserve with ankle

injury (December 26, 1987-remainder of season).... Traded by Saints to Denver Broncos for nose tackle Ted Gregory (August 29, 1988).... Released by Broncos (August 29, 1989).... Signed as free agent by Phoenix Cardinals (September 15, 1989). ... On injured reserve with dislocated shoulder (October 10-November 25, 1989).... Granted unconditional free agency (February 1, 1990).... Signed by Minnesota Vikings (March 30, 1990).... Released by Vikings (September 3, 1990).... Signed by WLAF (January 31, 1991).... Selected by Sacramento Surge in first round (second defensive lineman) of 1991 WLAF positional draft.... Signed by Kansas City Chiefs (June 14, 1991).... Released by Chiefs (August 12, 1991).
PLAYING EXPERIENCE: New Orleans NFL, 1987; Denver NFL, 1988; Phoenix NFL, 1989; Sacramento WLAF, 1991.... Games: 1987 (10), 1988 (14), 1989 (7), 1991 (10). Total NFL: 31. Total Pro: 41.
PRO STATISTICS: NFL: 1989—Recovered one fumble.... WLAF: 1991—Recovered three fumbles.

LANSFORD, MIKE
PK

PERSONAL: Born July 20, 1958, at Monterrey Park, Calif.... 6-0/190.... Full name: Michael John Lansford.
HIGH SCHOOL: Arcadia (Calif.).
COLLEGE: Pasadena City College (Calif.), then Washington.
TRANSACTIONS/CAREER NOTES: Selected by New York Giants in 12th round (312th pick overall) of 1980 NFL draft.... Released by Giants (August 3, 1980).... Awarded on waivers to San Francisco 49ers (August 5, 1980).... Released by 49ers (August 18, 1980).... Signed as free agent by Oakland Raiders (June, 1981).... Released by Raiders (August 18, 1981).... Signed as free agent by Los Angeles Rams (July 1, 1982).... On injured reserve with knee injury (August 24-November 23, 1983).... Activated after clearing procedural waivers (November 25, 1983).... Crossed picket line during players' strike (October 2, 1987).... Granted unconditional free agency (February 1, 1991).... Signed by Cleveland Browns (April 1, 1991).... Released by Browns after failing physical (April 2, 1991).
CHAMPIONSHIP GAME EXPERIENCE: Played in NFC championship game after 1985 and 1989 seasons.
RECORDS/HONORS: Named to THE SPORTING NEWS NFL All-Pro team, 1989.

| | | | — PLACE-KICKING — | | | |
Year	Team	G	XPM	XPA	FGM	FGA	Pts.
1982—L.A. Rams NFL		9	23	24	9	15	50
1983—L.A. Rams NFL		4	9	9	6	9	27
1984—L.A. Rams NFL		16	37	38	25	33	112
1985—L.A. Rams NFL		16	38	39	22	29	104
1986—L.A. Rams NFL		16	34	35	17	24	85
1987—L.A. Rams NFL		15	36	38	17	21	87
1988—L.A. Rams NFL		16	45	48	24	32	117
1989—L.A. Rams NFL		16	*51	51	23	30	120
1990—L.A. Rams NFL		16	42	43	15	24	87
Pro totals (9 years)		124	315	325	158	217	789

LAUFENBERG, BABE
QB

PERSONAL: Born December 5, 1959, at Burbank, Calif.... 6-3/214.... Full name: Brandon Hugh Laufenberg.
HIGH SCHOOL: Crespi Carmelite (Encino, Calif.).
COLLEGE: Stanford, Missouri, Los Angeles Pierce College, then Indiana (degree in business administration and marketing).
TRANSACTIONS/CAREER NOTES: Selected by Chicago Blitz in 20th round (235th pick overall) of 1983 USFL draft.... Selected by Washington Redskins in sixth round (168th pick overall) of 1983 NFL draft.... Signed by Redskins (June 17, 1983).... Active for 16 games with Redskins in 1983; did not play.... On injured reserve with rotator cuff injury (August 27, 1984-entire season).... Released by Redskins (September 2, 1985).... Signed as free agent by San Diego Chargers (September 30, 1985). ... Active for two games with Chargers in 1985; did not play.... Released by Chargers (October 15, 1985).... USFL rights traded by Arizona Outlaws to Memphis Showboats for quarterback John Conner (November 1, 1985).... Signed as free agent by Washington Redskins (November 20, 1985).... Active for five games with Redskins in 1985; did not play.... Released by Redskins (August 26, 1986).... Awarded on waivers to New Orleans Saints (August 27, 1986).... Released by Saints (September 1, 1986).... Re-signed by Saints (September 23, 1986).... Released by Saints (November 8, 1986).... Signed as free agent by Kansas City Chiefs (May 28, 1987).... Released by Chiefs (August 31, 1987).... Signed as free agent by Washington Redskins (September 16, 1987).... Active for one game with Redskins in 1987; did not play.... Released by Redskins (October 27, 1987).... Signed as free agent by San Diego Chargers (March 24, 1988).... Granted unconditional free agency (February 1, 1989).... Did not receive qualifying offer (April 15, 1989).... Signed by Dallas Cowboys (May 17, 1989).... On inactive list (September 9 and 16, 1990).... Released by Cowboys (July 30, 1990).
CHAMPIONSHIP GAME EXPERIENCE: Member of Washington Redskins for NFC championship game and Super Bowl XVIII after 1983 season; did not play.
PRO STATISTICS: Passer rating points: 1988 (59.3), 1990 (16.9). Career: 45.9.... 1988—Recovered three fumbles and fumbled twice for minus 10 yards. 1990—Recovered one fumble.

| | | | — PASSING — | | | | | | — RUSHING — | | | | — TOTAL — | | |
Year	Team	G	Att.	Cmp.	Pct.	Yds.	TD	Int.	Avg.	Att.	Yds.	Avg.	TD	TD	Pts.	F.
1986—New Orleans NFL		1	0	0		0	0	0		0	0		0	0	0	0
1988—San Diego NFL		8	144	69	47.9	778	4	5	5.40	31	120	3.9	0	0	0	2
1989—Dallas NFL		3	0	0		0	0	0		0	0		0	0	0	0
1990—Dallas NFL		4	67	24	35.8	279	1	6	4.16	2	6	3.0	0	0	0	1
Pro totals (4 years)		16	211	93	44.1	1057	5	11	5.01	33	126	3.8	0	0	0	3

DID YOU KNOW. . .

...that the New York Giants' 10-0 start in 1990 was their best ever?

LITTLE, DAVE

TE

PERSONAL: Born April 18, 1961, at Selma, Calif. . . . 6-2/230. . . . Full name: David Gene Little.
HIGH SCHOOL: Roosevelt (Fresno, Calif.).
COLLEGE: Kings River College (Calif.), then Middle Tennessee State.
TRANSACTIONS/CAREER NOTES: Signed as free agent by Memphis Showboats of USFL (January 11, 1984). . . . Released by Showboats (February 20, 1984). . . . Signed as free agent by Kansas City Chiefs (June 21, 1984). . . . On injured reserve with knee injury (November 6, 1984-remainder of season). . . . Released by Chiefs (August 19, 1985). . . . Signed as free agent by Philadelphia Eagles (September 11, 1985). . . . On injured reserve with knee injury (September 15-October 11, 1988). . . . Granted unconditional free agency (February 1, 1990). . . . Signed by Denver Broncos (March 28, 1990). . . . Traded by Broncos to Phoenix Cardinals for undisclosed draft pick (August 15, 1990). . . . On injured reserve with knee injury (November 27, 1990-remainder of season). . . . Released by Cardinals after failing physical (July 16, 1991).
PRO STATISTICS: 1985—Recovered fumble in end zone for a touchdown. 1986—Fumbled once. 1989—Returned two kickoffs for 14 yards and fumbled once for minus 14 yards.

			RECEIVING		
Year Team	G	No.	Yds.	Avg.	TD
1984— Kansas City NFL........	10	1	13	13.0	0
1985— Philadelphia NFL	15	7	82	11.7	0
1986— Philadelphia NFL	16	14	132	9.4	0
1987— Philadelphia NFL	12	1	8	8.0	0
1988— Philadelphia NFL	10	0	0		0
1989— Philadelphia NFL	16	2	8	4.0	1
1990— Phoenix NFL	11	0	0		0
Pro totals (7 years)	90	25	243	9.7	1

LOCKETT, DANNIE

LB

PERSONAL: Born July 11, 1964, at Fort Valley, Ga. . . . 6-3/255. . . . Full name: Dannie Key Lockett.
HIGH SCHOOL: Peach County (Fort Valley, Ga.).
COLLEGE: College of the Sequoias (Calif.), then Arizona.
TRANSACTIONS/CAREER NOTES: Selected by Detroit Lions in sixth round (148th pick overall) of 1987 NFL draft. . . . Signed by Lions (July 25, 1987). . . . Crossed picket line during players' strike (October 14, 1987). . . . Released by Lions (September 1, 1989). . . . Signed as free agent by San Francisco 49ers (March 20, 1990). . . . Released by 49ers (June 20, 1990). . . . Signed by WLAF (January 31, 1991). . . . Selected by London Monarchs in second round (17th linebacker) of 1991 WLAF positional draft. . . . Signed by New York Jets (June 18, 1991). . . . Released by Jets (August 6, 1991).
PLAYING EXPERIENCE: Detroit NFL, 1987 and 1988; London WLAF, 1991. . . . Games: 1987 (13), 1988 (16), 1991 (10). Total NFL: 29. Total Pro: 39.
PRO STATISTICS: NFL: 1987—Recovered one fumble. 1988—Recovered one fumble. . . . WLAF: 1991—Recovered three fumbles (including one for 65 yards and a touchdown).

LYLES, LESTER

S

PERSONAL: Born December 27, 1962, at Washington, D.C. . . . 6-3/200. . . . Full name: Lester Everett Lyles.
HIGH SCHOOL: St. Albans (Washington, D.C.).
COLLEGE: Virginia.
TRANSACTIONS/CAREER NOTES: Selected by Orlando Renegades in 1985 USFL territorial draft. . . . Selected by New York Jets in second round (40th pick overall) of 1985 NFL draft. . . . Signed by Jets (July 3, 1985). . . . On injured reserve with hip injury (August 27-November 16, 1985). . . . On injured reserve with knee injury (September 14-November 9, 1987). . . . On injured reserve with ankle injury (November 27, 1987-remainder of season). . . . Released by Jets (August 30, 1988). . . . Signed as free agent by Phoenix Cardinals (November 8, 1988). . . . Granted unconditional free agency (February 1, 1989). . . . Signed by San Diego Chargers (March 31, 1989). . . . Granted unconditional free agency (February 1, 1991).
PRO STATISTICS: 1985—Recovered one fumble for 13 yards. 1986—Recovered one fumble for 16 yards. 1989—Returned one punt for no yards, recovered one fumble and fumbled once. 1990—Returned one punt for no yards.

			INTERCEPTIONS		
Year Team	G	No.	Yds.	Avg.	TD
1985— N.Y. Jets NFL	6	0	0		0
1986— N.Y. Jets NFL	16	5	36	7.2	0
1987— N.Y. Jets NFL	4	0	0		0
1988— Phoenix NFL	6	2	0	.0	0
1989— San Diego NFL	16	2	28	14.0	0
1990— San Diego NFL	15	1	19	19.0	0
Pro totals (6 years)	63	10	83	8.3	0

MANUEL, LIONEL

WR

PERSONAL: Born April 13, 1962, at Rancho Cucamonga, Calif. . . . 5-11/180. . . . Full name: Lionel Manuel Jr.
HIGH SCHOOL: Bassett (La Puente, Calif.).
COLLEGE: Citrus College (Calif.), then Pacific.
TRANSACTIONS/CAREER NOTES: Selected by Los Angeles Express in 1984 USFL territorial draft. . . . Selected by New York Giants in seventh round (171st pick overall) of 1984 NFL draft. . . . Signed by Giants (June 4, 1984). . . . On injured reserve with pulled hamstring (November 30-December 28, 1985). . . . On injured reserve with knee injury (September 29, 1986-January 3, 1987). . . . On injured reserve with thumb injury (September 21-October 24, 1987). . . . Released by Giants (December, 1990). . . . Signed as free agent by Buffalo Bills (April 23, 1991). . . . Released by Bills (August 1, 1991).
CHAMPIONSHIP GAME EXPERIENCE: Played in NFC championship game after 1986 season. . . . Played in Super Bowl XXI after 1986 season.

PRO STATISTICS: 1984—Returned eight kickoffs for 62 yards. 1986—Returned three kickoffs for 22 yards. 1988—Recovered one fumble. 1989—Recovered one fumble.

Year	Team	G	RUSHING Att.	Yds.	Avg.	TD	RECEIVING No.	Yds.	Avg.	TD	TOTAL TD	Pts.	F.
1984—	N.Y. Giants NFL	16	3	2	.7	0	33	619	18.8	4	4	24	2
1985—	N.Y. Giants NFL	12	0	0		0	49	859	17.5	5	5	30	1
1986—	N.Y. Giants NFL	4	1	25	25.0	0	11	181	16.5	3	3	18	0
1987—	N.Y. Giants NFL	12	1	-10	-10.0	0	30	545	18.2	6	6	36	1
1988—	N.Y. Giants NFL	16	4	27	6.8	0	65	1029	15.8	4	4	24	1
1989—	N.Y. Giants NFL	16	0	0		0	33	539	16.3	1	1	6	0
1990—	N.Y. Giants NFL	14	0	0		0	11	169	15.4	0	0	0	0
	Pro totals (7 years)	90	9	44	4.9	0	232	3941	17.0	23	23	138	5

MAYES, RUEBEN
RB

PERSONAL: Born June 6, 1963, at North Battleford, Saskatchewan. . . . 5-11/200.
HIGH SCHOOL: Comprehensive (North Battleford, Saskatchewan).
COLLEGE: Washington State.
TRANSACTIONS/CAREER NOTES: Selected by Memphis Showboats in 1986 USFL territorial draft. . . . Selected by New Orleans Saints in third round (57th pick overall) of 1986 NFL draft. . . . Signed by Saints (June 20, 1986). . . . On injured reserve with Achilles' heel injury (September 5, 1989-entire season).
RECORDS/HONORS: Named THE SPORTING NEWS NFL Rookie of the Year, 1986. . . . Named to play in Pro Bowl after 1986 season; replaced due to injury by Gerald Riggs. . . . Named to play in Pro Bowl after 1987 season; replaced due to injury by Gerald Riggs.
PRO STATISTICS: 1987—Recovered one fumble.

Year	Team	G	RUSHING Att.	Yds.	Avg.	TD	RECEIVING No.	Yds.	Avg.	TD	KICKOFF RETURNS No.	Yds.	Avg.	TD	TOTAL TD	Pts.	F.
1986—	New Orleans NFL	16	286	1353	4.7	8	17	96	5.7	0	10	213	21.3	0	8	48	4
1987—	New Orleans NFL	12	243	917	3.8	5	15	68	4.5	0	0	0		0	5	30	8
1988—	New Orleans NFL	16	170	628	3.7	3	11	103	9.4	0	7	132	18.9	0	3	18	1
1990—	New Orleans NFL	15	138	510	3.7	7	12	121	10.1	0	2	39	19.5	0	7	42	1
	Pro totals (4 years)	59	837	3408	4.1	23	55	388	7.1	0	19	384	20.2	0	23	138	14

McDONALD, MIKE
LB

PERSONAL: Born June 22, 1958, at North Hollywood, Calif. . . . 6-1/235.
HIGH SCHOOL: John Burroughs (Burbank, Calif.).
COLLEGE: Southern California.
TRANSACTIONS/CAREER NOTES: Signed as free agent by Los Angeles Rams (December 21, 1983). . . . Released by Rams (August 27, 1984). . . . Re-signed by Rams (August 28, 1984). . . . Released by Rams (August 17, 1986). . . . Re-signed by Rams (September 24, 1986). . . . Released by Rams (February 1, 1987). . . . Signed as free agent by Kansas City Chiefs (August 28, 1987). . . . Released by Chiefs (August 31, 1987). . . . Signed as free-agent replacement player by Los Angeles Rams (October 15, 1987). . . . Granted unconditional free agency (February 1, 1991).
PLAYING EXPERIENCE: Los Angeles Rams NFL, 1984 and 1986-1990. . . . Games: 1984 (16), 1986 (13), 1987 (10), 1988 (16), 1989 (16), 1990 (16). Total: 87.
CHAMPIONSHIP GAME EXPERIENCE: Played in NFC championship game after 1989 season.
PRO STATISTICS: 1988—Returned three kickoffs for 34 yards and fumbled once. 1989—Returned two kickoffs for 22 yards. 1990—Returned one kickoff for 15 yards.

McKINNON, DENNIS
WR

PERSONAL: Born August 22, 1961, at Quitman, Ga. . . . 6-1/177. . . . Full name: Dennis Lewis McKinnon.
HIGH SCHOOL: South Miami Senior (Miami).
COLLEGE: Florida State (bachelor of arts degree in criminology, 1983).
TRANSACTIONS/CAREER NOTES: Signed as free agent by Chicago Bears (May 4, 1983). . . . On reserve/physically unable to perform list with knee injury (August 18, 1986-entire season). . . . Granted unconditional free agency (February 1, 1990). . . . Signed by Dallas Cowboys (March 3, 1990). . . . Released by Cowboys (November 14, 1990). . . . Signed by Miami Dolphins (November 16, 1990). . . . Released by Dolphins (November 19, 1990). . . . Re-signed by Dolphins (December 12, 1990). . . . Released by Dolphins (December 22, 1990). . . . Active for one game with Dolphins in 1990; did not play.
CHAMPIONSHIP GAME EXPERIENCE: Played in NFC championship game after 1984, 1985 and 1988 seasons. . . . Played in Super Bowl XX after 1985 season.
PRO STATISTICS: 1983—Recovered one fumble. 1984—Rushed twice for 12 yards. 1985—Rushed once for no yards. 1987—Recovered three fumbles. 1988—Rushed three times for 25 yards and a touchdown and recovered one fumble. 1989—Rushed three times for five yards and recovered one fumble. 1990—Rushed once for minus eight yards.

Year	Team	G	RECEIVING No.	Yds.	Avg.	TD	PUNT RETURNS No.	Yds.	Avg.	TD	KICKOFF RETURNS No.	Yds.	Avg.	TD	TOTAL TD	Pts.	F.
1983—	Chicago NFL	16	20	326	16.3	4	34	316	9.3	*1	2	42	21.0	0	5	30	2
1984—	Chicago NFL	12	29	431	14.9	3	5	62	12.4	0	0	0		0	3	18	1
1985—	Chicago NFL	14	31	555	17.9	7	4	44	11.0	0	1	16	16.0	0	7	42	1
1987—	Chicago NFL	12	27	406	15.0	1	40	405	10.1	*2	0	0		0	3	18	6
1988—	Chicago NFL	15	45	704	15.6	3	34	277	8.2	0	0	0		0	4	24	3
1989—	Chicago NFL	16	28	418	14.9	3	10	67	6.7	0	0	0		0	3	18	3
1990—	Dal.(9)-Mia.(0) NFL	9	14	172	12.3	1	2	20	10.0	0	0	0		0	1	6	1
	Pro totals (7 years)	94	194	3012	15.5	22	129	1191	9.2	3	3	58	19.3	0	26	156	17

McSWAIN, ROD
CB

PERSONAL: Born January 28, 1962, at Caroleen, N.C. . . . 6-1/198. . . . Full name: Rodney Mc-Swain. . . . Brother of Chuck McSwain, running back with Dallas Cowboys and New England Patriots, 1983, 1984 and 1987.
HIGH SCHOOL: Chase (Forest City, N.C.).
COLLEGE: Clemson.
TRANSACTIONS/CAREER NOTES: Selected by Washington Federals in 1984 USFL territorial draft. . . . Selected by Atlanta Falcons in third round (63rd pick overall) of 1984 NFL draft. . . . Signed by Falcons (May 16, 1984). . . . Traded by Falcons to New England Patriots for eighth-round pick in 1985 draft (August 27, 1984). . . . On injured reserve with shoulder separation (September 2-October 3, 1986). . . . On injured reserve with back and hamstring injuries (September 29-November 10, 1989). . . . On inactive list (September 9 and 16, 1990). . . . Granted unconditional free agency (February 1, 1991). . . . Rights relinquished by Patriots (April 26, 1991).
CHAMPIONSHIP GAME EXPERIENCE: Played in AFC championship game after 1985 season. . . . Played in Super Bowl XX after 1985 season.
PRO STATISTICS: 1984—Recovered one fumble. 1986—Returned blocked punt 31 yards for a touchdown. 1990—Returned one kickoff for no yards and recovered one fumble.

| | | | —— INTERCEPTIONS—— | | |
Year Team	G	No.	Yds.	Avg.	TD
1984— New England NFL......	15	0	0		0
1985— New England NFL......	16	1	0	.0	0
1986— New England NFL......	9	1	3	3.0	0
1987— New England NFL......	12	1	17	17.0	0
1988— New England NFL......	16	2	51	25.5	0
1989— New England NFL......	9	1	18	18.0	0
1990— New England NFL......	13	0	0		0
Pro totals (7 years)........	90	6	89	14.8	0

MEISNER, GREG
DE

PERSONAL: Born April 23, 1959, at New Kensington, Pa. . . . 6-3/271. . . . Full name: Gregory Paul Meisner.
HIGH SCHOOL: Valley (New Kensington, Pa.).
COLLEGE: Pittsburgh (bachelor of arts degree in psychology, 1981).
TRANSACTIONS/CAREER NOTES: Selected by Los Angeles Rams in third round (63rd pick overall) of 1981 NFL draft. . . . On non-football injury list with head injuries (August 18-October 24, 1981). . . . On injured reserve with knee injury (December 16, 1982-remainder of season). . . . Granted free agency (February 1, 1985). . . . Re-signed by Rams (September 18, 1985). . . . Granted roster exemption (September 18-September 20, 1985). . . . Crossed picket line during players' strike (October 2, 1987). . . . Granted unconditional free agency (February 1, 1989). . . . Signed by Kansas City Chiefs (March 14, 1989). . . . Granted unconditional free agency (February 1, 1991).
PLAYING EXPERIENCE: Los Angeles Rams NFL, 1981-1988; Kansas City NFL, 1989 and 1990. . . . Games: 1981 (9), 1982 (6), 1983 (16), 1984 (16), 1985 (14), 1986 (15), 1987 (15), 1988 (12), 1989 (12), 1990 (16). Total: 131.
CHAMPIONSHIP GAME EXPERIENCE: Played in NFC championship game after 1985 season.
PRO STATISTICS: 1981—Returned one kickoff for 17 yards. 1984—Recovered one fumble. 1986—Recovered one fumble for 15 yards. 1988—Intercepted one pass for 20 yards.

OSBORNE, ELDONTA
LB

PERSONAL: Born August 12, 1967. . . . 6-0/215. . . . Full name: Eldonta R. Osborne.
HIGH SCHOOL: Jonesboro-Hodge (Jonesboro, La.).
COLLEGE: Louisiana Tech (degree in business management).
TRANSACTIONS/CAREER NOTES: Signed as free agent by Phoenix Cardinals (April 30, 1990). . . . On injured reserve with back injury (December 5, 1990-remainder of season). . . . Released by Cardinals after failing physical (July 16, 1991).
PLAYING EXPERIENCE: Phoenix NFL, 1990. . . . Games: 1990 (12).

PALMER, PAUL
RB

PERSONAL: Born October 14, 1964, at Bethesda, Md. . . . 5-9/187. . . . Full name: Paul Woodrow Palmer.
HIGH SCHOOL: Winston Churchill (Potomac, Md.).
COLLEGE: Temple.
TRANSACTIONS/CAREER NOTES: Selected by Kansas City Chiefs in first round (19th pick overall) of 1987 NFL draft. . . . Signed by Chiefs (July 17, 1987). . . . On suspended list (November 27-November 30, 1988). . . . Released by Chiefs (September 4, 1989). . . . Awarded on waivers to Detroit Lions (September 5, 1989). . . . Traded by Lions to Dallas Cowboys for eighth-round pick in 1990 NFL draft (October 17, 1989). . . . Granted unconditional free agency (February 1, 1990). . . . Signed by Cincinnati Bengals (March 30, 1990). . . . Released by Bengals (preseason, 1990). . . . Signed by WLAF (January 31, 1991). . . . Selected by Barcelona Dragons in first round (third running back) of 1991 WLAF positional draft. . . . Signed by Philadelphia Eagles (June 27, 1991). . . . Released by Eagles (August 5, 1991).
RECORDS/HONORS: Tied NFL record for most kickoff returns, game (9), against Seattle Seahawks (September 20, 1987). . . . Named as running back on THE SPORTING NEWS college All-America team, 1986.
PRO STATISTICS: 1987—Attempted one pass with no completions. 1988—Recovered one fumble.

| | | —— RUSHING —— | | | | —— RECEIVING —— | | | | – KICKOFF RETURNS – | | | | —— TOTAL —— | | |
Year Team	G	Att.	Yds.	Avg.	TD	No.	Yds.	Avg.	TD	No.	Yds.	Avg.	TD	TD	Pts.	F.
1987— Kansas City NFL....	12	24	155	6.5	0	4	27	6.8	0	*38	*923	24.3	*2	2	12	2
1988— Kansas City NFL....	15	134	452	3.4	2	53	611	11.5	4	23	364	15.8	0	6	36	7
1989— Det.(5)-Dal.(9) NFL .	14	112	446	4.0	2	17	93	5.5	0	11	255	23.2	0	2	12	3
1991— Barcelona WLAF....	5	93	350	3.8	2	7	102	14.6	0	8	151	18.9	0	2	12	—
NFL totals (3 years)......	41	270	1053	3.9	4	74	731	9.9	4	72	1542	21.4	2	10	60	12
WLAF totals (1 year)......	5	93	350	3.8	2	7	102	14.6	0	8	151	18.9	0	2	12	—
Pro totals (4 years).......	46	363	1403	3.9	6	81	833	10.3	4	80	1693	21.2	2	12	72	12

PHILLIPS, KIM
DB

PERSONAL: Born October 28, 1966, at New Boston, Tex. . . . 5-10/190. . . . Full name: Kim Darnell Phillips.
HIGH SCHOOL: New Boston (Tex.).
COLLEGE: North Texas.
TRANSACTIONS/CAREER NOTES: Selected by New Orleans Saints in third round (79th pick overall) of 1989 NFL draft. . . . Signed by Saints (July 30, 1989). . . . On injured reserve with groin injury (December 15, 1989-remainder of season). . . . Released by Saints (August 28, 1990). . . . Signed by Buffalo Bills (September 26, 1990). . . . On inactive list (October 7, 1990). . . . Released by Bills (October 31, 1990). . . . Signed by Tampa Bay Buccaneers (June 3, 1991). . . . Released by Buccaneers (August 12, 1991).
PLAYING EXPERIENCE: New Orleans NFL, 1989; Buffalo NFL, 1990. . . . Games: 1989 (5), 1990 (1). Total: 6.
PRO STATISTICS: 1989—Returned one kickoff for 24 yards.

PIKE, CHRIS
DL

PERSONAL: Born January 13, 1964, at Washington, D.C. . . . 6-8/290. . . . Full name: Chris Holtz Pike.
HIGH SCHOOL: Calvin Coolidge (Washington, D.C.).
COLLEGE: North Carolina, then Tulsa.
TRANSACTIONS/CAREER NOTES: Selected by Philadelphia Eagles in sixth round (158th pick overall) of 1987 NFL draft. . . . On reserve/unsigned free agent list (August 31, 1987-entire season). . . . Rights traded by Eagles to Cleveland Browns for cornerback D.D. Hoggard, sixth-round pick in 1988 NFL draft and conditional pick in 1989 NFL draft (March 25, 1988). . . . Signed by Browns (March 25, 1988). . . . On injured reserve with knee injury (August 23, 1988-entire season). . . . On inactive list (December 9 and 16, 1990). . . . On injured reserve with knee injury (December 19, 1990-remainder of season). . . . Granted unconditional free agency (February 1, 1991). . . . Signed by San Diego Chargers (April 1, 1991). . . . Released by Chargers (April 25, 1991).
PLAYING EXPERIENCE: Cleveland NFL, 1989 and 1990. . . . Games: 1989 (12), 1990 (12). Total: 24.
CHAMPIONSHIP GAME EXPERIENCE: Played in AFC championship game after 1989 season.
PRO STATISTICS: 1990—Recovered one fumble.

PORTER, KERRY
RB

PERSONAL: Born September 23, 1964, at Vicenza, Italy. . . . 6-2/220.
HIGH SCHOOL: Great Falls (Mont.).
COLLEGE: Washington State.
TRANSACTIONS/CAREER NOTES: Selected by Buffalo Bills in seventh round (171st pick overall) of 1987 NFL draft. . . . Signed by Bills (July 23, 1987). . . . On injured reserve with shoulder injury (September 7-October 23, 1987). . . . Released by Bills (August 30, 1988). . . . Signed as free agent by Los Angeles Raiders (May 10, 1989). . . . Released by Raiders (September 3, 1990). . . . Signed by Denver Broncos (September 26, 1990). . . . Granted unconditional free agency (February 1, 1991). . . . Signed by Houston Oilers for 1991. . . . Left camp voluntarily (July 22, 1991).
PRO STATISTICS: 1989—Recovered one fumble.

		RUSHING				RECEIVING				TOTAL	
Year Team	G	Att.	Yds.	Avg.	TD	No.	Yds.	Avg.	TD	TD	Pts.	F.
1987—Buffalo NFL	6	2	0	.0	0	0	0		0	0	0	0
1989—L.A. Raiders NFL	16	13	54	4.2	0	0	0		0	0	0	0
1990—Denver NFL	13	1	3	3.0	0	4	44	11.0	0	0	0	0
Pro totals (3 years)	35	16	57	3.6	0	4	44	11.0	0	0	0	0

RICE, RODNEY
DB

PERSONAL: Born June 18, 1966, at Albany, Ga. . . . 5-8/180. . . . Full name: Rodney Donadrain Rice.
HIGH SCHOOL: Atwater (Calif.).
COLLEGE: Merced College (Calif.), then Brigham Young (degrees in sociology and psychology, 1989).
TRANSACTIONS/CAREER NOTES: Selected by New England Patriots in eighth round (210th pick overall) of 1989 NFL draft. . . . Signed by Patriots (July 22, 1989). . . . On injured reserve with hamstring injury (November 15, 1989-remainder of season). . . . Granted unconditional free agency (February 1, 1990). . . . Signed by Tampa Bay Buccaneers (March 20, 1990). . . . Released by Buccaneers (August 12, 1991).
PRO STATISTICS: 1989—Recovered one fumble.

		INTERCEPTIONS				KICKOFF RETURNS				TOTAL	
Year Team	G	No.	Yds.	Avg.	TD	No.	Yds.	Avg.	TD	TD	Pts.	F.
1989—New England NFL	10	0	0		0	11	242	22.0	0	0	0	0
1990—Tampa Bay NFL	16	2	7	3.5	0	0	0		0	0	0	0
Pro totals (2 years)	26	2	7	3.5	0	11	242	22.0	0	0	0	0

SMITH, DON
RB

PERSONAL: Born October 30, 1963, at Hamilton, Miss. . . . 5-11/200. . . . Full name: Donald Michael Smith.
HIGH SCHOOL: Hamilton (Miss.).
COLLEGE: Mississippi State.
TRANSACTIONS/CAREER NOTES: Selected by Tampa Bay Buccaneers in second round (51st pick overall) of 1987 NFL draft. . . . Signed by Buccaneers (July 18, 1987). . . . On injured reserve with leg injury (September 8-November 12, 1987). . . . Transferred to non-football injury list with back injury (November 13, 1987-remainder of season). . . . On injured reserve with knee injury (August 22-October 14, 1988). . . . On injured reserve with fractured fibula (November 22, 1989-remainder of season). . . . Granted unconditional free agency (February 1, 1990). . . . Signed by Buffalo Bills (March 29, 1990). . . . Granted unconditional free agency (February 1, 1991). . . . Signed by Miami Dolphins (April 1, 1991). . . . Released by Dolphins (July 11, 1991).

CHAMPIONSHIP GAME EXPERIENCE: Played in AFC championship game after 1990 season. . . . Played in Super Bowl XXV after 1990 season.

PRO STATISTICS: 1990—Attempted one pass with no completions.

Year	Team	G	Att.	Yds.	Avg.	TD	No.	Yds.	Avg.	TD	No.	Yds.	Avg.	TD	TD	Pts.	F.
				RUSHING				RECEIVING				KICKOFF RETURNS				TOTAL	
1988—	Tampa Bay NFL.....	10	13	46	3.5	1	12	138	11.5	0	9	188	20.9	0	1	6	0
1989—	Tampa Bay NFL.....	11	7	37	5.3	0	7	110	15.7	0	0	0			0	0	1
1990—	Buffalo NFL............	16	20	82	4.1	2	21	225	10.7	0	32	643	20.1	0	2	12	1
	Pro totals (3 years).......	37	40	165	4.1	3	40	473	11.8	0	41	831	20.3	0	3	18	2

SMITH, J.T.
WR

PERSONAL: Born October 29, 1955, at Leonard, Tex. . . . 6-2/185. . . . Full name: John Thomas Smith.
HIGH SCHOOL: Big Spring (Leonard, Tex.).
COLLEGE: North Texas State.
TRANSACTIONS/CAREER NOTES: Signed as free agent by Washington Redskins (May, 1978). . . . Released by Redskins (September 21, 1978). . . . Signed as free agent by Kansas City Chiefs (November 7, 1978). . . . On inactive list (September 19, 1982). . . . On injured reserve with knee injury (August 30-October 14, 1983). . . . On injured reserve with separated shoulder (December 10, 1984-remainder of season). . . . Released by Chiefs (August 26, 1985). . . . Signed as free agent by St. Louis Cardinals (September 17, 1985). . . . Crossed picket line during players' strike (October 2, 1987). . . . Franchise transferred to Phoenix (March 15, 1988). . . . On injured reserve with fractured fibula and torn ankle ligament (November 10, 1989-remainder of season). . . . Released by Phoenix Cardinals (April 15, 1991).
RECORDS/HONORS: Played in Pro Bowl after 1980 and 1988 seasons. . . . Named as punt returner on THE SPORTING NEWS NFL All-Pro team, 1980. . . . Named to THE SPORTING NEWS NFL All-Pro team, 1987.
PRO STATISTICS: 1979—Recovered one fumble for one yard. 1980—Recovered two fumbles. 1981—Recovered one fumble for 19 yards. 1985—Rushed three times for 36 yards. 1986—Recovered three fumbles. 1988—Rushed once for 15 yards and recovered one fumble. 1989—Rushed twice for 21 yards.

Year	Team	G	No.	Yds.	Avg.	TD	No.	Yds.	Avg.	TD	No.	Yds.	Avg.	TD	TD	Pts.	F.
				RECEIVING				PUNT RETURNS				KICKOFF RETURNS				TOTAL	
1978—	Was.(6)-K.C.(6) NFL	12	0	0		0	4	33	8.3	0	1	18	18.0	0	0	0	
1979—	Kansas City NFL.	16	33	444	13.5	3	58	*612	10.6	2	0	0		0	5	30	3
1980—	Kansas City NFL.	16	46	655	14.2	2	40	*581	*14.5	*2	0	0		0	4	24	1
1981—	Kansas City NFL.	16	63	852	13.5	2	50	528	10.6	0	0	0		0	2	12	2
1982—	Kansas City NFL.	5	10	168	16.8	1	3	26	8.7	0	0	0		0	1	6	0
1983—	Kansas City NFL.	9	7	85	12.1	0	26	210	8.1	0	1	5	5.0	0	0	0	0
1984—	Kansas City NFL.	15	8	69	8.6	0	39	332	8.5	0	19	391	20.6	0	0	0	1
1985—	St. Louis NFL	14	43	581	13.5	1	26	283	10.9	0	4	59	14.8	0	1	6	3
1986—	St. Louis NFL	16	80	1014	12.7	6	1	6	6.0	0	0	0		0	6	36	1
1987—	St. Louis NFL	15	*91	*1117	12.3	8	0	0		0	0	0		0	8	48	2
1988—	Phoenix NFL	16	83	986	11.9	5	17	119	7.0	0	0	0		0	5	30	4
1989—	Phoenix NFL	9	62	778	12.6	5	0	0		0	0	0		0	5	30	0
1990—	Phoenix NFL	13	18	225	12.5	2	3	34	11.3	0	0	0		0	2	12	0
	Pro totals (13 years) ..	172	544	6974	12.8	35	267	2764	10.4	4	25	473	18.9	0	39	234	17

TATE, LARS
RB

PERSONAL: Born February 2, 1966, at Indianapolis. . . . 6-2/215. . . . Full name: Lars Jamel Tate.
HIGH SCHOOL: North Central (Indianapolis).
COLLEGE: Georgia.
TRANSACTIONS/CAREER NOTES: Selected by Tampa Bay Buccaneers in second round (53rd pick overall) of 1988 NFL draft. . . . Signed by Buccaneers (July 15, 1988). . . . Released by Buccaneers (September 2, 1990). . . . Signed by Chicago Bears (September 26, 1990). . . . On injured reserve with neck injury (November 2, 1990-remainder of season). . . . Granted unconditional free agency (February 1, 1991).
PRO STATISTICS: 1990—Returned one kickoff for no yards.

Year	Team	G	Att.	Yds.	Avg.	TD	No.	Yds.	Avg.	TD	TD	Pts.	F.
				RUSHING				RECEIVING				TOTAL	
1988—	Tampa Bay NFL...............................	15	122	467	3.8	7	5	23	4.6	1	8	48	2
1989—	Tampa Bay NFL...............................	15	167	589	3.5	8	11	75	6.8	1	9	54	2
1990—	Chicago NFL	3	3	5	1.7	0	0	0		0	0	0	0
	Pro totals (3 years)	33	292	1061	3.6	15	16	98	6.1	2	17	102	4

WILLIAMS, ED
LB

PERSONAL: Born September 8, 1961, at Odessa, Tex. . . . 6-4/244. . . . Full name: Edward Eugene Williams.
HIGH SCHOOL: Ector (Odessa, Tex.).
COLLEGE: Texas.
TRANSACTIONS/CAREER NOTES: Selected by San Antonio Gunslingers in 1984 USFL territorial draft. . . . Selected by New England Patriots in second round (43rd pick overall) of 1984 NFL draft. . . . Signed by Patriots (July 13, 1984). . . . On injured reserve with groin injury (November 14, 1986-remainder of season). . . . On injured reserve with knee injury (August 15, 1988-entire season). . . . Granted unconditional free agency (February 1, 1989). . . . Did not receive qualifying offer (April 15, 1989). . . . Re-signed by Patriots (April 21, 1989). . . . On physically unable to perform list with knee injury (July 24, 1989-entire season). . . . Released by Patriots (September 3, 1990). . . . Re-signed by Patriots (September 4, 1990). . . . Granted unconditional free agency (February 1, 1991).
PLAYING EXPERIENCE: New England NFL, 1984-1987 and 1990. . . . Games: 1984 (14), 1985 (13), 1986 (8), 1987 (12), 1990 (15). Total: 62.

CHAMPIONSHIP GAME EXPERIENCE: Played in AFC championship game after 1985 season. . . . Played in Super Bowl XX after 1985 season.
PRO STATISTICS: 1987—Intercepted one pass for 51 yards and recovered two fumbles for eight yards. 1990—Recovered one fumble.

WILSON, MIKE
WR

PERSONAL: Born December 19, 1958, at Los Angeles. . . . 6-3/215. . . . Full name: Michael Ruben Wilson.
HIGH SCHOOL: Carson (Calif.).
COLLEGE: Washington State.
TRANSACTIONS/CAREER NOTES: Selected by Dallas Cowboys in ninth round (246th pick overall) of 1981 NFL draft. . . . Released by Cowboys (August 24, 1981). . . . Signed as free agent by San Francisco 49ers (August 27, 1981). . . . On injured reserve with broken finger (September 9-November 20, 1982). . . . On injured reserve with neck injury (November 21, 1986-remainder of season). . . . Granted unconditional free agency (February 1, 1991).
CHAMPIONSHIP GAME EXPERIENCE: Played in NFC championship game after 1981, 1983, 1984 and 1988-1990 seasons. . . . Played in Super Bowl XVI after 1981 season, Super Bowl XIX after 1984 season, Super Bowl XXIII after 1988 season and Super Bowl XXIV after 1989 season.
PRO STATISTICS: 1981—Returned four kickoffs for 67 yards and recovered one fumble. 1983—Fumbled once. 1984—Returned one kickoff for 14 yards. 1986—Returned one kickoff for 10 yards and recovered one fumble. 1988—Returned one kickoff for two yards. 1989—Recovered one fumble and fumbled twice. 1990—Returned one punt for one yard and recovered one fumble.

| | | | —— RECEIVING —— | | |
Year	Team	G	No.	Yds.	Avg.	TD
1981—	San Francisco NFL....	16	9	125	13.9	1
1982—	San Francisco NFL....	6	6	80	13.3	1
1983—	San Francisco NFL....	15	30	433	14.4	0
1984—	San Francisco NFL....	13	17	245	14.4	1
1985—	San Francisco NFL....	16	10	165	16.5	2
1986—	San Francisco NFL....	11	9	104	11.6	1
1987—	San Francisco NFL....	11	29	450	15.5	5
1988—	San Francisco NFL....	16	33	405	12.3	3
1989—	San Francisco NFL....	16	9	103	11.4	1
1990—	San Francisco NFL....	16	7	89	12.7	0
Pro totals (10 years)		**136**	**159**	**2199**	**13.8**	**15**

WINTER, BLAISE
DE

PERSONAL: Born January 31, 1962, at Blauvelt, N.Y.... 6-4/271.
HIGH SCHOOL: Tappan Zee (Orangeburg, N.Y.).
COLLEGE: Syracuse.
TRANSACTIONS/CAREER NOTES: Selected by New Jersey Generals in 1984 USFL territorial draft. . . . Selected by Indianapolis Colts in second round (35th pick overall) of 1984 NFL draft. . . . Signed by Colts (July 27, 1984). . . . On injured reserve with shoulder injury (August 27, 1985-entire season). . . . On injured reserve with knee injury (August 18-October 14, 1986). . . . Released by Colts (October 15, 1986). . . . Signed as free agent by San Diego Chargers (November 24, 1986). . . . Released by Chargers (August 29, 1987). . . . Re-signed as replacement player by Chargers (September 28, 1987). . . . On injured reserve with hand injury (October 27, 1987-remainder of season). . . . Traded by Chargers to Green Bay Packers for past considerations (April 28, 1988). . . . Released by Packers (August 28, 1990). . . . Re-signed by Packers (September 5, 1990). . . . On injured reserve with knee injury (December 14, 1990-remainder of season). . . . Granted unconditional free agency (February 1, 1991). . . . Rights relinquished by Packers (July 19, 1991).
PLAYING EXPERIENCE: Indianapolis NFL, 1984; San Diego NFL, 1986 and 1987; Green Bay NFL, 1988-1990. . . . Games: 1984 (16), 1986 (4), 1987 (3), 1988 (16), 1989 (16), 1990 (13). Total: 68.
PRO STATISTICS: 1984—Recovered one fumble. 1988—Returned one kickoff for seven yards and recovered two fumbles.

WRIGHT, ERIC
CB

PERSONAL: Born April 18, 1959, at St. Louis.... 6-1/185.
HIGH SCHOOL: Assumption (East St. Louis, Ill.).
COLLEGE: Missouri.
TRANSACTIONS/CAREER NOTES: Selected by San Francisco 49ers in second round (40th pick overall) of 1981 NFL draft. . . . On inactive list (September 19, 1982). . . . On injured reserve with pulled abdomen (December 24, 1985-remainder of 1985 season playoffs). . . . On injured reserve with groin injury (September 3-October 3, 1986). . . . On injured reserve with groin injury (October 29, 1986-remainder of season). . . . Crossed picket line during players' strike (October 7, 1987). . . . On injured reserve with groin injury (October 8, 1987-remainder of season). . . . Granted unconditional free agency (February 1, 1990). . . . Rights relinquished (April 13, 1990). . . . Re-signed by 49ers (May 9, 1990). . . . On inactive list reserve (October 7, 1990). . . . On injured reserve with knee injury (November 23, 1990-remainder of 1990 season playoffs). . . . Granted unconditional free agency (February 1, 1991).
CHAMPIONSHIP GAME EXPERIENCE: Played in NFC championship game after 1981, 1983, 1984 and 1989 seasons. . . . Member of

---

DID YOU KNOW. . .

. . .that when the Cleveland Browns drafted UCLA safety Eric Turner second overall in 1991, it was the highest a defensive back had been drafted since the Pittsburgh Steelers took Colorado State's Gary Glick No. 1 overall in 1956?

San Francisco 49ers for NFC championship game after 1988 season; did not play. . . . Played in Super Bowl XVI after 1981 season, Super Bowl XIX after 1984 season, Super Bowl XXIII after 1988 season and Super Bowl XXIV after 1989 season.
RECORDS/HONORS: Played in Pro Bowl after 1984 season. . . . Named to play in Pro Bowl after 1985 season; replaced due to injury by Gary Green. . . . Named to THE SPORTING NEWS NFL All-Pro team, 1985.
PRO STATISTICS: 1981—Recovered two fumbles. 1983—Recovered one fumble. 1988—Recovered one fumble. 1990—Recovered one fumble.

Year Team	G	No.	Yds.	Avg.	TD
			INTERCEPTIONS		
1981—San Francisco NFL....	16	3	26	8.7	0
1982—San Francisco NFL....	7	1	31	31.0	0
1983—San Francisco NFL....	16	7	*164	23.4	*2
1984—San Francisco NFL....	15	2	0	.0	0
1985—San Francisco NFL....	16	1	0	.0	0
1986—San Francisco NFL....	2	0	0		0
1987—San Francisco NFL....	2	0	0		0
1988—San Francisco NFL....	15	2	-2	-1.0	0
1989—San Francisco NFL....	11	2	37	18.5	0
1990—San Francisco NFL....	9	0	0		0
Pro totals (10 years)	109	18	256	14.2	2

HEAD COACHES

BELICHICK, BILL
BROWNS

PERSONAL: Born April 16, 1952, at Nashville, Tenn. . . . Full name: William Stephen Belichick. . . . Son of Steve Belichick, fullback with Detroit Lions (1941); head coach at Hiram College, 0. (1946-1949); assistant coach, Vanderbilt (1949-1953); assistant coach, North Carolina (1953-1956); assistant coach, Navy (1956-1983); administrative assistant, Navy (1983-1989).
HIGH SCHOOL: Annapolis (Md.) and Phillips Academy (Andover, Mass.).
COLLEGE: Wesleyan University (bachelor of arts degree in economics, 1975).
BACKGROUND: Special assistant, Baltimore Colts NFL (1975). . . . assistant coach, Detroit Lions NFL (1976 and 1977). . . . assistant coach, Denver Broncos NFL (1978). . . . assistant coach, New York Giants NFL (1979-1991).

BUGEL, JOE
CARDINALS

PERSONAL: Born March 10, 1940, at Pittsburgh. . . . Full name: Joseph John Bugel.
HIGH SCHOOL: Munholl (Pittsburgh).
COLLEGE: Western Kentucky (degree in physical education, 1963; master's degree in guidance and counseling, 1964).
BACKGROUND: Assistant coach, Western Kentucky (1964-1968). . . . assistant coach, Navy (1969-1972). . . . assistant coach, Iowa State (1973). . . . assistant coach, Ohio State (1974). . . . assistant coach, Detroit Lions NFL (1975 and 1976). . . . assistant coach, Houston Oilers NFL (1977-1980). . . . assistant coach, Washington Redskins NFL (1981-1989).

HEAD COACHING RECORD

					REGULAR SEASON	POST-SEASON	
	W	L	T	Pct.	Finish	W	L
1990 — Phoenix NFL	5	11	0	.313	5th/NFC Eastern Division	—	—
Pro totals (1 year)	5	11	0	.313			

BURNS, JERRY
VIKINGS

PERSONAL: Born January 24, 1927, at Detroit. . . . Full Name: Jerome Monahan Burns.
HIGH SCHOOL: Catholic Central (Detroit).
COLLEGE: Michigan (degree in physical education).
BACKGROUND: Assistant coach, Hawaii (1951). . . . assistant coach, Whittier College (1952). . . . head coach, St. Mary of Redford High School, Detroit (1953). . . . assistant coach, Iowa (1954-1960). . . . assistant coach, Green Bay Packers NFL (1966 and 1967). . . . assistant coach, Minnesota Vikings NFL (1968-1985).

HEAD COACHING RECORD

					REGULAR SEASON	POST-SEASON	
	W	L	T	Pct.	Finish	W	L
1961 — Iowa	5	4	0	.556	T7th/Big Ten Conference	—	—
1962 — Iowa	4	5	0	.444	T5th/Big Ten Conference	—	—
1963 — Iowa	3	3	2	.500	8th/Big Ten Conference	—	—
1964 — Iowa	3	6	0	.333	T9th/Big Ten Conference	—	—
1965 — Iowa	1	9	0	.100	10th/Big Ten Conference	—	—
1986 — Minnesota NFL	9	7	0	.563	2nd/NFC Central Division	—	—
1987 — Minnesota NFL	8	7	0	.533	2nd/NFC Central Division	2	1
1988 — Minnesota NFL	11	5	0	.688	2nd/NFC Central Division	1	1
1989 — Minnesota NFL	10	6	0	.625	T1st/NFC Central Division	0	1
1990 — Minnesota NFL	6	10	0	.375	T2nd/NFC Central Division	—	—
College totals (5 years)	16	27	2	.378			
Pro totals (5 years)	44	35	0	.557	**Pro totals (3 years)**	3	3

NOTES:
1987 — Won wild-card playoff game from New Orleans, 44-10; won conference playoff game from San Francisco, 36-24; lost NFC championship game to Washington, 17-10.
1988 — Won wild-card playoff game from Los Angeles Rams, 28-17; lost conference playoff game to San Francisco, 34-9.
1989 — Lost conference playoff game to San Francisco, 41-13.

COSLET, BRUCE
JETS

PERSONAL: Born August 5, 1946, at Oakdale, Calif. . . . Full name: Bruce Noel Coslet. . . . Played tight end.
HIGH SCHOOL: Joint Union (Oakdale, Calif.).
COLLEGE: Pacific (bachelor of arts degree in history and psychology).
TRANSACTIONS/CAREER NOTES: Signed as free agent by Cincinnati Bengals (1969).
PRO STATISTICS: 1971—Fumbled three times. 1973—Returned one kickoff for no yards and recovered one fumble. 1975—Rushed once for one yard and recovered two fumbles for two yards. 1976—Recovered two fumbles.

				RECEIVING		
Year Team	G	No.	Yds.	Avg.	TD	
1969 — Cincinnati AFL	8	1	39	39.0	1	
1970 — Cincinnati NFL	14	8	97	12.1	1	
1971 — Cincinnati NFL	14	21	356	17.0	4	

Year Team	G	No.	RECEIVING Yds.	Avg.	TD
1972— Cincinnati NFL	10	5	48	9.6	1
1973— Cincinnati NFL	13	9	123	13.7	0
1974— Cincinnati NFL	14	2	24	12.0	0
1975— Cincinnati NFL	14	10	117	11.7	0
1976— Cincinnati NFL	14	5	73	14.6	2
AFL totals (1 year)	8	1	39	39.0	1
NFL totals (7 years)	93	60	838	14.0	8
Pro totals (8 years)	101	61	877	14.4	9

BACKGROUND: Assistant coach, San Francisco 49ers NFL (1980).... assistant coach, Cincinnati Bengals NFL (1981- 1989).

HEAD COACHING RECORD

	W	L	T	Pct.	REGULAR SEASON Finish	POST- SEASON W	L
1990— New York Jets NFL	6	10	0	.375	4th/ AFC Eastern Division	—	—
Pro totals (1 year)	6	10	0	.375			

DITKA, MIKE

BEARS

PERSONAL: Born October 18, 1939, at Carnegie, Pa.... Full name: Michael Keller Ditka.... Played tight end.
HIGH SCHOOL: Aliquippa (Pa.).
COLLEGE: Pittsburgh.
TRANSACTIONS/CAREER NOTES: Selected by Chicago Bears in first round of 1961 NFL draft.... Traded by Bears to Philadelphia Eagles for quarterback Jack Concannon and a pick in 1968 draft (April 26, 1967).... Traded by Eagles to Dallas Cowboys for receiver Dave McDaniels (January 18, 1969).
CHAMPIONSHIP GAME EXPERIENCE: Played in NFL championship game after 1963 season.... Played in NFC championship game after 1970- 1972 seasons.... Played in Super Bowl V after 1970 season and Super Bowl VI after 1971 season.
RECORDS/HONORS: Named as end on THE SPORTING NEWS college All-America team, 1960.... Named THE SPORTING NEWS NFL Rookie of the Year, 1961.... Named to THE SPORTING NEWS NFL Western Conference All-Star team, 1961-1965.... Played in Pro Bowl after 1961- 1965 seasons.... Inducted into Pro Football Hall of Fame, 1988.
PRO STATISTICS: 1962—Recovered one fumble for a touchdown. 1964—Recovered one fumble for a touchdown. 1969—Fumbled once. 1971—Rushed twice for two yards, returned three kickoffs for 30 yards and recovered one fumble.

Year Team	G	No.	RECEIVING Yds.	Avg.	TD
1961— Chicago NFL	14	56	1076	19.2	12
1962— Chicago NFL	14	58	904	15.6	5
1963— Chicago NFL	14	59	794	13.5	8
1964— Chicago NFL	14	75	897	12.0	5
1965— Chicago NFL	14	36	454	12.6	2
1966— Chicago NFL	14	32	378	11.8	2
1967— Philadelphia NFL	9	26	274	10.5	2
1968— Philadelphia NFL	11	13	111	8.5	2
1969— Dallas NFL	12	17	268	15.8	3
1970— Dallas NFL	14	8	98	12.3	0
1971— Dallas NFL	14	30	360	12.0	1
1972— Dallas NFL	14	17	198	11.7	1
Pro totals (12 years)	158	427	5812	13.6	43

BACKGROUND: Assistant coach, Dallas Cowboys NFL (1973- 1981).
HONORS: Named THE SPORTING NEWS NFL Coach of the Year, 1985.

HEAD COACHING RECORD

	W	L	T	Pct.	REGULAR SEASON Finish	POST- SEASON W	L
1982— Chicago NFL	3	6	0	.333	T 11th/NFC	—	—
1983— Chicago NFL	8	8	0	.500	T2nd/ NFC Central Division	—	—
1984— Chicago NFL	10	6	0	.625	1st/NFC Central Division	1	1
1985— Chicago NFL	15	1	0	.938	1st/NFC Central Division	3	0
1986— Chicago NFL	14	2	0	.875	1st/NFC Central Division	0	1
1987— Chicago NFL	11	4	0	.733	1st/NFC Central Division	0	1
1988— Chicago NFL	10	4	0	.714	1st/NFC Central Division	1	1
1989— Chicago NFL	6	10	0	.375	4th/NFC Central Division	—	—
1990— Chicago NFL	11	5	0	.688	1st/NFC Central Division	1	1
Pro totals (9 years)	88	46	0	.657	Pro totals (6 years)	6	5

NOTES:
1984— Won conference playoff game from Washington, 23- 19; lost NFC championship game to San Francisco, 23-0.
1985— Won conference playoff game from New York Giants, 21-0; won NFC championship game from Los Angeles Rams, 24-0; won Super Bowl XX from New England, 46- 10.
1986— Lost conference playoff game to Washington, 27- 13.

1987 — Lost conference playoff game to Washington, 21-17.
1988 — Missed two games due to heart attack suffered on November 1, 1988; assistant coach Vince Tobin was 2-0 during that time. . . . Won conference playoff game from Philadelphia, 20-12; lost NFC championship game to San Francisco, 28-3.
1990 — Won conference playoff game from New Orleans, 16-6; lost conference playoff game to New York Giants, 31-3.

FONTES, WAYNE
LIONS

PERSONAL: Born February 2, 1940, at New Bedford, Mass. . . . Full name: Wayne Howard Joseph Fontes. . . . Name pronounced FONTS. . . . Played defensive back. . . . Brother of Len Fontes, assistant coach with Detroit Lions; and brother of John Fontes, assistant coach with Tampa Bay Storm of Arena Football League.
HIGH SCHOOL: Wareham (Mass.); and McKinley (Canton, O.).
COLLEGE: Michigan State (bachelor's degree in biological science, 1962; master's degree in administration, 1964).
TRANSACTIONS/CAREER NOTES: Selected (as future choice) by New York Titans in 22nd round of 1961 AFL draft.

Year	Team	G	No.	Yds.	Avg.	TD
				INTERCEPTIONS		
1962 — New York AFL		9	4	145	36.3	1
Pro totals (1 year)		9	4	145	36.3	1

BACKGROUND: Freshman coach, Michigan State (1965). . . . head coach, Visitation High School, Bay City, Mich. (1966 and 1967). . . . assistant coach, Dayton (1968). . . . assistant coach, Iowa (1969-1971). . . . assistant coach, Southern California (1972-1975). . . . assistant coach, Tampa Bay NFL (1976-1984). . . . assistant coach, Detroit NFL (1985-November 13, 1988).

HEAD COACHING RECORD

						POST-SEASON
			REGULAR SEASON			
	W	L	T	Pct.	Finish	W	L
1988 — Detroit NFL	2	3	0	.400	T4th/NFC Central Division	—	—
1989 — Detroit NFL	7	9	0	.438	3rd/NFC Central Division	—	—
1990 — Detroit NFL	6	10	0	.375	T2nd/ NFC Central Division	—	—
Pro totals (3 years)	15	22	0	.405			

NOTES:
1988 — Replaced Darryl Rogers as coach of Detroit on November 14, with 2-9 record and tied for fourth place.

GIBBS, JOE
REDSKINS

PERSONAL: Born November 25, 1940, at Mocksville, N.C. . . . Full name: Joe Jackson Gibbs.
HIGH SCHOOL: Spring (Santa Fe, Calif.).
COLLEGE: Cerritos Junior College (Calif.); and San Diego State (bachelor of science degree in physical education, 1964; master's degree, 1966).
BACKGROUND: Graduate assistant, San Diego State (1964 and 1965). . . . assistant coach, San Diego State (1966). . . . assistant coach, Florida State (1967 and 1968). . . . assistant coach, Southern California (1969 and 1970). . . . assistant coach, Arkansas (1971 and 1972). . . . assistant coach, St. Louis Cardinals NFL (1973-1977). . . . assistant coach, Tampa Bay Buccaneers NFL (1978). . . . assistant coach, San Diego Chargers NFL (1979 and 1980).
HONORS: Named THE SPORTING NEWS NFL Coach of the Year, 1982 and 1983.

HEAD COACHING RECORD

						POST-SEASON
			REGULAR SEASON			
	W	L	T	Pct.	Finish	W	L
1981 — Washington NFL	8	8	0	.500	4th/NFC Eastern Division	—	—
1982 — Washington NFL	8	1	0	.889	1st/ NFC	4	0
1983 — Washington NFL	14	2	0	.875	1st/NFC Eastern Division	2	1
1984 — Washington NFL	11	5	0	.688	1st/NFC Eastern Division	0	1
1985 — Washington NFL	10	6	0	.625	T1st/NFC Eastern Division	—	—
1986 — Washington NFL	12	4	0	.750	2nd/NFC Eastern Division	2	1
1987 — Washington NFL	11	4	0	.733	1st/NFC Eastern Division	3	0
1988 — Washington NFL	7	9	0	.438	T3rd/NFC Eastern Division	—	—
1989 — Washington NFL	10	6	0	.625	3rd/NFC Eastern Division	—	—
1990 — Washington NFL	10	6	0	.625	T2nd/ NFC Eastern Division	1	1
Pro totals (10 years)	101	51	0	.664	Pro totals (6 years)	12	4

NOTES:
1982 — Won conference playoff game from Detroit, 31-7; won conference playoff game from Minnesota, 21-7; won NFC championship game from Dallas, 31-17; won Super Bowl XVII from Miami, 27-17.
1983 — Won conference playoff game from Los Angeles Rams, 51-7; won NFC championship game from San Francisco, 24-21; lost Super Bowl XVIII to Los Angeles Raiders, 38-9.
1984 — Lost conference playoff game to Chicago, 23-19.
1986 — Won wild-card playoff game from Los Angeles Rams, 19-7; won conference playoff game from Chicago, 27-13; lost NFC championship game to New York Giants, 17-0.
1987 — Won conference playoff game from Chicago, 21-17; won NFC championship game from Minnesota, 17-10; won Super Bowl XXII from Denver, 42-10.
1990 — Won conference playoff game from Philadelphia, 20-6; lost conference playoff game to San Francisco, 28-10.

GLANVILLE, JERRY

FALCONS

PERSONAL: Born October 14, 1941, at Detroit.... Full name: Jerry Michael Glanville. **HIGH SCHOOL:** Reading (O.). **COLLEGE:** Montana State; Northern Michigan (bachelor of science degree, 1964); and Western Kentucky (master's degree in art western, 1966).

BACKGROUND: Assistant coach, Central Catholic High School, Lima, O. (1963 and 1964).... assistant coach, Reading High School, Reading, O. (1965).... assistant coach, Northern Michigan (1966).... assistant coach, Western Kentucky (1967). ... assistant coach, Georgia Tech (1968-1973).... assistant coach, Detroit Lions NFL (1974-1976).... assistant coach, Atlanta Falcons NFL (1977-1982).... assistant coach, Buffalo Bills NFL (1983).... assistant coach, Houston Oilers NFL (1984 and 1985).

HEAD COACHING RECORD

	W	L	T	Pct.	Finish	POST-SEASON W	L
1985— Houston NFL	0	2	0	.000	4th/AFC Central Division	—	—
1986— Houston NFL	5	11	0	.313	4th/AFC Central Division	—	—
1987— Houston NFL	9	6	0	.600	2nd/AFC Central Division	1	1
1988— Houston NFL	10	6	0	.625	T2nd/ AFC Central Division	1	1
1989— Houston NFL	9	7	0	.563	T2nd/ AFC Central Division	0	1
1990— Atlanta NFL	5	11	0	.313	T3rd/NFC Western Division	—	—
Pro totals (6 years)	**38**	**43**	**0**	**.469**	**Pro totals (3 years)**	**2**	**3**

NOTES:
1985— Replaced Hugh Campbell as coach of Houston on December 9, with 5-9 record and in fifth place.
1987— Won wild-card playoff game from Seattle, 23-20 (OT); lost conference playoff game to Denver, 34-10.
1988— Won wild-card playoff game from Cleveland, 24-23; lost conference playoff game to Buffalo, 17-10.
1989— Lost wild-card playoff game to Pittsburgh, 26-23 (OT).

HANDLEY, RAY

GIANTS

PERSONAL: Born October 8, 1944, at Artesia, N.M.... Full name: Robert Ray Handley. **HIGH SCHOOL:** Reno (Nev.). **COLLEGE:** Stanford (bachelor of arts degree in history). **BACKGROUND:** Assistant freshman coach, Stanford (1966).... assistant coach, Army (1968 and 1969).... assistant coach, Reno High School, Nev. (1970).... assistant coach, Stanford (1971-1974).... head coach, Edward C. Reed High School, Sparks, Nev. (1974-1977).... assistant coach, Air Force (1978).... assistant coach, Stanford (1979-1983).... assistant coach, New York Giants NFL (1984-1991).

HENNING, DAN

CHARGERS

PERSONAL: Born June 21, 1942, at Bronx, N.Y. ... Full name: Daniel Ernest Henning. ... Played quarterback. **HIGH SCHOOL:** St. Francis Prep (Fresh Meadows, N.Y.). **COLLEGE:** William & Mary.

TRANSACTIONS/CAREER NOTES: Signed as free agent by San Diego Chargers of AFL (February 19, 1964).... Released by Chargers (September 1, 1964).... Re-signed by San Diego Chargers (December 2, 1964).... Released by Chargers (August 2, 1965).... Re-signed by San Diego Chargers (July 2, 1966).... Released by Chargers (August 25, 1966).... Re-signed by Chargers and placed on taxi squad for 1966 season.... Active for one game in 1966; did not play.... Released by Chargers (August 29, 1967).... Played with Springfield, Mass., of Atlantic Coast Football League (1964) and with Norfolk Neptunes of Continental Football League (1965 and 1967).

BACKGROUND: Assistant coach, Homer L. Ferguson High School, Newport News, Va. (1967).... assistant coach, Florida State (1968-1970 and 1974).... assistant coach, Virginia Tech (1971 and 1973).... assistant coach, Houston Oilers NFL (1972). ... assistant coach, New York Jets NFL (1976-1978).... assistant coach, Miami Dolphins NFL (1979 and 1980).... assistant coach, Washington Redskins NFL (1981, 1982, 1987 and 1988).

HEAD COACHING RECORD

	W	L	T	Pct.	Finish	POST-SEASON W	L
1983— Atlanta NFL	7	9	0	.438	4th/ NFC Western Division	—	—
1984— Atlanta NFL	4	12	0	.250	4th/NFC Western Division	—	—
1985— Atlanta NFL	4	12	0	.250	4th/NFC Western Division	—	—
1986— Atlanta NFL	7	8	1	.469	3rd/NFC Western Division	—	—
1989— San Diego NFL	6	10	0	.375	5th/AFC Western Division	—	—
1990— San Diego NFL	6	10	0	.375	4th/AFC Western Division	—	—
Pro totals (6 years)	**34**	**61**	**1**	**.359**			

INFANTE, LINDY

PACKERS

PERSONAL: Born May 27, 1940, at Miami.... Full name: Gelindo Infante. **HIGH SCHOOL:** Miami. **COLLEGE:** Florida (bachelor of science degree in education, 1964). **TRANSACTIONS/CAREER NOTES:** Selected by Cleveland Browns in 12th round of 1963 NFL draft.... Selected by Buffalo Bills in 11th round of 1963 AFL draft.... Signed by Bills (1963).... Released by Bills (1963).... Signed by Hamilton Tiger-Cats of CFL (1963).

Year Team		G	Att	Yds	Avg	TD
			—RUSHING—			
1963— Hamilton CFL		1	3	12	4.0	0
Pro totals (1 year)		1	3	12	4.0	0

BACKGROUND: Assistant coach, Miami (Fla.) High School (1964).... head coach, Miami (Fla.) High School (1965).... assistant coach, Florida (1966-1971).... assistant coach, Memphis State (1972-1974).... assistant coach, Charlotte Hornets of WFL (1975).... assistant coach, Tulane (1976 and 1979).... assistant coach, New York Giants NFL (1977 and 1978).... assistant coach, Cincinnati Bengals NFL (1980-1982).... assistant coach, Cleveland Browns NFL (1986 and 1987).

HONORS: Named THE SPORTING NEWS NFL Coach of the Year, 1989.

HEAD COACHING RECORD

	REGULAR SEASON					POST-SEASON	
	W	L	T	Pct.	Finish	W	L
1984— Jacksonville USFL	6	12	0	.333	5th/Eastern Conference Southern Division	—	—
1985— Jacksonville USFL	9	9	0	.500	6th/Eastern Conference	—	—
1988— Green Bay NFL	4	12	0	.250	T4th/NFC Central Division	—	—
1989— Green Bay NFL	10	6	0	.625	T1st/NFC Central Division	—	—
1990— Green Bay NFL	6	10	0	.375	T2nd/NFC Central Division	—	—
USFL Totals (2 years)	15	21	0	.417			
NFL totals (3 years)	20	28	0	.417		—	—
Pro totals (5 years)	35	49	0	.417			

JOHNSON, JIMMY
COWBOYS

PERSONAL: Born July 16, 1943, at Port Arthur, Tex. ... Full name: James William Johnson.
HIGH SCHOOL: Thomas Jefferson (Port Arthur, Tex.).
COLLEGE: Arkansas (bachelor of arts degree in psychology, 1965).
BACKGROUND: Assistant coach, Louisiana Tech (1965).... assistant coach, Wichita State (1967).... assistant coach, Iowa State (1968 and 1969).... assistant coach, Oklahoma (1970-1972).... assistant coach, Arkansas (1973-1976).... assistant coach, Pittsburgh (1977 and 1978).

HEAD COACHING RECORD

	REGULAR SEASON					POST-SEASON	
	W	L	T	Pct.	Finish	W	L
1979— Oklahoma State	7	4	0	.636	3rd/Big Eight Conference	—	—
1980— Oklahoma State	3	7	1	.318	5th/Big Eight Conference	—	—
1981— Oklahoma State	7	4	0	.636	T3rd/Big Eight Conference	0	1
1982— Oklahoma State	4	5	2	.455	3rd/Big Eight Conference	—	—
1983— Oklahoma State	7	4	0	.636	T4th/Big Eight Conference	1	0
1984— Miami (Fla.)	8	4	0	.667	Independent	0	1
1985— Miami (Fla.)	10	1	0	.909	Independent	0	1
1986— Miami (Fla.)	11	0	0	1.000	Independent	0	1
1987— Miami (Fla.)	11	0	0	1.000	Independent	1	0
1988— Miami (Fla.)	10	1	0	.909	Independent	1	0
1989— Dallas NFL	1	15	0	.063	5th/NFC Eastern Division	—	—
1990— Dallas NFL	7	9	0	.438	4th/NFC Eastern Division	—	—
College totals (10 years)	78	30	3	.716	College totals (7 years)	3	4
Pro totals (2 years)	8	24	0	.250			

NOTES:
1980— Oklahoma State played to a 14-14 forfeited tie against Kansas on October 25.
1981— Lost Independence Bowl to Texas A&M, 33-16.
1983— Won Bluebonnet Bowl from Baylor, 24-14.
1984— Lost Fiesta Bowl to UCLA, 39-37.
1985— Lost Sugar Bowl to Tennessee, 35-7.
1986— Lost Fiesta Bowl to Penn State, 14-10.
1987— Won Orange Bowl from Oklahoma, 20-14.
1988— Won Orange Bowl from Nebraska, 23-3.

KNOX, CHUCK
SEAHAWKS

PERSONAL: Born April 27, 1932, at Sewickley, Pa. ... Full name: Charles Robert Knox Sr.
HIGH SCHOOL: Sewickley (Pa.).
COLLEGE: Juniata College, Pa. (bachelor of arts degree in history, 1954).
BACKGROUND: Assistant coach, Juniata College (1954). ... assistant coach, Tyrone High School, Pa. (1955).... head coach, Ellwood City High School, Pa. (1956-1958; record: 10-16-2).... assistant coach, Wake Forest (1959 and 1960).... assistant coach, Kentucky (1961 and 1962).... assistant coach, New York Jets AFL (1963-1966).... assistant coach, Detroit Lions NFL (1967-1972).

HONORS: Named THE SPORTING NEWS NFL Coach of the Year, 1973, 1980 and 1984.

			REGULAR SEASON					POST-SEASON	
	W	L	T	Pct.	Finish			W	L
1973— Los Angeles Rams NFL	12	2	0	.857	1st/NFC Western Division			0	1
1974— Los Angeles Rams NFL	10	4	0	.714	1st/NFC Western Division			1	1
1975— Los Angeles Rams NFL	12	2	0	.857	1st/NFC Western Division			1	1
1976— Los Angeles Rams NFL	10	3	1	.750	1st/NFC Western Division			1	1
1977— Los Angeles Rams NFL	10	4	0	.714	1st/NFC Western Division			0	1
1978— Buffalo NFL	5	11	0	.313	T4th/AFC Eastern Division			—	—
1979— Buffalo NFL	7	9	0	.438	4th/AFC Eastern Division			—	—
1980— Buffalo NFL	11	5	0	.688	1st/AFC Eastern Division			0	1
1981— Buffalo NFL	10	6	0	.625	3rd/AFC Eastern Division			1	1
1982— Buffalo NFL	4	5	0	.444	T8th/AFC			—	—
1983— Seattle NFL	9	7	0	.563	2nd/AFC Western Division			2	1
1984— Seattle NFL	12	4	0	.750	2nd/AFC Western Division			1	1
1985— Seattle NFL	8	8	0	.500	T3rd/AFC Western Division			—	—
1986— Seattle NFL	10	6	0	.625	T2nd/AFC Western Division			—	—
1987— Seattle NFL	9	6	0	.600	2nd/AFC Western Division			0	1
1988— Seattle NFL	9	7	0	.563	1st/AFC Western Division			0	1
1989— Seattle NFL	7	9	0	.438	4th/AFC Western Division			—	—
1990— Seattle NFL	9	7	0	.563	3rd/AFC Western Division			—	—
Pro totals (18 years)	**164**	**105**	**1**	**.609**	**Pro totals (11 years)**			**7**	**11**

NOTES:
1973— Lost conference playoff game to Dallas, 27-16.
1974— Won conference playoff game from Washington, 19-10; lost NFC championship game to Minnesota, 14-10.
1975— Won conference playoff game from St. Louis, 35-23; lost NFC championship game to Dallas, 37-7.
1976— Won conference playoff game from Dallas, 14-12; lost NFC championship game to Minnesota, 24-13.
1977— Lost conference playoff game to Minnesota, 14-7.
1980— Lost conference playoff game to San Diego, 20-14.
1981— Won conference playoff game from New York Jets, 31-27; lost conference playoff game to Cincinnati, 28-21.
1983— Won wild-card playoff game from Denver, 31-7; won conference playoff game from Miami, 27-20; lost AFC championship game to Los Angeles Raiders, 30-14.
1984— Won wild-card playoff game from Los Angeles Raiders, 13-7; lost conference playoff game to Miami, 31-10.
1987— Lost wild-card playoff game to Houston, 23-20 (OT).
1988— Lost conference playoff game to Cincinnati, 21-13.

KOTITE, RICH

EAGLES

PERSONAL: Born October 13, 1942, at Brooklyn, N.Y. . . . Full name: Richard Edward Kotite. . . . Played tight end.
HIGH SCHOOL: Poly Prep Country Day School (Brooklyn, N.Y.).
COLLEGE: Wagner College (bachelor of science degree in economics, 1967).
TRANSACTIONS/CAREER NOTES: Signed as free agent by New York Giants (1967). . . . Released by Giants (September 3, 1968). . . . Signed by Pittsburgh Steelers (September 27, 1968). . . . Released by Steelers (September 8, 1969). . . . Re-signed by New York Giants (September 23, 1969). . . . Released by Giants (September 7, 1970). . . . Re-signed by Giants (September 16, 1970). . . . Released by Giants (September 5, 1972). . . . Re-signed by Giants (September 13, 1972).

			RECEIVING			
Year	Team	G	No.	Yds.	Avg.	TD
1967— N.Y. Giants NFL		4	0	0		0
1968— Pittsburgh NFL		12	6	65	10.8	2
1969— N.Y. Giants NFL		3	1	2	2.0	1
1970— N.Y. Giants NFL		0	0	0		0
1971— N.Y. Giants NFL		14	10	146	14.6	2
1972— N.Y. Giants NFL		2	0	0		0
Pro totals (6 years)		**35**	**17**	**213**	**12.5**	**5**

BACKGROUND: Assistant coach, Tennessee-Chattanooga (1973-1976). . . . assistant coach, New Orleans Saints NFL (1977). . . . assistant coach, Cleveland Browns NFL (1978-1982). . . . assistant coach, New York Jets NFL (1983-1989). . . . assistant coach, Philadelphia Eagles NFL (1990).

LEVY, MARV

BILLS

PERSONAL: Born August 3, 1928, at Chicago. . . . Full name: Marvin Daniel Levy.
HIGH SCHOOL: South Shore (Chicago).
COLLEGE: Coe College, Ia. (received degree, 1950); and Harvard (master's degree in English History, 1951).
BACKGROUND: Head coach, St. Louis Country Day School, Mo. (1951 and 1952; record: 13-0-1). . . . assistant coach, Coe College (1953-1955). . . . assistant coach, New Mexico (1956 and 1957). . . . assistant coach, Philadelphia Eagles NFL (1969). . . . assistant coach, Los Angeles Rams NFL (1970). . . . assistant coach, Washington Redskins NFL (1971 and 1972).
HONORS: Named THE SPORTING NEWS NFL Coach of the Year, 1988.

	REGULAR SEASON					POST-SEASON	
	W	L	T	Pct.	Finish	W	L
1958— New Mexico	7	3	0	.700	2nd/Skyline Conference	—	—
1959— New Mexico	7	3	0	.700	3rd/Skyline Conference	—	—
1960— California	2	7	1	.250	4th/Athletic Assoc. of Western Universities	—	—
1961— California	1	8	1	.150	T4th/Athletic Assoc. of Western Universities	—	—
1962— California	1	9	0	.100	5th/Athletic Assoc. of Western Universities	—	—
1963— California	4	5	1	.450	4th/Athletic Assoc. of Western Universities	—	—
1964— William & Mary	4	6	0	.400	T4th/Southern Conference	—	—
1965— William & Mary	6	4	0	.600	1st/Southern Conference	—	—
1966— William & Mary	5	4	1	.550	T1st/Southern Conference	—	—
1967— William & Mary	5	4	1	.550	4th/Southern Conference	—	—
1968— William & Mary	3	7	0	.300	T3rd/Southern Conference	—	—
1973— Montreal CFL	7	6	1	.536	3rd/Eastern Conference	1	1
1974— Montreal CFL	9	5	2	.625	1st/Eastern Conference	2	0
1975— Montreal CFL	9	7	0	.563	2nd/Eastern Conference	2	1
1976— Montreal CFL	7	8	1	.469	T3rd/Eastern Conference	0	1
1977— Montreal CFL	11	5	0	.688	1st/Eastern Conference	2	0
1978— Kansas City NFL	4	12	0	.250	5th/AFC Western Division	—	—
1979— Kansas City NFL	7	9	0	.438	5th/AFC Western Division	—	—
1980— Kansas City NFL	8	8	0	.500	T3rd/AFC Western Division	—	—
1981— Kansas City NFL	9	7	0	.563	3rd/AFC Western Division	—	—
1982— Kansas City NFL	3	6	0	.333	11th/AFC	—	—
1984— Chicago USFL	5	13	0	.278	5th/Western Conference Central Division	—	—
1986— Buffalo NFL	2	5	0	.286	4th/AFC Eastern Division	—	—
1987— Buffalo NFL	7	8	0	.467	4th/AFC Eastern Division	—	—
1988— Buffalo NFL	12	4	0	.750	1st/AFC Eastern Division	1	1
1989— Buffalo NFL	9	7	0	.563	1st/AFC Eastern Division	0	1
1990— Buffalo NFL	13	3	0	.813	1st/AFC Eastern Division	2	1
CFL totals (5 years)	43	31	4	.577	**CFL totals (5 years)**	7	3
NFL totals (10 years)	74	69	0	.518	**NFL totals (3 years)**	3	3
USFL totals (1 year)	5	13	0	.278			
Pro totals (16 years)	122	113	4	.519	**Pro totals (8 years)**	10	6
College totals (11 years)	45	60	5	.432			

NOTES:

1973— Won conference playoff game from Toronto, 32-10; lost conference championship game to Ottawa, 23-14.

1974— Won conference championship game from Ottawa, 14-4; won Grey Cup (CFL championship game) from Edmonton, 20-7.

1975— Won conference playoff game from Hamilton, 35-12; won conference championship game from Ottawa, 20-10; lost Grey Cup to Edmonton, 9-8.

1976— Lost conference playoff game to Hamilton, 23-0.

1977— Won conference championship game from Ottawa, 21-18; won Grey Cup from Edmonton, 41-6.

1986— Replaced Hank Bullough as coach of Buffalo on November 3, with 2-7 record and in fourth place.

1988— Won conference playoff game from Houston, 17-10; lost AFC championship game to Cincinnati, 21-10.

1989— Lost conference playoff game to Cleveland, 34-30.

1990— Won conference playoff game from Miami, 44-34; won AFC championship game from Los Angeles Raiders, 51-3; lost Super Bowl XXV to New York Giants, 20-19.

MacPHERSON, DICK

PATRIOTS

PERSONAL: Born November 4, 1930, at Old Town, Me. . . . Full name Richard F. MacPherson.

HIGH SCHOOL: Maine Maritime Academy (Castine, Me.).

COLLEGE: Springfield College (bachelor of science degree in physical education, 1958); and Illinois (master's degree in physical education, 1959).

BACKGROUND: Assistant freshman coach, Illinois (1958). . . . assistant freshman coach, Massachusetts (1959 and 1960). . . . assistant coach, Cincinnati (1961-1965). . . . assistant coach, Maryland (1966). . . . assistant coach, Denver Broncos NFL (1967-1970). . . . assistant coach, Cleveland Browns NFL (1978-1980).

MISCELLANEOUS: Served in Air Force (1950-1953).

HEAD COACHING RECORD

	REGULAR SEASON					POST-SEASON		
	W	L	T	Pct.	Finish	W	L	T
1971— Massachusetts	4	4	1	.500	T1st/Yankee Conference	—	—	—
1972— Massachusetts	8	2	0	.800	1st/Yankee Conference	1	0	0
1973— Massachusetts	6	5	0	.545	3rd/Yankee Conference	—	—	—
1974— Massachusetts	5	6	0	.455	T1st/Yankee Conference	—	—	—
1975— Massachusetts	8	2	0	.800	2nd/Yankee Conference	—	—	—
1976— Massachusetts	5	5	0	.500	2nd/Yankee Conference	—	—	—
1977— Massachusetts	8	2	0	.800	1st/Yankee Conference	0	1	0
1981— Syracuse	4	6	1	.409	Independent	—	—	—
1982— Syracuse	2	9	0	.182	Independent	—	—	—

					REGULAR SEASON	POST-SEASON		
	W	L	T	Pct.	Finish	W	L	T
1983— Syracuse	6	5	0	.545	Independent	—	—	—
1984— Syracuse	6	5	0	.545	Independent	—	—	—
1985— Syracuse	7	4	0	.636	Independent	0	1	0
1986— Syracuse	5	6	0	.455	Independent	—	—	—
1987— Syracuse	11	0	0	1.000	Independent	0	0	1
1988— Syracuse	9	2	0	.818	Independent	1	0	0
1989— Syracuse	7	4	0	.636	Independent	1	0	0
1990— Syracuse	6	4	2	.583	Independent	1	0	0
College totals (17 years)	107	71	4	.599	College totals (7 years)	4	2	1

NOTES:
1972— Won Boardwalk Bowl from California-Davis, 35-14.
1977— Lost NCAA Division II playoff game to Lehigh, 30-23.
1985— Lost Cherry Bowl to Maryland, 35-18.
1987— Tied Auburn in Sugar Bowl, 16-16.
1988— Won Hall of Fame Bowl from Louisiana State, 23-10.
1989— Won Peach Bowl from Georgia, 19-18.
1990— Won Aloha Bowl from Arizona, 28-0.

MEYER, RON
COLTS

PERSONAL: Born February 17, 1941, at Columbus, O. . . . Full name: Ronald Shaw Meyer. **HIGH SCHOOL:** Westerville, O. **COLLEGE:** Purdue (bachelor of science degree in physical education, 1963; master's degree in physical education, 1965).
BACKGROUND: Graduate assistant, Purdue (1963). . . . Head coach at Penn Hill High School, Mishawaka, Ind. (1964; record: 5-4-1). . . . assistant coach, Purdue (1965-1970). . . . scout, Dallas Cowboys (1971 and 1972).

HEAD COACHING RECORD

					REGULAR SEASON	POST-SEASON	
	W	L	T	Pct.	Finish	W	L
1973— UNLV	8	3	0	.727		—	—
1974— UNLV	11	0	0	1.000		1	1
1975— UNLV	7	4	0	.636		—	—
1976— Southern Methodist	3	8	0	.273	T7th/Southwest Conference	—	—
1977— Southern Methodist	4	7	0	.364	T6th/Southwest Conference	—	—
1978— Southern Methodist	4	6	1	.409	T6th/Southwest Conference	—	—
1979— Southern Methodist	5	6	0	.455	6th/Southwest Conference	—	—
1980— Southern Methodist	8	3	0	.727	2nd/Southwest Conference	0	1
1981— Southern Methodist	10	1	0	.909	1st/Southwest Conference	—	—
1982— New England NFL	5	4	0	.556	7th/AFC	0	1
1983— New England NFL	8	8	0	.500	T2nd/AFC Eastern Division	—	—
1984— New England NFL	5	3	0	.625	3rd/AFC Eastern Division	—	—
1986— Indianapolis NFL	3	0	0	1.000	5th/AFC Eastern Division	—	—
1987— Indianapolis NFL	9	6	0	.600	1st/AFC Eastern Division	0	1
1988— Indianapolis NFL	9	7	0	.563	T2nd/AFC Eastern Division	—	—
1989— Indianapolis NFL	8	8	0	.500	T2nd/AFC Eastern Division	—	—
1990— Indianapolis NFL	7	9	0	.438	3rd/AFC Eastern Division	—	—
College totals (9 years)	60	38	1	.611	College totals (2 years)	1	2
Pro totals (8 years)	54	45	0	.545	Pro totals (2 years)	0	2

NOTES:
1974— Won NCAA Division II playoff game from Alcorn State, 35-22; lost NCAA Division II playoff game to Delaware, 49-11.
1980— Lost Holiday Bowl to Brigham Young, 46-45.
1982— Lost conference playoff game to Miami, 28-13.
1984— Replaced by Raymond Berry as coach of New England on October 25, 1984.
1986— Replaced Rod Dowhower as coach of Indianapolis on December 1, 1986, with 0-13 record and in fifth place.
1987— Lost conference playoff game to Cleveland, 38-21.

MORA, JIM
SAINTS

PERSONAL: Born May 24, 1935, at Los Angeles. . . . Full name: James Ernest Mora. . . . Father of Jim Mora Jr., assistant coach with San Diego Chargers. **HIGH SCHOOL:** University (Los Angeles). **COLLEGE:** Occidental College (bachelor of arts degree in physical education, 1957); and Southern California (master's degree in education, 1967).
MISCELLANEOUS: Played in U.S. Marines at Quantico (1957) and at Camp Lejeune (1958 and 1959).
BACKGROUND: Assistant coach, Occidental College (1960-1963). . . . assistant coach, Stanford (1967). . . . assistant coach, Colorado (1968-1973). . . . assistant coach, UCLA (1974). . . . assistant coach, Washington (1975-1977). . . . assistant coach, Seattle Seahawks NFL (1978-1981). . . . assistant coach, New England Patriots NFL (1982).
HONORS: Named THE SPORTING NEWS USFL Coach of the Year (1984). . . . Named THE SPORTING NEWS NFL Coach of the Year (1987).

HEAD COACHING RECORD

					REGULAR SEASON	POST-SEASON	
	W	L	T	Pct.	Finish	W	L
1964— Occidental	5	4	0	.556	3rd/Southern Calif. Intercollegiate Conference	—	—
1965— Occidental	8	1	0	.889	1st/Southern Calif. Intercollegiate Conference	—	—
1966— Occidental	5	4	0	.556	4th/Southern Calif. Intercollegiate Conference	—	—
1983— Philadelphia USFL	15	3	0	.833	1st/Atlantic Division	1	1
1984— Philadelphia USFL	16	2	0	.889	1st/Eastern Conference Atlantic Division	3	0
1985— Baltimore USFL	10	7	1	.583	4th/Eastern Conference	3	0
1986— New Orleans NFL	7	9	0	.438	4th/NFC Western Division	—	—
1987— New Orleans NFL	12	3	0	.800	2nd/NFC Western Division	0	1
1988— New Orleans NFL	10	6	0	.625	T 1st/NFC Western Division	—	—
1989— New Orleans NFL	9	7	0	.563	3rd/NFC Western Division	—	—
1990— New Orleans NFL	8	8	0	.500	2nd/NFC Western Division	0	1
USFL totals (3 years)	41	12	1	.769	USFL totals (3 years)	7	1
NFL totals (5 years)	46	33	0	.582	NFL totals (2 years)	0	2
Pro totals (8 years)	87	45	1	.658	Pro totals (5 years)	7	3
College totals (3 years)	18	9	0	.667			

NOTES:
1983— Won divisional playoff game from Chicago, 44-38 (OT); lost USFL championship game to Michigan, 24-22.
1984— Won conference playoff game from New Jersey, 28-7; won conference championship game from Birmingham, 20-10; won USFL championship game from Arizona, 23-3.
1985— Won conference playoff game from New Jersey, 20-17; won conference championship game from Birmingham, 28-14; won USFL championship game from Oakland, 28-24.
1987— Lost wild-card playoff game to Minnesota, 44-10.
1990— Lost conference playoff game to Chicago, 16-6.

NOLL, CHUCK
STEELERS

PERSONAL: Born January 5, 1932, at Cleveland. . . . Full name: Charles Henry Noll. . . . Played linebacker and offensive guard.
HIGH SCHOOL: Benedictine (Cleveland).
COLLEGE: Dayton (bachelor of science degree in education, 1953).
TRANSACTIONS/CAREER NOTES: Selected by Cleveland Browns in 21st round of 1953 NFL draft.
CHAMPIONSHIP GAME EXPERIENCE: Played in NFL championship game after 1953-1955 seasons.
PRO STATISTICS: 1954—Recovered two fumbles for 10 yards. 1955—Credited with one safety. 1956—Recovered one fumble for 39 yards and a touchdown.

		INTERCEPTIONS				KICKOFF RETURNS				TOTAL		
Year Team	G	No.	Yds.	Avg.	TD	No.	Yds.	Avg.	TD	TD	Pts.	F.
1953— Cleveland NFL	12	0	0		0	1	2	2.0	0	0	0	0
1954— Cleveland NFL	12	0	0		0	0	0		0	0	0	0
1955— Cleveland NFL	12	5	74	14.8	1	0	0		0	1	8	0
1956— Cleveland NFL	12	1	13	13.0	0	0	0		0	1	6	0
1957— Cleveland NFL	5	0	0		0	0	0		0	0	0	0
1958— Cleveland NFL	12	0	0		0	0	0		0	0	0	0
1959— Cleveland NFL	12	2	5	2.5	0	1	20	20.0	0	0	0	0
Pro totals (7 years)	77	8	92	11.5	1	2	22	11.0	0	2	14	0

BACKGROUND: Assistant coach, Los Angeles Chargers AFL (1960). . . . assistant coach, San Diego Chargers AFL (1961-1965). . . . assistant coach, Baltimore Colts NFL (1966-1968).

HEAD COACHING RECORD

					REGULAR SEASON	POST-SEASON	
	W	L	T	Pct.	Finish	W	L
1969— Pittsburgh NFL	1	13	0	.071	4th/Eastern Conference Century Division	—	—
1970— Pittsburgh NFL	5	9	0	.357	3rd/AFC Central Division	—	—
1971— Pittsburgh NFL	6	8	0	.429	2nd/AFC Central Division	—	—
1972— Pittsburgh NFL	11	3	0	.786	1st/AFC Central Division	1	1
1973— Pittsburgh NFL	10	4	0	.714	T 1st/AFC Central Division	0	1
1974— Pittsburgh NFL	10	3	1	.750	1st/AFC Central Division	3	0
1975— Pittsburgh NFL	12	2	0	.857	1st/AFC Central Division	3	0
1976— Pittsburgh NFL	10	4	0	.714	T 1st/AFC Central Division	1	1
1977— Pittsburgh NFL	9	5	0	.643	1st/AFC Central Division	0	1
1978— Pittsburgh NFL	14	2	0	.875	1st/AFC Central Division	3	0
1979— Pittsburgh NFL	12	4	0	.750	1st/AFC Central Division	3	0
1980— Pittsburgh NFL	9	7	0	.563	3rd/AFC Central Division	—	—
1981— Pittsburgh NFL	8	8	0	.500	2nd/AFC Central Division	—	—
1982— Pittsburgh NFL	6	3	0	.667	T4th/AFC	0	1
1983— Pittsburgh NFL	10	6	0	.625	1st/AFC Central Division	0	1
1984— Pittsburgh NFL	9	7	0	.563	1st/AFC Central Division	1	1
1985— Pittsburgh NFL	7	9	0	.438	T2nd/AFC Central Division	—	—
1986— Pittsburgh NFL	6	10	0	.375	3rd/AFC Central Division	—	—

	W	L	T	Pct.	REGULAR SEASON — Finish	POST-SEASON W	L
1987— Pittsburgh NFL	8	7	0	.533	3rd/AFC Central Division	—	—
1988— Pittsburgh NFL	5	11	0	.313	4th/AFC Central Division	—	—
1989— Pittsburgh NFL	9	7	0	.563	T2nd/AFC Central Division	1	1
1990— Pittsburgh NFL	9	7	0	.563	T1st/AFC Central Division	—	—
Pro totals (22 years)	186	139	1	.572	Pro totals (12 years)	16	8

NOTES:

1972— Won conference playoff game from Oakland, 13-7; lost AFC championship game to Miami, 21-17.

1973— Lost conference playoff game to Oakland, 33-14.

1974— Won conference playoff game from Buffalo, 32-14; won AFC championship game from Oakland, 24-13; won Super Bowl IX from Minnesota, 16-6.

1975— Won conference playoff game from Baltimore, 28-10; won AFC championship game from Oakland, 16-10; won Super Bowl X from Dallas, 21-17.

1976— Won conference playoff game from Baltimore, 40-14; lost AFC championship game to Oakland, 24-7.

1977— Lost conference playoff game to Denver, 34-21.

1978— Won conference playoff game from Denver, 33-10; won AFC championship game from Houston, 34-5; won Super Bowl XIII from Dallas, 35-31.

1979— Won conference playoff game from Miami, 34-14; won AFC championship game from Houston, 27-13; won Super Bowl XIV from Los Angeles, 31-19.

1982— Lost conference playoff game to San Diego, 31-28.

1983— Lost conference playoff game to Los Angeles Raiders, 38-10.

1984— Won conference playoff game from Denver, 24-17; lost AFC championship game to Miami, 45-28.

1989— Won wild-card game from Houston, 26-23 (OT); lost conference playoff game to Denver, 24-23.

PARDEE, JACK

OILERS

PERSONAL: Born April 19, 1936, at Exira, Ia. . . . Full name: John Perry Pardee. . . . Played linebacker.

HIGH SCHOOL: Christoval (Tex.).

COLLEGE: Texas A&M (bachelor of arts degree, 1957).

TRANSACTIONS/CAREER NOTES: Selected by Los Angeles Rams in second round of 1957 NFL draft. . . . Traded by Rams with defensive tackle Diron Talbert, guard John Wilbur, linebackers Myron Pottios and Maxie Baughn, running back Jeff Jordan and fifth-round pick in 1971 draft to Washington Redskins for linebacker Marlin McKeever, first- and third-round picks in 1971 draft and third-, fourth-, fifth-, sixth- and seventh-round picks in 1972 draft (January 28, 1971).

CHAMPIONSHIP GAME EXPERIENCE: Played in NFC championship game after 1972 season. . . . Played in Super Bowl VII after 1972 season.

RECORDS/HONORS: Played in Pro Bowl after 1963 season. . . . Named to THE SPORTING NEWS NFL Western Conference All-Star team, 1963.

PRO STATISTICS: 1957—Returned three kickoffs for 21 yards and recovered two fumbles. 1958—Recovered one fumble. 1960—Recovered one fumble. 1961—Recovered one fumble. 1962—Credited with a safety and recovered one fumble for 32 yards and a touchdown. 1963—Recovered two fumbles for 12 yards. 1966—Recovered two fumbles. 1967—Recovered one fumble. 1970—Recovered two fumbles for five yards. 1971—Recovered one fumble. 1972—Recovered two fumbles.

Year Team	G	INTERCEPTIONS No.	Yds.	Avg.	TD
1957— L.A. Rams NFL	12	0	0		0
1958— L.A. Rams NFL	12	0	0		0
1959— L.A. Rams NFL	12	0	0		0
1960— L.A. Rams NFL	8	1	10	10.0	0
1961— L.A. Rams NFL	13	1	2	2.0	0
1962— L.A. Rams NFL	14	0	0		0
1963— L.A. Rams NFL	14	2	5	2.5	0
1964— L.A. Rams NFL	14	1	32	32.0	0
1966— L.A. Rams NFL	14	2	0	.0	0
1967— L.A. Rams NFL	14	6	95	15.8	2
1968— L.A. Rams NFL	14	2	75	37.5	*2
1969— L.A. Rams NFL	14	1	19	19.0	0
1970— L.A. Rams NFL	14	1	9	9.0	0
1971— L.A. Rams NFL	14	5	58	11.6	1
1972— Washington NFL	13	0	0		0
Pro totals (15 years)	196	22	305	13.9	5

BACKGROUND: Assistant coach, Texas A&M (1965). . . . assistant coach, Washington Redskins NFL (1973). . . . assistant coach, San Diego Chargers NFL (1981).

HEAD COACHING RECORD

	W	L	T	Pct.	REGULAR SEASON — Finish	POST-SEASON W	L
1974— Florida WFL	14	6	0	.700	1st/Eastern Division	2	1
1975— Chicago NFL	4	10	0	.286	T3rd/NFC Central Division	—	—
1976— Chicago NFL	7	7	0	.500	2nd/NFC Central Division	—	—
1977— Chicago NFL	9	5	0	.643	T1st/NFC Central Division	0	1
1978— Washington NFL	8	8	0	.500	3rd/NFC Eastern Division	—	—

					REGULAR SEASON	POST-SEASON	
	W	L	T	Pct.	Finish	W	L
1979— Washington NFL	10	6	0	.625	3rd/NFC Eastern Division	—	—
1980— Washington NFL	6	10	0	.375	3rd/NFC Eastern Division	—	—
1984— Houston USFL	13	5	0	.722	1st/Western Conference Central Division	0	1
1985— Houston USFL	10	8	0	.556	3rd/Western Conference	0	1
1987— Univ. of Houston	4	6	1	409	7th/Southwest Conference	—	—
1988— Univ. of Houston	9	2	0	.818	2nd/Southwest Conference	0	1
1989— Univ. of Houston	9	2	0	.818	Southwest Conference/ineligible for title	—	—
1990— Houston NFL	9	7	0	.563	T1st/AFC Central Division	0	1
WFL totals (1 year)	14	6	0	.700	**WFL totals (1 year)**	2	1
NFL totals (7 years)	53	53	0	.500	**NFL totals (2 years)**	0	2
USFL totals (2 years)	23	13	0	.639	**USFL totals (2 years)**	0	2
Pro totals (10 years)	90	72	0	.556	**Pro totals (5 years)**	2	5
College totals (3 years)	22	10	1	.682	**College totals (1 year)**	0	1

NOTES:

1974— Won playoff game from Philadelphia, 18-3; won playoff game from Memphis, 18-15; lost WFL championship game to Birmingham, 22-21.

1977— Lost conference playoff game to Dallas, 37-7.

1984— Lost conference playoff game to Arizona, 17-16.

1985— Lost conference quarterfinal playoff game to Birmingham, 22-20.

1988— Lost Eagle Aloha Bowl to Washington State, 24-22.

1990— Lost conference playoff game to Cincinnati, 41-14.

REEVES, DAN
BRONCOS

PERSONAL: Born January 19, 1944, at Rome, Ga. . . . Full name: Daniel Edward Reeves. . . . Played running back.

HIGH SCHOOL: Americus, Ga.

COLLEGE: South Carolina.

TRANSACTIONS/CAREER NOTES: Signed as free agent by Dallas Cowboys (1965).

CHAMPIONSHIP GAME EXPERIENCE: Played in NFL championship game after 1966 and 1967 seasons. . . . Played in NFC championship game after 1970 and 1971 seasons. . . . Played in Super Bowl V after 1970 season and Super Bowl VI after 1971 season.

RECORDS/HONORS: Named to THE SPORTING NEWS NFL Eastern Conference All-Star team, 1966.

PRO STATISTICS: 1965—Returned two kickoffs for 45 yards. 1966—Returned three kickoffs for 56 yards and returned two punts for minus one yard.

			PASSING						RUSHING				RECEIVING				TOTAL		
Year Team	G	Att.	Cmp.	Pct.	Yds.	TD	Int.	Avg.	Att.	Yds.	Avg.	TD	No.	Yds.	Avg.	TD	TD	Pts.	F.
1965— Dallas NFL	13	2	1	50.0	11	0	0	5.50	33	102	3.1	2	9	210	23.3	1	3	18	0
1966— Dallas NFL	14	6	3	50.0	48	0	0	8.00	175	757	4.3	8	41	557	13.6	8	*16	96	6
1967— Dallas NFL	14	7	4	57.1	195	2	1	27.86	173	603	3.5	5	39	490	12.6	6	11	66	7
1968— Dallas NFL	4	4	2	50.0	43	0	0	10.75	40	178	4.5	4	7	84	12.0	1	5	30	0
1969— Dallas NFL	13	3	1	33.3	35	0	1	11.67	59	173	2.9	4	18	187	10.4	1	5	30	2
1970— Dallas NFL	14	3	1	33.3	14	0	1	4.67	35	84	2.4	2	12	140	11.7	0	2	12	4
1971— Dallas NFL	14	5	2	40.0	24	0	1	4.80	17	79	4.7	0	3	25	8.3	0	0	0	0
1972— Dallas NFL	14	2	0	.0	0	0	0	.00	3	14	4.7	0	0	0		0	0	0	0
Pro totals (8 years)	100	32	14	43.8	370	2	4	11.56	535	1990	3.7	25	129	1693	13.1	17	42	252	20

BACKGROUND: Player-coach, Dallas Cowboys NFL (1970 and 1971). . . . assistant coach, Dallas Cowboys NFL (1972 and 1974-1980).

HEAD COACHING RECORD

					REGULAR SEASON	POST-SEASON	
	W	L	T	Pct.	Finish	W	L
1981— Denver NFL	10	6	0	.625	T1st/AFC Western Division	—	—
1982— Denver NFL	2	7	0	.222	12th/AFC	—	—
1983— Denver NFL	9	7	0	.563	T2nd/AFC Western Division	0	1
1984— Denver NFL	13	3	0	.813	1st/AFC Western Division	0	1
1985— Denver NFL	11	5	0	.688	2nd/AFC Western Division	—	—
1986— Denver NFL	11	5	0	.688	1st/AFC Western Division	2	1
1987— Denver NFL	10	4	1	.700	1st/AFC Western Division	2	1
1988— Denver NFL	8	8	0	.500	2nd/AFC Western Division	—	—
1989— Denver NFL	11	5	0	.688	1st/AFC Western Division	2	1
1990— Denver NFL	5	11	0	.313	5th/AFC Western Division	—	—
Pro totals (10 years)	90	61	1	.595	**Pro totals (5 years)**	6	5

NOTES:

1983— Lost wild-card playoff game to Seattle, 31-7.

1984— Lost conference playoff game to Pittsburgh, 24-17.

1986— Won conference playoff game from New England, 22-17; won AFC championship game from Cleveland, 23-20 (OT); lost Super Bowl XXI to New York Giants, 39-20.

1987— Won conference playoff game from Houston, 34-10; won AFC championship game from Cleveland, 38-33; lost Super Bowl XXII to Washington, 42-10.

1989— Won conference playoff game from Pittsburgh, 24-23; won AFC championship game from Cleveland, 37-21; lost Super Bowl XXIV to San Francisco, 55-10.

ROBINSON, JOHN
RAMS

PERSONAL: Born July 25, 1935, at Chicago. . . . Full name: John Alexander Robinson.
HIGH SCHOOL: San Mateo (Calif.).
COLLEGE: Oregon (bachelor of science degree in education, 1958).
BACKGROUND: Assistant coach, Oregon (1960-1971). . . . assistant coach, Southern California (1972-1974). . . . assistant coach, Oakland Raiders (1975).

HEAD COACHING RECORD

	REGULAR SEASON					POST-SEASON	
	W	L	T	Pct.	Finish	W	L
1976— Southern California	10	1	0	.909	1st/Pacific-8 Conference	1	0
1977— Southern California	7	4	0	.636	T2nd/Pacific-8 Conference	1	0
1978— Southern California	11	1	0	.917	1st/Pacific-10 Conference	1	0
1979— Southern California	10	0	1	1.000	1st/Pacific-10 Conference	1	0
1980— Southern California	8	2	1	.773	3rd/Pacific-10 Conference	—	—
1981— Southern California	9	2	0	.818	T2nd/Pacific-10 Conference	0	1
1982— Southern California	8	3	0	.727	Pacific-10 Conference/ineligible for title	—	—
1983— Los Angeles Rams NFL	9	7	0	.563	2nd/NFC Western Division	1	1
1984— Los Angeles Rams NFL	10	6	0	.625	2nd/NFC Western Division	0	1
1985— Los Angeles Rams NFL	11	5	0	.688	1st/NFC Western Division	1	1
1986— Los Angeles Rams NFL	10	6	0	.625	2nd/NFC Western Division	0	1
1987— Los Angeles Rams NFL	6	9	0	.400	3rd/NFC Western Division	—	—
1988— Los Angeles Rams NFL	10	6	0	.625	T1st/NFC Western Division	0	1
1989— Los Angeles Rams NFL	11	5	0	.688	2nd/NFC Western Division	2	1
1990— Los Angeles Rams NFL	5	11	0	.313	T3rd/NFC Western Division	—	—
College totals (7 years)	63	13	2	.821	**College totals (5 years)**	4	1
Pro totals (8 years)	72	55	0	.557	**Pro totals (6 years)**	4	6

NOTES:
1976— Won Rose Bowl from Michigan, 14-6.
1977— Won Bluebonnet Bowl from Texas A&M, 47-28.
1978— Won Rose Bowl from Michigan, 17-10.
1979— Won Rose Bowl from Ohio State, 17-16.
1981— Lost Fiesta Bowl to Penn State, 26-10.
1983— Won wild-card playoff game from Dallas, 24-17; lost conference playoff game to Washington, 51-7.
1984— Lost wild-card playoff game to New York Giants, 16-13.
1985— Won conference playoff game from Dallas, 20-0; lost NFC championship game to Chicago, 24-0.
1986— Lost wild-card playoff game to Washington, 19-7.
1988— Lost wild-card playoff game to Minnesota, 28-17.
1989— Won wild-card playoff game from Philadelphia, 21-7; won conference playoff game from New York Giants, 19-13 (OT); lost NFC championship game to San Francisco, 30-3.

SCHOTTENHEIMER, MARTY
CHIEFS

PERSONAL: Born September 23, 1943, at Canonsburg, Pa. . . . Full name: Martin Edward Schottenheimer. . . . Played linebacker. . . . Brother of Kurt Schottenheimer, assistant coach with Kansas City Chiefs.
HIGH SCHOOL: McDonald (Pa.).
COLLEGE: Pittsburgh (bachelor of arts degree in English, 1964).
TRANSACTIONS/CAREER NOTES: Selected by Buffalo Bills in seventh round of 1965 AFL draft. . . . Released by Bills and signed by Boston Patriots (1969). . . . Traded by New England Patriots to Pittsburgh Steelers for offensive tackle Mike Haggerty and a draft choice (July 10, 1971). . . . Released by Steelers (1971).
CHAMPIONSHIP GAME EXPERIENCE: Played in AFL championship game after 1965 and 1966 seasons.
RECORDS/HONORS: Played in AFL All-Star Game after 1965 season.
PRO STATISTICS: 1969—Returned one kickoff for 13 yards. 1970—Returned one kickoff for eight yards.

			INTERCEPTIONS			
Year	Team	G	No.	Yds.	Avg.	TD
1965— Buffalo AFL		14	0	0		0
1966— Buffalo AFL		14	1	20	20.0	0
1967— Buffalo AFL		14	3	88	29.3	1
1968— Buffalo AFL		14	1	22	22.0	0
1969— Boston AFL		11	1	3	3.0	0
1970— Boston NFL		12	0	0		0
AFL totals (5 years)		67	6	133	22.2	1
NFL totals (1 year)		12	0	0		0
Pro totals (6 years)		79	6	133	22.2	1

BACKGROUND: Assistant coach, Portland Storm WFL (1974). . . . assistant coach, New York Giants NFL (1975-1977). . . . assistant coach, Detroit Lions NFL (1978 and 1979). . . . assistant coach, Cleveland Browns NFL (1980-1984).

HEAD COACHING RECORD

		REGULAR SEASON				POST-SEASON	
	W	L	T	Pct.	Finish	W	L
1984— Cleveland NFL	4	4	0	.500	3rd/AFC Central Division	—	—
1985— Cleveland NFL	8	8	0	.500	1st/AFC Central Division	0	1
1986— Cleveland NFL	12	4	0	.750	1st/AFC Central Division	1	1
1987— Cleveland NFL	10	5	0	.667	1st/AFC Central Division	1	1
1988— Cleveland NFL	10	6	0	.625	T2nd/AFC Central Division	0	1
1989— Kansas City NFL	8	7	1	.531	2nd/AFC Western Division	—	—
1990— Kansas City NFL	11	5	0	.688	2nd/AFC Western Division	0	1
Pro totals (7 years)	63	39	1	.617	Pro totals (5 years)	2	5

NOTES:
1984— Replaced Sam Rutigliano as coach of Cleveland on October 22, with 1-7 record and in third place.
1985— Lost conference playoff game to Miami, 24-21.
1986— Won conference playoff game from New York Jets, 23-20 (2 OT); lost AFC championship game to Denver, 23-20 (OT).
1987— Won conference playoff game from Indianapolis, 38-21; lost AFC championship game to Denver, 38-33.
1988— Lost wild-card playoff game to Houston, 24-23.
1990— Lost conference playoff game to Miami, 17-16.

SEIFERT, GEORGE
49ERS

PERSONAL: Born January 22, 1940, at San Francisco. . . . Full name: George Gerald Seifert. **HIGH SCHOOL:** Polytechnic (San Francisco). **COLLEGE:** Utah (bachelor of science degree in zoology, 1963; master's degree in physical education, 1966).
MISCELLANEOUS: Served six months in U.S. Army after college.
BACKGROUND: Graduate assistant, Utah (1964). . . . assistant coach, Iowa (1966). . . . assistant coach, Oregon (1967-1971). . . . assistant coach, Stanford (1972-1974 and 1977-1979). . . . assistant coach, San Francisco 49ers NFL (1980-1988).
HONORS: Named THE SPORTING NEWS NFL Coach of the Year (1990).

HEAD COACHING RECORD

		REGULAR SEASON				POST-SEASON	
	W	L	T	Pct.	Finish	W	L
1965— Westminster College (Utah)	3	3	0	.500	Independent	—	—
1975— Cornell	1	8	0	.111	8th/Ivy League	—	—
1976— Cornell	2	7	0	.222	T7th/Ivy League	—	—
1989— San Francisco NFL	14	2	0	.875	1st/NFC Western Division	3	0
1990— San Francisco NFL	14	2	0	.875	1st/NFC Western Division	1	1
College totals (3 years)	6	18	0	.250			
Pro totals (2 years)	28	4	0	.875	Pro totals (2 years)	4	1

NOTES:
1989— Won conference playoff game from Minnesota, 41-13; won NFC championship game from Los Angeles Rams, 30-3; won Super Bowl XXIV from Denver, 55-10.
1990— Won conference playoff game from Washington, 28-10; lost NFC championship game to New York Giants, 15-13.

SHELL, ART
RAIDERS

PERSONAL: Born November 26, 1946, at Charleston, S.C. . . . Full name: Arthur Shell. . . . Played offensive tackle. **HIGH SCHOOL:** Bonds-Wilson (North Charleston, S.C.). **COLLEGE:** Maryland State-Eastern Shore College (bachelor of science degree in industrial arts education, 1968).
TRANSACTIONS/CAREER NOTES: Selected by Oakland Raiders in third round (80th pick overall) of 1968 AFL-NFL. . . On injured reserve with knee injury (August 29-October 8, 1979).
PLAYING EXPERIENCE: Oakland AFL, 1968 and 1969; Oakland NFL, 1970-1981; Los Angeles Raiders NFL, 1982. . . . Games: 1968 (14), 1969 (14), 1970 (14), 1971 (14), 1972 (14), 1973 (14), 1974 (14), 1975 (14), 1976 (14), 1977 (14), 1978 (16), 1979 (11), 1980 (16), 1981 (16), 1982 (8). Total AFL: 28. Total NFL: 179. Total Pro: 207.
CHAMPIONSHIP GAME EXPERIENCE: Played in AFL championship game after 1969 season. . . . Played in AFC championship game after 1970, 1973-1977 and 1980 seasons. . . . Played in Super Bowl XI after 1976 season and Super Bowl XV after 1980 season.
RECORDS/HONORS: Played in Pro Bowl after 1972-1978 and 1980 seasons. . . . Named to THE SPORTING NEWS AFC All-Star team, 1974, 1975 and 1977. . . . Inducted into Pro Football Hall of Fame, 1989.
PRO STATISTICS: 1968—Returned one punt for no yards and fumbled once. 1970—Recovered one fumble. 1971—Recovered one fumble. 1977—Recovered one fumble. 1978—Recovered two fumbles. 1979—Recovered one fumble for five yards. 1980—Recovered three fumbles.
BACKGROUND: Assistant coach, Los Angeles Raiders NFL (1983-October 2, 1989).

HEAD COACHING RECORD

	W	L	T	Pct.	Finish		Post-Season W	L
1989— Los Angeles Raiders NFL	7	5	0	.583	3rd/AFC Western Division		—	—
1990— Los Angeles Raiders NFL	12	4	0	.750	1st/AFC Western Division		1	1
Pro totals (2 years)	19	9	0	.679	Pro totals (1 year)		1	1

NOTES:
1989— Replaced Mike Shanahan as coach of L.A. Raiders on October 3, with 1-3 record and tied for fourth place.
1990— Won conference playoff game from Cincinnati, 20-10; lost AFC championship game to Buffalo, 51-3.

SHULA, DON
DOLPHINS

PERSONAL: Born January 4, 1930, at Painesville, O. . . . Full name: Donald Francis Shula. . . . Played defensive back. . . . Father of David Shula, assistant coach with Cincinnati Bengals; and father of Mike Shula, coaches' assistant with Miami Dolphins.
HIGH SCHOOL: Harvey (Painesville, O.).
COLLEGE: John Carroll University (bachelor of arts degree in sociology, 1951).
TRANSACTIONS/CAREER NOTES: Selected by Cleveland Browns in ninth round of 1951 NFL draft. . . . Traded by Browns with quarterback Harry Agganis, defensive backs Bert Rechichar and Carl Taseff, end Gern Nagler, guards Elmer Willhoite, Ed Sharkey and Art Spinney and tackles Dick Batten and Stu Sheetz to Baltimore Colts for linebacker Tom Catlin, guard Herschel Forester, halfback John Petitbon and tackles Don Colo and Mike McCormack (March 25, 1953). . . . Sold by Colts to Washington Redskins (1957).
CHAMPIONSHIP GAME EXPERIENCE: Played in NFL championship game after 1951 and 1952 seasons.
PRO STATISTICS: 1951—Returned one kickoff for six yards. 1953—Caught one pass for six yards and recovered one fumble. 1954—Rushed twice for three yards. 1955—Recovered two fumbles for 26 yards. 1956—Returned one kickoff for no yards and recovered one fumble for six yards.

			INTERCEPTIONS		
Year Team	G	No.	Yds.	Avg.	TD
1951— Cleveland NFL	12	4	23	5.8	0
1952— Cleveland NFL	5	0	0		0
1953— Baltimore NFL	12	3	46	15.3	0
1954— Baltimore NFL	12	5	84	16.8	0
1955— Baltimore NFL	9	5	64	12.8	0
1956— Baltimore NFL	12	1	2	2.0	0
1957— Washington NFL	11	3	48	16.0	0
Pro totals (7 years)	73	21	267	12.7	0

BACKGROUND: Assistant coach, Virginia (1958). . . . assistant coach, Kentucky (1959). . . . assistant coach, Detroit Lions NFL (1960-1962).
HONORS: Named THE SPORTING NEWS NFL Coach of the Year (1964, 1968, 1970 and 1972).

HEAD COACHING RECORD

	W	L	T	Pct.	Finish		Post-Season W	L
1963— Baltimore NFL	8	6	0	.571	3rd/Western Conference		—	—
1964— Baltimore NFL	12	2	0	.857	1st/Western Conference		0	1
1965— Baltimore NFL	10	3	1	.750	2nd/Western Conference		0	1
1966— Baltimore NFL	9	5	0	.643	2nd/Western Conference		—	—
1967— Baltimore NFL	11	1	2	.857	2nd/Western Conference		—	—
1968— Baltimore NFL	13	1	0	.929	1st/Western Conference Coastal Division		2	1
1969— Baltimore NFL	8	5	1	.607	2nd/Western Conference Coastal Division		—	—
1970— Miami NFL	10	4	0	.714	2nd/AFC Eastern Division		0	1
1971— Miami NFL	10	3	1	.750	1st/AFC Eastern Division		2	1
1972— Miami NFL	14	0	0	1.000	1st/AFC Eastern Division		3	0
1973— Miami NFL	12	2	0	.857	1st/AFC Eastern Division		3	0
1974— Miami NFL	11	3	0	.786	1st/AFC Eastern Division		0	1
1975— Miami NFL	10	4	0	.714	T1st/AFC Eastern Division		—	—
1976— Miami NFL	6	8	0	.429	3rd/AFC Eastern Division		—	—
1977— Miami NFL	10	4	0	.714	T1st/AFC Eastern Division		—	—
1978— Miami NFL	11	5	0	.688	T1st/AFC Eastern Division		0	1
1979— Miami NFL	10	6	0	.625	1st/AFC Eastern Division		0	1
1980— Miami NFL	8	8	0	.500	3rd/AFC Eastern Division		—	—
1981— Miami NFL	11	4	1	.719	1st/AFC Eastern Division		0	1
1982— Miami NFL	7	2	0	.778	T2nd/AFC		3	1
1983— Miami NFL	12	4	0	.750	1st/AFC Eastern Division		0	1
1984— Miami NFL	14	2	0	.875	1st/AFC Eastern Division		2	1
1985— Miami NFL	12	4	0	.750	1st/AFC Eastern Division		1	1
1986— Miami NFL	8	8	0	.500	3rd/AFC Eastern Division		—	—
1987— Miami NFL	8	7	0	.533	T2nd/AFC Eastern Division		—	—
1988— Miami NFL	6	10	0	.375	5th/AFC Eastern Division		—	—
1989— Miami NFL	8	8	0	.500	T2nd/AFC Eastern Division		—	—
1990— Miami NFL	12	4	0	.750	2nd/AFC Eastern Division		1	1
Pro totals (28 years)	281	123	6	.693	Pro totals (16 years)		17	14

NOTES:
1964— Lost NFL championship game to Cleveland, 27-0.
1965— Lost conference playoff game to Green Bay, 13-10.
1968— Won conference playoff game from Minnesota, 24-14; won NFL championship game from Cleveland, 34-0; lost Super Bowl III to New York Jets, 16-7.
1970— Lost conference playoff game to Oakland, 21-14.
1971— Won conference playoff game from Kansas City, 27-24; won AFC championship game from Baltimore, 21-0; lost Super Bowl VI to Dallas, 24-3.
1972— Won conference playoff game from Cleveland, 20-14; won AFC championship game from Pittsburgh, 21-17; won Super Bowl VII from Washington, 14-7.
1973— Won conference playoff game from Cincinnati, 34-16; won AFC championship game from Oakland, 27-10; won Super Bowl VIII from Minnesota, 24-7.
1974— Lost conference playoff game to Oakland, 28-26.
1978— Lost conference playoff game to Houston, 17-9.
1979— Lost conference playoff game to Pittsburgh, 34-14.
1981— Lost conference playoff game to San Diego, 41-38 (OT).
1982— Won conference playoff game from New England, 28-13; won conference playoff game from San Diego, 34-13; won AFC championship game from New York Jets, 14-0; lost Super Bowl XVII to Washington, 27-17.
1983— Lost conference playoff game to Seattle, 27-20.
1984— Won conference playoff game from Seattle, 31-10; won AFC championship game from Pittsburgh, 45-28; lost Super Bowl XIX to San Francisco, 38-16.
1985— Won conference playoff game from Cleveland, 24-21; lost AFC championship game to New England, 31-14.
1990— Won conference playoff game from Kansas City, 17-16; lost conference playoff game to Buffalo, 44-34.

WILLIAMSON, RICHARD
BUCCANEERS

PERSONAL: Born April 13, 1941, at Fort Deposit, Ala.... Full name: Richard Alan Williamson.
HIGH SCHOOL: Lowndes County (Ala.).
COLLEGE: Alabama (bachelor of arts degree in education, 1962).
BACKGROUND: Assistant coach, Alabama (1963-1967).... assistant coach, Arkansas (1968 and 1969).... assistant coach, Alabama (1970 and 1971).... assistant coach, Arkansas (1972-1974).... assistant coach, Kansas City Chiefs NFL (1983-1986).... assistant coach, Tampa Bay Buccaneers NFL (1987-December 3, 1990).

HEAD COACHING RECORD

	W	L	T	Pct.	Finish	W	L
					REGULAR SEASON	POST-SEASON	
1975— Memphis State	7	4	0	.636	Independent	—	—
1976— Memphis State	7	4	0	.636	Independent	—	—
1977— Memphis State	6	5	0	.545	Independent	—	—
1978— Memphis State	4	7	0	.364	Independent	—	—
1979— Memphis State	5	6	0	.455	Independent	—	—
1980— Memphis State	2	9	0	.182	Independent	—	—
1990— Tampa Bay NFL	1	2	0	.333	T2nd/NFC Central Division	—	—
College totals (6 years)	31	35	0	.470			
Pro totals (1 year)	1	2	0	.333			

NOTES:
1990— Replaced Ray Perkins as coach of Tampa Bay on December 3, with 5-8 record and in fourth place.

WYCHE, SAM
BENGALS

PERSONAL: Born January 5, 1945, at Atlanta.... Full name: Samuel David Wyche.... Played quarterback.... Brother of Joseph (Bubba) Wyche, former quarterback with Saskatchewan Roughriders (CFL) and Detroit Wheels, Chicago Fire and Shreveport Steamer (WFL).
HIGH SCHOOL: North Fulton (Atlanta).
COLLEGE: Furman (bachelor of arts degree in business administration, 1966); and South Carolina (master's degree).
TRANSACTIONS/CAREER NOTES: Played in Continental Football League with Wheeling Ironmen (1966).... Signed as free agent by Cincinnati Bengals of AFL (1968).... Traded by Bengals to Washington Redskins for running back Henry Dyer (May 5, 1971).... Member of Redskins' taxi squad (1973).... Traded by Redskins to Detroit Lions for quarterback Bill Cappelman (August 17, 1974).... Released by Lions (September 2, 1975).... Signed by St. Louis Cardinals (1976).... Released by Cardinals (September 23, 1976).... Signed by Buffalo Bills (October 26, 1976).... Active for seven games with Bills in 1976; did not play.
CHAMPIONSHIP GAME EXPERIENCE: Played in Super Bowl VII after 1972 season.
PRO STATISTICS: CoFL: 1966—Intercepted three passes for nine yards.... AFL: 1968—Caught one pass for five yards.... NFL: 1970—Recovered one fumble for minus one yard.

				PASSING					RUSHING				TOTAL		
Year	Team	G	Att.	Cmp.	Pct.	Yds.	TD	Int.	Avg.	Att.	Yds.	Avg.	TD	TD	Pts.	F.
1966— Wheeling CoFL		—	18	9	50.0	101	0	1	5.61	5	-11	-2.2	0	0	0	0
1968— Cincinnati AFL		3	55	35	63.6	494	2	2	8.98	12	74	6.2	0	0	0	2
1969— Cincinnati AFL		7	108	54	50.0	838	7	4	7.76	12	107	8.9	1	1	6	1
1970— Cincinnati NFL		13	57	26	45.6	411	3	2	7.21	19	118	6.2	2	2	12	3
1971— Washington NFL		1	0	0		0	0	0		1	4	4.0	0	0	0	0
1972— Washington NFL		7	0	0		0	0	0		0	0		0	0	0	0

Year	Team	G	Att.	Cmp.	Pct.	Yds.	TD	Int.	Avg.	Att.	Yds.	Avg.	TD	TD	Pts.	F.
					PASSING						RUSHING				TOTAL	
1974— Detroit NFL		14	1	0	.0	0	0	1	.00	1	0	.0	0	0	0	0
1976— St.L.(1)-Buf.(0) NFL		1	1	1	100.0	5	0	0	5.00	0	0		0	0	0	0
AFL totals (2 years)		10	163	89	54.6	1332	9	6	8.17	24	181	7.5	1	1	6	3
NFL totals (5 years)		36	59	27	45.8	416	3	3	7.05	21	122	5.8	2	2	12	3
Pro totals (7 years)		46	222	116	52.3	1748	12	9	7.87	45	303	6.7	3	3	18	6

BACKGROUND: Graduate assistant, South Carolina (1967).... assistant coach, San Francisco 49ers NFL (1979-1982).

HEAD COACHING RECORD

						REGULAR SEASON	POST-SEASON	
		W	L	T	Pct.	Finish	W	L
1983— Indiana		3	8	.0	.273	T8th/Big Ten Conference	—	—
1984— Cincinnati NFL		8	8	0	.500	2nd/AFC Central Division	—	—
1985— Cincinnati NFL		7	9	0	.438	T2nd/AFC Central Division	—	—
1986— Cincinnati NFL		10	6	0	.625	2nd/AFC Central Division	—	—
1987— Cincinnati NFL		4	11	0	.267	4th/AFC Central Division	—	—
1988— Cincinnati NFL		12	4	0	.750	1st/AFC Central Division	2	1
1989— Cincinnati NFL		8	8	0	.500	4th/AFC Central Division	—	—
1990— Cincinnati NFL		9	7	0	.563	T1st/AFC Central Division	1	1
College totals (1 year)		3	8	0	.273			
Pro totals (7 years)		58	53	0	.523	Pro totals (2 years)	3	2

NOTES:
1988— Won conference playoff game from Seattle, 21-13; won AFC championship game from Buffalo, 21-10; lost Super Bowl XXIII to San Francisco, 20-16.
1990— Won conference playoff game from Houston, 41-14; lost conference playoff game to Los Angeles Raiders, 20-10.

RECENTLY RETIRED PLAYERS

BAKER, AL 'BUBBA'
DE

PERSONAL: Born December 9, 1956, at Jacksonville, Fla. . . . 6-6/280. . . . Full name: James Albert London Baker.
HIGH SCHOOL: Weequahic (Newark, N.J.).
COLLEGE: Colorado State.
TRANSACTIONS/CAREER NOTES: Selected by Detroit Lions in second round (40th pick overall) of 1978 NFL draft. . . . On reserve/retired list (August 19-September 11, 1980). . . . On physically unable to perform/active list with groin injury (July 29-August 31, 1982). . . . Traded by Lions to St. Louis Cardinals for defensive tackle Mike Dawson and third-round pick in 1984 draft (July 18, 1983). . . . Granted free agency (February 1, 1986). . . . Re-signed by Cardinals (August 26, 1986). . . . Granted roster exemption (August 26 and 27, 1986). . . . Traded by Cardinals to Cleveland Browns for fifth-round pick in 1988 draft (September 3, 1987). . . . Released by Browns (August 30, 1988). . . . Signed as free agent by Minnesota Vikings (September 10, 1988. . . . On suspended list (September 30-October 3, 1988). . . . Granted unconditional free agency (February 1, 1989). . . . Signed by Cleveland Browns (March 31, 1989). . . . On injured reserve with neck injury (November 14, 1990-remainder of season). . . . Granted unconditional free agency (February 1, 1991).
PLAYING EXPERIENCE: Detroit NFL, 1978-1982; St. Louis NFL, 1983-1986; Cleveland NFL, 1987, 1989 and 1990; Minnesota NFL, 1988. . . . Games: 1978 (16), 1979 (16), 1980 (15), 1981 (11), 1982 (9), 1983 (16), 1984 (15), 1985 (16), 1986 (16), 1987 (12), 1988 (14), 1989 (16), 1990 (9). Total: 181.
CHAMPIONSHIP GAME EXPERIENCE: Played in AFC championship game after 1987 and 1989 seasons.
RECORDS/HONORS: Named THE SPORTING NEWS NFC Rookie of the Year, 1978. . . . Played in Pro Bowl after 1978-1980 seasons.
PRO STATISTICS: 1978—Recovered one fumble. 1979—Recovered one fumble. 1980—Intercepted one pass for no yards and recovered one fumble. 1981—Intercepted one pass for nine yards. 1982—Recovered one fumble. 1983—Intercepted two passes for 24 yards and recovered two fumbles. 1985—Recovered one fumble. 1987—Recovered one fumble.

HAIRSTON, CARL
DE

PERSONAL: Born December 15, 1952, at Martinsville, Va. . . . 6-2/275. . . . Full name: Carl Blake Hairston.
HIGH SCHOOL: Martinsville (Va.).
COLLEGE: Maryland-Eastern Shore (bachelor of arts degree in education, 1985).
TRANSACTIONS/CAREER NOTES: Selected by Philadelphia Eagles in seventh round (191st pick overall) of 1976 NFL draft. . . . Traded by Eagles to Cleveland Browns for ninth-round pick in 1985 draft (February 9, 1984). . . . Crossed picket line during players' strike (October 7, 1987). . . . Granted unconditional free agency (February 1, 1989). . . . Re-signed by Browns (April 11, 1989). . . . Released by Browns (July 17, 1990). . . . Awarded on waivers to Phoenix Cardinals (July 20, 1990). . . . Granted unconditional free agency (February 1, 1991).
PLAYING EXPERIENCE: Philadelphia NFL, 1976-1983; Cleveland NFL, 1984-1989; Phoenix NFL, 1990. . . . Games: 1976 (14), 1977 (14), 1978 (16), 1979 (15), 1980 (16), 1981 (16), 1982 (9), 1983 (16), 1984 (16), 1985 (16), 1986 (16), 1987 (14), 1988 (16), 1989 (16), 1990 (16). Total: 224.
CHAMPIONSHIP GAME EXPERIENCE: Played in NFC championship game after 1980 season. . . . Played in Super Bowl XV after 1980 season. . . . Played in AFC championship game after 1986, 1987 and 1989 seasons.
PRO STATISTICS: 1977—Recovered one fumble. 1980—Intercepted one pass for no yards and recovered one fumble. 1981—Recovered one fumble. 1982—Recovered two fumbles for 24 yards. 1983—Recovered two fumbles. 1985—Recovered one fumble. 1986—Recovered one fumble. 1987—Ran 40 yards with lateral from interception and recovered one fumble.

HAMPTON, DAN
DT

PERSONAL: Born September 19, 1957, at Oklahoma City, Okla. . . . 6-5/274. . . . Full name: Daniel Oliver Hampton.
HIGH SCHOOL: Jacksonville (Ark.).
COLLEGE: Arkansas.
TRANSACTIONS/CAREER NOTES: Selected by Chicago Bears in first round (fourth pick overall) of 1979 NFL draft. . . . On injured reserve with knee injury (November 16-December 14, 1987). . . . On injured reserve with knee injury (October 4, 1989-remainder of season). . . . Granted free agency (February 1, 1990). . . . Re-signed by Bears (July 25, 1990). . . . On inactive list (December 9 and 16, 1990). . . . Granted unconditional free agency (February 1, 1991).
PLAYING EXPERIENCE: Chicago NFL, 1979-1990. . . . Games: 1979 (16), 1980 (16), 1981 (16), 1982 (9), 1983 (11), 1984 (15), 1985 (16), 1986 (16), 1987 (8), 1988 (16), 1989 (4), 1990 (14). Total: 157.
CHAMPIONSHIP GAME EXPERIENCE: Played in NFC championship game after 1984, 1985 and 1988 seasons. . . . Played in Super Bowl XX after 1985 season.
RECORDS/HONORS: Played in Pro Bowl after 1980, 1982, 1984 and 1985 seasons. . . . Named to THE SPORTING NEWS NFL All-Pro team, 1984.
PRO STATISTICS: 1979—Recovered two fumbles. 1984—Recovered three fumbles. 1985—Recovered three fumbles. 1986—Credited with a safety and recovered two fumbles.

LYONS, MARTY
DE

PERSONAL: Born January 15, 1957, at Tokoma Park, Md. . . . 6-5/269.
HIGH SCHOOL: Catholic (St. Petersburg, Fla.).
COLLEGE: Alabama.
TRANSACTIONS/CAREER NOTES: Selected by New York Jets in first round (14th pick overall) of 1979 NFL draft. . . . On injured reserve with shoulder injury (November 12-December 12, 1986). . . . Crossed picket line during players' strike (October 2, 1987). . . . On injured reserve with knee injury (December 7, 1989-remainder of season). . . . On in-

jured reserve with torn bicep muscle (August 27, 1990-entire season). . . . Granted unconditional free agency (February 1, 1991).
PLAYING EXPERIENCE: New York Jets NFL, 1979-1989. . . . Games: 1979 (16), 1980 (16), 1981 (12), 1982 (7), 1983 (16), 1984 (13), 1985 (16), 1986 (12), 1987 (13), 1988 (16), 1989 (10). Total: 147.
CHAMPIONSHIP GAME EXPERIENCE: Played in AFC championship game after 1982 season.
RECORDS/HONORS: Named as defensive lineman on THE SPORTING NEWS college All-America team, 1978.
PRO STATISTICS: 1979—Recovered three fumbles. 1981—Recovered one fumble. 1982—Recovered one fumble for 10 yards. 1986—Recovered one fumble. 1987—Credited with a safety. 1988—Credited with a safety and recovered two fumbles.

NEWSOME, OZZIE
TE

PERSONAL: Born March 16, 1956, at Muscle Shoals, Ala. . . . 6-2/225. . . . Cousin of Darrin Nelson, running back with Minnesota Vikings; and cousin of Kevin Nelson, running back with Los Angeles Express, 1984 and 1985.
HIGH SCHOOL: Colbert County (Leighton, Ala.).
COLLEGE: Alabama (bachelor of science degree in recreation and park management).
TRANSACTIONS/CAREER NOTES: Selected by Cleveland Browns in first round (23rd pick overall) of 1978 NFL draft. . . . Crossed picket line during players' strike (October 14, 1987). . . . Granted unconditional free agency (February 1, 1989). . . . Did not receive qualifying offer (April 15, 1989). . . . Re-signed by Cleveland Browns (May 24, 1989). . . . Granted unconditional free agency (February 1, 1991).
CHAMPIONSHIP GAME EXPERIENCE: Played in AFC championship game after 1986, 1987 and 1989 seasons.
RECORDS/HONORS: Established NFL record for most pass receptions by tight end, career (662). . . . Named as wide receiver on THE SPORTING NEWS college All-America team, 1977. . . . Named to THE SPORTING NEWS AFC All-Star team, 1979. . . . Played in Pro Bowl after 1981, 1984 and 1985 seasons. . . . Named to THE SPORTING NEWS NFL All-Pro team, 1984.
PRO STATISTICS: 1978—Returned two punts for 29 yards, rushed 13 times for 96 yards and two touchdowns and fumbled once. 1979—Rushed one for six yards. 1980—Rushed twice for 13 yards and fumbled twice. 1981—Rushed twice for 20 yards. 1985—Recovered one fumble.

			——— RECEIVING ———			
Year	Team	G	No.	Yds.	Avg.	TD
1978—	Cleveland NFL	16	38	589	15.5	2
1979—	Cleveland NFL	16	55	781	14.2	9
1980—	Cleveland NFL	16	51	594	11.6	3
1981—	Cleveland NFL	16	69	1002	14.5	6
1982—	Cleveland NFL	8	49	633	12.9	3
1983—	Cleveland NFL	16	89	970	10.9	6
1984—	Cleveland NFL	16	89	1001	11.2	5
1985—	Cleveland NFL	16	62	711	11.5	5
1986—	Cleveland NFL	16	39	417	10.7	3
1987—	Cleveland NFL	13	34	375	11.0	0
1988—	Cleveland NFL	16	35	343	9.8	2
1989—	Cleveland NFL	16	29	324	11.2	1
1990—	Cleveland NFL	16	23	240	10.4	2
Pro totals (13 years)		197	662	7980	12.1	47

QUICK, MIKE
WR

PERSONAL: Born May 14, 1959, at Hamlet, N.C. . . . 6-2/195. . . . Full name: Michael Anthony Quick.
HIGH SCHOOL: Richmond (Rockingham, N.C.) and Fork Union Military Academy (Fork Union, Va.).
COLLEGE: North Carolina State.
TRANSACTIONS/CAREER NOTES: Selected by Philadelphia Eagles in first round (20th pick overall) of 1982 NFL draft. . . . On did not report list (August 20-September 1, 1985). . . . Reported and granted roster exemption (September 2-September 5, 1985). . . . On injured reserve with broken leg (October 3-December 2, 1988). . . . On injured reserve with knee injury (October 18, 1989-remainder of season). . . . On injured reserve with leg injury (October 20, 1990-remainder of 1990 season). . . . Granted unconditional free agency (February 1, 1991).
RECORDS/HONORS: Tied NFL record for longest passing play from scrimmage when he caught a 99-yard touchdown pass from quarterback Ron Jaworski against Atlanta Falcons (November 10, 1985). . . . Played in Pro Bowl after 1983-1985 and 1987 seasons. . . . Member of Pro Bowl squad after 1986 season; did not play. . . . Named to THE SPORTING NEWS NFL All-Pro team, 1985.
PRO STATISTICS: 1982—Recovered one fumble. 1983—Fumbled once. 1984—Rushed once for minus five yards. 1985—Recovered one fumble and fumbled once. 1986—Returned two kickoffs for six yards, recovered one fumble and fumbled once. 1987—Recovered one fumble and fumbled three times.

			——— RECEIVING ———			
Year	Team	G	No.	Yds.	Avg.	TD
1982—	Philadelphia NFL	9	10	156	15.6	1
1983—	Philadelphia NFL	16	69	*1409	20.4	13
1984—	Philadelphia NFL	14	61	1052	17.2	9
1985—	Philadelphia NFL	16	73	1247	17.1	11
1986—	Philadelphia NFL	16	60	939	15.7	9
1987—	Philadelphia NFL	12	46	790	17.2	11
1988—	Philadelphia NFL	8	22	508	23.1	4
1989—	Philadelphia NFL	6	13	228	17.5	2
1990—	Philadelphia NFL	4	9	135	15.0	1
Pro totals (9 years)		101	363	6464	17.8	61

TURNER, KEENA
LB

PERSONAL: Born October 22, 1958, at Chicago. . . . 6-2/219.
HIGH SCHOOL: Vocational (Chicago).
COLLEGE: Purdue.
TRANSACTIONS/CAREER NOTES: Selected by San Francisco 49ers in second round (39th pick overall) of 1980 NFL draft. . . . On injured reserve with knee injury (December 17, 1989-remainder of season). . . . On injured reserve with pinched nerve in neck (November 19-December 31, 1988). . . . Granted unconditional free agency (February 1, 1990). . . . Rights relinquished (April 13, 1990). . . . Re-signed by 49ers (May 10, 1990). . . . Released by 49ers (September 3, 1990). . . . Re-signed by 49ers (September 4, 1990). . . . Granted unconditional free agency (February 1, 1991).
CHAMPIONSHIP GAME EXPERIENCE: Played in NFC championship game after 1981, 1983, 1984 and 1988-1990 seasons. . . . Played in Super Bowl XVI after 1981 season, Super Bowl XIX after 1984 season, Super Bowl XXIII after 1988 season and Super Bowl XXIV after 1989 season.
RECORDS/HONORS: Played in Pro Bowl after 1984 season.
PRO STATISTICS: 1981—Recovered three fumbles. 1983—Recovered one fumble. 1985—Returned two fumbles for 65 yards and a touchdown. 1988—Recovered two fumbles. 1990—Credited with a safety.

		INTERCEPTIONS			
Year Team	G	No.	Yds.	Avg.	TD
1980—San Francisco NFL....	16	2	15	7.5	0
1981—San Francisco NFL....	16	1	0	.0	0
1982—San Francisco NFL....	9	0	0		0
1983—San Francisco NFL....	15	0	0		0
1984—San Francisco NFL....	16	4	51	12.8	0
1985—San Francisco NFL....	15	0	0		0
1986—San Francisco NFL....	16	1	9	9.0	0
1987—San Francisco NFL....	10	1	15	15.0	0
1988—San Francisco NFL....	11	1	2	2.0	0
1989—San Francisco NFL....	13	1	42	42.0	0
1990—San Francisco NFL....	16	0	0		0
Pro totals (11 years)......	153	11	134	12.2	0

WEBSTER, MIKE
C

PERSONAL: Born March 18, 1952, at Tomahawk, Wis. . . . 6-2/260. . . . Full name: Michael Lewis Webster.
HIGH SCHOOL: Rhinelander (Wis.).
COLLEGE: Wisconsin.
TRANSACTIONS/CAREER NOTES: Selected by Pittsburgh Steelers in fifth round (125th pick overall) of 1974 NFL draft. . . . On injured reserve with dislocated elbow (September 3-October 3, 1986). . . . Crossed picket line during players' strike (September 30, 1987). . . . Granted unconditional free agency (February 1, 1989). . . . Signed by Kansas City Chiefs (March 30, 1989). . . . Granted unconditional free agency (February 1, 1991).
PLAYING EXPERIENCE: Pittsburgh NFL, 1974-1988; Kansas City NFL, 1989 and 1990. . . . Games: 1974 (14), 1975 (14), 1976 (14), 1977 (14), 1978 (16), 1979 (16), 1980 (16), 1981 (16), 1982 (9), 1983 (16), 1984 (16), 1985 (16), 1986 (12), 1987 (15), 1988 (16), 1989 (16), 1990 (9). Total: 245.
CHAMPIONSHIP GAME EXPERIENCE: Played in AFC championship game after 1974-1976, 1978, 1979 and 1984 seasons. . . . Played in Super Bowl IX after 1974 season, Super Bowl X after 1975 season, Super Bowl XIII after 1978 season and Super Bowl XIV after 1979 season.
RECORDS/HONORS: Played in Pro Bowl after 1978-1985 and 1987 seasons. . . . Named to THE SPORTING NEWS AFC All-Star team, 1978 and 1979. . . . Named to THE SPORTING NEWS NFL All-Pro team, 1980, 1981 and 1983.
PRO STATISTICS: 1976—Fumbled twice. 1979—Recovered two fumbles for two yards. 1983—Recovered two fumbles. 1985—Recovered one fumble. 1988—Fumbled twice for minus 58 yards. 1990—Recovered one fumble.

WINDER, SAMMY
RB

PERSONAL: Born July 15, 1959, at Madison, Miss. . . . 5-11/203.
HIGH SCHOOL: Ridgeland (Madison, Miss.).
COLLEGE: Southern Mississippi.
TRANSACTIONS/CAREER NOTES: Selected by Denver Broncos in fifth round (131st pick overall) of 1982 NFL draft. . . . Granted unconditional free agency (February 1, 1991).
CHAMPIONSHIP GAME EXPERIENCE: Played in AFC championship game after 1986, 1987 and 1989 seasons. . . . Played in Super Bowl XXI after 1986 season, Super Bowl XXII after 1987 season and Super Bowl XXIV after 1989 season.
RECORDS/HONORS: Played in Pro Bowl after 1984 and 1986 seasons.
PRO STATISTICS: 1982—Recovered one fumble. 1984—Recovered two fumbles. 1985—Attempted one pass with no completions and recovered one fumble. 1986—Recovered one fumble. 1987—Recovered two fumbles. 1988—Returned one kickoff for 11 yards. 1990—Returned four kickoffs for 55 yards.

		RUSHING				RECEIVING				TOTAL		
Year Team	G	Att.	Yds.	Avg.	TD	No.	Yds.	Avg.	TD	TD	Pts.	F.
1982—Denver NFL	8	67	259	3.9	1	11	83	7.5	0	1	6	1
1983—Denver NFL	14	196	757	3.9	3	23	150	6.5	0	3	18	7
1984—Denver NFL	16	296	1153	3.9	4	44	288	6.5	2	6	36	5
1985—Denver NFL	14	199	714	3.6	8	31	197	6.4	0	8	48	4
1986—Denver NFL	16	240	789	3.3	9	26	171	6.6	5	14	84	2
1987—Denver NFL	12	196	741	3.8	6	14	74	5.3	1	7	42	5
1988—Denver NFL	16	149	543	3.6	4	17	103	6.1	1	5	30	1
1989—Denver NFL	16	110	351	3.2	2	14	91	6.5	0	2	12	1
1990—Denver NFL	15	42	120	2.9	2	17	145	8.5	0	2	12	2
Pro totals (9 years)	127	1495	5427	3.6	39	197	1302	6.6	9	48	288	28

WOODRUFF, DWAYNE

CB

PERSONAL: Born February 18, 1957, at Bowling Green, Ky. . . . 6-0/198. . . . Full name: Dwayne Donzell Woodruff.
HIGH SCHOOL: New Richmond (O.).
COLLEGE: Louisville (bachelor of science degree in commerce, 1979); attended Duquesne Law School (received degree, 1988).
TRANSACTIONS/CAREER NOTES: Selected by Pittsburgh Steelers in sixth round (161st pick overall) of 1979 NFL draft. . . . USFL rights traded by Pittsburgh Maulers with rights to quarterback Jeff Hostetler to Arizona Wranglers for a draft pick (May 2, 1984). . . . On injured reserve with Steelers with dislocated elbow (October 15-November 15, 1985). . . . On injured reserve with knee injury (August 26, 1986-entire season). . . . Released by Steelers (September 4, 1990). . . . Re-signed by Steelers (September 5, 1990). . . . On inactive list (September 9, 1990). . . . Granted unconditional free agency (February 1, 1991).
CHAMPIONSHIP GAME EXPERIENCE: Played in AFC championship game after 1979 and 1984 seasons. . . . Played in Super Bowl XIV after 1979 season.
PRO STATISTICS: 1981—Recovered one fumble and fumbled once. 1984—Recovered one fumble for 65 yards and a touchdown. 1989—Recovered one fumble for 21 yards and a touchdown. 1990—Recovered one fumble for 13 yards.

Year	Team	G	No.	Yds.	Avg.	TD
			INTERCEPTIONS			
1979—	Pittsburgh NFL	16	1	31	31.0	0
1980—	Pittsburgh NFL	16	1	0	.0	0
1981—	Pittsburgh NFL	16	1	17	17.0	0
1982—	Pittsburgh NFL	9	5	53	10.6	0
1983—	Pittsburgh NFL	15	3	85	28.3	0
1984—	Pittsburgh NFL	16	5	56	11.2	1
1985—	Pittsburgh NFL	12	5	80	16.0	0
1987—	Pittsburgh NFL	12	5	91	18.2	1
1988—	Pittsburgh NFL	14	4	109	27.3	1
1989—	Pittsburgh NFL	16	4	57	14.3	0
1990—	Pittsburgh NFL	15	3	110	36.7	0
Pro totals (11 years)		157	37	689	18.6	3

YOUNG, FREDD

LB

PERSONAL: Born November 14, 1961, at Dallas. . . . 6-1/233.
HIGH SCHOOL: Woodrow Wilson (Dallas).
COLLEGE: New Mexico State.
TRANSACTIONS/CAREER NOTES: Selected by Arizona Wranglers in 1984 USFL territorial draft. . . . Selected by Seattle Seahawks in third round (76th pick overall) of 1984 NFL draft. . . . Signed by Seahawks (May 17, 1984). . . . Crossed picket line during players' strike (October 14, 1987). . . . Left Seahawks camp voluntarily (July 27, 1988). . . . Returned (August 27, 1988). . . . Granted roster exemption (August 27-September 8, 1988). . . . Traded by Seahawks to Indianapolis Colts for first-round picks in 1989 and 1990 drafts (September 9, 1988). . . . On inactive list (December 22 and 30, 1990). . . . Granted unconditional free agency (February 1, 1991).
PLAYING EXPERIENCE: Seattle NFL, 1984-1987; Indianapolis NFL, 1988-1990. . . . Games: 1984 (16), 1985 (16), 1986 (15), 1987 (13), 1988 (15), 1989 (15), 1990 (11). Total: 101.
RECORDS/HONORS: Played in Pro Bowl after 1984-1987 seasons. . . . Named to THE SPORTING NEWS NFL All-Pro team, 1987.
PRO STATISTICS: 1985—Recovered one fumble for 13 yards. 1987—Intercepted one pass for 50 yards and a touchdown and recovered four fumbles. 1989—Intercepted two passes for two yards. 1990—Recovered one fumble.

RECENTLY RETIRED COACH

PARCELLS, BILL

PERSONAL: Born August 22, 1941, at Englewood, N.J. . . . Full name: Duane Charles Parcells.

HIGH SCHOOL: River Dell (Oradell, N.J.).

COLLEGE: Wichita State (bachelor of arts degree in education, 1964).

BACKGROUND: Assistant coach, Hastings College, Neb. (1964). . . . assistant coach, Wichita State (1965). . . . assistant coach, Army (1966-1969). . . . assistant coach, Florida State (1970-1972). . . . assistant coach, Vanderbilt (1973 and 1974). . . . assistant coach, Texas Tech (1975-1977). . . . assistant coach, New England Patriots NFL (1980). . . . assistant coach, New York Giants NFL (1981 and 1982).

HONORS: Named THE SPORTING NEWS NFL Coach of the Year (1986).

HEAD COACHING RECORD

	W	L	T	Pct.	Finish	POST-SEASON W	L
1978 — Air Force	3	8	0	.273			
1983 — New York Giants NFL	3	12	1	.219	5th/NFC Eastern Division	—	—
1984 — New York Giants NFL	9	7	0	.563	T2nd/NFC Eastern Division	1	1
1985 — New York Giants NFL	10	6	0	.625	T1st/NFC Eastern Division	1	1
1986 — New York Giants NFL	14	2	0	.875	1st/NFC Eastern Division	3	0
1987 — New York Giants NFL	6	9	0	.400	5th/NFC Eastern Division	—	—
1988 — New York Giants NFL	10	6	0	.625	T1st/NFC Eastern Division	—	—
1989 — New York Giants NFL	12	4	0	.750	1st/NFC Eastern Division	0	1
1990 — New York Giants NFL	13	3	0	.813	1st/NFC Eastern Division	3	0
College totals (1 year)	3	8	0	.273			
Pro totals (8 years)	77	49	1	.610	**Pro totals (5 years)**	8	3

NOTES:

1984 — Won wild-card playoff game from Los Angeles Rams, 16-10; lost conference playoff game to San Francisco, 21-10.

1985 — Won wild-card playoff game from San Francisco, 17-3; lost conference playoff game to Chicago, 21-0.

1986 — Won conference playoff game San Francisco, 49-3; won NFC championship game from Washington, 17-0; won Super Bowl XXI from Denver, 39-20.

1989 — Lost conference playoff game to Los Angeles Rams, 19-13 (OT).

1990 — Won conference playoff game from Chicago, 31-3; won NFC championship game from San Francisco, 15-13; won Super Bowl XXV from Buffalo, 20-19.